Lecture Notes in Compute

Edited by G. Goos, J. Hartmanis and

Springer

Berlin
Heidelberg
New York
Barcelona
Budapest
Hong Kong
London
Milan
Paris
Singapore
Tokyo

Hans Burkhardt   Bernd Neumann (Eds.)

Computer Vision – ECCV'98

5th European Conference on Computer Vision
Freiburg, Germany, June 2-6, 1998
Proceedings, Volume I

 Springer

Series Editors

Gerhard Goos, Karlsruhe University, Germany
Juris Hartmanis, Cornell University, NY, USA
Jan van Leeuwen, Utrecht University, The Netherlands

Volume Editors

Hans Burkhardt
Computer Science Department, University of Freiburg
Am Flughafen 17, D-79085 Freiburg, Germany
E-mail: burkhardt@informatik.uni-freiburg.de

Bernd Neumann
Computer Science Department, University of Hamburg
Vogt-Koelln-Str. 30, D-22527 Hamburg, Germany
E-mail: neumann@informatik.uni-hamburg.de

Cataloging-in-Publication data applied for

Die Deutsche Bibliothek - CIP-Einheitsaufnahme

Computer vision : proceedings / ECCV '98, 5th European Conference on Computer
Vision, Freiburg, Germany, June 2 - 6, 1998. Hans Burkhardt ; Bernd Neumann
(ed.). - Berlin ; Heidelberg ; New York ; Barcelona ; Budapest ; Hong Kong ;
London ; Milan ; Paris ; Santa Clara ; Singapore ; Tokyo : Springer.

Vol. 1. - (1998)
(Lecture notes in computer science ; Vol. 1406)
ISBN 3-540-64569-1

CR Subject Classification (1991): I.3.5, I.5, I.2.9-10, I.4

ISSN 0302-9743
ISBN 3-540-64569-1 Springer-Verlag Berlin Heidelberg New York

© Springer-Verlag Berlin Heidelberg 1998
Printed in Germany

Typesetting: Camera-ready by author
SPIN 10637150   06/3142 – 5 4 3 2 1 0   Printed on acid-free paper

Preface

Following the highly successful conferences held in Antibes (ECCV '90), Santa Margherita Ligure (ECCV '92), Stockholm (ECCV '94), and Cambridge (ECCV '96), the Fifth European Conference on Computer Vision (ECCV '98) will take place from 2–6 June 1998 at the University of Freiburg, Germany. It is an honour for us to host this conference which has turned out to be one of the major events for the computer vision community. The conference will be held under the auspices of the European Vision Society (EVS) and the German Association for Pattern Recognition (DAGM).

ECCV is a single track conference consisting of highest quality, previously unpublished, contributed papers on new and original research on computer vision presented either orally or as posters. 223 manuscripts were reviewed double-blind each by three reviewers from the program committee. Forty-two papers were selected to be delivered orally and seventy to be presented at poster sessions.

Based on a generous donation from the OLYMPUS Europe Foundation "Science for Life" 10,000.- DM will be awarded for the best papers.

ECCV '98 is being held at the University of Freiburg, located in the lovely surroundings of the Black Forest. It is one of the oldest universities in Germany, founded in 1457, with an outstanding international reputation. This university with a long tradition has been recently enriched through the foundation of a new 15th Faculty for Applied Sciences consisting of two Institutes: the Institute of Computer Science which will host the ECCV '98 and the Institute of Microsystem Technology.

We wish to thank the members of the program committee and the conference board for their help in the reviewing process. It is their competence and hard work which provides the key for the continuing success of this conference series.

Our thanks are extended also to the University of Freiburg and its rector W. Jäger for hosting this conference; to Springer-Verlag in Heidelberg for their support of this conference through the proceedings; and to k&k for the local organization.

Finally we would like to express our appreciation to the members of our institutes and especially to Nikos Canterakis, to Christoph Schnörr, and to Helen Brodie for their never-ending patience and humour.

We wish all participants a successful and inspiring conference and a pleasant stay in Freiburg.

Freiburg, March 1998   Hans Burkhardt and Bernd Neumann

Contents of Volume I

Stereo Vision and Calibration II

Colour and Indexing

Tracking, CONDENSATION

Contents of Volume II

Shading and Shape

Appearance and Recognition

Motion Segmentation

Recognition / Robotics and Active Vision

Structure from Motion

Multiple View Geometry

A Common Framework for Multiple View Tensors *

Anders Heyden

Dept of Mathematics, Lund University
Box 118, S-221 00 Lund, Sweden
email: heyden@maths.lth.se

Abstract. *In this paper, we will introduce a common framework for the definition and operations on the different multiple view tensors. The novelty of the proposed formulation is to not fix any parameters of the camera matrices, but instead letting a group act on them and look at the different orbits. In this setting the multiple view geometry can be viewed as a four-dimensional linear manifold in $\mathbb{R}^{3m}$, where m denotes the number of images. The Grassman coordinates of this manifold are the epipoles, the components of the fundamental matrices, the components of the trifocal tensor and the components of the quadfocal tensor. All relations between these Grassman coordinates can be expressed using the so called quadratic p-relations, which are quadratic polynomials in the Grassman coordinates. Using this formulation it is evident that the multiple view geometry is described by four different kinds of projective invariants; the epipoles, the fundamental matrices, the trifocal tensors and the quadfocal tensors.*

As an application of this formalism it will be shown how the multiple view geometry can be calculated from the fundamental matrix for two views, from the trifocal tensor for three views and from the quadfocal tensor for four views. As a byproduct, we show how to calculate the fundamental matrices from a trifocal tensor, as well as how to calculate the trifocal tensors from a quadfocal tensor. It is, furthermore, shown that, in general, $n < 6$ corresponding points in four images gives $16n - n(n-1)/2$ linearly independent constraints on the quadfocal tensor and that 6 corresponding points can be used to estimate the tensor components linearly. Finally, it is shown that the rank of the trifocal tensor is 4 and that the rank of the quadfocal tensor is 9.

1 Introduction

There has been an intensive research on multiple view geometry during the last few years. Several different approaches to treat the case of many images, taken by uncalibrated cameras, of a 3D object have been proposed in the literature. These approaches ranges from using camera matrices, using multilinear forms to

---

* This work has been done within then ESPRIT Reactive LTR project 21914, CUMULI and the Swedish Research Council for Engineering Sciences (TFR), project 95-64-222

using multiple view tensors. In this paper we will concentrate on the tensorial description and show its relation to other descriptions.

One of the first approaches to multiple view geometry is to use the camera matrices directly, as in [12], where canonic representations for the multiple view geometry are given. The disadvantage of the use of camera matrices is that one has to choose a coordinate system in 3D in order to write down the camera matrices. This fixes some degrees of freedom that are natural in the uncalibrated case, which we argue is less intuitive than leaving these degrees of freedom unfixed.

The multilinear forms have been treated by many researchers. The bilinear form, expressed by the fundamental matrix, has been known for a long time. The trilinear forms was originally discovered by Spetsakis and Aloimonis in [16], in the calibrated case, and rediscovered by Shashua, in [13, 15] in the uncalibrated case. Faugeras and Mourrain, in [2, 1] use Grassman-Cayley algebra to derive relation between different multilinear forms. Heyden uses a reduced form of the multilinear constraints in [8]. In [9, 10] the algebraic relations between the different multilinear constraints have been explored in detail. One drawback of the multilinear forms is that one has to be careful about what can be estimated from image measurements and what can be calculated from the multilinear forms. These two things are often, unintentionally, mixed together.

The tensorial description was introduced, in the case of three images, by Hartley, in [6, 7] and in a general projective framework by Triggs, in [17]. Reduced forms of the multiple view tensors, together with necessary and sufficient conditions for the tensor components, have been introduced by Heyden, in [8]. Necessary and sufficient conditions for the ordinary trifocal tensor components have been found by Faugeras and Papadopoulo, in [3, 4]. These conditions are needed when estimating the tensor components using nonlinear methods. The advantages of using the multiple view tensors are that no coordinate system has to be fixed and that the difference between what entities that can be estimated from image measurements and what can be estimated from the tensor components are more evident.

In this paper we will present a common framework for the definition and manipulation of multiple view tensors. This will be done in Section 2. In Section 3 we will show how the camera matrices relate to the multiple view tensors and introduce a normal form for the representation of the multiple view geometry. The bifocal tensor will be studied in detail in Section 4, the trifocal tensor in Section 5 and the quadfocal tensor in Section 6. Here we show how to calculate lower order tensors from the quadfocal, trifocal or bifocal tensors and how to obtain a representative of the multiple view geometry. Finally, in Section 7, some conclusions will be given.

2   The Multiple View Tensors

In this section the multiple view tensors will be defined in a generic way. We start with the standard camera equation, for an uncalibrated pinhole camera:

$$\lambda \mathbf{x} = P\mathbf{X} , \qquad (1)$$

where $\mathbf{X} = [\,X\,Y\,Z\,1\,]^T$ denote extended object coordinates, $\mathbf{x} = [\,x\,y\,1\,]^T$ denote extended image coordinates, P denotes the camera matrix and λ a scale-factor.

Assume that we have m images of n points taken by a camera, modeled as in (1). Then we can write

$$\lambda_{i,j}\mathbf{x}_{i,j} = P_i\mathbf{X}_j, \ i = 1,\ldots,m, \ j = 1,\ldots n \ . \tag{2}$$

Consider one object point $\mathbf{X}_1$ and its images $\mathbf{x}_{i,1}$. Observing that (2) is linear in $\mathbf{X}_1$ and $\lambda_{i,j}$, it can be written, using the notation $\mathbf{X} = \mathbf{X}_1$, $\mathbf{x}_i = \mathbf{x}_{i,1}$ and $\lambda_{i,j} = \lambda_{i,1}$,

$$\underbrace{\begin{bmatrix} P_1 & \mathbf{x}_1 & 0 & 0 & \ldots & 0 \\ P_2 & 0 & \mathbf{x}_2 & 0 & \ldots & 0 \\ P_3 & 0 & 0 & \mathbf{x}_3 & \ldots & 0 \\ \vdots & \vdots & \vdots & \vdots & \ddots & \ldots \\ P_m & 0 & 0 & 0 & \ldots & \mathbf{x}_m \end{bmatrix}}_{M} \begin{bmatrix} \mathbf{X} \\ -\lambda_1 \\ -\lambda_2 \\ -\lambda_3 \\ \vdots \\ -\lambda_m \end{bmatrix} = \begin{bmatrix} 0 \\ 0 \\ 0 \\ \vdots \\ 0 \end{bmatrix} . \tag{3}$$

Since M has a nontrivial right nullspace

$$\mathrm{rank}\, M < m + 4 \tag{4}$$

holds, i.e. all $(m+4) \times (m+4)$ submatrices of M have vanishing determinants. Using Laplace expansions, see [5], of these minors, it can be seen that they can be written as sums of products of determinants of four rows taken from the first four columns of M and of image coordinates. Moreover, it can be seen from the structure of M that all such minors can be factorized as a product of image coordinates multiplied by an expression involving only rows taken from at most four different camera matrices. This observation leads us to study the special case of four images.

Consider the first four images and call the first four camera matrices A, B, C and D. The equations in (2) for one object point $\mathbf{X}_1$ can be written, again using the notation $\mathbf{X} = \mathbf{X}_1$, $\mathbf{x}_i = \mathbf{x}_{i,1}$ and $\lambda_{i,j} = \lambda_{i,1}$,

$$\underbrace{\begin{bmatrix} A & \mathbf{x}_1 & 0 & 0 & 0 \\ B & 0 & \mathbf{x}_2 & 0 & 0 \\ C & 0 & 0 & \mathbf{x}_3 & 0 \\ D & 0 & 0 & 0 & \mathbf{x}_4 \end{bmatrix}}_{M_4} \begin{bmatrix} \mathbf{X} \\ -\lambda_1 \\ -\lambda_2 \\ -\lambda_3 \\ -\lambda_4 \end{bmatrix} = \begin{bmatrix} 0 \\ 0 \\ 0 \\ 0 \end{bmatrix} . \tag{5}$$

In the same way as before we conclude that

$$\mathrm{rank}\, M_4 < 8 \tag{6}$$

and using Laplace expansions of suitable 8×8 minors from M_4 we observe that there are essentially three different types of such determinants.

The first type of minors from M_4 involves all three rows from one camera matrix and all three rows from another, e.g.

$$\det \begin{bmatrix} A^1 & x_1 & 0 \\ A^2 & y_1 & 0 \\ A^3 & 1 & 0 \\ B^1 & 0 & x_2 \\ B^2 & 0 & y_2 \\ B^3 & 0 & 1 \end{bmatrix} = 0 , \tag{7}$$

where A^i denotes the i:th row of A etc. To be precise the actual 8×8 minor from M_4 is a product of one image coordinate in image 3, one image coordinate in image 4 and the determinant in (7), but since these image coordinates can be factored out they are omitted in the sequel. This type of minors in (7) are bilinear forms in the image coordinates of the two images. These bilinear forms express the well-known **bilinear** or **epipolar constraints**, which also can be expressed using the **fundamental matrix**. In fact, the coefficients of the bilinear forms are the components of the bifocal tensor defined as follows.

Definition 1. *Let ϵ_{ijk} denote the permutation symbol, i.e. $\epsilon_{123} = \epsilon_{231} = \epsilon_{312} = 1$, $\epsilon_{321} = \epsilon_{213} = \epsilon_{132} = -1$ and $\epsilon_{ijk} = 0$ if two indices are equal, and let P_I^i denote the i:th row of the camera matrix P_I for image I. Then the tensor*

$$_{IJ}F_{ij} = \epsilon_{ii'i''}\epsilon_{jj'j''} \det \begin{bmatrix} P_I^{i'} \\ P_I^{i''} \\ P_J^{j'} \\ P_J^{j''} \end{bmatrix} ,$$

*where Einsteins' summation convention has been used, is called the **bifocal tensor** corresponding to views I and J.*

When the notation in (5) has been used, the bifocal tensors will be denoted by $_{AB}F$, $_{CB}F$ etc. Note that from Definition 1 it follows that $_{IJ}F_{ij} = {}_{JI}F_{ji}$.

In fact, $_{IJ}F_{ij}$ can be viewed as a tensor of degree 2, that are covariant in both indices, which alludes to how the tensor components change when making coordinate changes in the images. Choose new coordinate systems in image I and J, by changing coordinates from $\mathbf{x}_I$ to $\hat{\mathbf{x}}_I$ according to $\mathbf{x}_I = S\hat{\mathbf{x}}_I$, i.e. $x_I^i = s_{i'}^i \hat{x}_I^{i'}$, where $s_{i'}^i$ denotes $(S)_{i',i}$, i.e. the element with row-index i and column-index i' of S and similarly for image J using the U instead of S. Then the tensor $_{IJ}\hat{F}_{i'j'}$ describing the relations between the new coordinates in image I and the coordinates in image J can be written

$$_{IJ}\hat{F}_{i'j'} = s_{i'}^i u_{j'}^j {}_{IJ}F_{ij} .$$

Finally, the tensor can be used to transfer a point in one image, say the point $\mathbf{x}_I$ in image I, to the corresponding epipolar line, $\mathbf{l}^J$ in the second image according to

$$l_j^J = {}_{IJ}F_{ij}x_I^i , \tag{8}$$

where $\mathbf{x}_I^i$ denote coordinate number i of $\mathbf{x}_I$ and $\mathbf{l}_j^J$ denote the dual coordinates of $\mathbf{l}^J$. The following incidence relation, which can be used to estimate the bifocal tensor, follows from (8)

$$_{IJ}F_{ij}\mathbf{x}_I^i\mathbf{x}_J^j = 0 \ . \tag{9}$$

Thus each corresponding point in two images gives one linear constraint on the bifocal tensor components, which gives the well-known theorem:

Theorem 1. *The bifocal tensor can be linearly estimated from at least 8 corresponding points in two images.*

The second type of minors from M_4 involves three rows from one camera matrix, two rows from another camera matrix and two rows from a third camera matrix, e.g.

$$\det \begin{bmatrix} A^1 & x_1 & 0 & 0 \\ A^2 & y_1 & 0 & 0 \\ A^3 & 1 & 0 & 0 \\ B^1 & 0 & x_2 & 0 \\ B^2 & 0 & y_2 & 0 \\ C^1 & 0 & 0 & x_3 \\ C^2 & 0 & 0 & y_3 \end{bmatrix} = 0 \ . \tag{10}$$

This type of minors are trilinear forms in the image coordinates of the three images. These trilinear forms express the well-known **trilinear constraints**, which also can be expressed using the **trifocal tensor**. In fact, the coefficients of the trilinear forms are the components of the trifocal tensor defined as follows.

Definition 2. *Using the notations in Definition 1, the tensor*

$$^{JK}_{I}T_i^{jk} = \epsilon_{ii'i''} \det \begin{bmatrix} P_I^{i'} \\ P_I^{i''} \\ P_J^{j} \\ P_K^{k} \end{bmatrix} \ ,$$

*where again Einsteins' summation convention has been used, is called the **trifocal tensor** corresponding to views I, J and K.*

When the notation in (5) has been used, the trifocal tensors will be denoted by $^{BC}_{A}T$, $^{AD}_{C}T$ etc. Note that from Definition 2 it follows that $^{BC}_{A}T_i^{jk} = -^{CB}_{A}T_i^{kj}$. Unfortunately the relation between $^{BC}_{A}T_i^{jk}$ and $^{AC}_{B}T_i^{jk}$ are not so easy to express.

The numbers $^{JK}_{I}T_i^{jk}$ can be viewed as a tensor of degree 3, that are covariant in one index and contravariant in the other indices. This means that making changes of coordinates in image I, image J and image K using matrices S, U and V, respectively, change the components of the tensor according to

$$^{JK}_{I}\hat{T}_{i'}^{j'k'} = s_{i'}^{i}\,\tilde{u}_{j}^{j'}\,\tilde{v}_{k}^{k'}\,^{JK}_{I}T_i^{jk} \ , \tag{11}$$

where $\tilde{u}^i_{i'}$ denote the entries of the inverse of U, i.e. $\tilde{u}^j_i u^k_j = \delta^k_i$, where δ^k_i denote the Kronecker delta, i.e. $\delta^i_i = 1$ and $\delta^k_i = 0$ when $i \neq k$. Observe that the tensor components change differently when coordinate changes are made in image I (contraction with $s^i_{i'}$) than when coordinate changes are made in image J or K (contraction with $\tilde{u}^{j'}_j$ or $\tilde{v}^{k'}_k$). Finally, the tensor can be used to transfer two lines in image J and image K, $\mathbf{l}^J$ and $\mathbf{l}^K$ to the corresponding line in image I, $\mathbf{l}^I$, see [3, 18] according to

$$l^I_i = {}^{JK}_I T^{jk}_i l^J_j l^K_k \ . \tag{12}$$

From (12), the following transfer equations follows, see also [18],

$$\mathbf{x}^j_J = {}^{JK}_I T^{jk}_i \mathbf{x}^i_I l^K_k , \quad \mathbf{x}^k_K = {}^{JK}_I T^{jk}_i \mathbf{x}^i_I l^J_j \ .$$

The following incidence relation, which can be used to estimate the trifocal tensor, follows from (12)

$${}^{JK}_I T^{jk}_i \mathbf{x}^i_I l^J_j l^K_k = 0 \ . \tag{13}$$

In (12) l^J_j can be replaced by $\epsilon_{jj'j''} \mathbf{x}^{j'}_J$, representing all lines through $\mathbf{x}_J$, see also [18], and similarly for l^K_k, giving

$$\begin{aligned}
{}^{JK}_I T^{jk}_i \mathbf{x}^i_I \epsilon_{jj'j''} \mathbf{x}^J_{j'} l^K_k &= 0, \\
{}^{JK}_I T^{jk}_i \mathbf{x}^i_I l^J_{j'} \epsilon_{kk'k''} \mathbf{x}^{k'}_K &= 0, \\
{}^{JK}_I T^{jk}_i \mathbf{x}^i_I \epsilon_{jj'j''} \mathbf{x}^{j'}_J \epsilon_{kk'k''} \mathbf{x}^{k'}_K &= 0 \ .
\end{aligned} \tag{14}$$

Thus each corresponding point in three images gives 9 linear constraint on the trifocal tensor components. However, it can easily be seen that for each fixed j, the equations in (14) give only two linearly independent constraints on the trifocal tensor components. Thus (14) gives 4 linearly independent constraints, giving the well-known theorem:

Theorem 2. *The trifocal tensor can be linearly estimated from at least 7 corresponding points in three images.*

The third type of minors from M_4 involves two rows from each of four different camera matrices, e.g.

$$\det \begin{bmatrix} A^1 & x_1 & 0 & 0 & 0 \\ A^2 & y_1 & 0 & 0 & 0 \\ B^1 & 0 & x_2 & 0 & 0 \\ B^2 & 0 & y_2 & 0 & 0 \\ C^1 & 0 & 0 & x_3 & 0 \\ C^2 & 0 & 0 & y_3 & 0 \\ D^1 & 0 & 0 & 0 & x_4 \\ D^2 & 0 & 0 & 0 & y_4 \end{bmatrix} = 0 \ . \tag{15}$$

This type of minors are quadlinear forms in the image coordinates of the four images. These quadlinear forms express the well-known **quadlinear constraints**, which also can be expressed using the **quadfocal tensor**. In fact, the coefficients of the quadlinear forms are the components of the quadfocal tensor defined as follows.

Definition 3. *The tensor*

$$^{IJKL}Q^{ijkl} = \det \begin{bmatrix} P_I^i \\ P_J^j \\ P_K^k \\ P_L^l \end{bmatrix} ,$$

is called the **quadfocal tensor** *corresponding to views I, J, K and L.*

When the notation in (5) has been used, the quadfocal tensors will be denoted by ^{ABCD}T, ^{CBAD}T etc. Note that from Definition 3 it follows that $^{ABCD}T^{ijkl} = -^{BACD}T_{jikl}$, and similarly for other permutations of the images.

The numbers $^{IJKL}Q^{ijkl}$ can be viewed as a tensor of degree 4, that are contravariant in all indices. This means that making changes of coordinates, for example in image 1 using the matrix S, changes the components of the tensor according to

$$^{IJKL}\hat{Q}^{i'jkl} = \bar{s}_i^{i'} \, ^{IJKL}Q^{ijkl} , \tag{16}$$

where again $\bar{s}_i^{i'}$ denotes the components of the inverse of S^T. Finally, the tensor can be used to transfer three lines, say in images J, K and L, $\mathbf{l}^J$, $\mathbf{l}^K$ and $\mathbf{l}^L$ to the corresponding point in image I, $\mathbf{x}_I$ according to

$$\mathbf{x}_I^i = \, ^{IJKL}Q^{ijkl}\mathbf{l}_j^J\mathbf{l}_k^K\mathbf{l}_l^L \tag{17}$$

and similarly for any permutation of the image I, J, K and L. The corresponding point in image L is the image of the 3D-point obtained from the intersection of the three planes defined by the optical centers and the corresponding lines in the other images. The following incidence relation, which can be used to estimate the quadfocal tensor, follows from (17)

$$^{IJKL}Q^{ijkl}\mathbf{l}_i^I\mathbf{l}_j^J\mathbf{l}_k^K\mathbf{l}_l^L = 0. \tag{18}$$

Similarly to the incidence relations for the trifocal tensor each occurrence of a line in (18) can be replaced by a point, using the permutation symbol, e.g.

$$^{IJKL}Q^{ijkl}\epsilon_{ii'i''}\mathbf{x}_{i'}^I\epsilon_{jj'j''}\mathbf{x}_{j'}^J\epsilon_{kk'k''}\mathbf{x}_{k'}^K\epsilon_{ll'l''}\mathbf{x}_{l'}^L = 0. \tag{19}$$

Thus each corresponding point in three images gives 27 linear constraint on the quadfocal tensor components. However, it can easily be seen that for each fixed j, k and l (14) gives only two linearly independent constraints on the trifocal tensor components. Thus (14) gives 16 linearly independent constraints for one point alone. However, it turns out that there exists a linear dependency between the 32 constraints obtained for two different corresponding points. The coefficients of this linear dependency can be expressed in the image coordinates, giving one linear dependency for every pair of points.

Theorem 3. *From $n < 6$ corresponding points in 4 images $16n - n(n-1)/2$ linearly independent constraints on the quadfocal tensor components can be obtained . From $n \geq 6$ corresponding points 80 linearly independent constraints can be obtained. Thus the components of the quadfocal tensor can be linearly calculated from at least 6 corresponding points in 4 images.*

Looking at the three different tensors in Definition 1, Definition 2 and Definition 3 we observe that all determinants of the matrices obtained by picking four rows from the different camera matrices P_I, P_j, P_K and P_L have been used except for the case of all three rows from one camera matrix and one row from another, e.g.

$$
\begin{bmatrix} P_I^1 \\ P_I^2 \\ P_I^3 \\ P_J^j \end{bmatrix} . \tag{20}
$$

The reason for this is that there are no minors of M_4 where coefficients of this type appear. Note that (20) can be interpreted as the j:th component of the epipole from camera I in image J, which can not be estimated directly from image measurements in the same way as the bifocal, trifocal and quadfocal tensors can be estimated. For the sake of completeness we make the following definition:

Definition 4. *The tensor*

$$
_{IJ}e^j = \det \begin{bmatrix} P_I^1 \\ P_I^2 \\ P_I^3 \\ P_J^j \end{bmatrix} ,
$$

*is called the **monofocal tensor** corresponding to views I and J.*

Observe that $_{IJ}e^j$ is a contravariant tensor of degree 1, which again alludes to the fact that a change of coordinates in image J, using the matrix S, changes the tensor components according to

$$
_{IJ}\hat{e}^{j'} = s_j^{j'} \, _{IJ}e^j .
$$

3 Representation of the Multiple View Geometry

We now turn to the question of how to represent the multiple view geometry. Looking at (3) it can be seen that if a given set of camera matrices P_i, fulfil (2), also the camera matrices P_iH fulfil (2), where H denotes an arbitrary nonsingular 4×4 matrix, if $\mathbf{X}$ is replaced by $H^{-1}\mathbf{X}$. This ambiguity in representation corresponds to arbitrary projective transformations of the object.

One way to represent the multiple view geometry is by taking the first four columns of M in (3), containing all camera matrices, i.e.

$$\mathbf{P} = \begin{bmatrix} P_1 \\ P_2 \\ \vdots \\ P_m \end{bmatrix} . \tag{21}$$

The previously mentioned ambiguity corresponds in this representation to the fact that $\mathbf{P}$ and $\mathbf{P}H$ represents the same viewing geometry. Observe that all tensor components are minors taken from $\mathbf{P}$ and replacing $\mathbf{P}$ by $\mathbf{P}H$ changes the overall scale of all tensor components by the factor det H. Another ambiguity in representation is the scale for every camera matrix P_i, which can be chosen arbitrarily. This can be seen from (2) by changing P_i to $\mu_i P_i$ and λ_i to $\mu_i \lambda_i$ and still obtaining a solution.

Proposition 1. *Let $\mathcal{G}$ denote the group of all projective transformations in 3D, represented by 4×4 matrices defined up to scale. Then the multiple view geometry for m views can be uniquely represented as an equivalence class of m 3×4 matrices defined up to scale under the action of right multiplication with elements from the group $\mathcal{G}$.*

From the proposition follows that the minimal number of parameters needed to represent the multiple view geometry for m views is $11m - 15$.

Note that the tensor components, i.e. the minors of $\mathbf{P}$ in (21) are Grassman coordinates of the linear subspace in R^{3m} spanned by the columns of $\mathbf{P}$. This indicates another way to look at the multiple view geometry, that is as this subspace, represented by its Grassman coordinates. However, the ambiguity corresponding to rescaling the camera matrices has not been taken into account. One natural way to do that is to use a slight generalization of the Grassman coordinates obtained as follows. We divide the set of Grassman coordinates into different subsets, each corresponding to one of the multiple view tensors. Then we define each subset of Grassman coordinates up to an unknown scale and use these modified Grassman coordinates as a representation.

Definition 5. *The set of multiple view tensor components, defined up to an unknown scale for each tensor, will be called* **modified Grassman coordinates**.

Proposition 2. *The multiple view geometry for m views can be uniquely represented by the modified Grassman coordinates, i.e. by the different multiple view tensors each one defined up to scale.*

This representation is of course not minimal, i.e. there exist dependencies between the different tensor components. For the ordinary Grassman coordinates, all such dependencies can be written as so called **quadratic p-relations**, see [11]. These can be written

$$p_{i_1 i_2 i_3 i_4} p_{j_1 j_2 j_3 j_4} - p_{j_1 i_2 i_3 i_4} p_{i_1 j_2 j_3 j_4} +$$
$$p_{j_2 i_2 i_3 i_4} p_{j_1 i_1 j_3 j_4} - p_{j_3 i_2 i_3 i_4} p_{j_1 j_2 i_1 j_4} + p_{j_4 i_2 i_3 i_4} p_{j_1 j_2 j_3 i_1} = 0 , \tag{22}$$

where p_{ijkl} denotes the determinant of the matrix obtained from rows i, j, k and l from $\mathbf{P}$ in (21). One example is, using the notation $[A^2 A^3 B^1 B^2]$ for the determinant of the matrix formed by the rows A^2, A^3, B^1 and B^2,

$$[A^2 A^3 B^1 B^2][A^1 A^2 A^3 B^3] - [A^1 A^2 A^3 B^2][B^1 A^2 A^3 B^3] + [A^1 A^2 A^3 B^1][B^2 A^2 A^3 B^3]$$
$$= {}_{AB}F_{13} \cdot {}_{AB}e^3 + {}_{AB}F_{12} \cdot {}_{AB}e^2 + {}_{AB}F_{11} \cdot {}_{AB}e^1 = 0 \ ,$$

i.e. the well-known fact that the epipole in image 2 can be obtained as the left nullspace to the fundamental matrix between images 1 and 2.

A necessary and sufficient condition for numbers p_{ijkl} to be Grassman coordinates of a subspace is that they fulfil all quadratic p-relations. Thus given a subset of multiple view tensors, the relation between the components of this subset of tensors can be obtained by considering the ideal of all quadratic p-relations and then calculating the elimination ideal, where the tensor components outside the subset have been eliminated. Another application of the quadratic p-relations is to calculate one tensor from other tensor/tensors and to calculate a representation of the multiple view geometry in form of the camera matrices. These two applications will be described in the next sections.

From the representation $\mathbf{P}$ in (21) and the action of the group $\mathcal{G}$ of all projective transformations in 3D on $\mathbf{P}$, a unique representative of camera matrices can be obtained by setting $P_1 = [I \,|\, 0]$, P_2^1 proportional to $[0\,0\,0\,1]$ and fixing the scale of the other camera matrices arbitrarily. According to the definition of the multiple view tensors, this normal form can be written, in the case of 4 images, as

$$\mathbf{P}_n = \begin{bmatrix}
1 & 0 & 0 & 0 \\
0 & 1 & 0 & 0 \\
0 & 0 & 1 & 0 \\
0 & 0 & 0 & {}_{AB}e^1 \\
-{}_{AB}F_{13} & {}_{AB}F_{23} & -{}_{AB}F_{33} & {}_{AB}e^2 \\
{}_{AB}F_{12} & -{}_{AB}F_{22} & {}_{AB}F_{32} & {}_{AB}e^3 \\
{}_{A}^{BC}T_1^{11} & {}_{A}^{BC}T_2^{11} & {}_{A}^{BC}T_3^{11} & {}_{AC}e^1 \\
{}_{A}^{BC}T_1^{12} & {}_{A}^{BC}T_2^{12} & {}_{A}^{BC}T_3^{12} & {}_{AC}e^2 \\
{}_{A}^{BC}T_1^{13} & {}_{A}^{BC}T_2^{13} & {}_{A}^{BC}T_3^{13} & {}_{AC}e^3 \\
{}_{A}^{BD}T_1^{11} & {}_{A}^{BD}T_2^{11} & {}_{A}^{BD}T_3^{11} & {}_{AD}e^1 \\
{}_{A}^{BD}T_1^{12} & {}_{A}^{BD}T_2^{12} & {}_{A}^{BD}T_3^{12} & {}_{AD}e^2 \\
{}_{A}^{BD}T_1^{13} & {}_{A}^{BD}T_2^{13} & {}_{A}^{BD}T_3^{13} & {}_{AD}e^3
\end{bmatrix} . \tag{23}$$

Observe that the scale for the block containing ${}_{AB}F$ can be fixed independently of the scale of the block containing ${}_{AB}e$, giving $5 + 2 = 7$ parameters for the first two views and $7 + 11(n - 2)$ parameters for $n > 2$ views. It follows that the camera matrices are determined from the fundamental matrix between views 1 and 2, the trifocal tensors between views 1, 2 and $i \geq 3$ and the epipoles in image 1 from image $i \geq 2$, when the scales between ${}_{AB}F$ and ${}_{AB}e$ and between ${}_{1}^{2I}T$ and ${}_{11}e$ have been determined. These scales can easily be obtained by calculating suitable minors of $\mathbf{P}_n$, e.g. the expression for ${}_{A}^{BC}T_1^{21}$ gives one linear constraint on these scales. We conclude this section with the observation that minimal parametrizations of the multiple view geometry can easily be obtained from (23).

4 Two Views

In this section we will study the case of two images in detail. The only tensors appearing here are the bifocal tensors $_{AB}F$ and $_{BA}F$ and the two monofocal tensors $_{AB}e$ and $_{BA}e$. The relations between them can be obtained by exploring the quadratic p-relations. Putting $i_1 = 1$, $i_2 = 2$, $i_3 = 3$, $i_4 = 6$, $j_1 = 2$, $j_2 = 3$, $j_3 = 4$ and $j_4 = 5$ gives the quadratic p-relation

$$[A^1 A^2 A^3 B^3][A^2 A^3 B^1 B^2] - [B^1 A^2 A^3 B^3][A^1 A^2 A^3 B^2] + [B^2 A^2 A^3 B^3][A^1 A^2 A^3 B^1]$$
$$= {}_{AB}e^3 \cdot {}_{AB}F_{13} + {}_{AB}F_{12} \cdot {}_{AB}e^2 + {}_{AB}F_{11} \cdot {}_{AB}e^1 = 0 \ .$$

Similar quadratic p-relations give

$$_{AB}F_{ij} \cdot {}_{AB}e^i = 0, \quad {}_{AB}F_{ij} \cdot {}_{BA}e^j = 0 \tag{24}$$

and similarly for $_{BA}F$. From (24) it follows that $_{AB}F_{ij}$ constitute the components of a matrix, denoted $_{AB}F_{\bullet\bullet}$, which is singular and whose right nullspace is $_{BA}e$ and whose left nullspace is $_{AB}e$. This means that $_{BA}e$ and $_{AB}e$ can be found up to proportionality by considering suitable minors of $_{AB}F_{\bullet\bullet}$. In fact, putting $i_1 = 1$, $i_2 = 1$, $i_3 = 3$, $i_4 = 4$, $j_1 = 2$, $j_2 = 4$, $j_3 = 5$ and $j_4 = 6$ gives the quadratic p-relation

$$- [A^2 A^1 A^3 B^1][A^1 B^1 B^2 B^3] - [B^2 A^1 A^3 B^1][A^1 A^2 B^1 B^3] +$$
$$+ [A^1 A^3 B^1 B^3][A^1 A^2 B^1 B^2] = 0 \ .$$

Similar quadratic p-relations give

$$
\begin{array}{lll}
F_{22}F_{33} - F_{23}F_{32} = e^1 \bar{e}^1, & F_{23}F_{31} - F_{21}F_{33} = e^1 \bar{e}^2, & F_{21}F_{32} - F_{22}F_{31} = e^1 \bar{e}^3, \\
F_{13}F_{32} - F_{12}F_{33} = e^2 \bar{e}^1, & F_{11}F_{33} - F_{13}F_{31} = e^2 \bar{e}^2, & F_{12}F_{31} - F_{11}F_{32} = e^2 \bar{e}^3, \\
F_{12}F_{23} - F_{13}F_{22} = e^3 \bar{e}^1, & F_{13}F_{21} - F_{11}F_{23} = e^3 \bar{e}^2, & F_{11}F_{22} - F_{12}F_{21} = e^3 \bar{e}^3,
\end{array}
\tag{25}
$$

where $F = {}_{AB}F$, $e = {}_{AB}e$ and $\bar{e} = {}_{BA}e$ giving the proportionality factors from the minors. Let $\mathrm{adj}(F)$ denote the adjoint matrix to $_{AB}F_{\bullet\bullet}$. Then the equations in (25) can be interpreted as

$$\mathrm{adj}(F) = {}_{AB}e^T \cdot {}_{BA}e \ . \tag{26}$$

Thus the epipoles can be calculated directly from the fundamental matrix, with correct scale factors, using (26). From noisy data this can easily be established from the singular value decomposition of $\mathrm{adj}(F)$. Moreover this means that a representative for the multiple view geometry in the form of (23) can be written out directly. Finally, we conclude this section with the well known theorem:

Theorem 4. *The numbers $_{AB}F_{ij}$ constitute the components of a bifocal tensor if and only if $_{AB}F_{\bullet\bullet}$ is a singular matrix.*

Proof. The necessity of the conditions follows from (24). The sufficiency follows from the fact that a representative of the bifocal geometry can be obtained from such numbers $_{AB}F_{ij}$, with these numbers as Grassman coordinates.

Observe that in non-degenerate cases $\operatorname{rank}_{AB}F_{\bullet\bullet} = 2$.

5 Three Views

In this section we will study the case of three views in detail. The tensors appearing here are the six trifocal tensors $^{BC}_{A}T$, $^{CB}_{A}T$, $^{AC}_{B}T$, etc., the six bifocal tensors $_{BA}F$, $_{BA}F$, $_{AC}F$ etc., and the six monofocal tensors $_{AB}e$, $_{BA}e$, $_{AC}e$, etc. Taking the previously mentioned symmetries into account, we have essentially 3 trifocal tensors, 3 bifocal tensors and 6 monofocal tensors. The relations between them can be obtained by exploring the quadratic p-relations. We will show how these quadratic p-relations can be used to calculate one trifocal tensor from another, how the bifocal tensors can be calculated from the trifocal tensors and finally how a representative of the trifocal geometry can be obtained.

Studying quadratic p-relations of the type

$$[B^1A^1A^2B^3][A^1A^2B^2C^1] - [B^2A^1A^2B^3][A^1A^2B^1C^1] + [C^1A^1A^2B^3][A^1A^2B^1B^2]$$
$$= -_{AB}F_{32} \cdot {}^{BC}_{A}T^{21}_3 - _{AB}F_{31} \cdot {}^{BC}_{A}T^{11}_3 - {}^{BC}_{A}T^{31}_3 \cdot {}_{AB}F_{33} = 0$$

give the following relations, writing $F = {}_{AB}F$, $\bar{F} = {}_{AC}F$ and $T = {}^{BC}_{A}T$,

$$T^{j1}_i F_{1j} = 0, \quad T^{j2}_i F_{2j} = 0, \quad T^{j3}_i F_{3j} = 0,$$
$$T^{1k}_i \bar{F}_{1k} = 0, \quad T^{2k}_i \bar{F}_{2k} = 0, \quad T^{3k}_i \bar{F}_{3k} = 0 , \tag{27}$$

implying that $F_{i\bullet}$ and $\bar{F}_{i\bullet}$ can be obtained as the left and right nullspace respectively to the matrix $T^{\bullet\bullet}_i$. However, the scale between $F_{i\bullet}$ for different i can not be determined in this way. Since the monofocal tensor $_{AB}e$, according to (24), can be obtained from $F_{i\bullet}$, we can also calculate the epipoles $_{AB}e$ and $_{AC}e$ easily from $^{BC}_{A}T$. The simplest way to obtain the scale between the different $F_{i\bullet}$, as well as the other fundamental matrices and epipoles, is to calculate the other trifocal tensors from $^{BC}_{A}T$. For this calculation study the quadratic p-relation

$$[A^1A^3B^2C^1][A^2B^1B^2C^1] - [A^2A^3B^2C^1][A^1B^1B^2C^1] + [B^1A^3B^2C^1][A^1A^2B^2C^1]$$
$$= {}^{BC}_{A}T^{21}_2 \cdot {}^{AC}_{B}T^{21}_3 + {}^{BC}_{A}T^{21}_1 \cdot {}^{AC}_{B}T^{11}_3 + {}^{AC}_{B}T^{31}_3 \cdot {}^{BC}_{A}T^{21}_3 = 0 .$$

Similar quadratic p-relations give, using the notation $T = {}^{BC}_{A}T$ and $U = {}^{AC}_{B}T$,

$$T^{1K}_i U^{iK}_3, \quad T^{2K}_i U^{iK}_3, \quad T^{1K}_i U^{iK}_2, \quad T^{3K}_i U^{iK}_2, \quad T^{2K}_i U^{iK}_1, \quad T^{3K}_i U^{iK}_1 , \tag{28}$$

where $K = 1, 2, 3$ is fixed and summation is done over i only. Thus (28) implies that $U_j^{\bullet k}$ can be obtained up to an unknown scale from T as the cross products of $T_\bullet^{j'k}$ and $T_\bullet^{j''k}$, where j, j' and j'' are different. A correct scale between different $U_j^{\bullet k}$ can be obtained from the quadratic p-relations:

$$\begin{aligned}
T_\bullet^{1K} \times T_\bullet^{2K} &= {}_{AC}e^K U_3^{\bullet K}, \\
T_\bullet^{1K} \times T_\bullet^{3K} &= {}_{AC}e^K U_2^{\bullet K}, \\
T_\bullet^{2K} \times T_\bullet^{3K} &= {}_{AC}e^K U_1^{\bullet K},
\end{aligned} \tag{29}$$

where $a \times b$ denotes the cross-product of the vectors a and b. Since ${}_{AC}e^K$ can be calculated from T as described above, the scale between different $U_j^{\bullet k}$ can be recovered. Thus all trifocal tensors can be calculated from ${}_A^{BC}T$. Moreover, from ${}_B^{AC}T$, it is possible to calculate ${}_{AB}F_{\bullet j}$ from equations similar to (27). Finally, when both ${}_{AB}F_{i\bullet}$ and ${}_{AB}F_{\bullet j}$ are known, up to scale, it is possible to calculate ${}_{AB}F$. We have thus shown how to calculate everything from ${}_A^{BC}T$, using only polynomial equations of degree 2.

From (27) and (24), it follows that the components of the trifocal tensor must fulfil

$$\det T_i^{\bullet\bullet} = 0 \quad \text{and} \quad \det[\mathcal{N}(T_1^{\bullet\bullet})\mathcal{N}(T_2^{\bullet\bullet})\mathcal{N}(T_3^{\bullet\bullet})] = 0 \ . \tag{30}$$

Moreover, since T_i^{jk} is a third order tensor that transforms according to (11) and that the conditions on the tensor components in (30) are generic, i.e. independent of the chosen coordinate systems in the images, it follows that (30) are valid also when T_i are replaced by $\lambda_{ij}T_j$ for any nonsingular matrix with components λ_{ij}. In fact, we have

Theorem 5. *A necessary and sufficient condition for 27 numbers T_i^{jk} to constitute the components of a trifocal tensor is*

$$\det \lambda_i T_i^{\bullet\bullet} = 0, \quad \forall \lambda_i \quad and \quad \det[\mathcal{N}(T_1^{\bullet\bullet})\mathcal{N}(T_2^{\bullet\bullet})\mathcal{N}(T_3^{\bullet\bullet})] = 0 \ . \tag{31}$$

Proof. The necessity follows from the previous discussion. For the sufficiency see [3]. ∎

Another property of the trifocal tensor is that it has rank 4, where the rank of a tensor is defined as the minimal number of terms needed in order to write the tensor as a sum of rank 1 tensors and a rank 1 tensor is an outer product of three vectors. This fact has been proven in [14], however, a simpler proof will be given here.

Theorem 6. *The trifocal tensor, T, fulfils*

$$\operatorname{rank} T = 4 \ .$$

Proof. First observe that the rank of the trifocal tensor is a generic property, i.e. it does not depend on the chosen coordinate systems in the images. Thus, we may chose a representative for the multiple view geometry, using the camera matrices

$$P_1 = \begin{bmatrix} 1 & 0 & 0 & 0 \\ 0 & 1 & 0 & 0 \\ 0 & 0 & 1 & 0 \end{bmatrix}, \quad P_2 = \begin{bmatrix} 0 & 0 & 0 & 1 \\ 1 & 0 & 0 & 0 \\ 0 & 1 & 0 & 0 \end{bmatrix}, \quad P_3 = \begin{bmatrix} 0 & 0 & 1 & 0 \\ 0 & 0 & 0 & 1 \\ 1 & 0 & 0 & 0 \end{bmatrix}, \quad (32)$$

i.e. by choosing a 3D coordinate system such that the focal points of the three cameras have projective coordinates $(0, 0, 0, 1)$, $(0, 0, 1, 0)$ and $(0, 1, 0, 0)$, respectively and the 2D coordinate systems in the images have been chosen such that the remaining 3×3 part of the camera matrix becomes the identity matrix. Calculating the trifocal tensor from the camera matrices in (32) gives $T_i^{jk} = 0$ except for,

$$T_3^{11} = -1, \quad T_1^{22} = 1, \quad T_2^{32} = 1 \quad \text{and} \quad T_1^{13} = -1 , \quad (33)$$

which immediately implies that rank $T \leq 4$. Looking at the nonzero coefficients of T in (33), it is obvious that it is not possible to write T as a sum of less than 4 rank 1 tensors. This observation concludes the proof.

We conclude this section by showing how a representative of the multiple view geometry can be obtained from the trifocal tensor, T. Starting from T, we have shown how to calculate $_{AB}F$, $_{AB}e$ and $_{AC}e$, up to scale. Thus everything in (23) is known apart from the scale between T and $_{AC}e$, that has to be compatible with the other fixed scales (the ones for T, $_{AB}F$ and $_{AB}e$. This scale can be obtained from (23) by calculating minors corresponding to T_i^{jk}, when $j \neq 1$. The expressions obtained from these minors can also be derived from suitable quadratic p-relations.

6   Four Views

We now turn to the case of four views, where the tensors appearing are the quad-focal tensor, 12 trifocal tensors, 6 bifocal tensors and 12 monofocal tensors, when the symmetries have been taken into account. We will show how the quadratic p-relations can be used to calculate one trifocal tensor from the quadfocal tensor and how a representative of the quadfocal geometry can be obtained.

The quadratic p-relations of the type

$$[A^1 B^1 C^1 D^1][A^2 A^3 B^1 C^1] - [A^2 B^1 C^1 D^1][A^1 A^3 B^1 C^1] + [A^3 B^1 C^1 D^1][A^1 A^2 B^1 C^1]$$
$$= {}^{ABCD}Q^{1111} \cdot {}^{BC}_{A}T_1^{11} + {}^{ABCD}Q^{2111} \cdot {}^{BC}_{A}T_2^{11} + {}^{ABCD}Q^{3111} \cdot {}^{BC}_{A}T_3^{11} = 0 ,$$

imply that, writing $Q = {}^{ABCD}Q$,

$$
\begin{array}{lll}
Q^{iJKl} \cdot {}^{BC}_{A}T_i^{JK} = 0, & Q^{iJkL} \cdot {}^{BD}_{A}T_i^{JL} = 0, & Q^{ijKL} \cdot {}^{CD}_{A}T_i^{KL} = 0, \\
Q^{IjKl} \cdot {}^{AC}_{B}T_j^{IK} = 0, & Q^{IjkL} \cdot {}^{AD}_{B}T_j^{IL} = 0, & Q^{ijKL} \cdot {}^{CD}_{B}T_j^{KL} = 0, \\
Q^{IJkl} \cdot {}^{AB}_{C}T_k^{IJ} = 0, & Q^{IjkL} \cdot {}^{AD}_{C}T_k^{IL} = 0, & Q^{iJkL} \cdot {}^{BD}_{C}T_k^{JL} = 0, \\
Q^{IJkl} \cdot {}^{AB}_{D}T_l^{IJ} = 0, & Q^{IjKl} \cdot {}^{AC}_{D}T_l^{IK} = 0, & Q^{iJKl} \cdot {}^{BC}_{D}T_l^{JK} = 0 ,
\end{array}
\quad (34)
$$

where again capital letters denotes indices where no summation is done. Thus $_{BC}^{A}T_{\bullet}^{ij}$, etc. can be calculated, up to scale, from Q. A first step towards the fixation of these scales is to consider quadratic p-relations of the type

$$-[A^2 A^1 A^3 B^1][A^1 B^1 C^1 D^1] - [C^1 A^1 A^3 B^1][A^1 A^2 B^1 D^1] +$$
$$[D^1 A^1 A^3 B^1][A^1 A^2 B^1 C^1] =$$
$$= {}_{AB}e^1 \cdot {}^{ABCD}Q^{1111} - {}_{A}^{BC}T_2^{11} \cdot {}_{A}^{BD}T_3^{11} - {}_{A}^{BD}T_2^{11} \cdot {}_{A}^{BC}T_3^{11} = 0 \ .$$

Similar quadratic p-relations gives the following equations, writing $T = {}_{A}^{BC}T$, $U = {}_{A}^{BD}T$ and $e = {}_{AB}e$,

$$T_{\bullet}^{JK} \times U_{\bullet}^{JL} = e^J Q^{\bullet JKL} \ , \tag{35}$$

making it possible to recover the scale between $T_{\bullet}^{JK}$ for different K by fixing $U_{\bullet}^{JL}$. What remains to do is to calculate the scale between $T_{\bullet}^{J\bullet}$ for different J. This can be done from quadratic p-relations, similar to the ones in (35),

$$_{A}^{BC}T_{\bullet}^{JK} \times {}_{A}^{CD}T_{\bullet}^{KL} = e^K Q^{\bullet JKL} \ . \tag{36}$$

We have thus shown how to calculate the trifocal tensor $_{A}^{BC}T$ from the quadfocal tensor ^{ABCD}Q. This implies that all trifocal tensors can be calculated from the quadfocal tensor and also all bifocal and monofocal tensor using the methods presented in the previous sections.

Looking at (34) and using the transformation properties of the quadfocal tensor we get the following theorem.

Theorem 7. *A necessary condition for* 81 *numbers* Q^{ijkl} *to constitute the components of a quadfocal tensor is*

$$\det(\lambda_{ij}^1 Q^{ij\bullet\bullet}) = 0, \quad \det(\lambda_{ik}^2 Q^{i\bullet k\bullet}) = 0, \quad \det(\lambda_{il}^3 Q^{i\bullet\bullet l}) = 0,$$
$$\det(\lambda_{jk}^4 Q^{\bullet jk\bullet}) = 0, \quad \det(\lambda_{jl}^5 Q^{\bullet j\bullet l}) = 0, \quad \det(\lambda_{kl}^6 Q^{\bullet\bullet kl}) = 0 \ , \tag{37}$$

where λ_{ij}^m *denote the components of arbitrary nonsingular matrices.*

The question of whether or not the equations in (37) also are sufficient, is to our knowledge open.

Another property of the quadfocal tensor is that it has rank 9, where the rank of a fourth order tensor is defined similarly to the case of a third order tensor, described above.

Theorem 8. *The quadfocal tensor, Q, fulfils*

$$\text{rank } Q = 9 \ .$$

Proof. The proof is similar to the proof of rank of the trifocal tensor. Choose coordinate systems according to (32) and

$$P_3 = \begin{bmatrix} 0 & 1 & 0 & 0 \\ 0 & 0 & 1 & 0 \\ 0 & 0 & 0 & 1 \end{bmatrix} \tag{38}$$

calculate the quadfocal tensor. This gives $Q^{ijkl} = 0$ except for

$$Q^{1111} = -1, \quad Q^{3221} = -1, \quad Q^{3131} = 1,$$
$$Q^{1322} = -1, \quad Q^{2222} = 1, \quad Q^{2132} = -1, \tag{39}$$
$$Q^{1313} = 1, \quad Q^{2213} = -1 \quad \text{and} \quad Q^{3333} = -1 ,$$

which in the same way as for the trifocal tensor implies that rank $Q = 9$.

We conclude this section by showing how a representative of the multiple view geometry can be obtained from the quadfocal tensor, Q. Starting from Q, we have shown how to calculate ${}^{BC}_{A}T$, ${}^{BD}_{A}T$, ${}_{AB}F$, ${}_{AB}e$, ${}_{AC}e$ and ${}_{AD}e$, up to scale. Thus everything in (23) is known apart from the scale between ${}^{BC}_{A}T$ and ${}_{AC}e$ and the scale between ${}^{BD}_{A}T$ and ${}_{AD}e$ that has to be compatible with the other fixed scales. This scale can be obtained from (23) by calculating minors from (23) corresponding to Q^{ijkl}, for all i, j, k and l. The expressions obtained from these minors can also be derived from suitable quadratic p-relations.

7   Conclusions

In this paper we have presented a new framework for multiple view geometry and multiple view tensors, using Grassman coordinates and quadratic p-relations. Using this framework, relations between different tensors and constraints on tensor components can be derived. This has been exemplified by calculating bifocal tensors from a trifocal tensor and by calculating trifocal tensors from a quadfocal tensor. Having these tools available, it is possible to calculate a representative of the multiple view geometry, in the form of the camera matrices, from different combinations of multiple view tensors. It has also been shown that the rank of the trifocal tensor is 4 and that the rank of the quadfocal tensor is 9. Finally, we have proved that it is possible to recover the quadfocal tensor from at least 6 corresponding points in 4 images linearly. Using the previously mentioned methods, the camera matrices can be calculated from the tensor components and, finally, a reconstruction can be obtained.

References

1. O. Faugeras and B. Mourrain. About the correspondence of points between n images. In *IEEE Workshop on Representation of Visual Scenes, MIT, Boston, MA*, pages 37–44. IEEE Computer Society Press, 1995.
2. O. Faugeras and B. Mourrain. On the geometry and algebra of the point and line correspondences between n images. In *Proc. 5th Int. Conf. on Computer Vision, MIT, Boston, MA*, pages 951–956. IEEE Computer Society Press, 1995.
3. O. Faugeras and T. Papadopoulo. Grassman-cayley algebra for modeling systems of cameras and the algebraic equations of the manifold of trifocal tensors. Technical Report 3225, Institut national de recherche en informatique et en automatique, july 1997.

4. O. Faugeras and T. Papadopoulo. A nonlinear method for estimating the projective geometry of three views. In *Proc. 6th Int. Conf. on Computer Vision, Mumbai, India*, 1998. to appear.

5. B. Gelbaum. *Linear Algebra : Basic, Practice and Theory*. North-Holand, 1989.

6. R. Hartley. A linear method for reconstruction from points and lines. In *Proc. 5th Int. Conf. on Computer Vision, MIT, Boston, MA*, pages 882–887. IEEE Computer Society Press, 1995.

7. R. Hartley. Lines and points in three views and the trifocal tensor. *Int. Journal of Computer Vision*, 22(2):125–140, March 1997.

8. A. Heyden. Reconstruction from image sequences by means of relative depths. *Int. Journal of Computer Vision*, 24(2):155–161, September 1997. also in Proc. of the 5th International Conference on Computer Vision, IEEE Computer Society Press, pp. 1058-1063.

9. A. Heyden and K. Åström. Algebraic varieties in multiple view geometry. In B. Buxton and R. Cipolla, editors, *Proc. 4th European Conf. on Computer Vision, Cambridge, UK*, volume 1065 of *Lecture notes in Computer Science*, pages 671–682. Springer-Verlag, 1996.

10. A. Heyden and K. Åström. Algebraic properties of multilinear constraints. *Mathematical Methods in the Applied Scinces*, 20:1135–1162, 1997.

11. W. V. D. Hodge and D. Pedoe. *Methods of Algebraic Geometry*. Cambridge University Press, 1947.

12. Q.-T. Luong and T. Vieville. Canonic representations for the geometries of multiple projective views. In J.-O. Eklund, editor, *Proc. 4th European Conf. on Computer Vision, Cambridge, UK*, volume 800 of *Lecture Notes in Computer Science*, pages 589–599. Springer-Verlag, 1994.

13. A. Shashua. Trilinearity in visual recognition by alignment. In J.-O. Eklund, editor, *Proc. 4th European Conf. on Computer Vision, Cambridge, UK*, volume 800 of *Lecture Notes in Computer Science*, pages 479–484. Springer-Verlag, 1994.

14. A. Shashua and S. Maybank. Degenerate n point configurations of three views: Do critical surfaces exist? Technical Report TR 96-19, Hebrew University of Jerusalem, 1996.

15. A. Shashua and M. Werman. On the trilinear tensor of three perspective views and its associated tensor. In *Proc. 5th Int. Conf. on Computer Vision, MIT, Boston, MA*, pages 920–925. IEEE Computer Society Press, 1995.

16. M. E. Spetsakis and J. Aloimonos. A unified theory of structure from motion. In *Proc. DARPA IU Workshop*, pages 271–283, 1990.

17. B. Triggs. Matching constraints and the joint image. In *Proc. 5th Int. Conf. on Computer Vision, MIT, Boston, MA*, pages 338–343. IEEE Computer Society Press, 1995.

18. A. Zisserman. A users guide to the trifocal tensor. Draft, july 1996.

Computation of the Quadrifocal Tensor

Richard I. Hartley

G.E. Corporate Research and Development
1 Research Circle,
Niskayuna, NY 12309,
USA

Abstract. This paper gives a practical and accurate algorithm for the computation of the quadrifocal tensor and extraction of camera matrices from it. Previous methods for using the quadrifocal tensor in projective scene reconstruction have not emphasized accuracy of the algorithm in conditions of noise. Methods given in this paper minimize algebraic error either through a non-iterative linear algorithm, or two alternative iterative algorithms. It is shown by experiments with synthetic data that the iterative methods, though minimizing algebraic, rather than more correctly geometric error measured in the image, give almost optimal results.

Keywords

Calibration and Pose Estimation, Stereo and Motion, Image Sequence Analysis, Algebraic error, Quadrifocal tensor

1 Introduction

In the study of the geometry of multiple views, the fundamental matrix and more recently the trifocal tensor have proven to be essential tools. The quadrifocal tensor which relates coordinates measured in four views is the natural extension of these techniques to four views. Because of the added stability of a fourth view, and the more tightly it constrains the position of reconstructed points in space, use of the quadrifocal tensor should lead to greater accuracy than two and three-view techniques. This hypothesis is supported by the results of Heyden ([6, 5]). However, the four-view tensor has not been given much attention in the literature. One of the main impediments to its use is the fact that the quadrifocal tensor is very greatly overparametrized, using 81 components of the tensor to describe a geometric confuguration that depends only on 29 parameters. This can lead to severe inaccuracies if additional constraints are not applied. One method of doing this was proposed by Heyden, who defined the reduced quadrifocal tensor. This has the effect of partially constraining the solution, but still leaves many (in fact 32) unresolved constraints.

In this paper, a method is given for computing the quadrifocal tensor and extracting camera parameters in a way so as to satisfy all constraints on the tensor, while at the same time minimizing the algebraic measurement error. The results obtained prove to be near optimal in terms of minimizing residual error in the measured image coordinates.

2   The Quadrifocal Tensor

The quadrifocal tensor was discovered by Triggs ([8]) and an algorithm for using it for reconstruction was given by Heyden ([6,5]). However, because the quadrifocal tensor is not so widely understood as the fundamental matrix, or the trifocal tensor, a derivation of its properties and description of existing algorithms is given here. The only previously existing algorithm for computation of the quadrifocal tensor and extraction of the camera matrix is due to Heyden ([6,5]). This algorithm will be described below, since most of the material will be needed for the description of a new algorithm.

Consider four cameras P, P′, P″ and P‴, and let $\mathbf{x}$ be a point in space imaged by the four cameras. Let the corresponding image points in the four images be denoted by $\mathbf{u}$, $\mathbf{u}'$, $\mathbf{u}''$ and $\mathbf{u}'''$ respectively. We write $\mathbf{u} \approx \mathsf{P}\mathbf{x}$, and similarly for the other images. The notation $\approx$ indicated that the two sides of the equation are equal, up to an unknown scale factor. Taking account of the scale factor, there are constants k, k', k'' and k''' such that $k\mathbf{u} = \mathsf{P}\mathbf{x}$, $k'\mathbf{u}' = \mathsf{P}'\mathbf{x}$, and so on for the other two images. This set of equations may be written as a single matrix equation as follows:

$$
\begin{bmatrix}
\mathbf{a}^1 \ u^1 & & & \\
\mathbf{a}^2 \ u^2 & & & \\
\mathbf{a}^3 \ u^3 & & & \\
\hline
\mathbf{b}^1 & u'^1 & & \\
\mathbf{b}^2 & u'^2 & & \\
\mathbf{b}^3 & u'^3 & & \\
\hline
\mathbf{c}^1 & & u''^1 & \\
\mathbf{c}^2 & & u''^2 & \\
\mathbf{c}^3 & & u''^3 & \\
\hline
\mathbf{d}^1 & & & u'''^1 \\
\mathbf{d}^2 & & & u'''^2 \\
\mathbf{d}^3 & & & u'''^3
\end{bmatrix}
\begin{pmatrix}
\mathbf{x} \\ -k \\ -k' \\ -k'' \\ -k'''
\end{pmatrix} = 0
\tag{1}
$$

where vectors $\mathbf{a}^i$, $\mathbf{b}^i$, $\mathbf{c}^i$ and $\mathbf{d}^i$ are the row vectors of the matrices P, P′, P″ and P″ respectively.

Since this equation has a solution, the matrix X on the left has rank at most 7, and so all 8×8 determinants are zero. Any determinant containing fewer than two rows from each of the camera matrices gives rise to a trilinear or bilinear relation between the remaining cameras. A different case occurs when we consider 8×8

determinants containing two rows from each of the camera matrices. Expansion of the determinant leads directly to a quadrilinear relationship of the form

$$u^i u'^j u''^k u'''^l \epsilon_{ipw} \epsilon_{jqx} \epsilon_{kry} \epsilon_{lsz} Q^{pqrs} = 0_{wxyz} \tag{2}$$

where 0_{wxyz} is a zero tensor with four indices w, x, y and z, and the rank-4 tensor Q^{pqrs} is defined by

$$Q^{pqrs} = \det \begin{bmatrix} \mathbf{a}^p \\ \mathbf{b}^q \\ \mathbf{c}^r \\ \mathbf{d}^s \end{bmatrix} \tag{3}$$

The tensor ϵ_{ijk} is defined to be zero unless i, j and k are distinct, and otherwise equal to 1 or -1 depending on whether (ijk) is an even or odd permutation of (123). We use the tensor summation convention in which an index repeated in upper (contravariant) and lower (covariant) positions implies summation of all values $1, 2, 3$ of the index.

Note that the four indices of the four-view tensor are contravariant A discussion of tensors, contravariant and covariant indices is found in an appendix of [2]. Note that for this *quadrifocal tensor* there is no distinguished view as there is in the case of the trifocal tensor. There is only one quadrifocal tensor corresponding to four given views. More details of this derivation, and the equations that may be derived from it are given in [4].

Each point correspondence across four views gives rise via (2) to 81 equations in the entries of Q, one equation for each of the choices of indices w, x, y, z. Among these equations, there are 16 linearly independent equations in the 81 entries of the quadrifocal tensor Q. From a set of several point correspondences across four views one obtains a set of linear equations of the form $\mathbf{Aq} = 0$ where $\mathbf{q}$ is a vector containing the entries of Q. Since Q is defined only up to scale, it may appear that from 5 point correspondences there are enough equations to compute Q. However, the sets of equations arising from different point correspondences have a linear relationship, as shown in [4]. It turns out that 6 points are required to solve for Q. With 6 points or more, one may solve a linear least-squares problem to find Q.

It is also possible to derive equations involving the quadrifocal tensor from line correspondences, or mixed line-point correspondences, as explained in [4]. All the techniques of this paper are applicable to line or mixed point-line correspondences as well, but we omit further mention of this point.

2.1 Algebraic Error

In the presence of noise, one can not expect to obtain an exact solution to an overconstrained set of equations of the form $\mathbf{Aq} = \mathbf{0}$ such as those that arise from a point correspondence in 4 views. The linear least-squares algorithm instead finds the unit-norm vector $\mathbf{q}$ that minimizes $\|\mathbf{Aq}\|$. The vector $\epsilon = \mathbf{Aq}$ is the error vector and it is this error vector that is minimized. The solution is the unit singular vector corresponding to the smallest singular value of $\mathbf{A}$.

Consider an estimate for the quadrifocal tensor Q, represented by a vector $\mathbf{q}$, and let A be the matrix of equations corresponding to a set of point correspondences $\mathbf{u}_i \leftrightarrow \mathbf{u}'_i \leftrightarrow \mathbf{u}''_i \leftrightarrow \mathbf{u}'''_i$ across 4 views. The vector $\mathsf{A}\mathbf{q}$ is the *algebraic error vector* associated with the estimate $\mathbf{q}$, relative to the measurements. Thus, our goal is to find the unit norm vector $\mathbf{q}$ minimizing the algebraic error $\|\mathsf{A}\mathbf{q}\|$. In finding this minimum, the vector $\mathbf{q}$ may be allowed to vary freely over the whole linear space R^{81}, or be constrained to some subset of R^{81}. In any case, the principle is the same, namely that $\mathsf{A}\mathbf{q}$ is the algebraic error vector.

Constraints. The simplest manner of estimating the tensor Q is the linear least squares method, that finds the unit vector $\mathbf{q}$ that minimizes algebraic error, where $\mathbf{q}$ is allowed to vary over the whole space R^{81}. As with the fundamental matrix and the trifocal tensor, the tensor Q that one finds in this way will not in general correspond (as in (3)) to a set of four camera matrices. This will only be the case when Q is appropriately constrained. To be more precise, a quadrifocal tensor Q is determined by the four camera matrices. These have a total of 44 degrees of freedom. However, the quadrifocal tensor (just as the fundamental matrix and trifocal tensor) is unchanged by a projective transformation of space, since its value is determined only by image coordinates. Hence, we may subtract 15 for the degrees of freedom of a 3D projective transformation. The quadrifocal tensor depends on only 29 essential parameters. Thus, it must satisfy a total of $51 = 80 - 29$ constraints, in addition to the scale ambiguity. As one may see, the 81 entries of the quadrifocal tensor are very greatly redundant as far as describing the projective configuration of the cameras is concerned.

By constrast, the fundamental matrix has 8 entries up to scale, and must satisfy a single constraint ($\det F = 0$). The trifocal tensor has 27 entries and must satisfy 8 constraints, since the projective configuration of three cameras has $18 = 33 - 15$ degrees of freedom. Although one may perhaps hope to get reasonable results by ignoring the constraints on the fundamental matrix and even the trifocal tensor, it is clear that one can not ignore the 51 constraints of the quadrifocal tensor and hope to get reasonable results.

The method described in this paper for computation of the quadrifocal tensor is to find $\mathbf{q}$ that minimizes algebraic error, while at the same time being constrained to correspond to a set of four camera matrices, according to (3).

2.2 Minimization subject to constraints

In the case where the vector $\mathbf{q}$ is constrained to lie on a linear submanifold (an affine subspace) of R^{81}, a simple linear method exists for carrying out the minimization. The following algorithm was give in [3]. Since it is an essential part of our method for finding the quadrifocal tensor, it is repeated below for convenience.

Algorithm : Given a "measurement" matrix A and "constraint" matrix C find the unit norm vector $\mathbf{q}$ that minimizes $\|\mathsf{A}\mathbf{q}\|$ subject to constraints $\mathbf{q} = \mathsf{C}\mathbf{a}$ for some vector $\mathbf{a}$. Equivalently, minimize $\|\mathsf{A}\mathsf{C}\mathbf{a}\|$ subject to $\|\mathsf{C}\mathbf{a}\| = 1$, then set $\mathbf{q} = \mathsf{C}\mathbf{a}$.

Solution :

1. Compute the SVD $\mathtt{C} = \mathtt{UDV}^\top$ such that the non-zero values of D appear first down the diagonal.
2. Let $\mathtt{U}'$ be the matrix comprising the first r columns of U, where r is the rank of C. Further, let $\mathtt{V}'$ consist of the first r columns of V and $\mathtt{D}'$ consist of the r first rows and columns of D.
3. Find the unit vector $\mathbf{q}'$ that minimizes $\|\mathtt{AU}'\mathbf{q}'\|$. This is the singular vector corresponding to the smallest singular value of $\mathtt{AU}'$.
4. The required vector $\mathbf{q}$ is given by $\mathbf{q} = \mathtt{U}'\mathbf{q}'$, A vector $\mathbf{a}$ such that $\mathbf{q} = \mathtt{C}\mathbf{a}$ is given by $\mathbf{a} = \mathtt{V}'\mathtt{D}'^{-1}\mathbf{q}'$.

2.3 Geometric Distance

A common assumption is that measurement error is confined to image measurements, and image measurements conform to a gaussian error model. Given a set of measured correspondences $\mathbf{u}_i \leftrightarrow \mathbf{u}'_i \leftrightarrow \mathbf{u}''_i \leftrightarrow \mathbf{u}'''_i$, the optimal estimate for the quadrifocal tensor under this error model is the one that satisifies equations of the form

$$\hat{u}_i^a \hat{u}_i'^b \hat{u}_i''^c \hat{u}_i'''^d \epsilon_{apw} \epsilon_{bqx} \epsilon_{cry} \epsilon_{dsz} Q^{pqrs} = 0_{wxyz} \tag{4}$$

as in (3) for each matched point, where $\hat{\mathbf{u}}_i, \dots, \hat{\mathbf{u}}_i'''$ are estimated image points that minimize the geometric error

$$\sum_i d(\hat{\mathbf{u}}_i, \mathbf{u}_i)^2 + d(\hat{\mathbf{u}}'_i, \mathbf{u}'_i)^2 + d(\hat{\mathbf{u}}''_i, \mathbf{u}''_i)^2 + d(\hat{\mathbf{u}}'''_i, \mathbf{u}'''_i)^2 \tag{5}$$

subject to the condition that (4) is satisfied exactly. Here, $d(\cdot, \cdot)$ represents Euclidean distance in the image. The quantity $d(\mathbf{u}_i, \hat{\mathbf{u}}_i)$ is known as the *geometric distance* between $\mathbf{u}_i$ and $\hat{\mathbf{u}}_i$. Thus the error to be minimized is the sum of squares of geometric distances between measured and projected points.

Geometric error may be minimized using the technique of bundle adjustment, to carry out a projective reconstruction of the scene. A method for doing this using sparse techniques to minimize time complexity is given in [1]. In general, minimization of geometric error can be expected to give the best possible results (depending on how realistic the error model is). This algorithm is not implemented here for use in comparison with the algebraic minimization algorithm. Nevertheless, one may easily derive a theoretical bound (the Cramer-Rao lower bound) for the minimum error obtainable using the geometric error model. This bound is used to evaluate the algebraic minimization algorithms. Consider an estimation problem involving N measurements each of a Gaussian random variable with standard deviation σ, and d parameters, the minimum residual error (distance between measured and modelled values) is equal ([7]) to $\epsilon = \sigma(1 - d/N)^{1/2}$. In this particular case, with four images and n points, two coordinates per point, there are $8n$ measurement. Counting parameters, we count $3n$ for the coordinates of the points in space, plus 29 for the degrees of freedom of the quadrifocal tensor. Hence, the optimal residual error is

$$E = \sigma((5n - 29)/8n)^{1/2} \; . \tag{6}$$

2.4 The Reduced Measurement Matrix

In general, the matrix A may have a very large number of rows. As described in [3] it is possible to replace A by a square matrix Â such that $||\mathbf{Aq}|| = ||\hat{\mathbf{A}}\mathbf{q}||$ for any vector $\mathbf{q}$. Such a matrix Â is called a *reduced measurement matrix*. An efficient way of obtaining Â is to use the QR decomposition $\mathbf{A} = \mathbf{Q}\hat{\mathbf{A}}$, where Q has orthogonal columns and Â is upper-triangular and square.

In this way, all the information we need to keep about the set of matched data $\mathbf{u}_i \leftrightarrow \mathbf{u}'_i \leftrightarrow \mathbf{u}''_i \leftrightarrow \mathbf{u}'''_i$ is contained in the single matrix Â. If we wish to minimize algebraic error $||\mathbf{Aq}||$ as $\mathbf{q}$ varies over some restricted set of transforms, then this is equivalent to minimizing the norm $||\hat{\mathbf{A}}\mathbf{q}||$.

2.5 The reduced quadrifocal tensor

A method introduced by Heyden ([6, 5]) for reducing the number of unsatisfied constraints involving the quadrifocal tensor involves the *reduced quadrifocal tensor*. Heyden applied the same techniques to defined also a reduced fundamental matrix and reduced trifocal tensor, but these will not be considered in this paper.

Suppose that among the set of correspondences, three correspondences $\mathbf{u}_i \leftrightarrow \mathbf{u}'_i \leftrightarrow \mathbf{u}''_i \leftrightarrow \mathbf{u}'''_i$ for $i = 1, \ldots, 3$ are selected. This selection should be done in such a way that points $\mathbf{u}_1$, $\mathbf{u}_2$ and $\mathbf{u}_3$ are not collinear, and neither are the corresponding points in the other images. Now, a projective transformation T exists that maps the points represented in homogeneous coordinates as $\mathbf{e}_1 = (1,0,0)^\top$, $\mathbf{e}_2 = (0,1,0)^\top$ and $\mathbf{e}_3 = (0,0,1)^\top$. to the points $\mathbf{u}_1, \mathbf{u}_2, \mathbf{u}_3$. Note that T is not an affine transformation, since it does not keep the plane at infinity fixed. As such, it is not fully defined by three point correspondences. However, a simple choice of T is the one represented by a matrix

$$\mathbf{T} = \begin{bmatrix} u_1 & u_2 & u_3 \\ v_1 & v_2 & v_3 \\ w_1 & w_2 & w_3 \end{bmatrix} \tag{7}$$

where $(u_i, v_i, w_i)^\top$ are the coordinates of $\mathbf{u}_i$. One verifies easily that indeed $\mathbf{Te}_i = \mathbf{u}_i$. We assume that each point $\mathbf{u}_i$ in the image is subjected to the transformation $\mathbf{T}^{-1}$, resulting in a new set of points. Let us assume that this transformation has been carried out, and agree to denote the new transformed points by the same symbol $\mathbf{u}_i$. Thus, one has a set of image points $\mathbf{u}_i$ of which the first three points $\mathbf{u}_1$, $\mathbf{u}_2$ and $\mathbf{u}_3$ are equal to $\mathbf{e}_i$, $i = 1, \ldots, 3$.

Let the points in space mapping to the points $\mathbf{u}_i$ be denoted $\mathbf{x}_i$. Thus, $\mathbf{u}_i = \mathbf{Pu}_i$. We focus on the first three points $\mathbf{x}_1$, $\mathbf{x}_2$ and $\mathbf{x}_3$. Since image points $\mathbf{u}_1$, $\mathbf{u}_2$ and $\mathbf{u}_3$ are not collinear (by assumption), neither are the points $\mathbf{x}_i$ that project to them. It is possible, therefore to select a projective coordinate frame in which these points have coordinates $\mathbf{x}_1 = (1,0,0,0)^\top$, $\mathbf{x}_2 = (0,1,0,0)^\top$ and $\mathbf{x}_3 = (0,0,1,0)^\top$. Since these points map to image points $\mathbf{e}_i$, one verifies that the form of the projection matrix must be

$$P = \begin{bmatrix} p_1 & & q_1 \\ & p_2 & q_2 \\ & & p_3 \ q_3 \end{bmatrix}. \tag{8}$$

We may make the further assumption that the centre of the camera is at the point $(0,0,0,1)^\top$, which means that $P(0,0,0,1)^\top = (0,0,0)^\top$. Consequently, $q_1 = q_2 = q_3 = 0$.

Now, applying a similar argument to each of the other cameras, one sees that each of P, P', P'' and P''' has a similar form, consisting of a left hand diagonal block, plus an arbitrary 4-th column. Finally, one may multiply each of the camera matrices on the right by the matrix

$$\begin{bmatrix} p_1^{-1} & & & -p_1^{-1}q_1 \\ & p_2^{-1} & & -p_2^{-1}q_2 \\ & & p_2^{-1} & -p_3^{-1}q_3 \\ & & & 1 \end{bmatrix}.$$

This reduces the first matrix P to the particular simple form $[\mathrm{I} \mid \mathbf{0}]$ while retaining the form (8) of the other matrices. This is the reduced form for the camera matrices.

Notation : To avoid continually having to count the number of primes to distinguish the elements from the three cameras, we will write the four cameras as

$$P = [\mathrm{I} \mid \mathbf{0}] \quad ; \quad P' = \begin{bmatrix} a_1 & & a_1' \\ & a_2 & a_2' \\ & & a_3 \ a_3' \end{bmatrix}$$

$$P'' = \begin{bmatrix} b_1 & & b_1' \\ & b_2 & b_2' \\ & & b_3 \ b_3' \end{bmatrix} \quad ; \quad P''' = \begin{bmatrix} c_1 & & c_1' \\ & c_2 & c_2' \\ & & c_3 \ c_3' \end{bmatrix}. \tag{9}$$

We now consider the quadrifocal tensor Q^{ijkl} defined by (3), in terms of the matrices in (9). This tensor is known as the *reduced quadrifocal tensor*. Each entry is defined as a determinant made up of one row from each of the four camera matrices. Note that if one of the three indices 1, 2 or 3 is absent from the indices of Q^{ijkl}, then the corresponding column of the determinant contains only zeros, and the entry of Q^{ijkl} is zero. Thus, the only nonzero entries are those in which all three indices occur. Since in total there are four indices, one index must appear twice. Simple counting reveals that there are only 36 non-zero entries in the reduced quadrifocal tensor – 6 to account for the choice of which pair of the four indices i, j, k, l are the same, and 6 to account for the permutations of the indices $1, 2, 3$.

We may now summarize an algorithm due to Heyden ([6, 5]) for computing the reduced quadrifocal tensor from a set of point correspondences.

1. Select three point correspondences $\mathbf{u}_i \leftrightarrow \mathbf{u}_i' \leftrightarrow \mathbf{u}_i'' \leftrightarrow \mathbf{u}_i'''$ for $i = 1, \ldots, 3$ and compute transformations T, T', T'' and T''' that map points $\mathbf{e}_i$ $i = 1, \ldots, 3$ to these selected points. Apply the inverse transformation to the complete set of points in each image, to obtain a new set of transformed point correspondences.

2. Each transformed point correspondence gives a set of linear equations in the 36 non-zero entries of the quadrifocal tensor, according to (2). One ignores the first three point correspondences, since they give null equations. Solve these equations in a least-squares manner to find the entries of the quadrifocal tensor.

Transforming the quadrifocal tensor. The quadrifocal tensor corresponding to the original set of point correspondences (not the transformed set) may be retrieved by transforming the reduced quadrifocal tensor found by the above algorithm. To do that, we need to consider how the quadrifocal tensor transforms. Note that the quadrifocal tensor has 4 contravariant (upper) indices. Similarly, points, such as $\mathbf{u}_i$ have a contravariant index. This means that Q transforms in the same way as points. In particular, denote by $\hat{\mathbf{u}}_i$ the set of transformed points, $\hat{\mathbf{u}}_i = \mathbf{T}^{-1}\mathbf{u}_i$, and let $\hat{\mathbf{u}}_i'$, $\hat{\mathbf{u}}_i''$ and $\hat{\mathbf{u}}_i''$ be defined similarly. Suppose $\hat{Q}$ is the quadrifocal tensor corresponding to the set of correspondences $\hat{\mathbf{u}}_i \leftrightarrow \hat{\mathbf{u}}_i' \leftrightarrow \hat{\mathbf{u}}_i'' \leftrightarrow \hat{\mathbf{u}}_i'''$, and Q is derived from $\mathbf{u}_i \leftrightarrow \mathbf{u}_i' \leftrightarrow \mathbf{u}_i'' \leftrightarrow \mathbf{u}_i'''$. Since $\mathbf{u}_i = \mathbf{T}\hat{\mathbf{u}}_i$, the tensor $\hat{Q}$ also transforms via transform T. More precisely, one finds that

$$Q^{ijkl} = \hat{Q}^{abcd} T_a^i T_b'^j T_c''^k T_d'''^l \tag{10}$$

If $\hat{Q}$ is the tensor computed from the transformed points, then (10) allows us to retrieve the tensor corresponding to the original points.

2.6 Retrieving the Camera Matrices

Following Heyden, we give a method for computing the camera matrices once the reduced tensor has been computed. In contrast with the methods for computing the camera matrices from the fundamental matrix or the trifocal tensor, in which one computes first the epipoles, in the method to be described, one computes first the diagonal elements of the matrices in (9), and then computes the final columns, which represent the epipoles. To understand this, we consider the two entries Q^{2311} and Q^{3211}. From (3) one finds that

$$Q^{2311} = \det \begin{bmatrix} 1 & \\ & a_3 \, a_3' \\ b_1 & b_1' \\ c_1 & c_1' \end{bmatrix} = a_3(b_1 c_1' - c_1 b_1')$$

On the other hand, similarly, one finds that $Q^{3211} = -a_2(b_1 c_1' - c_1 b_1')$. Hence, one sees that the ratio $a_3 : a_2 = Q^{2311} : -Q^{3211}$. Continuing in this manner, one may solve for the diagonal elements of the matrices (9) by solving the following equations :

$$
\begin{bmatrix} 0 & Q^{2311} & Q^{3211} \\ Q^{1322} & 0 & Q^{3122} \\ Q^{1233} & Q^{2133} & 0 \end{bmatrix} \begin{pmatrix} a_1 \\ a_2 \\ a_3 \end{pmatrix} = \mathbf{0}
$$

$$
\begin{bmatrix} 0 & Q^{2131} & Q^{3121} \\ Q^{1232} & 0 & Q^{3212} \\ Q^{1323} & Q^{2313} & 0 \end{bmatrix} \begin{pmatrix} b_1 \\ b_2 \\ b_3 \end{pmatrix} = \mathbf{0} \tag{11}
$$

$$
\begin{bmatrix} 0 & Q^{2113} & Q^{3112} \\ Q^{1223} & 0 & Q^{3221} \\ Q^{1332} & Q^{2331} & 0 \end{bmatrix} \begin{pmatrix} c_1 \\ c_2 \\ c_3 \end{pmatrix} = \mathbf{0}
$$

These equations have a pattern to them, which the reader may easily discover. (The first index of Q^{ijkl} corresponds to the column of each matrix in (11), and the repeated index corresponds to the row.) In this way, one computes the diagonal elements of (9). Each of the solution vectors $(a_1, a_2, a_3)^\top$, $(b_1, b_2, b_3)^\top$ and $(c_1, c_2, c_3)^\top$ may be chosen to have unit norm.

2.7 Retrieving the epipoles

Once one knows the values of $(a_1, a_2, a_3)^\top$, $(b_1, b_2, b_3)^\top$ and $(c_1, c_2, c_3)^\top$, the values of the entries of Q are linear in the remaining entries

$$
a_1', a_2', a_3', b_1', b_2', b_3', c_1', c_2', c_3' \ .
$$

This is because these entries will all appear in the last column of the determinant (3) representing Q^{ijkl}. Hence the determinant expression can not contain higher order terms in these entries. The exact form of the linear relationship can be computed by cofactor expansion of the determinant expression (3) for Q^{ijkl} down the last column. We will be content to express it in the form $\hat{\mathbf{q}} = \mathtt{M}\mathbf{a}'$, where $\hat{Q}$ is the vector of entries of the reduced quadrifocal tensor, and $\mathbf{a}'$ is the vector $(a_1', a_2', a_3', b_1', b_2', b_3', c_1', c_2', c_3')^\top$. The unit-norm least-squares solution of this set of equations gives the entries of vector $\mathbf{a}'$. Along with the values of $\mathbf{a} = (a_1, a_2, a_3, b_1, b_2, b_3, c_1, c_2, c_3)^\top$ previously computed, this gives a complete solution for the camera matrices, according to (9).

The complete algorithm (due to Heyden) for computing the camera matrices from the reduced quadrifocal tensor is therefore as follows.

1. Compute the diagonal entries of the camera matrices (9) by solving (the unit norm least-squares solution) of the equations (11). Denote the vector of diagonal entries by $\mathbf{a}$.
2. Express the entries of the reduced quadrifocal tensor in terms of the vector $\mathbf{a}'$ of last-column entries of the matrices in (11). This gives a set of equations $\hat{\mathbf{q}} = \mathtt{M}\mathbf{a}'$, where the entries of $\mathtt{M}$ are quadratic expressions in the entries of $\mathbf{a}$. Solve this set of equations (once more the unit-norm least-squares solution) to find $\mathbf{a}'$.

3. If required, the reduced quadrifocal tensor may be computed using (3). Finally, the quadrifocal tensor corresponding to the original data may be computed using (10). Alternatively, if one requires only the original camera matrices, they may be obtained by transforming the reduced camera matrices found in steps 1 and 2.

It is important to note that this method, along with the algorithm for finding the reduced quadrifocal tensor together give a method for computing a quadrifocal tensor corresponding to a valid choice of camera matrices, and hence satisfying all needed constraints. This is done, of course, without explicitly finding the form of the constraints.

3 Minimizing Algebraic Distance

The algorithm given in the last section, though apparently performing adequately ([6, 5]) has various weaknesses, from a computational viewpoint.

1. In computing the transformations $T, \ldots, T'''$ according to (7) one risks encountering the case where the three points used to define the transforms are nearly collinear. In this case T may be close to being invertible. This means that the positions of the transformed points computed by applying T^{-1} to the original data points may not be very stable.
2. In solving for the epipoles, using (11) the matrices involved will not generally be singular. The solution is found in effect by computing the nearest singular matrix (in Frobenius norm) and taking the null space of that matrix. However, there is really no theoretical justification for finding the nearest singular matrix in Frobenius norm. The problem is analogous with that encountered when enforcing the singularity constraint for the fundamental matrix.
3. In the computation of the vector $\mathbf{a}'$, we solve a set of equations once more using a least-squared method. However, once more the quantity that we are minimizing has no meaningful interpretation in terms of errors in the original data.

It will now be shown how we may avoid these problems in a way so as to minimize algebraic error. The result is that in carrying out the three steps of the algorithm one is minimizing always the same algebraic cost function, and numerical performance is improved.

3.1 Minimizing Algebraic Error

Solving for the quadrifocal tensor. The transformation formula (10) is seen to be linear in the entries of $\hat{Q}$. More specifically, we may write $\mathbf{q} = \mathcal{T}\hat{\mathbf{q}}$. In this equation $\hat{\mathbf{q}}$ and $\mathbf{q}$ are vectors of entries of the reduced and full quadrifocal tensors, and $\mathcal{T}$ is an 81×36 matrix. Let A be the reduced measurement matrix computed from the *original* point correspondences. One wishes to compute the unit-norm vector $\mathbf{q}$ that minimizes the algebraic error $||A\mathbf{q}||$ subject to the constraint that $\mathbf{q}$ is derived from a reduced quadrifocal tensor according to the constraint $\mathbf{q} = \mathcal{T}\hat{\mathbf{q}}$. In other words, we wish to minimize $||A\mathcal{T}\hat{\mathbf{q}}||$ subject to the condition $||\mathcal{T}\hat{\mathbf{q}}|| = 1$. This is the type of constrained minimization problem considered in section 2.2. It is important to note here, that the transformation $\hat{Q} \mapsto Q$ given by (10) depends on the matrices $T, \ldots, T'''$ given by a formula such as (7) which is built from the coordinates of the matched points. It is not necessary ever to invert this matrix to find $T^{-1}, \ldots, T'''^{-1}$. In addition, the reduced measurement matrix A is formed from the coordinates of the original untransformed points. In fact, it is never necessary to invert the matrices $T, \ldots, T'''$ at all. Thus, one computes the reduced quadrifocal tensor, *while completely avoiding* the problem of inverting matrices, which could potentially be near-singular.

Solving for the epipoles. It does not seem to be possible to find the diagonal entries of the reduced camera matrices in a way so as to minimize algebraic error, in a linear manner. Therefore, we adopt the method of Heyden of finding the least-squares solution to equations (11). This leaves the problem of finding the final columns of the matrices, namely the vector $\mathbf{a}'$. As before, the reduced quadrifocal tensor $\hat{Q}$ may be expressed linearly in terms of the entries of $\mathbf{a}'$, writing $\hat{\mathbf{q}} = M\mathbf{a}'$, assuming as we do that the diagonals of the reduced camera matrices are known.

Now, we wish to find $\mathbf{q}$ of unit norm that minimizes $||A\mathbf{q}||$ subject to the additional constraints that $\mathbf{q} = \mathcal{T}\hat{\mathbf{q}}$ and $\hat{\mathbf{q}} = M\mathbf{a}'$. These last two constraints become a single constraint $\mathbf{q} = \mathcal{T}M\mathbf{a}'$. Thus, the problem may be cast as follows : minimize $||A(\mathcal{T}M)\mathbf{a}'||$ subject to the condition $||(\mathcal{T}M)\mathbf{a}'|| = 1$. Once more this is a minimization problem of the sort solved in section 2.2. The solution method provides values for either $\mathbf{a}'$ or $\mathbf{q}$. Thus, we may compute the quadrifocal tensor directly by computing $\mathbf{q}$, or we may retrieve the reduced camera matrices by computing $\mathbf{a}'$.

The complete proposed algorithm is therefore as follows.

1. Form the reduced measurement matrix A from the original data.
2. Obtain the transformation matrices $T, \ldots, T'''$ from three of the correspondences, using formula (7).
3. Compute the 81×36 transformation matrix $\mathcal{T}$ such that $\mathbf{q} = \mathcal{T}\hat{\mathbf{q}}$ from the transformation rule (10)
4. Solve the minimization problem : minimize $||A\mathcal{T}\hat{\mathbf{q}}||$ subject to $||\mathcal{T}\hat{\mathbf{q}}|| = 1$ to find $\hat{Q}$, an initial estimate of the reduced fundamental matrix.
5. Find the diagonal elements (vector $\mathbf{a}$) of the reduced camera matrices by solving (11).
6. Compute the 36×9 matrix M such that $\hat{\mathbf{q}} = M\mathbf{a}'$, where $\mathbf{a}'$ is the 9-vector containing the elements of the last columns (representing epipoles relative to the first camera) of the reduced camera matrices.

7. Solve the minimization problem : minimize $\|A\mathcal{T}Ma'\|$ subject to $\|\mathcal{T}M\hat{a}'\| = 1$. From this we may derive the vector $\mathbf{q} = \mathcal{T}M\hat{a}'$ corresponding to a full quadrifocal tensor.

8. If desired, we may compute the reduced camera matrices (9) from the vectors $\mathbf{a}$ and $\mathbf{a}'$. These may be transformed to camera matrices for the original set of data by left-multiplication by the transforms $T, \ldots, T'''$.

The quadrifocal tensor found in this way is a valid tensor satisfying all appropriate constraints, since it is derived from a set of camera matrices. In addition, it minimizes algebraic error subject to the two conditions :

1. The camera matrix diagonals have the value given by the 9-vector $\mathbf{a}$, computed at step 5 of the algorithm.

2. The three points used to compute transforms $T, \ldots, T'''$ correspond precisely.

3.2 Iterative Estimation

The algorithm of the last section gives a way of computing an algebraic error vector $A\mathbf{q}$ assuming that the 9-vector $\mathbf{a}$ representing the diagonals of the reduced camera matrices is known. This mapping $\mathbf{a} \mapsto A\mathbf{q}$ is a map from R^9 to R^{81}. This suggests an iterative approach in which the goal is to vary $\mathbf{a}$ in a way such as to minimize the algebraic error $\|A\mathbf{q}\|$. Such an iteration may be carried out using a parameter minimization program such as the Levenberg-Marquardt algorithm.

The solution that one obtains in this manner minimizes algebraic error subject to the the condition that the points $Te_i \leftrightarrow T'e_i \leftrightarrow T''e_i \leftrightarrow T'''e_i$ correspond exactly for $i = 1, \ldots, 3$, where transformations $T, \ldots, T'''$ are fixed during the computation. These transformations are derived (using (7)) from the coordinates of the first three measured points. One may further let the entries of the three transformation matrice T', T'', T''' vary to find an absolute minimum of algebraic error. Since $T', \ldots, T'''$ are determined by the coordinates $\mathbf{u}'_i, \mathbf{u}''_i, \mathbf{u}'''_i$ for $i = 1, \ldots 3$, this accounts for a further 18 variable parameters, a total of 27 in all. It is unnecessary to let the points $\mathbf{u}_i$ (or equivalently the transformation T) vary as well, since there must exist some points $\mathbf{u}'_i, \mathbf{u}''_i, \mathbf{u}'''_i$ that truly correspond to $\mathbf{u}_i$.

Note the advantage of this method of computing Q is that the iterative part of the algorithm is of fixed size independent of the number of point correspondences involved.

3.3 4 points on a plane

It may be observed that if 4 of the points are known to lie on a plane, then the minimization of algebraic error can succeed without iteration in a single step. (We do not consider the case where three of these points are collinear.) To be specific, one may choose the first three correspondences to have homogeneous image coordinates $\mathbf{e}_1 = (1,0,0)^\top$, $\mathbf{e}_2 = (0,1,0)^\top$, $\mathbf{e}_3 = (0,0,1)^\top$ as before and the fourth point can be chosen as $\mathbf{e}_4 = (1,1,1)$. In a real computation, one needs to find transformations $\mathtt{T}, \ldots, \mathtt{T}'''$ that map these basis points to the actual image points. Now, since the points are known to be coplanar, one may assume that they lie on the plane at infinity, as the points $(1,0,0,0)^\top$, $(0,1,0,0)^\top$, $(0,0,1,0)^\top$ and $(1,1,1,0)^\top$. One assumes further that the first camera centre is at the origin $(0,0,0,1)^\top$. In this case, it is easily verified that the camera matrices have the form (9) in which the diagonal elements are all equal to 1. This means that we can skip steps 4 and 5 of the algorithm of section 3.1. The complete algorithm is as follows :

1. Compute the reduced measurement matrix from the original data.
2. Compute the transforms $\mathtt{T}, \ldots, \mathtt{T}'''$ that take the image basis points $\mathbf{e}_1, \ldots, \mathbf{e}_4$ to the measured coordinate values.
3. Compute the 81×36 matrix $\mathcal{T}$ from (10) as before, such that $\mathbf{q} = \mathcal{T}\hat{\mathbf{q}}$.
4. Compute the 36×9 matrix $\mathtt{M}$ such that $\hat{\mathbf{q}} = \mathtt{M}\mathbf{a}'$, assuming that the diagonals of the reduced camera matrices (9) are all 1. This matrix has a given fixed form independent of the data.
5. Compute $\mathbf{a}'$ by solving the problem : minimize $\|\mathtt{A}\mathcal{T}\mathtt{M}\mathbf{a}'\|$ subject to $\|\mathcal{T}\mathtt{M}\mathbf{a}'\| = 1$. The quadrifocal tensor is given by $\mathbf{q} = \mathcal{T}\mathtt{M}\mathbf{a}'$.

The tensor derived in this way minimizes algebraic error, subject to the first four point correspondences (those for the coplanar points) being correct.

One should note that essentially the same technique works for the fundamental matrix and the trifocal tensor. If there exist four points known to lie in a plane, then there exists a straight-forward linear method that finds the matrix, or tensor, satisfying all constraints and minimizing algebraic error.

4   Experimental Results

The new algorithm for computation of the quadrifocal tensor was was tested with synthetic data. The data were created to simulate a standard 35mm camera with a 35mm focal length lens. A set of points were synthesized inside a sphere of radius 1m, and cameras were located at a distance of about 2.5m from the centre of the sphere aimed at the point set from random directions. The image is sampled so that the magnification factors are $\alpha_u = \alpha_v = 1000.0$, the same in each direction. This corresponds to a pixel size of $35\mu m$ for a $35mm$ camera. The expected optimum value of the residual error was computed using formula ((6)). The results are shown in Fig 1.

The results given in Fig 1 are for a set of arbitrarily placed cameras and arbitrarily chosen points. An experiment was carried out to determine how the algorithms performed in near-critical configurations. A similar configuration of points and cameras was chosen as in the previous test. However, the first camera centre was located on the line through the first two world points $\mathbf{x}_1$ and $\mathbf{x}_2$. The

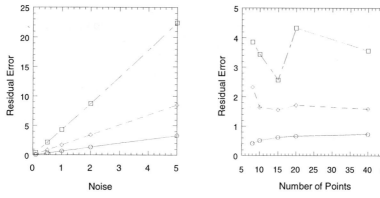

Fig. 1. *The residual error achieved by the algorithm of this paper is compared with the optimal value as well as with the algorithm of Heyden. Each of the graphs shows the residual error RMS-averaged over 200 runs. In the left hand graph, the residual error is plotted against the amount of injected noise, for a set of 20 points. The right hand graph shows the effect of varying the number of points used to compute the tensor. It starts with 7 points, since none of the algorithms seems to perform well with just 6 points. The noise level is fixed at 1 pixel (in each coordinate direction). In each case, the lower plot is the optimum error given by (6)) while the two upper plots are the residual error for the algorithm of this paper (middle curve) and for Heyden's algorithm (top curve). One sees that the presently considered algorithm performs significantly better than Heyden's algorithm, but misses the optimal result by about a factor of 2. Note that the error is closely proportional to the amount of injected noise.*

result of this is that the points $\mathbf{u}_1$ and $\mathbf{u}_2$ (the images with respect to the first camera) are close together (in fact without noise, they coincide). Thus the transformation $\mathbf{T}$ is close to being singular. The result of this experiment is shown in Fig 2.

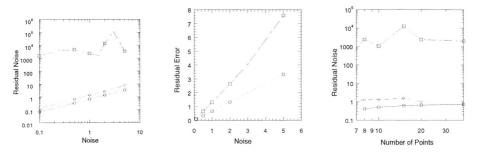

Fig. 2. *In near singular cases, the present algorithm still performs well, as shown in these graphs. On the left is shown the residual as a function of increasing noise, and on the right the residual is plotted against the number of points. These are shown as log-log plots, so that the top curve will fit on the graph. It is seen that in this case Heyden's algorithm (represented by the top curve) fails completely. The center graph is a linear plot of just the optimal and the present non-iterative algorithm results.*

Iterative Algorithms We now compare the iterative algorithms with the non-iterative algorithm. The results are shown if Fig 3. Two iterative algorithms are compared. In the first algorithm, the transformations $T, \ldots T'''$ are kept fixed, and the 9 diagonal entries of the reduced camera matrices vary. Thus, there are 9 varying parameters and 81 measured values. In the second method the transformation matrices T', T'', T''' are allowed to vary also. There are 27 varying parameters in this case. This second method should be expected to give better results.

5 Conclusion

The method of computing the quadrifocal tensor by minimizing algebraic error gives results almost indistinguishable from minimizing geometric error, and almost optimal. It avoids singular configurations in which Heyden's algorithm fails entirely, and in general gives numerically superior results. It is true that it is possible to be careful in selecting the three points used in Heyden's method for defining the reduced tensor. If this is done, then it is possible to avoid catastrophic failure of the algorithm. However this involves additional uncertainties in the algorithm. The present algorithm avoids such difficulties by avoiding the problems with singular configurations of points altogether.

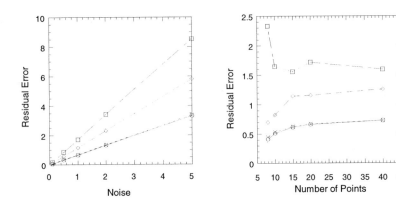

Fig. 3. *These graphs show the performance of iterative algorithms for computing the quadrifocal tensor. The data set used is the same as for Fig 1. Each graph shows 4 curves. From top to bottom they are (i) the non-iterative algorithm, (ii) the 9-parameter iterative method, (iii) the 27 parameter iterative method and (iv) the theoretical optimal method. As may be seen, the 27-parameter iterative method gives very nearly optimal results (in fact the two last curves are indistinguishable). The two graphs shown are for varying noise and 20 points (on the left), and for fixed noise of 1 pixel and varying numbers of points (right).*

References

1. Richard I. Hartley. Euclidean reconstruction from uncalibrated views. In *Applications of Invariance in Computer Vision : Proc. of the Second Joint European - US Workshop, Ponta Delgada, Azores – LNCS-Series Vol. 825, Springer Verlag*, pages 237–256, October 1993.
2. Richard I. Hartley. Lines and points in three views and the trifocal tensor. *International Journal of Computer Vision*, 22(2):125–140, March 1997.
3. Richard I. Hartley. Minimizing algebraic error in geometric estimation problems. In *Proc. International Conference on Computer Vision*, 1998.
4. Richard I. Hartley. Multilinear relationships between coordinates of corresponding image points and lines. to appear.
5. Anders Heyden. *Geometry and Algebra of Multiple Projective Transformations*. PhD thesis, Department of Mathematics, Lund University, Sweden, December 1995.
6. Anders Heyden. Reconstruction from multiple images using kinetic depths. *International Journal of Computer Vision*, to appear.
7. K. Kanatani. *Statistical Optimization for Geometric Computation : Theory and Practice*. North Holland, Amsterdam, 1996.
8. Bill Triggs. The geometry of projective reconstruction I: Matching constraints and the joint image. unpublished report, 1995.

Self-Calibration of a 1D Projective Camera and Its Application to the Self-Calibration of a 2D Projective Camera

Olivier FAUGERAS[1], Long QUAN[2], and Peter STURM[2]

[1] INRIA Sophia Antipolis, 2004, route des Lucioles – B.P. 93
06902 Sophia Antipolis Cedex, France
Olivier.Faugeras@sophia.inria.fr
http://www.inria.fr/robotvis/personnel/faugeras/faugeras-eng.html
[2] CNRS-GRAVIR-INRIA, ZIRST – 655 avenue de l'Europe
38330 Montbonnot, France
Long.Quan, Peter.Sturm@inrialpes.fr
http://www.inrialpes.fr/movi/people/Quan,Sturm/index.html

Abstract. We introduce the concept of self-calibration of a 1D projective camera from point correspondences, and describe a method for uniquely determining the two internal parameters of a 1D camera based on the trifocal tensor of three 1D images. The method requires the estimation of the trifocal tensor which can be achieved linearly with no approximation unlike the trifocal tensor of 2D images, and solving for the roots of a cubic polynomial in one variable. Interestingly enough, we prove that a 2D camera undergoing a planar motion reduces to a 1D camera. From this observation, we deduce a new method for self-calibrating a 2D camera using planar motions.

Both the self-calibration method for a 1D camera and its applications for 2D camera calibration are demonstrated on real image sequences. Other applications including 2D affine camera self-calibration are also discussed.

1 Introduction

A CCD camera is commonly modeled as a 2D projective device that projects a point in $\mathcal{P}^3$ (the projective space of dimension 3) to a point in $\mathcal{P}^2$. By analogy, we can consider what we call a 1D projective camera which projects a point in $\mathcal{P}^2$ to a point in $\mathcal{P}^1$. This 1D projective camera may seem very abstract, but many imaging systems using laser beams, infra-red or ultra-sounds acting only on a source plane can be modeled this way. What is less obvious, but more interesting for our purpose, is that in some situations, the usual 2D camera model is also closely related to this 1D camera model. One first example might be the case of the 2D affine camera model operating on line segments: The direction vectors of lines in 3D space and in the image correspond to each other via this 1D projective camera model [15, 14]. Other cases will be discussed later.

In this paper, we first introduce the concept of self-calibration of a 1D projective camera by analogy to that of a 2D projective camera which is a very active topic [11, 5, 9, 13, 1] since the pioneering work of [12]. It turns out that the theory of self-calibration of 1D camera is considerably simpler than the corresponding one in 2D. It is essentially determined in a unique way by a linear algorithm using the trifocal tensor of 1D cameras. After establishing this result, we further investigate the relationship between the usual 2D camera and the 1D camera. It turns out that a 2D camera undergoing a planar motion can be reduced to a 1D camera on the trifocal line of the 2D cameras. This remarkable relationship allows us to calibrate a real 2D projective camera using the theory of self-calibration of a 1D camera. The advantage of doing so is evident. Instead of solving complicated Kruppa equations for 2D camera self-calibration, exact linear algorithm can be used for 1D camera self-calibration. The only constraint is that the motion of the 2D camera should be restricted to planar motions. The other applications, including 2D affine camera calibration, are also briefly discussed.

Throughout the paper, vectors are denoted in lower case boldface $\mathbf{x}$, $\mathbf{u}$ ..., matrices and tensors in upper case boldface $\mathbf{A}$, $\mathbf{T}$ ...; Scalars are any plain letters or lower case Greek a, u, A, λ .... The geometric objects are sometimes denoted by plain or Greek letters like l for a 2D line and L for a 3D line whenever it is necessary to distinguish the geometric object l from its coordinate representation by a vector $\mathbf{l}$. Some basic tensor notation is used sometimes: Covariant indices are written as subscripts and contravariant indices as superscripts. e.g. the coordinates of a point $\mathbf{x}$ in $\mathcal{P}^3$ are written with an upper index $\mathbf{x} = (x^1, x^2, x^3, x^4)^T$. A matrix $\mathbf{A}$ is written with two indices like A^i_j, where i indexes rows and j columns. The implicit summation convention is also adopted.

2   1D projective camera and its trifocal tensor

We will first review the one-dimensional camera which was abstracted from the study of the geometry of lines under affine cameras [15, 14]. We can also introduce it directly by analogy to a 2D projective camera.

A 1D projective camera projects a point $\mathbf{x} = (x^1, x^2, x^3)^T$ in $\mathcal{P}^2$ (projective plane) to a point $\mathbf{u} = (u^1, u^2)^T$ in $\mathcal{P}^1$ (projective line). This projection may be described by a 2×3 homogeneous matrix $\mathbf{M}$ as $\lambda \mathbf{u} = \mathbf{M}_{2 \times 3} \mathbf{x}$.

We now examine the geometric constraints available for points seen in multiple views similar to the 2D camera case [17, 18, 9, 21, 7]. There is a constraint only in the case of 3 views, as there is no any constraint for 2 views (two projective lines always intersect in a point in a projective plane).

Let the three views of the same point $\mathbf{x}$ be given as follows:

$$\begin{cases} \lambda \mathbf{u} = \mathbf{M}\mathbf{x}, \\ \lambda' \mathbf{u}' = \mathbf{M}'\mathbf{x}, \\ \lambda'' \mathbf{u}'' = \mathbf{M}''\mathbf{x}. \end{cases} \tag{1}$$

These can be rewritten in matrix form as

$$\begin{pmatrix} \mathbf{M} & \mathbf{u} & 0 & 0 \\ \mathbf{M}' & 0 & \mathbf{u}' & 0 \\ \mathbf{M}'' & 0 & 0 & \mathbf{u}'' \end{pmatrix} \begin{pmatrix} \mathbf{x} \\ -\lambda \\ -\lambda' \\ -\lambda'' \end{pmatrix} = 0. \tag{2}$$

The vector $(\mathbf{x}, -\lambda, -\lambda', -\lambda'')^T$ cannot be zero, so

$$\begin{vmatrix} \mathbf{M} & \mathbf{u} & 0 & 0 \\ \mathbf{M}' & 0 & \mathbf{u}' & 0 \\ \mathbf{M}'' & 0 & 0 & \mathbf{u}'' \end{vmatrix} = 0. \tag{3}$$

The expansion of this determinant produces a trifocal constraint for the three views

$$T_{ijk} u^i u'^j u''^k = 0, \tag{4}$$

where T_{ijk} is a $2 \times 2 \times 2$ homogeneous tensor whose components T_{ijk} are 3×3 minors (involving all three views) of the 6×3 joint projection matrix by stacking $\mathbf{M}$, $\mathbf{M}'$ and $\mathbf{M}''$.

This trifocal tensor encapsulates exactly the information needed for projective reconstruction in $\mathcal{P}^2$. Namely, it is the unique matching constraint, it minimally parametrizes the three views and it can be estimated linearly. Contrast this to the 2D image case in which the multilinear constraints are algebraically redundant and the linear estimation is only an approximation based on over-parametrization.

Each point correspondence in 3 views $\mathbf{u} \leftrightarrow \mathbf{u}' \leftrightarrow \mathbf{u}''$ yields one homogeneous linear equation for the unknown vector $\mathbf{t_8}$ representing the 8 tensor components T_{ijk} for $i, j, k = 1, 2$:

$$(u^1 u'^1 u''^1, u^1 u'^1 u''^2, u^1 u'^2 u''^1, u^1 u'^2 u''^2, u^2 u'^1 u''^1, u^2 u'^1 u''^2, u^2 u'^2 u''^1, u^2 u'^2 u''^2) \mathbf{t_8} = 0.$$

With at least 7 point correspondences, we can solve for the tensor components linearly.

A careful normalisation of the measurement matrix is nevertheless necessary just like that stressed in [8] for the linear estimation of the fundamental matrix. The points at each image are first translated so that the centroid of the points is the origin of the image coordinates, then scaled so that the average distance of the points from the origin is $\sqrt{2}$. This is achieved by an affine transformation of the image coordinates in each image: $\bar{\mathbf{u}} = \mathbf{A}\mathbf{u}$, $\bar{\mathbf{u}}' = \mathbf{B}\mathbf{u}'$ and $\bar{\mathbf{u}}'' = \mathbf{C}\mathbf{u}''$.

With these normalised image coordinates, the normalised tensor components $\bar{T}_{ijk}$ are linearly estimated by SVD from $\bar{T}_{ijk} \bar{u}^i \bar{u}'^j \bar{u}''^k = 0$.

The original tensor components T_{ijk} are recovered by de-scaling the normalised tensor $\bar{T}_{ijk}$ as $T_{abc} = \bar{T}_{ijk} A_a^i B_b^j C_c^k$.

3 Self-calibration of a 1D camera from 3 views

The concept of camera self-calibration using only point correspondences became popular in computer vision community following Maybank and Faugeras [12] by solving the so-called Kruppa equations. The basic assumption is that the internal parameters of the camera remain invariant. In the case of the 2D projective camera, the internal calibration (the determination of the 5 internal parameters) is equivalent to the determination of the image ω of the absolute conic.

3.1 The internal parameters of a 1D camera and the circular points

For a 1D camera represented by a 2×3 projection matrix $\mathbf{M}_{2\times 3}$, this projection matrix can always be decomposed into

$$\mathbf{M}_{2\times 3} = \mathbf{K}_{2\times 2} \left(\mathbf{R}_{2\times 2} \; \mathbf{t}_{2\times 1}\right),$$

where

$$\mathbf{K}_{2\times 2} = \begin{pmatrix} \alpha & u_0 \\ 0 & 1 \end{pmatrix}$$

represents the two internal parameters: α the focal length in pixels and u_0 the position of the principal point; the external parameters are represented by a 2×2 rotation matrix $\mathbf{R}_{2\times 2}$,

$$\mathbf{R}_{2\times 2} = \begin{pmatrix} \cos \theta & \sin \theta \\ -\sin \theta & \cos \theta \end{pmatrix}$$

and the translation vector $\mathbf{t}_{2\times 1}$.

The object space for a 1D camera is a projective plane, and any rigid motion on the plane leaves the two circular points I and J invariant (a pair of complex conjugate points on the line at infinity) of the plane. Similar to the 2D camera case where the knowledge of the internal parameters is equivalent to that of the image of the absolute conic, the knowledge of the internal parameters of a 1D camera is equivalent to that of the image points $\mathbf{i}$ and $\mathbf{j}$ of the circular points in $\mathcal{P}^2$.

The relationship between the image of the circular points and the internal parameters of the 1D camera follows directly by projecting one of the circular points $I = (i, 1, 0)^T$, where $i = \sqrt{-1}$, by the camera $\mathbf{M}_{2\times 3}$:

$$\lambda \mathbf{i} = e^{-i\theta} \begin{pmatrix} u_0 + i\alpha \\ 1 \end{pmatrix} = \begin{pmatrix} \alpha & u_0 \\ 0 & 1 \end{pmatrix} \left(\mathbf{R}_{2\times 2} \; \mathbf{t}\right) \begin{pmatrix} i \\ 1 \\ 0 \end{pmatrix}.$$

It clearly appears that the real part of the ratio of the homogeneous coordinates of the image of the circular point $\mathbf{i}$ is the position of the principal point u_0 and the imaginary part is the focal length α.

3.2   Determination of the images of the circular points

Our next task is to locate the circular points in the images. Let us consider one of the circular points, say I. This circular point is projected onto **i**, **i**′ and **i**″ in the three views. As they should be invariant because of our assumption that the internal parameters of the camera are constant, we have:

$$\lambda \mathbf{i} = \lambda' \mathbf{i}' = \lambda'' \mathbf{i}'' \equiv \mathbf{u},$$

where $\mathbf{u} = (u^1, u^2)^T = \rho(a + ib, 1)^T$ for $\lambda, \lambda', \lambda'', \rho \in \mathcal{C}$.

The triplet of corresponding points $\mathbf{i} \leftrightarrow \mathbf{i}' \leftrightarrow \mathbf{i}''$ satisfies the trilinear constraint (4) as all corresponding points do, therefore,

$$T_{ijk} i^i i'^j i''^k = 0,$$

i.e.

$$T_{ijk} u^i u^j u^k = 0.$$

This yields the following cubic equation in the unknown $x = u^1/u^2$:

$$T_{111} x^3 + (T_{211} + T_{112} + T_{121}) x^2 + (T_{212} + T_{221} + T_{122}) x + T_{222} = 0. \quad (5)$$

A cubic polynomial in one unknown with real coefficients has in general either three real roots or one real root and a pair of complex conjugate roots. The latter case of one real and a pair of complex conjugates is obviously the case of interest here. In fact, Equation (5) characterizes all the points of the projective plane which have the same coordinates in three views. This is reminiscent of the 3D case where one is interested in the locus of all points in space that project onto the same point in two views (see Section 5.2). The result that we have just obtained is that in the case where the internal parameters of the camera are constant, there are in general three such points: the two circular points which are complex conjugate, and a real point with the following geometric interpretation.

Consider first the case of two views and let us ask the question, what is the set of points such that their images in the two views are the same? This set of points can be called the 2D horopter (h) of the set of two 1D views. Since the two cameras have the same internal parameters we can ignore them and assume that we work with the calibrated pixel coordinates. In that case, a camera can be identified to an orthonormal system of coordinates centered at the optical center, one axis is parallel to the retina, the other one is the optical axis. The two views correspond to each other via a rotation followed by a translation. This can always be described in general as a pure rotation around a point A. A simple computation then shows that the horopter (h) is the circle going through the two optical centers and A, as illustrated in Figure 1.a. In fact it is the circle minus the two optical centers. Note that since all circles go through the circular point (hence their name), they also belong to the horopter curve, as expected.

In the case of three views, the real point, when it exists, must be at the intersection of the horopter (h_{12}) of the first two views and the horopter (h_{23}) of the last two views. The first one is a circle going through the optical centers

C_1 and C_2, the second one is a circle going through the optical centers C_2 and C_3. Those two circles intersect in general at a second point C which is the real point we were discussing, and the third circle (h_{13}) corresponding to the first and third views must also go through this real point C, see Figure 1.b.

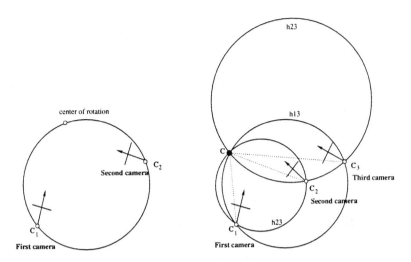

Fig. 1. (a) The two dimensional horopter which is the set of points having the same coordinates in the 2 views (see text). (b) The geometric interpretation of the real point C which has the same images in all three views (see text).

We have therefore established the interesting result that the internal parameters of a 1D camera can be uniquely determined through at least 7 point correspondences in 3 views: the seven points yield the trifocal tensor and Equation (5) yields the internal parameters.

4 Applications

The theory of self-calibration of 1D camera is considerably simpler than the corresponding one in 2D [12] and can be directly used whenever a 1D projective camera model occurs, for instance:

- self-calibration of some active systems using laser beams, infra-reds or ultra-sounds whose imaging system is basically reduced to a 1D camera on the source plane;
- self-calibration of a 2D affine camera using line segments,
- partial/full self-calibration of 2D projective camera using planar motions.

The first two types of applications are straightforward. The interesting observation is that the 1D calibration procedure can also be used for self-calibrating a real 2D projective camera if the camera motion is restricted to planar motions. This is discussed in detail in the remaining of this paper.

5 Calibrating a 2D projective camera using planar motions

A planar motion consists of a translation in a plane and a rotation about an axis perpendicular to that plane. Planar motion is often performed by a vehicle moving on the ground, and has been studied for camera self-calibration by Beardsley and Zisserman [3] and Armstrong et al. [1].

Recall that the self-calibration of a 2D projective camera [6, 12] consists of determining the 5 unchanging internal parameters of a 2D camera, represented by a 3×3 upper triangular matrix

$$\mathbf{K} = \begin{pmatrix} \alpha_u & s & u_0 \\ 0 & \alpha_v & v_0 \\ 0 & 0 & 1 \end{pmatrix}.$$

This is mathematically equivalent to the determination of the image of the absolute conic ω, which is a plane conic described by $\mathbf{x}^T (\mathbf{K}^{-1})^T (\mathbf{K}^{-1}) \mathbf{x} = 0$ for image point $\mathbf{x}$. Given the image of the absolute conic $\mathbf{x}^T \mathbf{C} \mathbf{x} = 0$, the calibration matrix $\mathbf{K}$ can be found using Cholesky decomposition of the conic matrix $\mathbf{C}$.

5.1 Using known planar motions

By *"known planar motion"*, it is meant that the plane of motion is known. The case of unknown planar motions will be treated in the next section.

Without loss of generality and to simplify the explanation, let us assume that the camera is moving on the natural horizontal ground, so the plane of motion is horizontal and the rotation axes are all vertical. We assume a 3D coordinate system with the x- and z-axes on the ground and the y-axis vertical, and a set of point correspondences has been established in 3 images as $(u_i, v_i, 1) \leftrightarrow (u_i', v_i', 1) \leftrightarrow (u_i'', v_i'', 1)$.

As the camera is moving on the plane of motion, therefore the trifocal plane—the plane through the camera centers—of the camera is also a plane parallel to the ground and coincident with the plane of motion. Obviously, if restricting the working space to the trifocal plane, we have a perfect 1D projective camera model which projects the points of the trifocal plane onto the trifocal line in the 2D image plane, as the trifocal line is the image of the trifocal plane. In practice, very few or no any points at all really lie on the trifocal plane. However, we may take the orthogonal projection onto the trifocal plane ($y = 0$) of all points $(x_i, y_i, z_i, 1)^T$ in space, i.e.

$$(x_i, y_i, z_i, 1)^T \mapsto (x_i, z_i, 1)^T = \mathbf{x}_i.$$

Since the camera plane is vertical and perpendicular to the trifocal plane, this orthogonal projection in the image plane is nothing but taking the horizontal coordinate u_i of the image point $(u_i, v_i, 1)^T$, i.e.

$$(u_i, v_i, 1)^T \mapsto (u_i, 1)^T = \mathbf{u}_i.$$

The points $\mathbf{x}_i = (x_i, z_i, 1)^T$ in $\mathcal{P}^2$ and the points $\mathbf{u}_i = (u_i, 1)^T$ in $\mathcal{P}^1$ are related by the following 1D projective camera model

$$\lambda \begin{pmatrix} u_i \\ 1 \end{pmatrix} = \mathbf{M} \begin{pmatrix} x_i \\ z_i \\ 1 \end{pmatrix}.$$

At this point, we have obtained the interesting result that a 1D projective camera model is obtained by considering only the horizontal pixel coordinate of the 2D image points if the camera undergoes a planar motion on the horizontal ground plane!

The 1D self-calibration method just described in the above will allow us to locate the image of the circular points common to all horizontal planes. The circular points are also the intersection points of the line at infinity of the pencil of parallel planes and the absolute conic. We can easily see how the image of the circular points are related to the internal parameters of the 2D camera. The horizontal planes $y = t$ meet the plane at infinity $t = 0$ at the line at infinity whose image is given by $(0, 1, 0)^T \mathbf{K}^{-1}(u, v, 1)^T = 0$, i.e. $v = v_0$. Hence, the location of the trifocal line determines the vertical position of the principal point v_0.

By intersecting the absolute conic given by

$$(u, v, 1)(\mathbf{K}^{-1})^T (\mathbf{K}^{-1})(u, v, 1)^T = 0.$$

and the trifocal line, we have

$$\frac{(u - u_0)^2}{\alpha_u^2} + 1 = 0,$$

i.e. the image of the circular points are given by $u_0 \pm i\alpha_u$. It follows that the internal parameters of the 1D camera are exactly two of the internal parameters of the 2D camera: the focal length α_u in horizontal pixels and the horizontal location of the principal point u_0.

If we assume that the image axes are perpendicular and the aspect ratio is known—this is almost always true in practice, this planar motion allows us to calibrate the 2D camera. For a general 2D camera with 5 internal parameters, additional planar motions will be necessary.

5.2 Using unknown planar motions

So far, we have used known planar motions. In the general case we would like a) to be able to determine from three arbitrary images whether they correspond to a planar motion, and b) if it is the case that the motion is planar, to locate the image of the motion plane, then to recover two points on the image of the absolute conic. The determination of the image of the motion plane from fundamental matrices has been reported in [1,3], to which the following paragraph on the planarity test of the motion is therefore closely.

Testing the planarity of the motion

We first estimate the three fundamental matrices of each pair of images which encode the epipolar geometry of each pair. Let e_{ij}, $i \neq j$, $i = 1, 2, 3$ be the epipole in view i with respect to view j. The trifocal lines t_i, $i = 1, 2, 3$ are the lines $e_{ij} \times e_{ik}$, $i \neq j \neq k$.

The locus of all points in space that projects onto the same points in two images is the well-known horopter curve (H) [4], in general a twisted cubic. This horopter curve has a very simple definition in terms of the fundamental matrix. Let $\mathbf{F}$ be the fundamental matrix and $\mathbf{x}$ a point in the first image. Its epipolar line in the second image is represented by $\mathbf{Fx}$ and since the image of the 3D point corresponding to $\mathbf{x}$ is the same in the second image, we must have $\mathbf{x}^T \mathbf{Fx} = 0$. Conversely, if $\mathbf{x}$ is a point in the first image such that $\mathbf{x}^T \mathbf{Fx} = 0$, it is the image of a point on the horopter, except if $\mathbf{Fx} = \mathbf{0}$ or $\mathbf{F}^T \mathbf{x} = \mathbf{0}$ because then one has $\mathbf{y}^T \mathbf{Fx} = 0$ or $\mathbf{x}^T \mathbf{Fy} = 0$ for all points $\mathbf{y}$.

The curve of equation $\mathbf{x}^T \mathbf{Fx} = 0$ is a conic (c). The matrix of this conic is $\mathbf{G} = \mathbf{F} + \mathbf{F}^T$ since the antisymmetric part of $\mathbf{F}$ is irrelevant. Note that we have two such identical conics, (c) and (c'), one for each view.

The horopter therefore appears as part of the intersection of two quadratic cones each one being defined by the optical center C (respectively C') and the conic (c) (respectively (c')). The intersection of two quadratic cones is a space curve of degree 4. But note that the points e and e' belong to (c) and (c'). This implies that the line (C, C') going through the two optical centers belongs to the curve of intersection since the points on this line project to e in the first view and to e' in the second view. But this line is not on the horopter curve since e satisfies $\mathbf{Fe} = \mathbf{0}$ and e' satisfies $\mathbf{F}^T e' = \mathbf{0}$. The remaining chunk is a curve of degree three, in general a twisted cubic. Note that because the images of this cubic in the two views are the conics (c) and (c'), the cubic has to go through the optical centers C and C' [4].

In the case of interest here where we rotate the camera with respect to an axis L, the horopter curve is simpler. Let us consider the images l and l' of L in the two views. They are clearly identical and therefore L belongs to (H). The remaining part must be a conic which can be easily determined.

Consider the plane Π going through the two optical centers C and C' and perpendicular to L. Such a plane is well defined if L does not meet the line (C, C') which we assume to be the case. The intersection of that plane with the two retinal planes determines two 1D cameras with optical centers C and C' and we can look for the points in that plane such that they have the same images in the two 1D cameras (this is the 2D horopter curve (h) for the system of two cameras described in Section 3.2). Let A be the point of intersection of L and Π. We saw in Section 3.2 that (h) is the circle going through C, C' and A.

The conclusion is that in the case of a rotation with respect to an axis L, the horopter curve (H) splits into the line L and the previous circle in the plane Π. Its image (c) (respectively (c')) therefore also splits into two lines, the image line l (respectively the line l') of L and the line p (respectively p') of intersection of Π with the retinal plane.

For a set of three views, we consider the plane Π_{12} corresponding to the first rotation and the plane Π_{23} corresponding to the second. The motion is planar if and only if the two planes Π_{12} and Π_{23} coincide with the trifocal plane.

This gives a test for the planarity of a motion. The three fundamental matrices yield the three trifocal lines l_i represented by $\mathbf{t}_i = \mathbf{e}_{ij} \times \mathbf{e}_{ik}\ i = 1, 2, 3,\ i \neq j \neq k$. The three matrices $\mathbf{G}_{ij} = \mathbf{F}_{ij} + \mathbf{F}_{ij}^T$, $i \neq j$ (note that $\mathbf{G}_{ij} = \mathbf{G}_{ji}$) define the three conics (c_{ij}) which must split each into two lines, hence the six lines $l_{12}, p_{12}, l_{23}, p_{23}, l_{31}, p_{31}$. A necessary condition for the motion to be planar is that the six lines $l_1, l_2, l_3,$ and l_{12}, l_{23}, l_{31} are "close" enough. The lines p_{ij} are the image lines of the rotation axes, hence generally different and intersect at a point which is the vanishing point of the direction of the rotation axes (the direction perpendicular to the common plane of motion).

Converting 2D images into 1D images

Now comes the central idea of our method: *the 2D images of a camera undergoing any planar motion reduce to 1D images by projecting the 2D image points onto the trifocal line.*

This can be achieved in at least two ways.

First, if the vanishing point $\mathbf{v}$ of the rotation axes is well-defined. Given a 3D point M with image $\mathbf{m}$, we mentally project it to $\hat{M}$ in the plane of motion, the projection being parallel to the direction of rotation. The image $\hat{\mathbf{m}}$ of this virtual point can be obtained in the image as the intersection of the line $\mathbf{v} \times \mathbf{m}$ with the trifocal line $\mathbf{t}$, i.e. $\hat{\mathbf{m}} = \mathbf{t} \times (\mathbf{v} \times \mathbf{m})$.

Since the vanishing point $\mathbf{v}$ of the axes of rotation and the trifocal line $\mathbf{t}$ are known, this is a well-defined construction, see Figure 2.a.

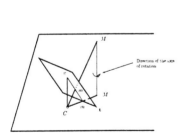 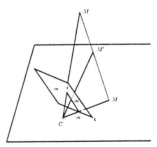

Fig. 2. (a) Creating a 1D image from a 2D image from the vanishing point of the rotation axis and the trifocal line (see text). (b) Creating a 1D image from any pairs of points or any line segments (see text).

Note this is also a projective projection from $\mathcal{P}^2$ (image plane) to $\mathcal{P}^1$ (trifocal line): $\mathbf{m} \mapsto \hat{\mathbf{m}}$.

Alternatively, if the vanishing point does not exist or is poorly defined, we can nonetheless create the virtual points in the trifocal plane. Given two points M and M' with images m and m', the line (M, M') intersects the plane of motion in $\hat{M}$. The image $\hat{m}$ of this virtual point can be obtained in the image as the intersection of the line (m, m') with the trifocal line $\mathbf{t}$, see Figure 2.b.

Another important consequence of this construction is that *2D image line segments can also be converted into 1D image points!* The construction is even simpler, as the resulting 1D image point is just the intersection of the line segment with the trifocal line.

1D Self-calibration

Once the 2D images are reduced to 1D images, we apply the 1D self-calibration method described in Section 3 to the 1D images.

Estimation of the image of the absolute conic for the 2D camera

Each planar motion generally gives us two points on the absolute conic, together with the vanishing point of the rotation axes as the pole of the trifocal line w.r.t. the absolute conic. The pole/polar relation between the vanishing point of the rotation axes and the trifocal line was introduced in [1]. As a whole, this provides 4 constraints on the absolute conic. Since a conic has 5 d.o.f., at least 2 different planar motions, yielding 8 linear constraints on the absolute conic (see Figure 3.a), will be sufficient to determine the full set of 5 internal parameters of a general 2D camera by fitting a general conic $\mathbf{x}^T \mathbf{C} \mathbf{x} = 0$.

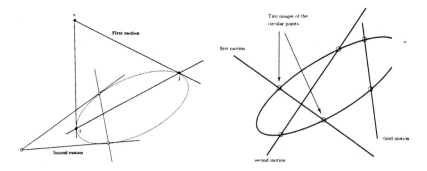

Fig. 3. (a) Computing the image of the absolute conic from two planar motions using the vanishing point of the rotation axes. (b) Computing the image of the absolute conic from three planar motions using only points lying on the conic.

If we assume a 4-parameter model for camera calibration with no image skew (i.e. $s = 0$), one planar motion yielding 4 constraints to determine the 4 internal parameters of the 2D camera is generally sufficient. However this is not true for the very common planar motions such as purely horizontal or vertical motions with the image plane perpendicular to the motion plane (for instance, the planar motion described in Section 5.1 typically belongs to this situation)! It can be easily proven that there are only 3 instead of 4 independent constraints on the absolute conic in these configurations. We need at least 2 different planar motions for determining the 4 internal parameters.

This also suggests that even the planar motion is not purely horizontal or vertical, but close to be, the vanishing point of the rotation axes only constrains loosely the absolute conic. Using only the circular points located on the absolute conic is preferable and numerically stable, but we may need at least 3 planar motions to determine the 5 internal parameters of the 2D camera (see Figure 3.b). Note that the numerical instability of the vanishing point for nearly horizontal trifocal line was already noticed by Armstrong in [2].

Obviously, if we work with a 3-parameter model for camera calibration with known aspect ratio and no image skew, one planar motion is sufficient as was illustrated in Section 5.1 and [1].

Summary and comparison

We can summarize our algorithm for self-calibrating a 2D camera as follows:

1. Take three views of a scene.
2. Estimate the three fundamental matrices [23, 20].
3. Verify that the motion is planar as described above. If it is not planar, stop.
4. Project the point and line correspondences in the retinal plane using either one of the two methods proposed above.
5. Estimate linearly the trifocal tensor of the 3 corresponding 1D images.
6. Solve for the three roots of (5). This yields two points on the image of the absolute conic.
7. If the number of constraints on the absolute conic is less than the number of internal parameters, go to step 1.
8. Fit a complex ellipse using all available constraints.

As we have mentioned at the beginning of this section the method described in this section is related to the work of Armstrong et al. [1], but there are some important differences which we explain now.

First, our approach gives an elegant insight of the intricate relationship between 2D and 1D cameras for a special kind of motion called planar motion.

Second, it allows us to use only the fundamental matrices of the 2D images and the trifocal tensor of 1D images to self-calibrate the camera instead of the trifocal tensor of 2D images. It is now well known that fundamental matrices can be very efficiently and robustly estimated [23, 20]. The same is true of the estimation of the 1D trifocal tensor [14] which is a *linear* process. Armstrong et al., on the other hand, use the trifocal tensor of 2D images which so far has been hard to estimate due to complicated algebraic constraints. Also, the trifocal tensor of 2D images takes a special form in the planar motion case [1] and the new constraints have to be included in the estimation process.

It may be worth mentioning that in the case of interest here, planar motion of the cameras, the Kruppa equations become degenerate [22] and do not allow to recover the internal parameters. Since it is known that the trifocal tensor of 2D images is algebraically equivalent to the three fundamental matrices plus the restriction of the trifocal tensor to the trifocal plane [16, 10], our method can be seen as an unexpensive way of estimating the full trifocal tensor of 2D images:

first estimate the three fundamental matrices (nonlinear but simple and well understood), then estimate the trifocal tensor in the trifocal plane (linear).

Although it looks superficially that both the 1D and 2D trifocal tensors can be estimated linearly with at least 7 image correspondences, this is misleading since the estimation of the 1D trifocal tensor is exactly linear for 7 d.o.f. whereas the linear estimation of the 2D trifocal tensor is only a rough approximation based on a set of 26 auxiliary parameters for its 18 d.o.f. and obtained by neglecting 8 complicated algebraic constraints.

Third, but this is a minor point, our method may not require the estimation of the vanishing point of the rotation axes.

6   Critical motions for self-calibration

In this section, we describe the camera motions that may defeat the self-calibration method developed in Section 3. We call these camera motions critical in that they give rise to ambiguous solutions to the location of the circular points, thus leading to ambiguous calibration and ambiguous metric reconstruction. More details and proofs are given in [19]. Here we only summarize the results.

- If the camera center remains fixed, but the camera may rotate arbitrarily, 2D reconstruction is obviously impossible while self-calibration is possible.
- If the camera undergoes pure translations, by analogy to the 2D camera case, affine reconstruction is possible, but self-calibration is impossible.
- If the camera moves on a circle, and is oriented in such a way that all points of the circle have fixed projections in all the views, neither affine reconstruction nor self-calibration are possible.

7   Experimental results

The theoretical results for 1D camera self-calibration and its applications to 2D camera calibration have been implemented and experimented on synthetic and real images.

We first used a regular square grid of 25 points to show the very strong stability of focal length w.r.t. high noise level. The principal point coordinate is set to 200 and the focal length to 400. The image resolution with such a setting of internal parameters is about 500 pixels. The 25 points of the grid are projected onto the three 1D images. Finally the positions of the projected points are perturbed by adding various amounts of uniformly distributed pixel noise. The results are presented in Table 1.

We note the very stable results of the estimated focal length. With noise levels up to ±10 pixels, the estimation remains extremely near to the true value. The degradation for the estimated positions of the principal point and the fixed point is also graceful, but more sensitive to noise.

For the real case, we consider a scenario of a real camera mounted on a robot's arm. Two sequences of images are acquired by the camera moving in two

Noise	±0	±1	±2	±3	±4	±5	±6	±7	±8	±9	±10
α	400	400.2	400.4	400.7	400.9	401.1	401.3	401.5	401.7	401.8	401.9
u_0	200	205.9	211.8	217.7	223.6	229.5	235.3	241.1	246.8	252.6	258.3
σ	0.0	0.03	0.06	0.09	0.1	0.2	0.3	0.3	0.5	0.6	0.9

Table 1. Table of the estimated internal parameters α and u_0 by 1D self-calibration method from 3 synthetic 1D images with uniform pixel errors of different levels. The fourth row σ shows the standard deviation of the reprojection error for the estimation of the trifocal tensor.

different planes. The first sequence contains 7 (indexed from 16 to 22) images (cf. Figure 4) and the second contains 8 (indexed from 8 to 15).

The calibration grid was used to have the ground truth for the internal camera parameters which have been measured as $\alpha_u = 1534.7$, $\alpha_v = 1539.7$, $u_0 = 281.3$ and $v_0 = 279.0$ using the standard calibration method.

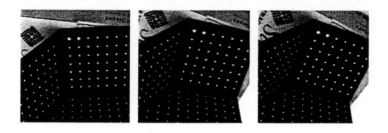

Fig. 4. Three images of the first planar motion.

We take triplets of images from the first sequence and for each triplet we estimate the trifocal line and the vanishing point of the rotation axes by the 3 fundamental matrices of the triplet. The 1D self-calibration is applied for estimating the images of the circular points along the trifocal lines. To evaluate the accuracy of the estimation, the images of the circular points of the trifocal plane are re-computed in the image plane from the known internal parameters by intersecting the image of the absolute conic with the trifocal line. Table 2 shows the results for different triplets of images of the first sequence.

Since we have more than 3 images for the same planar motion of the camera, we could also estimate the trifocal line and the vanishing point of the rotation axes by using all available fundamental matrices of the 7 images of the sequence. The results using redundant images are presented for different triplets in Table 3. We note the slight improvement of the results compared with those presented in Table 2.

The same experiment was carried out for the other sequence of images where the camera underwent a different planar motion. Similar results to the first image

Image triplet	Fixed point	Circular points by self-calibration	Circular points by calibration
$(16, 19, 22)$	493.7	$290.7 \pm i2779.1$	$310.3 \pm i2650.3$
$(16, 20, 22)$	421.8	$250.1 \pm i2146.3$	$273.9 \pm i2153.5$
$(17, 19, 21)$	533.1	$291.3 \pm i2932.4$	$241.3 \pm i2823.1$
$(16, 18, 20)$	617.8	$238.5 \pm i2597.6$	$238.1 \pm i2791.5$
$(18, 20, 22)$	368.3	$230.6 \pm i2208.2$	$272.1 \pm i2126.2$

Table 2. Table of the estimated positions of the images of the circular points by self-calibration with different triplets of images of the first sequence.

Image triplet	Circular points	Fixed point
$(16, 18, 20)$	$245.5 \pm i2490.5$	590.0
$(18, 20, 22)$	$221.4 \pm i2717.8$	384.4
$(16, 20, 22)$	$236.2 \pm i2617.3$	452.9
$(16, 19, 22)$	$240.0 \pm i2693.4$	488.0
$(17, 19, 21)$	$304.7 \pm i2722.7$	516.6
known position by calibration	$262.1 \pm i2590.6$	

Table 3. Table of the estimated positions of the image of circular points with different triplets of images. The trifocal line and the vanishing point of the rotation axes are estimated using 7 images of the sequence instead of the minimum of 3 images.

sequence are obtained, we give only the result for one triplet of images in Table 4 for this sequence.

Image triplet	Fixed point	Circular points by self-calibration	Circular points by calibration
$(8, 11, 15)$	927.2	$269.7 + i1875.5$	$276.5 + i1540.1$

Table 4. Table of the estimated position of the image of circular points with one triplet of second image sequence.

Now two sequences of images each corresponding to a different planar motion yield four distinct imaginary points on the image plane which must be on the image ω of the absolute conic. We therefore fit to those four points an imaginary ellipse using standard techniques and compute the resulting internal parameters. Note that we did not use the pole/polar constraint of the vanishing point of the rotation axes on the absolute conic as it was discussed in Section 5.2 that this constraint is not numerically reliable.

The ultimate goal of self-calibration is to get 3D metric reconstruction. 3D reconstruction from two images of the sequence is performed by using the estimated internal parameters as illustrated in Figure 5. To evaluate the reconstruction quality, we did the same reconstruction using the known internal parameters. Two such reconstructions differ merely by a 3D similarity transformation which could be easily estimated. The resulting normalised relative error of the reconstruction from two images by self-calibration with respect to the reconstruction by off-line calibration is 3.4 percent. More intensive experimental results could be found in the extended version which can be downloaded from http://www.inrialpes.fr/movi/people/Quan/publication.

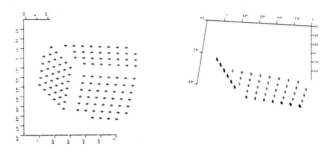

Fig. 5. Two views of the resulting 3D reconstruction by self-calibration.

8   Conclusions and other applications

We have first established that the 2 internal parameters of 1D camera can be uniquely determined through the trifocal tensor of three 1D images. Since the trifocal tensor can be estimated linearly from at least 7 points in three 1D images, the method of the 1D self-calibration is a real linear method (modulo the fact that we have to find the roots of a third degree polynomial in 1 variable), no any over-parameterisation was introduced.

Secondly, we have proven that if a 2D camera undergoes a planar motion, the 2D camera reduces to a 1D camera in the plane of motion. The reduction of a 2D image to a 1D image can be efficiently performed by using only the fundamental matrices of 2D images. Based on this relation between 2D and 1D images, the self-calibration of 1D camera can be applied for self-calibrating a 2D camera. Our experimental results based on real image sequences show the very large stability of the solutions yielded by the 1D self-calibration method and the accurate 3D metric reconstruction that can be obtained from the internal parameters of the 2D camera estimated by the 1D self-calibration method.

Acknowledgement This work has been supported in part by European project CUMULI. We would also like to thank R. Mohr for interesting discussion and the anonymous ECCV reviewers for the constructive comments.

References

1. M. Armstrong, A. Zisserman, and R. Hartley. Self-calibration from image triplets. ECCV, 3–16, 1996.
2. M. Armstrong. Self-calibration from image sequences. Ph.D. Thesis, University of Oxford, 1996.

3. P.A. Beardsley and A. Zisserman. Affine calibration of mobile vehicles. *Europe-China Workshop on GMICV*, 214–221. 1995.

4. T. Buchanan. The twisted cubic and camera calibration. CVGIP, 42(1):130–132, 1988.

5. O. Faugeras. Stratification of three-dimensional vision: Projective, affine and metric representations. JOSA, 12:465–484, 1995.

6. O. Faugeras and S. Maybank. Motion from point matches: Multiplicity of solutions. IJCV, 3(4):225–246, 1990.

7. O. Faugeras and B. Mourrain. About the correspondences of points between n images. *Workshop on Representation of Visual Scenes*, 37–44, 1995.

8. R. Hartley. In defence of the 8-point algorithm. ICCV, 1064–1070, 1995.

9. R.I. Hartley. A linear method for reconstruction from lines and points. ICCV, 882–887, 1995.

10. A. Heyden. *Geometry and Algebra of Multiple Projective Transformations*. Ph.D. thesis, Lund University, 1995.

11. Q.-T. Luong and O. Faugeras. Self-calibration of a moving camera from point correspondences and fundamental matrices. IJCV, 22(3):261–289, 1997.

12. S.J. Maybank and O.D. Faugeras. A theory of self calibration of a moving camera. IJCV, 8(2):123–151, 1992.

13. R. Mohr, B. Boufama, and P. Brand. Understanding positioning from multiple images. AI, (78):213–238, 1995.

14. L. Quan. Uncalibrated 1D projective camera and 3D affine reconstruction of lines. CVPR, 60–65, 1997.

15. L. Quan and T. Kanade. Affine structure from line correspondences with uncalibrated affine cameras. *Trans. PAMI*, 19(8):834–845, 1997.

16. L. Quan. Algebraic Relations among Matching Constraints of Multiple Images. Technical Report INRIA, RR-3345, Jan. 1998 (also TR Lifia-Imag 1995).

17. A. Shashua. Algebraic functions for recognition. *Trans. PAMI*, 17(8):779–789, 1995.

18. M. Spetsakis and J. Aloimonos. A unified theory of structure from motion. *DARPA Image Understanding Workshop*, 271–283, 1990.

19. P. Sturm. Vision 3D non calibrée : contributions à la reconstruction projective et étude des mouvements critiques pour l'auto-calibrage. Ph.D. Thesis, INPG, 1997.

20. P.H.S. Torr and A. Zissermann. Performance characterization of fundamental matrix estimation under image degradation. MVA, 9:321–333, 1997.

21. B. Triggs. Matching constraints and the joint image. ICCV, 338–343, 1995.

22. Cyril Zeller and Olivier Faugeras. Camera self-calibration from video sequences: the Kruppa equations revisited. Research Report 2793, INRIA, February 1996.

23. Z. Zhang, R. Deriche, O. Faugeras, and Q.T. Luong. A robust technique for matching two uncalibrated images through the recovery of the unknown epipolar geometry. AI, 78:87–119, 1995.

Stereo Vision and Calibration I

Multi Viewpoint Stereo
from Uncalibrated Video Sequences

Reinhard Koch, Marc Pollefeys, and Luc Van Gool

Katholieke Universiteit Leuven,
Kardinaal Mercierlaan 94, B-3001 Leuven, Belgium
Email: firstname.lastname@esat.kuleuven.ac.be
http://www.esat.kuleuven.ac.be/psi/visics.html

Abstract. This contribution describes an automatic 3D surface modeling system that extracts dense metric 3D surfaces from an uncalibrated video sequence. A static 3D scene is observed from multiple viewpoints by freely moving a video camera around the object. No restrictions on camera movement and internal camera parameters like zoom are imposed, as the camera pose and intrinsic parameters are calibrated from the sequence.

Dense surface reconstructions are obtained by first treating consecutive images of the sequence as stereoscopic pairs and computing dense disparity maps for all image pairs. All viewpoints are then linked by controlled correspondence linking for each image pixel. The correspondence linking algorithm allows for accurate depth estimation as well as image texture fusion from all viewpoints simultaneously. By keeping track of surface visibility and measurement uncertainty it can cope with occlusions and measurement outliers. The correspondence linking is applied to increase the robustness and geometrical resolution of surface depth as well as to remove highlights and specular reflections, and to create super-resolution texture maps for increased realism.

The major impact of this work is the ability to automatically generate geometrically correct and visually pleasing 3D surface models from image sequences alone, which allows the economic model generation for a wide range of applications. The resulting textured 3D surface model are highly realistic VRML representations of the scene.

1 Introduction

3D surface reconstruction from image sequences is an ongoing research topic in the computer vision society. For calibrated sequences good results were obtained by structure-from-motion algorithms or stereoscopic image sequences (see [10, 26, 16]). Contributions were made for multi baseline stereo [19], incremental depth estimation [18] and multi viewpoint analysis [9] from known camera positions.

Metric reconstruction from uncalibrated sequences is still under investigation. In the uncalibrated case all parameters - camera pose and intrinsic calibration as well as the 3D scene structure - have to be estimated from the 2D image sequence alone. Faugeras and Hartley first demonstrated how to obtain projective reconstructions from such image sequences [6, 11]. Since then, researchers tried to find ways to upgrade these reconstructions to metric (i.e. Euclidean but unknown scale, see for example [7, 22, 25]).

They mostly restricted themselves to constant intrinsic parameters. Recently, extensions of this work to varying intrinsic camera parameters were proposed [21, 12, 23].

To employ these self-calibration methods for sequence analysis they must be embedded in a complete scene reconstruction system. Beardsley et al. [1] proposed a scheme to obtain projective calibration and 3D structure by robustly tracking salient scene feature points throughout an image sequence. This sparse object representation outlines the object shape, but gives insufficient surface detail for visual reconstruction. Highly realistic 3D surface models need dense depth maps and can not rely on relatively few feature points.

In [23] the method of Beardsley et al. [1] was extended in two directions: On the one hand the projective reconstruction was updated to metric even for varying internal camera parameters. On the other hand a dense stereo matching technique [4] was applied between two selected images of the sequence to obtain a dense depth map for a single viewpoint. From this depth map a triangular surface wire-frame was constructed and texture mapping from one image was applied to obtain realistic surface models.

In this contribution we extend the dense surface reconstruction as proposed in [23] to sequence analysis. An algorithm is proposed that links image correspondences over the image sequence and allows to integrate both depth and image texture. Only weak restrictions are imposed on the camera motion and on scene geometry, and the approach is embedded in a completely uncalibrated and automatic framework. It will be shown how the analysis of surface depth and surface texture from the image sequence will improve the accuracy of the surface model. At the same time texture integration opens new means to enhance the object texture quality. The creation of super-resolution texture maps and removal of imaging artifacts or specular reflections are additional features of the proposed algorithm.

1.1 Overview of 3-D Reconstruction System

The complete 3-D surface reconstruction system consists of several modules to be executed in a processing pipeline. Some modules were discussed in earlier publications and will be sketched only. The system structure can be summarized as follows:

1. Sparse Point Tracking and Calibration. Section 2 reviews the feature point tracking algorithm. It uses a 2 step approach:
   (a) obtain projective calibration and 3D point reconstruction,
   (b) upgrade to metric calibration and structure through self-calibration based on constraints applied to the *absolute quadric*.

2. Pairwise Dense Disparity Matching. Section 3 deals with dense disparity measurements from image pairs. Adjacent images of the sequence are treated as stereo image pairs and dense correspondence maps are computed between these pairs [4].

3. Correspondence Linking Algorithm. In Sect. 4 the correspondence linking algorithm is developed which links all possible image point correspondences over the sequence, guided by a depth verification that allows to test for outliers and occlusions. Depth and texture fusion are derived from the basic linking scheme.

4. 3-D Surface Reconstruction. Textured triangular surface meshes are then generated from refined depth and texture maps to build highly realistic scene models, as described in Sect. 5.

2   Camera Calibration through Feature Point Tracking

Two things are needed to build a 3D model from an image sequence: (1) the calibration[1] of the sequence and (2) the correspondences between the images. Starting from an image sequence acquired by an uncalibrated video camera, both these prerequisites are unknown and therefore have to be retrieved from image data. Only a few but very reliable image correspondences are needed to retrieve the calibration of the camera setup. Salient feature points like strong intensity corners are robustly tracked throughout the image sequence for that purpose. In a two-step approach a projective calibration and feature point reconstruction is recovered from the image sequence which is then upgraded to metric calibration with a self-calibration approach.

2.1   Retrieving the Projective Framework

At first, feature correspondences are found by extracting intensity corners in different images and matching them using a robust corner matcher [24]. In conjunction with the matching of the corners a restricted calibration of the setup is calculated (i.e. only determined up to an arbitrary projective transformation). This allows to eliminate matches which are inconsistent with the calibration. The 3D position of a point is restricted to the line passing through its image point and the camera projection center. Therefore the corresponding point is restricted to the projection of this line in the other image. Using this constraint, more matches can easily be found and used to refine this calibration. The principle is explained in Fig. 1.

The matching is first carried out on the first two images. This defines a projective framework in which the projection matrices of the other views are retrieved one by one. In this approach we follow the procedure proposed by Beardsley et al. [1]. We therefore obtain projection matrices (3×4) of the form

---

[1] By *calibration* we mean the actual internal calibration of the camera as well as the relative position and orientation of the camera for the different viewpoints.

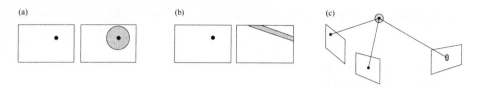

Fig. 1. Images with (a) a priori search region, (b) search region based on the epipolar constraint, (c) prediction of search region in the sequence after projective reconstruction of the point (used for refinement).

$$\mathbf{P}_1 = [\mathbf{I}|0] \text{ and } \mathbf{P}_i = [\mathbf{H}_{1i}|e_{1i}] \tag{1}$$

with $\mathbf{H}_{1i}$ the homography for some reference plane from view 1 to view i and e_{1i} the corresponding epipole.

2.2 Retrieving the Metric Framework

Such a projective calibration is certainly not satisfactory for the purpose of 3D modeling. A reconstruction obtained up to a projective transformation can differ very much from the original scene according to human perception: orthogonality and parallelism are in general not preserved, part of the scene can be warped to infinity, etc. To obtain a better calibration, constraints on the internal camera parameters can be imposed (e.g. absence of skew, known aspect ratio, ...). By exploiting these constraints, the projective reconstruction can be upgraded to metric (Euclidean up to scale).

In that case the camera projection matrices should have the following form:

$$\mathbf{P}_i = \mathbf{K}_i \, [\mathbf{R}_i|\text{-}\mathbf{R}_i\mathbf{t}_i] \text{ with } \mathbf{K}_i = \begin{bmatrix} f_x & s & u_x \\ & f_y & u_y \\ & & 1 \end{bmatrix} \tag{2}$$

where $\mathbf{R}_i$ and $\mathbf{t}_i$ indicate the orientation and position of the camera for view i, $\mathbf{K}_i$ contains the internal camera parameters, f_x and f_y stand for the horizontal and vertical focal length (in pixels), $\mathbf{u} = (u_x, u_y)$ is the principal point and s is a measure of the skew.

A practical way to obtain the calibration parameters from constraints on the internal camera parameters is through application of the concept of the absolute quadric [25,23]. In space, exactly one degenerate quadric of planes exists which has the property to be invariant under all rigid transformations. In a metric frame it is represented by the following 4×4 symmetric rank 3 matrix $\Omega = \begin{bmatrix} \mathbf{I} & 0 \\ 0 & 0 \end{bmatrix}$. If $\mathbf{T}$ transforms points $M \to \mathbf{T}M$ (and thus $\mathbf{P} \to \mathbf{P}\mathbf{T}^{-1}$), then it transforms $\Omega \to \mathbf{T}\Omega\mathbf{T}^\top$ (which can be verified to yield Ω when $\mathbf{T}$ is a similarity transformation)[2]. The projection of the absolute quadric onto the image yields

---

[2] Using (2) this can be verified for a metric basis. Transforming $\mathbf{P} \to \mathbf{P}\mathbf{T}^{-1}$ and $\Omega \to \mathbf{T}\Omega\mathbf{T}^\top$ will not change the projection.

the intrinsic camera parameters independent of the chosen projective basis:

$$\mathbf{K}_i \mathbf{K}_i^{\mathsf{T}} \propto \mathbf{P}_i \Omega \mathbf{P}_i^{\mathsf{T}} \tag{3}$$

where $\propto$ means equal up to an arbitrary non-zero scale factor. Therefore constraints on the internal camera parameters in $\mathbf{K}_i$ can be translated to constraints on the absolute quadric. If enough constraints are at hand, only one quadric will satisfy them all, i.e. the *absolute quadric*. At that point the scene can be transformed to the metric frame (which brings Ω to its canonical form).

3 Dense Stereo Pair Matching

With the camera calibration given for all viewpoints of the sequence, we can proceed with methods developed for calibrated structure from motion algorithms. The feature tracking algorithm already delivers a sparse surface model based on distinct feature points. This however is not sufficient to reconstruct geometrically correct and visually pleasing surface models. This task is accomplished by a dense disparity matching that estimates correspondences from the grey level images directly by exploiting additional geometrical constraints.

3.1 Exploiting Scene Constraints

The epipolar constraint obtained from calibration restricts corresponding image points to lie in the epipolar plane[3] which also cuts a 3D profile out of the surface of the scene objects. The profile projects onto the corresponding epipolar lines in the images $\mathbf{I_i}$ and $\mathbf{I_k}$ where it forms an ordered set of neighboring correspondences (see left of Fig. 2).

For well behaved surfaces this ordering is preserved and delivers an additional constraint, known as *ordering constraint*. Scene constraints like this can be applied by making weak assumptions about the object geometry. In many real applications the observed objects will be opaque and composed out of piecewise continuous surfaces. If this restriction holds then additional constraints can be imposed on the correspondence estimation. Kochan [17] listed as many as 12 different constraints for correspondence estimation in stereo pairs. Of them, the two most important apart from the epipolar constraint are:

1. *Ordering Constraint:* For opaque surfaces the order of neighboring correspondences on the corresponding epipolar lines is always preserved. This ordering allows the construction of a dynamic programming scheme which is employed by many dense disparity estimation algorithms [3, 4, 8].
2. *Uniqueness Constraint:* The correspondence between any two corresponding points is bidirectional as long as there is no occlusion in one of the images. A correspondence vector pointing from an image point to its corresponding point in the other image always has a corresponding reverse vector pointing back. This test is used to to detect outliers and occlusions.

---

[3] The epipolar plane is the plane defined by the the image point and the camera projection centers.

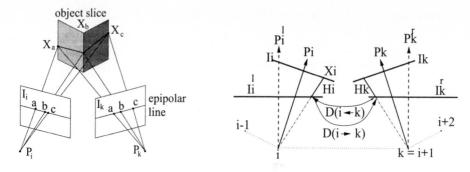

Fig. 2. Left: Object profile triangulation from ordered neighboring correspondences. Right: Rectification and correspondence between viewpoints i and k

3.2 Image Rectification

All above mentioned constraints operate along the epipolar lines which may have an arbitrary orientation in the image planes. The matching procedure is greatly simplified if the image pair is rectified to a standard geometry. In standard geometry both image planes are coplanar and the epipoles are projected to infinity. The rectified image planes can further be oriented such that the epipolar lines coincide with the image scan lines. Image rectification then involves a planar projective mapping from the original towards the rectified image planes. Note that the rectification process is under-determined and there is an additional degree of freedom to be set. Conveniently the projective mapping transformation $\mathbf{H}$ is chosen such that the resulting image distortions are minimized. Possible criteria can be to minimize the change of camera orientation [16] or the deviation of the image corner angles from right angles [5].

Figure 2 (right) clarifies the relation between the original and rectified images and cameras, as well as the correspondence matching process that links the viewpoints i and k. Viewpoint i is treated as the left member of the pair, k as right member. For identification purposes they are indexed with superscript (l,r), respectively. The camera and image $(\mathbf{I_i}, \mathbf{P_i})$ is then rectified to $(\mathbf{I_i^l}, \mathbf{P_i^l})$, while $(\mathbf{I_k}, \mathbf{P_k})$ is rectified to $(\mathbf{I_k^r}, \mathbf{P_k^r})$.

3.3 Constrained Matching

For dense correspondence matching a disparity estimator based on the dynamic programming scheme of Cox et al. [3], is employed that incorporates the above mentioned constraints. It operates on rectified image pairs where the epipolar lines coincide with image scan lines. The matcher searches at each pixel in image $\mathbf{I_i^r}$ for maximum normalized cross correlation in $\mathbf{I_k^l}$ by shifting a small measurement window (kernel size 5x5 or 7x7) along the corresponding scan line. The selected search step-size ΔD (usually 1 pixel) determines the search resolution. Matching ambiguities are resolved by exploiting the ordering constraint in the dynamic programming approach [16]. The algorithm was further adapted to employ extended neighborhood relationships and a pyramidal estimation scheme to reliably deal with very large disparity ranges of over 50% of the image size [4]. The estimate is stored in a disparity map $D_{(i,k)}$ with one of the following values:

- a valid correspondence $\mathbf{x}_k^l = D_{(i,k)}[\mathbf{x}_i^r]$,
- an undetected search failure which leads to an outlier,
- a detected search failure with no correspondence.

The matching algorithm was tested extensively on different scenes under laboratory and real outdoor conditions. To verify ground truth the system estimates were compared with synthetic data of known ground truth and with a high resolution active scanning system that projects coded light stripe patterns on the scene. It was found that the relative depth error of the matching system ranged between 0.3% to 1%. For further details see [16].

4 Multi Viewpoint Linking

The pairwise disparity estimation allows to compute image to image correspondence between adjacent rectified image pairs, and independent depth estimates for each camera viewpoint. An optimal joint estimate will be achieved by fusing all independent estimates into a common 3D model. The fusion can be performed in an economical way through controlled correspondence linking as described in this contribution. The approach utilizes a flexible multi viewpoint scheme by combining the advantages of small baseline and wide baseline stereo.

As *small baseline stereo* we define viewpoints where the baseline is much smaller than the observed average scene depth. This configuration is usually valid for image sequences were the images are taken as a spatial sequence from many slightly varying view points. The advantages (+) and disadvantages (−) are

+ easy correspondence estimation, since the views are similar,
+ small regions of viewpoint related occlusions[4],
− small triangulation angle, hence small depth accuracy.

The *wide baseline stereo* in contrast is used mostly with still image photographs of a scene where few images are taken from a very different viewpoint. Here the depth accuracy is better but correspondence and occlusion problems appear

− difficult correspondence estimation, since the views are not similar,
− large regions of viewpoint related occlusions,
+ big triangulation angle, hence high depth accuracy.

The *multi viewpoint linking* combines the virtues of both approaches. In addition it will produce denser depth maps than either of the other techniques,

---

[4] As view point related occlusions we consider those parts of the object that are visible in one image only, due to object self-occlusion.

and allows additional features for depth and texture fusion. Advantages of *multi viewpoint linking* are

- very dense depth maps for each viewpoint,
- no viewpoint dependent occlusions,
- high depth accuracy through viewpoint fusion,
- texture enhancement through texture fusion.

4.1 Correspondence Linking Algorithm

The correspondence linking is described in the following section. It concatenates corresponding image points over multiple viewpoints by correspondence tracking over adjacent image pairs.

Consider an image sequence taken from $i = [1, N]$ viewpoints with camera projection matrices calibrated as described in Sect. 2. Assume that the sequence is taken by a camera moving sideways while keeping the object in view. For any view point i let us consider the image triple $[I_{i-1}, I_i, I_{i+1}]$. The image pairs (I_{i-1}, I_i) and (I_i, I_{i+1}) form two stereoscopic image pairs with correspondence estimates as described above.

We can now create two chains of correspondence links for an image point $\mathbf{x_i}$, one up and one down the image index i.

Upwards linking: $\mathbf{x_{i+1}} = (\mathbf{H^r_{i+1}})^{-1} D_{(i,i+1)}[\mathbf{H^l_i x_i}],$

Downwards linking: $\mathbf{x_{i-1}} = (\mathbf{H^l_{i-1}})^{-1} D_{(i,i-1)}[\mathbf{H^r_i x_i}].$

$\mathbf{H}$ denotes the transformation for image rectification and $D_{(i,k)}$ the correspondence between the rectified images. The linking process is repeated along the image sequence to create a chain of correspondences upwards and downwards. Every correspondence link requires 2 mappings and 1 disparity lookup. Throughout the sequence of N images, $2(N-1)$ disparity maps are computed. The multi viewpoint linking is then performed efficiently via fast lookup functions on the pre-computed estimates.

Occlusions and Visibility. In a triangulation sensor with two viewpoints i and k two types of occlusion occur. If parts of the object are hidden in both viewpoints due to object self-occlusion, then we speak of *object occlusions* which cannot be resolved from this viewpoint. If a surface region is visible in viewpoint i but not in k, we speak of a *shadow occlusion*. The regions have a shadow-like appearance of undefined disparity values since the occlusions at view k cast a shadow on the object as seen from view i. Shadow occlusions are in fact detected by the uniqueness constraint discussed in Sect. 3. A solution to avoid shadow occlusions is to incorporate a symmetrical multi viewpoint matcher as proposed in this contribution. Points that are shadowed in the (right) view $i+1$ are normally visible in the (left) view $i-1$ and vice versa. The exploitation of up-and down-links will resolve for the shadow occlusions. A helpful measure in this context is the visibility V that defines for a pixel in view i the maximum number of possible correspondences in the sequence. $V = 1$ is caused by a shadow occlusion, $V >= 2$ allows a depth estimate.

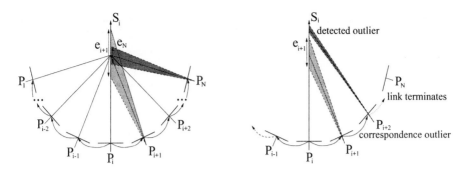

Fig. 3. Left: Depth fusion and uncertainty reduction from correspondence linking. Right: detection of correspondence outliers by depth interval testing.

Depth Estimation and Outlier Detection. Care must be taken to exclude invalid disparity values or outliers from the chain. If an invalid disparity value is encountered, the chain is terminated immediately. Outliers are detected by the statistics of the depth estimate computed from the correspondences. Inliers will update the depth estimate using a 1-D Kalman filter.

Depth and Uncertainty. Consider a 3D surface point $\mathbf{X}$ that is projected onto its corresponding image points $\mathbf{x_i} = \mathbf{P_i X}, \mathbf{x_k} = \mathbf{P_k X}$. The inverse process holds for triangulating $\mathbf{X}$ from the corresponding point pair $(\mathbf{x_i}, \mathbf{x_k})$. We can in fact exploit the calibrated camera geometry and express the 3D point $\mathbf{X}$ as a depth value d_x along the known line of sight $\mathbf{S_{xi}}$ that extends from the camera projection center through the image correspondence $\mathbf{x_i}$. Triangulation computes the depth as the length of $\mathbf{S_{xi}}$ between the camera projection center and the locus of minimum distance between the corresponding lines of sight. The triangulation is computed for each image point and stored in a depth map associated with the viewpoint.

The depth for each reference image point $\mathbf{x_i}$ is improved by the correspondence linking that delivers two lists of image correspondences relative to the reference, one linking down from $i \to 1$ and one linking up from $i \to N$. For each valid corresponding point pair $(\mathbf{x_i}, \mathbf{x_k})$ we can triangulate a consistent depth estimate $d(x_i, x_k)$ along $\mathbf{S_{xi}}$ with e_k representing the depth uncertainty. Figure 3(left) visualizes the decreasing uncertainty interval during linking. While the disparity measurement resolution ΔD in the image is kept constant (at 1 pixel), the reprojected depth error e_k decreases with the baseline.

Outlier Detection and Inlier Fusion. As measurement noise we assume a contaminated Gaussian distribution with a main peak within a small interval (of 1 pixel) and a small percentage of outliers. Inlier noise is caused by the limited resolution of the disparity matcher. Outliers are undetected correspondence failures and may be arbitrarily large. As threshold to detect the outliers we utilize the depth uncertainty interval e_k. The detection of an outlier at k terminates the linking at $k - 1$. All depth values $[d_i, d_{i+1}, ..., d_{k-1}]$ are inlier depth values that fall within the uncertainty interval around the mean depth estimate. They are fused by a simple 1-D kalman filter to obtain a mean depth estimate.

Figure 3 (right) explains the outlier selection and link termination. The outlier detection scheme is not optimal since it relies on the position of the outlier in the chain. Valid correspondences behind the outlier are not considered any more. It will, however, always be as good as a single estimate and in general superior to it. In addition, since we process bidirectionally up- and down-link, we always have two correspondence chains to fuse which allows for one outlier per chain.

4.2 Texture Enhancement

The correspondence linking builds a controlled chain of correspondences that can be used for texture enhancement as well. At each reference pixel one may collect a sorted list of image color values from the corresponding image positions. This allows to enhance the original texture in many ways by accessing the color statistics. Some features that are derived naturally from the linking algorithm are:

1. **Highlight and reflection removal**: A median or robust mean of the corresponding texture values is computed to discard imaging artifacts like sensor noise, specular reflections and highlights [20].
2. **Super-resolution texture**: The correspondence linking is not restricted to pixel-resolution, since each sub-pixel-position in the reference image can be used to start a correspondence chain. The correspondence values are obtained from the disparity map through interpolation. The object is viewed with a camera of limited pixel resolution but from many slightly displaced viewpoints. This can be exploited to create super-resolution texture by fusing all images on a finer resampling grid [13].
3. **Best view selection for highest texture resolution**: For each surface region around a pixel the image which has the highest possible texture resolution is selected, based on the object distance and viewing angle. The composite image takes the highest possible resolution from all images into account.

A detailed discussion of texture fusion is out of the scope of this contribution but we will give some examples of it in the experiment section.

5 3D Surface Modeling

The dense depth maps as computed by the correspondence linking need to be approximated by a 3D surface representation suitable for visualization. So far each object point was treated independently. To achieve spatial coherence and a connected surface, the depth map is spatially interpolated using a parametric surface model. We employ a bounded thin plate model with a second order spline to smooth the surface and to interpolate small surface gaps in regions that could not be measured. This spatially smoothed surface is then approximated by a triangular wire frame to reduce geometric complexity and tailor the model for visualization [15]. Texture mapping of the texture onto the wire frame model greatly enhances the realism of the models which are stored in VRML file format for easy exchange with visualization systems.

The mesh triangulation currently utilizes the reference view only to build the model. It can deal with shadow occlusions but not with true 3D object occlusions. In a next step a viewpoint independent mesh generation will be implemented to allow closure of the object surface. We will incorporate a surface registration scheme based on the Iterated Closest Point algorithm ICP [2] to fit surfaces from different view points. The surface parts that are overlapping are then retriangulated to allow for one consistent surface mesh [14].

Another problem to be tackled is the fusion of different projective frames into a global coordinate system. Often it is not possible to record a contiguous video stream of an extended object where all views are calibrated in the same projective frame. When moving around or inside of a building, for example, scene cuts are inevitable and the system will generate an independent calibration for each scene cut. Registration of the independent frames consists of 3D position and scale adaptation. We are developing an interactive 3D interface where the user can easily register those frames.

6 Experiments

In this section the performance of the algorithm is tested on the two outdoor sequences *Castle* and *Fountain*.

6.1 Castle Sequence

The *Castle* sequence consists of 22 images of 720x576 pixel resolution taken with a standard semi-professional camcorder that was moved freely in front of a building. Figure 4 shows results from camera tracking. Four of the images (left) and the estimated 3D-structure of the building with calibrated camera positions are displayed from a front view (right). The rectangular appearance of the building, the regular spacing of camera positions, and measurements on the reconstructed surface [23] confirm the metric qualities of the calibration.

To judge the geometric and visual quality of the reconstruction, different perspective views of the model were computed and displayed in Fig. 5. In the shaded view (left), the geometric details like the window and door niches are seen. A close-up look from a position that a human observer would take reveals the high visual quality of the model (center). To demonstrate the texture fusion capabilities of the algorithm, the specular reflection in the upper right window was removed by a texture median filtering and a super-resolution texture with zoom factor of 4 was generated from the image sequence (right). The region shows the reference image (above) and the generated median super-resolution texture without reflection (below).

Fig. 4. Left: 4 of 22 images of the castle which were used for the reconstruction. Right: a view of the 3D model with feature points superimposed in black and the calibrated camera positions visualized as pyramids.

Performance Evaluation for the Castle Sequence. The above reconstructions showed some qualitative results. The quantitative performance of correspondence linking can be tested in different ways. One measure already mentioned is the visibility of an object point. In connection with correspondence linking, we have defined visibility V as the number of views linked to the reference view. Another important feature of the algorithm is the density and accuracy of the depth maps. To describe its improvement over the 2-view estimator, we define the fill rate F and the average relative depth error E as additional measures.

Fig. 5. Left: shaded view. Center: close-up view. Right: 4x zoomed original region (above), generation of median-filtered super-resolution texture (below).

Visibility $V\,[views]$: average number of views linked to the reference image.

Fill Rate $F\,[\%]$: $\dfrac{\text{Number of valid pixels}}{\text{Total number of pixels}}$

Depth error $E\,[\%]$: relative depth error e_d for all valid pixels.

The 2-view disparity estimator is a special case of the proposed linking algorithm, hence both can be compared on an equal basis. The 2-view estimator operates on the image pair $(i, i+1)$ only, while the multi view estimator operates on a sequence $1 < i < N$ with $N >= 3$. The above defined statistical measures were computed for different sequence lengths N. Figure 6 displays visibility and relative depth error for sequences from 2 to 15 images, chosen symmetrically around the reference image. The average visibility V shows that for up to 5 images nearly all views are utilized. For 15 images, at average 9 images are linked. The amount of linking is reflected in the relative depth error that drops from 5% in the 2 view estimator to about 1.2% for 15 images.

Linking two views is the minimum case that allows triangulation. To increase the reliability of the estimates, a surface point should occur in more than two images. We can therefore impose a minimum visibility V_{min} on a depth estimate. This will reject unreliable depth estimates effectively, but will also reduce the fill-rate of the depth map.

The graphs in Fig. 6(center) show the dependency of the fill rate and depth error on minimum visibility for N=11. The fill rate drops from 92% to about 70%, but at the same time the depth error is reduced to 0.5% due to outlier rejection. The depth map and the relative error distribution over the depth map

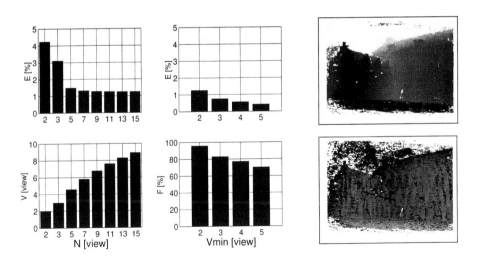

Fig. 6. Statistics of the castle sequence. Left: Influence of sequence length N on visibility V and relative depth error E. Center: Influence of minimum visibility V_{min} on fill rate F and depth error E for $N = 11$. Right: Depth map (above: dark=near, light=far) and error map (below: dark=large error, light=small error) for $N = 11$ and $V_{min} = 3$.

is displayed in Fig. 6(right). The error distribution shows a periodic structure that in fact reflects the quantization uncertainty of the disparity resolution when it switches from one disparity value to the next.

6.2 Fountain Sequence

The *Fountain* sequence consists of 5 images of the back wall of a fountain at the archaeological site of Sagalassos in Turkey, taken with a digital camera with 573x764 pixel resolution. It shows a concavity in which once a statue was situated. Figure 7 shows from left to right images 1 and 3 of the sequence, the depth map as computed with the 2-view estimator, and the depth map when using all 5 images. The white (undefined) regions in the 2-view depth map are due to shadow occlusions which are almost completely removed in the 5-view depth map. This is reflected in the fill rate that increases from 89 to 96%. It should be noted that for this sequence a very large search range of 400 pixels was used, which is over 70% of the image width. Despite this large search range only few matching errors occurred.

Fig. 7. Left: First and last image of sequence. Right: Depth maps from the 2-view and the 5-view estimator (from left to right) showing the very dense depth maps.

The performance characteristics are displayed in the Table 1. The fill rate is high and the relative error is rather low because of a fairly wide baseline between views. This is reflected in the high geometric quality of depth the map and the reconstruction.

Table 1. Statistics of fountain sequence for visibility V, fill rate F and depth error E.

N[view]	V[views]	F[%]	E[%]
2	2	89.8728	0.294403
3	2.85478	96.7405	0.208367
5	4.23782	96.4774	0.121955

The visual reconstruction quality for the fountain is displayed in Fig. 8. Even fine details like the relief carved into the stones are preserved. The side and top views of the overall model show the accurate and detailed structure due to the wide triangulation angle over the sequence, and the textured close-up view reveals a highly realistic sensation.

Fig. 8. Above: shaded and textured front view of model, Below: shaded top view and close-up of the textured model.

7   Conclusion

In this contribution we developed a correspondence linking scheme that computes dense and accurate depth maps based on the sequence linking of pairwise estimated disparity maps. The correspondence linking is the basic tool which allows to perform a variety of different operations on the image data. Depth and texture fusion, outlier detection and texture enhancement are some of the proposed applications.

The algorithm is embedded in a surface reconstruction system that allows for fully automatic generation of textured 3D surface models from image sequences, acquired with uncalibrated hand-held cameras. The performance analysis showed that very dense depth maps with fill rates of over 90% and a relative depth error of 0.1% can be measured with off-the-shelf cameras even in unrestricted outdoor environments such as an archaeological site.

Acknowledgments

We would like to thank Andrew Zisserman and his group from Oxford for supplying us with robust projective reconstruction software. I. Cox and L. Falkenhagen supplied versions of their disparity matching code. A specialization grant from the Flemish Institute for Scientific Research in Industry (IWT) and the financial support from the EU ACTS project AC074 VANGUARD are also gratefully acknowledged.

References

1. P. Beardsley, P. Torr and A. Zisserman: 3D Model Acquisition from Extended Image Sequences. In: B. Buxton, R. Cipolla(Eds.) Computer Vision - ECCV 96, Cambridge, UK., vol.2, pp.683-695. Lecture Notes in Computer Science, Vol. 1064. Springer Verlag, 1996.
2. Y. Chen and G. Medioni: Object Modeling by Registration of Multiple Range Images. Proceedings 1991 IEEE International Conference on Robotics and Automation, pp. 2724-2729, Sacramento (CA), 1991.
3. I. J. Cox, S. L. Hingorani, and S. B. Rao: A Maximum Likelihood Stereo Algorithm. Computer Vision and Image Understanding, Vol. 63, No. 3, May 1996.
4. L.Falkenhagen: Hierarchical Block-Based Disparity Estimation Considering Neighborhood Constraints. International Workshop on SNHC and 3D Imaging, September 5-9, 1997, Rhodes, Greece.
5. O.Faugeras: Three-Dimensional Computer Vision - a geometric viewpoint. MIT-Press, 1993.
6. O. Faugeras: What can be seen in three dimensions with an uncalibrated stereo rig. Proc. ECCV'92, pp.563-578.
7. O. Faugeras, Q.-T. Luong and S. Maybank: Camera self-calibration - Theory and experiments. Proc. ECCV'92, pp.321-334.
8. G.L.Gimel'farb: Symmetrical approach to the problem of automating stereoscopic measurements in photogrammetry. Cybernetics, 1979, 15(2), 235-247; Consultants Bureau, N.Y.

9. G.L.Gimel'farb and R.M.Haralick: Terrain reconstruction from multiple views. Proc. 7th Int. Conf. on Computer Analysis of Images and Patterns (CAIP'97), Kiel, Germany, Sept. 1997. (G.Sommer, K.Daniilidis, and J.Pauli, Eds.). Lecture Notes in Computer Science 1296, Springer: Berlin e.a., 1997, pp.694-701.

10. C.G. Harris and J.M. Pike: 3D Positional Integration from Image Sequences. 3rd Alvey Vision Conf, pp. 233-236, 1987.

11. R. Hartley: Estimation of relative camera positions for uncalibrated cameras. Proc. ECCV'92, pp.579-587.

12. A. Heyden and K. Åström: Euclidean Reconstruction from Image Sequences with Varying and Unknown Focal Length and Principal Point. Proc. CVPR'97.

13. M. Irani and S. Peleg: Super resolution from image sequences. Tenth International Conference on Pattern Recognition (Atlantic City, NJ, June 16-21, 1990), IEEE Catalog No. 90CH2898-5, 1990, subconference C, 115-120.

14. R. Koch: 3-D Modeling of Human Heads from Stereoscopic Image Sequences. Proc. DAGM'96, Informatik Aktuell, Springer Heidelberg, Germany, Sept. 1996.

15. R. Koch: Surface Segmentation and Modeling of 3-D Polygonal Objects from Stereoscopic Image Pairs. Proc. ICPR'96, Vienna 1996.

16. R. Koch: Automatische Oberflächenmodellierung starrer dreidimensionaler Objekte aus stereoskopischen Bildfolgen. Ph.D. Thesis, Fortschr.-Ber. 10/499. Düsseldorf: VDI Verlag 1997.

17. A. Kochan: Eine Methodenbank zur Evaluierung von Stereo-Vision-Verfahren. Ph.D. Thesis, TU Berlin, June 1991.

18. L. Matthies, T. Kanade, and R. Szeliski: Kalman filter-based algorithms for estimating depth from image sequences. International Journal of Computer Vision, vol. 3, 1989, 209-236.

19. M. Okutomi and T. Kanade: A multiple-baseline stereo. IEEE Transactions on Pattern Analysis and Machine Intelligence, vol. 15, no. 4, 1993, 353-363.

20. E. Ofek, E. Shilat, A. Rappoport, M. Werman: Highlight and Reflection-Independent Multiresolution Textures from Image Sequences. IEEE Computer Graphics and Applications vol. 17 (2), March-April 1997.

21. M. Pollefeys, L. Van Gool and M. Proesmans: Euclidean 3D Reconstruction from Image Sequences with Variable Focal Lengths. Proc. ECCV'96, vol.1, pp. 31-42.

22. M. Pollefeys and L. Van Gool: Self-calibration from the absolute conic on the plane at infinity. Proc. CAIP'97.

23. M. Pollefeys, R. Koch and L. Van Gool: Self-Calibration and Metric Reconstruction in spite of Varying and Unknown Internal Camera Parameters. Proc. ICCV'98, Bombay, India, 1998.

24. P.H.S. Torr: Motion Segmentation and Outlier Detection. PhD thesis, Dept. Eng. Science, University of Oxford, UK, 1995.

25. B. Triggs: The Absolute Quadric. Proc. CVPR'97.

26. Z. Zhang and O. Faugeras: 3D Dynamic Scene Analysis. Springer Verlag, 1992.

Recognition of Planar Point Configurations Using the Density of Affine Shape

Rikard Berthilsson and Anders Heyden

Dept of Mathematics, Lund University
Box 118, S-221 00 Lund, Sweden
{rikard,heyden}@maths.lth.se

Abstract. In this paper, we study the statistical theory of shape for ordered finite point configurations, or otherwise stated, the uncertainty of geometric invariants. Such studies have been made for affine invariants in e.g. [GHJ92], [Wer93], where in the former case a bound on errors are used instead of errors described by density functions, and in the latter case a first order approximation gives an ellipsis as uncertainty region. Here, a general approach for defining shape and finding its density, expressed in the densities for the individual points, is developed. No approximations are made, resulting in an exact expression of the uncertainty region. Similar results have been obtained for the special case of the density of the cross ratio, see [May95,Åst96].

In particular, we will concentrate on the affine shape, where often analytical computations are possible. In this case confidence intervals for invariants can be obtained from a priori assumptions on the densities of the detected points in the images. However, the theory is completely general and can be used to compute the density of any invariant (Euclidean, similarity, projective etc.) from arbitrary densities of the individual points. These confidence intervals can be used in such applications as geometrical hashing, recognition of ordered point configurations and error analysis of reconstruction algorithms. Another approach towards this problem, in the case of similarity transformations, can be found in [Ken89]. For the special case of normally distributed feature points in a plane and similarity transformations, see [Boo86], [MD89].

Finally, an example will be given, illustrating an application of the theory for the problem of recognising planar point configurations from images taken by an affine camera. This case is of particular importance in applications, where details on a conveyor belt are captured by a camera, with image plane parallel to the conveyor belt and extracted feature points from the images are used to sort the objects.

keywords: shape, invariants, densities, error analysis, recognition, distribution of invariants

1   Introduction

In many disciplines (technology, science, biology, etc), one often encounters a need to describe geometrical shapes. This is usually done by extracting a configuration of feature points for the object at hand. Once these points have been extracted, they have to be treated collectively, and not as individual points. For example, the location and orientation in space is in general irrelevant for the shape, which means that one should not distinguish between configurations that can be transformed into each other by rotations and translations. To achieve this one often defines a function from the set of possible point configurations, which is constant or invariant under rotations and translations of a point configuration.

Often there are other immaterial properties at hand, like for example scaling. To treat this quantitatively, a parametrisation of point configurations is needed, that only bothers about essential properties, 'the shape', of the application at hand. What is meant by 'essential' can often be described in terms of a group of transformations, by identifying objects that can be transformed into each other by elements of the group.

When using such parametrisations of shape in practice, one soon encounters the problem of how uncertainties in the measurements of individual feature points affect the shape parameters. This is the subject of the present study, i.e. to device a general, method for parametrisation of shape, taking only relevant information into account, and to investigate the statistical density of the shape parameters given the statistical density for the individual points of the configurations.

As an example of a specific field of applications in computer vision we have the structure and motion problem. When deriving the structure of a 3D-scene from a sequence of 2D-images, one often has little or none calibration information about the cameras. Fortunately, cf [Spa96], it is still often possible to derive structure information, but only up to some class of transformations, i.e. a situation similar to the one described above. The algorithms for this only use some kind of shape data, with respect to some group of transformations. This means that the data needed by the algorithms consists of shape parameters, which are 'packages' of measurement parameters. To analyse the stability and robustness of such algorithms, the densities of these shape parameters are needed.

Another computer vision application of the result of this paper, is model based recognition. Here a data base is built containing e.g. affine or projective shapes of a number of model objects. The recognition problem consists of matching measured image features to the right model object. To do this, shapes are computed from image data. Knowing the densities of shape, this can be done in a firm way, using quantitative hypothesis testing. We give the necessary densities, which will allow us to determine confidence sets for shape below.

In this paper we will outline a general framework for shape. The result will be explicit parametrisations of shape spaces together with formulas for the exact density of shape, given as integrals. The general theory will be illustrated by a number of examples of affine shape. Furthermore, we will show how the theory can be used to solve the problem of recognising point configurations taken by affine cameras, using real images.

The pioneer in the study of shape along these lines is Kendall, cf [Ken89], who dealt with the case of positive similarity transformations. Bookstein, cf [Boo86], introduced variables for size and shape to treat this problem when all feature points belongs to a plane. The density for the shape variables was later computed in [MD89], where the feature points were assumed to be normally distributed.

In computer vision, the density of affine shape has been studied in [GHJ92], [Wer93] and [Hey95]. In [GHJ92], the uncertainty of the affine coordinates of a planar four point configuration is treated. However, instead of errors described by a density function, a bound on errors is derived. In [Hey95] a first order approximation is used to compute the density of the affine shape to a planar four point configuration, when the points are normally distributed. A similar method is used in [Wer93]. A first order approximation has also been applied for the density of similarity invariants in [RH95].

Densities of projective shape have been studied in [Åst96] and [May95], where exact densities for the cross ratio for four points on a line are computed.

The approach of the present paper uses an abstract setting, which makes it possible to cover all these situations simultaneously. For a more thorough treatment of the contents of this paper, we refer the reader to [Ber97].

2   Shape of finite ordered point configurations

In this section, we will define a general notion for the shape of finite point configurations. To begin with, some terminology is needed.

Let C_m^n be the set of ordered m-point configurations

$$\mathcal{X} = (p_1, p_2, \ldots, p_m)$$

in $\mathbb{R}^n$, where $p_i \in \mathbb{R}^n$ is the coordinate vector of point number i in $\mathcal{X}$. Thus, there is a natural isomorphism between C_m^n and $\mathbb{R}^{mn}$. As topology on C_m^n, we will use the one inherited from $\mathbb{R}^{mn}$.

Let G be a group of transformations $C_m^n \to C_m^n$. By the **G-orbit** of $\mathcal{X} \in C_m^n$ is meant the set

$$\{\mathcal{Y} \mid \mathcal{Y} = g(\mathcal{X}), \; g \in G\} \; .$$

We write $\mathcal{X} \sim \mathcal{Y}$, when $\mathcal{X}$ and $\mathcal{Y}$ are in the same orbit. For a group G of transformations $\mathbb{R}^n \to \mathbb{R}^n$, let G^m be the group of product transformations, $C_m^n \to C_m^n$, defined by

$$g(\mathcal{X}) = (g(p_1), \ldots, g(p_m)), \text{ when } \mathcal{X} = (p_1, \ldots, p_m) \in C_m^n \text{ and } g \in G \; .$$

For our applications, this is the most usual situation, i.e. the same transformation is applied to all points of the configuration. By abuse of language, we write G instead of G^m.

For the geometric applications we are interested in, the following terminology is convenient.

Definition 1. *Let G be a group of transformations $\mathcal{C}_m^n \to \mathcal{C}_m^n$. The* **shape space** *is defined as the set of orbits $\mathcal{C}_m^n/G$. Let*

$$s : \mathcal{C}_m^n \to \mathcal{C}_m^n/G \ ,$$

be the natural projection. For $\mathcal{X} \in \mathcal{C}_m^n$, the orbit $s(\mathcal{X}) \in \mathcal{C}_m^n/G$ is called the **shape** *of $\mathcal{X}$ and each element of $s(\mathcal{X})$ is called a* **representative** *of $s(\mathcal{X})$. A function φ on $\mathcal{C}_m^n$, which is constant on each orbit is called an* **invariant**. *The functions $\varphi = (\varphi_1, \ldots, \varphi_k)$ form a* **complete set of invariants** *if $\varphi(\mathcal{X}) = \varphi(\mathcal{Y})$ if and only if $\mathcal{X} \sim \mathcal{Y}$. As topology on $\mathcal{C}_m^n/G$, we choose the strongest topology that makes s continuous.*

Since G forms a group, the orbits of $\mathcal{C}_m^n/G$ are disjoint. The space $\mathcal{C}_m^n$ can then be viewed as divided into disjoint strings, where each string is an orbit, see Figure 1.

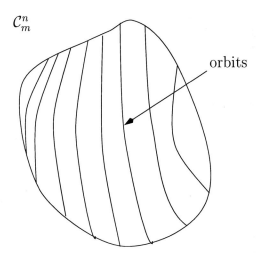

$\mathcal{C}_m^n$

orbits

Fig. 1. Orbits of $\mathcal{C}_m^n$.

According to Klein, in his Erlanger-program, geometry is the study of properties of geometric objects, which are invariant with respect to some class of transformation. This point of view fits with Definition 1, as is also illustrated by the following examples.

Example 1. Let G be the group of nonsingular Euclidean transformations, acting on $\mathcal{C}_m^n$. Euclidean invariants are distances between points in the point configurations. The orbits consist of configurations that are congruent, in the sense of classical Euclidean geometry.

Example 2. When G is the group of affine transformations, $\mathcal{C}_m^n/G$ is isomorphic to a Grassman manifold, consisting of linear subspaces of some ambient linear space, cf [Spa92]. These subspaces have been called affine shape, and can be described explicitly as

$$s(\mathcal{X}) = \left\{ \xi \;\middle|\; \sum_{i=1}^{m} \xi_i x_i = 0, \; \sum_{i=1}^{m} \xi_i = 0, \; \mathcal{X} = (x_1, \ldots, x_m) \right\} \;.$$

3 Density of shape, general theory

We now introduce a parametrisation of point configurations $\mathcal{C}_m^n$, by taking the transformation group G into account, which will enable us to write down a formula for a density function on the shape space $\mathcal{C}_m^n/G$, when a density function on $\mathcal{C}_m^n$, i.e. the individual points of the configurations is known. This parametrisation will be done by pulling $\mathcal{C}_m^n$ back to two parameter sets A and B, such that B labels the orbits $\mathcal{C}_m^n/G$ and A provides parameters along each orbit. Recall that a function is called a C^n-**diffeomorphism** if it is invertible and $f, f^{-1} \in C^n$.

Definition 2. *Let $A \subseteq \mathbb{R}^k$ and $B \subseteq \mathbb{R}^{k'}$ be two open subsets for some k and k' and let G be a group of transformations $\mathcal{C}_m^n \to \mathcal{C}_m^n$. Suppose that there exist open sets $A \subseteq \mathbb{R}^k$ and $B \subseteq \mathbb{R}^{k'}$, a bijection*

$$g : A \ni a \to g_a \in G \;,$$

and a function

$$\zeta : B \to \mathcal{C}_m^n \;,$$

such that the function

$$\gamma_\zeta : A \times B \to \mathcal{C}_m^n, \; \text{defined by } \gamma_\zeta(a, b) = g_a \circ \zeta(b) \;,$$

has a dense open range $U \subseteq \mathcal{C}_m^n$ and $\gamma_\zeta : A \times B \to U$, is a C^1-diffeomorphism. Then ζ is said to be a **parametrisation of shape** *and g a* **parametrisation of G.**

The reason for using a dense open subset of $\mathcal{C}_m^n$ instead of the whole set, is that it is in general not possible to parametrise the entire $\mathcal{C}_m^n$. However, the remaining set $\mathcal{C}_m^n \setminus U$ is of measure zero and are therefore irrelevant here.

The dimensions k, k' only depend on $\mathcal{C}_m^n$ and G, as γ_ζ is a C^1-diffeomorphism. The specific choices of parametrisations for shape and G merely represent a choice of coordinates on $U \subseteq \mathcal{C}_m^n$, such that ζ labels the orbits and g describes the location within each orbit, see Figure 2.

It can be shown that B and $s(U)$ are homeomorphic, see [Ber97]. Thus, $s(U)$ is also metrizable, since B is a metric space. We call $s(U)$ the **non-degenerate shape space**.

We now turn to the main question, to define densities on shape spaces. To this end assume that $\mathcal{C}_m^n$ has a density function $0 \le \phi \in L^1(\mathcal{C}_m^n)$, where $\int \phi d\mathcal{X} =$

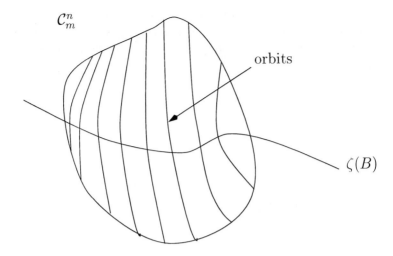

Fig. 2. Parametrisation of $\mathcal{C}_m^n$. Each orbit has a unique intersection with $\zeta(B)$.

1. Often it is obtained from density functions for the individual points of the configurations. We want to define a density function on $\mathcal{C}_m^n/G$, i.e. a density function for shapes. Let γ_ζ be as in Definition 2, then

$$\int_{\mathcal{C}_m^n} \phi(\mathcal{X})d\mathcal{X} = \int_B \left(\int_A \phi \circ \gamma_\zeta(a,b) \left| \det(\gamma_\zeta') \right| da \right) db \ ,$$

where $\det(\gamma_\zeta')$ is the functional determinant of $\gamma_\zeta(a,b)$. It is thus a determinant of order $k + k'$. Here the function

$$B \ni b \to \int_A \phi \circ \gamma_\zeta(a,b) \left| \det(\gamma_\zeta') \right| da \in L^1$$

is defined almost everywhere. As B and the non-degenerate shape space $s(U)$ are homeomorphic, it is natural to use this function when defining a density of shape.

Definition 3. *Let $\phi \in L^1(\mathcal{C}_m^n)$ be a density function, $\zeta : B \to \mathcal{C}_m^n$ a parametrisation of shape, $g : A \ni a \to g_a \in G$ a parametrisation of the group G and set $\gamma_\zeta(a,b) = g_a \circ \zeta(b)$. The function $\mathfrak{D}(\phi, \zeta) : B \to \mathbb{R}$, defined by*

$$\mathfrak{D}(\phi, \zeta) : b \to \int_A \phi \circ \gamma_\zeta(a,b) \left| \det \gamma_\zeta' \right| da \tag{1}$$

*is called the **density of shape** on $\mathcal{C}_m^n$, with respect to G.*

Observe that the density of shape depends on the parametrisation of shape, which can be chosen in many ways. This seems to bring in an ambiguity. Also the parametrisation of G can be done in many ways. However, it can be shown, see [Ber97] that the density of shape is independent of the parametrisation of G and that there exist canonical transformations between the density of shape for different parametrisations of shape. This canonical transformation implies that if we integrate over a set in $s(U)$ the result will be independent of the specific choice of parametrisation of shape ζ.

Example 3. As an illustration of Definition 2 and 3, let G be the group of nonsingular affine transformations $\mathbb{R}^2 \to \mathbb{R}^2$. Extend G to the space $\mathcal{C}_4^2$, which consist of all ordered four point configurations in $\mathbb{R}^2$. Using matrix notation, we write

$$\mathcal{X} = \begin{pmatrix} x_1 & x_2 & x_3 & x_4 \\ y_1 & y_2 & y_3 & y_4 \end{pmatrix} \in \mathcal{C}_4^2,$$

where each column represents a point in $\mathbb{R}^2$. Let

$$\zeta : \mathbb{R}^2 \ni b \to \begin{pmatrix} 1 & 0 & 0 & b_1 \\ 0 & 1 & 0 & b_2 \end{pmatrix} \in \mathcal{C}_4^2$$

be a parametrisation of shape and

$$g : A \ni a \to g_a(\cdot) = \begin{pmatrix} a_{11} & a_{12} \\ a_{21} & a_{22} \end{pmatrix} (\cdot) + \begin{pmatrix} a_1 \\ a_2 \end{pmatrix} \in G, \quad \det(\{a_{ij}\}) \neq 0 \ ,$$

be a parametrisation of G, where $A \subset \mathbb{R}^6$ is open and dense. Then γ_ζ in Definition 2 is given by

$$\gamma_\zeta : A \times \mathbb{R}^2 \ni (a, b) \to \begin{pmatrix} a_{11} & a_{12} & a_1 \\ a_{21} & a_{22} & a_2 \end{pmatrix} \begin{pmatrix} 1 & 0 & 0 & b_1 \\ 0 & 1 & 0 & b_2 \\ 1 & 1 & 1 & 1 \end{pmatrix} \in \mathcal{C}_4^2 \ .$$

Here γ_ζ has a dense open range in $\mathcal{C}_4^2$ and $\gamma_\zeta : A \times \mathbb{R}^2 \to \gamma_\zeta(A \times \mathbb{R}^2)$ is a C^1-diffeomorphism.

If $\phi \in L^1(\mathcal{C}_4^2)$ is a density function, inserting γ_ζ in (1) in Definition 3, gives us a density function of affine shapes for $\mathcal{C}_4^2$. Examples will be given below.

The following theorem shows how the density of $\phi \in \mathcal{C}_m^n$ can be transformed without changing the the density of shape.

Theorem 1. *Let* $\phi \in L^1(\mathcal{C}_m^n)$, *be a density function,* $g : A \to g_a \in G$ *a parametrisation of* G *and* ζ *a parametrisation of shape. If* $f \in G$ *is a* C^1*-diffeomorphism, then*

$$\mathfrak{D}(\phi, \zeta) = \mathfrak{D}(|\det f'| \phi \circ f, \zeta).$$

As a consequence of Theorem 1, neither scaling nor translation of the density $\phi \in L^1(\mathcal{C}_m^n)$, affect the density of affine or positive similarity shape.

4 Density of affine shape

We will now focus on the affine group of transformations. First the theory of densities of affine shape will be outlined, then these densities will be computed and the special case of affine shape of four planar points will be treated in detail.

4.1 Theory

Let us start with a parametrisation of C_m^n as in (1) in Definition 2, when $m \geq n+2$ and G is the group of affine transformations.

Proposition 1. *Let $\phi \in L^1(C_m^n)$ be a density function for C_m^n, where $m \geq n+2$, and let G be the group of nonsingular affine transformations $\mathbb{R}^n \to \mathbb{R}^n$ with the parametrisation*

$$g : A \ni a = (\{y_{ij}\}, \{t_k\}) \to g_a(\cdot) = \{y_{ij}\}(\cdot) + \{t_k\} \in G, \quad \det\{y_{ij}\} \neq 0 ,$$

where $\{y_{ij}\}$ is an $n \times n$ matrix, $\{t_k\}$ is an $n \times 1$ matrix and $A \subset \mathbb{R}^{n^2} \times \mathbb{R}^n$. Furthermore, let

$$\zeta : \mathbb{R}^{n(m-n-1)} \ni \{b_{ij}\} \to \left(I \; 0 \; \{b_{ij}\}\right) \in C_m^n$$

be a parametrisation of affine shape, where I is the $(n \times n)$ identity matrix and $\{b_{ij}\}$ is a $(n \times (m-n-1))$ matrix. Then the density of affine shape is given by

$$\mathfrak{D}(\phi, \zeta)(b) = \int |\det\{y_{ij}\}|^{m-n-1} \phi \circ \gamma_\zeta(a, b)\, da,$$

and

$$\mathfrak{D}(\phi, \zeta) = \mathfrak{D}(|\det C|^m \, \phi \circ f, \zeta)$$

for every nonsingular affine transformation $f(b) = Cb + d$.

It is easily seen that γ_ζ fulfills the conditions in Definition 2. All that has to been done then is to compute the functional determinant of γ'_ζ. The details are left to the reader.

4.2 Density of affine shape for four normally distributed planar points

In this subsection, we compute the density of affine shape for four points in a plane, when the points are distributed normally and independent. The densities will provide a useful tool for determining search areas in shape space, when comparing an objects shape with some shapes in a data base.

When the four points are distributed with the same mean, it is possible to obtain a closed form solution, and when the means are different, the density of shape is given as a one dimensional integral, which generally has to be evaluated numerically.

Let

$$\phi(x, y) = \prod_{i=1}^{4} \psi(x_i)\psi(y_i) ,$$

where $\psi(x) = \pi^{-1/2} e^{-x^2}$, is the density for four points in a plane, i.e. $\phi \in L^1(C_4^2)$ and $\int \phi \, dx dy = 1$. Let

$$g : A \ni \alpha = (\{y_{ij}\}, \{t_k\}) \to g_\alpha(\cdot) = \begin{pmatrix} y_{11} & y_{12} \\ y_{21} & y_{22} \end{pmatrix} (\cdot) + \begin{pmatrix} t_1 \\ t_2 \end{pmatrix}, \quad \det\{y_{ij}\} \neq 0 ,$$

$$\tag{2}$$

be a parametrisation of the group G of nonsingular affine transformations $\mathbb{R}^2 \to \mathbb{R}^2$, where $A \subset \mathbb{R}^6$ is open and dense. Choose

$$\zeta : \mathbb{R}^2 \ni (x_1, x_2) \to \begin{pmatrix} 1 & 0 & 0 & x_1 \\ 0 & 1 & 0 & x_2 \end{pmatrix} ,$$

as a parametrisation of shape. Set

$$\gamma_\zeta : A \times \mathbb{R}^2 \ni (\alpha, x) \to g_\alpha \circ \zeta(x) \in \mathcal{C}_4^2 .$$

Then the density of shape is

$$\mathfrak{D}(\phi, \zeta)(x) = \int_A |\det\{y_{ij}\}| \, \phi \circ \gamma_\zeta \, d\alpha . \tag{3}$$

After tedious symbolic computations, we obtain

$$\mathfrak{D}(\phi, \zeta)(x) = \frac{1}{2\pi\sqrt{2}} \left(1 - x_1 - x_2 + x_2^2 + x_1^2 + x_1 x_2\right)^{-3/2} .$$

Observe that the level curves of this density function are ellipses. A simulation was performed, where a sequence of point configurations were drawn, each with the density function ϕ. From the map γ_ζ, a unique $x = (x_1, x_2)$ was obtained and the plot for that variable is shown to the right. $\mathfrak{D}(\phi, \zeta)(x)$ is shown to the left. The results are shown in Figure 3, where the simulated data are shown to the right.

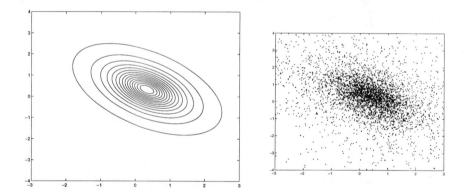

Fig. 3. Computed density function and simulated.

Now assume that the points are normally distributed and independent, with respective means $m_j \in \mathbb{R}^2$, $j = 1, 2, 3, 4$ but with the same standard deviation, i.e.

$$\phi(x, y) = \prod_{j=1}^{4} \psi(x_j - m_{x_j})\psi(y_j - m_{y_j}) , \tag{4}$$

where $\psi(x) = (2\pi\sigma^2)^{-1/2}e^{-x^2/(2\sigma^2)}$. By Theorem 1, with

$$g_{a_0} : \mathbb{R}^2 \ni v \mapsto \sigma R v - m \ ,$$

where R is a rotation matrix and $m \in \mathbb{R}^2$ is a vector, it is no restriction to assume that $\psi(x) = \pi^{-1/2}e^{-x^2}$ and that $m_{j_1} = (0,0)$, $m_{j_2} = (0, m_{y_{j_2}})$, for some $j_1 \neq j_2$.

It is possible to write the density of shape (3) as an integral in one dimension, which generally has to be evaluated numerically. As an example, assume that $m_1 = (0,0)$, $m_2 = (0,1)$ $m_3 = (1,1)$ and $m_4 = (1,0)$. The density of shape is then given by

$$\mathfrak{D}(\phi, \zeta) = \frac{1}{\pi^2} \int_0^\infty \frac{u(x_1, x_2, \omega)}{\omega} d\omega \ ,$$

where

$$u(x_1, x_2, \omega) = \frac{4\omega(3a + \omega^2 - b)\cos(\frac{c\omega}{a+\omega^2}) + 2c(a - \omega^2)\sin(\frac{c\omega}{a+\omega^2})}{(a^3 + 3a^2\omega + 3a\omega^4 + \omega^6)} e^{-\frac{b+2\omega^2}{a+\omega^2}} \ ,$$

$$a(x_1, x_2, \omega) = (x_1 + x_2)^2 + (x_1 - 1)^2 + (x_2 - 1)^2 \ ,$$

$$b(x_1, x_2, \omega) = (x_1 + x_2)^2 + (x_1 - 1)^2 \ ,$$

and

$$c(x_1, x_2, \omega) = 2(1 - x_2) \ .$$

The density function is illustrated in Figure 4. Note that the level curves are not ellipses in this case, indicating a deviation from the first order approximation.

In order to compute (3), with $\phi(x, y)$ given by (4), we use the Fourier transformation $\widehat{|t|}$ of $t \mapsto |t|$, where the Fourier transformation is taken in distribution sense according to Schwartz. It can be shown, c.f. [Ber97], that

$$\mathfrak{D}(\phi, \zeta) = -\frac{1}{\pi} \int_0^\infty \frac{\psi'(\omega) - \psi'(-\omega)}{\omega} d\omega, \tag{5}$$

where

$$\psi(x_1, x_2, \omega, m) = \int_A \phi \circ \gamma_\zeta e^{i\omega \det\{y_{ij}\}} d\alpha.$$

For general means m_j, $j = 1, \ldots, 4$, is straight forward, to compute ψ from the formula

$$\int e^{-(z_1 t^2 + z_2 t)} dt = e^{z_2^2/(4z_1)} \sqrt{\frac{\pi}{z_1}}, \qquad \Re(z_1) > 0,$$

which is obtained by changing the path of integration to the complex plane. As the left hand side is continuous in z_1, the principal branch is chosen for the square root.

Since $\lim_{\omega \to 0}\{\psi'(\omega) - \psi'(-\omega)\}\omega^{-1}$ is bounded, it follows, by partial integration of (5), that

$$\mathfrak{D}(\phi, \zeta) = -\frac{1}{\pi} \int_0^\infty \frac{\psi(\omega) + \psi(-\omega) - 2\psi(0)}{\omega^2} d\omega.$$

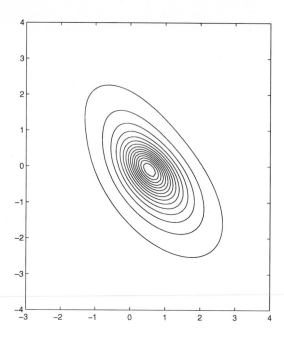

Fig. 4. Computed density function.

We will use this formula to compute a number of densities of shape below in Section 6. For general means, it is possible to obtain a closed form solution of the integrand, but the solution is very complicated. Instead we compute the integrand for each mean $m = (m_1, m_2, m_3, m_4)$, $m_j \in \mathbb{R}^2$.

4.3 Density of affine shape for four uniformly distributed planar points

An interesting situation is when we have four points in plane, which are uniformly and independently distributed in $[0,1] \times [0,1]$. This case corresponds to four randomly chosen points in an image. The density is important to know, when calculating false alarm rates, i.e. the possibility that four randomly chosen points $\mathcal{X}$ have shape $s(\mathcal{X})$ inside the confidence area for some of the model points.

Let

$$\phi(x, y) = \prod_{i=1}^{4} \psi(x_i)\psi(y_i),$$

where ψ is defined as

$$\psi(x) = \begin{cases} 0 & |x - 1/2| > 1/2, \\ 1 & |x - 1/2| \leq 1/2 \ , \end{cases}$$

be the uniform joint density in C_4^2 With the parametrisation of G in (2) and

$$\zeta : \mathbb{R}^2 \ni (x_1, x_2) \to \begin{pmatrix} 1 & 0 & x_1 & 0 \\ 0 & 1 & 0 & x_2 \end{pmatrix} \in C_4^2$$

as a parametrisation of shape, it is possible to compute the density of shape in closed form, though some effort is needed.

That ζ is in fact a parametrisation of shape can be seen if, given a point configuration $\mathcal{X} = (p_1, p_2, p_3, p_4) \in C_4^2$, we let $t^T = (t_1, t_2)$ be the intersection of the lines obtained by adjoining the points p_1 with p_3 and p_2 with p_4. Thus

$$\begin{pmatrix} y_{11} & y_{12} \\ y_{21} & y_{22} \end{pmatrix} = (p_1 - t \;\; p_2 - t)$$

and

$$\begin{pmatrix} x_1 & 0 \\ 0 & x_2 \end{pmatrix} = \begin{pmatrix} y_{11} & y_{12} \\ y_{21} & y_{22} \end{pmatrix}^{-1} (p_1 - t \;\; p_2 - t) \;\; .$$

This computation is possible for almost all $\mathcal{X} \in C_4^2$.

The density of affine shape, given as an integral, is

$$\mathfrak{D}(\phi, \zeta)(x_1, x_2) = |1 - x_1| |1 - x_2| \int |\det(A)| \, \phi \circ \gamma_\zeta(y, x) dy$$

and when computed, it turns out to be a piecewise rational function in $\mathbb{R}^2$. By Theorem 1, the density $\mathfrak{D}(\phi, \zeta)$ is independent of any non-singular affine transformation of ϕ.

5   Application of affine shape to recognition

The densities $\mathfrak{D}(\phi, \zeta)$ in Section 4.2 can be used to limit the search area in a data base, that is used for recognition. The problem is to identify an unknown object with some object in a reference set, by using affine shape of extracted feature points.

For a set of planar objects, four feature points are extracted from each to give a set of point configurations $\{\mathcal{X}_j\}_{j=1}^n$. The affine shape $s(\mathcal{X}_j) = (x_{1j}, x_{2j}) \in \mathbb{R}^2$ is computed and stored in a data base $\{s(\mathcal{X}_j)\}_{j=1}^n$. If we assume that the feature points $\mathcal{X}_j$ have a normal independent density function ϕ_j, it is possible to compute the density of shape $\mathfrak{D}(\phi_j, \zeta)$, by the method described in Section 4.2.

Set

$$\Omega_b(j) = \left\{ (x, y) \;\middle|\; \mathfrak{D}(\phi_j, \zeta) > a, \int_{\mathfrak{D}(\phi_j, \zeta) > a} \mathfrak{D}(\phi_j, \zeta) dx dy = b \right\} ,$$

where $0 \leq b \leq 1$ is set by a human operator. In the example illustrated in Figure 4, Ω_b is the set, such that when integrating $\mathfrak{D}(\phi_j, \zeta)$ over the set, which is bounded by a level curve, the integral should be equal to b. b gives the level of significance.

For an unknown object, four feature points are extracted, forming a point configuration $\mathcal{Y}$, and the shape $s(\mathcal{Y})$ is computed. We identify $\mathcal{Y}$ as object j in the data base if $\mathcal{Y} \in \Omega_b(j)$.

Moreover, let ϕ_u be the uniform and independent joint density for four points in a rectangular subset of $\mathbb{R}^2$. If the density of shape $\mathfrak{D}(\phi_u, \zeta)$ is integrated over the union of all $\Omega_b(j)$, $j = 1, 2, \ldots$, this will give the false alarm rate. The false alarm rate measures the probability that four randomly chosen points is decided to be an object in the database. Letting P_{FAR} denote the false alarm rate, we have

$$P_{FAR} = \int_{\cup \Omega_b(j)} \mathfrak{D}(\phi_u, \zeta) dx dy \ . \tag{6}$$

6 Experiments

In order to simulate objects arriving at a conveyor belt, five different quadrangles were cut out of a piece of black paper. These five quadrangles were then put on a larger piece of white paper in six different positions. One image for each position were captured, with image plane parallel to the papers, see Figure 5.

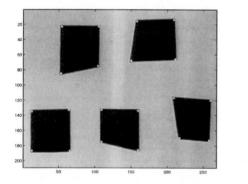

Fig. 5. Two of the images of quadrangles with detected corners.

The images were taken using a standard S-VHS video camera, giving images of size 500×700 pixels approximately. The sizes of the quadrangles were about 100 pixels. Each of these images were then subsampled giving images of half the size, with quadrangles of size about 50 pixels. Some of the images were then subsampled once more, giving quadrangles of size about 25 pixels.

The corners in the images were detected using Harris' corner detector, see Figure 5 again. The correspondence problem was solved by hand, but could easily be solved automatically, by identifying the corners belonging to each object and then walking around the contour. Since this is outside the scope of the present paper we chose to solve this problem manually.

The shape of each configuration in each image are plotted in Figure 6, where an asterisk is used for the original resolution, a circle for the subsampled resolution and a plus for the subsubsampled resolution. The 90% confidence areas for the five corresponding different densities of shape are shown in the same figure, when the points are assumed to be distributed as in Section 4.2 with $\sigma = 1/1.96$ and means

$$m_1 = \begin{pmatrix} 20 & 0 & 0 & 20 \\ 0 & 20 & 0 & 20 \end{pmatrix}, \quad m_2 = \begin{pmatrix} 20 & 0 & 0 & 16 \\ 0 & 20 & 0 & 20 \end{pmatrix}, \quad m_3 = \begin{pmatrix} 20 & 0 & 0 & 20 \\ 0 & 20 & 0 & 24 \end{pmatrix},$$

$$m_4 = \begin{pmatrix} 20 & 0 & 0 & 24 \\ 0 & 20 & 0 & 20 \end{pmatrix}, \quad m_5 = \begin{pmatrix} 20 & 0 & 0 & 20 \\ 0 & 20 & 0 & 16 \end{pmatrix},$$

respectively. The reason for using $\sigma = 1/1.96$ is that we assume that the errors in the measurements of the corners are normally distributed, with 95% of the measurements giving an error smaller than one pixel. The 90% confidence areas corresponds to an uncertainty of the measured points that is about $1/20$ of the side length of the quadrangle.

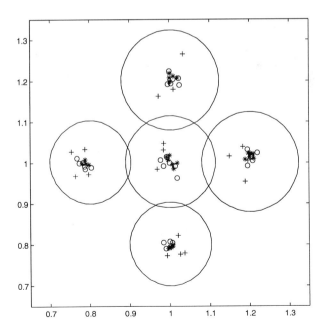

Fig. 6. 90% confidence areas for the shape of four point configurations with different means but with the same standard deviation, together with measured values.

In Figure 7, the points from the middle of Figure 6 are shown together with 90% confidence areas, when the means of the points are given by

$$\begin{pmatrix} 20 & 0 & 0 & 20 \\ 0 & 20 & 0 & 20 \end{pmatrix}, \quad \begin{pmatrix} 40 & 0 & 0 & 40 \\ 0 & 40 & 0 & 40 \end{pmatrix} \quad \text{and} \quad \begin{pmatrix} 80 & 0 & 0 & 80 \\ 0 & 80 & 0 & 80 \end{pmatrix},$$

and the standard deviation is $\sigma = 1/1.96$ for all points. This corresponds to an uncertainty of about $1/20$, $1/40$ and $1/80$ of the side length of the quadrangle respectively, which is in appliance with the actual sizes of the objects.

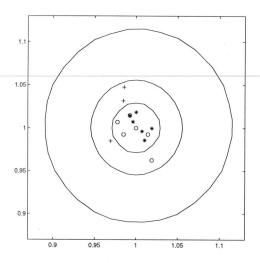

Fig. 7. 90% confidence areas for shape of four point configurations with different standard deviation but with the same mean.

Figure 7 indicates that the measured shapes are more accurate than the predicted, since all points lie well inside the 90% confidence area. There can be several reasons for this. Firstly, the measured corner positions, from Harris' corner detector, may be more accurate than one pixel. Secondly, the errors in the different corner positions may not be independent. It is well known that the position of a corner tends to move towards the interior of an object when the resolution diminishes. This bias in the measurements, gives highly correlated errors, when they are not modeled as a bias but rather as an error. Moreover, moving all points a little towards the center of the object does not affect the affine shape significantly. The false alarm rate given by (6), can be computed from results in [Ber97]. A computation gives that $P_{FAR} = 0.0420$.

In order to show that the confidence areas need not always be ellipses, Figure 8 shows the density of shape when

$$m = \begin{pmatrix} 0 & 10 & -7 & -16 \\ 0 & 0 & -2 & 2 \end{pmatrix} \tag{7}$$

and $\sigma = 1/\sqrt{2}$.

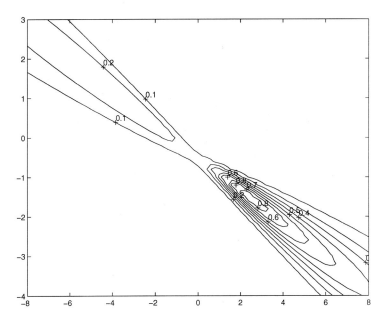

Fig. 8. Contour plot of $\mathfrak{D}(\phi, \zeta)^{1/4}$, when $\sigma = 1/\sqrt{2}$ and m is given by (7).

7 Conclusions

In this paper we have presented a theoretical framework for computing the density of different types of invariants, given the density of the underlying points. This framework is applied to affine invariants for planar four point configurations, especially for the case of normally distributed points and uniformly distributed points. From the density of shape, different kinds of levels of significance, can be calculated, as well as false alarm rates. The results are verified on real images of five different quadrangles, showing the applicability of the theory.

References

[Åst96] K. Åström. *Invariancy Methods for Points, Curves and Surfaces in Computer Vision.* PhD thesis, Lund University, Lund Institute of Technology, Department of Mathematics, 1996.

[Ber97] R. Berthilsson. A statistical theory of shape. Technical report, Department of Mathematics, Lund Institute of Technology, 1997. Licentiate Thesis, www.maths.lth.se/matematiklth/personal/rikard/index.html.

[Boo86] F. L. Bookstein. Size and shape spaces for landmark data in two dimensions. *Statistical Science*, 1(2):181–242, 1986.

[GHJ92] W Grimson, D Huttenlocher, and D Jacobs. A study of affine matching with bounded sensor error. In G. Sandini, editor, *Proc. 2nd European Conf. on Computer Vision*, volume 588, pages 291–306. Springer-Verlag, 1992.

[Hey95] Anders Heyden. *Geometry and Algebra of Multiple Projective Transforms*. PhD thesis, Lund University, Lund Institute of Technology, Department of Mathematics, 1995.

[Ken89] David G. Kendall. A survey of the statistical theory of shape. *Statistical Science*, 4(2):87–120, 1989.

[May95] S. J. Maybank. Probabilistic analysis of the application of the cross ratio to model based vision: Misclassification. *International Journal of Computer Vision*, 14(3), 1995.

[MD89] V. Mardia, K. and I. L. Dryden. Shape distribution for landmark data. *Adv. Appl. Prob.*, pages 742–755, 1989.

[RH95] I. Rigoutsos and R. Hummel. A bayesian approach to model matching with geometric hashing. *Computer Vision and Image Understanding*, 62(1):11–26, July 1995.

[Spa92] G. Sparr. Depth-computations from polyhedral images. In G. Sandini, editor, *Proc. 2nd European Conf. on Computer Vision*, pages 378–386. Springer-Verlag, 1992. Also in *Image and Vision Computing, Vol 10.*, 1992, pages 683-688.

[Spa96] G. Sparr. Simultaneous reconstruction of scene structure and camera locations from uncalibrated image sequences. In *13th International Conference on Pattern Recognition, Vienna, Austria*, volume 1, pages 328–333, 1996.

[Wer93] Carl-Gustav Werner. Selective geometric hashing, by means of determinants of transformations. In *SCIA '93, Proceedings of the 8th Scandinavian Conference on Image Analysis*, volume 2, pages 715–718. NOBIM, 1993.

Autocalibration from Planar Scenes

Bill Triggs

INRIA Rhône-Alpes, 655 avenue de l'Europe, 38330 Montbonnot St. Martin, France
Bill.Triggs@inrialpes.fr — http://www.inrialpes.fr/movi/people/Triggs

Abstract. This paper describes the theory and a practical algorithm for the autocalibration of a moving projective camera, from $m \geq 5$ views of a *planar* scene. The unknown camera calibration, motion and scene geometry are recovered up to scale, from constraints encoding the motion-invariance of the camera's internal parameters. This extends the domain of autocalibration from the classical non-planar case to the practically common planar one, in which the solution can not be bootstrapped from an intermediate projective reconstruction. It also generalizes Hartley's method for the internal calibration of a rotating camera, to allow camera translation and to provide 3D as well as calibration information. The basic constraint is that orthogonal directions (points at infinity) in the plane must project to orthogonal directions in the calibrated images. Abstractly, the plane's two circular points (representing its Euclidean structure) lie on the 3D absolute conic, so their projections must lie on the absolute image conic (representing the camera calibration). The resulting algorithm optimizes this constraint numerically over all circular points and all projective calibration parameters, using the inter-image homographies as a projective scene representation.

Keywords: Autocalibration, Euclidean structure, Absolute Conic & Quadric, Planar Scenes.

1 Introduction

This paper describes a method of autocalibrating a moving projective camera with general, unknown motion and unknown intrinsic parameters, from $m \geq 5$ views of a *planar* scene. Autocalibration is the recovery of metric information from uncalibrated images using geometric self-consistency constraints. For example, the internal and external calibration of a moving projective camera can be recovered from the knowledge that the internal parameters are constant during the motion, and the inter-image consistency constraints that this entails. Since the seminal work of Maybank & Faugeras [14, 3], a number of different approaches have been developed [5, 6, 1, 26, 25, 2, 13, 9, 16, 15, 22, 10]. For the 'classical' problem of a single perspective camera with constant but unknown internal

---

Work supported by Esprit LTR project CUMULI. Many thanks to P. Sturm for discussions, G. Csurka and A. Ruf for test images and calibration data, and the anonymous reviewers for comments. An extended version is available from my web page.

parameters moving with a general but unknown motion in a 3D scene, the original 'Kruppa equation' approach [14] seems to be being displaced by methods based on the 'rectification' of an intermediate projective reconstruction [5, 9, 15, 22, 10]. More specialized methods exist for particular types of motion and simplified calibration models [6, 23, 1, 16]. Stereo heads can also be autocalibrated [26, 11]. Limited variations of the intrinsic parameters can also be handled [9, 15]. Hartley [6] gives a particularly simple internal calibration method for a 'rotating camera' — *i.e.* whose translation is known to be negligible relative to $n \geq 4$ distant, identifiable, real or synthetic points in the scene. Faugeras [2] advocates a 'stratification' paradigm based on such 'plane at infinity' constructs. The numerical conditioning of autocalibration is historically delicate. Although recent algorithms have improved the situation significantly [9, 15, 22], classical autocalibration still has some restrictive intrinsic degeneracies — classes of motion for which no algorithm can recover a full unique solution. Sturm [18, 19] gives a catalogue of these. At least 3 views, some translation and some rotation about at least two non-aligned axes are required.

Planar Autocalibration: Existing approaches to classical autocalibration rely on information equivalent to a 3D projective scene reconstruction. In the Kruppa approach this is the fundamental matrices and epipoles, while for most other methods it is an explicit 3D reconstruction. This is a problem whenever planar or near-planar scenes occur, as projective reconstructions, fundamental matrices, *etc.*, can not be estimated stably in the near-planar case. In contrast, *calibrated* reconstruction from near-planar scenes is not difficult, so it is exactly here where projective methods fail, where autocalibration would be most useful. The current paper aims to rectify this, by providing methods which autocalibrate planar scenes by 'straightening' the inter-image homographies induced by the plane. A longer term goal is to find ways around the ill-conditioning of projective reconstruction for near-planar scenes, and also to develop 'structure-free' internal calibration methods similar to Hartley's rotating camera one [6], but which work for non-zero translations. The hope is that planar methods may offer one way to attack these problems.

Planar autocalibration has other potential advantages. Planes are very common in man-made environments, and often easily identifiable and rather accurately planar. They are simple to process and allow very reliable and precise feature-based or intensity-based matching, by fitting the homographies between image pairs. They are also naturally well adapted to the calibration of lens distortion, as some of the subtleties of 3D geometry are avoided[1].

The main *dis*advantage of planar autocalibration (besides the need for a nice, flat, textured plane) seems to be the number of images required. Generically, $m \geq \lceil \frac{n+4}{2} \rceil$ images are needed for an internal camera model with n free parameters, *e.g.* $m \geq 5$ for the classical 5 parameter projective model (focal length f, aspect ratio a, skew s, principal point (u_0, v_0)), or $m \geq 3$ if only focal length is

---

[1] We will ignore lens distortion throughout this paper. If necessary it can be corrected by a nominal model or — at least in theory — estimated up to an overall 3×3 projectivity by a bundled adjustment over all the inter-image homographies.

estimated. However for good accuracy and reliability, at least 8–10 images are recommended in practice. Almost any attempt at algebraic elimination across so many images rapidly leads to a combinatorial explosion. Hence, the approach is resolutely numerical, and it seems impracticable to initialize the optimization from a minimal algebraic solution. Although in many cases the numerical domain of convergence is sufficient to allow moderately reliable convergence from a fixed default initialization, and we have also developed several initialization search methods which may be useful in some cases, occasional convergence to false minima remains a problem.

Organization: Section 2 gives a direction-vector based formulation of autocalibration, and discusses how planar and non-planar autocalibration can be approached within this framework. Section 3 describes the statistically-motivated cost function we optimize. Section 4 discusses the numerical algorithm, and the method used to initialize it. Section 5 gives experimental results on synthetic and real images, and section 6 concludes the paper.

Notation will be introduced as required. Briefly we use bold upright $\mathbf{x}, \mathbf{M}$ for homogeneous 3D (4 component) vectors and matrices; bold italic $\boldsymbol{x}, \boldsymbol{M}$ for 3 component ones (homogeneous image, inhomogeneous 3D, 3-component parts of homogeneous 4-component objects); $\mathbf{P}$ for image projections and $\boldsymbol{H}$ for inter-image homographies; $\boldsymbol{K}$, $\boldsymbol{C} = \boldsymbol{K}^{-1}$ for upper triangular camera calibration and inverse calibration matrices; $\boldsymbol{\Omega}^*$ and $\boldsymbol{\Omega}$ for the absolute conic and dual (hyperplane) quadric; and $\boldsymbol{\omega}^{-1} = \boldsymbol{C}^\top \boldsymbol{C}, \boldsymbol{\omega} = \boldsymbol{K} \boldsymbol{K}^\top = \mathbf{P} \boldsymbol{\Omega} \mathbf{P}^\top$ for their images.

2 Euclidean Structure and Autocalibration

To recover the metric information implicit in projective images, we need a projective encoding of Euclidean structure. The key to this is the dot product between direction vectors ("points at infinity"), or dually the dot product between hyperplane normals. The former leads to the stratified "plane at infinity + absolute conic" (affine + metric structure) formulation [17], the latter to the "absolute dual quadric" one [22]. These are just dual ways of saying the same thing. The dual quadric formalism is preferable for 'pure' autocalibration where there is no prior decomposition into affine and metric strata, while the point one may be simpler if such a stratification is given.

Generalities: Consider k-dimensional Euclidean space. We will need the cases $k = 2$ (the planar scene and its 2D images) and $k = 3$ (ordinary 3D space). Introducing homogeneous Euclidean coordinates, points, displacement vectors and hyperplanes are encoded respectively as homogeneous $k + 1$ component column vectors $\mathbf{x} = (\boldsymbol{x}, 1)^\top$, $\mathbf{t} = (\boldsymbol{t}, 0)^\top$ and row vectors $\mathbf{p} = (\boldsymbol{n}, d)$. Here $\boldsymbol{x}, \boldsymbol{t}$ and $\boldsymbol{n}$ are the usual k-D coordinate vectors of the point, the displacement, and the hyperplane normal, and d is the hyperplane offset. Points and displacements on the plane satisfy respectively $\mathbf{p} \cdot \mathbf{x} = \boldsymbol{n} \cdot \boldsymbol{x} + d = 0$ and $\mathbf{p} \cdot \mathbf{t} = \boldsymbol{n} \cdot \boldsymbol{t} = 0$. Displacement directions can be appended to the point space, as a **hyperplane at infinity** $\mathbf{p}_\infty$ of **vanishing points**. Projectively, $\mathbf{p}_\infty$ behaves much like any other hyperplane. In Euclidean coordinates, $\mathbf{p}_\infty = (\boldsymbol{0}, 1)$ so that $\mathbf{p}_\infty \cdot \mathbf{t} = 0$ for any displacement $\mathbf{t} = (t, 0)$. **Projective transformations** mix finite and infinite points. Under a projective transformation encoded by an arbitrary nonsingular $(k+1) \times (k+1)$ matrix $\mathbf{T}$, points and directions (column vectors) transform **contravariantly**, *i.e.* by $\mathbf{T}$ acting on the left: $\mathbf{x} \to \mathbf{T}\mathbf{x}$, $\mathbf{v} \to \mathbf{T}\mathbf{v}$. To preserve the point-on-plane relation $\mathbf{p} \cdot \mathbf{x} = \mathbf{n} \cdot \mathbf{x} + d = 0$, hyperplanes (row vectors) transform **covariantly**, *i.e.* by $\mathbf{T}^{-1}$ acting on the right: $\mathbf{p} \to \mathbf{p}\mathbf{T}^{-1}$.

Absolute Conic & Dual Quadric: The Euclidean dot product between hyperplane normals is $\mathbf{n}_1 \cdot \mathbf{n}_2 = \mathbf{p}_1 \boldsymbol{\Omega} \mathbf{p}_2^{\top}$ where the symmetric, rank k, positive semidefinite matrix $\boldsymbol{\Omega} = \begin{pmatrix} I_{k \times k} & 0 \\ 0 & 0 \end{pmatrix}$ is called the **absolute dual quadric**. $\boldsymbol{\Omega}$ encodes the Euclidean structure in projective coordinates. Under projective transformations it transforms contravariantly (*i.e.* like a point) in each of its two indices so that the dot product between plane normals is invariant: $\boldsymbol{\Omega} \to \mathbf{T} \boldsymbol{\Omega} \mathbf{T}^{\top}$ and $\mathbf{p}_i \to \mathbf{p}_i \mathbf{T}^{-1}$, so $\mathbf{p}_1 \boldsymbol{\Omega} \mathbf{p}_2^{\top} = \mathbf{n}_1 \cdot \mathbf{n}_2$ is constant. $\boldsymbol{\Omega}$ is invariant under Euclidean transformations, but in a general projective frame it loses its diagonal form and becomes an arbitrary symmetric positive semidefinite rank k matrix. In any frame, the Euclidean angle between two hyperplanes is $\cos\theta = (\mathbf{p}\,\boldsymbol{\Omega}\,\mathbf{p}'^{\top})/\sqrt{(\mathbf{p}\,\boldsymbol{\Omega}\,\mathbf{p}^{\top})(\mathbf{p}'\,\boldsymbol{\Omega}\,\mathbf{p}'^{\top})}$, and the plane at infinity is $\boldsymbol{\Omega}$'s unique null vector: $\mathbf{p}_\infty \boldsymbol{\Omega} = \mathbf{0}$. When restricted to coordinates on $\mathbf{p}_\infty$, $\boldsymbol{\Omega}$ becomes nonsingular and can be dualized (inverted) to give the $k \times k$ symmetric positive definite **absolute (direction) conic** $\boldsymbol{\Omega}^*$. This measures dot products between displacement vectors, just as $\boldsymbol{\Omega}$ measures them between hyperplane normals. $\boldsymbol{\Omega}^*$ is defined *only* on direction vectors, not on finite points, and unlike $\boldsymbol{\Omega}$ it has no unique canonical form in terms of the *un*restricted coordinates.

Direction bases: In Euclidean coordinates, $\boldsymbol{\Omega}$ can be decomposed as a sum of outer products of any orthonormal (in terms of $\boldsymbol{\Omega}^*$) basis of displacement vectors: $\boldsymbol{\Omega} = \sum_{i=1}^{k} \boldsymbol{x}_i \boldsymbol{x}_i^{\top}$ where $\boldsymbol{x}_i \boldsymbol{\Omega}^* \boldsymbol{x}_j = \delta_{ij}$. For example in 2D, $\boldsymbol{\Omega} = \begin{pmatrix} I_{2 \times 2} & 0 \\ 0 & 0 \end{pmatrix} = \hat{\boldsymbol{x}}\,\hat{\boldsymbol{x}}^{\top} + \hat{\boldsymbol{y}}\,\hat{\boldsymbol{y}}^{\top}$ where $\hat{\boldsymbol{x}} = (1, 0, 0)^{\top}$, $\hat{\boldsymbol{y}} = (0, 1, 0)^{\top}$, are the usual unit direction vectors. Gathering the basis vectors into the columns of a $(k+1) \times k$ orthonormal rank k matrix $\mathbf{U}$ we have $\boldsymbol{\Omega} = \mathbf{U}\mathbf{U}^{\top}$, $\mathbf{p}_\infty \mathbf{U} = \mathbf{0}$ and $\mathbf{U}^{\top} \boldsymbol{\Omega}^* \mathbf{U} = I_{k \times k}$. The columns of $\mathbf{U}$ span $\mathbf{p}_\infty$. These relations remain valid in an arbitrary projective frame $\mathbf{T}$ and with an arbitrary choice of representative for $\boldsymbol{\Omega}^*$, except that $\mathbf{U} \to \mathbf{T}\mathbf{U}$ ceases to be orthonormal.

$\mathbf{U}$ is defined only up to an arbitrary $k \times k$ orthogonal mixing of its columns (redefinition of the direction basis) $\mathbf{U} \to \mathbf{U}\,R_{k \times k}$. In a Euclidean frame $\mathbf{U} = \begin{pmatrix} V \\ 0 \end{pmatrix}$ for some $k \times k$ rotation matrix V, so the effect of a Euclidean space transformation is $\mathbf{U} \to \begin{pmatrix} R & t \\ 0 & 1 \end{pmatrix}\mathbf{U} = \mathbf{U}\,R'$ where $R' = V^{\top} R V$ is the conjugate rotation: Euclidean transformations of direction bases (*i.e.* on the left) are equivalent to orthogonal re-mixings of them (*i.e.* on the right). This remains true in an arbitrary projective frame, even though $\mathbf{U}$ and the space transformation no longer *look* Euclidean. Given a projective frame, this mixing freedom can be used to choose an associated direction basis in which the columns of $\mathbf{U}$ are numerically orthonormal up to a diagonal rescaling: simply take the SVD $\mathbf{U}'D V^{\top}$ of $\mathbf{U}$ and discard the mixing rotation $V^{\top}$. Equivalently, the eigenvectors and square roots of eigenvalues of Ω can be used. Such orthogonal parametrizations of $\mathbf{U}$ make good sense numerically, and we will use them below.

Circular points: Given any two orthonormal direction vectors $\mathbf{x}, \mathbf{y}$, the complex conjugate vectors $\mathbf{x}_\pm \equiv \frac{1}{\sqrt{2}}(\mathbf{x} \pm i\mathbf{y})$ satisfy $\mathbf{x}_\mp^\top \Omega^* \mathbf{x}_\pm = 0$. Abstractly, these complex directions lie on the absolute conic. Conversely, given any complex projective point lying on Ω^*, its real and imaginary parts are two orthogonal direction vectors. In the 2D case there is only one such conjugate pair up to complex phase, and these **circular points** characterize the Euclidean structure of the plane. The phase freedom in $\mathbf{x}_\pm$ corresponds to the 2×2 orthogonal mixing freedom of $\mathbf{x}$ and $\mathbf{y}$. In the implementation we prefer to avoid complex numbers by using $\mathbf{x}$ and $\mathbf{y}$ rather than $\mathbf{x}_\pm$.

The above parametrizations of Euclidean structure are theoretically equivalent. Which is practically best depends on the problem. Ω is easy to use, except that constrained optimization is required to handle the rank k constraint $\det \Omega = 0$. Direction bases $\mathbf{U}$ eliminate the constraint at the cost of a $k \times k$ orthogonal gauge freedom. The absolute conic Ω^* has neither constraint nor gauge freedom, but has significantly more complicated image projection properties and can only be defined once the plane at infinity $\mathbf{p}_\infty$ is known and a projective coordinate system on it has been chosen (*e.g.* induced from one of the images). One can also use Cholesky-like decompositions $\Omega = \mathbf{L}\mathbf{L}^\top$ (*e.g.* the L part of the LQ decomposition of $\mathbf{U}$), although pivoting is needed to avoid singularities at maximally non-Euclidean frames.

Image Projections: Since the columns of a 3D direction basis $\mathbf{U}$ are *bona fide* 3D direction vectors, its image projection is simply $\mathbf{P}\,\mathbf{U}$, where $\mathbf{P}$ is the usual 3×4 point projection matrix. Hence, the projection of $\Omega = \mathbf{U}\mathbf{U}^\top$ is the 3×3 symmetric positive definite contravariant image matrix $\omega = \mathbf{P}\,\Omega\,\mathbf{P}^\top$. Abstractly, this is the image line quadric dual to the image of the absolute conic. Concretely, given any two image lines l_1, l_2, ω encodes the 3D dot product between their 3D visual planes $\mathbf{p}_i \equiv l_i\mathbf{P}$: $\mathbf{p}_1\,\Omega\,\mathbf{p}_2^\top = l_1\,\mathbf{P}\,\Omega\,\mathbf{P}^\top l_2^\top = l_1\,\omega\,l_2^\top$. With the traditional Euclidean decomposition $\mathbf{K}\,\mathbf{R}\,(\,\mathbf{I}\,|-\mathbf{t})$ of $\mathbf{P}$ into an upper triangular **internal calibration matrix** $\mathbf{K}$, a 3×3 **camera orientation** (rotation) $\mathbf{R}$ and an **optical centre** $\mathbf{t}$, ω becomes simply $\mathbf{K}\,\mathbf{K}^\top$. ω is invariant under camera displacements so long as $\mathbf{K}$ remains constant. $\mathbf{K}$ can be recovered from ω by Cholesky decomposition. Similarly, the Euclidean scene structure (in the form of a 'rectifying' projectivity) can be recovered from Ω. The upper triangular **inverse calibration matrix** $\mathbf{C} = \mathbf{K}^{-1}$ converts homogeneous pixel coordinates to optical ray directions in the Euclidean camera frame. $\omega^{-1} = \mathbf{C}^\top \mathbf{C}$ is the image of the absolute conic.

Autocalibration: Given several images taken with projection matrices $\mathbf{P}_i = \mathbf{K}_i\,\mathbf{R}_i(\mathbf{I}| - \mathbf{t}_i)$, and (in the same Euclidean frame) a orthogonal direction basis $\mathbf{U} = \binom{V}{0}$, we find that

$$\mathbf{C}_i\,\mathbf{P}_i\,\mathbf{U} = \mathbf{R}_i' \tag{1}$$

where $\mathbf{C}_i = \mathbf{K}_i^{-1}$ and $\mathbf{R}_i' = \mathbf{R}_i\,V$ is a rotation matrix depending on the camera pose. This is perhaps the most basic form of autocalibration constraint. It says that the calibrated images (*i.e.* 3D directions in the camera frame) of an orthogonal direction basis must remain orthogonal. It remains true in arbitrary projective 3D and image frames, as the projective deformations of $\mathbf{P}_i$ *vs.* $\mathbf{U}$ and C_i *vs.* $\mathbf{P}_i$ cancel each other out. Unfortunately, for projectively reconstructed projection matrices it is seldom possible to estimate scale factors consistent with those of their unknown Euclidean parents. So in practice the autocalibration constraint can only be applied up to an unknown scale factor: $C_i \, \mathbf{P}_i \, \mathbf{U} \sim R_i'$. As always, the direction basis $\mathbf{U}$ is only defined up to an arbitrary 3×3 orthogonal mixing $\mathbf{U} \to \mathbf{U} \, R$.

2.1 Autocalibration for Non-Planar Scenes

The simplest approaches to non-planar autocalibration are based on (1), an intermediate projective reconstruction $\mathbf{P}_i$, and some sort of knowledge about the C_i (classically that they are constant, $C_i = C$ for some unknown C). Non-linear optimization or algebraic elimination are used to estimate the Euclidean structure Ω or $\mathbf{U}$, and the free parameters of the C_i. Multiplying (1) either on the left or on the right by its transpose to eliminate the unknown rotation, and optionally moving the C's to the right hand side, gives several equivalent symmetric 3×3 constraints linking Ω or $\mathbf{U}$ to ω_i, K_i or C_i

$$\mathbf{U}^\mathsf{T} \mathbf{P}_i^\mathsf{T} \, \omega_i^{-1} \, \mathbf{P}_i \, \mathbf{U} \sim I_{3 \times 3} \tag{2}$$

$$C_i \, \mathbf{P}_i \, \Omega \, \mathbf{P}_i^\mathsf{T} \, C_i^\mathsf{T} \sim I_{3 \times 3} \tag{3}$$

$$\mathbf{P}_i \, \Omega \, \mathbf{P}_i^\mathsf{T} \sim \omega_i = K_i \, K_i^\mathsf{T} \tag{4}$$

In each case there are 5 independent constraints per image on the 8 non-Euclidean d.o.f. of the 3D projective structure[2] and the ≤ 5 d.o.f. per image of the internal calibrations C_i. For example, three images in general position suffice for classical constant-C autocalibration. In each case, the unknown scale factors can be eliminated by treating the symmetric 3×3 left and right hand side matrices as $\frac{3 \cdot 4}{2} = 6$ component vectors, and either (*i*) cross-multiplying, or (*ii*) projecting (say) the left hand side vectors orthogonally to the right hand ones (hence deleting the proportional components and focusing on the constraint-violating non-proportional ones). Cross-multiplication gives

$$\mathbf{u}_i \cdot \mathbf{v}_i = \mathbf{u}_i \cdot \mathbf{w}_i = \mathbf{v}_i \cdot \mathbf{w}_i = 0 \qquad \|\mathbf{u}_i\|^2 = \|\mathbf{v}_i\|^2 = \|\mathbf{w}_i\|^2 \tag{5}$$

$$(C_i \, \mathbf{P}_i \, \Omega \, \mathbf{P}_i^\mathsf{T} \, C_i^\mathsf{T})^{AA} = (C_i \, \mathbf{P}_i \, \Omega \, \mathbf{P}_i^\mathsf{T} \, C_i^\mathsf{T})^{BB}$$
$$(C_i \, \mathbf{P}_i \, \Omega \, \mathbf{P}_i^\mathsf{T} \, C_i^\mathsf{T})^{AB} = 0 \tag{6}$$

---

[2] These can be counted as follows: 15 for a 3D projective transformation modulo 7 for a scaled Euclidean one; or 12 for a 4×3 $\mathbf{U}$ matrix modulo 1 scale and 3 d.o.f. for a 3×3 orthogonal mixing; or $4 \cdot 5/2 = 10$ d.o.f. for a 4×4 symmetric quadric matrix Ω modulo 1 scale and 1 d.o.f. for the rank 3 constraint $\det \Omega = 0$; or 3 d.o.f. for $\mathbf{p}_\infty$ and 5 for the $3 \cdot 4/2 = 6$ components of Ω^* modulo 1 scale.

$$(\mathbf{P}_i \, \boldsymbol{\Omega} \, \mathbf{P}_i^\top)^{CD} \, (\boldsymbol{\omega})^{EF} = (\boldsymbol{\omega})^{CD} \, (\mathbf{P}_i \, \boldsymbol{\Omega} \, \mathbf{P}_i^\top)^{EF} \tag{7}$$

where $(\mathbf{u}_i, \mathbf{v}_i, \mathbf{w}_i) \equiv C_i \, \mathbf{P}_i \, \mathbf{U}$ and $A < B, C \le D, E \le F = 1 \ldots 3$. Several recent autocalibration methods (*e.g.* [22, 9]) are based implicitly on these constraints, parametrized by $\boldsymbol{K}$ or $\boldsymbol{\omega}$ and something equivalent[3] to $\boldsymbol{\Omega}$ or $\mathbf{U}$. All of these methods seem to work well provided the intrinsic degeneracies of the autocalibration problem [18] are avoided. In contrast, methods based on the Kruppa equations [14, 3, 25] are not recommended for general use, because they add a serious additional singularity to the already-restrictive ones intrinsic to the problem: if any 3D point projects to the same pixel and is viewed from the same distance in each image, one focal length parameter can not be recovered [19].

2.2   Autocalibration from Planar Scenes

Now consider autocalibration from *planar* scenes. Everything above remains valid, except that no intermediate 3D projective reconstruction is available from which to bootstrap the process. However autocalibration is still possible using the inter-image homographies. The Euclidean structure of the scene plane is given by any one of (*i*) a 3×3 rank 2 absolute dual (line) quadric $\boldsymbol{Q}$; (*ii*) a 3 component line at infinity $\boldsymbol{l}_\infty$ and its associated 2×2 absolute (direction) conic matrix; (*iii*) a 3×2 direction basis matrix $\boldsymbol{U} = (\boldsymbol{x} \ \boldsymbol{y})$; (*iv*) two complex conjugate circular points $\boldsymbol{x}_\pm = \frac{1}{\sqrt{2}}(\boldsymbol{x} \pm i\boldsymbol{y})$ which are also the two roots of the absolute conic on $\boldsymbol{l}_\infty$ and the factors of the absolute dual quadric $\boldsymbol{Q} = \boldsymbol{x} \, \boldsymbol{x}^\top + \boldsymbol{y} \, \boldsymbol{y}^\top = \boldsymbol{x}_+ \boldsymbol{x}_-^\top + \boldsymbol{x}_- \boldsymbol{x}_+^\top$. In each case the structure is the natural restriction of the corresponding 3D one, re-expressed in the planar coordinate system. In each case it projects isomorphically into each image, either by the usual 3×4 3D projection matrix (using 3D coordinates), or by the corresponding 3×3 world-plane to image-plane homography $\boldsymbol{H}$ (using scene plane coordinates). Hence, each image inherits a pair of circular points $\boldsymbol{H}_i \, \boldsymbol{x}_\pm$ and the corresponding direction basis $\boldsymbol{H}_i \, (\boldsymbol{x} \ \boldsymbol{y})$, line at infinity $\boldsymbol{l}_\infty \, \boldsymbol{H}_i^{-1}$ and 3×3 rank 2 absolute dual quadric $\boldsymbol{H}_i \, \boldsymbol{Q} \, \boldsymbol{H}_i^\top$. The columns of the planar $\boldsymbol{U}$ matrix still represent *bona fide* 3D direction vectors (albeit expressed in planar coordinates), so their images still satisfy the autocalibration constraints (1):

$$C_i \, \boldsymbol{H}_i \, \boldsymbol{U} \sim \boldsymbol{R}_{3 \times 2} \tag{8}$$

where $\boldsymbol{R}_{3 \times 2}$ contains the first two columns of a 3×3 rotation matrix. Left multiplication by the transpose eliminates the unknown rotation (*c.f.* (2)):

$$\boldsymbol{U}^\top \, \boldsymbol{H}_i^\top \, \boldsymbol{\omega}_i^{-1} \, \boldsymbol{H}_i \, \boldsymbol{U} \sim \boldsymbol{I}_{2 \times 2} \tag{9}$$

Splitting this into components gives the form of the constraints used by our planar autocalibration algorithm:

$$\|\boldsymbol{u}_i\|^2 = \|\boldsymbol{v}_i\|^2, \quad \boldsymbol{u}_i \cdot \boldsymbol{v}_i = 0 \quad \text{where} \quad (\boldsymbol{u}_i, \boldsymbol{v}_i) \equiv C_i \, \boldsymbol{H}_i \, (\boldsymbol{x}, \boldsymbol{y}) \tag{10}$$

---

[3] If the first camera projection is taken to be $(\,\boldsymbol{I}\,|\,\boldsymbol{0}\,)$ [5, 9], $\mathbf{U}$ can be chosen to have the form $\begin{pmatrix} \boldsymbol{I} \\ -\boldsymbol{p}^\top \end{pmatrix} \boldsymbol{K}$ where $\mathbf{p}_\infty \sim (\boldsymbol{p}^\top, 1)$, whence $\boldsymbol{\Omega} \sim \begin{pmatrix} \boldsymbol{\omega} & -\boldsymbol{\omega} \, \boldsymbol{p} \\ -\boldsymbol{p}^\top \boldsymbol{\omega} & \boldsymbol{p}^\top \boldsymbol{\omega} \, \boldsymbol{p} \end{pmatrix}$ and $\begin{pmatrix} \boldsymbol{C} & \boldsymbol{0} \\ \boldsymbol{p}^\top & 1 \end{pmatrix}$ is a Euclideanizing projectivity.

These constraints say that any two orthonormal directions in the world plane project (via $C_i H_i$) to orthonormal directions in the calibrated camera frame. Equivalently, the images of the circular points $x_\pm = \frac{1}{\sqrt{2}}(x \pm iy)$ lie on the image of the absolute conic:

$$(H_i\, x_\pm)^\top\, \omega^{-1}\, (H_i\, x_\pm) \;=\; \|u_{i\pm}\|^2 \;=\; 0 \qquad \text{where} \qquad u_{i\pm} \;\equiv\; C_i\, H_i\, x_\pm \qquad (11)$$

All of the above constraints are valid in arbitrary projective image and world-plane frames, except that $U = (x\ y)$ is no longer orthonormal. As always, (x, y) are defined only up to a 2×2 orthogonal mixing, and we can use this gauge freedom to require that $x \cdot y = 0$.

Our planar autocalibration method is based on direct numerical minimization of the residual error in the constraints (10) from several images, over the unknown direction basis (x, y) and any combination of the five intrinsic calibration parameters f, a, s, u_0 and v_0. The input data is the set of world plane to image homographies H_i, expressed with respect to an arbitrary projective frame for the world plane. In particular, if the plane is coordinatized by its projection into some key image (say image 1), the inter-image homographies H_{i1} can be used as input.

Four independent parameters are required to specify the Euclidean structure of a projective plane: the 6 components of (x, y) modulo scale and the phase of a 2×2 rotation; or the $3 \cdot 4/2 = 6$ components of a 3×3 absolute dual quadric Q modulo scale and det $Q = 0$; or the 2 d.o.f. of the plane's line at infinity, plus the 2 d.o.f. of two circular points on it. Since equations (9), (10) or (11) give two independent constraints for each image, $\lceil \frac{n+4}{2} \rceil$ images are required to estimate the Euclidean structure of the plane and n intrinsic calibration parameters. For known calibration, two images suffice (classical plane-based relative camera orientation). Three are required if the focal length is also estimated, four for the perspective f, u_0, v_0 model, and five if all 5 intrinsic parameters are unknown.

2.3   Camera Parametrization

We have not yet made the camera parametrization explicit, beyond saying that it is given by the upper triangular matrices K or $C = K^{-1}$. For autocalibration methods which fix some parameters while varying others, it makes a difference which parametrization is used. I prefer the following form motivated by a zoom lens followed by an affine image-plane coordinatization:

$$K = \begin{pmatrix} f & fs & u_0 \\ 0 & fa & v_0 \\ 0 & 0 & 1 \end{pmatrix} \qquad\qquad C = K^{-1} = \frac{1}{fa} \begin{pmatrix} a & -s & sv_0 - au_0 \\ 0 & 1 & -v_0 \\ 0 & 0 & fa \end{pmatrix}$$

Here, if standard pixel coordinates are used, $f = \alpha_u$ is the focal length in u-pixels, $s = -\tan\theta_{\text{skew}}$ is the dimensionless geometric skew, $a = \alpha_v/(\alpha_u \cos\theta_{\text{skew}})$ is the dimensionless $v : u$ aspect ratio, and (u_0, v_0) are the pixel coordinates of the principal point. However pixel coordinates are *not* used in the optimization routine below. Instead, a nominal calibration is used to standardize the parameters to nominal values $f = a = 1$, $s = u_0 = v_0 = 0$, and all subsequent fitting is done using the above model with respect to these values.

3 Algebraic *vs.* Statistical Error

Many vision problems reduce to minimizing the residual violation of some vector of nonlinear constraints $e(x, \mu) \approx 0$ over parameters μ, given noisy measurements x with known covariance V_x. Often, heuristic **algebraic error** metrics like $\|e(x, \mu)\|^2$ are minimized. However this is statistically sub-optimal, and if done uncritically can lead to both (*i*) very significant bias in the results and (*ii*) severe constriction of the domain of convergence of the optimization. Appropriate **balancing** or **preconditioning** (numerical scaling of the variables and constraints, as advocated in [7,8] and any numerical optimization text) is one step towards eliminating such problems, but it is not the whole story. In any case it begs the question of what *is* "balanced". It is *not* always appropriate to scale all variables to $\mathcal{O}(1)$. In fact, in the context of parameter estimation, balanced simply means "close to an underlying *statistical* error metric" such as $\chi_e^2 \approx e^\top V_e^{-1} e$, where $V_e \approx \frac{De}{Dx} V_x \frac{De}{Dx}^\top$ is the covariance[4] of e.

Ideally one would like to minimize the underlying statistical error, but this can be complicated owing to the matrix products and (pseudo-)inverse. Simple approximations often suffice, and I feel that this is the *only* acceptable way to introduce algebraic error measures — as explicit, controlled approximations to an underlying statistical metric. The extra computation required for a suitable approximation is usually minimal while the results can be substantially more accurate, so it makes little sense to use an arbitrary *ad hoc* error metric.

One useful simplification ignores the dependence of V_e^{-1} on μ in cost function derivatives. This gives **self-consistent** or **iterative re-weighting** schemes (*e.g.* [12]), where V_e is treated as a constant within each optimization step, but updated at the end of it. One can show that the missing terms effectively displace the cost derivative evaluation point from the measured x to a first order estimate of the true underlying value x_0 [20]. For the most part this makes little difference unless the constraints are strongly curved on the scale of V_x.

However, as I feel that a final bundle adjustment is an essential part of any reconstruction or autocalibration technique, my current implementation uses a rather simplistic error model for the H_i. Firstly, I ignore the fact that they are correlated through their mutual dependence on the base image, which is treated just like any other in the sum. This undoubtedly introduces some bias. Correcting it would significantly complicate the method, and require users to supply an inconvenient amount of inter-H_i covariance data. Secondly, the components of

---

[4] e is a random variable through its dependence on x. Assuming that the uncertainties are small enough to allow linearization and that x is centred on some underlying x_0 satisfying $e(x_0, \mu_0) = 0$ for underlying parameters μ_0, $e(x, \mu_0)$ has mean 0 and the above covariance. It follows that $e^\top V_e^{-1} e$ is approximately a $\chi_{\text{rank}(e)}^2$ variable near μ_0, which can be minimized to find a maximum likelihood estimate of μ.

H_i are assumed to be i.i.d. in the nominally calibrated coordinate system: $\mathbf{V}_H = \langle \Delta H_B^A \, \Delta H_D^C \rangle \sim \epsilon \cdot \delta^{AC} \cdot \delta_{BD}$ where ϵ is a noise level[5]. This could easily be corrected at the cost of a little extra linear algebra.

From here, it is straightforward to find and invert the constraint covariance. For the planar autocalibration constraint (10), and assuming that we enforce the gauge constraint $x \cdot y = 0$, the constraint covariance is

$$
\mathbf{V_e} \approx \epsilon \cdot \begin{pmatrix} x^2 \, a_i^2 + y^2 \, b_i^2 & (x^2 - y^2) \, a_i \cdot b_i \\ (x^2 - y^2) \, a_i \cdot b_i & x^2 \, b_i^2 + y^2 \, a_i^2 \end{pmatrix}, \qquad \begin{aligned} (a_i, b_i) &\equiv C_i^\top (u_i, v_i) \\ &= \omega_i^{-1} \, H_i (x, y) \end{aligned}
$$

In this case, numerical experience indicates that the off-diagonal term is seldom more than a few percent of the diagonal ones, which themselves are approximately equal for each image, but differ by as much as a factor of 2–3 between images[6]. Hence, we drop the off-diagonal term to give an autocalibration method based on self-consistent optimization of the diagonal cost function

$$
\sum_{i=1}^{m} \left(\frac{(\|u_i\|^2 - \|v_i\|^2)^2}{x^2 \, \|C_i^\top u_i\|^2 + y^2 \, \|C_i^\top v_i\|^2} + \frac{(u_i \cdot v_i)^2}{x^2 \, \|C_i^\top v_i\|^2 + y^2 \, \|C_i^\top u_i\|^2} \right) \tag{12}
$$

where $(u_i, v_i) \equiv C_i \, H_i (x, y)$. In our synthetic experiments, this statistically motivated cost function gives ground-truth standard deviations about 10% lower than even the most carefully normalized algebraic ones. This is a modest but useful improvement, obtained without any measurable increase in run time. The improvement would have been *much* larger had the error model been less uniform in the standardized coordinates. Perhaps most importantly, the statistical cost is almost completely immune to mis-scaling of the variables. This is certainly not true of the algebraic ones, which deteriorate very rapidly for mis-scaling factors greater than about 3.

4 Planar Autocalibration Algorithm

Numerical Method: Our planar autocalibration algorithm is based on direct numerical minimization of the m-image cost function (12), with respect to the direction basis (x, y) and any subset of the 5 internal calibration parameters focal length f, aspect ratio a, skew s, and principal point (u_0, v_0). There are 4 d.o.f. in (x, y) — 6 components defined up to an overall rescaling and a 2×2

---

[5] Although balancing should make their variances similar, in reality the components are unlikely to be independent. At very least we should subtract a 'scale' term $H_B^A H_D^C$, as variations proportional to H make no projective difference. However this makes no difference here. A correctly weighted error metric e must be insensitive to rescalings of its projective-homogeneous parameters H. Hence it has homogeneity 0 in H — $\frac{De}{DH} \cdot H = 0$ — and $\mathbf{V_e}$ is unaffected by the 'scale' term.

[6] This was to be expected: we chose everything to be well-scaled except that the H normalizations may differ somewhat from their 'correct' Euclidean ones, and our noise model is uniform in an approximately calibrated frame. Relaxing any of these conditions would make the differences *much* greater.

orthogonal mixing — so the optimization is over 5–9 parameters in all. Numerically, the 6 component $(\boldsymbol{x}, \boldsymbol{y})$ vector is projected onto the subspace orthogonal to its current scaling and mixing d.o.f. by Householder reduction (*i.e.* effectively a mini QR decomposition). As mentioned in section 2, the mixing freedom allows us to enforce the gauge condition $\boldsymbol{x} \cdot \boldsymbol{y} = 0$. Although not essential, this costs very little (one Jacobi rotation) and we do it at each iteration as an aid to numerical stability.

A fairly conventional nonlinear least squares optimization method is used: Gauss-Newton iteration based on Cholesky decomposition of the normal equations. As always, forming the normal equations gives a fast, relatively simple method but effectively squares the condition number of the constraint Jacobian. This is not a problem so long as intermediate results are stored at sufficiently high precision: double precision proves more than adequate here.

As with any numerical method, care is needed to ensure stability should the numerical conditioning become poor. Our parametrization guarantees that all variables are of $\mathcal{O}(1)$ and fairly well decoupled, so preconditioning is not necessary. The Cholesky routine uses diagonal pivoting and Gill & Murray's [4] minimum-diagonal-value regularization to provide local stability. The regularizer is manipulated in much the same way as a Levenberg-Marquardt parameter to ensure that each step actually reduces the cost function. We also limit the maximum step size for each variable, relatively for the positive, multiplicative parameters f and a and absolutely for the others. Both the regularizer and the step size limits are activated fairly often in practice, the regularizer at any time, and the step limit usually only during the first 1–2 iterations. The method terminates when the step size converges to zero, with additional heuristics to detect thrashing. Convergence within 5–10 iterations is typical.

Prior over Calibrations: We also allow for a simple user-defined prior distribution on the calibration parameters. Even if there is no strong prior knowledge, it is often advisable to include a weak prior in statistical estimation problems as a form of regularization. If there are nearly unobservable parameter combinations (*i.e.* which make little or no difference to the fit), optimal, unbiased estimates of these are usually extremely sensitive to noise. A weak prior has little influence on strong estimates, but significantly reduces the variability of weak ones by biasing them towards reasonable default values. A desire to keep the results unbiased is understandable, but limiting the impact of large fluctuations on the rest of the vision system is often more important in practice.

Priors can also be used to ensure that parameters retain physically meaningful values. For example, the multiplicative parameters f and a must lie in the range $(0, \infty)$, and we include weak heuristic priors of the form $(f/f_0 - f_0/f)^2$ (*i.e.* multiplicatively symmetric about f_0) to ensure this. This is particularly important for autocalibration problems, where degenerate motions occur frequently. In such cases the calibration can not be recovered uniquely and a numerical method will converge to an arbitrary member of the family of possible solutions. For sanity, it pays to ensure that this is a physically feasible solution not too far from the plausible range of values. A weak default prior is an effective means of achieving this, and seems no more unprincipled than any other method. (This is not to say that degeneracies should be left unflagged, simply that recovering from them is easier if it starts from reasonable default values).

Initialization: The domain of convergence of the numerical method is reasonable and for many applications it will probably be sufficient to initialize from fixed default values. The most critical parameters are the focal length f and the number and angular spread of the views. For example, if f can only be guessed within a factor of 2 and all 5 parameters f, a, s, u_0, v_0 are left free, about 9–10 images spread by more than about $10°$ seem to be required for reliable convergence to the true solution. Indeed, with 5 free parameters and the theoretical minimum of only 5–6 images, even an *exact* initialization is not always sufficient to eliminate false solutions (*i.e.* whose residuals happen to be slightly smaller than the true one). These figures assume that the direction basis x, y is completely unknown: constraints on it are potentially very valuable and should be used if available. Knowledge of the world-plane's horizon (line at infinity) removes 2 d.o.f. from x, y and hence reduces the number of images required by one, and knowledge of its Euclidean structure (but not the positions of points on it) eliminates another image. Even if not directly visible, horizons can be recovered from known 3D parallelism or texture gradients, or bounded by the fact that visible points on the plane must lie inside them. We will not consider such constraints further here.

If a default initialization is insufficient to guarantee convergence, several strategies are possible. One quite effective technique is simply to use a preliminary optimization over x, y or x, y, f to initialize a full one over all parameters. More global searches over f, x, y are also useful. Perhaps the easiest way to approach this is to fix nominal values for all of the calibration parameters except f, and to recover estimates for x, y as a function of f from a single pair of images as f varies. These values can then be substituted into the autocalibration constraints for the other images, and the overall most consistent set of values chosen to initialize the optimization routine. The estimation of $x(f), y(f)$ reduces to the classical photogrammetric problem of the relative orientation of two calibrated cameras from a planar scene, as the Euclidean structure is easily recovered once the camera poses are known. In theory this problem could be solved in closed form (the most difficult step being a 3×3 eigendecomposition) and optimized over f analytically. But in practice this would be rather messy and I have preferred to implement a coarse numerical search over f. The search uses a new SVD-based planar relative orientation method [21] related to Wunderlich's eigendecomposition approach [24]. The camera pose and planar structure are recovered directly from the SVD of the inter-image homography. As always with planar relative orientation, there is a two-fold ambiguity in the solution, so both solutions are tested. In the implemented routine, the solutions for each image against the first one, and for each f in a geometric progression, are substituted into the constraints from all the other images, and the most consistent overall values are chosen.

If the full 5 parameter camera model is to be fitted, Hartley's 'rotating camera' method [6] can also be used for initialization. It works well *provided* (i) the camera translations are smaller than or comparable to the distance to the plane; (ii) no point on the plane is nearly fixated from a constant distance. (For such a point $\boldsymbol{x}$, $\boldsymbol{\omega} + \mu \boldsymbol{x}\boldsymbol{x}^\top$ is an approximate solution of Hartley's equation $\boldsymbol{H}\boldsymbol{\omega}\boldsymbol{H}^\top = \boldsymbol{\omega}$ for any μ, *i.e.* $\boldsymbol{\omega}$ can not be estimated uniquely, even for small translations).

5 Experiments

Synthetic data: The method has been implemented in C and tested on both real and synthetic images. For the synthetic experiments, the camera roughly fixates a point on the plane from a constant distance, from randomly generated orientations varying by (by default) $\pm 30°$ in each of the three axes. The camera calibration varies randomly about a nominal focal length of 1024 pixels and unit aspect ratio, by $\pm 30\%$ in focal length f, $\pm 10\%$ in aspect ratio a, ± 0.01 in dimensionless skew s, and ± 50 pixels in principal point (u_0, v_0). (These values are standard deviations of log-normal distributions for f, a and normal ones for s, u_0, v_0). The scene plane contains by default 40 visible points, projected into the 512×512 images with a Gaussian noise of ± 1 pixel. Before the homographies are estimated and the method is run, the pixel coordinates are centred and scaled to a nominal focal length of 1: $(u, v) \rightarrow (u-256, v-256)/1024$. The output is classed as a 'success' or 'failure' according to fixed thresholds on the size of its deviation from the true value. Only successes count towards the accuracy estimates. The usual mode of failure is convergence to a false solution with extremely short focal length (say < 50 pixels). However when the angular spread of the views is small or there are only a few images, random fluctuations sometimes take a "correct" but highly variable solution outside the (generously set) thresholds. Conversely, there is occasionally convergence to a false solution within the threshold. Thus, when the failure rate is high, neither it nor the corresponding precision estimates are accurate. The optimization typically converges within 5–10 iterations, although more may be needed for degenerate problems. The run time is negligible: on a Pentium 133, about 0.5 milliseconds per image if the default initialization is used, or 2.0 with a fairly fine initialization search over f.

Figure 1 gives some illustrative accuracy and reliability results, concentrating on the estimation of focal length f. First consider the plots where all 5 calibration parameters are estimated. The error scales roughly linearly with noise and inversely with the angular spread of the views. It drops rapidly as the first few images are added, but levels off after about 10 images. The failure rate increases rapidly for more than about 2–3 pixels noise, and is also unacceptably high for near-minimal numbers of images (within 1–2 of the minimum) and small angular spreads (less than about 10°). however, it decreases rapidly as each of these variables is increased. It seems to be difficult to get much below about 1% failure rate with the current setup. Some of the failures probably result from degeneracies in the randomly generated problems, but most of them are caused by convergence to a false solution with implausible parameters, either very small f

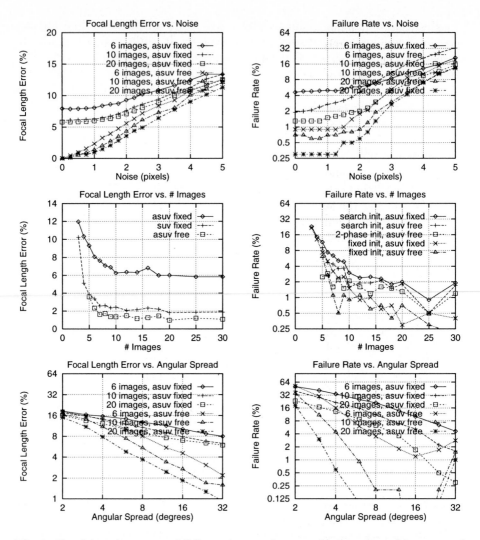

Fig. 1. Focal length error and failure rate *vs.* image noise, number of images and angular spread of cameras, averaged over 1000 trials. The aspect ratio a, skew s, and principal point (u_0, v_0) are either fixed at their nominal values, or allowed to vary freely, as indicated. The method is initialized from the nominal calibration, except that in the failure *vs.* images plot we also show the results for initialization by numerical search over f, and by a preliminary fit over f alone ('2-phase').

(less than about 50) or a far from 1. The initialization method has little impact on the reliability. In fact, in these experiments the default initialization proved more reliable than either numerical search over f, or an initial optimization over f alone. The reason is simply that we do not assume prior knowledge of *any* of the calibration parameters. An initialization search over f must fix a, s, u_0, v_0 at their inaccurate nominal values, and this is sometimes enough to make it miss the true solution entirely. This also explains the poor performance of the methods which hold a, s, u_0, v_0 fixed and estimate f alone. As the graphs of error *vs.* noise and number of images show, errors in a, s, u_0, v_0 lead to a significant bias in f, but most of this can be eliminated by estimating a as well as f. The initialization search over f also becomes much more reliable (*e.g.* 0.05% failure rate for 10 images, 30° spread and 1 pixel noise) if a and s are accurate to within a few percent. Here and elsewhere, it is only worthwhile to fix parameters if they are reliably known to an accuracy better than their measured variabilities, *e.g.* here for 1 pixel noise and 10 images, to about 0.003 for a, s or 20 pixels for u_0, v_0.

For conventional calibration, f is often said the most difficult parameter to estimate, and also the least likely to be known *a priori*. In contrast, a and s are said to be estimated quite accurately, while u_0 and v_0 — although variable — are felt to have little effect on the overall results. A more critical, quantitative view is to compare the *relative* accuracy $|\Delta f/f|$ to the dimensionless quantities $|\Delta a|$, $|\Delta s|$, $|\Delta u_0/f|$ and $|\Delta v_0/f|$. Errors in these contribute about equally to the overall geometric accuracy (*e.g.* reconstruction errors of 3D visual ray directions). Conversely, other things being equal, geometric constraints such as the autocalibration ones typically constrain each of these quantities to about the same extent. A good rule of thumb is that for auto- (and many other types of) calibration, $|\Delta u_0/f|$ and $|\Delta v_0/f|$ are of the same order of magnitude as $|\Delta f/f|$, while $|\Delta a|$ and $|\Delta s|$ are usually somewhat smaller if there are strong aspect ratio constraints (*e.g.* cyclotorsion), but larger if there are none (*e.g.* motions that leave a direction in the optical plane fixed). These rules are well borne out in all of the experiments reported here: we always find $|\Delta u_0| \approx |\Delta v_0| \approx |\Delta f|$, while $|\Delta a|$ and $|\Delta s|$ are respectively about one fifth, one half, and one tenth of $|\Delta f/f|$ for the synthetic experiments, the real experiments below, and the Faugeras-Toscani calibration used in the real experiments.

Real data: We have also run the method on parts of a sequence of about 40 real images of our tri-planar calibration grid. Only the 49 (at most) points on the base plane of the grid are used. (The algorithm could easily be expanded to handle several planes, but there seems little point as a non-planar method could be used in this case). The motion was intended to be general within the limits of the 5 d.o.f. robot used to produce it, but is fairly uniform within each subsequence. Visibility considerations limited the total angular displacement to about 40°, and significantly less within each subsequence. Here are the sample means and standard deviations over a few non-overlapping subsequences for (*i*) f alone, and (*ii*) all 5 parameters. The errors are observed sample scatters, *not* estimates of absolute accuracy.

	f only	f	a	s	u_0	v_0
calibration	-	1515 ± 4	0.9968 ± 0.0002	-	271 ± 3	264 ± 4
6 images	1584 ± 63	1595 ± 63	0.9934 ± 0.0055	0.000 ± 0.001	268 ± 10	271 ± 22
8 images	1619 ± 25	1614 ± 42	0.9890 ± 0.0058	-0.005 ± 0.005	289 ± 3	320 ± 26
10 images	1612 ± 19	1565 ± 41	1.0159 ± 0.0518	-0.004 ± 0.006	273 ± 5	286 ± 27

The 'calibrated' values are the averaged results of several single-image Faugeras-Toscani calibrations using all visible points on the grid. Looking at the table, the results of the autocalibration method seem usable but not quite as good as I would have expected on the basis of the synthetic experiments. This may just be the effect of the small angular range within each subsequence, but the estimates of f seem suspiciously high and it may be that some small systematic error has occurred during the processing. Further work is required to check this. Note that in this case, fixing a, s, u_0, v_0 appears to have the desired effect of decreasing the variability of the estimated f without perturbing its value very much.

6   Summary

In summary, we have shown how autocalibration problems can be approached using a projective representation of orthogonal 3D direction frames, and used this to derive a practical numerical algorithm for the autocalibration of a moving projective camera viewing a planar scene. The method is based on the 'rectification' of inter-image homographies. It requires a minimum of 3 images if only the focal length is estimated, or 5 for all five internal parameters. Using 9–10 images significantly increases both reliability and accuracy. An angular spread between the cameras of at least 15–20° is recommended.

Priorities for future work are the initialization problem and the detection of false solutions (or possibly the production of multiple ones). Although the current numerical method is stable even for degenerate motions (and hence gives a possible solution), it does not attempt to detect and flag the degeneracy. This can be done, *e.g.* by extracting the null space of the estimated covariance matrix. It would also be useful to have autocalibration methods that could estimate lens distortion. This should be relatively simple in the planar case, as distortion can be handled during homography estimation.

References

1. M. Armstrong, A. Zisserman, and R. Hartley. Self-calibration from image triplets. In B. Buxton and R. Cipolla, editors, *European Conf. Computer Vision*, pages 3–16, Cambridge, U.K., April 1996.
2. O. Faugeras. Stratification of 3-d vision: Projective, affine, and metric representations. *J. Optical Society of America*, A 12(3):465–84, March 1995.
3. O. Faugeras, Q.-T. Luong, and S. J. Maybank. Camera self calibration: Theory and experiments. In *European Conf. Computer Vision*, Santa Margherita Ligure, Italy, May 1992. Springer-Verlag.
4. P. Gill, W. Murray, and M. Wright. *Practical Optimization*. Academic Press, 1981.
5. R. Hartley. Euclidean reconstruction from multiple views. In 2nd *Europe-U.S. Workshop on Invariance*, pages 237–56, Ponta Delgada, Azores, October 1993.
6. R. Hartley. Self-calibration from multiple views with a rotating camera. In *European Conf. Computer Vision*, pages 471–8. Springer-Verlag, 1994.
7. R. Hartley. In defence of the 8-point algorithm. In E. Grimson, editor, *IEEE Int. Conf. Computer Vision*, pages 1064–70, Cambridge, MA, June 1995.

8. R. Hartley. Minimizing algebraic error. In *IEEE Int. Conf. Computer Vision*, Bombay, January 1998.

9. A. Heyden and K. Åström. Euclidean reconstruction from constant intrinsic parameters. In *Int. Conf. Pattern Recognition*, pages 339–43, Vienna, 1996.

10. A. Heyden and K. Åström. Euclidean reconstruction from image sequences with varying and unknown focal length and principal point. In *IEEE Conf. Computer Vision & Pattern Recognition*, Puerto Rico, 1997.

11. R. Horaud and G. Csurka. Self-calibration and euclidean reconstruction using motions of a stereo rig. In *IEEE Int. Conf. Computer Vision*, January 1998.

12. K. Kanatani. *Statistical Optimization for Geometric Computation: Theory and Practice*. Elsevier Science, Amsterdam, 1996.

13. Q.-T. Luong and T. Viéville. Canonic representations for the geometries of multiple projective views. Technical Report UCB/CSD-93-772, Dept. EECS, Berkeley, California, 1993.

14. S. J. Maybank and O. Faugeras. A theory of self calibration of a moving camera. *Int. J. Computer Vision*, 8(2):123–151, 1992.

15. M. Pollefeys and L Van Gool. A stratified approach to metric self-calibration. In *IEEE Conf. Computer Vision & Pattern Recognition*, pages 407–12, San Juan, Puerto Rico, June 1997.

16. M. Pollefeys, L Van Gool, and M. Proesmans. Euclidean 3d reconstruction from image sequences with variable focal length. In B. Buxton and R. Cipolla, editors, *European Conf. Computer Vision*, pages 31–42, Cambridge, U.K., April 1996.

17. J. G. Semple and G. T. Kneebone. *Algebraic Projective Geometry*. Oxford University Press, 1952.

18. P. Sturm. Critical motion sequences for monocular self-calibration and uncalibrated Euclidean reconstruction. In *IEEE Conf. Computer Vision & Pattern Recognition*, Puerto Rico, 1997.

19. P. Sturm. *Vision 3D non calibrée : contributions à la reconstruction projective et étude des mouvements critiques pour l'auto-calibrage*. Ph.D. Thesis, Institut National Polytechnique de Grenoble, December 1997.

20. B. Triggs. A new approach to geometric fitting. Available from http://www.inrialpes.fr/movi/people/Triggs.

21. B. Triggs. SVD based relative orientation from planar scenes. Available from http://www.inrialpes.fr/movi/people/Triggs.

22. B. Triggs. Autocalibration and the absolute quadric. In *IEEE Conf. Computer Vision & Pattern Recognition*, Puerto Rico, 1997.

23. T. Viéville and O. Faugeras. Motion analysis with a camera with unknown and possibly varying intrinsic parameters. In E. Grimson, editor, *IEEE Int. Conf. Computer Vision*, pages 750–6, Cambridge, MA, June 1995.

24. W. Wunderlich. Rechnerische rekonstruktion eines ebenen objekts aus zwei photographien. In *Mittsilungen Geodät. Inst. TU Gras,* Folge 40 (festschrift K. Rimmer sum 70. Geburstag), pages 365–77, 1982.

25. C. Zeller and O. Faugeras. Camera self-calibration from video sequences: the Kruppa equations revisited. Technical Report 2793, INRIA, INRIA Sophia-Antipolis, France, 1996.

26. Z. Zhang, Q.-T. Luong, and O. Faugeras. Motion of an uncalibrated stereo rig: Self-calibration and metric reconstruction. Technical Report 2079, INRIA, Sophia-Antipolis, France, 1993.

Multiple View Geometry
Stereo Vision and Calibration
Geometry and Invariance
Structure from Motion

A New Characterization of the Trifocal Tensor*

Théodore Papadopoulo and Olivier Faugeras

INRIA Sophia Antipolis
2004 Route des Lucioles, BP 93
06902 SOPHIA-ANTIPOLIS Cedex
FRANCE
Name.Surname@sophia.inria.fr

Abstract. This paper deals with the problem of characterizing and parametrizing the manifold of trifocal tensors that describe the geometry of three views like the fundamental matrix characterizes the geometry of two. The paper contains two new results. First a new, simpler, set of algebraic constraints that characterizes the set of trifocal tensors is presented. Second, we give a new parametrization of the trifocal tensor based upon those constraints which is also simpler than previously known parametrizations. Some preliminary experimental results of the use of these constraints and parametrization to estimate the trifocal tensor from image correspondences are presented.

1 Introduction

This article deals with the problem of finding a minimal representation of the trifocal tensor and using the representation to estimate the tensor from feature correspondences in three views.

Given three views, it has been shown originally by Shashua [Sha94] that the coordinates of three corresponding points satisfied a set of algebraic relations of degree 3 called the trilinear relations. It was later on pointed out by Hartley [Har94] that those trilinear relations were in fact arising from a tensor that governed the correspondences of lines between three views which he called the trifocal tensor. Hartley also correctly pointed out that this tensor had been used, if not formally identified as such, by researchers working on the problem of the estimation of motion and structure from line correspondences [SA90]. Given three views, there are of course three such tensors, depending upon which view is selected as the one one wants to predict to.

The trinocular tensors play the same role in the analysis of scenes from three views as the fundamental matrix play in the two-view case, therefore the question of their estimation from feature correspondences arise naturally. The question of estimating the fundamental matrix between two views has received considerable attention in the last few years and robust algorithms have been proposed by a number of researchers [DZLF94,ZDFL95,TZ97b,Har95]. The main difficulty of the estimation arises from the fact that the fundamental matrix must satisfy one nonlinear constraint, i.e. that its determinant is equal to 0, which prevents the straightforward application of quadratic least-squares methods.

* This work was partially supported by the EEC under the reactive LTR project 21914-CUMULI.

The related question for the trinocular tensor has received much less attention except for the obvious application of quadratic least-squares methods [Har94,Sha95]. What makes the use of these methods even more questionable in the case of the trinocular tensor is the fact that it is much more constrained than the fundamental matrix: even though it superficially seems to depend upon 26 parameters (27 up to scale), these 26 parameters are not independent since the number of degrees of freedom of three views has been shown to be equal to 18 in the projective framework (33 parameters for the 3 perspective projection matrices minus 15 for an unknown projective transformation) [LV94]. Therefore the trifocal tensor can depend upon at most 18 independent parameters and therefore its 27 components must satisfy a number of algebraic constraints, some of them have been elucidated [SW95,Hey95,AS96].

The contributions of this paper are three-folds. First we give a new set of algebraic constraints that characterize the set of trifocal constraints. Those constraints are simpler than the ones we derived in [FP97] and used in [FP98]. Second we derive a new minimal parametrization of the trifocal tensor that does not suffer from the problems of previous ones. Third we present some preliminary experimental results where we use this new parametrization to estimate the trifocal tensor from image correspondences.

We assume that the reader is familiar with elementary Grassmann-Cayley algebra since the necessary ingredients have already been presented to the Computer Vision community in a number of publications such as, for example, [Car94,FM95].

2 A New Formulation of the Trifocal Tensor Constraints

2.1 The Trifocal Tensors

Let us consider three views, with projection matrices $\mathcal{P}_n, n = 1, 2, 3$, a 3D line L with images l_n. We denote by $\boldsymbol{\Gamma}_n$, $\boldsymbol{\Lambda}_n$, $\boldsymbol{\Theta}_n$ the row vectors of $\mathcal{P}_n$. They define three planes called the *principal planes* of camera n. The three lines of intersection $\boldsymbol{\Lambda}_n \, \Delta \, \boldsymbol{\Theta}_n$, $\boldsymbol{\Theta}_n \, \Delta \, \boldsymbol{\Gamma}_n$, $\boldsymbol{\Gamma}_n \, \Delta \, \boldsymbol{\Lambda}_n$ of those three planes are three optical rays, i.e. lines going through the optical center C_n, called the *principal rays*.

Given two images l_j and l_k of L, L can be defined as the intersection (the meet) of the two planes $\mathcal{P}_j^T l_j$ and $\mathcal{P}_k^T l_k$: $\mathbf{L} \simeq \mathcal{P}_j^T l_j \, \Delta \, \mathcal{P}_k^T l_k$, where the vector $\mathbf{L}$ is the 6×1 vector of Plücker coordinates of the line L.

Let us write the right-hand side of this equation explicitly in terms of the row vectors of the matrices $\mathcal{P}_j$ and $\mathcal{P}_k$ and the coordinates of l_j and l_k:

$$\mathbf{L} \simeq (l_j^1 \boldsymbol{\Gamma}_j + l_j^2 \boldsymbol{\Lambda}_j + l_j^3 \boldsymbol{\Theta}_j) \, \Delta \, (l_k^1 \boldsymbol{\Gamma}_k + l_k^2 \boldsymbol{\Lambda}_k + l_k^3 \boldsymbol{\Theta}_k)$$

By expanding the meet operator and applying the matrix $\tilde{\mathcal{P}}_i$ defined in [FP97,FP98] to the Plücker coordinates of L, we obtain the coordinates of the image l_i of L:

$$l_i \simeq \tilde{\mathcal{P}}_i (\mathcal{P}_j^T l_j \, \Delta \, \mathcal{P}_k^T l_k) \tag{1}$$

which is valid for $i \neq j \neq k$. Note that if we exchange view j and view k, we just change the sign of l_i and therefore we do not change l_i. A geometric interpretation of this is shown in Fig. 1. For convenience, we rewrite (1) in a more compact form:

$$l_i \simeq \mathcal{T}_i(l_j, l_k) .$$

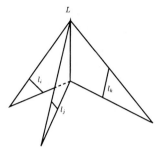

Fig. 1. The line l_i is the image by camera i of the 3D line L intersection of the planes defined by the optical centers of the cameras j and k and the lines l_j and l_k, respectively.

This expression can be also put in a slightly less compact form with the advantage of making the dependency on the projection planes of the matrices $\mathcal{P}_n, n = 1, 2, 3$ explicit: $\mathbf{l}_i \simeq \left[\mathbf{l}_j^T \mathbf{G}_i^1 \mathbf{l}_k \; \mathbf{l}_j^T \mathbf{G}_i^2 \mathbf{l}_k \; \mathbf{l}_j^T \mathbf{G}_i^3 \mathbf{l}_k \right]^T$. This is, in the projective framework, the exact analog of the equation used in the work of Spetsakis and Aloimonos [SA90] to study the structure from motion problem from line correspondences.

The three 3×3 matrices $\mathbf{G}_i^n, n = 1, 2, 3$ will play an important role in the sequel. We do not give their explicit forms which will not be needed in this paper [FP97,FP98].

Note that (1) allows us to predict the coordinates of a line l_i in image i given two images l_j and l_k of an unknown 3D line in images j and k, except in two cases where $\mathcal{T}_i(\mathbf{l}_j, \mathbf{l}_k) = \mathbf{0}$ detailed in [FP98]. Except in those cases, we have defined an application $\mathcal{T}_i$ from $\mathbb{P}^{*2} \times \mathbb{P}^{*2}$, the Cartesian product of two duals of the projective plane, into $\mathbb{P}^{*2}$. A pictorial view is shown in Fig. 2: the tensor is represented as a 3×3 cube, the three horizontal planes representing the matrices $\mathbf{G}_i^n, n = 1, 2, 3$. It can be thought of as a black box which takes as its input two lines, l_j and l_k and outputs a third one, l_i. Hartley

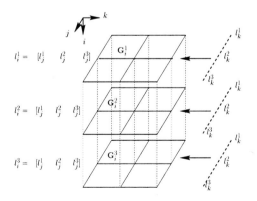

Fig. 2. A three-dimensional representation of the trifocal tensor.

has shown [Har94,Har97] that the trifocal tensors can be very simply parameterized by the perspective projection matrices $\mathcal{P}_n$, $n = 1, 2, 3$ of the three cameras. This result is summarized in the following proposition:

Proposition 1 (Hartley). *Let $\mathcal{P}_n$, $n = 1, 2, 3$ be the three perspective projection matrices of three cameras in general viewing position. After a change of coordinates, those matrices can be written, $\mathcal{P}_1 = [\mathbf{I}_3\,\mathbf{0}]$, $\mathcal{P}_2 = [\mathbf{X}\,\mathbf{e}_{2,1}]$ and $\mathcal{P}_3 = [\mathbf{Y}\,\mathbf{e}_{3,1}]$ and the matrices $\mathbf{G}_1^n$ can be expressed as:*

$$\mathbf{G}_1^n = \mathbf{e}_{2,1}\mathbf{Y}^{(n)T} - \mathbf{X}^{(n)}\mathbf{e}_{3,1}^T \quad n = 1, 2, 3 \tag{2}$$

where the vectors $\mathbf{X}^{(n)}$ and $\mathbf{Y}^{(n)}$ are the column of the matrices $\mathbf{X}$ and $\mathbf{Y}$, respectively.

We use this proposition as a definition:

Definition 1. *Any tensor of the form (2) is a trifocal tensor.*

2.2 Algebraic and Geometric Properties of the Trifocal Tensors

The matrices $\mathbf{G}_i^n$, $n = 1, 2, 3$ have interesting properties which are closely related to the epipolar geometry of the views j and k. We start with the following proposition, which was proved for example in [Har97]. The proof hopefully gives some more geometric insight of what is going on:

Proposition 2 (Hartley). *The matrices $\mathbf{G}_i^n$ are of rank 2 and their nullspaces are the three epipolar lines, noted l_k^n in view k of the three projection rays of camera i. These three lines intersect at the epipole $e_{k,i}$. The corresponding lines in view i are represented by $\mathbf{e}_n \times \mathbf{e}_{i,k}$ and can be obtained as $\mathcal{T}_i(l_j, l_k^n), n = 1, 2, 3$ for any l_j not equal to l_j^n (see proposition 3).*

Proof. The nullspace of $\mathbf{G}_i^n$ is the set of lines l_k^n such that $\mathcal{T}_i(l_j, l_k^n)$ has a zero in the n-th coordinate for all lines l_j. The corresponding lines l_i such that $l_i = \mathcal{T}_i(l_j, l_k^n)$ all go through the point represented by $\mathbf{e}_n, n = 1, 2, 3$ in the i-th retinal plane. This is true if and only if l_k^n is the image in the k-th retinal plane of the projection ray $\Lambda_i \,\Delta\,\Theta_i\,(n = 1)$, $\Theta_i\,\Delta\,\Gamma_i\,(n = 2)$ and $\Gamma_i\,\Delta\,\Lambda_i\,(n = 3)$: l_k^n is an epipolar line with respect to view i. Moreover, it is represented by $\mathbf{e}_n \times \mathbf{e}_{i,k}$. □

A similar reasoning applies to the matrices $\mathbf{G}_i^{nT}$:

Proposition 3 (Hartley). *The nullspaces of the matrices $\mathbf{G}_i^{nT}$ are the three epipolar lines, noted $l_j^n, n = 1, 2, 3$, in the j-th retinal plane of the three projection rays of camera i. These three lines intersect at the epipole $e_{j,i}$, see Fig. 3. The corresponding lines in view i are represented by $\mathbf{e}_n \times \mathbf{e}_{i,j}$ and can be obtained as $\mathcal{T}_i(l_j^n, l_k), n = 1, 2, 3$ for any l_k not equal to l_k^n.*

This provides a geometric interpretation of the matrices $\mathbf{G}_i^n$: they represent mappings from the set of lines in view k to the set of points in view j located on the epipolar line l_j^n defined in proposition 3. This mapping is geometrically defined by taking the intersection of the plane defined by the optical center of the kth camera and any line

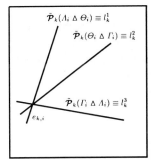 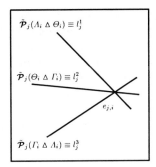

Fig. 3. The lines l_j^n (resp. l_k^n), $n = 1, 2, 3$ in the nullspaces of the matrices $\mathbf{G}_i^{nT}$ (resp. $\mathbf{G}_i^n$) are the images of the three projection rays of camera i. Hence, they intersect at the epipole $e_{j,i}$ (resp. $e_{k,i}$). The corresponding epipolar lines in camera i are obtained as $T_i(l_j^n, l_k)$ (resp. $T_i(l_j, l_k^n)$) for $l_k \neq l_k^n$ (resp. $l_j \neq l_j^n$).

of its retinal plane with the nth projection ray of the ith camera and forming the image of this point in the jth camera. This point does not exist when the plane contains the projection ray. The corresponding line in the kth retinal plane is the epipolar line l_k^n defined in proposition 2. Moreover, the three columns of $\mathbf{G}_i^n$ represent three points which all belong to the epipolar line l_j^n.

We can go a little further in the interpretation of the matrices $\mathbf{G}_i^n$. They also define each a collineation from the line l_k^n to the line l_j^n: given a point a_k of l_k^n, the pencil of lines going through a_k defines a pencil of planes whose axis is the 3D line (C_k, A_k) (A_k is the point of the corresponding optical ray of the ith camera). The corresponding point b_k on l_j^n is the image of A_k. The correspondence (a_k, b_k) is the analog for $\mathbf{G}_i^n$ of the correspondence between two epipolar lines for the fundamental matrix. Indeed, there is a very strong analogy between the matrices $\mathbf{G}_i^n$ and fundamental matrices: both are of rank two and both, as we just showed, define collineations between $\mathbb{P}^1$.

Since each matrix $\mathbf{G}_i^n$, $n = 1, 2, 3$ defines a collineation from l_k^n to l_j^n, we have three such collineations that we denote by h^n. Those three collineations are not independent and we have the following proposition:

Proposition 4. *The three collineations h^n satisfy the relations:*

$$h^n(e_{k,i}) = e_{j,i} \quad n = 1, 2, 3 \tag{3}$$

Proof. We know that the three lines l_k^n (respectively l_j^n) go through the epipole ek,i (respectively $e_{j,i}$) and from the definition of h^n, when the point a_k coincides with the epipole $e_{k,i}$, the point b_k coincides with the epipole $e_{j,i}$, hence (3). □

Similarly, the matrices $\mathbf{G}_i^{nT}$ represent mappings from the set of lines in view j to the set of points in view k located on the epipolar line l_k^n. From the previous discussion we deduce that:

Proposition 5. *The rank of the matrices $\left[1_k^1 \; 1_k^2 \; 1_k^3 \right]$ and $\left[1_j^1 \; 1_j^2 \; 1_j^3 \right]$ is 2 in general.*

Algebraically, this implies that the three determinants $det(\mathbf{G}_i^n)$, $n = 1, 2, 3$ are equal to 0. Another constraint implied by proposition 5 is that the 3×3 determinants formed with the three vectors in the nullspaces of the $\mathbf{G}_i^n$, $n = 1, 2, 3$ (resp. of the $\mathbf{G}_i^{nT}$, $n = 1, 2, 3$) are equal to 0. It turns out that the applications $\mathcal{T}_i$, $i = 1, 2, 3$ satisfy other algebraic constraints which are relevant for this paper.

To simplify a bit the notations, we assume in the sequel that $i = 1, j = 2, k = 3$ and ignore the ith index everywhere, e.g. denote $\mathcal{T}_1$ by $\mathcal{T}$.

We have already seen several such constraints when we studied the matrixes $\mathbf{G}^n$. Let us summarize those constraints in the following proposition:

Proposition 6. *Under the general viewpoint assumption, the trifocal tensor* $\mathcal{T}$ *satisfies the three constraints, called the* rank *constraints:*

$$rank(\mathbf{G}^n) = 2 \Rightarrow det(\mathbf{G}^n) = 0 \quad n = 1, 2, 3$$

The trifocal tensor $\mathcal{T}$ *satisfies the two constraints, called the* epipolar *constraints:*

$$rank([\mathbf{l}_2^1 \, \mathbf{l}_2^2 \, \mathbf{l}_2^3]) = rank([\mathbf{l}_3^1 \, \mathbf{l}_3^2 \, \mathbf{l}_3^3]) = 2 \Rightarrow \mid \mathbf{l}_2^1 \, \mathbf{l}_2^2 \, \mathbf{l}_2^3 \mid = \mid \mathbf{l}_3^1 \, \mathbf{l}_3^2 \, \mathbf{l}_3^3 \mid 0$$

Those five constraints on the form of the matrices $\mathbf{G}^n$ are clearly algebraically independent since the rank constraints say nothing about the way the kernels are related.

There is a further set of constraints that are satisfied by any trifocal tensor and are of great interest for this paper. They are described in the next proposition.

Proposition 7. *The trifocal tensor* $\mathcal{T}$ *satisfies the ten algebraic constraints, called the* extended rank constraints*:*

$$rank(\sum_{n=1}^{3} \lambda_n \mathbf{G}^n) \leq 2 \; \forall \lambda_n \; n = 1, 2, 3$$

Proof. Notice that for fixed values (not all zero) of the λ_n's, and for a given line l_3 in view 3, the point which is the image in view 2 of line l_3 by $\sum_{n=1}^{3} \lambda_n \mathbf{G}^n$ is the image of the point defined by: $\lambda_1 \mathcal{P}_2^T \mathbf{l} \triangle (\mathbf{\Lambda} \triangle \mathbf{\Theta}) + \lambda_2 \mathcal{P}_2^T \mathbf{l} \triangle (\mathbf{\Theta} \triangle \mathbf{\Gamma}) + \lambda_3 \mathcal{P}_2^T \mathbf{l} \triangle (\mathbf{\Gamma} \triangle \mathbf{\Lambda})$
This expression can be rewritten as:

$$\mathcal{P}_2^T \mathbf{l} \triangle (\lambda_1 \mathbf{\Lambda} \triangle \mathbf{\Theta} + \lambda_2 \mathbf{\Theta} \triangle \mathbf{\Gamma} + \lambda_3 \mathbf{\Gamma} \triangle \mathbf{\Lambda}) \tag{4}$$

The line $\lambda_1 \mathbf{\Lambda} \triangle \mathbf{\Theta} + \lambda_2 \mathbf{\Theta} \triangle \mathbf{\Gamma} + \lambda_3 \mathbf{\Gamma} \triangle \mathbf{\Lambda}$ is an optical ray of the first camera, and when l varies in view 3, the point defined by (4) is well defined except when l is the image of that line in view 3. In that case the meet in (4) is zero and the image of that line is in the nullspace of $\sum_{n=1}^{3} \lambda_n \mathbf{G}^n$. $\square$

Proposition 7 is equivalent to the vanishing of the 10 coefficients of the homogeneous polynomial of degree 3 in the three variables λ_n, $n = 1, 2, 3$ equal to $det(\sum_{n=1}^{3} \lambda_n \mathbf{G}^n)$. The coefficients of the terms λ_n^3, $n = 1, 2, 3$ are the determinants $det(\mathbf{G}^n)$, $n = 1, 2, 3$. Therefore the extended rank constraints contain the rank constraints.

To be complete, we give the expressions of the seven extended rank constraints which are different from the three rank constraints:

Proposition 8. *The seven extended rank constraints are given by:*

$$\lambda_1^2\lambda_2 \quad |\, \mathbf{G}_1^1\,\mathbf{G}_2^1\,\mathbf{G}_3^2\,| + |\,\mathbf{G}_1^1\,\mathbf{G}_2^2\,\mathbf{G}_3^1\,| + |\,\mathbf{G}_1^2\,\mathbf{G}_2^1\,\mathbf{G}_3^1\,| = 0 \tag{5}$$

$$\lambda_1^2\lambda_3 \quad |\, \mathbf{G}_1^1\,\mathbf{G}_2^1\,\mathbf{G}_3^3\,| + |\,\mathbf{G}_1^1\,\mathbf{G}_2^3\,\mathbf{G}_3^1\,| + |\,\mathbf{G}_1^3\,\mathbf{G}_2^1\,\mathbf{G}_3^1\,| = 0 \tag{6}$$

$$\lambda_2^2\lambda_1 \quad |\, \mathbf{G}_1^2\,\mathbf{G}_2^2\,\mathbf{G}_3^1\,| + |\,\mathbf{G}_1^2\,\mathbf{G}_2^1\,\mathbf{G}_3^2\,| + |\,\mathbf{G}_1^1\,\mathbf{G}_2^2\,\mathbf{G}_3^2\,| = 0 \tag{7}$$

$$\lambda_2^2\lambda_3 \quad |\, \mathbf{G}_1^2\,\mathbf{G}_2^2\,\mathbf{G}_3^3\,| + |\,\mathbf{G}_1^2\,\mathbf{G}_2^3\,\mathbf{G}_3^2\,| + |\,\mathbf{G}_1^3\,\mathbf{G}_2^2\,\mathbf{G}_3^2\,| = 0 \tag{8}$$

$$\lambda_3^2\lambda_1 \quad |\, \mathbf{G}_1^3\,\mathbf{G}_2^3\,\mathbf{G}_3^1\,| + |\,\mathbf{G}_1^3\,\mathbf{G}_2^1\,\mathbf{G}_3^3\,| + |\,\mathbf{G}_1^1\,\mathbf{G}_2^3\,\mathbf{G}_3^3\,| = 0 \tag{9}$$

$$\lambda_3^2\lambda_2 \quad |\, \mathbf{G}_1^3\,\mathbf{G}_2^3\,\mathbf{G}_3^2\,| + |\,\mathbf{G}_1^3\,\mathbf{G}_2^2\,\mathbf{G}_3^3\,| + |\,\mathbf{G}_1^2\,\mathbf{G}_2^3\,\mathbf{G}_3^3\,| = 0 \tag{10}$$

$$\lambda_1\lambda_2\lambda_3 \quad |\, \mathbf{G}_1^1\,\mathbf{G}_2^2\,\mathbf{G}_3^3\,| + |\,\mathbf{G}_1^1\,\mathbf{G}_2^3\,\mathbf{G}_3^2\,| + |\,\mathbf{G}_1^2\,\mathbf{G}_2^1\,\mathbf{G}_3^3\,| +$$
$$|\, \mathbf{G}_1^2\,\mathbf{G}_2^3\,\mathbf{G}_3^1\,| + |\,\mathbf{G}_1^3\,\mathbf{G}_2^1\,\mathbf{G}_3^2\,| + |\,\mathbf{G}_1^3\,\mathbf{G}_2^2\,\mathbf{G}_3^1\,| = 0 \tag{11}$$

2.3 New Constraints that Characterize the Tensor

We now show the new result that the ten extended constraints and the epipolar constraints characterize the trifocal tensors:

Theorem 1. *Let $\mathcal{T}$ be a bilinear mapping from $\mathbb{P}^{*2} \times \mathbb{P}^{*2}$ to $\mathbb{P}^{*2}$ which satisfies the twelve extended rank and epipolar constraints. Then this mapping is a trifocal tensor, i.e. it satisfies definition 1. Those twelve algebraic equations are another set of implicit equations of the manifold of trifocal tensors.*

The proof of this theorem is the subject of the rest of this section. We start with a proposition that will be used to prove that the three rank constraints and the two epipolar constraints are not sufficient to characterize the set of trifocal tensors. Its proof that can be found in [FP97].

Proposition 9. *If a tensor $\mathcal{T}$ satisfies the three rank constraints and the two epipolar constraints, then its matrices $\mathbf{G}^n, n = 1, 2, 3$ can be written:*

$$\mathbf{G}^n = a_n\mathbf{X}^{(n)}\mathbf{Y}^{(n)T} + \mathbf{X}^{(n)}\mathbf{e}_{3,1}^T + \mathbf{e}_{2,1}\mathbf{Y}^{(n)T}, \tag{12}$$

where $e_{2,1}$ (resp. $e_{3,1}$) is a fixed point of image 2 (resp. of image 3), the three vectors $\mathbf{X}^{(n)}$ represent three points of image 2, and the three vectors $\mathbf{Y}^{(n)}$ represent three points of image 3.

What about the ten extended rank constraints: Are they sufficient to characterize the trilinear tensor? the following proposition answers this question negatively.

Proposition 10. *The ten extended rank constraints do not imply the epipolar constraints.*

Proof. The proof consists in exhibiting a counterexample. The tensor $\mathcal{T}$ defined by:

$$\mathbf{G}^1 = \begin{bmatrix} 0 & 0 & 0 \\ -1 & -1 & 0 \\ 1 & 0 & 1 \end{bmatrix} \qquad \mathbf{G}^2 = \begin{bmatrix} -1 & -1 & 0 \\ 0 & 0 & 0 \\ 0 & 1 & 0 \end{bmatrix} \qquad \mathbf{G}^3 = \begin{bmatrix} -1 & 0 & -1 \\ 0 & 1 & 0 \\ 0 & 0 & 0 \end{bmatrix}$$

satisfies the ten extended rank constraints but the corresponding three left nullspaces do not satisfy the left epipolar constraint. □

We are now ready to prove Theorem 1:

Proof. The proof consists in showing that any bilinear application $\mathcal{T}$ that satisfies the five rank and epipolar constraints, i.e. whose matrices $\mathbf{G}^n$ can be written as in (12) and the remaining seven extended rank constraints (5-11) can be written as in (2), i.e. is such that $a_n = 0$, $n = 1, 2, 3$.

If we use the parametrization (12) and evaluate the constraints (5-10), we find:

$$-a_2 \mid \mathbf{e}_{2,1} \, \mathbf{X}^{(1)} \, \mathbf{X}^{(2)} \mid \, \| \, \mathbf{e}_{3,1} \, \mathbf{Y}^{(1)} \, \mathbf{Y}^{(2)} \mid \tag{13}$$

$$-a_3 \mid \mathbf{e}_{2,1} \, \mathbf{X}^{(1)} \, \mathbf{X}^{(3)} \mid \, \| \, \mathbf{e}_{3,1} \, \mathbf{Y}^{(1)} \, \mathbf{Y}^{(3)} \mid \tag{14}$$

$$-a_1 \mid \mathbf{e}_{2,1} \, \mathbf{X}^{(1)} \, \mathbf{X}^{(2)} \mid \, \| \, \mathbf{e}_{3,1} \, \mathbf{Y}^{(1)} \, \mathbf{Y}^{(2)} \mid \tag{15}$$

$$-a_3 \mid \mathbf{e}_{2,1} \, \mathbf{X}^{(2)} \, \mathbf{X}^{(3)} \mid \, \| \, \mathbf{e}_{3,1} \, \mathbf{Y}^{(2)} \, \mathbf{Y}^{(3)} \mid \tag{16}$$

$$-a_1 \mid \mathbf{e}_{2,1} \, \mathbf{X}^{(1)} \, \mathbf{X}^{(3)} \mid \, \| \, \mathbf{e}_{3,1} \, \mathbf{Y}^{(1)} \, \mathbf{Y}^{(3)} \mid \tag{17}$$

$$-a_2 \mid \mathbf{e}_{2,1} \, \mathbf{X}^{(2)} \, \mathbf{X}^{(3)} \mid \, \| \, \mathbf{e}_{3,1} \, \mathbf{Y}^{(2)} \, \mathbf{Y}^{(3)} \mid \tag{18}$$

In those formulas, our attention is drawn to determinants of the form $\mid \mathbf{e}_{2,1} \, \mathbf{X}^{(i)} \, \mathbf{X}^{(j)} \mid$, $i \neq j$ (type 2) and $\mid \mathbf{e}_{3,1} \, \mathbf{Y}^{(i)} \, \mathbf{Y}^{(j)} \mid$, $i \neq j$ (type 3). The nullity of a determinant of type 2 (resp. type 3) implies that the epipole $e_{2,1}$ (resp. $e_{3,1}$) is on the line defined by the two points $X^{(i)}$, $X^{(j)}$ (resp. $Y^{(i)}$, $Y^{(j)}$), if the corresponding points are distinct. If all determinants are non zero, the constraints (13-18) imply that all a_n's are zero. Things are slightly more complicated if some of the determinants are equal to 0.

We prove that if the matrices $\mathbf{G}^n$ are of rank 2, no more than one of the three determinants of each of the two types can equal 0. We consider several cases. • The first case is when all points of one type are different. Suppose that the three points represented by the three vectors $\mathbf{X}^{(n)}$ are not aligned. Having two of the determinants of type 2 equal to 0 implies that the point $e_{2,1}$ is identical to one of the points $X^{(n)}$ since it is at the intersection of two of the lines they define. But, according to (12), this implies that the corresponding matrix $\mathbf{G}^n$ is of rank 1, contradicting the hypothesis that this rank is 2. Similarly, if the three points $X^{(n)}$ are aligned, if one determinant is equal to 0, the epipole $e_{2,1}$ belongs to the line $(X^{(1)}, X^{(2)}, X^{(3)})$ which means that the three epipolar lines l_2^1, l_2^2, l_2^3 are identical contradicting the hypothesis that they form a matrix of rank 2. Therefore, in this case, all three determinants are non null. • The second case is when two of the points are equal, e.g. $\mathbf{X}^{(1)} \simeq \mathbf{X}^{(2)}$. The third point must then be different, otherwise we would only have one epipolar line contradicting the rank 2 assumption on those epipolar lines, and, if it is different, the epipole $e_{2,1}$ must not be on the line defined by the two points for the same reason. Therefore in this case also at most one of the determinants is equal to 0.

Having at most one determinant of type 2 and one of type 3 equal to 0 implies that at least two of the a_n are 0. This is seen by inspecting the constraints (13-18). If we now express the seventh constraint:

$$a_1 a_2 a_3 \mid \mathbf{Y}^{(1)} \, \mathbf{Y}^{(2)} \, \mathbf{Y}^{(3)} \parallel \mathbf{X}^{(1)} \, \mathbf{X}^{(2)} \, \mathbf{X}^{(3)} \mid$$

$$- (\mid \mathbf{e}_{2,1} \, \mathbf{X}^{(1)} \, \mathbf{X}^{(2)} \parallel \mathbf{e}_{3,1} \, \mathbf{Y}^{(1)} \, \mathbf{Y}^{(3)} \mid + \mid \mathbf{e}_{3,1} \, \mathbf{Y}^{(1)} \, \mathbf{Y}^{(2)} \parallel \mathbf{e}_{2,1} \, \mathbf{X}^{(1)} \, \mathbf{X}^{(3)} \mid) a_1$$

$$+ (\mid \mathbf{e}_{3,1} \, \mathbf{Y}^{(1)} \, \mathbf{Y}^{(2)} \parallel \mathbf{e}_{2,1} \, \mathbf{X}^{(2)} \, \mathbf{X}^{(3)} \mid + \mid \mathbf{e}_{3,1} \, \mathbf{Y}^{(2)} \, \mathbf{Y}^{(3)} \parallel \mathbf{e}_{2,1} \, \mathbf{X}^{(1)} \, \mathbf{X}^{(2)} \mid) a_2$$

$$- (\mid \mathbf{e}_{2,1} \, \mathbf{X}^{(2)} \, \mathbf{X}^{(3)} \parallel \mathbf{e}_{3,1} \, \mathbf{Y}^{(1)} \, \mathbf{Y}^{(3)} \mid + \mid \mathbf{e}_{3,1} \, \mathbf{Y}^{(2)} \, \mathbf{Y}^{(3)} \parallel \mathbf{e}_{2,1} \, \mathbf{X}^{(1)}, \mathbf{X}^{(3)} \mid) a_3$$

$$+ (\mid \mathbf{e}_{2,1} \, \mathbf{X}^{(1)} \, \mathbf{X}^{(2)} \parallel \mathbf{Y}^{(1)} \, \mathbf{Y}^{(2)} \, \mathbf{Y}^{(3)} \mid + \mid \mathbf{e}_{3,1} \, \mathbf{Y}^{(1)} \, \mathbf{Y}^{(2)} \parallel \mathbf{X}^{(1)} \, \mathbf{X}^{(2)} \, \mathbf{X}^{(3)} \mid) a_1 a_2$$

$$+ (\mid \mathbf{e}_{3,1} \, \mathbf{Y}^{(2)} \, \mathbf{Y}^{(3)} \parallel \mathbf{X}^{(1)} \, \mathbf{X}^{(2)} \, \mathbf{X}^{(3)} \mid + \mid \mathbf{e}_{2,1} \, \mathbf{X}^{(2)} \, \mathbf{X}^{(3)} \parallel \mathbf{Y}^{(1)} \, \mathbf{Y}^{(2)} \, \mathbf{Y}^{(3)} \mid) a_2 a_3$$

$$- (\mid \mathbf{e}_{2,1} \, \mathbf{X}^{(1)} \, \mathbf{X}^{(3)} \parallel \mathbf{Y}^{(1)} \, \mathbf{Y}^{(2)} \, \mathbf{Y}^{(3)} \mid + \mid \mathbf{X}^{(1)} \, \mathbf{X}^{(2)} \, \mathbf{X}^{(3)} \parallel \mathbf{e}_{3,1} \, \mathbf{Y}^{(1)} \, \mathbf{Y}^{(3)} \mid) a_1 a_3,$$

we find that it is equal to the third a_n multiplied by two of the nonzero determinants, implying that the third a_n is null and completing the proof.

Let us give a few examples of the various cases. Assume first that $\mid \mathbf{e}_{2,1} \, \mathbf{X}^{(1)} \, \mathbf{X}^{(2)} \mid = \mid \mathbf{e}_{3,1} \, \mathbf{Y}^{(1)} \, \mathbf{Y}^{(2)} \mid = 0$. Then (17), (18) and (16) imply $a_1 = a_2 = a_3 = 0$. The second situation occurs if we assume for example $\mid \mathbf{e}_{2,1} \, \mathbf{X}^{(1)} \, \mathbf{X}^{(2)} \mid = \mid \mathbf{e}_{3,1} \, \mathbf{Y}^{(1)} \, \mathbf{Y}^{(3)} \mid = 0$. Then (18) and (16) imply $a_2 = a_3 = 0$. Equation (11) takes then the form $- \mid \mathbf{e}_{2,1} \, \mathbf{X}^{(1)} \, \mathbf{X}^{(3)} \parallel \mathbf{e}_{3,1} \, \mathbf{Y}^{(1)} \, \mathbf{Y}^{(2)} \mid a_1$, and implies $a_1 = 0$. $\qquad \square$

Practically, Theorem 1 provides a simpler set of sufficient constraints than those used in [FP98]: The ten extended constraints are of degree 3 in the elements of $\mathcal{T}$ whereas the other constraints are of degree 6 as are the two epipolar constraints.

3 A New Parameterization

Having minimal parameterizations of the trifocal tensor is very useful:
• first, the canonical elements emphasized by such parameterizations may help to have a better geometrical understanding of the mathematical concept of the trifocal tensor (some results of this articles were obtained in this way).
• if we want to use general non-constrained optimization techniques to estimate trifocal tensors that are optimal with respect to the data. In the absence of such parameterizations, one has either to rely on constrained optimization, or to optimize only over a subset of the parameters defining the trifocal tensor [Har97]. However, finding a good minimal parameterization of the trifocal tensor is not an easy task and to our knowledge only two have been proposed to date [TZ97a,FP98].
This section presents a new minimal parameterization of the trifocal tensor, that overcomes some problems that arise with those.

3.1 A Few Notations

There is a common point to the objects introduced to deal with multiple view geometry such as fundamental matrices or trifocal tensor: they all involve at some point matrices of rank 2. Furthermore, in most cases, the left and right kernels of these matrices are attached to geometrical properties of the system of cameras. This suggests that the set

$\mathcal{M}(\mathbf{L}, \mathbf{R})$ of all the matrices that have a given left kernel $\mathbf{L} = [l_1, l_2, l_3]^T \neq \mathbf{0}$ and right kernel $\mathbf{R} = [r_1, r_2, r_3]^T \neq \mathbf{0}$ is of some importance, and it indeed received a lot of attention with the study and parameterization of the fundamental matrix. Most of this section is just a slightly different formulation of a well-known parameterization of the fundamental matrix, which uses the 2 epipoles and 4 coefficients of the original matrix that describe the homography relating the epipolar lines in the two images [LF96].

Obviously, $\mathcal{M}(\mathbf{L}, \mathbf{R})$ is a linear space of dimension 4. Thinking in terms of linear spaces, a basis can be found and the coordinates of a given matrix of $\mathcal{M}(\mathbf{L}, \mathbf{R})$ in that basis correspond to the 4 coefficients of the fundamental matrix parameterization. Unfortunately, there is no systematic way to define a basis for $\mathcal{M}(\mathbf{L}, \mathbf{R})$ that would be valid for all choices of $\mathbf{L}$ and $\mathbf{R}$: different maps cannot be avoided as long as we want a minimal basis. To simplify the presentation, we assume that the highest components in magnitude of both $\mathbf{L}$ and $\mathbf{R}$ are in first position: in this case, the four matrices of rank 1 $\mathbf{M}_1$, $\mathbf{M}_2$, $\mathbf{M}_3$ and $\mathbf{M}_4$ constitute a basis of $\mathcal{M}(\mathbf{L}, \mathbf{R})$.

$$\mathbf{M}_1 = \begin{bmatrix} r_3 l_3 & 0 & -r_1 l_3 \\ 0 & 0 & 0 \\ -r_3 l_1 & 0 & r_1 l_1 \end{bmatrix}, \mathbf{M}_2 = \begin{bmatrix} -r_2 l_3 & r_1 l_3 & 0 \\ 0 & 0 & 0 \\ r_2 l_1 & -r_1 l_1 & 0 \end{bmatrix},$$

$$\mathbf{M}_3 = \begin{bmatrix} -r_3 l_2 & 0 & r_1 l_2 \\ r_3 l_1 & 0 & -r_1 l_1 \\ 0 & 0 & 0 \end{bmatrix}, \mathbf{M}_4 = \begin{bmatrix} r_2 l_2 & -r_1 l_2 & 0 \\ -r_2 l_1 & r_1 l_1 & 0 \\ 0 & 0 & 0 \end{bmatrix} \qquad (19)$$

This basis is valid as long as $l_1 \neq 0$ and $r_1 \neq 0$. This explains our choice of having maximal magnitudes for those coefficients. The 8 other maps that correspond to different choices for the positions of the highest components are obtained similarly.

The coordinates of a matrix $\mathbf{M}$ of $\mathcal{M}(\mathbf{L}, \mathbf{R})$ in this basis are called a_1, a_2, a_3 and a_4: $\mathbf{M} = a_1 \mathbf{M}_1 + a_2 \mathbf{M}_2 + a_3 \mathbf{M}_3 + a_4 \mathbf{M}_4$. $\mathbf{M}$ is of rank 1 iff $a_2 a_3 - a_1 a_4 = 0$.

3.2 The Extended Rank Constraints Revisited

The 3 matrices $\mathbf{G}^i$, $i = 1 \dots 3$ being rank-2, we note $\mathbf{L}^i$ and $\mathbf{R}^i$ their respective left and right kernels. Each $\mathbf{G}^i$ can thus be represented by its coordinates a_1^i, a_2^i, a_3^i and a_4^i in a basis of $\mathcal{M}(\mathbf{L}^i, \mathbf{R}^i)$. We assume hereafter that the first coordinates of $\mathbf{L}^i$ and $\mathbf{R}^i$ are those of highest magnitude, so that we work in the basis described by (19).

Since $\mathbf{L}^i$, $i = 1 \dots 3$ and $\mathbf{R}^i$, $i = 1 \dots 3$ are orthogonal to $\mathbf{e}_{2,1}$ and $\mathbf{e}_{3,1}$ respectively, we can write $\mathbf{L}^i = \mathbf{e}_{2,1} \times \mathbf{X}^{(i)}$, $i = 1 \dots 3$ and $\mathbf{R}^i = \mathbf{e}_{3,1} \times \mathbf{Y}^{(i)}$, $i = 1 \dots 3$, where $\mathbf{X}^{(i)}$ and $\mathbf{Y}^{(i)}$ are the vectors of formula 2. Plugging these values into the extended rank constraints 5–11 and using computer algebra to factorize the results leads to the following result which is an algebraic translation of proposition 4:

Theorem 2. *Assuming that the first coordinates of $\mathbf{L}^i$ and $\mathbf{R}^i$ are those of highest magnitude, The four coefficients a_j^i, $j = 1 \dots 4$ representing $\mathbf{G}^i$ in $\mathcal{M}(\mathbf{L}^i, \mathbf{R}^i)$ satisfy the following linear relation:*

$$e_{2,1}^2 e_{3,1}^2 a_1^i + e_{2,1}^2 e_{3,1}^3 a_2^i + e_{2,1}^3 e_{3,1}^2 a_3^i + e_{2,1}^3 e_{3,1}^3 a_4^i = 0, \qquad (20)$$

where $\mathbf{e}_{2,1} = \begin{bmatrix} e_{2,1}^1, e_{2,1}^2, e_{2,1}^3 \end{bmatrix}^T$ *and* $\mathbf{e}_{3,1} = \begin{bmatrix} e_{3,1}^1, e_{3,1}^2, e_{3,1}^3 \end{bmatrix}^T$.

Remarks:
- Equations 20 are only factors that appear in the extended rank constraints, but it can be shown that it is the only one that must generically vanish.
- In general, the first coordinates of $\mathbf{L}^i$ and $\mathbf{R}^i$ are not those of highest magnitude, but (20) remains essentially the same with the substitution of $e_{2,1}^j$ and $e_{3,1}^k$ by $e_{2,1}^{\lambda^i(j)}$ and $e_{3,1}^{\rho^i(k)}$, where λ^i and ρ^i are the circular permutations that bring respectively the coordinates of highest magnitude of $\mathbf{L}^i$ and $\mathbf{R}^i$ into first position.
- It is not difficult to show that (20) are never degenerated provided that the proper permutations λ^i and ρ^i have been made.

3.3   A Minimal Parameterization of the Trifocal Tensor

Let us first assume that the 6 vectors $\mathbf{L}^i, i = 1 \ldots 3$ and $\mathbf{R}^i, i = 1 \ldots 3$ are given, we show that the three matrices $\mathbf{G}^i, i = 1 \ldots 3$ can be parameterized by 8 coefficients. To do so, consider the 12 coordinates $a_j^i, i = 1 \ldots 3, j = 1 \ldots 4$. Since for each i the $a_j^i, j = 1 \ldots 4$ are satisfying (20), it is possible to drop one of those four coordinates: for numerical stability, the best choice is to drop the coordinate which has the highest coefficient in magnitude in (20). Moreover, since the $\mathbf{G}^i$ are only defined up to a global scale factor, we can drop one more of the 9 remaining coordinates by normalizing it to 1. This leaves us with 8 coefficients that completely describe the $\mathbf{G}^i, i = 1 \ldots 3$, given the $\mathbf{L}^i, i = 1 \ldots 3$ and $\mathbf{R}^i, i = 1 \ldots 3$. Since 8 parameters have been used, only 10 parameters remain to parameterize the $\mathbf{L}^i, i = 1 \ldots 3$ and $\mathbf{R}^i, i = 1 \ldots 3$.

We can assume without loss of generality that $\|\mathbf{L}^i\| = 1, i = 1 \ldots 3$. These 3 vectors are orthogonal to the epipole $\mathbf{e}_{2,1}$ which can be parameterized by 2 coordinates by normalizing its biggest coordinate to 1 (there are thus 3 maps). The vectors $\mathbf{L}^i$ are conveniently represented by 3 angles in a canonical basis of the plane orthogonal to the direction defined by $\mathbf{e}_{2,1}$. All the $\mathbf{L}^i$ can thus be represented by 5 parameters. A similar parameterization is obtained for the $\mathbf{R}^i, i = 1 \ldots 3$, which gives the desired result.

As a consequence, we have obtained a minimal parameterization of the trifocal tensor, i.e by 18 parameters. As the reader may have noticed, the number of maps of this parameterization is very large ($9 \times 3^2 \times 3^6$) but it is nonetheless easy to define a general routine that chooses the best map and computes the parameterization.

3.4   Relationship with Projection Matrices (Hartley Parameterization)

Following Hartley's work as described in proposition 1, we choose without loss of generality a projective basis of the 3D space such that the projection matrix of the first camera $\mathbf{P}_1 = [\mathbf{I}|\mathbf{0}]$. In this basis, we note $\mathbf{P}_2 = \begin{bmatrix} \alpha_j^i \end{bmatrix}$ and $\mathbf{P}_3 = \begin{bmatrix} \beta_j^i \end{bmatrix}$ the projection matrices of the two other cameras. With these notations, the matrices $\mathbf{G}^i, i = 1 \ldots 3$ of the trifocal tensor T_1 can be written as $G_{jk}^i = \alpha_i^j \beta_4^k - \alpha_4^j \beta_i^k$. Although not minimal (22 parameters), this parameterization is interesting because it establishes a link between the trifocal tensors and the projection matrices. We now give expressions for the parameters introduced in the previous section in terms of those projection matrices.

$$\mathbf{L}^i = \left[\alpha_4^3\alpha_i^2 - \alpha_4^2\alpha_i^3, \alpha_4^1\alpha_i^3 - \alpha_4^3\alpha_i^1, \alpha_4^2\alpha_i^1 - \alpha_4^1\alpha_i^2\right]^T,$$
$$\mathbf{R}^i = \left[\beta_4^3\beta_i^2 - \beta_4^2\beta_i^3, \beta_4^1\beta_i^3 - \beta_4^3\beta_i^1, \beta_4^2\beta_i^1 - \beta_4^1\beta_i^2\right]^T.$$

Using the permutations λ^i and ρ^i of Sect. 3.2, we can express the coordinates $a_j^i, j = 1 \ldots 4$ of $\mathbf{G}^i$ in the basis of $\mathcal{M}(\mathbf{L}^i, \mathbf{R}^i)$ defined by those permutations:

$$a_1^i = \frac{\alpha_i^{\lambda^i(3)}\beta_4^{\rho^i(3)} - \alpha_4^{\lambda^i(3)}\beta_i^{\rho^i(3)}}{D}, \quad a_2^i = \frac{\alpha_i^{\lambda^i(3)}\beta_4^{\rho^i(2)} - \alpha_4^{\lambda^i(3)}\beta_i^{\rho^i(2)}}{D},$$

$$a_3^i = \frac{\alpha_i^{\lambda^i(2)}\beta_4^{\rho^i(3)} - \alpha_4^{\lambda^i(2)}\beta_i^{\rho^i(3)}}{D}, \quad a_4^i = \frac{\alpha_i^{\lambda^i(2)}\beta_4^{\rho^i(2)} - \alpha_4^{\lambda^i(2)}\beta_i^{\rho^i(2)}}{D},$$

where $D = L^i_{\lambda^i(1)} R^i_{\rho^i(1)} = (\alpha_4^{\lambda^i(3)}\alpha_i^{\lambda^i(2)} - \alpha_4^{\lambda^i(2)}\alpha_i^{\lambda^i(3)})(\beta_4^{\lambda^i(3)}\beta_i^{\lambda^i(2)} - \beta_4^{\lambda^i(2)}\beta_i^{\lambda^i(3)})$
is the product of the two highest coordinates in magnitude of $\mathbf{L}^i$ and $\mathbf{R}^i$ respectively. Since the parameters of the parameterization are ratios of coordinates of $\mathbf{L}^i$ and $\mathbf{R}^i$ and of $a_j^i, j = 1 \ldots 4$, they are projective invariants of the original projection matrices.

3.5 Comparison with Previous Minimal Parameterizations

Previously, only two minimal parameterizations have been proposed: in [TZ97a], Torr and Zisserman propose a parameterization **TZ** that is based on 6 corresponding points in the 3 images, in [FP98], Faugeras and Papadopoulo use a minimal parameterization **FP** that is based directly on the coefficients of the trifocal tensor.

In both cases, the parameterization is not one to one, i.e. one vector parameter parameterizes more than one trifocal tensor (up to three with **TZ** and up to two with **FP**). This arises because a polynomial equations of degree 3 for **TZ** and degree 2 for **FP** has to be solved in order to recover the trifocal tensor. This has two practical consequences:
• The multiple trifocal tensors parameterized by a single vector of 18 values can be distinguished only by using the image data. Although, the authors never experienced such a behavior, it might be possible to have situations for which this distinction is difficult.
• With a minimization process that updates "blindly" the vector of parameters, it is possible to "lose" the trifocal tensor when the solution designated by the data "disappears" in the complex plane leaving only one potential candidate with **TZ** and none with **FP**. In both cases, this is bad and there is no good solution to the problem. This should be a rare event but could result in a really bad solution when it happens. The authors experienced this problem in one case with the **FP** parameterization.

Since the new parameterization is one to one (one parameter code for only one trifocal tensor), such problems should never happen. Finally, none of the two parameterizations **TZ** or **FP** deals very well with map problems: in both case, there is no clear way to choose the map to minimize the numerical problems (i.e. what is the best choice of point for **TZ** apart from being in general position, and what columns of the trifocal tensor to take as parameters with **FP**). On the contrary, with our new parameterization, there is always a well-defined way to choose the best map for a given trifocal tensor.

4   Experimental Results

We have used our new parameterization in a minimisation process, similar to the one described in [FP98]. We start with a set of point of three corresponding images for which triplets of corresponding points have been extracted. From an initial linear estimate that, in general, does not verify the trifocal constraint, we compute an initial tensor that satisfies them[1]. Then, this initial trifocal tensor is parameterized and this minimal description of the tensor is used in a non-linear optimization process that refines the tensor by minimizing a criterion defined as the sum of the squared euclidean distances between the predicted and measured points in all the three images. For more details on this criterion see [FP98].

Fig. 4. One image excerpted of each triplet used for the experiments. In each case, the point matches used for the experiments are shown. Notice that the first of these triplets is actually a triplet of mosaics made from different pictures. Starting from top to bottom and from left to right these experimental sets are called **Triplet 1**, **Triplet 2** and **Triplet 3** respectively.

Figure 4 shows one image of each of the three triplets **Triplet 1**, **Triplet 2** and **Triplet 3** of real images that we used for our experiments. Each triplet contains about 30 point matches that are used to estimate the trifocal tensor. Those points were obtained using an interactive tool and are of good quality (reasonable accuracy, of the order of .5 pixels, and no false matches). To check the behavior of the minimizations in less perfect situations, we have also rounded to the closest integer value the pixels coordinates for the second and third triplets which are referred to as **Triplet 2'** and **Triplet 3'**.

Table 1 show the residual errors after minimization. For comparison purposes, we have also included the results obtained with the **FP** parameterization. As it can be seen,

---

[1] There are many reliable ways to achieve this step: we can use either a parameterization or a minimisation process over the trifocal constraints. The quality of the result varies with the method but this is not the topic of this paper.

	Triplet 1		Triplet 2		Triplet 2'		Triplet 3		Triplet 3'	
	Average	Max.	Average	Max.	Average	Max.	Average	Max.	Average	Max.
FP	$3.9e^{-3}$	2.2	$4.5e^{-4}$	0.1	$6.9e^{-3}$	1.7	$3.3e^{-4}$	0.1	$6.2e^{-4}$	0.2
	$3.6e^{-3}$	1.6	$9.5e^{-4}$	0.2	$8.1e^{-3}$	1.9	$1.7e^{-4}$	0.1	$6.8e^{-4}$	0.7
	$8.4e^{-3}$	3.6	$7.4e^{-4}$	0.1	$3.0e^{-3}$	0.6	$2.4e^{-4}$	0.1	$7.3e^{-4}$	0.3
New	$4.7e^{-3}$	1.3	$7.4e^{-4}$	0.2	$7.9e^{-3}$	2.0	$4.3e^{-4}$	0.1	$1.0e^{-3}$	0.3
	$2.1e^{-3}$	0.6	$8.2e^{-4}$	0.2	$1.1e^{-2}$	2.4	$2.9e^{-4}$	0.1	$6.0e^{-4}$	0.3
	$5.2e^{-3}$	2.2	$6.5e^{-4}$	0.1	$2.7e^{-3}$	0.5	$3.5e^{-4}$	0.2	$1.5e^{-3}$	0.8

Table 1. Prediction errors in pixels for all experiments. The rows labelled **FP** corresponds to the minimization process using the **FP** parameterization, whereas **New** corresponds to the one using the new parameterization. For each experiment, both average and maximal errors for each image are shown.

the results are quite comparable even though those obtained with the new method seem to be be generally of slightly lower quality. It should be said that during the tunning of the whole minimization process (test with different initializations and with different setup for the minimization processes), the results were consistently of lower quality (sometimes slightly worse than what is happening with the options that have been used for the results shown here). However, we have also seen among the hundreds of tests, at least three cases for which the **FP** based method fails miserably with NaN values for the trifocal tensors coefficients. This is because of the phenomenon explained in Sect. 3.5. On the contrary, the **New** method has always given a plausible result.

5 Conclusion

We have given a new set of algebraic constraints that characterize the set of trifocal constraints (Theorem 1). Those constraints are simpler than the ones we derived in [FP97] and used in [FP98]. We have used those constraints to derive a new minimal parametrization of the trifocal tensor that does not suffer from the problems of previous ones. Finally we have presented some experimental results where we use this new parametrization to estimate the trifocal tensor from image correspondences.

References

[AS96]   S. Avidan and A. Shashua. Tensorial transfer: Representation of $n > 3$ views of 3d scenes. In *Proceedings of the ARPA Image Understanding Workshop*. darpa, morgan-kaufmann, February 1996.

[Car94]   Stefan Carlsson. Multiple image invariance using the double algebra. In Joseph L. Mundy, Andrew Zissermann, and David Forsyth, editors, *Applications of Invariance in Computer Vision*, volume 825 of *Lecture Notes in Computer Science*, pages 145–164. Springer-Verlag, 1994.

[DZLF94] R. Deriche, Z. Zhang, Q.-T. Luong, and O. Faugeras. Robust recovery of the epipolar geometry for an uncalibrated stereo rig. In Eklundh [Ekl94], pages 567–576, Vol. 1.

[Ekl94]   J-O. Eklundh, editor. volume 800-801 of *Lecture Notes in Computer Science*, Stockholm, Sweden, May 1994. Springer-Verlag.

[FM95]   Olivier Faugeras and Bernard Mourrain. On the geometry and algebra of the point and line correspondences between n images. In *Proceedings of the 5th International Conference on Computer Vision* [icc95], pages 951–956.

[FP97]   Olivier Faugeras and Théodore Papadopoulo. A nonlinear method for estimating the projective geometry of three views. RR 3221, INRIA, July 1997.

[FP98]   Olivier Faugeras and Théodore Papadopoulo. A nonlinear method for estimating the projective geometry of three views. In *Proceedings of the 6th International Conference on Computer Vision*, pages 477–484, Bombay, India, January 1998. IEEE Computer Society Press.

[Har94]   Richard Hartley. Lines and points in three views-an integrated approach. In *Proceedings of the ARPA Image Understanding Workshop*. Defense Advanced Research Projects Agency, Morgan Kaufmann Publishers, Inc., 1994.

[Har95]   R.I. Hartley. In defence of the 8-point algorithm. In *Proceedings of the 5th International Conference on Computer Vision* [icc95], pages 1064–1070.

[Har97]   Richard I. Hartley. Lines and points in three views and the trifocal tensor. *The International Journal of Computer Vision*, 22(2):125–140, March 1997.

[Hey95]   Anders Heyden. Reconstruction from image sequences by means of relative depths. In *Proceedings of the 5th International Conference on Computer Vision* [icc95], pages 1058–1063.

[icc95]   Boston, MA, June 1995. IEEE Computer Society Press.

[LF96]   Quang-Tuan Luong and Olivier D. Faugeras. The fundamental matrix: Theory, algorithms and stability analysis. *The International Journal of Computer Vision*, 1(17):43–76, January 1996.

[LV94]   Q.-T. Luong and T. Viéville. Canonic representations for the geometries of multiple projective views. In Eklundh [Ekl94], pages 589–599.

[SA90]   Minas E. Spetsakis and Y. Aloimonos. A unified theory of structure from motion. In *Proc. DARPA IU Workshop*, pages 271–283, 1990.

[Sha94]   Amnon Shashua. Trilinearity in visual recognition by alignment. In Eklundh [Ekl94], pages 479–484.

[Sha95]   Amnon Shashua. Algebraic functions for recognition. *IEEE Transactions on Pattern Analysis and Machine Intelligence*, 17(8):779–789, 1995.

[SW95]   A. Shashua and M. Werman. On the trilinear tensor of three perspective views and its underlying geometry. In *Proceedings of the 5th International Conference on Computer Vision* [icc95].

[TZ97a]   P.H.S. Torr and A. Zisserman. Robust parameterization and computation of the trifocal tensor. *Image and Vision Computing*, 15:591–605, 1997.

[TZ97b]   P.H.S. Torr and A. Zissermann. Performance characterization of fundamental matrix estimation under image degradation. *Machine Vision and Applications*, 9:321–333, 1997.

[ZDFL95]   Z. Zhang, R. Deriche, O. Faugeras, and Q.-T. Luong. A robust technique for matching two uncalibrated images through the recovery of the unknown epipolar geometry. *Artificial Intelligence Journal*, 78:87–119, October 1995.

Threading Fundamental Matrices

Shai Avidan and Amnon Shashua

Institute of Computer Science, The Hebrew University,
91904 Jerusalem, Israel.
email:{avidan,shashua}@cs.huji.ac.il

Abstract

We present a new function that operates on Fundamental matrices across a sequence of views. The operation, we call "threading", connects two consecutive Fundamental matrices using the Trilinear tensor as the connecting thread. The threading operation guarantees that consecutive camera matrices are consistent with a unique 3D model, without ever recovering a 3D model. Applications include recovery of camera ego-motion from a sequence of views, image stabilization (plane stabilization) across a sequence, and multi-view image-based rendering.

1 Introduction

Consider the problem of recovering the (uncalibrated) camera trajectory from an extended sequence of images. Since the introduction of multi-linear forms across three or more views (see Appendix) there have been several attempts to put together a coherent algebraic framework that would produce a sequence of camera matrices that are consistent with the same 3D (projective) world [25, 4, 23]. The consistency requirement arises from the simple fact that from an algebraic standpoint a camera trajectory must be *concatenated* from pairs or triplet of images. Therefore, a sequence of independently computed Fundamental matrices or Trilinear tensors, maybe optimally consistent with the image data, but not necessarily consistent with a unique camera trajectory (see Figure 1). There are two basic approaches to the problem:

1. Recover (incrementally or batch-wise) the most (statistically) optimal 3D structure from the image measurements across the extended sequence. Then, given the 3D and 2D correspondences recover the corresponding camera matrix.
2. Recover a sequence of camera matrices whose homography matrices all correspond to the same reference plane.

The first approach is intuitive and fairly amenable to recursive estimation. Example of recent implementations of this approach for uncalibrated camera include the incremental method of [4] who recover Fundamental matrices or Trilinear tensors to ensure the quality of matching points, and then estimate the camera matrices from the 3D structure which is built-up incrementally. Likewise, [23]

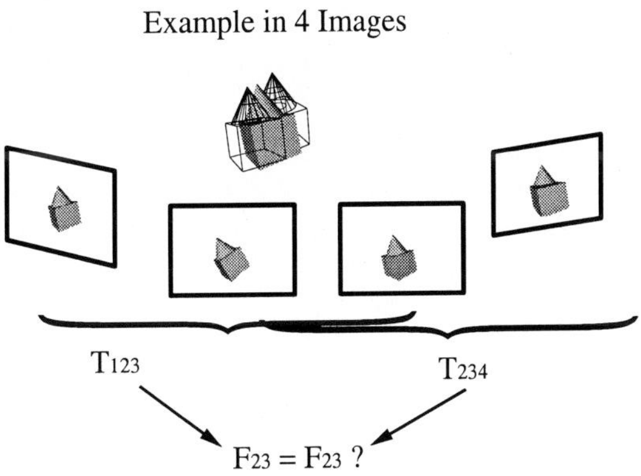

Example in 4 Images

$$T_{123} \qquad T_{234}$$

$$F_{23} = F_{23} \ ?$$

(a)

Fig. 1. One can compute two tensors T_{123}, T_{234} from the four images of the 3D scene. However, each tensor can give rise to a different reconstruction of the 3D structure due to noise or errors in measurments, and therefor the camera trajectory between images 2 and 3, as captured by the fundamental matrix F_{23}, is inconsistent between the two tensors. The "threading" operator described in the text guarantees a consistent recovery of the camera trajectory.

recovers independently the Fundamental matrices of every consecutive pair of images, and relies on a 3D-structure to put them all in a single measurement matrix that is used to recover the camera parameters.

The second approach is more challenging since it requires a deeper investigation into the connections between camera matrices. If a simple connection exists then there is the advantage of avoiding 3D structure, as an intermediate variable in the process. The only attempt we know of is of [25] who seeks a sequence of camera matrices in which the homography matrices all correspond to the plane at infinity. However, the method resorts to a large non-linear optimization problem, where one alternatively recovers 3D structure from motion and motion from structure (thus not avoiding the 3D structure as an intermediate variable).

In this paper we introduce a new result on the connection between Fundamental matrices and Trilinear tensors. As a byproduct, this result provide a principaled method for concatenating camera matrices along an extended sequence without resorting to 3D structure. The connection is based on a representation of the tensor as a function of the elements of two consecutive Fundamental matrices and a homography matrix of some arbitrary reference plane (Eqn. 1). An interesting byproduct of this representation is that we are guaranteed to recover (linearly) two *consistent* camera matrices. By repeated application of the basic result, we call a *threading operation*, on a sliding window of triplets of views, we obtain a consistent sequence of camera matrices (and the Fundamental matrix and Trilinear tensors as well). The immediate byproducts (applications) of the threading operation include:

– **Ego-Motion**
  The algorithm recovers a consistent camera trajectory along the image sequence without recovering 3D structure.

– **Image stabilization**
  The algorithm recovers a sequence of camera matrices that are due to the same plane. By selecting a reference plane in the first pair of images, we ensure that the same plane is stabilized throughout the sequence.

– **Multi-view Image-Based Rendering**
  The algorithm puts all the images in a single projective coordinate framework and therefor all the images can contribute to the synthesis of a novel image, using a technique such as [3].

The paper is organized as follows. Section 2 provides the general notations and conventions used in the paper. The main results are stated and proven in Section 3. The outline of the algorithm is given in Section 4 and results are shown in Section 5. The Appendix contains a brief overview of the necessary elements assumed including the Fundamental matrix, Plane + Parallax representation, the Trilinear tensor, and the tensorial form of the Fundamental matrix.

2 Notations

A point x in the 3D projective space $\mathcal{P}^3$ is projected onto the point p in the 2D projective space $\mathcal{P}^2$ by a 3×4 camera projection matrix $\mathbf{A} = [A, v']$ that satisfies $p \cong \mathbf{A}x$, where $\cong$ represents equality up to scale. The left 3×3 minor of $\mathbf{A}$, denoted by A, stands for a 2D projective transformation of some arbitrary plane (the reference plane) and the fourth column of $\mathbf{A}$, denoted by v', stands for the epipole (the projection of the center of camera 1 on the image plane of camera 2). In a calibrated setting the 2D projective transformation is the rotational component of camera motion (the reference plane is at infinity) and the epipole is the translational component of camera motion. Since only relative camera positioning can be recovered from image measurements, the camera matrix of the first camera position in a sequence of positions can be represented by $[I; 0]$.

We will occasionally use tensorial notations as described next. We use the covariant-contravariant summation convention: a point is an object whose coordinates are specified with superscripts, i.e., $p^i = (p^1, p^2, ...)$. These are called contravariant vectors. An element in the dual space (representing hyper-planes — lines in $\mathcal{P}^2$), is called a covariant vector and is represented by subscripts, i.e., $s_j = (s_1, s_2, ...)$. Indices repeated in covariant and contravariant forms are summed over, i.e., $p^i s_i = p^1 s_1 + p^2 s_2 + ... + p^n s_n$. This is known as a contraction. An outer-product of two 1-valence tensors (vectors), $a_i b^j$, is a 2-valence tensor (matrix) c_i^j whose i, j entries are $a_i b^j$ — note that in matrix form $C = ba^\mathsf{T}$. Further details on the necessary background can be found in the Appendix.

The Threading Step

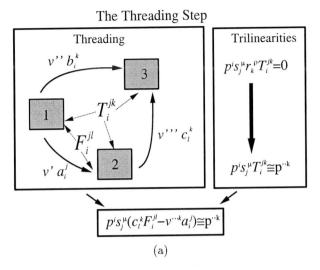

(a)

Fig. 2. The threading step is plugged into the trilinearities to obtain the threading equation.

3   Threading Fundamental Matrices Using Trilinear Tensors

Given an extended sequence of images we wish to recover a unique camera trajectory which is the most consistent with the image measurements. We wish to do so in a principaled manner, i.e., see first what can be done at the algebraic level. On that level, a necessary condition for trajectory consistency is that the recovered camera matrices all refer to the same common reference plane (which could be virtual), see Appendix. The two theorems below are the essence of this paper and include:

- Providing an equation for representing the Trilinear tensor as a function of the Fundamental matrix (represented in its trivalent tensorial form), the reference plane homography between views 1 and 2, and the camera motion between images 2 and 3.
- Given the equation discussed above, the Fundamental matrix between views 1 and 2, and at least 6 matching points across images 1,2,3, one can linearly recover the camera motion between views 2 and 3.
- The recovered camera motion between views 2 and 3, is guaranteed to be consistent (i.e., the corresponding homography matrix is associated with the same reference plane).

By repeatedly applying these results on a sliding window of triplets of views we obtain a camera trajectory which is consistent with a single 3D reconstruction of the world — because all the homography matrices correspond to a single reference plane (see Figure 2).

Theorem 1. *The following equation holds:*

$$T_i^{jk} = c_l^k \mathcal{F}_i^{jl} - v'''^k a_i^j \tag{1}$$

where T_i^{jk} is the tensor of views 1,2,3, the matrix A, whose elements are a_i^j, is a homography from image 1 to 2 via some arbitrary plane π, $\mathcal{F}_i^{jl}$ is the 2-view tensor of views 1,2, and $\mathbf{C} = [C; v''']$ is the camera motion from image 2 to 3 where c_l^k is a homography matrix from image 2 to 3 via the (same) plane π.

Proof: We know that

$$T_i^{jk} = v'^j b_i^k - v''^k a_i^j$$

where the parameters $[A, v'] = [a_i^j, v'^j]$ and $[B, v''] = [b_i^k, v''^k]$ are the camera matrices from 3D to views 2,3 respectively:

$$\lambda p' = Ap + \rho v'$$
$$p'' \cong Bp + \rho v''$$

where p, p', p'' are the matching points in views 1,2,3 respectively, and A, B are homography matrices due to the *same* (arbitrary) reference plane π (uniqueness issue discussed in [14]). Clearly,

$$p'' \cong BA^{-1}p' + \frac{\rho}{\lambda}(v'' - BA^{-1}v')$$

Therefore, the camera motion from view 2 to 3 is represented by,

$$[C; v'''] = [BA^{-1}; v'' - BA^{-1}v']$$

and,

$$\begin{aligned} b_i^k &= c_l^k a_i^l \\ v''^k &= c_l^k v'^l + v'''^k. \end{aligned} \tag{2}$$

By substituting the expressions above instead of b_i^k and v''^k in T_i^{jk}, we obtain:

$$\begin{aligned} T_i^{jk} &= v'^j(c_l^k a_i^l) - (c_l^k v'^l + v'''^k)a_i^j \\ &= c_l^k(v'^j a_i^l - v'^l a_i^j) - v'''^k a_i^j \\ &= c_l^k \mathcal{F}_i^{jl} - v'''^k a_i^j, \end{aligned} \tag{3}$$

where $\mathcal{F}_i^{jl}$ is the trivalent tensor form of the Fundamental matrix, i.e., $\mathcal{F}_i^{jl} = \epsilon^{sjl} F_{si}$ where F_{li} is the Fundamental matrix and ϵ^{ljk} is the cross-product tensor (see Appendix). Finally, because of the group property of projective transformations, since A, B are transformations due to some plane π, then so is $C = BA^{-1}$.
□

Theorem 2. *Given the Fundamental matrix of views 1,2 and the tensor T_i^{jk}, then the Fundamental matrix between views 2,3 can be recovered linearly from 6 matching points across the three views.*

Proof: The basic tensorial contraction, a trilinearity, is

$$p^i s_j r_k T_i^{jk} = 0,$$

where s and r are lines coincident with p' and p'', respectively (see Appendix). Thus, the tensor and two views uniquely determine the third view (the reprojection equation) as follows:

$$p^i s_j T_i^{jk} \cong p''^k,$$

where the choice of the line s is immaterial as long as it is coincident with p'. By substitution we obtain,

$$p^i s_j (c_l^k \mathcal{F}_i^{jl} - v'''^k a_i^j) \cong p''^k \tag{4}$$

which provides two linear equations for the unknowns c_l^k and v'''. We next show that different choices of the line s do not produce new (linearly independent) equations, and thus 6 matching points are required for a linear system for the unknowns.

Just as the Trilinear tensor T_i^{jk} satisfies the reprojection equation, so does the 2-view tensor $\mathcal{F}_i^{jl}$:

$$p^i s_j \mathcal{F}_i^{jl} \cong p'^l,$$

where the choice of the orientation of the line s_j is immaterial (see Appendix). Thus, Eqn. 4 reduces to (in matrix form):

$$p'' \cong Cp' + \rho(s)v''',$$

where $\rho(s)$ is a scalar (depends also on s) that determines the ratio between p'' and Cp' and v''', thus is unique (invariant to the choice of s). $\square$

It is worthwhile to note that the homography matrix A that appears in Eqn. 3 can be generated using the following two observations. First, the space of all homography matrices between two fixed views lives in a 4-dimensional space [17], thus we can span A from 4 primitive homography matrices. Second, three of the primitive homography matrices can be generated from the "homography contraction" property of the tensors (see Appendix), i.e., $\delta_k \mathcal{F}_i^{jk}$ is a homography matrix indexed by δ_k, thus by setting δ_k to be $(1,0,0), (0,1,0)$ and $(0,0,1)$ we obtain three primitive homography matrices, the fourth homography matrix is composed of the elements of the epipole. In matrix form we have:

$$\begin{bmatrix} 0 & 0 & 0 \\ 0 & 0 & -1 \\ 0 & 1 & 0 \end{bmatrix} F \quad \begin{bmatrix} 0 & 0 & 1 \\ 0 & 0 & 0 \\ -1 & 0 & 0 \end{bmatrix} F \quad \begin{bmatrix} 0 & -1 & 0 \\ 1 & 0 & 0 \\ 0 & 0 & 0 \end{bmatrix} F \quad \begin{bmatrix} v_1' & 0 & 0 \\ v_2' & 0 & 0 \\ v_3' & 0 & 0 \end{bmatrix} \tag{5}$$

where F is the Fundamental matrix and v' is the epipole statisfying $F^\top v' = 0$. The left three homography matrices correspond to planes coincident with the center of projection of the second camera (thus are rank 2 matrices). The fourth primitive homography corresponds to a plane coincident with the center of projection of the first camera (thus is rank 1), therefore is not linearly spanned by the three homography contractions of the 2-view tensor. Taken together, any linear combination (that includes the fourth primitive homography matrix) of the above four matrices will provide an admissible homography matrix A that can be used in Eqn. 3.

4 The Online algorithm

The online algorithm threads together the Fundamental matrices of consecutive images, by applying the threading operation on a sliding window of triplets of images. The algorithm starts with computing the Fundamental matrix of the first pair of images and recovering an initial homography matrix. The initial homography matrix can be recovered either from the primitive homography matrices constructed from the Fundamental matrix, or by using any method for the recovery of a homography matrix by plane stabilization [11]. The rest of the images are added one by one by applying the threading operation on a sliding window of triplets of images. Figure 3 gives a block diagram of the proposed algorithm.

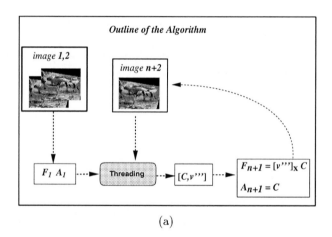

(a)

Fig. 3. The algorithm starts with recovering the Fundamental matrix F_1 of the first pair of images in the sequence. The Fundamental matrix is then used to construct the initial homography matrix A_1. For image $n + 2$, the current Fundamental matrix F_n and homography A_n are used to recover the camera parameters of the new image - $[C, v''']$, using the threading operation. This parameters are then used to construct $F_{n+1} = [v''']_\times C$ and $A_{n+1} = C$.

In detail, the algorithm is as follows:

1. Recover the Fundamental matrix F_1 of the first pair of images in the sequence.

2. Recover the epipole v' from the null-space of $F_1{}^T$.

3. Construct the initial homography A_1 as a linear combination of the four homography matrices in Eqn. 5. For the sake of numerical stability we wish to find a linear combination that will approximate the form of a rotation matrix. In particular we use the method described in [13] which is suitable for small-angle rotations.

For image $n + 2$:

1. Apply the threading operation for recovering the camera matrix $\mathbf{C} = [C, v''']$. The input to the operation is 6 point matches across three images, the Fundamental matrix F_n and homography matrix A_n, using Equation 4.

2. The new Fundamental matrix $F_{n+1} = [v''']_\times C$ and homography $A_{n+1} = C$ are the parameters for the recovery of the camera matrix of the next image.

5 Experiments

Experiments were conducted on synthetic data and several different real images with different cameras and different motion parameters. No information about camera internal parameters or motion is known or used. The point correspondence, for the real images, were extracted automatically by our system. In a nutshell, the system computes a bi-directional optical flow and searches for points with high gradient that have a matching optical flow in both direction. Typically we obtain around 200 matching points.

5.1 Test on Synthetic Data

We measured the error of the threading operation along an image sequence. The 3D world consisted of a set of 50 points that were projected on a sequence of 21 images, using randomly generated camera matrices. All image measurements were normalized to the range $[0..1]$ and white noise (of up to 2 pixels in a $512{\times}512$ pixels image) was added. We recovered the Fundamental matrix of the first pair of images, using the 8-point algorithm, and used the fourth homography matrix in Equation 5 as the initial homography matrix. The rest of the camera matrices were recovered according to the algorithm described in Section 4 and we denote the recovered epipoles by e_T. For comparison, we computed the Fundamental matrix from every consecutive pair of images and recovered the epipole from it and denote it by e_F. Figure 4 shows the ratio $\frac{d(e_T)}{d(e_F)}$, where $d(\cdot)$ measures the distance, in parameter space, between the recovered epipole and correct epipole. The test was repeated for 30 times and the median of the errors, for white noise of 2 pixels, is shown. As can be seen, the error rate of the threading operation is almost identical to that achieved by the Fundamental matrix, and does not degrade with the number of images.

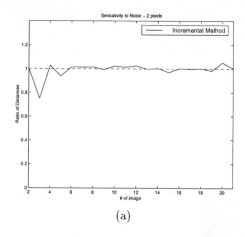

(a)

Fig. 4. The quality of the recovered camera matrices on a sequence of 21 synthetic images of size 512×512 with added white noise of 2 pixels. The graph shows the ratio between the error of the threading operation and the error of the Fundamental matrix of every consecutive pair of images. The error term is defined as the distance, in parameter space, between the recovered epipole and the ground truth epipole. A value smaller than 1 means the threading operation performed better than the Fundamental matrix. Note that the threading operation does not accumulate errors and remains close to the error rate obtained when using the Fundamental matrix.

5.2 Real Data

Tests on two real sequences were conducted. The first test presents a possible use of our method for the purpose of multi-camera image-based rendering mechanism and the second test demonstrates the ability to stabilize a plane.

Test 1 A sequence of 28 images of size 320×240 pixels was used with the camera moving in a semi-circle motion forward and to the right. The initial homography matrix was recovered with the method described in [13, 2]. The camera matrices of images 2 through 28 were recovered with the threading operation and used to construct two tensors - $< 1, 2, 28 >, < 26, 27, 28 >$. Since the threading operation prodcues the camera matrix of image $n + 2$ in the coordinate system of image $n + 1$ we had to concatenate the camera matrices to bring them all into the a single coordinate system. The image pairs $(1, 2)$ and $(26, 27)$, together with their respective tensors, were used to reproject image 28. The results are shown in Figure 5.

Test 2 A sequence of 7 images of size 384×288 pixels was used, with the camera moving mainly to the left. The images contain a collection of toy animals placed on a table covered with a picture of a fruit salad. We manually selected the plane of the table as our initial homography matrix and applied the threading

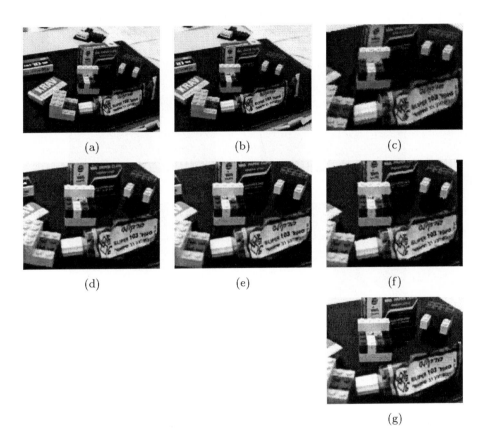

Fig. 5. Accumulating the camera matrices along a sequence of 28 images to construct the tensors $< 1, 2, 28 >, < 26, 27, 28 >$. The two tensors are then used to reproject image 28. (a),(b) show images 1 and 2, respectively and (d),(e) show images 26 and 27, respectively. (c),(f) show how image 28 was reprojected from the two pairs, respectively, using the reconstructed tensors. (g) is the original image 28, shown here for comparison.

operation to recover the camera matrices. From Theorem 1, the homography matrix between images 6 and 7 should be due to the same plane defined in images 1 and 2. To verify this, we marked the plane in image 6 by comparing the optical flow between images 6 and 7 with the recovered homography matrix. All the pixels with optical flow not equal to the homography matrix are considered as coming from outside the reference plane and are marked with black. Note that the threading operation does not need the plane to be present in the sequence and that the plane is used here only for the purpose of verifying the consistency of the recovered camera matrices. Figure 6 shows the results of this test.

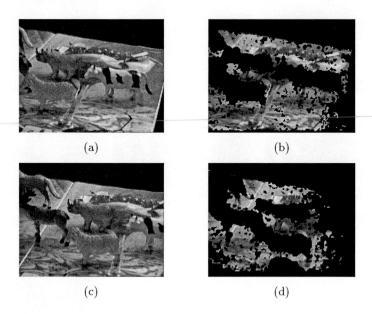

(a)

(b)

(c)

(d)

Fig. 6. Stabilizing the plane in the first image over a sequence of 7 images. (a),(c) are images 1 and 6 in the sequence. (b), (d) are the same images with the pixels outside the plane marked with black pixels.

6 Conclusion

We have presented a new result on the connection between Fundamental matrices and Trilinear tensors. This result is used to thread Fundamental matrices of consecutive images into a consistent camera trajectory. The threading operation is applied on a sliding window of triplets of images to construct a consistent camera trajectory along an extended sequence of (uncalibrated) images, without recovering 3D structure. Immediate application of the threading operation are:

- **Ego-Motion**
  The algorithm recovers a consistent camera trajectory along the image sequence without recovering 3D structure.
- **Image stabilization**
  The algorithm recovers a sequence of camera matrices that are due to the same plane. By selecting a reference plane in the first pair of images, we ensure that the same plane is stabilized throughout the sequence.
- **Multi-view Image-Based Rendering**
  The algorithm puts all the images in a single projective coordinate framework and therefor all the images can contribute to the synthesis of a novel image, using a technique such as [3].

References

1. S. Avidan and A. Shashua. Tensorial transfer: On the representation of $n > 3$ views of a 3D scene. In *Proceedings of the ARPA Image Understanding Workshop*, Palm Springs, CA, February 1996.
2. S. Avidan and A. Shashua. Unifying two-view and three-view geometry. In *ARPA, Image Understanding Workshop*, 1997.
3. S. Avidan and A. Shashua. View synthesis in tensor space. In *Proceedings of the IEEE Conference on Computer Vision and Pattern Recognition*, Puerto Rico, June 1997.
4. P.A. Beardsley, A. Zisserman, and D.W. Murray. Sequential updating of projective and affine structure from motion. *International Journal of Computer Vision, 23(3):235-260*, 1997.
5. O.D. Faugeras. What can be seen in three dimensions with an uncalibrated stereo rig? In *Proceedings of the European Conference on Computer Vision*, pages 563–578, Santa Margherita Ligure, Italy, June 1992.
6. O.D. Faugeras and B. Mourrain. On the geometry and algebra of the point and line correspondences between N images. In *Proceedings of the International Conference on Computer Vision*, Cambridge, MA, June 1995.
7. R. Hartley. Lines and points in three views — a unified approach. In *Proceedings of the ARPA Image Understanding Workshop*, Monterey, CA, November 1994.
8. R. Hartley. In defence of the 8-point algorithm. In *Proceedings of the International Conference on Computer Vision*, 1995.
9. R. Hartley. A linear method for reconstruction from lines and points. In *Proceedings of the International Conference on Computer Vision*, pages 882–887, Cambridge, MA, June 1995.
10. A. Heyden. Reconstruction from image sequences by means of relative depths. In *Proceedings of the International Conference on Computer Vision*, pages 1058–1063, Cambridge, MA, June 1995.
11. M. Irani, B. Rousso, and S. Peleg. Recovery of ego-motion using image stabilization'. In *Proceedings of the IEEE Conference on Computer Vision and Pattern Recognition*, pages 454–460, Seattle, Washington, June 1994.
12. H.C. Longuet-Higgins. A computer algorithm for reconstructing a scene from two projections. *Nature, 293:133–135*, 1981.
13. B. Rousso, S. Avidan, A. Shashua, and S. Peleg. Robust recovery of camera rotation from three frames. In *Proceedings of IEEE Conference on Computer Vision and Pattern Recognition*, 1996.

14. A. Shashua. Algebraic functions for recognition. *IEEE Transactions on Pattern Analysis and Machine Intelligence*, 17(8):779–789, 1995.

15. A. Shashua. Trilinear tensor: The fundamental construct of multiple-view geometry and its applications. Submitted for journal publication. A short version has appeared in International Workshop on Algebraic Frames For The Perception Action Cycle (AFPAC97), Kiel Germany Sep. 8–9, 1997, 1997.

16. A. Shashua and P. Anandan. The generalized trilinear constraints and the uncertainty tensor. In *Proceedings of the ARPA Image Understanding Workshop*, Palm Springs, CA, February 1996.

17. A. Shashua and S. Avidan. The rank4 constraint in multiple view geometry. In *Proceedings of the European Conference on Computer Vision*, Cambridge, UK, April 1996.

18. A. Shashua and N. Navab. Relative affine structure: Canonical model for 3D from 2D geometry and applications. *IEEE Transactions on Pattern Analysis and Machine Intelligence*, 18(9):873–883, 1996.

19. A. Shashua and M. Werman. Trilinearity of three perspective views and its associated tensor. In *Proceedings of the International Conference on Computer Vision*, June 1995.

20. M.E. Spetsakis and J. Aloimonos. Structure from motion using line correspondences. *International Journal of Computer Vision*, 4(3):171–183, 1990.

21. M.E. Spetsakis and J. Aloimonos. A unified theory of structure from motion. In *Proceedings of the ARPA Image Understanding Workshop*, 1990.

22. G. Stein and A. Shashua. Model based brightness constraints: On direct estimation of structure and motion. In *Proceedings of the IEEE Conference on Computer Vision and Pattern Recognition*, Puerto Rico, June 1997.

23. P. Sturm and B. Triggs. A factorization based algorithm for multi-image projective structure and motion. In *Proceedings of the European Conference on Computer Vision*, 1996.

24. B. Triggs. Matching constraints and the joint image. In *Proceedings of the International Conference on Computer Vision*, pages 338–343, Cambridge, MA, June 1995.

25. T. Vieville, O. Faugeras, and Q.T. Loung. Motion of points and lines in the uncalibrated case. *International Journal of Computer Vision, 17(1):7–42*, 1996.

26. J. Weng, T.S. Huang, and N. Ahuja. Motion and structure from line correspondences: Closed form solution, uniqueness and optimization. *IEEE Transactions on Pattern Analysis and Machine Intelligence*, 14(3), 1992.

A Background

The background material of this paper includes (i) the Fundamental matrix, (ii) the "plane + parallax" representation, (iii) the Trilinear tensor and its contraction properties, and (iv) the reduction of the Trilinear tensor into the 2-view tensor whose components include the elements of the Fundamental matrix.

A.1 The Fundamental Matrix of Two Views

Two views $p = [I; 0]x$ and $p' \cong Ax$ are known to produce a bilinear matching constraint whose coefficients are arranged in a 3×3 matrix F known as the "Essential matrix" of

[12] described originally in an Euclidean setting, or the "Fundamental matrix" of [5] described in the setting of Projective Geometry (uncalibrated cameras):

$$F = [v']_\times A \tag{6}$$

where $\mathbf{A} = [A; v']$ (a_j^l are the elements of A - the left 3×3 minor of $\mathbf{A}$, and v' is the fourth column, the epipole, of $\mathbf{A}$). $[v']_\times$ denotes the skew-symmetric matrix of v'. i.e., the product with some vector u, $[v']_\times u$, produces the cross product between v' and u, $v' \times u$. The minor A is a 2D projective transformation from the first view onto the second via some *arbitrary* plane. In an affine setting the plane is at infinity, and in an Euclidean setting it is the rotational component of camera motion. The epipole v' is the projection of the camera center of the first camera onto the second view, and in an Euclidean setting it is the translational component of camera motion.

The Fundamental matrix satisfies the constraint $p'^\top F p = 0$ for all pairs of matching points p, p' in views 1 and 2, respectively. This bilinear form in image coordinates arises from the fact that the points v', Ap and p' are collinear, thus $p'^\top (v' \times Ap) = 0$. The matrix F can be recovered linearly from 8 matching points, and $F^\top v' = 0$.

A.2 Plane + Parallax Representation

The claim that recovering a consistent camera trajectory is equivalent to recovering camera matrices that are all due to the same reference plane relies on the *Relative Affine Structure* representation.

The collinearity of v', Ap and p', where A is the homography matrix due to *some* reference plane π, can be used to describe p' as follows:

$$p' \cong Ap + \rho v' \tag{7}$$

The coefficient ρ depends on the point p and the position of the plane π, is *invariant* to the choice of the second camera position (see Figure 7). Thus, by fixing the same plane along an image sequence we obtain the same relative affine structure - ρ for all the images. This is analogous to recovering the *same* 3D structure from all the images. Further details can be found in [18].

A.3 The Trilinear Tensor of Three Views

Matching image points across three views will be denoted by p, p', p''; the homogeneous coordinates will be referred to as p^i, p'^j, p''^k, or alternatively as non-homogeneous image coordinates $(x, y), (x', y'), (x'', y'')$ — hence, $p^i = (x, y, 1)$, etc.

Three views, $p = [I; 0]x, p' \cong \mathbf{A}x$ and $p'' \cong \mathbf{B}x$, are known to produce four trilinear forms whose coefficients are arranged in a tensor representing a bilinear function of the camera matrices $\mathbf{A}, \mathbf{B}$:

$$\mathcal{T}_i^{jk} = v'^j b_i^k - v''^k a_i^j \tag{8}$$

where $\mathbf{A} = [a_i^j, v'^j]$ (a_i^j is the 3×3 left minor and v' is the fourth column of $\mathbf{A}$) and $\mathbf{B} = [b_i^k, v''^k]$. The tensor acts on a triplet of matching points in the following way:

$$p^i s_j^\mu r_k^\rho \mathcal{T}_i^{jk} = 0 \tag{9}$$

where s_j^μ are any two lines (s_j^1 and s_j^2) intersecting at p', and r_k^ρ are any two lines intersecting p''. Since the free indices are μ, ρ each in the range 1,2, we have 4 trilinear

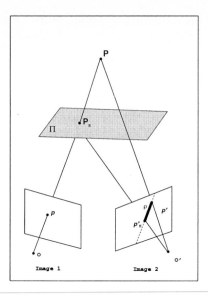

Fig. 7. The Relative Affine Structure ρ (the bold line) measures how much does the point p deviates from the plane π. ρ is invariant to the position of the second camera. Stabilizing the *same* plane along a sequence of images is therefore analogous to recovering the *same* 3D structure from all the images.

equations (unique up to linear combinations). If we choose the *standard* form where s^μ (and r^ρ) represent vertical and horizontal scan lines, i.e.,

$$s_j^\mu = \begin{bmatrix} -1 & 0 & x' \\ 0 & -1 & y' \end{bmatrix}$$

then the four trilinear forms, referred to as *trilinearities*[14], have the following explicit form:

$$x'' T_i^{13} p^i - x'' x' T_i^{33} p^i + x' T_i^{31} p^i - T_i^{11} p^i = 0,$$
$$y'' T_i^{13} p^i - y'' x' T_i^{33} p^i + x' T_i^{32} p^i - T_i^{12} p^i = 0,$$
$$x'' T_i^{23} p^i - x'' y' T_i^{33} p^i + y' T_i^{31} p^i - T_i^{21} p^i = 0,$$
$$y'' T_i^{23} p^i - y'' y' T_i^{33} p^i + y' T_i^{32} p^i - T_i^{22} p^i = 0.$$

These constraints were first derived in [14]; the tensorial derivation leading to Eqns. 8 and 9 was first derived in [16]. The Trilinear tensor has been well known in disguise in the context of Euclidean line correspondences and was not identified at the time as a tensor but as a collection of three matrices (a particular contraction of the tensor known as correlation contractions) [20, 21, 26]. The link between the two and the generalization to projective space was identified later in [7, 9]. Additional work in this area can be found in [19, 6, 24, 10, 17, 1, 3, 22].

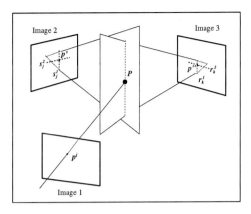

Fig. 8. Each of the four trilinear equations describes a matching between a point p in the first view, some line s_j^μ passing through the matching point p' in the second view and some line r_k^ρ passing through the matching point p'' in the third view. In space, this constraint is a meeting between a ray and two planes.

A.4 Contraction Properties of the Tensor

The lines s_j^μ coincident with p' and the lines r_k^ρ coincident with p'' for a basis for all lines coincident with p' and p'', thus we readily have the "point+line+line" property:

$$p^i s_j r_k T_i^{jk} = 0 \tag{10}$$

where s_j is *some* line through p' and r_k is *some* line through p''. Similarly, since $s_j r_k T_i^{jk}$ is a line (coincident with p), then a triplet of matching lines provides two constraints:

$$s_j r_k T_i^{jk} \cong q_i \tag{11}$$

for all lines q, s, r coincident with the points p, p', p'' (in particular, matching lines). The third point-line property is the "reprojection" constraint:

$$p^i s_j T_i^{jk} \cong p''^k \tag{12}$$

which provides a direct means for "transfer" of image measurements from views 1,2 onto view 3 (prediction of p'' from views 1,2).

The tensor has certain contraction properties and can be sliced in three principled ways into matrices with distinct geometric properties divided into two families: *Homography Contractions* and *Correlation Contractions*. We will briefly introduce the Homography contractions described originally in [19] — further details on that and on Correlation contractions can be found in [15].

Consider the matrix arising from the contraction,

$$\delta_k T_i^{jk} \tag{13}$$

which is a 3×3 matrix, we denote by E, obtained by the linear combination $E = \delta_1 T_i^{j1} + \delta_2 T_i^{j2} + \delta_3 T_i^{j3}$ (which is what is meant by a contraction), and δ_k is an *arbitrary* covariant vector. The matrix E has a general meaning introduced in [19]:

Proposition 1 (Homography Contractions). *The contraction $\delta_k \mathcal{T}_i^{jk}$ for some arbitrary δ_k is a homography matrix from image one onto image two determined by the plane containing the third camera center C'' and the line δ_k in the third image plane. Generally, the rank of E is 3. Likewise, the contraction $\delta_j \mathcal{T}_i^{jk}$ is a homography matrix from image one onto image three.*

For proof see [19]. Clearly, since δ is spanned by three vectors, we can generate up to at most three distinct homography matrices by contractions of the tensor. We define the *Standard Homography Slicing* as the homography contractions associated by selecting δ be $(1,0,0)$ or $(0,1,0)$ or $(0,0,1)$, thus the three standard homography slices between image one and two are $\mathcal{T}_i^{j1}, \mathcal{T}_i^{j2}$ and $\mathcal{T}_i^{j3}$, and we denote them by E_1, E_2, E_3 respectively, and likewise the three standard homography slices between image one and three are $\mathcal{T}_i^{1k}, \mathcal{T}_i^{2k}$ and $\mathcal{T}_i^{3k}$, and we denote them by W_1, W_2, W_3 respectively.

A.5   The 2-view Tensor

We return to Equation 8 and consider the case where the third image coincide with the second. The camera matrices for both images are $\mathbf{A} = [A; v']$ and this special tensor can be written as:

$$\mathcal{F}_i^{jk} = v'^j a_i^k - v'^k a_i^j \tag{14}$$

which is composed of the elements of the Fundamental matrix, as the following lemma shows.

Lemma 1. *The two-view-tensor $\mathcal{F}_i^{jk}$ is composed of the elements of the Fundamental matrix:*

$$\mathcal{F}_i^{jk} = \epsilon^{ljk} F_{li}$$

where F_{li} is the Fundamental matrix and ϵ^{ljk} is the cross-product tensor.

Proof: We consider Equation 8 with $\mathcal{F}_i^{jk} = \epsilon^{ljk} F_{li}$ to derive the following equalities:

$$\begin{aligned} p^i s_j r_k \mathcal{F}_i^{jk} &= \\ p^i s_j r_k (\epsilon^{ljk} F_{li}) &= \\ p_i \underbrace{\left(s_j r_k \epsilon^{ljk} \right)}_{p'^l} F_{li} &= 0 \end{aligned} \tag{15}$$

▯

The two-view-tensor is an admissible tensor that embodies the Fundamental matrix in a three-image-framework. Algorithm that works with the Trilinear tensor of three views can work with this tensor as well. In particular, the point-line contractions and the Homography contractions hold, for example:

$$p^i s_j \mathcal{F}_i^{jk} \cong p'^k$$

which takes p and a line s coincident with p' and produces p'. The contraction $\delta_k \mathcal{F}_i^{jk}$ is a homography contraction, i.e., produces a homography matrix from view 1 onto view 2 given by the plane coincident with the center of projection of camera 2 and the line δ in view 2. Similarly to the 3-view tensor, the Standard Homography Slices correspond to setting δ to $(1,0,0)$ or $(0,1,0)$ or $(0,0,1)$. Further details can be found in [2].

Use Your Hand as a 3-D Mouse,
or,
Relative Orientation from Extended Sequences of Sparse Point and Line Correspondences Using the Affine Trifocal Tensor[*]

Lars Bretzner and Tony Lindeberg

Computational Vision and Active Perception Laboratory (CVAP)
Dept. of Numerical Analysis and Computing Science,
KTH, S-100 44 Stockholm, Sweden

Abstract. This paper addresses the problem of computing three-dimensional structure and motion from an unknown rigid configuration of point and lines viewed by an affine projection model. An algebraic structure, analogous to the trilinear tensor for three perspective cameras, is defined for configurations of three centered affine cameras. This centered affine trifocal tensor contains 12 non-zero coefficients and involves linear relations between point correspondences and trilinear relations between line correspondences. It is shown how the affine trifocal tensor relates to the perspective trilinear tensor, and how three-dimensional motion can be computed from this tensor in a straightforward manner. A factorization approach is also developed to handle point features and line features simultaneously in image sequences. This theory is applied to a specific problem in human-computer interaction of capturing three-dimensional rotations from gestures of a human hand. Besides the obvious application, this test problem illustrates the usefulness of the affine trifocal tensor in a situation where sufficient information is not available to compute the perspective trilinear tensor, while the geometry requires point correspondences as well as line correspondences over at least three views.

1   Introduction

The problem of deriving structural information and motion cues from image sequences arises as an important subproblem in several computer vision tasks. In this paper, we are concerned with the computation of three-dimensional structure and motion from point and line correspondences extracted from a rigid three-dimensional object of unknown shape, using the affine camera model.

Early works addressing this problem domain based on point correspondences from perspective and orthographic projection have been presented by (Ullman

---

[*] The support from the Swedish Research Council for Engineering Sciences, TFR, is gratefully acknowledged. Email: bretzner@nada.kth.se, tony@nada.kth.se

1979, Maybank 1992, Huang & Lee 1989, Huang & Netravali 1994) and others. With the introduction of the affine camera model (Koenderink & van Doorn 1991, Mundy & Zisserman 1992) a large number of approaches have been developed, including (Shapiro 1995, Beardsley et al. 1994, McLauchlan et al. 1994, Torr 1995) to mention just a few. Line correspondences have been studied by (Spetsakis & Aloimonos 1990, Weng et al. 1992), and factorization methods for points and lines constitute a particularly interesting development (Tomasi & Kanade 1992, Morita & Kanade 1997, Quan & Kanade 1997, Sturm & Triggs 1996). These directions of research have recently been combined with the ideas behind the fundamental matrix (Longuet-Higgins 1981, Faugeras 1992, Xu & Zhang 1997) and have lead to the trilinear tensor (Shashua 1995, Hartley 1995, Heyden 1995) as a unified model for point and line correspondences for three cameras, with interesting applications (Beardsley et al. 1996) as well as a deeper understanding of the relations between point features and line features over multiple views (Faugeras & Mourrain 1995, Heyden et al. 1997).

The subject of this paper is to build upon the abovementioned works, and to develop a framework for handling point and line features simultaneously for three or more affine views. Initially, we shall focus on image triplets and show how an *affine trifocal tensor* can be defined for three centered affine cameras. This tensor has a similar algebraic structure as the trilinear tensor for three perspective cameras. Compared to the trilinear tensor, however, it has the advantage that it contains a smaller number of coefficients, which implies that fewer feature correspondences are required to determine this tensor. It will also be shown that motion estimation from this tensor is more straightforward.

This theory will then be applied to the problem of computing changes in three-dimensional orientation from a sparse set of point and line correspondences. Specifically, it will be demonstrated how a straightforward man-machine interface for 3-D orientation interaction (Lindeberg & Bretzner 1998) can be designed based on the theory presented and using no other user equipment than the operator's own hand. For more details, see (Bretzner & Lindeberg 1998).

2 Geometric problem and extraction of image features

A specific application we are interested in is to measure changes in the orientation of a human hand, as a straightforward interface to transfer 3-D rotational information to a computer using no other user equipment than the operator's own hand. In contrast to previous approaches for human–computer interaction that are based on detailed geometric hand models (such as (Lee & Kunii 1995, Heap & Hogg 1996)) we shall here explore a model based on qualitative features only. This model involves the thumb, the index finger and the middle finger, and for each finger the position of the finger tip and the orientation of the finger are measured in the image domain. Successful tracking of these image features over time leads to three point correspondences and three line correspondences, and the task is to compute changes in the 3-D orientation of such a configuration, which is assumed to be rigid. It is worth noting that neither the trajectories of point features or line features *per se* are sufficient to compute the motion information we are interested in. The problem requires the combination of point and line features. Moreover, due to the small number of image features, the information is not sufficient to compute the trilinear tensor for perspective projection (see the next section). For this reason, we shall use an affine projection model, and the affine trifocal tensor will be a key tool.

The trajectories of image features used as input are extracted using a framework for feature tracking with automatic scale selection reported in (Bretzner & Lindeberg 1996, Bretzner & Lindeberg 1997). Blob features corresponding to the finger tips are computed from points $(x, y; t)$ in scale-space (Koenderink 1984, Lindeberg 1994) at which the squared normalized Laplacian

$$(\nabla^2_{norm} L)^2 = t^2 (L_{xx} + L_{yy})^2 \tag{1}$$

assumes maxima with respect to scale and space simultaneously (Lindeberg 1994). Such points are referred to as scale-space maxima of the normalized Laplacian. In a similar way, ridge features are detected from scale-space maxima of a normalized measure of ridge strength defined by (Lindeberg 1996)

$$\mathcal{AL}^2_{\gamma-norm} = t^{4\gamma} (L^2_{pp} - L^2_{qq})^2 = t^{4\gamma} \left((L_{xx} - L_{yy})^2 + 4L^2_{xy}\right)^2 , \tag{2}$$

where L_{pp} and L_{qq} are the eigenvalues of the Hessian matrix and the normalization parameter $\gamma = 0.875$. At each ridge feature, a windowed second moment matrix (Förstner & Gülch 1987, Bigün et al. 1991, Lindeberg 1994)

$$\mu = \int \int_{(\xi,\eta)\in\mathbb{R}^2} \begin{pmatrix} L^2_x & L_x L_y \\ L_x L_y & L^2_y \end{pmatrix} g(\xi, \eta; \ s) \, d\xi \, d\eta \tag{3}$$

is computed using a Gaussian window function $g(\cdot, \cdot; \ s)$ centered at the spatial maximum of $\mathcal{AL}_{\gamma-norm}$ and with the integration scale s tuned by the detection scale of the scale-space maximum of $\mathcal{AL}_{\gamma-norm}$. The eigenvector of μ corresponding to the largest eigenvalue gives the orientation of the finger.

The left column in figure 3 shows an example of image trajectories obtained in this way. An attractive property of this feature tracking scheme is that the scale selection mechanism adapts the scale levels to the local image structure. This gives the ability to track image features over large size variations, which is particularly important for the ridge tracker. Provided that the contrast to the background is sufficient, this scheme gives feature trajectories over large numbers of frames, using a conceptually very simple interframe matching mechanism.

3 The trifocal tensor for three centered affine cameras

To capture motion information from the projections of an unknown configuration of lines in 3-D, it is necessary to have at least three independent views. A canonical model for describing the geometric relationships between point correspondences and line correspondences over three perspective views is provided by the trilinear tensor (Shashua 1995, Shashua 1997, Hartley 1995, Heyden et al. 1997).

For affine cameras, a compact model of point correspondences over multiple frames can be obtained by factorizing a matrix with image measurements to the product of two matrices of rank 3, one representing motion, and the other one representing shape (Tomasi & Kanade 1992, Ullman & Basri 1991). Frameworks for capturing line correspondences over multiple affine views have been presented by (Quan & Kanade 1997) and for point features under perspective projection by (Sturm & Triggs 1996).

The subject of this section is to combine the idea behind the trilinear tensor for simultaneous modelling of point and line correspondences over three views with the affine projection model. It will be shown how an algebraic structure closely related to the trilinear tensor can be defined for three centered affine cameras. This *centered affine trifocal tensor* involves linear relations between the point features and trilinear relationships between the line features.

3.1 Perspective camera and three views

Consider a point $P = (x, y, 1, \lambda)^T$ which is projected by three camera matrices $M = [I, 0]$, $M' = [A, u']$ and $M'' = [B, u'']$ to the image points p, p' and p'':

$$
p = \begin{pmatrix} x \\ y \\ 1 \end{pmatrix} = \begin{pmatrix} 1 & 0 & 0 & 0 \\ 0 & 1 & 0 & 0 \\ 0 & 0 & 1 & 0 \end{pmatrix} \begin{pmatrix} x \\ y \\ 1 \\ \lambda \end{pmatrix},
\tag{4}
$$

$$
p' = \alpha \begin{pmatrix} x' \\ y' \\ 1 \end{pmatrix} = \begin{pmatrix} a_1^1 & a_2^1 & a_3^1 & u'^1 \\ a_1^2 & a_2^2 & a_3^2 & u'^2 \\ a_1^3 & a_2^3 & a_3^3 & u'^3 \end{pmatrix} \begin{pmatrix} x \\ y \\ 1 \\ \lambda \end{pmatrix} = \begin{pmatrix} a^{1^T} p + \lambda u'^1 \\ a^{2^T} p + \lambda u'^2 \\ a^{3^T} p + \lambda u'^3 \end{pmatrix},
\tag{5}
$$

$$
p'' = \beta \begin{pmatrix} x'' \\ y'' \\ 1 \end{pmatrix} = \begin{pmatrix} b_1^1 & b_2^1 & b_3^1 & u''^1 \\ b_1^2 & b_2^2 & b_3^2 & u''^2 \\ b_1^3 & b_2^3 & b_3^3 & u''^3 \end{pmatrix} \begin{pmatrix} x \\ y \\ 1 \\ \lambda \end{pmatrix} = \begin{pmatrix} b^{1^T} p + \lambda u''^1 \\ b^{2^T} p + \lambda u''^2 \\ b^{3^T} p + \lambda u''^3 \end{pmatrix}.
\tag{6}
$$

Following (Faugeras & Mourrain 1995) and (Shashua 1997), let us introduce the following two matrices

$$
r_j^\mu = \begin{pmatrix} -1 & 0 & x' \\ 0 & -1 & y' \end{pmatrix}, \qquad s_k^\nu = \begin{pmatrix} -1 & 0 & x'' \\ 0 & -1 & y'' \end{pmatrix}.
\tag{7}
$$

Then, in terms of tensor notation (where $i, j, k \in [1, 3]$, $\mu, \nu \in [1, 2]$ and we throughout follow the Einstein summation convention that a double occurrence of an index implies summation over that index) the relations between the image coordinates and the camera geometry can be written

$$
\lambda r_j^\mu u'^j + r_j^\mu a_i^j p^i = 0, \qquad \lambda s_k^\nu u''^k + s_k^\nu b_i^k p^i = 0.
\tag{8}
$$

By introducing the trifocal tensor (Shashua 1995, Hartley 1995)

$$
T_i^{jk} = a_i^j u''^k - b_i^k u'^j,
\tag{9}
$$

the relations between the point correspondences lead to the trifocal constraint

$$r_j^\mu s_k^\nu T_i^{jk} = 0. \tag{10}$$

Written out explicitly, this expression corresponds to the following four relations between the projections p, p' and p'' of P (Shashua 1997):

$$
\begin{aligned}
x''T_i^{13}p^i - x''x'T_i^{33}p^i + x'T_i^{31}p^i - T_i^{11}p^i &= 0, \\
y''T_i^{13}p^i - y''x'T_i^{33}p^i + x'T_i^{32}p^i - T_i^{12}p^i &= 0, \\
x''T_i^{23}p^i - x''y'T_i^{33}p^i + y'T_i^{31}p^i - T_i^{21}p^i &= 0, \\
y''T_i^{23}p^i - y''y'T_i^{33}p^i + y'T_i^{32}p^i - T_i^{22}p^i &= 0.
\end{aligned}
\tag{11}
$$

Given three corresponding lines, $l^T p = 0$, $l'^T p' = 0$ and $l''^T p'' = 0$, each image line defines a plane through the center of projection, given by $L^T P = 0$, $L'^T P = 0$ and $L''^T P = 0$, where

$$
\begin{aligned}
L^T &= l^T M = (l_1, l_2, l_3\, 0), \\
L'^T &= l'^T M' = (l'_j a_1^j, l'_j a_2^j, l'_j a_3^j, l'_j u'^j), \\
L''^T &= l''^T M'' = (l''_k b_1^k, l''_k b_2^k, l''_k b_3^k, l''_k u''^k).
\end{aligned}
\tag{12}
$$

Since l, l' and l'' are assumed to be projections of the same three-dimensional line, the intersection of the planes L, L' and L'' must degenerate to a line and

$$
\text{rank}
\begin{pmatrix}
l_1 & l'_j a_1^j & l''_k b_1^k \\
l_2 & l'_j a_2^j & l''_k b_2^k \\
l_3 & l'_j a_3^j & l''_k b_3^k \\
0 & l'_j u'^j & l''_k u''^k
\end{pmatrix}
= 2.
\tag{13}
$$

All 3×3 minors must be zero, and removal of the three first lines respectively, leads to the following trilinear relationships, out of which two are independent:

$$
\begin{aligned}
(l_2 T_3^{jk} - l_3 T_2^{jk}) l'_j l''_k &= 0, \\
(l_1 T_3^{jk} - l_3 T_1^{jk}) l'_j l''_k &= 0, \\
(l_1 T_2^{jk} - l_2 T_1^{jk}) l'_j l''_k &= 0.
\end{aligned}
\tag{14}
$$

These expressions provide a compact characterization of the trilinear line relations first introduced by (Spetsakis & Aloimonos 1990).

In summary, each point correspondence gives four equations, and each line correspondence two. Hence, K points and L lines are (generically) sufficient to express a linear algorithm for computing the trilinear tensor (up to scale) if $4K + 2L \geq 26$ (Shashua 1995, Hartley 1995).

3.2 Affine camera and three views

Consider next a point $Q = (x, y, \lambda, 1)^T$ which is projected to the image points q, q' and q'' by three affine camera matrices M, M' and M'', respectively:

$$q = \begin{pmatrix} x \\ y \\ 1 \end{pmatrix} = MQ = \begin{pmatrix} 1 & 0 & 0 & 0 \\ 0 & 1 & 0 & 0 \\ 0 & 0 & 0 & 1 \end{pmatrix} \begin{pmatrix} x \\ y \\ \lambda \\ 1 \end{pmatrix}, \tag{15}$$

$$q' = \begin{pmatrix} x' \\ y' \\ 1 \end{pmatrix} = M'Q = \begin{pmatrix} c_1^1 & c_2^1 & c_3^1 & v'^1 \\ c_1^2 & c_2^2 & c_3^2 & v'^2 \\ 0 & 0 & 0 & 1 \end{pmatrix} \begin{pmatrix} x \\ y \\ \lambda \\ 1 \end{pmatrix}, \tag{16}$$

$$q'' = \begin{pmatrix} x'' \\ y'' \\ 1 \end{pmatrix} = M''Q = \begin{pmatrix} d_1^1 & d_2^1 & d_3^1 & v''^1 \\ d_1^2 & d_2^2 & d_3^2 & v''^2 \\ 0 & 0 & 0 & 1 \end{pmatrix} \begin{pmatrix} x \\ y \\ \lambda \\ 1 \end{pmatrix}. \tag{17}$$

Here, the parameterization of Q differs from P, since for an image point $q = (x, y, 1)^T$ the projection (15) implies that the three-dimensional point is on the ray $Q = (x, y, \lambda, 1)^T$ for some λ. By eliminating λ, we obtain the following linear relationships between the image coordinates of q, q' and q'':

$$
\begin{aligned}
(c_3^1 d_1^1 - c_1^1 d_3^1)x + (c_3^1 d_2^1 - c_2^1 d_3^1)y + d_3^1 x' - c_3^1 x'' + (c_3^1 v''^1 - d_3^1 v'^1) &= 0, \\
(c_3^1 d_1^1 - c_1^2 d_3^1)x + (c_3^1 d_2^1 - c_2^2 d_3^1)y + d_3^1 y' - c_3^2 x'' + (c_3^2 v''^1 - d_3^1 v'^2) &= 0, \\
(c_3^2 d_1^2 - c_1^1 d_3^2)x + (c_3^1 d_2^2 - c_2^1 d_3^2)y + d_3^2 x' - c_3^1 y'' + (c_3^1 v''^2 - d_3^2 v'^2) &= 0, \\
(c_3^2 d_1^2 - c_1^2 d_3^2)x + (c_3^2 d_2^2 - c_2^2 d_3^2)y + d_3^2 y' - c_3^2 y'' + (c_3^2 v''^2 - d_3^2 v'^2) &= 0.
\end{aligned}
\tag{18}
$$

This structure corresponds to the trilinear constraint (11) for perspective projection, and we shall refer to it as the affine trifocal point constraint.

Three lines $l^T q = 0$, $l'^T q' = 0$ and $l''^T q'' = 0$ in the three images define three planes $L^T Q = 0$, $L'^T Q = 0$ and $L''^T Q = 0$ in three-dimensional space with

$$L^T = l^T M = (l_1, l_2, 0, l_3),$$

$$L'^T = l'^T M' = (l'_1 c_1^1 + l'_2 c_1^2, \; l'_1 c_2^1 + l'_2 c_2^2, \; l'_1 c_3^1 + l'_2 c_3^2, \; l'_1 v'^1 + l'_2 v'^2 + l'_3),$$

$$L'^T = l''^T M'' = (l''_1 d_1^1 + l''_2 d_1^2, \; l''_1 d_2^1 + l''_2 d_2^2, \; l''_1 d_3^1 + l''_2 d_3^2, \; l''_1 v''^1 + l''_2 v''^2 + l''_3).$$

Since l, l' and l'' are projections of the same three-dimensional line, the intersection of L, L' and L'' must degenerate to a line and

$$
\text{rank} \begin{vmatrix}
l_1 & l'_1 c_1^1 + l'_2 c_1^2 & l''_1 d_1^1 + l''_2 d_1^2 \\
l_2 & l'_1 c_2^1 + l'_2 c_2^2 & l''_1 d_2^1 + l''_2 d_2^2 \\
0 & l'_1 c_3^1 + l'_2 c_3^2 & l''_1 d_3^1 + l''_2 d_3^2 \\
l_3 & l'_1 v'^1 + l'_2 v'^2 + l'_3 & l''_1 v''^1 + l''_2 v''^2 + l''_3
\end{vmatrix} = 2. \tag{19}
$$

All 3×3 minors must be zero, and deletion of the first, second and fourth rows, respectively, results in the following relationships between l, l' and l'':

$$
\begin{aligned}
l_2 \, (c_3^j v''^k - d_3^k v'^j) \, l_j' l_k'' - l_3 \, (c_3^j d_2^k - c_2^j d_3^k) \, l_j' l_k'' &= 0, \\
l_1 \, (c_3^j v''^k - d_3^k v'^j) \, l_j' l_k'' - l_3 \, (c_3^j d_1^k - c_1^j d_3^k) \, l_j' l_k'' &= 0, \\
l_1 \, (c_2^j d_3^k - c_3^j d_2^k) \, l_j' l_k'' - l_2 \, (c_1^j d_3^k - c_3^j d_1^k) \, l_j' l_k'' &= 0,
\end{aligned}
\tag{20}
$$

where $c_j^3 = d_k^3 = 0$, $v'^3 = v''^3 = 1$ and only two of the relations are independent.

This treatment, which largely derives similar results as (Torr 1995) while using another formalism, shows that point and line correspondences are captured by 16 coefficients. Each point correspondence gives four equations, and each line correspondence two. Thus, K point correspondences and L line correspondences are sufficient to compute this *affine trifocal tensor* (up to scale) if $4K + 2L \geq 15$.

3.3 The centered affine camera and its relations to perspective

Let us next consider the case when image coordinates in the affine camera are measured relative to the center of gravity of a point configuration. This centered affine camera is obtained by setting $(v'^1, v'^2) = (v''^1, v''^2) = (0,0)$ in (16) and (17) and corresponds to disregarding the translational motion. Then, the expressions (18) and (20) for the point and line correspondences reduce to:

$$
\begin{aligned}
(c_3^1 d_1^1 - c_1^1 d_3^1)x + (c_3^1 d_2^1 - c_2^1 d_3^1)y + d_3^1 x' - c_3^1 x'' &= 0, \\
(c_3^2 d_1^1 - c_1^2 d_3^1)x + (c_3^2 d_2^1 - c_2^2 d_3^1)y + d_3^1 y' - c_3^2 x'' &= 0, \\
(c_3^1 d_1^2 - c_1^1 d_3^2)x + (c_3^1 d_2^2 - c_2^1 d_3^2)y + d_3^2 x' - c_3^1 y'' &= 0, \\
(c_3^2 d_1^2 - c_1^2 d_3^2)x + (c_3^2 d_2^2 - c_2^2 d_3^2)y + d_3^2 y' - c_3^2 y'' &= 0, \\
l_1(l_j' c_3^j)l_3'' - l_1 l_3'(l_k'' d_3^k) + l_3(l_j' c_1^j)(l_k'' d_3^k) - l_3(l_j' c_3^j)(l_k'' d_1^k) &= 0, \\
l_2(l_j' c_3^j)l_3'' - l_2 l_3'(l_k'' d_3^k) + l_3(l_j' c_2^j)(l_k'' d_3^k) - l_3(l_j' c_3^j)(l_k'' d_2^k) &= 0, \\
l_1(l_j' c_2^j)(l_k'' d_3^k) - l_1(l_j' c_3^j)(l_k'' d_2^k) + l_2(l_j' c_3^j)(l_k'' d_1^k) - (l_j' c_1^j)(l_k'' d_3^k) &= 0.
\end{aligned}
\tag{21}
$$

Structurally, there is a strong similarity between these relationships for the centered affine camera and the corresponding relationships (11) and (14) for the perspective camera. Let us make the following formal replacements between the affine camera model (15)–(17) and the perspective camera model (4)–(6):

– Interchange rows 3 and 4 in the coordinate vectors in the 3-D domain:

$$
Q = (x, y, \lambda, 1)^T \quad \Rightarrow \quad P = (x, y, 1, \lambda)^T,
\tag{22}
$$

– Interchange columns 3 and 4 in the camera matrices:

$$
\begin{pmatrix}
a_1^1 & a_2^1 & a_3^1 & u'^1 \\
a_1^2 & a_2^2 & a_3^2 & u'^2 \\
a_1^3 & a_2^3 & a_3^3 & u'^3
\end{pmatrix}
=
\begin{pmatrix}
c_1^1 & c_2^1 & 0 & c_3^1 \\
c_1^2 & c_2^2 & 0 & c_3^2 \\
0 & 0 & 0 & 1
\end{pmatrix},
\quad
\begin{pmatrix}
b_1^1 & b_2^1 & b_3^1 & u''^1 \\
b_1^2 & b_2^2 & b_3^2 & u''^2 \\
b_1^3 & b_2^3 & b_3^3 & u''^3
\end{pmatrix}
=
\begin{pmatrix}
d_1^1 & d_2^1 & 0 & d_3^1 \\
d_1^2 & d_2^2 & 0 & d_3^2 \\
0 & 0 & 0 & 1
\end{pmatrix}.
\tag{23}
$$

Then, the algebraic structure between corresponding points and lines will be the same for the two projection models. This implies that the relations between point and line correspondences in (21) for three centered cameras can be expressed on the form (11) and (14) with the *centered affine trifocal tensor* defined by

$$T_i^{jk} = a_i^j u''^k - b_i^k u'^j = \{(23)\} = c_i^j d_3^k - d_i^k c_3^j. \tag{24}$$

Written out explicitly, the components of T_i^{jk} are given by

$$
\begin{array}{llll}
T_1^{11} = c_1^1 d_3^1 - d_1^1 c_3^1, & T_1^{12} = c_1^1 d_3^2 - d_1^2 c_3^1, & T_1^{13} = c_1^1 d_3^3 - d_1^3 c_3^1 & = 0, \\
T_1^{21} = c_1^2 d_3^1 - d_1^1 c_3^2, & T_1^{22} = c_1^2 d_3^2 - d_1^2 c_3^2, & T_1^{23} = c_1^2 d_3^3 - d_1^3 c_3^2 & = 0, \\
T_1^{31} = c_1^3 d_3^1 - d_1^1 c_3^3 = 0, & T_1^{32} = c_1^3 d_3^2 - d_1^2 c_3^3 = 0, & T_1^{33} = c_1^3 d_3^3 - d_1^3 c_3^3 & = 0, \\
T_2^{11} = c_1^1 d_3^1 - d_1^1 c_3^1, & T_2^{12} = c_1^1 d_3^2 - d_1^2 c_3^1, & T_2^{13} = c_1^1 d_3^3 - d_1^3 c_3^1 & = 0, \\
T_2^{21} = c_1^2 d_3^1 - d_1^1 c_3^2, & T_2^{22} = c_1^2 d_3^2 - d_1^2 c_3^2, & T_2^{23} = c_1^2 d_3^3 - d_1^3 c_3^2 & = 0, \\
T_2^{31} = c_1^3 d_3^1 - d_1^1 c_3^3 = 0, & T_2^{32} = c_1^3 d_3^2 - d_1^2 c_3^3 = 0, & T_2^{33} = c_1^3 d_3^3 - d_1^3 c_3^3 & = 0, \\
T_3^{11} = c_1^1 d_3^1 - d_1^1 c_3^1 = 0, & T_3^{12} = c_1^1 d_3^2 - d_1^2 c_3^1 = 0, & T_3^{13} = c_1^1 d_3^3 - d_1^3 c_3^1 = -c_3^1, \\
T_3^{21} = c_1^2 d_3^1 - d_1^1 c_3^2 = 0, & T_3^{22} = c_1^2 d_3^2 - d_1^2 c_3^2 = 0, & T_3^{23} = c_1^2 d_3^3 - d_1^3 c_3^2 = -c_3^2, \\
T_3^{31} = c_1^3 d_3^1 - d_1^1 c_3^3 = d_3^1, & T_3^{32} = c_1^3 d_3^2 - d_1^2 c_3^3 = d_3^2, & T_3^{33} = c_1^3 d_3^3 - d_1^3 c_3^3 & = 0, \quad (25)
\end{array}
$$

and the relations between point and line correspondences in (21) can be written

$$
\begin{aligned}
T_3^{13} x'' + T_3^{31} x' - T_1^{11} x - T_2^{11} y &= 0, \\
T_3^{13} y'' + T_3^{32} x' - T_1^{12} x - T_2^{12} y &= 0, \\
T_3^{23} x'' + T_3^{31} y' - T_1^{21} x - T_2^{21} y &= 0, \\
T_3^{23} y'' + T_3^{32} y' - T_1^{22} x - T_2^{22} y &= 0,
\end{aligned} \tag{26}
$$

$$
\begin{aligned}
l_3(l_1' l_1'' T_1^{11} + l_1' l_2'' T_1^{12} + l_2' l_1'' T_1^{21} + l_2' l_2'' T_1^{22}) & \\
- l_1(l_1' l_3'' T_3^{13} + l_2' l_3'' T_3^{23} + l_3' l_1'' T_3^{31} + l_3' l_2'' T_3^{32}) &= 0, \\
l_3(l_1' l_1'' T_2^{11} + l_1' l_2'' T_2^{12} + l_2' l_1'' T_2^{21} + l_2' l_2'' T_2^{22}) & \\
- l_2(l_1' l_3'' T_3^{13} + l_2' l_3'' T_3^{23} + l_3' l_1'' T_3^{31} + l_3' l_2'' T_3^{32}) &= 0.
\end{aligned} \tag{27}
$$

The centered affine trifocal tensor has 12 non-zero entries. Due to the centering of the equations, one point correspondence is redundant. Thus, K point correspondences and L line correspondences are (generically) sufficient to compute T_i^{jk} (up to scale) provided that $4(K - 1) + 2L \geq 11$.

4 Orientation from the centered affine trifocal tensor

To compute the camera parameters from the affine trifocal tensor, we largely follow the approach that (Hartley 1995) uses for three perspective cameras. The calculations can, however, be simplified with affine cameras. From (25) we directly get

$$c_3^1 = -T_3^{13}, \qquad d_3^1 = T_3^{31}, \qquad c_3^2 = -T_3^{23}, \qquad d_3^2 = T_3^{32}. \tag{28}$$

Given these c_3^j and d_3^k, the remaining c_i^j and d_i^k can be computed from (25) using

$$\begin{pmatrix} d_3^1 & & & & -c_3^1 & & & \\ d_3^2 & & & & & -c_3^1 & & \\ & d_3^1 & & & -c_3^2 & & & \\ & d_3^2 & & & & -c_3^2 & & \\ & & d_3^1 & & & & -c_3^1 & \\ & & d_3^2 & & & & & -c_3^1 \\ & & & d_3^1 & & & -c_3^2 & \\ & & & d_3^2 & & & & -c_3^2 \end{pmatrix} \begin{pmatrix} c_1^1 \\ c_1^2 \\ c_2^1 \\ c_2^2 \\ d_1^1 \\ d_1^2 \\ d_2^1 \\ d_2^2 \end{pmatrix} = \begin{pmatrix} T_1^{11} \\ T_1^{12} \\ T_1^{21} \\ T_1^{22} \\ T_2^{11} \\ T_2^{12} \\ T_2^{21} \\ T_2^{22} \end{pmatrix}. \tag{29}$$

The camera matrices are, however, not uniquely determined. The centered affine trifocal tensor T_i^{jk} in (24) is invariant under transformations of the type

$$\tilde{c}_i^j = c_i^j + \gamma_i c_3^j, \qquad \tilde{d}_i^k = d_i^k + \gamma_i d_3^k. \tag{30}$$

With N' and N'' denoting the upper left 2×3 submatrices of M' and M'' respectively, this ambiguity implies that both $\{\tilde{N}', \tilde{N}''\}$ and $\{N', N''\}$ are possible solutions (with $\tilde{N}''$ analogously)

$$\tilde{N}' = \begin{pmatrix} \tilde{c}_1^1 & \tilde{c}_2^1 & \tilde{c}_3^1 \\ \tilde{c}_1^2 & \tilde{c}_2^2 & \tilde{c}_3^2 \end{pmatrix} = \begin{pmatrix} c_1^1 & c_2^1 & c_3^1 \\ c_1^2 & c_2^2 & c_3^2 \end{pmatrix} \begin{pmatrix} 1 & & \\ & 1 & \\ \gamma_1 & \gamma_2 & \gamma_3 \end{pmatrix} = N' \Gamma. \tag{31}$$

To determine Γ, let us assume that the affine camera model corresponds to scaled orthographic projection, and that internal calibration is available. Then, the camera matrices can be written (with $\tilde{N}''$ analogously)

$$\tilde{N}' = \sigma' \begin{pmatrix} 1 & 0 & 0 \\ 0 & 1 & 0 \end{pmatrix} \qquad R' = \sigma' \begin{pmatrix} \rho'^1_1 & \rho'^1_2 & \rho'^1_3 \\ \rho'^2_1 & \rho'^2_2 & \rho'^2_3 \end{pmatrix}, \tag{32}$$

where $\rho'^{jT} = (\rho'^j_1, \rho'^j_2, \rho'^j_3)$ are the row vectors in the three-dimensional rotation matrix R', while σ' is a scaling factor. Since the rows of R' are orthogonal, $\rho_i'^{jT} \rho_i'^k = \delta_{jk}$, where δ_{jk} is the Kronecker delta symbol, we have

$$\tilde{N}' \tilde{N}'^T = N' \Gamma \Gamma^T N'^T = (\sigma')^2 I_{2 \times 2}, \tag{33}$$

where $I_{2 \times 2}$ represents a unit matrix of size 2×2. With

$$\Gamma \Gamma^T = \begin{pmatrix} 1 & 0 & \gamma_1 \\ 1 & 0 & \gamma_2 \\ \gamma_1 & \gamma_2 & \gamma_1^2 + \gamma_2^2 + \gamma_3^2 \end{pmatrix} = \begin{pmatrix} 1 & 0 & \xi \\ 0 & 1 & \eta \\ \xi & \eta & \zeta \end{pmatrix} \tag{34}$$

we rewrite (33) as

$$
\begin{pmatrix}
2c_1^1 c_3^1 & 2c_2^1 c_3^1 & (c_3^1)^2 & -1 & 0 \\
c_1^1 c_3^2 + c_3^1 c_1^2 & c_2^1 c_3^2 + c_3^1 c_2^2 & c_3^1 c_3^2 & 0 & 0 \\
2c_1^2 c_3^2 & 2c_2^2 c_3^2 & (c_3^2)^2 & -1 & 0 \\
2d_1^1 d_3^1 & 2d_2^1 d_3^1 & (d_3^1)^2 & 0 & -1 \\
d_1^1 d_3^2 + d_3^1 d_1^2 & d_2^1 d_3^2 + d_3^1 d_2^2 & d_3^1 d_3^2 & 0 & 0 \\
2d_1^2 d_3^2 & 2d_2^2 d_3^2 & (d_3^2)^2 & 0 & -1
\end{pmatrix}
\begin{pmatrix}
\xi \\ \eta \\ \zeta \\ (\sigma')^2 \\ (\sigma'')^2
\end{pmatrix}
= -
\begin{pmatrix}
(c_1^1)^2 + (c_2^1)^2 \\
c_1^1 c_1^2 + c_2^1 c_2^2 \\
(c_1^2)^2 + (c_2^2)^2 \\
(d_1^1)^2 + (d_2^1)^2 \\
d_1^1 d_1^2 + d_2^1 d_2^2 \\
(d_1^2)^2 + (d_2^2)^2
\end{pmatrix}.
$$

$$(35)$$

Solving this system of equations in the least squares sense gives $(\xi, \eta, \zeta, (\sigma')^2, (\sigma'')^2)$ as function of c_i^j and d_i^k determined from (28) and (29). Then, Γ is given by

$$
\Gamma =
\begin{pmatrix}
1 & 0 & 0 \\
0 & 1 & 0 \\
\gamma_1 & \gamma_2 & \gamma_3
\end{pmatrix}
=
\begin{pmatrix}
1 & 0 & 0 \\
0 & 1 & 0 \\
\xi & \eta & \pm\sqrt{\zeta - \xi^2 - \eta^2}
\end{pmatrix},
$$

$$(36)$$

and we estimate the first two rows of R' in (32) by $\tilde{N}' = \sigma' N' \Gamma$. The third row is then easily obtained as the cross product of the first two rows: $\rho'^3 = \rho'^1 \times \rho'^2$. The ambiguity in the determination of γ_3 in Γ corresponds to a sign change in the last component of the first two rows of R' and R'', and a corresponding sign change in the last row, i.e., the following solutions:

$$
\rho =
\begin{pmatrix}
\rho_1^1 & \rho_2^1 & \rho_3^1 \\
\rho_1^2 & \rho_2^2 & \rho_3^2 \\
\rho_1^3 & \rho_2^3 & \rho_3^3
\end{pmatrix},
\qquad
\bar{\rho} =
\begin{pmatrix}
\rho_1^1 & \rho_2^1 & -\rho_3^1 \\
\rho_1^2 & \rho_2^2 & -\rho_3^2 \\
-\rho_1^3 & -\rho_2^3 & \rho_3^3
\end{pmatrix}.
$$

$$(37)$$

This ambiguity reflects the fact that for scaled orthographic projection we cannot distinguish between positive rotation of a point in front of the center of rotation and negative rotation of a similar point behind the center of rotation. To choose between the two possible solutions, we can either assume similarity between adjacent rotations, or use the size variations of the tracked image features.

The matrices obtained from (37) depend upon Γ and $(\xi, \eta, \zeta, (\sigma')^2, (\sigma'')^2)$ and are not guaranteed to be orthogonal matrices, since $(\xi, \eta, \zeta, (\sigma')^2, (\sigma'')^2)$ is computed from an overdetermined system of equations. Given an estimate ρ of the rotation matrix R, a singular value decomposition is carried out of ρ, and R is determined from $\rho = U\Sigma V^T$, which gives $R = UV^T$. This choice minimizes the difference between ρ and R in the Frobenius norm.

5 Joint factorization of point and line correspondences

The treatment so far shows how changes in the orientation of an unknown three-dimensional point and line configuration can be computed from three affine views. To derive corresponding motion descriptors from time sequences, we shall in this section develop a factorization approach, which treats point features and line features together. In this way, we shall combine several of the ideas in the factorization methods for either point features or line features (Tomasi & Kanade 1992, Quan & Kanade 1997, Sturm & Triggs 1996). It should be noticed, however, that the main intention here is not to separate the motion information from structural information a priori as in (Tomasi & Kanade 1992). The goal is to exploit the redundancy between point features and line features over multiple frames, and to avoid the degenerate cases that are likely to occur if we compute three-dimensional motion using image triplets only.

Let us introduce a slightly different notion (and do away with the Einstein summation convention). The centered affine projection of a three-dimensional point $P_k = (X_k, Y_k, Z_k)^T$ in image n shall be written

$$\begin{pmatrix} x_k^n \\ y_k^n \end{pmatrix} = M^n P_k = \begin{pmatrix} - \alpha^{nT} - \\ - \beta^{nT} - \end{pmatrix} \begin{pmatrix} X_k \\ Y_k \\ Z_k \end{pmatrix}, \tag{38}$$

while the (centered) affine projection of a line $P_l = (X_{l,0}, Y_{l,0}, Z_{0,l})^T + \tau(U_l, V_l, W_l)^T = P_{l,0} + \tau Q_l$ in image n shall be represented by the directional vector

$$\lambda_l^n \begin{pmatrix} u_l^n \\ v_k^n \end{pmatrix} = M^n Q_l = \begin{pmatrix} - \alpha^{nT} - \\ - \beta^{nT} - \end{pmatrix} \begin{pmatrix} U_l \\ V_l \\ W_l \end{pmatrix}, \tag{39}$$

where the suppression of $(X_{l,0}, Y_{l,0}, Z_{0,l})^T$ and the introduction of the scale factor λ_l^n account for the fact that the position of the line is unimportant, the length of (u_l^n, v_k^n) is unknown, and only the orientation of the line is significant.

Given K point correspondences and L line correspondences over N image frames, we model these measurements together by a matrix G

$$\begin{pmatrix} x_1^1 & \cdots & x_K^1 & \lambda_1^1 u_1^1 & \cdots & \lambda_L^1 u_L^1 \\ y_1^1 & \cdots & y_K^1 & \lambda_1^1 v_1^1 & \cdots & \lambda_L^1 v_L^1 \\ \vdots & & \vdots & \vdots & & \vdots \\ x_1^N & \cdots & x_K^N & \lambda_1^N u_1^N & \cdots & \lambda_L^N u_L^N \\ y_1^N & \cdots & y_K^N & \lambda_1^N v_1^N & \cdots & \lambda_L^N v_L^N \end{pmatrix} = \begin{pmatrix} - \alpha^{1T} - \\ - \beta^{1T} - \\ \vdots \\ - \alpha^{NT} - \\ - \beta^{NT} - \end{pmatrix} \begin{pmatrix} X_1 & \cdots & X_K & U_1 & \cdots & U_L \\ Y_1 & \cdots & Y_K & V_1 & \cdots & V_L \\ Z_1 & \cdots & Z_K & W_1 & \cdots & W_L \end{pmatrix}. \tag{40}$$

Since the rank of the matrices on the right hand side is maximally three, it follows that any 4×4-minor must be zero, and we can, for example, form selections of $k, k', k'' \in [1..K]$, $l \in [1..L]$ and $n, n' \in [1..N]$, with

$$\begin{vmatrix} x_k^n & x_{k'}^n & x_{k''}^n & \lambda_l^n u_l^n \\ y_k^n & y_{k'}^n & y_{k''}^n & \lambda_l^n v_l^n \\ x_k^{n'} & x_{k'}^{n'} & x_{k''}^{n'} & \lambda_l^{n'} u_l^{n'} \\ y_k^{n'} & y_{k'}^{n'} & x_{k''}^{n'} & \lambda_l^{n'} v_l^{n'} \end{vmatrix} = 0. \tag{41}$$

If we would have $K \geq 4$ point correspondences, this would give us up to $\binom{K}{3}\binom{N}{2}L$ linear relationships, out of which a subset could be selected for determining the scale factors λ_l^n from an overdetermined system of homogeneous linear equations. Approaches closely related to this have been applied to line features by (Quan & Kanade 1997) and to point features by (Sturm & Triggs 1996).

Given only three points, however, as in our test problem, these linear relationships degenerate, since any minor with $K = 3$ point features is zero (due to centering, all the K points together will be linearly dependent).

To determine λ_l^n (totally NL scaling factors) in this case, we instead apply the affine trifocal tensor to a set of randomly selected triplets of image frames as a preprocessing stage. In analogy with (Quan & Kanade 1997) let us for each such triplet $n, n', n'' \in [1..N]$, insert the following shape matrix

$$\begin{pmatrix} X_1 & X_2 & X_3 \\ Y_1 & Y_2 & Y_3 \\ Z_1 & Z_2 & Z_3 \end{pmatrix} = \begin{pmatrix} 1 & 0 & 0 \\ 0 & 1 & 0 \\ 0 & 0 & 1 \end{pmatrix} \tag{42}$$

into the projection equation (40) for $K = 3$ point features:

$$H^{n,n',n''} = \begin{pmatrix} - & \alpha^{nT} & - & \lambda_1^n u_1^n & \dots & \lambda_L^n u_L^n \\ - & \beta^{nT} & - & \lambda_1^n v_1^n & \dots & \lambda_L^n v_L^n \\ - & \alpha^{n'T} & - & \lambda_1^{n'} u_1^{n'} & \dots & \lambda_L^{n'} u_L^{n'} \\ - & \beta^{n'T} & - & \lambda_1^{n'} v_1^{n'} & \dots & \lambda_L^{n'} v_L^{n'} \\ - & \alpha^{n''T} & - & \lambda_1^{n''} u_1^{n''} & \dots & \lambda_L^{n''} u_L^{n''} \\ - & \beta^{n''T} & - & \lambda_1^{n''} v_1^{n''} & \dots & \lambda_L^{n''} v_L^{n''} \end{pmatrix}. \tag{43}$$

Then, since the rank of the right hand side in (40) is maximally three, it follows that any 4×4-minor of this matrix must be zero. For each line feature $l \in [1..L]$, we consider three algebraically independent minors. Given three camera matrices M^n, $M^{n'}$ and $M^{n''}$, these minors define three homogeneous linear relations between λ_l^n, $\lambda_l^{n'}$ and $\lambda_l^{n''}$ for each $l \in [1..L]$. The camera matrices for stating these relations are determined by computing the trifocal tensor for the corresponding triplets of image features as described in section 4.

From a set of such (randomly selected) triplets, we then for each l define a homogeneous system of equations of the following type for determining λ_l^n:

$$D_l \Lambda_l = \begin{pmatrix} * & \dots & * \\ \vdots & \ddots & \vdots \\ * & \dots & * \end{pmatrix} \begin{pmatrix} \lambda_l^1 \\ \vdots \\ \lambda_l^N \end{pmatrix} = \begin{pmatrix} 0 \\ \vdots \\ 0 \end{pmatrix}.$$

Three consecutive rows in D_l correspond to one image triplet, and the entries in the matrix D_l have just been indicated by '∗' symbols. In practice, we let the number of triplets be substantially larger than the number of image frames (by a factor from 2 to 4). Moreover, a ranking of the image triplets is carried out based on sorting and thresholding with respect to a condition number.

Then, Λ_l is determined from the overconstrained system of equations using a singular value decomposition of D_l:

$$D_l = U_l \Sigma_l V_l^T \quad \Rightarrow \quad \Lambda_l = \text{the last row of } V_l. \tag{44}$$

The λ_l^n values are inserted into G in (40) and a singular value decomposition is computed $G = U_G \Sigma_G V_G^T$. All elements except the three first ones in Σ_G are set to zero to reduce the rank to three, and finally the ambiguity in the separation of motion information from structure information $G = MS = \hat{M}LL^{-1}\hat{S}$ is resolved in a similar fashion as in (Tomasi & Kanade 1992, Quan & Kanade 1997).

6 Experiments

To investigate the properties of this framework for computing relative orientation, let us first apply it to synthetic data, which will be generated by the following procedure: A three-dimensional point and line model is generated from three lines and three points with the approximate shape of the thumb, the index finger and the middle finger of a hand. This configuration is subjected to a smooth rotation, where the mean of the three directional vectors rotates by $\Delta\phi \approx 2$ degrees between each frame, while the configuration also rotates by $\Delta\psi \approx 2$ degrees per frame around this moving axis. For each frame, an affine projection is computed involving variations in scale and translation. White Gaussian noise with zero mean and standard deviation Σ is added to the image projections, where s is determined from a noise level ν according to $s = \nu D/2$ and D is the diameter of the circle that interpolates the three (undistorted) image points.

The difference between the orientation estimates and the true orientation is measured in the following ways: (i) the Frobenius norm of the difference between the true and the estimated rotation matrix, (ii) two geometric angles defined as follows: θ is the angle between the true and the estimate rotation axis (this rotation axis is the real eigenvector of the rotation matrix), and ϕ is the difference between the estimated and the real rotation around this rotation axis.

Figure 1 shows the result of estimating rotations from these point and line features using the affine trifocal tensor applied to triplets of frames only. The distance between adjacent frames varies from $\Delta n = 2$ to 20 frames, and all results are average values over 10 experiments.

Figure 2 shows a corresponding evaluation of the joint factorization approach. Here, the error is shown as function of the number of frames for computing the

Noise level	Error measure in 3-D			Noise level	Error measure in 3-D		
$\nu = 0.002$	Frobenius	θ	ϕ	$\nu = 0.005$	Frobenius	θ	ϕ
$\Delta n = 2$	0.22	31.00	5.92	$\Delta n = 2$	0.27	48.74	6.18
$\Delta n = 5$	0.39	20.35	13.15	$\Delta n = 5$	0.50	35.33	17.18
$\Delta n = 10$	0.11	2.69	3.35	$\Delta n = 10$	0.29	11.58	8.85
$\Delta n = 20$	0.02	0.46	0.30	$\Delta n = 20$	0.08	1.58	1.30

Fig. 1: Experimental evaluation of the noise sensitivity when computing 3-D orientation estimates by determining the affine trifocal tensor from three point correspondences and three line correspondences over three affine views. From left to right, the tables show the following error measures: (left) the Frobenius norm, (middle) the rotation axis θ, and (right) the rotation angle ϕ. The results are shown for two noise levels.

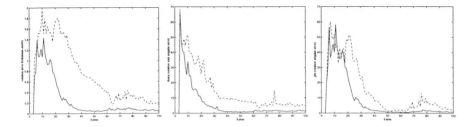

Fig. 2: Experimental evaluation of the noise sensitivity when computing 3-D orientation using the joint factorization of point features and line features. From left to right, the graphs how the following error measures depend on the number of frames: (left) the Frobenius norm, (middle) the rotation axis θ, and (right) the rotation angle ϕ. Three curves are shown in each graph, for noise levels $\nu = 0.002$ and 0.005, respectively.

factorization. (The results are averages over 8 experiments with incremental computations.) As expected, the error decreases with the number of image frames.

Finally, figure 3 shows the result of computing corresponding estimates by applying the joint factorization approach to the feature trajectories obtained by tracking blob and ridge features of a human hand as described in section 2. Here, since no ground truth is available, the result is illustrated by subjecting a synthetic cube to the rotation estimates computed from the feature trajectories.

7   Summary and discussion

We have presented a framework for capturing point and line correspondences over multiple affine views. This framework is closely connected to and builds upon several previous works concerning the affine projection model (Koenderink & van Doorn 1991, Mundy & Zisserman 1992, Shapiro 1995, Faugeras 1995), perspective point correspondences (Ullman 1979, Huang & Netravali 1994) and line correspondences (Spetsakis & Aloimonos 1990, Weng et al. 1992) as can be modelled by the trilinear tensor (Shashua 1995, Hartley 1995, Faugeras & Mourrain 1995, Shashua 1997). It also builds upon factorization approaches for affine (Tomasi & Kanade 1992, Quan & Kanade 1997, Morita & Kanade 1997) and perspective (Sturm & Triggs 1996) projection.

We propose that the (centered) affine trifocal tensor constitutes a canonical tool to model point and line correspondences in triplets of affine views (section 3). This extends the advances by (Torr 1995) as well as the abovementioned works, and we show how the trifocal affine tensor relates to the perspective trilinear tensor. Indeed, the algebraic structure of the affine trifocal tensor can be mapped to the algebraic structure of the perspective trilinear tensor. The centered affine trifocal tensor makes it possible to explore sparse sets of point and line features, since it contains 12 non-zero coefficients compared to the 27 coefficients in the trilinear tensor. The computation of motion parameters from the affine trifocal sensor (section 4) is also more straightforward.

To capture point and line correspondences in dense time sequences, we have also applied a factorization approach (section 5), to which the affine trifocal

Feature trajectories   Estimated rotation

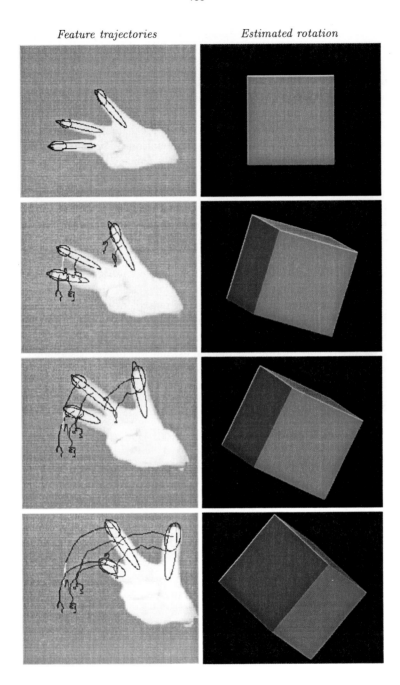

Fig. 3: Estimates of relative orientation from hand gestures. The left column shows point features and line features obtained from a feature tracker with automatic scale selection (Bretzner & Lindeberg 1997). The right column shows the result of computing changes in 3-D orientation using the joint factorization of point and line features in section 5. The results are illustrated by subjecting a three-dimensional cube to the estimated rotations.

tensor serves as an important processing step for computing the scaling factors of line correspondences when three or less point correspondences are available. When four or more point correspondences are given, these scaling factors can be determined directly from a system of linear equations.

The abovementioned theory has been combined with a framework for feature tracking with automatic scale selection (section 2), which has the attractive property that it adapts the scale levels to the local image structure and allows image features to be tracked over large size variations. The extended feature trajectories obtained in this way allow for higher accuracy in the motion estimates, since the relative influence of position errors decreases as the motion gets larger over time. The scale information associated with the image features also resolves the inherent reversal ambiguity of scaled orthographic projection.

Specifically, we have considered a problem in human-computer interaction of transferring three-dimensional orientation to a computer using no other equipment than the operator's own hand (Lindeberg & Bretzner 1998). Contrary to the more common approach of using detailed geometric hand models (Lee & Kunii 1995), we have here illustrated how changes in three-dimensional orientation can be computed using a qualitative model, based on blob features and ridge features from three fingers. Whereas a more detailed model could possibly allow for higher accuracy in the motion estimates, the simplicity and the generic nature of this module for motion estimation makes it straightforward to implement and lends itself easily to extensions to other problems.

References

Beardsley, P., Torr, P. & Zisserman, A. (1996), 3D model acquistions from extended image sequences, *in* '4th ECCV', 683–695.

Beardsley, P., Zisserman, A. & Murray, D. (1994), Navigation using affine structure from motion, *in* '3th ECCV', 85–96.

Bigün, J., Granlund, G. H. & Wiklund, J. (1991), 'Multidimensional orientation estimation with applications to texture analysis and optical flow', *PAMI* **13**(8), 775–790.

Bretzner, L. & Lindeberg, T. (1996), Feature tracking with automatic selection of spatial scales, ISRN KTH/NA/P--96/21--SE, KTH, Stockholm, Sweden.

Bretzner, L. & Lindeberg, T. (1997), On the handling of spatial and temporal scales in feature tracking, *in* 'Proc. 1st Scale-Space'97', Utrecht, Netherlands, 128–139.

Bretzner, L. & Lindeberg, T. (1998), Use your hand as a 3-d mouse, or, relative orientation from extended sequences of sparse point and line correspondences using the affine trifocal tensor. Technical report to be published at KTH.

Faugeras, O. (1992), What can be seen in three dimensions with a stereo rig?, *in* '2nd ECCV', 563–578.

Faugeras, O. (1995), 'Stratification of three-dimensional vision: Projective, affine and metric reconstructions', *JOSA* **12**(3), 465–484.

Faugeras, O. & Mourrain, B. (1995), On the geometry and algebra of the point and line correspondences between N images, *in* '5th ICCV', Cambridge, MA, 951–956.

Förstner, W. A. & Gülch, E. (1987), A fast operator for detection and precise location of distinct points, corners and centers of circular features, *in* 'ISPRS'.

Hartley, R. (1995), A linear method for reconstruction from points and lines, *in* '5th ICCV', Cambridge, MA, 882–887.

Heap, T. & Hogg, D. (1996), Towards 3D hand tracking using a deformable model, *in* 'Int. Conf. Autom. Face and Gesture Recogn., Killington, Vermont, 140–145.

Heyden, A. (1995), Reconstruction from image sequences by means of relative depth, *in* '5th ICCV', Cambridge, MA, 57–66.

Heyden, A., Sparr, G. & Åström, K. (1997), Perception and action using multilinear forms, *in* 'Proc. AFPAC'97', Kiel, Germany, 54–65.

Huang, T. S. & Lee, C. H. (1989), 'Motion and structure from orthographic projection', *IEEE-PAMI* **11**(5), 536–540.

Huang, T. S. & Netravali, A. N. (1994), 'Motion and structure from feature correspondences: A review', *Proc. IEEE* **82**, 251–268.

Koenderink, J. J. (1984), 'The structure of images', *Biol. Cyb.* **50**, 363–370.

Koenderink, J. J. & van Doorn, A. J. (1991), 'Affine structure from motion', *JOSA* 377–385.

Lee, J. & Kunii, T. L. (1995), 'Model-based analysis of hand posture', *Computer Graphics and Applications* pp. 77–86.

Lindeberg, T. (1994), *Scale-Space Theory in Computer Vision*, Kluwer, Netherlands.

Lindeberg, T. (1996), Edge detection and ridge detection with automatic scale selection, *in* 'CVPR'96', 465–470.

Lindeberg, T. & Bretzner, L. (1998), Visuellt människa-maskin-gränssnitt för tredimensionell orientering. Patent application.

Longuet-Higgins, H. C. (1981), 'A computer algorithm for reconstructing a scene from two projections', *Nature* **293**, 133–135.

Maybank, S. (1992), *Theory of Reconstruction from Image Motion*, Springer-Verlag.

McLauchlan, P., Reid, I. & Murray, D. (1994), Recursive affine structure and motion from image sequences, *in* '3th ECCV', Vol. 800, 217–224.

Morita, T. & Kanade, T. (1997), 'A sequential factorization method for recovering shape and motion from image streams', *IEEE-PAMI* **19**(8), 858–867.

Mundy, J. L. & Zisserman, A., eds (1992), *Geometric Invariance in Computer Vision*, MIT Press.

Quan, L. & Kanade, T. (1997), 'Affine structure from line correspondences with uncalibrated affine cameras', *IEEE-PAMI* **19**(8), 834–845.

Shapiro, L. S. (1995), *Affine analysis of image sequences*, Cambridge University Press.

Shashua, A. (1995), 'Algebraic functions for recognition', *IEEE-PAMI* **17**(8), 779–789.

Shashua, A. (1997), Trilinear tensor: The fundamental construct of multiple-view geometry and its applications, *in* 'Proc. AFPAC'97', Kiel, Germany, 190–206.

Spetsakis, M. E. & Aloimonos, J. (1990), 'Structure from motion using line correspondences', *IJCV* **4**(3), 171–183.

Sturm, P. & Triggs, B. (1996), A factorization based algorithm for multi-image projective structure and motion, *in* '4th ECCV', Vol. 1064, 709–720.

Tomasi, C. & Kanade, T. (1992), 'Shape and motion from image streams under orthography: A factorization method', *IJCV* **9**(2), 137–154.

Torr, P. H. S. (1995), Motion Segmentation and Outlier Detection, PhD thesis, Univ. of Oxford.

Ullman, S. (1979), *The Interpretation of Visual Motion*, MIT Press.

Ullman, S. & Basri, R. (1991), 'Recognition by linear combinations of models', *IEEE-PAMI* **13**(10), 992–1006.

Weng, J., Huang, T. S. & Ahuja, N. (1992), 'Motion and structure from line correspondences: Closed form solution and uniqueness results', *IEEE-PAMI* **14**(3), 318–336.

Xu, G. & Zhang, Z., eds (1997), *Epipolar Geometry in Stereo, Motion and Object Recognition: A Unified Approach*, Kluwer, Netherlands.

Do We Really Need an Accurate Calibration Pattern to Achieve a Reliable Camera Calibration?

* Jean-Marc Lavest, † Marc Viala, * M.Dhome

* LASMEA
LAboratoire des Sciences et Matériaux pour l'Electronique, et d'Automatique
UMR 6602 du CNRS, Université Blaise-Pascal de Clermont-Ferrand
63177 Aubière cedex. France
lavest@lasmea.univ-bpclermont.fr
† CEA-LETI, Département d'Electronique et d'Instrumentation Nucléaire
Service Logiciels et Architecture
CEA/SACLAY, 91191 Gif-sur-Yvette cedex

Abstract. This article raises the problem of errors caused by the metrology of a calibration pattern to the accurate estimation of the intrinsic and extrinsic calibration parameters modeling the video system. In order to take into account these errors a new approach is proposed that enables us to compute in the same time the traditional calibration parameters and the 3D geometry of the calibration pattern using a multi-images calibration algorithm. Experimental results shows that the proposed algorithm leads to reliable calibration results and proves that calibration errors no longer depend on the accuracy of calibration point measurement, but on the accuracy of calibration point detection in the image plane.

Keys Words
  Camera calibration, Calibration pattern, Photogrammetry, Metrology.

1 Introduction

Video cameras are becoming more and more widely used in Computer Vision for 3D measurements. To obtain accurate results, calibration is often necessary in order to determine the intrinsic parameters modeling the video camera system.

Well known calibration technics [Bro71], [Tsa86], [FT87] usually require a 3D known object, called the *calibration target*. This object has to be well defined and accurately measured to insure that the calibration parameters are stable. Nowadays, the wide range of application tasks in robotics has encouraged the use of long focal lengths (i.e. zooming applications [LL96]) as well as very short ones (3.5mm fish-Eye) to obtain a large inspection field. By doing so, it is almost impossible to use the same calibration pattern in the experimental set-up for both zoom and fish-eye applications. Specific patterns have to be setout for a given range of focal lengths.

In order to achieve accurate measurements and calibration results, particular care has to be taken in the way that a 3D calibration pattern is constructed and also the way the calibration points are measured. This is expensive and time consuming.

In this article we shall examine the influence of errors induced by the metrology of calibration points on the accuracy of the intrinsic calibration parameters. First, we briefly outline the photogrammetric calibration approach used in the article and the way the correlation matrix associated to each camera parameter is estimated. Then, in the second part, the accuracy of the intrinsic camera parameters is analyzed with respect to measurement errors introduced in the 3D calibration points, and also with respect to the 2D errors introduced by the target detection in the camera image plane.

As a result of the conclusions deduced from the previous analysis, a new calibration approach is proposed so that the traditional calibration parameters and the 3D geometry of the calibration pattern can be estimated. Experimental results using first synthetic, then real data, show that the proposed approach enables us to take into account large errors in 3D calibration point measurements.

2 Mathematical Tools for Simultaneous Calibration Using a Least Squares Technique

In our study we use a simplified camera model, i.e., the *pin-hole* model, as depicted in Figure 1. Through this section, the following notations are used:

- W–XYZ is a right-handed 3–D coordinate system as the world reference coordinate system.
- o–uv is the 2–D image pixel system with the origin at the top-left corner of the image.
- o–xy is a 2–D image coordinate system with x and y parallel to those of o–uv and with origin at the principal point o.
- c–xyz is the 3–D camera coordinate system with origin at the optical center c and z-axis coincides with the optical axis and x, y parallel to those of o–xy.

The intrinsic parameters we need to calibrate are: the principal point (u_0, u_0), the focal length f, the pixel sizes of the CCD array or their aspect ratio and the distortion parameters of the optical system.

The extrinsic parameters are the rotation matrix $\boldsymbol{R}$ as well as the translation vector $\boldsymbol{T}$ between W–XYZ and c–xyz.

The method presented in this section is strictly a least squares technique in the sense that we minimize the errors of the measurements. Notations and reference systems are those used in Photogrammetry.

2.1 The Mathematical Model

We assume a perspective projection between a 2–D image and a 3–D object (under the pin-hole camera model). The relationship between a 3–D point and its 2–D image is described by the following equations:

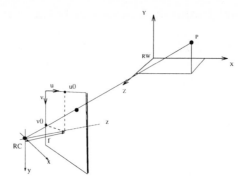

Fig. 1. *The pin-hole camera model, image geometry and coordinate systems.*

$$
\begin{pmatrix} x_i \\ y_i \\ z_i \end{pmatrix} = \lambda_i \left[\boldsymbol{R} \begin{pmatrix} X_i \\ Y_i \\ Z_i \end{pmatrix} + \boldsymbol{T} \right]
\tag{1}
$$

where in (1), (x_i, y_i, z_i) is the image point in the camera system as defined in Figure 1 and $\bar{z}_i \equiv f$, i.e., the focal length of the camera, (u_0, v_0) the coordinates of the principal point, λ_i is a scale factor which maps a point in the camera coordinate system to the image plane, (X_i, Y_i, Z_i) is the object point in the world-coordinate system $W\text{–}XYZ$, (T_x, T_y, T_z) is the translation vector, and $\boldsymbol{R}$ is the rotation matrix, which is constructed by three *independent* rotation angles: α rotating around X-axis, β around Y-axis, and γ around Z-axis:

If we eliminate λ_i in (1) and omit the subscript i, we have the following so-called *collinearity equations* in photogrammetry:

$$
\left.
\begin{aligned}
x &= f \frac{r_{11}X + r_{12}Y + r_{13}Z + T_x}{r_{31}X + r_{32}Y + r_{33}Z + T_z} \\[2mm]
y &= f \frac{r_{21}X + r_{22}Y + r_{23}Z + T_y}{r_{31}X + r_{32}Y + r_{33}Z + T_z}
\end{aligned}
\right\}
\tag{2}
$$

If we transform (x, y) into the pixel coordinate system (u, v), that is

$$
\left.
\begin{aligned}
x &= (u + v_x - u_0)dx - do_x \\
y &= (v + v_y - v_0)dy - do_y
\end{aligned}
\right\}
\tag{3}
$$

Here v_x, v_y are errors of the measurements x and y, i.e., corrections to the measurements so that they fit the function values. do_x, do_y are the lens distortion components, which consist of two parts: *radial* and *tangential* distortions, i.e., $do_x = do_{xr} + do_{xt}$ and $do_y = do_{yr} + do_{yt}$. We use two models which are often used in photogrammetry [Ame84]:

$$
\left.
\begin{aligned}
do_{xr} &= (u - u_0)dx(a_1 r^2 + a_2 r^4 + a_3 r^6) \\
do_{yr} &= (v - v_0)dy(a_1 r^2 + a_2 r^4 + a_3 r^6)
\end{aligned}
\right\}
\tag{4}
$$

$$
\left.
\begin{aligned}
do_{xt} &= p_1[r^2 + 2(u - u_0)^2 dx^2] + 2p_2(u - u_0)dx(v - v_0)dy \\
do_{yt} &= p_2[r^2 + 2(v - v_0)^2 dy^2] + 2p_1(u - u_0)dx(v - v_0)dy
\end{aligned}
\right\}
\tag{5}
$$

where in (3), (4), and (5), u, v are the image coordinates in the pixel system, u_0, v_0 define the principal point in the pixel system, a_1, a_2, a_3 are the radial lens distortion parameters, p_1, p_2 are the tangential distortion parameters, and d_x, d_y are the scale factors of the pixel system in x and y directions respectively, and $r = \sqrt{(u - u_0)^2 + (v - v_0)^2}$, is the radial distance from the principal point.

Substituting (3), (4) and (5) into (2), we have the following:

$$\left. \begin{array}{l} u + v_x = u_0 + (do_{xr} + do_{xt})/dx + (\frac{f}{dx})\frac{r_{11}X + r_{12}Y + r_{13}Z + T_x}{r_{31}X + r_{32}Y + r_{33}Z + T_z} = P(\boldsymbol{\Phi}) \\[3mm] v + v_y = v_0 + (do_{yr} + do_{yt})/dy + (\frac{f}{dy})\frac{r_{21}X + r_{22}Y + r_{23}Z + T_y}{r_{31}X + r_{32}Y + r_{33}Z + T_z} = Q(\boldsymbol{\Phi}) \end{array} \right\} \quad (6)$$

that can also be rewritten,

$$\left. \begin{array}{l} v_x = P(\boldsymbol{\Phi}) - u \\ v_y = Q(\boldsymbol{\Phi}) - v \end{array} \right\} F(\boldsymbol{\Phi}) \quad (7)$$

As the perspective projection is always defined up to a scale factor, we usually set dx parameter to 1. If we define $f_x = \frac{f}{d_x}$ and $f_y = \frac{f}{d_y}$, the calibration parameters to be estimated have the following expression:

$$\boldsymbol{\Phi} = [u_0, v_0, a_1, a_2, a_3, p_1, p_2, f_x, f_y, T_x, T_y, T_z, \alpha, \beta, \gamma]^T$$

2.2 Solving the Problem

The problem is to estimate the vector $\boldsymbol{\Phi}$ by minimizing $\sum_{i=1}^{n} (v_{x_i}^2 + v_{y_i}^2)$. In (6) $P(\boldsymbol{\Phi})$ and $Q(\boldsymbol{\Phi})$ are non-linear functions of $\boldsymbol{\Phi}$, the minimization is a non-linear optimization problem. One way of solving the problem is to linearize (6) with some initial value $\boldsymbol{\Phi}_0$ and solve for $\Delta\boldsymbol{\Phi}$. Then by adding $\Delta\boldsymbol{\Phi}$ to $\boldsymbol{\Phi}_0$ as the new initial value and repeating the process until a certain convergency is satisfied.

Given n 3D points and their corresponding 2D image points, we can write the $2 \times n$ linearized measurement or error equations in matrix form:

$$\boldsymbol{V} = \boldsymbol{L} + \boldsymbol{A} \, \Delta\boldsymbol{\Phi} \quad (8)$$

$$with \qquad \boldsymbol{L} = \boldsymbol{V}(\boldsymbol{\Phi}_0) \qquad and \qquad \boldsymbol{A} = \boldsymbol{F}'_{\Phi_0} = \frac{\delta F}{\delta \boldsymbol{\Phi}}\Big|_{\Phi = \Phi_0}$$

Let the weight matrix of the measurements be $\boldsymbol{W}$, the least squares solution to (8) is a minimization problem of

$$\min_{\Delta\boldsymbol{\Phi} \in \Re^{15}} \left(\boldsymbol{V}^T \boldsymbol{W} \boldsymbol{V} \right) \quad (9)$$

The solution to (9) can be obtained as:

$$\Delta\boldsymbol{\Phi} = (\boldsymbol{A}^T \boldsymbol{W} \boldsymbol{A})^{-1}(\boldsymbol{A}^T \boldsymbol{W} \boldsymbol{L}) \quad (10)$$

2.3 Multi-image Calibration

One major source of calibration errors is the results of measurement errors. These errors can be located on the 3d coordinates of the calibration points but also in the image plane when the target point coordinates are estimated.

One way to improve this is to combine more than one image taken by the same camera but from different (rotated and/or translated) positions. In such a case, the intrinsic parameters remain the same for all images and the calibration task means computing a parameter vector of

$$\boldsymbol{\Phi}_{9+6m} = \Big[u_0, u_0, a_1, a_2, a_3, p_1, p_2, f_x, f_y, T_x^1, T_y^1, T_z^1, \alpha^1, \beta^1, \gamma^1,$$
$$\cdots, T_x^m, T_y^m, T_z^m, \alpha^m, \beta^m, \gamma^m \Big]^T$$

If m is the number of images and n is the number of points on each image, the total number of equations will be $(2mn)$ and the total number of parameter is $(9 + 6m)$. The redundancy number r is $r = 2mn - 9 - 6m$, which is much larger than the one in the single-image calibration case. As we will show in the next subsection, the larger the redundancy the higher the reliability.

An important advantage of the multiple images approach is to provide a better estimate of distorsion paramaters when a short focal length has to be calibrated. Actually, in most application cases, the calibration target only covers a short part of the image. Using a multiple images approach, you can move the camera to obtain measurement information in all the CCD matrix surface and insure the radial parameters are more reliable.

3 Accuracy Assessment

3.1 Theoretical point of view

From the least squares estimation of (8) and (9), we can compute the estimates of the residual vector $\boldsymbol{V}$ as

$$\hat{\boldsymbol{V}} = [\boldsymbol{I} + \boldsymbol{A}(\boldsymbol{A}^T \boldsymbol{W} \boldsymbol{A})^{-1} \boldsymbol{A}^T \boldsymbol{W}] \boldsymbol{L} \tag{11}$$

and the estimate of the so called *standard error of unit weight*, which is the posteriori estimation of the noises σ_0 of the image coordinates if the model is correct and there are no system errors:

$$\hat{\sigma}_0^2 = \frac{\boldsymbol{V}^T \boldsymbol{W} \boldsymbol{V}}{N - r} \tag{12}$$

and the estimate of the *covariance* matrix of the parameters $\boldsymbol{\Phi}$:

$$C_\Phi = (\boldsymbol{A}^T \boldsymbol{W} \boldsymbol{A})^{-1} \tag{13}$$

And for each individual parameter ϕ_i, we can then compute the estimate of its precision, or the standard deviation:

$$\hat{\sigma}_{\phi_i}^2 = \hat{\sigma}_0^2 c_{ii} \tag{14}$$

3.2   Experimental factors

There are many factors which affect the accuracy of the computed parameters, and thus the reconstructed 3D data using these parameters. In the previous paragraph we have shown some error sources. Let us summarize the major factors:

- The number and accuracy of the measurements. How well we can measure 2D points in the image, and the accuracy of the 3D object points are the main factor which effect the accuracy of the calibration. Usually, we assume the 3D points are free of error, which is not quite true. Assuming both errors are random errors (with a certain distribution), this type of error will result in a random residual error in the image after the least squares adjustment.
- Geometrical configuration of the set up, i.e., the relation between the camera and the calibration object. This factor determines the internal strength of the least squares solution, i.e., the design matrix A of the system. Improper geometrical configuration will result in poor accuracy and reliability [LL96].
- The mathematical models used for the calibration. We model the camera lens as a *pin-hole* model, which is just an approximation, and so the lens distortion is modelled as radial and tangential distortion. The lens system is a very complicated optical and mechanical construction, and there is no exact model for it. The imperfect model will result in a systematic error in the image after the calibration.
- Jitter effects can also be underlined. They are directly influenced by with the electronic stability of the frame grabber, and [Bey92] shows that their influence can induce systematic errors in the video images - up to 0.5 pixel.

3.3   Influence of the calibration pattern

The influence of the calibration pattern on the parameters estimated during the calibration process can be analysed in different ways.

In [LL96] the authors show that the geometrical configuration of the calibration pattern (several grids, cubes ...) is highly connected to the correlation matrix form of the computed parameters.

In this section we want to analyse the influence of random errors introduced in the coordinates of the calibration points, on the accuracy of the computed parameters.

Experimental setup

Let us define a set of 11 synthetic images, that represents a calibration pattern of 11 points observed with a video camera equipped with a 10mm lens. The image set is computed in order to allow the calibration pattern to be observed from highly different view points.

Table 1 describes the calibration results obtained for different ranges of noise (in millimeters) introduced in the coordinates (x,y,z) of the calibration points. The total dimensions of the calibration object are approximately $(0.6 \times 0.6 \times 0.4m^3)$. The target is observed at a mean distance of $1.5m$.

Table 1. Calibration results in relation to a gaussian noise added to the coordinates x, y, z of the calibration points

noise (x,y,z) 0.0 mm^3	
$\sigma_0 = 0.0$ (pix)	
$fx(pix) = 1670.0$	$\sigma fx = 1.0\text{e-}9$
$fy(pix) = 1671.0$	$\sigma fy = 1.0\text{e-}9$
$u0(pix) = 391.0$	$\sigma u0 = 1.0\text{e-}9$
$v0(pix) = 278.0$	$\sigma v0 = 1.0\text{e-}9$

noise (x,y,z) 0.01mm^3		noise (x,y,z) 0.1mm^3	
$\sigma_0 = 0.006$ (pix)		$\sigma_0 = 0.05$ (pix)	
$fx = 1668.92$	$\sigma fx = 0.21$	$fx = 1659.68$	$\sigma fx = 2.12$
$fy = 1669.98$	$\sigma fy = 0.21$	$fy = 1661.24$	$\sigma fy = 2.15$
$u0 = 391.27$	$\sigma u0 = 0.15$	$u0 = 393.66$	$\sigma u0 = 1.55$
$v0 = 277.89$	$\sigma v0 = 0.17$	$v0 = 277.10$	$\sigma v0 = 1.72$

noise (x,y,z) 0.5mm^3		noise (x,y,z) 2.0mm^3	
$\sigma_0 = 0.28$ (pix)		$\sigma_0 = 1.16$ (pix)	
$fx = 1626.55$	$\sigma fx = 10.26$	$fx = 1610.26$	$\sigma fx = 44.04$
$fy = 1630.40$	$\sigma fy = 10.36$	$fy = 1623.36$	$\sigma fy = 44.59$
$u0 = 402.47$	$\sigma u0 = 7.42$	$u0 = 422.83$	$\sigma u0 = 30.01$
$v0 = 276.10$	$\sigma v0 = 8.13$	$v0 = 296.10$	$\sigma v0 = 32.00$

$\sigma 0$ represents the standard deviation of unit weight estimated from expression (12). The standard deviation associated to each parameter of the calibration vector is estimated from expression (14). The first experiment is performed without adding any noise. It gives the synthetical calibration results according to the images set.

Through these tables, we can notice the major infuence of the metrological quality of the calibration target on the accuracy of the calibration results.

It can be underlined:

– on the one hand that the intrinsic parameters are soon affected by a random noise added on target points,
– moreover that an error greater than ($2mm^3$) leads to the non-convergence of the optimization process. This critical value is conditionned by the experimental setup. For example the calibration of a fish-eye lens will lead to the non covergence of the algorithm for a smaller value of measurement errors.

Noise added to each calibration point coordinates, was generated during this experimental setup, under a uniform law. The influence of the calibration pattern metrology could also be analysed with systhematic errors introduced, for example by the non orthogonality between the different faces of a calibration cube.

3.4 Influence of calibration point detection

Table 2. Calibration results in relation to a gaussian noise added to calibration point detection in the image plane

noise (u,v) 0.0 pix^2	
$\sigma_0 = 0.0$ (pix)	
$fx(pix) = 1670.0$	$\sigma fx = $ 1.0e-9
$fy(pix) = 1671.0$	$\sigma fy = $ 1.0e-9
$u0(pix) = 391.0$	$\sigma u0 = $ 1.0e-9
$v0(pix) = 278.0$	$\sigma v0 = $ 1.0e-9

noise (u,v) 0.02 pix^2		noise (u,v) 0.05 pix^2	
$\sigma_0 = 0.02$ (pix)		$\sigma_0 = 0.05$ (pix)	
$fx= 1670.16$	$\sigma fx = 0.77$	$fx= 1670.58$	$\sigma fx = 1.94$
$fy= 1671.24$	$\sigma fy = 0.78$	$fy= 1671.79$	$\sigma fy = 1.96$
$u0= 391.66$	$\sigma u0 = 0.56$	$u0= 392.63$	$\sigma u0 = 1.41$
$v0= 278.76$	$\sigma v0 = 0.63$	$v0= 279.93$	$\sigma v0 = 1.58$

noise (u,v) 0.5 pix^2		noise (u,v) 1.0 pix^2	
$\sigma_0 = 0.51$ (pix)		$\sigma_0 = 1.06$ (pix)	
$fx= 1704.82$	$\sigma fx = 20.63$	$fx= 1837.14$	$\sigma fx = 51.85$
$fy= 1708.11$	$\sigma fy = 20.77$	$fy= 1842.94$	$\sigma fy = 52.00$
$u0= 402.92$	$\sigma u0 = 14.70$	$u0= 400.93$	$\sigma u0 = 33.58$
$v0= 303.34$	$\sigma v0 = 16.53$	$v0= 346.98$	$\sigma v0 = 40.94$

Experimental setup

The experimental setup remains similar to the previous one. In this section the 3D coordinate of the calibration points are supposed to be noise free.

Table 2 describes experimental calibration results obtained for different ranges of noise (in pixel) added to each coordinate (u, v) of the calibration points projected in the image plane.

The first table, which is noise free, gives the theoretical solution according to the synthetic data. The noise ranges used in this experiment are classified from an accurate subpixel detector ($\sigma0 = 0.02pix$) to a rough estimate of the calibration point coordinates ($\sigma0 = 1.0pix$) .

A precise analysis of the table shows that accurate calibration results can only be achieved with a **subpixel detector**. Errors greater than $0.5pix$ in coordinate point estimates lead to significant variation in the calibration parameters.

4 New Calibration Formulation

High quality calibration patterns are often difficult to achieve. They have to be mechanically stable in time (compared with the temperature change), and an accurate measurement of the location of points carried out by a metrology company is expensive. Futhermore, the large range of application fields in robotics means we use short as well as long focal lengths. This implies that the laboratory must have several calibration patterns associated to specified applications.

Is it possible inside a multiple images calibration approach to estimate the calibration point coordinates in space at the same time as the intrinsic and extrinsic calibration parameters ?

Let us rewrite the colinearity equations:

$$\left. \begin{array}{l} u + v_x = u_0 + (do_{xr} + do_{xt})/dx + (\frac{f}{dx})\frac{r_{11}X+r_{12}Y+r_{13}Z+T_x}{r_{31}X+r_{32}Y+r_{33}Z+T_z} = P(\boldsymbol{\Phi}) \\[2mm] v + v_y = v_0 + (do_{yr} + do_{yt})/dy + (\frac{f}{dy})\frac{r_{21}X+r_{22}Y+r_{23}Z+T_y}{r_{31}X+r_{32}Y+r_{33}Z+T_z} = Q(\boldsymbol{\Phi}) \end{array} \right\} \quad (15)$$

The new calibration vector to be determined, if the 3D coordinates of calibration points have to be estimated with the traditional calibration parameters, takes the following form:

$$\boldsymbol{\Phi}_{9+6m+3*n} = \Big[u_0, v_0, a_1, a_2, a_3, p_1, p_2, f_x, f_y, X^1, Y^1, Z^1, \cdots, X^n, Y^n, Z^n,$$
$$T_x^1, T_y^1, T_z^1, \alpha^1, \beta^1, \gamma^1, \cdots, T_y^m, T_z^m, \alpha^m, \beta^m, \gamma^m \Big]^T$$

where n represents the total number of target points and m the total number of images taken during the calibration setup.

4.1 Redundancy

Total number of unknown parameters :
9 (intrinsic parameters) + 3*n (calibration point coordinates) + 6*m (extrinsic parameters).
Number of equations : 2*m*n.
The redundancy of the system to be solved, $r = 2*m*n - (9 + 3*n + 6*m)$, can be obtained easily. According to the the synthetic experiments previously used, in which the calibration pattern was achieved with 11 points ($n = 11$), a minimal set of 3 images is sufficient to over-determine the system.

4.2 Initial conditions to insure algorithm convergency

The system to be solved is a non-linear optimisation. It requires an initial value of the calibration vector not too far from the solution in order to insure algorithm convergency.

In the final experimental results, we will show that this initial value is not really difficult to obtain, and that a good convergency can be achieved if the calibration views of the pattern are taken from different orientation observations. This is equivalent to insuring very constrained triangulation angles in space for the 3D point reconstruction. As underlined in [Bro71], we have noticed that multiple views taken with a 90 degree rotation around the optical axis leads to a better estimate (better convergency and better accuracy) of the calibration parameters.

4.3 Calibration solution determined up to a scale factor

1. Intrinsic parameters
   In the traditional approach to photogrammetric calibration, the intrinsic parameters are always determined up to a scale factor. The usual assignation of the x-size of the CCD matrix to one ($dx = 1$), means the other parameters can be expressed in an arbitrary unit defined in pixels.
2. Extrinsic parameters
   Since the 3D coordinates of the calibration points are simultaneously estimated with the calibration parameters, the extrinsic geometry of the vision system is also determined up to a scale factor. Actually, in these conditions the reconstruction of a bigger calibration pattern observed from a farther distance will provide an identical image.

   This loss of metric dimension does not have great consequences on a single camera calibration. Key information for further application tasks are only contained in the intrinsic parameters. Let us recall that extrinsic parameters gives the 3D location of the calibration pattern, expressed in the camera frame, and in accordance with a given view of the image set. However if a stereo (or more) vision system has to be calibrated it will be necessary to introduce a metric dimension to fix the extrinsic geometry of the camera configuration. Such a task can easily be performed with the accurate knowledge of the euclidian distance between 2 points among n.

5 Experimental results

In this section, an experimental study is performed. It is divided into two parts. first, synthetic data previously used is tested with the new calibration approach. Then, the algorithm is evaluated with real data taken from camera devices equipped with different fixed focal-lens lenses.

5.1 Synthetic data

Without noise on image point detection

In this sub-section the experimental conditions used to create the synthetic data set remain the same as those defined in section 3.2. A random noise (inside a given standard deviation) is added to each coordinate of the 3D calibration points. Point detection in the image plane is first of all supposed to be noise free.

Table 3. Calibration results from synthetic data in relation to a gaussian noise added to the calibration point coordinates

				Starting conditions (fx=3000 fy=3000) (u0=300 v0=300)			
noise	*convergency*			*results*			
xyz mm^3	*nb itera*	*k*	σ_k	*fx* (*pix*)	*fy* (*pix*)	*u0* (*pix*)	*v0* (*pix*)
0.01	45	0.9838	0.0	1670	1671	391	278
0.1	45	0.9838	0.0	1670	1671	391	278
1.0	47	0.9832	0.0	1670	1671	391	278
10.0	48	0.9767	0.0	1670	1671	391	278

Table 3 shows that the new calibration formula enables us to take into account errors (up to $10.0mm^3$) introduced into the calibration pattern and converges at any time to the same values of intrinsic parameters. Note, that the starting conditions are far from the true solution and are directely correlated to the number of iterations required by the process to find the solution.

Parameter k indicates the scale factor of the extrinsic geometry obtained at the convergency. It is estimated as followed

$$k = \frac{1}{n-1} \sum_{i=2}^{n} \frac{|P_i - P_{i-1}|}{|\hat{P}_i - \hat{P}_{i-1}|} \tag{16}$$

where P_i is a reconstructed points of the calibration pattern and $\hat{P}_i$ its corresponding point in the true solution.

σ_k gives the standard deviation of this distribution. In table 3 it can be noted that σ_k is systematically equal to zero, because the algorithm has accurately estimated the calibration target geometry, as well as the intrinsic and extrinsic parameters that give the perfect correspondance of colinearity equations (6). Results described in this table have to be compared with experiment Table 1 using the traditional calibration formulation.

Adding noise to image point detection

For this experiment two different noises added on each image coordinate have been considered (respectively 0.01 pix and 0.1 pix). Given an image noise, the 3d coordinates of all the calibration points have been modified using a gaussian distribution with a standard deviation of respectively $0.1mm^3$ and $10.0mm^3$.

For a given range of image noise (0.01 and 0.1 pix), the analysis in table 4 shows that the algorithm computes the same extrinsic geometry of the calibration set-up (up to a scale factor) and converges to the same values of the intrinsic parameters (focal length, principal point).

Table 4. Calibration results from synthetic data in relation to a gaussian noise added to the calibration points coordinates and the image point detection

Initial conditions (results in pixel) (fx=3000 fy=3000) (u0=300 v0=300)			
image noise (u,v) 0.01 pix			
calib. target noise (x,y,z) 0.1mm³		calib. target noise (x,y,z) 10.0mm³	
fx= 1666.64	σ = 0.35	fx= 1666.64	σ = 0.35
fy= 1668.03	σ = 0.36	fy= 1668.03	σ = 0.36
u0= 391.49	σ = 0.26	u0= 391.49	σ = 0.26
v0= 278.73	σ = 0.31	v0= 278.73	σ = 0.31
nb itera=47		nb itera=48	
σ0=0.01		σ0=0.01	
k = 0.97538	σ = 0.000101	k= 0.97433	σ = 0.000103
image noise (u,v) 0.1 pix			
calib. target noise (x,y,z) 0.1mm³		calib. target noise (x,y,z) 10.0mm³	
fx= 1651.35	σ = 3.50	fx= 1651.35	σ = 3.50
fy= 1652.99	σ = 3.54	fy= 1652.99	σ = 3.54
u0= 396.03	σ = 2.60	u0= 396.03	σ = 2.60
v0= 285.10	σ = 3.01	v0= 285.10	σ = 3.01
nb itera=48		nb itera=49	
σ0=0.094		σ0=0.094	
k = 0.97538	σ = 0.000910	k= 0.97433	σ = 0.000910

Conclusion

The calibration errors compared with the true synthetic solution no longer depend on the accuracy of the calibration point measurement, but on the accuracy of calibration point detection in the image plane. The first part of table 4 indiquates that a subpixel (0.01pix) point detector leads to calibration results very close to the true solution even if the 3d calibration points are estimated roughly. It can be underlined that a good numerical convergency of the algorithm greatly depends on the choice of the target observation points of view.

5.2 Real Data

Test sequence n-1 Table 5 describes the results of a traditional multiple-images calibration algorithm, experimented on a set of 11 images. The target pattern is composed of 30 points. The tridimensional geometry of the calibration points is known with an accuracy of $0.02mm^3$. The total volume of the calibration pattern is equal to $(0.6 \times 0.6 \times 0.4m^3)$. Each calibration point is obtained using

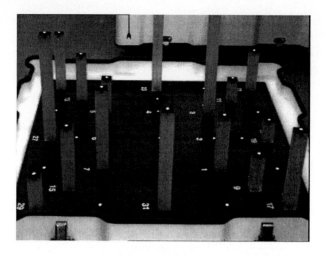

Fig. 2. CEA calibration pattern

a photo-reflector material to insure an accurate detection.

Data was tested in two different laboratories and algorithms were also implemented in C and Fortran with two different numerical optimisation librairies (Numerical Recipies and dMinPack).

The classical calibration approach leads to a residual value of 0.033 and 0.026 pixel respectively along the coordinates (u,v) of the 289 measurement points. According to a recent experiment performed by the European Space Agency (ESA) [Pa97], these results seem quite good.

Table 6 describes results obtained with the new calibration algorithm. Solution of intrinsic parameters are quite similar. The residual value at convergency is slightly smaller. Even if calibration points coordinates are modified (noise up to $10.0mm^3$), the solution at convergency remains the same.

As the true values of the calibration points are known in this section, the factor σk gives us information about the relationship between the reconstructed target and the true one. We can notice that modification of $1.2e - 4\%$ has been found by the algorithm to allows a better fitting of the colinearity equations.

Conclusion

To conclude, we can say that while accurate observation of n points from a set of m different points of view is possible, an accurate knowledge of the 3d calibration point coordinates does not seem to be necessary to achieve accurate values of intrinsic calibration parameters.

Test sequence n-2 In this experiment, our aim is to achieve calibration of a fisheye lens (3.8mm) that induces a high radial distorsion in the image plane. The target used for calibration was rapidely setup using two little circular objects composed of 12 photo-reflector points.

Table 5. Calibration results on real data

camera	: Sony XC75CE
lens	: 10mm Angénieux
frame grabber	: Silicon Graphics
algorithm	: Traditional multiple image calibration
calibration target	: CEA-Saclay

Number of images	: 11
Number of measurements	: 289

vx residual: mean and std-dev (pix)	-9.150e-06	3.344e-02
vy residual: mean and std-dev (pix)	1.233e-05	2.634e-02
Std error of unit weight (pix)		3.686107e-02

		σ				σ
fx(pix)	1672.89	2.08e-01		a1	1.538e-01	5.12e-03
fy(pix)	1676.03	2.09e-01		a2	-8.758e-01	1.44e-0
u0(pix)	386.74	4.26e-01		a3	6.121e+00	1.23e+00
v0(pix)	276.86	3.65e-01		p1	6.478e-04	7.12e-05
				p2	7.684e-05	6.41e-05

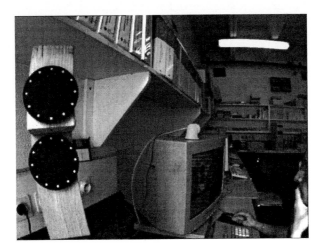

Fig. 3. Fish-eye calibration

The geometry of each elementary target was roughly known ($\simeq 1mm$). The relative location between the two objects was set to zero at the begining of the process convergency. Figure 3 shows one of the eight views used during the

Table 6. Calibration results on real data with added noise on the 3D coordinates of the calibration points

New approach				
camera : Sony XC75CE				
lens : 10mm Angénieux				
frame grabber : Silicon Graphic				
algorithm : New Approach.				

Number of images   : 11
Number of measurements : 271

vx residual: mean and std-dev (pix)	2.934e-07	1.875e-02
vy residual: mean and std-dev (pix)	-5.486e-09	1.337e-02
Std error of unit weight (pix)		1.972624e-02
scale factor ($\bar{k}$ and σk)	0.98733	0.00012

		σ				σ
fx(pix)	1672.85	1.33e-01	a1	1.458e-01	3.20e-03
fy(pix)	1675.96	1.34e-0	a2	-6.749e-01	9.02e-0
u0(pix)	386.48	2.68e-01	a3	4.685e+00	7.69e-01
v0(pix)	277.26	2.34e-01	p1	5.960e-04	4.44e-05
			p2	5.599e-05	4.04e-05

calibration setup and shows the radial distorsion phenomenon. During the images sequence the camera is moved to obtain measurement points throughout all the CCD surface.

We must underline that approximate knowledge of the circular object allows us to compute an initial value of rotation and translation parameters (R_i, T_i) that locates the target in each image. We hope in further works to improve this point using shape from motion approaches as those proposed by Kanade [PK94].

In this experiment (table 7), the new calibration approach enables us to reconstruct the calibration pattern and provides a solution of intrinsic parameters leading to quite small residual values (0.030 et 0.026 pix). The standard deviation for this last experiment is larger than for the previous data set (Tab 6). The difference is mainly due to the less accurate adequation of the distorsion model in this case.

Table 7. Calibration results with real data

New approach						
camera : JAI M50 lens : 3.8mm Ernitec frame grabber : Silicon Graphics algorithm :new approach.						
Number of images : 8 Number of measurements : 185						
vx residual mean and std-dev (pix)			-7.135e-05	3.080e-02		
vy residual mean and std-dev (pix)			-6.216-05	2.663e-02		
Std error of unit weight (pix)				3.565e-02		
		σ				σ
fx(pix)	459.70	2.65e-01	a1	3.746e-01	1.56e-03	
fy(pix)	460.44	2.67e-01	a2	1.120e-01	4.58e-03	
u0(pix)	365.97	2.26e-01	a3	1.729e-01	4.68e-03	
v0(pix)	299.96	2.49e-01	p1	4.635e-04	1.03e-04	
			p2	-1.232e-03	1.15e-04	

6 Discussion and Conclusion

Calibration point detection

Accuracy of calibration parameters achieved by the algorithm described in this article is greatly dependent on the quality of calibration point detection in the image plane. We have shown with synthetic data that a sub-pixel detector (0.01 or 0.02 accurate) leads to almost perfect calibration parameters.

In practice, we have noticed that the sub-pixel detection of image dots gives more reliable results than cross detection. In [Pa97] the authors arrive at the same conclusions. Experimental results described in the paper use a subpixel spot detector based on an affine transformation associated with a scale factor, that transform the photonic response of a theoretical spot to fit the image content. Experimental accuracy achieved by this way is less than 0.02 pixel.

Introduction of a metric distance

As previously stated the extrinsic geometry between the different points of view of the calibration set-up is determined up to a scale factor. To eliminate this unknown factor, it is sufficient to introduce among the n calibration points the distance between 2 points. Actually, we can imagine that each calibration pattern is roughtly achieved in connection with the adopted focal-length. An accurate metric distance determined by two photoreflector points in a very stable material (invar) could be added in the set of calibration images. The final cost of the calibration pattern is limited to the accurate measurement of the distance between these two points. Most optical firms can provide this kind of calibration metrics.

Convenient to use

The calibraton algorithm described in this article is really convenient to use, and makes it possible to obtain rapid, perfectly defined calibration targets for short as well as long focal-lengths. The residual values obtained during the experiments are similar to those given by traditional algorithms, and show the reliability of the proposed algorithm. In practice, the convergency is assured without problem if the 3d geometry of the target is approximately known. For critical cases where no 3D information is available, we usually start the process with a flat model located in front of the camera. This case could be improved by starting the algorithm with an initial value given by a shape from motion estimator.

Further works

Instead of using photo-reflector calibration points that are well defined in the images, we should like to experiment the same approach on natural scenes. Using texture information contained about specific points of interest, we are working on accurate matching between these points along the set of calibration images. In this way we hope to perform accurate camera calibration with natural textured objects.

References

[Ame84] American Society for Photogrammetry. *Manual of Photogrammetry*, 4th edition, 1984.

[Bey92] H.A. Beyer. *Geometric and Radiometric Analysis of a CCD-Camera Based Photogrammetric Close-Range System*. PhD thesis, Institut fur Geodasie und Photogrammetrie, Nr 51, ETH, Zurich., May 1992.

[Bro71] D.C. Brown. Close-range camera calibration. *Photogrammetric Engineering*, Vol 8(Nr 37):pp 855–866, 1971.

[FT87] O. Faugeras and G. Toscani. Camera calibration for 3d computer vision. In *Proc. of CVPR*, Tokyo, japan, 1987.

[LL96] M. Li and JM. Lavest. Some aspects of zoom lens calibration. *IEEE PAMI*, Vol 18(Nr 11), 1996.

[Pa97] P. Plancke and al. Calibration of vision system (calvin). *Final Report of European Space Agency*, (WPB5-T1), 1997.

[PK94] C.J. Poelman and T. Kanade. A paraperspective factorisation method for shape and motion recovery. *Third European Conference on Computer Vision,ECCV94,Stockholm*, Vol 2:pp 97–108, May 1994.

[Tsa86] R.Y. Tsai. An efficient ansd accurate calibration technique for 3d machine vision. In *In proc. of CVPR*, pages pp 364–374, Miami, UsA, 1986.

Optimal Estimation of Three-Dimensional Rotation and Reliability Evaluation*

Naoya Ohta and Kenichi Kanatani

Department of Computer Science, Gunma University,
Kiryu, Gunma 376-8515 Japan
{ohta|kanatani}@cs.gunma-u.ac.jp

Abstract. We discuss optimal rotation estimation from two sets of 3-D points in the presence of anisotropic and inhomogeneous noise. We first present a theoretical accuracy bound and then give a method that attains that bound, which can be viewed as describing the reliability of the solution. We also show that an efficient computational scheme can be obtained by using quaternions and applying renormalization. Using real stereo images for 3-D reconstruction, we demonstrate that our method is superior to the least-squares method and confirm the theoretical predictions of our theory by applying the bootstrap procedure.

1 Introduction

Determining a rotational relationship between two sets of 3-D points is an important task for 3-D object reconstruction and recognition. For example, if we use stereo vision or range sensing, the 3-D shape can be reconstructed only for visible surfaces. Hence, we need to fuse separately reconstructed surfaces into one object [13]. For this task, we need to determine the rigid transformation between two sets of points. If one set is translated so that its centroid coincides with that of the other, the problem reduces to estimating a rotation.

Let $\{r_\alpha\}$ and $\{r'_\alpha\}$, $\alpha = 1, ..., N$, be the sets of three-dimensional vectors before and after a rotation, respectively. A conventional method for determining the rotation is the following least squares method:

$$\sum_{\alpha=1}^{N} \|r'_\alpha - Rr_\alpha\|^2 \to \min. \tag{1}$$

In this paper, $\|a\|$ denotes the norm of a vector a.

The solution of the minimization (1) can be obtained analytically: Horn [3] proposed a method using quaternions; Arun et al. [1] used the singular value decomposition; Horn et al. [4] used the polar decomposition. The method of Horn [3] is guaranteed to yield a rotation matrix, while the methods of Arun et al. [1] and Horn et al. [4] may yield an orthogonal matrix of determinant -1.

---

* This work was in part supported by the Ministry of Education, Science, Sports and Culture, Japan under a Grant in Aid for Scientific Research C(2) (No. 09680352).

This drawback was later remedied by Umeyama [14] by introducing a Lagrange multiplier for that constraint; Kanatani [8] restated it from a group-theoretical viewpoint.

From a statistical point of view, the above least-squares method implicitly assumes the following noise model:

- Points $\{r_\alpha\}$ are observed without noise, while the rotated points $\{Rr_\alpha\}$ are observed with noise $\{\Delta r'_\alpha\}$.
- The noise $\{\Delta r'_\alpha\}$ is subject to an isotropic, identical, and independent Gaussian distribution of zero mean.

The least-squares solution is optimal for this model. However, this model is not realistic in many situations:

- The noise is often neither isotropic nor identical [10, 11]. 3-D points measured by stereo vision or range sensing usually have errors that are very large along the viewing direction as compared with the directions perpendicular to it. In addition, the noise characteristics differ from point to point; usually, points near the sensor are more accurate than points far away.
- The 3-D points in both sets suffer noise. If the 3-D points are measured by a sensor before and after a rotation, it is unreasonable to assume that noise exists only in one set.

In this paper, we first introduce a realistic noise model and present a *theoretical accuracy bound*, which can be evaluated *independently* of particular solution techniques involved. Then, we describe an estimation method that attains the accuracy bound; such a method alone can be called "optimal".

Since the solution attains the accuracy bound, we can view it as quantitatively describing the reliability of the solution; in the past, the reliability issue has attracted little attention.

The optimal method turns out to be highly nonlinear. However, we show that an efficient computational scheme can be obtained by using quarternions and applying the *renormalization* technique proposed by Kanatani [9]. Using real stereo images for 3-D reconstruction, we demonstrate that our method is indeed superior to the least-squares method and confirm the theoretical predictions of our theory by applying the bootstrap procedure [2].

2   Noise Model

Let $\bar{r}_\alpha$ and $\bar{r}'_\alpha$, $\alpha = 1, ..., N$, denote the true 3-D positions before and after a rotation, respectively, and let r_α and r'_α be their respective positions observed in the presense of noise. We write

$$r_\alpha = \bar{r}_\alpha + \Delta r_\alpha, \qquad r'_\alpha = \bar{r}'_\alpha + \Delta r'_\alpha, \tag{2}$$

and assume that Δr_α and $\Delta r'_\alpha$ are independent Gaussian random variables of mean zero. Their covariance matrices are defined by

$$V[r_\alpha] = E[\Delta r_\alpha \Delta r_\alpha^\top], \qquad V[r'_\alpha] = E[\Delta r'_\alpha \Delta r'^{\top}_\alpha], \tag{3}$$

where $E[\cdot]$ denotes expectation and the superscript $\top$ denotes transpose. The problem is formally stated as follows:

Problem 1. Estimate the rotation matrix $\boldsymbol{R}$ that satisfies

$$\bar{\boldsymbol{r}}'_\alpha = \boldsymbol{R}\bar{\boldsymbol{r}}_\alpha, \qquad \alpha = 1, ..., N, \tag{4}$$

from the noisy data $\{\boldsymbol{r}_\alpha\}$ and $\{\boldsymbol{r}'_\alpha\}$.

In practice, it is often very difficult to predict the covariance matrices $V[\boldsymbol{r}_\alpha]$ and $V[\boldsymbol{r}'_\alpha]$ precisely. In many cases, however, we can estimate their relative scales. If the 3-D positions are computed by stereo vision for example, the distribution of errors can be computed up to scale from the geometry of the camera configuration [10]. In view of this, we decompose the covariance matrices into an unknown constant ϵ and known matrices $V_0[\boldsymbol{r}_\alpha]$ and $V_0[\boldsymbol{r}'_\alpha]$ in the form

$$V[\boldsymbol{r}_\alpha] = \epsilon^2 V_0[\boldsymbol{r}_\alpha], \qquad V[\boldsymbol{r}'_\alpha] = \epsilon^2 V_0[\boldsymbol{r}'_\alpha]. \tag{5}$$

We call ϵ the *noise level*, and $V_0[\boldsymbol{r}_\alpha]$ and $V_0[\boldsymbol{r}'_\alpha]$ the *normalized covariance matrices*.

3 Theoretical Accuracy Bound

The reliability of an estimator can be evaluated by its covariance matrix if the set of parameters to be estimated can be identified with a point in a Euclidean space. However, a rotation is an element of the group of rotations $SO(3)$, which is a three-dimensional Lie group. Hence, we cannot define the covariance matrix of a rotation in the usual sense.

Let $\hat{\boldsymbol{R}}$ be an estimator of the true rotation $\bar{\boldsymbol{R}}$. Let $\boldsymbol{l}_r$ and $\Delta\Omega$ be, respectively, the axis (unit vector) and the angle of the relative rotation $\hat{\boldsymbol{R}}\bar{\boldsymbol{R}}^\top$. We define a three-dimensional vector

$$\Delta\boldsymbol{\Omega} = \Delta\Omega\boldsymbol{l}_r, \tag{6}$$

and regard this as the measure of deviation of the estimator $\hat{\boldsymbol{R}}$ from the true rotation $\bar{\boldsymbol{R}}$. We define the covariance matrix of $\hat{\boldsymbol{R}}$ by

$$V[\hat{\boldsymbol{R}}] = E[\Delta\boldsymbol{\Omega}\Delta\boldsymbol{\Omega}^\top]. \tag{7}$$

The group of rotations $SO(3)$ has the topology of the three-dimensional projective space P^3, which is locally homeomorphic to a 3-sphere S^3 [6]. If the noise is small, the deviation $\Delta\boldsymbol{\Omega}$ is also small and identified with an element of the Lie algebra $so(3)$, which can be viewed as a Euclidean space. This is equivalent to regarding errors as occurring in the tangent space to the 3-sphere S^3 at $\bar{\boldsymbol{R}}$.

With this definition of the covariance matrix, we can apply the theory of Kanatani (Sect. 14.4.3 of [9]) to obtain a theoretical accuracy bound, which he called the *Cramer-Rao lower bound* in analogy with the corresponding bound in traditional statistics. In the present case, it reduces to

$$V[\hat{\boldsymbol{R}}] \succ \epsilon^2 \left(\sum_{\alpha=1}^{N} (\bar{\boldsymbol{R}}\bar{\boldsymbol{r}}_\alpha) \times \bar{\boldsymbol{W}}_\alpha \times (\bar{\boldsymbol{R}}\bar{\boldsymbol{r}}_\alpha) \right)^{-1}, \tag{8}$$

$$\bar{\boldsymbol{W}}_\alpha = \left(\bar{\boldsymbol{R}} V_0[\boldsymbol{r}_\alpha] \bar{\boldsymbol{R}}^\top + V_0[\boldsymbol{r}'_\alpha] \right)^{-1}. \tag{9}$$

Here, $\boldsymbol{A} \succ \boldsymbol{B}$ means that $\boldsymbol{A} - \boldsymbol{B}$ is a positive semi-definite symmetric matrix. The product $\boldsymbol{v} \times \boldsymbol{A} \times \boldsymbol{v}$ of a vector $\boldsymbol{u} = (u_i)$ and a matrix $\boldsymbol{A} = (A_{ij})$ is the matrix whose (ij) element is $\sum_{k,l,m,n=1}^{3} \varepsilon_{ikl}\varepsilon_{jmn} v_k v_m A_{ln}$, where ε_{ijk} is the *Eddington epsilon*, taking 1 when (ijk) is an even permutation of (123), -1 when it is an odd permutation of (123), and 0 otherwise.

If the noise is isotropic and identical, we have $V_0[\boldsymbol{r}_\alpha] = V_0[\boldsymbol{r}'_\alpha] = \boldsymbol{I}$ (unit matrix). In this case, Eq. (8) corresponds to the result obtained by Oliensis [12].

4 Optimal Estimation

Applying the general theory of Kanatani [9] (Sect. 14.5.2 of [9]), we can obtain a computational scheme for solving Problem 1 in such a way that the resulting solution attains the accuracy bound (8) in the first order (i.e., ignoring terms of $O(\epsilon^4)$): we minimize the sum of squared *Mahalanobis distances*, i.e.,

$$J = \sum_{\alpha=1}^{N} (\boldsymbol{r}_\alpha - \bar{\boldsymbol{r}}_\alpha, V_0[\boldsymbol{r}_\alpha]^{-1}(\boldsymbol{r}_\alpha - \bar{\boldsymbol{r}}_\alpha))$$
$$+ \sum_{\alpha=1}^{N} (\boldsymbol{r}'_\alpha - \bar{\boldsymbol{r}}'_\alpha, V_0[\boldsymbol{r}'_\alpha]^{-1}(\boldsymbol{r}'_\alpha - \bar{\boldsymbol{r}}'_\alpha)) \to \min, \tag{10}$$

subject to the constraint (4). Throughout this paper, $(\boldsymbol{a}, \boldsymbol{b})$ denotes the inner product of vectors $\boldsymbol{a}$ and $\boldsymbol{b}$. Note that Eq. (10) involves the normalized covariance matrices $V_0[\boldsymbol{r}_\alpha]$ and $V_0[\boldsymbol{r}'_\alpha]$ alone; no knowledge of the noise level ϵ is required.

If $\boldsymbol{R}$ is fixed, the values of $\bar{\boldsymbol{r}}_\alpha$ and $\bar{\boldsymbol{r}}'_\alpha$ that minimize J subject to Eq. (4) can be obtained analytically. Introducing Lagrange multipliers, we obtain

$$\bar{\boldsymbol{r}}_\alpha = \boldsymbol{r}_\alpha + V_0[\boldsymbol{r}_\alpha]\boldsymbol{R}^\top \boldsymbol{W}_\alpha (\boldsymbol{r}'_\alpha - \boldsymbol{R}\boldsymbol{r}_\alpha), \tag{11}$$
$$\bar{\boldsymbol{r}}'_\alpha = \boldsymbol{r}'_\alpha - V_0[\boldsymbol{r}'_\alpha]\boldsymbol{W}_\alpha (\boldsymbol{r}'_\alpha - \boldsymbol{R}\boldsymbol{r}_\alpha), \tag{12}$$

where

$$\boldsymbol{W}_\alpha = \left(\boldsymbol{R} V_0[\boldsymbol{r}_\alpha] \boldsymbol{R}^\top + V_0[\boldsymbol{r}'_\alpha] \right)^{-1}. \tag{13}$$

The resulting minimum is then minimized with respect to $\boldsymbol{R}$. If Eqs. (11) and (12) are substituted into Eq. (10), the problem reduces to

$$J = \sum_{\alpha=1}^{N} (\boldsymbol{r}'_\alpha - \boldsymbol{R}\boldsymbol{r}_\alpha, \boldsymbol{W}_\alpha (\boldsymbol{r}'_\alpha - \boldsymbol{R}\boldsymbol{r}_\alpha)) \to \min. \tag{14}$$

If $V_0[\boldsymbol{r}_\alpha] = V_0[\boldsymbol{r}'_\alpha] = \boldsymbol{I}$, Eq. (14) reduces to Eq. (1). This proves that the least-squares method (1) is optimal for isotropic and identical noise even if $\boldsymbol{r}_\alpha$ and $\boldsymbol{r}'_\alpha$ both contain noise. This corresponds to the result of Goryn and Hein [5].

5 Reliability of the Solution

The unknown noise level ϵ can be estimated *a posteriori*. Let $\hat{J}$ be the *residual*, i.e., the minimum of J. Since $\hat{J}/\epsilon^2$ is subject to a χ^2 distribution with $3(N-1)$ degrees of freedom in the first order (Sect. 7.1.4 of [9]), we obtain an unbiased estimator of the squared noise level ϵ^2 in the following form:

$$\hat{\epsilon}^2 = \frac{\hat{J}}{3(N-1)}. \tag{15}$$

Because the solution $\hat{\boldsymbol{R}}$ of (14) attains the accuracy bound (8) in the first order, we can evaluate its covariance matrix $V[\hat{\boldsymbol{R}}]$ by optimally estimating the true positions $\{\bar{\boldsymbol{r}}_\alpha\}$ (we discuss this in Section 9) and substituting the solution $\hat{\boldsymbol{R}}$ and the estimator (15) for their true values $\bar{\boldsymbol{R}}$ and ϵ^2 in Eq. (8).

The minimization (14) must be conducted subject to the constraint that $\boldsymbol{R}$ be a rotation matrix. This means we need to parameterize $\boldsymbol{R}$ appropriately and do numerical search in the parameter space. Such a technique is often inefficient. Kanatani [9] proposed an efficient computational scheme called *renormalization* for maximum likelihood estimation with *linear* constraints. Here, the constraint is nonlinear, so Kanatani's technique cannot be applied directly. However, we can show that the constraint can be converted into a *linear* equation in terms of *quaternions*.

6 Quaternion Optimization

Consider a rotation by angle Ω around axis $\boldsymbol{l}$ (unit vector). Define a scalar q_0 and a three-dimensional vector $\boldsymbol{q}_l$ by

$$q_0 = \cos\frac{\Omega}{2}, \qquad \boldsymbol{q}_l = \boldsymbol{l}\sin\frac{\Omega}{2}. \tag{16}$$

Note that $q_0^2 + \|\boldsymbol{q}_l\|^2 = 1$ by definition. Conversely, a scalar q_0 and a three-dimensional vector $\boldsymbol{q}_l$ such that $q_0^2 + \|\boldsymbol{q}_l\|^2 = 1$ uniquely determine a rotation $\boldsymbol{R}$ around axis $\boldsymbol{l}$ by angle Ω $(0 \le \Omega < \pi)$ in the form

$$\boldsymbol{R} = (q_0^2 - \|\boldsymbol{q}_l\|^2)\boldsymbol{I} + 2(\boldsymbol{q}_l\boldsymbol{q}_l^\top + q_0\boldsymbol{q}_l \times \boldsymbol{I}), \tag{17}$$

where the product $\boldsymbol{a} \times \boldsymbol{A}$ of a vector $\boldsymbol{a}$ and a matrix $\boldsymbol{A}$ is the matrix whose columns are vector products of $\boldsymbol{a}$ and the corresponding columns of $\boldsymbol{A}$. Hence, a rotation is uniquely represented by a pair $\{q_0, \boldsymbol{q}_l\}$, which is called a *quaternion* [6].

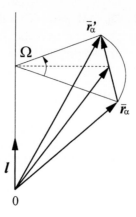

Fig. 1. 3-D rotation by angle Ω around axis l.

Suppose a point $\bar{r}_\alpha$ undergoes a rotation R by angle Ω around axis l and moves to a new position $\bar{r}'_\alpha$. From Fig. 1, we can see that the displacement $\bar{r}'_\alpha - \bar{r}_\alpha$ and the midpoint $(\bar{r}_\alpha + \bar{r}'_\alpha)/2$ are related by

$$\bar{r}'_\alpha - \bar{r}_\alpha = 2\tan\frac{\Omega}{2}l \times \frac{\bar{r}_\alpha + \bar{r}'_\alpha}{2}. \tag{18}$$

Solving this for $\bar{r}'_\alpha$ in terms of $\bar{r}_\alpha$, we can obtain a relation equivalent to Eq. (4) expressed in terms of the angle Ω and axis l of rotation R. Hence, Eq. (18) is equivalent to Eq. (4). Multiplying Eq. (18) by $\cos(\Omega/2)$ on both sides, we obtain after some manipulations

$$q_0(\bar{r}'_\alpha - \bar{r}_\alpha) + (\bar{r}'_\alpha + \bar{r}_\alpha) \times q_l = 0. \tag{19}$$

Define a 3×4 matrix X_α and a four-dimensional unit vector q by

$$X_\alpha = \left(r'_\alpha - r_\alpha \ (r'_\alpha + r_\alpha) \times I \right), \qquad q = \begin{pmatrix} q_0 \\ q_l \end{pmatrix}. \tag{20}$$

Let $\bar{X}_\alpha$ be the value of X_α obtained by replacing r_α and r'_α by $\bar{r}_\alpha$ and $\bar{r}'_\alpha$, respectively, in the first of Eqs. (20). Then, Eq. (19) can be expressed as a *linear* equation in q in the form

$$\bar{X}_\alpha q = 0. \tag{21}$$

Now the problem is to minimize Eq. (10) subject to the constraint (21). Introducing Lagrange multipliers for this constraint and eliminating $\bar{r}_\alpha$ and $\bar{r}'_\alpha$, we can reduce the problem to the following minimization with respect to q:

$$J = (q, Mq) \to \min. \tag{22}$$

Here, M is a 4×4 matrix defined by

$$M = \sum_{\alpha=1}^{N} X_\alpha^\top W_\alpha X_\alpha, \tag{23}$$

where W_α is a 3×3 matrix given by

$$W_\alpha = \Big(q_0{}^2 \left(V_0[r_\alpha] + V_0[r'_\alpha] \right) - 2q_0 S[q_l \times \left(V_0[r_\alpha] - V_0[r'_\alpha] \right)]$$
$$+ q_l \times \left(V_0[r_\alpha] + V_0[r'_\alpha] \right) \times q_l \Big)^{-1}. \tag{24}$$

Here, the operation $S[\cdot]$ designates symmetrization: $S[A] = (A + A^\top)/2$.

If noise is isotropic and identical, Eq. (22) reduces to the method implied by Zhang and Faugeras [16] and Weng et al. [15]. In this sense, Eq. (22) can also be viewed as an extension of their methods to cope with anisotropic noise.

7 Renormalization

Since the constraint (21) is linear, the renormalization technique of Kanatani [9] can be applied to the optimization (22). In order to do so, we first evaluate the statistical bias of the moment matrix M defined by Eq. (23).

Let $\bar{X}_\alpha$ be the true value of X_α, and write $X_\alpha = \bar{X}_\alpha + \Delta X_\alpha$. From the first of Eqs. (20), we see that the error term ΔX_α is given by

$$\Delta X_\alpha = \Big(\Delta r'_\alpha - \Delta r_\alpha \left(\Delta r'_\alpha + \Delta r_\alpha \right) \times I \Big). \tag{25}$$

Similarly, let $\bar{M}$ be the true value of M, and write $M = \bar{M} + \Delta M$. From Eq. (23), we see that the error term ΔM has the following expression:

$$\Delta M = \sum_{\alpha=1}^{N} \Big(\Delta X_\alpha^\top W_\alpha X_\alpha + X_\alpha^\top W_\alpha \Delta X_\alpha + \Delta X_\alpha^\top W_\alpha \Delta X_\alpha \Big). \tag{26}$$

It follows that the moment matrix M has the following statistical bias.

$$E[\Delta M] = \sum_{\alpha=1}^{N} E[\Delta X_\alpha^\top W_\alpha \Delta X_\alpha]$$
$$= \sum_{\alpha=1}^{N} E\Big[\begin{pmatrix} (\Delta r'_\alpha - \Delta r_\alpha, W_\alpha(\Delta r'_\alpha - \Delta r_\alpha)) \\ -(\Delta r'_\alpha + \Delta r_\alpha) \times W_\alpha(\Delta r'_\alpha - \Delta r_\alpha) \end{pmatrix}$$
$$\begin{pmatrix} ((\Delta r'_\alpha + \Delta r_\alpha) \times W_\alpha(\Delta r'_\alpha - \Delta r_\alpha))^\top \\ (\Delta r'_\alpha + \Delta r_\alpha) \times W_\alpha \times (\Delta r'_\alpha + \Delta r_\alpha) \end{pmatrix} \Big]. \tag{27}$$

Define a 4×4 matrix N by

$$N = \begin{pmatrix} n_0 & n^\top \\ n & N' \end{pmatrix}, \tag{28}$$

where

$$n_0 = \sum_{\alpha=1}^{N} (\boldsymbol{W}_\alpha; V_0[\boldsymbol{r}_\alpha] + V_0[\boldsymbol{r}'_\alpha]), \tag{29}$$

$$\boldsymbol{n} = -2 \sum_{\alpha=1}^{N} t_3 [A[\boldsymbol{W}_\alpha (V_0[\boldsymbol{r}_\alpha] - V_0[\boldsymbol{r}'_\alpha])]], \tag{30}$$

$$\boldsymbol{N}' = \sum_{\alpha=1}^{N} [\boldsymbol{W}_\alpha \times (V_0[\boldsymbol{r}_\alpha] + V_0[\boldsymbol{r}'_\alpha])]. \tag{31}$$

The inner product $(\boldsymbol{A}; \boldsymbol{B})$ of matrices $\boldsymbol{A} = (A_{ij})$ and $\boldsymbol{B} = (B_{ij})$ is defined by $(\boldsymbol{A}; \boldsymbol{B}) = \sum_{i,j=1}^{3} A_{ij} B_{ij}$. The exterior product $[\boldsymbol{A} \times \boldsymbol{B}]$ is the matrix whose (ij) element is $\sum_{k,l,m,n=1}^{3} \varepsilon_{ikl} \varepsilon_{jmn} A_{km} B_{ln}$. The operation $A[\cdot]$ designates antisymmetrization: $A[\boldsymbol{A}] = (\boldsymbol{A} - \boldsymbol{A}^\top)/2$. For an antisymmetric matrix $\boldsymbol{C} = (C_{ij})$, we define $t_3[\boldsymbol{C}] = (C_{32}, C_{13}, C_{21})^\top$. Then, the statistical bias $E[\Delta \boldsymbol{M}]$ is expressed as follows:

$$E[\Delta \boldsymbol{M}] = \epsilon^2 \boldsymbol{N}. \tag{32}$$

Applying the recipe of Kanatani [9], we obtain the following renormalization procedure:

1. From the data $\{\boldsymbol{r}_\alpha\}$ and $\{\boldsymbol{r}'_\alpha\}$, compute $\boldsymbol{X}_\alpha$, $\alpha = 1, \dots, N$, by the first of Eqs. (20).
2. Set $c = 0$ and $\boldsymbol{W}_\alpha = \boldsymbol{I}$, $\alpha = 1, \dots, N$.
3. Compute the moment matrix $\boldsymbol{M}$ by Eq. (23).
4. Compute the matrix $\boldsymbol{N}$ by Eq. (28).
5. Compute the smallest eigenvalue λ of matrix

$$\hat{\boldsymbol{M}} = \boldsymbol{M} - c\boldsymbol{N} \tag{33}$$

and the corresponding unit eigenvector $\boldsymbol{q} = (q_0 \ q_1 \ q_2 \ q_3)^\top$.
6. If $|\lambda| \approx 0$, return $\boldsymbol{q}$ and stop. Otherwise, update c and $\boldsymbol{W}_\alpha$ as follows and go back to Step 3:

$$c \leftarrow c + \frac{\lambda}{(\boldsymbol{q}, \boldsymbol{N}\boldsymbol{q})}, \tag{34}$$

$$\boldsymbol{W}_\alpha \leftarrow \Big(q_0{}^2 (V_0[\boldsymbol{r}_\alpha] + V_0[\boldsymbol{r}'_\alpha]) - 2q_0 S[\boldsymbol{q}_l \times (V_0[\boldsymbol{r}_\alpha] - V_0[\boldsymbol{r}'_\alpha])]$$
$$+ \boldsymbol{q}_l \times (V_0[\boldsymbol{r}_\alpha] + V_0[\boldsymbol{r}'_\alpha]) \times \boldsymbol{q}_l \Big)^{-1}. \tag{35}$$

Here, we put $\boldsymbol{q}_l = (q_1 \ q_2 \ q_3)^\top$.

Table 1. Estimated rotations.

	Axis	Angle
Renormalization	$(0.9999, 0.0003, 0.0123)$	$29.769°$
Least squares	$(0.9985, -0.0545, 0.0040)$	$26.790°$
True values	$(1.0000, 0.0000, 0.0000)$	$30.000°$

8 Rotation Estimation from Stereo Images

We conducted experiments for 3-D data obtained by stereo vision. Figures 2(a) and (b) are pairs of stereo images of an object before and after a rigid rotation around a vertical axis. We manually selected the feature points marked by black dots and computed their 3-D positions r_α and normalized covariance matrices $V_0[r_\alpha]$ by the method described in [10], assuming that image noise was isotropic and homogeneous (but the resulting errors in the reconstructed 3-D positions were highly anisotropic and inhomogeneous). We thus obtained two sets of 3-D points.

After translating one set so that its centroid coincides with that of the other, we computed the rotation by renormalization. As a comparison, we also tried the conventional least-squares method (the schemes described in [1, 3, 4, 8, 14, 15, 16] all yield the same solution). Table 1 lists the computed values together with the true values. We can see from this that our method considerably improves accuracy as compared with the least-squares method. However, this result is for just one occurrence of noise. In order to assert the superiority of our method, we need to examine the reliability of the solution for *all possible occurrences* of noise.

9 Reliability Analysis

We evaluated the reliability of the computed solution $\hat{R}$ in the following two ways:

- Theoretical analysis.
- Random noise simulation.

The former is straightforward: since our method attains the theoretical accuracy bound (8) in the first order, we can evaluate the reliability of the solution by approximating the true values by their estimates in Eq. (8).

A well known method to the latter is (parametric) *bootstrap* [2], which can be applied to any solution method. In the present case, we do not know the true positions $\{\bar{r}_\alpha\}$, but we know the true rotation $\bar{R}$ (see Table 1). So, we first estimate $\{\bar{r}_\alpha\}$ by optimally correcting the data $\{r_\alpha\}$ and $\{r'_\alpha\}$ into $\{\hat{r}_\alpha\}$ and $\{\hat{r}'_\alpha\}$, respectively, so that the constraint $\hat{r}'_\alpha = \bar{R}\hat{r}_\alpha$ is exactly satisfied. From Eqs. (11) and (12), this optimal correction is done as follows[2] [9]:

$$\hat{r}_\alpha = r_\alpha + V_0[r_\alpha]\bar{R}^\top \bar{W}_\alpha(r'_\alpha - \bar{R}r_\alpha), \tag{36}$$

---

[2] If the true value $\bar{R}$ is not known, its estimate $\hat{R}$ is used.

(a) Before rotation.

(b) After rotation.

Fig. 2. Stereo images.

$$\hat{r}'_\alpha = r_\alpha - V_0[r'_\alpha]\bar{W}_\alpha(r'_\alpha - \bar{R}r_\alpha), \tag{37}$$

$$\bar{W}_\alpha = \left(\bar{R}V_0[r_\alpha]\bar{R}^\top + V_0[r'_\alpha]\right)^{-1}. \tag{38}$$

Estimating the variance ϵ^2 by Eq. (15), we generated random independent Gaussian noise that has the estimated variance $\hat{\epsilon}^2$ and added it to the projections of the corrected positions $\{\hat{r}_\alpha\}$ and $\{\hat{r}'_\alpha\}$ $(= \{\bar{R}\hat{r}_\alpha\})$ on the image planes of the left and the right cameras independently. Then, we computed the rotation R^* and the error vector $\Delta\Omega^*$ in the form given by Eq. (6).

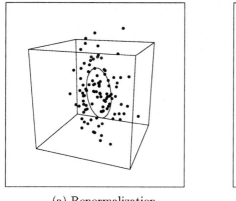
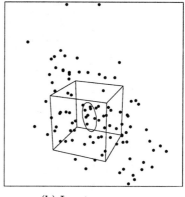

(a) Renormalization.   (b) Least squares.

Fig. 3. Error distribution.

Figure 3(a) shows three-dimensional plots of the error vector $\Delta\Omega^*$ for 100 trials. The ellipsoid in the figure is defined by

$$(\Delta\Omega^*, \hat{V}[\hat{R}]^{-1}\Delta\Omega^*) = 1, \tag{39}$$

where $\hat{V}[\hat{R}]$ is the covariance matrix computed by approximating $\bar{R}$, $\{\bar{r}_\alpha\}$, and ϵ^2 by $\hat{R}$, $\{\hat{r}_\alpha\}$, and $\hat{\epsilon}^2$, respectively, on the right-hand side of Eq. (8). This ellipsoid indicates the standard deviation of the errors in each orientation [9]; the cube in the figure is displayed merely as a reference. Figure 3(b) is the corresponding figure for the least-squares method (the ellipsoid and the cube are the same as in Fig. 3(a)).

Comparing Figs. 3(a) and (b), we can confirm that our method improves the accuracy of the solution considerably as compared with the least-squares method. We can also see that errors for our method distribute around the ellipsoid defined by Eq. (39), indicating that our method already attains the theretical accuracy bound; no further improvement is possible.

The above visual observation can be given quantitative measures. We define the *bootstrap mean* m^*_Ω and the *bootstrap covariance matrix* $V[\hat{R}^*]$ by

$$m^*_\Omega = \frac{1}{B}\sum_{b=1}^{B}\Delta\Omega^*_b, \tag{40}$$

$$V[\hat{R}^*] = \frac{1}{B}\sum_{b=1}^{B}(\Delta\Omega^*_b - m^*_\Omega)(\Delta\Omega^*_b - m^*_\Omega)^\top, \tag{41}$$

where B is the number of bootstrap samples and $\Delta\Omega^*_b$ is the error vector for the bth sample. The *bootstrap mean error* E^*_Ω and the *bootstrap standard deviation* S^*_Ω are defined by

$$E^*_\Omega = \|m^*_\Omega\|, \qquad S^*_\Omega = \sqrt{\mathrm{tr}V[\hat{R}^*]}, \tag{42}$$

Table 2. Bootstrap errors and the theoretical lower bound.

	E_Ω^*	S_Ω^*
Renormalization	0.0277°	1.1445°
Least squares	0.0468°	3.0868°
Lower bound	0°	1.1041°

where tr A denotes the trace of matrix A. The corresponding standard deviation for the (estimated) theoretical lower bound $\hat{V}[\hat{R}]$ is $\sqrt{\mathrm{tr}\hat{V}[\hat{R}]}$. Table 2 lists the values of E_Ω^* and S_Ω^* for our method and the least-squares method ($B = 2000$) together with their theoretical lower bounds. We see from this that although the mean errors are very small for both methods, the standard deviation of our solution is almost 1/3 that of the least-squares solution and very close to the theoretical lower bound.

This observation confirms that the reliability of the solution computed by our method can indeed be evaluated by (approximately) computing the theoretical accuracy bound given by Eq. (8).

10   Concluding Remarks

We have discussed optimal rotation estimation from two sets of 3-D points in the presence of anisotropic and inhomogeneous noise. We have first presented a theoretical accuracy bound defined independently of solution techniques and then given a method that attains it; our method is truly "optimal" in that sense. This optimal method is highly nonlinear, but we have shown that an efficient computational scheme can be obtained by using quaternions and applying the renormalization technique.

Since the solution attains the accuracy bound, we can view it as describing the reliability of the solution; the computation does not require any knowledge about the noise magnitude. Using real stereo images for 3-D reconstruction, we have demonstrated that our method is considerably more accurate than the conventional least-squares method. We have also confirmed the theoretical predictions of our theory by applying bootstrap procedure.

References

1. K. S. Arun, T. S. Huang and S. D. Blostein, Least-squares fitting of two 3-D point sets, *IEEE Trans. Patt. Anal. Mach. Intell.*, **9**-5 (1987), 698–700.
2. B. Efron and R. J. Tibshirani, *An Introduction to Bootstrap*, Chapman-Hall, New York, 1993.
3. B. K. P. Horn, Closed-form solution of absolute orientation using unit quaternions, *J. Opt. Soc. Am.*, A4 (1987), 629–642.
4. B. K. P. Horn, H. M. Hilden and S. Negahdaripour, Closed-form solution of absolute orientation using orthonormal matrices, *J. Opt. Soc. Am.*, A5 (1988), 1127–1135.

5. D. Goryn and S. Hein, On the estimation of rigid body rotation from noisy data, *IEEE Trans. Patt. Anal. Mach. Intell.*, **17**-12 (1995), 1219–1220.

6. K. Kanatani, *Group-Theoretical Methods in Image Understanding*, Springer, Berlin, 1990,

7. K. Kanatani, *Geometric Computation for Machine Vision*, Oxford University Press, Oxford, 1993.

8. K. Kanatani, Analysis of 3-D rotation fitting, *IEEE Trans. Patt. Anal. Mach. Intell.*, **16**-5 (1994), 543–5490.

9. K. Kanatani, *Statistical Optimization for Geometric Computation: Theory and Practice*, Elsevier, Amsterdam, 1996.

10. Y. Kanazawa and K. Kanatani, Reliability of 3-D reconstruction by stereo vision, *IEICE Trans. Inf. & Syst.*, **E78-D**-10 (1995), 1301–1306.

11. Y. Kanazawa and K. Kanatani, Reliability of fitting a plane to range data, *IEICE Trans. Inf. & Syst.*, **E78-D**-12 (1995), 1630–1635.

12. J. Oliensis, Rigorous bounds for two-frame structure from motion, *Proc. 4th European Conf. Computer Vision*, April 1996, Cambridge, Vol. 2, pp. 184–195.

13. I. Shimizu and K. Deguchi, A method to register multiple range images from unknown viewing directions, *Proc. MVA '96*, Nov. 1996, Tokyo, pp. 406–409.

14. S. Umeyama, Least-squares estimation of transformation parameters between two point sets, *IEEE Trans. Patt. Anal. Mach. Intell.*, **13**-4 (1991), 379–380.

15. J. Weng, T. S. Huang and N. Ahuja, *Motion and Structure from Image Sequences*, Springer, Berlin, 1993.

16. Z. Zhang and O. Faugeras, *3D Dynamic Scene Analysis*, Springer, Berlin, 1992.

From Regular Images to Animated Heads: A Least Squares Approach

P. Fua and C. Miccio

Computer Graphics Lab (LIG)
EPFL
CH-1015 Lausanne
Switzerland
fua@lig.di.epfl.ch

Abstract. We show that we can effectively fit arbitrarily complex animation models to noisy image data. Our approach is based on least-squares adjustment using of a set of progressively finer control triangulations and takes advantage of three complementary sources of information: stereo data, silhouette edges and 2–D feature points.

In this way, complete head models—including ears and hair—can be acquired with a cheap and entirely passive sensor, such as an ordinary video camera. They can then be fed to existing animation software to produce synthetic sequences.

1 Introduction

In this paper, we show that we can effectively fit a complex head animation model, including ears and hair, to image data obtained using simple video or CCD cameras as opposed to sophisticated sensors such as laser range finders.

In recent years much work has been devoted to the modelling of faces from image and range data. There are many effective approaches to recovering face geometry. They rely on stereo [5], shading [14], structured light [19], silhouettes [20] or low-intensity lasers. Some of these systems such as the C3D^{tm1} or the Cyberware^{tm} scanner are commercially available. However, recovering a head as a simple triangulated mesh does not suffice: To animate the face, one must further fit an actual animation model to the data.

Automated approaches to this task can be roughly classified into the following two categories:

- Some concentrate on tracking the head motion and some features. They typically use a fairly coarse face model that is too simple for realistic face animation (e.g. [4]).
- Others use sophisticated face models with large numbers of degrees of freedom that are suitable for animation purposes but require very clean data—the kind produced by a laser scanner or structured light—to instantiate them (e.g. [15]).

---

[1] Turing Institute, Glasgow

The approach proposed here bridges the gap between these two classes by fitting to actual image data a detailed face model that has successfully been used to animate virtual actors. We can generate with very limited manual intervention a physical model of the surface—that is, one that includes both geometry and reflectance properties—that can then be used to animate the face.

Our contribution is twofold:

- Because we use robust fitting techniques and take advantage of our rough knowledge of a face's shape, we obtain reliable results even from noisy data acquired with a cheap and entirely passive technique. In particular, we will show that a complete model can be constructed from a sequence acquired with a simple hand-held video camera.
- The least-squares framework we have developed allows us to pool several kinds of heterogeneous information sources—stereo or range, silhouettes and 2–D feature locations—without deterioration in the convergence properties of the algorithm. This is in contrast to typical optimization approaches whose convergence properties tend to degrade when using an objective function that is the sum of many incommensurate terms [10, 9].

These attributes of our approach allow us to derive convincing models even from relatively low-resolution images.

We typically start with a set of stereo image pairs or a video sequence. In this work, we assume that the monochrome images we use are registered and that precise camera models are available. This assumption is reasonable because there are well established photogrammetric techniques, such as bundle-adjustment, that allow the computation of these models as needed. Furthermore recent work in the area of autocalibration [6, 21, 17] could be brought to bear to automate the process. We then go through the following three steps:

- We compute disparity maps for each stereo pair or each consecutive pair in the video sequences, fit local surface patches to the corresponding 3–D points, and use these patches to compute a central 3–D point and a normal vector. Optionally, we also use semi-automated techniques to extract silhouettes and a small number of feature points.
- We attach a coarse control mesh to the animation model and perform a least squares adjustment of this control mesh so that the model matches the previously computed data. We weigh the data points according to how close—in the least squares sense—they are to the model and use an iterative reweighting technique to eliminate the outliers. We then subdivide the control mesh and repeat the procedure to refine the result.
- We use the original images to compute an optimal facet albedo for each facet of the model to achieve the closest possible resemblance to those images.

In the remainder of the paper, we first introduce our optimization framework. We then show how the various sources of information are handled. Finally we present reconstruction and animation results on a number of different heads.

2   Least Squares Framework

In this work, we use the facial animation model that has been developed at University of Geneva and EPFL [12]. It can produce the different facial expressions arising from speech and emotions. Its multilevel configuration reduces complexity and provides independent control for each level. At the lowest level, a deformation controller simulates muscle actions using rational free form deformations. At a higher level, the controller produces animations corresponding to abstract entities such as speech and emotions.

The corresponding skin surface is shown in its rest position in Figure 1(a). We will refer to it as the *surface triangulation*. From a fitting point of view, this model embodies a rough knowledge about the face's shape and can be used to constrain the search space. Our goal is to deform the surface—without changing its topology—so that it conforms to the image data. In standard least-squares fashion, we will use this data to write *nobs* observation equations of the form

$$f_i(P) = obs_i + \epsilon_i \ , 1 \leq i \leq nobs \ , \tag{1}$$

where P is a parameter vector that defines the shape of the surface and ϵ_i is the deviation from the model. We will then minimize

$$\sum_{1 \leq i \leq nobs} w_i \epsilon_i^2 \ , \tag{2}$$

where w_i is a weight associated to each observation. The optimization is then performed using the Levenberg-Marquardt algorithm [18].

In theory we could take the parameter vector P to be the vector of all x, y, and z coordinates of the surface triangulation. However, because the image data is very noisy, we would have to impose a very strong regularization constraint. For example, we have tried to treat the surface triangulation as finite element mesh. Due to its great irregularity and its large number of vertices, we have found the fitting process to be very brittle and the smoothing coefficients difficult to adjust. Therefore, we have developed the following scheme to achieve robustness.

2.1   Control Triangulation

Instead of directly modifying the vertex positions during the minimization, we introduce *control triangulations* such as the ones shown in Figure 1(b,c,d). The vertices of the surface triangulation are "attached" to the control triangulation and the range of allowable deformations of the surface triangulation is defined in terms of weighted averages of displacements of the vertices of the control triangulation. The triangulation can thus be deformed to fit image data and to produce results such as those shown in the second row of Figure 1.

More specifically, we project each vertex of the surface triangulation onto the control triangulation. If this projection falls in the middle of a control facet, we "attach" the vertex to the three vertices of the control facets and compute the corresponding barycentric coordinates. If this projection falls between two

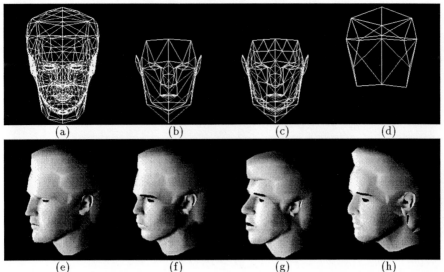

Fig. 1. Animation model. (a) The model used to animate complete heads. (b,c) Two
levels of refinement of the control mesh used to deform the face. (d) The control
mesh used to deform the hair. (e) A shaded view of the model in its default
state. (f,g,h) Shaded views of the model deformed to resemble three of the
people shown in the result section.

facets, we "attach" the vertex to the vertices of the corresponding edge. In effect,
we take one of the barycentric coordinates to be zero.

Given these attachments, the surface triangulation's shape is defined by deformation vectors associated to the vertices of the control triangulation. The
3–D position P_i of vertex i of the surface triangulation is taken to be

$$P_i = P_i^0 + l_1^i \delta_{j1} + l_2^i \delta_{j2} + l_3^i \delta_{j3} \quad , \tag{3}$$

where P_i^0 is its initial position, $\delta_{j1}, \delta_{j2}, \delta_{j3}$ are the deformation vectors associated
to the control triangulation vertices to which vertex i is attached, and l_1^i, l_2^i, l_3^i
are the precomputed barycentric coordinates.

In this fashion, the shape of the surface triangulation becomes a function of
the δ_j and the parameter vector P of Equation 1 is taken to be the vector of the
x, y and z components of these δ_j. Because the control triangulations have fewer
vertices that are more regularly spaced than the surface triangulation, the least-
squares optimization has better convergence properties. Of course the finer the
control triangulation, the less smoothing it provides. By using a precomputed set
of increasingly refined control triangulations, we implement a hierarchical fitting
scheme that has proved very useful when dealing with noisy data, as shown in
Section 3. Two levels of refinement of the control mesh used to deform the face
and the coarsest level of the control mesh used to deform the hair are shown in
the top row of Figure 1.

2.2 Stiffness Matrix

Because there may be gaps in the image data, it is necessary to add a small stiffness term into the optimization to ensure that the δ_j of the control vertices located where there is little or no data are consistent with their neighbors. If the surface was continuous, we could take this term to be

$$\iint \left(\frac{\partial}{\partial u} \delta(u, v) \right)^2 + \left(\frac{\partial}{\partial v} \delta(u, v) \right)^2 du\, dv \ .$$

However, because our control triangulation is discrete, we can treat its facets as C^0 finite elements and write our stiffness term as

$$E_S = \Delta_x^t K \Delta_x + \Delta_y^t K \Delta_y + \Delta_z^t K \Delta_z \tag{4}$$

where K is a stiffness matrix and Δ_x, Δ_y and Δ_z are the vectors of the x, y and z coordinates of the displacements δ. The term we actually optimize becomes

$$E = \sum_{1 \leq i \leq nobs} w_i \epsilon_i^2 + \lambda_S E_S \ , \tag{5}$$

where λ_S is a small positive constant. This is achieved very simply in the least squares framework by incrementing the appropriate elements of the matrix that appears in the normal equations by those of the stiffness matrix K.

2.3 Weighing the Observations

As will be discussed in Section 3, our system must be able to deal with many observations coming from different sources that may not be commensurate with each other. Formally we can rewrite the observations equations of Equation 1 as

$$f_i^{type}(P) = obs_i^{type} + \epsilon_i \ , 1 \leq i \leq nobs \ , \tag{6}$$

with weight w_i^{type}, where $type$ is one of the possible types of observations we use. In this paper, $type$ may be stereo, silhouette position or 2–D feature location. The least-squares minimization procedure involves iteratively solving normal equations and solving linear systems of the form

$$A^t A X = A^t Y$$

where the A matrix is formed by summing the elements of the gradient vectors $w_i^{type} \nabla f_i^{type}(P)$. To ensure that these matrices are well conditioned and that the minimization proceeds smoothly we multiply the weight w_i^{type} of the n_{type} individual observations of a given type by a global coefficient w_{type} computed as follows:

$$G_{type} = \frac{\sqrt{\sum_{1 \leq i \leq nobs, j = type} w_i^{type} \| \nabla f_i^j(P) \|^2}}{n_{type}}$$

$$w_{type} = \frac{\lambda_{type}}{G_{type}} \tag{7}$$

where λ_{type} is a user supplied coefficient between 0 and 1 that indicates the relative importance of the various kinds of observations. This guarantees that, initially at least, the magnitudes of the gradient terms for the various types have the appropriate relative values.

As shown in Section 4, the final result is relatively insensitive to the exact values of the λ_{type} and we have used the same set of values to generate all of our results. Because the complete objective function is not convex, no numerical optimization technique can be guaranteed to find the global optimum at each level of refinement of the control triangulations. The experiments described in Section 4, however, indicate that the Levenberg-Marquardt optimizer consistently yields better minima and needs fewer iterations at each level than other methods such as the Euler-Lagrange methods that have been extensively used in the Computer Vision field [13]—the so-called snake approaches—and one of the best known implementations of a quasi-newton approach in the field of Operations Research [16].

3   From Image Data to Observations

In this section we focus on stereo range data and silhouettes because they can be readily acquired from image sequences and form two complementary sources of information: Stereo can be expected to give good results where the surface more or less faces the cameras while silhouettes appear where the surfaces slopes away from the camera planes. We also use a few key feature points to pin down some of the crucial elements of the model.

3.1   Stereo Data

We use several sets of stereo pairs or triplets of a given face as our input data such as those of Figure 2. We assume that the images are monochrome and registered so that their relative camera models are known *a priori*. Since we are interested in reconstructing surfaces, we start the process by using a simple correlation-based algorithm [7] to compute a disparity map for each pair or triplet and by turning each valid disparity value into a 3–D point. If other sources of range data were available, they could be used in a similar fashion. Because, these 3–D points typically form an extremely noisy and irregular sampling of the underlying global 3–D surface, we begin by robustly fitting surface patches to the raw 3–D points. This first step eliminates some of the outliers and generates meaningful local surface information for arbitrary surface orientation and topology. Figure 2(e) depicts the result of this procedure. For additional details, we refer the interested reader to an earlier publication [8].

The center of each patch is treated as an attractor. The easiest way to handle is to model it as a spring attached to the mesh vertex closest to it. This, however, is inadequate if one wishes to use facets that are large enough so that attracting the vertices, as opposed to the surface point closest to the attractor, would cause unwarranted deformations of the mesh. This is especially important when using

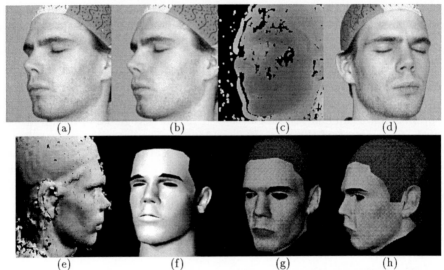

Fig. 2. Modeling a head from a video sequence of forty images (Courtesy of IGP, ETHZ). (a,b) Consecutive images treated as a stereo pair. (c) Corresponding disparity map. Black indicates that no disparity value was computed; lighter areas are further away than darker ones. Note that the disparities around the occluding contour on both the left and right sides of the head are erroneous. (d) Image taken from a different viewpoint. (e) Planar patches extracted from the stereo data represented as disks and shaded according to the orientation of their normals. The shape is recovered but there still are a number of spurious patches and the model cannot be animated as this stage of the processing. (f) Shaded view of the animation model fitted to the face only. (g,h) Shaded views using the facet reflectances derived from the images for the complete head.

a sparse set of attractors. In our implementation, this is achieved by writing the observation equation as

$$d_i^a = 0 + \epsilon_i \quad , \tag{8}$$

where d_i^a is the orthogonal distance of the attractor to the closest facet and can be computed as a function of the x,y, and z coordinates of the vertices of the facet closest to the attractor.

The normal vector to a facet can be computed as the normalized cross product of the vectors defined by two sides of that facet, and d_i^a as the dot product of this normal vector with the vector defined by one of the vertices and the attractor. Letting $(x_i, y_i, z_i)_{1 \leq i \leq 3}$ be the three vertices of a facet, consider the polynomial D defined as

$$D = \begin{vmatrix} x_1 & y_1 & z_1 & 1 \\ x_2 & y_2 & z_2 & 1 \\ x_3 & y_3 & z_3 & 1 \\ x_a & y_a & z_a & 1 \end{vmatrix} = C_x x_a + C_y y_a + C_z z_a \tag{9}$$

where C_x, C_y, and C_z are polynomial functions of x_i, y_i, and z_i for $1 \leq i \leq 3$. It is easy to show that the facet normal is parallel to the vector (C_x, C_y, C_z) and that the orthogonal distance d_i^a of the attractor to the facet becomes

$$d^a = D / \sqrt{C_x^2 + C_y^2 + C_z^2}$$

Finding this "closest facet" is computationally expensive if we exhaustively search the list of facets for the one that initially minimizes the observation error of Equation 8. However, the search can be made efficient and fast if we assume that the 3–D points can be identified by their projection in an image, as is the case with stereo data. For each image, we use the Z-buffering capability of our machines to compute what we call a "Facet-ID image:" We encode the index i of each facet f_i as a unique color, and project the surface into the image plane, using a standard hidden-surface algorithm. We can then trivially look up the facet that projects at the same place as a given point.

We recompute these attachments at each stage of the hierarchical fitting scheme of Section 2, that is each time we introduce a new control triangulation. Because some of the patches derived from stereo may be spurious, we use a variant of the Iterative Reweighted Least Squares [1] technique. Each time we recompute the attachments, we also recompute the weight w_i^{stereo} of observation i and take it to be inversely proportional to the initial distance d_i^a of the data point to the surface triangulation. More specifically we compute w_i^{stereo} as

$$w_i^{stereo} = exp(\frac{-d_i^a}{\overline{d^a}}) \quad \text{for } 1 \leq i \leq n \tag{10}$$

where $\overline{d^a}$ is the median value of the d_i. In effect, we use $\overline{d^a}$ as an estimate of the noise variance and we discount the influence of points that are more than a few standard deviations away.

Robustness can be further increased by multiplying the w_i by the dot product of the normal of the surface patches used to derive the attractors with the current estimate of the normal vector of the facet to which the facet is attached. In this manner, the influence of patches whose orientation is very different from that of the attached facet is discounted.

3.2 Silhouette Data

Contrary to 3–D edges, silhouette edges are typically 2–D features since they depend on the viewpoint and cannot be matched across images. However, they constrain the surface tangent. Each point of the silhouette edge defines a line that goes through the optical center of the camera and is tangent to the surface at its point of contact with the surface. The points of a silhouette edge therefore define a ruled surface that is tangent to the surface. In terms of our facetized representation, this can be expressed as follows. Given a silhouette point (u_s, v_s) in an image, there must be a facet with vertices $(x_i, y_i, z_i)_{1 \leq i \leq 3}$ whose image projections $(u_i, v_i)_{1 \leq i \leq 3}$, as well as (u_s, v_s), all lie on a single line. This can be enforced by writing for each silhouette point three observation equations:

$$\begin{vmatrix} u_i & u_j & u_s \\ v_i & v_j & v_s \\ 1 & 1 & 1 \end{vmatrix} = 0 + \epsilon_{ij} \quad , 1 \leq i \leq 3 \, , \, i \leq j \leq 3 \tag{11}$$

where the (u_i, v_i) are derived from the (x_i, y_i, z_i) using the camera model.

As with the 3–D attractors of Section 3.1, we can use the iterative reweighting scheme described above and the main problem is to find the "silhouette facet" to which the constraint applies. As before, we can exhaustively search the facets of the surface triangulation for those that initially are close to being parallel to the ruled surface defined by the silhouette and minimize the observations errors of Equation 11. Alternatively, we can use the Facet-ID image to speed up the process: Since the silhouette point (u_s, v_s) can lie outside the projection of the current estimate of the surface, we must search the Facet-ID image in a direction normal to the silhouette edge for a facet that minimizes the initial observation error. This, in conjunction with our coarse-to-fine optimization scheme, has proved a robust way of determining which facets correspond to silhouette points.

3.3   2–D Location of Features

In order to ensure proper animation, it is important to guarantee that important features of the model—mouth and corners of the eyes especially—project at the correct locations in the face. Because there now are automated techniques to effectively extract those [2, 3, 11], a system likes ours must be able to take advantage of those whenever available. For each vertex x_i, y_i, z_i of the *surface triangulation* whose 2–D projection u_i, v_i is known, we can write two observation equations:

$$Pr_u(x_i, y_i, z_i) = u_i + \epsilon_i^u \tag{12}$$
$$Pr_v(x_i, y_i, z_i) = v_i + \epsilon_i^v \quad ,$$

where Pr_u and Pr_v stand for the projection in u and v. In this way we do not need the explicit 3–D position of these feature points, only their 2–D image location.

3.4   Reflectance Data

To estimate the reflectance of the facets of the model, we project them into the images and compute the mean gray-level of the pixels belonging to these projections. Here again we take advantage of the Z-buffering capability of our machines to perform this operation quickly while taking occlusions into account.

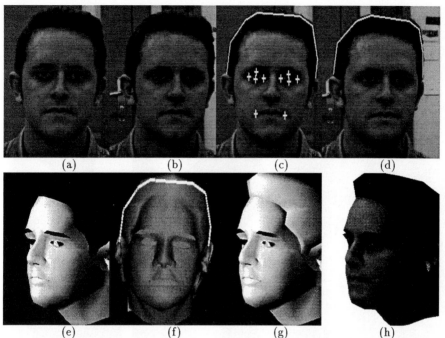

Fig. 3. Modelling the complete head. (a,b) Two images from a triplet. (c,d) 2–D feature points and hair outlines (e) Reconstructed face. (f) Hair optimized to conform to the outlines of (c) and (d). (g) Shaded view of the complete head. (h) Shaded view using the albedoes computed from the images.

4 Results

Figures 2(f,g,h) demonstrates the effectiveness of the fitting technique using only high-quality stereo data as described in Section 3.1.

To illustrate the use of silhouettes and feature points, we use the images of Figure 3. By supplying a small number of feature points and providing an outline for the hair—where stereo fails—we were able to reconstruct both the complete face and the hairdo as follows: We start with three image triplets and use stereo and feature data to reconstruct the face to yield the result shown in Figure 3(e). The hair outlines of Figure 3(c) and (d) can then be treated as silhouettes. They are used, in conjunction with the stereo data and the *hair control triangulation* of Figure 1(d) to deform the part of *the surface triangulation* that corresponds to hair and yield the results of Figure 3(f,g,h) Using the same approach and the same parameters and three stereo pairs for each person, we obtained the three complete heads of Figure 4.

In all cases the heads can be animated by invoking the animation controller [12], as depicted by Figure 5.

The results of Figures 2, 3, and 4 have all been computed using the same value (0.005) for the stiffness parameter λ_S of Equation 5. In the general case,

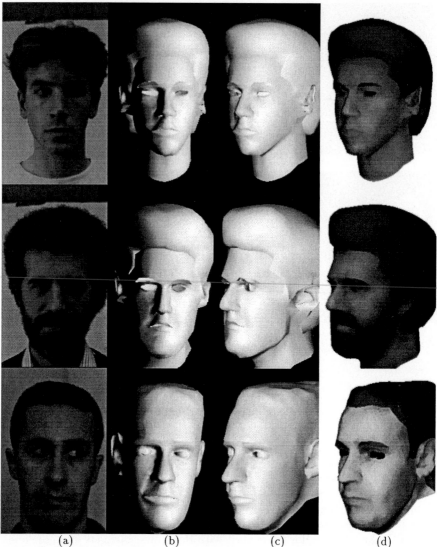

(a)   (b)   (c)   (d)

Fig. 4. Three LIG researchers. (a) Left images of one of the three stereo pairs used for each person. (b,c) Shaded views of the complete head. (d) Shaded view using the albedoes computed from the images. All the models have the same topology and can be animated as those of Figure 1.

these results may involve the combination of several sources of information—stereo, silhouette position and 2–D feature location—and require the setting of relative weights, the λ_{type} of Section 3.2. In all cases we have used $\lambda_{stereo} = 1.0$ and $\lambda_{silhoutte} = \lambda_{features} = 0.3$. To demonstrate the relative insensitivity of the results to the precise value of these weighing parameters, we have run the face re-

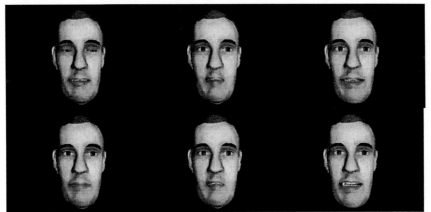

Fig. 5. Animating the face: the third character of Figure 4 opens his eyes and talks.

construction algorithm on the images of Figure 6(a) several times with different parameters setting. We have used both chin silhouettes and feature points, with values of $\lambda_{silhoutte}$ and $\lambda_{features}$ ranging from 0.0 to 0.5 and λ_{stereo} remaining equal to 1.0. In Figure 6(b), we histogram the distances of the 3-D data points derived from stereo to the resulting face surfaces. Note that for each face, the five plots are almost indistinguishable. In other words, the observations derived from the points and the silhouettes affect the result for the surface vertices on which they act, without negatively affecting the convergence properties of the remaining parts the surface. For comparison's sake, we have tried to recompute the face surface's shape using the *same* weighing parameters and the *same* schedule for refining the control triangulations but different optimization techniques:

1. the Euler Lagrange approach found in many snake-like approaches,
2. the MINOS nonlinear optimizer [16] which is considered as one of the most effective such algorithm in the field of operations-research.

We plot the results in Figure 6(c) and (d).

A perfect result is one where the majority of 3-D data points are very close to the recovered surface and therefore their distance to it is almost zero and where a minority of points, the outliers in the stereo data, are much further. The plots of Figure 6(b) are closer to that ideal than those of Figure 6(c,d), especially those derived using MINOS. Although the difference is less obvious, the graphs derived using the Euler-Lagrange approach also exhibit slightly worse convergence properties: there are fewer points whose distance to the surface is almost zero. Furthermore, as shown in Figure 7, the median value of the distances of those points to the surface is also slightly higher. A theoretical understanding of this behavior would require a very sophisticated applied mathematics treatment of the objective function and is therefore beyond the scope of this paper. We conjecture that the use of a stiffness matrix by both the standard least squares approach and the Euler-Lagrange one allows a rapid propagation of the

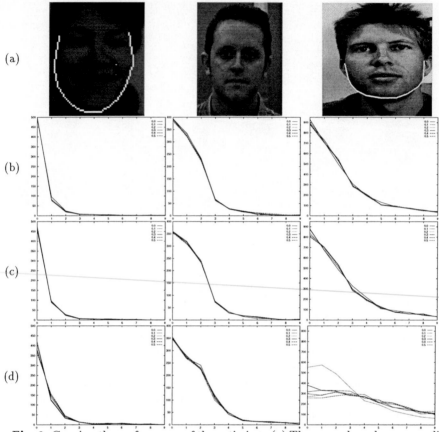

Fig. 6. Gauging the performance of the optimizer: (a) Three people and corresponding silhouette data for the chin. For all three, we have used the feature points depicted by Figure 3(c). (b) For each person's face, we histogram in the distance of the optimized face surface to the 3–D data-points derived from stereo for $\lambda_{stereo} = 1.0$ and $\lambda_{silhouette} = \lambda_{feature} = x$, $0.0 \leq x \leq 0.5$. Note that for each of the three images, the various plots are almost indistinguishable thereby illustrating the relative insensitivity of the result to exact value of $\lambda_{silhouette}$ and $\lambda_{feature}$. (c) Graphs similar to those shown in row (b) but derived by performing the optimization using the Euler-Lagrange approach instead of the Levenberg-Marquardt approach. There are fewer points in the histogram bins that denote a distance close to zero than in the corresponding ones in row (b). (d) Graphs derived using the MINOS optimizer.

smoothness constraints across the triangulation and thus improves convergence, as was claimed in the original snake paper [13]. We further hypothesize that the difference between these two methods, lies in the fact that the Levenberg-Marquardt algorithm does not explicitly compute the gradient of the sum of the squares of the observations. Instead, it computes the individual gradients of the observations—and not their squares—and uses them to construct the matrices that appear in the normal equations.

Levenberg-Marquardt	2.33	6.38	0.55
Euler-Lagrange	2.58	6.87	0.60
MINOS	2.95	7.40	1.40

Fig. 7. Median distance. For the three images of Figure 6(a), we indicate the median distance of the 3–D points derived from stereo to the final face surface for $\lambda_{stereo} = 1.0$ and $\lambda_{silhouette} = \lambda_{feature} = 0.0$.

5 Conclusion

We have presented a technique that allows us to fit a complex animation model to noisy image data with very limited manual intervention. As a result, these models can be produced cheaply and fast. Furthermore, because our approach relies on the use of a coarse to fine control triangulation, it can be used to fit arbitrarily complex models whose topology is designed for animation purposes and are not necessarily well suited for surface reconstruction.

In future work, we intend to extend the approach to the modelling of dynamic faces and more importantly to the estimation not only of the parameters that control the shape of the surface but also of those that control the various facial expressions. We will also incorporate self-calibration techniques into our framework so that we can achieve this result using ordinary video sequences filmed using regular camcorders.

Furthermore, the face model we use has been one of the starting points for the facial animation parameters defined in the MPEG-4 FBA work. When standardization is complete, it will therefore be easy to make the parameters of our model conformant with the MPEG-4 norm for facial animation and the work presented here will become directly relevant to video transmission.

Acknowledgements

We wish to thank Prof. Nadia Magnenat Thalmann, Prof. Daniel Thalmann and Dr. Prem Kalra for having made their facial animation model available to us. We are also indebted to Prof. Grün for sharing with us his insights about least-squares technology.

References

1. A. E. Beaton and J.W. Turkey. The Fitting of Power Series, Meaning Polynomials, Illustrated on Band-Spectroscopic Data. *Technometrics*, 16:147–185, 1974.
2. A. Blake and M. Isard. 3D Position Attitude and Shape Input Using Video Tracking of Hands and Lips. In *Computer Graphics, SIGGRAPH Proceedings*, pages 71–78, July 1994.

3. T.F. Cootes and C.J. Taylor. Locating Objects of Varying Shape Using Statistical Feature Detectors. In *European Conference on Computer Vision*, Cambridge, England, April 1996.

4. D. DeCarlo and D. Metaxas. The Integration of Optical Flow and Deformable Models with Applications to Human Face Shape and Motion Estimation. In *Conference on Computer Vision and Pattern Recognition*, pages 231–238, 1996.

5. F. Devernay and O. D. Faugeras. Computing Differential Properties of 3–D Shapes from Stereoscopic Images without 3–D Models. In *Conference on Computer Vision and Pattern Recognition*, pages 208–213, Seattle, WA, June 1994.

6. O.D. Faugeras, Q.-T. Luong, and S.J. Maybank. Camera self-calibration: theory and experiments. In *European Conference on Computer Vision*, pages 321–334, Santa-Margerita, Italy, 1992.

7. P. Fua. A Parallel Stereo Algorithm that Produces Dense Depth Maps and Preserves Image Features. *Machine Vision and Applications*, 6(1):35–49, Winter 1993.

8. P. Fua. From Multiple Stereo Views to Multiple 3–D Surfaces. *International Journal of Computer Vision*, 24(1):19–35, 1997.

9. P. Fua and C. Brechbühler. Imposing Hard Constraints on Deformable Models Through Optimization in Orthogonal Subspaces. *Computer Vision and Image Understanding*, 24(1):19–35, February 1997.

10. P.E. Gill, W. Murray, and M.H. Wright. *Practical Optimization*. Academic Press, London a.o., 1981.

11. T.S. Jebara and A. Pentland. Parametrized Structure from Motion for 3D Adaptive Feedback Tracking of Faces. In *Conference on Computer Vision and Pattern Recognition*, pages 144–150, Porto Rico, June 1997.

12. P. Kalra, A. Mangili, N. Magnenat Thalmann, and D. Thalmann. Simulation of Facial Muscle Actions Based on Rational Free Form Deformations. In *Eurographics*, 1992.

13. M. Kass, A. Witkin, and D. Terzopoulos. Snakes: Active Contour Models. *International Journal of Computer Vision*, 1(4):321–331, 1988.

14. Y. G. Leclerc and A. F. Bobick. The Direct Computation of Height from Shading. In *Conference on Computer Vision and Pattern Recognition*, Lahaina, Maui, Hawaii, June 1991.

15. Y. Lee, D. Terzopoulos, and K. Waters. Realistic Modeling for Facial Animation. In *Computer Graphics, SIGGRAPH Proceedings*, pages 191–198, Los Angeles, CA, August 1995.

16. B. Murtagh and M.A. Saunders. Minos 5.4 User's Guide. Technical Report SOL 83-20R, Department of Operations Research, Stanford University, 1983.

17. M. Pollefeys, R. Koch, and L. VanGool. Self-Calibration and Metric Reconstruction In Spite of Varying and Unknown Internal Camera Parameters. In *International Conference on Computer Vision*, 1998.

18. W.H. Press, B.P. Flannery, S.A. Teukolsky, and W.T. Vetterling. *Numerical Recipes, the Art of Scientific Computing*. Cambridge U. Press, Cambridge, MA, 1986.

19. M. Proesmans, L. Van Gool, and A. Oosterlinck. Active acquisition of 3D shape for Moving Objects. In *International Conference on Image Processing*, Lausanne, Switzerland, September 1996.

20. L. Tang and T.S. Huang. Analysis-based facial expression synthesis. *ICIP-III*, 94:98–102.

21. B. Triggs. Autocalibration and the Absolute Quadric. In *Conference on Computer Vision and Pattern Recognition*, pages 609–614, 1997.

Stereo Vision-Based Navigation in Unknown Indoor Environment

O. Schreer

Dipl.-Ing. Oliver Schreer, Sekr. EN11, Einsteinufer 17
D-10587 Berlin
e-mail: schreer@rtws18.ee.TU-Berlin.DE

Abstract. Different applications in the field of vision-based navigation of autonomous mobile robots depend on the degree of knowledge of the environment. Indoor environment applications often use landmarks or maps for navigation. Others have only knowledge of known and expected objects. In such applications, parts of the scene are classified in these objects, e.g. road junctions, doors, walls, furniture, and a possible path will be estimated. In case of a lack of *a priori* knowledge of the environment, we propose an approach for vision-based navigation, considering any reconstructed 3D point of the scene. A line segment stereo algorithm and a reconstruction procedure lead to uncertain 3D points of the scene in front of the mobile system. All these 3D points are regarded as obstacles and a following trace estimation will be applied on this 3D data. In order to increase the reliability of reconstructed 3D points, a validation step excludes impossible 3D points, exploiting the stereo geometry of the vision system. After validation a two-step analysis is applied, which contains the minimum distance method and point distribution analysis method. This analysis leads to a possible trace for the mobile robot, resulting in values for steering angle and velocity given to the mobile system. The method has been implemented on the experimental system MOVILAR (MObile VIsion and LAser based Robot) which is based on a multi-processor network. It achieves actually process cycles of approximately 1.5s and a velocity of about 10 cm/s, i.e. a slow walking speed. Experimental results of the above mentioned methods are presented.

1 Introduction

Different applications in the field of vision-based navigation of autonomous mobile robots depend on the degree of knowledge of the environment. Indoor environment applications often use landmarks or maps to navigate. In [9] a method is proposed which recognizes objects like doors, using them as landmarks. In applications like navigating in the middle of the road or in a corridor, the scene is analysed for road junctions [3] or bounds of a hallway [7]. With these methods, known objects are expected in the scene. In case of a lack of *a priori* knowledge of the environment or expected objects we propose an approach for vision-based navigation, considering any reconstructed 3D point as an obstacle.

The basis of our investigation is a line segment stereo algorithm and a 3D reconstruction procedure which is illustrated in the next chapter. This step leads to uncertain 3D points of the scene in front of the mobile system which are the basis for the trace estimation. In order to increase the reliability of reconstructed 3D points, a validation step is applied which is explained in chapter 3. The stereo geometry of the vision system is exploited to exclude impossible 3D points, i.e. false matches. In chapter 4, the two-step trace estimation procedure is proposed which contains the minimum distance method and the point distribution analysis method. The assumption for this algorithm is a local navigation task, i.e. the search for the closest possible path in front of the mobile system with respect to the dimension of the system while avoiding obstacles. Both methods work with all reconstructed 3D points. The analysis of the distribution of 3D points in space leads to a possible trace for the mobile robot, resulting in values for steering angle and velocity given to the mobile system.

The method is implemented on the experimental system MOVILAR (MObile VIsion and LAser based Robot) which is based on a multi processor network. This experimental system achieves actually process cycles of approximately 1.5s and a velocity of about 10 cm/s, i.e. a slow walking speed and is briefly described in chapter 5. Experimental results of the trace estimation procedure in different real scenes are presented in chapter 6.

2 Reconstruction of 3D Points

To get 3D information from images, two different views of the same scene are required. The two views can be obtained from one camera at two different times, called axial motion stereo, or by two or more cameras at the same time. The advantage of polyocular vision systems is the reconstruction of depth information without moving the mobile system in dynamic scenes. On the other hand more hardware equipment and complex algorithms are necessary.

The classical pinhole camera model is the basis for the mapping of the 3D world into a 2D image. This mapping is described with the projective matrix P_i which contains the intrinsic and extrinsic camera parameters. The reconstruction of the 3D point M for two corresponding points I_1 and I_2 in the left and right image is possible, if the projective matrix is known for both cameras as the result of a calibration procedure [5], [6]. The index i refers to cameras 1 and 2. In figure 1, the scheme of a general stereo rig is shown.

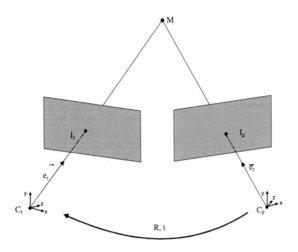

Fig. 1. Stereo geometry for the general case

The 4×3 projective matrix P_i contains the matrix A_i with the intrinsic camera parameters, the rotation matrix R_i and translation vector t_i from camera coordinate system to world coordinate system. In the figure above, the world coordinate system is defined in the optical centre of the left camera. The elements of matrix A_i are the focal length measured in horizontal and vertical pixels α_u, α_v ; the angle θ which describes a non-orthogonality of the retinal coordinate system; and the principal point (μ_0, v_0).

$$A_i = \begin{bmatrix} a_u & -a_u \cdot \cot\theta & u_0 \\ 0 & \frac{a_v}{\sin\theta} & v_0 \\ 0 & 0 & 1 \end{bmatrix}. \tag{1}$$

$$P_i = A_i \cdot \begin{bmatrix} R_i & t_i \end{bmatrix} \tag{2}$$

In the following equations p^i_{jk} denotes the (j,k)-element of the projective matrix of camera i . The first three elements of each row of P_i are composed to the vector $p^i_j = (p^i_{j1}, p^i_{j2}, p^i_{j3})^T$. If the two image points $I_i = (u_i, v_i)^T$ for camera 1 and 2 are known, four equations in three unknowns $M = (x, y, z)^T$ are obtained.

$$\begin{aligned}
(p^1_1 - u_1 \cdot p^1_3)^T \cdot M + p^1_{14} - u_1 \cdot p^1_{34} &= 0 \\
(p^1_2 - v_1 \cdot p^1_3)^T \cdot M + p^1_{24} - v_1 \cdot p^1_{34} &= 0 \\
(p^2_1 - u_2 \cdot p^2_3)^T \cdot M + p^2_{14} - u_2 \cdot p^2_{34} &= 0 \\
(p^2_2 - v_2 \cdot p^2_3)^T \cdot M + p^2_{24} - v_2 \cdot p^2_{34} &= 0
\end{aligned} \tag{3}$$

The optimum 3D point M which is closest to both optical rays of each image point has to be estimated by least squares or other optimization methods [1], [6], [10].

For two cameras, set

$$A \cdot a = b, \quad \text{with} \quad A = \begin{pmatrix} A_1 \\ A_2 \end{pmatrix}, \quad a = (x, y, z)^T \quad \text{and} \quad b = \begin{pmatrix} b_1 \\ b_2 \end{pmatrix} \tag{4}$$

and

$$A_i = \begin{pmatrix} \left(p_1^i - u_i \cdot p_3^i\right)^T \\ \left(p_2^i - v_i \cdot p_3^i\right)^T \end{pmatrix} \quad \text{and} \quad b_i = \begin{pmatrix} u_i \cdot p_{34}^i - p_{14}^i \\ v_i \cdot p_{34}^i - p_{24}^i \end{pmatrix} \tag{5}$$

The least squares solution is then given by

$$a = \left(A^T \cdot A\right)^{-1} \cdot A^T \cdot b \tag{6}$$

The problem in stereo vision is to solve the correspondence problem between distinct tokens of the left and right image [6]. In our approach, a line segment stereo algorithm is used, based on a prediction, propagation and validation strategy [1]. We have choosen line segments as tokens because they describe scenes of man-made indoor environment in an adequate manner, and supply geometrical and structural features for a succesful match. The algorithm was extended by additional grey-level features like the gradient and the mean grey value at each edge. These additional features increase the amount of correct matches and the reliability of the solution [3]. It is important to say that the kind of token, e.g. points or lines is no prerequisite for the subsequent trace estimation algorithm.

The matching and reconstruction algorithm assumes a parallel stereo geometry which results in faster algorithms, e.g. there is no necessity for rectification. On the other hand, the reconstruction results are less accurate, yet a small uncertainty in relation to the dimension of the mobile system is acceptable.

Finally, the 3D points will be obtained by considering the starting and end points of each corresponding segment pair. Unfortunately, the matching result is not entirely correct, due to errors of the previous line segmentation algorithm and the occurence of many parallel straight line segments. In order to reduce the amount of incorrect matches, the result of 3D reconstruction is compared to the stereo geometry.

3 Validation by Using Stereo Geometry

The stereo geometry defines boundaries which have to be fulfilled by the reconstructed 3D points. These boundaries are based on physical limitations, but also on assumptions regarding the navigation process. In the following explanations, the parallel stereo geometry is considered. The notation in the subsequent chapters is sometimes similiar to the previous one, but is selfexplaining in the context.

3.1 The Horizontal Case

First, the horizontal x/z-plane is shown in figure 2. The cameras are placed on the x-axis, the left one at $B/2$ and the right at $-B/2$, at which B is the base length of the stereo system. The cameras are arranged parallel to each other and oriented towards positive z-direction. The origin of the x/z-plane is equal to the origin of the local platform coordinate system and placed at the front side of the mobile system.

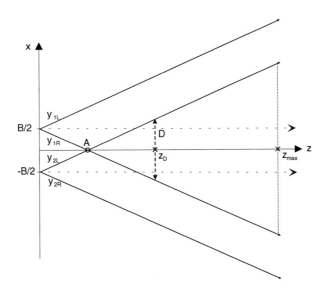

Fig. 2. The visual area of a parallel stereo geometry in top view (x/z-plane)

In x-direction, the area of view from both cameras is bounded on the left side by the left ray of the right camera and on the right side vice versa. It is expressed in the following equation, at which m_χ is the slope of left rays, depending on the focal distance f and the CCD-chip dimension Δx :

$$y_{2L}(z) = m_\chi \cdot z - \frac{B}{2}, \quad y_{1R}(z) = -m_\chi \cdot z + \frac{B}{2}, \quad \text{with } m_\chi = \frac{\Delta x}{2 \cdot f} \tag{7}$$

Observing this area of view, all reconstructed 3D points outside this area have to be excluded. In z-direction, the closest point to the vision system is A. If we consider the width D of the mobile system, a resulting minimum distance z_D is obtained.

$$z_D = \frac{D + B}{2 \cdot m_\chi} \tag{8}$$

The area in front of the mobile system up to the distance z_D is not completly observable. Consequently, 3D points lying in this security area are also excluded.

3.2 The Vertical Case

In the vertical x/y-plane, 3D points should lie above the ground plane and under a maximum height, that depends on the height of the mobile system and a security distance. This assumption is realistic for indoor environment. In natural outdoor environment obstacles below the ground plane may occur and the assumption will be no longer valid.

This validation procedure leads to a set of 3D points which lie within the 3D boundaries explained before. There is no guarantee that all reconstructed 3D points correspond to real 3D points of the scene, and the trace estimation algorithm described below has to take this fact into account.

4 Trace Estimation

The task of the mobile system is to move straight ahead or search the next possible path in the area of view and to avoid obstacles. In order to solve this problem, the trace estimation procedure works with all valid 3D points. The movement is only horizontal in the x/z-plane, therefore the x- and z-coordinates are observed. The orientation of the vehicle is in positive z-direction.

The uncertainty in 3D point reconstruction prohibits a trace estimation from single points. The main goal of the proposed methods is to deal with this uncertainty by means of a statistical analysis of the whole 3D point distribution in order to reduce the influence of false 3D points.

4.1 Minimum Distance Method

The following assumption is made:

> If there is a possible path between two obstacles, and if edges of these obstacles are found, there are two pairs of 3D points with a distance greater than a maximum width d_w.

The value of d_w is determined by the dimension of the mobile system. The line between these two points is called *trace segment*, and the point in the middle of the line is called *trace point* Tr_k. 3D points of the same 3D edge are excluded from the analysis in pairs, because a path through the 3D edge is impossible. Since the mobile system has to move straight ahead, the angle β between each trace segment and the x-axis should be less than $\pm 45°$. This boundary is no restriction to any given path, and will be explained at the end of the chapter.

The previous considerations are expressed in the following manner:

$$\left|P_i(x,z)-P_j(x,z)\right|>d_w \quad \text{and} \quad |\beta|<45°$$

$$\forall i,j\in N,\quad i\neq j,\quad i \text{ and } j \text{ from different edges,}\quad N=\text{number of 3D - points} \tag{9}$$

$$Tr_k(x,z)=\left(P_i(x,z)-P_j(x,z)\right)/2 \tag{10}$$

In [2], a confidence measure for 3D line segments is proposed which depends on the distance to the robot and some other elements of the processing chain. The uncertainty in the distance depends on less resolution of the disparity by computing 3D edges far away from the vision system. This weighting is introduced in our 3D point-approach in a similiar way. We compute the distance-dependent weighted sum of all trace points, which leads to the resulting mean trace.

$$Tr_{mean}(x,z)=\sum_{k=1}^{M}Tr_k(x,z)\cdot w(d_k),\quad d_k:\ \text{distance of } Tr_k(x,z)$$

$$w(r):\text{weighting - function} \tag{11}$$

$$M:\quad \text{number of trace points}$$

The polar coordinates of the mean trace point contain the steering angle α for the mobile system. The figure below illustrates the idea.

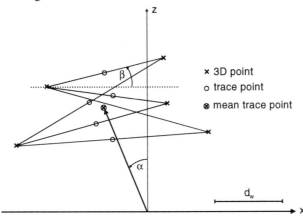

Fig. 3. The minimum distance method applied on five 3D points

This criterion works well if the obstacles are distributed in two parts which the mobile system is able to pass. In the case of aligned 3D points resulting from e.g. a wall, an additional criterion is introduced by analysing the neighbourhood of the 3D points. If a trace segment is found that fulfils the criteria in (9), an area around the trace segment is observed, marked grey-shaded in figure 4 . The width of the area is determined by a constant d_v, describing a minimum distance of trace points in depth of x/z-space.

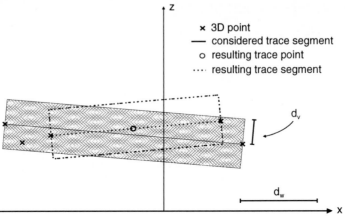

Fig. 4. The case of aligned 3D points

If one or more other 3D points are found within the area, the current observed trace segment and resulting trace point will be rejected. In the example above, one possible trace point is found at the end of the procedure. Now, we define a minimum amount of trace points required for estimating a mean trace. In the example above no trace estimation is possible. Nevertheless, the trace estimation problem will be solved by applying a second analysis, explained in the next chapter.

The boundary for the angle β between each trace segment and the x-axis is no restriction for paths with a larger angle, because it is applied locally at time t_i. At time t_{i+1}, the mobile system was moved in a new position with a new orientation, observing new 3D points with a new resulting mean trace. The behaviour is shown in the figures below.

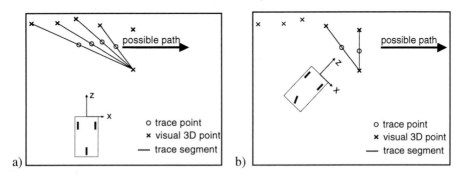

Fig. 5. a) Position and orientation at time t_i, b) Position and orientation at time t_{i+1}

4.2 Point Distribution Method

In case of rejection by the previous method, the distribution of the 3D points in the x/z-plane will be analysed. The 2D covariance matrix of the points is calculated by

$$\vec{p}_i = P_i(x, z) \tag{12}$$

$$\underline{C} = \sum_{i=1}^{N} (\vec{p}_i - \vec{m}_0) \cdot (\vec{p}_i - \vec{m}_0)', \vec{m}_0 = \text{mean of the point distribution} \tag{13}$$

The eigenvectors represent the orientation of the distribution and the roots of the eigenvalues correspond to the standard deviation in each main axis. In order to extract trace information of different point distribution ellipsoids, classifying of position and orientation is necessary.

For a reliable analysis, small and concentrated point distributions should be excluded, as no main direction is detectable. The position and orientation of the point distribution ellipsoid are determined by the centre of gravity m_0 and the angle φ between the main axis of the distribution and the z-axis. The steering angle α depends on the end-point of the main axis adding a security distance d_s perpendicular to the main axis or in horizontal direction. The different possibilities of orientation and position on the left hand side of the z-axis with the resulting steering angle are shown in figure 6. The coherence for point distributions with a centre of gravity on the right hand side of the z-axis is equal.

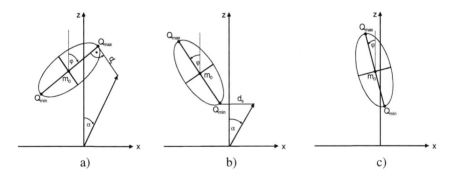

Fig. 6. Different cases of point distribution ellipsoids

We observe three different cases depending on the orientation, the centre of gravity m_0, the point Q_{min} with smaller z-coordinate and Q_{max} with larger z-coordinate related to the mobile system:

a) If the angle is positive, the aiming point is found next to Q_{max}, taking into account the security distance d_s perpendicular to the main axis.

b) If the angle is negativ, the aiming point is found next to Q_{min} , taking into account the security distance d_s as a horizontal shift.

c) If the centre of gravity m_0 and the point Q_{min} are located on different sides of the z-axis and the absolut value of the angle φ is less then a pre-set threshold, it is difficult to decide whether the obstacles are on the left or right side of the mobile system. In this case, no steering angle will be estimated, the mobile system takes the previous value and reduces its speed.

5 The Experimental System

The above mentioned methods have been investigated on our experimental mobile system MOVILAR (MObile VIsion and LAser based Robot). It is a three-wheel vehicle with rear drive. The steering motor and the drive motor are DC-motors, each of them is driven by a PWM power module (Pulse Width Modulation). A controller-card, based on a microcontroller 80C537, provides the link between the vehicle hardware and the control computer.

Fig. 7. The mobile system MOVILAR

A stereo vision head with two CCD-cameras provides a resolution of 512 x 604 pixels. Both cameras are mounted on rotating discs on a splint at the head of the vehicle. They can be shifted along this splint which enables different stereo geometries, with regard to the distance between the cameras (baselength) and the angle between the axes of the two cameras. The image processing runs on a multi-transputer system. The kernel of the system consists of two transputer frame grabbers (TFG), digitizing the images in real time and providing a digital image in the video memory. Furthermore, for algorithms with high computational expense, e.g. image preprocessing, two PowerPC-moduls with an MPC 601 processor are available. For further investigations, a laser scanner PLS-200 is installed in front of the mobile platform.

6 Experimental Results

The system moves with a mean velocity of about 10 cm/s in our lab and finds a possible path without collision. In order to illustrate the performance of the estimation procedure, a part of real scenes is presented, showing all steps of processing in the subsequent figures. The basis is a stereo segment image as input for the stereo algorithm, shown in the top left window. The left and right line segments are marked with dashed and solid lines. The homologous segments as a result of matching can be seen in the window top right, where the corresponding segments are equally numbered. On bottom left hand side, the 3D data in the x/z-plane are displayed. The reconstructed 3D points are marked with a cross, the computed trace points with circles, and the estimated trace is displayed with a straight line. The point distribution ellipsoids are also visualized. The length of both main axes is three times the standard deviation of the distribution.

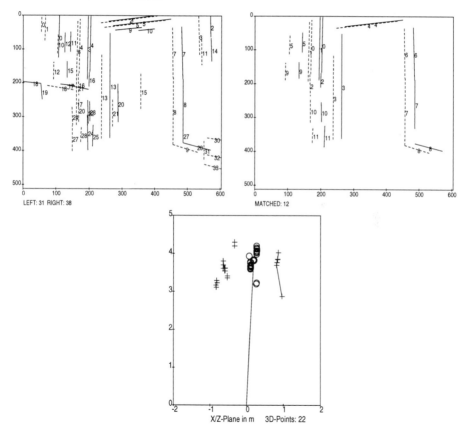

Fig. 8. The minimum distance method

In the figure above, the minimum distance method was applied, since 3D points were found on the left and right hand side, with a possible path between them.

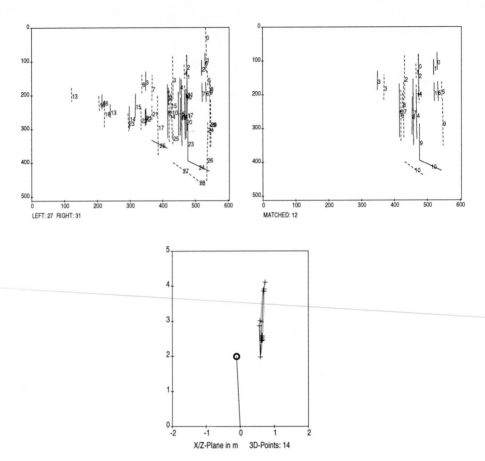

Fig. 9. An example for moving along a wall by applying the point distribution method

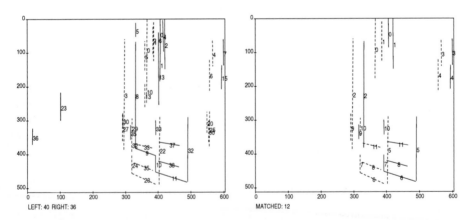

Fig. 10. Stereo segments and matching result for obstacles found on the right side

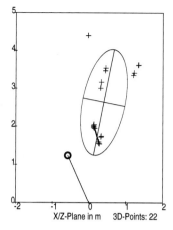

Fig. 11. Obstacles found on the right side by applying the point distribution method based on the stereo segments in figure 10

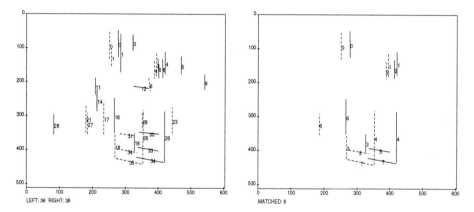

Fig. 12. Stereo segments and matching result for obstacles in front of the mobile system

In figure 9 and 11, the minimum distance method did not lead to a result, but a reliable trace could be established through the point distribution analysis. The examples correspond to the cases a) and b) of figure 6. An example for rejection by the trace estimation algorithm i.e. the case c), is given in figure 13. The angle φ is less than a pre-set threshold, and the point distribution is closed to the z- axis.

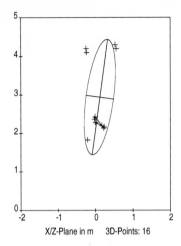

Fig. 13. Rejection by the trace estimation algorithm based on the stereo segments in figure 12

7 Conclusion

We have proposed a method for stereo vision based navigation of autonomous mobile robots. This method does not require any knowledge of the environment (like maps, landmarks or objects). The main idea is to consider every reconstructed 3D point as an obstacle. A validation procedure uses the knowledge of the stereo geometry to eliminate impossible 3D points. The remaining uncertainty of the 3D points is taken into account by two successive statistical methods. In case of point distributions in two parts of the space which the mobile system is able to pass, the minimum distance method leads to a robust trace angle estimation. This method takes into account the uncertainty related to the distance of considered 3D points.

In case of failure of this method, the point distribution analysis method is applied. The method results in an adequate estimation of the steering angle when obstacles are seen only at one side of the mobile system, e.g. in case of moving along a wall. The main goals of this approach was to deal with the uncertainty of 3D point reconstruction, to find a reliable trace, and to avoid collisions while navigating the mobile system.

Acknowledgement

The author would like to thank Prof. Dr. I. Hartmann for his contribution to this research.

References

[1] N. Ayache: „Artificial Vision for Mobile Robots", MIT Press, Cambridge, Massachusetts, 1991.

[2] M. Buffa, O. Faugeras, Z. Zhang: „A Stereovision-Based System for a Mobile Robot", Research Report No. 1895, Institut National de Recherche en Informatique et en Automatique (INRIA), April 1993, Sophia-Antipolis.

[3] M. Ekinci, B.T. Thomas: „Road Junction Recognition and Turn-Offs for Autonomous Road Vehicle Navigation", Int. Conf. on Pattern Recognition, Aug. 1996, Austria.

[4] O. D. Faugeras: „Three-Dimensional Computer Vision", The MIT Press, Cambridge, Massachusetts, London, England, 1993.

[5] O. D. Faugeras and G. Toscanini: „The Calibration Problem for Stereo", Proc. of Conf. Comput. Vision and Pattern Recognition, Florida, 1986.

[6] R. K. Lenz and R. Y. Tsai: „Calibrating a Cartesian Robot with Eye-on-Hand Configuration Independent of Eye-to-Hand Relationship", PAMI Vol.11, No.9, September 1989.

[7] L. Robert, C. Zeller, O. Faugeras: „Applications of Non-metric Vision to Some Visually Guided Robotics Tasks", Research Report No. 2584, Institut National de Recherche en Informatique et en Automatique (INRIA), June 1995, Sophia-Antipolis.

[8] O. Schreer, I. Hartmann and R. Adams: „Analysis of Grey-Level Features for Line Segment Stereo Matching", Int. Conf. on Image Analysis and Processing, Sept. 1997, Florence, Italy.

[9] P. Weckesser, F. Wallner, R. Dillmann: „Position Correction of a Mobile Robot Using Predictive Vision", Int. Conf. on Intelligent Autonomous Systems, IAS-4, 1995.

[10] Z. Zhang, G. Xu: „Epipolar Geometry in Stereo, Motion and Object Recognition", Kluwer Academic Publisher, 1996, Netherlands.

Epipolar Geometry for Panoramic Cameras [*]

Tomáš Svoboda, Tomáš Pajdla and Václav Hlaváč

Center for Machine Perception
Czech Technical University, Faculty of Electrical Engineering
121 35 Prague 2, Karlovo náměstí 13, Czech Republic
http://cmp.felk.cvut.cz

Abstract. This paper presents fundamental theory and design of *central panoramic cameras*. Panoramic cameras combine a convex hyperbolic or parabolic mirror with a perspective camera to obtain a large field of view. We show how to design a panoramic camera with a tractable geometry and we propose a simple calibration method. We derive the image formation function for such a camera. The main contribution of the paper is the derivation of the epipolar geometry between a pair of panoramic cameras. We show that the mathematical model of a central panoramic camera can be decomposed into two central projections and therefore allows an epipolar geometry formulation. It is shown that epipolar curves are conics and their equations are derived. The theory is tested in experiments with real data.

Keywords: omnidirectional vision, epipolar geometry, panoramic cameras, hyperbolic mirror, stereo, catadioptric sensors.

1   Introduction

It is well known that egomotion estimation algorithms in some cases cannot well distinguish a small pure translation of the camera from a small rotation. An example is a translation parallel to the image plane and a rotation around an axis perpendicular to the direction of the translation [6]. The confusion becomes dominant when the depth variations in the scene are small or if the field of view is narrow.

The confusion can be removed if a camera with a large field of view is used [6]. Ideally, one would like to use a panoramic camera which has complete 360° field of view and sees in all directions. Such panoramic camera can, in principle, obtain correspondences from everywhere independently of the direction of egomotion. The uncertainty of the motion estimation will therefore also become independent of the motion direction. The above intuitive reasoning has been formalized by

[*] This research was supported by the Czech Ministry of Education grant VS96049, the internal grant of the Czech Technical University 3097472/335, the Grant Agency of the Czech Republic, grants 102/97/0480, 102/97/0855 and European Union grant Copernicus CP941068.

the result of Brodský et al. [3] who show that the motion estimation is almost never ambiguous for the spherical imaging surface.

This work was motivated by improving stability of egomotion estimation by enlarging field of view of the camera. However, the results concerning epipolar geometry are general and can be used also for looking for stereo correspondences in panoramic images or reconstruction of a scene. In the sequel, we introduce a mathematical model of central panoramic cameras and derive epipolar geometry between a pair of them.

1.1 Work related to panoramic stereo

Though other researchers have already realized that the use of panoramic cameras improves egomotion estimation, little attention has been given to developing the geometry of moving panoramic images as is the *epipolar geometry* [7] for perspective camera. The closest related works by others are by Benosman et al. [2], Yagi et al. [19, 20], Southwell et al. [17], Chahl et al. [4], and most recently by Nene et al. [15] and [9]. Benosman et al. use two 1024×1 line cameras rotating around a vertical axis. They get two panoramic images but does not calculate epipolar geometry since the corresponding features lie trivially in the same column. The disadvantage is the complicated construction of the sensor. Yagi at al. [19] developed a panoramic camera with a conic mirror. They use it for the detection of an azimuth of vertical lines. An acoustics sensor with an optical one is integrated and the trajectory of a mobile robot is found. In [20] a hyperbolic mirror is used, however swiveling motion is detected by analyzing an optical flow and no epipolar geometry is presented. Southwell et al. [17] propose an idea of the stereo with one camera and concentric double lobed mirror but they do not present solid mathematical background. Chahl and Srinivasan [4] draw a method for range estimation using panoramic sensor with the conic mirror. The approach is based on range dependency of motion–induced deformation of the panoramic image. Most recently, Nene and Nayar [15] offer a stereo sensor built from one standard camera and two mirrors. They establish the epipolar geometry for limited case of pure rotation (translation in the case of using parabolic mirror and orthographic camera) of the mirror around the camera. Gluckman and Nayar [9] estimate ego-motion of the omnidirectional cameras by an optical flow algorithm.

A number of authors use panoramic cameras for fast visualization of a complete surroundings of the observer or as a source of images in order to construct a scene representation for virtual reality [5, 8, 10, 13, 14].

2 Design of a panoramic camera

Several different designs of panoramic camera emerged recently. We do not consider panoramic vision systems with moving parts since they are not applicable for real time imaging due to considerable time needed to capture a panoramic image. Fleck [8] uses wide–angle lenses to capture a panoramic image covering a hemisphere. However, such lenses are large and expensive [5]. A panoramic camera covering almost a whole imaging sphere can be obtained by combining a classical perspective (pinhole) camera with a convex mirror. Yagi uses a conic–shaped mirror [19] and hyperbolic mirror [20]. Hamit [10] describes various approaches to obtain panoramic images using different types of mirrors. Nayar presents [14, 10] several prototypes of panoramic cameras using a parabolic mirror in combination with orthographic cameras. Chahl and Srinivasan [5] study reflective surfaces preserving a linear relationship between the angle of incidence of light on the surface and the angle of reflection onto the imaging device. Most recently, independently of this work, Baker and Nayar [1] describe the class of convex mirrors preserving the single effective viewpoint.

The cameras based on convex mirrors offer large field of view (approx. 360° × 150°), instant image acquisition at video rate, compact design, cheap (US$220 for our hyperbolic mirror) production, and the freedom to choose the shape of the mirror in order to yield a nice mathematical model of the camera.

2.1   Shape of the mirror

A panoramic camera with a mirror, see Figure 1, consists of a perspective camera looking into a convex mirror. The ray p_1 proceeding from (or incoming into) the camera is reflected by the mirror as a ray p_1'. Each ray p has to pass through the camera center of projection C. Reflected rays p' can but need not intersect at the same point. Figure 1(a) shows a panoramic camera with a spherical mirror in which case the reflected rays do not intersect at the same point. Figure 1(b) shows the upper part of hyperboloid of two sheets, further called hyperbolic mirror, where all the reflected rays intersect at the focal point of the mirror F'. The camera center of projection C coincides with the second focal point of the mirror, F. Figure 1(c) shows the parabolic mirror. Reflected rays p_1', p_2' intersect in the focal point F' of the mirror and the second mirror focus F is at infinity thus the *orthographic* projection has to be used.

We further focus on the case when all reflected rays intersect at a single point. *This is an important property which is a necessary condition for the existence of epipolar geometry inherent to the moving sensor and independent of the scene structure.* Panoramic cameras with this property shall be called *central panoramic cameras*. In this case the model of the panoramic camera can be decomposed into a central projection from space onto a curved surface of the mirror and a central projection from the surface of the mirror into the image plane.

2.2   Model of a panoramic camera with a hyperbolic mirror

Figure 2 shows the composition of a perspective camera with a hyperbolic mirror so that the camera projection center C coincides with the focal point of the mirror F. The perspective camera can be modeled by an *internal camera calibration matrix* K which relates 3D coordinates $X = [x, y, z]^T$ into retinal coordinates $\mathbf{q} = [q_u, q_v, 1]^T$.

$$\mathbf{q} = \frac{1}{z} K X, \tag{1}$$

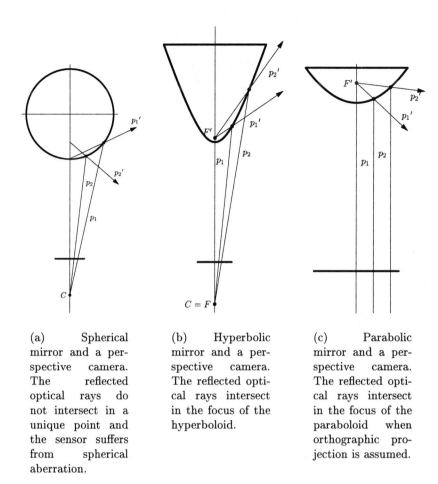

(a) Spherical mirror and a perspective camera. The reflected optical rays do not intersect in a unique point and the sensor suffers from spherical aberration.

(b) Hyperbolic mirror and a perspective camera. The reflected optical rays intersect in the focus of the hyperboloid.

(c) Parabolic mirror and a perspective camera. The reflected optical rays intersect in the focus of the paraboloid when orthographic projection is assumed.

Fig. 1. Three combinations lens–mirror.

See [7] for more information about camera calibration.

In the "mirror coordinate system", which is centered at the focal point F', a hyperbolic mirror is defined by the equation

$$\frac{(z + \sqrt{a^2 + b^2})^2}{a^2} - \frac{x^2 + y^2}{b^2} = 1, \tag{2}$$

where a, b are parameters of the mirror. The image formation can be expressed as a composition of the coordinate transformations and projections. We want to find the relationship between a point X in the world coordinates and the camera point $\mathbf{q}$ in the retinal coordinate system. The derivation of the image formation is omitted here due to lack of space, details can be found in [18]. Complete model

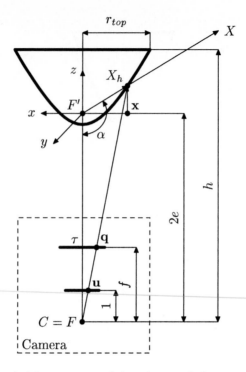

Fig. 2. The geometry of the mirror and the camera.

can be written concisely as

$$\mathbf{q} \simeq K R_C \Big(\mathcal{F}^-(R_M(X - \mathbf{t}_M)) R_M(X - \mathbf{t}_M) - \mathbf{t}_C \Big), \tag{3}$$

where $\simeq$ denotes equality up to nonzero scale. $R_C, \mathbf{t}_C$ express the rotation and translation between the mirror coordinate system and the camera coordinate system. $R_M, \mathbf{t}_M$ denote the transformation between the world and the mirror coordinate frames. $\mathcal{F}^-$ is the following nonlinear function of a 3D vector $\mathbf{v} = [v_1, v_2, v_3]^T$, which is in this case equal to $R_M(X - \mathbf{t}_M)$

$$\mathcal{F}^\pm(\mathbf{v}) = \frac{b^2(\pm e v_3 + a\|\mathbf{v}\|)}{b^2 v_3^2 - a^2 v_1^2 - a^2 v_2^2}, \quad \text{where } e = \sqrt{a^2 + b^2}. \tag{4}$$

Mapping (3) contains 6 external calibration parameters (3 for $\mathbf{t}_M$ and 3 for R_M) and 9 internal parameters (a, b for the mirror, 2 for the rotation R_C, and 5 for K) [18]. The translation vector $\mathbf{t}_C = [0, 0, -2e]^T$ is indispensable, since the projection center of the camera has to coincide with the second focus of the hyperboloid.

In order to establish the equations for the epipolar geometry, it is necessary to find the coordinates of the point on the mirror X_h, see Figure 2, for each image point $\mathbf{q}$. The formula for computing X_h from pixel coordinates $\mathbf{q}$ reads as

$$X_h = \mathcal{F}^+(R_C^T K^{-1} \mathbf{q}) R_C^T K^{-1} \mathbf{q} + \mathbf{t}_C, \tag{5}$$

where $\mathcal{F}^+(\mathbf{v})$ is given by equation (4).

3 Epipolar geometry of central panoramic cameras

3.1 Epipolar geometry for perspective cameras

Epipolar geometry of two perspective cameras [7], see Figure 3, assigns to each point q_1 in one image an epipolar line l_2 in the second image. All epipolar lines in each image intersect in the epipoles e_1 and e_2. Coordinates of an epipolar line

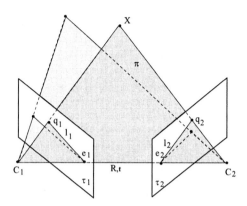

Fig. 3. The epipolar geometry of two perspective cameras.

can be defined as

$$l_1 = q_1 \wedge e_1, \qquad (6)$$

where the symbol $\wedge$ denotes a crossproduct. The equation (6) can be rewritten in a matrix form as

$$l_1 = B(e_1)q_1. \qquad (7)$$

The vector l_1 is perpendicular to the line joining points e_1 and q_1 and points on this line satisfy $l_1 q = 0$. Since the epipolar lines l_1 and l_2 are coplanar, the transformation between them is a collineation, defined by a 3×3 matrix A.

$$l_2 = Al_1. \qquad (8)$$

By combining equations (8) and (7) together, we get

$$l_2 = AB(e_1)q_1 = Qq_1, \qquad (9)$$

where Q denotes the *fundamental matrix* [7]. Multiplying equation (9) by the q_2^T from the right side leaves us with

$$q_2^T Q q_1 = 0, \qquad (10)$$

This equation says that the vector t connecting the centers of the cameras C_1 and C_2 is coplanar with the corresponding vectors q_1 and q_2.

3.2 Epipolar geometry for panoramic cameras

Let us define the translation $\mathbf{t}$ and the rotation R between sensors as the translation and the rotation between local coordinate systems centered at mirror foci F_1' and F_2' , see Figure 4. Let points on the mirrors related to the a single 3D point be denoted X_{h1} resp. X_{h2}, see Figure 4. The coplanarity of vectors X_{h1}, X_{h2}, and $\mathbf{t}$ can be written as

$$X_{h2} R(\mathbf{t} \wedge X_{h1}) = 0. \tag{11}$$

Introducing an antisymmetric matrix S

$$S = \begin{bmatrix} 0 & -t_z & t_y \\ t_z & 0 & -t_x \\ -t_y & t_x & 0 \end{bmatrix}, \tag{12}$$

we can rewrite the coplanarity constraint (11) in the matrix form as

$$X_{h2}^T E X_{h1} = 0, \text{ where } E = RS \tag{13}$$

stands for the *essential matrix*. The essential matrix E can be used here instead of the fundamental matrix since vectors X_{hi} are metric entities. Vectors X_{h1}, X_{h2}, and $\mathbf{t}$ form the *epipolar plane* π. This plane intersects the mirrors in space conics. These conics are then projected onto another conics in the image planes by a central (perspective) projection. A conic is uniquely assigned in the second image to a point $\mathbf{q}_1$ in the first image

$$\mathbf{q}_2^T A_2(E, \mathbf{q}_1) \, \mathbf{q}_2 = 0. \tag{14}$$

In general case, the matrix $A_2(E, \mathbf{q}_1)$ is a nonlinear function of the essential matrix E, point $\mathbf{q}_1$, and the calibration parameters of the panoramic cameras and the mirrors.

The shape of the conic, i.e. whether they are lines, ellipses, parabolas or hyperbolas, depends on the shape of mirrors, on motion of the cameras as well as on which pair of corresponding points in the images is considered. It holds that there is at least one line among all epipolar conics. It is the line which corresponds to the epipolar plane passing through the axis of the mirror. The corresponding epipolar curves are both lines iff the motion is a translation, i.e. the axes of the mirrors remain parallel. Moreover, if the translation is along the axis of the mirror, all epipolar curves become lines. It is clear that epipolar curves form a one-parameter family of conics which is parameterized by the angle of rotation of the epipolar planes around the vector $\mathbf{t}$.

All epipolar conics pass through two points which are the images of the intersection of mirrors with the line $F_1' F_2'$. Therefore, there are usually two epipoles, denoted e_1 and e_1' resp. e_2 and e_2' in Figure 4. The epipoles can degenerate into one double epipole if the camera is translated along the rotation axis of the rotation of the mirror.

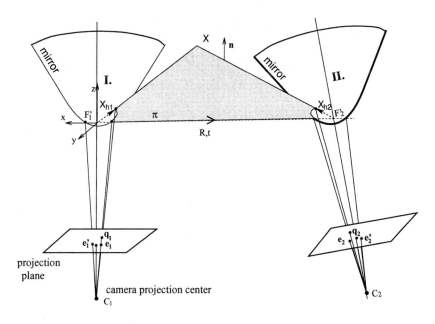

Fig. 4. The epipolar geometry of two panoramic cameras with hyperbolic mirrors.

3.3 Formula of epipolar conics

We look for the $A_2(E, \mathbf{q}_1)$ from equation (14). Let us find the equation of an orthographic projection of the space conic given by the intersection of the epipolar plane with the mirror to xy plane of the mirror coordinate system, see Figure 4.

$$\mathbf{x}_2^T A_{\mathbf{x}_2} \mathbf{x}_2 = 0, \tag{15}$$

where

$$\mathbf{x}_2 = [x, y, 1]^T \text{ and } X_{h2} = [x, y, z]^T. \tag{16}$$

The focus of the first mirror F_1', vectors X_{h1} and $\mathbf{t}$ define the epipolar plane π. This plane intersects the second mirror in a planar conic. The normal vector of the plane π expressed in the coordinate system of the first mirror is

$$\mathbf{n_1} = \mathbf{t} \wedge X_{h1}, \tag{17}$$

Normal vector $\mathbf{n}_1$ can be expressed in the coordinate system of the second mirror by using E, equation (13), as

$$\mathbf{n_2} = R\mathbf{n_1} = R(\mathbf{t} \wedge X_{h1}) = RSX_{h1} = EX_{h1}. \tag{18}$$

Writing $\mathbf{n_2} = [p, q, s]^T$, the equation of the plane π can be written in the second coordinate system as

$$px + qy + sz = 0. \tag{19}$$

We can express z as a function of x, y from the equation (19) and substitute it into the equation (2) yielding us a polynomial in x, y

$$(p^2b^2 - s^2a^2)x^2 + 2pqb^2xy + (q^2b^2 - s^2a^2)y^2 - 2spb^2ex - 2sqb^2ey - s^2b^4 = 0, \quad (20)$$

which is actually the quadratic form of the conic (15). Parameters a, b in equation (20) are related to the second mirror, since the epipolar plane, defined by the first mirror, intersects the second mirror. Consequently the matrix $A_{\mathbf{x}_2}$ from (15) has the form

$$A_{\mathbf{x}_2} = \begin{bmatrix} p^2b^2 - s^2a^2 & pqb^2 & -pseb^2 \\ pqb^2 & q^2b^2 - s^2a^2 & -qseb^2 \\ -pseb^2 & -qseb^2 & s^2b^4 \end{bmatrix}. \quad (21)$$

Let $s \neq 0$, i.e. the epipolar plane does not contain the axis of the mirror. Corresponding point in the second mirror X_{h2} lies on the epipolar plane π. Substituting x, y coordinates of $\mathbf{x}_2$ into equation (19), the coordinates of the point X_{h2} can be expressed as a linear function of $\mathbf{x}_2$

$$X_{h2} = \begin{bmatrix} x \\ y \\ \frac{-px-qy}{s} \end{bmatrix} = \begin{bmatrix} 1 & 0 & 0 \\ 0 & 1 & 0 \\ -\frac{p}{s} & -\frac{q}{s} & 0 \end{bmatrix} \mathbf{x}_2. \quad (22)$$

It follows then from equations (5) and (22) that[1]

$$\mathcal{F}^+(R_C^T K^{-1}\mathbf{q}_2)R_C^T K^{-1}\mathbf{q}_2 = \left(X_{h2} + \begin{bmatrix} 0 \\ 0 \\ 2e \end{bmatrix}\right) = \begin{bmatrix} 1 & 0 & 0 \\ 0 & 1 & 0 \\ -\frac{p}{s} & -\frac{q}{s} & 2e \end{bmatrix} \mathbf{x}_2. \quad (23)$$

Since $\mathcal{F}^+(R_C^T K^{-1}\mathbf{q}_2) \neq 0$ for $s \neq 0$ we can write

$$\mathbf{x}_2 \simeq N R_C^T K^{-1}\mathbf{q}_2, \text{ where } N = \begin{bmatrix} 1 & 0 & 0 \\ 0 & 1 & 0 \\ \frac{p}{2se} & \frac{q}{2se} & \frac{1}{2e} \end{bmatrix}. \quad (24)$$

$\mathbf{x}_2$ can be then substituted into equation (15) yielding the desired equation of the epipolar conic in the image plane

$$\mathbf{q}_2^T K^{-T} R_C N^T A_{\mathbf{x}_2} N R_C^T K^{-1}\mathbf{q}_2 = 0, \quad (25)$$

leaving us with $A_2 = K^{-T} R_C B_2 R_C^T K^{-1}$, where

$$B_2 = N^T A_{\mathbf{x}_2} N = \begin{bmatrix} -4s^2a^2e^2 + p^2b^4 & pqb^4 & psb^2(-2e^2 + b^2) \\ pqb^4 & -4s^2a^2e^2 + q^2b^4 & qsb^2(-2e^2 + b^2) \\ psb^2(-2e^2 + b^2) & qsb^2(-2e^2 + b^2) & s^2b^4 \end{bmatrix} \quad (26)$$

---

[1] In (5), we use $\mathbf{t}_C = [0, 0, -2e]^T$ since the center of the camera has to coincide with the second focal point of the mirror.

is a nonlinear function of a, b, and

$$[p, q, s]^T = E \left(\mathcal{F}^+ (R_C^T K^{-1} \mathbf{q}_1) R_C^T K^{-1} \mathbf{q}_1 - [0, 0, 2e]^T \right). \qquad (27)$$

$\mathcal{F}^+ (R_C^T K^{-1} \mathbf{q}_1)$ is defined by equation (4). Though we have assumed that $s \neq 0$ in the above development, equation (25) holds even for $s = 0$ as it can be verified by repeating the development for $X_{h2} = [x, y, 0]^T$ instead of equation (22) and comparing with the substitution of $s = 0$ into the equation (25).

Equation (25) defines the curve on which the projected corresponding point has to lie and it is indeed an equation of a conic as alleged by equation (14).

3.4 Using the epipolar geometry

The epipolar geometry presented above can be exploited similarly as in the case of standard perspective cameras. Once the epipolar geometry between two panoramic images is established, the search for correspondences is nicely reduced to 1 degree of freedom problem. At least 8 correspondences are needed to solve essential matrix linearly (13), using method [12], for instance. If the essential matrix E is known we can compute epipolar conic for each point of interest in the first image, on which the corresponding point has to lie in the second image. We can then employ an iterative algorithm to establish epipolar geometry and to find correspondences more robustly [21].

Let the essential matrix E be robustly estimated, from equation (13). Recall that $E = RS$, where R is a rotation matrix and matrix S is formed by elements of the translation vector $\mathbf{t}$, see equation (12). The *motion parameters* R and $\mathbf{t}$ can be recovered using the approach described in [11], for instance.

4 Experiments

Our panoramic (omnidirectional) camera is intended for use in our mobile robot. The camera is below the mirror. We designed the mirror that the high vertical angle of view with the values $a = 28.1851$ mm and $b = 9.3950$ mm was obtained, see [18]. The mirror was manufactured by ASTRO—Telescope, Přerov, Czech Republic.

Assembly. We calibrated the standard CCD camera off–line, using the method and the equipment from [16]. The focal length f of the camera used is 8.5 mm and the camera resolution is 768×512 pixels. To position camera correctly, we projected the calibration circle and the calibration axes into the image and moved the mirror until the axis of the mirror fits the calibration axes and the mirror rim fits the calibration circle.

Sequence. We captured a sequence by moving the panoramic sensor through our laboratory. The area, in which the sensor moved, was approximately 6×6

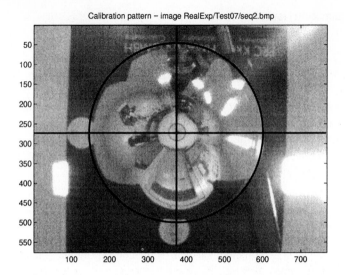

Calibration pattern – image RealExp/Test07/seq2.bmp

Fig. 5. Assembly of the sensor. The mirror fits the projected calibration circle and the calibration cross.

meters. The camera is below the mirror and the sensor is moving near the floor. Two consecutive images are shown in Fig 6. The points of interest were selected manually. There is no rotation between the two positions, because it is difficult to rotate the real sensor in a controlled way. The translation between two positions is $\mathbf{t} = [60, 60, 0]$ cm.

Although we used a very simple method to adjust the camera and mirror so that $C = F$, and no correction to radial distortion of the lens was used, the results are acceptable, see Figure 7. The epipolar conics pass very close to their corresponding point, see Figure 7. The inaccuracy is about two pixels, what is sufficient to find correspondences along conics. Three conics intersect in the epipole exactly.

5 Summary

This paper presented the fundamental theory and design of the central panoramic cameras. We presented an approach to design of a useful panoramic camera and we proposed a simple adjustment method. We defined the image formation function for such a camera. *Our main contribution is the derivation of epipolar geometry for panoramic cameras.*

Even when a simple adjustment method of the sensor was used, results corroborate our theory. The epipolar conics lie close to the corresponding points. The errors were about two pixels.

There are severeal questions which remain beyond the scope of this paper. It is a question how will the lower resolution affect the quality of motion estimation. Special care needs to be taken to finding an automatic calibration and

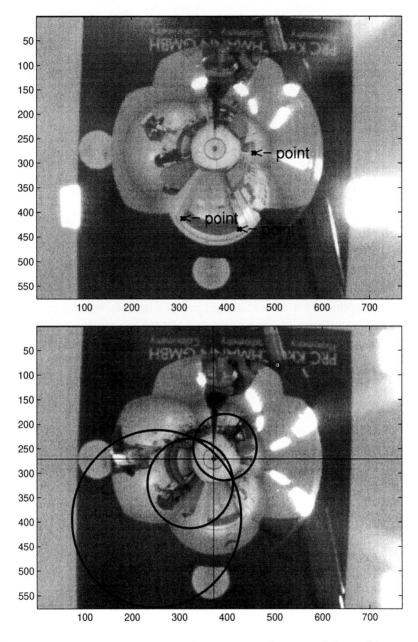

Fig. 6. Two panoramic images. Translation in x and y axis. Points of interest are marked in the upper image. Related epipolar conics are drawn in the bottom image. The conics pass through the corresponding points and intersect in two epipoles.

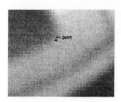

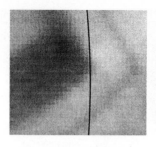

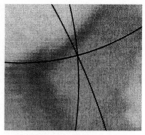

(a) Point in the corner of the jamb of the laboratory door.

(b) Related epipolar conics passes close to the corner in the second image. The error is less than 2 pixels.

(c) The epipolar conics intersect in the epipole.

Fig. 7. Details from the real images, shown in Figure 6.

adjustment method for real mirrors and perspective cameras. An analysis how an incorrect adjustment of the camera and the mirror influences the precision of the epipolar geometry need to be further worked out. More experiment with the stability of ego-motion computation are needed.

References

1. Simon Baker and Shree K. Nayar. A theory of catadioptric image formation. *Submitted to IJCV*, 1997. Also appears in ICCV98, and exists as TR CUCS-015-97, and it was presented in Darpa IUW 1997.
2. R. Benosman, T. Maiere, and J. Devars. Multidirectional stereovision sensor, calibration and scenes reconstruction. In *International Conference on Pattern Recognition 1996, Vienna, Austria*, pages 161–165. IEEE Computer Society Press, September 1996.
3. T. Brodský, C. Fernmüller, and Y. Aloimonos. Directions of motion fields are hardly ever ambiguous. In Buxton. B. and R. Cipola, editors, *4th European Conference on Computer Vision, Cambridge UK*, volume 2, pages 119–128, 1996.
4. J.S. Chahl and M.V. Srinivasan. Range estimation with a panoramic visual sensor. *Journal of the Optical Society of America*, 14(9):2144–2151, September 1997.
5. J.S. Chahl and M.V. Srinivasan. Reflective surfaces for panoramic imaging. *Applied Optics*, 36(31):8275–8285, November 1997.
6. K. Daniilidis and H.-H. Nagel. The coupling of rotation and translation in motion estimation of planar surfaces. In *IEEE Conf. on Computer Vision and Pattern Recognition*, pages 188–193, New York, NY, June 1993.
7. Olivier Faugeras. *3-D Computer Vision, A Geometric Viewpoint*. MIT Press, 1993.
8. Margaret M. Fleck. Perspective projection: The wrong imaging model. Research report 95-01, Department of Computer Science, University of Iowa, Iowa City, USA, 1995.

9. Joshua Gluckman and Shree K. Nayar. Ego-motion and omnidirectional cameras. In Sharat Chandran and Uday Desai, editors, *The Sixth International Conference on Computer Vision in Bombay, India*, pages 999–1005, 6 Community Centre, Pansheel Park, New Delhi 110 017, January 1998. N. K. Mehra for Narosa Publishing House.

10. Francis Hamit. New video and still cameras provide a global roaming viewpoint. *Advance Imaging*, pages 50–52, March 1997.

11. Richard I. Hartley. Euclidean reconstruction from uncalibrated views. In *Workshop on Invariants in Computer Vision*, pages 187 – 202, October 1993.

12. Richard I. Hartley. In defence of the 8-point algorithm. In *Fifth International Conference on Computer Vision, MIT Cambridge Massachusetts*, pages 1064–1070. IEEE Copmuter Society Press, 1995.

13. Hiroshi Ishiguro, Masashi Yamamoto, and Saburo Tsuji. Omni–directional stereo. *IEEE Transactions on Pattern Analysis and Machine Inteligence*, 14(2):257–262, February 1992.

14. Shree K. Nayar. Catadioptric omnidirectional camera. In *International Conference on Computer Vision and Pattern Recognition 1997, Puerto Rico USA*, pages 482–488. IEEE Computer Society Press, June 1997.

15. Sameer A. Nene and Shree K. Nayar. Stereo with mirrors. In Sharat Chandran and Uday Desai, editors, *The Sixth International Conference on Computer Vision in Bombay, India*, pages 1087–1094, 6 Community Centre, Pansheel Park, New Delhi 110 017, January 1998. N. K. Mehra for Narosa Publishing House.

16. Tomáš Pajdla. BCRF - Binary Illumination Coded Range Finder: Reimplementation. ESAT MI2 Technical Report Nr. KUL/ESAT/MI2/9502, Katholieke Universiteit Leuven, Belgium, April 1995.

17. David Southwell, Anup Basu, Mark Fiala, and Jereome Reyda. Panoramic stereo. In *International Conference on Pattern Recognition 1996, Vienna, Austria*, volume A, pages 378–382. IEEE Computer Society Press, August 1996.

18. Tomáš Svoboda, Tomáš Pajdla, and Václav Hlaváč. Central panoramic cameras: Geometry and design. Research report K335/97/147, Czech Technical University, Faculty of Electrical Engineering, Center for Machine Perception, December 1997. Available at ftp://cmp.felk.cvut.cz/pub/cmp/articles/svoboda/TR-K335-97-147.ps.gz.

19. Yasushi Yagi, Yoshimitsu Nishizawa, and Masahiko Yachida. Map-based navigation for a mobile robot with omnidirectional images sensor COPIS. *IEEE Transaction on Robotics and Automation*, 11(5):634–648, October 1995.

20. Yasushi Yagi, Kazuma Yamazawa, and Masahiko Yachida. Rolling motion estimation for mobile robot by using omnidirectional image sensor hyperomnivision. In *International Conference on Pattern Recognition 1996, Vienna, Austria*, pages 946–950. IEEE Computer Society Press, September 1996.

21. Zhengyou Zhang, Rachid Deriche, Olivier Faugeras, and Quang-Tuang Luog. A robust technique for matching two uncalibrated images through the recovery of the unknown epipolar geometry. *Artificial Inteligence*, 78:87–119, October 1995. Also Research Report No.2273, INRIA Sophia-Antipolis.

Occlusions, Discontinuities, and Epipolar Lines in Stereo*

Hiroshi Ishikawa and Davi Geiger

Department of Computer Science, Courant Institute of Mathematical Sciences
New York University, 251 Mercer Street, New York, NY 10012, U.S.A.
ishikawa@cs.nyu.edu, geiger@cs.nyu.edu

Abstract. Binocular stereo is the process of obtaining depth information from a pair of left and right views of a scene. We present a new approach to compute the disparity map by solving a global optimization problem that models occlusions, discontinuities, and epipolar-line interactions.

In the model, geometric constraints require every disparity discontinuity along the epipolar line in one eye to *always* correspond to an occluded region in the other eye, while at the same time encouraging smoothness across epipolar lines. Smoothing coefficients are adjusted according to the edge and junction information. For some well-defined set of optimization functions, we can map the optimization problem to a maximum-flow problem on a directed graph in a novel way, which enables us to obtain a global solution in a polynomial time. Experiments confirm the validity of this approach.

1 Introduction

Binocular stereo is the process of obtaining depth information from a pair of left and right images, which may be obtained biologically or via a pair of cameras. The fundamental issues in stereo are: (i) how the geometry and calibration of the stereo system are determined, (ii) what primitives are matched between the two images, (iii) what a priori assumptions are made about the scene to determine the disparity, (iv) how the disparity map is computed, and (v) how the depth is calculated from the disparity.

Here we assume that (i) is solved, and hence the correspondence between epipolar lines (see Fig.1) in the two images are known. Answering question (v) involves determining the camera parameters, triangulation between the cameras, and an error analysis, for which we refer the reader to [10]. We focus on problems (ii), (iii), and (iv) in this paper.

Main contributions of this paper to these problems are summarized as follows:

(ii) A stereo algorithm solely based on matching pixels from the left and right views tends to have difficulties precisely locating the discontinuities. To remedy this problem, we use intensity edges and junctions as cues for the depth discontinuities. The significance of junctions to stereo has been pointed out in [1, 16]. Our new approach uses edges and junctions in a uniform manner where "ordinary" pixels, edge pixels, and junction pixels increasingly suggest discontinuities in this order. Although

---

* This work was supported in part by NSF under contract IRI-9700446.

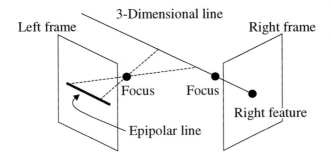

Fig. 1. A pair of frames (eyes) and an epipolar line in the left frame.

a use of window features can also accommodate for this problem, it requires another set of parameters to estimate their size and shape [15].

(iii) Various algorithms, as in the cooperative stereo [17], have proposed a priori assumptions on the solution, including *smoothness* to bind nearby pixels and *uniqueness* to inhibit multiple matches. Occlusions and discontinuities must also be modeled to explain the geometry of the multiple-view image formation [3, 11]. Another aspect of stereo geometry is the interdependence between epipolar lines. This topic is often neglected because of a lack of optimal algorithms. We show that it is possible to account for all of these assumptions, including occlusions, discontinuities, and epipolar-line interactions, in computing the optimal solution. However, this result is under some restricted set of optimization functions and we discuss the scope of its applicability.

(iv) Our method is a new use of the maximum-flow algorithm to find a globally optimal solution, which is represented by a cut of a *directed* graph that models a symmetric stereo (symmetric with respect to the left and right views.) We will describe the limitations imposed on the prior knowledge of surfaces to allow the use of the maximum-flow algorithm. More precisely, it can be shown that, to model interactions between epipolar lines, or discontinuities and occlusions along them, only convex functions can be used in the way described in this paper. Thus, for instance, the cost for discontinuities must be at least linear on the size of the discontinuities. Roy and Cox [22] introduced maximum-flow algorithms on *undirected* graphs for stereo, a more limited set than directed graphs, to compute disparity maps. They also claimed the approach to be a generalization of the dynamic programming algorithm. While our approach is also motivated by their work, we will show that their algorithm has several limitations in the ability to model stereo, e.g., no guarantee of ordering or uniqueness, no model for occlusions and discontinuities, and that it cannot be called a generalization of the dynamic programming algorithms in a strict sense.

1.1 Testing Stereo Algorithms

Evaluation of stereo theories and algorithms is a difficult task. Stereo must deliver accurate disparity maps. While obtaining real image results that "look" good is a definite necessity, looking good is not enough to guarantee a high stereo quality. A careful examination of the disparity map is necessary.

One method of comparison would be to test all current stereo algorithms against each other. However, not only is it difficult to have access to most stereo algorithms, the criteria of comparisons are also unclear.

Alternatively, let us assume we have a ground-truth solution. Then we can compare the disparity map resulting from the algorithm against the ground truth by computing some measure of the error. Usually, ground truth is available only for synthetic examples. Synthetic examples can be created to capture geometrical scene properties, such as occlusions, discontinuities, and junctions, to maximize the information they provide about a stereo theory/algorithm. On the other hand, synthetic images generally lack realistic intensity information that accurately reflects such properties as textures, reflectivity, and illuminations. Thus, while it would take very sophisticated measures to study illumination and reflectivity-related issues with synthetic images, even the simplest synthetic examples using only black and white pixels can be quite instrumental to study the prior models of stereo geometry and the role of edges and junctions.

Two kinds of synthetic imagery are of special interest.

1. Random-dot stereograms (see Fig.7): They remove intensity considerations and essentially lack any features. The disambiguation and solution are derived by the prior model of surfaces. It is interesting to note that an occluded region in one of the pair of images is created by adding random dots to an empty region and, therefore, does not have a good correspondence in the other image.
2. Illusory Surfaces (see Fig.6): These are very important synthetic images to complement the random-dot stereograms, since they crucially require the study of edge and junction features as well as the way in which they relate to occlusions and discontinuities. The following issues deserve our attention: (a) the formation of discontinuities where no intensity edges are present, (b) the choice between front parallel panes with discontinuities and tilted planes, and (c) the role of epipolar-line interactions. In contrast to the random-dot stereograms, occluded regions are composed of pixels that in terms of feature match can have good correspondences, which however the geometrical constraints would not allow.

Finally, let us emphasize that the ultimate test of a stereo algorithm is its performance on real image pairs. We do address all these experimental issues in this paper.

1.2   Background and Comparison to Previous Work

A number of researchers, including Julesz [14]; Marr and Poggio [17]; Pollard, Mayhew and Frisby [21]; Grimson [13]; Kanade and Okutomi [15]; Ayache [2]; Roy and Cox [22], have addressed the problem of binocular stereo matching without explicitly modeling occlusions and its relation to discontinuities.

There is now abundant psychophysical evidence [1, 12, 19] that the human visual system does take advantage of the detection of occluded regions to obtain depth information. The earliest attempts to model occlusions and its relation to discontinuities, in Geiger, Ladendorf and Yuille [11], and independently in Belhumeur and Mumford [3], had a limitation that they restrict the optimization function to account only for interactions along the epipolar lines. Malik [16] brought attention to the role of junctions in stereo, together with Anderson's experiments [1]. Our use of junctions in this paper is limited to the detection of discontinuities.

As for optimization, Roy and Cox [22] presented the study of epipolar-line interaction through the use of maximum-flow algorithm, where they claimed that the algorithm provides a generalization of the dynamic programming algorithm to the two-dimensional stereo. We point out that their algorithm does not model discontinuities and occlusions and that their algorithm obliges occlusion regions to have a match. Thus, for example, their algorithm would have difficulties with random-dot stereograms, where occluded regions do not have any good correspondence. Also, their method provides no guarantee of unique match, but almost always results in undesirable multiple matches, which it eliminates in an ad-hoc way. Moreover, contrary to their claim, the maximum-flow algorithms cannot be a generalization of the dynamic programming. We show that this way of using maximum-flow algorithm cannot model non-convex functions and, as a result, it cannot use sublinear penalties for discontinuities. Though our proposed maximum-flow algorithm is still limited in the same way, it guarantees the ordering constraint (or monotonicity of the solution) and uniqueness of the match, and can model occlusions, discontinuities, and epipolar-line interactions. When non-convex costs are needed, we propose the use of the dynamic programming algorithms, but at the expense of approximate solution when accounting for the epipolar-line interactions.

2 Matching and Surface Reconstruction

Here we describe our stereo model so that in the next section we can discuss the optimization issues.

2.1 Matching Features

We use gray-level pixels, edgeness, and cornerity as features. While we assume the error in the correspondence is solely based on gray-level values, the detection of discontinuities is helped by the intensity edges (edgeness) and, even more, by junctions (cornerity). That is, our model assumes that depth discontinuities are more likely to occur in the presence of edges, and of junctions even more.

If feature $I_{e,l}^{L}$ at pixel l on epipolar line e, or pixel (e,l), in the left image matches feature $I_{e,r}^{R}$ at pixel (e,r) in the right image, then $\| I_{e,l}^{L} - I_{e,r}^{R} \|$ should be small, where $\| \cdot \|$ is some measure of feature distance. We assume a dense set of features, though it would be easy to extend the model to include sparse features like edges.

As in [11, 17], we use a matching process $M_{l,r}^{e}$ that is 1 if the feature at pixel (e,l) in the left eye matches the feature at pixel (e,r) in the right eye, and 0 otherwise. Given a pair of left and right image I^{L} and I^{R}, we define the input cost of the matching process M by

$$E_{\text{input}}(M \,|\, I^{L}, I^{R}) = \sum_{l,r,e} M_{l,r}^{e} \| I_{e,l}^{L} - I_{e,r}^{R} \| , \tag{1}$$

where $l = 0, \ldots, N-1$ and $r = 0, \ldots, N-1$ are indices that scan the left and right images along the epipolar lines $e = 0, \ldots, N-1$ for $N \times N$ square images.

This model, in principle, can be derived from an image formation model. For example, in the case where $\| \cdot \|$ is the Euclidean norm, (1) assumes that the pixels $I^L_{e,l}$ and $I^R_{e,r}$ are related by the relation $I^L_{e,l} = I^R_{e,r} + x$ for corresponding points l and r, where x is a random variable distributed with $P(x) = e^{-x^2}/\sqrt{2\pi}$.

2.2 Uniqueness, Occlusion and Disparity

In order to prohibit multiple matches, we impose a *uniqueness* constraint:

$$\sum_{l=0}^{N-1} M^e_{l,r} \leq 1 \quad \text{for all } r \quad \text{and} \quad \sum_{r=0}^{N-1} M^e_{l,r} \leq 1 \quad \text{for all } l. \tag{2}$$

Notice that this guarantees that there can be at most one match per feature, while also allowing unmatched features to exist.

Remark: It is important to account for scenes composed of tilted planes. In the discretized setting, image pairs of tilted planes exhibit less pixels in one image than in the other. This property will force the pairing to break the uniqueness constraint. When thinking in a continuous setting, the concept of uniqueness is not broken by tilted planes, but in the discrete setting it is. When we describe the mapping of the model to the maximum-flow problem, we will account for multiple matching in the presence of tilted plane.

Occlusion and Disparity: For a stereoscopic image pair we define occlusions to be regions in one image that have no match in the other image. These may occur as a result of occlusions in the 3-D scene (see Fig.2.) We first define an occlusion field $O^L_{e,l}$ and $O^R_{e,r}$ as

$$O^L_{e,l}(M) = 1 - \sum_{r=0}^{N-1} M^e_{l,r} \quad \text{and} \quad O^R_{e,r}(M) = 1 - \sum_{l=0}^{N-1} M^e_{l,r} \; .$$

Due to uniqueness constraint (2), the occluded pixels are the ones with this field 1, when no matches occur.

Now, we define a disparity field $D^L_{e,l}$ and $D^R_{e,r}$ as

$$D^L_{e,l}(M) = \sum_{r=0}^{N-1} M^e_{l,r}(r-l) \quad \text{if} \quad O^L_{e,l} = 0 \quad \text{and}$$

$$D^R_{e,r}(M) = \sum_{l=0}^{N-1} M^e_{l,r}(r-l) \quad \text{if} \quad O^R_{e,r} = 0 \; ,$$

for unoccluded pixels and then linearly interpolate for occluded pixels, assuming the boundary condition $D^L_{e,-1}(M) = D^L_{e,N}(M) = D^R_{e,-1}(M) = D^R_{e,N}(M) = 0$. Then, it can be shown that the following holds:

$$\sum_{l=0}^{N-1} D^L_{e,l}(M) = \sum_{r=0}^{N-1} D^R_{e,r}(M) \; .$$

Since these two variables $O(M)$ and $D(M)$ are functions of the matching process M, our model is completely determined by M.

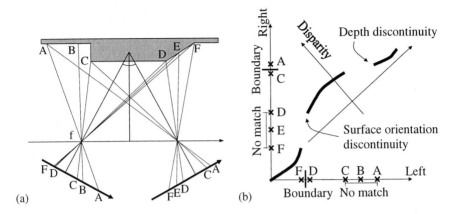

Fig. 2. (a) A polyhedron (shaded area) with self-occluding regions and with a discontinuity in the surface-orientation at feature D and a depth discontinuity at feature C. (b) A diagram of left and right images (1D slice) for the image of the ramp above. Notice that occlusions always correspond to discontinuities. Dark lines indicates where match occurs

2.3 The Monotonicity / Ordering constraint

The *monotonicity* constraint is a variant of the ordering constraint. It differs slightly from the standard ordering constraint because it requires neighboring points to match.

The monotonicity constraint is defined as follows:

Monotonicity Constraint: For every match (e,l,r) such that $M^e_{lr} = 1$,

$$M^e_{N^L_{e,l}, N^R_{e,r}} = 1 \qquad (3)$$

holds, where

$$N^L_{e,l} = \max(\{l' | l' < l, O^L_{e,l'} = 0\})$$
$$N^R_{e,r} = \max(\{r' | r' < r, O^R_{e,r'} = 0\}) \ .$$

We call the match $N^e_{l,r} = (e, N^L_{e,l}, N^R_{e,r})$ the *neighbor match* to match (e,l,r).

The criteria to choose the optimal matching are based on the prior knowledge of surfaces as well as on the data matching term. We will formalize it next.

2.4 Surface Reconstruction

We now specify a prior model for surfaces in the scene. Depth changes are usually small compared to the viewer distance, except at depth discontinuities. Thus, we would like surfaces to be smooth, yet like to allow for large depth changes to occur. Since there is a simple trigonometric relation between disparity and depth, we consider the same constraint to hold for disparities. This can be modeled by some cost function E_{surface} depending upon the disparity change $\nabla_{\text{v}}D(M)$ and $\nabla_{\text{h}}D(M)$. We define the disparity change $\nabla_{\text{v}}D(M)$ along the epipolar line, which is defined only at unoccluded pixels, as follows:

$$\nabla_{\text{v}}D_{l,r}^e = D_{e,l}^L - D_{e,N_{e,l}^L}^L = (l - N_{e,l}^L) + (r - N_{e,r}^R) = D_{e,r}^R - D_{e,N_{e,r}^R}^R \quad,$$

and we define the terms as:

$$\nabla_{\text{v}}D_{e,l}^L = l - N_{e,l}^L \qquad \nabla_{\text{v}}D_{e,r}^R = r - N_{e,r}^R \quad.$$

Next, we define the disparity change $\nabla_{\text{h}}D(M)$ across the epipolar line as:

$$\nabla_{\text{h}}D_{e,l}^L = D_{e,l}^L - D_{e-1,l}^L \;, \text{ and}$$

$$\nabla_{\text{h}}D_{e,r}^R = D_{e,r}^R - D_{e-1,r}^R \;.$$

We can now define the cost function E_{surface} as

$$E_{\text{surface}}(M \,|\, I^L, I^R) = \sum_{e,l,r} M_{l,r}^e \Big\{ \; \mu_{e,l,r}^{\text{vL}} F(\nabla_{\text{v}}D_{e,l}^L) + \mu_{e,l,r}^{\text{vR}} F(\nabla_{\text{v}}D_{e,r}^R)$$

$$+ \; \mu_{e,l,r}^{\text{hL}} F(\nabla_{\text{h}}D_{e,l}^L) + \mu_{e,l,r}^{\text{hR}} F(\nabla_{\text{h}}D_{e,r}^R) \Big\} \;, \qquad (4)$$

where the function $F(x)$ penalizes for the size of the disparity changes x. The parameters μ^{vL} and μ^{hL} control the smoothing in the left image along and across epipolar lines, respectively. Analogously, μ^{vR} and μ^{hR} control the smoothing in the right image along and across epipolar lines.

These smoothing parameters vary according to intensity edges and junction information. The edge information affects the parameters as

$$\mu_{e,l,r}^{\text{vL}} \propto \frac{\gamma}{\gamma + (\Delta_{\text{v}}I_{e,r}^R)^2} \;, \qquad \mu_{e,l,r}^{\text{hL}} \propto \frac{\gamma}{\gamma + (\Delta_{\text{h}}I_{e,r}^R)^2} \;,$$

$$\mu_{e,l,r}^{\text{vR}} \propto \frac{\gamma}{\gamma + (\Delta_{\text{v}}I_{e,l}^L)^2} \;, \qquad \mu_{e,l,r}^{\text{hR}} \propto \frac{\gamma}{\gamma + (\Delta_{\text{h}}I_{e,l}^L)^2} \;.$$

where γ is a parameter to be estimated, and $\Delta_{\text{v}}I_{e,l}^L = I_{e,l}^L - I_{e,l-1}^L$, $\Delta_{\text{h}}I_{e,l}^L = I_{e,l}^L - I_{e-1,l}^L$, $\Delta_{\text{v}}I_{e,r}^R = I_{e,r}^R - I_{e,r-1}^R$, and $\Delta_{\text{h}}I_{e,r}^R = I_{e,r}^R - I_{e-1,r}^R$.

Large image gradients in one image reduce the smoothing coefficients and facilitate discontinuities in the other image to occur. To further reduce the cost of discontinuities occurring at junctions (without affecting the edge information,) we write

$$\mu_{e,l,r}^{\text{vL}} = \mu \frac{\gamma}{\gamma + (\Delta_{\text{v}}I_{e,r}^R)^2} \Big\{ \; \frac{\gamma}{\gamma + (\Delta_{\text{h}}I_{e,r}^R)^2} + \frac{\gamma}{\gamma + (\Delta_{\text{h}}I_{e,r-1}^R)^2}$$

$$+ \; \frac{\gamma}{\gamma + (\Delta_{\text{h}}I_{e-1,r}^R)^2} + \frac{\gamma}{\gamma + (\Delta_{\text{h}}I_{e-1,r-1}^R)^2} \Big\} \;,$$

so that corners have even lower cost for discontinuities along either direction. We define the other smoothing parameters analogously.

The final optimization cost is then given by

$$E(M \mid I^{\mathrm{L}}, I^{\mathrm{R}}) = E_{\mathrm{input}}(M \mid I^{\mathrm{L}}, I^{\mathrm{R}}) + E_{\mathrm{surface}}(M \mid I^{\mathrm{L}}, I^{\mathrm{R}}) \ . \tag{5}$$

We can see this cost as the energy of a Gibbs probability distribution

$$P_{\mathrm{stereo}}(M \mid I^{\mathrm{L}}, I^{\mathrm{R}}) = \frac{1}{Z} e^{-E(M \mid I^{\mathrm{L}}, I^{\mathrm{R}})} \ ,$$

where Z is a normalization constant.

Observe that our theory, given by (1) and (4), is symmetric with respect to the two eyes. This is necessary to ensure that the full information can be extracted from occlusions. Moreover, the monotonicity constraint (3) will be applied as a hard constraint to simplify the optimization of the cost.

We will show in Sect.3 that the maximum-flow algorithm naturally lands to this theory but it restricts the function $F(x)$ to be a convex function. To account for this limitation, we will consider $F(x) = |x|$, since, among the convex functions, it penalizes least for large $|x|$.

3 Mapping the Optimization Problem to a Maximum-flow Problem

In this section, we explain the stereo-matching architecture that utilizes the maximum-flow algorithm to obtain the globally optimal matching, with respect to the energy (5), between left and right image.

3.1 The Directed Graph

We devise a directed graph and let a cut represent a matching so that the minimum cut corresponds to the optimal matching. The formulation explicitly handles the occlusion and is completely symmetric with respect to left and right, up to the reversal of all edges, under which the solution is invariant.

Let $\mathcal{M}$ be the set of all possible matching between pixels, i.e., $\mathcal{M} = \{(e,l,r) \mid e,l,r \in [0,\ldots N-1]\}$. We define a directed graph $G = (V,E)$ as follows:

$$V = \{u_{lr}^e \mid (e,l,r) \in \mathcal{M}\} \cup \{v_{lr}^e \mid (e,l,r) \in \mathcal{M}\} \cup \{s,t\}$$
$$E = E_{\mathrm{M}} \cup E_{\mathrm{C}} \cup E_{\mathrm{P}} \cup E_{\mathrm{E}}.$$

In addition to the source s and the sink t, the graph has two vertices u_{lr}^e and v_{lr}^e for each possible matching $(e,l,r) \in \mathcal{M}$. The set E of edges is divided into subsets E_{M}, E_{C}, E_{P}, and E_{E}, each associated with a capacity with a precise meaning in terms of the model (5), which we will explain in the following subsections.

We denote a directed edge from vertex u to vertex v as (u,v). Each edge (u,v) has a nonnegative capacity $c(u,v) \geq 0$. A *cut* of G is a partition of V into subsets S and

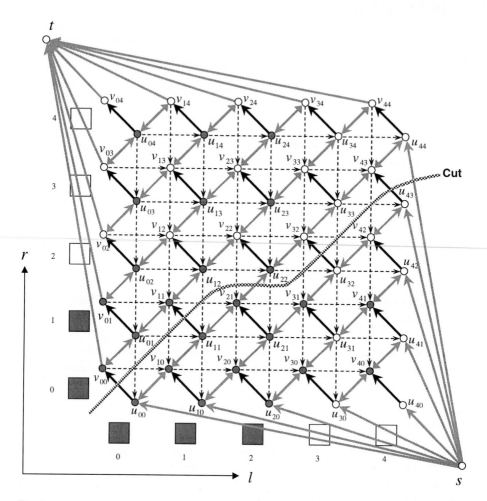

Fig. 3. An epipolar slice of the graph representing the stereo model, where we perform a maximum-flow algorithm. The full graph is naturally represented as three dimensional, with the third axis parametrizing epipolar lines. Edges are given by pairs of graph nodes (u, v). A cut of the graph can be thought of as a surface that separates the two parts, and restrict to a curve (a path) in an epipolar slice. The optimal cut is the one that minimizes the sum of the capacities associated with the cut edges. In this example, we illustrate a cut (solution) that yields the matches $(l, r) = (0, 0), (1, 1), (3, 2)$, and $(4, 3)$ and assign an occlusion to gray (white) pixel 2 (4) in the left (right) image. In the following figures we explain each type of edge/capacity.

$T = V \setminus S$ such that $s \in S$ and $t \in T$ (see Fig.3). When two vertices of an edge (u,v) is separated by a cut with $u \in S$ and $v \in T$, we say that the edge is cut. This is the only case that the cost $c(u,v)$ of the edge contributes to the total cost, i.e., if the cut is through the edge (u,v) with $u \in T$ and $v \in S$, the cost is $c(v,u)$, which is in general different from $c(u,v)$. It is well known that by solving a maximum-flow problem one can obtain a *minimum cut*, a cut that minimizes the total cost $\sum_{u \in S, v \in T} c(u,v)$ over all cuts. (See [9] for details.)

Note that, in this formulation, we use a directed graph while in the method of [22] it suffices to use an undirected graph. The use of the directed graph is crucial to enforce the uniqueness constraint (2) and the ordering/monotonicity constraint (3).

Let us now explain each set of edges E_M, E_C, E_P, and E_E.

3.2 Matching Edges

Each pair of vertices are connected by a directed edge (u_{lr}^e, v_{lr}^e) with a capacity $\| I_{e,l}^L - I_{e,r}^R \|$. This edge is called a *matching edge* and we denote the set of matching edges by E_M:

$$E_M = \{(u_{lr}^e, v_{lr}^e) \mid (e,l,r) \in \mathcal{M}\} \ .$$

If a matching edge (u_{lr}^e, v_{lr}^e) is cut, we interpret this to represent a match between pixels (e,l) and (e,r), i.e., $M_{l,r}^e = 1$. Thus, the sum of the capacities associated with the cut matching edges is exactly E_{input} in (5), which is defined in (1). Figure 3 shows the nodes and matching edges on an epipolar line. The cut shown represents a match $\{(l,r)\} = \{(0,0),(1,1),(3,2),(4,3)\}$.

Note that pixel 2 in the left image has no matching pixel in the right image, as well as pixel 4 in the right image, that is, these pixels are occluded. This is how the formulation represents occlusions and discontinuities, whose costs are accounted for by *penalty edges*.

3.3 Penalty Edges (Discontinuity, Occlusions, and Tilts)

Penalty edges are classified in four categories:

$$E_P = E_L \cup E_L' \cup E_R \cup E_R'$$
$$E_L = \{(v_{lr}^e, u_{l(r+1)}^e) \mid (e,l,r) \in \mathcal{M}, r < N-1\} \cup$$
$$\{(s, u_{l0}^e) \mid e, l \in [0 \ldots N-1]\} \cup$$
$$\{(v_{l(N-1)}^e, t) \mid e, l \in [0 \ldots N-1]\}$$
$$E_L' = \{(u_{l(r+1)}^e, v_{lr}^e) \mid (e,l,r) \in \mathcal{M}, r < N-1\}$$
$$E_R = \{(v_{lr}^e, u_{(l-1)r}^e) \mid (e,l,r) \in \mathcal{M}, l > 0\} \cup$$
$$\{(s, u_{(N-1)r}^e) \mid e, r \in [0 \ldots N-1]\} \cup$$
$$\{(v_{0r}^e, t) \mid e, r \in [0 \ldots N-1]\}$$
$$E_R' = \{(u_{(l-1)r}^e, v_{lr}^e) \mid (e,l,r) \in \mathcal{M}, l > 0\}$$

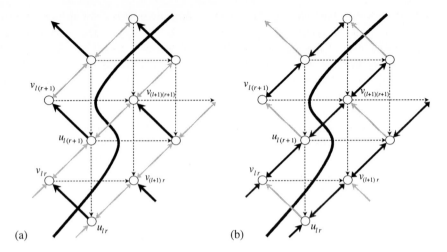

Fig. 4. (a) A *matching edge* is here represented by a black arrow, and we show a cut through a matching edge (u^e_{lr}, v^e_{lr}). This capacity, given by $\| I^L_{e,l} - I^R_{e,r} \|$, provides the cost for the first term of the stereo-energy cost. (b) Penalty edges are represented by dark arrows. Every time a cut crosses these edges the cost is given by its capacity, which are given by either $\mu^{vL}_{e,l,r}$ or $\mu^{vR}_{e,l,r}$. By crossing consecutive penalty capacities, the cost is added linearly, accounting for the function $F(x) = |x|$. Here, the cut crosses the penalty edge $(v_{(l+1)(r+1)}, u_{l(r+1)})$ with cost $\mu^{vR}_{e,l+1,r+1}$, accounting for the occlusion of pixel $r+1$ on the right image.

These edges are for paying for discontinuities and occlusions. Edges in E_L are cut whenever a pixel in the left image has no matching pixel in the right image. For instance, if pixel (e,l) in the left image has no match, exactly one of the edges of the form $(v^e_{lr}, u^e_{l(r+1)})$, (s, u^e_{l0}), or $(v^e_{l(N-1)}, t)$ is cut (see Fig.4(b).) By setting the capacity for these edges, we control the smoothness along the epipolar line. Similarly, an edge in E_R corresponds to an occlusion in the right image. The penalty is given by the smoothing coefficients $\mu^{vL}_{e,l,r}$ for a edge $(v^e_{l(r-1)}, u^e_{lr})$ in E_L and $\mu^{vR}_{e,l,r}$ for a edge $(v^e_{lr}, u^e_{(l-1)r})$ in E_R. By crossing consecutive penalty capacities the cost is added linearly, accounting for the function $F(x) = |x|$.

Edges in E'_L are cut when a pixel in the left image matches two or more pixels in the right image. This corresponds to a tilted surface. Since every edge $(u^e_{l(r+1)}, v^e_{lr})$ in E'_L has an opposite edge $(v^e_{lr}, u^e_{l(r+1)})$ in E_L, by setting the capacity of $(u^e_{l(r+1)}, v^e_{lr})$ higher or lower than the capacity of $(v^e_{lr}, u^e_{l(r+1)})$, we can favor or disfavor tilted surface solution over occlusion/discontinuity solution. To strictly enforce the uniqueness constraint (2), we can make the capacity of the edge infinity, which cannot be done in an undirected graph.

$F(x)$ must be convex: We briefly outline a proof that $F(x)$ has to be convex. We assume a uniformity of the cost, i.e., $F(x)$ is the same everywhere in the system. The cost of a cut is the sum of the capacities of the edges crossed by the cut. This sum can only increase the cost by the amount of each capacity, since the capacity is non-negative. The size of the discontinuity defines the minimum number of edges that is crossed,

and as the graph becomes more connected, the number of edges only increases, adding up the cost of a discontinuity more. The sum guarantees at least a linear cost, for the minimum connectivity used here, which represents the function $F(x) = |x|$. This proves that we cannot use non-convex functions as $F(x)$ and in particular cannot penalize for discontinuities or occlusions sublinearly.

In a graph with more connectivity, this cost can grow faster than lineality and so other convex functions can be created. Our interest is to have costs that increase the least with the discontinuity size and hence to have as few edges as possible, which also is helpful to improve the efficiency of the algorithm. This is a limitation of the use of the maximum-flow algorithm that is not present in dynamic programming algorithms (e.g., [11]). While there is this limitation, our experiments do yield good solution with the linear cost $F(x) = |x|$.

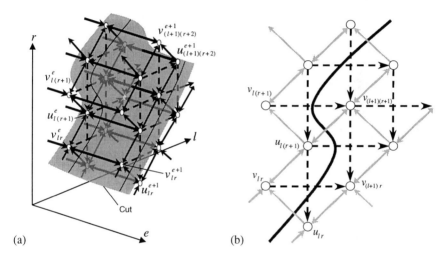

(a)   (b)

Fig. 5. (a) This figure shows a piece of the full three dimensional graph. Epipolar edges account for the epipolar-line interactions. They are represented by thick arrows. A cut is shown through two epipolar edges. (b) Constraint edges are depicted as dashed arrows. They enforce the monotonicity or ordering constraint (3), i.e., the edge capacity are set to infinity so that the optimal (minumum) cut does not cut them.

3.4 Epipolar edges

Epipolar edges are the only edges across epipolar lines. They simply connects vertices with the same (l,r) in both directions:

$$
\begin{aligned}
E_{\mathrm{E}} = {} & \{(u_{lr}^e, u_{lr}^{e+1}) \mid (e,l,r) \in \mathcal{M}, e < N-1\} \cup \\
& \{(u_{lr}^{e+1}, u_{lr}^e) \mid (e,l,r) \in \mathcal{M}, e < N-1\} \cup \\
& \{(v_{lr}^e, v_{lr}^{e+1}) \mid (e,l,r) \in \mathcal{M}, e < N-1\} \cup \\
& \{(v_{lr}^{e+1}, v_{lr}^e) \mid (e,l,r) \in \mathcal{M}, e < N-1\} \ .
\end{aligned}
$$

The capacity of an epipolar edge controls the smoothness of the solution across epipolar lines. In one extreme, if the cost is zero, the matching on epipolar lines have no influence to each other. In the other extreme, if the cost is infinity, all epipolar lines must have the same matching (see Fig.5(a).)

3.5 Constraint Edges

Constraint edges are for enforcing the monotonicity constraint (3) and defined as follows:

$$
\begin{aligned}
E_C = \ & \{(u^e_{lr}, u^e_{(l+1)r}) \mid (e,l,r) \in \mathcal{M}, l < N-1\} \cup \\
& \{(u^e_{lr}, u^e_{l(r-1)}) \mid (e,l,r) \in \mathcal{M}, r > 0\} \cup \\
& \{(v^e_{lr}, v^e_{(l+1)r}) \mid (e,l,r) \in \mathcal{M}, l < N-1\} \cup \\
& \{(v^e_{lr}, v^e_{l(r-1)}) \mid (e,l,r) \in \mathcal{M}, r > 0\} \ .
\end{aligned}
$$

The capacity of each constraint edge is set to infinity. Therefore, any cut with a finite total flow cannot cut these edges. Note that, because the edges have directions, a constraint edge prevents only one of two ways to cut them. In Fig.5(b), constraint edges are depicted as dashed arrows, and none is cut. This cannot be done with undirected graphs, where having an edge with an infinite capacity is equivalent to merging two vertices, and thus meaningless. This is why the algorithm in [22] cannot guarantee the monotonicity/ordering constraint.

4 Implementation and Results

We implemented the architecture explained in the last section, with window features of small size for the real-image experiments. For the maximum-flow algorithm, we used the standard push-relabel method with global relabeling [8]. It took about 1 hour on 266Mhz Pentium II machine to compute the results on real images (512×512 pixels).

To see how the algorithm handles occlusions and discontinuities, we experimented with both random-dot stereogram and illusory surface images. These experiments were particularly important on the early phases of the work, when we needed to understand the role of each kind of edges and capacities in the graph. For instance, letting disparity discontinuity more likely to be present at intensity edges and junctions, as well as the epipolar-line interactions, was crucial for the performance of the algorithm on the illusory figures. The experiments on random-dot stereograms were important as they made it apparent that occluded regions do not match any region, and therefore having multiple matches at these points as the algorithm in [22] does cannot possibly be right. Results are shown in Fig.6 and Fig.7. In both cases, the program successfully found the occluded regions in both left and right images. The correspondence diagram in Fig.7 shows the symmetric nature of our result.

We also tested the algorithm on real images. Figure 8 shows the result for images Pentagon and Fruits. The results are in support of the model – they "look good". Notice that the small variance of the height of the ground around the Pentagon can clearly be seen.

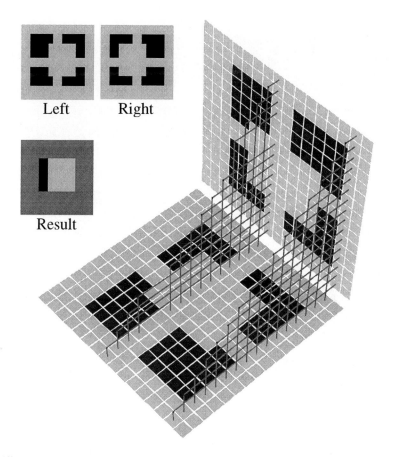

Fig. 6. Illusory surface. Shown as result is the disparity map for the left image. The diagram on the right shows the correspondence between left and right pixels for two epipolar lines. Note the symmetric nature of the result.

Fig. 7. Random-dot stereogram. Shown as result is the disparity map for the left image. Note the occluded region (black) at the left of the rectangle.

Left   Right   Left

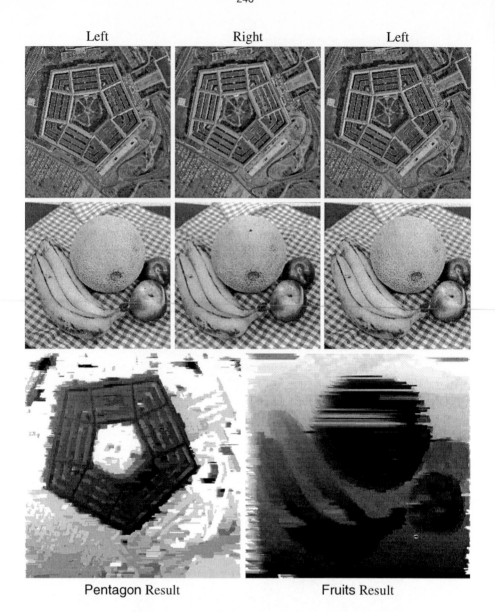

Pentagon Result   Fruits Result

Fig. 8. Results (disparity maps for the left image) on real images **Pentagon** and **Fruits**. Notice the small variance of the height of the ground around the Pentagon can clearly be seen. Also, in **Pentagon**, the disparity map is slightly darker toward the bottom, suggesting that the pictures were not taken exactly over the site. In **Fruits**, one can check by doing stereo with own eyes that even the region in the middle of the cantaloupe that is giving a background disparity is correct, i.e., there is some correlating noise present in both images.

5 Conclusion

We have presented a new approach to compute the disparity map, by modeling occlusions, discontinuities, and epipolar-line interactions, then optimally solving the problem in a polynomial time. We have modeled binocular stereo, including the monotonicity/ordering constraint, mapped the model to a directed graph and used a maximum-flow algorithm to globally optimize the problem. We have improved on previous work, which either (i) models occlusion/discontinuities and ordering constraints, but does not incorporates epipolar-line interactions, with, e.g., as the dynamic programming does, or (ii) models epipolar-line interactions, but not ordering constraint or discontinuities, as in the case of maximum-flow approach on undirected graphs. We have shown that the discontinuities/occlusions cost have to be modeled by a convex function in order to map stereo to a directed graph, and thus used the linear function, since it least penalizes for large discontinuities and offers simplicity (fewer edges in the graph). The experiments support the model.

References

1. B. Anderson. The role of partial occlusion in stereopsis. *Nature*, 367:365–368, 1994.
2. N. Ayache. *Artificial Vision for Mobile Robots*. MIT Press. Cambridge, Mass., 1991.
3. P. N. Belhumeur and D. Mumford. A bayesian treatment of the stereo correspondence problem using half-occluded regions. In *Proc. IEEE Conf. on Computer Vision and Pattern Recognition*, 1992.
4. A. Blake and A. Zisserman. *Visual Reconstruction*. MIT Press, Cambridge, Mass., 1987.
5. P. Burt and B. Julesz. A disparity gradient limit for binocular fusion. *Science*, 208:615–617, 1980.
6. B. Cernushi-Frias, D. B. Cooper, Y. P. Hung, and P. Belhumeur. Towards a model-based bayesian theory for estimating and recognizing parameterized 3d objects using two or more images taken from different positions. *IEEE Transactions on Pattern Analysis and Machine Intelligence*, PAMI-11:1028–1052, 1989.
7. A. Champolle, D. Geiger, and S. Mallat. Un algorithme multi-échelle de mise encorrespondance stéréo basé sur les champs markoviens. In *13th GRETSI Conference on Signal and Image Processing*, Juan-les-Pins, France, Sept. 1991.
8. B. V. Cherkassky and A. V. Goldberg On Implementing Push-Relabel Method for the Maximum Flow Problem. In *Proc. 4th Int. Programming and Combinatorial Optimization Conf.*, pages 157-171, 1995.
9. T. H. Cormen, C. E. Leiserson, and R. L. Rivest. *Introduction to Algorithms*. McGrow-Hill, New York, 1990.
10. O. Faugeras *Three-Dimensional Computer Vision*. MIT Press. Cambridge, Mass., 1993.
11. D. Geiger and B. Ladendorf and A. Yuille Occlusions and binocular stereo. *International Journal of Computer Vision*, 14, pp 211-226 March, 1995.
12. B. Gillam and E. Borsting. The role of monocular regions in stereoscopic displays. *Perception*, 17:603–608, 1988.
13. W. E. L. Grimson. *From Images to Surfaces*. MIT Press. Cambridge, Mass., 1981.
14. B. Julesz. *Foundations of Cyclopean Perception*. The University of Chicago Press, Chicago, 1971.
15. T. Kanade and M. Okutomi. A stereo matching algorithm with an adaptive window: theory and experiments. In *Proc. Image Understanding Workshop DARPA*, PA, September 1990.

16. J. Malik. On Binocularly viewed occlusion Junctions. In *Fourth European Conference on Computer Vision*, vol.1, pages 167–174, Cambridge, UK, 1996. Springer-Verlag.

17. D. Marr and T. Poggio. Cooperative computation of stereo disparity. *Science*, 194:283–287, 1976.

18. D. Marr and T. Poggio. A computational theory of human stereo vision. *Proceedings of the Royal Society of London B*, 204:301–328, 1979.

19. K. Nakayama and S. Shimojo. Da vinci stereopsis: depth and subjective occluding contours from unpaired image points. *Vision Research*, 30:1811–1825, 1990.

20. Y. Ohta and T. Kanade. Stereo by intra- and inter-scanline search using dynamic programming. *IEEE Transactions on Pattern Analysis and Machine Intelligence*, PAMI-7(2):139–154, 1985.

21. S. B. Pollard, J. E. W. Mayhew, and J. P. Frisby. Disparity gradients and stereo correspondences. *Perception*, 1987.

22. S. Roy and I. Cox. A Maximum-Flow Formulation of the N-camera Stereo Correspondence Problem In *Proc. Int. Conf. on Computer Vision, ICCV'98*, Bombay, India 1998.

Symmetry in Perspective

Stefan Carlsson

Numerical Analysis and Computing Science, Royal Institute of Technology, (KTH), S-100 44 Stockholm, Sweden, stefanc@bion.kth.se, http://www.nada.kth.se/~stefanc

Abstract. When a symmetric object in 3D is projected to an image, the symmetry properties are lost except for specific relative viewpoints. For sufficiently complex objects however, it is still possible to infer symmetry in 3D from a single image of an uncalibrated camera. In this paper we give a general computational procedure for computing 3D structure and finding image symmetry constraints from single view projections of symmetric 3D objects. For uncalibrated cameras these constraints take the form of polynomials in brackets (determinants) and by using projectively invariant shape constraints relating 3D and image structure, the symmetry constraints can be derived easily by considering the effects of the corresponding symmetry transformation group in 3D. The constraints can also be given a useful geometric interpretation in terms of projective incidence using the Grassmann-Cayley algebra formalism. We demonstrate that in specific situations geometric intuition and the use of GC-algebra is a very simple and effective tool for finding image symmetry constraints.

1 Introduction

The detection and analysis of symmetry is a problem that has many aspects and levels of complexity depending on e.g. the geometry of the imaging process and the shape of the objects being imaged. An object that is symmetric in 3D will only give rise to a symmetric image for specific viewing positions. It is however in general still possible to decide whether an image is a view of a symmetric object. This has been studied most extensively for the case of planar objects in parallel projection [6] [10] [15], but also for projections of 3D symmetric objects [8] [11]. Comparatively less work has been concerned with the more general and difficult case of *perspective* projection with some exceptions [14], [17]. For the case of 3D symmetric objects in perspective projection [17] gives an extensive overview of the possibility of computing projective 3D structure from single images of a symmetric object by exploiting properties of rotationally symmetric objects and the fact that the imaging of a bilaterally symmetric object is formally equivalent to the case of two cameras looking at one non-symmetric object.

So far there seems to exist no general procedure however for deciding whether a given image is the projection of a specific 3D symmetric object with no prior information about viewpoint. In this paper we will therefore give a formal method that can compute view invariant image symmetry constraints as well as 3D structure from a single view of a 3D symmetric object. These constraints will be necessary but in general not sufficient for detecting 3D symmetry. We will work in a projectively invariant framework which means that all constraints derived will be independent of camera calibration.

Our approach will be based on the projective shape constraints [3], [5] [12], [16] that can be derived for an arbitrary number of points in a single image, relating the projective structure of a point set in 3D to that of the projected 2D point set in the image. Imposing symmetry constraints on the shape in 3D , will generate auxiliary shape - image constraint relations. The 3D shape can therefore be eliminated from the shape-image constraints leaving constraints on projective image structure that have to be fulfilled in the case of specific 3D symmetric objects.

The fact that these image symmetry constraints are expressed in terms of the projective image structure means that they can be given an intuitive interpretation as geometric incidence constraints by using the Grassmann-Cayley algebra [1] [2] [7] [13]. For a given complex object we will see that the GC-algebra formalism is actually a superior and simple tool for finding symmetry constraints.

2 Planar shapes

With an uncalibrated camera we can only talk about relations between projective structure in 3D and the image. For planar shapes in 3D, projective structure is invariant over the perspective viewing transformation and changes of viewpoint. We will start by considering planar shapes and the continue with the non-planar case. In both cases we will exploit the fact that symmetry transformations in 3D such as reflexions and rotations are part of the general symmetric group, i.e. permutations of coordinates. Using the bracket (determinant) expressions for projective structure therefore leads to a very simple analysis of the effect of symmetry.

2.1 Symmetry constraints from projective structure and the symmetric group

Projective structure of a set of points in 2D (projective 2-space) can be described by the projective coordinates. These can be defined using four points p_1, p_2, p_3, p_4 in projective 2-space as a basis in the following way. An arbitrary point p_n can be expressed in this basis as [1]:

$$p_n = x_n^p [234] p_1 - y_n^p [134] p_2 + w_n^p [124] p_3 \qquad (1)$$

Where the factors $[ijk]$ are used to make p_n homogeneous,i.e arbitrary scalings of the homogeneous coordinates p_i imply the same scaling of p_n.

---

[1] We will use the notation $[ijk]$ for the bracket $[p_i \ p_j \ p_k]$ with lower case numbers denoting image coordinates and upper case denoting 3D-coordinates

x_n^p, y_n^p, w_n^p are the homogeneous projective coordinates of the point p_n in the basis p_1, p_2, p_3, p_4. They can be expressed explicitly in terms of the cartesian coordinates p_i by considering eq. (1) as a linear system and solving it. We can directly compute the determinants:

$$
\begin{aligned}
[23n] &= x_n^p \, [234] \, [123] \\
[13n] &= y_n^p \, [134] \, [123] \\
[12n] &= w_n^p \, [124] \, [123]
\end{aligned}
\tag{2}
$$

By taking ratios we can form the absolute projective coordinates:

$$
\frac{x_n^p}{w_n^p} = \frac{[23n]\,[124]}{[234]\,[12n]} \qquad \frac{y_n^p}{w_n^p} = \frac{[13n]\,[124]}{[134]\,[12n]}
\tag{3}
$$

A set of points in 3D has a symmetry if there is a transformation $\mathbf{T}$ e.g. a rotation or reflexion, that maps the point set into itself, i.e. for every point p_i there is another point p_{i*} in the set such that:

$$
p_{i*} = \mathbf{T} p_i
\tag{4}
$$

Any symmetry transformation corresponds to a permutation of the points making up the shape. The group of symmetry transformation is therefore equivalent to the group of permutations, known as the symmetric group.

Rotations and reflexions can be modeled as linear transformations of homogeneous coordinates. A bracket is therefore transformed as:

$$
[p_{i*} p_{j*} p_{k*}] = [\mathbf{T} p_i \; \mathbf{T} p_j \; \mathbf{T} p_k] = [\mathbf{T}] \, [p_i \; p_j \; p_k]
\tag{5}
$$

In an arbitrary perspective mapping the projective invariants (3) are conserved. If we use the shorter notation $[i\; j\; k] = [p_i\; p_j\; p_k]$ we get for five points:

$$
\frac{[2\;3\;5][1\;2\;4]}{[2\;3\;4][1\;2\;5]} = \frac{[2^*3^*5^*][1^*2^*4^*]}{[2^*3^*4^*][1^*2^*5^*]}
\tag{6}
$$

which can be written as a constraint polynomial:

$$
[2\;3\;5\;][1\;2\;4\;][2^*3^*4^*][1^*2^*5^*] - [2\;3\;4\;][1\;2\;5\;][2^*3^*5^*][1^*2^*4^*] = 0
\tag{7}
$$

The symmetry transformation $i \rightarrow i^*$ therefore induces a constraint (7) on the coordinates of the points in any perspective mapping. This constraint is in the form of bracket polynomials and will be a necessary condition for the symmetry to be present. The fact that the constraint is in the form of a bracket polynomial ensures that the incidence in preserved over projective transformations, e.q. perspective mappings between planar surfaces.

As an example, consider the five coplanar points in fig (1) that have a vertical bilateral symmetry axis. A reflexion in the symmetry axis produces the following permutation of the points:

$$
\begin{array}{lccccc}
i: & 1 & 2 & 3 & 4 & 5 \\
i^*: & 2 & 1 & 4 & 3 & 5
\end{array}
\tag{8}
$$

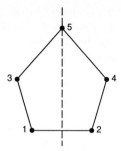

Fig. 1. *Bilateral symmetry five coplanar points*

If the permutated coordinates are substituted in the constraint equation (7) we get after cancelling common factors:

$$[2\ 3\ 5\ ][1\ 2\ 4\ ][1\ 3\ 4]-[2\ 3\ 4\ ][1\ 4\ 5][1\ 2\ 3] = 0 \qquad (9)$$

This constraint, expressed in image coordinates of an arbitrary frame, will be satisfied for arbitrary perspective views of the five point bilateral symmetry configuration of fig (1)

Introducing more symmetry into the five point configuration implies more algebraic image constraints. Fig (2) shows five points with a rotational symmetry around the center.

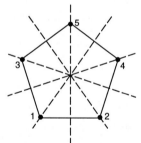

Fig. 2. *Rotational symmetry five coplanar points*

Any cyclic permutation of the points will produce a new image constraint. From eq. (9) we then get get

$$[2\ 3\ 5][1\ 2\ 4][1\ 3\ 4] - [2\ 3\ 4][1\ 4\ 5][1\ 2\ 3] = 0$$
$$[1\ 3\ 4][2\ 4\ 5][1\ 2\ 5] - [1\ 4\ 5][2\ 3\ 5][1\ 2\ 4] = 0$$
$$[1\ 2\ 5][3\ 4\ 5][2\ 3\ 4] - [2\ 3\ 5][1\ 3\ 4][2\ 4\ 5] = 0$$
$$[2\ 3\ 4][1\ 3\ 5][1\ 4\ 5] - [1\ 3\ 4][1\ 2\ 5][3\ 4\ 5] = 0$$
$$[1\ 4\ 5][1\ 2\ 3][2\ 3\ 5] - [1\ 2\ 5][2\ 3\ 4][1\ 3\ 5] = 0 \qquad (10)$$

Given a pentagon as in (2) these constraints will be satisfied in an image from an arbitrary viewpoint in an arbitrarily chosen coordinate system in the image. Since five points in the plane have 2 projective degrees of freedom, these constraints will not be independent. This can be seen by choosing the first four points as a projective basis. The fifth point will then have the two projective invariants as coordinates. This means that any choice of three equations from equations (10) will be dependent.

The limited projective degrees of freedom of a set of points means that in general, homogeneous bracket expressions will have dependencies. These are known as the Plücker - Grassmann relations [9] and for five points a, b, c, d, e in projective 2-space they can be expressed as:

$$[a\ b\ c][a\ d\ e]\ -\ [a\ b\ d][a\ c\ e]\ +\ [a\ b\ e][a\ c\ d] = 0$$

$$[a\ b\ c][b\ d\ e]\ -\ [a\ b\ d][b\ c\ e]\ +\ [a\ b\ e][b\ c\ d] = 0 \tag{11}$$

By using these relations, bracket expressions can often be simplified (straightened) which we will find use for in the coming sections.

2.2 Geometric Interpretation Using the Grassmann - Cayley Algebra

The bracket algebra constraints induced by the symmetry of the shape can be given a simple geometric interpretation using some simple Grassmann - Cayley algebra formalism. The Grassmann - Cayley algebra [1] can be described as the algebra of unions and intersections of linear subspaces. In the case of planar points, i.e. points in projective 2-space, two points can be joined to a line and two lines can be intersected to give a point. If we have four points we can form the lines p_1p_2 and p_3p_4. The point q of intersection of these lines, can be expressed in terms of the coordinates of the points $p_1 \ldots p_4$ as:

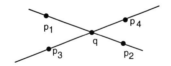

Fig. 3. *Intersection of lines*

$$q\ =\ p_1p_2 \wedge p_3p_4\ =\ [p_1\ p_2\ p_3]p_4 - [p_1\ p_2\ p_4]p_3 \tag{12}$$

where the symbol $\wedge$ is called the meet operation. The point of intersection is a linear combination of the points p_3p_4 on one of the lines.

Using this operation we will see how symmetry constraints can be derived directly from geometric considerations. Fig. (4) shows a perspective view of the five point bilateral symmetry configuration of fig. (1). The point q_1 is the intersection of the lines 13 and 24 and the point q_2 is the intersection of the lines 23 and 14. Using the intersection formula (12) we get:

$$q_1\ =\ 13 \wedge 24 = [1\ 3\ 2]4 - [1\ 3\ 4]2 = [1\ 2\ 3]4 + [1\ 3\ 4]2$$

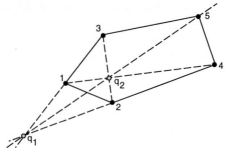

Fig. 4. *Five point bilateral symmetry configuration in perspective. The collinearity of q_1, q_2 and point 5 is induced by the symmetry*

$$q_2 \;=\; 23 \wedge 14 = [2\ 3\ 1]4 - [2\ 3\ 4]1 = [1\ 2\ 3]4 - [2\ 3\ 4]1 \qquad (13)$$

Where the last equality is just a permutation of points in the bracket to get lexicographic ordering. (Note that any permutation in a bracket changes its sign and the overall sign of a homogeneous expression is irrelevant.) The bilateral symmetry implies that both q_1 and q_2 lie on the symmetry axis that passes through the point 5. q_1, q_2 and 5 are therefore collinear, which means that their bracket vanishes:

$$[q_1\ q_2\ 5] \;=\; 0 \qquad (14)$$

If we substitute the expressions (13) for q_1 and q_2 in this we get:

$$[q_1\ q_2\ 5] \;=\; [\ [1\ 2\ 3]4 + [1\ 3\ 4]2,\ [1\ 2\ 3]4 - [2\ 3\ 4]1,\ 5\ ] =$$

$$= -[1\ 2\ 3][2\ 3\ 4][1\ 4\ 5] + [1\ 2\ 3][1\ 3\ 4][2\ 4\ 5] + [1\ 3\ 4][2\ 3\ 4][1\ 2\ 5] \;=\; 0 \qquad (15)$$

The last two terms in this expression can be simplified using the Plücker - Grassmann relations eq. (11):

$$[1\ 2\ 3][1\ 3\ 4][2\ 4\ 5] + [1\ 3\ 4][2\ 3\ 4][1\ 2\ 5] \;=$$

$$= [1\ 3\ 4]\ (\ [1\ 2\ 3][2\ 4\ 5] + [2\ 3\ 4][1\ 2\ 5]\ )\ =\ [1\ 3\ 4][1\ 2\ 4][2\ 3\ 5] \qquad (16)$$

The bilateral symmetry therefore implies:

$$[q_1\ q_2\ 5] \;=\; -[1\ 2\ 3][2\ 3\ 4][1\ 4\ 5] + [1\ 3\ 4][1\ 2\ 4][2\ 3\ 5] \;=\; 0 \qquad (17)$$

which is identical to that in eq. (9). Grassmann - Cayley algebra therefore provides us with a nice intuitive tool for deriving image constraints induced by symmetry in 3D. We see that given a projective constraint such as collinearity, the formulation of the appropriate Grassmann-Cayley expression and its expansion in a bracket algebra expression is straightforward. The inverse problem of starting with a bracket algebra expression and derive a corresponding Grassmann-Cayley expression and projective constraint, known as Cayley-factorization, is in general much harder.

3 3D Shapes

The fact that projective image structure for planar shapes is view invariant greatly simplified the analysis of symmetry. For non-planar 3D shapes projective image structure is no longer invariant over changes of viewpoint. The analysis of the effect and possibility of inferring symmetry in 3D from image data is therefore more complicated. However, we will see that just as in the planar case, symmetry of non-planar 3D objects induces view invariant image constraints in the form of bracket polynomials for the case of uncalibrated perspective viewing. In order to see this we will exploit constraint relations between projective 3D and image structure of a set of points and the viewpoint. By selecting sufficiently many points,the viewpoint can be eliminated leaving relations between projective 3D and image structure known as shape constraints. [4], [5], [12], [16] Symmetry properties of the 3D object can then be used to generate more shape constraints from which projective 3D structure can be eliminated, leaving constraint relations on projective image structure.

3.1 Projective Shape Constraints

For s set of points in 3D we can choose four points as basis points and a fifth for normalization to get projective coordinates X_n, Y_n, Z_n, W_n for an arbitrary point. If the image points of the four basis points are used as a projective basis for all image points x_n, y_n, w_n the projective 3D and image structure for points $5, 6, 7 \ldots$ satisfy the constraint equations [4], [5]:

$$
\begin{pmatrix}
0 & w_5 Y_5 & -y_5 Z_5 & (y_5 - w_5)W_5 \\
w_5 X_5 & 0 & -x_5 Z_5 & (x_5 - w_5)W_5 \\
0 & w_6 Y_6 & -y_6 Z_6 & (y_6 - w_6)W_6 \\
w_6 X_6 & 0 & -x_6 Z_6 & (x_6 - w_6)W_6 \\
0 & w_7 Y_7 & -y_7 Z_7 & (y_7 - w_7)W_7 \\
w_7 X_7 & 0 & -x_7 Z_7 & (x_7 - w_7)W_7 \\
& & \vdots &
\end{pmatrix}
\begin{pmatrix}
X_0^{-1} \\
Y_0^{-1} \\
Z_0^{-1} \\
W_0^{-1}
\end{pmatrix}
= 0
\qquad (18)
$$

Where (X_0, Y_0, Z_0, W_0) are the projective coordinates of the viewpoint.

Since this system has rank < 4 any determinant formed by taking four arbitrary rows of the system must vanish giving the shape constraint relations. [3], [5], [16], These constraints are dual to the multiple view matching constraints obtained in the same way, [7] Using the fact that $(X_5, Y_5, Z_5, W_5) = (1, 1, 1, 1)$

and taking the determinant of the first four rows of eq. (18) we get the shape constraint for six points [12].

$$(w_5y_6 - x_5y_6)X_6Z_6 + (x_5y_6 - x_5w_6)X_6W_6 + (x_5w_6 - y_5w_6)X_6Y_6+$$

$$+ (y_5x_6 - w_5x_6)Y_6Z_6 + (y_5w_6 - y_5x_6)Y_6W_6 + (w_5x_6 - w_5y_6)Z_6W_6 = 0$$

If the projective coordinates of the sixth point in 3D are expressed in terms of brackets of cartesian basis coordinates in arbitrary frames in the same way as in the 2D case:

$$\frac{X_6}{W_6} = \frac{[2346][1235]}{[2345][1236]} \qquad \frac{Y_6}{W_6} = \frac{[1346][1235]}{[1345][1236]} \qquad \frac{Z_6}{W_6} = \frac{[1246][1235]}{[1245][1236]}$$

and these are straightened using the Plucker-Grassmann relations, this constraint can be written as the bracket polynomial:

$$[125]\,[346]\,[1236]\,[1246]\,[1345]\,[2345] \qquad -$$

$$[126]\,[345]\,[1235]\,[1245]\,[1346]\,[2346] \qquad +$$

$$[135]\,[246]\,[1236]\,[1245]\,[1346]\,[2345] \qquad -$$

$$[136]\,[245]\,[1235]\,[1246]\,[1345]\,[2346] \qquad + \tag{19}$$

$$[145]\,[236]\,[1235]\,[1246]\,[1346]\,[2345] \qquad -$$

$$[146]\,[235]\,[1236]\,[1245]\,[1345]\,[2346] \qquad = 0$$

3.2 Symmetry Inference

The shape constraint (19) is of the form

$$i_1I_1 + i_2I_2 + i_3I_3 + i_4I_4 + i_5I_5 + i_6I_6 = 0 \tag{20}$$

where i_k and I_k are products of image and 3D point brackets respectively. Just as in 2D, a symmetry relation between a set of points in 3D implies a transformation that maps every point to another point in the set:

$$[P_{i*}P_{j*}P_{k*},P_{l*}] = [\mathbf{T}P_i\,\mathbf{T}P_j\,\mathbf{T}P_k\,\mathbf{T}P_l] = [\mathbf{T}]\,[P_i\,P_j\,P_k\,P_l] \tag{21}$$

Since the transformation can be factored out, this means that a homogeneous bracket polynomial such as (19) is transformed as: as:

$$i_1I_1^* + i_2I_2^* + i_3I_3^* + i_4I_4^* + i_5I_5^* + i_6I_6^* = 0 \tag{22}$$

where I_k^* is the bracket product I_k with permuted coordinates according to the symmetry transformation. Since the shape constraint (19) is generic, i.e. independent of the numbering of the points, we can renumber *both* the image and 3D coordinates in eq. (22) so that the products I_k^* are transformed back into I_k. The image point brackets i_k are then transformed into permutated brackets i^* and we get the constraint:

$$i_1^* I_1 + i_2^* I_2 + i_3^* I_3 + i_4^* I_4 + i_5^* I_5 + i_6^* I_6 = 0 \qquad (23)$$

The symmetry constraint therefore generates an extra constraint on the projective 3D structure $I_1 \ldots I_6$ of the point set. The effect can be seen to be equivalent to that of adding an extra image. Symmetry constraints can have a more direct constraining effect on projective structure in the sense that they induce coplanarity constraints. If the four points i, j, k and l are related by a reflexion symmetry in the sense that i and j are symmetrically related to k and l respectively we have:

$$P_i = \mathbf{T} P_k \qquad P_j = \mathbf{T} P_l \qquad P_k = \mathbf{T} P_i \qquad P_l = \mathbf{T} P_j$$

$$[P_i\ P_j\ P_k\ P_l] = [\mathbf{T} P_k\ \mathbf{T} P_l\ \mathbf{T} P_i\ \mathbf{T} P_j] = [\mathbf{T}]\ [P_k\ P_l\ P_i\ P_j] = \mathbf{T}[P_i\ P_j\ P_k\ P_l]$$

but for a reflexion we will have $[\mathbf{T}] = -1$ which implies:

$$[P_i\ P_j\ P_k\ P_l] = 0$$

which just states the simple fact that any four points that are pairwise reflexions will be coplanar.

Using the projective shape constraints we will see how symmetry constraints in 3D induces invariant image constraints in terms of bracket polynomials. We will also see how these bracket polynomials can be interpreted as invariant geometric image constraints using the Grassmann-Cayley algebra. We will consider the case of 6 points in space with various symmetry constraints.

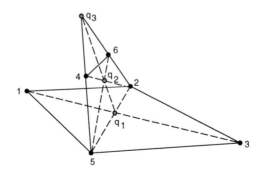

Fig. 5. *Six point 3D bilateral symmetry configuration in perspective. Points 4 6 and 5 2 are reflexions in symmetry plane containing points 1 and 3*

6 point 3D symmetry configuration The configuration in fig (5) has a symmetry plane through the points 1 and 3. Points 1235 and 2456 are constrained to be coplanar. This implies $[1235] = 0$ and $[2456] = 0$. Using the P-G relation:

$$[1246][2345] - [1245][2346] + [1234][2456] = 0 \tag{24}$$

we have

$$[1246][2345] - [1245][2346] = 0 \tag{25}$$

The coplanarities therefore imposes the following constraints on the bracket products:

$$\begin{aligned}
[1235] &= 0 \Rightarrow I_2, I_4, I_5 = 0 \\
[2456] &= 0 \Rightarrow I_1 - I_6 = 0
\end{aligned} \tag{26}$$

We therefore get the shape constraints:

$$\begin{aligned}
i_1 I_1 + i_3 I_3 + i_6 I_6 &= 0 \\
I_1 - I_6 &= 0
\end{aligned} \tag{27}$$

Note that these constraints permit the computations of relative projective invariants I_1, I_3, I_6 from image data i_1, i_2, i_3. The two coplanarity constraints are sufficient for this. Adding the symmetry constraint will give an invariant image constraint. The symmetry implies the permutations:

$$\begin{matrix}
1 & 2 & 3 & 4 & 5 & 6 \\
1 & 5 & 3 & 6 & 2 & 4
\end{matrix} \tag{28}$$

The bracket products i_1, i_3 are therefore transformed as:

$$\begin{aligned}
i_1 &= [125][346] \Rightarrow [125][346] = i_1 \\
i_3 &= [135][246] \Rightarrow -[123][456] = i^* \\
i_6 &= -[146][235] \Rightarrow -[146][235] = i_6
\end{aligned} \tag{29}$$

The symmetry constraint therefore gives us:

$$i_1 I_1 + i^* I_3 + i_6 I_6 = 0 \tag{30}$$

Together with the constraints (27) we get that:

$$\begin{vmatrix}
i_1 & i_3 & i_6 \\
1 & 0 & -1 \\
i_1 & i^* & i_6
\end{vmatrix} = (i_3 - i^*)(i_1 + i_6) = 0 \tag{31}$$

If this is expressed as brackets we get:

$$\big([135][246] + [123][456]\big)\big([125][346] - [146][235]\big) = 0 \tag{32}$$

The first factor can be shown to be non-zero. We therefore get the invariant symmetry constraint:

$$[125][346] - [146][235] = 0 \tag{33}$$

Geometric incidence from GC-algebra As in the previous examples, this expression can be given a geometric incidence explanation using the G-C algebra. Consider the intersection points q_1, q_2 and q_3 in fig (5):

$$
\begin{aligned}
q_1 &= 13 \wedge 25 = [135]2 - [123]5 \\
q_2 &= 24 \wedge 56 = [245]6 - [246]5 \\
q_3 &= 26 \wedge 45 = [246]5 - [256]4
\end{aligned}
\tag{34}
$$

By the construction and the symmetry constraint, these points are collinear. We therefore have $[q_1 \, q_2 \, q_3] = 0$. Substituting the bracket expressions for q_1, q_2 and q_3 we get after cancelling common terms and factoring out common brackets:

$$
[q_1 \, q_2 \, q_3] = [125] \, [346] - [146][235] = 0
\tag{35}
$$

which is exactly the same constraint that was derived using the shape constraint equations.

Fig. (6) shows two more examples of symmetric 3D six-point configurations and their associated geometric GC-algebra and bracket image constraints.

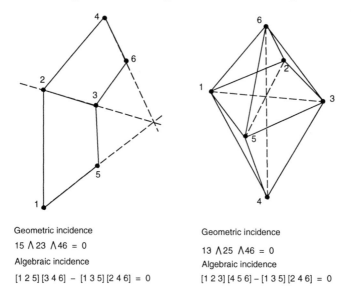

Geometric incidence

$15 \wedge 23 \wedge 46 = 0$

Algebraic incidence

$[1\,2\,5]\,[3\,4\,6] - [1\,3\,5]\,[2\,4\,6] = 0$

Geometric incidence

$13 \wedge 25 \wedge 46 = 0$

Algebraic incidence

$[1\,2\,3]\,[4\,5\,6] - [1\,3\,5]\,[2\,4\,6] = 0$

Fig. 6. *Symmetric 3D six-point configurations and image constraints*

3.3 Symmetry inference and figural completion from partial data

Example 1 If an object is sufficiently constrained, we will be able to infer symmetry even when some features are missing from the image. Using the symmetry constraints, the missing features can be recovered. Using the GC-algebra, these computations can be made very intuitive and simple. As a simple example consider the image of a rectangular block in fig (7) where we assume that only the outline of the block is visible in the image, i.e the corner points $p_1 \ldots p_6$. The remaining corner points points q_1 and q_2 are assumed to be missing from the image , but we will see that symmetry can be inferred from existing data and the missing data can be computed using the symmetry properties of the block.

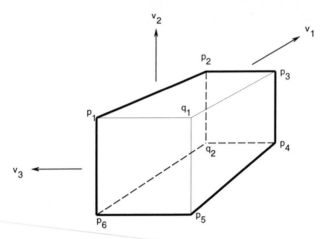

Fig. 7. *Image of rectangular block with missing and hidden lines*

The fact that several lines on the block are mutually parallel implies that their images intersect at vanishing points. There are three vanishing points and they can be computed by intersecting lines as:

$$
\begin{aligned}
v_1 &= p_1 p_2 \wedge p_4 p_5 = [124]5 - [125]4 \\
v_2 &= p_1 p_6 \wedge p_3 p_4 = [136]4 - [146]3 \\
v_3 &= p_2 p_3 \wedge p_5 p_6 = [235]6 - [236]5
\end{aligned}
\tag{36}
$$

The missing points q_1 and q_2 can then be computed using the vanishing points and a corner point:

$$
\begin{aligned}
q_1 &= v_1 p_3 \wedge v_2 p_5 \\
q_2 &= v_1 p_6 \wedge v_2 p_2
\end{aligned}
\tag{37}
$$

The missing points are actually over constrained since we have not used the vanishing point v_3. We can therefore compute image constraints on the visible points $p_1 \ldots p_6$ that can be used to verify the symmetry constraints on the rectangular block.

The vanishing point v_3 satisfies the constraint:

$$
[q_1 \ p_1 \ v_3] = 0
\tag{38}
$$

If the expression for q_1 is substituted into this we get:

$$
[q_1 \ p_1 \ v_3] = [v_1 \ p_3 \ p_5][v_2 \ p_1 \ v_3] - [v_1 \ p_3 \ v_2][p_5 \ p_1 \ v_3] =
$$

$$
= [124][136][235] - [125][134][236] = 0
\tag{39}
$$

This is the invariant constraint on the points $p_1 \ldots p_6$ for them to be the images of the visible corners of a rectangular block.

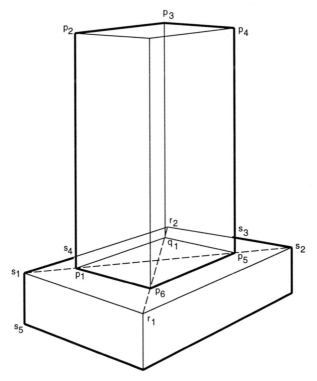

Fig. 8. *One rectangular block symmetrically placed on top of another*

Example 2 Fig (8) shows the image of a rectangular block symmetrically placed on top of another. It is possible to derive necessary conditions on the corner points using only visible points on the outlines of the two objects. The vanishing points v_1, v_2, v_3 can be computed in the same way as in (36). The points r_1 and r_2 on the lower block can be expressed as intersections, using these vanishing points as

$$r_1 = s_1 v_2 \wedge s_2 v_3 \tag{40}$$
$$r_2 = s_1 s_4 \wedge s_2 s_3 \tag{41}$$

For a symmetric placement we have that:

$$[p_6 \ r_1 \ r_2] = 0 \tag{42}$$

Substituting the expressions for r_1 and r_2 in this we get eventually:

$$\begin{aligned}
[p_6 \ r_1 \ r_2] = {} & [s_1 \ s_2 \ v_2][s_1 \ s_2 \ s_4][v_3 \ s_3 \ p_6] - \\
& [s_1 \ s_2 \ v_2][s_1 \ s_2 \ s_3][v_3 \ s_4 \ p_6] + \\
& [s_1 \ v_2 \ v_3][s_1 \ s_2 \ s_3][s_2 \ s_4 \ p_6] = 0
\end{aligned} \tag{43}$$

The parallel alignment oft he blocks implies:

$$[s_1 \ s_5 \ v_1] = [p_1 \ p_2 \ p_4][p_5 \ s_1 \ s_5] - [p_1 \ p_2 \ p_5][p_4 \ s_1 \ s_5] = 0$$

$$[s_2\ s_3\ v_2] = [p_1\ p_3\ p_6][p_4\ s_2\ s_3] - [p_1\ p_4\ p_6][p_3\ s_2\ s_3] = 0$$
$$[s_1\ s_4\ v_3] = [p_2\ p_3\ p_5][p_6\ s_1\ s_4] - [p_2\ p_3\ p_6][p_5\ s_1\ s_4] = 0 \qquad (44)$$

and correct centering of the blocks means:

$$[p_1\ s_1\ s_2] = 0$$
$$[p_5\ s_1\ s_2] = 0 \qquad (45)$$

Conditions (43), (44) and (45) are all necessary invariant conditions for the two blocks to be symmetrically placed. The fact that we are dealing with constrained objects and placements implies that theses conditions can be derived from the limited information of visible points on the outlines of the objects.

4   Summary and conclusions

We have derived calibration and viewpoint independent constraints on perspective images of point sets that are induced by 3D symmetry properties of the points. They can therefore be used to infer symmetry in 3D from image data. The constraints are in the form of homogeneous bracket (determinant) polynomials and can be given a nice intuitive interpretation by using the Grassmann–Cayley algebra. The possibility of inferring symmetry from images has potential applications in object recognition and robot vision.

Acknowledgment

This work was supported by the Swedish Foundation for Strategic Research under the "Center for Autonomous Systems" contract.

References

1. Barnabei M. , Brini A. and Rota G-C. 1985, On the exterior calculus of invariant theory, *J. of Algebra*, vol. 96, pp 120-160.
2. Carlsson, S. 1994, The double algebra: an effective tool for computing invariants in computer vision *"Applications of Invariance in Computer Vision" Springer LNCS 825* pp. 145 - 164 Zisserman and Mundy eds.
3. Carlsson, S. 1995a, View variation and linear invariants in 2-D and 3-D *Tech. rep. Royal Institute of Technology, ISRN KTH/NA/P–95/22–SE*, Dec. 1995
4. Carlsson, S. 1995b, Duality of reconstruction and positioning from projective views. In *Proceedings of the IEEE Workshop on Representations of Visual Scenes*, Cambridge, Mass, June 1995
5. Carlsson S. & Weinshall D. 1996 Dual computation of projective shape and camera positions from multiple images Tech. Rep. ISRN KTH/NA/P–96/19–SE, May 1996. *Int. J. Comp. Vision* (To appear)
6. Cham T.J, and R. Cipolla, Symmetry detection through local skewed symmetries, Image and Vision Computing, vol. 13, no. 5, 1995, 439-450.
7. Faugeras, O.D. & Mourrain, B. 1995 Algebraic and geometric properties of point correspondences between N images, *Proc 5:th ICCV*, 951-956,

8. Fawcett R, Zisserman A., and Brady,J.M. Extracting structure from an affine view of a 3D point set with one or 2 bilateral symmetries, Image and Vision Computing, vol. 12, no. 9, 1994, 615-622.

9. Hodge W. V. and Pedoe D., 1947 *Methods of algebraic geometry, Vol 1,* Cambridge University Press

10. Kanade T, Recovery of the three dimensional shape of an object from a single view, Artif. Intell. Vol. 17, (1981), 409-460

11. Mukherjee,D.P Zisserman A., and Brady,J.M Shape from Symmetry - Detecting and Exploiting Symmetry in Affine Images Phil. Trans. Royal Society, London, 351, 77-106, 1995.

12. Quan L. 1994 Invariants of 6 points from 3 uncalibrated images, *Proc. 3:rd ECCV, pp. Vol. II* 459 - 470

13. Svensson L. (1993), On the use of the double algebra in computer vision, Technical. rep. TRITA-NA-P9310

14. van Gool, L.J., Proesmans, M.[Marc], Moons, T.[Theo], Mirror and Point Symmetry under Perspective Skewing, CVPR96(285-292). BibRef 9600

15. van Gool L. J. , T. Moons, D. Ungureanu, and A. Oosterlinck, The characterization and detection of skewed symmetry, Computer Vision and Image Understanding, vol. 61, no. 1, 1995, 138-150.

16. Weinshall D. , Werman M. & Shashua A. 1995 Shape tensors for efficient and learnable indexing. *Proceedings of the IEEE Workshop on Representations of Visual Scenes*, Cambridge, Mass, June 1995

17. Zisserman, A., Forsyth, D., Mundy, J., Rothwell, C., Liu, J. and Pillow, N. 3D Object Recognition Using Invariance Technical Report No. 2027/94, Oxford University Department of Engineering Science, 1994.

Projective and Illumination Invariant Representation of Disjoint Shapes[1]

Sergei Startchik, Ruggero Milanese, Thierry Pun

Dept. of Computer Science (CUI), University of Geneva
24, rue General Dufour, 1211 Geneva 4, Switzerland
e-mail: <FirstName>.<LastName>@cui.unige.ch

Abstract. A projectively invariant representation for groups of planar disjoint contours is proposed as a simultaneous polar reparametrization of multiple curves. Its origin is an invariant point and for each ray orientation, the cross-ratio of the intersections with its closest curves is taken as a value associated to the radius. The sequence of cross-ratio values for all orientations represents a signature. With respect to other methods this representation is less reliant on single curve properties, both for the construction of the projective basis and for calculating the signature. The proposed representation has been originally developed for planar shapes, but an extension is proposed and validated for trihedral corners. Illumination invariant measures are introduced into the representation to increase it discrimination capability. The whole approach is applied to shape-based retrieval from image databases. Experiments are reported on a database of real trademarks.

1. Introduction

The emerging field of image databases [6,10,21,27] has created a demand for new querying techniques. Such techniques must cope with large amounts of image data, without restrictions on the image content. Computer vision methods can be employed, provided that they do not rely on application-specific constraints [12].

Content-based, or similarity-based retrieval requires some semantic description. We hypothesize that this can be extracted in terms of image properties. For example, searching for images containing a particular trademark amounts to searching for properties like colour [7] or shape [6,10]. However, all such properties are influenced by the viewing conditions. The geometric changes introduced by varying viewing conditions can be modelled by either projective or affine transformations, while linear transformations can be used to model chromatic changes under different illuminants. The reliability of a search method depends on how well it can separate information influenced by viewing conditions from object properties, and use the latter. Separable object properties are called invariants and their application to computer vision was first broadly reviewed in [18].

For mathematical reasons, invariants are obtained more easily for planar geometric structures [3,23]. This has limited their use to object facets and trademark recognition.

---

1. This work is supported by a grant from the Swiss National Fund for Scientific Research 20-40239.94

Some studies have proposed the use of algebraic invariants, i.e. measures that are obtained from *regular* geometric structures, like a group of lines [26] or conics [19]. The difficulty of characterizing any object with such structures has constrained the use of algebraic invariants to specific (mostly industrial) classes of objects. Also, as pointed out in [15], the small number of these invariants fails to provide sufficient discriminative capability when the amount of objects increases.

Differential invariants (based on derivatives) were designed to generalize previous approaches to a larger class of objects and consist of expressing the local behaviour of a shape in a reference frame, defined by some regular invariant geometric structures [29,28]. Such structures could be invariant points [2], tangents [17,23], lines [9] and the represented curve should have a sufficient number of them. A simplified version of these invariants can be achieved by replacing the projective camera model by an affine model [20,25].

In practice, when invariant representations are used for shape-based retrieval, two major weaknesses can be observed. First, they focus on single-curve properties, thereby neglecting the fact that shapes are generally defined over a neighbourhood containing multiple curves. A lot of geometric information is thus lost. The second weakness is the tendency of purely geometric and local representations to produce a large number of false matches. The present article proposes a technique improving these two points. A geometric shape representation integrating multiple curves is combined with chromatic information invariant to illumination conditions.

The rest of this paper is structured as follows: section 2 outlines the idea of the proposed representation and shows its projective invariance; Section 3 focuses on the problem of finding reference lines, necessary for invariant reparametrization; in Section 4 the method is extended with illumination invariance. Finally, in section 5 experimental results on invariance and database aspects such as shape comparison and indexing are reported.

2. Projectively Invariant Description of Disjoint Curves

In this section we express invariant relationships between multiple disjoint curves. A representation is derived and used for further experiments. Special attention is paid to guaranteeing projective invariance at each step of the representation construction.

2.1 Building Multi-Curve Descriptors

In order to represent geometric arrangements of multiple planar curves, one needs to represent relations between points on those curves. Let us suppose that each curve c in an image has its associated length parameter t and each of its points is defined as a point vector $c(t)$ for some value of $t \in [0,1]$. Let us take N_c such curves into account with one point per curve, so that each point is allowed to move freely along its corresponding curve. The dimensionality of the representation space for the relationship between those points will be N_c. In the case of three such curves, the 3D parameter space is already too large to search for relationships between the curves and to extract invariants.

This dimensionality can be reduced by imposing some constraints on the free points taken from different curves. The simplest such relationship is collinearity of points. Any two points from two curves uniquely specify one line and therefore all other points are uniquely defined with respect to this line. So, with the collinearity condition, the dimensionality of the representation space is two, whatever the number of curves. It should be noted that collinearity is a projectively invariant condition.

As the number of curves in an image approaches a few hundred, two-dimensional descriptions for each pair of curves are still not a promising approach. We can reduce this description space to one dimension by constraining the line to pass through one point (e.g. C_0 in figure 1.b). By selecting this point as one extreme of the line, one obtains a one-parameter family of rays, uniquely defined by their orientation angle θ.

For each ray $r(\theta)$, we can detect its intersection points P_1, P_2,.... with all image curves (cf. figure 1.c). It is now possible to characterize this set of points with some function and plot this function against the parameter θ. This provides a "signature" $s(C_0)$ for any choice of the origin C_0, which is based on *multiple* curves and describes information about their spatial arrangement. The number of rays N_r cast from C_0 over the interval $[0, 2\pi]$ defines the signature's resolution, and can be defined a priori.

This representation scheme will be of interest only if it guarantees projective invariance of the signature. For this to be true, all stages of the signature construction method should be projectively invariant. Collinearity of intersection points is already so. The invariance of the position of the centre point C_0 is provided by construction methods addressed in Section 3. Also, the way rays are cast from C_0 should be invariant. This is equivalent to the invariance of the parametrization $r(\theta)$, and is studied in the following subsection. Subsection 2.3 then describes how to obtain an invariant value for a set of intersection points on the ray, and how to construct a shape signature.

2.2 Reparametrization of Rays

Let N_r be the total number of rays originating from C_0. A configuration where C_0 is the centre of coordinates and the distribution of the orientation parameter α is uniform over the 2π interval is referred to as *canonical* and is shown in figure 1.a. In figure 1.b a projectively transformed version of these rays is presented. This configuration will be referred to as *image* coordinate frame and corresponds to the unknown projective transformation of the canonical frame. C_0 corresponds to the invariant point detected in the image.

Let θ be a new orientation parameter which now describes the unknown, projectively distorted, distribution of rays in the image. This non-uniform distribution has to be compensated for projective transformation or, in other words, a correspondence between the canonical and the projected rays should be found.

Let M denote the 3x3 matrix of the unknown 2D projective transformation from canonical to image frame. This matrix is expressed in homogeneous coordinates up to a scale factor which can be fixed by setting the value of one of its elements. The transformation thus has *eight* degrees of freedom (DOFs). As already pointed out, C_0 is by construction an invariant point detected in the image, whose coordinates are thus known. Establishing the correspondence between C_0 and the centre of coordinates in the canonical frame gives the equation: $M \begin{bmatrix} 0 & 0 & 1 \end{bmatrix}^T = \begin{bmatrix} C_0^x & C_0^y & 1 \end{bmatrix}^T$. This equation gives two elements of the matrix M which, after their substitution, leaves six DOFs.

Once the correspondence between centres is established, the transformation between canonical and image rays can be seen as a transformation between two pencils of rays.

Although in the canonical frame the orientation is already given by the angle , in the image system the parameter θ has to be determined. Each of these pencils is a one-dimensional projective space and the transformation between them can be described by a 1D projective transformation with three DOFs [13]. This means that *three* reference rays are needed to establish the full correspondence between rays in canonical and projected frames. Its explicit form is derived using the duality of lines and points in the projective space.

In figure 1.a. the first and second homogeneous coordinates of the 1D projective space are respectively the vertical and horizontal axes. The projective line l corresponds to all points with second coordinate equal to 1. A point with coordinate t_α on the line is dual to the ray with angle α and because the distance from l to the centre is 1, then $t_\alpha = \tan\alpha$. Let us take three reference rays $\alpha_1, \alpha_2, \alpha_3$ and one unknown ray α in the canonical pencil and their corresponding rays in the image frame: $\theta_1, \theta_2, \theta_3, \theta$. For the canonical frame the respective dual points on the line are: $t_{\alpha_1}, t_{\alpha_2}, t_{\alpha_3}, t_\alpha$. Under a 1D projective transformation a well-known invariant value called cross-ratio can be defined for *four* points in terms of distances between them [3,13,18]. This value, will thus be the same in both frames. Equating the expressions for the cross-ratio of points in the canonical frame and for the corresponding points in the image frame gives:

$$\frac{(t_{\theta_3} - t_{\theta_2})(t_\theta - t_{\theta_1})}{(t_\theta - t_{\theta_2})(t_{\theta_3} - t_{\theta_1})} = \frac{(t_{\alpha_3} - t_{\alpha_2})(t_\alpha - t_{\alpha_1})}{(t_\alpha - t_{\alpha_2})(t_{\alpha_3} - t_{\alpha_1})} \tag{1}$$

Taking three rays with predefined orientations α_1, α_2, α_3 in the canonical frame and three corresponding rays invariantly identified in the image space with orientations θ_1, θ_2, θ_3 allows their tangents to be computed and substituted into eq.1. We thus obtain an expression relating tangents of any image orientation θ and canonical orientation α.

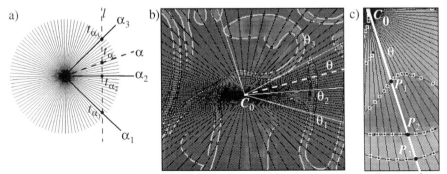

Fig. 1. Canonical (a) and image (b) coordinate frames with reference and sampling rays for $N_r = 100$. In (b), the fourth ray indicates the symmetry frontier. The sampling rays (black) follow the projective transformation determined by the reference rays θ_1, θ_2, θ_3. (c) Intersection of image curves with rays originating from a point C_0. White squares represent the intersections points.

In practice, let us take the canonical reference orientations as $[\alpha_1, \alpha_2, \alpha_3] = [-\pi/4, 0, \pi/4]$ (cf. figure 1.a) which correspond to tangents $[t_{\alpha_1}, t_{\alpha_2}, t_{\alpha_3}] = [-1, 0, 1]$ (interval of highest tangent stability). By substituting them into eq.1, we obtain the mapping between the tangents t_α and t_θ in the canonical and image frames:

$$t_\theta = \frac{(t_{\theta_3} t_{\theta_2})(t_\alpha + 1) + (t_{\theta_1} t_{\theta_2})(t_\alpha - 1) - 2 t_\alpha t_{\theta_3} t_{\theta_1}}{(t_{\theta_3}(1 - t_\alpha) - t_{\theta_1}(t_\alpha + 1) + 2 t_\alpha t_{\theta_2})} \qquad (2)$$

Once this correspondence is established, we construct rays with a uniform distribution in the canonical frame and transform them to the image frame with the above formula (cf. figure 1.b). All rays so defined in the image space are projectively invariant with respect to the reference rays. They are fully invariant provided that reference rays were invariantly identified. It should be noted that working with tangents in eq.2 provides correspondence only up to the central symmetry. This direction ambiguity is removed during ray construction. As will be shown later, at least one point is available on one reference ray, thereby allowing the selection of the positive direction.

To summarize, we now possess a method for projective normalization of ray orientations from an invariant point, given three reference rays. This normalization has removed five DOFs from the projective transformation matrix thus leaving only three.

2.3 Calculating the Signature

In this section we show how to attribute an invariant value to a given ray using its points of intersection with image curves. The three remaining DOFs correspond to a 1D projective transformation *along* each ray which lets us focus on the projective line. The cross-ratio invariant requires a minimum of four points on this line. By taking the centre point and the *first* three other points on one ray, one can compute their cross-ratio, providing an invariant value for *that* ray. Using the notation of figure 1.c the cross-ratio will be computed as: $cr(\theta) = (|C_0 P_2||P_1 P_3|)/(|P_1 P_2||C_0 P_3|)$ where $|xy|$ denotes the distance $\|x - y\|$ or the determinant of the corresponding homogeneous coordinate vectors. The fact that only the three closest curves to the point C_0 will be used is an attractive property. Indeed, the signature will be based on multiple curves, expressing their relative position, but this will be done locally, without going beyond the three closest curves.

Projective invariance is now achieved. To construct a signature, we take in the canonical frame N_r uniformly spaced rays and transform them, with the help of the reference lines, to the image domain. For each ray obtained, a cross ratio of three intersection points gives the signature value. In practice, cross-ratio values are bound. If curves can not be closer that d_{min} pixels due to edge detector properties and the image size does not exceed d_{max} pixels, then the upper bound for the cross-ratio is: $cr_{max} = (d_{max} - d_{min})^2 / (4(d_{max} d_{min}))$. With $d_{min} = 3$ and $d_{max} = 600$ the cr_{max} we have $cr_{max} = 50$ which can be used as a normalization factor for signature comparison. When the number of intersections is less than three, the signature value is undefined and arbitrarily set to zero.

To compare the signatures of two patterns, we need a matching measure. Let $cr_1(\alpha)$, $cr_2(\alpha)$ be the signature values at orientation α for two different patterns. In order to emphasize the suitability of the signature itself, we consider the simplest function between signatures s_1 and s_2, given by the normalized sum of Euclidean distances across all rays:

$$d(s_m, s_n) = 1/(cr_{max}N_r)\sum_{\alpha=0}^{N_r-1}\|cr_1(\alpha) - cr_2(\alpha)\| \tag{3}$$

where $\|x\|$ denotes in this case the absolute value but could be extended to the L_2 norm for multidimensional signatures (cf. section 5).

The following example illustrates the invariance of these signatures. In figure 2 (a) and (b) the same group of curves is viewed from two different viewpoints (they are projectively equivalent). For both images, one invariant point and three reference rays (gray) are shown. In this case, $N_r = 100$ and the two corresponding signatures are shown in figure 2.c. Their normalized difference, according to eq.3, is 0.03. More extensive tests with variations of distance under projective transformation are presented in the experimental results section.

a)   b)   c)   d)

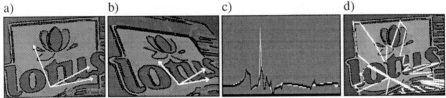

Fig. 2. Projectively equivalent shapes (a), (b). Example of signatures (c) computed from these shapes. In (d) The "cover zone" of the signature in the original image is shown.

It should be noticed that for the simpler case of affine projection the number of DOFs is six, which is two degrees less than in the projective case. The equivalent representation for affine case would then require two reference rays and three points on each ray. This configuration can be used for angles but is not further studied in this paper.

Given a triplet of lines representing the reference frame, it is possible to define a region of the image whose outline is formed by the last curves participating in the signature (i.e. the third point for each ray). An example of such outline is shown in figure 2.d. leading to two interesting observations. First, the signature remains local for objects presenting a high density of curves while spanning multiple curves. Second, attention should be paid to gaps in some curves which produced unpredictable variations in the signature values. This also suggests a possible way to improve our definition of distance between signatures, namely the possibility to disregard *small* intervals of α where two signatures clearly diverge.

3. Construction of Invariant Reference Frames

In the previous section we have shown that exactly three projectively invariant lines passing through one point are necessary to build an invariant signature for such a point. The present section addresses the issue of constructing these reference lines from such invariant curve properties as points and tangents.

3.1 Construction of New Lines

Projectively invariant properties of a curve include points and straight lines. Points on the curve are projectively invariant if they are cusps, inflections or bitangent points of contact. A straight line, given either by a bitangent line, inflection tangent or by a piece of straight curve is also projectively invariant [23]. Cusps are not considered, due to their relatively high instability. For bitangents and inflections either tangents or points can be used but tangents are used first whenever possible because of their higher stability [18, 29].

Unfortunately, none of these properties has a configuration where three lines meet in one point. Therefore, different invariant properties should be combined to build a frame. By taking the intersection of *two* tangents of invariant properties on the curve, one obtains an invariant point C_0 and two lines. Linking one further invariant point and C_0 by a line would complete the construction with the third line.

In order to reduce the number of combinations, the grouping operation underlying the construction of invariant frames should respect the order of invariant components along the curve. All invariant lines are associated with some points on the curve. Bitangents have two points of contact with the curve and can be considered as two separate points with equal tangents (of course their intersection will in this case be avoided). The straight part of a curve can be approximated by a line segment. For grouping purposes, its two endpoints can be considered as points of contact for this line. All invariant properties of one curve are thus ordered and their *successive* triples can be used for frame construction. The unknown direction of a curve still leads to an ambiguity about the global order of points, i.e. the same frame should be obtained if the order of points in the triple is reversed. To achieve this in a local fashion, we suggest to construct the centre point C_0 as the intersection of tangents of the two *external* points of the triple. The third line would then pass through C_0 and the *middle* invariant point.

Let us take, for example, a triple of invariant points, such as the bitangent point B_1 and the two inflections I_1, I_2 of figure 3.a with their respective tangents b_1, l_1, l_2. Taking the intersection of tangents from the first and third points (I_1 and I_2) gives the centre point C_0. The third line l_3 is passed through C_0 and the middle point in the triple which is B_1. The order between the three constructed rays is selected in correspondence with canonical rays and becomes the following: l_1, l_3, l_2.

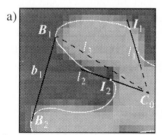
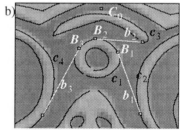

Fig. 3. (a) Three-line configuration constructed from a bitangent and two inflections. A bitangent b_1 and two inflections I_1, I_2 are used to construct a reference frame of three lines: l_1, l_3, l_2. (b) Constructing a reference frame using bitangents that have been fitted to multiple curves.

The constructive approach described above is a general method for constructing reference frames by selecting successive triples of invariant properties. The only exception is the particular case when a straight line is the middle invariant property in the triple. Indeed, taking the intersection of *external* (rather than neighbouring) points in the triple places in general the centre point rather far from the curve. This prevents points on the ray from being too close to the centre point and thus from producing degenerate values of the signature for a whole range of orientations.

3.2 Bitangents of Multiple Curves

As mentioned above, curves play the role of grouping operator for invariant points. However, practice shows that the topology of curves in the image is affected by perspective projection and image noise. In curve zones where a particular projective transformation increases the curvature, a potential gap can be expected because of the fixed geometry and finite resolution of edge detectors. Thus, curve topology depends on the transformation and can not be relied on for grouping remote invariant properties. To overcome this problem, more invariant properties are needed to increase their density along the curves. We make the assumption that within a local neighbourhood curved contours belong to the same object and so are coplanar. In the case of trademarks, curved contours rarely correspond to 3D edges and we expect this hypothesis to hold. Quantitatively, this assumption depends on the number of planar facets in the scene and on the number of curves belonging to each facet. To validate it experimentally we have found that for our database of trademarks (cf. section 5) approximately 4% of neighbouring curve pairs do not belong to the same object.

If neighbouring curves do belong to the same rigid object, their *joint* projectively invariant properties can be used. In this case, only bitangents are suitable since they have two-point contact and so can be fitted to a pair of curves. For each curve a subset of neighbouring curves is thus constructed and bitangents are fitted to them. We impose the condition that such bitangents do not intersect other curves so as to keep properties local.

Figure 3.b illustrates this stage. The curve c_1 does not have any invariant points of its own; therefore no invariant frame could be found for it. However, several invariant properties can be found in common with its neighbours c_2, c_3 and c_4, such as the three bitangents b_1, b_2, b_3. These lines are sufficient to construct at least one reference frame for c_1. Taking the intersection of b_1 and b_3 produces the centre point C_0 and the third line would pass through B_2.

We statistically estimated the advantage of using multi-curve properties for signature construction with respect to methods based on a single curve. For our database we found an average of 0.19 bitangents, 0.62 lines, and 0.17 inflections per curve. This gives a total of 0.98 invariant properties per curve while the number of triplets of these properties, necessary for frame construction is on average below 0.24 for each individual curve. However, if we consider bitangents spanning two curves, their occurrence per curve is 1.7 and the average number of triples increases to 0.76. This affects the density of reference frames in the image making it high enough to not only cover the whole object with invariant descriptors, but also to provide sufficient level of redundancy to deal with noise and occlusion.

3.3 Extension to 3D Faceted Objects

The construction of the invariant signature described above has been defined for shapes such as trademarks located on a planar surface. However, trademarks are often placed on pack boxes that have orthogonal sides. If a box corner is visible from the camera, two or three facets are visible simultaneously. Trademarks located on each facet can be represented independently, but in this case the integration of the information from different facets would also be of considerable interest. In this section we address the issue of finding a reference frame of three rays for *each* facet using the assumption of facet orthogonality. In this work we assume that the corner point is lying on the optical axis.

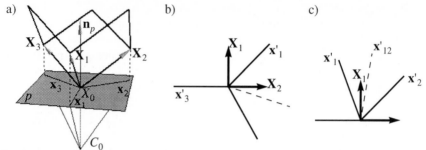

Fig. 4. (a) Projective configuration for the case of an orthogonal corner with three visible facets (seen from C_0). (b) Three-ray configuration recovered for the facet $\mathbf{X}_1 \mathbf{X}_2$. (c) Three-ray configuration reconstructed for facet $\mathbf{X}_1 \mathbf{X}_2$ with correct definition of the midray

Figure 4.a illustrates a homogeneous projective configuration, corresponding to a visible orthogonal corner. In this case p is the projective plane (image plane) and C_0 is the optical centre. The corner point X_0 will be selected as coordinate centre for convenience. Let the basis unit vectors $\mathbf{X}_1$, $\mathbf{X}_2$, $\mathbf{X}_3$ lay on 3D corner edges. For now we will study the case when all the three facets are visible.

The vectors $\mathbf{X}_1$, $\mathbf{X}_2$, $\mathbf{X}_3$ will project onto vectors $\mathbf{x}_1$, $\mathbf{x}_2$, $\mathbf{x}_3$ on the plane p. As we are interested only in *rays* corresponding to the edges of the corner, only the orientation of the vectors $\mathbf{x}_1$, $\mathbf{x}_2$, $\mathbf{x}_3$ is important, and not their length. This corresponds to an arbitrary depth of the corner in the scene or, equivalently, to arbitrary position of the projective plane along the line $C_0 X_0$. Thus we can consider that it passes through X_0 and it is defined by its normal $\mathbf{n}_p$ in the $\mathbf{X}_1$, $\mathbf{X}_2$, $\mathbf{X}_3$ frame. Let $\mathbf{n}_p$ be defined as the vector $\mathbf{X}_3 = \begin{bmatrix} 0 & 0 & 1 \end{bmatrix}$ rotated around $\mathbf{X}_1$ by the angle β and then around $\mathbf{X}_3$ by the angle γ. The corresponding rotation matrices are denoted by R_{X_1} and R_{X_3} thus $\mathbf{n}_p = R_{X_1} R_{X_3} \mathbf{X}_3$.

Let us take the facet spanned by $\mathbf{X}_1$ and $\mathbf{X}_2$ as an example. As we saw in section 3, ray normalization in the plane requires three reference rays. The two vectors spanning the facet already give two such rays and so we need to find the third one. One excellent candidate is the bisector of the angle between $\mathbf{X}_1$ and $\mathbf{X}_2$ because the triple of rays will then correspond to the canonical frame $[\alpha_1, \alpha_2, \alpha_3]$ defined in section 2.2. Since $\mathbf{X}_1$ and $\mathbf{X}_2$ are orthogonal and of unit length, their bisector is spanned by the vector $\mathbf{X}_1 + \mathbf{X}_2$. Let $\mathbf{X}_{12}$ denote this vector and $\mathbf{x}_{12}$ its projection on the plane p (not shown on the figure). In the following, we shall show that orthogonality of facets imposes a rigidity constraint on the orientation of three rays and exploit this to derive a closed-form expression for the orientation of $\mathbf{x}_{12}$.

The vector $\mathbf{x}_1$ which defines the ray of projection of $\mathbf{X}_1$ on p is defined by:

$$\mathbf{x}_1 = (\mathbf{n}_p \times \mathbf{X}_1) \times \mathbf{n}_p \tag{4}$$

and the same formula applies to three other vectors $\mathbf{x}_2$, $\mathbf{x}_3$, $\mathbf{x}_{12}$. By definition, all these vectors lay on the p plane in space. Let x_i denote the *orientation* (tangent) of any such vector $\mathbf{x}_i$ in the projective plane with respect to some basis, we then need to find x_{12} from x_1, x_2, x_3. Together with x_1 and x_2, x_{12} will become the third reference ray for the facet $\mathbf{X}_1 \mathbf{X}_2$ and will complete the construction of projectively invariant frame described in the previous section. The same reasoning applies to the other two facets.

The orientation x_i of a vector $\mathbf{x}_i$ lying in the projective plane, can be measured only with respect to a selected basis in this plane. The coordinates of vectors $\mathbf{x}_i$ are already expressed with respect to the three unit vectors $\mathbf{X}_1$ $\mathbf{X}_2$ $\mathbf{X}_3$. Keeping the same basis we rotate the projective plane p together with the four orientation vectors $\mathbf{x}_i$ around the centre X_0 so as to align it with one facet. Selecting, for example, the one spanned by vectors $\mathbf{X}_1$ and $\mathbf{X}_2$, these latter vectors become the basis of the transformed plane (cf. figure 4.b). So, we can use the coordinates of the transformed vectors to calculate their orientations (tangents).

In practice, the rotation of the plane p can be sought as a rotation of its normal $\mathbf{n}_p$ so that after the transformation the normal is aligned with $\mathbf{X}_3$. This rotation is in fact the inverse transformation of $\mathbf{n}_p$ definition i.e. the two rotations R_{X_3}, R_{X_1} applied in the reverse order. Multiplying these two matrices together gives the final transformation matrix. By applying this transformation to four vectors $\mathbf{x}_i$ in the projective plane defined by (eq.4) we obtain new vectors $\mathbf{x'}_i$ all belonging to the $\mathbf{X}_1$ $\mathbf{X}_2$ plane (cf. figure 4.b). Taking the ratio of the *first* and *second* coordinates of each vector gives a tangent for each ray as follows: $x_1 = 1/(c_\gamma t_\beta)$, $x_2 = -t_\beta/c_\gamma$, $x_{12} = (t_\beta - 1)/((t_\beta + 1)c_\gamma)$ where $t_\beta = \tan\beta$ and $c_\gamma = \cos\gamma$. By construction, $\mathbf{x}_3$ is aligned with the $\mathbf{X}_2$ axis and so its orientation x_3 is zero. By rearranging terms we obtain an expression for x_{12}:

$$x_{12} = \frac{k(x_1 - k)}{x_1 + k}, \tag{5}$$

where $k = \sqrt{-x_1 x_2}$. The first observation is that x_{12} depends only on two rays spanning the facet it belongs to. This is true as long as $\mathbf{x}_3$ is aligned with the horizontal axis and the order between x_1 and x_2 is correct. Selecting the correct order, however, can not be done in the absence of x_3 and should be done in the *clockwise* direction as illustrated in figure 4.b. A second remark is that x_1 and x_2 should be of different sign. This condition is a consequence of the rigidity imposed by the orthogonality of facets and it is always satisfied when $\mathbf{x}_3$ is aligned with the horizontal axis. So, if we find a Y-junction in the image, we align one ray with the horizontal axis and evaluate the midray for the other two according to the proposed formula.

Let us consider now the case when only two facets are visible. The rays projected onto the image plane are shown in figure 4.c. This case differs from the previous one by the fact that all pairwise angles between rays in the image plane are less than $\pi/2$ and thus can be easily detected in the image. The same rotations are applied to align $\mathbf{x}_3$ with the horizontal axis. However, two other rays, due to the rigidity constraint, are now placed on the opposite sides of $\mathbf{X}_1$. However, the expression in eq.5 will give a correct midray orientation only when the orientations of rays $\mathbf{x}_1, \mathbf{x}_2$ are measured with first and second coordinates reversed.

Let us consider figure 5 for a practical example. A box corner can be detected in the image by searching for Y-junctions of lines. Three rays were detected, shown in the figure 5.a. For the facet S a bisector was detected according to the proposed method and a signature evaluated. This operation was also performed with a different view of the same box, shown in figure 5.b. Again, a signature was evaluated and a comparison between the two is provided in figure 5.c. It can be seen that except for few points, the signature profiles match rather well.

Fig. 5. (a) A bisector ray found for the facet S. In (b) the same ray is found for an image of the same corner viewed from another viewpoint. In (c) the signatures constructed from the two corresponding facets are shown.

It should be noticed that, unlike the planar case, in 3D signatures for all facets correspond to three $\pi/2$ intervals in the canonical frame. There is no circular order for these intervals. A comparison technique that takes the best distance over 3 circular permutations of intervals should thus be considered.

4. Illumination Invariance for Indexing

The method presented above for computing a pattern signature is purely geometric. In order to increase its discriminating capability some chromatic information could be added to the signature. In line with the whole approach, this information is required to be invariant to illumination changes. Several models exist to describe chromatic changes under illuminant variations [5,7]. Invariance to illumination must be seeked as invariance to a specific transformation model. One of the optimal approximations is the scaling model [5] where, under illuminant change, each colour channel changes its intensity according to a separate scale factor. In this case chromatic values measured one point under one illuminant $[R\ G\ B]$ change to $[R'\ G'\ B']$ according to the following expression: $\begin{bmatrix} R' & G' & B' \end{bmatrix} = \begin{bmatrix} s_R R & s_G G & s_B B \end{bmatrix}$. Let us assume that two neighbouring pixels 1 and 2 belong to the same surface. Due to their proximity we consider them as subject to the same illuminant. In this case, the following relation [7] allow the scaling factors of the previous expression to be discarded: $(R'_1 G'_2)/(R'_2 G'_1) = (R_1 G_2)/(R_2 G_1)$.

Such ratios are therefore locally invariant to illumination. In chromatically uniform image areas, this ratio should be approximately constant. The disadvantage of this method is that local changes of colours occurring at the border of two surfaces result in large variations of this ratio, making recognition unstable.

In our case, we have an invariantly constructed ray with four points. It would be interesting if we could complement the geometric information represented by their cross-ratio with a more stable chromatic measure computed on *intervals* between such points. Since curves in an image correspond to chromatic variations, the areas they enclose tend to be more uniform or textured and can thus be well described by simple functions.

The simplest method to model their variations is to take averages over the profile between points of intersection and work with these values to find a possible invariant to illumination. Such an illumination invariant value can be stored with each geometric signature point and used as an additional dimension for discrimination.

Let b_L^f denote the average value of the part of the chromatic profile under some canonical illuminant. Here the index $L = \{1, 2, 3\}$ indicates the interval and the index

$F = \{R, G, B\}$ indicates the chromatic channel. Under a change of illumination each point in the interval and therefore also the average will be subject to a vertical scaling with a factor s_F. For instance, b_1^R will become $s_R b_1^R$.

Due to the unknown projective transformation along the ray the density of points in each interval changes. For the operation of averaging this amounts to weighting differently the chromatic value of each point over the interval. The net effect on the average value is a change that can be modelled also by a scale factor a_L. So, under a change of illumination, a chromatic average b_L^F becomes $s_F a_L b_L^F$ and can be denoted as $b_L'^F$. Given nine intervals with their averages, three unknown chromatic factors and three unknown factors a_L this leaves three independent invariant values. Using ratios eliminates all parameters, providing the following three expressions: $b_2'^R b_1'^G / (b_1'^R b_2'^G)$, $b_3'^G b_2'^B / (b_3'^B b_2'^G)$, $b_1'^R b_3'^B / (b_3'^R b_1'^B)$. These can be used to characterize the signature from a chromatic point of view in addition to the geometric invariant descriptors. Overall, the proposed invariant signature consists of N_c vectors containing the cross-ratio of points detected on each ray, plus three chromatic invariants.

5. Experimental Results

In this section, we first test the stability of the proposed invariant representation under different types of image noise. Second, we assess its usefulness for image database applications with standard performance measures used in information retrieval.

A database of 203 images of 41 planar objects (c.f. figure 6 for a few samples) was collected using different acquisition devices (camcoder and two digital cameras). Images were taken from different viewpoints under various illumination conditions (daylight, neon/bulb lamp). The signature extraction process was run fully automatic and produced an average 40 valid signatures for each image. For each image we computed the cover zone (cf. section 2.3) of all its signatures which, on average, amounts to 2.1 times the image surface. The average overlap is thus 50% of the cover zone.

Fig. 6. Thirteen typical images from the database. The last row features faceted objects.

Separate tests were conducted for faceted objects. A database of 170 corner views of 53 boxes was collected under the same conditions as described above. Retrieval tests are presented at the end of this section.

5.1 Stability of the Invariant Representation

The construction of the invariant representation can be divided into three steps: curve detection, extraction of invariant properties, grouping and signature evaluation. The stability of each step is estimated with respect to "image noise" produced from various sources. These include viewpoint transformation and resolution changes. The latter can be modelled by a scaling transformation while viewpoint change can be approximated by a general projective transformation (cf. section 2.2). Illumination changes are produced by different lamps, and their effects are only estimated with respect to database retrieval (cf. section 5.2).

In order to make curve extraction less sensitive to changes in resolution, scale and illumination, we use a multiscale edge detector [14] on the RGB colour planes. In this way we considerably reduce curve gaps. Furthermore a multiscale approach prevents from detecting spurious curves as the resolutions increases. Because of this multiscale analysis the edge detector cannot separate two curves if they are less than 5 pixels apart.

The scaling range that a shape can withstand depends on the smallest distance between its curves with respect to its full size. Let r be such a ratio and s be the image size (maximum camera resolution in pixels). It is straightforward to express the maximum resolution reduction after which the closest curves can still be discriminated, which is: $sr/5$. Given typical values, such as $r = 0.06$ and $s = 512$ the maximum scaling factor allowed for full-image objects amounts to 6.1 and will be used as a reference scale for resolution stability tests.

A similar reasoning can be made about the allowed range of the projective transformation (change in viewpoint). In this case, for the same viewpoint position, remote parts of the object are subject to stronger contraction. Thus, distance reduction depends not only on the transformation parameters, but also on the image position of the point to be transformed. To quantify this reduction, a value that combines both parameters and position should be used. For this purpose we use "homogeneous depth" i.e. the value of the third homogeneous coordinate after the transformation M (cf. section 2.2).

The depth for the frontal view of the object is equal to 1.0 and under any projective transformation the maximum reduction will occur at object corners. For the same values of r and s introduced above, the average maximum distance between closest curves at highest resolutions is 15 pixels. If two curves, separated by this distance are found in the corner of the image, the distance between their transformed versions can be expressed as a function of the "depth". The upper bound for the range of allowed projective transformations is equal to 1.68 (homogeneous coordinates). This value is obtained by setting the obtained distance equal to the minimal allowed distance of 5 pixels and by solving for the "depth". For the real images of the database the viewpoint position with respect to the object was unknown and so the depth is estimated by recovering transformation with respect to a reference frontal image.

Next, we evaluate the robustness of the recovery of invariant properties. As long as curves are detected, the detection of bitangents, inflections and lines presents no major problems. However these properties exhibit different degree of numerical stability, as can be seen in figure 7.a for scaling and in figure 7.b for the projective transformation. Each graph represents the proportion of detected features (manually verified a posteriori) with respect to ideal situation, averaged over the database. It can be seen that up to 75% of the allowed transformation range we still obtain 80% of the same invariant properties. In figure 7.c we show an example image of an object taken from a viewpoint at the extreme of the allowed interval.

Finally, we consider the stability of the grouping and signature construction process. The grouping operation is clearly sensitive to curve gaps. The decreasing number of detected reference frames as a function of viewpoint transformation is also shown in figure 7.b (triples). This can be explained by the fact that extreme viewpoints increase the number of curve gaps at high curvature points.

By definition, the stage of signature construction itself is not sensitive to gaps in curves (cf. section 5). These might cause a change in the signature values only within limited intervals and their influence on the distance between signatures can be neutralized by the use of robust estimators [11]. Nevertheless, the presence of spurious curves can undermine a large part of the signature. That is why the *same* curves should be detected when viewed from different viewpoints. This is achieved by the use of multiscale detector, as illustrated by variation of the proportion of curves in figure 7.b.

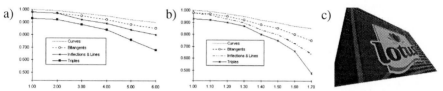

Fig. 7. Robustness of the signature construction process. Proportion of detected features as a function of resolution changes (a) and projective transformations (b). (c) Example of the extreme projective image transformation withstood by the method, for a typical shape.

For the case of orthogonal facets, reference frame detection is greatly simplified. Detection of lines is facilitated by specular reflections on box edges, by different illumination conditions for each facet (higher contrast on the edge) and finally by the relatively long edges of the box that are hardly subject to projective distortion. The grouping operation is performed by selecting line triples and by verifying that three criteria are satisfied. First, three lines rarely intersect at one unique point, but rather form a "triangle of intersection". Therefore, the surface of this triangle should be small. The second condition is on the orientation of rays. Orthogonality of facets imposes a condition on the rays orientation that should be satisfied. Finally, lines often do not reach the "corner" point, introducing gaps between their endpoint and the corner point. Therefore the third constraint imposes that the sum of these gaps should not exceed a fixed percentage of the three lines total length.

5.2 Evaluation of the Content-Based Retrieval Capabilities

In this section we present two types of experiments in order to assess the suitability of the proposed invariant signature for content-based shape retrieval. Initially, an individual signature is used as a query to the database while in the second stage all signatures, automatically extracted from the same image are used as queries. In both cases, separate tests with four different subsets of the database are performed. In case one, only one version of each image is included in the database (frontal view). In case two, close views of the same object but under different illumination conditions are considered. In the third case, object views from different viewpoints are included within the allowed range. The fourth case combines the images of the last two.

Shape-based retrieval was performed by pairwise comparison between signatures, using the Euclidean distance on the whole equally-weighted vector including geometric and chromatic information (cf. eq. 8). The search process is thus linear in the database size, although faster approaches can easily be introduced 1.. Given a query signature, the retrieval performance was assessed using standard information retrieval measures on the ranked hits, namely precision and recall. *Precision* is the proportion of correct hits in the set of retrieved items up to the last correct one. *Recall* is the proportion of target images that have been retrieved among the top N hits, $N \geq 1$.

In the first experiment, individual signatures were used for matching with the contents of four datasets. However, only the signatures for which a correct answer exist in the database were used. Table 1 shows the average values of the precision for all signatures of the frontal view, matched against all other signatures in the four separate datasets. Images from which the query was extracted were removed from their corresponding "front-view" dataset.

Table 1: Performance results

	Frontal views only	Illumination changes	Viewpoint variation	Both
Querying using individual signatures from frontal views				
Precision	69%	65%	58%	56%
Recall (N=15)	78%	73%	65%	61%
Querying with frontal views				
Precision	73%	70%	66%	62%
Recall (N=15)	82%	75%	69%	64%
Performance of image querying using facet signatures				
Precision			78%	72%
Recall (N=10)			85%	78%

On average, most of the correct signatures are among the $N = 15$ top-ranked hits, for all types of allowed transformations. In general, if at least one signature of an object (complex objects may provide several signatures) is detected in the image its discriminative power is sufficient enough to perform shape-based retrieval.

In the second experiment, the same four datasets are used as the database contents, but the way to define a query is different. For all objects in the database, other frontal views (different from those already in the database) are used for signature extraction. All automatically extracted signatures are used for separately querying the database. The $N = 15$ top-ranked hits were retained for each case. By using a simple voting scheme for all signatures of the same object, the rank of each signature was accumulated into an *object* rank. The central part of Table 1 shows the precision results using this rank, averaged across all queries.

Using the same procedure, we then performed retrieval test for faceted objects. Similar datasets were constructed. Views taken from different points in space but under the same illumination conditions were included in the first set. Views with all conditions allowed to vary were gathered in the second set ("Both"). Retrieval was performed by comparing three signatures of a test image with the whole collection of signatures. It can be seen (cf. Table 1) that retrieval performance is more stable and better than in a mere planar case. This stability can be explained by the more robust extraction of reference rays and by the fact that when one facet becomes hardly visible, the others automatically offers a good view to the camera.

6. Conclusions

In this article we have presented an approach for representing planar complex shapes. The proposed representation is projectively invariant and describes the local arrangement of neighbouring curves with respect to the invariant properties of one or move curves. This method presents two major advantages. First, less information is required with respect to previous approaches for one curve to produce a reference frame. Only three concurrent rays are necessary, against four points in a general projective case. Second, the local arrangement of neighbouring curves is incorporated into the description. This makes curves without any invariant properties at all also useful. Both advantages can be exploited to extend the application of invariant methods to a broad class of shapes found in the real-world situations and its extension to 3D faceted objects broadens its field of application to package boxes.

The proposed geometric construction is appropriate for the integration of chromatic information. Together with projective invariance, illumination invariant measures are associated with the shape description. This helps discriminate geometrically similar cases and leads to a more complete object representation.

The applicability of the proposed invariant representation to database retrieval has been validated with statistical tests. The representation maintains, within small variations, the property of projective invariance under reasonable viewpoint changes. At the same time, it allows discrimination among a few hundreds three-ray configurations selected from a database of real flat or faceted trademarks.

References

1. S. Arya, D.M. Mount, N.S. Netanyahu, R. Silverman, A.Y. Wu, An optimal algorithm for approximate nearest neighbour searching in fixed dimensions. Department of Computer Science, University of Maryland, College Park, Technical report CS-TR-3568, Dec. 1995.
2. S. Carlsson, R. Mohr, T. Moons, L. Morin, C. Rothwell, M. Van Diest, L. Van Gool, F. Veillon, A. Zissermann, "Semi-local projective invariants for the recognition of smooth plane curve", Intern. J. Comput. Vis. 19(3), 1996, p. 211-236.
3. C. Coelho, A. Heller, J.L. Mundy, D. A. Forsyth, A. Zisserman, "An Experimental Evaluation of Projective Invariants", In [56], p. 87-104.
4. F. S. Cohen, J.-Y. Wang, "Part I: Modeling image curves using invariant 3-D object curve models - a path to 3-D recognition and shape estimation from image contours", IEEE Trans. Patt. Anal. Mach. Intell., 1994, vol. 16, No. 1, p. 1-12.
5. G. D. Finlayson, "Color constancy in diagonal chromaticity space", Intern. Conf. Comp. Vis., MIT, 1995, p. 218-223.
6. M. Flickner, H. Sawhney, W. Niblack, J. Ashley, Q. Huang, B. Dom, M. Gorkani, J. Hafner, D. Lee, D. Petkovic, D. Steele, and P. Yanker (1995). Query by image and video content: the QBIC system. IEEE Computer, September, 23-32.
7. T. Gevers, A. W. M. Smeulders, "A comparative study of several color models for color image invariant retreival", Proc. 1st Int. Workshop on Image Databases & Multimedia Search, Amsterdam, Netherlands, 1996, p. 17.
8. A. Goshtasby, "Design and Recovery of 2-D and 3-D shapes using rational gaussian curves and surfaces", Intern. J. Comput. Vis. 10:3, 1993, pp. 233-256.

9. R. Hartley, "Projective reconstruction and invariants from multiple images", IEEE Trans. Patt. Anal. Mach. Intell., 1994, vol. 16, No. 10.

10. K. Hirata and T. Kato, *Query by Visual Example: Content-Based Image Retrieval*. A. Pirotte, C. Delobel and Gottlob (Eds.), Proc. E. D. B. T.'92 Conf. on Advances in Database Technology. Lecture Notes in Computer Science Vol. 580, Springer-Verlag, 1994, 56-71.

11. P.J. Huber, "Robust statistics", Wiley, 1981

12. R. Jain, "Image databases and multimedia search", Invited talk, Proc. 1st Int. Workshop on Image Databases & Multimedia Search, Amsterdam, Netherlands, 1996.

13. K. Kanatani, "Computational cross-ratio for computer vision", CVGIP: Image Understanding, Vol. 60, No. 3, 1994, p. 371-381.

14. D. G. Lowe, "Perceptual Organization and Visual Recognition", Kluwer Academic, Norwell, Ma, 1985.

15. S. Maybank, "Probabilistic analysis of the application of the cross ratio to model based vision: misclassification", Intern. J. Comput. Vis. 14, 1995, p. 199-210.

16. R. Milanese, D. Squire and T. Pun, *Correspondence analysis and hierarchical indexing for content-based image retrieval*. IEEE Intl. Conference on Image Processing, Lausanne, Switzerland, Sept 16-19, 1996.

17. T.Moons, E.J. Pauwels, L.J. Van Gool, A. Oosterlinck, "Foundations of semi-differential invariants", Intern. J. Comput. Vis. 14, 1993, p. 25-47.

18. J.L. Mundy and A. Zisserman (editors), "Geometric Invariance in Computer Vision", MIT Press, Cambridge Ma, 1992.

19. J.L. Mundy, D. Kapur, S. J. Maybank, P. Gros and L. Quan, "Geometric Interpretation of Joint Conic Invariants", In [56], p. 77-86.

20. E.J. Pauwels, T.Moons, L.J. Van Gool, P. Kempenaers, A. Oosterlinck, "Recognition of planar shapes under affine distortion", Intern. J. Comput. Vis. 14, 1993, p. 49-65.

21. A. Pentland, R.W. Picard, and S. Sclaroff (1994). Photobook: tools for content-based manipulation of image databases. (Storage and Retrieval for Image and Video Databases II, San Jose, CA, USA, 7-8 Feb. 1994). *Proc. of the SPIE-The Int. Soc. for Optical Eng.*, 2185, 34-47.

22. T. Pun, D. Squire, *Statistical structuring of pictorial databases for content-based image retrieval systems*. Pattern Recognition Letters, 17, 12, October 1996, 1299-1310.

23. T. H. Reiss, "Recognizing planar objects using invariant image features", Lecture Notes in Computer Science, Springer-Verlag, 676, 1993.

24. E. Rivlin, I. Weiss, "Local invariants for recognition", IEEE Trans. Patt. Anal. Mach. Intell., 1995, vol. 17, No. 3.

25. S. Startchik, R. Milanese, C. Rauber, T. Pun, "Planar shape databases with affine invariant search", Workshop on Image Databases & Multimedia Search, Amsterdam, 1996, p.202.

26. S. Startchik, C. Rauber, T. Pun, "Recognition of planar objects over complex backgrounds using line invariants and relevance measures", Workshop on Geometric Modeling & Invariants for Computer Vision, Xian, China , 1995, p. 301-307.

27. VIRAGE web site, http://www.virage.com.

28. I. Weiss, "Geometric Invariants and Object Recognition", Intern. J. Comput. Vis. 10:3, 1993, pp. 209.

29. A. Zissermann, D.A. Forsyth, J.L. Mundy, C.A. Rothwell, "Recognizing general curved objects efficiently", In 18., p. 228-251

Robust Techniques for the Estimation of Structure from Motion in the Uncalibrated Case

Michael J. Brooks,[1] Wojciech Chojnacki,[1] Anton van den Hengel,[1]
Luis Baumela[2]

[1] Department of Computer Science, University of Adelaide
Adelaide, SA 5005, Australia
{mjb,wojtek,hengel}@cs.adelaide.edu.au

[2] Departamento de Inteligencia Artificial, Universidad Politécnica de Madrid
Campus de Montegancedo s/n, 28660 Boadilla del Monte, Madrid, Spain
lbaumela@fi.upm.es

Abstract. Robust techniques are developed for determining structure from motion in the uncalibrated case. The structure recovery is based on previous work [7] in which it was shown that a camera undergoing unknown motion and having an unknown, and possibly varying, focal length can be self-calibrated via closed-form expressions in the entries of two matrices derivable from an instantaneous optical flow field. Critical to the recovery process is the obtaining of accurate numerical estimates, up to a scalar factor, of these matrices in the presence of noisy optical flow data. We present techniques for the determination of these matrices via least-squares methods, and also a way of enforcing a dependency constraint that is imposed on these matrices. A method for eliminating outlying flow vectors is also given. Results of experiments with real-image sequences are presented that suggest that the approach holds promise.

1 Introduction

In this paper we present robust techniques for estimating structure from motion in the uncalibrated case. The structure recovery is based on a method for self-calibrating a single moving camera from instantaneous optical flow, as developed in [7]. Here, self-calibration amounts to automatically determining the unknown instantaneous ego-motion and intrinsic parameters of the camera, and is analogous to self-calibrating a stereo vision set-up from corresponding points [9, 17]. The method of self-calibration rests on an equation that we term the *differential epipolar equation for uncalibrated optical flow*, which relates optical flow to the ego-motion and intrinsic parameters of the camera. This equation incorporates two matrices which encode information about the ego-motion and internal geometry of the camera. Any sufficiently large subset of an optical flow field determines the composite ratio of some of the entries of these matrices, and, under certain assumptions, the moving camera can be self-calibrated by means of closed-form expressions evolved from this ratio.

Once self-calibration is completed, scene reconstruction, up to a scalar factor, can be carried out by employing a procedure, also described in [7], based on the results of self-calibration and the optical flow data. In this way, the structure recovery is essentially reduced to the determination of the critical composite ratio.

In this paper, we present various least-squares techniques and an outlier rejection scheme that facilitate robust estimation of the critical composite ratio. The self-calibration and reconstruction methods are tested on sparse optical flow fields derived from real-world image sequences of a calibration grid and an office.

The present work is most closely related to that of Viéville and Faugeras [25], which was the first to tackle the problem of interpreting optical flow arising from an uncalibrated camera. The approach of Ohta and Kanatani [18] is also related to this work, but is concerned with the calibrated case and hence is not immediately applicable to our more general situation. For examples of other work dealing with the ego-motion of a calibrated camera see [10, 11]. A contrasting approach is given by Beardsley et al. [5], involving the computation of projective and affine (rather than Euclidean) structure from motion. Other related papers include [1–4, 15, 19, 23, 26, 27].

2 Differential epipolar equation and a cubic constraint

Consider a camera with an associated coordinate frame such that the origin of the frame coincides with the camera's optical centre, two basis vectors span the focal plane, and the other basis vector passes through the optical axis. Suppose that the camera undergoes smooth motion. Denote by v and ω the camera's instantaneous *translational velocity* and instantaneous *angular velocity* with respect to the camera frame. Let P be a static point in space, let $x = [x_1, x_2, x_3]^T$ be the coordinates of the vector connecting C with P in the vector basis of the camera frame, and let $p = [p_1, p_2, p_3]^T$ be the coordinates of the perspective projection of P, through C, onto the image plane $\{x \in \mathbb{R}^3 \mid x_3 = -f\}$, relative to the camera frame; here f is the focal length. To account for the characteristics of the camera, we adopt a separate coordinate frame in the image plane. Let $[m_1, m_2]^T$ be the coordinates of the image of P in the vector basis of this frame. If we append to $[m_1, m_2]^T$ an extra entry equal to 1 to yield the vector $m = [m_1, m_2, 1]^T$, then the relation between p and m can be written as $p = Am$, where A is a 3×3, possibly time-dependent, invertible matrix called the *intrinsic-parameter matrix*. As the camera moves, the position of P relative to the image frame will change accordingly and will be recorded in the function $t \mapsto m(t)$. The associated function $t \mapsto [m^T(t), \dot{m}(t)^T]^T$ satisfies the *differential epipolar equation for uncalibrated optical flow*

$$m^T W \dot{m} + m^T C m = 0, \tag{1}$$

where C and W are 3×3 matrices explicitly expressible in terms of v, ω, A and $\dot{A}$. The function $t \mapsto [m^T(t), \dot{m}(t)^T]^T$ is a single trajectory of an *optical flow field*. An optical flow field at a given instant t is a set of vectors of the form $[m(t)^T, \dot{m}(t)^T]^T$ that describe the instantaneous position and velocity of the images of various elements of the scene. More precisely, such a set constitutes a *true image motion field* which, as is usual, we assume to correspond to an *observed image velocity field* or optical flow field. Eq. (1) relates optical flow, ego-motion and camera parameters. A similar constraint, termed the *first-order expansion of the fundamental motion equation*, was derived using quite different means by Viéville and Faugeras [25]. In contrast with the above, however, it takes the form of an approximation rather than a strict equality. A simpler form of (1), applying to the calibrated case, was first derived by Maybank [16] and was subsequently exploited by many authors (cf. [2, 3, 12]).

The matrix C is symmetric, and hence it is uniquely determined by the entries $c_{11}, c_{12}, c_{13}, c_{22}, c_{23}, c_{33}$. The matrix W is antisymmetric, and so it is uniquely determined by the entries w_{12}, w_{13}, w_{23}. Define the *joint projective form* $\pi(C, W)$ of C and W to be the composite ratio $(c_{11} : c_{12} : c_{13} : c_{22} : c_{23} : c_{33} : w_{12} : w_{13} : w_{23})$. Eq. (1) is essentially a constraint on $\pi(C, W)$, the equation remaining valid whenever C and W are multiplied by a common scalar factor. It turns out that

$$w^T C w = 0, \tag{2}$$

where $w = [-w_{23}, w_{13}, -w_{12}]^T$. Again (2) can be interpreted as a constraint on $\pi(C, W)$—more precisely, as a cubic constraint. It implies that $\pi(C, W)$ lies on a seven-dimensional manifold that does not depend on the optical flow entering (1), a fact already noted in [25].

As indicated in the Introduction, the differential epipolar equation (1) forms the basis for a method of self-calibration. We use this equation along with (2) to determine $\pi(C, W)$ from noisy optical flow. Knowing $\pi(C, W)$ allows in turn recovery of some of the parameters describing the ego-motion and internal geometry of the camera. For details, the reader is referred to [7].

3 Estimating $\pi(C, W)$

We now turn to the problem of estimating $\pi(C, W)$ from optical flow that is perturbed by noise and outliers.

Ohta and Kanatani [18] (see also [13, Chap. 12]) present a method for estimating ego-motion and structure from noise-contaminated calibrated optical flow. It relies on a model of noise in the measurement of flow velocity adopted from the outset, and takes the form of an optimal estimation algorithm accompanied by a measure of the reliability of the estimates. Our problem is not directly amenable to Ohta and Kanatani's sophisticated analysis for two reasons. First, we deal with uncalibrated flow, and, second, we cannot assume the position of a flow vector to be unperturbed. Our goal is to develop methods capable of dealing with sparse optical flow obtained via the tracking of features, and not only with dense optical flow calculated across a grid. Nevertheless, we draw upon various ideas present in [18].

Let $\mathcal{S} = \{[m_i^T, \dot{m}_i^T]^T \mid i = 1, \dots, n\}$ with $n \geq 7$ be a data set representing measurements of a portion of instantaneous optical flow. We shall consider ways in which estimates of $\pi(C, W)$ can be derived from $\mathcal{S}$. Note that a pair of matrices (C, W) is uniquely determined by the vector

$$\theta_{C, W} = [c_{11}, c_{12}, c_{13}, c_{22}, c_{23}, c_{33}, w_{12}, w_{13}, w_{23}]^T.$$

When (C, W) is understood, $\theta_{C, W}$ will often be contracted to θ. Furthermore, observe that the ratio $\pi(C, W)$ can be identified, to within sign, with the vector $\theta_{C, W}$ satisfying the normalisation condition $\|\theta_{C, W}\| = 1$, where $\|\theta_{C, W}\| = (c_{11}^2 + c_{12}^2 + $

$\cdots + w_{23}{}^2)^{1/2}$. It is therefore always possible to represent an estimate of $\pi(C, W)$ as a normalised vector $\widehat{\theta} = \theta_{\widehat{C}, \widehat{W}}$ for some pair $(\widehat{C}, \widehat{W})$. Here, adhering to a custom in statistics, we use $\widehat{x}$ to denote an estimate of x.

3.1 Seven-point estimator

If $n = 7$, then an estimate of $\pi(C, W)$ can be obtained by solving a system of seven equations

$$m_i^T W \dot{m}_i + m_i^T C m_i = 0 \tag{3}$$

and equation (2). All these equations are homogeneous in the components of θ, and effectively provide seven constraints for the ratio $\pi(C, W)$. Note that $m^T W \dot{m} + m^T C m$ depends linearly on θ, being expressible as

$$m^T W \dot{m} + m^T C m = \theta^T u_{m, \dot{m}}, \tag{4}$$

where

$$u_{m, \dot{m}} = \begin{bmatrix} m_1^2 \\ 2m_1 m_2 \\ 2m_1 m_3 \\ m_2^2 \\ 2m_2 m_3 \\ m_3^2 \\ m_1 \dot{m}_2 - m_2 \dot{m}_1 \\ m_1 \dot{m}_3 - m_3 \dot{m}_1 \\ m_2 \dot{m}_3 - m_3 \dot{m}_2 \end{bmatrix}.$$

Therefore the space of solutions to system (3) is spanned by two normalised linearly independent solutions $\widehat{\theta}_1$ and $\widehat{\theta}_2$. Accordingly, an un-normalised solution $\widehat{\eta}$ to the full system of equations can be represented as $\alpha \widehat{\theta}_1 + (1 - \alpha) \widehat{\theta}_2$ for some scalar parameter α. Substituting $\alpha \widehat{\theta}_1 + (1 - \alpha) \widehat{\theta}_2$ into (2) leads to a cubic constraint on α. This equation has either one or three real solutions, which in turn give rise to one or three normalised estimates $\widehat{\theta} = \widehat{\eta} / \|\widehat{\eta}\|$.

3.2 Least squares estimator based on algebraic distances

If $n \geq 8$, then the linear homogeneous equations forming system (3) provide $n - 1 \geq 7$ constraints for $\pi(C, W)$. We can use these equations to estimate $\pi(C, W)$ without immediate recourse to the cubic constraint (2). The redundancy in system (3) suggests a least squares solution. In order to develop such a solution, a cost function has to be specified. Given a single piece of data $[m^T, \dot{m}^T]^T$ and a parameter θ to be fit, we take the *algebraic distance* $|m^T W \dot{m} + m^T C m|$ between $[m^T, \dot{m}^T]^T$ and the hypersurface

$$\mathcal{M}_\theta = \{[n^T, \dot{n}^T]^T \mid n^T W \dot{n} + n^T C n = 0\}$$

for the *residual* or the measure of the agreement between $[m^T, \dot{m}^T]^T$ and θ. The *residual square error*

$$J_1(\theta; \mathcal{S}) = \sum_{i=1}^{n} |m_i^T W \dot{m}_i + m_i^T C m_i|^2$$

then serves as a natural cost function. This choice can be viewed as a generalisation of the criterion used by Bookstein [6] for conic fitting. The J_1-based *best-fit estimate* of $\pi(C, W)$ is a unique (up to a sign) normalised vector $\hat{\theta}$ such that

$$J_1(\hat{\theta}; \mathcal{S}) = \min_{\|\theta\| = 1} J_1(\theta; \mathcal{S}). \tag{5}$$

With errors ascribed to the $u_{m_i, \dot{m}_i}$, the J_1-based minimisation can be viewed as a method of *orthogonal regression*, also termed *total least squares regression* or *principal component regression*. The estimate $\hat{\theta}$ can be computed explicitly. In fact, in view of (4),

$$|m^T W \dot{m} + m^T C m|^2 = \theta^T M_{m, \dot{m}} \theta, \tag{6}$$

where

$$M_{m, \dot{m}} = u_{m, \dot{m}} u_{m, \dot{m}}{}^T$$

and further

$$J_1(\theta; \mathcal{S}) = \theta^T D \theta,$$

where

$$D = \sum_{i=1}^{n} M_{m_i, \dot{m}_i}.$$

The gradient of J_1 with respect to θ, traditionally written as a row vector,

$$\nabla_\theta J_1(\theta; \mathcal{S}) = \left[\frac{\partial J_1}{\partial c_{11}}(\theta; \mathcal{S}), \frac{\partial J_1}{\partial c_{12}}(\theta; \mathcal{S}), \ldots, \frac{\partial J_1}{\partial w_{23}}(\theta; \mathcal{S}) \right]$$

is given by

$$[\nabla_\theta J_1(\theta; \mathcal{S})]^T = 2 D \theta. \tag{7}$$

The minimisation condition (5) implies that

$$[\nabla_\theta J_1(\hat{\theta}; \mathcal{S})]^T = 2 \lambda \hat{\theta}$$

for some (unknown) scalar *Lagrange multiplier* λ. This together with (7) shows that $\hat{\theta}$ is an eigenvector of D with eigenvalue λ. If ξ is a normalised eigenvector of D with eigenvalue μ, then

$$\mu = \mu \xi^T \xi = J_1(\xi; \mathcal{S}) \geq J_1(\hat{\theta}; \mathcal{S}) = \hat{\theta}^T \lambda \hat{\theta} = \lambda,$$

showing that λ is the smallest eigenvalue of D. Therefore $\hat{\theta}$ is recognised as the normalised eigenvector (or the principal component) corresponding to the smallest eigenvalue of D. Both $\hat{\theta}$ and λ can be efficiently calculated by employing the method of singular value decomposition.

3.3 Least squares estimator based on Euclidean distances

The algebraic distance underlying the J_1-based estimation method has no geometric significance. In contrast, the expression

$$\delta(\boldsymbol{\theta}; \boldsymbol{m}, \dot{\boldsymbol{m}}) = \frac{|\boldsymbol{m}^T \boldsymbol{W} \dot{\boldsymbol{m}} + \boldsymbol{m}^T \boldsymbol{C} \boldsymbol{m}|}{\sqrt{\|2\boldsymbol{C}\boldsymbol{m} + \boldsymbol{W}\dot{\boldsymbol{m}}\|^2 + \|\boldsymbol{W}\boldsymbol{m}\|^2}} \tag{8}$$

is geometrically meaningful being an approximation of the *Euclidean distance* between $[\boldsymbol{m}^T, \dot{\boldsymbol{m}}^T]^T$ and $\mathcal{M}_\theta$. More generally, if $\mathcal{M}$ is a hypersurface in $\mathbb{R}^k$ defined by $\mathcal{M} = \{x \in \mathbb{R}^k \mid f(x) = 0\}$ and $z \in \mathbb{R}^k$ is a point close to $\mathcal{M}$, then the Euclidean distance between z and $\mathcal{M}$ is to a first order approximation equal to $|f(z)|/\|\nabla f(z)\|$—a fact exploited in vision-related statistical formulations first by Sampson [22] and later by a number of authors (cf. [13, 14, 24, 28]). Adopting $\delta(\boldsymbol{\theta}; \boldsymbol{m}, \dot{\boldsymbol{m}})$ as a statistically more adequate residual, we introduce a cost function

$$J_2(\boldsymbol{\theta}; \mathcal{S}) = \sum_{i=1}^{n} |\delta(\boldsymbol{\theta}; \boldsymbol{m}_i, \dot{\boldsymbol{m}}_i)|^2.$$

A similar cost function can be devised starting from the principles underpinning Kanatani's approach to statistical optimisation (cf. [13, Chap. 12] and [18]). With errors ascribed to the $[\boldsymbol{m}_i^T, \dot{\boldsymbol{m}}_i^T]^T$ rather than to the $\boldsymbol{u}_{\boldsymbol{m}_i, \dot{\boldsymbol{m}}_i}$, the J_2-based minimisation can be viewed as a variant of the method of orthogonal regression. Due to the complicated way in which $\boldsymbol{C}$ and $\boldsymbol{W}$ enter J_2, it is not clear whether the J_2-based estimate of $\pi(\boldsymbol{C}, \boldsymbol{W})$ can be given an explicit form. To evolve a numerical estimate, various standard iterative techniques can be employed like the Newton-Raphson method, the steepest descent method, the Levenberg-Marquardt method, the downhill simplex method, and various direction set methods of Powell (cf. [20]). Alternatively, one might attempt to develop algorithms especially adopted to cope with the task of minimisation of J_2. Two such algorithms are proposed next.

3.4 Iteratively reweighted least squares estimator

Let $\widehat{\boldsymbol{\theta}}$ be a normalised estimate corresponding to a pair $(\widehat{\boldsymbol{C}}, \widehat{\boldsymbol{W}})$, and let

$$J_3(\boldsymbol{\theta}; \widehat{\boldsymbol{\theta}}, \mathcal{S}) = \sum_{i=1}^{n} |\tilde{\delta}(\boldsymbol{\theta}; \widehat{\boldsymbol{\theta}}, \boldsymbol{m}_i, \dot{\boldsymbol{m}}_i)|^2,$$

where

$$\tilde{\delta}(\boldsymbol{\theta}; \widehat{\boldsymbol{\theta}}, \boldsymbol{m}, \dot{\boldsymbol{m}}) = \frac{|\boldsymbol{m}^T \boldsymbol{W} \dot{\boldsymbol{m}} + \boldsymbol{m}^T \boldsymbol{C} \boldsymbol{m}|}{\sqrt{\|2\widehat{\boldsymbol{C}}\boldsymbol{m} + \widehat{\boldsymbol{W}}\dot{\boldsymbol{m}}\|^2 + \|\widehat{\boldsymbol{W}}\boldsymbol{m}\|^2}}.$$

The denominator in the expression for $\tilde{\delta}$ does not depend on $\boldsymbol{\theta}$, and so minimisation of $J_3(\boldsymbol{\theta}; \mathcal{S})$ subject to the constraint $\|\boldsymbol{\theta}\|^2 = 1$ leads to an estimator falling into the category of weighted least squares techniques. Let

$$\boldsymbol{D}_{\widehat{\boldsymbol{\theta}}} = \sum_{i=1}^{n} \lambda_i(\widehat{\boldsymbol{\theta}}) \boldsymbol{M}_{\boldsymbol{m}_i, \dot{\boldsymbol{m}}_i} \tag{9}$$

where

$$\lambda_i(\widehat{\boldsymbol{\theta}}) = \left(\|2\widehat{\boldsymbol{C}}\boldsymbol{m}_i + \widehat{\boldsymbol{W}}\dot{\boldsymbol{m}}_i\|^2 + \|\widehat{\boldsymbol{W}}\boldsymbol{m}_i\|^2 \right)^{-1}.$$

Employing Lagrange multipliers, we verify at once that the J_3-based estimate can be identified with the eigenvector of $\boldsymbol{D}_{\widehat{\boldsymbol{\theta}}}$ corresponding to the smallest eigenvalue. Using this observation, we can now propose the following iteratively reweighted least squares estimator that seeks to minimise J_2:

1. Compute $\widehat{\boldsymbol{\theta}}_0$ using least-square fitting based on J_1.
2. Assuming that $\widehat{\boldsymbol{\theta}}_{k-1}$ is known, compute the matrix $\boldsymbol{D}_{\widehat{\boldsymbol{\theta}}_{k-1}}$.
3. Compute a normalised eigenvector of $\boldsymbol{D}_{\widehat{\boldsymbol{\theta}}_{k-1}}$ corresponding to the smallest eigenvalue and take this eigenvector for $\widehat{\boldsymbol{\theta}}_k$.
4. If $\widehat{\boldsymbol{\theta}}_k$ is sufficiently close to $\widehat{\boldsymbol{\theta}}_{k-1}$, then terminate the procedure; otherwise increment k and return to Step 2.

3.5 Modified iteratively reweighted least squares estimator

Typically, an estimate evolved by the algorithm in the previous subsection will be different from the sought-after estimate based on minimisation of J_2—the iteratively reweighted least squares techniques are susceptible to statistical bias (cf. [13, Chap. 9], [29]). In an attempt to eliminate this shortcoming, we put forward a modified algorithm. While in some aspects the proposed technique resembles Kanatani's technique of renormalisation [13, Chap. 9], it is different from the latter in that it is formulated in a purely deterministic, probability-free fashion, and that it impinges on the standard, rather than generalised, eigenvalue analysis.

Let

$$\boldsymbol{\rho}_1 = \begin{bmatrix} 1\,0\,0\,0\,0\,0\,0\,0\,0 \\ 0\,1\,0\,0\,0\,0\,0\,0\,0 \\ 0\,0\,1\,0\,0\,0\,0\,0\,0 \end{bmatrix}, \quad \boldsymbol{\sigma}_1 = \begin{bmatrix} 0\,0\,0\,0\,0\,0\,0\,0\,0 \\ 0\,0\,0\,0\,0\,0\,1\,0\,0 \\ 0\,0\,0\,0\,0\,0\,0\,1\,0 \end{bmatrix},$$

$$\boldsymbol{\rho}_2 = \begin{bmatrix} 0\,1\,0\,0\,0\,0\,0\,0\,0 \\ 0\,0\,0\,1\,0\,0\,0\,0\,0 \\ 0\,0\,0\,0\,1\,0\,0\,0\,0 \end{bmatrix}, \quad \boldsymbol{\sigma}_2 = \begin{bmatrix} 0\,0\,0\,0\,0\,0\,-1\,0\,0 \\ 0\,0\,0\,0\,0\,0\,\,0\,0\,0 \\ 0\,0\,0\,0\,0\,0\,\,0\,0\,1 \end{bmatrix},$$

$$\boldsymbol{\rho}_3 = \begin{bmatrix} 0\,0\,1\,0\,0\,0\,0\,0\,0 \\ 0\,0\,0\,0\,1\,0\,0\,0\,0 \\ 0\,0\,0\,0\,0\,1\,0\,0\,0 \end{bmatrix}, \quad \boldsymbol{\sigma}_3 = \begin{bmatrix} 0\,0\,0\,0\,0\,0\,0\,-1\,\,0 \\ 0\,0\,0\,0\,0\,0\,0\,\,0\,-1 \\ 0\,0\,0\,0\,0\,0\,0\,\,0\,\,0 \end{bmatrix}.$$

A fundamental property of these matrices is that, for each $\alpha \in \{1, 2, 3\}$,

$$\boldsymbol{\rho}_\alpha \boldsymbol{\theta} = [c_{\alpha 1}, c_{\alpha 2}, c_{\alpha 3}]^T \quad \text{and} \quad \boldsymbol{\sigma}_\alpha \boldsymbol{\theta} = [w_{\alpha 1}, w_{\alpha 2}, w_{\alpha 3}]^T.$$

Using this property, we find that

$$\boldsymbol{m}^T \boldsymbol{C}^2 \boldsymbol{m} = \sum_{\alpha,\beta,\gamma=1}^{3} m_\beta c_{\beta\alpha} c_{\alpha\gamma} m_\gamma = \sum_{\alpha,\beta,\gamma=1}^{3} c_{\beta\alpha} m_\beta m_\gamma c_{\alpha\gamma} = \sum_{\alpha=1}^{3} \boldsymbol{\theta}^T \boldsymbol{\rho}_\alpha{}^T \boldsymbol{m} \boldsymbol{m}^T \boldsymbol{\rho}_\alpha \boldsymbol{\theta}.$$

Likewise

$$m^T C W \dot{m} = \sum_{\alpha=1}^{3} \theta^T \rho_\alpha^{\ T} m \dot{m}^T \sigma_\alpha \theta,$$

$$\dot{m}^T W^2 \dot{m} = \sum_{\alpha=1}^{3} \theta^T \sigma_\alpha^{\ T} \dot{m} \dot{m}^T \sigma_\alpha \theta,$$

$$m^T W^2 m = \sum_{\alpha=1}^{3} \theta^T \sigma_\alpha^{\ T} m m^T \sigma_\alpha \theta.$$

Combining the last four identities with

$$\|2Cm + W\dot{m}\|^2 + \|Wm\|^2$$
$$= 4m^T C^2 m + 4m^T C W \dot{m} - \dot{m}^T W^2 \dot{m} - m^T W^2 m,$$

we see that

$$\|2Cm + W\dot{m}\|^2 + \|Wm\|^2 = \theta^T N_{m,\dot{m}} \theta, \tag{10}$$

where

$$N_{m,\dot{m}} = 4 \sum_{\alpha=1}^{3} \rho_\alpha^{\ T} m m^T \rho_\alpha + 4 \sum_{\alpha=1}^{3} \rho_\alpha^{\ T} m \dot{m}^T \sigma_\alpha$$
$$- \sum_{\alpha=1}^{3} \sigma_\alpha^{\ T} \dot{m} \dot{m}^T \sigma_\alpha - \sum_{\alpha=1}^{3} \sigma_\alpha^{\ T} m m^T \sigma_\alpha.$$

Now, in view of (6) and (10),

$$\delta(\theta; m, \dot{m}) = \frac{\theta^T M_{m,\dot{m}} \theta}{\theta^T N_{m,\dot{m}} \theta}$$

implying that

$$J_2(\theta; \mathcal{S}) = \sum_{i=1}^{n} \frac{\theta^T M_{m_i, \dot{m}_i} \theta}{\theta^T N_{m_i, \dot{m}_i} \theta}.$$

Hence, immediately,

$$[\nabla_\theta J_2(\theta; \mathcal{S})]^T = 2 X_\theta \theta, \tag{11}$$

where

$$X_\theta = \sum_{i=1}^{n} \frac{M_{m_i, \dot{m}_i}}{\theta^T N_{m_i, \dot{m}_i} \theta} - \sum_{i=1}^{n} \frac{\theta^T M_{m_i, \dot{m}_i} \theta}{(\theta^T N_{m_i, \dot{m}_i} \theta)^2} N_{m_i, \dot{m}_i}. \tag{12}$$

Again the minimiser $\widehat{\theta}$ satisfies $[\nabla_\theta J_2(\widehat{\theta}; \mathcal{S})]^T = 2\lambda\widehat{\theta}$ for some Lagrange multiplier λ. Combining this with (11), we conclude that $\widehat{\theta}$ is an eigenvector of $X_{\widehat{\theta}}$ with λ as the associated eigenvalue. Now

$$\widehat{\theta}^T X_{\widehat{\theta}} \widehat{\theta} = \lambda \widehat{\theta}^T \widehat{\theta} = \lambda.$$

On the other hand, recourse to (12) reveals that $\widehat{\theta}^T X_{\widehat{\theta}} \widehat{\theta} = 0$. Therefore $\lambda = 0$ and, consequently,

$$X_{\widehat{\theta}} \widehat{\theta} = 0. \tag{13}$$

This is a non-linear constraint on $\widehat{\theta}$ which one might hope to resolve by employing a method of successive approximations of some kind. The following scheme for solving (13) suggests itself naturally:

1. Compute $\widehat{\theta}_0$ using least-square fitting based on J_1.
2. Assuming that $\widehat{\theta}_{k-1}$ is known, compute the matrix $X_{\widehat{\theta}_{k-1}}$.
3. Compute a normalised eigenvector of $X_{\widehat{\theta}_{k-1}}$ corresponding to the smallest eigenvalue and take this eigenvector for $\widehat{\theta}_k$.
4. If $\widehat{\theta}_k$ is sufficiently close to $\widehat{\theta}_{k-1}$, then terminate the procedure; otherwise increment k and return to Step 2.

Observe that, on account of (9) and (12),

$$X_\theta = D_\theta - E_\theta,$$

where

$$E_\theta = \sum_{i=1}^n \frac{\theta^T M_{m_i, \dot{m}_i} \theta}{(\theta^T N_{m_i, \dot{m}_i} \theta)^2} N_{m_i, \dot{m}_i}.$$

Therefore X_θ can be viewed a modification of D_θ. Accordingly, the estimator embodied by the above algorithm can be viewed as a modification of the iteratively reweighted least squares estimator from the previous subsection.

Note that other more refined schemes for solving (13) may readily be developed. One such scheme may be obtained by linearising the left-hand side of (13) to incorporate the matrix-valued derivative of the mapping $\theta \mapsto X_\theta$.

3.6   Enforcing the cubic constraint

An estimate $\widehat{\theta}$ obtained by any of the methods considered above may fail to satisfy equation (2). A corrective procedure for modifying estimates to accommodate this constraint is therefore needed.

Given a (normalised) estimate $\widehat{\theta} = \theta_{\widehat{C}, \widehat{W}}$, possibly failing to satisfy (2), define $\widehat{\theta}_\rho = \theta_{\widehat{C}_\rho, \widehat{W}_\rho}$ by

$$\widehat{C}_\rho = \frac{\widehat{C} - P\widehat{C}P}{\|\theta_{\widehat{C} - P\widehat{C}P, \widehat{W}}\|} \quad \text{and} \quad \widehat{W}_\rho = \frac{\widehat{W}}{\|\theta_{\widehat{C} - P\widehat{C}P, \widehat{W}}\|},$$

Fig. 1. Image sequence of a calibration grid.

where

$$P = I + \|\widehat{w}\|^{-2}\widehat{W}^2.$$

Note that the vector $\widehat{\theta}_\rho$ comes automatically normalised. It is easily verified that if $\widehat{\theta}$ satisfies (2), then $P\widehat{C}P = 0$ and hence $\widehat{\theta} = \widehat{\theta}_\rho$. Since $P\widehat{w} = \widehat{w}$ and $\widehat{w}^T P = \widehat{w}^T$, it follows that $\widehat{w}^T \widehat{C}_\rho \widehat{w} = 0$, which in turn immediately implies that $\widehat{w}_\rho{}^T \widehat{C}_\rho \widehat{w}_\rho = 0$. Thus passing from $\widehat{\theta}$ to $\widehat{\theta}_\rho$ gives a sought-after modification procedure.

3.7 Robust estimation

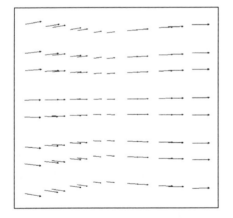

Fig. 2. Optical flow for calibration grid.

Typically, a data set comprises two subsets: a large, dominant subset of valid data or *inliers*, and a relatively small subset of *outliers* or *contaminants*. Least squares minimisation is by nature global and hence vulnerable to distortion by outliers. To obtain robust estimates, outliers have to be detected and rejected. To identify the outliers, we employ Rousseeuw's *least median of squares regression* (LMS), as presented in [21].

The LMS technique is applied to a collection of samples, each being a seven-element subset of S. The size of samples is such that it is minimal to allow an estimate of $\pi(C, W)$ to be determined from a single sample. The collection is assumed to be large enough to comprise a sample containing no outlying data. Ideally, the estimator should consider the set of all seven-element samples. In practice, to make the search computationally feasible, the sample space is reduced to a family of q randomly chosen samples.[1] The number q is determined as follows. Assume that the proportion of outliers in S does not exceed ϵ,

---

[1] It is important that such a family be chosen so that points forming samples are evenly spread throughout the whole image.

where $0 < \epsilon < 1$. The probability P that a family of q samples contains at least one sample that is outlier-free is then approximately given by

$$P = 1 - (1 - (1 - \epsilon)^7)^q.$$

Consequently,

$$q = \left[\frac{\log(1 - P)}{\log(1 - (1 - \epsilon)^7)} \right],$$

where $[x]$ denotes the integral part of x. We exploit this formula by assuming that $P = 0.95$ and $\epsilon = 0.5^2$. If after a first run the LMS estimator finds out that the level of contamination is essentially different from the initial value 0.5, we re-run the LMS procedure taking the estimated contamination level for an updated value of ϵ.

With q fixed, the LMS estimate of $\pi(C, W)$ is obtained by executing the following steps:

1. Using a random selection scheme[3], choose a family $\mathcal{S}_0$ consisting of q subsets of $\mathcal{S}$, each subset containing seven elements.
2. For each $s \in \mathcal{S}_0$, compute three estimates $\widehat{\theta}_{s,k}$ ($k \in \{1, 2, 3\}$) by using the seven-point algorithm from Subsection 3.1 (all three estimates may coincide).
3. For each $(s, k) \in \mathcal{S}_0 \times \{1, 2, 3\}$, determine the median

$$M_{s,k} = \operatorname*{med}_{i=1,\ldots,n} \delta(\widehat{\theta}_{s,k}; m_i, \dot{m}_i)^2.$$

4. Letting $(s_q, k_q) \in \mathcal{S}_0 \times \{1, 2, 3\}$ be such that

$$M_{s_q, k_q} = \min_{(s,k) \in \mathcal{S}_0 \times \{1,2,3\}} M_{s,k},$$

take $\widehat{\theta}_{s_q, k_q}$ for the LMS estimate of $\pi(C, W)$.

With the LMS estimate at hand, outliers within $\mathcal{S}$ are identified by using the following procedure:

1. Take $\hat{\sigma} = 1.4826 \left(1 + \frac{5}{n-7}\right) \sqrt{M_{s_q, k_q}}$ for the *robust standard deviation* of the measurements.
2. Declare $[m_i{}^T, \dot{m}_i{}^T]^T$ to be an outlier if and only if $\delta(\widehat{\theta}_{s_q, k_q}; m_i, \dot{m}_i) > 2.5\hat{\sigma}$.

Finally, an overall algorithm for generating a robust estimate of $\pi(C, W)$ can be formulated as follows:

---

1. Extract outliers from $\mathcal{S}$ by using the above procedure.
2. Compute an estimate $\widehat{\theta}$ by applying to the remaining elements of $\mathcal{S}$ (a refinement of) the iterative algorithm from Subsection 3.5 to solve (13).
3. Modify $\widehat{\theta}$ to $\widehat{\theta}_\rho$ by using the procedure from Subsection 3.6.

---

[2] 0.5 is roughly the *breakdown point* of the LMS estimator. The breakdown point of an estimator is the smallest proportion of the data that can have an arbitrarily large effect on its value.

[3] Such a scheme should be sufficiently regular to avoid clustered outcomes.

Fig. 3. Grid reconstruction from various views.

4 Experimental results

In order to assess the applicability of the approach, two tests with real image sequences were performed. The three images shown in Figure 1 were captured by a Phillips CCD camera with a 12.5-mm lens. Corners were localised to sub-pixel accuracy with the use of a corner detector, correspondences between the images were obtained, and the optical flow depicted in Figure 2 was computed by exploiting these correspondences (thus no use was made of intensity-based methods of flow computation). The LMS procedure was used to eliminate outliers, and a general solver was then employed to resolve (13), which resulted in an estimate of $\pi(C, W)$. Finally, closed-form expressions were employed to self-calibrate the system. With self-calibration completed, the pleasing reconstruction displayed in Figure 3 was finally obtained.

The images in Figure 4 were captured using a Nikon-N90/Kodak-DCS420 camera. The process outlined above produced the reconstruction depicted in Figure 5. To convey clearly the patterns of the calibration grid, reconstructed points in 3-space have been connected by line segments. Note that coplanarity of three dimensional points on the wall and table is well preserved, as is the orthogonality of groups of points on the different faces of the pillar. This simple reconstruction is again visually pleasing and suggests that the approach holds promise.

Acknowledgments

This research was in part funded by the Australian Research Council and the Cooperative Research Center for Sensor Signal and Information Processing.

References

1. M. Armstrong, A. Zisserman, and R. Hartley, *Self-calibration from image triplets*, In Buxton and Cipolla [8], pp. 3–16.
2. K. Åström and A. Heyden, *Continuous time matching constraints for image streams*, International Journal of Computer Vision, to appear.

Fig. 4. Extract from an office image sequence.

3. _____, *Multilinear forms in the infinitesimal-time case*, Proceedings, CVPR '96, IEEE Computer Society Conference on Computer Vision and Pattern Recognition (San Francisco, CA, June 18–20, 1996), IEEE Computer Society Press, Los Alamitos, CA, 1996, pp. 833–838.

4. J. L. Barron and R. Eagleson, *Recursive estimation of time-varying motion and structure parameters*, Pattern Recognition **29** (1996), no. 5, 797–818.

5. P. A. Beardsley, A. Zisserman, and D. W. Murray, *Sequential updating of projective and affine structure from motion*, International Journal of Computer Vision **23** (1997), no. 3, 235–259.

6. F. Bookstein, *Fitting conic sections to scattered data*, Computer Vision, Graphics, and Image Processing **9** (1979), no. 1, 56–71.

7. M. J. Brooks, W. Chojnacki, and L. Baumela, *Determining the egomotion of an uncalibrated camera from instantaneous optical flow*, Journal of the Optical Society of America A **14** (1997), no. 10, 2670–2677.

8. B. Buxton and R. Cipolla (eds.), *Computer Vision—ECCV '96*, Lecture Notes in Computer Science, vol. 1064, Fourth European Conference on Computer Vision, Cambridge, UK, April 14–18, 1996, Springer, Berlin, 1996.

9. O. D. Faugeras, Q. T. Luong, and S. J. Maybank, *Camera self-calibration: Theory and experiments*, Computer Vision—ECCV '92 (Second European Conference on Computer Vision, Santa Margherita Ligure, Italy, May 19–22, 1992) (G. Sandini, ed.), Springer, Berlin, 1992, pp. 321–334.

10. N. C. Gupta and L. N. Kanal, *3-D motion estimation from motion field*, Artificial Intelligence **78** (1995), no. 1-2, 45–86.

11. D. J. Heeger and A. D. Jepson, *Subspace methods for recovering rigid motion I: algorithm and implementation*, International Journal of Computer Vision **7** (1992), no. 2, 95–117.

12. K. Kanatani, *3-D interpretation of optical flow by renormalization*, International Journal of Computer Vision **11** (1993), no. 3, 267–282.

13. _____, *Statistical Optimization for Geometric Computation: Theory and Practice*, Elsevier, Amsterdam, 1996.

14. Q.-T. Luong and O. D. Faugeras, *The fundamental matrix: theory, algorithms, and stability analysis*, International Journal of Computer Vision **17** (1996), no. 1, 43–75.

15. _____, *Self-calibration of a moving camera from point correspondences and fundamental matrices*, International Journal of Computer Vision **22** (1997), no. 3, 261–289.

16. S. J. Maybank, *The angular velocity associated with the optical flowfield arising from motion through a rigid environment*, Proceedings of the Royal Society of London Ser. A **401** (1985), 317–326.

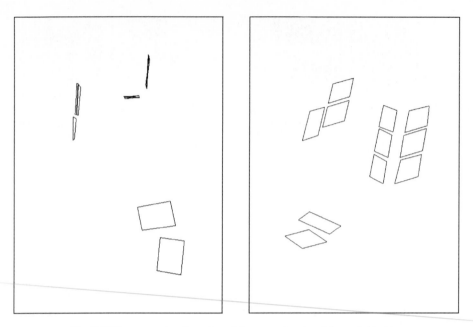

Fig. 5. Office reconstruction viewed from overhead and from right-side.

17. S. J. Maybank and O. D. Faugeras, *A theory of self-calibration of a moving camera*, International Journal of Computer Vision **8** (1992), no. 2, 123–151.

18. N. Ohta and K. Kanatani, *Optimal structure-from-motion algorithm for optical flow*, IEICE Transactions on Information and Systems **E78-D** (1995), no. 12, 1559–1566.

19. M. Pollefeys, M. Van Gool, and M. Proesmans, *Euclidean 3D reconstruction from image sequences with variable focal length*, In Buxton and Cipolla [8], pp. 31–42.

20. W. H. Press, S. A. Teukolsky, W. T. Vetterling, and B. P. Flannery, *Numerical Recipes in C*, Cambridge University Press, Cambridge, 1995.

21. P. J. Rousseeuw and A. M. Leroy, *Robust Regression and Outlier Regression*, John Wiley & Sons, New York, 1987.

22. P. D. Sampson, *Fitting conics sections to 'very scattered' data: An iterative refinement of the Bookstein algorithm*, Computer Graphics and Image Processing **18** (1982), no. 1, 97–108.

23. S. Soatto and P. Perona, *Recursive 3D visual motion estimation using subspace constraints*, International Journal of Computer Vision **22** (1997), no. 3, 235–259.

24. P. H. S. Torr and D. W. Murray, *The development and comparison of robust methods for estimating the fundamental matrix*, International Journal of Computer Vision **24** (1997), no. 3, 271–300.

25. T. Viéville and O. D. Faugeras, *Motion analysis with a camera with unknown, and possibly varying intrinsic parameters*, Proceedings of the Fifth International Conference on Computer Vision (Cambridge, MA, June 1995), IEEE Computer Society Press, Los Alamitos, CA, 1995, pp. 750–756.

26. T. Viéville, O. D. Faugeras, and Q.-T. Luong, *Motion of points and lines in the uncalibrated case*, International Journal of Computer Vision **17** (1996), no. 1, 7–41.

27. T. Viéville, C. Zeller, and L. Robert, *Using collineations to compute motion and structure in an uncalibrated image sequence*, International Journal of Computer Vision **20** (1996), no. 3, 213–242.

28. J. Weng, T. S. Huang, and N. Ahuja, *Motion and structure from two perspective views: algorithms, error analysis, and error estimation*, IEEE Transactions on Pattern Analysis and Machine Intelligence **11** (1989), no. 5, 451–476.

29. Z. Zhang, *Parameter estimation techniques: a tutorial with application to conic fitting*, Image and Vision Computing **15** (1997), no. 1, 57–76.

A Factorization Method for Projective and Euclidean Reconstruction from Multiple Perspective Views via Iterative Depth Estimation

Toshio Ueshiba and Fumiaki Tomita

Electrotechnical Laboratory
1-1-4 Umezono, Tsukuba, Ibaraki, 3058568 Japan
{ueshiba|tomita}@etl.go.jp

Abstract. A factorization method is proposed for recovering camera motion and object shapes from point correspondences observed in multiple images with perspective projection. For any factorization-based approaches for perspective images, scaling parameters called *projective depth*s must be estimated in order to obtain a *measurement matrix* that could be decomposed into motion and shape. One possible approach, proposed by Sturm and Triggs[11], is to compute projective depths from fundamental matrices and epipoles. The estimation process of the fundamental matrices, however, might be unstable if the measurement noise is large or the cameras and the object points are nearly in critical configurations. In this paper, the authors propose an algorithm by which the projective depths are iteratively estimated so that the measurement matrix is made to be as close as possible to rank 4. This estimation process requires no fundamental matrix computation and is therefore robust against measurement noise. Camera motion and shape in 3D projective space are then recovered by factoring the measurement matrix computed from the obtained projective depths. The authors also derive metric constraints for a perspective camera model in the case where the intrinsic camera parameters are available and show that these constraints can be linearly solved for a projective transformation which relates projective and Euclidean descriptions of the scene structure. Using this transformation, the projective motion and shape obtained in the previous factorization step is upgraded to metric descriptions, that is, represented with respect to the Euclidean coordinate frame. The validity of the proposed method is confirmed by experiments with real images.

1 Introduction

Structure-from-motion, i.e. recovering both camera motion and object shapes from multiple images, has been one of the most fundamental problems in computer vision and has attracted much attention in the vision community for a long time. Among the numerous techniques proposed over the past years, a factorization method developed by Tomasi and Kanade[12] is both elegant and useful because of its simplicity and stability. Although their work was based on the orthographic projection model of cameras, extensions to weak perspective[14] and paraperspective[9] projections have been made. All these methods utilize a distinctive characteristic in that the measurement matrix constructed from 2D coordinates of image points can be decomposed into two matrices representing camera motion and object shape with *affine* projections .

In recent years, several techniques extending the factorization method to perspective camera models have been proposed[1, 11, 13]. The essential difference between the affine and perspective factorization methods is that since the scaling factors (we call here *projective depths*) for each of the homogeneous coordinates of image points are unknown, the measurement matrix is also unknown. This means that we cannot apply conventional affine factorization techniques immediately to the obtained image data. Therefore the most crucial point in projective factorization is how to estimate these depth parameters.

Christy and Horaud[1] proposed a method for shape recovery from perspective images in which the depth parameters were iteratively estimated by repeating factorization of the measurement matrix starting from the paraperspective camera model. In each iteration step, they computed Euclidean motion and shape by solving *metric constraints*[12, 9] and updated the depths using these parameters. To apply metric constraints, however, one must know the intrinsic parameters of cameras, which limits this method only to use with calibrated cameras.

On the other hand, Sturm and Triggs[11] proposed a non-iterative factorization method for uncalibrated perspective views. The strategy of their algorithm is as follows; first several pairs of two images are sampled and fundamental matrices and epipoles are estimated for each pair independently. Projective depths for each image point are then computed from those fundamental matrices and epipoles so that the homogeneous coordinates of the image points overall satisfy some internal consistency. This strategy, however, depends highly on the accurate estimation of the fundamental matrices. If large errors are produced in the estimation, they would propagate to the measurement matrix and significantly degrade the accuracy of the final motion and shape. As it is well known that estimating a fundamental matrix from point correspondences between two images is quite sensitive to localization errors in the corresponding image points, we have to pay special attention to obtain reliable results[15]. Although Hartley[5] reported that the numerical stability of fundamental matrix estimation can be dramatically improved by normalizing the input image data, i.e. origin shift and scaling, this technique, in our experience, does not always yield satisfactory results. Moreover, if the two viewing points and object points happened to be in or nearly be in a special configuration, i.e. lying on a *critical surface*[8], the fundamental matrix would not be uniquely determined and the estimation process would break down. We believe that the original and inherent advantage of the factorization techniques lies in the uniform and simultaneous treatment of the total data obtained from all of the images, rather than in its linearity.

Such a method using fundamental matrix estimation could not fully utilize this advantage.

In this paper, we propose a method in which we first estimate the projective depths and then factor the measurement matrix constructed from these depth parameters into camera motion and scene shape. When estimating the projective depths, we do not compute any fundamental matrices. In contrast, we iteratively estimate the projective depths so that the measurement matrix achieves rank 4. Since the measurement matrix cannot strictly be rank 4 in the presence of noise, we define a measure representing the "rank 4 proximity" of the measurement matrix and formulate the estimation process as a non-linear optimization problem which minimizes this measure. This strategy is similar to the subspace method proposed by Heyden[6] where projection matrices onto row spaces of the measurement matrix corresponding to each view are computed in each iteration step and the depth parameters are updated so that the sum of these projections is made to be close to rank 4. Our strategy instead makes the measurement matrix rank 4 and allows much simpler formulation which requires no computation of the projection matrices. Following this approach, we can stably estimate projective depths utilizing the information from all of the views simultaneously and uniformly. Once the projective depths are available, we construct the measurement matrix and then factor it into camera motion and scene shape with respect to the projective coordinate frame, that is, *projective reconstruction*.

We also derive metric constraints for perspective camera models in the case where the intrinsic camera parameters are available, and show that these constraints can be linearly solved for a projective transformation which relates projective and Euclidean descriptions of the scene structure. Using this transformation, we can upgrade the projective motion and shape obtained in the previous factorization step to descriptions represented with respect to the Euclidean coordinate frame, that is, *Euclidean reconstruction*.

This paper is organized as follows; In Sect. 2, the relationships between perspective and affine camera models are clarified. The affine camera model can be viewed as a special case of the perspective camera model in which all the depth parameters are taken as unity. In Sect. 3, a new projective reconstruction method which iteratively estimates projective depths is proposed. We upgrade this projective reconstruction to Euclidean reconstruction by applying metric constraints in Sect. 4. We validate the proposed method by experiments with real image data in Sect. 5. Finally we give concluding remarks and the future direction of our work.

Notation

Throughout this article, vectors and matrices are denoted in bold-face. Especially, $\mathbf{0}_n$ and $\mathbf{I}_n$ represent n-dimensional zero vector and $n \times n$ identity matrix, respectively. Symbol $\top$ represents the transposition of vectors or matrices. Therefore $\mathbf{x}^\top \mathbf{y}$ is a scalar product of two vectors, $\mathbf{x}$ and $\mathbf{y}$. Any vector representing a homogeneous coordinate of a 2D or 3D point is underlined, e.g. $\underline{\mathbf{x}}$.

2   Camera Models

Assuming that P 3D object points are observed from F views, we let $\mathbf{x}_j$ ($j = 1, 2, \cdots, P$) be the j-th 3D object point which projects onto a 2D image point $\mathbf{m}_{ij}$ in the i-th ($i = 1, 2, \cdots, F$) frame. If each camera accurately provides perspective projection, each object point is mapped to an image point according to the following projection equation:

$$\lambda_{ij} \begin{bmatrix} \mathbf{m}_{ij} \\ 1 \end{bmatrix} = \mathbf{K}_i \left[\mathbf{R}_i^{\top} \ -\mathbf{R}_i^{\top} \mathbf{t}_i \right] \begin{bmatrix} \mathbf{x}_j \\ 1 \end{bmatrix} \tag{1}$$

where $\mathbf{t}_i$ and $\mathbf{R}_i$ are a 3D vector and a 3×3 orthogonal matrix that represent the position and orientation of i-th camera, and $\mathbf{K}_i$ is a 3×3 upper triangular matrix giving intrinsic camera parameters[3]. The scaling factor λ_{ij} represents the depth of the point $\mathbf{x}_j$ from i-th camera. By introducing a 2×3 matrix $\mathbf{P}_i^{\top}$ and a 3D vector $\mathbf{p}_i^{\top}$ which are composed from first two rows and third row of $\mathbf{K}_i \mathbf{R}_i^{\top}$, respectively, we rewrite (1) as

$$\lambda_{ij} \begin{bmatrix} \mathbf{m}_{ij} \\ 1 \end{bmatrix} = \begin{bmatrix} \mathbf{P}_i^{\top} & -\mathbf{P}_i^{\top} \mathbf{t}_i \\ \mathbf{p}_i^{\top} & -\mathbf{p}_i^{\top} \mathbf{t}_i \end{bmatrix} \begin{bmatrix} \mathbf{x}_j \\ 1 \end{bmatrix} . \tag{2}$$

Now we pick up one arbitrary point $\overline{\mathbf{x}}$ from $\mathbf{x}_1, \cdots, \mathbf{x}_P$ and let $\overline{\mathbf{m}}_i$ be the image of $\overline{\mathbf{x}}$ observed by i-th camera. We call $\overline{\mathbf{x}}$ a *reference point*. Then we shift the world coordinate system so that its origin coincides with this reference point $\overline{\mathbf{x}}$. Similarly, we translate the origin of each camera coordinate system to the image point $\overline{\mathbf{m}}_i$:

$$\Delta \mathbf{m}_{ij} = \mathbf{m}_{ij} - \overline{\mathbf{m}}_i, \qquad \Delta \mathbf{x}_j = \mathbf{x}_j - \overline{\mathbf{x}} . \tag{3}$$

After this translation, we rewrite (2) as

$$\begin{aligned} \lambda_{ij} \begin{bmatrix} \Delta \mathbf{m}_{ij} \\ 1 \end{bmatrix} &= \begin{bmatrix} \mathbf{I}_2 & -\overline{\mathbf{m}}_i \\ \mathbf{0}_2^{\top} & 1 \end{bmatrix} \begin{bmatrix} \mathbf{P}_i^{\top} & -\mathbf{P}_i^{\top} \mathbf{t}_i \\ \mathbf{p}_i^{\top} & -\mathbf{p}_i^{\top} \mathbf{t}_i \end{bmatrix} \begin{bmatrix} \mathbf{I}_3 & \overline{\mathbf{x}} \\ \mathbf{0}_3^{\top} & 1 \end{bmatrix} \begin{bmatrix} \Delta \mathbf{x}_j \\ 1 \end{bmatrix} \\ &= \begin{bmatrix} \mathbf{P}_i^{\top} - \overline{\mathbf{m}}_i \mathbf{p}_i^{\top} & (\mathbf{P}_i^{\top} - \overline{\mathbf{m}}_i \mathbf{p}_i^{\top})(\overline{\mathbf{x}} - \mathbf{t}_i) \\ \mathbf{p}_i^{\top} & \mathbf{p}_i^{\top}(\overline{\mathbf{x}} - \mathbf{t}_i) \end{bmatrix} \begin{bmatrix} \Delta \mathbf{x}_j \\ 1 \end{bmatrix} . \end{aligned}$$

Since $\overline{\mathbf{m}}_i$ is an image of $\overline{\mathbf{x}}$, we have $\overline{\mathbf{m}}_i = \mathbf{P}_i^{\top}(\overline{\mathbf{x}} - \mathbf{t}_i)/\mathbf{p}_i^{\top}(\overline{\mathbf{x}} - \mathbf{t}_i)$ which means $(\mathbf{P}_i^{\top} - \overline{\mathbf{m}}_i \mathbf{p}_i^{\top})(\overline{\mathbf{x}} - \mathbf{t}_i) = \mathbf{0}_2$. Therefore,

$$\left(1 + \frac{\Delta \lambda_{ij}}{\overline{\lambda}_i} \right) \begin{bmatrix} \Delta \mathbf{m}_{ij} \\ 1 \end{bmatrix} = \begin{bmatrix} (\mathbf{P}_i^{\top} - \overline{\mathbf{m}}_i \mathbf{p}_i^{\top})/\overline{\lambda}_i & \mathbf{0}_2 \\ \mathbf{p}_i^{\top}/\overline{\lambda}_i & 1 \end{bmatrix} \begin{bmatrix} \Delta \mathbf{x}_j \\ 1 \end{bmatrix} \tag{4}$$

where $\overline{\lambda}_i \equiv \mathbf{p}_i^{\top}(\overline{\mathbf{x}} - \mathbf{t}_i)$ and $\Delta \lambda_{ij} \equiv \mathbf{p}_i^{\top} \Delta \mathbf{x}_j$. This equation is called a *perspective camera model*.

If the depth variations, $\Delta \lambda_{ij}$, are sufficiently smaller than the depth of the reference point, $\overline{\lambda}_i$, the term $\Delta \lambda_{ij}/\overline{\lambda}_i$ in the left side of the above equation can be ignored to produce

$$\Delta \mathbf{m}_{ij} = \frac{1}{\overline{\lambda}_i} (\mathbf{P}_i^{\top} - \overline{\mathbf{m}}_i \mathbf{p}_i^{\top}) \Delta \mathbf{x}_j \tag{5}$$

as an approximation of (4) which we call an *affine camera model*.

3 Projective Reconstruction: From Affine to Perspective Projection

3.1 The Measurement Matrix and Projective Depths

Let us define the homogeneous coordinate vectors of the object point and its image as $\underline{\mathbf{x}}_j \equiv [\Delta \mathbf{x}_j^\top, 1]^\top$ and $\underline{\mathbf{m}}_{ij} \equiv [\Delta \mathbf{m}_{ij}^\top, 1]^\top$, respectively. In addition, we define a 3×4 projection matrix as

$$\mathbf{Q}_i^\top \equiv \begin{bmatrix} (\mathbf{P}_i^\top - \overline{\mathbf{m}}_i \mathbf{p}_i^\top)/\overline{\lambda}_i & \mathbf{0}_2 \\ \mathbf{p}_i^\top/\overline{\lambda}_i & 1 \end{bmatrix} . \tag{6}$$

Then we write (4) with the all views and object points as follows:

$$\underbrace{\begin{bmatrix} \mu_{11}\underline{\mathbf{m}}_{11} & \cdots & \mu_{1P}\underline{\mathbf{m}}_{1P} \\ \vdots & \ddots & \vdots \\ \mu_{F1}\underline{\mathbf{m}}_{F1} & \cdots & \mu_{FP}\underline{\mathbf{m}}_{FP} \end{bmatrix}}_{\mathbf{W}} = \underbrace{\begin{bmatrix} \mathbf{Q}_1^\top \\ \vdots \\ \mathbf{Q}_F^\top \end{bmatrix}}_{\mathbf{Q}^\top} \underbrace{\begin{bmatrix} \underline{\mathbf{x}}_1 & \cdots & \underline{\mathbf{x}}_P \end{bmatrix}}_{\mathbf{X}} . \tag{7}$$

where $\mu_{ij} \equiv 1 + \Delta\lambda_{ij}/\overline{\lambda}_i$. The $3F \times P$ matrix $\mathbf{W}$ is called the *measurement matrix* and (7) means that this matrix can be decomposed into $3F \times 4$ matrix $\mathbf{Q}^\top$ representing camera motion and $4 \times P$ matrix $\mathbf{X}$ representing the object shape.

The parameters μ_{ij} are called the *projective depths* of the j-th point in i-th view. Since these parameters are unknown with the perspective camera model, the measurement matrix is also unknown. This means that we cannot apply the conventional affine factorization technique directly to the observed image points. Estimating μ_{ij} is therefore the crucial step in factorization using perspective projections.

3.2 Factorization of the Measurement Matrix and its Projective Ambiguity

Now let us assume that projective depths μ_{ij} are given by some means. We can then construct the measurement matrix $\mathbf{W}$ and factor it into camera motion $\mathbf{Q}^\top$ and the object shape $\mathbf{X}$ (see (7)) as follows; Let

$$\begin{aligned} \mathbf{W} &= \mathbf{V}\text{diag}(\sigma_1, \cdots, \sigma_N)\mathbf{U}^\top \\ &= \mathbf{V}_1\text{diag}(\sigma_1, \cdots, \sigma_4)\mathbf{U}_1^\top + \underbrace{\mathbf{V}_2\text{diag}(\sigma_5, \cdots, \sigma_N)\mathbf{U}_2^\top}_{\Delta\mathbf{W}} \end{aligned} \tag{8}$$

be singular value decomposition (SVD) of the measurement matrix $\mathbf{W}$ with $N \equiv \min(3F, P)$ and singular values $\sigma_1 \geq \sigma_2 \geq \cdots \geq \sigma_n \geq 0$. The column vectors of the $P \times N$ ($3F \times N$) matrix $\mathbf{U} \equiv [\mathbf{U}_1, \mathbf{U}_2]$ ($\mathbf{V} \equiv [\mathbf{V}_1, \mathbf{V}_2]$) are mutually orthogonal, which means $\mathbf{U}^\top\mathbf{U} = \mathbf{I}_N$ ($\mathbf{V}^\top\mathbf{V} = \mathbf{I}_N$). If there is no noise in the 2D image coordinates $\mathbf{m}_{ij}$, $\mathbf{W}$ is rank 4 and $\Delta\mathbf{W}$ in (8) is zero. Therefore one possible factorization of $\mathbf{W}$ can be given by

$$\mathbf{Q}^{\mathsf{T}} = \mathbf{V}_1, \quad \mathbf{X} = \operatorname{diag}(\sigma_1, \cdots, \sigma_4)\mathbf{U}_1^{\mathsf{T}} . \tag{9}$$

However, this factorization is not unique; Letting μ_{ij} $(i = 1, \cdots, F; j = 1, \cdots, P)$ be the projective depths which give a measurement matrix that can be decomposed into motion and shape as in (7). Then the following equation holds for any 4×4 non-singular matrix $\mathbf{H}$ and any non-zero scalars α_i $(i = 1, \cdots, F)$ and β_j $(j = 1, \cdots, P)$:

$$\begin{bmatrix} \mu'_{11}\underline{\mathbf{m}}_{11} & \cdots & \mu'_{1P}\underline{\mathbf{m}}_{1P} \\ \vdots & \ddots & \vdots \\ \mu'_{F1}\underline{\mathbf{m}}_{F1} & \cdots & \mu'_{FP}\underline{\mathbf{m}}_{FP} \end{bmatrix} = \begin{bmatrix} \alpha_1\mathbf{Q}_1^{\mathsf{T}} \\ \vdots \\ \alpha_F\mathbf{Q}_F^{\mathsf{T}} \end{bmatrix} \mathbf{H}^{-1}\mathbf{H} \begin{bmatrix} \beta_1\underline{\mathbf{x}}_1 & \cdots & \beta_P\underline{\mathbf{x}}_P \end{bmatrix} \tag{10}$$

where

$$\mu'_{ij} = \alpha_i \mu_{ij} \beta_j \quad (i = 1, \cdots, F; j = 1, \cdots, P) . \tag{11}$$

From equations (10) and (11), we can observe two things:

Ambiguity of projective depths: If one family of projective depths $\{\mu_{ij}\}$ yields a measurement matrix that can be decomposed into motion and shape, another family $\{\mu'_{ij}\}$ given by (11) also yields a decomposable measurement matrix[11].

Ambiguity of reconstruction: Assuming that we obtain two solutions $\{\mathbf{Q}_i^{\mathsf{T}}, \underline{\mathbf{x}}_j\}$ and $\{\mathbf{Q}'^{\mathsf{T}}, \underline{\mathbf{x}}'_j\}$ by factoring two measurement matrices constructed from two depth families $\{\mu_{ij}\}$ and $\{\mu'_{ij}\}$, these two solutions are then related by using an unknown non-singular matrix $\mathbf{H}$ and unknown scalars α_i $(i = 1, \cdots, F)$ and β_i $(j = 1, \cdots, P)$ as

$$\mathbf{Q}_i'^{\mathsf{T}} = \alpha_i\mathbf{Q}_i^{\mathsf{T}}\mathbf{H}^{-1}, \quad \underline{\mathbf{x}}'_j = \beta_j\mathbf{H}\underline{\mathbf{x}}_j . \tag{12}$$

Equation (12) means that we can recover shape and motion only up to an unknown projective transformation and can arbitrarily choose a 3D projective coordinate frame in terms of which structure of the motion and shape are described[2, 4]. We call this kind of recovery *projective reconstruction*.

3.3 Estimation of Projective Depths by Conjugate Gradient Method

Now the key part of our proposed algorithm, the estimation of projective depths μ_{ij}, is described.

If there is no noise in $\mathbf{m}_{ij}$, the measurement matrix is rank 4 and $\Delta\mathbf{W}$ is zero for correct values of projective depths. With the presence of noise, $\mathbf{W}$ is not exactly rank 4. If the noise is small, however, $\mathbf{W}$ is still nearly rank 4 and

$\Delta \mathbf{W}$ is almost zero. So, we define a measure indicating the rank 4 proximity of $\mathbf{W}$ as

$$J \equiv \|\Delta \mathbf{W}\|^2 = \sum_{n=5}^{N} \sigma_n^2 \tag{13}$$

and estimate projective depths $\{\mu_{ij}\}$ which minimize this measure as a criterion.

Minimizing the criterion (13) is a non-linear optimization problem which requires iterative computation. We here adopt a conjugate gradient method[10], one of the general minimization techniques. When applying this method, we consider the following:

Initial guess: Making an initial guess sufficiently close to the optimal solution is essential for nonlinear optimization. Fortunately, we can use the affine projection to approximate perspective projection. As mentioned in Sect. 2, the affine camera model is obtained by putting $\Delta \lambda_{ij}/\bar{\lambda}_i = 0$, which means $\mu_{ij} = 1$. Therefore, we initialize the minimization process by taking μ_{ij} as unity for all i and j.

Gradient of the criterion: In order to apply a conjugate gradient method, we have to compute first order derivatives (i.e. gradient) of the criterion with respect to the parameters to be estimated. Letting $\mathbf{u}_n$ ($\mathbf{v}_n$) be n-th column of $\mathbf{U}$ ($\mathbf{V}$) in (8), and differentiating both sides of $\sigma_n = \mathbf{v}_n^\top \mathbf{W} \mathbf{u}_n$ and using relations $\mathbf{W} \mathbf{u}_n = \sigma_n \mathbf{v}_n$, $\mathbf{W}^\top \mathbf{v}_n = \sigma_n \mathbf{u}_n$ and $\mathbf{u}_n^\top \mathbf{u}_n = \mathbf{v}_n^\top \mathbf{v}_n = 1$, we obtain

$$\frac{\partial \sigma_n}{\partial \mu_{ij}} = \frac{\partial \mathbf{v}_n^\top}{\partial \mu_{ij}} \mathbf{W} \mathbf{u}_n + \mathbf{v}_n^\top \frac{\partial \mathbf{W}}{\partial \mu_{ij}} \mathbf{u}_n + \mathbf{v}_n^\top \mathbf{W} \frac{\partial \mathbf{u}_n}{\partial \mu_{ij}}$$

$$= \sigma_n \frac{\partial \mathbf{v}_n^\top}{\partial \mu_{ij}} \mathbf{v}_n + \mathbf{v}_n^\top \frac{\partial \mathbf{W}}{\partial \mu_{ij}} \mathbf{u}_n + \sigma_n \mathbf{u}_n^\top \frac{\partial \mathbf{u}_n}{\partial \mu_{ij}}$$

$$= \mathbf{v}_n^\top \frac{\partial \mathbf{W}}{\partial \mu_{ij}} \mathbf{u}_n .$$

From this, we compute the gradient of J as

$$\frac{1}{2} \frac{\partial J}{\partial \mu_{ij}} = \sum_{n=5}^{N} \sigma_n \frac{\partial \sigma_n}{\partial \mu_{ij}} = \sum_{n=5}^{N} \sigma_n \mathbf{v}_n^\top \frac{\partial \mathbf{W}}{\partial \mu_{ij}} \mathbf{u}_n = \sum_{n=5}^{N} \sigma_n \mathbf{v}_{in}^\top \underline{\mathbf{m}}_{ij} u_{jn} \tag{14}$$

with $\mathbf{u}_n = [u_{1n}, \cdots, u_{Pn}]^\top$ and $\mathbf{v}_n = [\mathbf{v}_{1n}^\top, \cdots, \mathbf{v}_{Fn}^\top]^\top$, where each $\mathbf{v}_{in}$ is a 3D vector corresponding to i-th frame.

Fixing some of the projective depths: Projective depths have the ambiguity represented by (11). Without loosing generality, we can choose one view, say $i = 1$, and one object point, say $j = 1$, and fix the depths associated with this view and this point to unity:

$$\mu_{1j} = \mu_{i1} = 1 \quad (i = 1, \cdots, F; j = 1, \cdots, P)$$

Therefore, the number of independent depth parameters is $(F-1) \times (P-1)$.

Normalizing the image coordinates: The optimization process is sometimes very unstable due to the unbalanced elements of the measurement matrix. Normalizing the image coordinates[5] is very effective for avoiding this numerical instability. Since we have already shifted each image coordinate system in (3), we change only the scale of each image coordinate. In our current implementation, for each frame, $\Delta\mathbf{m}_{ij}$ $(j = 1, \cdots, P)$ are multiplied with a common scale factor so that their average norm is equal to $\sqrt{2}$.

Considering these points, we can iteratively compute projective depths that minimize the criterion (13) and perform projective reconstruction in the steps summarized below:

1. Track P points through F frames and extract their image coordinates $\mathbf{m}_{ij}$ $(i = 1, \cdots, F; j = 1, \cdots, P)$.
2. Pick an arbitrary reference point from these points and then shift each image coordinate system by (3) so that its origin coincides with the image of this reference point.
3. Normalize the image coordinates for each frame.
4. Initialize all the projective depths with $\mu_{ij} = 1 (i = 1, \cdots, F; j = 1, \cdots, P)$.
5. Construct the measurement matrix $\mathbf{W}$ by (7) and compute its SVD.
6. Compute the gradient of the criterion J by (14) and estimate the increments $\Delta\mu_{ij}$ for μ_{ij} $(i = 2, \cdots, F; j = 2, \cdots, P)$ in the conjugate direction of the gradient[10]. If each $\Delta\mu_{ij}$ is sufficiently small, go to step 7. Otherwise update the projective depths by $\mu_{ij} \leftarrow \mu_{ij} + \Delta\mu_{ij}$ and go back to step 5.
7. Decompose $\mathbf{W}$ into projective motion $\mathbf{Q}^\top$ and shape $\mathbf{X}$ by (9). Finally recover the scale of the original image coordinates altered in step 3.

4 Euclidean Reconstruction: The Case of Known Intrinsic Camera Parameters

In this section, we consider a case in which the intrinsic parameters of all cameras are available. Under this condition, we describe that the projective description of the camera motion and object shape obtained in Sect. 3 can be upgraded to a description in terms of the Euclidean coordinate frame.

4.1 Metric Constraints in Perspective Camera Model

If the intrinsic camera parameters are given, we can regard $[\mathbf{P}_i, \mathbf{p}_i]$ in (2) in the same light as $\mathbf{R}_i$ in (1) by rewriting $\mathbf{K}_i^{-1}[\mathbf{m}_{ij}^\top, 1]^\top$ as $[\mathbf{m}_{ij}^\top, 1]^\top$. Therefore we assume that $[\mathbf{P}_i, \mathbf{p}_i]$ is a 3×3 orthogonal matrix from now on without loss of generality.

Letting $\mathbf{Q}_i'^\top$ $(i = 1, \cdots, F)$ and $\underline{\mathbf{x}}_j'$ $(j = 1, \cdots, P)$ be the projective motion and shape obtained by the perspective factorization proposed in Sect. 3, and on the other hand, letting $\mathbf{Q}_i^\top$ and $\underline{\mathbf{x}}_j$ be the motion and shape described in Euclidean space, we then relate these two descriptions by a 3D projective transformation as (12). Our purposes are to obtain a 4×4 non-singular matrix **H** representing this projective transformation and to correct the projective description $\{\mathbf{Q}_i^{'\mathsf{T}}, \mathbf{x}_j'\}$ to Euclidean description $\{\mathbf{Q}_i^\mathsf{T}, \mathbf{x}_j\}$.

Letting $\bar{\mathbf{x}}'$ be homogeneous coordinate vector of the reference point $\bar{\mathbf{x}}$, which is one of P coordinate vectors $\mathbf{x}_j'$ $(j = 1, \cdots, P)$, we set the origin of the Euclidean coordinate system to this point. Then the origin $[\mathbf{0}_3^\mathsf{T}, 1]^\mathsf{T}$ should be mapped to $\bar{\mathbf{x}}'$ by the projective transformation **H**, which means that the fourth column of **H** is equal to $\bar{\mathbf{x}}'$ multiplied by an unknown scalar. Since **H** is defined only up to a scale, we set the fourth column exactly to $\bar{\mathbf{x}}'$ without loosing generality. Then **H** can be written as:

$$\mathbf{H} = \begin{bmatrix} \mathbf{A} & \bar{\mathbf{x}}' \end{bmatrix} \tag{15}$$

where **A** is an unknown 4×3 matrix. Substituting equations (15) and (6) into the first equation of (12), we have

$$\mathbf{Q}_i^{'\mathsf{T}} \begin{bmatrix} \mathbf{A} & \bar{\mathbf{x}}' \end{bmatrix} = \frac{\alpha_i}{\lambda_i} \begin{bmatrix} \mathbf{P}_i^\mathsf{T} - \overline{\mathbf{m}}_i \mathbf{p}_i^\mathsf{T} & \mathbf{0}_2 \\ \mathbf{p}_i^\mathsf{T} & \lambda_i \end{bmatrix}. \tag{16}$$

Since we have set the origin of each image coordinate system to the projection of the reference point in Sect. 2, the first and second elements of $\mathbf{Q}_i^{'\mathsf{T}} \bar{\mathbf{x}}'$ are zero. This means that (1,4) and (2,4) elements of (16) have already been satisfied. We can also satisfy the (3,4) element by making α_i the third element of $\mathbf{Q}_i^{'\mathsf{T}} \bar{\mathbf{x}}'$.

As for first three columns, eliminating $[\mathbf{P}_i, \mathbf{p}_i]$ using its orthogonality, we have

$$\mathbf{Q}_i^{'\mathsf{T}} \mathbf{A} \mathbf{A}^\mathsf{T} \mathbf{Q}_i' = \frac{\alpha_i^2}{\lambda_i^2} \begin{bmatrix} \mathbf{I}_2 + \overline{\mathbf{m}}_i \overline{\mathbf{m}}_i^\mathsf{T} & -\overline{\mathbf{m}}_i \\ -\overline{\mathbf{m}}_i^\mathsf{T} & 1 \end{bmatrix} \tag{17}$$

which represents a constraint imposed on the projective transformation **H**. Following the usage in an affine camera model, we will call this the *metric constraints* for the perspective camera model.

4.2   Recovery of the Projective Transformation

Let us define a 4×4 positive semi-definite matrix $\mathbf{B} \equiv \mathbf{A}\mathbf{A}^\mathsf{T}$. Eliminating $\alpha_i^2/\overline{\lambda}_i^2$ from the metric constraints (17), we have

$$\begin{cases} \mathbf{a}_i^\mathsf{T} \mathbf{B} \mathbf{a}_i - (1 + \overline{m}_i^2) \mathbf{c}_i^\mathsf{T} \mathbf{B} \mathbf{c}_i = 0 \\ \mathbf{b}_i^\mathsf{T} \mathbf{B} \mathbf{b}_i - (1 + \overline{n}_i^2) \mathbf{c}_i^\mathsf{T} \mathbf{B} \mathbf{c}_i = 0 \\ \mathbf{a}_i^\mathsf{T} \mathbf{B} \mathbf{b}_i - \overline{m}_i \overline{n}_i \mathbf{c}_i^\mathsf{T} \mathbf{B} \mathbf{c}_i = 0 \\ \mathbf{a}_i^\mathsf{T} \mathbf{B} \mathbf{c}_i + \overline{m}_i \mathbf{c}_i^\mathsf{T} \mathbf{B} \mathbf{c}_i = 0 \\ \mathbf{b}_i^\mathsf{T} \mathbf{B} \mathbf{c}_i + \overline{n}_i \mathbf{c}_i^\mathsf{T} \mathbf{B} \mathbf{c}_i = 0 \end{cases} \tag{18}$$

where $\mathbf{a}_i^\mathsf{T}$, $\mathbf{b}_i^\mathsf{T}$ and $\mathbf{c}_i^\mathsf{T}$ are three rows of $\mathbf{Q}_i^{'\mathsf{T}}$, and $\overline{m}_i$ and $\overline{n}_i$ are two elements of $\overline{\mathbf{m}}_i$. One view gives five linear homogeneous equations (18), in terms of 10 elements of the 4×4 symmetric matrix **B**. If two or more views are available, we can obtain a least-square solution determined up to a scale as a solution of the ordinary eigenvalue problem.

Now we extract the matrix $\mathbf{A}$ from $\mathbf{B}$. Since $\mathbf{A}$ is a 4×3 matrix, $\mathbf{B}$ cannot be full rank and one of its eigenvalues is zero. Therefore the eigenvalue decomposition of $\mathbf{B}$ has the form: $\mathbf{B} = \mathbf{T}\,\mathrm{diag}(\nu_1, \nu_2, \nu_3, 0)\mathbf{T}^\top$ where ν_1, ν_2 and ν_3 are non-zero eigenvalues of $\mathbf{B}$, and $\mathbf{T}$ is a 4×4 orthogonal matrix. Letting $\mathbf{T}_1$ be a 4×3 matrix taking first three columns of $\mathbf{T}$, we then obtain $\mathbf{A}$ as

$$\mathbf{A} = \mathbf{T}_1\mathrm{diag}(\sqrt{\nu_1}, \sqrt{\nu_2}, \sqrt{\nu_3}) \ . \tag{19}$$

Since $\mathbf{B}$ is determined only up to a scale, so is $\mathbf{A}$. Therefore the scaling ratio between $\mathbf{A}$ and $\overline{\mathbf{x}}'$ in (15) is indeterminate. This means that the overall scale of the 3D Euclidean space is arbitrary. The sign of $\mathbf{A}$ is determined so that the determinant of the each rotation matrix $[\mathbf{P}_i, \mathbf{p}_i]$ is positive.

5 Experimental Results

5.1 The Scene "blocks"

To begin with, we applied our method to a sequence of three images of blocks. First we extracted edge points from each image and linked together the contiguous ones. Then we detected and localized feature points by extracting points with high curvature values. The localization was made at pixel accuracy, that is, no subpixel processing was performed. The correspondences between images were established manually and input to the proposed algorithm. We detected 35 feature points in this sequence.

First we performed projective reconstruction without the intrinsic camera parameters. Figure 1 shows some of the epipolar lines computed from the projective motion parameters of the camera. It can be observed that the two epipolar lines between each feature point and its corresponding points in two other images intersect at this point. Table 1 shows the reconstruction errors evaluated by the distance from each image point to its corresponding epipolar line. The mean error is within 1 pixel. The average distance error between the reprojections of the computed 3D points and the original image points was 0.719 pixel.

Fig. 1. Projective reconstruction of the scene "blocks": *Epipolar geometry was recovered using the proposed factorization algorithm. For each feature point (indicated by '×'), two corresponding epipolar lines intersect at this point.*

Next we performed Euclidean reconstruction by providing the intrinsic camera parameters (Fig. 2). For viewing convenience, we reconstructed not only the feature points but also other edge points using a trinocular stereo vision system developed in our research group to which we gave camera motion parameters obtained by this Euclidean reconstruction.

Table 1. Errors in projective reconstruction of the scene "blocks": *Errors are evaluated in terms of image distances from the feature points to their corresponding epipolar lines.*

Combination of frames	Mean error (pixel)	Max. error (pixel)
1 - 2	0.718	2.22
1 - 3	0.904	3.07
2 - 3	0.709	4.34

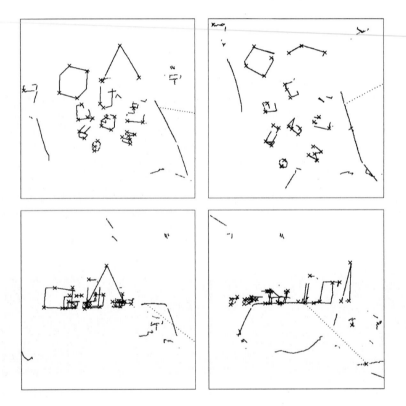

Fig. 2. Euclidean reconstruction of the scene "blocks": *3D positions of the feature points (indicated by 'x') were reconstructed using the proposed method. The obtained Euclidean motion parameters were supplied to a trinocular stereo vision system and 3D information of edge points was recovered as well.*

5.2 The Scene "building"

Figure 3 shows a sequence of five images capturing a building by lateral motion of the camera. Twenty correspondences of feature points were established. Since the localization accuracy of the feature points was poor, it was difficult to estimate the fundamental matrices correctly between two adjacent frames.

Figure 4 shows the epipolar lines between the second and third frames estimated in two ways;

Fig. 3. An image sequence of the scene "building" captured by lateral camera movement

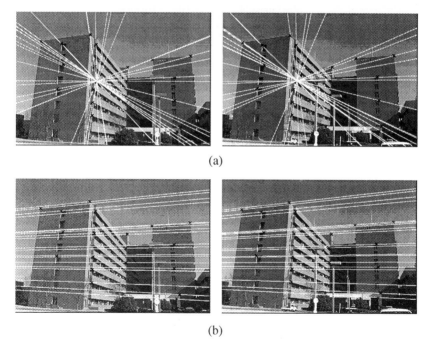

(a)

(b)

Fig. 4. Estimation of epipolar lines between the second and third frames of the scene "building": *(a) An initial guess of the fundamental matrix was computed using 8-point algorithm accompanied with Hartley's normalization and then improved via a non-linear minimization technique. (b) The proposed factorization method was used.*

In (a), we computed an initial guess of the fundamental matrix using an 8-point algorithm accompanied with Hartley's normalization[5] and then improved it via a non-linear minimization technique imposing a rank-2 constraint on the fundamental matrix. The epipole is located within the image in spite of the lateral camera movement, which is apparently a wrong result. Hence it seems difficult to apply the projective factorization method with fundamental matrix estimation[11] to this sequence.

In (b), the proposed factorization method is used. Since the epipolar lines were estimated utilizing all the information from all of the images, the estimation process was very robust. We can observe that the directions of the estimated epipolar lines coincide with the horizontal boundaries of the building, which is compatible with the lateral camera motion.

Table 2 shows the errors in projective reconstruction. The average distance error between the reprojections of the computed 3D points and the original image points was 0.788 pixel.

Table 2. Errors in projective reconstruction of the scene "building": *See caption of Table 1.*

Combination of frames	Mean error (pixel)	Max. error (pixel)
1 - 2	0.737	2.89
1 - 3	0.614	1.98
1 - 4	0.655	1.68
1 - 5	0.899	2.29
2 - 3	0.803	1.87
2 - 4	0.874	2.01
2 - 5	0.786	3.07
3 - 4	0.486	1.81
3 - 5	0.703	2.43
4 - 5	0.455	1.59

In addition, the result of Euclidean reconstruction is displayed in Fig. 5. In this figure, 3D information of edge points was also recovered from the second, fourth and fifth frames using a trinocular stereo vision system as with the scene "blocks". It can be observed that angles are preserved which means Euclidean reconstruction was successfully attained.

6   Conclusion

In this paper, we have described our proposed factorization method for recovering camera motion and object shape when using a perspective camera model. In order to construct a measurement matrix that can be decomposed into motion and shape, we need scaling parameters, called projective depths, for each image point. We define a measure of the "rank 4 proximity" of the measurement

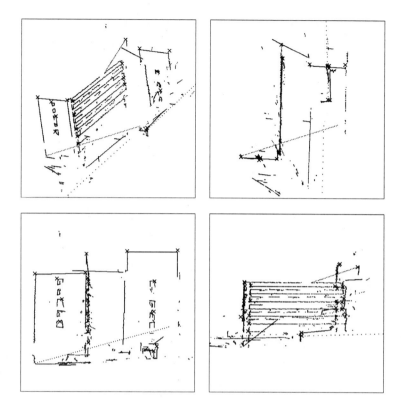

Fig. 5. Euclidean reconstruction of the scene "building": *See caption of Fig. 2.*

matrix and estimate a family of projective depths which minimizes this measure. Although this minimization process requires non-linear iteration, the affine camera model provides a good initial guess and we had little convergence problems. Less than fifteen iteration steps were enough to obtain the final solution. Following this approach, we can treat all the feature points in all of the images simultaneously in an uniform manner and recover the projective structure of the scene without using fundamental matrix estimation which is often unstable with measurement noise.

We have also shown that the projective motion and shape obtained by factoring the measurement matrix can be upgraded to Euclidean values if the intrinsic camera parameters are available. We have derived constraints imposed on a projective transformation relating the projective and Euclidean descriptions. These constraints can be viewed as a natural extension of metric constraints for affine projections to those for perspective projections, and as they can be linearly solved for the projective transformation, Euclidean reconstruction is possible.

Although the proposed measure of "rank 4 proximity" is quite effective for estimating projective depths, it is not physically or statistically meaningful. In-

troducing a new measure that reflects statistical optimality[7] of the solution to
the estimation process seems to be an important future direction for our work.

References

1. S. Christy, R. Horaud, "Euclidean Reconstruction: from Paraperspective to Perspective", Proc. 4th European Conf. on Computer Vision, Cambridge, vol.2,
   pp.129–140, 1996
2. O. D. Faugeras, "What can be seen in three dimensions with an uncalibrated stereo
   rig?", Proc. 2nd European Conf. on Computer Vision, Santa Margherita Ligure,
   pp.563–578, 1992
3. O. D. Faugeras, "Three-Dimensional Computer Vision", MIT Press, Cambridge,
   1993
4. R. Hartley, R. Gupta, and T. Chang, "Stereo from Uncalibrated Cameras", Proc.
   Computer Vision and Pattern Recognition, Champaign, pp.761–764, 1992
5. R. I. Hartley, "In Defense of the 8-point Algorithm", Proc. 5th Int. Conf. on Computer Vision", Cambridge, pp.1064–1070, 1995
6. A. Heyden, "Projective Structure and Motion from Image Sequences Using Subspace Methods", Proc. 10th Scandinavian Conference on Image Analysis, Lappen-
   raanta, 1997
7. K. Kanatani, "Statistical Optimization for Geometric Computation: Theory and
   Practice", Elsevier Science, Amsterdam, 1996
8. S. J. Maybank, "The projective geometry of ambiguous surface", Phil. Trans. of
   the Royal Society of London: A, vol.332, pp.1–47, 1990
9. C. J. Poelman and T. Kanade, "A Paraperspective Factorization Method for Shape
   and Motion Recovery", Proc. 3rd European Conference on Computer Vision, vol.2,
   pp.97–108, 1994
10. W. H. Press, B. P. Flannery, S. A. Teukolsky, and W. T. Vetterling, "Numeri-
    cal Recipes in C: The Art of Scientific Computing", Cambridge University Press,
    Cambridge, 1988
11. P. Sturm and B. Triggs, "A Factorization Based Algorithm for Multi-Image Pro-
    jective Structure and Motion", Proc. 4th European Conf. on Computer Vision,
    Cambridge, vol.2, pp.709–720, 1996
12. C. Tomasi and T.Kanade, "Shape and Motion from Image Streams under Orthog-
    raphy: a Factorization Method", International Journal of Computer Vision, vol.9,
    no.2, pp.137–154, 1992
13. B. Triggs, "Factorization Methods for Projective Structure and Motion", Proc.
    Computer Vision and Pattern Recognition, San Francisco, pp.845–851, 1996
14. D. Weinshall and C. Tomasi, "Linear and Incremental Acquisition of Invariand
    Shape Models from Image Sequences", Proc. 4th International Conference on Com-
    puter Vision", pp.675–682, 1993
15. Z. Zhang, "Determining the Epipolar Geometry and its Uncertainty: A Review",
    Technical Report RR-2927, INRIA, 1996

Automatic Camera Recovery for Closed or Open Image Sequences

Andrew W. Fitzgibbon and Andrew Zisserman

Robotics Research Group, Department of Engineering Science,
University of Oxford, 19 Parks Road, Oxford OX1 3PJ, United Kingdom
{awf,az}@robots.ox.ac.uk

Abstract. We describe progress in completely automatically recovering 3D scene structure together with 3D camera positions from a sequence of images acquired by an unknown camera undergoing unknown movement.

The main departure from previous structure from motion strategies is that processing is *not* sequential. Instead a hierarchical approach is employed building from image triplets and associated trifocal tensors. This is advantageous both in obtaining correspondences and also in optimally distributing error over the sequence.

The major step forward is that closed sequences can now be dealt with easily. That is, sequences where part of a scene is revisited at a later stage in the sequence. Such sequences contain additional constraints, compared to open sequences, from which the reconstruction can now benefit.

The computed cameras and structure are the backbone of a system to build texture mapped graphical models directly from image sequences.

1   Introduction

The goal of this work is to obtain camera projection matrices and 3D structure from long sequences of uncalibrated images. Once obtained the cameras and structure are the basis for building 3D graphical models directly from images. This competence is also required for many other structure-from-motion applications, for example ego-motion determination.

There are two main aspects. The first is establishing corresponding image tokens (corners here) over all the images. This problem is exasperated because a corner feature will generally not appear in all of the images, and often will be missing from consecutive images. Sequential matchers have proved the most successful [1, 2, 3, 4, 13, 26, 27, 33].

The second aspect is distributing camera and structure "error" in an optimal manner over all the images. Optimal here is defined as minimizing the reprojection error over the sequence. In the case of affine cameras (e.g. weak perspective) the factorization method of Tomasi and Kanade [26] is optimal [18]. In the case of general perspective (which is the only case considered from here on) factorization-like methods have been developed [9, 22, 25] but these minimize an algebraic error rather than reprojection error. Furthermore, all factorization methods are limited to features for which there are correspondences in every

Fig. 1. Example sequences: Dinosaur on turntable (36 frames); Castle, hand-held camera (25 frames); Basement, camera on AGV (12 frames).

image, a problem that is addressed in [10]. Bundle adjustment [6, 15] involves varying the structure and cameras in order to minimize reprojection error. This is optimal, and is not hindered by missing correspondences. However, bundle adjustment does not have a direct solution (such as the SVD solution in factorization) and involves a non-linear optimization which requires a good starting point. A sub-optimal alternative to bundle adjustment is a recursive (Kalman like) filter in sequential processing [1, 3, 4, 14]. However a poor two view or three view structure initialization severely affects the accuracy of subsequent camera and structure recovery for sequential systems. The problem of distributing error over many measurements of a 3D scene is a recurring one in computer vision. Ikeuchi [21] dealt with it for range images, and Porrill [17] for a calibrated stereo head.

The starting point for the work described here is the competence in computing multiple view relations for consecutive frames of a sequence — the fundamental matrix F for image pairs and trifocal tensor [7, 20, 23] $\mathcal{T}$ for image triplets can be computed *well*. Their computation is automatic and reliable, and the estimated tensor is extremely accurate. The key idea here is to always build on this competence. As will be demonstrated in the sequel, building on this strength allows the detection and avoidance of many of the problems that plague both sequential matching and the initialization of bundle adjustment.

The building block used is an image triplet. A triplet consists of three elements: image corner correspondences between the three views; the trifocal tensor for the triplet; and the 3D structure in an arbitrary projective frame defined by three camera matrices consistent with the trifocal tensor. This basic unit is optimal in the sense that the projection matrices and 3D structure are refined by bundle adjustment. Its computation is described in section 2. Using triplets as the building block confers a number of important advantages: the strong geometric constraint means that very few false corner correspondences are encountered, line matches can also be included, and the problem of critical surfaces is reduced [12].

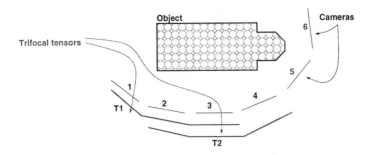

Fig. 2. Overview of the problem. A rigid object is observed by unknown cameras. Camera positions and the structure of the object are computed automatically using image triplets as the basic building block. The triplets/trifocal tensors are registered into sub-sequences.

To proceed from triplets to a complete description of a sequence it is necessary to *register* all the triplets into the same coordinate frame. One possible strategy is to register triplets directly and thence build up common 3D structure and consistent camera matrices for all views. It will be shown that there are significant advantages in instead using a hierarchical approach where triplets are registered into sub-sequences, (figure 2), followed by registering sub-sequences into the entire sequence. The overall process is summarised in figure 3. Of course, if the sub-sequence is the entire sequence then triplets are registered directly. Similar approaches to ours have been developed by Laveau [11] and Sturm [24].

---

1. *Optimally estimate trifocal tensors* $\mathcal{T}$ *for all consecutive image triplets.*
2. *Compute structure points* $\{\mathbf{X}_i\}$ *and camera positions* $\{P_1, P_2, P_3\}$ *for each triplet.*
3. *Register triplets into consistent sub-sequences using 3-space homographies* $\mathbf{H}$.
4. *Bundle adjust sub-sequences.*
5. *Optional hierarchical registration of sub-sequences into longer sub-sequences.*
6. *Register sub-sequences, again using homographies, to obtain cameras and structure for the complete sequence.*
7. *Bundle adjust the cameras and 3D structure for the complete sequence.*

Fig. 3. Algorithm overview: Hierarchically compute correspondences, cameras and 3D structure over a sequence.

The advantages conferred by proceeding in this hierarchical fashion, as opposed to a sequential approach, are five fold, and are the main contributions of this paper. First, erroneous processing in particular sub-sequences can be dealt with locally before the frames are combined; second, the dependency on a good estimate from the early frames of the sequence is reduced; third, the overall process can sometimes be more computationally efficient; fourth, the reconstruction after bundle adjustment is more accurate because a closer starting point is provided; finally, closed sequences can be processed easily in this framework.

Registration of triplets and sub-sequences is achieved by computing the homography of 3-space which results in the best overlap (where "best" will be defined later) of the two projective structures. Section 3 describes and compares a number of strategies for determining this homography, and the registration of triplets. Section 4 describes the registration of sub-sequences. Finally, appendix A overviews the bundle adjustment algorithm which is used at a number of stages throughout this work.

In order to be able to visually assess the reconstruction quality all cameras and 3D structure are Euclidean corrected. The auto-calibration method for this Euclidean correction proceeds from the computed camera matrices, and is based on the dual of the absolute conic parametrization of Triggs [31] together with the algorithm of Pollefeys *et al.* [16].

2   Estimation of $\mathcal{T}$ for image triplets

The foundation of the methods described in this paper is the ability to automatically and reliably compute an accurate trifocal tensor for consecutive frames of a sequence. Trifocal tensor computation has greatly improved over the computational method described in [2]. This improvement is not due solely to one factor, but to a combination of many incremental changes. As $\mathcal{T}$ estimation is not the main contribution of this paper the algorithm will not be described in detail, but the important incremental improvements are summarised.

Briefly, putative point matches (Harris corners[5]) are first obtained for the consecutive image pairs, one/two and two/three, by simultaneously computing epipolar geometry and matches consistent with this estimated geometry using a robust estimation algorithm. This is now fairly standard [2, 28, 32]. From these seed matches the trifocal tensor is robustly fitted, and new matches are found (*guided matching*) which are consistent with the fitted $\mathcal{T}$. Fitting and guided matching are repeated until the number of matched points stabilises. The improvements over [2] include:

1. Parametrizing the trifocal tensor such that it obeys all the constraints between the tensor elements [30].

2. Maximum-Likelihood Estimation (MLE) of $\mathcal{T}$ via bundle adjustment (appendix A). The use of a cost function which corresponds to reprojection error [30] rather than transfer error is one of the most important improvements, as the transfer error tends to accept points which are large outliers to the MLE distance and vice-versa.

3. Point pairs are transferred for guided matching by first Hartley-Sturm [8] correcting the pair. This ensures that the guided matching stage does not lose inliers.

4. Point triplets are accepted during guided matching based on reprojection error rather than transfer distance. This is also an important modification: if the guided matching stage uses a different distance measure to the fitting stage, the number of matches oscillates with each iteration and heuristic termination criteria are needed to decide when to stop the procedure. When the same error is used for both stages, the number of matches increases monotonically until convergence.

5. The RANSAC procedure uses the adaptive termination criterion detailed in [29, p. 286] which allows safe early termination for simple scenes without prejudicing more complex ones.

Together, these modifications result in more accurate tensors with more inliers and fewer false matches. Although some of the modifications appear expensive, the improvement in convergence properties means that the total time to estimate $\mathcal{T}$ is substantially reduced.

3 From triplets to sub-sequences

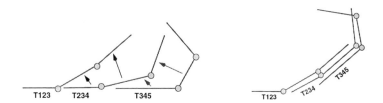

Fig. 4. Registration of trifocal tensors into consistent projective frames. Homographies of $\mathcal{P}^3$ are computed which place tensors $\mathcal{T}_{234}$ and $\mathcal{T}_{345}$ in the frame of $\mathcal{T}_{123}$.

This section describes the registration of image triplets to form sub-sequences (see figure 4). To be specific the case of registering two triplets will be considered, but the issues that arise are common to all the registration problems in the following sections.

We are given a pair of image triplets, each with an estimated trifocal tensor and a set of 3D points corresponding to image points in all views of the triplet. It is assumed that some of the 3D points are common to both sets. The goal is to obtain a common set of 3D points and a camera for each view, such that the reprojection error is minimized.

In more detail we have a set of 3D points represented in the two projective frames provided by the trifocal tensor of each triplet. Suppose a point has coordinates $\mathbf{X}_i$ in the first triplet and $\mathbf{X}'_i$ in the second. If all measurements were perfect then there would exist a homography H of 3-space between the two projective frames such that

$$P_j = P'_j H^{-1} \tag{1}$$

$$\mathbf{X}_i = H\mathbf{X}'_i \tag{2}$$

where P_j, P'_j are the corresponding camera matrices for images common to the triplets. Of course, with real image sequences the relationship will not be obeyed exactly, and an error-minimizing estimate must be found.

Registration will always proceed in two steps: first, a homography of 3 space is computed which approximately registers the triplets; second, an optimal registration is obtained by bundle adjustment (see appendix A). The different strategies are targetted on how best to obtain the approximate homography.

Zisserman *et al.* [34] and Laveau [11, §3.4] describe two ways in which this homography may be obtained. The first is to minimize a "distance" between the 3D points:

$$\min_{H} \epsilon_D = \sum_i D^2(\mathbf{X}_i, H\mathbf{X}'_i) \tag{3}$$

where the distance $D(\cdot, \cdot)$ is either *algebraic* distance

$$D_A(\mathbf{X}, \mathbf{Y}) = \sum_{k=1}^{3} (X_k Y_4 - Y_k X_4)^2 \tag{4}$$

or *Euclidean* distance

$$D_E(\mathbf{X}, \mathbf{Y}) = \sum_{k=1}^{3} (\frac{X_k}{X_4} - \frac{Y_k}{Y_4})^2 \tag{5}$$

which is only strictly meaningful if the 3D projective frame has been corrected to metric. The second estimator minimizes *reprojection error* to the original corners from which the 3D points were triangulated

$$\min_{H} \epsilon_d = \sum_{ij} d^2(P_j H\mathbf{X}'_i, \mathbf{x}_{ij}) + d^2(P'_j H^{-1}\mathbf{X}_i, \mathbf{x}_{ij}) \tag{6}$$

where $d(\mathbf{x}, \mathbf{y})$ is a Euclidean image distance between the inhomogeneous points corresponding to $\mathbf{x}$ and $\mathbf{y}$.

3.1 The degree of overlap and establishing correspondences

Two triplets can share zero, one or two images so that after registration the sub-sequences consist of six, five or four images respectively. We start with the correspondence problem when there is no overlap. Suppose, I, the last image of triplet one is the neighbour of I', the first image of triplet two. Then correspondences can be computed by simultaneously estimating F and corner matches consistent with F between images I and I'. The corners in I will index some points in the 3D structure $\{\mathbf{X}_i\}$ of triplet one, and corners in I' will index some points in $\{\mathbf{X}'_i\}$. Thus the corner correspondence provides a partial correspondence between the two 3D point sets $\{\mathbf{X}_i\}$ and $\{\mathbf{X}'_i\}$.

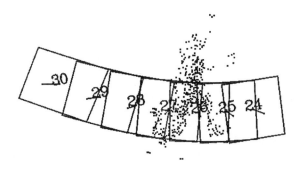

Fig. 5. Registered subsequence. Registered cameras and point structure for a 7-frame sub-sequence of the Dinosaur sequence. The cameras (numbered) are represented by their image planes and principal axes.

A much simpler solution has been suggested by Laveau [11]. Suppose there is an overlap of one view. Then image I is image I'. Consequently corner points in I/I' directly supply partial correspondences between the two 3D point sets $\{\mathbf{X}_i\}$ and $\{\mathbf{X}'_i\}$. The correspondence is only partial because a 3D point is only instantiated in a triplet if there are corner correspondences in all 3 images. So a particular corner might have an associated 3D point in one triplet but not the other. An analogous simplification in establishing correspondences applies if there is a two view overlap.

3.2 Obtaining the initial homography

We now describe methods of computing H which allow direct solutions (such as SVD). These solutions generally minimize an algebraic error with no direct geometric or statistical meaning. Furthermore, the solutions are not covariant with the choice of projective frame. However these methods are necessary for initialization of the bundle adjustment that follows, and of interest in themselves. In some cases the direct solution can be further refined by a nonlinear stage (to use reprojection error rather than algebraic distance for example) before the final bundle adjustment.

Method I: Direct 3D point registration The 3D algebraic distance (4) is readily minimized using linear algebraic methods. The Euclidean distance (5) can be solved in closed form when H is limited to similarity transformations, but requires a nonlinear minimization when the homography is allowed to be a general projectivity. This method is applicable for any number of overlapping views, including zero.

Method II: Enforcing camera consistency: one-view overlap Since a homography has 15 degrees of freedom and a camera matrix only 11, two cameras P and P' can be exactly registered, by (1). This constrains all but four of the parameters of H. The determination of the remaining parameters will now be described.

We seek a homography H which minimizes $\epsilon_D = \sum_i D^2(\mathbf{X}_i, \mathtt{H}\mathbf{X}_i')$ subject to the constraint $\mathtt{PH} = \mathtt{P}'$. The solution is a member of the 4-parameter family of homographies:

$$\mathtt{H}(\mathbf{v}) = \mathtt{P}^+\mathtt{P}' + \mathbf{h}\mathbf{v}^\top$$

where $\mathbf{h}$ is the nullvector and $\mathtt{P}^+$ the pseudoinverse of P. When D is the algebraic distance, a direct solution for $\mathbf{v}$ is obtained, leading to a system of 3 equations for $\mathbf{v}$ per 3D point:

$$\mathbf{b}\mathbf{X}'^\top\mathbf{v} = \mathbf{c}$$

where the 3-vectors $\mathbf{b}$ and $\mathbf{c}$ are defined by $b_k = h_k X_4 - h_4 X_k$, $c_k = X_k a_4 - X_4 a_k$ and $\mathbf{a} = \mathtt{P}^+\mathtt{P}'\mathbf{X}'$. When D is Euclidean distance or reprojection error, a nonlinear minimization over $\mathbf{v}$ is required.

Method III: Maximizing camera consistency: two-view overlap In this case, there is a pair of overlapping projection matrices, say $\mathtt{P}_1, \mathtt{P}_2$ which overlap with $\mathtt{P}_1', \mathtt{P}_2'$. Each overlapping matrix $\mathtt{P}_i, \mathtt{P}_i'$ provides 11 linear constraints on the elements of H and therefore two or more overlapping views are sufficient to over determine H in (1), without recourse to the 3D point information. In general, this process is followed by a minimization of reprojection error before proceeding to bundle adjustment.

3.3   Comparison of triplet registration methods

In this section we compare registration methods in terms of accuracy, reliability and computational cost. First the one-view and two-view methods are compared and then experimental results are provided.

One-view overlap

Update based on single-view overlap is fast because trifocal tensors are required only for triplets which begin every second image. Conversely, however, it is not clear how one might use the alternate triplets. For example, having combined triplets 123, 345 and 567, how can use be made of triplets 234 and 456? On the other hand, the one-view version requires that 3D point matches be available, which implies that some feature tracking must be maintained for five images. Although this imposes stringent robustness requirements on the trifocal tensor computation, it has not proved a problem in the hundreds of images on which the algorithm has been tested. Typically 400 corners are extracted from each image which yields on average 50 to 100 correspondences over the five views. On the positive side, such tracks correspond to the most reliably located and detected 3D points, so that registration accuracy is maintained. Of course, the

Abbreviation	Overlap	Algorithm
lin	1 view	II, linear algebraic
linc	1 view	"lin", conditioned
euc	1 view	II, nonlinear 3D distance
eucc	1 view	"euc", conditioned
2view	2 views	III + Reprojection error

Sequence	Algorithm	Initial Error	Final Error	Iterations
	lin	0.319	0.198	9
	linc	0.323	0.198	8
	euc	0.329	0.198	20
	eucc	0.336	0.198	8
	2view	0.357	0.205	8
	lin	0.417	0.197	10
	linc	0.574	0.197	23
	euc	0.538	0.197	25
	eucc	0.516	0.197	23
	2view	0.309	0.215	18
	lin	0.261	0.197	18
	linc	0.264	0.197	18
	euc	0.262	0.197	18
	eucc	0.263	0.197	18
	2view	0.366	0.225	20
	lin	0.773	0.229	19
	linc	0.562	0.228	17
	euc	0.627	0.224	24
	eucc	0.441	0.226	17
	2view	0.482	0.244	16
	lin	1.213	0.461	10
	linc	1.218	0.461	22
	euc	1.209	0.461	10
	eucc	1.213	0.461	22
	2view	0.920	0.124	23

Table 1. Comparison of triplet registration algorithms. The first three tables are for subsequences 0-6, 6-12 and 12-18 of the Dinosaur sequence. The others are for the first seven frames of the Basement and Castle sequences. The initial and final error columns are the (average) reprojection errors in pixels before and after bundle adjustment. The iterations column shows the number of bundle adjustment steps required for each algorithm.

final bundle adjustment uses all correspondences (not just the 5-view ones) to obtain greater accuracy.

If using Method I, at least five 3D point correspondences are required to constrain H, and many more are needed to obtain a reliable least squares estimate. Using Method II, just two correspondences are required, meaning that the estimate is more reliable, 50 corresponding points providing a reasonable basis for the least squares computation.

Two-view overlap

With two-view overlap 3D points are not required, at least for the linear algorithm. Therefore there is no dependence on the distance metric in 3D. However, it is again difficult both to interpret the measure being minimized in terms of maximum likelihood estimation and indeed to define a ML estimator for H without recourse to the 3D point information. The two-view overlap has the advantage that shorter tracks are needed—four views rather than five—and that any false inliers to the trifocal tensors may be identified because their tracks are inconsistent. For example, a 3D point in the triplet $(1-2-3)$ may be matched to image corners numbered $(100, 200, 300)$, say, in each frame. If the corner match $(200, p, q)$ appears in the second triplet and $p \neq 300$, then one of the two triplet matches is incorrect. In the current implementation, the absence of further information means that both should be rejected. Finally, two view overlap means that all tensors in the sequence are used, which can lead to an improvement in accuracy at the expense of computational effort.

Experimental results

Table 1 compares the triplet registration strategies on a number of sequences. Each strategy was used to sequentially register seven images, and the RMS reprojection error before and after bundle adjustment was recorded. Seven images were registered in order to reflect the use to which they will be put in the following sections. An example of the registered views and structure is shown in figure 5.

The algorithms were compared using the direct linear algorithms, in both preconditioned versions (for which the 3D points were centered on the unit cube prior to computation) and non-preconditioned versions. Execution time for all algorithms is very similar: about one tenth of a second for 200 points on a Sun Ultra 170. Non-linear minimization is carried out using the Levenberg-Marquardt algorithm.

The table shows that the one-view algorithms all perform similarly, with the linear algorithm the cheapest (in terms of the number of bundle-adjustment steps subsequently needed) on high-quality laboratory sequences. However, the best all-round choice is the conditioned nonlinear algorithm. The performance of the two-view algorithm is more variable than the single view techniques, but in some cases it can lead to significantly better results. In the light of this, the recommended strategy is to use both approaches and select whichever yields lower reprojection error for each sub-sequence. If speed is more important than reliability, the single-view linear approach is indicated.

4   From sub-sequences to sequences

The previous section describes and compares methods for the registration of triplets. Here we describe the subsequence pasting. Clearly the triplet registration approaches extend perfectly naturally to the registration of longer subsequences, being defined purely in terms of the camera projection matrices and 3D points. This can be extended to the entire input sequence, giving an algorithm similar in spirit to the earlier purely sequential approaches. On occasion however, a more hierarchical approach can yield superior results. One such situation occurs when the sequence is *closed*, visiting the same points of the object at the beginning and end of (or at any other times during) the sequence. Even with an open sequence, the hierarchical approach confers advantages in terms of speed and accuracy.

4.1   Closed sequences

In the case of a closed sequence, for example if the camera completely circumnavigates an object, there is a very tight constraint available — if there is a single overlapping frame then the camera at the head of the sequence coincides with the camera at the tail. The extent to which the computed cameras differ is a clear measure of the success of the camera recovery.

Furthermore, by explicitly enforcing the constraint that the cameras are the same, a significant improvement in accuracy is obtained. Although bundle adjustment should theoretically be able to distribute the error in such a way as to close the sequence, the point from which it starts is often sufficiently far from the true solution that the bundle adjustment converges to a local minimum.

Using the sub-sequence registration paradigm, we can solve this problem easily. Conceptually we break the full sequence into sub-sequences which are then "hinged" together using homographies. Each subsequence is then allowed to deform under a homography in order to minimize the 3D error. Because the entire system can be transformed by a homography without changing the relative positioning of the sub-sequences, one sub-sequence is chosen as a basis and remains unchanged through the minimization. Taking as an example the case of four sub-sequences numbered 1 through 4, with sub-sequence 1 as the basis, the error to be minimized is

$$\sum D^2(\mathbf{X}_1, \mathrm{H}_2\mathbf{X}_2) + \sum D^2(\mathrm{H}_2\mathbf{X}_2, \mathrm{H}_3\mathbf{X}_3) + \sum D^2(\mathrm{H}_3\mathbf{X}_3, \mathrm{H}_4\mathbf{X}_4) + \sum D^2(\mathrm{H}_4\mathbf{X}_4, \mathbf{X}_1)$$

where the sums are taken over the overlapping subsets of the 3D points in each frame. With this error function the choice of basis sequence will affect the result. If instead reprojection error is used, the basis is immaterial as the error function is invariant to homographies of space. However an advantage of the 3-space error

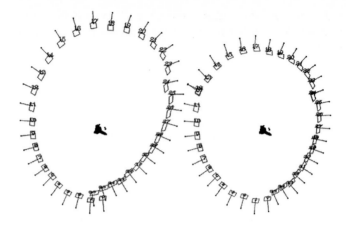

Fig. 6. Closed sequence before and after imposition of closure constraint.
The left figure shows a plan view of the cameras for the Dinosaur scene as recovered by
the hierarchical process. The right figure shows the same cameras after closure. Frames
0-12 are in exactly the same position in both models. The double cameras at positions
12 and 24 show where the structure was "hinged".

distance is that the camera centres may be included as part of the overlapping
point sets, which assists the process when the cameras are far from the object
as they are in the dinosaur sequence.

Solving the closure problem in this way has the effect of distributing the
closure constraint over the entire sequence in an approximate—but computationally tractable—manner. A final bundle adjustment completes the procedure. Figure 6 illustrates the efficacy of this approach on a sequence taken using
a rotating turntable.

4.2 Open sequences

Although the above technique was described as a solution to the closure problem,
it is also of use in the case where no constraint is available. By hierarchically
building sub-sequences using trifocal tensor registration, and then registering
these sub-sequences together we can improve the speed and accuracy of the
overall strategy. The m-view bundle adjustment problem is broken down into a
number of smaller subproblems followed by a final m-view pass. The reason for
the improvement is that the final pass generally converges much more quickly
and to a better minimum if preceded by the hierarchical approach. To give some
example costs: if the sequence is broken into 3 parts, each of $m/3$ views, the cost
to process each part[1] is $m^2/9$, and the cost of processing all subparts is $m^2/3$. If

---

[1] Although bundle adjustment of many views is dominated by an m^3 cost, the small
number of views used here means that the overall cost is approximately m^2

the final adjustment is made faster by a factor of more than $\frac{1}{3}$, the hierarchical strategy is faster. Table 2 shows typical results from our implementation: the costs are roughly offset, meaning that both approaches take approximately the same time, but the hierarchical approach achieves a lower reprojection error.

		Timings (sec)			RMS Errors	
Number of views	subseq	full	Total	Initial	Final
19	-	285	285	0.638	0.175
3 × 7	74	222	296	0.332	0.161

Table 2. **Hierarchical versus monolithic processing**. Comparison for one example sequence. The hierarchical approach is slightly slower on this short sequence, but is more accurate.

5 Discussion

We have presented a system for structure and motion recovery which overcomes many of the problems with previous methods. The system builds on the maturity and robustness of the estimation algorithm for the trifocal tensor, and extends these algorithms to sequence matching in a similarly robust manner. In addition, the approach makes it easy to solve some other difficult problems, notably employing the extra information provided in a closed sequence.

Computational complexity is placed on the shoulders of the trifocal tensor computations, which are independent of each other. This independence means that it is easy to continue processing if one of the triplet computations fails. Also, the independence of these (very) large-grain processes means that parallel computation is immediately useful.

In summary the range of applicability of the approach is largely that of the traditional sequential systems, but it is markedly superior in terms of reliability, accuracy, ease of use, and possibly speed. Figures 7 and 8 show results of the system.

A Bundle Adjustment

A key component of the system described here is the ability to quickly compute maximum likelihood estimates of cameras and structure via bundle adjustment. The description of the process is relatively simple: For m views of n 3D points, we wish to estimate projection matrices $\{\hat{P}_i\}_{i=1}^{m}$ and 3D points $\hat{X}_j$ which project exactly to image points $\hat{x}_{ij}$ as $\hat{x}_{ij} = \hat{P}_i\hat{X}_j$. The projection matrices and 3D points which we seek are those that minimize the image distance between the

(a)   (b)

Fig. 7. Results: 3D point structure for the dinosaur sequence (a). The castle sequence (b) is shown in plan view with the estimated cameras.

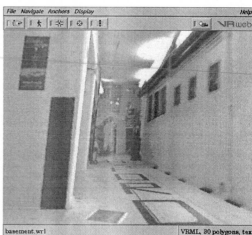

Fig. 8. Basement: Texture mapped planar model built from 11 views of the basement sequence. Left: VRML model of the scene with the cameras represented by their image planes. Right: a rendering of the scene from a novel viewpoint different from any in the sequence. The planar structure was built from 3D lines extracted by the algorithm of Schmid [19] using projection matrices computed by our algorithm.

reprojected point and detected (measured) image points $\mathbf{x}_{ij}$ for every view in which the 3D point appears, i.e.

$$\min_{\hat{\mathsf{P}}_i, \hat{\mathbf{X}}_j} \epsilon = \sum_{ij} d^2(\hat{\mathsf{P}}_i \hat{\mathbf{X}}_j, \mathbf{x}_{ij})$$

where $d(\mathbf{x}, \mathbf{y})$ is the Euclidean image distance between the homogeneous points $\mathbf{x}$ and $\mathbf{y}$. If the image error is Gaussian then bundle adjustment is the MLE. While simply expressed, the size of this optimization problem in a typical sequence of 30 images of 3000 points means that particular care must be taken to ensure a computationally tractable solution. Following [6], efficient use is made of the block structure of the matrices involved, and the sparsity of the problem.

Acknowledgements

We are grateful for the castle sequence supplied by the University of Leuven, and the dinosaur sequence supplied by the University of Hannover. Financial support was supplied by EU ACTS Project VANGUARD.

References

1. N. Ayache. *Artificial vision for mobile robots.* MIT Press, Cambridge, 1991.
2. P. Beardsley, P. Torr, and A. Zisserman. 3D model acquisition from extended image sequences. In *Proc. ECCV*, LNCS 1064/1065, pages 683–695. Springer-Verlag, 1996.
3. P. Beardsley, A. Zisserman, and D. W. Murray. Navigation using affine structure and motion. In *Proc. ECCV*, LNCS 800/801, pages 85–96. Springer-Verlag, 1994.
4. C. J. Harris. Determination of ego-motion from matched points. In *Alvey Vision Conf.*, pages 189–192, 1987.
5. C. J. Harris and M. Stephens. A combined corner and edge detector. In *Alvey Vision Conf.*, pages 147–151, 1988.
6. R. I. Hartley. Euclidean reconstruction from uncalibrated views. In J. Mundy, A. Zisserman, and D. Forsyth, editors, *Applications of Invariance in Computer Vision*, LNCS 825, pages 237–256. Springer-Verlag, 1994.
7. R. I. Hartley. A linear method for reconstruction from lines and points. In *Proc. ICCV*, pages 882–887, 1995.
8. R. I. Hartley and P. Sturm. Triangulation. In *American Image Understanding Workshop*, pages 957–966, 1994.
9. A. Heyden and K. Åström. Euclidean reconstruction from image sequences with varying and unknown focal length and principal point. In *Proc. CVPR*, 1997.
10. D. Jacobs. Linear fitting with missing data: Applications to structure from motion and to characterizing intensity images. In *Proc. CVPR*, pages 206–212, 1997.
11. S. Laveau. *Géométrie d'un système de N caméras. Théorie, estimation et applications.* PhD thesis, INRIA, 1996.
12. S. J. Maybank and A. Shashua. Ambiguity in reconstruction from images of six points. In *Proc. ICCV*, pages 703–708, 1998.
13. P. F. McLauchlan and D. W. Murray. A unifying framework for structure from motion recovery from image sequences. In *Proc. ICCV*, pages 314–320, 1995.
14. P. F. McLauchlan, I. D. Reid, and D. W. Murray. Recursive affine structure and motion from image sequences. In *Proc. ECCV*, volume 1, pages 217–224, May 1994.
15. R. Mohr, B. Boufama, and P. Brand. Accurate projective reconstruction. In J. Mundy, A. Zisserman, and D. Forsyth, editors, *Applications of Invariance in Computer Vision*, LNCS 825. Springer-Verlag, 1994.
16. M. Pollefeys, R. Koch, and L. Van Gool. Self calibration and metric reconstruction in spite of varying and unknown internal camera parameters. In *Proc. ICCV*, pages 90–96, 1998.

17. J. Porrill. Optimal combination and constraints for geometrical sensor data. *Intl. J. of Robotics Research*, 7(6):66–77, 1988.
18. I. D. Reid and D. W. Murray. Active tracking of foveated feature clusters using affine structure. *Intl. J. of Computer Vision*, 18(1):41–60, 1996.
19. C. Schmid and A. Zisserman. Automatic line matching across views. In *Proc. CVPR*, pages 666–671, 1997.
20. A. Shashua. Trilinearity in visual recognition by alignment. In *Proc. ECCV*, volume 1, pages 479–484, May 1994.
21. H. Y. Shum, M. Hebert, K. Ikeuchi, and R. Reddy. An integral approach to free-form object modeling. In *Proc. ICCV*, pages 870–875, 1995.
22. G. Sparr. Simultaneous reconstruction of scene structure and camera locations from uncalibrated image sequences. In *Proc. ICPR*, 1996.
23. M. E. Spetsakis and J. Aloimonos. Structure from motion using line correspondences. *Intl. J. of Computer Vision*, 4(3):171–183, 1990.
24. P. Sturm. *Vision 3D non calibrée: Contributions à la reconstruction projective et étude des mouvements critiques pour l'auto calibrage*. PhD thesis, INRIA Rhône-Alpes, 1997.
25. P. Sturm and W. Triggs. A factorization based algorithm for multi-image projective structure and motion. In *Proc. ECCV*, pages 709–720, 1996.
26. C. Tomasi and T. Kanade. Shape and motion from image streams under orthography: A factorization approach. *Intl. J. of Computer Vision*, 9(2):137–154, 1992.
27. P. H. S. Torr, A. W. Fitzgibbon, and A. Zisserman. Maintaining multiple motion model hypotheses over many views to recover matching and structure. In *Proc. ICCV*, pages 485–491, January 1998.
28. P. H. S. Torr and D. W. Murray. Statistical detection of independent movement from a moving camera. *Image and Vision Computing*, 1(4):180–187, May 1993.
29. P. H. S. Torr and D. W. Murray. The development and comparison of robust methods for estimating the fundamental matrix. *Intl. J. of Computer Vision*, 24(3):271–300, 1997.
30. P. H. S. Torr and A. Zisserman. Robust parameterization and computation of the trifocal tensor. *Image and Vision Computing*, 15:591–605, 1997.
31. W. Triggs. Auto-calibration and the absolute quadric. In *Proc. CVPR*, pages 609–614, 1997.
32. Z. Zhang, R. Deriche, O. Faugeras, and Q. Luong. A robust technique for matching two uncalibrated images through the recovery of the unknown epipolar geometry. *Artificial Intelligence*, 78:87–119, 1995.
33. Z. Zhang and O. Faugeras. *3D Dynamic Scene Analysis*. Springer-Verlag, 1992.
34. A. Zisserman, P. Beardsley, and I. Reid. Metric calibration of a stereo rig. In *IEEE Workshop on Representation of Visual Scenes, Boston*, pages 93–100, 1995.

Structure and Motion from Points, Lines and Conics with Affine Cameras

Fredrik Kahl[*], Anders Heyden[**]

Dept of Mathematics, Lund University
Box 118, S-221 00 Lund, Sweden
email: {fredrik,heyden}@maths.lth.se

Abstract. *In this paper we present an integrated approach that solves the structure and motion problem for affine cameras. Given images of corresponding points, lines and conics in any number of views, a reconstruction of the scene structure and the camera motion is calculated, up to an affine transformation. Starting with three views, two novel concepts are introduced. The first one is a quasi-tensor consisting of 20 components and the second one is another quasi-tensor consisting of 12 components. These tensors describe the viewing geometry for three views taken by an affine camera. It is shown how correspondences of points, lines and conics can be used to constrain the tensor components. A set of affine camera matrices compatible with the quasi-tensors can easily be calculated from the tensor components. The resulting camera matrices serve as an initial guess in a factorisation method, using points, lines and conics concurrently, generalizing the well-known factorisation method by Tomasi-Kanade. Finally, examples are given that illustrate the developed methods on both simulated and real data.*

1 Introduction

One of the main problems in computer vision is to recover the scene structure and the camera motion from a set of images. In the last few years there has been an intense research on this subject, especially concentrated on point features. Recently, attention has also turned to the use of other features such as lines, conics, general curves or even silhouettes of surfaces, see [11, 10, 1, 7].

For points, the viewing geometry can be estimated linearly in two, three and four images, see [2, 5, 19]. For more images, a major breakthrough was made in [17] where a factorisation method was developed in the case of an orthographic camera. This has later been generalized to the projective camera, cf. [16, 15, 6].

The next natural step is to use line correspondences. Linear algorithms exist for the case of three images obtained by a projective camera, see [20, 4]. In the latter algorithm, it is possible to combine points and lines in order to estimate

---

[*] Supported by the ESPRIT Reactive LTR project 21914, CUMULI

[**] Supported by the Swedish Research Council for Engineering Sciences (TFR), project 95-64-222

the viewing geometry. With the projective camera at least 13 line correspondences are needed to estimate the trifocal tensor linearly. However, with the affine camera it is possible to recover the viewing geometry from a minimum of seven line correspondences in three views, cf. [12].

In the case of conics, the situation is more complicated. In [11] a conic in space was reconstructed from two views with known epipolar geometry. A further step was taken in [8], where conic correspondences in two images were used to estimate the epipolar geometry, but the methods rely on non-linear algorithms that require initialisations.

In this paper we present an integrated approach for structure and motion from corresponding points, lines and conics. From any number of views with any number of image features, we show how to recover the scene structure and the camera motion with an affine camera. First, we derive and analyse two different parametrisations describing the viewing geometry for three cameras. The components of these parametrisations are combinations of different tensors and therefore called quasi-tensors. Specializing the projective trifocal tensor directly to the affine case leads to a larger number of parameters, cf. [18]. The corresponding image features impose constraints on the coefficients of the quasi-tensor, making it possible to estimate it when a sufficient number of correspondences is available. When a quasi-tensor is known the camera matrices for these three views are easily determined up to an unknown affine transformation. Then, a factorisation algorithm is presented that uses all points, lines and conics in all images concurrently to estimate structure and motion. The reconstruction can optionally be refined with bundle adjustment.

The motivation for using affine cameras instead of projective ones is manyfold. Firstly, in most practical applications, the affine camera model is a good approximation to the projective one. In addition, an affine reconstruction of the scene is obtained, whilst in the projective case only projective structure is recovered. Secondly, algorithms using the full projective model are inherently unstable in situations where the depth of the scene is small compared to the viewing distance. In such situations, it is even advisable to use the affine model to get more robust results. Thirdly, there is a lack of satisfactory algorithms for non-point features for projective cameras. Another advantage is that the minimum number of corresponding image features required is substantially smaller.

2   The Affine Camera

In this section we give a brief review of the affine camera model and describe how points and lines are projected onto the image. For a more thorough treatment, see [14] for points and [12] for lines. Then, we analyse how quadrics in the scene are projected to conics in the image.

The projective/perspective camera is modeled by

$$\lambda \begin{bmatrix} \mathbf{x} \\ 1 \end{bmatrix} = P \begin{bmatrix} \mathbf{X} \\ 1 \end{bmatrix} , \quad \lambda \neq 0 , \tag{1}$$

where P denotes the standard 3×4 camera matrix and λ a scale factor. Here $\mathbf{X} = [XYZ]^T$ and $\mathbf{x} = [xy]^T$ denote point coordinates in the 3D scene and in the image respectively.

The affine camera model, first introduced by Mundy and Zisserman in [9], has the same form as in (1), but the camera matrix is restricted to

$$P = \begin{bmatrix} p_{11} & p_{12} & p_{13} & p_{14} \\ p_{21} & p_{22} & p_{23} & p_{24} \\ 0 & 0 & 0 & p_{34} \end{bmatrix} \tag{2}$$

and the homogeneous scale factors λ are the same for all points. It is an approximation of the projective camera and it generalizes the orthographic, the weak perspective and the para-perspective camera models. The affine camera has eight degrees of freedom, since (2) is only defined up to a scalar factor, and it can be seen as a projective camera with its optical center on the plane at infinity.

Rewriting (1) with the affine camera matrix (2) results in

$$\mathbf{x} = A\mathbf{X} + b \ , \tag{3}$$

where

$$A = \frac{1}{p_{34}} \begin{bmatrix} p_{11} & p_{12} & p_{13} \\ p_{21} & p_{22} & p_{23} \end{bmatrix} \text{ and } b = \frac{1}{p_{34}} \begin{bmatrix} p_{14} \\ p_{24} \end{bmatrix} \ .$$

By using relative coordinates with respect to some reference point $\mathbf{X_0}$ in the object and to the point $\mathbf{x_0} = A\mathbf{X_0} + b$ in the image, (3) simplifies to

$$\Delta\mathbf{x} = A\Delta\mathbf{X} \ , \tag{4}$$

where $\Delta\mathbf{x} = \mathbf{x} - \mathbf{x_0}$ and $\Delta\mathbf{X} = \mathbf{X} - \mathbf{X_0}$. Normally, the reference point is chosen as the centroid of the set of points. This is possible since the centroid of the 3D points projects onto the centroid of the image points.

A line in the scene through a point $\mathbf{X}$ with direction $\mathbf{D}$ can be written

$$\mathbf{L} = \mathbf{X} + \mu\mathbf{D} \ , \quad \mu \in \mathbb{R} \ .$$

With the affine camera, this line is projected to the image line $\mathbf{l}$ according to

$$\mathbf{l} = A\mathbf{L} + b = A(\mathbf{X} + \mu\mathbf{D}) + b = A\mathbf{X} + \mu A\mathbf{D} + b = \mathbf{x} + \mu A\mathbf{D} \ , \tag{5}$$

where $\mathbf{x} = A\mathbf{X} + b$. From (5), it follows that the direction $\mathbf{d}$ of the image line is obtained as

$$\lambda\mathbf{d} = A\mathbf{D}, \quad \lambda \in \mathbb{R} \ . \tag{6}$$

In [12], it was noted that this equation is nothing but a projective transformation from $\mathbb{P}^2$ to $\mathbb{P}^1$ if the directions are regarded as points in $\mathbb{P}^2$ and $\mathbb{P}^1$, respectively. Notice that the only difference between the projection of points in (4) and the projection of directions of lines in (6) is the scale factor λ present in (6), but not in (4). Thus, with known scale factor λ, a direction can be treated as an ordinary point. This fact will be used later on in the factorisation algorithm.

A general *conic curve* in the plane can be represented by its dual form, the *conic envelope*,

$$\mathbf{u}^T l \mathbf{u} = 0 \; , \tag{7}$$

where l denotes a 3×3 symmetric matrix and $\mathbf{u} = [\, u \, v \, 1 \,]^T$ denotes extended dual coordinates in the image plane. In the same way, a general *quadric surface* in the scene can be represented by its dual form, the *quadric envelope*,

$$\mathbf{U}^T L \mathbf{U} = 0 \; , \tag{8}$$

where L denotes a 4×4 symmetric matrix and $\mathbf{U} = [\, U \, V \, W \, 1 \,]^T$ denotes extended dual coordinates in the 3D space. For more details, see [13].

The image, under a perspective projection, of a quadric L is a conic l. This relation is expressed by

$$\lambda l = P L P^T \; , \tag{9}$$

where P is the camera matrix and λ a scale factor. Introducing

$$l = \begin{bmatrix} l_1 & l_2 & l_4 \\ l_2 & l_3 & l_5 \\ l_4 & l_5 & l_6 \end{bmatrix} \quad \text{and} \quad L = \begin{bmatrix} L_1 & L_2 & L_4 & L_7 \\ L_2 & L_3 & L_5 & L_8 \\ L_4 & L_5 & L_6 & L_9 \\ L_7 & L_8 & L_9 & L_{10} \end{bmatrix} \tag{10}$$

and specializing (9) to an affine camera matrix gives

$$\lambda \begin{bmatrix} l_1 & l_2 & l_4 \\ l_2 & l_3 & l_5 \\ l_4 & l_5 & l_6 \end{bmatrix} = \begin{bmatrix} A & b \\ 0 & 1 \end{bmatrix} \begin{bmatrix} L_1 & L_2 & L_4 & L_7 \\ L_2 & L_3 & L_5 & L_8 \\ L_4 & L_5 & L_6 & L_9 \\ L_7 & L_8 & L_9 & L_{10} \end{bmatrix} \begin{bmatrix} A^T & 0 \\ b^T & 1 \end{bmatrix} \; . \tag{11}$$

These equations can be divided into two sets of equations. The first set is

$$\lambda \begin{bmatrix} l_1 & l_2 \\ l_2 & l_3 \end{bmatrix} = A \begin{bmatrix} L_1 & L_2 & L_4 \\ L_2 & L_3 & L_5 \\ L_4 & L_5 & L_6 \end{bmatrix} A^T + A \begin{bmatrix} L_7 & L_8 & L_9 \end{bmatrix}^T b^T + b \begin{bmatrix} L_7 & L_8 & L_9 \end{bmatrix} A^T + b L_{10} b^T \; , \tag{12}$$

containing three nonlinear equations in A and b. The second set is

$$\lambda \begin{bmatrix} l_4 \\ l_5 \\ l_6 \end{bmatrix} = \begin{bmatrix} A & b \\ 0 & 1 \end{bmatrix} \begin{bmatrix} L_7 \\ L_8 \\ L_9 \\ L_{10} \end{bmatrix} \; , \tag{13}$$

containing three linear equations in A and b.

Normalising l such that $l_6 = 1$ and L such that $L_{10} = 1$, the linear equations in (13) can be written

$$\begin{bmatrix} l_4 \\ l_5 \end{bmatrix} = A \begin{bmatrix} L_7 \\ L_8 \\ L_9 \end{bmatrix} + b \ . \tag{14}$$

Observe that this equation is of the same form as (3), which implies that conics can be treated in the same way as points, when the nonlinear equations in (12) are omitted. The geometrical interpretation of (14) is that the center of the quadric projects onto the center of the conic in the image, since indeed $[\, l_4/l_6 \ l_5/l_6 \,]^T$ corresponds to the center of the conic.

3 Three views

In the projective case, the trifocal tensor plays a fundamental role in reconstruction from three views. In this section, we derive the analogous tensor for the affine camera. Furthermore, we show how this tensor can be linearly estimated from points, lines and conics.

3.1 The affine quasi-tensor

We start by looking at points. Assume that relative coordinates are used and denote the three camera matrices by A, B and C. A point $\mathbf{X}$ is projected onto the three views as

$$\mathbf{x} = A\mathbf{X}, \quad \mathbf{x}' = B\mathbf{X} \quad \text{and} \quad \mathbf{x}'' = C\mathbf{X} \ ,$$

or equivalently

$$M \begin{bmatrix} \mathbf{X} \\ -1 \end{bmatrix} = \begin{bmatrix} A & \mathbf{x} \\ B & \mathbf{x}' \\ C & \mathbf{x}'' \end{bmatrix} \begin{bmatrix} \mathbf{X} \\ -1 \end{bmatrix} = 0 \ . \tag{15}$$

From the above equation, it follows that rank $M \leq 3$ since the nullspace of M is non-empty and, in turn, this implies that all 4×4 minors of M vanish. There are in total $\binom{6}{4} = 15$ such minors and they are linear expressions in the coordinates of $\mathbf{x}$, $\mathbf{x}'$ and $\mathbf{x}''$. By using Laplace expansions, see [3], on these minors it can be seen that they are built up by sums of terms that are products of an image coordinate and a 3×3 minor formed by three rows from the camera matrices A, B and C. Let

$$T = \begin{bmatrix} A \\ B \\ C \end{bmatrix} \ . \tag{16}$$

The minors from (16) are the Grassman coordinates of the subspace of $\mathbb{R}^6$ spanned by the columns of T. We will use a slightly different terminology and notation, according to the following definition.

Definition 1. *The minors built up by the rows* i, j *and* k *from* T *in (16) will be called the* **affine quasi-tensor** *and its* $\binom{6}{3} = 20$ *components will be denoted by* t_{ijk}. ∎

Observe that t_{ijk} is not a tensor, since the components transform differently depending on which rows that are selected from T. The components arising from the selection of one row from each of A, B and C can be reordered to constitute a tri-valent tensor that is contravariant in all indices, whereas the components arising from two rows from A and one row from C can be reordered into a two-valent tensor that is covariant in one index and contravariant in the other.

Given the image coordinates in all three images the minors obtained from M in (15) give linear constraints on the 20 components of the affine quasi-tensor. As an example, the minor obtained by picking the first, second, third and fifth row from M can be written

$$t_{123}x'' - t_{125}x' + t_{135}y - t_{235}x = 0 \ .$$

There are in total 15 such linear constraints on the components of the affine quasi- tensor. These can be written

$$Rt = 0 \ , \tag{17}$$

where R is a 15×20 matrix containing relative image coordinates of the image point and t is a vector containing the 20 components of the affine quasi-tensor. From (17), it follows that the overall scale of the tensor components can not be determined. This means that if t_{ijk} constitute the components of an affine quasi-tensor, then λt_{ijk}, where $0 \neq \lambda \in \mathbb{R}$, also constitute components of an affine quasi-tensor corresponding to the same viewing geometry. This undetermined scale factor corresponds to the possibility to rescale both the reconstruction and the camera matrices, keeping (4) valid. Observe that since relative coordinates are used, one point alone gives no constraints on the tensor, because its relative coordinates are all zero. The number of linearly independent constraints for different number of point correspondences are given in the following proposition.

Proposition 1. *Two corresponding points in 3 images give 10 linearly independent constraints on the components of the affine quasi-tensor. Three points give 16 constraints and four or more points give 19 constraints. Thus the components of the affine quasi-tensor can be linearly recovered from at least four point correspondences in 3 images.*

Proof. Use MAPLE or some other symbolic system to compute the rank of the matrices obtained by stacking a different number of R:s as in (17) above each other.

The next question is how to calculate the camera matrices A, B and C from the 20 components of the affine quasi-tensor. Observe first that the camera matrices can never be recovered uniquely from the quasi-tensor, since a multiplication by an arbitrary non-singular 3×3 matrix to the right of T in (16) only changes the common scale of the tensor components. Thus, a natural representation for the three camera matrices is to set

$$A = \begin{bmatrix} 1 & 0 & 0 \\ a_1 & a_2 & a_3 \end{bmatrix}, \quad B = \begin{bmatrix} 0 & 1 & 0 \\ b_1 & b_2 & b_3 \end{bmatrix} \quad \text{and} \quad C = \begin{bmatrix} 0 & 0 & 1 \\ c_1 & c_2 & c_3 \end{bmatrix}. \tag{18}$$

Using this parametrisation of the three camera matrices, the unknown parameters a_i, b_j and c_k can easily be calculated according to the following proposition.

Proposition 2. *Given an affine quasi-tensor normalised such that $t_{135} = 1$, the camera matrices in the form of (18) can be calculated as*

$$A = \begin{bmatrix} 1 & 0 & 0 \\ t_{235} & t_{125} & -t_{123} \end{bmatrix}, \quad B = \begin{bmatrix} 0 & 1 & 0 \\ -t_{345} & t_{145} & t_{134} \end{bmatrix} \quad \text{and} \quad C = \begin{bmatrix} 0 & 0 & 1 \\ t_{356} & -t_{156} & t_{136} \end{bmatrix}.$$

Notice that only 9 of the 20 components of the affine quasi-tensor have been used to calculate the camera matrices. This indicates that the 20 components (defined up to a common scale factor) obey 10 polynomial constraints in order to form the components of the affine quasi-tensor. In fact, we have the following theorem.

Theorem 1. *The 20 numbers t_{ijk}, normalised such that $t_{135} = 1$ constitute the components of an affine quasi-tensor if and only if*

$$t_{146} = t_{136}t_{145} + t_{134}t_{156}, \quad t_{236} = t_{136}t_{235} + t_{123}t_{356}, \quad t_{245} = t_{145}t_{235} + t_{345}t_{125},$$
$$t_{124} = t_{125}t_{134} + t_{123}t_{145}, \quad t_{126} = t_{125}t_{136} - t_{123}t_{156}, \quad t_{234} = t_{235}t_{134} - t_{345}t_{123},$$
$$t_{346} = t_{345}t_{136} + t_{356}t_{134}, \quad t_{256} = t_{235}t_{156} + t_{356}t_{125}, \quad t_{456} = t_{356}t_{145} - t_{345}t_{156},$$
$$t_{246} = t_{345}(t_{136}t_{125} - t_{123}t_{156}) + t_{134}(t_{235}t_{156} + t_{356}t_{125}) +$$
$$t_{145}(t_{136}t_{235} + t_{123}t_{356}).$$

Proof. The theorem follows immediately by calculating suitable minors from (16), using the camera matrices in Proposition 2.

We now turn to the use of line correspondences to constrain the components of the affine quasi-tensor. Consider (6) for three different images of a line with direction $\mathbf{D}$ in 3D space, i.e.

$$\lambda \mathbf{d} = A\mathbf{D}, \quad \lambda'\mathbf{d}' = B\mathbf{D} \quad \text{and} \quad \lambda''\mathbf{d}'' = C\mathbf{D}. \tag{19}$$

Since these equations are linear in the scalar factors and in $\mathbf{D}$, they can be written

$$N \begin{bmatrix} \mathbf{D} \\ -\lambda \\ -\lambda' \\ -\lambda'' \end{bmatrix} = \begin{bmatrix} A & \mathbf{d} & 0 & 0 \\ B & 0 & \mathbf{d}' & 0 \\ C & 0 & 0 & \mathbf{d}'' \end{bmatrix} \begin{bmatrix} \mathbf{D} \\ -\lambda \\ -\lambda' \\ -\lambda'' \end{bmatrix} = 0. \tag{20}$$

Thus the nullspace of N is non-empty, hence $\det N = 0$. Developing this determinant, we see that it is a trilinear expression in $\mathbf{d}$, $\mathbf{d}'$ and $\mathbf{d}''$ with coefficients that are suitable minors of T in (16). The coefficients appearing here is a subset of the components of the affine quasi-tensor. The subset consists of the minors formed by picking one row from each of A, B and C, i.e. t_{ijk}, where $i \in \{1,2\}$, $j \in \{3,4\}$ and $k \in \{5,6\}$. This subset constitutes a tensor and it is the one used in [12]. Finally, we conclude that the direction of each line gives one constraint on the viewing geometry and that both points and lines can be used to constrain the components of the affine quasi-tensor.

It is evident from (13) that conics can be used in the same way as points, when the nonlinear equations for conics are omitted. In this way each conic correspondence acts as a point correspondence and gives the same number of constraints on the viewing geometry.

3.2   The reduced affine quasi-tensor

It may seem superfluous to use 20 numbers to describe the viewing geometry of three affine cameras, since specializing the trifocal tensor (which has 27 components) for the projective camera, to the affine case, the number of components reduces to only 16, cf. [18]. However, this comparison is not fair, because our 20 number describes *all* trilinear functions between three affine views and should be compared to the $3 \times 16 = 48$ and $3 \times 27 = 81$ components of all trilinear tensors between three affine views and three projective views, respectively. However, it is possible to use a tensor with only 12 components to describe the viewing geometry in our case.

In order to obtain a smaller number of parameters, start again from (15) and rank $M \leq 3$. This time we will only consider the 4×4 minors of M that contain both rows one and two, one of rows three and four, and one of rows five and six. There are in total 4 such minors and they are linear in the coordinates of $\mathbf{x}$, $\mathbf{x}'$ and $\mathbf{x}''$. Again, these linear expressions have coefficients that are 3×3 minors of T in (16), but this time the only minors occurring are the ones containing both rows from A and one from B and one from C.

Definition 2. *The minors built up by the rows i, j and k, where either $i \in \{1,2\}$, $j \in \{3,4\}$, $k \in \{5,6\}$ or $i = 1$, $j = 2$, $k \in \{3,4,5,6\}$, from T in (16) will be called the* **reduced affine quasi-tensor** *and its 12 components will be denoted by t_{ijk}.*   ∎

Observe once more that t_{ijk} is not a real tensor since different components transform differently.

Given the image coordinates in all three images, the minors of the chosen rows obtained from M give linear constraints on the 12 components of the reduced affine quasi-tensor. There are in total 4 such linear constraints on the components of the affine quasi-tensor. These can be written

$$R^r t^r = 0 \ , \tag{21}$$

where R^r is a 4×12 matrix containing relative image coordinates of the image point and t^r is a vector containing the 12 components of the reduced affine quasi-tensor. Observe again that the overall scale of the tensor components can not be determined. In the same manner as in the previous section, we can prove the following.

Proposition 3. *Two corresponding points in 3 images give 4 linearly independent constraints on the components of the reduced affine quasi-tensor. Three points give 8 constraints and four or more points give 11 constraints. Thus the components of the affine quasi-tensor can be linearly recovered from at least four point correspondences in 3 images.*

Again the camera matrices can be calculated from the 12 components of the reduced affine quasi-tensor. The parametrisation in (18) will be used again.

Proposition 4. *Given a reduced affine quasi-tensor normalised such that $t_{135} = 1$, the camera matrices in the form of (18) can be calculated as*

$$A = \begin{bmatrix} 1 & 0 & 0 \\ t_{235} & t_{125} & -t_{123} \end{bmatrix}, \quad B = \begin{bmatrix} 0 & 1 & 0 \\ (t_{145}t_{235} - t_{245})/t_{125} & t_{145} & (t_{136} - t_{123}t_{145})/t_{125} \end{bmatrix}$$

$$and \quad C = \begin{bmatrix} 0 & 0 & 1 \\ (t_{236} - t_{136}t_{235})/t_{123} & (t_{126} - t_{125}t_{136})/t_{123} & t_{136} \end{bmatrix} .$$

Theorem 2. *The 12 numbers t_{ijk}, normalised such that $t_{135} = 1$ constitute the components of a reduced affine quasi-tensor if and only if*

$$(t_{146} - t_{136}t_{145})t_{123}t_{125} = (t_{124} - t_{123}t_{145})(t_{126} - t_{125}t_{136}),$$

$$t_{246}t_{125}t_{123} = (t_{123}t_{245}t_{126} + t_{125}t_{124}t_{236} - t_{235}t_{124}t_{126}) .$$

Proof. Follows immediately by calculating suitable minors from (16), using the camera matrices in Proposition 4.

Corresponding lines and conics can be used in the same way as before to constrain the components of the reduced quasi-tensor.

Using these tensors, a number of minimal cases appear for recovering the viewing geometry. In order to solve these minimal cases one has to take also the nonlinear properties, given in Theorem 1 and Theorem 2, of the tensor components into account. However, in the present work, we concentrate on developing a method to use points, lines and conics in a unified manner, when there is a sufficient number of corresponding features available to avoid the minimal cases.

4 Many views

In the landmark paper [17] a factorisation method was presented for the orthographic camera using point features. In this section we generalize this algorithm for the affine camera using not only points, but lines and conics as well. The algorithm takes any number of points, lines and conics in any number of images as input and the result is a reconstruction of the scene structure as well as the camera motion.

4.1 The factorisation algorithm

In Section 2 we derived how points, lines and conics project onto the image. Now consider m points or conics, and n lines in p images. From equations (4) and (6) we see that this can be written as one single matrix equation (with relative coordinates),

$$S = \begin{bmatrix} \mathbf{x}_{11} & \cdots & \mathbf{x}_{1m} & \lambda_{11}\mathbf{d}_{11} & \cdots & \lambda_{1n}\mathbf{d}_{1n} \\ \vdots & \ddots & \vdots & \vdots & \ddots & \vdots \\ \mathbf{x}_{p1} & \cdots & \mathbf{x}_{pm} & \lambda_{p1}\mathbf{d}_{p1} & \cdots & \lambda_{pn}\mathbf{d}_{pn} \end{bmatrix} = \begin{bmatrix} A_1 \\ \vdots \\ A_p \end{bmatrix} \begin{bmatrix} \mathbf{X}_1 & \cdots & \mathbf{X}_m & \mathbf{D}_1 & \cdots & \mathbf{D}_n \end{bmatrix} . \quad (22)$$

The right-hand side of (22) is the product of a $2p \times 3$ matrix and a $3 \times (m+n)$ matrix, which gives the following theorem.

Theorem 3. *The matrix S in (22) must obey*

$$\text{rank } S \leq 3 .$$

Observe that the matrix S contains entries obtained from measurements in the images, as well as the unknown scalar factors λ_{ij}, which have to be estimated. Assuming that these are known, the camera matrices, the 3D points and the 3D directions can be obtained by factorising S. This can be done from the singular value decomposition of S, $S = U\Sigma V^T$, where U and V are orthogonal matrices and Σ is a diagonal matrix containing the singular values, σ_i, of S. Let $\tilde{\Sigma} = \text{diag}(\sigma_1, \sigma_2, \sigma_3, 0, \ldots, 0)$ and let $\tilde{U}$ and $\tilde{V}$ denote the first three columns of U and V, respectively. Then

$$\begin{bmatrix} A_1 \\ \vdots \\ A_p \end{bmatrix} = \tilde{U}\sqrt{\tilde{\Sigma}} \quad \text{and} \quad \begin{bmatrix} X_1 & \cdots & X_m & D_1 & \cdots & D_n \end{bmatrix} = \sqrt{\tilde{\Sigma}}\tilde{V}^T \quad (23)$$

fulfil (22). Observe that the whole singular value decomposition of S is not needed. It is sufficient to calculate the three largest eigenvalues and the corresponding eigenvectors of SS^T.

4.2 The initialisation

We now turn to the initialisation of the scalar factors, where the previously defined tensors will be useful. Assume that the (reduced) affine quasi-tensors have been calculated. Then the camera matrices can be calculated from Proposition 2 or Proposition 4. It follows from (20) that once the camera matrices for three images are known, the scalar factors for each direction can be calculated up to an unknown scalar factor. It remains to estimate the scalar factors for all images with a consistent scale. We have chosen the following method. Consider the first three views with camera matrices A_1, A_2 and A_3. Rewriting (20) as

$$M \begin{bmatrix} \mathbf{D} \\ -1 \end{bmatrix} = \begin{bmatrix} A_1 & \lambda_1\mathbf{d}_1 \\ A_2 & \lambda_2\mathbf{d}_2 \\ A_3 & \lambda_3\mathbf{d}_3 \end{bmatrix} \begin{bmatrix} \mathbf{D} \\ -1 \end{bmatrix} = 0 , \quad (24)$$

shows that M in (24) has rank less than 4 which implies that all 4×4 minors are equal to zero. These minors give linear constraints on the scale factors. However, only 3 of them are independent. So we get a system with the following appearance,

$$
\begin{bmatrix} * & * & * \\ * & * & * \\ * & * & * \end{bmatrix} \begin{bmatrix} \lambda_1 \\ \lambda_2 \\ \lambda_3 \end{bmatrix} = 0 \ , \tag{25}
$$

where $*$ indicates a matrix entry that can be calculated from A_i and $\mathbf{d}_i$. It is evident from (25) that the scalar factors λ_i only can be calculated up to an unknown common scale factor. By considering another triplet, with two images in common with the first triple, say the last two, we can obtain consistent scale factors for both triplets by solving a system with the following appearance,

$$
\begin{bmatrix} * & * & * & 0 \\ * & * & * & 0 \\ * & * & * & 0 \\ 0 & * & * & * \\ 0 & * & * & * \\ 0 & * & * & * \end{bmatrix} \begin{bmatrix} \lambda_1 \\ \lambda_2 \\ \lambda_3 \\ \lambda_4 \end{bmatrix} = 0 \ .
$$

This procedure is easy to systematize such that all scale factors from the direction of one line can be computed as the nullspace of a single matrix. The drawback is of course that we first need to compute all camera matrices of the sequence.

4.3 Summary

In summary, the following algorithm is proposed:

1. Calculate the scalar factors λ_{ij} using an affine quasi-tensor.
2. Calculate S in (22) from λ_{ij} and the image measurements.
3. Calculate the singular value decomposition of S.
4. Estimate the camera matrices and the reconstruction of points and line directions according to (23).
5. Reconstruct 3D lines and 3D quadrics.

The last step needs a further comment. From the factorisation the 3D directions of the lines and the centers of the quadrics are obtained. The remaining unknowns can be recovered linearly from (5) and (12).

If further accuracy is required, the reconstruction can be refined with bundle adjustment techniques.

5 Experiments

In this section we present some experimental results on the developed theory. The experiments have been performed on both synthetic and real data.

5.1 Simulated Data

The synthetic data was produced in the following. First, points and line segments were randomly distributed within a sphere. Then, views corresponding to camera positions on the sphere were randomly chosen and the features were projected to these views. In each view, the coordinate system was chosen so that the data lies within the range $[-1, 1]$ to improve numerical conditioning. In order to test the stability of the proposed methods, different levels of noise were added to the data. Points were perturbed with uniform, independent Gaussian noise. In order to incorporate the higher accuracy of the line segments, a number of evenly sampled points on the line segment were perturbed with independent Gaussian noise in the normal direction of the line. Then, the line parameters were estimated with least-squares. The residual error for points was chosen as the distance between the true point position and the reprojected reconstructed 3D point. For lines, the residual errors were chosen as the smallest distances between the endpoints of the true line segment and the reprojected 3D line. These settings are close to real life situations (up to scale). A noise level of 0.005 corresponds approximately to a perturbation of 1 pixel for a 512×512 image.

STD of noise	0	0.005	0.01	0.02
Red. quasi-tensor				
RMS of points	0.0	0.015	0.030	0.068
RMS of lines	0.0	0.012	0.026	0.057
Quasi-tensor				
RMS of points	0.0	0.0045	0.0086	0.017
RMS of lines	0.0	0.0031	0.0060	0.013
Factorisation				
RMS of points	0.0	0.0043	0.0088	0.017
RMS of lines	0.0	0.0029	0.0060	0.012

Table 1. Result of simulations of 10 points and 10 lines in 3 images for different levels of noise using the affine quasi-tensor, the reduced affine quasi-tensor and the factorisation approach. The root mean square (RMS) errors are shown for the different approaches.

In Table 1 it can be seen that the 20-parameter formulation of the three views is consistently superior to the 12-parameter formulation. For three views, nothing is gained by applying the factorisation method. All three methods handle moderate noise perturbations well. In Table 2 the number of points and lines are varied. The more points and lines used the better results as expected. Finally, in Table 3 the number of views is varied. In spite of the rather high noise level, the factorisation method manages to keep the residuals low.

5.2 Real Data

The presented methods have been tested on real data as well. In this section an experiment is presented that was performed on an outdoor statue, which is

#points, #lines	3,3	10,10	20,20	30,30
Red. quasi-tensor				
RMS of points	0.0094	0.030	0.024	0.021
RMS of lines	0.024	0.026	0.018	0.015
Quasi-tensor				
RMS of points	0.0094	0.0086	0.0082	0.0080
RMS of lines	0.021	0.0060	0.0055	0.0053
Factorisation				
RMS of points	0.0091	0.0088	0.0081	0.0079
RMS of lines	0.028	0.0060	0.0054	0.0054

Table 2. Results of simulation of 3 views with a different number of points and lines and with a standard deviation of noise equal to 0.05. The table shows the resulting error (RMS) after using the differnt approaches.

#views	3	5	10	20
Factorisation				
RMS of points	0.017	0.019	0.019	0.026
RMS of lines	0.013	0.015	0.016	0.022

Table 3. Table showing simulated results for 10 points and 10 lines in a different number of views, with an added error of standard deviation 0.02 .

in fact built up by conics and lines. More precisely, the statue consists of two ellipses lying on two different planes in space and the two ellipses are connected by straight lines, almost like a hyperboloid, see Figure 1(a).

In the experiment, 5 different images (768 × 575) of the statue were taken. In these images, the two ellipses, 17 lines and 17 points were picked out by hand and for the ellipses and lines, least-squares were used to compute the appropriate representations. The residual errors are shown in Table 4 in pixels with the same definitions of residual errors (between measured and reprojected quantities) as in the previous experiments. The results are clearly plausible, see Figure 1(b).

Factorisation	Points	Lines	Conics(center)
RMS pixels	4.3	0.56	6.6

Table 4. Table showing the result of statue experiment with five real images.

6 Conclusions

In this paper a novel scheme that can handle any number of corresponding points, lines and conics in any number of images, taken by affine cameras has been presented. Two novel concepts have been introduced; the affine quasi-tensor

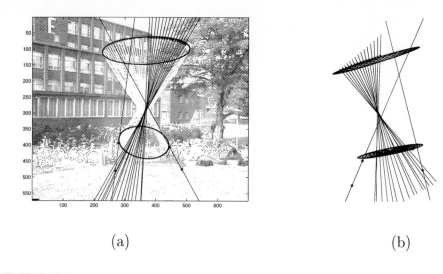

(a)   (b)

Fig. 1. (a) Image of a statue. (b) Reconstructed 3D model

and the reduced affine quasi-tensor. Using these concepts, the camera matrices in a triplet of affine views can be estimated linearly from corresponding points, lines and conics. First, the tensor components (20 or 12) are estimated from image data and then the camera matrices are obtained from the tensor components. A slight generalization of this procedure gives also the scale factors for all line directions, needed to initialise the factorisation method. Furthermore, it has been shown that this approach works well on both simulated and real data.

References

1. R. Berthilsson and K. Åström. Reconstruction of 3d-curves from 2d-images using affine shape methods for curves. In *Proc. Conf. Computer Vision and Pattern Recognition*, 1997.
2. O. Faugeras and B. Mourrain. On the geometry and algebra of the point and line correspondences between n images. In *Proc. 5th Int. Conf. on Computer Vision, MIT, Boston, MA*, pages 951–956, 1995.
3. B. Gelbaum. *Linear Algebra : Basic, Practice and Theory.* North-Holand, 1989.
4. R. I. Hartley. A linear method for reconstruction from lines and points. In *Proc. 5th Int. Conf. on Computer Vision, MIT, Boston, MA*, pages 882–887, 1995.
5. R. I. Hartley. Lines and points in three views and the trifocal tensor. *Int. Journal of Computer Vision*, 22(2):125–140, 1997.
6. A. Heyden. Projective structure and motion from image sequences using subspace methods. In *Proc. 10th Scandinavian Conf. on Image Analysis, Lappeenranta, Finland*, pages 963–968, 1997.
7. F. Kahl and K. Åström. Motion estimation in image sequences using the deformation of apparent contours. In *Proc. 6th Int. Conf. on Computer Vision, Mumbai, India*, 1998.

8. F. Kahl and A. Heyden. Using conic correspondences in two images to estimate the epipolar geometry. In *Proc. 6th Int. Conf. on Computer Vision, Mumbai, India*, 1998.

9. J. L. Mundy and A. Zisserman, editors. *Geometric invariance in Computer Vision*. MIT Press, Cambridge Ma, USA, 1992.

10. T. Papadopoulo and O. Faugeras. Computing structure and motion of general 3d curves from monocular sequences of perspective images. In B Buxton and R. Cipolla, editors, *Proc. 4th European Conf. on Computer Vision, Cambridge, UK*, pages 696–708. Springer-Verlag, 1996.

11. L. Quan. Conic reconstruction and correspondence from two views. *IEEE Trans. Pattern Analysis and Machine Intelligence*, 18(2):151–160, February 1996.

12. L. Quan and T. Kanade. Affine structure from line correspondences with uncalibrated affine cameras. *IEEE Trans. Pattern Analysis and Machine Intelligence*, 19(8), August 1997.

13. J. G. Semple and G. T. Kneebone. *Algebraic Projective Geometry*. Clarendon Press, Oxford, 1952.

14. L. S. Shapiro. *Affine Analysis of Image Sequences*. Cambridge University Press, 1995.

15. G. Sparr. Simultaneous reconstruction of scene structure and camera locations from uncalibrated image sequences. In *Proc. Int. Conf. on Pattern Recognition, Vienna, Austria*, 1996.

16. P. Sturm and B. Triggs. A factorization based algorithm for multi-image projective structure and motion. In *Proc. 4th European Conf. on Computer Vision, Cambridge, UK*, pages 709–720, 1996.

17. C. Tomasi and T. Kanade. Shape and motion from image streams under orthography: a factorization method. *Int. Journal of Computer Vision*, 9(2):137–154, 1992.

18. P. Torr. *Motion Segmentation and Outlier Detection*. PhD thesis, Department of Engineering Science, University of Oxford, 1995.

19. B. Triggs. Matching constraints and the joint image. In *Proc. 5th Int. Conf. on Computer Vision, MIT, Boston, MA*, pages 338–343, 1995.

20. J. Weng, T.S. Huang, and N. Ahuja. Motion and structure from line correspondances: Closed-form solution, uniqueness, and optimization. *IEEE Trans. Pattern Analysis and Machine Intelligence*, 14(3), 1992.

Simultaneous Estimation of Viewing Geometry and Structure

Tomáš Brodský, Cornelia Fermüller, and Yiannis Aloimonos

Computer Vision Laboratory, Center for Automation Research,
University of Maryland, College Park, MD 20742-3275, USA
{brodsky,fer,yiannis}@cfar.umd.edu

Abstract. Up to now, structure from motion algorithms proceeded in two well defined steps, where the first and most important step is recovering the rigid transformation between two views, and the subsequent step is using this transformation to compute the structure of the scene in view. This paper introduces a novel approach to structure from motion in which both aforementioned steps are accomplished in a synergistic manner. Existing approaches to 3D motion estimation are mostly based on the use of optic flow which however poses a problem at the locations of depth discontinuities. If we knew where depth discontinuities were, we could (using a multitude of approaches based on smoothness constraints) estimate accurately flow values for image patches corresponding to smooth scene patches; but to know the discontinuities requires solving the structure from motion problem first. In the past this dilemma has been addressed by improving the estimation of flow through sophisticated optimization techniques, whose performance often depends on the scene in view. In this paper we follow a different approach. The main idea is based on the interaction between 3D motion and shape which allows us to estimate the 3D motion while at the same time segmenting the scene. If we use a wrong 3D motion estimate to compute depth, then we obtain a distorted version of the depth function. The distortion, however, is such that the worse the motion estimate, the more likely we are to obtain depth estimates that are locally unsmooth, i.e., they vary more than the correct ones. Since local variability of depth is due either to the existence of a discontinuity or to a wrong 3D motion estimate, being able to differentiate between these two cases provides the correct motion, which yields the "smoothest" estimated depth as well as the image location of scene discontinuities. Although no optic flow values are computed, we show that our algorithm is very much related to minimizing the epipolar constraint and we present a number of experimental results with real image sequences indicating the robustness of the method.

1 Introduction and Motivation

One of the biggest challenges of contemporary computer vision is to create robust and automatic procedures for recovering the structure of a scene given multiple views. This is the well known problem of structure from motion (SFM) [4] [10].

Here the problem is treated in the differential sense, that is, assuming that a camera moving in an unrestricted rigid manner in a static environment continuously takes images. Regardless of particular approaches, the solution always proceeds in two steps: first, the rigid motion between the views is recovered and, second, the motion estimate is used to recover the scene structure.

Traditionally, the problem has been treated by first finding the correspondence or optic flow and then optimizing an error criterion based on the epipolar constraint. Although considerable progress has been made in minimizing deviation from the epipolar constraint [11] [13] [14], the approach is based on the values of flow whose estimation is an ill-posed problem.

The values of flow are obtained by applying some sort of smoothing to the locally computed image derivatives. When smoothing is done in an image patch corresponding to a smooth scene patch, accurate flow values are obtained. When, however, the patch corresponds to a scene patch containing a depth discontinuity, the smoothing leads to erroneous flow estimates there. This can only be avoided if a priori knowledge about the locations of depth discontinuities is available. Thus, flow values close to discontinuities often contain errors (and these affect the flow values elsewhere) and when the estimated 3D motion (containing errors) is used to recover depth, it is unavoidable that an erroneous scene structure will be computed. The situation presents itself as a chicken-and-egg problem. If we had information about the location of the discontinuities, then we would be able to compute accurate flow and subsequently accurate 3D motion. Accurate 3D motion implies, in turn, accurate location of the discontinuities and estimation of scene structure. Thus 3D motion and scene discontinuities are inherently related through the values of image flow and the one needs the other to be better estimated. Researchers avoid this problem by attempting to first estimate flow using sophisticated optimization procedures that could account for discontinuities, and although such techniques provide better estimates, their performance often depends on the scene in view, they are in general very slow and require a large number of resources [7] [12] [15].

In this paper, instead of attempting to estimate flow at all costs before proceeding with structure from motion, we ask a different question: Would it be possible to utilize any available local image motion information, such as normal flow for example, in order to obtain knowledge about scene discontinuities which would allow better estimation of 3D motion? Or, equivalently, would it be possible to devise a procedure that estimates scene discontinuities while at the same time estimating 3D motion? We show here that this is the case and we present a novel algorithm for 3D motion estimation. The idea behind our approach is based on the interaction between 3D motion and scene structure that only recently has been formalized [3]. If we have a 3D motion estimate which is wrong and we use it to estimate depth, then we obtain a distorted version of the depth function. Not only do incorrect estimates of motion parameters lead to incorrect depth estimates, but the distortion is such that the worse the motion estimate, the more likely we are to obtain depth estimates that locally vary much more than the correct ones. The correct motion then yields the "smoothest" estimated depth and we can define a measure whose minimization yields the correct ego-motion parameters. The measure can be computed from normal flow only, so the computation of optical flow is not needed by the algorithm. Intuitively, the proposed algorithm proceeds as follows: first, the image is divided into small patches and a search — for the 3D motion — which as explained in Sect. 3 takes place in the two-dimensional space of translations — is performed. For each candidate 3D motion, using the local normal flow measurements in each patch, the depth of the scene corresponding to the patch is computed. If the variation of depth for all patches is small, then the candidate 3D motion is close to the correct one. If, however, there is a significant variation of depth in a patch, this is either because the candidate 3D motion is inaccurate or because there is a discontinuity in the patch. The second situation is differentiated from the first if the distribution of the depth values inside the patch is bimodal with the two classes of values spatially separated. In such a case the patch is subdivided into two new ones and the process is repeated. When the depth values computed in each patch are smooth functions, the corresponding motion is the correct one and the procedure has at the same time given rise to the location of a number of discontinuities. The rest of the paper formalizes these ideas and presents a number of experimental results.

1.1 Organization of the Paper

Sect. 2 defines the imaging model and describes the equations of the motion field induced by rigid motion; it also develops certain constraints that will be of use later and makes explicit the relationship between distortion of depth and errors in 3D motion. Sect. 3 is devoted to the description of the algorithm and Sect. 4 describes a number of experimental results with real image sequences. It also formalizes the relationship of the approach to algorithms utilizing the epipolar constraint.

2 Preliminaries

We consider an observer moving rigidly in a static environment. The camera is a standard calibrated pinhole with focal length f and the coordinate system $OXYZ$ is attached to the camera, with Z being the optical axis.

Image points are represented as vectors $\mathbf{r} = [x, y, f]^{\mathrm{T}}$, where x and y are the image coordinates of the point and f is the focal length in pixels. A scene point $\mathbf{R}$ is projected onto the image point

$$\mathbf{r} = f \frac{\mathbf{R}}{\mathbf{R} \cdot \hat{\mathbf{z}}} \tag{1}$$

where $\hat{\mathbf{z}}$ is the unit vector in the direction of the Z axis.

Let the camera move in a static environment with instantaneous translation $\mathbf{t}$ and instantaneous rotation $\boldsymbol{\omega}$ (measured in the coordinate system $OXYZ$). Then a scene point $\mathbf{R}$ moves with velocity (relative to the camera)

$$\dot{\mathbf{R}} = -\mathbf{t} - \boldsymbol{\omega} \times \mathbf{R} . \tag{2}$$

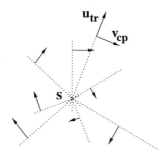

Fig. 1. The copoint directions corresponding to $\hat{\mathbf{t}}$

The image motion field is then the usual [9]

$$\dot{\mathbf{r}} = -\frac{1}{(\mathbf{R} \cdot \hat{\mathbf{z}})}(\hat{\mathbf{z}} \times (\mathbf{t} \times \mathbf{r})) + \frac{1}{f}\hat{\mathbf{z}} \times (\mathbf{r} \times (\boldsymbol{\omega} \times \mathbf{r})) = \frac{1}{Z}\mathbf{u}_{\mathrm{tr}}(\mathbf{t}) + \mathbf{u}_{\mathrm{rot}}(\boldsymbol{\omega}) \qquad (3)$$

where Z is used to denote the scene depth $(\mathbf{R} \cdot \hat{\mathbf{z}})$, and $\mathbf{u}_{\mathrm{tr}}, \mathbf{u}_{\mathrm{rot}}$ the direction of the translational and the rotational flow respectively. Due to the scaling ambiguity, only the direction of translation (focus of expansion—FOE, or focus of contraction—FOC, depending on whether the observer approaches or moves away from the scene) and the three rotational parameters can be estimated from monocular image sequences.

2.1   Projections of Motion Fields

The search for candidate 3D motions is achieved by searching for the translational component, i.e., the FOE. Given a candidate FOE, the rotation that best fits image data can be obtained by examining normal flow vectors that are perpendicular to lines passing from the FOE, since these flow values would not contain any translational part. For this we need to formalize properties of motion fields projected onto particular directions. Indeed, by projecting the motion field vectors $\dot{\mathbf{r}}$ onto certain directions, it is possible to gain some very useful insights [5] [6] [8] [1]. Of particular interest, are the *copoint* projections [5], where the flow vectors are projected onto directions perpendicular to a certain translational flow field (see Fig. 1). Let point $\hat{\mathbf{t}}$ be the FOE in the image plane of this translational field and consider the vectors emanating from $\hat{\mathbf{t}}$. Vectors perpendicular to such vectors are $\mathbf{v}_{\mathrm{cp}}(\mathbf{r}) = \hat{\mathbf{z}} \times \mathbf{u}_{\mathrm{tr}}(\hat{\mathbf{t}}) = \hat{\mathbf{z}} \times (\hat{\mathbf{z}} \times (\hat{\mathbf{t}} \times \mathbf{r}))$.

Let the camera motion be $(\mathbf{t}, \boldsymbol{\omega})$. Projection of the flow (3) onto $\mathbf{v}_{\mathrm{cp}}$ is

$$\dot{\mathbf{r}} \cdot \frac{\mathbf{v}_{\mathrm{cp}}}{\|\mathbf{v}_{\mathrm{cp}}\|} = \frac{1}{\|\mathbf{v}_{\mathrm{cp}}\|}\left(\frac{1}{Z}p_t(\mathbf{t}, \hat{\mathbf{t}}, \mathbf{r}) + p_\omega(\boldsymbol{\omega}, \hat{\mathbf{t}}, \mathbf{r})\right) \qquad (4)$$

where the functions p_t, p_ω are:

$$p_t(\mathbf{t}, \hat{\mathbf{t}}, \mathbf{r}) = f\,(\mathbf{t} \times \hat{\mathbf{t}}) \cdot \mathbf{r}$$
$$p_\omega(\boldsymbol{\omega}, \hat{\mathbf{t}}, \mathbf{r}) = (\boldsymbol{\omega} \times \mathbf{r}) \cdot (\hat{\mathbf{t}} \times \mathbf{r}) .$$

In particular, if we let $\hat{\mathbf{t}} = \mathbf{t}$, the translational component of the copoint projection becomes zero and (4) simplifies into

$$\dot{\mathbf{r}} \cdot \frac{\mathbf{v}_{\mathrm{cp}}}{\|\mathbf{v}_{\mathrm{cp}}\|} = \frac{1}{\|\mathbf{v}_{\mathrm{cp}}\|} p_\omega(\boldsymbol{\omega}, \hat{\mathbf{t}}, \mathbf{r}) . \tag{5}$$

2.2 Estimating Rotation from Known Translation

If we can estimate the translation of the camera, it is quite simple to estimate the rotational component of the camera motion. Let us for now assume that the translation $\mathbf{t}$ is known. Then the rotation can be estimated based on (5), as long as there are some normal flow measurements in the direction of the appropriate copoint vectors. Since (5) is linear in the elements of $\boldsymbol{\omega}$, we can setup a least squares minimization to estimate $\boldsymbol{\omega}$ based on the appropriate normal flow measurements.

Specifically at points with suitable normal flow direction, we have equations

$$\dot{\mathbf{r}} \cdot \frac{\mathbf{v}_{\mathrm{cp}}}{\|\mathbf{v}_{\mathrm{cp}}\|} = \left(\frac{1}{\|\mathbf{v}_{\mathrm{cp}}\|} (\mathbf{t} \times \mathbf{r})^{\mathrm{T}} \right) \boldsymbol{\omega}$$

that are linear in $\boldsymbol{\omega}$.

2.3 Depth Estimation from Motion Fields

This section introduces the novel criterion of "smoothness of depth" which is used to evaluate the consistency of the normal flow field with the estimated 3D motion and also to segment the scene at its depth boundaries. The idea is based on the interrelationship of estimated 3D motion $(\hat{\mathbf{t}}, \hat{\boldsymbol{\omega}})$ and estimated depth of the scene $\hat{Z}$.

The structure of the scene, i.e., depth computed, can be expressed as a function of the estimated translation $\hat{\mathbf{t}}$ and the estimated rotation $\hat{\boldsymbol{\omega}}$. At an image point $\mathbf{r}$ where the normal flow direction is $\mathbf{n}$, the inverse scene depth can be estimated from (3) as

$$\frac{1}{\hat{Z}} = \frac{\dot{\mathbf{r}} \cdot \mathbf{n} - \mathbf{u}_{\mathrm{rot}}(\hat{\boldsymbol{\omega}}) \cdot \mathbf{n}}{\mathbf{u}_{\mathrm{tr}}(\hat{\mathbf{t}}) \cdot \mathbf{n}} \tag{6}$$

where $\mathbf{u}_{\mathrm{rot}}(\hat{\boldsymbol{\omega}}), \mathbf{u}_{\mathrm{tr}}(\hat{\mathbf{t}})$ refer to the estimated rotational and translational flow respectively.

Substituting into (6) from (3), we obtain:

$$\frac{1}{\hat{Z}} = \frac{\frac{1}{Z}\mathbf{u}_{\mathrm{tr}}(\mathbf{t}) \cdot \mathbf{n} - \mathbf{u}_{\mathrm{rot}}(\delta\boldsymbol{\omega}) \cdot \mathbf{n}}{\mathbf{u}_{\mathrm{tr}}(\hat{\mathbf{t}}) \cdot \mathbf{n}} \quad \text{or}$$

$$\frac{1}{\hat{Z}} = \frac{1}{Z} \frac{\mathbf{u}_{\mathrm{tr}}(\mathbf{t}) \cdot \mathbf{n} - Z\mathbf{u}_{\mathrm{rot}}(\delta\boldsymbol{\omega}) \cdot \mathbf{n}}{\mathbf{u}_{\mathrm{tr}}(\hat{\mathbf{t}}) \cdot \mathbf{n}}$$

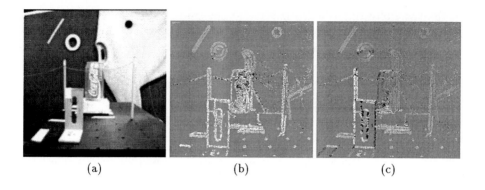

(a)　　　　　　　　　(b)　　　　　　　　　(c)

Fig. 2. (a) One frame of the NASA Coke can sequence. (b) Inverse depth estimated for the correct FOE in the middle of the image. (c) Inverse depth for an incorrect FOE 100 pixels to the left of the correct FOE (the image size was 512×512 pixels). The grey-level value represents inverse estimated depth with mid-level grey representing zero, white representing large positive $1/Z$ and black representing large negative $1/Z$

where $\mathbf{u}_{\mathrm{rot}}(\delta\boldsymbol{\omega})$ is the rotational flow due to the rotational error $\delta\boldsymbol{\omega} = (\hat{\boldsymbol{\omega}} - \boldsymbol{\omega})$. To make clear the relationship between actual and estimated depth we write

$$\hat{Z} = Z \cdot D \tag{7}$$

with

$$D = \frac{\mathbf{u}_{\mathrm{tr}}(\hat{\mathbf{t}}) \cdot \mathbf{n}}{(\mathbf{u}_{\mathrm{tr}}(\mathbf{t}) - Z\mathbf{u}_{\mathrm{rot}}(\delta\boldsymbol{\omega})) \cdot \mathbf{n}}$$

hereafter termed the distortion factor. Equation (7) shows how wrong depth estimates are produced due to inaccurate 3D motion values. The distortion factor for any direction $\mathbf{n}$ corresponds to the ratio of the projections of the two vectors $\mathbf{u}_{\mathrm{tr}}(\hat{\mathbf{t}})$ and $\mathbf{u}_{\mathrm{tr}}(\mathbf{t}) + Z\mathbf{u}_{\mathrm{rot}}(\delta\boldsymbol{\omega})$ on $\mathbf{n}$. The larger the angle between these two vectors is the more the distortion will be spread out over the different directions. Thus, considering a patch of a smooth surface in space and assuming that normal flow measurements are taken along many directions, a rugged (i.e., unsmooth) surface will be computed on the basis of wrong 3D motion estimates. To give an example, we show the estimated depth for the NASA Coke can sequence (one frame is shown in Fig. 2 (a)). For two different translations we estimate the rotation as in Sect. 2.2 and then plot the estimated values of (6). Notice the reasonably smooth depth estimates for the correct FOE in Fig. 2 (b) and compare with sharp changes in the depth map (neighboring black and white regions) in Fig. 2 (c).

The above observation constitutes the main idea behind our algorithm. For a candidate 3D motion estimate we evaluate the smoothness of estimated depth within image patches. If the chosen image patches correspond to smooth 3D scene patches the correct 3D motion will certainly give rise to the overall smoothest image patches. To obtain such situation we attempt a segmentation of scene on the basis of estimated depth while at the same time testing the candidate 3D motions. As all computations are based on normal flow and we thus have available the full statistics of the raw data a good segmentation generally is possible.

3 Finding the Focus of Expansion

3.1 Algorithm Description

The focus of expansion is found by localizing the minimum of function $\Phi(\hat{\mathbf{t}})$, which constitutes a measure of the estimated depth variation. Let $\hat{\mathbf{t}}$ be a candidate translation, and estimate the scene depth we would obtain if $\hat{\mathbf{t}}$ were the correct translation. To obtain $\Phi(\hat{\mathbf{t}})$ we examine variation of the estimated depth over small image regions and compute a weighted sum of the local results.

We first summarize the computation of $\Phi(\hat{\mathbf{t}})$ and then explain the algorithm. To obtain $\Phi(\hat{\mathbf{t}})$

1. Estimate the camera rotation $\hat{\boldsymbol{\omega}}$ from the copoint vectors corresponding to $\hat{\mathbf{t}}$.
2. Compute the depth estimates $1/\hat{Z}$ from (6) and multiply them by the average size of $\mathbf{u}_{\mathrm{tr}}(\hat{\mathbf{t}})$ in the region.
3. Partition the image into small regions, for each region $\mathcal{R}$ check whether it needs to be segmented as described in Sect. 3.2. If the region cannot be segmented, the error measure $\Theta(\hat{\mathbf{t}}, \mathcal{R})$ is the variance of all the estimated $1/\hat{Z}$ values. Otherwise, compute the variances of $1/\hat{Z}$ in each subregion separately and let $\Theta(\hat{\mathbf{t}}, \mathcal{R})$ be the sum of the variances.
4. The depth variation measure $\Phi(\hat{\mathbf{t}})$ is the sum of $\Theta(\hat{\mathbf{t}}, \mathcal{R})$ over all image regions $\mathcal{R}$.

Several steps of the algorithm need additional explanation. The scaling of the inverted depth values in step 2 corresponds to making $\mathbf{u}_{\mathrm{tr}}(\hat{\mathbf{t}})$ a unit vector and it is equivalent to the proper scaling of the epipolar constraint.

The smoothness measure used here corresponds to deviations of the inverse depth from a fronto-parallel plane. If more precision is required or if large image regions are used, we may fit a plane through the estimated $1/\hat{Z}$ values and replace each $1/\hat{Z}$ by its distance from the plane. Then we reduce the errors caused by small changes of the flow field within the image region.

As shown in Sect. 3.4, the smoothness measure gives provably correct results for any image patch that corresponds to a single smooth scene surface. In order to obtain only such image patches we perform a segmentation of the scene, as described in the next section. Of course, a correct segmentation at all locations cannot be guaranteed. This, however, should not influence much the solution of the 3D motion estimation, as even for patches that contain depth discontinuity, in many cases the smoothness measure is smaller for the correct 3D motion than for incorrect ones.

To find the minimum of Φ and thus the FOE/FOC, we perform a hierarchical search over the two-dimensional space of FOE positions. In practice, the function Φ is quite smooth, that is small changes in $\hat{\mathbf{t}}$ give rise to only small changes in Φ. One of the reasons for this is that for any $\hat{\mathbf{t}}$, the value of $\Phi(\hat{\mathbf{t}})$ is influenced by all the normal flow measurements and not only by a small subset.

For most motion sequences, the motion of the camera does not change abruptly. Then the FOE position does not change much between frames and a complete search only has to be performed for the first flow field. In the successive flow fields, we can search only in a smaller area centered around the previously estimated FOE.

3.2 Patch Segmentation

By segmenting a patch, we decrease its contribution to $\Phi(\hat{\mathbf{t}})$. Ideally, an image patch should be segmented if it contains two smooth scene surfaces separated by a depth discontinuity and the depth is estimated using the correct 3D motion and it should not be segmented if it corresponds to one smooth surface and the depth is estimated on the basis of incorrect 3D motion. If that is the case, we decrease $\Phi(\hat{\mathbf{t}})$ for the correct translation while keeping the measure large for incorrect translations.

We use a simple segmentation criterion. First of all, segmentation is attempted only for patches where the estimated depth is not smooth. If the histogram of depth values in the region is bimodal and the region can be divided into two spatially coherent regions that correspond to the two modes of the histogram, we divide the patch into the two subregions.

It is simple to show that this strategy can be expected to yield good patch segmentation. When the motion estimate is correct, also the depth estimates are correct and patches with large amount of depth variation contain depth discontinuities.

For incorrect motions, the distortion factor depends on the direction of normal flow. While for any patch we can split the depth estimates into two groups and decrease the variance, it is highly unlikely that the two groups of measurements define two spatially coherent separate subregions. More likely, the depth estimates from both groups are randomly distributed within the patch.

However, as the segmentation is based on local information only, we cannot expect it to perfectly distinguish the depth discontinuities from depth variation due to incorrect 3D motion. Sometimes, if a patch contains two subregions with different distributions of normal flow directions, we may split the patch even for incorrect 3D motion. An improvement, however, could be achieved by taking into account also the distribution of normal flow directions in relation to the estimated depth.

The local results are used in a global measure and occasional segmentation errors are unlikely to change the overall results. For the segmentation to cause an incorrect motion to yield the smallest $\Phi(\hat{\mathbf{t}})$, special normal flow configurations would have to occur in many patches in the image.

3.3   The Estimated Rotation

The analysis of $\Phi(\hat{\mathbf{t}})$ should start by relating the estimated rotation $\hat{\omega}$ and the true motion parameters $(\mathbf{t}, \omega)$. When $\hat{\omega}$ is computed, the measurements used in (5) are given by (4), i.e.,

$$\dot{\mathbf{r}} \cdot \mathbf{n} = \frac{1}{\|\mathbf{v}_{\mathrm{cp}}\|} p_\omega(\omega, \hat{\mathbf{t}}, \mathbf{r}) + \frac{1}{\|\mathbf{v}_{\mathrm{cp}}\|} \frac{1}{Z} p_{\mathrm{t}}(\mathbf{t}, \hat{\mathbf{t}}, \mathbf{r}) .$$

Note that unless $\hat{\mathbf{t}}$ is the correct translation, values of the flow along the copoint vectors are influenced by the translational component of the flow field. Due to linearity, the estimated rotation is (ignoring measurement errors):

$$\hat{\omega} = \omega + \delta\omega \tag{8}$$

where ω is the true rotation and $\delta\omega$ is the rotation of a field that best fits the translational component of the copoint projections.

The residual of the estimate is one possible source of information about the true FOE. If $\hat{\mathbf{t}}$ is the correct solution, then $\delta\omega = 0$ and the residual is small regardless of the scene depth. If $\hat{\mathbf{t}}$ is an incorrect estimate, then the residual, in general, will be large; the residual could still be small, but only under special circumstances; for the residual to be zero, the depth Z has to satisfy

$$\mathbf{u}_{\mathrm{rot}}(\delta\omega) \cdot \mathbf{v}_{\mathrm{cp}} = p_\omega(\delta\omega, \hat{\mathbf{t}}, \mathbf{r}) = \frac{1}{Z} p_{\mathrm{t}}(\mathbf{t}, \hat{\mathbf{t}}, \mathbf{r}) . \tag{9}$$

Multiplying by Z^2 and substituting $Z\mathbf{r} = f\mathbf{R}$, we obtain a second order equation for the scene points $\mathbf{R}$

$$p_\omega(\delta\omega, \hat{\mathbf{t}}, \mathbf{R}) - p_{\mathrm{t}}(\mathbf{t}, \hat{\mathbf{t}}, \mathbf{R}) = (\delta\omega \times \mathbf{R}) \cdot (\hat{\mathbf{t}} \times \mathbf{R}) - f(\mathbf{t} \times \hat{\mathbf{t}}) \cdot \mathbf{R} = 0 . \tag{10}$$

Therefore, the residual is a measure of the difference between the surface in view and the quadric given by (10), but only at points where suitable normal flow measurements are available.

Assuming the scene cannot be approximated sufficiently well by a single second order surface, one might try to use the copoint residual to find the correct FOE. Such approaches can be found in [2]. In practice, however, this method may run into problems. Only a small and changing subset of measurements is used to compute the rotation, the measurements are noisy and the noise level may vary across the image. It is very difficult to weigh the residuals for different candidate translations so that they can be compared.

The main problem is that the residuals only provide negative information about the FOE. If the residual is large, we can be quite sure that the candidate translation is incorrect. However, a small residual may be caused by the lack of data and does not necessarily imply that the solution is correct. Thus, our method tests for the correct translation by going through the estimation of depth and analyzing how it is varying locally.

3.4 Algorithm Analysis

The function $\Phi(\hat{\mathbf{t}})$ depends not only on the true and the estimated motion parameters, but also on the actual distribution of normal flow directions as well as the unknown scene depth. Therefore only a statistical analysis of Φ is possible. What we study here is $\Theta(\hat{\mathbf{t}}, \mathcal{R})$, a contribution to $\Phi(\hat{\mathbf{t}})$ from a single image region $\mathcal{R}$.

We substitute both $\hat{\boldsymbol{\omega}}$ and the true motion parameters into (6) and simplify the expression

$$
\frac{1}{\hat{Z}} = \frac{(1/Z)\mathbf{u}_{\mathrm{tr}}(\mathbf{t}) \cdot \mathbf{n} + \mathbf{u}_{\mathrm{rot}}(\boldsymbol{\omega}) \cdot \mathbf{n} - \mathbf{u}_{\mathrm{rot}}(\boldsymbol{\omega} + \delta\boldsymbol{\omega}) \cdot \mathbf{n}}{\mathbf{u}_{\mathrm{tr}}(\hat{\mathbf{t}}) \cdot \mathbf{n}}
$$
$$
= \frac{(1/Z)\mathbf{u}_{\mathrm{tr}}(\mathbf{t}) \cdot \mathbf{n} - \mathbf{u}_{\mathrm{rot}}(\delta\boldsymbol{\omega}) \cdot \mathbf{n}}{\mathbf{u}_{\mathrm{tr}}(\hat{\mathbf{t}}) \cdot \mathbf{n}} .
$$

The vectors $\mathbf{u}_{\mathrm{tr}}(\mathbf{t})$, $\mathbf{u}_{\mathrm{rot}}(\delta\boldsymbol{\omega})$, and $\mathbf{u}_{\mathrm{tr}}(\hat{\mathbf{t}})$ are polynomial functions of image position $\mathbf{r}$ and can usually be approximated by constants within a small image region.

Consider a local coordinate system where $\mathbf{u}_{\mathrm{tr}}(\hat{\mathbf{t}})$ is parallel to $[1,0,0]^{\mathrm{T}}$. Because the computed depths are scaled in step 2 of the algorithm, we can equivalently set the length of $\mathbf{u}_{\mathrm{tr}}(\hat{\mathbf{t}})$ to one and write $\mathbf{u}_{\mathrm{tr}}(\hat{\mathbf{t}}) = [1,0,0]^{\mathrm{T}}$. In the coordinate system, we denote

$$
\begin{aligned}
\mathbf{u}_{\mathrm{rot}}(\delta\boldsymbol{\omega}) &= u_r\left[\cos\varphi_r, \sin\varphi_r, 0\right]^{\mathrm{T}} \\
\mathbf{u}_{\mathrm{tr}}(\mathbf{t}) &= u_t\left[\cos\varphi_t, \sin\varphi_t, 0\right]^{\mathrm{T}} \\
\mathbf{n} &= \left[\cos\psi, \sin\psi, 0\right]^{\mathrm{T}} .
\end{aligned}
\tag{11}
$$

Then $\mathbf{u}_{\mathrm{tr}}(\hat{\mathbf{t}}) \cdot \mathbf{n} = \cos\psi$ and

$$
\begin{aligned}
1/\hat{Z} &= (1/Z)u_t\left(\cos\varphi_t + \sin\varphi_t \tan\psi\right) - u_r\left(\cos\varphi_r + \sin\varphi_r \tan\psi\right) = \\
&= \left((1/Z)u_t\cos\varphi_t - u_r\cos\varphi_r\right) + \tan\psi\left((1/Z)u_t\sin\varphi_t - u_r\sin\varphi_r\right) .
\end{aligned}
\tag{12}
$$

As $u_r\cos\varphi_r$ is approximated by a constant, it does not influence the variance of $1/\hat{Z}$ and it is thus sufficient to study the variance of $1/\hat{Z}'$:

$$
\frac{1}{\hat{Z}'} = (1/Z)u_t\cos\varphi_t + \tan\psi\left((1/Z)u_t\sin\varphi_t - u_r\sin\varphi_r\right) .
\tag{13}
$$

For the correct translation, we have $\delta\boldsymbol{\omega} = \mathbf{0}$, i.e., $u_r = 0$, and $\varphi_t = 0$, i.e., $\sin\varphi_t = 0$. Therefore $1/\hat{Z}'$ simplifies into

$$
\frac{1}{\hat{Z}'} = \frac{1}{Z}u_t
\tag{14}
$$

and the variance of $1/\hat{Z}'$ is proportional to the variance of the inverse real depth $1/Z$ and is independent of $\tan\psi$.

For incorrect translation estimates, on the other hand, $\varphi_t \neq 0$ except for points on a certain line. Unless the surface is special so that $\delta\boldsymbol{\omega} = \mathbf{0}$, also $u_r \neq 0$

at most points in the image. In most cases $1/\hat{Z}'$ depends on $\tan\psi$ and it can become very large (or very small) when there are normal flow measurements in the region such that ψ is close to $\pm\pi/2$.

Obviously, large variance of $\tan\psi$ will lead to large $\Theta(\hat{\mathbf{t}}, \mathcal{R})$ only if expression $(1/Z)u_t \sin\varphi_t - u_r \sin\varphi_r$ is not small.

Consider now a typical image patch corresponding to a smooth scene patch, where the variance of $1/Z$ is small. For the correct motion estimate also the variance of $1/\hat{Z}'$ is small. For other translations, the variance of $1/\hat{Z}'$ is proportional to the variance of $\tan\psi$. It can be small if all the normal flow measurements in the patch have approximately the same direction, or if the scene patch is close to the ambiguous quadric (10).

If the depth of the scene patch varies significantly, the exact distribution of normal flow directions as well as their correlation with the scene depth will determine the 3D motion yielding the smallest depth variance. However, on average it can be expected that the depth variance for the correct 3D motion is smaller than the variances for most incorrect motions.

If the image region contain sufficiently many different directions of normal flow so that the value of $\tan\psi$ changes significantly, the variance of $1/\hat{Z}$ is dominated by

$$\tan\psi((1/Z)u_t \sin\varphi_t - u_r \sin\varphi_r) . \tag{15}$$

Expression (15) is zero for the correct motion and non-zero for most incorrect motions. Only a scene patch close to the ambiguous quadric can give small depth variance for an incorrect 3D motion.

3.5   The Epipolar Constraint

The depth smoothness measure is closely related to the traditional epipolar constraint and we examine the relationship here. In the instantaneous form the epipolar constraint can be written as

$$(\hat{\mathbf{z}} \times \mathbf{u}_{\mathrm{tr}}(\hat{\mathbf{t}})) \cdot (\dot{\mathbf{r}} - \mathbf{u}_{\mathrm{rot}}(\hat{\boldsymbol{\omega}})) = 0 \tag{16}$$

or in the usual simplified form as

$$(\hat{\mathbf{t}} \times \mathbf{r}) \cdot (\dot{\mathbf{r}} + (\hat{\boldsymbol{\omega}} \times \mathbf{r})) = 0 .$$

Usually, the distance of the flow vector $\dot{\mathbf{r}}$ from the epipolar line (determined by $\mathbf{u}_{\mathrm{tr}}(\hat{\mathbf{t}})$ and $\mathbf{u}_{\mathrm{rot}}(\hat{\boldsymbol{\omega}})$) is computed, and the sum of the squared distances, i.e.,

$$\sum \left((\hat{\mathbf{z}} \times \mathbf{u}_{\mathrm{tr}}(\hat{\mathbf{t}})) \cdot (\dot{\mathbf{r}} - \mathbf{u}_{\mathrm{rot}}(\hat{\boldsymbol{\omega}}))\right)^2 \tag{17}$$

is minimized.

Methods based upon (17) suffer from bias, however, and a scaled epipolar constraint has been used to give an unbiased solution:

$$\sum \frac{\left(\mathbf{u}_{\mathrm{tr}}(\hat{\mathbf{t}}) \cdot (\dot{\mathbf{r}} - \mathbf{u}_{\mathrm{rot}}(\hat{\boldsymbol{\omega}}))\right)^2}{\|\mathbf{u}_{\mathrm{tr}}(\hat{\mathbf{t}})\|^2} . \tag{18}$$

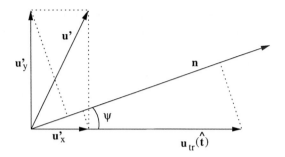

Fig. 3. The relationship between the epipolar constraint and the estimated depth

To relate the epipolar constraint and the depth smoothness measure, we rewrite (16) and substitute the true motion parameters to obtain

$$\mathbf{v}_{\mathrm{cp}} \cdot \left(\frac{1}{Z}\mathbf{u}_{\mathrm{tr}}(\mathbf{t}) - \mathbf{u}_{\mathrm{rot}}(\delta\boldsymbol{\omega}) \right) = \frac{1}{Z}p_t(\mathbf{t}, \hat{\mathbf{t}}, \mathbf{r}) - p_\omega(\delta\boldsymbol{\omega}, \hat{\mathbf{t}}, \mathbf{r}) = 0 \ .$$

Since $\|\mathbf{v}_{\mathrm{cp}}\| = \|\mathbf{u}_{\mathrm{tr}}(\hat{\mathbf{t}})\|$, the properly scaled epipolar constraint can be written as

$$\frac{1}{\|\mathbf{v}_{\mathrm{cp}}\|} \left(\frac{1}{Z}p_t(\mathbf{t}, \hat{\mathbf{t}}, \mathbf{r}) - p_\omega(\delta\boldsymbol{\omega}, \hat{\mathbf{t}}, \mathbf{r}) \right) = 0 \ . \tag{19}$$

Consider now the local coordinate system used in Sect. 3.4. In the rotated coordinate system, $\mathbf{v}_{\mathrm{cp}} = [0, 1, 0]^\mathrm{T}$ and thus

$$(1/Z)p_t(\mathbf{t}, \hat{\mathbf{t}}, \mathbf{r}) - p_\omega(\delta\boldsymbol{\omega}, \hat{\mathbf{t}}, \mathbf{r}) = (1/Z)u_t \sin\varphi_t - u_r \sin\varphi_r \ . \tag{20}$$

We see that one part of the estimated depth (12) is proportional to the epipolar distance (20).

The geometric relationship of the two quantities is illustrated in Fig. 3. We denote the derotated flow $\dot{\mathbf{r}} - \mathbf{u}_{\mathrm{rot}}(\hat{\boldsymbol{\omega}})$ by $\mathbf{u}'$ and decompose it into two components, $\mathbf{u}'_x$ parallel to $\mathbf{u}_{\mathrm{tr}}(\hat{\mathbf{t}})$, and $\mathbf{u}'_y$ perpendicular to $\mathbf{u}_{\mathrm{tr}}(\hat{\mathbf{t}})$.

In the figure, the epipolar distance is just $\|\mathbf{u}'_y\|$.

The estimated depth (12) is the sum of

$$\frac{\mathbf{u}'_x \cdot \mathbf{n}}{\mathbf{u}_{\mathrm{tr}}(\hat{\mathbf{t}}) \cdot \mathbf{n}} + \frac{\mathbf{u}'_y \cdot \mathbf{n}}{\mathbf{u}_{\mathrm{tr}}(\hat{\mathbf{t}}) \cdot \mathbf{n}} \ .$$

Since $\mathbf{u}'_x$ is parallel to $\mathbf{u}_{\mathrm{tr}}(\hat{\mathbf{t}})$, the first part of the sum is $\|\mathbf{u}'_x\|/\|\mathbf{u}_{\mathrm{tr}}(\hat{\mathbf{t}})\|$, i.e., independent of $\mathbf{n}$. This is the first part of (12).

The angle between vectors $\mathbf{n}$ and $\mathbf{u}_{\mathrm{tr}}(\hat{\mathbf{t}})$ is ψ, so for the second part of the sum, $\mathbf{u}'_y \cdot \mathbf{n} = \|\mathbf{u}'_y\| \cos(\pi/2 - \psi)$ and $\mathbf{u}_{\mathrm{tr}}(\hat{\mathbf{t}}) \cdot \mathbf{n} = \|\mathbf{u}_{\mathrm{tr}}(\hat{\mathbf{t}})\| \cos(\psi) = \cos\psi$, since $\mathbf{u}_{\mathrm{tr}}(\hat{\mathbf{t}})$ is scaled to be a unit vector. Consequently, the second part of the sum is

$$\|\mathbf{u}'_y\| \tan\psi \ .$$

Consider now a constant depth patch, where $\mathbf{u}'$ is approximately constant. Then the variance of $1/\hat{Z}'$ is equal to the epipolar constraint multiplied by the variance of $\tan \psi$.

The above analysis makes clear the close relationship of the smoothness measure to the traditional epipolar constraint. Indeed, in a smooth patch, $(1/Z)u_t$ is approximately constant and the variance of $1/\hat{Z}$ can be written (using (20)) as

$$\Theta(\hat{\mathbf{t}}, \mathcal{R}) = \text{Var}(1/\hat{Z}) = \text{Var}(\tan \psi) \left((1/Z)p_t(\mathbf{t}, \hat{\mathbf{t}}, \mathbf{r}) - p_\omega(\delta\boldsymbol{\omega}, \hat{\mathbf{t}}, \mathbf{r})\right)^2 . \quad (21)$$

Therefore, in a smooth patch

$$\frac{\text{Var}(1/\hat{Z})}{\text{Var}(\tan \psi)}$$

is a good approximation of the epipolar constraint

$$\left((1/Z)p_t(\mathbf{t}, \hat{\mathbf{t}}, \mathbf{r}) - p_\omega(\delta\boldsymbol{\omega}, \hat{\mathbf{t}}, \mathbf{r})\right)^2 .$$

We thus define a scaled measure

$$\Theta'(\hat{\mathbf{t}}, \mathcal{R}) = \frac{\Theta(\hat{\mathbf{t}}, \mathcal{R})}{\text{Var}(\tan \psi)}$$

and the corresponding global smoothness measure

$$\Phi'(\hat{\mathbf{t}}) = \sum_{\mathcal{R}} \Theta'(\hat{\mathbf{t}}, \mathcal{R}) .$$

Measure $\Phi'(\hat{\mathbf{t}})$ is approximately equal to the epipolar measure if the scene patches are smooth (or successfully segmented). However, when measure $\Phi'(\hat{\mathbf{t}})$ is used as opposed to a measure evaluating the deviation from the epipolar constraint, no computation of optical flow is required. Furthermore, as discussed above, measure $\Phi'(\hat{\mathbf{t}})$ is advantageous in its ability to handle depth discontinuities as even for discontinuous patches that weren't successfully segmented, in many cases the depth smoothness measure gives the correct solution.

4 Experimental Results

Experiment 1. The depth segmentation described in Sect. 3.2 was tested for the Coke can sequence. Fig. 4 shows the image patches that were segmented for the correct FOE. Many depth discontinuities in the scene are such that computed normal flow measurements appear only on one side of the discontinuity. Consequently, such patches are not segmented and pose no problem for the motion estimation algorithm.

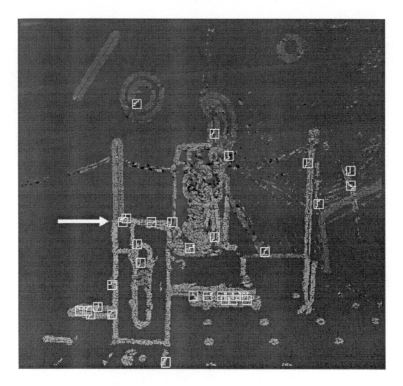

Fig. 4. Patch segmentation of the Coke can sequence overlayed on the computed inverse depth. The correct FOE (in the middle of the image) was used. The arrow points to the patch used in experiment 2

Experiment 2. The effects of the patch segmentation are best demonstrated by showing for varying $\hat{t}$ function $\Theta'(\hat{t}, \mathcal{R})$ for a fixed image region $\mathcal{R}$. The results are shown in Fig. 5. In particular, Fig. 5 (a) shows for all positions $\hat{t}$ the smoothness measure $\Theta'(\hat{t})$ for a fixed image region when segmentation was performed and Fig. 5 (b) shows the smoothness measure when no segmentation took place. Fig. 5 (c) shows all the FOE positions for which a segmentation was performed.

Experiment 3. The Yosemite fly-through sequence (one frame is shown in Fig. 6) contains independently moving clouds. Each image frame was thus clipped to contain only the mountain range.

We tested both depth smoothness measures $\Phi(\hat{t})$ and $\Phi'(\hat{t})$. For comparison, we estimated optical flow by assuming it locally to be constant and computed the epipolar constraint measure, using (18). The FOE voting results are shown in Fig. 7. Since the depth of the scene is changing slowly, the scaled depth smoothness measure $\Phi'(\hat{t})$ gives results that are very close to the results using the epipolar constraint.

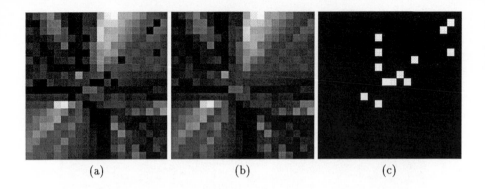

(a)   (b)   (c)

Fig. 5. Function $\Theta(\hat{t}, \mathcal{R})$ for a fixed region $\mathcal{R}$ marked in Fig. 4. The area shown is three times the image size with the image in the center of the area. Black denotes the smallest and white largest values of $\Theta(\hat{t}, \mathcal{R})$. (a) The patch was segmented if possible. (b) No patch segmentation was performed. (c) White blocks denote candidate FOE positions for which the patch was segmented

Fig. 6. One frame from the Yosemite fly-through sequence. Only the lower part of the image was used in the algorithm

In the coordinate system centered in the middle of the image, the correct focus of expansion was at $(-20, -100)$ in pixels.

The following FOE positions were found using hierarchical search:

- Using $\Phi(\hat{t})$: $(21, -87)$
- Using $\Phi'(\hat{t})$: $(-24, -104)$
- Using the epipolar constraint : $(-21, -116)$

5 Conclusions

There exists a lot of structure in the world. With regard to shape, this structure manifests itself in surface patches that are smooth, separated by abrupt discontinuities. This paper exploited this fact in order to provide an algorithm that estimates 3D motion while at the same time it recovers scene discontinuities.

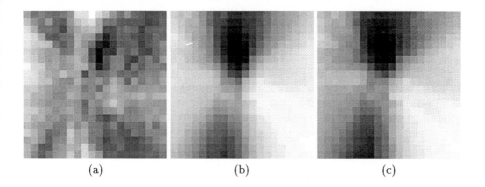

$$(a) \qquad\qquad (b) \qquad\qquad (c)$$

Fig. 7. The results of the FOE voting. The voting area is three times the image size with the image in the center of the area. The gray value of the bin represents the value of the depth smoothness measure with black representing the smallest value. (a) The smoothness measure $\Phi(\hat{t})$. (b) The scaled smoothness measure $\Phi'(\hat{t})$. (c) The epipolar constraint measure

The basis of the technique lies in the understanding of the interaction between 3D shape and motion. Wrong 3D motion estimates give rise to depth values that are locally unsmooth, i.e., they vary more than the correct ones. This was exploited in order to obtain the 3D motion that locally provides the "smoothest" depth while recovering scene discontinuities. Finally, it was shown that the technique is very much related to epipolar minimization since the function to be minimized in image areas corresponding to smooth scene patches takes the same values as deviation from the epipolar constraint. The function used here, however, is obtained from normal flow measurements. The fact that values of the flow are not needed in the approach, along with the aforementioned equivalence of our objective function to the epipolar constraint, demonstrates that the presented algorithm is an improvement over existing techniques.

References

1. T. Brodsky, C. Fermüller, and Y. Aloimonos. Directions of motion fields are hardly ever ambiguous. *International Journal of Computer Vision*, 26:5–24, 1998.
2. S. Carlsson. Sufficient image structure from motion and shape estimation. In *Proc. European Conference on Computer Vision*, pages 83–94, Stockholm, Sweden, 1994.
3. L. Cheong, C. Fermüller, and Y. Aloimonos. Effects of errors in the viewing geometry on shape estimation. *Computer Vision and Image Understanding*, 1998. In press. Earlier version available as Technical Report CAR-TR-773, June 1996.
4. O. D. Faugeras. *Three-Dimensional Computer Vision*. MIT Press, Cambridge, MA, 1992.
5. C. Fermüller. Navigational preliminaries. In Y. Aloimonos, editor, *Active Perception*, Advances in Computer Vision, pages 103–150. Lawrence Erlbaum Associates, Hillsdale, NJ, 1993.

6. C. Fermüller and Y. Aloimonos. Direct perception of three-dimensional motion from patterns of visual motion. *Science*, 270:1973–1976, 1995.

7. S. Geman and D. Geman. Stochastic relaxation, Gibbs distribution and Bayesian restoration of images. *IEEE Transactions on Pattern Analysis and Machine Intelligence*, 6:721–741, 1984.

8. B. K. P. Horn. Motion fields are hardly ever ambiguous. *International Journal of Computer Vision*, 1:259–274, 1987.

9. B. K. P. Horn and E. J. Weldon, Jr. Direct methods for recovering motion. *International Journal of Computer Vision*, 2:51–76, 1988.

10. J. J. Koenderink and A. J. van Doorn. Affine structure from motion. *Journal of the Optical Society of America*, 8:377–385, 1991.

11. Q.-T. Luong and O. D. Faugeras. The fundamental matrix: Theory, algorithms, and stability analysis. *International Journal of Computer Vision*, 17:43–75, 1996.

12. J. Marroquin. *Probabilistic Solution of Inverse Problems*. PhD thesis, Massachusetts Institute of Technology, 1985.

13. S. J. Maybank. Algorithm for analysing optical flow based on the least-squares method. *Image and Vision Computing*, 4:38–42, 1986.

14. S. J. Maybank. *A Theoretical Study of Optical Flow*. PhD thesis, University of London, England, 1987.

15. D. Mumford and J. Shah. Boundary detection by minimizing functionals. In *Proc. IEEE Conference on Computer Vision and Pattern Recognition*, pages 22–25, 1985.

What Is Computed by
Structure from Motion Algorithms?

Cornelia Fermüller and Yiannis Aloimonos

Computer Vision Laboratory, Center for Automation Research,
University of Maryland, College Park, MD 20742-3275, USA
{fer,yiannis}@cfar.umd.edu

Abstract. In the literature we find two classes of algorithms which, on the basis of two views of a scene, recover the rigid transformation between the views and subsequently the structure of the scene. The first class contains techniques which require knowledge of the correspondence or the motion field between the images and are based on the epipolar constraint. The second class contains so-called direct algorithms which require knowledge about the value of the flow in one direction only and are based on the positive depth constraint. Algorithms in the first class achieve the solution by minimizing a function representing deviation from the epipolar constraint while direct algorithms find the 3D motion that, when used to estimate depth, produces a minimum number of negative depth values. This paper presents a stability analysis of both classes of algorithms. The formulation is such that it allows comparison of the robustness of algorithms in the two classes as well as within each class. Specifically, a general statistical model is employed to express the functions which measure the deviation from the epipolar constraint and the number of negative depth values, and these functions are studied with regard to their topographic structure, specifically as regards the errors in the 3D motion parameters at the places representing the minima of the functions. The analysis shows that for algorithms in both classes which estimate all motion parameters simultaneously, the obtained solution has an error such that the projections of the translational and rotational errors on the image plane are perpendicular to each other. Furthermore, the estimated projection of the translation on the image lies on a line through the origin and the projection of the real translation.

1   Introduction

Structure from motion (SFM), one of the central problems in computational vision, amounts to the following problem: Given multiple views of a scene, to recover the rigid transformation between any two views and the structure of the imaged scene. Existing publications treat the problem using two broad classes of approaches, *differential* (where the views are close together) and *discrete* (where the views are far apart). Although the formalisms used in these two approaches are not identical, the underlying geometric structure of the problem remains essentially the same. Here the analysis is done in the framework of the differential case, assuming that a camera is moving in an unrestricted rigid manner while imaging a static scene. Although a solution to the SFM problem may involve several information sources which are fused, it always proceeds in two steps, first estimating the rigid motion between the views and second using the estimated 3D motion to compute the structure of the scene. The first step of estimating 3D motion is treated in many research papers using approaches that appear different. The purpose of this paper is to unify existing approaches to the problem into a single framework, and, in so doing, to explain why the problem is difficult and what approaches have the potential to provide a robust solution. Existing algorithms fall into two classes: approaches that utilize the epipolar constraint and the more recent approaches that utilize the "positive depth" constraint, the so-called direct algorithms.

In the first case, it is assumed that the motion field is available or has been computed from the image sequence, i.e., that points in the images that are the projections of the same point in the scene have been identified. Algorithms in this class attempt to find the 3D motion that best satisfies the epipolar constraint for all corresponding points. In technical terms, the epipolar constraint gives rise to a function whose global minimization provides the desired 3D motion. The high dimensionality (there are five motion parameters, three for the rotation and two for the direction of translation) and nonlinearity of this function have made it difficult to understand the behavior of existing algorithms. In addition, algorithms that first find the rotation and then on the basis of the rotational result find the translation often behave differently from algorithms that acquire the translation first and then the rotation, or from algorithms that attempt to find all motion parameters simultaneously. Many techniques can be found in the literature. These include algorithms that first estimate the rotation using either nonlinear equations [19] or search in the space of rotational parameters [4], [20]; algorithms that first estimate the translation [1], [3], [9], [10], [15], [18], [21] either through the optimization of an error function or by the employment of the motion parallax constraint; and algorithms that solve simultaneously for the rotation and translation which are mostly based on the linearization introduced in [14].

Algorithms based on the epipolar constraint require that an estimate of the motion field or correspondence be available. Motivated by the difficulty of estimating accurate correspondence, the so-called direct algorithms employ only the component of the flow along the gradient direction (normal flow), which can be derived solely from local image information. On the basis of flow information in only one direction, the epipolar constraint cannot be used. The only constraint that can be utilized, without making any assumptions about the scene, is that the depth of the scene is positive (since the scene lies in front of the camera). Direct motion algorithms thus attempt to find the 3D motion which, when used with the values of the normal flow to compute depth, yields the smallest number of image points with negative depths. As in the case of the epipolar constraint, the minimization of negative depth is quite difficult due to high dimensionality and nonlinearity.

The constraint of negative depth has been used for 3D motion estimation in the case of a general rigid motion in [7]. The techniques proposed there solve simultaneously for both the translation and rotation, and are implemented as search procedures in lower-dimensional subspaces. Earlier techniques which employ normal flow measurements only have assumed purely rotational flow fields [11] or purely translational flow fields [11]. One might employ the first class of algorithms for flow fields which contain small translations, and the second class for flow fields which contain small rotations; or one might use inertial sensor information to estimate rotation. In these cases one deals with the situation of having an error in either the translation or the rotation, on the basis of which 3D motion estimation must be achieved.

What is it that makes 3D motion estimation difficult? What is the relationship between solutions obtained from minimization of the epipolar constraint and from minimization of negative depth? Is one approach better than the other with respect to some criterion? Why is it that algorithms that compute translation and rotation in different orders have different behaviors? These are the questions addressed in this paper. On the basis of a statistical model for the scene we derive functions representing deviation from the epipolar constraint or the amount of negative depth, and we study these functions with regard to their topographic structure. To be more precise, we are interested in the relationships between the errors in 3D motion at the points representing the minima of the functions. Our analysis is performed both in the absence of error in the image measurements—in which case it becomes a geometric analysis of the inherent confusion between rotation and translation—and in the case where the image measurements are corrupted by noise that satisfies an appropriate model. The next section reviews the basic image formation model, introduces the probabilistic models used, describes the ideas underlying the analysis, and finishes by summarizing the results and comparing them with earlier studies.

2 Overview and Problem Statement

2.1 Prerequisites

We describe the motion of the observer by its translational velocity $\mathbf{t} = (U, V, W)$ and its rotational velocity $\boldsymbol{\omega} = (\alpha, \beta, \gamma)$ with respect to a coordinate system $OXYZ$ fixed to the nodal point of the camera. Image formation is modeled as perspective projection on a plane orthogonal to the Z axis at distance f from the nodal point. Thus the image points p with coordinates $\mathbf{r} = (x, y)$ are related to the scene points $P = (X, Y, Z)$ through the relation $(x, y) = \left(\frac{Xf}{Z}, \frac{Yf}{Z} \right)$. As a consequence of the well-known scaling ambiguity, only the direction of translation expressed through the image coordinates $(x_0, y_0) = \left(\frac{Uf}{W}, \frac{Vf}{W} \right)$ (referred to as the focus of expansion (FOE) or focus of contraction, depending on whether W is positive or negative) and the scaled depth W/Z are obtainable from image information. If we also allow a noise term $\mathbf{N} = (N_x, N_y)$ we obtain the following equations for the flow measurements $(\mathbf{v}(\mathbf{r}) = (u(x, y), v(x, y))$:

$$u(x, y) = \frac{u_{\text{tr}}(x,y)}{Z} + u_{\text{rot}}(x, y) = (x - x_0)\frac{W}{Z} + \alpha\frac{xy}{f} - \beta\left(\frac{x^2}{f} + f\right) + \gamma y + N_x$$

$$v(x, y) = \frac{v_{\text{tr}}(x,y)}{Z} + \frac{v_{\text{rot}}(x,y)}{Z} = (y - y_0)\frac{W}{Z} + \alpha\left(\frac{y^2}{f} + f\right) - \beta\frac{xy}{f} - \gamma x + N_y,$$

$$(1)$$

where $\frac{\mathbf{v}_{\text{tr}}(\mathbf{r})}{Z} = \left(\frac{u_{\text{tr}}(x,y)}{Z}, \frac{v_{\text{tr}}(x,y)}{Z}\right)$ and $\mathbf{v}_{\text{rot}}(\mathbf{r}) = (u_{\text{rot}}(x, y), v_{\text{rot}}(x, y))$ are the translational and rotational flow components, respectively. Therefore, the component of flow $u_n(x, y)$ along any direction $\mathbf{n}(\mathbf{r}) = (n_x(x, y), n_y(x, y))$ is

$$u_n(x, y) = \left(\frac{u_{\text{tr}}(x, y)}{Z} + u_{\text{rot}}(x, y) + N_x\right) n_x(x, y)$$

$$+ \left(\frac{v_{\text{tr}}(x, y)}{Z} + v_{\text{rot}}(x, y) + N_y\right) n_y(x, y). \qquad (2)$$

2.2   The Model

In its instantaneous form the epipolar constraint is obtained from (1) by subtraction of the rotational components and projection on the vector perpendicular to the translational component. Assuming noiseless flow measurements, that is, $\mathbf{N} = 0$, and dropping in the notation the dependence of vectors on (x, y), the epipolar constraint amounts to $(u - u_{\text{rot}})v_{\text{tr}} - (v - v_{\text{rot}})u_{\text{tr}} = 0$. The Euclidean norm is usually used as error norm, leading to least square error minimization. It is assumed that estimates for the full flow (u, v) have been obtained. Let $(\hat{u}_{\text{tr}}, \hat{v}_{\text{tr}})$ denote the estimates of the direction of the translational component and let $(\hat{u}_{\text{rot}}, \hat{v}_{\text{rot}})$ denote the estimates of the rotational components, and let FV denote the field of view. The estimates of interest are those which minimize

$$\iint\limits_{\text{FV}} \left((u - \hat{u}_{\text{rot}})\, \hat{v}_{\text{tr}} - (v - \hat{v}_{\text{rot}})\, \hat{u}_{\text{tr}}\right)^2 dx\, dy. \qquad (3)$$

If negative depth estimates are considered, it is assumed that not the full flow vectors, but only a component, u_n, of the flow vectors along some direction (n_x, n_y) is available (usually the normal flow). From this flow component the estimated depth, $\hat{Z}$, is derived (from (2)) as $\hat{Z} = \frac{\hat{u}_{\text{tr}}n_x + \hat{v}_{\text{tr}}n_y}{u_n - \hat{u}_{\text{rot}}n_x - \hat{v}_{\text{rot}}n_y}$, and it is negative if the numerator and denominator have opposite sign. Thus, for given translational and rotational estimates, a negative depth value is estimated at point (x, y) with flow estimate in the direction (n_x, n_y) if $(u_n - \hat{u}_{\text{rot}}n_x - \hat{v}_{\text{rot}}n_y)(\hat{u}_{\text{tr}}n_x + \hat{v}_{\text{tr}}n_y) < 0$. As a measure of the minimization of negative depth values the sum of all points $p(x, y)$ yielding negative depth estimates is considered, that is,

$$\iint\limits_{\text{FV}} \{p(x, y) \mid ((u_n - \hat{u}_{\text{rot}}n_x - \hat{v}_{\text{rot}}n_y)(\hat{u}_{\text{tr}}n_x + \hat{v}_{\text{tr}}n_y)) < 0\} dx\, dy. \qquad (4)$$

We need a statistical model for the scene which does justice to our goal of providing a comparison between the different minimizations. In particular, we are interested in the expected values of 3D motion estimates resulting from the different minimizations. Therefore, we assume that the depth of the scene is uniformly distributed between certain minimum and maximum values. For the minimization of negative depth values we further assume that the directions in which flow measurements are made are uniformly distributed in every direction for every depth.

Considering (u, v) as functions of x, y, Z and u_n as a function of $x, y, Z, \mathbf{n}$, where we parameterize $\mathbf{n}$ by ψ, the angle between $\mathbf{n}$ and the x axis, the function studied in the case of epipolar constraint minimization therefore amounts to

$$\int_{Z=Z_{\min}}^{Z_{\max}} \iint_{FV} \left((u - \hat{u}_{\mathrm{rot}})\,\hat{v}_{\mathrm{tr}} - (v - \hat{v}_{\mathrm{rot}})\,\hat{u}_{\mathrm{tr}}\right)^2 dx\,dy\,dZ \tag{5}$$

and the function studied in the case of minimization of negative depth values amounts to

$$\int_{\psi=0}^{\pi} \int_{Z=Z_{\min}}^{Z_{\max}} \iint_{FV}$$
$$\{p(x, y) \mid ((u_n - \hat{u}_{\mathrm{rot}} n_x - \hat{v}_{\mathrm{rot}} n_y)(\hat{u}_{\mathrm{tr}} n_x + \hat{v}_{\mathrm{tr}} n_y)) < 0\} dx\,dy\,dZ\,d\psi . \tag{6}$$

The desired model for the noise should be such that no specific directions are favored and that there is a dependence between noise and depth, because the translational flow component is proportional to the inverse depth. Therefore we define noise using two stochastic variables $\boldsymbol{\epsilon} = (\epsilon_x, \epsilon_y)$ and $\boldsymbol{\delta} = (\delta_x, \delta_y)$:

$$(N_x, N_y) = (\epsilon_x, \epsilon_y)\frac{1}{Z} + (\delta_x, \delta_y) , \tag{7}$$

with the first and second moments being $E(\epsilon_x) = E(\epsilon_y) = E(\delta_x) = E(\delta_y) = 0, E(\delta_x^2) = E(\delta_y^2) = \sigma_\delta^2, E(\delta_x \delta_y) = 0, E(\epsilon_x^2) = E(\epsilon_y^2) = \sigma_\epsilon^2, E(\epsilon_x \epsilon_y) = 0$, and all stochastic variables being independent of each other, independent of image position, and independent of the depth.

In the following sections we first study the functions as they arise from noiseless flow. The idea behind this is that noise which is of no specific bias does not alter the qualitative structure of the function. To be more precise, we are interested in certain local minima of the function, which can explain the behavior of different minimization techniques. For our purpose, we view the functions as five-dimensional in the three rotational and two translational error parameters. Clearly, if there is no noise in the image measurements the functions have their global minima at 0, the point where all motion errors are zero.

A technique which attempts 3D motion estimation in two steps, for example, by first estimating the rotational parameters, probably with some error, is confined in the second step to the subspace of translational parameters corresponding to the rotational error occurring in the first step. Thus our functions characterize these techniques through their local minima in the space of translational error parameters corresponding to a fixed rotational error. To characterize techniques which attempt global minimization, we consider the lowest valleys of the functions in two-dimensional subspaces which pass through 0. In the image processing literature, such local minima are often referred to as ravine lines or courses.

2.3 Negative Depth and Distortion of Depth

We consider as image measurements the projections of the flow field on certain directions (e.g., the normal flow field). If the 3D motion is estimated correctly, and there is no noise in the image measurements, the depth of the scene in view can be derived correctly from (2). However, an error in the estimation of the 3D motion parameters and the image measurements will result in computation of a distorted version of the depth. We use letters with hat signs to represent estimated quantities, unmarked letters to represent the actual quantities, and the subscript "ϵ" to denote errors, where we define the error quantity to be the actual quantity minus the estimated one (e.g., $u_{tr_\epsilon} = u_{tr} - \hat{u}_{tr}$, $x_{0_\epsilon} = x_0 - \hat{x}_0$, $\alpha_\epsilon = \alpha - \hat{\alpha}$, etc.).

The estimated depth can be derived from (2) as $\hat{Z} = \frac{\hat{u}_{tr}n_x + \hat{v}_{tr}n_y}{u_n - (\hat{u}_{rot}n_x + \hat{v}_{rot}n_y)}$ or

$$\hat{Z} = Z \left(\frac{\hat{u}_{tr}n_x + \hat{v}_{tr}n_y}{u_{tr}n_x + v_{tr}n_y + Z \left(u_{rot_\epsilon}n_x + v_{rot_\epsilon}n_y + N_x n_x + N_y n_y \right)} \right). \quad (8)$$

If we set $W = 1$ and $\hat{W} = 1$ this amounts to $\hat{Z} = Z \cdot D$, with

$$D = \frac{\hat{u}_{tr}n_x + \hat{v}_{tr}n_y}{u_{tr}n_x + v_{tr}n_y + Z \left(u_{rot_\epsilon}n_x + v_{rot_\epsilon}n_y \right) + Z \left(N_x n_x + N_y n_y \right)}.$$

This equation describes for any fixed direction (n_x, n_y) a surface in xyZ space which we have called an iso-distortion surface. Any such surface is to be understood as a locus of points in space which are distorted in depth by the same multiplicative factor if the image measurements are in direction (n_x, n_y). The iso-distortion surfaces of a family intersect in a curve and they change continuously as we vary D. Thus all scene points giving rise to negative depth estimates lie between the 0 and $-\infty$ distortion surfaces. The integral over all points (for all directions) giving rise to negative depth estimates we call the negative depth volume.

Let us now consider a single image point (x, y). For any depth value Z, the range of directions yielding negative depth estimates is defined by the angle α between the estimated and the actual image flow vector, or equivalently the two vectors $\hat{\mathbf{v}}_{tr}$ and $\mathbf{v}_{tr} + Z(\mathbf{v}_{rot_\epsilon} + \mathbf{N})$ (see Fig. 1). Thus, the angle α describes for every Z the contribution of the point to the negative depth volume.

The distortion factor for any direction $\mathbf{n}$ corresponds to the ratio of the projections of the two vectors $\hat{\mathbf{v}}_{tr}$ and $\mathbf{v}_{tr} + Z(\mathbf{v}_{rot_\epsilon} + \mathbf{N})$ on $\mathbf{n}$. The larger α is, the more the distortion will be spread out over the different directions, and probabilistically the more distorted the computed depth of the scene. Thus, the number of negative depth values corresponding to a wrong motion estimate is proportional to how well the actual depth of the scene in view is computed.

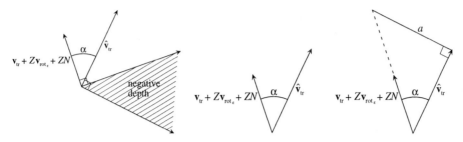

Fig. 1. The angle α between $\hat{\mathbf{v}}_{\text{tr}}$ and $\mathbf{v}_{\text{tr}} + Z\mathbf{v}_{\text{rot}_\epsilon}$ can be considered as a measure of the number of negative depth values, and also as a measure of the smoothness of the depth for a surface patch

Fig. 2. Different measures used in minimization constraints. (a) $\angle\alpha$ in the minimization of negative depth values from projections of motion fields. (b) a^2 in the epipolar constraint

2.4 Minimization Constraints and Summary of Results

Let us examine the different minimization terms considered here from a geometrical perspective.

When deriving the deviation from the epipolar constraint we consider integration over all points and depth values of the expression $((u - \hat{u}_{\text{rot}})\hat{v}_{\text{tr}} - (v - v_{\text{rot}_\epsilon})\hat{u}_{\text{tr}})^2$ or, equivalently, $((\mathbf{v}_{\text{tr}} + Z(\mathbf{v}_{\text{rot}_\epsilon} + \mathbf{N})) \cdot \hat{\mathbf{v}}_{\text{tr}}^{\perp})^2$, where $\hat{\mathbf{v}}_{\text{tr}}^{\perp}$ denotes the vector perpendicular to $\hat{\mathbf{v}}_{\text{tr}}$. When deriving the number of negative depth values we consider integration over all points and depth values of the angle α between the two vectors $\hat{\mathbf{v}}_{\text{tr}}$ and $\mathbf{v}_{\text{tr}} + Z(\mathbf{v}_{\text{rot}_\epsilon} + \mathbf{N})$. An illustration is given in Fig. 2. The two measures considered in the two different minimizations are clearly related to each other. In the case of negative depth we consider the angle α, whereas in the case of the epipolar constraint we consider the squared distance a^2, which amounts to $(\tan \alpha \|\hat{\mathbf{v}}_{\text{tr}}\|)^2$.

The major difference in using the two measures arises for angles $\alpha > 90°$. The measure for negative depth is monotonic in α, but the measure for the deviation from the epipolar constraint is not, because it does not differentiate between depth estimates of positive and negative value. The main constraints obtained from the minimization of the functions in (5) and (6) are as follows:

1. Considering the epipolar constraint as a minimization criterion:
   (a) For a fixed rotational error we obtain a translational error which depends on all the rotational error parameters as well as the actual translation.
   (b) For a fixed translational error we obtain a rotational error of the form $\gamma_\epsilon = 0$ and $\frac{-\beta_\epsilon}{\alpha_\epsilon} = \frac{x_{0_\epsilon}}{y_{0_\epsilon}}$, that is, there is no error in the estimate of the cyclotorsion, and the projection of the translational error on the image plane is perpendicular to the projection of the rotational error on the image plane.
   (c) The minima characterizing global minimization are also defined by the constraints, $\gamma_\epsilon = 0$ and $\frac{-\beta_\epsilon}{\alpha_\epsilon} = \frac{x_{0_\epsilon}}{y_{0_\epsilon}}$. In addition, we have the constraints

$\frac{x_0}{y_0} = \frac{\hat{x_0}}{\hat{y_0}}$ and $\text{sgn}(x_0) = \text{sgn}(x_{0_e})$, that is, the projection of the actual translation and the projection of the estimated translation lie on a line passing through the image center, and the estimated FOE is biased toward the image center.

To make future discussions easier, we will refer to the constraint $\frac{x_{0_e}}{y_{0_e}} = \frac{-\beta_e}{\alpha_e}$ as the "orthogonality constraint," and to $\frac{x_0}{y_0} = \frac{\hat{x_0}}{\hat{y_0}}$ as the "line constraint."

2. Considering the number of negative depth values estimated on the basis of normal flow as a minimization criterion:

   (a, b) Whether there is a fixed rotational error or a fixed translational error, we always have $\frac{x_{0_e}}{y_{0_e}} = \frac{-\beta_e}{\alpha_e}$. For a fixed translational error, in addition, $\gamma_e = 0$.

   (c) Global minimization is characterized, as for the epipolar constraint, by the two constraints $\frac{x_{0_e}}{y_{0_e}} = \frac{-\beta_e}{\alpha_e}$ and $\frac{x_0}{y_0} = \frac{\hat{x_0}}{\hat{y_0}}$, but here $\text{sgn}(x_0) = -\text{sgn}(x_{0_e})$, that is, the estimated FOE is further from the image center than the actual FOE.

A large number of error analyses have been carried out [2], [6], [12], [23] in the past. None of the existing studies, however, has attempted a topographic characterization of the function to be minimized for the purpose of analyzing different motion techniques. All the studies consider optical flow or correspondence as image measurements and investigate minimizations based on the epipolar constraint. Often, restrictive assumptions about the structure of the scene or the estimator have been made, but the main results obtained are in accordance with our findings. In particular, the following results already occur in the literature: (a) Translation along the x axis can be easily confounded with rotation around the y axis, and translation along the y axis can be easily confounded with rotation around the x axis, for small fields of view and insufficient depth variation. This fact has long been known from experimental observation, and has been proved for planar scene structures and unbiased estimators [5]. The orthogonality constraint found here confirms these findings, and imposes even more restrictive constraints. It shows, in addition, that the x-translation and y-rotation, and y-translation and x-rotation, are not decoupled. Furthermore, we have found that rotation around the Z axis can be most easily distinguished from the other motion components. (b) If the error metric of (3) is used in the minimization, the translation is biased toward the viewing direction. This is because the metric is not appropriately normalized [22]. (c) Maybank [17], [18] and Jepson and Heeger [12] established the line constraint, but under more restrictive assumptions. In particular, they showed that for a small field of view, a translation $\mathbf{t}$ far away from the image center and an irregular surface, the function in (3) has its minima along a line in the space of translation directions which passes through the true translation and the viewing direction. Under fixation the viewing direction becomes the image center.

The next two sections provide the analysis for the functions resulting from the minimization of deviation from the epipolar constraint (Sect. 3) and minimization of the number of negative depth values from projections of flow (Section 4).

3 Minimization of Deviation from the Epipolar Constraint

In the analyses throughout this paper we consider a small field of view. Since the quadratic terms in the image coordinates are small relative to the linear and constant terms, we perform the simplification of dropping the quadratic terms.

If we consider a circular aperture of radius e, and set the focal length $f = 1$, we obtain from (5) the function E to be minimized in the form

$$E = \int_{Z=Z_{\min}}^{Z_{\max}} \int_{r=0}^{e} \int_{\phi=0}^{2\pi} \left\{ r \left(\left(\frac{x - x_0}{Z} - \beta_\epsilon + \gamma_\epsilon y + N_x \right) (y - \hat{y}_0) \right. \right.$$
$$\left. \left. - \left(\frac{y - y_0}{Z} + \alpha_\epsilon - \gamma_\epsilon x + N_y \right) (x - \hat{x}_0) \right) \right\} dr \, d\phi \, dZ ,$$

where (r, ϕ) are polar coordinates.

We first study the function E_{NF} resulting from a noise-free flow field. Setting $N_x = N_y = 0$ and substituting for $x = r \cos \varphi$ and $y = r \sin \varphi$ we obtain

$$E_{\mathrm{NF}} = \pi e^2 \left((Z_{\max} - Z_{\min}) \left(\frac{1}{3} \gamma_\epsilon^2 e^4 + \frac{1}{4} \left(\gamma_\epsilon^2 (\hat{x}_0^2 + \hat{y}_0^2) + 6\gamma_\epsilon (\hat{x}_0 \alpha_\epsilon + \hat{y}_0 \beta_\epsilon) + \alpha_\epsilon^2 \right. \right. \right.$$
$$\left. + \beta_\epsilon^2 \right) e^2 + (\hat{x}_0 \alpha_\epsilon + \hat{y}_0 \beta_\epsilon)^2 \Big) + (\ln(Z_{\max}) - \ln(Z_{\min})) \left(\frac{1}{2} (3\gamma_\epsilon (x_{0_\epsilon} y_0 \right.$$
$$- y_{0_\epsilon} x_0) + x_{0_\epsilon} \beta_\epsilon - y_{0_\epsilon} \alpha_\epsilon) e^2 + 2(x_{0_\epsilon} y_0 - y_{0_\epsilon} x_0)(\hat{x}_0 \alpha_\epsilon + \hat{y}_0 \beta_\epsilon) \Big)$$
$$+ \left(\frac{1}{Z_{\min}} - \frac{1}{Z_{\max}} \right) \left(\frac{1}{4} (y_{0_\epsilon}^2 + x_{0_\epsilon}^2) e^2 + (x_{0_\epsilon} y_0 - y_{0_\epsilon} x_0)^2 \right) \Bigg) . \tag{9}$$

To illuminate the behavior of different motion estimation techniques we study the function E_{NF} with regard to the minimization of different sets of errors in the 3D motion parameters.

We start the analysis with techniques which as a first step estimate the rotation. Let us assume a rotational error $(\alpha_\epsilon, \beta_\epsilon, \gamma_\epsilon)$. Solving for $\frac{\partial E_{\mathrm{NF}}}{\partial x_{0_\epsilon}} = 0$ and $\frac{\partial E_{\mathrm{NF}}}{\partial y_{0_\epsilon}} = 0$, we obtain elaborate expressions for $x_{0_\epsilon}, y_{0_\epsilon}$. The translational error depends on all the other parameters, that is, the rotational error, the actual translation, the image size, and the depth interval. All the parameters of the rotational error are coupled with the actual translation.

To understand the behavior of techniques which estimate the translation as a first step, assuming a certain translational error $(x_{0_\epsilon}, y_{0_\epsilon})$, we solve for $\frac{\partial E_{\mathrm{NF}}}{\partial \alpha_\epsilon} = 0$, $\frac{\partial E_{\mathrm{NF}}}{\partial \beta_\epsilon} = 0$ and $\frac{\partial E_{\mathrm{NF}}}{\partial \gamma_\epsilon} = 0$ and obtain

$$\alpha_\epsilon = \frac{y_{0_\epsilon} (\ln(Z_{\max}) - \ln(Z_{\min}))}{Z_{\max} - Z_{\min}}, \quad \beta_\epsilon = \frac{-x_{0_\epsilon} (\ln(Z_{\max}) - \ln(Z_{\min}))}{Z_{\max} - Z_{\min}}, \quad \gamma_\epsilon = 0 .$$
$$\tag{10}$$

From (10) follows the orthogonality constraint, $\alpha_\epsilon / \beta_\epsilon = -x_{0_\epsilon} / y_{0_\epsilon}$.

Often 3D motion estimation is achieved by searching for the correct translation in the two-dimensional space of directions of translation [9], [17]. Such techniques estimate the 3D motion by evaluating for every possible candidate translation a minimization of the error term described in (3) or a similar one with regard to the rotation. To investigate the behavior of such techniques, we ask what direction of translational error minimizes E_{NF} for a given amount of translational error $\sqrt{x_{0_\epsilon}^2 + y_{0_\epsilon}^2}$. Substituting (10) into (9) and expressing the translational error as $x_{0_\epsilon} = K \cos\varphi$ and $y_{0_\epsilon} = K \sin\varphi$, we solve for $\frac{\partial E_{\mathrm{NF}}}{\partial \varphi} = 0$ and obtain: $x_{0_\epsilon} / y_{0_\epsilon} = x_0 / y_0$. This means that for such techniques the estimated translation is described by the line constraint: The projection of the translational error and the projection of the actual translation, and thus the projection of the estimated translation, lie on a line passing through the image center.

To understand the behavior of techniques that minimize simultaneously for both the translation and rotation, we study the subspaces in which E_{NF} changes the least at its absolute minimum; that is, we are interested in the direction of the smallest second derivative at 0, the point where all motion errors are zero. To find this direction, we compute the Hessian at 0, that is, the matrix of the second derivatives of E_{NF} with regard to the five motion error parameters, and compute the eigenvector corresponding to the smallest eigenvalue.

The scaled components of this vector amount to

$$x_{0_\epsilon} = x_0, \quad y_{0_\epsilon} = y_0, \quad \beta_\epsilon = -\alpha_\epsilon \frac{x_0}{y_0}, \quad \gamma_\epsilon = 0,$$

$$\alpha_\epsilon = 2 y_0 Z_{\min} Z_{\max} \left(\ln\left(Z_{\max}\right) - \ln\left(Z_{\min}\right) \right) \Big/ \Big(\left(Z_{\max} - Z_{\min}\right) \left(Z_{\max} Z_{\min} - 1\right)$$

$$+ \Big(\left(Z_{\max} - Z_{\min}\right)^2 \left(Z_{\max} Z_{\min} - 1\right)^2$$

$$+ 4 Z_{\max}^2 Z_{\min}^2 \left(\ln\left(Z_{\max}\right) - \ln\left(Z_{\min}\right) \right)^2 \Big)^{1/2} \Big) .$$

As can be seen, for points defined by this direction, the translational and rotational error are characterized by the orthogonality constraint and the line constraint.

Next we consider noise in the flow measurements. We model the noise (N_x, N_y) as defined in (7) and derive $E(E)$, the expected value of E, which amounts to

$$E(E) = E_{\mathrm{NF}} + \int\limits_{Z=Z_{\min}}^{Z_{\max}} \int\limits_{\phi=0}^{2\pi} \int\limits_{r=0}^{e} \left\{ \left(\sigma_\epsilon^2 \frac{1}{Z^2} \left[(\hat{y}_0 - y)^2 + (\hat{x}_0 - x)^2 \right] \right. \right.$$

$$\left. \left. + \sigma_\delta^2 \left[(\hat{y}_0 - y)^2 + (\hat{x}_0 - x)^2 \right] \right) r \right\} dr \, d\phi \, dZ , \tag{11}$$

and thus

$$E(E) = E_{\mathrm{NF}} + e^2 \pi \left(\sigma_\epsilon^2 \left(\frac{1}{Z_{\min}} - \frac{1}{Z_{\max}} \right) + \sigma_\delta^2 \left(Z_{\max} - Z_{\min} \right) \right) \left(\hat{y}_0^2 + \hat{x}_0^2 + \frac{e^2}{2} \right) .$$

If we fix α_ϵ, β_ϵ, and γ_ϵ, and solve for $\frac{\partial E(E)}{\partial x_{0_\epsilon}} = 0$ and $\frac{\partial E(E)}{\partial y_{0_\epsilon}} = 0$, we obtain as before a complicated relationship between the translational error, the actual translation, and the rotational error.

If we fix x_{0_ϵ} and y_{0_ϵ} and solve for $\frac{\partial E(E)}{\partial \alpha_\epsilon} = 0$, $\frac{\partial E(E)}{\partial \beta_\epsilon} = 0$ and $\frac{\partial E(E)}{\partial \gamma_\epsilon} = 0$, we obtain the same relationship as for noiseless flow described in (10).

This shows that the noise does not alter the expected behavior of techniques which in a first step minimize either the rotation or the translation.

To analyze the behavior of techniques which minimize for all 3D motion parameters, we study the global minimum of $E(E)$. From minimization with regard to the rotational parameters, we obtained (10). Substituting (10) into (11) and solving for $\frac{\partial E(E)}{\partial x_{0_\epsilon}} = 0$ and $\frac{\partial E(E)}{\partial y_{0_\epsilon}} = 0$, we get, in addition,

$$x_{0_\epsilon} = 4x_0(Z_{\max} - Z_{\min})^2 \left(\sigma_\epsilon^2 + \sigma_\delta^2 Z_{\max} Z_{\min}\right) / \qquad y_{0_\epsilon} = x_{0_\epsilon} \frac{y_0}{x_0} .$$
$$\left((Z_{\max} - Z_{\min})^2 \left(4\sigma_\epsilon^2 + 4\sigma_\delta^2 Z_{\max} Z_{\min} + e^2\right)\right.$$
$$\left. - Z_{\max} Z_{\min} e^2 (\ln(Z_{\max}) - \ln(Z_{\min}))^2\right)$$

Thus the absolute minimum of $E(E)$ is to be found in the direction of smallest increase in E_{NF}, and is described by the constraint $\gamma_\epsilon = 0$, by the orthogonality constraint, and by the line constraint. Furthermore, it can be verified from the above equations that $\mathrm{sgn}(x_0) = \mathrm{sgn}(x_{0_\epsilon})$, that is, the estimated FOE is closer to the image center than the actual FOE.

4   Minimization of Negative Depth Volume

In the following analysis we study the function describing the negative depth values geometrically, by means of the negative depth volumes, that is, the points corresponding to negative depth distortion as defined in Sect. 2.3. This allows us to incrementally derive properties of the function without considering it with respect to all its parameters at once. For simplicity, we assume that the FOE and the estimated FOE are inside the image, and we do not consider the exact effects resulting from volumes of negative depth in different directions being outside the field of view.

We first concentrate on the noiseless case. If, as before, we ignore terms quadratic in the image coordinates, the 0 distortion surface becomes

$$(x - \hat{x}_0) n_x + (y - \hat{y}_0) n_y = 0 \qquad (12)$$

and the $-\infty$ distortion surface takes the form

$$(x - x_0)n_x + (y - y_0)n_y + Z\left((-\beta_\epsilon + \gamma_\epsilon y) n_x + (\alpha_\epsilon - \gamma_\epsilon x) n_y\right) = 0 . \qquad (13)$$

The flow directions (n_x, n_y) can alternatively be written as $(\cos\psi, \sin\psi)$, with $\psi \in [0, \pi]$ denoting the angle between $[n_x, n_y]^T$ and the x axis.

To simplify the visualization of the volumes of negative depth in different directions, we perform the following coordinate transformation to align the flow direction with the x axis: for every ψ we rotate the coordinate system by angle ψ, to obtain the new coordinates

$$[x', y']^T = R[x, y]^T, [x_0', y_0']^T = R[x_0, y_0]^T$$
$$[\hat{x}_0', \hat{y}_0']^T = R[\hat{x}_0, \hat{y}_0]^T, [\alpha_\epsilon', \beta_\epsilon']^T = R[\alpha_\epsilon, \beta_\epsilon]^T \quad \text{where} \quad R = \begin{bmatrix} \cos\psi & \sin\psi \\ -\sin\psi & \cos\psi \end{bmatrix}.$$

Thus, (12) and (13) become $(x' - \hat{x}_0') = 0$ and $(x' - x_0') + Z(-\beta_\epsilon' + \gamma_\epsilon y') = 0$.

To investigate techniques which, as a first step, estimate the rotation, we first study the case of $\gamma_\epsilon = 0$ and then extend the analysis to the general case.

If $\gamma_\epsilon = 0$, the volume of negative depth values for every direction ψ lies between the surfaces $(x' - \hat{x}_0') = 0$ and $(x' - x_0') - \beta_\epsilon' Z = 0$.

The equation $(x' - \hat{x}_0') = 0$ describes a plane parallel to the $y'Z$ plane at distance $\hat{x}_0'$ from the origin, and $(x' - x_0') - \beta_\epsilon' Z = 0$ describes a plane parallel to the y' axis of slope $\frac{1}{\beta_\epsilon'}$, which intersects the $x'y'$ plane in the x' coordinate x_0'. Thus we obtain a wedge-shaped volume parallel to the y' axis. Fig. 3 illustrates the volume through a slice parallel to the $x'Z$ plane.

The scene in view extends between the depth values $Z_{\min}$ and $Z_{\max}$. We denote by A_ψ the area of the cross section parallel to the $x'Z$ plane through the negative depth volume in direction ψ.

If x_0' lies between $x_0' + \beta_\epsilon' Z_{\min}$ and $x_0' + \beta_\epsilon' Z_{\max}$, then $A_\psi = \int_{Z=Z_{\min}}^{Z_{\max}} |x_0' - \hat{x}_0' - \beta_\epsilon' Z| dZ$, which amounts to

$$A_\psi = \left| x_{0_\epsilon}' (Z_{\max} + Z_{\min}) + \frac{\beta_\epsilon'}{2} (Z_{\max}{}^2 + Z_{\min}{}^2) + \frac{x_{0_\epsilon}'^2}{\beta_\epsilon} \right|. \tag{14}$$

If we fix β_ϵ' and solve $\partial A_\psi / \partial x_{0_\epsilon}' = 0$ for x_{0_ϵ}' we obtain:

$$x_{0_\epsilon}' = -\frac{\beta_\epsilon'}{2} (Z_{\max} + Z_{\min}), \tag{15}$$

that is, the 0 distortion surface has to intersect the $-\infty$ distortion surface in the middle of the depth interval in the plane $Z = \frac{(Z_{\max} + Z_{\min})}{2}$.

$\frac{x_{0_\epsilon}'}{\beta_\epsilon'}$ depends only on the depth interval, and thus is independent of the direction, ψ. Therefore, the negative depth volume is minimized if (15) holds for every direction. Since $\beta_\epsilon' = \cos\psi\beta_\epsilon - \sin\psi\alpha_\epsilon$ and $x_{0_\epsilon}' = \cos\psi x_{0_\epsilon} + \sin\psi y_{0_\epsilon}$, we obtain $\frac{x_{0_\epsilon}}{y_{0_\epsilon}} = \frac{-\beta_\epsilon}{\alpha_\epsilon}$.

For the case of $\gamma_\epsilon \neq 0$ the same result is true. Before, we found that for a given rotational error $(\alpha_\epsilon, \beta_\epsilon)$ and $\gamma_\epsilon = 0$ the smallest volume of negative depth values is obtained if $\hat{x}_0' = x_0' + \beta_\epsilon' \frac{Z_{\max} + Z_{\min}}{2}$, which we express as $x_0' + \beta_\epsilon' Z_I$. In this case of $\gamma_\epsilon \neq 0$, we study the change of volume V_c as $\hat{x}_0'$ changes from $x_0' + \beta_\epsilon' Z_I$. In particular, a change in the position of $\hat{x}_0'$ to $\hat{x}_0' + d$ causes a change in negative depth volume for any direction which amounts to:

$$V_c = -\text{sgn}(\gamma_\epsilon) \frac{d}{\gamma_\epsilon} (2\beta_\epsilon' (Z_{\max} - Z_{\min}) - (2\beta_\epsilon' Z_I + d)(\ln(Z_{\max}) - \ln(Z_{\min}))).$$
$$\tag{16}$$

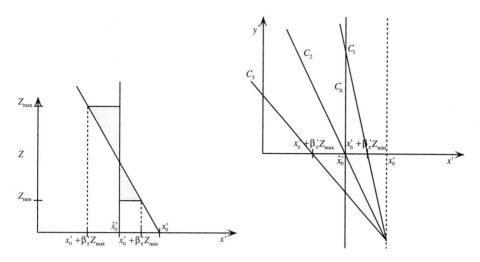

Fig. 3. Slice parallel to the $x'Z$ plane through the volume of negative estimated depth for a single direction

Fig. 4. Slices parallel to the $x'y'$ plane through the 0 distortion surface (C_0) and the $-\infty$ distortion surface at depth values $Z = Z_{\min}$ (C_1), $Z = -\frac{x'_{0_\epsilon}}{\beta'_\epsilon}$ (C_2), and $Z = Z_{\max}$ (C_3)

By solving $\frac{\partial V_\epsilon}{\partial d} = 0$ it is found that the minimum negative depth volume is obtained if $x'_{0_\epsilon} = -\beta'_\epsilon \frac{(Z_{\max} - Z_{\min})}{\ln(Z_{\max}) - \ln(Z_{\min})}$ holds for every direction, which means $\frac{x_{0_\epsilon}}{y_{0_\epsilon}} = -\frac{\beta_\epsilon}{\alpha_\epsilon}$ independent of γ_ϵ.

Next let us consider techniques which first estimate the translation. We fix the translational error. Using Fig. 4, it can be seen that for every direction ψ the area of negative depth values for every depth Z increases as γ_ϵ increases. Thus $\gamma_\epsilon = 0$.

By solving $\frac{\partial A_\psi}{\partial \beta'_\epsilon} = 0$ we obtain

$$x_{0_\epsilon}' = -\beta_\epsilon' f \sqrt{\frac{\left(Z_{\max}^2 + Z_{\min}^2\right)}{2}}, \tag{17}$$

that is, the 0 distortion surface and the $-\infty$ distortion surface intersect in the plane $Z = \sqrt{\frac{(Z_{\max}^2 + Z_{\min}^2)}{2}}$. Again, since $\frac{x'_{0_\epsilon}}{\beta'_\epsilon}$ depends only on the depth interval, the total negative depth volume is minimized if $\frac{x_{0_\epsilon}}{y_{0_\epsilon}} = \frac{-\beta_\epsilon}{\alpha_\epsilon}$. There exists a symmetry in the function defined by the negative depth values that doesn't exist in the function arising from the epipolar constraint. Whether we consider a fixed rotational error or whether we consider a fixed translational error, we obtain the orthogonality constraint.

Next we investigate techniques which minimize both the translation and rotation at once. We know that $\gamma_\epsilon = 0$ and $\frac{x_{0_\epsilon}}{y_{0_\epsilon}} = \frac{-\beta_\epsilon}{\alpha_\epsilon}$. The exact relationship of β'_ϵ to x'_{0_ϵ} is characterized by the locations of local minima of the function

A_ψ, which in the image processing literature are often referred to as "courses." (These are not courses in the topographical sense [13].) To be more precise, we are interested in the local minima of A_ψ in the direction corresponding to the largest second derivative. We compute the largest eigenvalue, λ_1, of the Hessian, H, of A_ψ, that is the matrix of the second derivatives of A_ψ with respect to x'_{0_ϵ} and β'_ϵ, which amounts to $H = \begin{bmatrix} \frac{2}{\beta'_\epsilon} & \frac{-2x_{0_\epsilon}'}{\beta_\epsilon'^2} \\ \frac{-2x_{0_\epsilon}'}{\beta_\epsilon'^2} & \frac{2x_{0_\epsilon}'}{\beta_\epsilon'^3} \end{bmatrix}$ and obtain $\lambda_1 = \frac{2}{\beta'_\epsilon} + \frac{2x_{0_\epsilon}'^2}{\beta_\epsilon'^3}$. The corresponding eigenvector, $\mathbf{e}_1$, is $(\beta'_\epsilon, -x'_{0_\epsilon})$. Solving for $\mathbf{e}_1 \cdot \nabla A_\psi = 0$, we obtain

$$
\begin{aligned}
x'_{0_\epsilon} = \beta'_\epsilon 6^{-2/3} &\left(\left(-18(Z_{\max} + Z_{\min}) \right.\right. \\
&\left. +6^{1/2} \left(54(Z_{\max} + Z_{\min})^2 - (Z_{\max}^2 + Z_{\min}^2 - 4)^3 \right)^{1/2} \right)^{2/3} \\
&\left. -6^{1/3} \left(Z_{\max}^2 + Z_{\min}^2 - 4 \right) \right) \Big/ \left(-18(Z_{\max} + Z_{\min}) \right. \\
&\left. +6^{1/2} \left(54(Z_{\max} + Z_{\min})^2 - (Z_{\max}^2 + Z_{\min}^2 - 4) \right)^{1/2} \right)^{1/3}. \quad (18)
\end{aligned}
$$

Last in our analysis of the noiseless case, we consider the effects due to the finiteness of the aperture. As before, we consider a circular aperture. We assume a certain amount of translational error $\sqrt{x_{0_\epsilon}^2 + y_{0_\epsilon}^2}$, and we seek the direction of translational error that results in the smallest negative depth volume.

Independent of the direction of translation, (18) describes the relationship of x_{0_ϵ} and β_ϵ for the smallest negative depth volume. Substituting (18) into (14), we obtain the cross-section through the negative depth volume as a function of x_{0_ϵ}' and the depth interval. The negative depth volume for every direction ψ amounts to $A_\psi l_\psi$, where l_ψ denotes the average extent of the wedge-shaped negative depth volume in direction ψ. The total negative depth volume is minimized if $\int_0^\pi A_\psi l_\psi d\psi$ is minimized. Considering a circular aperture, this minimization is achieved if the largest A_ψ corresponds to the smallest extent l_ψ and the smallest A_ψ corresponds to the largest l_ψ. This happens when the line constraint holds, that is, $\frac{x_0}{y_0} = \frac{x_{0_\epsilon}}{y_{0_\epsilon}}$, and $\text{sgn}(x_0) = -\text{sgn}(x_{0_\epsilon})$, that is, when the estimated FOE is further from the image center than the actual FOE (see Fig. 5).

It remains to be shown that noise in the flow measurements does not alter the qualitative characteristics of the negative depth volume and thus the results obtained. First we analyze the orthogonality constraint. The analysis for the general case is carried out without considering the size of the aperture; as will be shown, this analysis leads to the orthogonality constraint. To begin, let $\gamma_\epsilon = 0$. Ignoring the image size, we are interested in $E(V)$, the expected value of the

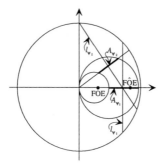

Fig. 5. Cross-sectional view of the wedge-shaped negative depth volumes in a circular aperture. The minimization of the negative depth volume for a given amount of translational error occurs when $\frac{x_0}{y_0} = \frac{x_0'}{y_0'}$. A_{ψ_i} and l_{ψ_i} denote the areas of the cross sections and average extents respectively, for two angles ψ_1 and ψ_2. The two circles bounding A_{ψ_i} are given by the equations $x' = x_{0_\epsilon}' + \beta_\epsilon' Z_{\min}$ and $x' = x_{0_\epsilon}' + \beta_\epsilon' Z_{\max}$

integral of the cross sections A_ψ, which amounts to

$$E(V) = E\left(2 \int\limits_{Z=Z_{\min}}^{Z_{\max}} \left((x_{0_\epsilon} + Z\beta_\epsilon - Z\delta_x - \epsilon_x)^2 + (y_{0_\epsilon} - Z\alpha_\epsilon - Z\delta_y - \epsilon_y)^2\right)^{1/2}\right).$$

Approximating the expectation of the inner integral through a Taylor expansion at 0 up to second order, we obtain an expression for $E(V)$ (see [8]). We are interested in the angle μ between the translational and rotational error which minimizes the negative depth volume. If we align the translational error with the x axis, $y_{0_\epsilon} = 0$, and if we express the rotational error as $(-\beta_\epsilon, \alpha_\epsilon) = (K\cos\mu, K\sin\mu)$, we obtain a new expression for $E(V)$ and, solving for $\frac{\partial E(V)}{\partial \mu} = 0$, we obtain $\mu = 0$, which shows$(x_{0_\epsilon}, y_{0_\epsilon})$ to be perpendicular to $(\alpha_\epsilon, \beta_\epsilon)$, if $\gamma_\epsilon = 0$, for all minimizations considered.

Next, we allow γ_ϵ to be different from zero. For the case of a fixed translational error, again, the volume increases as γ_ϵ increases, and thus the smallest negative depth volume occurs for $\gamma_\epsilon = 0$. For the case of a fixed rotational error we have to extend the previous analysis (studying the change of volume when changing the estimated translation) to noisy motion fields: The $-\infty$ distortion surface becomes $x' - x_0' - Z\beta_\epsilon' + Z\gamma_\epsilon y' + Z\delta' + \epsilon'$ and the 0 distortion surfaces remain the same. Therefore, V_C becomes $-\text{sgn}(\gamma_\epsilon)\frac{d}{\gamma_\epsilon}(2(\beta_\epsilon' - \delta')(Z_{\max} - Z_{\min}) - (2\beta_\epsilon' Z_I + 2\epsilon' + d)(\ln(Z_{\max}) - \ln(Z_{\min})))$, and $E(V_C)$ takes the same form as V_C in (16). We thus obtain the orthogonality constraint for $\gamma_\epsilon \neq 0$.

Finally, we take into account the limited extent of a circular aperture for the case of global minimization. As noise does not change the structure of the iso-distortion surfaces, as shown in Fig. 5, in the presence of noise, too, the smallest negative depth volume is obtained if the FOE and the estimated FOE lie on a line passing through the image center. This proves the orthogonality constraint for the full model as well as the line constraint. The global minimum of the negative depth volume is thus described by the constraint $\gamma_\epsilon = 0$, the orthogonality constraint, the line constraint, and $\text{sgn}(x_0) = -\text{sgn}(x_{0_\epsilon})$.

5   Conclusions and Future Directions

The goal of this study was to uncover inherent ambiguities in the computation of structure from motion using a geometric methodology that allowed us to identify specific biases in a variety of published 3D motion estimation algorithms. These algorithms attempt to estimate 3D motion from multiple views by optimizing a criterion or an objective function. The question we asked was: If an optimization technique provides an answer, i.e., it yields a point satisfying the properties of a global minimum, have we then computed the correct answer for the 3D motion parameters? The answer is, in general, no. We arrived at this result by studying the topographic structure of the objective functions to be minimized. This topographic structure reveals how rotation and translation can be confused while still satisfying the objective optimization criterion, both in the presence of noise in the image measurements and in the absence of noise.

The nature of the present study is such that it allows us to draw a number of general conclusions that are of interest to computer vision practitioners and developers of algorithms for recovering the rigid transformation relating different views: (a) Algorithms based on the epipolar constraint that first recover the rotation and subsequently, on the basis of the rotational result, recover the translation, should in general be avoided, because the dependence of the error on the actual translation, as well as the form of that dependence, may result in unpredictable results. (b) Algorithms based on the epipolar constraint that first estimate the translation or estimate all parameters simultaneously, and all possible direct algorithms, have solutions at which the errors satisfy the orthogonality constraint, whose consequences are more predictable. Actually, algorithms that estimate all parameters together, such as those based on estimating the fundamental matrix [16], yield solutions for which the error satisfies both the orthogonality and line constraints. This means that even if solutions are obtained with some error, a number of statistical properties of this error are available, making further developments possible. (c) The line constraint shows that the tilt of the FOE (or epipole) is more reliably estimated than its slant. (d) Epipolar minimization based on correspondence or optic flow turns out to have the same properties as direct algorithms that minimize the amount of negative depth based on normal flow.

References

1. G. Adiv. Determining 3D motion and structure from optical flow generated by several moving objects. *IEEE Transactions on Pattern Analysis and Machine Intelligence*, 7:384–401, 1985.
2. G. Adiv. Inherent ambiguities in recovering 3-D motion and structure from a noisy flow field. *IEEE Transactions on Pattern Analysis and Machine Intelligence*, 11:477–489, 1989.

3. A. Bruss and B. K. P. Horn. Passive navigation. *Computer Vision, Graphics, and Image Processing*, 21:3–20, 1983.

4. W. Burger and B. Bhanu. Estimating 3-D egomotion from perspective image sequences. *IEEE Transactions on Pattern Analysis and Machine Intelligence*, 12:1040–1058, 1990.

5. K. Daniilidis. *On the Error Sensitivity in the Recovery of Object Descriptions*. PhD thesis, Department of Informatics, University of Karlsruhe, Germany, 1992. In German.

6. K. Daniilidis and M. E. Spetsakis. Understanding noise sensitivity in structure from motion. In Y. Aloimonos, editor, *Visual Navigation: From Biological Systems to Unmanned Ground Vehicles*, chapter 4. Lawrence Erlbaum Associates, Hillsdale, NJ, 1997.

7. C. Fermüller. Passive navigation as a pattern recognition problem. *International Journal of Computer Vision*, 14:147–158, 1995.

8. C. Fermüller and Y. Aloimonos. What is computed by structure from motion algorithms? Technical Report CAR-TR-863, Center for Automation Research, University of Maryland, 1997.

9. D. J. Heeger and A. D. Jepson. Subspace methods for recovering rigid motion I: Algorithm and implementation. *International Journal of Computer Vision*, 7:95–117, 1992.

10. B. K. P. Horn. Relative orientation. *International Journal of Computer Vision*, 4:59–78, 1990.

11. B. K. P. Horn and E. J. Weldon. Computationally efficient methods for recovering translational motion. In *Proc. International Conference on Computer Vision*, pages 2–11, 1987.

12. A. D. Jepson and D. J. Heeger. Subspace methods for recovering rigid motion II: Theory. Technical Report RBCV-TR-90-36, University of Toronto, 1990.

13. J. J. Koenderink and A. J. van Doorn. Two-plus-one-dimensional differential geometry. *Pattern Recognition Letters*, 15:439–443, 1994.

14. H. C. Longuet-Higgins. A computer algorithm for reconstructing a scene from two projections. *Nature*, 293:133–135, 1981.

15. H. C. Longuet-Higgins and K. Prazdny. The interpretation of a moving retinal image. *Proc. Royal Society, London B*, 208:385–397, 1980.

16. Q.-T. Luong and O. D. Faugeras. The fundamental matrix: Theory, algorithms, and stability analysis. *International Journal of Computer Vision*, 17:43–75, 1996.

17. S. J. Maybank. Algorithm for analysing optical flow based on the least-squares method. *Image and Vision Computing*, 4:38–42, 1986.

18. S. J. Maybank. *A Theoretical Study of Optical Flow*. PhD thesis, University of London, England, 1987.

19. K. Prazdny. Egomotion and relative depth map from optical flow. *Biological Cybernetics*, 36:87–102, 1980.

20. K. Prazdny. Determining instantaneous direction of motion from optical flow generated by a curvilinear moving observer. *Computer Vision, Graphics, and Image Processing*, 17:238–248, 1981.

21. J. H. Rieger and D. T. Lawton. Processing differential image motion. *Journal of the Optical Society of America A*, 2:354–359, 1985.

22. M. E. Spetsakis. Models of statistical visual motion estimation. *Computer Vision, Graphics, and Image Processing*, 60:300–312, 1994.

23. J. I. Thomas, A. Hanson, and J. Oliensis. Understanding noise: The critical role of motion error in scene reconstruction. In *Proc. DARPA Image Understanding Workshop*, pages 691–695, 1993.

Stereo Vision and Calibration II

Complete Dense Stereovision Using Level Set Methods

Olivier Faugeras[1] and Renaud Keriven[2]

[1] INRIA, France and MIT AI-Lab, USA (`Olivier.Faugeras@inria.fr`)
[2] CERMICS-ENPC, France (`Renaud.Keriven@cermics.enpc.fr`)

Abstract. We present a novel geometric approach for solving the stereo problem for an arbitrary number of images (greater than or equal to 2). It is based upon the definition of a variational principle that must be satisfied by the surfaces of the objects in the scene and their images. The Euler-Lagrange equations which are deduced from the variational principle provide a set of PDE's which are used to deform an initial set of surfaces which then move towards the objects to be detected. The level set implementation of these PDE's potentially provides an efficient and robust way of achieving the surface evolution and to deal automatically with changes in the surface topology during the deformation, i.e. to deal with multiple objects. Results of an implementation of our theory also dealing with occlusion and vibility are presented on synthetic and real images.

1 Introduction and preliminaries

The idea that is put forward in this paper is that the methods of curve and surface evolutions which have been developed in computer vision under the name of snakes [19] and then reformulated by Caselles, Kimmel and Sapiro [1] and Kichenassamy et al. [21] in the context of PDE driven evolving curves can be used effectively for solving 3D vision problems such as stereo and motion analysis.

As a first step in this direction we present a mathematical analysis of the stereo problem in this context as well as a partial implementation. The problem of curve evolution driven by a PDE has been recently studied both from the theoretical standpoint [13, 14, 26] and from the viewpoint of implementation [23, 28, 29] with the development of level set methods that can efficiently and robustly solve those PDE's. A nice recent exposition of the level set methods and of many of their applications can be found in [27]. The problem of surface evolution has been less touched upon even though some preliminary results have been obtained [29, 2]. The path we will follow to attack the stereo problem from that angle is, not surprisingly, a variational one. In a nutshell, we will describe the stereo problem (to be defined more precisely later) as the minimisation of a functional (we will explore several such functionals) with respect to some parameters (describing the geometry of the scene); we will compute the Euler-Lagrange equations of this functional, thereby obtaining a set of necessary conditions, in effect a set of partial differential equations, which we will solve as a time evolution problem by a level set method. Stereo is a problem that has received considerable attention for decades in the psychophysical, neurophysiological and, more recently, in the computer vision literatures. It is impossible to cite all the published work here, we will simply refer the reader to some basic books on the subject [18, 15–17, 7]. To explain the problem of stereo from the computational standpoint, we will refer the reader to Fig. 1.a. Two, may be more, images of the world are taken simultaneously. The problem is, given those images, to recover the geometry of the scene. Given the fact that the relative positions and orientations and the internal parameters of the cameras are known which we will assume in this article (the cameras are then said to be calibrated [7]), the problem is essentially (but not only) one of establishing correspondences between the views: one talks about the matching problem. The matching problem is usually solved by setting up a matching functional for which one then tries to find extrema. Once a pixel in view i has been identified as being the image of the same scene point as another pixel in view j, the 3D point can then be reconstructed by intersecting the corresponding optical rays (see Fig. 1.a again). In order to go any further,

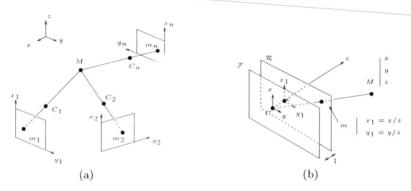

(a)   (b)

Fig. 1. (a) The multicamera stereo vision problem is, given a pixel m_1 in image 1, to find the corresponding pixel m_2 in image 2, ... , the corresponding pixel m_n in image n, i.e. the ones which are the images of the same 3D point M. Once such a correspondence has been established, the point M can be reconstructed by intersecting the optical rays $\langle m_i, C_i \rangle$, $i = 1, \cdots, n$. (b) The focal plane (x, y) is parallel to the retinal plane (x_1, y_1) and at a distance of 1 from it.

we need to be a little more specific about the process of image formation. We will assume here that the cameras perform a perspective projection of the 3D world on the retinal plane as shown in Fig. 1.b. The optical center, noted C in the figure, is the center of projection and the image of the 3D point M is the pixel m at the intersection of the optical ray $\langle C, m \rangle$ and the retinal plane $\mathcal{R}$. As described in many recent papers in computer vision, this operation can be conveniently described in projective geometry by a matrix operation. The projective coordinates of the pixel m (a 3×1 vector) are obtained by applying a 3×4 matrix $\mathbf{P}_1$ to the projective coordinates of the 3D point M (a 4×1 vector).

This matrix is called the perspective projection matrix. If we express the matrix $\mathbf{P}_1$ in the coordinate system (C, x, y, z) shown in the Fig. 1.b, it then takes a very simple form:

$$\mathbf{P}_1 = [\mathbf{I}_3\,\mathbf{0}]$$

where $\mathbf{I}_3$ is the 3×3 identity matrix. If we now move the camera by applying to it a rigid transformation described by the rotation matrix $\mathbf{R}$ and the translation vector $\mathbf{t}$, the expression of the matrix $\mathbf{P}$ changes accordingly and becomes:

$$\mathbf{P}_2 = [\mathbf{R}^T\,-\,\mathbf{R}^T\mathbf{t}]$$

With these preliminaries in mind we are ready to proceed with our program which we will do by progressing along two related axes. The first axis is that of object complexity, the second axis is that of matching functional complexity. They are related in the sense that an increase along one axis usually implies a corresponding increase along the other. We start the paper with a short comparison of our work to previous work. In the next two sections we will consider a simple object model which is well adapted to the binocular stereo case where it is natural to consider that the objects in the scene can be considered mathematically as forming the graph of an unknown smooth function (the depth function in the language of computer vision). In Sect. 3 we consider an extremely simplified matching criterion which will allow us to convey to the reader the flavor of the ideas that we are trying to push here. We then move in Sect. 4 to a more sophisticated albeit classical matching criterion which is at the heart of the techniques known in computer vision as correlation based methods. Within the framework of this model we study two related shape models. In the Section 5 we introduce a more general shape model in which we do not assume anymore that the objects are the graph of a function and model them as a set of general smooth surfaces in three space. The next step would of course be to relax the smoothness assumption but we will postpone this to a future paper.

Let us decide on some definitions and notations. Images are denoted by I_k, k taking some integer values which indicate the camera with which the image has been acquired. They are considered as smooth (i.e. C^2, twice continuously differentiable) functions of pixels m_k whose coordinates are defined in some orthonormal image coordinate systems (x_k, y_k) which are assumed to be known. We note $I_k(m_k)$ or $I_k(x_k, y_k)$ the intensity value in image k at pixel m_k. We will use the first and second order derivatives of these functions, i.e. the gradient ∇I_k, a 2×1 vector equal to $[\frac{\partial I_k}{\partial x_k}, \frac{\partial I_k}{\partial y_k}]^T$, and the Hessian $\mathbf{H}_k$, a 2×2 symmetric matrix. The pixels in the images are considered as functions of the 3D geometry of the scene, i.e. of some 3D point M on the surface of an object in the scene, and of the unit normal vector $\mathbf{N}$ to this surface. Vectors and matrixes will generally be indicated in boldfaces, e.g. $\mathbf{x}$. The dot or inner product of two vectors $\mathbf{x}$ and $\mathbf{y}$ is denoted by $\mathbf{x} \cdot \mathbf{y}$. The cross-product of two 3×1 vectors $\mathbf{x}$ and $\mathbf{y}$ is noted $\mathbf{x} \times \mathbf{y}$. Partial derivatives will be indicated either using the ∂ symbol, e.g. $\frac{\partial f}{\partial \mathbf{x}}$, or as a lower index, e.g. $f_{\mathbf{x}}$.

2   Comparison with previous work

Our approach is an extension of previous work by Robert et al. and Robert and Deriche, [25, 24], where the idea of using a variational approach for solving the stereo problem was proposed first in the classical Tikhonov regularization framework and then by using regularization functions more proper to preserve discontinuities. Our work can be seen as a 3D extension of the approach proposed in [5] where we limit ourselves to the binocular case, to finding cross-sections of the objects with a fixed plane, and do not take into account the orientation of the tangent plane to the object.

Our work is also connected to that of Fua and Leclerc [12] and Fua [11] who have developed techniques and programs to integrate multiple stereo views. They use meshes and/or systems of particles to represent the surfaces of the objects and deform the mesh or move the particles to minimize a criterion that is not unlike the one we are using. The problems with this approach are well-known and described for example in [23, 27]: vertices of the mesh or particles tend to cluster in areas of high curvature and the evolution may become unstable; moreover, the representation of complicated shapes with several connected components or nonzero genus as in the two tori of figure 4. The level set methods which we use to implement the evolution of the objects' surface was invented precisely because it solves elegantly those two problems [23, 27]. Another main departure from Fua and Leclerc's approach is the use of a partial differential equation to drive this evolution. This puts our method on firmer mathematical grounds. We can potentially derive proofs of uniqueness of solutions in various functional spaces as well, prove convergence to the real scene as in [2] as well as benefit from the power of the level set method in our implementation.

There is also a connection to the work of Takeo Kanade and colleagues [22]. They build 3-D models of scenes from multiple cameras by merging the depth maps from different cameras into a common volumetric space. Just like in the case of the previous authors, we believe that their method suffers from the use of a mesh-like representation of the surface of the objects of the scene which makes merging difficult and unstable, the representation of objects with nonzero genus problematical and does not allow set the stage for proofs of correctness of the algorithm.

3   A simple object and matching model

This section introduces in a simplified framework some of the basic ideas of this paper. We assume, and it is the first important assumption, that the objects which are being imaged by the stereo rig (a binocular stereo system) are modelled as the graph of an unknown smooth function $z = f(x, y)$ defined in the first retinal plane which we are trying to estimate. A point M of coordinates $[x, y, f(x, y)]^T$ is seen as two pixels m_1 and m_2 whose coordinates $(g_i(x, y), h_i(x, y)), i = 1, 2$, can be easily computed as functions of $x, y, f(x, y)$ and the coefficients of the perspective projection matrices $\mathbf{P}_1$ and $\mathbf{P}_2$. Let I_1

and I_2 be the intensities of the two images. Assuming, and it is the second important assumption, that the objects are perfectly Lambertian, we must have $I_1(m_1) = I_2(m_2)$ for all pixels in correspondence, i.e. which are the images of the same 3D point.

This reasoning immediately leads to the variational problem of finding a suitable function f defined, to be rigorous, over an open subset of the focal plane of the first camera which minimizes the following integral:

$$C_1(f) = \int \int (I_1(m_1(x,y)) - I_2(m_2(x,y)))^2 dxdy \qquad (1)$$

computed over the previous open subset. Our first variational problem is thus to find a function f in some suitable functional space that minimizes the error measure $C_1(f)$. The corresponding Euler-Lagrange equation is readily obtained:

$$(I_1 - I_2)(\nabla I_1 \cdot \frac{\partial \mathbf{m}_1}{\partial f} - \nabla I_2 \cdot \frac{\partial \mathbf{m}_2}{\partial f}) = 0 \qquad (2)$$

The values of $\frac{\partial \mathbf{m}_1}{\partial f}$ and $\frac{\partial \mathbf{m}_2}{\partial f}$ are functions of f which are easily computed. The terms involving I_1 and I_2 are computed from the images. In order to solve (2) one can adopt a number of strategies.

One standard strategy is to consider that the function f is also a function $f(x, y, t)$ of time and to solve the following PDE:

$$f_t = \varphi(f)$$

where $\varphi(f)$ is equal to the left hand side of (2), with some initial condition $f(x, y, 0) = f_0(x, y)$. We thus see appear for the first time the idea that the shape of the objects in the scene, described by the function f, is obtained by allowing a surface of equation $z = f(x, y, t)$ to evolve over time, starting from some initial configuration $z = f(x, y, 0)$, according to some PDE, to hopefully converge toward the real shape of the objects in the scene when time goes to infinity. This convergence is driven by the data, i.e. the images, as expressed by the error criterion (1) or the Euler-Lagrange term $\varphi(f)$. It is known that if care is not taken, for example by adding a regularizing term to (1), the solution f is likely not to be smooth and therefore any noise in the images may cause the solution to differ widely from the real objects. This is more or less the approach taken in [25, 24]. We will postpone the solution of this problem until Sect. 5 and in fact solve it differently from the usual way which consists in adding a regularization term to $C_1(f)$.

Another strategy is to apply the level set idea [23, 27]. Consider the family of surfaces S defined by $\mathbf{S}(x, y, t) = [x, y, f(x, y, t)]^T$. The parameters x and y are used to parameterize the surface, t is the time. The unit normal to this surface is the vector $\mathbf{N} = \pm \frac{1}{\sqrt{1+|\nabla f|^2}}[\nabla f^T, 1]^T$, the velocity vector is $\mathbf{S}_t = [0, 0, f_t]^T$ and hence the evolution of the surface can be written

$$\mathbf{S}_t = \frac{\varphi(f)}{\sqrt{1+|\nabla f|^2}} \mathbf{N} \qquad (3)$$

This expression of the evolution of the surface directly leads to a straightforward application of the level set methods. Consider a function $u(x, y, z, t)$ whose zero level set is the surface S, i.e. at each time instant t, the set of points (x, y, z) such that $u(x, y, z, t) = 0$ is identical to the surface S. Note that the function u can be considered a temporal sequence of volumetric images. The next question is, given the fact that the time evolution of S is given by (3), what should the evolution of u be? This question has been answered in [23] and the answer is:

$$u_t = \frac{\varphi(f)}{\sqrt{1 + |\nabla f|^2}} \; |\nabla u|$$

where ∇u is the gradient of u with respect to the first three variables. There are a couple of subtle points here. The first is that the level set methods have been designed for closed manifolds (curves or surfaces, say) but here the surface S is not closed in general, being a graph. This problem can be solved, as described for example in [3, 27]. The second point is that the coefficient of the term $|\nabla u|$ in the previous equation is defined only on the surface S and not in the whole (x, y, z) volume. But this term is needed at all points to solve for u.

We will not delve further into the last issue because it will be solved as we proceed toward better models.

4   A better functional for matching

It is clear that the error measure (1) is a bit simple for practical applications. We can extend in at least two ways. The first is to replace the difference of intensities by a measure of correlation, the hypothesis being that the scene is made of fronto parallel planes. The second is to relax this hypothesis and to take into account the orientation of the tangent plane to the surface of the object. In the first case we move along the matching criterion axis, in the second we move both along the shape and matching criterion complexity axes.

We explore those two avenues in the next sections.

4.1   Fronto parallel correlation functional

To each pair of values (x, y), corresponds a 3D point M, $\mathbf{M} = [x, y, f(x, y)]^T$ which defines two image points m_1 and m_2 as in the previous section. We can then classically define the unnormalized cross-correlation between I_1 and I_2 at the pixels m_1 and m_2. We note this cross-correlation $\langle I_1, I_2 \rangle (f, x, y)$ to acknowledge its analogy with an inner product and the fact that it depends on M:

$$\langle I_1, I_2 \rangle (f, x, y) = \frac{1}{4pq} \int_{-p}^{+p} \int_{-q}^{+q} (I_1(m_1 + m) - \overline{I_1}(m_1)) \tag{4}$$
$$(I_2(m_2 + m) - \overline{I_2}(m_2))dm,$$

equation where the averages $\overline{I_1}$ and $\overline{I_2}$ are classically defined as:

$$\overline{I_k}(m_k) = \frac{1}{4pq} \int_{-p}^{+p} \int_{-q}^{+q} I_k(m_k + m')dm' \quad k = 1, 2 \tag{5}$$

Finally, we note $\mid I \mid^2$ the quantity $\langle I, I \rangle$. Note that $\langle I_1, I_2 \rangle = \langle I_2, I_1 \rangle$.

To simplify notations we write $\int^*$ instead of $\frac{1}{4pq} \int_{-p}^{+p} \int_{-q}^{+q}$ and define a matching functional which is the integral with respect to x and y of minus the normalized cross-correlation score:

$$C_2(f) = - \int \int \frac{\langle I_1, I_2 \rangle}{\mid I_1 \mid \cdot \mid I_2 \mid} dxdy = \int \int {}_2\Phi(f, x, y)dxdy \tag{6}$$

the integral being computed, as in the previous section, over an open set of the focal plane of the first camera. The functional ${}_2\Phi$ is $-\frac{\langle I_1, I_2 \rangle}{\mid I_1 \mid \cdot \mid I_2 \mid}(f, x, y)$. This quantity varies between -1 and +1, -1 indicating the maximum correlation. We have to compute its derivative with respect to f in order to obtain the Euler-Lagrange equation of the problem. The computations are simple but a little fastidious. They can be found in [8]. We can then proceed to solve the Euler-Lagrange equation as described in the previous section. But we will not pursue this task and explore rather a better functional.

4.2 Taking into account the tangent plane to the object

We now take into account the fact that the rectangular window centered at m_2 is not rectangular but is the image in the second retina of the backprojection on the tangent plane to the object at the point $M = (x, y, f(x, y))$ of the rectangular window centered at m_1 (see Fig. 2.a). In esssence, we approximate the object S in a neighbourhood of M by its tangent plane but without assuming, as in the previous section, that this plane is fronto parallel, and in fact also that the retinal planes of the two cameras are identical. Let us first study the correspondence induced by this plane between the two images.

Image correspondences induced by a plane Let us consider a plane of equation $\mathbf{N}^T \mathbf{M} - d = 0$ in the coordinate system of the first camera. d is the algebraic distance of the origin of coordinates to that plane and $\mathbf{N}$ is a unit vector normal to the plane. This plane induces a projective transformation between the two image planes. This correspondence plays an essential role in the sequel.

To see why we obtain a projective transformation, let M be a 3D point in that plane, $\mathbf{M}_1$ and $\mathbf{M}_2$ be the two 3D vectors representing this point in the coordinate systems attached to the first and second cameras, respectively. These two 3×1 vectors are actually coordinate vectors of the two pixels m_1 and m_2 seen as projective points (see Sect. 1). Furthermore, they are related by the following equation:

$$\mathbf{M}_2 = \mathbf{R}^T(\mathbf{M}_1 - \mathbf{t})$$

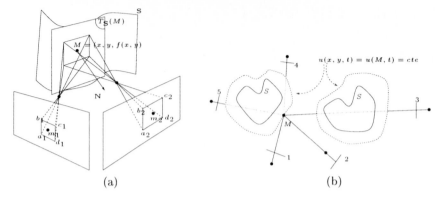

(a)   (b)

Fig. 2. (a) The square window (a_1, b_1, c_1, d_1) in the first image is back projected onto the tangent plane to the object S at point M and reprojected in the retinal plane of the second camera where it is generally not square. The observation is that the distortion between (a_1, b_1, c_1, d_1) and (a_2, b_2, c_2, d_2) can be described by a collineation which is function of M and the normal $\mathbf{N}$ to the surface of the object. (b) Occlusion is taken into account: only the cameras viewing the point according to the current surface are used,thus avoiding any irrelevant correlation.

Since M belongs to the plane, $\mathbf{N}^T \mathbf{M}_1 = d$, and we have:

$$\mathbf{M}_2 = (\mathbf{R}^T - \frac{\mathbf{R}^T \mathbf{t} \mathbf{N}^T}{d}) \mathbf{M}_1$$

which precisely expresses the fact that the two pixels m_1 and m_2 are related by a collineation, or projective transformation K. The 3×3 matrix representing this collineation is $(\mathbf{R}^T - \frac{\mathbf{R}^T \mathbf{t} \mathbf{N}^T}{d})$. This transformation is one to one except when the plane goes through one of the two optical centers when it becomes degenerate. We will assume that it does not go through either one of those two points and since the matrix of K is only defined up to a scale factor we might as well take it equal to:

$$\mathbf{K} = d\mathbf{R}^T - \mathbf{R}^T \mathbf{t} \mathbf{N}^T \tag{7}$$

The new criterion and its Euler-Lagrange equations   We just saw that a plane induces a collineation between the two retinal planes. This is the basis of the method proposed in [5] although for a very different purpose. The window alluded to in the introduction to this section is therefore the image by the collineation induced by the tangent plane of the rectangular window in image 1. This collineation is a function of the point M and of the normal to the object at M. It is therefore a function of f and ∇f that we denote by K. It satisfies the condition $K(m_1) = m_2$. The inner product (4) must be modified as follows:

$$\langle I_1, I_2 \rangle (f, \nabla f, x, y) = \int^* (I_1(m_1+m) - \overline{I_1}(m_1))(I_2(K(m_1+m)) - \overline{I_2}(m_2)) dm, \tag{8}$$

Note that, the definition of $\langle I_1, I_2 \rangle$ is no longer symmetric, because of K. In order to make it symmetric, we should define it as:

$$\langle I_1, I_2 \rangle (f, \nabla f, x, y) = \int^* (I_1(m_1 + m) - \overline{I_1}(m_1))(I_2(K(m_1 + m)) - \overline{I_2}(m_2))dm$$

$$+ \int^* (I_1(K^{-1}(m_2 + m')) - \overline{I_1}(m_1))(I_2(m_2 + m') - \overline{I_2}(m_2))dm' \quad (9)$$

The definition (5) of $\overline{I_1}$ (resp. of $\overline{I_2}$) is not modified in the first (resp. second) integral of the right hand side, that of $\overline{I_2}$ (resp. of $\overline{I_1}$), on the other hand, must be modified as follows:

$$\overline{I_2}(m_2) = \int^* I_2(K(m_1 + p))dp, \quad \overline{I_1}(m_1) = \int^* I_1(K^{-1}(m_2 + p'))dp' \quad (10)$$

Since this new definition does not modify the fundamental ideas exposed in this paper but makes the computations significantly more complex, we will assume the definition (8) in what follows, acknowledging the fact that in practice (9) should be used.

We now want to minimize the following error measure:

$$C_3(f, \nabla f) = - \int \int {}_3\Phi(f, \nabla f, x, y)dxdy, \quad {}_3\Phi = \frac{\langle I_1, I_2 \rangle}{|I_1| \cdot |I_2|}(f, \nabla f, x, y) \quad (11)$$

Since the functional ${}_3\Phi$ now depends on both f and ∇f, its Euler-Lagrange equations have the form ${}_3\Phi_f - div({}_3\Phi_{\nabla f}) = 0$. We must therefore recompute ${}_3\Phi_f$ to take into account the new dependency of K upon f and compute ${}_3\Phi_{\nabla f}$.

We will simplify the computations by assuming that the collineation K can be well approximated by an affine transformation. Because of the condition $K(m_1) = m_2$, this transformation can be written:

$$K(m_1 + m) \approx m_2 + \mathbf{A}m$$

where $\mathbf{A}$ is a 2×2 matrix depending upon f and ∇f.

In practice this approximation is often sufficient and we will assume that it is valid in what follows. We will not pursue this computation (see [8] for details) since we present in Sect. 5 a more elaborate model that encompasses this one and for which we will perform the corresponding computation.

5   An even more refined model

In this section we consider the case when the objects in the scene are not defined as the graph of a function of x and y as in the previous sections, but as the zero level set of a function $\hat{u} : \mathbf{R}^3 \to \mathbf{R}$ which we assume to be smooth, i.e. C^2. The coordinates (x, y, z) of the points in the scene which are on the surface of the objects present are thus defined by the equation $\hat{u}(x, y, z) = 0$. This approach has at least two advantages. First, by relaxing the graph assumption, it potentially allows us to use an arbitrary number of cameras to analyze the scene and second, it leads very naturally to an implementation of a surface evolution scheme through the level set method as follows.

Let us consider a family of smooth surfaces $S : (v, w, t) \to \mathbf{S}(v, w, t)$ where (v, w) parameterize the surface and t is the time. It is in general not possible to find a single mapping S from $\mathbf{R}^2$ to $\mathbf{R}^3$ that describes the entire surface of the objects (think of the sphere for example where we need at least two) but we do not have to worry about this since our results will in fact be independent of the parametrization we choose. The objects in the scene correspond to a surface $\hat{\mathbf{S}}(v, w)$ and our goal is, starting from an initial surface $\mathbf{S}_0(v, w)$, to derive a partial differential equation

$$\mathbf{S}_t = \beta \mathbf{N}, \tag{12}$$

where $\mathbf{N}$ is the inner unit normal to the surface, which, when solved with initial conditions $\mathbf{S}(v, w, 0) = \mathbf{S}_0(v, w)$, will yield a solution that closely approximates $\hat{\mathbf{S}}(v, w)$. The function β is determined by the matching functional that we minimize in order to solve the stereo problem. We define such a functional in the next paragraph. An interesting point is that the evolution equation (12) can be solved using the level set method which has the advantage of coping automatically with several objects in the scene. In detail, the surfaces $\mathbf{S}$ are at each time instant the zero level sets of a function $u : \mathbf{R}^4 \to \mathbf{R}$:

$$u(\mathbf{S}, t) = 0$$

Taking derivatives with respect to v, w, t, noticing that $\mathbf{N}$ can be chosen such that $\mathbf{N} = -\frac{\nabla u}{|\nabla u|}$, where ∇ is the gradient operator for the first three coordinates of u, one finds easily that the evolution equation for u is:

$$u_t = \beta \, | \, \nabla u \, | \tag{13}$$

Using the same ideas as in the section 4.2, we can define the following error measure:

$$C_4(\mathbf{S}, \mathbf{N}) = \int \int \, _4\Phi(\mathbf{S}, \mathbf{N}, v, w) d\sigma, \quad _4\Phi = - \sum_{i,j=1, i \neq j}^{n} \frac{1}{|\, I_i \,| \cdot |\, I_j \,|} \langle I_i, I_j \rangle \tag{14}$$

In this equation, the indexes i and j range from 1 to n, the number of views. In practice it is often not necessary to consider all possible pairs but it does not change our analysis of the problem. In (14), the integration is carried over with respect to the area element $d\sigma$ on the surface S. With the previous notations, we have

$$d\sigma = |\, \mathbf{S}_v \times \mathbf{S}_w \,| \, dv dw = h(v, w) dv dw$$

$d\sigma$ plays the role of $dx \, dy$ in our previous analysis, $\mathbf{S}$ that of f, and $\mathbf{N} = \frac{\mathbf{S}_v \times \mathbf{S}_w}{|\mathbf{S}_v \times \mathbf{S}_w|}$, the unit normal vector to the surface S, that of ∇f.

Note that this is a significant departure from what we had before because we are multiplying our previous normalized cross-correlation score with the term

$| \mathbf{S}_v \times \mathbf{S}_w |$. This has two dramatic consequences: (i) It automatically regularizes the variational problem like in the geodesic snakes approach [1], and (ii) it makes the problem intrinsic, i.e. independent of the parametrization of the objects in the scene.

Note also that each integral that appears in (14) is only computed for those points of the surface S which are visible in the two concerned images. Thus, *visibility and occlusion* are modelled in this approach (fig. 2.b). This is essential not to pretend the surface is at a wrong place when it actually is at the right place.

The rest of the derivation is extremely similar, although technically more complicated, to the derivations in the previous section, namely we write the Euler-Lagrange equations of the variational problem (14), consider their component β along the normal to the surface, set up a surface evolution equation (12) and implement it by a level-set method. This is all pretty straightforward except for the announced result that the resulting value of β is *intrinsic* and does not depend upon the parametrization of the surface S.

We will in fact prove a more general result. Let $\Phi : \mathbf{R}^3 \times \mathbf{R}^3 \longrightarrow S_2$ be a smooth function of class at least C^2 defined on the product of the three-dimensional space $\mathbf{R}^3$ where the surface S "lives" and the two-dimensional unit-radius sphere S_2 of $\mathbf{R}^3$ where the unit normal $\mathbf{N}$ to the surface S "lives". We note $\Phi(\mathbf{X}, \mathbf{N})$ the value of Φ at the point $\mathbf{X}$ of $\mathbf{R}^3$ and the point $\mathbf{N}$ of S_2. Let us now consider the following error measure:

$$C(\mathbf{S}, \mathbf{S}_v, \mathbf{S}_w) = \int \int \Phi(\mathbf{S}(v, w), \mathbf{N}(v, w)) h(v, w) dv \, dw \qquad (15)$$

where the integral is taken over the surface S.

We prove in [8] the following theorem:

Theorem 1. *Under the assumptions of smoothness that have been made for the function Φ and the surface S, the component of the Euler-Lagrange equations for criterion (15) along the normal to the surface is the product of h with an intrinsic factor, i.e. which does not depend upon the parametrization (v, w). Furthermore, this component is equal to*

$$h(\Phi_\mathbf{X} \mathbf{N} - 2H(\Phi - \Phi_\mathbf{N} \mathbf{N}) + Trace((\Phi_{\mathbf{XN}})_{T_S} + d\mathbf{N} \circ (\Phi_{\mathbf{NN}})_{T_S})) \qquad (16)$$

where all quantities are evaluated at the point $\mathbf{S}$ of normal $\mathbf{N}$ of the surface, T_S is the tangent plane to the surface at the point $\mathbf{S}$. $d\mathbf{N}$ is the differential of the Gauss map of the surface, H is its mean curvature, $\Phi_{\mathbf{XN}}$ and $\Phi_{\mathbf{NN}}$ are the second order derivatives of Φ, $(\Phi_{\mathbf{XN}})_{T_S}$ and $(\Phi_{\mathbf{NN}})_{T_S}$ their restrictions to the tangent plane T_S of the surface at the point S.

The symbol $\circ$ represents the composition of applications. Note that the error criterion (14) is of the form (15) if we define Φ to be

$$-\sum_{i,j=1, i \neq j}^{n} \frac{1}{| I_i | \cdot | I_j |} \langle I_i, I_j \rangle$$

According to the theorem 1, in order to compute the velocity β along the normal in the evolution equations (12) or (13) we only need to compute Φ_S, Φ_N, Φ_{SN} and Φ_{NN} as well as the second order intrinsic differential properties of the surface S. Using the fact that the function Φ is a sum of functions $\Phi_{ij} = -\frac{1}{|I_i| \cdot |I_j|} \langle I_i, I_j \rangle$, the problem is broken down into the problem of computing the corresponding derivatives of the Φ_{ij}'s, which, for the first order derivatives is extremely similar to what we have done in the Sect. 4.2. The computations are carried out in [8]. In terms of the level set implementation, we ought to make a few remarks. The first is to explain how we compute β in (13) at each point (x, y, z) rather than on the surface S. It should be clear that we do not have any problem for computing $\mathbf{N} = -\frac{\nabla u}{|\nabla u|}$ and $2H = div(\frac{\nabla u}{|\nabla u|})$ and $d\mathbf{N}$ which is the differential of the Gauss map of the level set surface going through the point (x, y, z). The vectors $\Phi_\mathbf{X}$, $\Phi_\mathbf{N}$, the matrices $\Phi_\mathbf{XN}$, $\Phi_\mathbf{NN}$ are computed as explained in [8].

The second remark is that we can now write (13) as follows:

$$u_t = |\nabla u| \ div(\Phi \frac{\nabla u}{|\nabla u|}) - \Phi_\mathbf{N}(D\mathbf{N} + trace(D\mathbf{N})\mathbf{I}_3)\nabla u$$
$$- Trace((\Phi_\mathbf{XN})_{T_S} + d\mathbf{N} \circ (\Phi_\mathbf{NN})_{T_S}) |\nabla u| \qquad (17)$$

where $D\mathbf{N}$ is the 3×3 matrix of the derivatives of the normal with respect to the space coordinates, $\mathbf{I}_3$ the identity matrix, and at each point (x, y, z) the tangent plane T_S is that of the level set surface $u = constant$ going through that point. Note that $trace(D\mathbf{N}) = -div(\frac{\nabla u}{|\nabla u|})$. The first term $|\nabla u| \ div(\Phi \frac{\nabla u}{|\nabla u|})$ is identical to the one in the work of Caselles, Kimmel, Sapiro and Sbert [2] on the use of minimal surfaces or geodesic snakes to segment volumetric images. Our other terms come from the particular process that we are modelling, i.e. stereo. We believe and hope that we can prove in the near future that, under some reasonable assumptions, (17) is well-posed. As a first step in that direction, we report on some important implementation details: (i) Near the solution, Φ is close to -1 and the term $|\nabla u| \ div(\Phi \frac{\nabla u}{|\nabla u|})$ becomes anti-diffusive! As a consequence, we used $\Phi' = \Phi + 1$ instead of Φ, which takes values between 0 and $+2$, as a new error measure. This is equivalent to introducing in the criterion a term that tends to minimize the total area of the objects since it has the effect of adding to our original criterion the term $\int \int d\sigma$ which is precisely equal to that area. (ii) Regarding the image smoothness assumptions, a Gaussian modulated correlation could be used [10]. Actually, image intensities and their derivatives are extracted using recursively implemented Gaussian filters [4]. (iii) Concerning the problems of visibility and occlusion, the total error measure C_4 assumes the choice of certain camera pairs. Due to lack of place, we will not go into the details and just say that our implementation handles this problem such that C_4 is at least continuous. For more details, see [20] and [9].

6   Results

We now present some results obtained from both synthetic and real images. The corresponding animated recovering processes as well as other results can be downloaded at: `http://cermics.enpc.fr/~keriven/stereo.html`. We first synthesized two crossing tori, shot from enough points of views so that each part was seen at least twice (actually 24 images – fig. 3). See how the surface splits after some iterations and how even the internal parts are recovered (fig. 4). We also used real images of a real objet (two human heads) that was rotated before the cameras (fig. 4). All viewed parts (ie. neither the top nor the bottom) are correctly recovered (fig. 5). In both cases the image textures are mapped on the surface by standard texture mapping techniques.

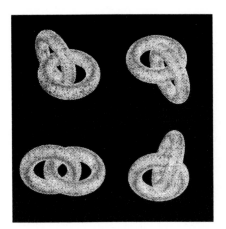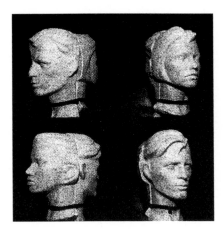

Fig. 3. Multicamera images of 3D objets. On the left hand side, two crossing synthetic tori (24 images). On the right hand side, real images: two human heads (18 images).

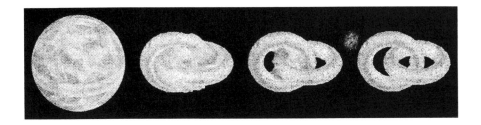

Fig. 4. Evolution of the surface for the two tori.

7 Conclusion

We have presented a novel geometric approach for solving the stereo problem from an arbitrary number of views. It is based upon writing a variational prin-

Fig. 5. Evolution of the surface for the two heads.

ciple that must be satisfied by the surfaces of the objects to be detected. The design of the variational principle allows us to clearly incorporate the hypotheses we make about the objects in the scene and how we obtain correspondences between image points. The Euler-Lagrange equations which are deduced from the variational principle provide a set of PDE's which are used to deform an initial set of surfaces which then move towards the objects to be detected. The level set implementation of these PDE's provides an efficient and robust way of achieving the surface evolution and to deal automatically with changes in the surface topology during the deformation. The whole objects (at least parts seen from two or more cameras) are recovered and visibility and occlusion are taken into account.

References

1. V. Caselles, R. Kimmel, and G. Sapiro. Geodesic active contours. In *Proceedings of the International Conference on Computer Vision*, pages 694–699, 1995.
2. V. Caselles, R. Kimmel, G. Sapiro, and C. Sbert. 3d active contours. In M-O. Berger, R. Deriche, I. Herlin, J. Jaffre, and J-M. Morel, editors, *Images, Wavelets and PDEs*, volume 219 of *Lecture Notes in Control and Information Sciences*, pages 43–49. Springer, June 1996.
3. David L. Chopp. Computing minimal surfaces via level set curvature flow. *Journal of Computational Physics*, 106:77–91, 1993.
4. R. Deriche. Recursively implementing the gaussian and its derivatives. Technical Report 1893, INRIA, Unité de Recherche Sophia-Antipolis, 1993.
5. Rachid Deriche, Stéphane Bouvin, and Olivier Faugeras. A level-set approach for stereo. In *Fisrt Annual Symposium on Enabling Technologies for Law Enforcement and Security - SPIE Conference 2942 : Investigative Image Processing.*, Boston, Massachusetts USA, November 1996.
6. M. P. DoCarmo. *Differential Geometry of Curves and Surfaces*. Prentice-Hall, 1976.
7. Olivier Faugeras. *Three-Dimensional Computer Vision: a Geometric Viewpoint*. MIT Press, 1993.
8. Olivier Faugeras and Renaud Keriven. Variational Principles, Surface Evolution, PDE's, Level Set Methods and the Stereo Problem. Technical Report 3021, INRIA, November 1996.

9. Olivier Faugeras, Renaud Keriven, and Imahd Eddine Srairi. A first implementation of a complete dense surface reconstruction from 2D images. Technical report, ENPC-CERMICS, October 1997.

10. L.M.J. Florack. *The syntactical structure of scalar images.* PhD thesis, Utrecht University, 1993.

11. Pascal Fua. From multiple stereo views to multiple 3-d surfaces. *The International Journal of Computer Vision,* 24(1):19–35, August 1997.

12. Pascal Fua and Yves G. Leclerc. Object-centered surface reconstruction: Combining multi-image stereo and shading. *The International Journal of Computer Vision,* 16(1):35–56, September 1995.

13. M. Gage and R.S. Hamilton. The heat equation shrinking convex plane curves. *J. of Differential Geometry,* 23:69–96, 1986.

14. M. Grayson. The heat equation shrinks embedded plane curves to round points. *J. of Differential Geometry,* 26:285–314, 1987.

15. W.E.L. Grimson. *From Images to Surfaces.* MIT Press : Cambridge, 1981.

16. H. L. F. von Helmholtz. *Treatise on Physiological Optics.* New York: Dover, 1925. Translated by J.P. Southall.

17. Berthold Klaus Paul Horn. *Robot Vision.* MIT Press, 1986.

18. Bela Julesz. *Foundations of Cyclopean perception.* The University of Chicago Press, Chicago and London, 1971.

19. M. Kass, A. Witkin, and D. Terzopoulos. SNAKES: Active contour models. *The International Journal of Computer Vision,* 1:321–332, January 1988.

20. Renaud Keriven. *Equations aux Dérivées Partielles, Evolutions de Courbes et de Surfaces et Espaces d'Echelle: Applications à la Vision par Ordinateur.* PhD thesis, Ecole Nationale des Ponts et Chaussées, Dec. 1997.

21. S. Kichenassamy, A. Kumar, P. Olver, A. Tannenbaum, and A. Yezzi. Gradient flows and geometric active contour models. In *Proc. Fifth International Conference on Computer Vision,* Boston, MA, June 1995. IEEE Computer Society Press.

22. P.J. Narayanan, P.W. Rander, and Takeo Kanade. Constructing virtual worlds using dense stereo. In *Proceedings of the 6th International Conference on Computer Vision,* Bombay, India, January 1998. IEEE Computer Society Press.

23. S. Osher and J. Sethian. Fronts propagating with curvature dependent speed : algorithms based on the Hamilton-Jacobi formulation. *Journal of Computational Physics,* 79:12–49, 1988.

24. L. Robert and R. Deriche. Dense depth map reconstruction: A minimization and regularization approach which preserves discontinuities. In Bernard Buxton, editor, *Proceedings of the 4th European Conference on Computer Vision,* Cambridge, UK, April 1996.

25. L. Robert, R. Deriche, and O.D. Faugeras. Dense depth recovery from stereo images. In *Proceedings of the European Conference on Artificial Intelligence,* pages 821–823, Vienna, Austria, August 1992.

26. Guillermo Sapiro and Allen Tannenbaum. Affine Invariant Scale Space. *The International Journal of Computer Vision,* 11(1):25–44, August 1993.

27. J. A. Sethian. *Level Set Methods.* Cambridge University Press, 1996.

28. J.A. Sethian. Numerical algorithms for propagating interfaces: Hamilton-jacobi equations and conservation laws. *Journal of Differential Geometry,* 31:131–161, 1990.

29. J.A. Sethian. Theory, algorithms, and applications of level set methods for propagating interfaces. Technical Report PAM-651, Center for Pure and Applied Mathematics, University of California, Berkeley, August 1995. To appear Acta Numerica.

The Geometry and Matching of Curves in Multiple Views

Cordelia Schmid[1] and Andrew Zisserman[2]

[1] INRIA Rhône-Alpes,655 av. de l'Europe, 38330 Montbonnot,France
[2] Dept of Engineering Science, 19 Parks Rd, Oxford OX1 3PJ, UK

Abstract. In this paper there are two innovations. First, the geometry of imaged curves is developed in two and three views. A set of results are given for both conics and non-algebraic curves. It is shown that the homography between the images induced by the plane of the curve can be computed from two views given only the epipolar geometry, and that the trifocal tensor can be used to transfer a conic or the curvature from two views to a third.

The second innovation is an algorithm for automatically matching individual curves between images. The algorithm uses both photometric information and the multiple view geometric results. For image pairs the homography facilitates the computation of a neighbourhood cross-correlation based matching score for putative curve correspondences. For image triplets cross-correlation matching scores are used in conjunction with curve transfer based on the trifocal geometry to disambiguate matches. Algorithms are developed for both short and wide baselines. The algorithms are robust to deficiencies in the curve segment extraction and partial occlusion.

Experimental results are given for image pairs and triplets, for varying motions between views, and for different scene types. The method is applicable to curve matching in stereo and trinocular rigs, and as a starting point for curve matching through monocular image sequences.

1   Introduction

This paper has two strands. The first is set of novel geometric results for curves in two and three views. The results are developed for both algebraic (conics) and non-algebraic curves. The key unifying idea is that the plane of the geometric entity can be computed from two views. The plane can then be used to transfer that entity into a third view via the trifocal tensor [8, 22, 23]. The transfer of points and lines via the trifocal tensor is well known and explored. This paper extends transfer to conics and curvature.

The second strand is an application of these results to the automatic matching of curves over multiple views. The idea here is that in addition to the geometric constraints that must be satisfied by matched curves, there are also photometric constraints on the intensity neighbourhood of the curve. These constraints are realised by computing intensity neighbourhood cross-correlation mediated by the homography (projective transformation) induced by the plane of the curve.

This paper can justly be seen as extending two papers by Faugeras and Roberts. The first, [7], dealt with the transfer of conics and curvature from two views to a third via epipolar transfer; in this paper the transfer is via the trifocal tensor and so does not suffer from the failings of epipolar transfer [28]. The second, [18], dealt with the trinocular matching of curves using only geometric constraints; in this paper these constraints are augmented by photometric constraints based on neighbourhood intensity correlation. In our previous work [20] this photometric constraint was shown to be a powerful disambiguation measure for line matches over two and three views.

1.1   Related literature on curve matching

Curve matching is a reoccurring topic in the stereo and motion literature, with the main application being the recovery of 3D geometry. A subsidiary goal has been to qualitatively distinguish between surface curves and apparent contours [2, 25]. Curves are a natural next step after lines, since they are a more faithful representation of a contour which would otherwise be represented by a polygonal chain. In this paper we are not considering closely spaced views where snake tracking is viable.

Basic criteria for curve matching in stereo pairs were established by Pollard *et al* in the PMF Stereo Algorithm [16]. Their primary criteria were the epipolar and ordering constraints, but these were supplemented by figural continuity to overcome problems where curves coincide with epipolar lines (since if the curve coincides with an epipolar line, point correspondences cannot be determined). Zhang and Gerbrands [27] again used epipolar geometry as their primary constraint, but followed this with criteria on the variation in disparity along the putatively matched curves. Brint and Brady [4] matched curves in trinocular views. Their primary matching constraint was a similarity measure based on the deformation between a curve and its putative match in another view. This measure was used to eliminate many potential mismatches. Trinocular consistency constraints were only used as a final verification. An alternative to matching curves individually is to first carry out a monocular grouping, and then match the groups. This is the approach adopted by Chung and Nevatia [5], and continued in work at USC by Havaldar and Medioni [10]. In this paper we match curves individually without first grouping.

Nayar and Bolle [15] developed a photometric matching constraint based on the ratio of intensities across region boundaries. This ratio of intensities has good invariance to lighting conditions. However, it is less general than the neighbourhood intensity correlation presented in this paper because it only applies to homogeneous regions, and it is also less discriminating.

1.2   Overview

Section 2 describes the geometry of conics and general curves in two and three views. Conic and curvature transfer methods are given, and these methods are assessed in section 3 by an implementation on real images. Matching is described in section 4. Algorithms are given for two and three views, and for short and wide baselines.

Two sequences are used to evaluate the geometry and matching. These are: a "plate" sequence, figure 2; and a "bottle" sequence, figure 3. Examples on other sequences are given in [21]. Frames are selected from these sequences to form image pairs or triplets. The camera motion between the frames is fairly uniform, so that the frame number is a good indicator of the distance between views.

The matching method developed in this paper requires only projective multiple view relations: the fundamental matrix for two views and the trifocal tensor for three. Camera calibration is not required. These relations are computed automatically from point (corner) correspondences [1, 24, 26].

2 Geometry

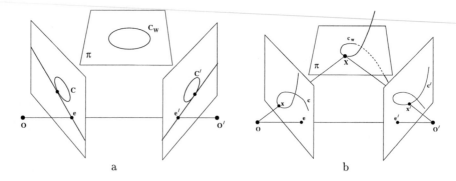

Fig. 1. (a) A conic defines a unique plane in 3-space. This plane is determined up to a two-fold ambiguity from the image of the conic in two views. One of the epipolar tangents is also shown. (b) The osculating plane of a (non-planar) curve varies, but is always defined in 3-space provided the curvature is not zero. This plane is determined uniquely from the image of the curve in two views. In both cases the plane induces a homography between the images.

2.1 Conic planes and homography

In this section we consider the reconstruction of a conic in 3-space given its image in two views and the epipolar geometry of the views represented by the fundamental matrix F. An explicit and simple expression is given for the plane of the conic and the homography it induces. The geometry is illustrated in figure 1a.

Several previous authors have investigated this geometry [12, 17, 19]. The most elegant is the approach of Quan [17] who shows, by reasoning on the back projected cones from each image conic, that there is a two fold ambiguity in the plane of the space conic. However, Quan's expressions are over complicated because he did not explicitly write the two camera matrices in terms of the epipolar geometry. Instead he derived correspondence conditions for the conics which are, actually, equivalent to the condition that the epipolar tangents to the conic must correspond (as in the Kruppa equations [13]).

We now give the main result of this section:

Given two perspective images of a conic (i.e. not a quadric), and the fundamental matrix between the views, then the plane of the conic (and consequently the homography induced by this plane) is defined up to a two fold ambiguity.

Suppose the image conics are represented by 3×3 symmetric matrices C and C' and the 3×4 camera matrices are chosen as

$$P = [I|0] \qquad P' = [A|e']$$

where e' is the epipole in the second view (e is the epipole in the first view). Then for the plane $\pi^\top = (a^\top, 1)$ and homography $x' = Hx$ where [11]

$$H = A + e'a^\top$$

and provided $e'^\top C'e' \neq 0$ and $e^\top Ce \neq 0$,

$$a(\mu) = -\left(\mu Ce + A^\top C'e'\right) / \left(e'^\top C'e'\right)$$

$$H(\mu) = \left(I - \frac{e'e'^\top C'}{e'^\top C'e'}\right) A - \mu \frac{e'e^\top C}{e'^\top C'e'}$$

and the two values of μ are obtained from

$$\mu^2 \left[(e^\top Ce)C - (Ce)(Ce)^\top\right] = A^\top \left[(e'^\top C'e')C' - (C'e')(C'e')^\top\right] A$$

If A is chosen as $A = [C'e']_\times F$ then simpler expressions are obtained:

$$H(\mu) = [C'e']_\times F - \mu e'(Ce)^\top$$

with

$$\mu^2 \left[(e^\top Ce)C - (Ce)(Ce)^\top\right] (e'^\top C'e') = -F^\top [C'e']_\times C'[C'e']_\times F$$

where the notation $[x]_\times$ means the 3×3 skew matrix with null space x, representing the vector cross product: $[x]_\times y = x \times y$.

The proof is omitted for lack of space but simply involves solving for a in $H = A + e'a^\top$ such that the image conics map as $C' = H^{-\top}CH^{-1}$. Note that when $e'^\top C'e' = e^\top Ce = 0$ the epipole is on the conic in each image, and the baseline intersects the space conic. In this case the plane is determined uniquely.

2.2 Curve osculating planes

In this section we first show how Euclidean curvature is mapped by a homography, and then how this result is used to determine the osculating plane of the curve. The geometry is illustrated in figure 1b.

Suppose a plane curve is imaged in two views, then the image curves are related by a homography induced by the curve plane. If the curve is not planar (it has non-zero torsion) then the image curves are not related globally by a homography, but *locally* they are related by a homography induced by the osculating plane of the space curve.

If corresponding curve points are related as $\mathbf{x}' = \mathrm{H}\mathbf{x}$. Then the Euclidean curvature at these points is related by

$$\kappa' = \kappa \left(\frac{ds}{ds'}\right)^3 \left(\frac{1}{\mathbf{h}_3.\mathbf{x}}\right)^3 |\mathrm{H}| \tag{1}$$

where $|\mathrm{H}|$ is the determinant of H, and $\mathbf{h}_i{}^\top$ is the ith row of H, i.e.

$$\mathrm{H} = \begin{bmatrix} \mathbf{h}_1{}^\top \\ \mathbf{h}_2{}^\top \\ \mathbf{h}_3{}^\top \end{bmatrix}$$

and $\frac{ds}{ds'}$ is the ratio of arc lengths given by

$$\frac{ds'}{ds} = \sqrt{\frac{[(\mathbf{h}_1.\dot{\mathbf{x}})\,(\mathbf{h}_3.\mathbf{x}) - (\mathbf{h}_1.\mathbf{x})\,(\mathbf{h}_3.\dot{\mathbf{x}})]^2 + [(\mathbf{h}_2.\dot{\mathbf{x}})\,(\mathbf{h}_3.\mathbf{x}) - (\mathbf{h}_2.\mathbf{x})\,(\mathbf{h}_3.\dot{\mathbf{x}})]^2}{(\mathbf{h}_3.\mathbf{x})^4\,(\dot{x}_1^2 + \dot{x}_2^2)}}$$

the notation $\dot{\mathbf{x}}$ indicates the derivative of the homogeneous vector $\mathbf{x} = (x_1, x_2, x_3)^\top$ by a curve parameter which need not be arc length and will *not*, in general, be the same in each image. The proof is omitted through lack of space, but starts from the formula of Brill *et al* [14], page 205.

We now show that the known curvatures at corresponding points, $\mathbf{x} \leftrightarrow \mathbf{x}'$, of the curves in each image determine the homography H. Suppose the tangent lines at $\mathbf{x}, \mathbf{x}'$, are $\mathbf{l}$ and $\mathbf{l}'$ respectively. These lines are related by $\mathbf{l} = \mathrm{H}^{-\top}\mathbf{l}'$. Given the epipolar geometry, there is a one parameter family of homographies which map a line in one image to a line in the other. This family may be written [20]

$$\mathrm{H}(\mu) = [\mathbf{l}']_\times \mathrm{F} + \mu \mathbf{e}'\mathbf{l}^\top$$

The remaining degree of freedom, μ, is determined *uniquely* using the relation (1) between image curvatures κ' and κ. We introduce the notation $\mathrm{A} = [\mathbf{l}']_\times \mathrm{F}$. Note that since $\mathbf{l} = \mathbf{x} \times \dot{\mathbf{x}}$, it follows that $\mathrm{H}(\mu)\mathbf{x} = \mathrm{A}\mathbf{x}$ and $\mathrm{H}(\mu)\dot{\mathbf{x}} = \mathrm{A}\dot{\mathbf{x}}$, so that $\mathbf{h}_i.\mathbf{x} = \mathbf{a}_i.\mathbf{x}$ etc. After some algebra:

$$\mu \left\{ l_1 |\mathbf{e}'\mathbf{a}^2\mathbf{a}^3| + l_2 |\mathbf{a}^1\mathbf{e}'\mathbf{a}^3| + l_3 |\mathbf{a}^1\mathbf{a}^2\mathbf{e}'| \right\} = \frac{\kappa'}{\kappa} \left(\frac{ds'}{ds}\right)^3 (\mathbf{a}_3.\mathbf{x})^3$$

where $\mathbf{a}^i$ is the ith column of A, and $|\mathbf{x}\mathbf{y}\mathbf{z}|$ is the determinant of the matrix with columns $\mathbf{x}, \mathbf{y}, \mathbf{z}$.

To summarise, we have shown that

Given two perspective images of a plane curve, and the fundamental matrix between the views, then the plane of the curve (and consequently the homography induced by this plane) is defined uniquely from the corresponding tangent lines and curvatures at one point.

There are two types of degenerate points at which the plane/homography cannot be uniquely determined by this method. The first is at epipolar tangents, where the tangent lines contain the epipole (i.e. if $l.e = l'.e' = 0$), since in this case the line in 3-space which projects to l and l' can not be determined as it lies in an epipolar plane. The second is at zero's of curvature (inflections) since then the curvature cannot be used to determine μ.

2.3 Transfer to a third view

The previous two sections have shown how the curve plane can be computed from two views. In this section we show that this plane, together with the trifocal tensor of the triplet, defines the mapping of the curve into a third view. This will be illustrated for a conic. The transfer of curvature via the osculating plane follows by analogy. In detail we show that

Given two perspective images of a conic and the trifocal tensor, the image of the conic in the third view is computed up to a two fold ambiguity

Suppose the (known) image conics are C and C' in views one and two, and the sought conic in view three is C''. The following steps determine C''

1. Obtain the three P matrices from the trifocal tensor as described by Hartley [9]
   $P = [I|0], \quad P' = [A|e'], \quad P'' = [B|e'']$.
2. Compute the plane of the homography $\mathbf{a}$ (two solutions) from the corresponding conics $C \leftrightarrow C'$ as described in section 2.1.
3. Then the homography $\mathbf{x}'' = H_{13}\mathbf{x}$ is $H_{13} = B + e''\mathbf{a}^\top$, and the conic C is transferred as $C'' = H_{13}^{-\top} C H_{13}^{-1}$.

3 Geometry Assessment

In this section we assess the performance of the methods of section 2 for an implementation on real images. The accuracy is evaluated from three views of a curve as follows: the plane of the curve is estimated from views one and two, and the curve and curvature are then transferred by the induced homography into the third view. The *transfer error* is assessed by comparing the transferred curve/curvature with that of the (veridical) curve imaged in the third view.

Assessment Criteria The transfer is assessed by two error measures. The first, $\epsilon_\mathbf{x}$, is the average Euclidean distance between the curves

$$\epsilon_\mathbf{x} = < d_\perp(\mathbf{c}(s), \mathbf{c}_t(s)) >$$

where $d_\perp$ is the distance between the curves in the normal direction from the imaged curve $\mathbf{c}$ to the transferred curve $\mathbf{c}_t$, and the average is performed over an arc length curve parameter s for the curve $\mathbf{c}$. The correspondence between the curves is established by intersecting the curve $\mathbf{c_t}$ with the normal of $\mathbf{c}(s)$. The second measure, ϵ_κ, is the average relative curvature difference of the curves

$$\epsilon_\kappa = < \frac{|\kappa(s) - \kappa_t(s)|}{\kappa(s)} >$$

where κ is the curvature of the imaged curve, and κ_t the curvature of the transferred curve. Points at which transfer is not possible, due to degeneracies in determining the osculating plane (see section 2.2), are excluded from the average.

The method is assessed for both conics (i.e. plane curves), and space curves. A conic allows the conic-specific method of section 2.1 to be compared to the general curve method of section 2.2 based on curvature. A conic also allows the curvature method to be assessed in two ways. In the first case a conic is fitted to the extracted conic boundary (edge chain) and intersections, tangents, and curvature are determined from the algebraic curve. This is a *global* method of estimation. In the second case the curve, its tangent, and curvature are determined locally (by spline fitting) using only this *local* information. In general we would expect the global estimates to be superior to the local.

For the plane curves the evaluation images consist of the two image triplets shown in figure 2, with the plate providing a conic. The triplets share the same first two views, but differ in the third. In triplet II the baseline between the second and third views is four times larger than that in triplet I. Space curves are evaluated using the image triplet shown in figure 3. The space curves used for the evaluation are superimposed; one is on the bottle, the second on the mug.

a   b   c   d

Fig. 2. Frames 3, 6, 7 and 10 from the "plate" sequence. The extracted conics are superimposed in black. Test triplet I consists of images (a), (b), (c); and test triplet II of images (a), (b), (d).

Implementation details Conic outlines are extracted using a subpixel Canny edge detector, and the conic estimated by Bookstein's fitting algorithm [3]. The local estimate of curvature is obtained by fitting cubic B-splines to the edgel chains. The average involved in both error measures, ϵ_x and ϵ_κ, is computed by sampling the conic/B-spline curve at one pixel arc length intervals.

Fig. 3. The "bottle" sequence (images 11,15 and 19). Two of the extracted contour chains are superimposed.

3.1 Assessing conic transfer

The conic plane is computed using conics from views one and two and the method of section 2.1. In order to have conics consistent with the epipolar geometry, a correction is required to ensure that the epipolar tangents to the conic (the tangent lines from the epipole to the conic) correspond between the images. This correction is achieved by applying the algorithm of [6]. The corrected conic is then transferred into the third image as described in section 2.3. The distance error and the relative curvature error are computed between the transferred and the extracted conic in the third image. The second solution for the conic plane can easily be ruled out as the distance error is very large.

For triplet I, $\epsilon_x = 0.15$ pixels, and $\epsilon_\kappa = 0.0024$. For triplet II, $\epsilon_x = 0.28$ pixels, and $\epsilon_\kappa = 0.0074$. Clearly, the transfer is excellent (visually the conics are indistinguishable.).

3.2 Assessing Curvature Transfer

Global curvature estimation Tangent lines and curvatures are obtained for the conics in each view by implicit differentiation of the fitted conics. The correspondence between points on the conic in the first and second view is obtained by intersecting the conic in the second view with the epipolar line of the point in the first view. The conic epipolar tangents and their neighbours are excluded from the error measures since curvature cannot be transferred for these points.

For triplet I, $\epsilon_x = 0.15$ pixels, and $\epsilon_\kappa = 0.0016$. For triplet II, $\epsilon_x = 0.34$ pixels, and $\epsilon_\kappa = 0.0047$. These results are almost identical to those of the previous section where conic transfer is used (section 2.1), as opposed to conic curvature transfer. They demonstrate that given almost perfect curvature (from the fitted conic) the curvature transfer is similarly almost perfect. The method of the next section investigates the deterioration when the curvature measurement is local and inferior.

Local curvature estimation The conics in image one and two are here represented by B-splines fitted to the edgel chain. The tangents, curvatures and epipolar line intersections are then computed from the B-splines, as opposed to the conics. The transferred curvature is compared to the curvature computed implicitly from C''. For triplet I, $\epsilon_x = 0.24$ pixels, and $\epsilon_\kappa = 0.046$. For triplet II, $\epsilon_x = 0.29$ pixels, and $\epsilon_\kappa = 0.074$.

3.3 Comparison of the different methods

The position error ϵ_x is of similar value over all methods. This is not surprising because the point transfer error only arises because of the difference between the fitted curves (conic or B-spline) and the veridical conic. This will be consistently sub-pixel because of the sub-pixel acuity of the Canny edge detector used. The curvature error ϵ_κ is more illuminating. The error is an order of magnitude larger when using local estimation of curvatures (via B-splines). This increased error is a direct consequence of the error in curvature estimation as can be seen from figure 4 which compares (a) the curvatures measured by the two methods in view one, and then (b) the resulting transferred curvatures in view three.

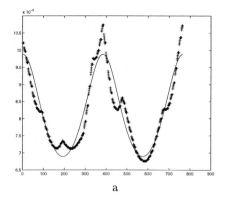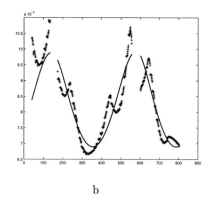

a   b

Fig. 4. (a) Comparison of curvature computed from a local B-spline fit (dashed curve), and a global conic fit (continuous curve) to the conic edgel chain. (b) Comparison of the transferred curvature using these two fitting methods for triplet I. In both cases curvature is plotted against arc length in pixels. The missing curve segments are at epipolar tangents where the curvature cannot be transferred.

3.4 Space curves

Figure 3 shows the two space curves used for assessing point and curvature transfer. For the curve on the bottle, $\epsilon_x = 0.43$ pixels, and $\epsilon_\kappa = 0.037$. For the curve on the mug, $\epsilon_x = 0.71$ pixels, and $\epsilon_\kappa = 0.097$. This is a very similar performance to the case of B-spline curvature computation for plane curves. Again the transfer accuracy is limited by the accuracy of the curvature measurement.

3.5 Rejection of the incorrect solution

Two solutions for the conic plane are obtained in practice using either of the two view methods. In the algebraic method of section 2.1, the two solutions arise because algebraic properties alone do not distinguish the front and back faces of the conic plane [17]. In the local curvature method of section 2.2 the two solutions arise because a curve point in the first view has two potential matches in the second view (since the epipolar line, corresponding to a point on the conic in the first view, intersects the conic in the second view twice). Thus the fallacious solutions originate for different reasons in the two methods. Consequently, the fallacious algebraic solution can be eliminated by simply testing one point with the curvature method: the correct solutions from both methods will be the same, but in general the fallacious solutions differ.

4 Matching curves over multiple views

The algorithm for automatic curve matching uses both photometric information and multiple view constraints. It is an extension to curves of the short and wide baseline algorithms for lines described in [20]. Short and wide base line cases are distinguished by the severity of the differing perspective distortions in the images. In both cases a photometric similarity measure between putatively matched contours is obtained from an aggregated neighbourhood cross-correlation score. In the short baseline case simple neighbourhood cross-correlation of corresponding points suffices; in the wide baseline case corresponding points for the cross-correlation are determined by a local planar projective transformation. The projective transformation is obtained here using the geometric relations of section 2. In the three view case curve matches are also verified using the geometric constraints provided by the trifocal geometry.

4.1 Short baseline between two views

Implementation details Each contour chain is treated as a list of edgels to which neighbourhood correlation is applied as a measure of similarity. The similarity score for a pair of contour chains c and c' is computed as the average of the individual edgel correlation values. Point correspondences are determined by the epipolar geometry. In detail, for an image point x which is an edgel of the contour chain c, the epipolar line in the second image is $l'_e = Fx$. This line l'_e is intersected with the potentially matching edgel chain c' (using linear interpolation between edgels). The correlation is between the neighbourhood of x and the neighbourhood of the intersection. Here a correlation window of 15x15 is used. In the case of multiple intersections the best correlation value is included in the overall score, and if there is no intersection, because the chains have different lengths, then no value is added to the score. To be robust to occlusion an individual correlation value is only included if above a threshold (here 0.6). If there are fewer than a minimum number (here 15) of matched edgels for a putative curve match, then that match is eliminated. No disparity threshold is used. Having determined similarity scores between contour pairs, the matches are selected using a winner take all scheme.

For a given pair of contours which have been deemed matched the parts of the curve for which there are corresponding edgels in both views are determined by only including edgels with correlation above threshold. When moving along a curve figural continuity is used to bridge gaps in the edgel correspondence arising from epipolar tangencies. If the parts of the curve for which there are corresponding edgels are non-contiguous, then only the three longest parts are retained.

Matching performance In the following we present a number of results using the short baseline algorithm. At present the ground-truth matches are assessed by hand. The performance varies with the parameters used for contour extraction and these are now described.

The algorithm used for contour extraction is the 'CannyOx' edge detector and linker from the Targetjr[1] software package. The low and high Canny thresholds for the edge detection are the same in all cases (2 and 12 respectively). The edgel linker parameters are varied, with their values given in table 1. The two parameters are the minimum gradient at which edgels are included in the linked chain (min gradient), — a high value excludes weak edges; and the minimum number of edgels in the linked chain (min length) — a high value excludes short chains. An example of extracted contours using a minimum gradient of 60 and a minimum length of 60 is displayed in figure 5 for the first two bottle images of figure 3.

The matched contours are shown in figure 5 in two ways. First, the complete contour chain matches are shown; second, only the parts of the matched contours for which there are corresponding edgels in both views are shown. The latter choice excludes the parts of the chains along epipolar lines, and also those parts of the chain which are detected as edgels in one view but not in the other. Only corresponding parts are shown for the rest of the examples in this paper.

The number of matched contour chains for different parameters for contour extraction are given in table 1. The matching results are extremely good, with most of the mismatches arising from specularities on the bottle: For the 60/30 case there is one false match, the other three are due to specularities; and for the 30/30 case there are two false matches, the other four are due to specularities. Curves arising from specularities can be removed by a pre-process. It is evident that there is little loss in matching performance when the number of contours is increased, i.e. when the parameter values are decreased.

As a second example contours are matched for the first two images of the "plate" sequence (cf. figure 2). Results are displayed in figure 6. 80 and 89 contours chain are obtained for the left and right image, respectively (using min grad 30 and min length 30); 100% of the 40 matched contour chains are correct.

---

[1] http://www.esat.kuleuven.ac.be/~targetjr

min grad	min length	number left	number right	number matched	correct
60	60	37	47	29	97%
60	30	59	72	41	90%
30	30	85	85	41	85%

Table 1. Edge detection parameters and curve matching results for the short baseline algorithm applied to an image pair of the "bottle" sequence.

Fig. 5. Short baseline matching. Upper pair : Contours extracted with CannyOx (parameters: min grad 60, min length 60). 37 and 47 contours are obtained for the left and right images respectively; Middle pair : Contours which are matched between views. Lower pair : Matched contours showing only the parts which have corresponding edgels in both views. 97% of the 29 matches are correct.

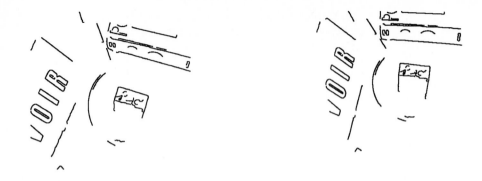

Fig. 6. Short baseline matching. 100% of the 40 matched contour chains are correct.

4.2 Large baseline algorithm between two views

In the case of a large baseline or significant rotation simple correlation based on square neighbourhoods will fail. However, the mapping between neighbourhood points can be determined from a homography based on the local tangent plane of the surface. In the case of line matching [20] this homography can only be determined up to a one parameter family because a line in 3D only determines the plane inducing the homography up to a one parameter family. This means that for lines a one dimensional search is required. However, in the case of curves the osculating plane determines a local plane uniquely (or up to a two-fold ambiguity for conics), and no search is required.

Thus there are two cases: if the curve has sufficient curvature the plane is computed as described in section 2.2; however, if the contour chain is straight or almost straight, curvature is close to zero and the osculating plane cannot be determined. In this case the algorithm developed for long range motion line matching (cf. [20]) is used. Lines here are the tangent lines to the contour chain. A threshold on local curvature is used to decide which case applies.

Images 11 and 19 of the "bottle" sequence (cf. figure 3) are matched; results are displayed in figure 7. 37 and 48 contour chains were extracted for the left and right images, respectively. 88% of the 16 matched contour chains are correct.

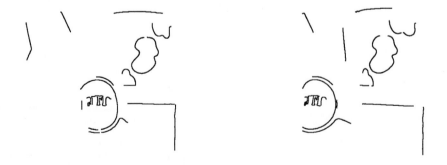

Fig. 7. Wide base line matching. 88% of the 16 matched contour chains are correct.

4.3 Three view matching

In the three view case there are three geometric constraints available for matching curves [18]: the curve point, its tangent, and its curvature. Here only the point is used directly as a geometric constraint. The tangent and curvature are used indirectly to determine the osculating plane, and hence provide a strong photometric constraint based on neighbourhood cross-correlation via the homography induced by the plane.

The three view matching builds on the curve matches provided by the two view algorithm. The point correspondences for matched chains in the first and second view are transferred into the third view using the trifocal tensor and are checked for coincidence with a contour chain in the third image (geometric constraint). A photometric score is then computed by correlating the point pair between images 2 and 3. If sufficient corresponding point triples are obtained for a putative contour triple, its mean correlation score is used to rank the match; otherwise the putative match is eliminated. This score is used in a winner take all scheme over three views which rules out multiple matches.

In the following results are given for two image triplets: "bottle" (images 11, 15, 17 of figure 3), and "plate" (images 3, 6, 7 of figure 2). Results on other triplets are given in [21]. Contours are extracted using the same parameters in all cases (min grad 30, min length 30).

Fig. 8. Three view matching. 25 contour chains are matched. There is only one incorrect match which arises from a specularity on the bottle.

Figure 8 shows results for three view matching for the "bottle" images (cf. figure 3). 85, 85 and 90 contour chains are obtained for the left, middle and right image, respectively. 25 contour chains were matched. Note, that the outline of the bottle is correctly *not* matched over the three views since it is an apparent contour and not rigidly attached to the scene. Annoyingly, the non-rigidity was insufficient to eliminate the only incorrect match which arose from the specularity on the bottle. In figure 9 matched contours are displayed for the "plate" images (cf. figure 2). 80, 89 and 84 contour chains are obtained for the left, middle and right image, respectively. 100% of the 30 matched contour chains are correct.

The three view matching gives excellent results. These matches will now form the foundation for a second pass where curves broken by the contour extraction

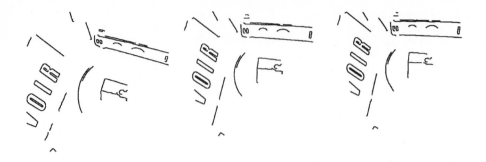

Fig. 9. Three view matching. 100% of the 30 matched contour chains are correct.

can be rejoined, and edge evidence sought for curve portions which are matched in only two of the three views. Such post processing substantially reduces curve fragmentation [20].

5 Discussion and extensions

We have derived and implemented new geometric results for conics and general curves over multiple views. These results have been applied to automatic curve matching over two and three views using a combination of geometric and photometric constraints.

The short baseline algorithm gives substantial disambiguation and generally excellent results being extremely robust with three views. The wide baseline algorithm also gives very good results, but relies on computing the osculating plane of the curve in order to determine a homography to map intensity neighbourhoods for correlation. There are two potential problems here: first, the osculating plane is only estimated accurately if the torsion of the curve is sufficiently small. However, this condition holds in many practical cases; second, the osculating plane of the curve may not coincide with the local tangent plane of the surface (think of the circular curve at the mouth of a mug). Fortunately, the intensity cross correlation is quite forgiving, and provides disambiguation even if the plane is imprecise.

Acknowledgements
We are very grateful to Andrew Fitzgibbon for both discussions and software. Financial support for this work was provided by EU Esprit Project IMPACT.

References

1. P. Beardsley, P. Torr, and A. Zisserman. 3D model acquisition from extended image sequences. In *Proc. ECCV*, pages 683–695, 1996.
2. A. Blake and R. Cipolla. Robust estimation of surface curvature from deformation of apparent contours. In *Proc. ECCV*, pages 465–474, 1990.
3. F.L. Bookstein. Fitting conic sections to scattered data. In *Computer Graphics and Image Processing*, 9:56–71, 1979.
4. A.T. Brint and M. Brady. Stereo matching of curves by least deformation. In *International Workshop on Intelligent Robots and Systems*, pages 163–170, 1989.

5. R. C. K. Chung and R. Nevatia. Use of monocular groupings and occlusion analysis in a hierarchical stereo system. In *Proc. CVPR*, pages 50–56, 1991.

6. G. Cross and A. Zisserman. Quadric surface reconstruction from dual-space geometry. In *Proc. ICCV*, pages 25–31, 1998.

7. O. Faugeras and L. Robert. What can two images tell us about a third one? *International Journal of Computer Vision*, 18:5–19, 1996.

8. R.I. Hartley. A linear method for reconstruction from lines and points. *Proc. ICCV*, pages 882–887, 1995.

9. R.I. Hartley. Lines and points in three views and the trifocal tensor. *International Journal of Computer Vision*, 22(2):125–140, 1997.

10. P. Havaldar and G. Medioni. Segmented shape-descriptions from 3-view stereo. *Proc. ICCV*, pages 102–108, 1995.

11. Q. Luong and T. Vieville. Canonic representations for the geometries of multiple projective views. Technical report, University of California, Berkeley, 1993.

12. S. Ma. Conics-based stereo, motion estimation, and pose determination. *International Journal of Computer Vision*, 10(1):7–25, 1993.

13. Maybank S. and Faugeras O. A theory of self-calibration of a moving camera. *International Journal of Computer Vision*, 8(2):123–151, 1992.

14. J.L. Mundy and A. Zisserman, editors. *Geometric Invariance in Computer Vision*. The MIT Press, Cambridge, MA, USA, 1992.

15. S.K. Nayar and R.M. Bolle, Reflectance Based Object Recognition. *International Journal of Computer Vision*, 17(3):219–240, 1996.

16. S.B. Pollard, J.E.W. Mayhew, and J.P. Frisby. PMF: A stereo correspondence algorithm using a disparity gradient constraint. *Perception*, 14:449–470, 1985.

17. L. Quan. Conic reconstruction and correspondence from two views. IEEE *Transactions on Pattern Analysis and Machine Intelligence*, 18(2):151–160, 1996.

18. L. Robert and O.D. Faugeras. Curve-based stereo: Figural continuity and curvature. In *Proc. CVPR*, pages 57–62, 1991.

19. R. Safaee-Rad, I. Tchoukanov, B. Benhabib, and K.C. Smith. 3D pose estimation from a quadratic curved feature in two perspective views. In *Proc. ICPR*, pages 341–344, 1992.

20. C. Schmid and A. Zisserman. Automatic line matching across views. In *Proc. CVPR*, pages 666–671, 1997.

21. C. Schmid and A. Zisserman. The geometry and matching of lines and curves over multiple views. Research Report, 1998.

22. A. Shashua. Trilinearity in visual recognition by alignment. In *Proc. ECCV*, pages 479–484, 1994.

23. M. Spetsakis and J. Aloimonos. Structure from motion using line correspondences. *International Journal of Computer Vision*, pages 171–183, 1990.

24. P. Torr and A. Zisserman. Robust parameterization and computation of the trifocal tensor. *Image and Vision Computing*, 15:591–605, 1997.

25. R. Vaillant. Using occluding contours for 3D object modeling. In *Proc. ECCV*, pages 454–464, 1990.

26. Z. Zhang, R. Deriche, O. Faugeras, and Q. Luong. A robust technique for matching two uncalibrated images through the recovery of the unknown epipolar geometry. *Artificial Intelligence*, 78:87–119, 1995.

27. Y. Zhang and J.J. Gerbrands. Method for matching general stereo planar curves. *Image and Vision Computing*, 13(8):645–655, 1995.

28. Zisserman A. and Maybank S. A case against epipolar geometry. In *Applications of Invariance in Computer Vision LNCS 825*. Springer-Verlag, 1994.

Automatic Modelling and 3D Reconstruction of Urban House Roofs from High Resolution Aerial Imagery

Theo Moons[1], David Frère[1], and Jan Vandekerckhove[1] and Luc Van Gool[1]

Katholieke Universiteit Leuven, ESAT / PSI,
Kard. Mercierlaan 94, B-3001 Leuven, BELGIUM
Firstname.Lastname@esat.kuleuven.ac.be

Abstract. Many tasks in modern urban planning require 3-dimensional (3D) spatial information, preferably in the form of 3D city models. Constructing such models requires automatic methods for reliable 3D building reconstruction. House roofs encountered in residential areas in European cities exhibit a wide variety in their shapes. This limits the use of predefined roof models for their reconstruction. The strategy put forward in this paper is, first, to construct a polyhedral model of the roof structure, which captures the topology of the roof, but which might not be very accurate in a metric sense; and then, in a second step, to improve the metric accuracy by fitting this model to the data. This decoupling of topology extraction from metric reconstruction allows a more efficient roof modelling involving less criteria. And, restricting the processing, at all stages, to one or just a few roof structures, by using a colour-based segmentation of the images, allows to use constraints that are not very tight. The approach has been tested on a state-of-the-art dataset of aerial images of residential areas in Brussels.

1 Introduction

Automatic generation of 3D models of buildings and other man-made structures from aerial images has become a topic of increasing importance. Although man-made objects generally exhibit quite a bit of regularity in their geometry, extracting and reconstructing buildings from aerial images is hampered by the lack of a generic 'building template'. In industrial areas or sites for official use, many flat roof and gable roof buildings are encountered. In the literature much attention has been paid to the extraction of such structures (see e.g. [3, 12–14]). House roofs encountered in residential areas in urban sites, on the other hand, show a much wider variety in their shapes. Many roofs neither are flat nor are composed of simple rectangular shapes. Model-based reconstruction now critically depends on the selection of the correct building model. Different strategies have been proposed in the literature, ranging from model selection by a human operator [7] to indexing in a model database [17]. In [5] it is observed that quite a variety of building models can be generated from a relatively small class of predefined building parts. Reconstruction is then performed by a 2-step process of hypothesis generation and verification: First, 3D feature points are grouped and related to building part primitives; and, in a second stage, these parts are combined into a building model. An alternative is to define very generic and free-form roof primitives that can be generated from the image data. In this respect, the observation that the 3D geometry of a house roof can be described as collections of line segments which tend to combine into planar structures, was used in [2] to model a house roof as a set of planar *polygonal patches*, each of which encloses a compact area with consistent photometric and chromatic properties, and that mutually adjoin along common boundaries. Since there are no constraints on the number of edges of the constituting polygons, nor on their lengths or angles, such an approach allows to model both simple as well as complicated roof structures. The strategy presented in this paper combines ideas from both approaches: First, we build, from the images, a polyhedral model of the roof structure — which captures the topology of the roof, but which might not be very accurate in a metric sense — using an hypothesis generation and verification procedure; and then, in a second step, we improve the metric accuracy by fitting this model to the data.

For the roof modelling step, we adopt the same methodology as in [2], but our implementation of the individual parts differs from that in [2] in the following respects: Firstly, it starts by delineating in the images regions that correspond to house roofs or house roof structures. Matching line segments across different views is simplified by restricting the search space to corresponding regions. Only line segments that are matched across three or more views are used for reconstruction. Moreover, coplanar grouping and polygonal patch formation also are initialized from 3D line segments that are reconstructed from those regions. In particular, polygon hypotheses are formed in 3D and verified both in 3D and by back-projecting in the images; and, if necessary, corrected accordingly. By processing one region at the time, we are able to keep the combinatorics under control. Secondly, in this paper all available views equally contribute to the reconstruction process, both on the level of 3D reconstruction itself as for polygon generation. In a next stage the different polygons are glued together into a roof model. As in [2], none of the constraints used for grouping and consistency verification are very tight. But, because the processing is restricted to regions that correspond to roof structures, we are able to retain valid object candidates. Moreover, in contradistinction to [2], the emphasis during the modelling stage is on extracting the correct topology of the roof structure, rather than on the metric accuracy of the reconstruction. This allows a more efficient roof modelling involving less criteria. Metric accuracy is obtained in an additional step by back-projecting the recovered (wireframe) model of the roof structure onto the images and minimizing the total reprojection error. This approach has been tested on a state-of-the-art dataset of aerial images of residential areas in Brussels.

The paper is organized as follows: Section 2 gives a brief overview of the different stages in the reconstruction process. Sections 3, 4 and 5 describe each of these parts in more detail. Each step is also illustrated on a real example.

Planned improvements for the implementation and possible extensions of the method are discussed in Section 6.

2 Method Overview

The roof modelling process is formulated as a feed-forward scheme in which 4 stages can be recognized: *2D edge detection and region selection, line segment matching and 3D reconstruction, 3D grouping and polygonal patch formation,* and finally, *roof model generation and model fitting.* Observe that the first part and half of the second are purely 2D, whereas the other parts are purely 3D in nature. Obviously, these parts are not completely separate entities, but the 2D components mutually exchange data and attribute to the 3D modules. Each part will be described in more detail in the subsequent sections.

The strategy presented in this paper is tested on a state-of-the-art dataset, produced by Eurosense Blefotop n.v.. It consists of high resolution colour images of residential areas in Brussels. The image characteristics are: 1:4000 image scale and geometrically accurate film scanning with 20 microns pixel size, four-way image overlap, and precise sensor orientation. The image overlap guarantees that each building is visible in 4 to 6 images. Our method requires at least 3 views of the scene to be present.

3 From Images to 3D Line Segments

3.1 2D Edge Detection and Region Selection

The image features used in this approach are straight line segments, which are extracted from the images by running the Canny edge detector followed by straight line fitting. Due to the nature of the scene and the large size (typically $3\,K \times 5\,K$ pixels) of the aerial images, an enormous number of straight line segments is found in every image. For an efficient further processing, it is desirable to segment the image(s) or to divide the set of line segments into relatively small parts containing only a few buildings. In the literature, this is done in many different ways, ranging from manual delineation [2], possibly combined with epipolar constraints and flight information [4, 14], via perceptual grouping techniques [3, 13], to the introduction of external knowledge which, in most cases, is available from Geographical Information Systems (GIS) or digital cadaster maps [10, 15]). For the moment, we solve this problem by navigating through a constraint triangulation network which has been constructed from the line segments extracted in the image(s). Such a constraint triangulation has the advantage that the extracted line segments coincide with edges of the triangles and that the colour content of a triangle's interior is fairly homogeneous. As a house roof generally is constructed from the same roofing material, roof structures are likely to correpond to image regions with a fairly homogeneous colour distribution. Therefore, image segmentation is performed by selecting a triangle in the triangulation and growing a region from it by merging adjacent triangles that have the same mean colour vector as the selected triangle. In our implementation, the generating triangle is selected manually (with a mouse click) in each image, but this process can be automated by selecting a triangle in one image and using epipolar and trifocal constraints to delineate a window in the other images, in which a triangle with a similar mean colour vector is to be found. Since at this stage only corresponding regions are needed, it is not crucial to find the exact triangle in the other images that corresponds to the selected one. These triangles will probably not be part of the triangulation of the other images anyway. A house roof generally is composed of more than one region.

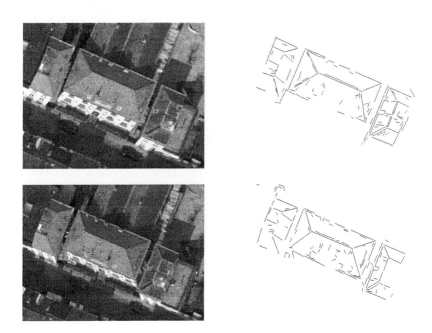

Fig. 1. Left : *A detail from two images in the dataset.* Right : *The edges contained in the selected regions.*

Fig. 1 (left) shows a small part of two aerial images of the same area in Brussels. The right views show the line segments which are contained in the regions that were generated by selecting 5 triangles (2 for the left building and 3 for the right one) in each image. These line segments will be used for matching and possible reconstruction in the next steps of the algorithm. Observe that the extracted regions correspond well to the actual roof surfaces and are quite stable over the images.

3.2 Line Segment Matching and 3D Reconstruction

Once a region of interest is constructed in every image, the longer ones among the line segments in each region are identified. As the regions are relatively small, only a small number of line segments will be selected in a region; and, because a constraint triangulation has been used, most line segments will occur at the region boundaries. Using epipolar geometry and flight information, matching line segments between corresponding regions in different images is rather easy. A complicating factor, however, is that a relatively long line segment in one image may correspond to a number of relatively short edges in another one. So, a line segment in one image must be allowed to correspond to more than one line segment in the other image. Most mismatches are then ruled out by using the trifocal constraints [11, 16] that must hold between any three views of a stationary scene. For all line segments that are matched across 3 or more views, a 3D reconstruction is computed by bundle adjustment [4] using the flight information and the calibration data of the camera.

4 3D Grouping and Polygonal Patch Formation

4.1 Coplanar Grouping

Next, the reconstructed 3D line segments are to be grouped into coplanar configurations. As the selected regions correspond to roof structures in the images, the grouping process can be restricted to the 3D line segments from one (or a few adjacent) region(s). Starting with the longest ones, 2 line segments are selected in the region(s). If the orthogonal distance between the corresponding reconstructed lines is small, a plane is constructed that fits to the line segments in a least-squares sense. In that case, the other line segments in the region(s) are tested for coplanarity with the hypothesized plane. Coplanarity is assumed if the line segment is almost parallel to the plane and if both its end points are close to the plane. All segments that satisfy these constraints are included in the defining set of the plane and the plane's equation is updated. This process is repeated until no more plane hypotheses can be formed form the selected region(s).

4.2 Polygon Hypothesis Generation

Subsequently, every line segment in the defining set of an hypothesized plane is projected orthogonally onto that plane. As the regions correspond well to roof structures, most plane hypotheses will correspond to planar patches of the roof structure. Thus, polygonal patch hypotheses can be formed directly from the projected segments. Unfortunately, the polygonal shapes encountered in the roof structures of urban and suburban houses — and consequently also the extracted regions — seldomly are convex, due to roof structures such as chimneys, attics, dormer-windows, etc.. So, great care should be taken when constructing the polygons. In particular, the polygon construction algorithm must try to involve as many 3D line segments in the region as possible. An initial hypothesis is formed by constructing the convex hull of the (projected) line segments. Then an initial boundary is generated by adapting the hull to include the line segments of which one of the end points contributes to the convex hull. In a next step it

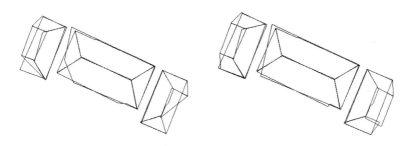

Fig. 2. *Initial polygon hypotheses* (left) *and after consistency verification* (right) *of selected houses in Fig. 1.*

is investigated whether this initial boundary can be adapted to incorporate line segments in the region's interior, one of whose end points is close to the boundary.

Fig. 2 (left) shows the result of coplanar grouping and the initial polygon hypotheses that are generated for two of the houses in Fig. 1. Five polygons are found for the middle house in Fig. 1: 2 triangular ones and 2 trapezia corresponding to the actual roof structure, and a horizontal plane that is formed by (parts of) the gutters of the building. Apart from a relatively small defect in the lower left corner of the horizontal plane — caused by short edge segments that could not be reconstructed properly (cf. Fig. 1 (lower right)) — the extracted polygons correspond quite well to the actual shape of the building. For the left building, also 5 polygons are constructed: 2 horizontal and 3 slanted ones. Clearly, 4 of the 5 polygons are correct, but the triangular shape of the lower side patch does not correspond to reality. The reason is that, only 1 of the 4 images used for reconstruction contains relatively complete edge information for that patch. Hence, no 3D line segments could be reconstructed for the lower left part of the patch, and the polygon construction algorithm was forced to insert wrong edge hypotheses. Similarly, only 3 of the 5 polygons that are constructed for the building on the right are correct. The 2 triangular shapes do not correspond to reality. Again, this is caused by the fact that, except in the upper image in Fig. 1, edges for the upper right corner in the other 3 views are either missing or to short to be reconstructed properly (cf. Fig. 1 (lower right)). Before glueing the polygons together, their edges should be compared with the data, and erroneous edges should be corrected. This is done in the next step.

4.3 Consistency Verification and Edge Correction

For each polygon that is constructed, every one of its edges is subjected to a consistency verification with respect to the 3D and 2D data. If the edge is one of the original (projected) 3D line segments, then the edge hypothesis is accepted. Otherwise, it is investigated whether the hypothesized edge is close to some reconstructed 3D line segments and has significant overlap with them. If the outcome is negative again, the edge hypothesis is back-projected into the images, and one looks for supporting information in at least 1 image. With supporting information, we mean original (possibly small) 2D line segments that are close to the projected edge and that cover at least half of the extent of the edge. It should be emphasized that the error tolerances in none of the above constraints may be very tight, in order not to rule out simple (but possibly correct) polygonal patches such as triangles, etc. too early in the process. Also observe that, since the processing is restricted to relatively small regions that correspond to actual roof structures, the number of polygons is kept under control at every stage of the reconstruction process.

Next, one tries to replace the edge hypotheses that failed for the previous consistency tests by better ones. For the moment, new hypotheses are only generated in case of a non-consistent edge for which both adjacent edges were found consistent with the data. In that case, the algorithm tries to construct a right angle. Depending on the geometric configuration of the adjacent edges, different possibilities occur, as can be seen in Fig. 3. For each possibility, its consistency with the data is verified by back-projection into the images as before, and the possibility that gets the most 2D edge support is accepted. The edges that fail for all of the previous tests finally are labeled as *doubtful*.

Fig. 2 (right) shows the result of consistency verification and edge correction of the initial polygon hypotheses of the houses in Fig. 1. Recall that the erroneous triangular shapes of the original polygon hypotheses for the left and the right roofs in Fig. 2 (left) were caused by the lack of 3D edge information among the reconstructed line segments. On the other hand, the upper image in Fig. 1 yields clear edges — and consequently, also sufficient 2D edge support — for both triangular patches of the right roof to correct the polygon hypotheses by the described procedure. And, similarly, the lower image in Fig. 1 together with another view yield sufficient 2D edge support to correct the erroneous lower left patch. Note also that the shape of the horizontal polygon of the middle house has been corrected, at least qualitatively. The orientation of the leftmost edge still deviates from reality, due to the lack of information about the position of the leftmost corner and because this edge actually connects the outer ridge of the gutter at the back of the house with the inner ridge of the gutter in the front. This, however, will be corrected in the last step of the method (cf. Section 5.3), when metric accuracy is retrieved.

5   Roof Model Generation and Model Fitting

The last step in the roof modelling process consists of combining the extracted polygons into roof models. A logical way to proceed would be to glue any 2 polygons together that have an edge which is the projection of one and the same reconstructed 3D line segment. Unfortunately, this is not feasible in practice. Indeed, because the polygons are constructed one region at the time, line segments at region boundaries may contribute to polygon hypotheses that are formed at different iterations of the reconstruction process. Hence, it would require a complicated data structure to record the history of every consistent polygon edge and to group the polygons accordingly. Furthermore, there not necessarily is

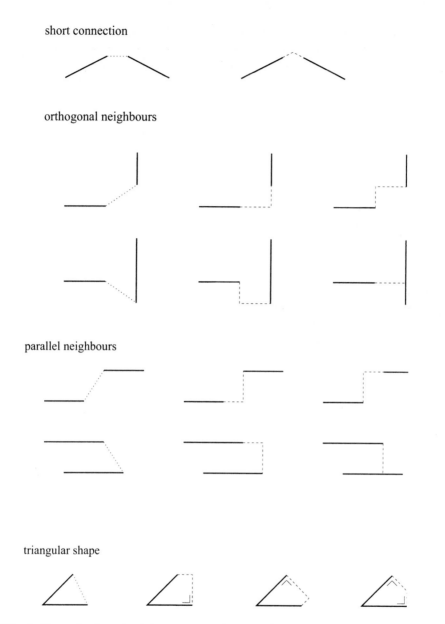

Fig. 3. *If an edge hypothesis is not accepted, it is replaced by new ones. The dotted line is the original edge hypothesis, full lines are its (accepted) neighbours, dashed lines are the alternative edge hypotheses.*

a reconstructed 3D line segment for every consistent edge that is constructed during the replacement of a non-consistent one. Therefore, we adopt another strategy that starts from the set of polygons *per se*. The key idea is to provide each edge of the polygons with a functional label, and to link polygons along edges bearing the same label and which nearly coincide.

5.1 Labeling the Edges of a Polygon

To each edge of the polygon, a label is attached according to its 3D position in the polygon. Edges whose end points have a significant difference in height above the ground level or edges that have a significant angle with the ground plane are called *slanted*. The remaining (horizontal) edges are divided into ridges and gutters. A *ridge* is a horizontal edge whose adjacent edges are both slanted and pointing downwards; whereas a *gutter* is a horizontal edge both whose adjacent edges are slanted and pointing upwards. If the plane of the polygon is horizontal, then all edges are labeled both *gutter* as well as *ridge*. Finally, a horizontal edge that does not satisfy one of the previous constraints is labeled as *ridge* (resp. as *gutter*) in case the average of the heights of its end points is greater (resp. smaller) than the average of the heights of the vertices of the polygon. If the labeling of the edges is completed, the topology of the labeled polygons is simplified by replacing any 2 adjacent edges that have the same label and are nearly collinear by one edge connecting the outer end points and having the same label.

5.2 Combining Polygons into Roof Surfaces

The final step in the roof modelling process is the combination of the polygons into roof models. To this end, the polygons are ordered by their area and linking starts with the polygons having the largest area. The underlying philosophy is that larger polygons generally consist of more and larger edges; and thus are more likely to correspond to actual scene structures. Two polygons will be glued together if they are not parallel, and if in both polygons an edge can be found with the same label and such that these two edges nearly coincide and have a significant mutual overlap. The actual glueing of the polygons is done by replacing these 2 edges by a segment of the line of intersection of the planes of the 2 polygons. Generally, the orthogonal projections of the end points of the 2 edges on the intersection line will not coincide. Therefore, the longest line segment that can be formed from these projections is taken as the common joint of the 2 polygons (cf. Fig. 4). This process is repeated until no more polygons can be glued together. However, there is an important geometric constraint to be taken into account, viz. each polygon can be glued *only once* to another polygon *along a given edge*. Indeed, it is unlikely for large roof structure to contain three planar faces intersecting in the same line segment. Since the larger — and hence more reliable — polygons are glued first, this constraint allows to rule out small polygons, which mostly correspond to polygonal roof structures that only have partially been recovered. Finally, all polygons that have not been joined to

Fig. 4. *Two polygons are glued together along the (dashed) line of intersection of the planes of the polygons. The resulting wireframe (bold) is shown on the right.*

another one, are removed; except for large isolated horizontal planes, which may correspond to a flat roof. Their analysis will be discussed in a subsequent paper.

Fig. 5 shows the roof models that are obtained by applying this procedure to the polygon hypotheses depicted in Fig. 2 (right). The resulting wireframe models clearly are topologically correct.

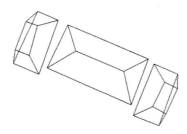

Fig. 5. *The roof models obtained by combining the polygonal patches shown in Fig. 2.*

5.3   Fitting the Wireframe Model to the Image Data

During the 3D grouping and the roof modelling stages of the algorithm, the metric accuracy of the reconstruction has been neglected. Indeed, a 3D line segment that originally was reconstructed from the images by bundle adjustment, first is orthogonally projected onto one or more planes in order to form polygonal patches, and then in the glueing process it is replaced by the line of intersection of the planes of the polygons to which it contributes. Moreover, the strategy expounded above fully exploits the polyhedral structure of the observed scene, an assumption that may not strictly be satisfied in reality. As a consequence, the computed roof model generally will deviate from the actual roof structure in the scene. This can clearly be observed when back-projecting the roof model into the images. For example, the left image in Fig. 6 shows the back-projection of one of the models in Fig. 5 into the lower image of Fig. 1. It immediately catches the eye that the projected gutters of the model do not coincide with those of the house in the image. But there also is a deviation in the position of the projected ridge and in the orientation of the projected rafters at the back of the roof model

Fig. 6. Left: *Back-projecting the roof model of Fig. 5 into the original images illustrates the loss of metric accuracy during the 3D grouping and roof modelling process.* Right: *Metric accuracy can be restored by changing the wireframe model so as to minimize the reprojection error in all the available images.*

with respect to those in the image. However, if the roof models constructed by the above procedure are primarily considered as wireframe models capturing the topological structure of the building, then a metric 3D reconstruction of the scene is to be obtained by fitting these models to the data. Generally speaking, there are two alternatives for fitting a 3D model: either the model is fitted directly to a 3D reconstruction of the scene, or the model is projected into the images and adjusted to fit the image data. Since our roof model has been constructed from the reconstructed 3D line segments, fitting must be done with respect to the original image data in order to use maximally independent information. Therefore, the roof model, as computed in the previous sections, is converted into a *wireframe model*, meaning that it is represented by a set of 3D points, called *vertices*, that are connected by straight line segments, called *edges*. Recall that the roof model constructed above actually has a polyhedral structure. Therefore, for each vertex not only a list of all the edges ending in that vertex is constructed, but also a list of all the planes of the polygonal faces that contain the given vertex is provided. This wireframe is then projected into all the images by using the flight information and the calibration data of the camera. The idea now is to adapt the 3D position of the vertices of the wireframe so as to bring the projected edges in as good as possible accordance with the observed image data. To this end, an *energy functional* is introduced, which measures the average image gradient along the projected edges of the wireframe. More precisely, for each vertex V_j of the wireframe, let $\mathcal{E}_j$ be the set of edges of which V_j is an end point, and let $\mathcal{P}_j$ denote the set of the planes of the polygonal faces that contain V_j. Furthermore, let L_i denote the intensity distribution (luminance function) of the ith image ($i = 1, \ldots, m$). Then the *total mean gradient energy* $G(V_j)$ of the vertex V_j is given by

$$G(V_j) = \frac{1}{m} \sum_{i=1}^{m} \left\{ \frac{1}{|\mathcal{E}_j|} \sum_{E \in \mathcal{E}_j} \frac{1}{\ell(\pi_i(E))} \int_{\pi_i(E)} \|\nabla L_i\| \right\} , \qquad (1)$$

where $|\mathcal{E}_j|$ is the number of elements in the set $\mathcal{E}_j$ (i.e. the number of edges ending in V_j), $\pi_i(E)$ is the projection of the line segment E in the ith image, $\ell(\pi_i(E))$ is the length of the projected line segment $\pi_i(E)$, and $\|\nabla L_i\|$ is the norm of the gradient ∇L_i of the image intensity function L_i. To meet the image data, the vertices of the wireframe model should be placed at those 3D positions for which the total mean gradient energy $\frac{1}{n}\sum_{j=1}^{n} G(V_j)$ is maximal. Here n is the number of vertices in the wireframe model. An important observation here is that, as each vertex is free to move in any 3D direction, the resulting wireframe that maximizes the total mean gradient energy generally will not define a polyhedral roof structure anymore. Theoretically, this need not to be a disadvantage, as most house roofs probably are not strictly polyhedral either. From a practical point of view, however, it is not advisable to allow the wireframe to deviate too much from a polyhedral shape; the reason being that in case a vertex of the wireframe happens to be occluded in one or more views, the 3D position of that vertex may drift away in order to bring the projected edges closer to (non-corresponding) image contours. One way to avoid this undesired behaviour is to use the median instead of the mean in the definition of the gradient energy $G(V_j)$. However, in practice this results in fitting the wireframe model to just one or two images, whereas our strategy is to use information from as many image as possible. Instead, we introduce an extra energy functional which measures the deviation of the vertex position from its polyhedral position. In particular, the *distance energy* $D(V_j)$ of the vertex V_j is defined as the sum of the distances $d(V_j, P)$ of V_j to each of the planes $P \in \mathcal{P}_j$ to which it originally belonged:

$$D(V_j) = \frac{1}{|\mathcal{P}_j|} \sum_{P \in \mathcal{P}_j} d(V_j, P) \ . \tag{2}$$

Another possibility is to update the equation of the planes $\mathcal{P}$ at each step of the iteration. This is computationally more demanding, and, in practice, yields the same results.

Together, G and D yield the following *energy functional* E that has to be maximized in order for the constructed wireframe to fit the image data:

$$E(V_1, V_2, \ldots, V_n) = \frac{1}{n} \sum_{j=1}^{n} \{ G(V_j) - \beta\, D(V_j) \} \ , \tag{3}$$

where $0 < \beta < 1$ is a real number that regulates the strength of the distance energy D in the energy functional E. To find the maximum of the energy functional E, the maximization problem is replaced by a dynamical system whose equilibrium states coincide with the critical points of the energy functional E. The critical points of E are the point positions $(V_1, V_2, \ldots, V_n)$ at which the gradient ∇E vanishes: $\nabla E(V_1, V_2, \ldots, V_n) = 0$; or equivalently, those points V_j for which

$$\nabla G(V_j) - \beta \nabla D(V_j) = 0 \qquad (j = 1, \ldots, n). \tag{4}$$

The same equations give the equilibrium states of the dynamical system

$$\frac{\partial V_j}{\partial t} = \alpha\, [\nabla G(V_j) - \beta \nabla D(V_j)] \qquad (j = 1, \ldots, n), \tag{5}$$

with α a positive real number. Since by construction the vertices of the wireframe computed in the previous sections are relatively close to a maximum of the energy functional E, starting the dynamical process (5) from these vertex positions will lead the vertices of the wireframe to those positions that correspond to the desired maximum of E. The main advantage of this approach is that it can be implemented as an iterative process by using a finite difference approximation of the system (5). At each iteration step, the vertex positions $V_j^{(p)}$ are all updated to new positions

$$V_j^{(p+1)} = V_j^{(p)} + \alpha \left[\Delta G_j^{(p)} - \beta \, \Delta D_j^{(p)} \right] \, , \tag{6}$$

where $\Delta G_j^{(p)}$ and $\Delta D_j^{(p)}$ are the finite difference approximations of the gradients ∇G and ∇D at vertex position $V_j^{(p)}$. Note that the computation of $\Delta G_j^{(p)}$ involves the evaluation of the functional G, and hence, the calculation of the line integrals $\int_{\pi_i(E)} \|\nabla L_i\|$ (cf. eq. (1)). These integrals are computed by sampling the gradient image along the given line segment and using Gaussian interpolation for obtaining sub-pixel accuracy.

The right image in Fig. 6 illustrates the effect of applying this procedure to one of the wireframes in Fig. 5. The resulting 3D reconstruction agrees much better with the image data, as can be seen in Fig. 6 (right) which shows the back-projection of the optimized wireframe into the second image of Fig. 1. In particular, the horizontal edges of the reconstruction coincide quite well now with the outer edges of the gutters in the image(s); and the projections of the ridge and the rafters of the model coincide with those in the image(s) as well.

From the reconstructed roofs a 3D model of the buildings can be generated by adding artificial vertical walls. This is done by constructing vertical line segments that connect the end points of the gutters with the ground plane. The ground plane is extracted automatically by selecting regions (i.e. triangle(s)) in the images that correspond to the street level, reconstructing the line segments contained in it as described in Section 3, and performing a coplanar grouping as outlined in Section 4.1. Fig. 7 illustrates the result of this operation by showing two views from different viewing directions of the houses in the images of Fig. 1, whose roofs were reconstructed by the method described above. The texture of the roof surface, as seen in the first image of Fig. 1, has been mapped onto the roofs in the reconstruction.

Fig. 8 (upper left) shows another detail of (one of) the aerial image(s). Observe the a-symmetrical shape of the corner building. Its roof is reconstructed from three regions: one large region covering the roof patches along the street sides, and two small ones corresponding to the upper right faces. Note that the patches contained in the large region actually belong to 3 different planes. Moreover, no 3D line segments could be recovered for the triangular patch at the corner, because its projection in the images consists of short edge segments only. So, initially, only two polygons are constructed: a trapesium for the left part of the roof, and a triangle for the lower right patch at the street side. The scattered edge information of the corner patch, however, provides sufficient support for the

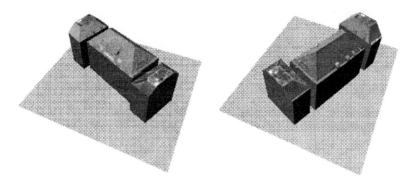

Fig. 7. *Two views of the houses reconstructed from the images in Fig. 1.*

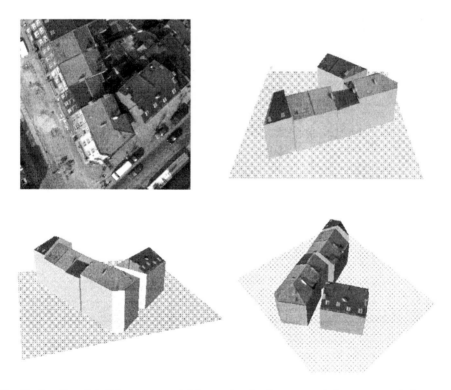

Fig. 8. *Another detail from an aerial image in the dataset and three views of the re-constructed houses.*

hypothesized rafters to pass the consistency verification step, thus leading to a topologically correct wireframe for the corner house. The extraction of the other roofs is straightforward. The 3D building models that are obtained by adding artificial vertical walls to the reconstructed roofs can also be seen in Fig. 8.

6   Conclusion and Future Work

A method is presented that automatically generates 3D models of generic house roofs from aerial images of residential areas in urban sites. Describing the 3D geometry of a house roof as collections of line segments which tend to combine into planar structures allows to model both simple as well as complicated roof structures by the same approach. Crucial to the method is the possibility of delineating regions in the images that correspond well to actual roof structures. This can be automatically done by introducing external information which often is available from Geographical Information Systems (GIS) or digital cadaster maps (cf. [15]). In our current implementation, colour-based image segmentation is performed by navigating through a constraint triangulation network that has been constructed from the line segments extracted in the image(s). Restricting the processing to relatively small regions allows at all stages of the algorithm to use constraints that are not very tight, and, at the same time, to keep the combinatorics under control. Furthermore, all modelling is done by reasoning in 3D. By adopting a strategy of hypothesis generation and verification, we not only are capable of using all the available image data at every step in the algorithm, but also to treat all views at the same level. Moreover, by decoupling the retrieval of the topology of the roof structure from the metric accuracy of the reconstruction, it is possible to generate and test combinations which otherwise would have been ruled out by more tight constraints.

The method is implemented and the first tests are performed on a state-of-the-art dataset containing aerial images of residential areas in Brussels. As can be seen from the examples above, it yields acceptable results. Of course, there still is a lot of work to be done. First of all, attention will be paid to optimizing and finetuning each of the different steps in the algorithm. On the theoretical level, more sophisticated techniques which have proven successful in a lot of other applications will be considered. Examples include the use of the Minimum Description Length principle for coplanar grouping and the exploitation of observed symmetry relations between different polygons in the glueing process. Another important issue that will be investigated is the formulation of a set of consistent geometric adjacency relations both for the 3D model and its projections in the images in order to obtain a quantitative assessment of the correctness and completeness of the constructed roof model. But the final test, of course, is an extensive evaluation of the accuracy and the completeness of the reconstructed house roof models with respect to the ground truth. Such a test is planned for the near future.

Acknowledgements

This work is support by the EU ESPRIT ltr 20.243 'IMPACT' project. The authors thank Eurosense Belfotop n.v. (Wemmel, Belgium) for providing the dataset of aerial images. Special thanks also goes to Marc Proesmans for valuable discussions and advice on the implementation of the wireframe fitting algorithm.

References

1. E.P. Baltsavias, W. Eckstein, E. Gülch, M. Hahn, D. Stallmann, K. Tempfli, and R. Welch (eds.), *3D Reconstruction and Modelling of Topographic Objects*, International Archives of Photogrammetry and Remote Sensing, Vol. **32** Part **3-4W2**, International Society of Photogrammetry and Remote Sensing, Sydney, 1997.
2. F. Bignone, O. Henricsson, P. Fua and M. Stricker, Automatic extraction of generic house roofs from high resolution aerial imagery, in : B. Buxton and R. Cipolla (eds.), *Computer Vision – ECCV'96*, Lecture Notes in Computer Science **1064**, Springer-Verlag, Berlin, 1996, pp. 85–96.
3. R.T. Collins, A.R. Hanson, M.R. Riseman and H. Schultz, Automatic extraction of buildings and terrain from aerial images, pp. 169–178, in [8].
4. O. Faugeras, S. Laveau, L. Robert, G. Csurka and C. Zeller, 3-D reconstruction of urban scenes from sequences of images, pp. 145–168, in [8].
5. A. Fischer, T.H. Kolbe and F. Lang, F., Integration of 2D and 3D Reasoning for Building Reconstruction Using a Generic Hierarchical Model, pp. 159–180, in [6].
6. W. Förstner, F. and L. Plümer, *Semantic Modeling for the Acquisition of Topographic Information from Images and Maps*, Birkhäuser-Verlag, Basel, 1997.
7. E. Gülch, Application of semi-automatic building acquisition, pp. 129–138, in [9].
8. A. Grün, O. Kübler and P. Agouris, *Automatic Extraction of Man-Made Objects from Aerial and Space Images*, Birkhäuser-Verlag, Basel, 1995.
9. A. Grün, E.P. Baltsavias and O. Henricsson, *Automatic Extraction of Man-Made Objects from Aerial and Space Images (II)*, Birkhäuser-Verlag, Basel, 1997.
10. N. Haala, C. Brenner and K.-H. Anders, Generation of 3D city models from Digital Surface Models and 2D GIS, pp. 68–76, in [1].
11. R. Hartley, Lines and points in three views — a unified approach, *Proc. ARPA Image Understanding Workshop* (IUW '94), Monterey, CA, 1994, pp. 1009–1016.
12. J. Mc Glone and J. Shuffelt, Projective and object space geometry for monocular building extraction, *Proc. of the IEEE Conference on Computer Vision and Pattern Recognition* (CVPR '94), Seattle, Washington, June 1994, pp. 54–61.
13. R. Nevatia, C. Lin and A. Huertas, A system for building detection from aerial images, pp. 77–86, in [9].
14. M. Roux and D. Mc Keown, Feature matching for building extraction from multiple views, *Proc. ARPA Image Understanding Workshop (IUW'94)*, Monterey, CA, 1994, pp. 331–349.
15. M. Roux and H. Maître, Three-dimensional description of dense urban areas using maps and aerial images, pp. 311–322, in [9].
16. A. Shashua, Algebraic functions for recognition, *IEEE Trans. on Pattern Analysis and Artificial Intelligence* (T-PAMI), Vol. **17** (1995), no. 8, pp. 779–789.
17. F. Stolle, A. Hanson, C. Jaynes, E. Riseman, and H. Schultz, Scene Reconstruction research — towards an automatic system, pp. 33–42, in [9].

Closed-Form Solutions for the Euclidean Calibration of a Stereo Rig

G. Csurka, D. Demirdjian, A. Ruf, and R. Horaud

INRIA Rhône-Alpes, 655 Av. de l'Europe, 38330 Montbonnot Saint Martin, France

Abstract. In this paper we describe a method for estimating the internal parameters of the left and right cameras associated with a stereo image pair. The stereo pair has known epipolar geometry and therefore 3-D projective reconstruction of pairs of matched image points is available. The stereo pair is allowed to move and hence there is a collineation relating the two projective reconstructions computed before and after the motion. We show that this collineation has similar but different parameterizations for general and ground-plane rigid motions and we make explicit the relationship between the internal camera parameters and such a collineation. We devise a practical method for recovering four camera parameters from a single general motion or three camera parameters from a single ground-plane motion. Numerous experiments with simulated, calibrated and natural data validate the calibration method.

1   Introduction

Traditional stereo vision systems use a single image pair to provide projective, affine, or Euclidean reconstruction. It has been clear that redundancy offered by further image pairs can significantly increase the quality and stability of visual reconstructions. Nevertheless, if the visual task is to recover metric structure, there are problems because both the intrinsic parameters (of the left and right cameras) and extrinsic ones (relative position and orientation of the two cameras) can vary over time. This is particularly critical when an active stereo head is being used. It is therefore important to be able to re-calibrate the stereo rig over time and over a small number of motions without using any special purpose calibration device.

A number of authors investigated the relationship between projective, affine, and metric spaces in conjunction with a single camera undergoing rigid motions [10,6,7,13,15]. In [14] it is shown that there are many critical situations for which metric structure cannot be recovered. When image pairs are available one may use additional constraints. Affine structure can be recovered from either pure translations [12], pure rotations [2] or ground-plane motions [1] of a stereo rig. For general motions, affine structure can be estimated from the eigenvector of a 3-D collineation [17] and metric structure can be estimated from two general motions [3]. Furthermore, in [8] it is shown that affine structure is an intrinsic property of a rigid stereo rig and that it can be easily recovered by combining any number of general motions.

In this paper we develop closed-form solutions for the self-calibration of a stereo rig from a **single** general or ground-plane motion. The basic assumption is that the stereo rig has the same internal and external parameters before and after the motion. More precisely, let $\mathcal{P}_1$ and $\mathcal{P}_2$ be two projective reconstructions obtained with an uncalibrated stereo rig before and after a rigid motion. These two reconstructions, i.e., a set of 3-D points, are related by a 4×4 collineation $\mathbf{H}_{12}$ which is related to the rigid motion $\mathbf{D}_{12}$ by ([17,3]):

$$\mathbf{H}_{12} \simeq \mathbf{H}_{PE}^{-1}\mathbf{D}_{12}\mathbf{H}_{PE} \qquad (1)$$

As it will be shown below, an immediate consequence of this similarity relationship is that $\mathbf{H}_{12}$ can be factorized as $\mathbf{\Lambda J\Lambda}^{-1}$ where $\mathbf{J}$ is a real Jordan canonical form. We prove that this factorization is not unique and we show how to parameterize all such factorizations and how to estimate them in practice. Furthermore, we show that there exists a relationship between the left (or right) camera parameters and all possible factorizations of $\mathbf{H}_{12}$.

More precisely, let $\mathbf{K}$ be the upper triangular matrix associated with the left camera such that $K_{33} = 1$. We will show that (i) in the case of a general motion the matrix $\mathbf{KK}^\top$ is parameterized by a pencil of conics and that (ii) for a ground-plane motion $\mathbf{KK}^\top$ is parameterized by a linear combination of three conics. Therefore, one constraint onto the entries of $\mathbf{K}$ is sufficient to estimate four intrinsic parameters from a single motion and two constraints onto the entries of $\mathbf{K}$ are necessary for estimating three intrinsic parameters from a single planar motion. As a consequence, a camera with zero image skew can be calibrated from a general motion and a camera with zero image skew and known aspect ratio can in turn be calibrated from one ground-plane motion.

The method described in this paper has several advantages over previous stereo calibration approaches. The first advantage is that affine calibration is not necessary prior to metric calibration as it is done with stratified approaches. This is particularly important for ground-plane motions for which affine structure has proved difficult to obtain. The second advantage is that all the computations are based on linear algebra techniques such as singular value decomposition. The third advantage is that, while a single motion is sufficient to calibrate, several motions can be combined in conjunction with a standard outliers rejection method in order to estimate the calibration parameters more robustly.

1.1 Paper organization

The remainder of the paper is organized as follows. Section 2 briefly recalls the camera model and makes explicit the structure of $\mathbf{KK}^\top$ for a camera with zero skew and for a camera with zero skew and known aspect ratio. Section 3 recalls the mathematical properties associated with equation (1). Section 4 describes the real Jordan factorization of matrix $\mathbf{H}_{12}$, analyses this factorization from a geometrical point of view, shows how to parameterize all possible factorizations, and describes a method to compute these factorizations in practice. Section 5 shows how to perform Euclidean calibration from the real Jordan factorization of $\mathbf{H}_{12}$ for general and ground-plane motions. Section 6 validates the method with simulated and real data and Section 7 discusses the method in the light of the experimental results obtained so far.

2 Camera model and the absolute conic

A pinhole camera projects a point M from the 3-D projective space onto a point m of the 2-D projective plane. This projection can be written as $m \simeq \mathbf{P}M$, where $\mathbf{P}$ is a $3{\times}4$ homogeneous matrix of rank equal to 3 and the sign $\simeq$ designates the projective equality – equality up to a scale factor. If we restrict the 3-D projective space to the Euclidean space, then it is well known that $\mathbf{P}$ can be written as:

$$\mathbf{P}_E = \mathbf{K}\left(\mathbf{R}\,t\right) = \left(\mathbf{KR}\ \mathbf{K}t\right) \tag{2}$$

where $\mathbf{R}$ and t describe the orientation and the position of the camera in the chosen Euclidean frame. If we consider the standard camera frame as the 3-D Euclidean frame (the origin is the center of projection, the xy-plane is parallel to the image plane and the z-axis points towards the visible scene), the projection matrix becomes[1] $\mathbf{P}_E = \left(\mathbf{K}\ \mathbf{0}_3\right)$.

The most general form for the matrix of intrinsic parameters $\mathbf{K}$ is:

$$\mathbf{K} = \begin{pmatrix} \alpha & r & u_0 \\ 0 & k\alpha & v_0 \\ 0 & 0 & 1 \end{pmatrix} \tag{3}$$

where α is the horizontal scale factor, k is the ratio between the vertical and horizontal scale factors, r is the image skew and u_0 and v_0 are the image coordinates of the center of projection.

The relation between the matrix $\mathbf{K}$ and the image of the absolute conic is $\mathbf{C} \simeq \mathbf{K}^{-\top}\mathbf{K}^{-1}$ [4]. Let us make explicit the dual of this conic, i.e., $\mathbf{A} = \mathbf{C}^{-\top}$:

$$\mathbf{A} \simeq \mathbf{KK}^\top = \begin{pmatrix} \alpha^2 + r^2 + u_0^2 & rk\alpha + u_0v_0 & u_0 \\ rk\alpha + u_0v_0 & k^2\alpha^2 + v_0^2 & v_0 \\ u_0 & v_0 & 1 \end{pmatrix} \tag{4}$$

This means that $\mathbf{A}$ is symmetric and if we want to fix the scale factor ($\mathbf{A}$ is defined up to a scale) such that $\mathbf{A} = \mathbf{KK}^\top$, we need that $A_{33} = 1$.

Equation (3) describes a five-parameter camera. It will be useful to consider camera models with a reduced set of intrinsic parameters, as follows:

– *four-parameter camera* with $r = 0$ (image skew), which means that the image is a rectangle – a sensible assumption. In this case the dual conic becomes:

$$\mathbf{A} \simeq \mathbf{KK}^\top = \begin{pmatrix} \alpha^2 + u_0^2 & u_0v_0 & u_0 \\ u_0v_0 & k^2\alpha^2 + v_0^2 & v_0 \\ u_0 & v_0 & 1 \end{pmatrix} \tag{5}$$

---

[1] We denote by $\mathbf{0}_n$ the n-vector containing n zeros.

which provides an additional constraint on the entries of $\mathbf{A}$, i.e. $A_{12} - A_{13}A_{23} = 0$.

- *three-parameter camera* with $r = 0$ and k (aspect ratio) having a known value; for instance the value of k can be obtained from the physical size of a pixel. Therefore there is an additional constraint on the entries of $\mathbf{A}$:

$$k^2(A_{11} - A_{12}^2) - (A_{23}^2 - A_{22}) = 0$$

3 Rigid motion of a stereo rig

A stereo rig is composed of two cameras fixed together. Let $\mathbf{P}$ and $\mathbf{P}'$ be the projection matrices of the left and right cameras. We can choose without loss of generality a projective basis $\mathcal{B}_P$ such that[2] $\mathbf{P} = (\mathbf{I}_3 \; \mathbf{0}_3)$. In this case $\mathbf{P}' = (\mathbf{H}_\infty + e'a^\top, \lambda e')$ [11], where $\mathbf{H}_\infty$ is the infinite homography between the left and right images, e' is the right epipole, a an arbitrary 3-vector and λ is an arbitrary scale factor. It was shown in [8] that the 4-vector $(a^\top \; \lambda)$ has a simple but important geometric interpretation, namely it is the plane of infinity associated with the stereo pair. However, this plane is not used throughout this paper.

Given a stereo rig with two projection matrices $\mathbf{P}$ and $\mathbf{P}'$, it is possible to compute the 3-D projective coordinates of a point M in the basis $\mathcal{B}_P$ from the equations $m \simeq \mathbf{P}M$ and $m' \simeq \mathbf{P}'M$, where m and m' are the projections of M onto the left and right images.

If we restrict the projective space to the Euclidean space and choose as basis $\mathcal{B}_E$ the standard camera frame associated with the first camera, $\mathbf{P}$ and $\mathbf{P}'$ are given by:

$$\mathbf{P}_E = (\mathbf{K} \; \mathbf{0}_3) \qquad \text{and} \qquad \mathbf{P}'_E = (\mathbf{K}'\mathbf{R} \; \mathbf{K}'t)$$

where $\mathbf{K}$ and $\mathbf{K}'$ are the matrices of left and right intrinsic camera parameters, $\mathbf{R}$ and t describe the orientation and position of the right camera frame with respect to the left camera frame. The equations $m \simeq \mathbf{P}_E M_E$ and $m' \simeq \mathbf{P}'_E M_E$ allow the estimation of M_E – the 3-D Euclidean coordinates of a 3-D point in the basis $\mathcal{B}_E$.

It is straightforward to show that, if $\mathbf{H}_{PE}$ represents the collineation between the projective basis $\mathcal{B}_P$ and the Euclidean frame $\mathcal{B}_E$, i.e., $M_E \simeq \mathbf{H}_{PE}M$, we have the followings relations:

$$\mathbf{P} \simeq \mathbf{P}_E \mathbf{H}_{PE} \qquad \text{and} \qquad \mathbf{P}' \simeq \mathbf{P}'_E \mathbf{H}_{PE}$$

Indeed, from $\mathbf{P}M \simeq m \simeq \mathbf{P}_E M_E \simeq \mathbf{P}_E \mathbf{H}_{PE}M$ it results that $\mathbf{P} \simeq \mathbf{P}_E \mathbf{H}_{PE}$.

The basic assumption throughout the paper is that the stereo rig performs a series of rigid motions and that during these motions $\mathbf{K}, \mathbf{K}'$, $\mathbf{R}$, and t remain constant, as shown in Figure 1. As the bases $\mathcal{B}_P$ and $\mathcal{B}_E$ are related to the

---

[2] We denote by $\mathbf{I}_n$ the $n \times n$ matrix of identity.

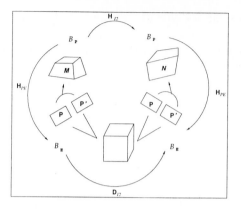

Fig. 1. Rigid motion of a stereo rig.

stereo rig we can again use them to compute N and N_E, the projective and Euclidean representations of the same physical point after the motion. Clearly, the relationship between the projective and Euclidean representations before the motion holds after the motion, $N_E \simeq H_{PE}N$.

Let $\mathbf{D}_{12}$ be the 4×4 matrix describing the rigid motion performed by the stereo rig. We have $N_E = \mathbf{D}_{12}M_E$ and by substituting M_E and N_E with $H_{PE}M$ and $H_{PE}N$ we obtain:

$$N \simeq H_{PE}^{-1}\mathbf{D}_{12}H_{PE}M$$

Consequently, the collineation between the two projective reconstructions (before and after the motion) (M and N) is related to the rigid motion by the following formula:

$$\mathbf{H}_{12} \simeq \mathbf{H}_{PE}^{-1}\mathbf{D}_{12}\mathbf{H}_{PE} \qquad (6)$$

In order to get rid of the scale factor one may normalize $\mathbf{H}_{12}$ by dividing each term with $sign(trace(\mathbf{H}_{12})) \sqrt[4]{det(\mathbf{H}_{12})}$. With this normalization "$\simeq$" becomes "$=$" and the eigenvalues of $\mathbf{H}_{12}$ and of $\mathbf{D}_{12}$ are the same. In what follows we assume that $\mathbf{H}_{12}$ has been normalized.

The following proposition proved in [8] makes explicit the structure of $\mathbf{H}_{PE}$ under the choice of the bases $\mathcal{B}_P$ and $\mathcal{B}_E$:

Proposition 1. *The 4×4 collineation* $\mathbf{H}_{PE}$ *allowing the conversion of a projective reconstruction (basis $\mathcal{B}_P$) obtained with a stereo rig into an Euclidean reconstruction (basis $\mathcal{B}_E$) has the following structure:*

$$\mathbf{H}_{PE} = \begin{pmatrix} \mathbf{K}^{-1} & \mathbf{0}_3 \\ \mathbf{a}^\top & \lambda \end{pmatrix} \qquad (7)$$

where $\mathbf{K}$ *is the matrix of intrinsic parameters of the left camera and* $\left(\mathbf{a}^\top \ \lambda\right)$ *is the equation of the plane at infinity in the projective basis $\mathcal{B}_P$.*

4   Algebraic preliminaries

In this section we make explicit some algebraic properties of the 4×4 collineation $\mathbf{H}_{12}$ which are direct consequences of equation (6).

The displacement matrix $\mathbf{D}_{12}$ has the form:

$$\mathbf{D} = \begin{pmatrix} \mathbf{R}_{12} & \mathbf{t}_{12} \\ \mathbf{0}_3^\top & 1 \end{pmatrix} \tag{8}$$

where $\mathbf{R}_{12}$ is a 3×3 rotation matrix and $\mathbf{t}_{12}$ represents the translation. Therefore the eigenvalues of $\mathbf{D}_{12}$ are $\{e^{i\theta}, e^{-i\theta}, 1, 1\}$.

A key issue with our approach is the distinction between the *algebraic multiplicity* of an eigenvalue and its *geometric multiplicity*. We recall the following definitions (see [16,9]):

Definition 2. Let λ be an eigenvalue of a matrix. Its **algebraic multiplicity** is the number of times that it occurs as a root of the corresponding characteristic polynomial.

Definition 3. The **geometric multiplicity** of an eigenvalue λ is the dimension of the eigenspace associated with the eigenvalue λ.

In the case of a rigid displacement the algebraic multiplicity of the eigenvalue $\lambda = 1$ is, in general, equal to 2 (it is equal to 4 if $\theta = 0$). However its geometric multiplicity depends on whether the rigid motion is a screw or not and is equal to:

- 1 in the case of general displacement, i.e., there is a translation along the screw axis
- 2 in the case of planar motion (there is no translation along the axis or rotation).

Therefore there are distinct calibration solutions for these two types of motion.

Given matrix $\mathbf{H}_{12}$ similar to $\mathbf{D}_{12}$, its eigenvalues are $\{e^{i\theta}, e^{-i\theta}, 1, 1\}$ as well. From [9] we have the following proposition.

Proposition 4. *Let Ω be a matrix with its eigenvalues equal to $\{e^{i\theta}, e^{-i\theta}, 1, 1\}$. Then there exists a non-singular matrix Λ such that:*

$$\Omega = \Lambda \begin{pmatrix} \cos(\theta) & -\sin(\theta) & 0 & 0 \\ \sin(\theta) & \cos(\theta) & 0 & 0 \\ 0 & 0 & 1 & \varepsilon \\ 0 & 0 & 0 & 1 \end{pmatrix} \Lambda^{-1} = \Lambda \mathbf{J}_\varepsilon \Lambda^{-1} \tag{9}$$

where $\varepsilon = 1$, if the geometric multiplicity of the double eigenvalue $\lambda = 1$ is 1, $\mathbf{J}_\varepsilon = \mathbf{J}_1$, and $\varepsilon = 0$ if the geometric multiplicity of the double eigenvalue $\lambda = 1$ is equal to 2, $\mathbf{J}_\varepsilon = \mathbf{J}_0$.

Furthermore, if $\Omega = \mathbf{D}$ is a displacement, $\Lambda = \Sigma$ is of form:

$$\Sigma = \begin{pmatrix} \mathbf{Q}_\Sigma & t_\Sigma \\ 0_3^\top & 1 \end{pmatrix} \tag{10}$$

where $\mathbf{Q}_\Sigma$ is an orthogonal matrix, i.e Σ is a rotation or a reflection followed by a translation.

Since $\mathbf{J}_\varepsilon$ is the matrix associated with the *real Jordan canonical form*, the factorizations introduced in the proposition above are called *real Jordan factorizations*.

4.1 Non uniqueness of the real Jordan factorization

The real Jordan factorization described above is not unique. This non unicity is of crucial importance for our calibration method and we are going to give some insights into this property.

Proposition 5. *The real Jordan factorization of a matrix Ω is not unique. Moreover, $\Omega = \Lambda \mathbf{J}_\varepsilon \Lambda^{-1}$ and $\Omega = \Lambda' \mathbf{J}_\varepsilon \Lambda'^{-1}$ are real Jordan factorizations if and only if there exists a matrix $\mathbf{M}$ commuting with $\mathbf{J}_\varepsilon$, i.e. $\mathbf{MJ}_\varepsilon = \mathbf{J}_\varepsilon \mathbf{M}$, such that $\Lambda' = \Lambda \mathbf{M}$.*

Proof: For any $\mathbf{M}$ commuting with $\mathbf{J}_\varepsilon$, we have $\Omega = \Lambda \mathbf{J}_\varepsilon \mathbf{MM}^{-1}\Lambda^{-1} = \Lambda \mathbf{MJ}_\varepsilon (\Lambda \mathbf{M})^{-1}$.

Conversely, if $\Omega = \Lambda \mathbf{J}_\varepsilon \Lambda^{-1} = \Lambda' \mathbf{J}_\varepsilon \Lambda'^{-1}$, results that $\Lambda^{-1}\Lambda' \mathbf{J}_\varepsilon = \mathbf{J}_\varepsilon (\Lambda^{-1}\Lambda')^{-1}$. Hence $\Lambda^{-1}\Lambda' = \mathbf{M}$ commutes with $\mathbf{J}_\varepsilon$.

∎

By making explicit the matrix equality $\mathbf{MJ}_\varepsilon = \mathbf{J}_\varepsilon \mathbf{M}$, it is easy to derive the structure of $\mathbf{M}$:

- if $\varepsilon = 1$ (general motion), $\mathbf{M} = \mathbf{M}_g$ has 4 degrees of freedom and can be written as:

$$\mathbf{M}_g = \begin{pmatrix} \alpha & -\beta & 0 & 0 \\ \beta & \alpha & 0 & 0 \\ 0 & 0 & \gamma & \omega \\ 0 & 0 & 0 & \gamma \end{pmatrix} \tag{11}$$

- if $\varepsilon = 0$ (planar motion), $\mathbf{M} = \mathbf{M}_p$ has 6 degrees of freedom and the form:

$$\mathbf{M}_p = \begin{pmatrix} \alpha & -\beta & 0 & 0 \\ \beta & \alpha & 0 & 0 \\ 0 & 0 & \gamma & \omega \\ 0 & 0 & \delta & \eta \end{pmatrix} \tag{12}$$

– if $\boldsymbol{\Omega}$ is a displacement, i.e. $\boldsymbol{\Omega} = \boldsymbol{\Sigma}\mathbf{J}_\varepsilon\boldsymbol{\Sigma}^{-1}$, $\boldsymbol{\Sigma}\mathbf{M}$, must be of form (10). Using this constraint we obtain:

$$\mathbf{M}_d = \begin{pmatrix} \cos(\psi) & \sin(\psi) & 0 & 0 \\ -\sin(\psi) & \cos(\psi) & 0 & 0 \\ 0 & 0 & \pm 1 & \omega \\ 0 & 0 & 0 & 1 \end{pmatrix} = \begin{pmatrix} \mathbf{Q}_z & t_z \\ \mathbf{0}_3^\top & 1 \end{pmatrix} \tag{13}$$

4.2 The real Jordan factorization of a collineation

The real Jordan factorization will be used to decompose matrix $\mathbf{H}_{12}$ which maps two projective reconstructions obtained with the stereo rig before and after the motion. It is therefore important to describe how to obtain **one** such a factorization.

Proposition 6. *Let $\{e^{i\theta}, e^{-i\theta}, 1, 1\}$ be the eigenvalues of $\mathbf{H}_{12}$ and let v_1, v_2 be the eigenvectors associated with $e^{i\theta}$ and $e^{-i\theta}$.*

(i) If the eigenvalue $\lambda = 1$ has geometric multiplicity equal to 1, let u_3 be the eigenvector associated with this eigenvalue and we obtain the following real Jordan factorization:

$$\mathbf{H}_{12} = \begin{pmatrix} u_1 & u_2 & u_3 & w \end{pmatrix} \mathbf{J}_1 \begin{pmatrix} u_1 & u_2 & u_3 & w \end{pmatrix}^{-1} = \boldsymbol{\Lambda}_g \mathbf{J}_1 \boldsymbol{\Lambda}_g^{-1} \tag{14}$$

where $u_1 = v_1 + v_2$, $u_2 = i(v_1 - v_2)$ are two real vectors and vector w is defined by[3]

$$w = \begin{pmatrix} (\overline{\mathbf{H}}_{12} - \mathbf{I}_3)^{-1}\overline{u}_3 \\ w_4 \end{pmatrix} \tag{15}$$

with w_4 chosen such that $\det(u_1, u_2, u_3, w) \neq 0$.

(ii) If the eigenvalue $\lambda = 1$ has geometric multiplicity equal to 2 let the vectors $\{u_3, u_4\}$ be a basis of the associated eigenspace and in this case the following real Jordan factorization is obtained:

$$\mathbf{H}_{12} = \begin{pmatrix} u_1 & u_2 & u_3 & u_4 \end{pmatrix} \mathbf{J}_0 \begin{pmatrix} u_1 & u_2 & u_3 & u_4 \end{pmatrix}^{-1} = \boldsymbol{\Lambda}_p \mathbf{J}_0 \boldsymbol{\Lambda}_p^{-1} \tag{16}$$

Proof: We show (ii) first. From $\mathbf{H}_{12}v_1 = (\cos(\theta) + i\sin(\theta))v_1$ and $\mathbf{H}_{12}v_2 = (\cos(\theta) - i\sin(\theta))v_2$, by simple addition and subtraction results:

$$\begin{cases} \mathbf{H}_{12}u_1 = \cos(\theta)u_1 + \sin(\theta)u_2 \\ \mathbf{H}_{12}u_2 = -\sin(\theta)u_1 + \cos(\theta)u_2 \end{cases} \tag{17}$$

Furthermore $\mathbf{H}_{12}u_3 = u_3$, $\mathbf{H}_{12}u_4 = u_4$ and writing together with (17), using matrix notation, gives:

$$\mathbf{H}_{12} \begin{pmatrix} u_1 & u_2 & u_3 & u_4 \end{pmatrix} = \begin{pmatrix} u_1 & u_2 & u_3 & u_4 \end{pmatrix} \begin{pmatrix} \cos(\theta) & -\sin(\theta) & 0 & 0 \\ \sin(\theta) & \cos(\theta) & 0 & 0 \\ 0 & 0 & 1 & 0 \\ 0 & 0 & 0 & 1 \end{pmatrix}$$

which is equivalent to (16).

---

[3] We denoted by $\overline{\mathbf{A}}$ the 3×3 upper left block of a 4×4 matrix $\mathbf{A}$ and by $\overline{a}$ the first 3 components ot the 4 vector a.

Second we prove (i). By combining equation (17) with $\mathbf{H}_{12}\boldsymbol{u}_3 = \boldsymbol{u}_3$ we obtain:

$$\mathbf{H}_{12}\begin{pmatrix} \boldsymbol{u}_1 & \boldsymbol{u}_2 & \boldsymbol{u}_3 \end{pmatrix} = \begin{pmatrix} \boldsymbol{u}_1 & \boldsymbol{u}_2 & \boldsymbol{u}_3 \end{pmatrix}\begin{pmatrix} \cos(\theta) & -\sin(\theta) & 0 \\ \sin(\theta) & \cos(\theta) & 0 \\ 0 & 0 & 1 \end{pmatrix}$$

By inspecting equation (14), we notice that $\boldsymbol{w}$ must verify:

$$\mathbf{H}_{12}\boldsymbol{w} = \boldsymbol{u}_3 + \boldsymbol{w} \tag{18}$$

The rank of $\mathbf{H}_{12} - \mathbf{I}_4$ is equal to 3. We can assume that $det(\overline{\mathbf{H}}_{12} - \mathbf{I}_3) \neq 0$ and construct the vector given by equation (15). If $det(\overline{\mathbf{H}}_{12} - \mathbf{I}_3) = 0$, we can consider an other 3×3 block of the matrix $\mathbf{H}_{12}$ and apply the same method.

∎

Consequently, one way to compute a real Jordan factorization of a 4×4 collineation $\mathbf{H}_{12}$ is to compute its eigenvalues and associated eigenvectors. In practice $\mathbf{H}_{12}$ is estimated from image measurements and therefore it is corrupted by noise. This noise can considerably perturbate the eigenvalues and eigenvectors of $\mathbf{H}_{12}$ [16].

Therefore we devised a simple method for computing the column vectors of matrix $\boldsymbol{\Lambda}$ without computing explicitly the eigenvalues of $\mathbf{H}_{12}$. The latter is estimated up to a scale factor but after normalization one may notice that the trace has a simple form $trace\ (\mathbf{H}_{12}) = 2 + 2\cos(\theta)$. Therefore, we have $\cos(\theta) = \frac{trace(\mathbf{H})-2}{2}$ and $\sin(\theta) = \sqrt{1 - \cos(\theta)^2}$. Finally, from equation (17) we obtain:

$$\begin{pmatrix} \mathbf{H}_{12} - \cos(\theta)\mathbf{I}_4 & -\sin(\theta)\mathbf{I}_4 \\ \sin(\theta)\mathbf{I}_4 & \mathbf{H}_{12} - \cos(\theta) \end{pmatrix}\begin{pmatrix} \boldsymbol{u}_1 \\ \boldsymbol{u}_2 \end{pmatrix} = \mathbf{0}_8$$

which yields a solution for $\boldsymbol{u}_1$ and $\boldsymbol{u}_2$.

The eigenspace corresponding to the eigenvalue 1 is given by $(\mathbf{H}_{12} - \mathbf{I}_4)\boldsymbol{u} = \mathbf{0}_4$. In the noise-less case the rank of $\mathbf{H}_{12} - \mathbf{I}_4$ is equal to 3. However, when the data are corrupted by noise $det(\mathbf{H}_{12} - \mathbf{I}_4) \neq 0$ and an approximate solution must be found. In practice the singular value decomposition of $\mathbf{H}_{12} - \mathbf{I}_4$ allows to compute the eigenspace associated with the unit eigenvalue. If there is one small singular value, the geometric multiplicity is one and $\boldsymbol{u}_3$ is the vector corresponding to this singular value. If there are two small singular values, the geometric multiplicity is 2 and the two associated vectors are $\boldsymbol{u}_3$ and $\boldsymbol{u}_4$.

5 Euclidean calibration

We come back now to the basic equation associated with the rigid motion of a stereo rig $\mathbf{H}_{12} = \mathbf{H}_{PE}^{-1}\mathbf{D}_{12}\mathbf{H}_{PE}$. Consider first a real Jordan factorization of

$\mathbf{D}_{12}$, i.e $\mathbf{D}_{12} = \mathbf{\Sigma}\mathbf{J}\mathbf{\Sigma}^{-1}$. We obtain **all** the factorization by multiplying $\mathbf{\Sigma}$ with $\mathbf{M}_d$, equation (13):

$$\mathbf{D}_{12} = \mathbf{\Sigma}\mathbf{M}_d\mathbf{J}_\varepsilon(\mathbf{\Sigma}\mathbf{M}_d)^{-1}$$

Consider now a real Jordan factorization of $\mathbf{H}_{12}$ obtained as described in Section **4.2**. Again we multiply by matrix $\mathbf{M}$ to obtain all possible factorizations of $\mathbf{H}_{12}$, i.e. $\mathbf{H}_{12} = \mathbf{\Lambda}\mathbf{M}\mathbf{J}_\varepsilon(\mathbf{\Lambda}\mathbf{M})^{-1}$.

Replacing $\mathbf{D}_{12}$ and $\mathbf{H}_{12}$ in $\mathbf{H}_{12} = \mathbf{H}_{PE}^{-1}\mathbf{D}_{12}\mathbf{H}_{PE}$, results:

$$\mathbf{\Lambda}\mathbf{M}\mathbf{J}_\varepsilon(\mathbf{\Lambda}\mathbf{M})^{-1} = \mathbf{H}_{PE}^{-1}\mathbf{\Sigma}\mathbf{M}_d\mathbf{J}_\varepsilon(\mathbf{H}_{PE}^{-1}\mathbf{\Sigma}\mathbf{M}_d)^{-1}$$

We immediately obtain $\mathbf{H}_{PE}^{-1}\mathbf{\Sigma}\mathbf{M}_d = \mathbf{\Lambda}\mathbf{M}$ and, from equations (7), (10) and (13), results:

$$\begin{pmatrix} \mathbf{K} & \mathbf{0}_3 \\ -\frac{1}{\lambda}\mathbf{a}^\top\mathbf{K} & \frac{1}{\lambda} \end{pmatrix} \begin{pmatrix} \mathbf{Q}_\Sigma & \mathbf{t}_\Sigma \\ \mathbf{0}_3^\top & 1 \end{pmatrix} \begin{pmatrix} \mathbf{Q}_z & \mathbf{t}_z \\ \mathbf{0}_3^\top & 1 \end{pmatrix} = \begin{pmatrix} \mathbf{K}\mathbf{Q}_\Sigma\mathbf{Q}_z & \bullet \\ \bullet & \bullet \end{pmatrix}$$

Furthermore, by considering only the upper-left 3×3 block matrices in this equation one obtains $\mathbf{K}\mathbf{Q}_\Sigma\mathbf{Q}_z = (\overline{\mathbf{\Lambda}\mathbf{M}})$ and finally the orthogonality of matrices $\mathbf{Q}_\Sigma$ and $\mathbf{Q}_z$ leads to the following relationship:

$$\mathbf{K}\mathbf{K}^\top = (\mathbf{K}\mathbf{Q}_\Sigma\mathbf{Q}_z)(\mathbf{K}\mathbf{Q}_\Sigma\mathbf{Q}_z)^\top = (\overline{\mathbf{\Lambda}\mathbf{M}})\,(\overline{\mathbf{\Lambda}\mathbf{M}})^\top \tag{19}$$

5.1 General motion

For a general motion the structure of matrix $\mathbf{M}$ is given by equations (14) and (11) and we have:

$$\mathbf{\Lambda}_g\mathbf{M}_g = \begin{pmatrix} \alpha\mathbf{u}_1 + \beta\mathbf{u}_2 & \alpha\mathbf{u}_2 - \beta\mathbf{u}_1 & \gamma\mathbf{u}_3 & \omega\mathbf{u}_3 + \gamma\mathbf{w} \end{pmatrix}$$

The dual of the image of the absolute conic becomes in this case:

$$\mathbf{K}\mathbf{K}^\top = (\overline{\mathbf{\Lambda}_g\mathbf{M}_g})(\overline{\mathbf{\Lambda}_g\mathbf{M}_g})^\top = \underbrace{(\alpha^2 + \beta^2)}_{\tau}(\overline{\mathbf{u}}_1\overline{\mathbf{u}}_1^\top + \overline{\mathbf{u}}_2\overline{\mathbf{u}}_2^\top) + \underbrace{\gamma^2}_{\sigma}\,\overline{\mathbf{u}}_3\overline{\mathbf{u}}_3^\top \tag{20}$$

where $\overline{\mathbf{u}}_i = (u_{i1}, u_{i2}, u_{i3})^\top$ for each $\mathbf{u}_i = (u_{i1}, u_{i2}, u_{i3}, u_{i4})^\top$, $i = 1, 2, 3$.

Note that $\mathbf{K}\mathbf{K}^\top$ depends merely on vectors $\overline{\mathbf{u}}_1, \overline{\mathbf{u}}_2, \overline{\mathbf{u}}_3$ which have already been estimated and on two further positive parameters $\tau \geq 0$ and $\sigma \geq 0$. Therefore, in order to estimate $\mathbf{A} = \mathbf{K}\mathbf{K}^\top$ *from a single movement* two additional constraints are needed. As it was shown in Section **2**, a four-parameter camera has exactly two constraints associated with the entries of $\mathbf{A}$, namely:

$$\begin{cases} A_{33} = 1 \\ A_{12} - A_{13}A_{23} = 0 \end{cases} \tag{21}$$

By combining (20) with (21) obtain the following solutions for τ and σ:

$$\sigma = -\frac{\prod_{j=1}^{2}(u_1^j u_2^3 - u_1^3 u_2^j)}{\prod_{j=1}^{2}(u_3^3(u_1^j u_1^3 + u_2^j u_2^3) - u_3^j((u_1^3)^2 + (u_2^3)^2))}$$

$$\tau = \frac{1 - \sigma(u_3^3)^2}{(u_1^3)^2 + (u_2^3)^2} \tag{22}$$

where u_i^j is the jth component of u_i. Notice that one must check the sign of σ and τ since they must be, strictly positives by definition.

Once σ and τ are computed, one may determine $\mathbf{KK}^\top$ and compute the intrinsic parameters either directly from equation (5) or by Cholesky factorization.

5.2 Planar motion

We consider now the case of a planar motion. In this case the structure of matrix $\mathbf{M}$ is defined by equation (12) and the structure of matrix $\mathbf{\Lambda}$ is given by equation (16), i.e., matrices $\mathbf{M}_p$ and $\mathbf{\Lambda}_p$. Hence:

$$\mathbf{\Lambda}_p\mathbf{M}_p = \begin{pmatrix} \alpha u_1 + \beta u_2 & \alpha u_2 - \beta u_1 & \gamma u_3 + \delta u_4 & \omega u_3 + \eta u_4 \end{pmatrix}$$

and we obtain for the dual of the image of the absolute conic:

$$\mathbf{KK}^\top = (\mathbf{\Lambda}_p\mathbf{M}_p)(\mathbf{\Lambda}_p\mathbf{M}_p)^\top = \underbrace{(\alpha^2 + \beta^2)}_{\tau}(\overline{u}_1\overline{u}_1^\top + \overline{u}_2\overline{u}_2^\top) \tag{23}$$

$$+ \underbrace{\gamma^2}_{\sigma}\left(\overline{u}_3\overline{u}_3^\top + \underbrace{\left(\frac{\delta}{\gamma}\right)}_{\mu}(\overline{u}_3\overline{u}_4^\top + \overline{u}_4\overline{u}_3^\top) + \underbrace{\left(\frac{\delta^2}{\gamma^2}\right)}_{\mu^2}\overline{u}_4\overline{u}_4^\top\right)$$

In this case, $\mathbf{A} = \mathbf{KK}^\top$ is defined by vectors $\overline{u}_1, \overline{u}_2, \overline{u}_3, \overline{u}_4$ and by three undetermined parameters τ, σ and μ. Since we have three unknown parameters, we need 3 constraints on $\mathbf{A}$ in order to calibrate the camera with a single motion. A three-parameter camera has the following three constraints associated with it (see Section 2):

$$\begin{cases} A_{33} = 1 \\ A_{12} - A_{13}A_{23} = 0 \\ k^2(A_{11} - A_{12}^2) - (A_{23}^2 - A_{22}) = 0 \end{cases} \tag{24}$$

By combining (23) with (24) we obtain the following formulae for $\tau > 0$, $\sigma > 0$ and $\mu \neq 0$:

$$\mu = -\frac{k^2 n^1(u_3^3 m^1 - u_3^1 m^3) + n^2(u_3^3 m^2 - u_3^2 m^3)}{k^2 n^1(u_4^3 m^1 - u_4^1 m^3) + n^2(u_4^3 m^2 - u_4^2 m^3)}$$

$$\sigma = \left(\frac{k^2 m^3 n^1 u_4^1 + m^3 n^2 u_4^2 - u_4^3(m^1 n^1 k^2 + m^2 n^2)}{km^3(u_3^1(u_4^3 m^1 - u_4^1 m^3) - u_3^2(u_4^3 m^2 - u_4^2 m^3) + u_3^3(u_4^2 m^1 - u_4^1 m^2))}\right)^2$$

$$\tau = \frac{1 - \sigma(u_3^3 + \mu u_4^3)^2}{m^3} \tag{25}$$

with $j \in \{1, 2, 3\}$, $m^j = u_1^j u_1^3 + u_2^j u_2^3$ and $n^j = u_1^j u_2^3 - u_1^3 u_2^j$.

Once τ, σ and μ are thus computed and if the constraint $\tau > 0$ is verified, one can determine the three camera parameters either in closed-form or by Cholesky factorization.

6 Experimental results

In a first series of experiments, the above developed methods are evaluated on synthetic image data in order to quantitatively study the accuracy of calibration as a function of image noise, and the type of movements considered. A second experiment compares the results of self-calibration and standard off-line calibration on images of a particular calibration grid. The third experiment is to validate the use of our method for self-calibration of a stereo rig in an unknown real-word scene.

6.1 Synthetic data

Synthetic stereo images showing a scene of about 40 3-D points are generated for five different points of view. The internal parameters of the two cameras were kept fixed, such that projective reconstruction using [5] with the same projection matrices results in a representation of the scene in one and the same projective frame related to the stereo rig.

The different viewpoints are related by rigid motions of the rig and the conjugate collineations $\mathbf{H}_{ii+1}$ from position i to $i+1$ of projective space are estimated by the linear method presented in [8]. General screw motions and restricted planar motions are considered as camera motions, in order to comparatively study the performance of the respective methods of self-calibration.

The influence of image noise is evaluated by adding artificial Gaussian noise with standard deviation varying from 0.3 to 2 pixels. In order to obtain significant results, closed-form self-calibration is performed for each single movement in the sequence and the average value of each parameter over the sequence is considered. For each parameter we compute the relative error between the estimated values $\alpha_u^*, k^*, u_0^*, v_0^*$ and the true values α_u, k, u_0, v_0:

$$\epsilon_\alpha = \frac{|\alpha_u - \alpha_u^*|}{|\alpha_u|}, \quad \epsilon_k = \frac{|k - k^*|}{|k|}, \quad \epsilon_u = \frac{|u_0 - u_0^*|}{|u_0|} \quad \text{and} \quad \epsilon_v = \frac{|v_0 - v_0^*|}{|v_0|}$$

and for the principal point additionally the relative Euclidean distance between the points (u_0^*, v_0^*) and (u_0, v_0) is considered:

$$\epsilon_{u,v} = \sqrt{\frac{(u_0 - u_0^*)^2 + (v_0 - v_0^*)^2}{u_0^2 + v_0^2}}$$

The median of the relative errors over 100 trial runs is depicted in Figure 2 which demonstrates that accuracy of self-calibration degrades monotonically nicely with increasing measurement noise. Furthermore, calibration in the case of planar motion compares favorably with the case of general motion, given that a priori estimates of the fixed parameters (skew and aspect ratio) are in the vicinity of the true values.

Obviously, the estimates of the principal point (u_0, v_0) are less stable than those of the scale factors (α_u, k). On the one hand, the instability of the principal

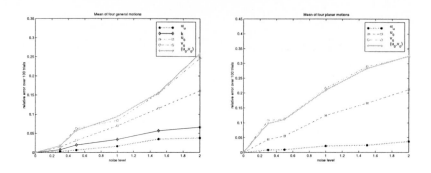

Fig. 2. Relative error in estimates of the intrinsic parameter from four general displacements (left) and four planar motions (right) at different noise levels.

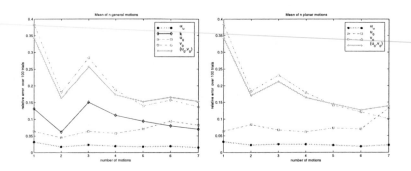

Fig. 3. The relative error in intrinsic parameters using an increasing number of motions.

point is an intrinsic problem of camera calibration from noisy image measurements and was observed with most of the existing algorithms. On the other hand, an inaccurate principal point barely affects Euclidean reconstruction, as outlined in [8].

To quantify the possible gain in accuracy from combining several motions, closed-form self-calibration is performed over one to seven movements out of trajectories consisting of either a general motion or a planar motion. From 100 trial at a noise level of 1 pixel, the first i movements of the trajectory were taken to calibrate and estimate the parameters by their average values. Figure 3 shows the evolution of the relative errors as a function of the number of motions which are considered.

Obviously, using several motions instead of a of a single motion does not improve the accuracy associated with the estimation of α_u and barely improves the accuracy associated with u_0, v_0 or k.

Method	left camera				right camera			
	α	k	u_0	v_0	α	k	u_0	v_0
Off-line calibration	1534	.996	270	265	1520	.996	264	271
General motion	1550	.988	278	300	1533	.988	256	277
Planar motion	1570	$k^\star$	261	291	1561	$k^\star$	291	296

Table 1. Results for the left and right camera parameters using off-line calibration and self-calibration. The results shown are means of several motions. We used $k^\star = .996$ as known value for planar motions.

6.2 Self-calibration with image pairs of a calibration grid

To justify the applicability of our method for camera self-calibration and to compare its effectiveness with that of standard off-line methods, calibration is executed on images of a 3-D calibration grid. It consists of 100 circular target points, that are evenly distributed on three planes. Their 3-D positions are known with an accuracy of 0.02 mm, and their image projection are detected and localized at an accuracy of 0.05 pixel. The results of off-line calibration using [4] and the results of applying our self-calibration methods to eight stereo image pairs of the grid are compared in Table 1, for the left and right cameras, respectively. Even-though no knowledge about 3D scene structure is required, self-calibration performs, for both types of motions, as well as off-line calibration.

6.3 On-line self-calibration from image pairs of a 3-D scene

In order to validate the applicability of our method for camera self-calibration during runtime of a vision-system, i.e. for on-line calibration, we gathered 45 stereo images of a real-world scene from viewpoints which differ merely by small motions of the stereo pair. To obtain point correspondences we used the following stereo tracking algorithm. Interest points are extracted from the first pair and matched between the left and right images. Next, the points in the left image are tracked, as the stereo rig moves, over the sequence of images associated with the left camera motion. To obtain point matches associated with the image pair after the motion, the tracking is guided by the epipolar geometry. This algorithm makes use of the fact that the epipolar geometry remains unchanged during the motion of the stereo rig. Figure 4 shows the matches obtained with two image pairs.

In contrast to the previous experiments, the matched points are no longer evenly distributed, neither in the image, nor in space. Even worse, mismatches may be present in the data. Additionally, interest points are no longer extracted with 0.05 pixel accuracy. Nevertheless, the camera parameters resulting from self-calibration are within the expected range and the behaviour of the method is consistent with the results obtained for synthetic data. Figure 5 depicts the distribution of parameter estimates obtained by closed-form calibration for about 1000 planar or general motions. Table 2 shows the average values of each parameter set.

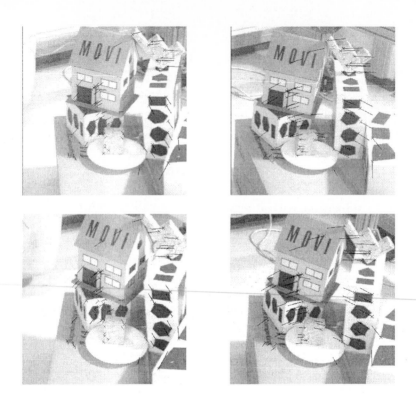

Fig. 4. Two image pairs and their matched points.

7   Conclusion

We proposed a method for self-calibration of a stereo rig from a single general or ground-plane motion. The basic assumption is that the stereo rig has the same internal and external parameters before and after the motion. In this case the collineation relating the two projective reconstructions performed at each position is conjugated to a displacement. By making explicit the algebraic properties of such a collineation, we derived a closed-form solution to recover four camera parameters from a single general motion or three camera parameters from a single ground-plane motion.

One of the advantages of this approach is that calibration was done without explicitly computing affine structure. The second advantage is that all the computations are based on linear algebra techniques such as singular value decomposition, and hence it is easy to implement and has low computation cost. Therefore, it can be included in on-line perception-action cycle, such as visual servoing.

One remarkable feature of our method is that it performs as well with small motions as with large ones. This has a crucial practical importance because it is much easier to find matches between images that differ by a small motion

	left camera				right camera			
Method	α	k	u_0	v_0	α	k	u_0	v_0
Off-line calibration	1534	.996	270	265	1520	.996	264	271
General motion	1531	1.01	255	323	1508	1.05	211	334
Planar motion	1462	$k^\star$	154	246	1464	$k^\star$	143	259

Table 2. Results for the left and right camera parameters using off-line calibration and self-calibration. The results shown are means of several motions. We used $k^\star = .996$ as known value for planar motions.

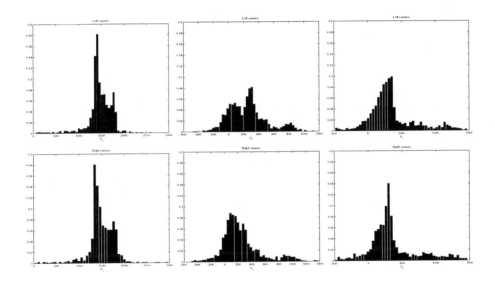

Fig. 5. The distributions of the estimated intrinsic parameters.

than for images that are far apart. One inconvenience is, however, that small motions may sometimes give rise to bad results simply because a rotation matrix which is closed to the identity matrix does not have the algebraic properties that are expected by the method. Nevertheless, these "bad" motions can be easily eliminated by simply checking the conditioning of the collineation $\mathbf{H}_{12}$.

Another source of errors is the sensitivity of the method to the accuracy with which the interest points are located and matched as well as the 3-D distribution of these points. This problem has been observed with both synthetic and real data. Interesting enough, the matrix conditioning analysis outlined above works well to eliminate such badly distributed data.

In the future we plan to investigate more thoroughly the relationship between bad calibration and the numerical conditioning of the problem and to combine closed-form calibration methods with statistically robust methods.

References

1. P. A. Beardsley and A. Zisserman. Affine calibration of mobile vehicles. In *Proceedings of Europe-China Workshop on Geometrical Modelling and Invariants for Computer Vision*, pages 214–221, Xi'an, China, April 1995. Xidan University Press.

2. P.A. Beardsley, I.D. Reid, A. Zisserman, and D.W. Murray. Active visual navigation using non-metric structure. In E. Grimson, editor, *Proceedings of the 5th International Conference on Computer Vision, Cambridge, Massachusetts, USA*, pages 58–64. IEEE Computer Society Press, June 1995.

3. F. Devernay and O. Faugeras. From projective to Euclidean reconstruction. In *Proceedings Computer Vision and Pattern Recognition Conference*, pages 264–269, San Francisco, CA., June 1996.

4. O. D. Faugeras. *Three Dimensional Computer Vision: A Geometric Viewpoint*. MIT Press, Boston, 1993.

5. R. Hartley and P. Sturm. Triangulation. *Computer Vision and Image Understanding*, 68(2):146–157, 1997.

6. R. I. Hartley. Euclidean reconstruction from uncalibrated views. In Mundy Zisserman Forsyth, editor, *Applications of Invariance in Computer Vision*, pages 237–256. Springer Verlag, Berlin Heidelberg, 1994.

7. A. Heyden and K. Åström. Euclidean reconstruction from constant intrinsic parameters. In *Proceedings of the 13th International Conference on Pattern Recognition, Vienna, Austria*, volume I, pages 339–343, August 1996.

8. R. Horaud and G. Csurka. Self-calibration and euclidean reconstruction using motions of a stereo rig. In *Proceedings of the 6th International Conference on Computer Vision, Bombay, India*, pages 96–103, January 1998.

9. R.A. Horn and C.R. Johnson. *Matrix analysis*. Cambridge University Press, 1985.

10. Q-T. Luong and O. D. Faugeras. Self-calibration of a moving camera from point correspondences and fundamental matrices. *International Journal of Computer Vision*, 22(3):261–289, 1997.

11. Q.T. Luong and T. Vieville. Canonic representations for the geometries of multiple projective views. In *Proceedings of the 3rd European Conference on Computer Vision, Stockholm, Sweden*, pages 589–599, May 1994.

12. T. Moons, L. Van Gool, M. Proesmans, and E Pauwels. Affine reconstruction from perspective image pairs with a relative object-camera translation in between. *IEEE Transactions on Pattern Analysis and Machine Intelligence*, 18(1):77–83, January 1996.

13. M. Pollefeys and L. Van Gool. A stratified approach to metric self-calibration. In *Proceedings of the Conference on Computer Vision and Pattern Recognition, Puerto Rico, USA*, pages 407–412. IEEE Computer Society Press, June 1997.

14. P. Sturm. Critical motion sequences for monocular self-calibration and uncalibrated euclidean reconstruction. In *Proceedings of IEEE Computer Society Conference on Computer Vision and Pattern Recognition*, pages 1100–1105, Puerto-Rico, June 1997.

15. B. Triggs. Autocalibration and the absolute quadric. In *Proceedings of the Conference on Computer Vision and Pattern Recognition, Puerto Rico, USA*, pages 609–614. IEEE Computer Society Press, June 1997.

16. J.H. Wilkinson. *The algebraic eigenvalue problem*. Clarendon Press - Oxford, 1965.

17. A. Zisserman, P. A. Beardsley, and I. D. Reid. Metric calibration of a stereo rig. In *Proc. IEEE Workshop on Representation of Visual Scenes*, pages 93–100, Cambridge, Mass., June 1995.

Colour and Indexing

Is Machine Colour Constancy Good Enough?

Brian Funt, Kobus Barnard and Lindsay Martin
School of Computing Science,
Simon Fraser University
Burnaby, British Columbia
Canada V5A 1S6
{funt, kobus, colour}@cs.sfu.ca

Abstract. This paper presents a negative result: current machine colour constancy algorithms are *not* good enough for colour-based object recognition. This result has surprised us since we have previously used the better of these algorithms successfully to correct the colour balance of images for display. Colour balancing has been the typical application of colour constancy, rarely has it been actually put to use in a computer vision system, so our goal was to show how well the various methods would do on an obvious machine colour vision task, namely, object recognition. Although all the colour constancy methods we tested proved insufficient for the task, we consider this an important finding in itself. In addition we present results showing the correlation between colour constancy performance and object recognition performance, and as one might expect, the better the colour constancy the better the recognition rate.

1 Introduction

We set out to show that machine colour constancy had matured to the point where it would be useful in other aspects of machine vision. Since all the different colour constancy algorithms require only a fraction of a second to run, they could be practical so long as their results were sufficiently accurate. 'Sufficiently accurate' begs the question—"Accurate enough for what?"—so we needed to choose a representative task that would provide an answer to the question and simultaneously give us a way to measure accuracy.

In the past the performance of colour constancy algorithms has been reported in terms of average angular error or RMS error between the predicted and target images [1]. In this paper, we test colour constancy by putting it to use in colour-based object recognition. The object recognition strategy is Swain and Ballard's "colour indexing" method [2], which is based on comparing histograms of the distribution of image colours. Colour indexing fails miserably when the ambient light illuminating the object to be recognized differs from that used in constructing the database of model images. Swain and Ballard suggest using colour constancy preprocessing as a way of addressing this problem; however, it has since been solved by introducing illumination-independent representations (e.g., relative colour instead of absolute colour [3] or by moment-based representations of colour histograms [4]). Nonetheless, if colour constancy methods work then it seems a natural task for them to be used in preprocessing images prior to indexing as Swain and Ballard originally suggested.

Clearly, the fact that colour indexing is sensitive to variations in the ambient scene illumination is to be expected since its an entirely colour-based method and the scene illumination directly affects the image RGB colour[1]. The question we address here is whether or not existing colour constancy algorithms are effective enough at generating illumination-independent colour descriptors that colour indexing will work under the typical range of scene illuminations that are encountered in practice such as daylight, tungsten light, and fluorescent office lighting. Since our goal is to test colour constancy, not to develop a new and improved object-recognition scheme, we use colour indexing without modification.

The outline of the paper is as follows: first colour indexing and the importance of colour constancy for it will be discussed; then the method for colour correction given a good estimate of the illumination will be considered; this will be followed by a brief description of each of the colour constancy methods (greyworld, white-patch retinex, neural net, 2D gamut-constraint, and 3D gamut-constraint); next is the experimental setup and a description of the database of test images; following this are results and discussion.

2 Colour Indexing and Colour Constancy

The task for a machine *colour constancy* algorithm is to generate illumination-independent descriptors of the scene colours measured in terms of the camera RGB coordinates. The camera output is affected by the surface reflectance and the illumination. For the red channel we have

$$R(x,y) = \int E(\lambda)S(x,y,\lambda)C_R(\lambda) \tag{1}$$

where $C_R(\lambda)$ is the spectral sensitivity of the camera's red channel (similar equations for the green and blue channels $G(x,y)$ and $B(x,y)$), $E(\lambda)$ is the spectrum of the incident illumination, and $S(x,y,\lambda)$ is the spectral reflectance of the surface.

We assume that the relative spectral power distribution of $E(\lambda)$ is spatially invariant (its intensity may vary), although some colour constancy methods have been developed that exploit spatial variation in illumination [5]. Surface colours as they would have appeared under some chosen 'canonical' illuminant will be used as illumination-independent colour descriptors. Hence the machine colour constancy problem can be expressed as that of deriving an image of the scene as it would appear under the canonical illuminant $RGB_{canonical}(x,y)$ given the image of the scene $RGB_{unknown}(x,y)$ under the unknown illuminant. The mapping has only to account for the change in relative spectral power distribution between the unknown and canonical illuminants.

---

[1] RGB space defined as the output of our SONY DXC-930 3-CCD colour video camera. Strictly speaking 'colour' is what a human observer perceives, but in this paper we will also use it to refer to a pixel's RGB.

Many colour constancy methods estimate only the chromaticity of the colours under the canonical illuminant and ignore the intensity component. There are many ways of normalizing the RGB to eliminate the effect of intensity of which we will use two different ones here. Colour indexing will be based on the standard chromaticity coordinate space:

$$r=R/(R+G+B); \quad g=G/(R+G+B) \tag{2}$$

For colour correction and the 2D gamut-constraint algorithm discussed below, we will use

$$r=R/B; \quad g=G/B \tag{3}$$

Colour constancy algorithms will be used to convert between chromaticity 'images', in other words from the chromaticity under the unknown illumination $rg_{unknown}(x,y)$ they will provide an estimate of what the chromaticity $rg_{canonical}(x,y)$ would have been under the canonical illumination.

Colour indexing is performed using 2-dimensional chromaticity histograms. Swain and Ballard did the majority of their tests using RGB but they included some tests with rg-chromaticity space. The method is quite simple. First a database of model (chromaticity) histograms is created from images of the objects that we wish the system to recognize. The objects need to be separated from the background before the database is built. This segmentation can be done manually if need be. Given an image of an object to be recognized—call it the 'test' object—its chromaticity histogram is determined. Unlike the case for the model objects, the test object does not need to be separated from the image background. The test histogram T is then intersected with each model histogram M in the database, where intersection is defined as,

$$H(T,M) = \sum_{j=1} \min(T_j, M_j) / \sum_{j=1} M_j \tag{4}$$

The model with the highest histogram intersection score is used to identify the unknown object.

In our implementation the chromaticity histograms are 16x16. This sampling might be too coarse for a very large image database, but for our purposes the coarse sampling should help tolerate inaccuracies in colour constancy.

3 Colour Constancy and Colour Correction

We test 5 different colour constancy algorithms: greyworld, white-patch retinex, 2D gamut-constraint, 3D gamut-constraint and neural network. These algorithms all either estimate the colour of the incident illumination and then use that estimate to transform the image colours to canonical colour descriptors, or as in the case of the gamut-constraint algorithms, they estimate the transformation directly. We do not test the Maloney-Wandell [6] algorithm since previous tests [7] have shown it to perform very poorly, often worse than doing no colour constancy at all.

The colour correction step is in each case based on a diagonal model of illumination change. Other names for the diagonal model are von Kries adaptation and coefficient rule [8] . The diagonal model simply states that the effect of moving from one scene illuminant to another can be modeled by scaling the R, G, and B channels by independent scale factors. These scale factors can be written as the elements of a diagonal matrix. Previous work has shown that the diagonal model works almost as well as a full 3x3 linear model for typical scene illuminants [9]. In particular, for the type sensors found in our video camera, which have relatively narrow band and non-overlapping sensitivity functions, the diagonal model works very well.

Some of the algorithms work in a 2-dimensional chromaticity space. In this case a 2x2 diagonal transform can still model the change in chromaticity caused by moving between illuminants. For the diagonal model to hold, the two-dimensional chromaticity coordinates must be those defined by Equation 3. Finlayson [10] shows that this choice of chromaticity coordinates is crucial in preserving, in 2-dimensional coordinates, the diagonal model of illumination change that was present in the original 3-dimensional coordinates.

Each of the colour constancy algorithms we test will be described briefly in turn. The version of the greyworld algorithm we use compares the average of all the RGB in the image to a 50% ideal grey under the canonical, i.e., to RGB_{grey} given by $RGB_{grey} = (^1/_2) * RGB_{canonical}$. The diagonal scale factors for colour correction then are simply $R_{grey}/R_{average}$, $G_{grey}/G_{average}$ and $B_{grey}/B_{average}$.

The white-patch retinex algorithm compares the RGB of white under the canonical to the maximum found in each of the 3 image bands separately. There are many different variants of retinex and our white-patch version corresponds to the infinite-path-without-reset case described by Brainard and Wandell [11]. It differs from the retinex described by McCann et al. [12] Once the maximum in each colour channel is found, the diagonal scale factors for colour correction are simply $R_{canonical}/R_{max}$, $G_{canonical}/G_{max}$ and $B_{canonical}/B_{max}$.

Previously studies [1] have shown the various gamut-constraint methods [8, 10, 13] to be some of the best performing machine colour constancy methods. The gamut-constraint method derives constraints on the ambient illumination by evaluating the differences between the gamut of colours found in the image and those of a canonical gamut. For our experiments we constructed the canonical gamut from a database of hundreds of reflectance spectra from a wide variety of common objects. The canonical gamut is given by the convex hull of the set of RGB values that would have arisen if these reflectances were to be illuminated by the canonical illuminant. To understand the gamut-constraint method, consider an RGB triple **a** arising in an image of a scene under some unknown illumination. What does **a**'s presence reveal about the illumination? Since the canonical gamut represents the full set of RGB's ever expected to occur, the same spot under the canonical illuminant must correspond to some RGB inside the canonical gamut. However, since **a** has been obtained under an illuminant different from the canonical one, it may no longer lie within the canonical gamut. The set of diagonal transformations mapping **a** back to the canonical gamut represents the set of possible unknown illuminations.

Consider as a simple example a database having only 4 reflectances resulting in the 4 chromaticities (1,2), (2,5), (4,4), (4,3) under the canonical illuminant. The canonical gamut is defined by the convex hull of these 4 points, which in this example happen to all be on the hull. Intensity in this case is eliminated by moving to the two-dimensional chromaticity coordinates defined in Equation 3.

Consider an image RGB triple, **a**=(6,10,2), converted to chromaticity coordinates (3,5), which turns out not to lie within the canonical gamut. What does it take to map it to the canonical gamut? If we suppose that **a** corresponds to one of the 4 known reflectances, say that represented by (1,2) in the canonical gamut, then to map it there requires a scaling of the first component by 0.33 and the second component by 0.4. On the other hand, it might correspond to the canonical gamut point (2,5) in which case a scaling of 0.67 and 1.0 is needed. The other 2 canonical gamut points yield 2 more scaling pairs. Figure 1 plots the four mappings as filled diamonds.

Of course it might have been the case that **a** corresponds to one of the points inside the convex hull of the canonical gamut. However, only linear scalings are involved, so mapping to those interior gamut points would only result in scalings within the interior of the convex hull (solid lines) of the mappings in Figure 1. The convex hull of the set of mappings, therefore, represents the complete set of mappings that could take **a** into the canonical gamut. . Each point within the convex hull in Figure 1 represents a different hypothesis about the unknown illumination. Each point models the change in (r,g) created by moving from the canonical illumination to a possible unknown illumination.

The convex hull in Figure 1 therefore expresses the constraints that finding **a** in the image imposed on what the unknown illumination might be. The illumination must be represented by one of the points within the convex hull because these are all the illuminations that could possibly have resulted in one of the colours in the canonical gamut appearing as **a**.

One RGB **a** yields constraints on the unknown illumination and a second one **b** will yield further constraints. Suppose the second chromaticity is (2,4), then the mappings taking **b** to the hull vertices of the canonical gamut are as shown by the

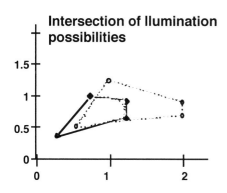

Intersection of Ilumination possibilities

Figure 1. Solid lines show the convex hull of four diagonal mappings (0.33,0.4), (0.67,1.0), (1.33,0.8) and (1.33,0.6) that transform chromaticity (3,5) to the 4 vertices of the canonical gamut. Dashed lines show convex hull of mappings taking (2,4) to the canonical gamut. The mappings describing the unknown illumination are therefore restricted to the intersection (shaded) of the two convex sets

open circles in Figure 1 superimposed on the mappings for **a**. Since both **a** and **b** appear in the image, and by assumption, both scene points are lit by the same unknown illumination, the unknown illumination must be represented by one of the mappings in the intersection of the two convex hulls. All other candidate illuminations are eliminated from consideration.

The convex hull of the set of distinct rg's in the image is called the *image gamut*. Each vertex of the image gamut will yield some new constraints on the unknown illumination that can be intersected with the constraints obtained from the other vertices. Once the mapping constraint set has been established some heuristic method must be used to pick one of the remaining candidates as the estimate of the unknown illumination. We have used the hull centroid as the final estimate.

Forsyth's CRULE [8] gamut-constraint method does not consider the possibility of illumination constraints. The experimental results reported below are based on the gamut-constraint method with added illumination constraints [10]. Measurement of lots of different light sources reveals quite a restricted gamut. Our sampling of illuminants includes 100 measurements of illumination around the university campus, including both indoor and outdoor illumination. Some inter-reflected light was included such as that from concrete buildings and light filtering through trees, but illumination that was obviously unusual was excluded. The resulting illumination gamut is reformulated in terms of the set of diagonal transformations mapping each illuminant to the canonical illuminant. In this form it can be intersected with the constraints from the image gamut to further constrain the estimate of the unknown illumination.

Gamut-constraint methods can be carried out either in a 2D chromaticity space or a 3D RGB space. The 3D gamut-constraint method is just like the 2D case except that the constraint sets are now polyhedral convex hulls. Potentially the 3D case can be used to estimate the surface brightness in addition to surface chromaticity, but for our experiments we do not require the brightness information, so after running the 3D method we convert back to 2D chromaticity space. It should be noted that carrying out the gamut-constraint method in 3D and converting the result to 2D is not equivalent to carrying it out in 2D in the first place. In addition, when the 3D method is being used to estimate chromaticity, the final estimate is made by maximizing the volume of the intersection set. This method of choosing the final estimate originates in [8] and gives better chromaticity estimates than the hull centroid in the 3D case.

4 Neural Network Colour Constancy

Previously reported results [1] have shown good performance using a neural network for colour constancy. The network estimates the illuminant chromaticity based on the gamut of colours present in the image. The neural network is a Perceptron [14] with one hidden layer and an input layer consisting of 1000 to 2000 binary inputs representing the chromaticity of the RGB's present in the scene. The hidden layer has a much smaller size, usually about 16-32 neurons and the output layer is composed of only two neurons. Each image RGB from a scene is transformed into standard rg-chromaticity space (Equation 2) which then is coarsely, but uniformly, discretized and presented to the network's input layer. The input is binary indicating either the presence or absence of the corresponding chromaticity in the image. The output layer of the neural network produces the values r and g (in the chromaticity space) of the illuminant. The output values are real numbers ranging from 0 to 1.

We trained the network using a back-propagation algorithm without momentum[15] on thousands of synthetic images generated by randomly selecting 1 illuminant and from 1 to 60 reflectances from our database of surface reflectances and illuminants, and then integrating them with the with the spectral sensitivity functions of our camera in accordance with Equation 1. During the learning phase the network is provided the image data along with the chromaticity of its illuminant.

5   The Test Images

The images used for our experiments are of 11 different, relatively colourful objects. (Figure 2 shows the objects). The pictures were taken with a Sony DXC-930 3-CCD colour video camera balanced for 3200K lighting with the gamma correction turned off so that its response is essentially a linear function of luminance. The RGB response of the camera was calibrated against a Photoresearch 650 spectraradiometer. The aperture was set so that no pixels were clipped in any of the three bands (i.e. R,G,B<255). Since most of the images had some specular highlights, reducing the aperture in this manner left much of each image quite dark. To overcome this problem we also extended the dynamic range of the images roughly 5-fold by averaging 25 frames (and storing the result as floating point images). Recording the images in this way produced a more versatile image database since it can then be used to simulate both the effect of brightening the images by increasing the aperture and the effect of clipping bright spots.

We took images under 5 different illuminants using the top section (the part where the lights are mounted) of a Macbeth Judge II light booth. The illuminants were the Macbeth Judge II illuminant A, a Sylvania Cool White Fluorescent, a Philips Ultralume Fluorescent, the Macbeth Judge II 5000 Fluorescent, and the Macbeth Judge II 5000 Fluorescent together with a Roscolux 3202 full blue filter, which produced a illuminant similar in colour temperature to a very deep blue sky. The effect created by changing between these illuminants can be seen in Figure 3 where the same ball is seen under each of the illuminants. The illuminant spectra are plotted in Figure 4.

Two sets of images were taken. For the "model" set, we took images of each object under each of the five illuminants, without moving the object. In other words, we have 11 groups of 5 registered images. The "test" set is similar, except that the object was purposefully moved before taking each image. With these two sets of images we are then able both to evaluate colour indexing under different scene illuminants with and without changes in object position. In total, 110 images were used.

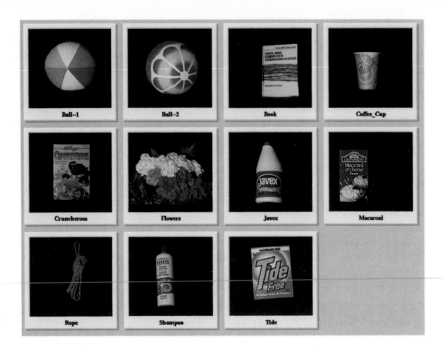

Figure 2. The 11 objects in the image database as seen under a single illuminant.

Figure 3. Ball-2 as seen under 4 of the 5 different illuminants.

Spectra of the illuminants

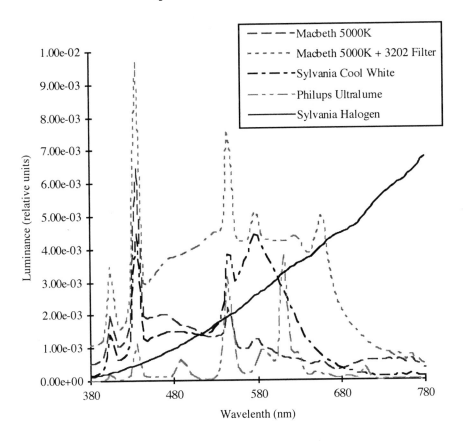

Figure 4. Spectra of the five test illuminants as measured by a Photoresearch spectrometer

Before using the images, they were first adjusted according to our camera calibration model. To do this we first subtract the variation of the background from the average background level, as determined by averaging a large number of images with the lens cap on. Then we adjusted pixels darker than a certain amount with a pre-established look-up table to make up for a small non-linearity in the camera. Finally, we subtracted the per-channel intercept of the camera linearity data from the images. The result is an image which is closer to one taken by an "ideal" camera, under the model that the RGB values are simply integrals as in Equation 1 of the incoming spectra multiplied by sensor sensitivity functions. When computing image histograms, the data is further cleaned up by averaging 5-by-5 blocks of pixels and excluding very dark pixels.

6 Results

Our experiments confirm the obvious hypothesis that colour constancy is likely to improve colour indexing in situations where the illumination impinging on the test object is different from that used in constructing the model database. Figure 5 shows a clear correlation between colour indexing performance and colour constancy error.

The recognition performance measure used in Figure 5 is based on a weighted average of colour indexing's rankings. During the recognition phase, colour indexing calculates match strengths for each model in the database. If the strongest match is in fact the correct object, then we say that we have a rank one match. If the correct object

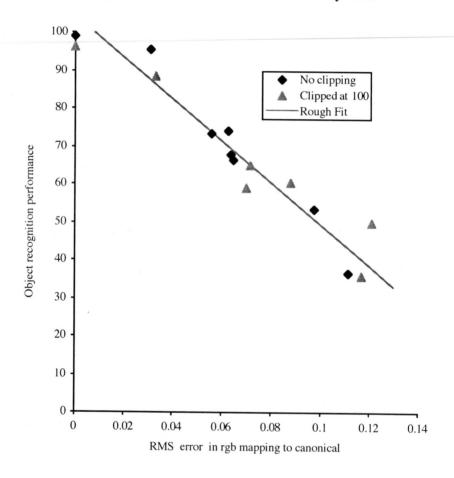

Figure 5. Object recognition performance as a function of colour constancy error.

is the algorithm's second choice, then we have a rank two match, and so on. For each algorithm, we obtain a percentage of the total (220 possible) matches by rank. To distill these results into a single representative value, we use a weighted sum of the percentages of the first three ranks: the weight for rank one is one, the weight for rank two is 1/2, and the weight for rank three is 1/3. Matches beyond rank 3 are considered failures and count as zero.

The measure for colour constancy error is based on a comparison of corrected and "target" images. Using the set of registered model images, we compute the root mean square difference on a pixel-by-pixel basis taken across the entire image in chromaticity between the target image—the one taken under the canonical illuminant—and the colour corrected image. Of the 5 illuminants, 4 are adequate for use as a canonical illuminant. One illuminant creates such a blue cast in the images that many of the red and green intensities are very low and possibly less reliable. As result for each colour constancy algorithm we obtain 4x55=220 colour constancy results, which are averaged to produce the data plotted as filled diamonds in Figure 5.

As noted above, our data set has an extended dynamic range with the images being purposefully underexposed in order to prevent any clipping. Visual checking by an impartial colleague suggested that exposure levels for normal viewing would be on average 2.5 times higher. Thus we simulated image capture at this level by scaling by 2.5 and thresholding anything greater than to 255 to 255. We then re-ran the matching experiments; the results are plotted with filled triangles in Figure 5.

Part of our motivation for experimenting with the clipping level was the unexpectedly good performance of the white-patch retinex method which was comparable to the gamut-constraint and neural net methods This was surprising given comparative results reported by Funt et al. [1]. Upon reflection, however, one might expect retinex to do relatively well given the special unclipped nature of our images. Clipping often is the cause of Retinex's failure because it relies on the brightest pixels being accurate, and clipped pixels clearly are not accurate. Specular highlights provide excellent clues to retinex as to the colour of the illuminant, again, providing they are not clipped. Our images generally do contain unclipped specularities. Even without specularities, preserving the maxima in each channel definitely will increase the performance of white-patch Retinex.

Under the more usual case, where either the human user or automatic aperture control has adjusted the capture process to obtain a pleasing image, there are invariably clipped pixels. In this case retinex starts to break down because by definition, the maximum value in at least one channel is a bad data point. To verify that this degradation does occur, we simulated clipping at various levels. The result is plotted in Figure 6. Here it is clear that as the clipping level increases, the retinex algorithm degrades much more quickly than the others, and when clipping is at the level of 75-100—consistent with the scaling of 2.5 used above—then its performance is close to previously reported results. The performance of all the algorithms in the non-clipped case is shown in Table 1.

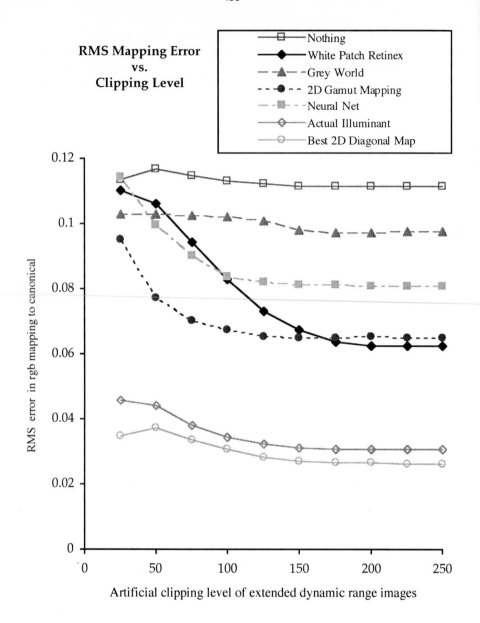

Figure 6. The RMS mapping error versus the artificially imposed clipping level. The RMS mapping error is the RMS difference between the chromaticity of the corrected images and the target image. The curve for the "algorithms" which do not explicitly depend on the data, such as "nothing" are almost flat, but not exactly flat, because as the clipping increases, we take the RMS difference between fewer and noisier data points. As conjectured, the white-patch Retinex method degrades much faster than the other algorithms.

Our original question was: Is machine colour constancy good enough? Based on our results, we feel that the answer is no. Table 2 shows the indexing performance of colour indexing using each algorithm for preprocessing. The best performer finds only 67% of the objects (rank 1 matches); whereas, the results (92% rank 1) based on using the actual illuminant RGB for colour correction indicate that both colour indexing and the diagonal model of illumination change will together support much better performance. Thus we conclude that we still have some distance still to go before machine colour constancy is up to the task of supporting object recognition.

In terms of our methodology, we feel that we gave machine colour constancy every reasonable chance, and thus the results should be considered closer to the "best case" than the "worst case". For example, we used illumination with spatially

Algorithm	RMS Error
Nothing	0.1114
Actual	0.0306
White-Patch Retinex	0.0625
Greyworld	0.0975
2D Gamut-Constraint	0.0649
3D Gamut-Constraint	0.0555
Neural Net	0.0634

Table 1: Colour Constancy Error by Algorithm: The error is the RMS difference in chromaticity between mapped image and registered target image. The results are the average of 220 results, being the estimated maps for 55 images to each of 4 illuminants. "Nothing" denotes doing no colour constancy and simply using the input image as the output image. "Actual" denotes using the true unknown illuminant RGB to do colour correction based on the diagonal model.

Rank	1	2	3	4	5	6	7	8	9	10	11
Nothing	28.4	10.2	9.1	9.1	8.5	6.8	4.5	6.2	5.7	4.5	6.8
Perfect	97.7	2.3									
Actual	92.3	5.5	1.4	0.9							
Retinex	67.7	8.6	5.9	1.8	2.7	1.8	1.4	3.2	5.5	0.9	0.5
Grey world	46.4	9.1	7.3	8.2	2.3	5.0	1.8	2.3	5.9	9.5	2.3
2D Gamut	60.0	10.9	8.6	5.5	1.8	3.6	2.3	2.3	1.8	1.4	1.8
3D Gamut	67.3	8.6	5.5	2.3	2.7	3.2	3.2	1.8	2.3	0.5	2.7
Neural net	61.4	7.7	7.7	4.1	1.8	2.3	1.4	1.4	1.8	5.9	4.5

Table 2: Number of matches by rank in percent. The total number of attempted matches is 220 for each except for "perfect" where only 44 matches make sense. "Perfect" indicates the case where the test illumination is the same as the canonical illumination and hence there is exact "colour constancy."

uniform chromaticity and were careful to remove noise through temporal and spatial averaging. We have also taken some trouble to develop a good camera model as required by some of the algorithms. Finally, the database was relatively small, and we avoided bad matches due to colours appearing coincidentally in the background by placing the objects on black cloth.

Having said that, we wish to emphasize some aspects of the experiment that were not open to compromise. First, and foremost, the data is real image data, and the objects are random everyday objects as opposed to, for example, planer non-specular "Mondrians". In particular, the object database includes several objects with a significant fluorescent component (e.g., the Tide box image). The fluorescent component does not change in the same way as the matte component which presents a problem for the diagonal model. It is perhaps also of some significance that the images were taken by a research assistant who had little understanding of the intended purpose of the experiment—possibly eliminating any unintended bias in the choice of objects to test. Finally, the illuminants represent quite a dramatic range in terms of what is usually encountered in common natural lighting and standard man-made lighting situations without adding the unusual effects of things like heavily filtered theater lights.

7   Conclusion

We tested machine colour constancy algorithms using the computer vision task of colour-based object recognition based on colour histogram intersection. The colour constancy algorithms did not perform as well as expected based on previous results with colour balancing images. We expected that colour constancy processing would provide colour descriptors that would be accurate enough that colour indexing performance would be close to that obtained when there is no change in the ambient illumination. As shown in Table 2, this is did not turn out to be the case. Colour constancy pre-processing did, however, yield a significant improvement over doing no pre-processing, it simply was not enough of an improvement. Figure 5 shows that the degree of improvement in histogram matching appears almost linearly related to the RMS error in colour prediction.

The results of Brainard et al. [16] indicate that human colour constancy is not all that accurate and state (p. 2101) "Our results represent neither complete constancy nor a complete absence of constancy." The results of our experiments raise the question as to whether or not human colour constancy would be sufficiently accurate for histogram-based object recognition?

We take the current state of machine colour constancy performance as a challenge for future research. It is clear that without RMS errors in colour prediction under 0.04, a typical vision task such as object recognition can not be based on absolute descriptors (as opposed to relative ones, like ratios) of colour.

References

1. Funt, B.V. and Cardei, V., Barnard, K., Learning Color Constancy, *IS&T Fourth Color Imaging Conference*, Scottsdale, Nov. 1996.
2   Swain, M., and Ballard, D., "Color Indexing," *Int. J. Comp Vision*, 7:11-32, 1991.
3. Funt, B.V., and Finlayson G.D., Color Constant Color Indexing, *IEEE Trans. Patt. Anal. and Mach. Intell*, 17(5), May 1995.
4. Healey, G. and Slater, D. "Global Color Constancy: recognition of objects by use of illumination invariant properties of color distributions," *J. Opt. Soc. Am. A*, 11(11):3003-3010, Nov. 1994.
5. Barnard. K., Finlayson, G., Funt, B., Colour Constancy for Scenes with Spectrally Varying Illumination, *ECCV'96 Fourth European Conference on Computer Vision*, Vol. II, pages 3-15, April 1996.
6. Maloney, L. and Wandell, B., "Color constancy: a method for recovering surface spectral reflectance," *J. Opt. Soc. Am. A*, 3:29-33, 1986.
7. Finlayson, G., Funt, B. and Barnard, J., Colour Constancy Under a Varying Illumination, *Proc. Fifth Intl. Conf. on Comp. Vis.*, Jun 1995.
8. Forsyth, D., A novel algorithm for color constancy, *Intl. Journal of Computer Vision* 5:5-36, 1990.
9. Finlayson, G., Drew, M., and Funt., B., Color Constancy: Generalized Diagonal Transforms Suffice, *J. Opt. Soc. Am. A*, 11(11):3011-3020,1994
10. Finlayson, G. Color in Perspective, PAMI Oct. 1996. Vol. 18 number 10, p1034-1038
11. Wandell, B.A. Analysis of the Retinex Theory of Color Vision, *Journal of the Optical Society of America A*, V 3, pp.1651-1661, Oct. 1986.
12. McCann, J.J., McKee, P., and A Taylor, T.H., Quantitative Studies in Retinex Theory, *Vision Res. Vol.* 16 pp. 445-458, 1976.
13. Kobus Barnard, "Computational colour constancy: taking theory into practice," MSc thesis, Simon Fraser University, School of Computing (1995).
14. Hertz, J., Krogh, A., and Palmer, R.G. *Introduction to the Theory of Neural Computation*, Addison-Wesley Publishing Company, 1991.
15. Rumelhart, D.E., Hinton, G.E., and. Williams, R.J, Learning Internal Representations by Error Propagation in D.E. Rumelhart & J.L. McClelland (Eds.), *Parallel Distributed Processing: Explorations in the Microstructure of Cognition.* Vol.1: Foundations. MIT
16 Brainard, D., Brunt, W., and Speigle, J., Color Constancy in the nearly natural image. I. Asymmetric matches, *Journal of the Optical Society of America A*, V 14, pp.2091-2110, Sept. 1997.

Colour Model Selection and Adaptation in Dynamic Scenes

Yogesh Raja[1], Stephen J. McKenna[2], and Shaogang Gong[1]

[1] Department of Computer Science, Queen Mary and Westfield College, England
{jpmetal,sgg}@dcs.qmw.ac.uk
[2] Department of Applied Computing, University of Dundee, Scotland
stephen@dcs.qmw.ac.uk

Abstract. We use colour mixture models for real-time colour-based object localisation, tracking and segmentation in dynamic scenes. Within such a framework, we address the issues of model order selection, modelling scene background and model adaptation in time. Experimental results are given to demonstrate our approach in different scale and lighting conditions.

1 Introduction

Colour has been used in machine vision for tasks such as segmentation [1, 2], tracking [3] and recognition [4, 5]. Colour offers many advantages over geometric information in dynamic vision such as robustness under partial occlusion, rotation in depth, scale changes and resolution changes. Furthermore, using colour enables real-time performance on modest hardware platforms [1].

Swain and Ballard [5] described a scheme which used histograms for modelling the colours of an object. The colour space was quantised through the histogram's structure which comprised a number of "bins". An algorithm known as "histogram intersection" was used for matching image histograms with model histograms. Although colour histograms can be used to estimate densities in colour space, the level of quantisation imposed on the colour space influences the resulting density. If the number of bins n is too high, the estimated density will be "noisy" and many bins will be empty. If n is too low, density structure is smoothed away. Histograms are effective only when n can be kept relatively low and where sufficient data are available. A potentially more effective semi-parametric [6] approach for colour density estimation is to use Gaussian mixture models. With this approach, a number of Gaussian functions are taken as an approximation to a multi-modal distribution in colour space and conditional probabilities are then computed for colour pixels [1, 3]. Gaussian mixture models can also be viewed as a form of generalised radial basis function network in which each Gaussian component is a basis function or 'hidden' unit. The component priors can be viewed as weights in an output layer. Finite mixture models have also been discussed at length elsewhere [6–12] although most of this work has concentrated on the general studies of the properties of mixture models rather than developing vision models for use with real data from dynamic scenes.

However, the use of colour mixture models in dynamic scenes is not without its difficulties. A common problem associated with density-based modelling of statistical data involves the selection of the number of parameters for a model, known as the *model order selection* problem [6]. With colour mixture models, this involves the selection of the number of Gaussian components. The goal is to generate a model that provides accurate predictions for new data. Too few parameters can lead to a poor model which over-generalises the data (high bias), while too many parameters can result in an overfit of the model to the training data (high variance) [13]. In either case, the underlying distribution responsible for the training data is not reflected accurately and performance on new data will be poor. Existing methods for model selection are usually rather *ad hoc*. An exception is the recursive algorithm of Priebe and Marchette [10]. It was extended to model non-stationary data series through the use of temporal windowing. Their algorithm adds new components dynamically when the mixture model fails to account well for a new data point. The approach in this paper is different in that an iterative algorithm is used to determine model order based on a fixed data set. The mixture model is then adapted on-line by updating components' parameters while keeping the number of components fixed. The assumption made here is that the number of components needed to accurately model an object's colour does not alter significantly with changing viewing conditions.

Methods have been proposed for colour-based detection and tracking of skin-coloured objects (e.g. [1, 14–17]). In particular, a system constructed by Wren *et al.* [18] enabled tracking of entire people in controlled environments with static cameras. Each pixel in an image had an associated feature vector comprising spatial and colour components. These feature vectors were clustered, which led to a collection of "blobs" defined by spatial and spectral similarity. A collection of blobs constituted a representation of a person. This limited tracking to people with homogeneously coloured regions with an unchanging background.

Most colour cameras provide an RGB (red, green, blue) signal. In order to model objects' colour distributions, the RGB signal is first transformed to make the intensity or brightness explicit so that it can be discarded in order to obtain a high level of invariance to the intensity of ambient illumination. Here the HSV (hue, saturation, value) representation was used and colour distributions were modelled in the 2D hue-saturation space. Hue corresponds to our intuitive notion of 'colour' whilst saturation corresponds to our idea of 'vividness' or 'purity' of colour. At low saturation, measurements of hue become unreliable and are discarded. Likewise, pixels with very high intensity are discarded. It should be noted that the HSV system does not relate well to human vision. In particular, the usual definition of intensity as $max(R+G+B)$ is at odds with our perception of intensity. However, this is not important for the tracking application described here. If in other applications it was deemed desirable to relate the colour models to human perception then perceptually-based systems like CIE $L^*u^*v^*$ and CIE $L^*a^*b^*$ should be used instead of HSV.

The main difficulty in modelling colour robustly is the *colour constancy* problem which arises due to variation in colour values brought about by lighting changes. This problem is addressed here by employing colour adaptation.

For the remaining sections of the paper, we first describe briefly in Section 2 colour mixture models in HS-space for dynamic scene segmentation and object tracking. In Section 3, we describe a method for automatic model selection in multi-colour mixture models. Section 4 focuses on the issue of modelling object colour in the context of a given scene. We then introduce a mechanism for model adaptation over time and under changing lighting conditions in Section 6. We discuss some experimental results in Section 7 before drawing conclusions in Section 8.

2   Colour Mixture Models

Colour histograms [5] are a simple non-parametric method for modelling. However, the use of histograms for estimating colour densities is only possible because n can be kept relatively small and because there are many data points (pixels) available. A more effective approach is to use Gaussian mixture models. Let the conditional density for a pixel $\boldsymbol{\xi}$ belonging to a multi-coloured object $\mathcal{O}$ be a mixture with M component densities:

$$p(\boldsymbol{\xi}|\mathcal{O}) = \sum_{j=1}^{M} p(\boldsymbol{\xi}|j)P(j) \tag{1}$$

where a mixing parameter $P(j)$ corresponds to the prior probability that pixel $\boldsymbol{\xi}$ was generated by component j and where $\sum_{j=1}^{M} P(j) = 1$. Each mixture component is a Gaussian with mean $\boldsymbol{\mu}$ and covariance matrix $\boldsymbol{\Sigma}$, i.e. in the case of a 2D colour space:

$$p(\boldsymbol{\xi}|j) = \frac{1}{2\pi|\boldsymbol{\Sigma}_j|^{\frac{1}{2}}} \exp^{-\frac{1}{2}(\boldsymbol{\xi}-\boldsymbol{\mu}_j)^T \boldsymbol{\Sigma}_j^{-1}(\boldsymbol{\xi}-\boldsymbol{\mu}_j)} \tag{2}$$

Expectation-Maximisation (EM) provides an effective maximum-likelihood algorithm for fitting such a mixture to a data set [6, 19]. Figure 1 shows an example of a Gaussian mixture model of a multi-coloured object in HS-space. Outlier points, which can be caused by image noise and specular highlights, have little influence upon the mixture model. Pixels with very low intensity were discarded because the observed hue and saturation became unstable for such pixels. Likewise, pixels with very high intensity were discarded. Once a model has been estimated it can be converted into a look-up table for efficient on-line indexing of colour probabilities.

Given a colour mixture model of an object, the object can then be effectively located and tracked in the scene by computing a probability map for the pixels in the image within a search window. The size and position of the object are then estimated from the resulting distribution in the image plane. Although the HS-space representation permits a degree of robustness against limited brightness

 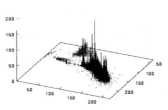 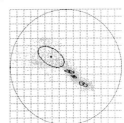

Fig. 1. *Left: a multi-coloured object (a PEPSI can). Centre: its colour histogram in HS-space. It can be noted that such a histogram representation is only viable when a large amount of data is available due to being non-parametric. Right: its Gaussian mixture model. The mixture components are shown as elliptical contours of equal probability.*

change, tracking is only reliable provided that the lighting conditions are relatively stable. Object position at frame t is taken to be the mean $\boldsymbol{m}_t = (m_x, m_y)$ and object size is estimated from the standard deviation $\boldsymbol{\sigma}_t = (\sigma_x, \sigma_y)$. More precisely, for a given frame t, the object position $\boldsymbol{m}_t$ is estimated as an offset from the position $\boldsymbol{m}_{t-1}$:

$$\boldsymbol{m}_t = \boldsymbol{m}_{t-1} + \frac{\sum_{\mathbf{x}} p(\boldsymbol{\xi}_{\mathbf{x}})(\mathbf{x} - \boldsymbol{m}_{t-1})}{\sum_{\mathbf{x}} p(\boldsymbol{\xi}_{\mathbf{x}})}$$

where $\mathbf{x}$ ranges over all image coordinates in the region of interest and $\boldsymbol{\xi}_{\mathbf{x}}$ is the colour point at image position $\mathbf{x}$. To improve accuracy, probabilities $p(\boldsymbol{\xi}_{\mathbf{x}})$ are thresholded. Values lower than the threshold are taken to be background and are consequently set to zero in order to nullify their influence on the estimation of $\boldsymbol{m}_t$ and $\boldsymbol{\sigma}_t$.

The size of the object is estimated by computing the standard deviation of the image probability density:

$$\sigma_t = \sqrt{\frac{\sum_{\mathbf{x}} p(\boldsymbol{\xi}_{\mathbf{x}})\{(\mathbf{x} - \boldsymbol{m}_{t-1}) - \boldsymbol{m}_t\}^2}{\sum_{\mathbf{x}} p(\boldsymbol{\xi}_{\mathbf{x}})}}$$

3 Model Order Selection

Model order selection is the problem of choosing the number of parameters that facilitates the accurate modelling of an underlying distribution for a set of data. In this section, we describe a constructive method for automatic determination of the number of components for a colour mixture model.

A standard technique employed for model training, known as *cross validation*, attempts to find the model order that provides the best trade-off between bias and variance. A number of models of different order are trained by minimising an error function for a training set. These models are then evaluated by computing the error function for an independent *validation set*. The model with the lowest error for the validation set is considered to exhibit the best generalisation and its order is taken to be optimal.

This concept is applied to the generation of mixture models through an iterative scheme of splitting components and monitoring generalisation ability. The available data set is partitioned into disjoint training and validation sets. A mixture model is initialised with a small number of components, typically one. Model order is then adapted by iteratively applying EM and splitting components. The likelihood for the validation set is computed after every iteration, and it is assumed that the optimal model order corresponds to the peak in this likelihood function over time. Here, the techniques for selecting and splitting components are outlined.

3.1 Splitting Components

For each component j, let us define a total responsibility r_j as:

$$r_j = \sum_{\xi} p(j|\xi) = \sum_{\xi} \frac{p(\xi|j)P(j)}{\sum_{i=1}^{M} p(\xi|i)P(i)} \tag{3}$$

Then the component k with the lowest total responsibility for the validation set is selected for splitting:

$$k = \arg\min_{j}(r_j)$$

Once the component k to be split has been selected, two new components with means μ_{new1} and μ_{new2}, and covariance matrices Σ_{new1} and Σ_{new2} are computed by:

$$\mu_{new1} = \mu_k + \frac{\lambda_1}{2}\mathbf{u}_1$$

$$\mu_{new2} = \mu_k - \frac{\lambda_1}{2}\mathbf{u}_1$$

$$\Sigma_{new1} = \Sigma_{new2} = \Sigma_k$$

where λ_1 is the largest eigenvalue of the covariance matrix Σ_k and $\mathbf{u}_1$ is the corresponding eigenvector.

The prior probabilities for the new components are assigned like so:

$$\pi_{new1} = \pi_{new2} = \frac{\pi_k}{2}$$

3.2 A Constructive Algorithm for Model Order Selection

Let i denote the iteration, M_i the number of components in a model at iteration i and $\mathcal{L}_i$ the likelihood of the validation set with respect to the model at iteration i. The initial number of components M_0 may be set to a low number (here $M_0 = 1$). With a validation set generated for the generalisation test, a constructive algorithm for model order selection is as follows:

```
1. Apply Expectation-Maximisation for model with M_i components.
2. Compute L_i for validation set
3. IF (L_i < L_{i-1}) STOP.
4. Save model
5. Find component j with lowest total responsibility
6. Split component j
7. Restart from step 1 with M_{i+1} = M_i + 1 and i = i + 1.
```

The algorithm terminates when a peak is located in the likelihood measurements for the validation set. The application of this algorithm to a data set for a multi-coloured object (the PEPSI can as shown in Figure 1) is illustrated in Figure 2.

4   Modelling Colour in Context: Foreground and Background Models

Thresholding probabilities generated by a foreground model alone is often ineffective due to severe overlap between background and foreground colour distributions. For dealing with multi-coloured objects in dynamic scenes, it is computationally desirable to model the colour distribution of the background scene in addition to the objects to be tracked. Given density estimates for both an object, $\mathcal{O}$, and the background scene, $\mathcal{S}$, the probability that a pixel, $\boldsymbol{\xi}$, belongs to the object is given by the posterior probability $P(\mathcal{O}|\boldsymbol{\xi})$:

$$P(\mathcal{O}|\boldsymbol{\xi}) = \frac{p(\boldsymbol{\xi}|\mathcal{O})P(\mathcal{O})}{p(\boldsymbol{\xi}|\mathcal{O})P(\mathcal{O}) + p(\boldsymbol{\xi}|\mathcal{S})P(\mathcal{S})} \qquad (4)$$

The prior probability, $P(\mathcal{O})$, is set to reflect the expected size of the object within the search area of the scene $[P(\mathcal{S}) = 1 - P(\mathcal{O})]$. Pixels can be classified by assigning them to the class with the maximum posterior probability. This minimises the probability of misclassification error in a Bayesian sense. However, it is preferable to use the posterior probabilities directly in order to estimate the spatial extent of the object. Furthermore, the density estimates provide a measure of confidence. Pixels in areas of colour space where both foreground and background likelihoods are low are classified with low confidence.

Modelling foreground and background separately has the practical advantage that the object and scene data can be acquired independently. A single background scene model can subsequently be used with many different objects. This is useful in a virtual studio application, for example, where it enables a single studio model to be subsequently used with many different people.

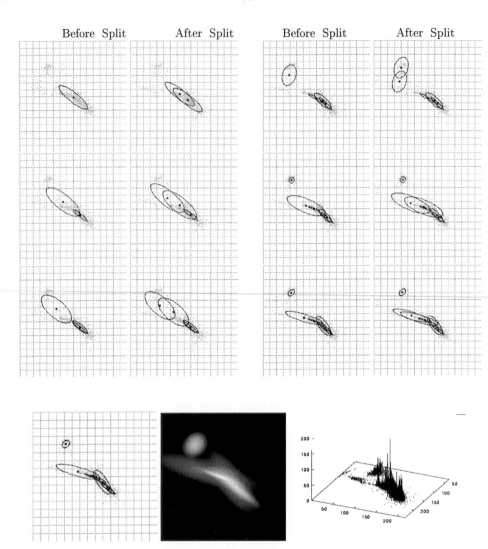

Before Split   After Split   Before Split   After Split

Fig. 2. *Automatic model selection for the colours of a PEPSI can. The top part illustrates the splitting process, with each pair of images showing convergence followed by the splitting of a component. The bottom part shows the final seven component model and the resulting probability density function. Finally, a histogram of the training data is shown.*

5 Modelling Colour in Time: Coping with Change

Colour appearance is often unstable due to changes in both background and foreground lighting. The colour constancy problem has been addressed mainly through the formulation of physics-based models (e.g.[20]). Colour appearance also varies over time due to changes in viewing geometry and changes in camera parameters (auto-iris adjustment). Under the assumption that viewing conditions change gradually over time, statistical colour models can be adapted to reflect the changing colour appearance of a tracked object (or the background scene against which it is tracked). The remainder of this section describes a method for adapting the Gaussian mixture colour models over time.

5.1 Model Adaptation Over Time

At each frame, t, a new set of pixels, $X^{(t)}$, is sampled from the object and used to update the mixture model[1]. These new data sample a slowly varying non-stationary signal. Let $r^{(t)}$ denote the sum of the posterior probabilities of the data in frame t, $r^{(t)} = \sum_{\xi \in X^{(t)}} p(j|\xi)$. The parameters are first estimated for each mixture component, j, using only the new data, $X^{(t)}$, from frame t:

$$\mu^{(t)} = \frac{\sum p(j|\xi)\xi}{r^{(t)}}, \qquad \pi^{(t)} = \frac{r^{(t)}}{N^{(t)}}$$

$$\Sigma^{(t)} = \frac{\sum p(j|\xi)(\xi - \mu_{t-1})^T(\xi - \mu_{t-1})}{r^{(t)}}$$

where $N^{(t)}$ denotes the number of pixels in the new data set and all summations are over $\xi \in X^{(t)}$. The mixture model components then have their parameters updated using weighted sums of the previous recursive estimates, $(\mu_{t-1}, \Sigma_{t-1}, \pi_{t-1})$, estimates based on the new data, $(\mu^{(t)}, \Sigma^{(t)}, \pi^{(t)})$, and estimates based on the old data, $(\mu^{(t-L-1)}, \Sigma^{(t-L-1)}, \pi^{(t-L-1)})$:

$$\mu_t = \mu_{t-1} + \frac{r^{(t)}}{D_t}(\mu^{(t)} - \mu_{t-1}) - \frac{r^{(t-L-1)}}{D_t}(\mu^{(t-L-1)} - \mu_{t-1})$$

$$\Sigma_t = \Sigma_{t-1} + \frac{r^{(t)}}{D_t}(\Sigma^{(t)} - \Sigma_{t-1}) - \frac{r^{(t-L-1)}}{D_t}(\Sigma^{(t-L-1)} - \Sigma_{t-1})$$

$$\pi_t = \pi_{t-1} + \frac{N^{(t)}}{\sum_{\tau=t-L}^{t} N^{(\tau)}}\left(\pi^{(t)} - \pi_{t-1}\right) - \frac{N^{(t-L-1)}}{\sum_{\tau=t-L}^{t} N^{(\tau)}}\left(\pi^{(t-L-1)} - \pi_{t-1}\right)$$

---

[1] Throughout this paper, superscript $^{(t)}$ denotes a quantity based only on data from frame t. Subscripts denote recursive estimates.

where $D_t = \sum_{\tau=t-L}^{t} r^{(\tau)}$. The following approximations are used for efficiency:

$$r^{(t-L-1)} \approx \frac{D_{t-1}}{L+1}$$

$$D_t \approx (1 - 1/(L+1))D_{t-1} + r^{(t)}$$

The parameter L controls the adaptivity of the model[2].

During the processing of a sequence, new samples of data for adaptation are gathered from a region of appropriate aspect ratio centred on the estimated object centroid. It is assumed that these data form a representative sample of the objects' colours. This will hold for a large class of objects.

5.2   Selective Adaptation

An obvious problem with adapting a colour model over time is the lack of ground-truth. Any colour-based tracker can lose the object it is tracking due, for example, to occlusion. If such errors go undetected the colour model will adapt to image regions which do not correspond to the object. This is clearly undesirable. In order to help alleviate this problem, observed log-likelihood measurements were used to detect erroneous frames. Colour data from these frames were not used to adapt the object's colour model. In order to boot-strap the tracker for object detection and re-initialisation after a tracking failure, a set of predetermined generic object colour models which perform reasonably in a wide range of illumination conditions are used. Once an object is being tracked, the model adapts and improves tracking performance by becoming specific to the observed conditions.

The adaptive mixture model seeks to maximise the log-likelihood of the colour data over time. The normalised log-likelihood, $\mathcal{L}$, of the data, $X^{(t)}$, observed from the object at time t is given by:

$$\mathcal{L} = \frac{1}{N^{(t)}} \sum_{\xi \in X^{(t)}} \log p(\xi|\mathcal{O})$$

At each time frame, $\mathcal{L}$ is evaluated. If the tracker loses the object there is often a sudden, large drop in the value of $\mathcal{L}$. This provides a way to detect tracker failure. Adaptation is suspended when such an error is detected. The tracker is then re-bootstrapped by increasing the search space to the maximum size. Adaptation is re-activated when the object is again tracked with sufficiently high likelihood.

A temporal median filter was used to compute a threshold, T. Adaptation was only performed when $\mathcal{L} > T$. The median, ν, and standard deviation, σ, of $\mathcal{L}$ were computed for the n most recent above-threshold frames, where $n \leq L$. The threshold was set to $T = \nu - k\sigma$, where k was a constant.

---

[2] Setting $L = t$ and ignoring terms based on frame $t-L-1$ gives a stochastic algorithm for estimating a Gaussian mixture for a stationary signal [6, 21].

6 Experiments

In the following we describe a set of experiments in which colour mixture models were applied to object segmentation and tracking in dynamic scenes. All the experiments ran in real-time (15-20Hz) on a standard 200MHz PC with a Matrox Meteor board.

6.1 Experiment 1: Colour-based Tracking

Figure 3 shows samples from one continuous sequence where a skin colour mixture model was used on an active camera with pan, tilt and zoom capabilities for tracking a face with occlusion, lighting and scale changes. It is clear that the model copes well with the changes in object appearance. Here the colour mixture model is relatively simple in the sense that the object of interest has almost a uniform colour. Therefore, the number of components can be easily determined.

Fig. 3. *A face is tracked against a cluttered background by an active camera which pans, tilts and zooms.*

6.2 Experiment 2: Modelling Colour in Context

Model selection becomes more difficult with multi-coloured objects. Figure 4 illustrates the multi-coloured object foreground and background models in HS colour space. These resulted from running the constructive algorithm with automatic model selection. A context-dependent object model can be given by a combined posterior density (shown in the bottom right) which defines decision boundaries between object foreground and scene background, even when significant overlap exists between the object and the background.

Figure 5 shows an application of the context-dependent object (person) model in segmentation and tracking. Pixels in the scene were classified as person or background using Equation (4) with the prior probabilities set to $P(\mathcal{S}) = P(\mathcal{O}) = 0.5$. A multi-resolution approach was taken in which segmentation was performed in a coarse-to-fine manner. The segmented object was superimposed

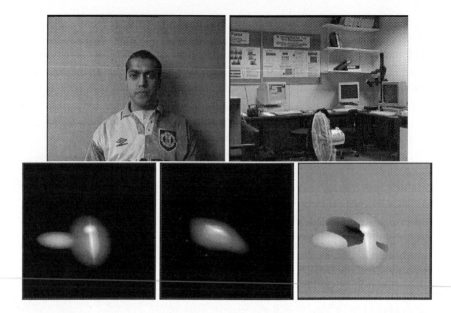

Fig. 4. *Colour mixture models of a multi-coloured object (person model) and the context (scene model). The first row shows the data used to build the foreground (person) and the background (laboratory) models. The second row illustrates the probability density estimated from mixture models for the object foreground and scene background. The rightmost image is the combined posterior density in the HS colour space. Here the "bright" regions represent foreground whilst the "dark" regions give the background. The "grey" areas are regions of uncertainty.*

onto another dynamic scene. Only pixels inside the search area of the tracker were classified. All pixels outside this area were rendered as background. The results are surprisingly good for individual pixel classification alone, but imperfect. However, geometrical models such as PDMs may be integrated into the current setup to exploit the classification results and generate boundary estimates for a more accurate segmentation result.

6.3   Experiment 3: Coping with Change

Results shown in Figures 6 and 7 illustrate the advantage in using an adaptive model. In this sequence the illumination conditions coupled with the camera's auto-iris mechanism resulted in large changes in the apparent colour of the object of interest (the face of a person) as it approached the window. Towards the end of the sequence, the face became very dark, making hue and saturation measurements unreliable. In Figure 6, a non-adaptive model was estimated based on the first image of the sequence only and was used throughout. It was unable to cope with the varying conditions and failure eventually occurred. In Figure 7, the model was allowed to adapt and successfully maintained lock on the face.

Fig. 5. Segmentation results. The top row outlines the tracked region for segmentation and the second row illustrates superimposition onto an alternative sequence.

Fig. 6. *Five frames from a sequence in which a face was tracked using a non-adaptive model. The apparent colour of the face changes due to (i) varying illumination and (ii) the camera's auto-iris mechanism which adjusts to the bright exterior light.*

The experiment shown in Figure 8 illustrates the advantage of selective adaptation. The person moved through challenging tracking conditions, before approaching the camera at close range (frames 50-60). Since the camera was placed in the doorway of another room with its own lighting conditions, the person's face underwent a large, sudden and temporary change in apparent colour. When adaptation was performed in every frame, this sudden change had a drastic effect on the model and ultimately led the tracker to fail when the person receded into the corridor. With selective adaptation, these sudden changes were treated as outliers and adaptation was suspended, permitting the tracker to recover.

Fig. 7. *The sequence depicted in Figure 6 tracked with an adaptive colour model. Here, the model adapts to cope with the change in apparent colour.*

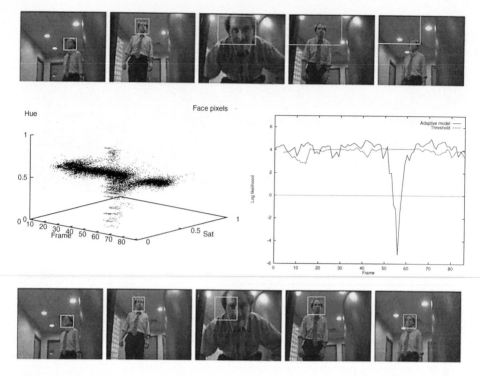

Fig. 8. *At the top are frames 35, 45, 55, 65 and 75 from a sequence. There is strong directional and exterior illumination. The walls have a fleshy tone. At around frame 55, the subject rapidly approaches the camera which is situated in a doorway, resulting in rapid changes in illumination, scale and auto-iris parameters. This can be seen in the 3D plot of the hue-saturation distribution over time. In the top sequence, the model was allowed to adapt in every frame, resulting in failure at around frame 60. The lower sequence illustrates the use of selective adaptation. The right-hand plot shows the normalised log-likelihood measurements and the adaptation threshold .*

7 Conclusion

We have described how the colour distributions of multi-coloured objects can be modelled using mixtures of Gaussians. A constructive algorithm based on maximum-likelihood EM was presented for training a Gaussian mixture model. This algorithm selects an appropriate model order automatically. It avoids the need for initialisation of component means, a procedure which is usually performed using rather *ad hoc* methods. Cross-validation was used to perform early stopping during training.

The colour mixture models were used to perform robust object detection and tracking in real-time using only modest hardware. The use of separate colour models for foreground objects and the background scene was described. Successful tracking was thus performed even when there was significant overlap between object and background colour distributions. Combined foreground and background models were also used for segmentation to facilitate the virtual studio application described. Segmentation quality is insufficient for broadcasting requirements with pixel-wise colour classification. However, it can be exploited to facilitate the application of geometrical models.

The apparent colour of an object varies over time due to changes in illumination, viewing geometry and camera parameters. Rather than attempt to model these changes directly, they were accommodated by allowing the colour models to adapt over time. An algorithm for adapting colour mixture models on-line was presented including a mechanism for detecting tracking errors. This was shown to improve tracking performance under large changes in apparent colour.

We are currently investigating on-line adaptation of model order. This involves both splitting and merging of Gaussian components during tracking. Work is also being done to integrate motion and colour to enable real-time tracking of multiple targets for dynamic gesture recognition. The integration of shape and colour for robust contour tracking and accurate segmentation is also being pursued. This involves the application of Point Distribution Models to colour probabilities to recover good estimates of object boundaries. Colour edges are then used to refine boundary estimates and enable highly accurate segmentation for broadcasting requirements.

References

1. Y. Raja, S. McKenna, and S. Gong, "Segmentation and tracking using colour mixture models," in *Asian Conference on Computer Vision*, Hong Kong, January 1998.
2. W. Skarbek and A. Koschan, "Colour image segmentation - a survey," Tech. Rep., Tech. Univ. of Berlin, 1994.
3. S. McKenna, S. Gong, and Y. Raja, "Face recognition in dynamic scenes," in *BMVC*, 1997.
4. J. Matas, R. Marik, and J. Kittler, "On representation and matching of multi-coloured objects," in *ICCV*, 1995, pp. 726–732.
5. M. J. Swain and D. H. Ballard, "Colour indexing," *IJCV*, pp. 11–32, 1991.
6. C. Bishop, *Neural Networks for Pattern Recognition*, Oxford University Press, 1995.
7. B. S. Everitt and D. J. Hand, *Finite Mixture Distributions*, Chapman and Hall, New York, 1981.
8. G. J. McLachlan and K. E. Basford, *Mixture Models: Inference and Applications to Clustering*, Marcel Dekker Inc., New York, 1988.
9. C. E. Priebe, "Adaptive mixtures," *J. Amer. Stat. Assoc.*, vol. 89, no. 427, pp. 796–806, 1994.
10. C. E. Priebe and D. J. Marchette, "Adaptive mixtures: Recursive nonparametric pattern recognition," *Pattern Recognition*, vol. 24, no. 12, pp. 1197–1209, 1991.
11. C. E. Priebe and D. J. Marchette, "Adaptive mixture density estimation," *Pattern Recognition*, vol. 26, no. 5, pp. 771–785, 1993.
12. D. M. Titterington, A. F. M. Smith, and U. E. Makov, *Statistical Analysis of Finite Mixture Distributions*, John Wiley, New York, 1985.
13. S. Geman, E. Bienenstock, and R. Doursat, "Neural networks and the bias/variance dilemma," *Neural Computation*, 1992.

14. R. Kjeldsen and J. Kender, "Finding skin in color images," in *2nd Int. Conf. on Auto. Face and Gest. Recog.*, 1996.

15. D. Saxe and R. Foulds, "Toward robust skin identification in video images," in *2nd Int. Conf. on Auto. Face and Gest. Recog.*, 1996.

16. B. Schiele and A. Waibel, "Gaze tracking based on face-color," in *IWAFGR*, 1995, pp. 344–349.

17. H. Wu, Q. Chen, and M. Yachida, "An application of fuzzy theory: face detection," in *IWAFGR*, Zurich, June 1995, pp. 314–319.

18. C.R. Wren, A. Azarbayejani, T. Darrell, and A.P. Pentland, "Pfinder:real-time tracking of the human body," *IEEE PAMI*, vol. 19, no. 7, pp. 780–785, 1997.

19. R. A. Redner and H. F. Walker, "Mixture densities, maximum likelihood and the EM algorithm," *SIAM Review*, vol. 26, no. 2, pp. 195–239, 1984.

20. D. A. Forsyth, *Colour Constancy and its Applications in Machine Vision*, Ph.D. thesis, University of Oxford, 1988.

21. H. G. C. Traven, "A neural network approach to statistical pattern classification by "semiparametric" estimation of probability density functions," *IEEE Trans. Neural Networks*, vol. 2, no. 3, pp. 366–378, 1991.

Comprehensive Colour Image Normalization

Graham D. Finlayson[1], Bernt Schiele[2], and James L. Crowley[3]

[1] The Colour & Imaging Institute
The University of Derby
United Kingdom

[2] MIT Media Lab
Cambridge MA
USA

[3] INRIA Rhônes Alpes
38330 Montbonnot
France

Abstract. The same scene viewed under two different illuminants induces two different colour images. If the two illuminants are the same colour but are placed at different positions then corresponding rgb pixels are related by simple scale factors. In contrast if the lighting geometry is held fixed but the colour of the light changes then it is the individual colour channels (e.g. all the red pixel values or all the green pixels) that are a scaling apart. It is well known that the image dependencies due to lighting geometry and illuminant colour can be respectively removed by normalizing the magnitude of the rgb pixel triplets (e.g. by calculating chromaticities) and by normalizing the lengths of each colour channel (by running the 'grey-world' colour constancy algorithm). However, neither normalization suffices to account for changes in both the lighting geometry and illuminant colour.

In this paper we present a new **comprehensive image normalization** which removes image dependency on lighting geometry and illumination colour. Our approach is disarmingly simple. We take the colour image and normalize the rgb pixels (to remove dependence on lighting geometry) and then normalize the r, g and b colour channels (to remove dependence on illuminant colour). We then repeat this process, normalize rgb pixels then r, g and b colour channels, and then repeat again. Indeed we repeat this process until we reach a stable state; that is reach a position where each normalization is idempotent. Crucially this iterative normalization procedure always converges to the same answer. Moreover, convergence is very rapid, typically taking just 4 or 5 iterations.

To illustrate the value of our "comprehensive normalization" procedure we considered the object recognition problem for three image databases that appear in the literature: Swain's database, the Simon Fraser database, Sang Wok Lee's database. In all cases, for recognition by colour distribution comparison, the comprehensive normalization improves recognition rates (the results are near perfect and in all cases improve on results reported in the literature). Also recognition for the composite database (comprising almost 100 objects) is also near perfect.

1   Introduction

The light reaching our eye is a function of surface reflectance, illuminant colour and lighting geometry. Yet, the colours that we perceive depend almost exclusively on surface reflectance; the dependencies due to lighting geometry **and** illuminant colour are removed through some sort of image normalization procedure. As an example, the white page of a book looks white whether viewed under blue sky or under artificial light and remains white, independent of the position of the light source. While analogous normalizations exist in computer vision for discounting lighting geometry **or** illuminant colour there does not exist a normalization which can do both, together at the same time. Yet, such a **comprehensive normalization** is clearly needed since both lighting geometry and illuminant colour can be expected to change from image to image. A comprehensive normalization is developed in this paper.

Image normalization research in computer vision generally proceeds in two stages and we will adopt the same strategy here. First, the physics of image formation are characterized and the dependency due to a given physical variable is made explicit. In a second stage, methods for removing this dependency (that is, canceling dependent variables) are developed. As an example of this kind of reasoning, it is well known that, assuming a linear camera response, if light intensity is scaled by a factor s then the image scales by the same factor: each captured (r, g, b) pixel becomes (sr, sg, sb). Relative to this simple physical model it is easy to derive a normalization procedure which is independent of the intensity of the viewing illuminant:

$$\frac{r}{r+g+b}, \frac{g}{r+g+b}, \frac{b}{r+g+b} \tag{1}$$

The normalized image colours are sometimes represented using only the *chromaticities* $\frac{r}{r+g+b}$ and $\frac{g}{r+g+b}$ (since $\frac{b}{r+g+b} = \frac{1-r-g}{r+g+b}$).

The normalization shown in (1) is well used, and well accepted, in the computer vision literature (e.g. [SW95,CB97,MMK95,FDB91,Hea89]) and does an admirable job of rendering image colours independent of the power of the viewing illuminant. As we shall see later, lighting geometry in general (this includes the notions of light source direction and light source power) affects only the magnitude of a captured rgb and so the normalization shown in (1) performs well in diverse circumstances.

Dependency due to illumination colour is also very simple to model (subject to certain caveats which are explored later). If (r_1, g_1, b_1) and (r_2, g_2, b_2) denote camera responses corresponding to two scene points viewed under one colour of light then $(\alpha r_1, \beta g_1, \gamma b_1)$ and $(\alpha r_2, \beta g_2, \gamma b_2)$ denote the responses induced by the same points viewed under a different colour of light[WB86] (the red, green and blue colour channels scale by the factors α, β and γ). Clearly, it is easy to derive algebraic expressions where α, β and γ cancel:

$$\left(\frac{2r_1}{r_1+r_2}, \frac{2g_1}{g_1+g_2}, \frac{2b_1}{b_1+b_2}\right), \left(\frac{2r_2}{r_1+r_2}, \frac{2g_2}{g_1+g_2}, \frac{2b_2}{b_1+b_2}\right) \tag{2}$$

The two pixel case summarized in (2) naturally extends to N-pixels: the denominator term becomes the sum of all pixels and numerators are scaled by N. Notice that after normalization, the mean image colour maps to $(1,1,1)$; that is, to 'grey'. For this reason, Equation (2) is sometimes called 'grey-world' normalization[Hun95,GJT88,Buc80].

Unfortunately, neither normalization (1) or (2) suffices to remove dependency on both lighting geometry and illuminant colour. To see that this is so, it is useful to step through a worked example. Let $(s_1\alpha r_1, s_1\beta g_2, s_1\gamma b_1)$ and $(s_2\alpha r_2, s_2\beta g_2, s_2\gamma b_2)$ denote image colours corresponding to two scene points where (s_1, s_2) and (α, β, γ) are scalars that model lighting geometry and illuminant colour respectively. Under lighting geometry normalization, Equation (1), the pixels become:

$$\left(\frac{\alpha r_1}{\alpha r_1 + \beta g_1 + \gamma b_1}, \frac{\beta g_1}{\alpha r_1 + \beta g_1 + \gamma b_1}, \frac{\gamma b_1}{\alpha r_1 + \beta g_1 + \gamma b_1}\right),$$
$$\left(\frac{\alpha r_2}{\alpha r_2 + \beta g_2 + \gamma b_2}, \frac{\beta g_2}{\alpha r_2 + \beta g_2 + \gamma b_2}, \frac{\gamma b_2}{\alpha r_2 + \beta g_2 + \gamma b_2}\right) \tag{3}$$

and under illuminant colour normalization, Equation (2):

$$\left(\frac{2s_1 r_1}{s_1 r_1 + s_2 r_2}, \frac{2s_1 g_1}{s_1 g_1 + s_2 g_2}, \frac{2s_1 b_1}{s_1 b_1 + s_2 b_2}\right), \left(\frac{2s_2 r_2}{s_1 r_1 + s_2 r_2}, \frac{2s_2 g_2}{s_1 g_1 + s_2 g_2}, \frac{2s_2 b_2}{s_1 b_1 + s_2 b_2}\right) \tag{4}$$

In both cases only some of the dependent variables cancel. This is unsatisfactory since both lighting geometry and illuminant colour will change from image to image.

Lin an Lee[LL97] proposed that this problem (cancellation failure) could be solved using normalized colour distribution manifolds. In their method images are normalized for lighting geometry and the variation due to illuminant colour is modelled explicitly. They show that the lighting geometry normalized distribution of colours in a scene viewed under all illuminant colours occupies a continuous manifold in distribution space. In later work by Berwick and Lee[BL98] this manifold is represented implicitly. Here a pair of lighting geometry normalized image colour distributions are defined to be the same if they can be 'matched' by a shift in illuminant colour; this matching effectively reconstructs the manifold 'on the fly'. Unfortunately both these solutions incur a substantial computational overhead. A high dimensional manifold is, at the best of times, unwieldy and implies costly indexing (i.e. to discover if a distribution belongs to a given manifold). Similarly the distribution matching solution, which operates by exhaustive distribution correlation, is very expensive.

In this paper we develop a new comprehensive normalization which can normalize away variation due to illuminant colour **and** lighting geometry together at the same time. Our approach is simplicity itself. We take an input image and normalize for lighting geometry using Equation (1). We then normalize for illuminant colour using Equation (2). We then iterate on this theme, successively normalizing away lighting geometry and light colour until each normalization step is idempotent.

We prove two very important results. First, that this process always converges. Second, that the convergent image is unique: the same scene viewed under any lighting geometry and under any illuminant colour has the same comprehensively normalized image. We also found that convergence is very rapid, typically taking just 4 or 5 iterations.

To illustrate the power of the comprehensive normalization procedure we generated synthetic images of a yellow/grey wedge viewed under white, blue and orange coloured lights which were placed at angles of 45° (close to the surface normal for grey), 90° (halfway between both surfaces) and 135° (close to the normal of yellow). The image capture conditions are illustrated at the top of Figure 1 (a blue light at 80° is shown). The 9 generated synthetic images are shown at the bottom of the figure together with corresponding normalized images. Lighting geometry normalization (Equation (1)) suffices to remove variation due to lighting position but not illuminant colour. Conversely, illuminant colour normalized images (Equation 2) are independent of light colour but depend on lighting position. Only the comprehensive normalization suffices to remove variation due to lighting geometry and illuminant colour.

Examples of the comprehensive normalization acting on real images are shown in Figure 2. The top two images are of the same object viewed under a pair of lighting geometries and illuminant colours. Notice how different the images appear. After comprehensive normalization the images, shown underneath, are almost the same. This experiments is repeated on a second image pair with similar results[1].

As a yet more rigorous test of comprehensive normalization we carried out several object recognition experiments using real images. We adopted the recognition paradigm suggested by Swain and Ballard[SB91] (which is widely used e.g. [SO95], [NB93] and [LL97]) where objects are represented by image colour distributions (or in the case of our experiments by the distribution of colours in comprehensively normalized images). Recognition proceeds by distribution comparison: query distributions are compared to object distributions stored in a database and the closest match identifies the query.

For the image databases of Swain (66 database objects, 31 queries), Chatterjee (13 database, 26 queries), Brewster and Lee (8 objects and 9 queries) and a composite set 87 objects and 67 queries, comprehensive normalization facilitated almost perfect recognition. For the composite database all but 6 of the objects are correctly identified and those that are not are identified in second place. This performance is quite startling in its own right (it is a large database compiled by a variety of research groups). Moreover, recognition performance surpasses, by far, that supported by the lighting geometry or illuminant colour normalizations applied individually.

In section 2 of this paper we discuss colour image formation and derive the normalizations shown above in equations (1) and (2). The comprehensive normalization is presented in section 3 together with proofs of uniqueness and

---

[1] All four input images shown in Figure 2 were taken by Berwick and Lee[BL98]

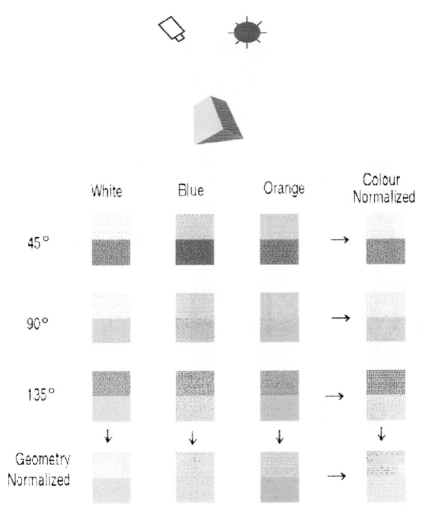

Fig. 1. A yellow/grey wedge, shown top of figure, is imaged under 3 lighting geometries and 3 light colours. The resulting 9 images comprise the 3 × 3 grid of images shown top left above. When illuminant colour is held fixed, lighting geometry normalization suffices (first 3 images in the last row). For fixed lighting geometry, illuminant colour normalization suffices (top 3 images in the last column). The comprehensive normalization removes the effects of both illuminant colour and lighting geometry (the single image shown bottom right)

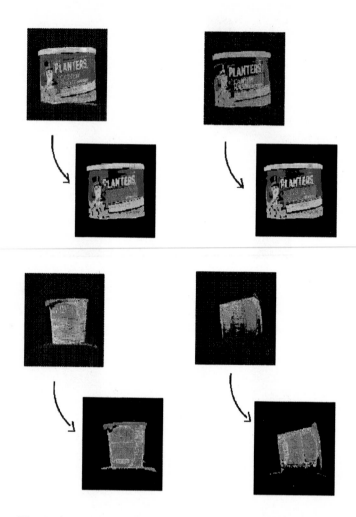

Fig. 2. A peanut container is imaged under two different lighting geometries and illuminant colours (top of figure). After comprehensive normalization the images appear the same (2nd pair of images). A pair of 'split-pea' images (third row) are comprehensively normalized (bottom pair of images). Notice how effectively comprehensive normalization removes dependence illuminant colour and lighting geometry

convergence. In section 4 the object recognition experiments are described and results presented. The paper finishes with some conclusions in section 5.

2   Colour Image Formation

The light reflected from a surface depends on the spectral properties of the surface reflectance and of the illumination incident on the surface. In the case of Lambertian surfaces (the only ones we consider here), this light is simply the product of the spectral power distribution of the light source with the percent spectral reflectance of the surface. Assuming a single point source light, illumination, surface reflection and sensor function, combine together in forming a sensor response:

$$\underline{p}^{\hat{x},E} = \underline{e}^x.\underline{n}^x \int_\omega S^x(\lambda)E(\lambda)\underline{F}(\lambda)d\lambda \tag{5}$$

where λ is wavelength, $\underline{p}$ is a 3-vector of sensor responses (*rgb* pixel value), $\underline{F}$ is the 3-vector of response functions (red-, green and blue- sensitive), E is the illumination striking surface reflectance S^x at location x. Integration is over the visible spectrum ω. Here, and throughout this paper, underscoring denotes vector quantities. The light reflected at x, is proportional to $E(\lambda)S^x(\lambda)$ and is projected onto $\hat{x}$ on the sensor array. The precise power of the reflected light is governed by the dot-product term $\underline{e}^x.\underline{n}^x$. Here, $\underline{n}^x$ is the unit vector corresponding to the surface normal at x and $\underline{e}^x$ is in the *direction* of the light source. The length of $\underline{e}^x$ models the power of the incident light at x. Note that this implies that the function $E(\lambda)$ is actually constant across the scene. Substituting $q^{x,E}$ for $\int_\omega S^x(\lambda)E(\lambda)\underline{F}(\lambda)$ allows us to simplify (5):

$$\underline{p}^{\hat{x},E} = \underline{q}^{x,E}\underline{e}^x.\underline{n}^x \tag{6}$$

It is now understood that $\underline{q}^{x,E}$ is that part of a scene that does not vary with lighting geometry (but does change with illuminant colour). Equation (6), which deals only with point-source lights is easily generalized to more complex lighting geometries. Suppose the light incident at x is a combination of m point source lights with lighting direction vectors equal to $\underline{e}^{x,i}$ $(i = 1, 2, \cdots, m)$. In this case the camera response is equal to:

$$\underline{p}^{\hat{x},E} = \underline{q}^{x,E} \sum_{i=1}^{m} \underline{e}^{x,i}.\underline{n}^x \tag{7}$$

Of course, all the lighting vectors can be combined into a single *effective* direction vector (and this takes us back to Equation (6)):

$$\underline{e}^x = \sum_{i=1}^{m} \underline{e}^{x,i} \Rightarrow \underline{p}^{\hat{x},E} = \underline{q}^{x,E}\underline{e}^x.\underline{n}^x \tag{7a}$$

Equation (7) conveys the intuitive idea that the camera response to m light equals the sum of the responses to each individual light. Simple though (7) is, it suffices to model extended light sources such as fluorescent lights[Pet93].

Since we now understand the dependency between camera response and lighting geometry, it is a scalar relationship dependent on $\underline{e}^x.\underline{n}^x$, it is a straightforward matter to normalize it away:

$$\frac{\underline{p}^{\hat{x},E}}{\sum_{i=1}^{3} p_i^{\hat{x},E}} = \frac{\underline{q}^{x,E}\underline{e}^x.\underline{n}^x}{\underline{e}^x.\underline{n}^x \sum_{i=1}^{3} q_i^{x,E}} = \frac{\underline{q}^x}{\sum_{i=1}^{3} q_i^{x,E}} \tag{8}$$

When $\underline{p}^{\hat{x},E} = (r,g,b)$ then the normalization returns: $(\frac{r}{r+g+b}, \frac{g}{r+g+b}, \frac{b}{r+g+b})$.

It is useful to view the dynamics of this normalization in terms of a complete image. Let us place the N image rgb pixels in rows of an $N \times 3$ image matrix $\mathcal{I}$. It is clear that (8) scales the rows of $\mathcal{I}$ to sum to one. The function $R()$ row-normalizes an image matrix according to (8):

$$R(\mathcal{I})_{i,j} = \frac{\mathcal{I}_{i,j}}{\sum_{k=1}^{3} \mathcal{I}_{i,k}} \tag{8a}$$

Here, and henceforth, a double subscript $_{i,j}$ indexes the ijth element of a matrix.

Let us now consider the effect of illuminant colour on the rgbs recorded by a camera. Here we hold lighting geometry, the vectors $\underline{e}^x$, fixed. To simplify matters still further camera sensors are delta functions: $F(\lambda) = \delta(\lambda - \lambda_i)$ $(i = 1, 2, 3)$. Under $E(\lambda)$ the camera response is equal to:

$$p_i^{\hat{x},E} = \underline{e}^x.\underline{n}^x \int_\omega S^x(\lambda)E(\lambda)\delta(\lambda - \lambda_i)d\lambda = \underline{e}^x.\underline{n}^x S^x(\lambda_i)E(\lambda_i) \tag{9}$$

and under $E_1(\lambda)$:

$$p_i^{\hat{x},E_1} = \underline{e}^x.\underline{n}^x \int_\omega S^x(\lambda)E_1(\lambda)\delta(\lambda - \lambda_i)d\lambda = \underline{e}^x.\underline{n}^x S^x(\lambda_i)E_1(\lambda_i) \tag{10}$$

Combining (9) and (10) together we see that:

$$p_i^{\hat{x},E_1} = \frac{E_1(\lambda_i)}{E(\lambda_i)} p_i^{\hat{x},E} \tag{11}$$

Equation (11) informs us that, as the colour of the light changes, the values recorded in each colour channel scale by a multiplicative factor (one factor per colour channel). If $\underline{R}$, $\underline{G}$ and $\underline{B}$ denote the N values recorded in an image (for each of the red, green and blue colour channels) then under a change in light colour the captured image becomes $\alpha\underline{R}$, $\beta\underline{G}$ and $\gamma\underline{B}$ (where α, β and γ are scalars). It is a simple matter to remove dependence on illumination colour:

$$\frac{\alpha N/3\,R}{\alpha \sum_{i=1}^{N} R_i} = \frac{N/3\,R}{\sum_{i=1}^{N} R_i}$$

$$\frac{\beta N/3\,G}{\beta \sum_{i=1}^{N} G_i} = \frac{N/3\,G}{\sum_{i=1}^{N} G_i} \qquad (12)$$

$$\frac{\gamma N/3\,B}{\gamma \sum_{i=1}^{N} B_i} = \frac{N/3\,B}{\sum_{i=1}^{N} B_i}$$

In terms of the $N \times 3$ image matrix $\mathcal{I}$, the normalization acts to scale each column to sum to $N/3$. This $N/3$ tally is far from arbitrary, but rather ensures that the total sum of all pixels post- column normalization is N which is the same as the total image sum calculated post row normalization. Thus, in principle, an image can be in both row- and column-normal form (and the goal of comprehensive normalization, discussed in the next section, is feasible). The function $C()$ column normalizes $\mathcal{I}$ according to (12a):

$$C(\mathcal{I})_{i,j} = \frac{N/3\,\mathcal{I}_{i,j}}{\sum_{k=1}^{N} \mathcal{I}_{k,j}} \qquad (12a)$$

It is prudent to remind the reader that in order to arrive at the simple normalization presented in (12) delta function sensitivities were selected for our camera. While such a selection is not generally applicable, studies[FF96,FDF94b,FDF94a] have shown that most camera sensors behave, or can be made to behave, like delta functions.

3   The Comprehensive Normalization

The **comprehensive normalization** procedure is defined below:

$$
\begin{aligned}
&1.\ \mathcal{I}_0 = \mathcal{I} && \text{Initialization} \\[1em]
&2.\ \mathcal{I}_{i+1} = C(R(\mathcal{I}_i)) && \text{Iteration step} \\[1em]
&3.\ \mathcal{I}_{i+1} = \mathcal{I}_i && \text{Termination condition}
\end{aligned}
\qquad (13)
$$

The comprehensive procedure iteratively performs row and column normalizations until the termination condition is met. In practice the process will terminate when a normalization step induces a change less than a criterion amount.

Obviously this iterative procedure is useful if and only if we can show convergence and uniqueness. The procedure is said to converge, if for all images termination is guaranteed. If the convergent image is always the same (for any fixed scene) then uniqueness follows.

As a step towards proving uniqueness it is useful to examine the effects of lighting geometry and illuminant colour using the tools of matrix algebra. From the discussion in section 2, we know that viewing the same scene under a different lighting geometry results in an image where pixels, that is **rows** of $\mathcal{I}$, are scaled. This idea can be expressed as an $N \times N$ diagonal matrix $\mathcal{D}^r$ premultiplying $\mathcal{I}$:

$$\mathcal{D}^r \mathcal{I} \tag{14}$$

Similarly, a change in illuminant colour results in a scaling of individual colour channels; that is, a scaling of the columns of $\mathcal{I}$. This may be written as $\mathcal{I}$ post multiplied by a 3×3 matrix $\mathcal{D}^c$:

$$\mathcal{I} \mathcal{D}^c \tag{15}$$

Equations (14) and (15) taken together inform us that the same scene viewed under a pair of lighting geometries and illuminant colours induces the image matrices: $\mathcal{I}$ and $\mathcal{D}^r \mathcal{I} \mathcal{D}^c$.

By definition, each iteration of the comprehensive normalization procedure scales the rows and then the columns of $\mathcal{I}$ by pre- and post-multiplying with the appropriate diagonal matrix. The operations of successive normalizations can be cascaded together and so we find that an image and its comprehensively normalized counterpart are related:

$$comprehensive(\mathcal{I}) = \mathcal{D}^{r*} \mathcal{I} \mathcal{D}^{c*} \tag{16}$$

where $comprehensive()$ is a function implementing the iterative procedure shown in (13) and the symbol $*$ conveys the idea of a sequence of diagonal matrices.

Theorem 1. *If $\mathcal{C}^1 = comprehensive(\mathcal{I})$ and $\mathcal{C}^2 = comprehensive(\mathcal{D}^r \mathcal{I} \mathcal{D}^c)$ then $\mathcal{C}^1 = \mathcal{C}^2$ (proof of uniqueness).*

Proof. Let us assume that $\mathcal{C}^1 \neq \mathcal{C}^2$. By (16), $\mathcal{C}^1 = \mathcal{D}_1^r \mathcal{I} \mathcal{D}_1^c$ and $\mathcal{C}^2 = \mathcal{D}_2^r \mathcal{D}^r \mathcal{I} \mathcal{D}^c \mathcal{D}_2^c$ for some diagonal matrices $\mathcal{D}_1^r$, $\mathcal{D}_2^r$, $\mathcal{D}_1^c$ and $\mathcal{D}_2^c$. It follows that:

$$\mathcal{C}^2 = \mathcal{D}^a \mathcal{C}^1 \mathcal{D}^b \tag{17}$$

where $\mathcal{D}^a = \mathcal{D}_2^r \mathcal{D}^r [\mathcal{D}_1^r]^{-1}$ and $\mathcal{D}^b = [\mathcal{D}_1^c]^{-1} \mathcal{D}^c \mathcal{D}_2^c$. By the assumption that $\mathcal{C}^1 \neq \mathcal{C}^2$, $\mathcal{D}^a$ and $\mathcal{D}^b$ are not equal to identity (or scaled identity) matrices. Clearly, for any $\mathcal{D}^a$ and $\mathcal{D}^b$ satisfying (17) so do $k\mathcal{D}^a$ and $\frac{1}{k}\mathcal{D}^b$ so, without loss of generality we assume that $\mathcal{D}_{i,i}^b > 1$. We also assume that $\mathcal{D}_{1,1}^b > \mathcal{D}_{2,2}^b > \mathcal{D}_{3,3}^b$ (since if this is not the case it can be made true by interchanging the columns of $\mathcal{C}^1$). Since $\mathcal{C}^2$ is comprehensively normalized we can express the components of $\mathcal{D}^a$ in terms of $\mathcal{D}^b$ and $\mathcal{C}^1$. In particular the ith diagonal term of $\mathcal{D}^a$ is, and must be, the reciprocal of the sum of the ith row of $\mathcal{C}^1 \mathcal{D}^b$:

$$\mathcal{D}_{i,i}^a = \frac{1}{\mathcal{D}_{1,1}^b \mathcal{C}_{i,1}^1 + \mathcal{D}_{2,2}^b \mathcal{C}_{i,2}^1 + \mathcal{D}_{3,3}^b \mathcal{C}_{i,3}^1} \tag{18}$$

From which it follows that:

$$\mathcal{C}_{i,1}^2 = \frac{\mathcal{D}_{1,1}^b \mathcal{C}_{i,1}^1}{\mathcal{D}_{1,1}^b \mathcal{C}_{i,1}^1 + \mathcal{D}_{2,2}^b \mathcal{C}_{i,2}^1 + \mathcal{D}_{3,3}^b \mathcal{C}_{i,3}^1} \tag{19}$$

Since have assumed that $\mathcal{D}^b_{1,1} > \mathcal{D}^b_{2,2} > \mathcal{D}^b_{3,3}$, it follows that

$$\frac{\mathcal{D}^b_{1,1}\mathcal{C}^1_{i,1}}{\mathcal{D}^b_{1,1}\mathcal{C}^1_{i,1} + \mathcal{D}^b_{1,1}\mathcal{C}^1_{i,2} + \mathcal{D}^b_{1,1}\mathcal{C}^1_{i,3}} < \frac{\mathcal{D}^b_{1,1}\mathcal{C}^1_{i,1}}{\mathcal{D}^b_{1,1}\mathcal{C}^1_{i,1} + \mathcal{D}^b_{2,2}\mathcal{C}^1_{i,2} + \mathcal{D}^b_{3,3}\mathcal{C}^1_{i,3}} \tag{20}$$

which implies that

$$\frac{\mathcal{C}^1_{i,1}}{\mathcal{C}^1_{i,1} + \mathcal{C}^1_{i,2} + \mathcal{C}^1_{i,3}} < \frac{\mathcal{D}^b_{1,1}\mathcal{C}^1_{i,1}}{\mathcal{D}^b_{1,1}\mathcal{C}^1_{i,1} + \mathcal{D}^b_{2,2}\mathcal{C}^1_{i,2} + \mathcal{D}^b_{3,3}\mathcal{C}^1_{i,3}} \equiv \mathcal{C}^1_{i,1} < \mathcal{C}^2_{i,1} \tag{21}$$

Equation (21) informs us that every element in the first column of C^1 is strictly less than the corresponding element in in C^2. However, this cannot be the case since both $\mathcal{C}_1$ and $\mathcal{C}_2$ are comprehensively normalized which implies that the sum of their respected first columns must be the same (and this cannot be the case if the inequality in (21) holds).

We have a contradiction and so, $C^1 = C^2$ and uniqueness is proven. $\qquad\square$

Theorem 2. *The comprehensive normalization procedure always converges.*

Proof. Our proof follows directly from **Sinkhorn's** thoerem[Sin64] which we invoke here as a Lemma.

Lemma. Let $\mathcal{B}$ denote an arbitrary $n \times n$ all positive matrix. Sinkhorn showed that the process where the rows of $\mathcal{B}$ are iteratively scaled to sum to $n/3$ and then the columns are scaled to sum to $n/3$ (in an analogous process to (13)) is guaranteed to converge[2].

First, note that images, under any imaging conditions, are all positive. Now, let matrix $\mathcal{B}$ be a $3N \times 3N$ where the $N \times 3$ image matrix $\mathcal{I}$ is copied N times in the horizontal and 3 times in the vertical direction:

$$\mathcal{B} = \begin{bmatrix} \mathcal{I}\,\mathcal{I}\,\cdots\,\mathcal{I} \\ \mathcal{I}\,\mathcal{I}\,\cdots\,\mathcal{I} \\ \mathcal{I}\,\mathcal{I}\,\cdots\,\mathcal{I} \end{bmatrix} \tag{22}$$

Suppose that $\mathcal{D}^r$ and $\mathcal{D}^c$ are diagonal matrices such that the rows of $\mathcal{D}^r\mathcal{B}$ sum to N and the columns of $\mathcal{B}\mathcal{D}^c$ sum to N (note $N = 3N/3$). From the block structure of $\mathcal{B}$, it follows that $\mathcal{D}^r_{i,i} = \mathcal{D}^r_{i+kN,i+kN}$ $(i = 1, 2, \cdots, N)$ $(k = 2,3)$. Similarly because columns sum to N, $\mathcal{D}^c_{i,i} = \mathcal{D}^c_{i+kN,i+kN}$ $(i = 1,2,3)$ and $k = (2, \cdots, N)$. Setting $\mathcal{D}^a = \mathcal{D}^r_{i,i}$ $(i = 1, 2, \cdots, N)$ and $\mathcal{D}^b = \mathcal{D}^c_{i,i}$ $(i = 1,2,3)$, we can write $\mathcal{D}^r\mathcal{B}$ and $\mathcal{B}\mathcal{D}^c$ as:

$$\mathcal{D}^r\mathcal{B} = \begin{bmatrix} \mathcal{D}^a\mathcal{I}\,\mathcal{D}^a\mathcal{I}\,\cdots\,\mathcal{D}^a\mathcal{I} \\ \mathcal{D}^a\mathcal{I}\,\mathcal{D}^a\mathcal{I}\,\cdots\,\mathcal{D}^a\mathcal{I} \\ \mathcal{D}^a\mathcal{I}\,\mathcal{D}^a\mathcal{I}\,\cdots\,\mathcal{D}^a\mathcal{I} \end{bmatrix} \quad , \quad \mathcal{B}\mathcal{D}^c = \begin{bmatrix} \mathcal{I}\mathcal{D}^b\,\mathcal{I}\mathcal{D}^b\,\cdots\,\mathcal{I}\mathcal{D}^b \\ \mathcal{I}\mathcal{D}^b\,\mathcal{I}\mathcal{D}^b\,\cdots\,\mathcal{I}\mathcal{D}^b \\ \mathcal{I}\mathcal{D}^b\,\mathcal{I}\mathcal{D}^b\,\cdots\,\mathcal{I}\mathcal{D}^b \end{bmatrix} \tag{23}$$

Each row in $\mathcal{D}^a\mathcal{I}$ sums to $\frac{3}{3N} * N = 1$ and each column in $\mathcal{I}\mathcal{D}^b$ sums to $\frac{N}{3N} * N = N/3$. That is each $\mathcal{I}$ in $\mathcal{B}$ is normalized according to the functions $R()$

---

[2] In fact we could choose any positive number here; $n/3$ will work well for our purposes.

and $C()$ and so after sufficient iterations, Sinkhorn's iterative process converges to:

$$Sinkhorn(\mathcal{B}) \;=\; \begin{bmatrix} comprehensive(\mathcal{I}) & comprehensive(\mathcal{I}) & \cdots & comprehensive(\mathcal{I}) \\ comprehensive(\mathcal{I}) & comprehensive(\mathcal{I}) & \cdots & comprehensive(\mathcal{I}) \\ comprehensive(\mathcal{I}) & comprehensive(\mathcal{I}) & \cdots & comprehensive(\mathcal{I}) \end{bmatrix}$$

(24)

Clearly, Sinkhorn's theorem implies the convergence of the comprehensive normalization procedure and our proof is complete. □

Experimentally, we found that the comprehensive normalization converges very rapidly: 4 or 5 iterations generally suffices.

4 Object Recognition Experiments

We carried out image indexing experiments for the Swain and Ballard[SB91], Simon Fraser[Cha95,GFF95], Berwick and Lee[BL98] image sets and a set of all images combined. Swain and Ballard's image set comprises 66 database and 31 query images. All images are taken under a fixed colour light source and there are only small changes in lighting geometry. Because there are, effectively, no confounding factors in Swain's images, we expect good indexing performance for lighting geometry, illuminant colour and comprehensive normalizations. The Simon Fraser dataset comprises a small database of 13 object images and 26 query images. Query images contain the same objects but viewed under large changes in lighting geometry and illuminant colour. In Lee and Berwick's image set there are 8 object images and 9 query images. Again queries images are captured under different conditions (viewing geometry and light colour change). The composite set comprises 87 database images and 67 queries.

To test the efficacy of each normalization we proceed as follows. For all images, database and query, we separately carried out lighting geometry, illuminant colour and comprehensive normalizations. At a second stage colour histograms, representing the colour distributions, of the variously normalized images are constructed. This involves histogramming only the (g, b) tuples in the normalized images. The pixel value r is discarded because $r + g + b = 1$ after lighting geometry and comprehensive normalizations, and so is a dependent variable. After illuminant colour normalization *on average* $r + g + b = 1$. A 16×16 partition of (G, B) colour space (which have values between 0 and 1) define the bins for the colour histograms. If H_i and Q denotes the histograms for the ith database and query images then the similarity of the ith image to the query image is defined as:

$$||H_i - Q||_1 \tag{25}$$

where $||.||_1$ denotes the L1 (or city-block distance) between the colour distributions. This distance is equal to the sum of absolute differences of corresponding histogram bins. Reassuringly, if $H_i = Q$ then $||H_i - Q||_1 = 0$; closeness corresponds to small distances.

For each query colour distribution, we calculate the distance to all distributions in the database. These distances are sorted into ascending order and the rank of the correct answer is recorded (ideally the image ranked in first place should contain the same object as the query image). Tables 1, 2 and 3 summarize indexing performance for all three normalizations operating on all four data sets. Two performance measures are shown: the % of queries that were correctly matched (% in 1st place) and the rank of the worst case match.

Image Set	% correct	worst ranking
Swain's	96.7	2nd out of 66
Simon Fraser	42.3	13th out of 13
Lee and Berwick	33.33	6th out of 8
Composite	58.2	86th out of 87

Table 1. Indexing performance of lighting geometry normalization

Image Set	% correct	worst ranking
Swain's	87.1	5th out of 66
Simon Fraser	80.8	6th out of 13
Lee and Berwick	67.7	4th out of 9
Composite	79.1	16th out of 87

Table 2. Indexing performance of illuminant normalization

Image Set	% correct	worst ranking
Swain's	80.6	2nd out of 66
Simon Fraser	100	1st out of 13
Lee and Berwick	100	1st out of 9
Composite	93.1	2nd out of 87

Table 3. Indexing performance of comprehensive normalization

A cursory look at the matching performance for Swain's images appears to suggest that lighting geometry normalization works best and the comprehensive normalization worst. This is, in fact, not the case: all three normalizations work very well. Notice that only the comprehensive normalization and lighting geometry normalizations place the correct answers in the top two ranks and this is an admirable level of performance given such a large database. For the Simon Fraser Database the comprehensive normalization procedure is vastly superior, 100% recognition is supported compared with 42.3% and 80.8% for lighting geometry and illuminant colour normalizations. The latter normalizations also perform very poorly in terms of the worst case rankings which are 13th and 6th respectively. This is quite unacceptable given the very small size (just 13 objects) of the Simon Fraser database. It is worth noting that no other colour distribution comparison method has come close to delivering 100% recognition on this dataset[FCF96] (these methods include, colour-angular indexing[FCF96], affine-invariants of colour histograms[HS94] and Colour constant colour indexing[FF95]). The same recognition story is repeated for the Berwick and Lee database. Comprehensive normalization supports 100% recognition and the other normalization perform very poorly.

Perhaps the recognition results for the composite data set are the most interesting. Over 93% (of 67) queries are correctly identified using comprehensive normalization and the worst case match is in second place. Such recognition performance is quite startling. The database is large comprising 87 objects and these were compiled by three different research groups. Also the means of recognition is a simple colour distribution comparison which is bound to fail when images, or objects, have the same mixture of colours. Indeed, most of the, 2nd place matches that are recorded have colour distributions which are similar to the overall best match. For example an image of 'Campbell's chicken soup' is confused with an image of 'Campbell's special chicken soup'. Both images are predominantly red and white (as we expect with Campbell's soup).

In comparison the lighting geometry and illuminant colour normalizations, used individually, perform very poorly. The former succeeds just 58% of the time and the worst case ranking is an incredibly poor 86th (out of 87). Illuminant colour normalization performs better, a recognition rate of 79% but again the worst case match is unacceptable: 16th placed out of 87.

5   Conclusion

The colours recorded in an image depend on both the lighting geometry and the colour of the illuminant. Unless these confounding factors can be discounted, colours cannot be meaningfully compared across images (and so object recognition by colour distribution comparison cannot work). In this paper we developed a new comprehensive normalization procedure which can remove dependency due to lighting geometry **and** illuminant colour and so can facilitate cross-image colour comparison.

Our approach is simplicity itself. We simply invoke normalization procedures which discount either lighting geometry **or** illuminant colour and apply them together and iteratively. We prove that this iterative process always converges to a unique *comprehensively normalized* image.

The power of our comprehensive normalization procedure was illustrated in a set the object recognition experiments. For four image databases: Swain's database, the Simon Fraser database, Sang Wok Lee's database, and a composite set (with almost 100 objects), recognition by colour distribution comparison, post-comprehensive normalization was found to be near perfect. Importantly, performance greatly surpassed that achievable using the lighting geometry or illuminant colour normalizations individually.

Acknowledgements

Graham Finlayson is grateful for support from the EC SMART TMR network and from EPSRC grant GR/L60852.

References

[BL98]   D. Berwick and S.W. Lee. A chromaticity space for specularity-, illumination color- and illumination pose-invariant 3-d object recognition. In *ICCV98*, page Session 2.3, 1998.

[Buc80]   G. Buchsbaum. A spatial processor model for object colour perception. *Journal of the Franklin Institute*, 310:1–26, 1980.

[CB97]   J.L. Crowley and F. Berard. Multi-modal tracking of faces for video communications. In *CVPR 97*, pages 640–645, 1997.

[Cha95]   S.S. Chatterjee. Color invariant object and texture recognition, 1995. MSc thesis, Simon Fraser University, School of Computing Science.

[FCF96]   G.D. Finlayson, S.S. Chatterjee, and B.V. Funt. Color angular indexing. In *The Fourth European Conference on Computer Vision (Vol II)*, pages 16–27. European Vision Society, 1996.

[FDB91]   B.V. Funt, M.S. Drew, and M. Brockington. Recovering shading in color images. In *The Second European Conference on Computer Vision*, pages 124–132. Springer Verlag, 1992.

[FDF94a]   G.D. Finlayson, M.S. Drew, and B.V. Funt. Color constancy: Generalized diagonal transforms suffice. *J. Opt. Soc. Am. A*, 11:3011–3020, 1994.

[FDF94b]   G.D. Finlayson, M.S. Drew, and B.V. Funt. Spectral sharpening: Sensor transformations for improved color constancy. *J. Opt. Soc. Am. A*, 11(5):1553–1563, May 1994.

[FF95]   B.V. Funt and G.D. Finlayson. Color constant color indexing. *IEEE transactions on Pattern analysis and Machine Intelligence*, 1995.

[FF96]   G.D. Finlayson and B.V. Funt. Coefficient channels: Derivation and relationship to other theoretical studies. *COLOR research and application*, 21(2):87–96, 1996.

[GFF95]   S.S. Chatterjee G.D. Finlayson and B.V. Funt. Color angle invariants for object recognition. In *3rd IS&T and SID Color Imaging Conference*, pages 44–47. 1995.

[GJT88]   R. Gershon, A.D. Jepson, and J.K. Tsotsos. From $[r, g, b]$ to surface reflectance: Computing color constant descriptors in images. In *International Joint Conference on Artificial Intelligence*, pages 755–758, 1987.

[Hea89]   G. Healey. Using color for geometry-insensitive segmentation. *J. Opt. Soc. Am. A*, 6:920–937, 1989.

[Hun95]   R.W.G. Hunt. *The Reproduction of Color*. Fountain Press, 5th edition, 1995.

[LL97]   S. Lin and S.W. Lee. Using chromaticity distributions and eigenspace analysis for pose-, illumination- and specularity-invariant recognition of 3d object. In *CVPR97*, pages 426–431, 1997.

[MMK95]   J. Matas, R. Marik, and J. Kittler. On representation and matching of multi-coloured objects. In *Proceedings of the fifth International Conference on Computer Vision*, pages 726–732. IEEE Computer Society, June 1995.

[NB93]   W. Niblack and R. Barber. The QBIC project: Querying images by content using color, texture and shape. In *Storage and Retrieval for Image and Video Databases I, volume 1908 of SPIE Proceedings Series*. 1993.

[Pet93]   A.P. Petrov. On obtaining shape from color shading. *COLOR research and application*, 18(4):236–240, 1993.

[SB91]   M.J. Swain and D.H.. Ballard. Color indexing. *International Journal of Computer Vision*, 7(11):11–32, 1991.

[Sin64]   R. Sinkhorn. A relationship between arbitrary positive matrices and doubly stochastic matrices. *Annals of Mathematical Statistics*, 35:876–879, 1964.

[SO95]   M. A. Stricker and M. Orengo. Similarity of color images. In *Storage and Retrieval for Image and Video Databases III*, volume 2420 of *SPIE Proceedings Series*, pages 381–392. Feb. 1995.

[SW95]   B. Schiele and A. Waibel. Gaze tracking based on face-color. In *International Workshop on Automatic Face- and Gesture-Recognition*, June 1995.

[WB86]   J.A. Worthey and M.H. Brill. Heuristic analysis of von Kries color constancy. *Journal of The Optical Society of America A*, 3(10):1708–1712, 1986.

Invariant-Based Shape Retrieval in Pictorial Databases

Michael Kliot and Ehud Rivlin

Computer Science Department, Technion - Israel Institute of Technology, Haifa 32000, Israel. Tel.: 972-4-8294304. E-Mail: {michk,ehudr}@cs.technion.ac.il

Abstract. One of the strongest cues for retrieval of content information from images is shape. However, due to the wide range of transformations that an object might undergo, this is also the most difficult one to handle. It seems that shape retrieval is one of the major barriers nowadays on the way of image databases to become commonly used. Common approaches use global attributes (Faloutsos et al. [1]), feature points (Pentland et al. [2]), histograms (Jain and Vailaya [3]), or physical models of deformations (Del Bimbo and Pala [4]). We present an approach for shape retrieval from pictorial databases which is based on invariant features of the image. In particular we use a combination of semi-local multi-valued invariant signatures and global features. Spatial relations and global properties are used to eliminate non-relevant images before similarity is computed. Common approaches usually don't handle viewpoint transformations more complex than similarity and require the full shape in order to compute image features. The advantages of the proposed approach are its ability to handle images distorted by different viewpoint transformations, its ability to retrieve images even in situations in which part of the shape is missing (i.e., in case of occlusion or sketch-based queries), and its ability to support efficient indexing. We have implemented our approach in a heterogeneous database having a SQL-like user interface augmented with sketch-based queries. The system is built on top of a commercial database system, and can be activated from the Web. We present experimental results demonstrating the effectiveness of the proposed approach.

1 Introduction

The area of pictorial databases has become recently a subject of extensive research. Large databases of images are used in different applications including multimedia systems, medical imaging systems, documents systems and so forth. The most common form of retrieval is based on image content. For most of the applications content is defined in terms of three basic components: color, shape and texture. This paper concentrates on shape-based retrieval.

Various approaches for shape retrieval differ by the features used for representing the image and for indexing, as by the different ways in which the pictorial information is organized to allow effective retrieval. Several works use *global numerical attributes* for indexing and retrieval shapes [1, 5, 6]. The distance between two images is obtained as the weighted Euclidean distance in a *n*-dimensional space of features. Another form of shape description is based on *feature points*, like corners and high-curvature points, detected from the image [2, 7, 8]. Other approaches use symbolic string representation of the images [9], histogram of the edge directions of the image [3], or elastic matching of user-drawn sketches [4].

Common approaches, while providing good accuracy and efficiency, still suffer from instability as a result of viewpoint transformations. An additional disadvantage is the requirement of the full, unoccluded shape in order to compute the needed image features. Some approaches (e.g. [4]) try to overcome the different deformations by using physical models (e.g elastic deformation energy). As they do not address the general geometric transformation it will be hard for them to handle the full spectrum of the transformations, as well as situations where part of the shape is missing. In order to handle such situations *local* invariant features should be used. The most popular and well-studied kind of local invariants are the *differential* invariants, i.e. invariants that are based on derivatives of different order. The main disadvantage of this kind of invariants is their sensitivity to noise, resulting from their differential character. Hybrid, or semi-differential invariants try to combine the advantages of the global and local approaches. Moons et al. [10] present a general theory of local semi-differential invariants. Bruckstein et al. [11, 12] use locally applied global geometric invariants.

In this work we attempt to overcome the limitations of the common approaches, namely a restriction of the viewing transformation to similarity, and a requirement for a complete, unoccluded input image. We use features, invariant for wide range of viewpoint transformations, including affine and perspective. Shape similarity is measured using semi-local multivalued invariant signatures, that allow to handle situations in which part of the shape information is missing (i.e occlusion or sketch-based retrieval). To efficiently handle such cases we introduce a data structure, the *containment tree* , that exploits the topological structure of the image. This structure supports indexing mostly in sketch-based retrieval. In this paper we present a series of experiments done on a heterogeneous database system which we build to test our approach. The system allows to query images by logical or shape descriptions (query by example), or combination of both. It has an interface to the Web, providing a convenient user interface.

The paper is organized as follows. In Sections 2 and 3 we present our approach for invariant-based retrieval. Section 2 presents the machinery needed for indexing and retrieval with full and partial shape information, while Section 3 describes the query processing itself. Section 4 presents variety of results using our approach for retrieving images from three different databases. Section 5 contains the concluding remarks.

2 Indexing and invariants

The purpose of indexing is to support fast retrieval from the database. Usually, two requirements are imposed on features used for indexing: the features should allow for substantial reduction in the number of candidates from the database, and a feature-based distance function should exist which supports ranking of images according to their distance from the input image.

As primitives for shape description we use various geometric entities. We exploit these entities for filtering the database while searching for a candidates set of images which answer a query. Features on which the description is based include various properties varying from the number of the different geometric entities, their dimensions and positions, to some topological relationships. Our approach emphasizes the use of *geometric invariants* which provide a good mean for indexing while supporting ranking. Different features are used for extraction of descriptors that are invariant under various transformations. Note that different applications may allow for different kinds of invariants. In applications that use images of trademarks, for example, similarity invariants are usually enough. For some other applications, however, a wider set of transformations, affine or projective, may be required. The applicability of a certain feature for indexing can be adjusted as well to the class of transformations derived from the application at hand.

Our invariant representation of objects is based mainly on *semi-local multivalued invariant signatures*. These signatures provide a measure of distance between two curves, which allows us to rank images according to their distance from the input image. Below we describe the extraction and matching of such invariant signatures.

2.1 Semi-local multivalued invariant signatures

Invariant signature is a function of a curve, calculated pointwise, and invariant for a given set of transformations. Invariant signatures can be used for recognition of planar curves. The important property of invariant signatures is their applicability in situations where the input curve is partially occluded. Having an invariant signature, curve matching reduces to matching signatures.

In order to calculate an invariant signature, one should find a local invariant for the given set of transformations, and apply it at each point of the curve. Our approach follows the one presented in [11, 12]. First, the curve (object boundary), given in arbitrary parameterization, is reparameterized invariantly, using the lowest possible order of derivatives. Formally, for a given planar shape transformation set $\mathbf{T}_\psi : \mathbf{R}^2 \to \mathbf{R}^2$, and for a given curve $\mathbf{P}(t)$, having an arbitrary parameterization, the target is to find an *invariant reparameterization* $\mathbf{P}(\tau)$ so that if $\mathbf{P}(t)$ and $\tilde{\mathbf{P}}(\tilde{t})$ are related via $\tilde{\mathbf{P}}(\tilde{\tau}) = \mathbf{T}_\psi[\mathbf{P}(t(\tilde{t}))]$ then $\tilde{\mathbf{P}}(\tilde{\tau}) = \mathbf{T}_\psi[\mathbf{P}(\tau + \tau_0)]$. In other words, the reparameterization is invariant if the corresponding points have the corresponding parameter value, up to some constant cyclic shift.

The equations for invariant reparameterization are obtained using the differential properties of the viewpoint transformations. Let's define $K^{n,m}[x, y|t] \triangleq x^{(n)}y^{(m)} - x^{(m)}y^{(n)}$. For the similarity transformation $\mathbf{T}_\psi(\mathbf{u}) = \tilde{\mathbf{u}} = \alpha \mathbf{U}_\omega \mathbf{u} + \mathbf{v}$, where $\mathbf{U}_\omega$ is a rotation matrix, we obtain that $d\tau = \dfrac{K^{1,2}[x, y|t]}{|\dot{\mathbf{P}}|^2} dt$ is an invariant, generalized arc length, reparameterization.

For the affine transformation $\mathbf{T}_\psi(\mathbf{u}) = \tilde{\mathbf{u}} = \mathbf{A}u + \mathbf{v}$ we obtain that for $d\tau^* = \left|K^{1,2}[x,y|t]\right|^{\frac{1}{3}} dt, d\tilde{\tau}^* = \left|K^{1,2}[\tilde{x},\tilde{y}|\tilde{t}]\right|^{\frac{1}{3}} d\tilde{t}$ we have $\tilde{\tau}^* = |det\mathbf{A}|^{\frac{1}{3}} \tau^* + \tau_0^*$. This gives us linear scaled invariant reparameterization. In the particular case $|det\mathbf{A}| = 1$, the reparameterization is absolutely invariant. Exploring further the properties of affine transformation, we obtain that $d\tau = \left|\dfrac{d}{d\tau^*}\left|\dfrac{K^{2,4}[x,y|\tau^*]}{K^{2,3}[x,y|\tau^*]^{3/2}}\right|\right| d\tau^*$ is a non-scaled affine invariant reparameterization.

The implementation of the reparameterization process intends to reduce the influence of the noise. First, the contour is transferred to a parametric form by B-spline approximation. Since we want the spline value at a certain point to depend on the coordinates of the contour points in a sufficiently large region, so that the influence of a small error in the edge detection is diminished, we adopted the technique used in [13]. The solution subsamples the contour, computes the spline values and averages the results for different positions of samples on the contour. So, the first sampling set consists of each l-th point on the contour, the points next to the chosen ones form the second set, etc. Thus, no information is lost, because each point participates in some sample. After the B-spline representation of the curve is obtained, the reparameterization is straightforward.

The computation of the semi-local signature is based on geometric features, that stay invariant under the viewpoint transformation. Under similarity transformation, ratios of lengths, ratios of areas and angles stay invariant. Thus, we can use those invariants locally to generate signature functions of various types. After the invariant reparameterization is completed, the two curves $\mathbf{P}(\tau)$ and $\tilde{\mathbf{P}}(\tilde{\tau})$ are related by $\tilde{\mathbf{P}}(\tilde{\tau}) = \mathbf{T}_\psi[\mathbf{P}(\tilde{\tau} + \tilde{\tau}_0)]$. This equation shows that one can compute the ratio of lengths, or the angle between, the segments defined by $(\mathbf{P}(\tau - s_B), \mathbf{P}(\tau))$ and $(\mathbf{P}(\tau), \mathbf{P}(\tau + s_F))$ for a priori chosen values s_B and s_F (locality parameters). Thus $\dfrac{\delta[\mathbf{P}(\tau),\mathbf{P}(\tau + s_F)]}{\delta[\mathbf{P}(\tau),\mathbf{P}(\tau - s_B)]}$ and the angle formed by the points as functions of τ are invariant signature functions (see Fig. 1(left)).

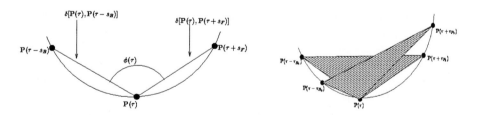

Fig. 1. Semi-local invariants. On the left - invariants for similarity transformation. On the right - invariants for the affine transformation.

Under affine transformation, areas are uniformly scaled by $det\ \mathbf{A}$. This fact implies that the ratio of areas is affine invariant. Assuming that an invariant parameterization was already obtained for the curve, we can choose four values for τ: $\tau_{B_1}, \tau_{B_2}, \tau_{F_1}, \tau_{F_2}$, and calculate at each point $\mathbf{P}(\tau)$ the ratio of areas, $\dfrac{Area_\triangle(\mathbf{P}_{B_1}, \mathbf{P}(\tau), \mathbf{P}_{F_1})}{Area_\triangle(\mathbf{P}_{B_2}, \mathbf{P}(\tau), \mathbf{P}_{F_2})}$, where $\mathbf{P}_{B_1}, \mathbf{P}_{F_1}, \mathbf{P}_{B_2}, \mathbf{P}_{F_2}$ are defined using locality parameters as for similarity case. This quantity is an invariant signature as a function of the invariant "arc length" τ (see Fig. 1(right)).

If the locality parameters set is let to be free parameters rather than setting them in advance, we obtain a whole range of invariants at each point rather than a single value (Bruckstein et al. [12]). The signature functions for curves become signature vectors or even continuum of values, i.e., surfaces or hypersurfaces. Matching them is less sensitive to peculiarities that may exist at some fixed pre-set value of the locality parameters.

It is important to note that since, in the general case, there is no correspondence between the initial points of the curves, the corresponding points on the curves have, after the invariant reparameterization, the same parameter value up to unknown constant cyclic shift value. This fact adds to the complexity of the matching process.

We designed an effective automatic matching procedure, that can handle images distorted by affine and similarity transformations, and situations in which image is partially occluded. To match two signatures, we map them to the matrices with the number of rows equal to the number of signatures in the multivalued signature, and the number of columns equal to the number of the samples. In order to estimate the unknown value of relative cyclic shift, we exploit reference points. As a reference point we use the signature extrema. Minimizing the difference between the matrices over all checked shift values provides a measure for the distance between the signatures.

Values of the invariant perimeters of the same curves, up to transformation, may differ due to possible error in the edge detection process (see Fig. 2). We map the signatures having different invariant perimeters to matrices with the same number of columns and calculate the difference, while taking the difference between the invariant perimeters into account. The differences between two multivalued signatures is given by

$$Diff(\mathbf{S}_{inp}, \mathbf{S}_{lib}) = \min_{sh \in Sh} \frac{\sum_{i=0}^{L-1} \sum_{j=0}^{N-1} (M_{inp}(i, \tilde{j}) - M_{lib}(i, j))^2}{L \times N} \times \left(\frac{max(p1, p2)}{min(p1, p2)}\right)^{\mathbf{p}}$$

where $\mathbf{N}$ is the number of signatures in the multivalued signature, $\mathbf{L}$ is the number of samples, $\mathbf{s1}$ and $\mathbf{s2}$ are the compared signatures, $\tilde{\mathbf{j}} = (j + sh) \, mod \, Lev$, $\mathbf{Sh}$ is the set of all the checked shift values, $\mathbf{p1}$ and $\mathbf{p2}$ are invariant perimeters, and $\mathbf{p}$ is a positive constant.

In order to speed up the matching process, we exploit the signature histogram. This feature is independent on the starting point. The low-dimensional histogram allows for using of efficient data structures, like R-trees, for the database organization. First, signature histograms are compared. Only items close enough to the input curve are matched using the whole signature.

The total difference between the images is taken to be the average of the distances between the corresponding curves:

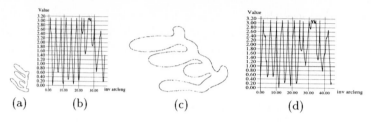

Fig. 2. Reparameterization inaccuracy. (a) & (b) Library image and its invariant signature. (c) & (d) The transformed library image and its invariant signature. Note the differentce of the domains of (b) and (d).

$$d(im_1, im_2) = \frac{\sum_{\{Maximal\ curves\}} \sqrt{diff(c_{1_i}, c_{2_i})}}{N},$$

where N is the number of compared curves, and c_{1_i} and c_{2_i} are corresponding curves of im_1 and im_2, respectively. In order to find pairs of corresponding curves we sort the curves of each image with respect to some invariant criterion. In case of similarity transformation, the curve's area serves as an ordering criterion. Curves that can not be sorted by area are ordered by their perimeters. Under affine transformation, perimeters can not be used any longer; however, the ratio of areas is still invariant and areas can used for ordering.

The following example illustrates extraction and matching of invariant signatures. The input image (Figure 3(a)) is an affine transformed version of the library image (Figure 3(b)). The extracted contours are presented on Fig. 3(c). The size of the biggest contour is about 300 pixels. The contours were ordered (by area) and invariant signatures were extracted. We use the invariant signature described above - the ratio of areas, with 4 parameters, each having 5 sample points. While for similarity invariants we used the angle, which is relatively stable characteristic, the ratio of areas can suffer from numerical instability. If the points $\mathbf{P}(\tau - \tau_{B_2})$, $\mathbf{P}(\tau)$ and $\mathbf{P}(\tau + \tau_{F_2})$ (see Fig.1(right)) become near collinear, the signature becomes unstable. Figure 4 presents the affine invariant signature for curve No. 5 from Fig. 3. The instability points force us to put a threshold on the signature values. While the resulting signature (see Fig. 4(b)) can still be used for the matching process, some of the information apparently is lost. Another possibility is to exchange the values of τ_{B_1} with τ_{B_2}, and τ_{F_1} with τ_{F_2}, respectively, and use the signature $\frac{1}{f(t)}$ instead of $f(t)$ (Figure 4(c)) .

The matching results for the trademarks presented on Fig. 3 are presented on Fig. 5. Each grey-level map, consisting of five strips, corresponds to the multivalued signature, while each strip corresponds to the singular signature. Each pair of the grey-level maps presents the signatures of the input (above) and library (below) contours at the shift position giving the best match (the numbering of the contours is as in Fig. 3(c)). Good match is achieved for all the curves. Note, that the signatures of curves No. 4 and 5 are very similar as the curves are almost identical when going under affine transformation.

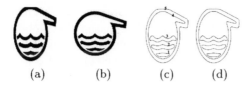

Fig. 3. (a) The input image (b) The source library image (c) The contours of the input image (numbered) (d) The fitted contours

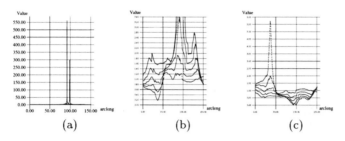

Fig. 4. Numerical instability of an affine invariant signature. (a) – Multivalued affine invariant signature $f(t)$ for curve No. 5 from Fig. 3. The signature is based on the areas ratio. (b) – $f(t)$ after putting a threshold. (c) – The signature $\frac{1}{f(t)}$.

2.2 Indexing while some shape information is missing

One of the main advantages of the proposed approach is its ability to handle situations in which part of shape information is missing. We handle separately two different cases: partial occlusion and user-generated sketch-based queries. In both cases the indexing is based on the same geometric features which are used regularly. However, the indexing algorithms will be used in accordance with the appropriate context.

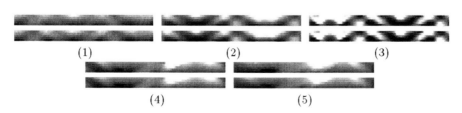

Fig. 5. The best match for each curve presented in Fig. 3. Grey-level maps are used for signatures. The curves are numbered as in Fig. 3. Good match is achieved for all the curves.

Partial occlusion. Partially occluded images are treated in the same way as regular images. Since both the reparameterization and signature extraction stages are absolutely local, the signature values for the part of the contour should match the values computed for the whole curve. The only difference is the need for *partial matching*, i.e. matching of the occluded contour to the part of the library curve. If the input curve is occluded, we map it to a matrix with number of columns proportional to the width of the signature domain. The domain of the multivalued signature is the minimal domain of its components (for open curve, the bigger the locality parameter, the smaller the signature domain). Thus, the number of columns in the matrix is

$$\tilde{Lev} = Lev * \min_{i=0}^{Num-1}\{\|domain(S_i)\|\}/Per_{lib},$$

where **Per**$_{lib}$ is the invariant perimeter of the library signature and **Lev** is the number of columns of the library matrix. The matrix of the occluded signature is then matched to a part of the library matrix.

Figure 6(a) is a rotated, scaled, and occluded version of the library image presented in Fig. 6(b). We use the angle $\phi(\tau)$, formed by the points $\mathbf{P}(\tau - s_B), \mathbf{P}(\tau)$ and $\mathbf{P}(\tau + s_F)$, as an invariant signature (as in Fig. 1(left)). Figure 6(lower) presents the best matchings between the input and the library curves. The signature domain is reduced as a result of the occlusion.

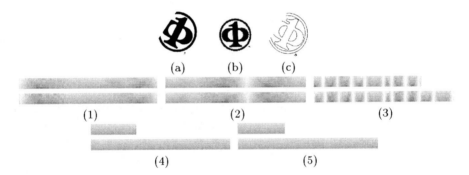

Fig. 6. Above: (a) The input image (occluded) (b) The source library image (c) The contours of the input image. Below: Best matches for the curves presented in (a). (1) and (2) Best matches for the signatures of the inner contours of the Φ letter. (3) The best matches for the external contour of the Φ letter. (4) The best match for the inner circle. (5) The best match for the external circle.

Sketch-based queries. We consider sketch-based retrieval as retrieval that uses the gross shape structure, while the fine details can be omitted. For sketch-based retrieval we exploit a topological invariant which we define here, that is based on the following simple and effective invariant property:

Given the same contour decomposition for an image P and a transformed image $\mathbf{T}_\psi(P)$, the contour C_1 of P resides inside the contour C_2 if and only if the same relation holds for the corresponding contours in the transformed image. This holds for any projective transformation $\mathbf{T}_\psi$.

In other words, the property that one contour is an inner contour of another is a projective invariant given the same contour representation. This property allows us to represent images exploiting the relations of internal-external between contours. Each image is represented as a tree which we term the *containment tree* . The vertices of the tree are curves. For two curves, C_1 and C_2, the edge $(C_1 \to C_2)$ exists if C_2 is inside C_1, and there is no C_3 such that C_2 is inside C_3 and C_3 is inside C_1. The root of the tree is a "dummy" contour which includes all the contours. This representation can easily be obtained after curves extraction (see Figure 7). The representation is unique up to the order between the vertices on the same level. Thus tree-matching algorithms can be used to compare the representation of the input image with the library images. This problem of tree matching has a polynomial solution [14]. The discrimination power of the containment tree is illustrated on Fig. 8.

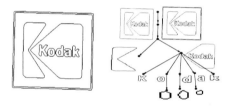

Fig. 7. The input image after curves extraction is presented on the left. The containment tree , representing the containment relationships between the curves is presented on the right. For each subtree, the corresponding curve and all its internal curves are presented.

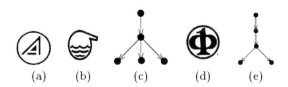

Fig. 8. The discrimination power of a containment tree . (a) & (b) Two images having the same containment tree . (c) The containment tree of (a). (d) The image has the same number of curves as in (a), but a different containment tree . (e) The containment tree of (d).

We exploit the containment tree for sketch-based retrieval. The matching algorithm is presented as Alg. 1. The algorithm requires that for each contour of the specified sketch all its sub-contours should be either omitted or specified. In this way we allow for queries that uses gross structure while omitting details (from some level of the tree).

Algorithm 1
Sketch matching.
Given: An input sketch S, and a database image I,

1. Build a containment tree T_1 for S, and a containment tree T_2 for I. In each containment tree the contours on the same level are ordered in descending order using the area – affine invariant geometric criterion.
2. Check if T_1 matches T_2.

The match is defined in the following manner:
The containment tree T_1 for the sketch S matches the containment tree T_2 for the image I if:

1. T_1 is a leaf **or**
2. The number of subtrees of T_1 equals that of T_2 and the corresponding sons of T_1 and T_2 match.

A flexible version of this algorithm which allows to omit small sub-contours of the specified sketch is presented as Alg. 2. Changing a threshold R allows us to control the retrieval flexibility. As the flexibility threshold R gets bigger, more candidates will pass the threshold and will match the input sketch, giving higher retrieval time. Setting R, therefore, presents a tradeoff between false alarms and misses. Algorithms 1 and 2 serve as pre-selections in the retrieval process. If the containment trees of the sketch and the image match according to the appropriate algorithm, the final verification is performed using multivalued signatures.

Figure 9 presents an example of sketch-based query. The lower row presents the distance values for the database items. One can see that the values confirm the intuitive measure of the similarity between the sketch and the images.

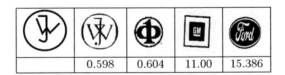

| | 0.598 | 0.604 | 11.00 | 15.386 |

Fig. 9. Sketch query example. The input sketch is on the left.

Algorithm 2
Flexible sketch matching.
Given: An input sketch S, and a database image I,

1. Build T_1 and T_2 as in Alg. 1.
2. Check if T_1 flexibly matches T_2.

We define a flexible match in the following manner:
The containment tree T_1 for the sketch S flexibly matches the containment tree T_2 for the image I if:

1. T_1 is a leaf **or**
2. The number of subtrees of T_1 equals that of T_2 and the corresponding sons of T_1 and T_2 flexibly match **or**
3. The number of subtrees of T_1, n, is less than that of T_2, but the $(n+1)^{th}$ son of T_2 corresponds to a contour which is much smaller than the contour corresponding to the nth son of T_2 (that is, the ratio of their areas is less than some predefined threshold R), and the first n corresponding sons of T_1 and T_2 flexibly match.

---

3 Shape retrieval

Our shape retrieval scheme consists of two main phases: filtering the database in order to drop the irrelevant images, and ranking the *candidates subset* according to the distance from the input image. For indexing we use geometric entities, such as circles, ellipses, etc. The number of these entities can serve for efficient filtering of the image collection. Final ranking within the set is based mainly on the semi-local multi-valued invariant signatures.

The general scheme of query processing is presented on Fig. 10. After edge detection and curves extraction from the input image, geometric entities are detected. This global features extraction is used as a basis for the filtering process. Relational database is used in this stage in order to retrieve the candidates subset. Features used for indexing to the relational database and eventually for pruning the candidates set vary from the number of the curves and the geometric entities, their relative dimensions, etc. The relational database includes alpha-numerical data as well. The query may contain this kind of information, like the organization name (for the trademarks database) etc., and this part of the query will be processed as a regular query (further pruning the set). The candidates obtained at this stage go to a matching with the input image. The final set, ordered according to the similarity measure is given as an answer.

4 Experiments

To show the applicability of our approach we tested it first on a database of 500 constrained 3D objects, namely surfaces of revolution. Using the KBS bottles collection ([15]) we present queries showing good retrieving ability for a specific,

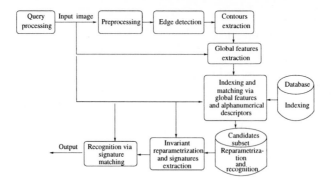

Fig. 10. Query processing.

and similar, objects. The effectiveness of the filtering process and the ability to handle different transformations are demonstrated in the second part in which a database of 100 trademarks is tested. We give results for sketch-based queries on a database of more than 300 "road signs". For all the four databases we used the same system. The system is implemented using ORACLE/SQL environment, and has a WWW interface. The user is allowed to query images by example, logical description or the combination of both. The example image can be the database image or the image provided by the user.

4.1 Invariant signatures for surfaces of revolution

An interesting practical application field for multivalued signatures is recognition in a database of 3-D objects which are surfaces of revolution (see also Mundy et al. [16]). We can treat such objects as planar under a controlled change of the viewpoint (which is common in industrial settings, e.g. in assembly lines). In this case, we can approximately describe the viewpoint change by affine transformation and apply our algorithms. In our experiment, the database contains more than 500 items some of which are photographed objects that are surfaces of revolution and the rest are bottles from the KBS bottles collection ([15]). Given an input image (one of the database objects under rotation and zoom), we compared it with the database by using multivalued signatures. Figure 11(a-c) presents an input image, its external contour and its multi-valued invariant signature. This input image was checked against all the images in the database. A good match was achieved retrieving the right database image in the first place. Figure 11(d) presents the grey-level maps of the input (above) and the database (below) contours at the shift position giving the best match. Retrieval results are presented next (first four of the set). Figure 11 (right) presents a number of queries performed using the surfaces of revolution database.

Figure 12(a) presents our HTML interface. The input scene and the processing results are presented on Fig. 12(b).

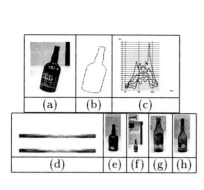

Fig. 11. Left: retrieval process. (a) The input image. (b) The external contour of the input image. (c) The invariant signature for the input image. (d) The best match for the input image. (e) – (h) Retrieval results. Right: results of queries on the bottles database.

4.2 Filtering the candidates set

Next we illustrate the effective filtering obtained by using invariant features. We run our queries on a database which contains more than 100 trademarks. In the first example (Figure 13(1)), the input image is a rotated and scaled version of one of the database trademarks. The user operated with the query
select title ordered by dist(logo30-trans.tiff) where (context = text).
The query looks for images having textual strings in them. Both alpha-numerical information and geometric features are used for filtering the database. Exploiting geometric features is especially effective for images with a large number of curves, because of their complicated structure. One can see that the number of candidates is rather small. In the following example (Figure 13(2)), the user operated with
select title where (N_circles = 1 and N_curv $\geq$ N_curv(logo55.tiff)),
directly specifying the number of geometric entities (circles). The input image is one of the database trademarks. One can see that the candidates comply with the given condition. The user has the freedom to limit the transformation which the images are allowed to undergo by stating the transformation explicitly in the query. In the next example (Figure 13(3)), the user limited the transformations to the affine case, operating with the query
select title ordered by dist(logo50-transf.tiff) under affine.
Both the filtering and the ranking are based on features that are invariant under the affine transformation. The input image is an occluded version of one of the database trademarks.

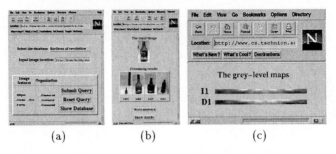

(a) (b) (c)

Fig. 12. (a) Querying the database using html interface (b) The input image and processing results (c) The grey-level maps, presenting multivalued signatures: above - the map corresponding to the input image; below - the map, corresponding to the image which took the first place.

The next example presents sketch-based retrieval (Figure 13(4)). The sketch was drawn using curves-drawing software (Xfig). Here we allow to omit some small objects within the image, while preserving its general structure. In this case we used algorithm 2 for filtering the database.

	Input image	Retrieval results			
1	*Kellogg's*	Place 1 0.128	Place 2 9.57	. . . . . .	Place 5 1492.57
2		Place 1	Place 2	. . .	Place 10
3	PHILLIPS 66	Place 1 0.233	Place 2 0.804	. . . . . .	Place 23 1347.148
4		Place 1 0.526	Place 2 0.632	Place 3 0.961	Place 4 0.961

Fig. 13. Queries results

Note that in all the examples the number of the images in the candidates set is sufficiently smaller than the number of the items in the database. The filtering is still effective even where occlusion is present (see, for example Fig. 13(3)). When the filtering is based on the containment tree we expect it to be more effective (see, for example, Fig. 13(4), where only 4 candidates left).

4.3 Sketch-based queries

Figure 14 presents a number of sketch-based queries and retrieval results. In addition, we present the queries in SQL-like notation (See Appendix A). The queries are performed on the database of "road signs", containing about 300 images. After filtering based on Alg. 1 or 2, the candidates passed matching with the input sketch, based on invariant signatures. For each query, the resulting candidates set contains no more than 15 images. One can see that the distance measure reflects the similarity between the sketch and the candidate image.

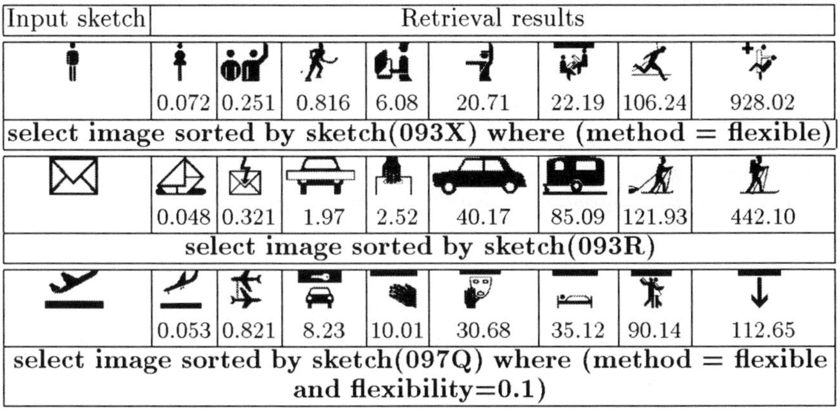

Input sketch	Retrieval results						
	0.072	0.251	0.816	6.08	20.71	22.19	106.24	928.02
select image sorted by sketch(093X) where (method = flexible)							
	0.048	0.321	1.97	2.52	40.17	85.09	121.93	442.10
select image sorted by sketch(093R)							
	0.053	0.821	8.23	10.01	30.68	35.12	90.14	112.65
select image sorted by sketch(097Q) where (method = flexible and flexibility=0.1)							

Fig. 14. Results of queries on the "road signs" database.

4.4 Efficiency analysis

In this section we used the combined database which included both the database of the trademarks and the "road signs". Figure 15(a) presents the average processing time (averaging on 100 queries) for a query as a function of the number of the curves in the input image. The upper curve corresponds to a sequential matching, i.e. a full signatures matching against the entries in the database. The middle presents average processing time for a query using the number of geometric entities for pruning the database. The lower curve corresponds to retrieval using the containment tree. The middle and lower curves are non-monotonous, a direct consequence of a tradeoff between a shorter query execution time as a result of the pruning and the extra time needed for matching more signatures. The graphs demonstrate that geometric entities and especially the containment tree are effective means for database pruning and their efficiency grows with the number of contours.

Figure 15(b) demonstrates the scalability of our approach. Queries have been run to retrieve an image from a subset of the database. The queries used the

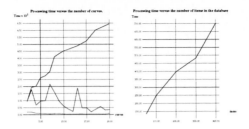

Fig. 15. Left: average evaluation time versus a number of curves. Right: scalability - processing time versus the number of database items.

number of geometric entities for pruning the subset. When the subset grows, processing time increases approximately as a linear function.

Table 1 illustrates the influence of the flexibility threshold R (See Alg. 2) on the number of retrieved images for sketch-based retrieval. The number of the answers depends on the complexity of the input sketch.

Table 1. The number of retrieved images as a function of the flexibility threshold R. For the presented input sketch, the number of retrieved images is given for different values of R.

R			
0.01	2	4	10
0.02	3	6	12
0.04	6	15	18
0.08	10	16	18
0.16	14	25	20

5 Conclusions

In this paper we have addressed the problem of shape-based retrieval from image databases. Our approach emphasizes the use of invariants as shape descriptors. Specifically, we have used geometric invariant features for efficient indexing, while local multi-valued invariant signatures have been used for ranking the answers. The substantial reduction of the candidates set due to the filtering stage guarantees the efficient retrieval. The approach supports image retrieval while part of the shape is missing, can handle images distorted by different viewpoint transformations, and can flexibly answers queries based on logical descriptions, shape (query by example), or combination of both.

We have implemented our approach in a heterogeneous database system having a SQL-like user interface augmented with sketch-based queries. The system is built on top of a commercial database system (Oracle), and can be activated from the Web. We have presented experimental results demonstrating the effectiveness of the proposed approach under various conditions using three different databases.

References

1. C. Faloutsos, R. Barber, M. Flickner, J. Hafner, W. Niblack, D. Petkovich, and W. Equitz, Efficient and effective querying by image content, *Journal of Intelligent Information Systems* **3**, 1994, 231–262.
2. A. Pentland, R. Picard, and S. Sclaroff, Photobook: Tools for content-base manipulation of image databases, in *Proceedings, SPIE Conf. on Storage and Retrieval of Image Databases II*, 1994, pp. 37–50.
3. A. Jain and A. Vailaya, Image retrieval using color and shape, *Pattern Recognition* **29**, 1996, 1233–1244.
4. A. D. Bimbo and P. Pala, Visual image retrieval by elastic matching of user sketches, *IEEE Trans. Patt. Anal. Mach. Intell.* **19**, 1997, 121–132.
5. S.-F. Chang, J. Smith, and H. Wang, Automatic feature extraction and indexing for content-based visual query, Tech. Rep. 408-95-14, Columbia University Center for Telecommunications Research, New York, NY, 1995.
6. S.-F. Chang and J. Smith, Extracting multi-dimensional signal features for content-based visual query, in *SPIE Int. Symp. on Visual Communications and Image Processing*, 1995.
7. R. Mehrotra and J. Gary, Similar-shape retrieval in shape data management, *IEEE Computer* **28**, 1995, 57–62.
8. K. Shields, J. Eakins, and J. Boardman, Automatic image retrieval using shape features, *New Review of Document and Text Management* **1**, 1995, 183–198.
9. S. Lee and F.J.Hsu, Spatial reasoning and similarity retrieval of images using 2D-C string knowledge representation, *Pattern Recognition* **25**, 1992, 305–318.
10. T. Moons, E. Pauwels, L. V. Gool, and A. Oosterlinck, Foundations of semi-differential invariants, *Int. Journal Of Comput. Vision* **14**, 1995, 25–47.
11. A. Bruckstein, J. Holt, A. Netravali, and T. Richardson, Invariant signatures for planar shape recognition under partial occlusion, *CVGIP:Image Understanding* **58**, 1993, 49–65.
12. A. Bruckstein, E. Rivlin, and I. Weiss, Recognizing objects using scale space local invariants, in *Int. Conf. on Pattern Recognition*, Vienna, 1996, p. A9M.6.
13. T. Moons, E. Pauwels, L. V. Gool, and A. Oosterlinck, Recognition of planar shapes under affine distortion, *Int. Journal Of Comput. Vision* **14**, 1995, 49–65.
14. J. Köbler, U. Schöning, and J. Torán, *The graph isomorphism problem.* Birkhäuser, Boston, 1993.
15. Kbs beer bottle collection, *URL: http://tuoppi.oulu.fi/kbs/beer/kbsbeer.htm*
16. A. Zisserman, D. Forsyth, J. Mundy, C. Rothwell, J. Liu, and N. Pillow, 3d object recognition using invariance, *Artificial Intelligence* **78**, 1995, 239–288.

Grouping and Segmentation

Concerning Bayesian Motion Segmentation, Model Averaging, Matching and the Trifocal Tensor

P. H. S. Torr and A. Zisserman

[1] Microsoft Research, One Microsoft Way, Redmond, WA 98052, USA,
philtorr@microsoft.com,
WWW home page: http://research.microsoft.com/research/vision/
[2] Dept. of Engineering Science, Oxford University, England
az@robots.ox.ac.uk,
WWW home page: http://www.robots.ox.ac.uk/vanguard/

Abstract. Motion segmentation involves identifying regions of the image that correspond to independently moving objects. The number of independently moving objects, and type of motion model for each of the objects is unknown *a priori*.

In order to perform motion segmentation, the problems of model selection, robust estimation and clustering must all be addressed simultaneously. Here we place the three problems into a common Bayesian framework; investigating the use of *model averaging*-representing a motion by a combination of models—as a principled way for motion segmentation of images. The final result is a fully automatic algorithm for clustering that works in the presence of noise and outliers.

1   Introduction

Detection of independently moving objects is an essential but often neglected precursor to problems in computer vision e.g. efficient video compression [3], video editing, surveillance, smart tracking of objects etc. The work in this paper stems from the desire to develop a general motion segmentation and grouping algorithm. That is, given two or more views of a scene, determine any of the objects within the scene which change their relative dispositions. Both the camera and objects' motion are presumed unknown as is the camera calibration. Consider figure 1 (a)-(c), a robot translating across a table as the camera moves down, causing apparent motion upwards in the image. Given this image triplet as input the ultimate goal would be to identify that the robot has moved independently of the background.

Motion segmentation turns out to be a most demanding problem and has received considerable attention over the years (see [5, 14, 13, 22, 30, 35, 41, 45] for a review). Many previous approaches to motion clustering have failed because the motion models that they employ are inappropriate. For instance, if one tries to group based purely on similarity of image velocities then any stream of images from a static scene viewed by a camera undergoing cyclotorsion would be incorrectly segmented. Schemes based on linear variation of the motion flow field will produce false segmentations at depth discontinuities when the camera is translating. Segmentation under the assumption of orthographic or weak perspective imaging conditions will fragment scenes with strong perspective effects, even if no independent motion is present. In contrast to these simplified motion models even the use of the most general model for segmentation can produce poor results; as it can lead to over fitting and hence a bad segmentation in which smaller objects might be missed [45]. Thus the need for a more general framework is apparent; one that can adaptively select the motion model for each object in the course of fitting.

There have been a few methods that have combined segmentation and model selection including Darrell *et al* [7], Gu *et al* [15], and the layered representation of Ayer & Sawhney [3], but none of these methods supports completely general models that may be of differing *dimensions* (see Section 2). Traditionally, all the potential models are fitted and a model selection procedure is used to select which *one* is best [23, 48]. When many models are initially considered, it often happens that several of them fit the data almost equally well, or that different models are arrived at by different model selection methods. It can then happen that different models, all of them defensible, lead to different answers to the main questions of interest (here the segmentation of images). Furthermore in the case of motion segmentation the model may change through time, and too early a commitment to a particular motion model of an object might lead to poor segmentation in subsequent frames.

There are two options. The first is to pick one model (as done traditionally) and adopt the segmentation that flows from it rather than from the other defensible models; this is somewhat arbitrary, first admitting model uncertainty by searching for a "best" model and then ignoring this uncertainty by making inferences and forecasts as if it were certain that his chosen model is actually correct. Selection of just one model means that the uncertainty on some parameters is underestimated [32]. The second option is to take account explicitly of model uncertainty by representing each independently moving object by a combination of models [9, 20, 27, 33, 25]. This is the option employed in this paper. A complete Bayesian solution to the model selection problem is given, which involves averaging over all possible models when making the segmentation, i.e. rather than use one motion model for each object a standard Bayesian formalism is adopted which averages the posterior distributions of the prediction under each model, weighted by their posterior model probabilities.

Corner and line features [16] are most amenable to geometric and statistical analysis, which is the flavour of this work. Furthermore corner features indicate pixels where both components of image motion might be recovered with reasonable accuracy; providing a strong constraint on the motion model. Corner features can provide good initial estimates of the motion of each object, unfortunately they only give a sparse representation: most pixels are not corners, so they will not be a member of a cluster or have a match in the other image(s). Here the models that are estimated from the corner features are used to flesh out the description of the segmentation, by predicting the motion of non-corner pixels near to classified matched corner pixels. In [28] it is shown that Bayesian model averaging provides optimal predictive results, superior to just selecting one of the competing models, hence it seems natural to use the Bayesian formalism for calculating the probabilities of cluster membership.

The paper is laid out as follows. Section 2 describes four classes of motion model. Section 3 describes a maximum likelihood/EM approach to clustering. Section 4 introduces model averaging and Section 5 describes its application to the problem of motion segmentation.

Notation: A 3D scene point projects to $\mathbf{x}$, $\mathbf{x}' = \mathbf{x}^2$ and $\mathbf{x}'' = \mathbf{x}^3$ in the first, second and third images respectively, and similarly the image of a line is l, l^2 and l^3. Where $\mathbf{x} = (x_1, x_2, x_3)^\top$ and $l = (l_1, l_2, l_3)^\top$ are homogeneous three vectors. The inhomogeneous coordinate of an image point is $(x, y) = (x_1, x_2)$. The correspondence $\mathbf{x} \leftrightarrow \mathbf{x}^2$ in two images and $\mathbf{x} \leftrightarrow \mathbf{x}^2 \leftrightarrow \mathbf{x}^3$ in three will also be represented by the shorthand notation $\mathbf{m}$, whether it is a correspondence through two or three images should be apparent from the context. Noise free (true data) will be denoted by an underscore $\underline{x}$, estimates $\hat{x}$, noisy (i.e. measured) data as x. The probability density function (p.d.f.) of x given y is $\Pr(x|y)$.

2   Putative Motion Models

This section describes the motion models which are deployed in the segmentation process. Each motion model is a *relation* $\mathcal{R}$ described by a set of *parameters* $\boldsymbol{\theta}$ which define one or more *implicit functional relationships* $\mathbf{g}(\mathbf{m}, \boldsymbol{\theta}) = \mathbf{0}$ ($\mathbf{0}$ is the zero vector) between the image coordinates i.e. $g_i(x, y, x', y'; \boldsymbol{\theta}) = 0$.

There are four types of relations $\mathcal{R}$ described in this section. Firstly, the relations can be divided between motions for which structure can be recovered—3D relations; and motions for which it cannot; for instance when all the points lie on a plane, or the camera rotates about its optic centre—2D relations. A second division is between projective and orthographic (affine) viewing conditions.

Two Views: Suppose that the viewed features arise from a 3D object which has undergone a rotation and non-zero translation. After the motion, the set of homogeneous image points $\{\mathbf{x}_i\}, i = 1, \ldots n$, is transformed to the set $\{\mathbf{x}'_i\}$. The two sets of features are related by an implicit functional relationship $\mathbf{x}'^\top_i \mathbf{F} \mathbf{x}_i = 0$ where $\mathbf{F}$ is the rank 2, 3×3 [10, 17] fundamental matrix, this is relation $\mathcal{R}_1$. The fundamental matrix encapsulates the epipolar geometry. It contains all the information on camera motion and internal camera parameters available from image feature correspondences alone.

When there is degeneracy in the data such that we cannot obtain a unique solution for $\mathbf{F}$ it is desirable to use a simpler motion model. For small independently moving objects, there may be an insufficient spread of features to enable a unique estimate of the Fundamental Matrix. Three other models are considered: $\mathcal{R}_2$, which is the affine camera model of Mundy & Zisserman [34] with linear fundamental matrix $\mathbf{F}_A$; $\mathcal{R}_3$, which is image projectivities; and $\mathcal{R}_4$, which is affinities as induced by planar homographies. The affine camera is applicable when the data is viewed under orthographic conditions and gives rise to a fundamental matrix with zeroes in the upper 2 by 2 submatrix. The homography $\mathbf{x}' = \mathbf{H}\mathbf{x}$, and affinity $\mathbf{x}' = \mathbf{A}\mathbf{x}$ arise when the viewed points all lie on a plane or the camera is rotating about its optic centre between images, the homography being in the projective case, the affinity in the orthographic.

Model Complexity: Following the maxim of Occam "Entities are not to be multiplied without necessity" [1] model selection typically scores models by a cost function that penalises models with more parameters. It is convenient at this point to introduce the number of explicit degrees of freedom in each model. The fundamental matrix has 7 degrees of freedom, the homography has 8, and yet the fundamental matrix is more general. The affine fundamental matrix has 4 degrees of freedom, affinity 6, again the affine fundamental matrix is more general; this seeming paradox can be resolved by considering the dimension of the model.

In addition to the degrees of freedom in the parameters we shall see that the complexity of a model is also determined by its dimension, which is defined now. Each pair of corresponding points $\mathbf{x}$, $\mathbf{x}'$ defines a single point $\mathbf{m}$ in a measurement space $\mathcal{R}^4$, formed by joining the coordinates in each image. These image correspondences, which are induced by a rigid motion, have an associated algebraic variety V in $\mathcal{R}^4$. The fundamental matrix, and affine fundamental matrix for two images are dimension 3 varieties of degree 2 (quadratic) and 1 (linear) respectively. The homography and affinity between two images are dimension 2 varieties of degree 2 (quadratic) and 1 (linear) respectively. The properties of the relations $\mathcal{R}$ are summarized in table 1.

In the case of general motion two views provide no constraint on the location of lines in those images, for this three views are needed, which are now described.

Three Views: The four classifications apply to the three view case and are now briefly summarized. Corresponding points in three images, and corresponding lines in three images, satisfy trilinear relations which are encapsulated in the trifocal tensor [18, 42, 43].

When the scene is viewed under orthographic conditions the affine camera model is most appropriate and the image correspondences can be well fitted by relation $\mathcal{R}_2$ the affine trifocal tensor $\mathbf{T}_A$ [45]. If the camera motion is pure rotation, or a plane is observed, then the line and point correspondences are determined by relation $\mathcal{R}_3$ and $\mathcal{R}_4$ image-image homographies. If the homography between image one and three is given by $\mathbf{x}^3 = \mathbf{H}_{13}\mathbf{x}$ then for lines $\mathbf{l} = \mathbf{H}^\top \mathbf{l}^3$. We shall make a simplifying assumption: As the segmentation methods are designed to take consecutive images from a sequence, we assume that the same motion model may be used between the first and second, and second and third image. This assumption is made to reduce the amount of computation necessary, it is a

---

[1] In fact Occam did not actually say this, but said something which has much the same effect, namely: 'It is vain to do with more what can be done with fewer'. That is to say, if everything in some science (here computer vision) can be interpreted without assuming this or that entity, there is no ground for assuming it [38].

triviality to generalise the system, but good results have been obtained without this resort. Thus if the projectivity model is selected we assume the following relations hold: $\mathbf{x}^3 = \mathbf{H}_{13}\mathbf{x}$, $\mathbf{x}^3 = \mathbf{H}_{23}\mathbf{x}^2$, and $\mathbf{x}^2 = \mathbf{H}_{12}\mathbf{x}$.

More on varieties and complexity: In three views, although the relations describe varieties in a six dimensional space of image coordinates the respective dimensions of the relations are unchanged i.e. three for the trifocal tensor $\mathcal{R}_1$ and affine trifocal tensor $\mathcal{R}_2$ and two for the homographies, $\mathcal{R}_3$ and $\mathcal{R}_4$. For the 2D relations the implicit functional relationships can be written consistently in terms of a homography between a point on an arbitrary plane $\hat{\mathbf{x}}$ and the point in each image i.e. $\mathbf{x}^1 = \hat{\mathbf{H}}_1\hat{\mathbf{x}}$, $\mathbf{x}^2 = \hat{\mathbf{H}}_2\hat{\mathbf{x}}$, and $\mathbf{x}^3 = \hat{\mathbf{H}}_3\hat{\mathbf{x}}$. In the next section it will be shown how to estimate each relation using maximum likelihood estimation.

Table 1. Motion Models Used *A description of the reduced models that are fitted to degenerate sets of correspondences. k is the number of parameters in the model, given I images; d is the dimension of the constraint.*

	3D Models		2D Models	
	$\mathcal{R}_1$	$\mathcal{R}_2$	$\mathcal{R}_3$	$\mathcal{R}_4$
	Projective	Affine	Projective	affine
2 view	Fund Matrix	Affine **F** Matrix	Homography	Affinity
3 view	Trifocal Tensor	Affine **T** Tensor	2 Homographies	2 affinities
k	$11I$ -15	$8I$ -12	$8I$ -8	$6I$ -6
d	3	3	2	2

3 Maximum Likelihood Estimation

Within this section the maximum likelihood estimate of the parameters $\boldsymbol{\theta}$ of a given relation $\mathcal{R}$ is derived. Although this is a standard result the derivation will reveal that there are more parameters to be considered in the model formulation than just the explicit parameters of $\boldsymbol{\theta}$ given in the last section and Table 1. These additional parameters are sometimes referred to as nuisance parameters [40]. This is important as in Section 4 it will be seen that the prior distribution of $\mathcal{R}$ is related to the number of parameters that need to be estimated. Furthermore deriving the maximum likelihood error from first principles is a useful exercise as there is a long history of researchers using *ad hoc* error measures to estimate multiple view relations which are sub optimal.

Let $\mathbf{m}$ be a vector of the observed x, y coordinates in each image of a correspondence over I images i.e. $\mathbf{m} = \left(x_1^1, x_2^1, \ldots x_1^I, x_2^I \right)^\top$, thus for two images $\mathbf{m} = (x, y, x'y')^\top$. It is assumed that the noise on $\mathbf{m}$ is Gaussian: $\mathbf{m} = \underline{\mathbf{m}} + \boldsymbol{\epsilon}$. with covariance matrix Λ. The covariance matrix for a set of correspondences, represented by a stacked vector $\kappa = (\mathbf{m}_1^\top, \ldots \mathbf{m}_n^\top)^\top$, is $\Lambda_\kappa = \text{diag}(\Lambda, \ldots \Lambda)$. In this paper it is assumed that the noise in the location of features in all the images is Gaussian on each image coordinate with zero mean and uniform standard deviation σ, thus $\Lambda = \mathbf{I}\sigma^2$ (extension to the more general case is not difficult and is described by Kanatani [24]). Recall that the true value $\underline{\mathbf{m}}$ of $\mathbf{m}$ satisfies the q implicit functional relationships (e.g. nine trilinearities for $\mathbf{T}$) $\mathbf{g}(\mathbf{m}; \boldsymbol{\theta}) = (g_1(\mathbf{m}; \boldsymbol{\theta}) \dots g_q(\mathbf{m}; \boldsymbol{\theta}))^\top$,

$$g_i(\mathbf{m}; \mathcal{R}) = 0 \qquad i = 1 \dots q \ . \tag{1}$$

Given $\boldsymbol{\theta}, \mathcal{R}, \hat{\boldsymbol{\kappa}}, \hat{\sigma}^2$ (the last being the estimated variance of the noise) the probability density function of a set of observed correspondences $\boldsymbol{\kappa}$ is:

$$\Pr(\boldsymbol{\kappa}|\hat{\boldsymbol{\theta}}, \mathcal{R}, \hat{\boldsymbol{\kappa}}, \hat{\sigma}^2) = \prod \left(\frac{1}{\sqrt{2\pi}\hat{\sigma}} \right)^{2In} e^{-((\boldsymbol{\kappa}_i - \hat{\boldsymbol{\kappa}}_i)^\top \Lambda_{\boldsymbol{\kappa}}^{-1} (\boldsymbol{\kappa}_i - \hat{\boldsymbol{\kappa}}_i))/(2\hat{\sigma}^2)} \ , \tag{2}$$

where $\mathbf{g}(\boldsymbol{\kappa}; \hat{\boldsymbol{\theta}}) = \mathbf{0}$. To find the maximum likelihood solution, the negative log-likelihood

$$L = -\log \Pr(\boldsymbol{\kappa}|\hat{\boldsymbol{\theta}}, \mathcal{R}, \hat{\boldsymbol{\kappa}}, \hat{\sigma}^2) \tag{3}$$

is minimized subject to the restrictions of $\mathbf{g}$. To accomplish this Lagrange multipliers are used, the derivatives of

$$L = nI \log \hat{\sigma}^2 + \frac{1}{2\hat{\sigma}^2} (\boldsymbol{\kappa}_i - \hat{\boldsymbol{\kappa}}_i)^\top \Lambda_{\boldsymbol{\kappa}}^{-1} (\boldsymbol{\kappa}_i - \hat{\boldsymbol{\kappa}}_i) + \boldsymbol{\lambda}^\top \mathbf{g}(\hat{\boldsymbol{\kappa}}; \hat{\boldsymbol{\theta}}) \tag{4}$$

with respect to[2] $\hat{\boldsymbol{\theta}}, \hat{\boldsymbol{\kappa}}, \hat{\sigma}^2$ [26] are equated to zero. The solution of this set of equations are the maximum likelihood estimates of the noise σ, the parameters θ for the relation, and the best fitting correspondences $\boldsymbol{\kappa}$. Assuming σ is given, the number of free parameters in this system is the number of degrees of freedom k in $\hat{\theta}$ given in Table 1, plus number of degrees of freedom in $\hat{\boldsymbol{\kappa}}_i$. Each correspondence $\hat{\mathbf{m}}$ obeys the constraints given by $\mathbf{g}$ and hence lies in the variety defined by $\mathcal{R}$; thus each correspondence $\hat{\mathbf{m}}$ has d degrees of freedom as given by Table 1; thus the number of degrees of freedom in $\hat{\boldsymbol{\kappa}}_i$ is nd (the extra number of nuisance parameters—although in this problem these parameters are far from being a nuisance as they implicitly define the estimated structure of the scene). The total number of parameters to be estimated (discounting σ) is $k + nd$, which is important in Section 4.

Given that $\Lambda = \mathbf{I}\sigma^2$, then the negative log likelihood (3) of all the correspondences $\mathbf{m}_i$, $i = 1..n$ where n is the number of correspondences is:

$$L(\boldsymbol{\kappa}, \mathcal{R}) = \sum_{ij} \left(\hat{x}_i^j - x_i^j \right)^2 = |\boldsymbol{\kappa} - \hat{\boldsymbol{\kappa}}| = \sum_i |\mathbf{m} - \hat{\mathbf{m}}| = \sum_i e_i^2 \tag{5}$$

where the log likelihood of a given match is $l(\mathbf{m}, \mathcal{R}) = e_i^2 = \sum_j \left(\hat{x}_i^j - x_i^j \right)^2$ discounting the constant terms (which is equivalent to the reprojection error

---

[2] At this juncture the selection of the functional form of the data—the most appropriate motion model $\mathcal{R}$ is assumed known.

of Hartley and Sturm [19]). If the type of relation $\mathcal{R}$ is known then, observing the data, we can estimate the parameters of $\mathcal{R}$ to minimize this log likelihood. This inference is called 'Maximum Likelihood Estimation' (Fisher 1936 [11]). Numerical methods for finding these two and three view relations are given in [4].

Robust Estimation The above derivation assumes that the errors are Gaussian, often however features are mismatched and the error on $\mathbf{m}$ is not Gaussian. Thus a a robust log likelihood error function $\rho(e_i^2)$ is used in place of $l(\mathbf{m}, \mathcal{R})$. To correctly determine $\rho(e_i^2)$ entails some knowledge of the outlier distribution; here it is assumed–without *a priori* knowledge–that the outlier distribution is uniform, with negative log likelihood $l_o = \lambda_3$ for error dimension one. For higher dimensional errors $l_o = (r - d)\lambda_3$ where $r - d$ is the codimension. The minimum of these two log likelihoods defines $\rho(e_i^2)$,

$$\rho(e^2) = \left\{ \begin{array}{ll} \frac{e^2}{\sigma^2} & \frac{e^2}{\sigma^2} < T(r-d) \\ \lambda_3(r-d) & \frac{e^2}{\sigma^2} \geq T(r-d) \end{array} \right\} = \min\left(\frac{e^2}{\sigma^2}, \lambda_3(r-d) \right) . \quad (6)$$

where σ is the standard deviation of the error on each coordinate. The form of $\rho()$ is derived to behave like a Gaussian for data with low residuals and a uniform distribution for data with high residuals. Here we choose $T = 4$, but experiments have shown that the solution remains unchanged for a range of T; in the case that the codimension is 1, this choice incorrectly rejects inliers 5% of the time.

Problems with MLE: If the type of relation $\mathcal{R}$ is unknown then we cannot use maximum likelihood estimation to decide the form of $\mathcal{R}$ as the most general model will always be most likely i.e. have lowest L. Fisher was aware of the limitations of maximum likelihood estimation and admits the possibility of a wider form of inductive argument that would determine the functional form of the data (Fisher 1936 p. 250 [11]); but then goes on to state 'At present it is only important to make clear that no such theory has been established'. This was because Fisher took a steadfastly non-Bayesian viewpoint, a Bayesian suggestion for this wider form of inductive argument is given in Section 4; before this the maximum likelihood solution for multiple motion case is considered using a mixture model.

Optimal Clustering: The initial set of matches κ is obtained by cross correlation as described in [4]. The problem is to optimally group them into sets consistent with the different motion models. This involves finding the most probable underlying interpretation ϕ, being a classification into several motion models together with the parameters of those models. The most likely partition is obtained by maximizing the probability of the interpretation given the data: $\max_\phi \Pr[\phi|\kappa]$, which may be rewritten using Bayes theorem,

$$\Pr[\phi|\kappa] = \frac{\Pr[\kappa|\phi] \Pr[\phi]}{\Pr[\kappa]} . \quad (7)$$

Thus clustering is defined as a Bayesian decision process that minimizes the Bayes risk incurred in choosing a partition of κ. As $\Pr[\kappa]$ does not depend on ϕ

it may be dropped from the exposition, and the problem becomes that of finding $\max_\phi \Pr[\boldsymbol{\kappa}|\phi] \Pr[\phi]$.

Each match $\mathbf{m}$ is modelled by a prior mixture model, such that $\mathbf{m}$ belongs to one of s clusters C_j with probabilities $\pi_1, \ldots \pi_s$ such that $\sum_{a=1}^{a=s} \pi_a = 1$ and $\pi_a \geq 0$. Adopting the notation of McLachlan [29] the p.d.f. of any match $\mathbf{m}$ given interpretation $\phi = ((\pi_1 \ldots \pi_s); (C_1 \ldots C_s))^\top$ is given by the finite mixture form

$$\Pr(\mathbf{m}|\phi) = \sum_{a=1}^{a=s} \pi_a \Pr(\mathbf{m}|C_a) \tag{8}$$

where $\Pr(\mathbf{m}|C_a)$ is the p.d.f. of the match given that it belongs to cluster C_a.

Once the clusters have been estimated (a method of initialisation is given in Section 5), estimates of the posterior probabilities of population membership are formed for each match $\mathbf{m}_i$ based on the estimated $\hat{\phi}$. The posterior probability $\tau_{ij}(\mathbf{m}|\phi)$ is given by

$$\tau_{ij}(\mathbf{m}|\phi) = \Pr[\mathbf{m}_i \in C_j | \mathbf{m}; \phi] = \pi_j \Pr(\mathbf{m}_i|C_j) / \sum_{k=1}^{k=s} \pi_k p_k(\mathbf{m}_i|C_k) \ . \tag{9}$$

A partitioning of $\mathbf{m}_1 \ldots \mathbf{m}_n$ into s non-overlapping clusters is effected by assigning each $\mathbf{m}_j$ to the population to which it has the highest estimated posterior probability $\tau_{ij}(\mathbf{m}|C_j)$ of belonging. That is $\mathbf{m}$ is assigned to cluster C_t if

$$\tau_{it}(\mathbf{m}|\hat{\phi}) > \tau_{ij}(\mathbf{m}|\hat{\phi}) \qquad (j = 1 \ldots s; j \neq t) \ . \tag{10}$$

To make this procedure robust a threshold must be made on $\Pr(\mathbf{m}_i|C_j)$ in order to eliminate outliers. If $-\log(\Pr(\mathbf{m}_i|C_j)) > l_o$ for $j = 1 \ldots s$ then the match is redesignated an outlier. This threshold is the value T discussed above.

To calculate the complete log likelihood

$$L_C = \log(\Pr[\boldsymbol{\kappa}|\phi]) \tag{11}$$

account must be taken of the fact that each match can only belong to one cluster. For this purpose, for each match an s dimensional vector of unknown indicator variables $\mathbf{c}_i = (c_{1i} \ldots c_{si})$ is introduced, where

$$c_{ij} \begin{cases} 1 \ \mathbf{m}_i \in C_j \\ 0 \ \mathbf{m}_i \notin C_j \end{cases} \tag{12}$$

Then following standard texts (McLachlan [29]) the complete log likelihood is given by

$$L_C = \sum_{i=1}^{i=n} \sum_{j=1}^{j=s} c_{ij} (\log \pi_j + \log(\Pr(\mathbf{m}_i|C_j))) \tag{13}$$

This may be maximized by treating the c_{ij} as missing data from the mixture model and using the EM algorithm [8], or some suitable gradient descent algorithm.

Thus far there has been no discussion of either how to determine the type of motion model appropriate for each cluster or the number of such clusters. In order to go about estimating this, the province of model selection must be entered, which is considered in the next section.

4   Bayesian Model Selection and Model Averaging

Usually only one model is fitted to the data. But what if the data might have arisen from one of several possible models? For instance any of the relations described in Section 2 could describe a given set of matches. Traditionally, all the potential models are fitted and a model selection procedure is used to select which is best. Generally in previous work, using an information criterion—AIC [1] to select a relation, we found that the method determined the dimension of the model varieties quite stably, but that their degree was more difficult to ascertain. Thus the decision between $\mathbf{F}$ and $\mathbf{H}$ was more reliable than that between $\mathbf{F}$ and $\mathbf{F}_A$ or $\mathbf{H}$ and $\mathbf{A}$; suggesting that adoption of one model is a poor policy. Commitment to just one model for each object has a distinct disadvantage in motion segmentation. Suppose that each independently moving object is initialized with some model, perhaps by using AIC, and then the EM algorithm, described in the previous section, and used to determine a segmentation. It might be that after several iterations of the EM algorithm, with consequent readjustment of cluster membership, that the initial relations selected were incorrect and the segmentation algorithm has irrevocably converged to the wrong solution as a result.

The next two subsections explore the use of several putative motion models rather than one for determining $\Pr(\mathbf{m}_i | C_j)$.

A Bayesian Predictive Approach by Model Averaging: Thus far the probability $\Pr(\mathbf{m}_i | C_j)$ in (13) has been left unspecified. Suppose that there are K competing motion models with relations $\mathcal{R}_1 \ldots \mathcal{R}_K$ with parameter vectors $\boldsymbol{\theta}_1 \ldots \boldsymbol{\theta}_K$, that could describe C_j. Then Bayesian inference about $\mathbf{m}_i$ is based its posterior distribution, which is

$$\Pr(\mathbf{m}_i | \boldsymbol{\kappa}) = \sum_{i=1}^{i=K} \Pr(\mathbf{m}_i | \mathcal{R}_k, \boldsymbol{\kappa}) \Pr(\mathcal{R}_k | \boldsymbol{\kappa}) \tag{14}$$

by the law of total probability [27]. Thus the full posterior probability of $\mathbf{m}_i$ is a weighted average of its posterior distribution under each of the models, where the weights are the posterior model probabilities, $\Pr(\mathcal{R}_k | \boldsymbol{\kappa})$ derived below. Equation (14) provides inference about $\mathbf{m}_i$ that takes into full account the uncertainty between models, and is particularly useful when two of the models describe the data equally well. Indeed it has been shown that model averaging can produce superior results in predictive performance than commitment to a single model [28].

Bayesian Estimation of the Posterior Probabilities: Suppose that the set of matches $\boldsymbol{\kappa}$ is to be used to determine between K competing motion models with relations $\mathcal{R}_1 \ldots \mathcal{R}_K$ with parameter vectors $\boldsymbol{\theta}_1 \ldots \boldsymbol{\theta}_K$. Then by Bayes' theorem, the posterior probability that $\mathcal{R}_k$ is the correct relation is

$$\Pr(\mathcal{R}_k|\boldsymbol{\kappa}) = \frac{\Pr(\boldsymbol{\kappa}|\mathcal{R}_k)\Pr(\mathcal{R}_k)}{\sum_{i=1}^{i=K} \Pr(\boldsymbol{\kappa}|\mathcal{R}_i)\Pr(\mathcal{R}_i)} \tag{15}$$

note that by construction $\sum_{i=1}^{i=K} \Pr(\mathcal{R}_i|\boldsymbol{\kappa}) = 1$. All the probabilities are implicitly conditional on the set of relations $\{\mathcal{R}_1, \ldots \mathcal{R}_K\}$ being considered. In the case of motion segmentation the models given in Table 1 should suffice to completely describe most situation. The marginal probability $\Pr(\boldsymbol{\kappa}|\mathcal{R}_k)$ is obtained by integrating out $\boldsymbol{\theta}_k$,

$$\Pr(\boldsymbol{\kappa}|\mathcal{R}_k) = \int \Pr(\boldsymbol{\kappa}|\mathcal{R}_k, \boldsymbol{\theta}_k)\Pr(\boldsymbol{\theta}_k|\mathcal{R}_k)d\boldsymbol{\theta}_k$$
$$= \int \text{likelihood} \times \text{prior } d\boldsymbol{\theta}_k \ .$$

$\Pr(\boldsymbol{\theta}_k|\mathcal{R}_k)$ is the prior density of $\boldsymbol{\theta}_k$ under the relation $\mathcal{R}_k$ (encapsulated in the covariance matrix $\Lambda_{\boldsymbol{\theta}_k}$ of the estimated parameters, obtained numerically from the inverse Hessian of $-\log(\boldsymbol{\theta}_k|\boldsymbol{\kappa}, \mathcal{R}_k)$). This integral is typically of a high dimension and difficult to evaluate, but can be adequately approximated if it is assumed that $\boldsymbol{\theta}_k$ can be approximated as a multivariate Gaussian $N(\boldsymbol{\theta}_k, \Lambda_{\boldsymbol{\theta}_k}^{-1})$, by Laplace's method [37] following the derivation given in [39] as

$$\log(\boldsymbol{\kappa}|\mathcal{R}_k) \approx \log(\boldsymbol{\kappa}|\hat{\boldsymbol{\theta}}_k) - \frac{D}{2}\log N \tag{16}$$

where $D = dn + k$ is the total number of parameters in the system, and $N = 2nI$ is the total number of observations, n the number of matches, I the number of images and d the dimension of R. This is sometimes referred to as the Bayesian Information Criterion or BIC and can be used to compare the likelihood of competing models, it originated in the work of Jeffreys [21]. Denoting the BIC for the kth model by

$$B_k = \log(\boldsymbol{\kappa}|\hat{\boldsymbol{\theta}}_k) - \frac{D}{2}\log N \tag{17}$$

then, assuming that the prior on the models $\Pr(\mathcal{R}_k)$ is uniform

$$\Pr(\mathcal{R}_k|\boldsymbol{\kappa}) = \frac{\exp(B_k)}{\sum_{i=1}^{i=K} \exp(B_i)} \tag{18}$$

Given two views, simpler models will be favoured over more complex ones as the $\frac{D}{2}\log N$ term will dominate, but as the number of images increases the likelihood function $\log(\boldsymbol{\kappa}|\hat{\boldsymbol{\theta}}_k)$ will take precedence.

5 Motion Segmentation

The final cost function to be maximized is given by L_C. It would be too computationally expensive to search every possible ϕ in order to minimize (13) hence a random sampling type algorithm is used, in which solutions are grown from minimal subsets of points within the image. The segmentation algorithm extracts models using RANSAC [12] to grow solutions from propinquintal sets. The two view phase is described in table 2. Once a set of matches has been established across two views; the same process is used for three views but using the three view constraints, and matched lines using the line matcher described in [31].

Once the clusters are identified a dense segmentation is made, for each pixel in image 1 its location in image 2 is predicted using each motion model, and the squared difference in image intensity calculated. The pixel is assigned to the cluster which minimizes this difference, matches may be reassigned at this juncture. For F and F_A pixel transfer is not defined, in order to accomplish the transfer the nearest three optimally estimated matches $\hat{m}$ consistent with the cluster to the pixel are found, and using these three matches and the estimate of F or F_A for the cluster, a homography is computed to transfer that pixel from image 1 to 2; similarly for images 2 to 3.

5.1 Results of The Segmentation Algorithm

Two example sequences of images are shown, the robot scene Figure 1, and the jeep scene Figure 2. The dense segmentation for both sequences are shown in Figure 3. The posterior probabilities of the clusters are given in Table 3. The dense segmentation method is still in the initial stage of development, the results are reasonable, but over two and three views there are still a large number of homogeneous regions where the segmentation is ambiguous. It is expected that the use of more images in the scheme will improve this, as would a prior on ϕ that favours spatially cohesive clusters. This could be achieved by using a Markov Random Field, we avoided this approach here as we were interested in seeing how far the predictive approach could be carried before more prior information is brought in. Future research will examine the improvement, relative to this work, furnished by the use of priors encouraging spatial cohesion. It might prove desirable to adjust the way that the motion models are determined to incorporate information from all pixels, not just highly textured areas. This is the approach followed by Ayer & Sawhney [3]; although they use only projectivities as motion models; and it is not clear how much extra advantage to the estimation of the motion models is gained by including non-textured regions of pixels in the minimization. But information from edges could be used to explicitly improve the detected motion discontinuities and this would be an interesting avenue for future research.

The convergence of the EM algorithm is notoriously slow [36] and it may be better to use some sort of conventional numerical optimization technique. Methods such as gradient descent have the added advantage of automatically supplying the covariance matrix as part of the algorithm. Comparison of EM and other algorithms for optimising a motion segmentation is an interesting vein of future work.

Table 2. *Clustering Algorithm for two views, the three view algorithm proceeds along the same lines.*

---

1. Cluster Extraction Stage:
   (a) Initialize the number of clusters extracted to $j = 0$.
   (b) RANSAC followed by a robust non-linear estimator are used to extract the best estimate of $\mathbf{F}$ from the set of matches κ not assigned to any cluster (all of them at start) as described in [46, 47] to give a set of inliers C_j. Information about spatial proximity is used to exploit the spatial cohesion of moving objects, by sampling correspondence sets that are close to each other (propinquintal) in the image.
   (c) If the number of inliers in C_j is below a threshold (determined from [44]), such that it is more likely to have arisen by a chance combination of outliers than an independently moving object, then stop extracting clusters and begin the dense segmentation stage.
   (d) RANSAC and a robust non-linear estimator are used to estimate the best sub models $\mathbf{F}_A$, $\mathbf{H}$, $\mathbf{A}$ from C_j.
   (e) Using the established clusters as input, calculate the probabilities π_j based on the proportion of matches in each cluster C_j.
   (f) The EM algorithm is applied to maximize (13), also re-estimating all cluster $C_1 \ldots C_j$. If the new estimate of the cost function L_C is below the previous estimate then accept cluster j, otherwise stop extracting clusters and begin the dense segmentation stage.
   (g) Increment j by one; repeat cluster extraction stage.
2. Dense Segmentation Stage:
   (a) Reassign matches $\mathbf{m}$ to their optimal estimates $\hat{\mathbf{m}}$.
   (b) For each pixel that is unmatched across the images estimate its match under each model of each cluster.
   (c) Determine which cluster it belongs to by use of equation (10).

Table 3. Clustering Results: *Posterior probabilities of the relations $\mathcal{R}$ for each of the clusters, after two views.*

2 Views	3D Models		2D Models	
	Projective	Affine	Projective	affine
Large Cluster Robot	0.001	0.35	0.1	0.55
Small Cluster Robot	0	0	0.13	0.87
Large Cluster Jeep	0	0	0.27	0.73
Small Cluster Jeep	0	0.000019	0.82	0.18
3 Views	3D Models		2D Models	
	Projective	Affine	Projective	affine
Large Cluster Robot	0.12	0.62	0.05	0.21
Small Cluster Robot	0	0	0.16	0.84
Large Cluster Jeep	0	0	0.31	0.69
Small Cluster Jeep	0	0	0.84	0.16

Fig. 1. Robot Scene *(a) (b) (c) three consecutive views of a robot translating to the left as the camera descends. Observe the approach of the robot to the heap of books. (d) point (e) line correspondences in the most substantial group. In (f) point (g) line correspondences in the second group Point matches shown for all three images, joined together, and superimposed onto the third image; line matches for all three images shown superimposed on the third image.*

(a) (b) (c)

(d) (e)

(f) (g)

Fig. 2. Jeep Scene. *(a) (b) (c) three consecutive views of a jeep translating to the right as the camera pans to keep it in view. Observe the cyclo-rotation of the jeep as its front wheel hits a pot hole. (d) point (e) line correspondences in the most substantial group. In (f) point (g) line correspondences in the second group Point matches shown for all three images, joined together, and superimposed onto the third image; line matches for all three images shown superimposed on the third image. It can be seen that the line segments are correctly partitioned between the jeep and background.*

(a)   (b)   (c)

(d)   (e)

(f)   (g)

Fig. 3. Dense Segmentation. *Dense Segmentation of robot (left) and jeep (right). The results given are without any post processing such as spatial clustering or morphological operators, which is the subject of separate work.*

6   Summary and Conclusions

There have been two contributions contained within this paper. The first contribution is to develop the Bayesian methods of model averaging for multiple view geometry. This is a very general purpose tool and may be used for things other than motion segmentation. For instance [2, 6] it is shown that when the fundamental matrix or trifocal tensor take on special forms that self calibration of the camera is possible. The BIC method can be used to calculate how likely it is that such a special case has occurred. There has also been some recent research interest in the plane plus parallax representation of a scene, the Bayesian approach extends naturally to such a combination of motion models.

The second contribution is to provide a new method of motion segmentation using the constraints enforced by rigid motion. This method uses mixture models in an optimal statistical framework to estimate the number and type of motion models as well as their parameters. To achieve this the use of Bayesian methods has been explored. A new general method has been presented for robust model selection, and its application to two and three view motion model fitting demonstrated. The method is highly robust and simultaneously flushes outliers and selects the type of model that best fits the data.

Acknowledgements We gratefully acknowledge A. Fitzgibbon, Dr. K. Kanatani, Dr. P. McLauchlan, Dr. D. Murray and W. Triggs. ACTS Project VANGUARD provided financial support.

References

1. H. Akaike. A new look at the statistical model identification. *IEEE Trans. on Automatic Control*, Vol. AC-19(6):716–723, 1974.
2. M. Armstrong, A. Zisserman, and R. Hartley. Self-calibration from image triplets. In *Proc. 4th ECCV*, pages 3–16. Springer–Verlag, 1996.

3. S. Ayer and H. Sawhney. Layered representation of motion video using robust maximum-likelihood estimation of mixture models and mdl encoding. In *Proc. 5th ICCV*, pages 777–784, 1995.

4. P. Beardsley, P. H. S. Torr, and A. Zisserman. 3D model aquisition from extended image sequences. In *4th ECCV*, pages 683–695. Springer–Verlag, 1996.

5. A. Black and P. Anandan. The robust estimation of multiple motions: Parametric and piecewise-smooth flow fields. *CVIU*, 63(1):75–104, 1996.

6. M. Brooks, L. Agapito, D. Huynh, and L. Baumela. Direct methods for self-calibration of a moving head. In *Proc. 4th ECCV*, pages 97–108. Springer–Verlag, 1996.

7. T. Darrell, S. Sclaroff, and A. Pentland. Segmentation by minimal description. In *Proc. 3rd ICCV*, pages 112–116. IEEE, 1990.

8. A. P. Dempster, N. M. Laird, and D. B. Rubin. Maximum likelihood from incomplete data via the em algorithm. *J. R. Statist. Soc.*, 39 B:1–38, 1977.

9. D. Draper. Assessment and propagation of model uncertainty (with discussion). *Journal of the Royal Statistical Society series B*, 57:45–97, 1995.

10. O.D. Faugeras. What can be seen in three dimensions with an uncalibrated stereo rig? In G. Sandini, editor, *Proc. 2nd ECCV*, pages 563–578. Springer–Verlag, 1992.

11. R. A. Fisher Uncertain Inference *Proc. Amer. Acad. Arts and Sciences*, 71 245–258, 1936.

12. M. Fischler and R. Bolles. Random sample consensus: a paradigm for model fitting with application to image analysis and automated cartography. *Commun. Assoc. Comp. Mach.*, vol. 24:381–95, 1981.

13. E. François and P. Bouthemy. Multiframe based identification of mobile components of a scene with a moving camera. In *Proc. CVPR.*, 1991.

14. E. Francois and P. Bouthemy. Derivation of qualitative information in motion analysis. *IVC*, vol. 8(4):279–287, Nov 1990.

15. H. Gu, S. Yoshiaki, and Asada M. MDL-based segementation and motion modeling in a long image sequence of scene with multiple independently moving objects. *PAMI*, 18:58–64, 1996.

16. C. Harris and M. Stephens. A combined corner and edge detector. In *Proc. Alvey Conf.*, pages 189–192, 1987.

17. R. I. Hartley. Estimation of relative camera positions for uncalibrated cameras. In *Proc. 2nd ECCV*, pages 579–87. Springer–Verlag, 1992.

18. R. I. Hartley. Lines and points in three views – a unified approach. In *ARPA Image Understanding Workshop, Monterey*, 1994.

19. R. I. Hartley and P. Sturm. Triangulation. In *American Image Understanding Workshop*, pages 957–966, 1994.

20. J. S. Hodges. Uncertainty, policy analysis and statistics (with discussion). *Statistical Science*, 2:259–291, 1987.

21. H. Jeffreys. *Theory of Probability*. Clarendon Press, Oxford, third edition, 1961.

22. A. Jepson and M. Black. Mixture models for optical flow computation. In *cvpr-93*, pages 760–766. IEEE, 1993.

23. K. Kanatani. Automatic singularity test for motion analysis by an information criterion. In *Proc. 4th ECCV*, pages 697–708, Springer–Verlag, 1996.

24. K. Kanatani. *Statistical Optimization for Geometric Computation: Theory and Practice*. Elsevier Science, Amsterdam, 1996.

25. R. E. Kass and A. E. Raftery. Bayes factors. *Journal of the American Statistical Association*, 90:733–795, 1995.

26. M. Kendall and A. Stuart. *The Advanced Theory of Statistics*. Charles Griffin and Company, London, 1983.

27. E. E. Leamer. *Specification searches: ad hoc inference with nonexperimental data.* Wiley, New York, 1978.

28. D. Madigan and A. E. Raftery. Model selection and accounting for model uncertainty in graphical models using Occam's window. *Journal of the American Statistical Association*, 89:1535–1546, 1994.

29. G.I. McLachlan and K. Basford. *Mixture models: inference and applications to clustering.* Marcel Dekker. New York, 1988.

30. P. F. McLauchlan, I. Reid, and D. W. Murray. Coarse image motion for saccade control. In *Proc. BMVC*. Springer-Verlag, Sept 1992. Leeds.

31. P. F. McLauchlan, I. Reid, and D. W. Murray. Recursive affine structure and motion from image sequences. In *Proc. 3rd ECCV*, volume 1, pages 217–224, May 1994.

32. A. J. Miller. Selection of subsets of regression variables (with discussion). *Journal of the Royal Statistical Society (Series A)*, 147:389–425, 1984.

33. B. R. Moulton. A Bayesian-approach to regression selection and estimation with application to a price-index for radio services. *Journal of Econometrics*, 49:169–193, 1991.

34. J. Mundy and A. Zisserman. *Geometric Invariance in Computer Vision.* MIT press, 1992.

35. R.C. Nelson. Qualitative detection of motion by a moving observer. *IJCV*, pages 33–46, 1991.

36. R. A. Redner and H. F. Walker. Mixture densities, maximum likelihood and the EM algorithm. *SIAM Review*, 26:195–239, 1984.

37. B. D. Ripley. *Pattern recognition and neural networks.* Cambridge University Press, Cambridge, 1996.

38. B. Russell. *History of Western Philosophy.* Routledge, 1961.

39. G. Schwarz. Estimating dimension of a model. *Ann. Stat.*, 6:461–464, 1978.

40. G.A.F. Wild C. J. Seber. *Non-Linear Regression.* Wiley, New York, 1989.

41. L. S. Shapiro. *Affine Analysis of Image Sequences.* PhD thesis, Oxford University, 1993.

42. A. Shashua. Trilinearity in visual recognition by alignment. In *Proc. 3rd ECCV*, volume 1, pages 479–484, May 1994.

43. M. Spetsakis and J. Aloimonos. A multi-frame approach to visual motion perception. *IJCV*, 6:245–255, 1991.

44. C. V. Stewart. Minpran; a new robust estimator for computer vision. *IEEE Trans. PAMI*, vol.PAMI-17,no.10:925–938, 1995.

45. P. H. S. Torr. *Outlier Detection and Motion Segmentation.* PhD thesis, Dept. of Engineering Science, University of Oxford, 1995.

46. P. H. S. Torr and D. W. Murray. The development and comparison of robust methods for estimating the fundamental matrix. *Int Journal of Computer Vision*, 24(3):271–300, 1997.

47. P. H. S. Torr and A Zisserman. Robust parameterization and computation of the trifocal tensor. *Image and Vision Computing*, 15:591–607, 1997.

48. P. H. S. Torr, A Zisserman, and S. Maybank. Robust detection of degenerate configurations for the fundamental matrix. To Appear CVIU, 1998.

Self Inducing Relational Distance and Its Application to Image Segmentation

Jianbo Shi and Jitendra Malik

Department of EECS, Computer Science Division
University of California at Berkeley, Berkeley, CA 94720, USA
{jshi,malik}@cs.berkeley.edu

Abstract. *We propose a new feature distance which is derived from an optimal relational graph matching criterion. Instead of defining an arbitrary similarity measure for grouping, we will use the criterion of reducing instability in the relational graph to induce a similarity measure. This similarity measure not only improves the stability of the matching, but more importantly, also captures the relative importance of relational similarity in the feature space for the purpose of grouping. We will call this similarity measure the* self-induced relational distance. *We demonstrate the distance measure on a brightness-texture feature space and apply it to the segmentation of complex natural images.*

1 Introduction

In any grouping algorithm, two crucial subproblems need to be addressed: (1) the similarity measure between the features, and (2) the grouping criterion and efficient algorithm to solve it.

In our previous paper[20], we have addressed the latter problem with *normalized cuts*. In the normalized cut scheme, the grouping problem is transformed into a graph partitioning problem. The nodes in the graph are feature points, such as pixels, and the weight on each graph edge reflects the similarity between the two nodes connected by that edge. The grouping problem then becomes the problem of finding the best hierarchical sub-partition of the graph according to a global partitioning criterion called *normalized cut*. The *normalized cut* criterion favors sub-partitioning of a graph such that the total similarity among the subgraphs is high and the total dissimilarity across the subgraphs is low. We have shown that this graph partitioning problem can be solved efficiently using a generalized eigenvalue system, and good results have been obtained on segmenting brightness and color images with a simple Euclidean distance in the HSV color space.

In the case of brightness and color segmentation, such simple similarity measures between the pixels are sufficient. Distance measures on combined texture and brightness-color space, however, are harder to define. Figure (1) illustrates some of the difficulties. The difficulties in scenes like those shown in figure (1a) is that although the cheetah has coherent texture, the tree branches in the background are essentially random with each branch differing from the others. One

Fig. 1. Two complex textured scenes in natural world. What is the right texture similarity measure?

would like the texture similarity measure not to overly emphasize the difference in that region. Defining a simple texture distance in figure (1b) could also be difficult because it is hard to judge whether the "stripe-ness" of the zebra skin is a more important similarity measure than the orientation of the stripes. In principle, one can claim that any distance measure can and should be induced by modeling the distribution of all the objects in the world. We will illustrate in this paper, however, that by analyzing relationships between the elements in a single scene, one can induce a very reasonable distance measure.

We extend the definition of texture to include invariant relational structural properties of the image features, rather than only the first or second order local statistics of filter outputs. In particular, we will construct a relational graph on an image, and study the invariant relational substructure in the context of self-matching.

A relational graph is a graph representation of image objects, their parts and the relationships among them. Typically, relational graph matching is used in the object recognition setting, where we would like to map the parts of an unknown object to those of a known object in a database, such that both the properties of the parts as well as the relationship among the parts are preserved. This requirement of preserving structural relationship is particularly useful when the parts themselves are not very descriptive. However, the ambiguities in the matching of the parts can not be completely removed by enforcing relational integrity. One could imagine cases where several parts share the same unary as well as binary relationships among them. One way of solving this problem is through a judicious selection of the parts and the relationship defined between them. In this paper, we will show that given any relational graph, the ambiguity in the graph matching is related to eigenvectors of its relational attribute graph. These eigenvectors can in turn be used to define a similarity measure. By grouping nodes that are similar with respect to this measure, one can detect the invariant substructure of the relational graph, as well as maximize the stability of graph matching process.

In particular, for defining texture similarity in image segmentation, we will build a relational graph for the image by taking each pixel as a node where the attribute values on the nodes are set to be the histograms of the image response to a filter bank on the pixels. We will then use the instability in matching this texture relational graph to itself to define a new texture similarity measure for grouping. We will call this new distance measure the *self induced relational distance*, for it pools not only local feature information, but also more global relationships among them. For image 1(a), one can see that although the tree branches look different from one another, their relative differences to other image parts are similar. In image 1(b), the relationship measured using the "stripe-ness" factor are more stable and prominent in this image than those using the stripe orientation. As we will see in sections 3 and 4(figure 6 and 7), our proposed distance measure can indeed capture this intuition.

This paper is organized as follows. In section 2, we will study the problem of relational graph matching, in particular the instability in the graph matching and how the *self-induced relational distance* can be used to reduce such instability. In sections 3 and 4, we will illustrate how such distance can be used in the case of texture segmentation. We conclude in section 5.

2 Relational Graph Matching

The use of relational graph matching in computer vision starts with the seminal work of Barrow and Popplestone[2], and is subsequently followed up by the works of [1, 8, 19, 17, 3, 6, 24, 9, 23]. For relational structural matching, an object is described by its attribute graph, and the mapping of the object parts can be performed by using relational graph matching. An attribute graph is a graph $G=(V,E)$, with attributes A attached to each of the nodes in V and edges in E. For example, figure (2) shows how an attribute graph can be constructed for an object in figure (2a).

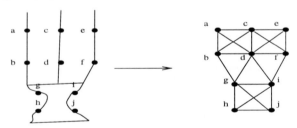

Fig. 2. An attribute graph representation(b) of the object on the left(a). The nodes in the graph are the landmark points. An attribute on each of the nodes could be the curvature at each point, and the attribute on edge (i, j) could the the distance between points i and j.

To match two attribute graphs $G = (V_G, E_G)$, and $H = (V_H, E_H)$, we seek a mapping $f : V_G \rightarrow V_H$ of the vertices, such that if $f(v_G) = v_H$, and $f(u_G) = u_H$, for v_G, u_G in G and v_H, u_H in H, then attributes of the nodes v_G,

u_G should match those of nodes v_H and u_H, and the attributes on the graph edge (v_G, u_G) should match those on graph edge (v_H, u_H).

Let us first consider a simpler case where graphs **G** and **H** are of the same size, and the attributes on the nodes and edges are real numbers. Given a graph **G** of size N, define $\boldsymbol{A}_G$ to be the $N \times N$ attribute matrix, where $\boldsymbol{A}_G(i, i)$ is the attribute on node i, and $\boldsymbol{A}_G(i, j)$ is the attribute of the graph edge (i, j). Furthermore, we will assume the attribute graph **G** is undirected. Let P be the $N \times N$ permutation matrix with $P(i, j) = 1$ iff $f(v_i) = v_j$ for v_i in **G** and v_j in **H**. We can define the cost function of the relational graph matching to be the L_2 norm of the total error on each of the nodes and edges:

$$
\boldsymbol{E}_1(P) = \sum_{i=1}^{N} \sum_{j=1}^{N} (\boldsymbol{A}_G(v_i, v_j) - \boldsymbol{A}_H(f(v_i), f(v_j)))^2
$$
$$
= \|P\boldsymbol{A}_G P^T - \boldsymbol{A}_H\|^2
$$

A similar cost function can be also defined using an inner product norm:

$$
\boldsymbol{E}_2(P) = \sum_{i=1}^{N} \sum_{j=1}^{N} \boldsymbol{A}_G(v_i, v_j) \times \boldsymbol{A}_H(f(v_i), f(v_j))
$$
$$
= \sum_{i=1}^{N} \sum_{j=1}^{N} P\boldsymbol{A}_G P^T(i, j) \times \boldsymbol{A}_H(i, j)
$$
$$
= tr(P^T \boldsymbol{A}_G P \boldsymbol{A}_H).
$$

In fact these two definitions of the error function are equivalent, since:

$$
\|P\boldsymbol{A}_G P^T - \boldsymbol{A}_H\|^2 = \|P\boldsymbol{A}_G P^T\|^2 + \|\boldsymbol{A}_H\|^2 - 2tr(P^T \boldsymbol{A}_G P \boldsymbol{A}_H)
$$
$$
= \|\boldsymbol{A}_G\|^2 + \|\boldsymbol{A}_H\|^2 - 2tr(P^T \boldsymbol{A}_G P \boldsymbol{A}_H).
$$

But $\|\boldsymbol{A}_G\|^2 + \|\boldsymbol{A}_H\|^2$ is a constant, thus minimizing E_1 is same as maximizing E_2. However, as we shall see later, some properties of relational graph matching can be seen more readily with one of the cost functions.

The graph isomorphism problem, that is finding the P that minimizes $\boldsymbol{E}_1$, is a difficult problem to solve exactly. In fact, it is one of the open problems which is not known to be **NP**-complete or in **P**[14]. There have been various efforts to find a close approximate solution using relaxation methods[16, 8], as well as variants of such methods in probabilistic settings[6, 24], or in energy minimization settings[9]. Also there are tree-search based methods such as[23]. In defining relational distance, Shapiro and Haralick[19] and Sanfelu and Fu[17] proposed a distance that will accommodate missing parts in the graphs. Boyer and Kak[3] and Vosselman[23] used information-theoretic approaches to take into consideration the different likelihoods of mis-matches in different attributes.

In this paper, however, we will be mostly interested in the possible uncertainties in the matching arising from the structure of the relational graph. Instead of looking at the discrete group of permutation matrices, we will study the continuous group of orthogonal matrices, of which the permutation matrix is a subgroup. As shown in the work of Brockett[4, 5] and Umeyama[21], in the space of orthogonal matrices, the convergence and stability properties of the matching problem are better understood.

2.1 Instability and Self-inducing Distance

The following two theorems capture the key properties of the solutions of the minimization problem (1) over the space of orthogonal matrices.

Theorem 1 [Umeyama 1988, Brockett 1991][21, 4] *Let* $A_G = V_G \Sigma_G V_G^T$, *and* $A_H = V_H \Sigma_H V_H^T$, *be the singular value decomposition of* A_G *and* A_H. *The matrix* $Q = V_H D \Pi V_G^T$ *minimizes* $E_1(Q) = \|QA_GQ^T - A_H\|^2$ *over all orthogonal matrices* Q, *where* $D = diag(d_1, d_2, ..., d_n)$ *with* $d_i = \pm 1$, *and* Π *is some permutation matrix. In the case where the eigenvalues in* Σ_G *and* Σ_H *are sorted,* $\Pi = I$.

Theorem 2 [von Neumann 1937, Brockett 1991][22, 4] *Let* $\{\lambda_1^G, \lambda_2^G, ..., \lambda_n^G\}$ *and* $\{\lambda_1^H, \lambda_2^H, ..., \lambda_n^H\}$ *be the sorted eigenvalues of* A_G *and* A_H. *The eigenvalues of the Hessian of* $E_2(Q) = tr(Q^T A_G Q A_H)$ *at the* $Q = V_H D \Pi V_G^T$, *are* $n(n-1)/2$ *products of form* $r_{ij} = (\lambda_j^G - \lambda_i^G)(\lambda_{\pi(i)}^H - \lambda_{\pi(j)}^H)$. *In particular, they are all negative for just one choice of* π, *which is when* $\pi(i) = i$.

Proofs of both theorem can be found in[4, 21], we shall only briefly[1] repeat the proof for Theorem 1. Suppose $Q = V_H D V_G^T$, we have

$$
\begin{aligned}
E_1(Q) &= \|QA_GQ^T - A_H\|^2 \\
&= \|V_H D V_G^T A_G V_G D V_H^T - A_H\|^2 \\
&= \|V_H D V_G^T V_G \Sigma_G V_G^T V_G D V_H^T - V_H \Sigma_H V_H^T\|^2 \\
&= \|V_H D \Sigma_G D V_H^T - V_H \Sigma_H V_H^T\|^2 \\
&= \|D \Sigma_G D - \Sigma_H\|^2 = \|\Sigma_G - \Sigma_H\|^2
\end{aligned}
$$

But since for any orthogonal matrix Q, we also have $\|QA_GQ^T - A_H\|^2 \geq \|\Sigma_G - \Sigma_H\|^2$, the above Q must also be the minimum of $E_1(Q)$.

Since the orthogonal matrix Q is an approximation of the permutation matrix P, ideally the entry in $Q(i, j)$ should be large if node v_i in **G** is matched to v_j in **H**. Simple inspection of the definition of Q in theorem 1 shows that the entry in $Q(i, j)$ is large if the ith row of V_H matches with jth row of DV_G. In another words, two nodes, where each node is represented by the corresponding row or column in A_G and A_H, are more likely to match each other if their projections onto the eigenvectors of the relational graphs are similar. The multiplication of

---

[1] Space limitations prevent us from developing the motivation and approach behind these results. We urge the reader to study the Umeyama and Brockett paper for a gentler introduction.

V_G on the left by D is necessary because the eigenvectors of $\boldsymbol{A}_G$ and $\boldsymbol{A}_H$ can take on arbitrary positive or negative direction. The closest permutation P to the orthogonal matrix Q can be then found by maximizing

$$\sum_i \sum_j P(i,j)Q(i,j) = tr(P^T Q).$$

However in general, D is unknown, we have to maximize $tr(P^T |V_H||V_G^T|)$ instead. The problem of maximizing $tr(P^T Q)$ or $tr(P^T |V_H||V_G^T|)$ is an instance of bipartite maximum weighted graph matching, with $Q(i,j)$ being the weight of the bipartite graph edges. The bipartite graph matching can be solved efficiently using max-flow or the Hungarian method[7]. Alternatively, we can use the method of Scott and Longuet-Higgins[18] to produce a quick approximation.

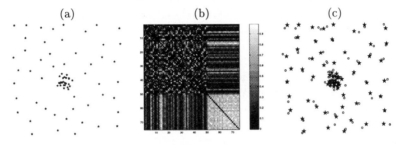

Fig. 3. Subplot (a) shows the spatial layout of the points in the graph **G**. The points are formed by overlapping two point sets sampled from Poisson distributions of different densities. The attribute value on the graph edge (v_i, v_j), shown in subplot (b), is defined as $e^{-d(i,j)/\sigma_s}$, where $d(i,j)$ is the spatial distance between the two points, and $\sigma_s = 4.0$ in this case. For purposes of visual illustration, we ordered the point set such that the points in the sparse set are numbered 1 to 50, and the points in the denser set are numbered 50 to 75. Note that the similarity measures among the sparse point sets are considerably weaker than those of the denser set. The points in Graph **H**, shown as circles in (c), are obtained by adding random Gaussian noise($\sigma = 0.2$) to the spatial location of points in graph **G**, shown as stars.

To see how such a method would work, we will look at an example shown in figure (3). The nodes in the graph (**G**) are constructed by overlaying two spatial point sets of different densities. The attribute relationship is a function of the spatial proximity of the nodes.

To test the sensitivity of the graph matching, we will construct a graph **H** by adding random Gaussian noise to the spatial location of the points in **G**. The performance of this matching algorithm as we increase the noise level in the spatial location of the point set can be seen in figure (4). As shown in figure (4), the computed permutation matrix is quite sensitive to noise in this particular example.

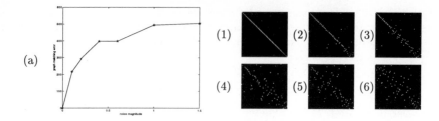

Fig. 4. Subplot (a) shows the error cost $\mathbf{E}_1(P)$ as a function of the noise added to points in graph $\mathbf{H}$. Subplots (1) to (6) show the permutation matrix computed with Gaussian noise of variance of $0, 0.1, 0.2, 0.4, 0.6, 1.0$ added to the spatial location of points in $\mathbf{G}$. Note that as the noise level increases, the ambiguity in the matching increases. However, most of the mismatches occur for the points within each of their own respective point sets.

Upon closer inspection of the graph $\mathbf{G}$, this problem should not be too surprising. The points in the dense cluster have very similar attribute relationships to all other points around it, hence each point can be mapped to other points in the dense cluster without affecting the matching cost. The same statement can also be made about the sparse set of points in the background. Furthermore, from this example, one notes that the uncertainties in matching occur in a structured way– the points in the sparse set are less likely to be mismatched with the points in the denser set.

This degree of uncertainty can in fact be quantified more precisely by theorem (2), which says the instability of Q at its minimum will be high in the dimension where the term $r_{ij} = (\lambda_j^G - \lambda_i^G)(\lambda_i^H - \lambda_j^H)$ is small. The difference in the singular values, $\lambda_i - \lambda_j$, is also often called the gap_i.

One way to remove this instability is to use only the set of eigenvectors whose gaps are large. One could define $Q^* = V_H^* D^* V_G^{*T}$, where V_H^* and V_G^* are the first k columns of V_H and V_G such that for all $j > k$, gap_j^G and gap_j^H are all less than some threshold, δ_{gap}. However, Q^* will no longer be an orthogonal matrix, for rows in V_H and V_G are not independent of each other. To solve this problem, we would like to group together nodes whose corresponding rows in V_H and V_G are similar. We can quantify this similarity by the inner product norm of the rows in V_G and V_H:

$$O_G = V_G^* V_G^{*T}. \tag{1}$$

By grouping nodes with this similarity measure, we can optimally remove the uncertainty in the matching of relational graphs.

Note that the similarity measure O_G depends only on the relationship of the nodes in one graph. Given a graph matching criteria we can perform the grouping of the nodes independently. We will call this distance measure the *self-induced relational distance*.

To test our concept of the *self-induced relational distance*, we shall return to the example in figure (3). Figure (5a) shows the value of gap_i for the eigenvalues of the attribute graph $\mathbf{A}_G$, normalized by the first eigenvalue. Note that gap_i becomes very small after the fourth eigenvector. We will define the self induced distance measure O_G by taking the first four eigenvectors of $\mathbf{A}_G$, shown in figure (5b). As one can see from figure (5), the new distance measure O_G favors condensing the dense point set in the middle into one node, and closely related points in the sparse set into small numbers of nodes. With this small set of nodes, the relational graph matching become more stable, though at the expense of a reduction of the matching resolution.

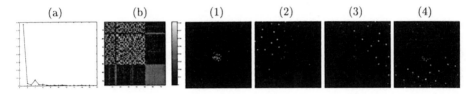

Fig. 5. Subplot (a) shows gap_i for the eigenvalues computed from the attribute graph $\mathbf{A}_G$ in 3(b). Subplot (b) shows the self induced distance matrix O_G computed using the first four eigenvectors of $\mathbf{A}_G$. The self induced distances from a point in the dense set and three other points in the sparse set to all other points are shown in subplots (1) to (4) respectively. The brightness value indicates the similarity strength between the points. Note the new distance measure more strongly connects up the sparse points, without blurring the connections from the dense set to the sparse set.

2.2 Relational Graph on Multi-valued Attributes

So far, we have focused on the case where the attribute value on each graph edge is just a scalar. In general, however, we could have a vector of real numbers representing the attribute relationship between two nodes. Let $[\mathbf{A}_G(v_i, v_j, 1), \mathbf{A}_G(v_i, v_j, 2), ..., \mathbf{A}_G(v_i, v_j, L)] = \mathbf{A}_G(v_i, v_j)$ denote the vector attribute relating node v_i and v_j. We can define a similar graph matching cost function with this new attribute graph:

$$\mathbf{E}_v = \sum_{i=1}^{N} \sum_{j=1}^{N} \sum_{k=1}^{L} \mathbf{A}_G(v_i, v_j, k) \times \mathbf{A}_H(f(v_i), f(v_j), k) \tag{2}$$

Although the problem of finding an approximate solution in the space of orthogonal matrices is more complicated, for the purpose of inducing a relational similarity measure, we can define a simpler cost function $\mathbf{E}_v^*$ which serves as an upper bound on $\mathbf{E}_v$:

$$\mathbf{E}_v^* = \sum_{i=1}^{N} \sum_{j=1}^{N} (\sum_{k=1}^{L} \mathbf{A}_G(v_i, v_j, k)^2)^{1/2} (\sum_{k=1}^{L} \mathbf{A}_H(v_i, v_j, k)^2)^{1/2}$$

$$\geq \sum_{i=1}^{N} \sum_{j=1}^{N} (\sum_{k=1}^{L} \mathbf{A}_G(v_i, v_j, k) \times \mathbf{A}_H(f(v_i), f(v_j), k)) = \mathbf{E}_v,$$

by Schwartz Inequality of $\langle \mathbf{x}, \mathbf{y} \rangle \leq \|\mathbf{x}\| \|\mathbf{y}\|$.

For the case where graphs **G** and **H** are isomorphic, the maxima of each cost function are the same, hence any orthogonal matrix that maximizes E_v^* also maximizes E_v. In the general case, however, the orthogonal matrix that maximizes E_v^* is only an optimistic approximation of the one that maximizes E_v. Even so, we found in practice, that this approximation often does a good job. We shall show this in the case of texture segmentation,

2.3 Summary of the self induced relational distance

Let us review the main thread of the argument in this section. Relational graph matching is studied in an algebraic setting, where finding the best match reduces to finding a permutation matrix that optimally reorders the nodes of one graph to correspond to the other. For mathematical convenience, the discrete search problem in the space of permutation matrices is transformed to a continuous problem by embedding it in the space of orthogonal matrices. Results derived by Umeyama[21] and Brockett[4, 5] reveal that the optimal matching orthogonal matrix and its instability is related to the eigenvectors(V) and eigenvalues(λ) of the relational attribute graphs. To ensure stability of the graph matching, graph nodes are clustered based on their projections in the space spanning the first few eigenvectors(V^*) whose *gaps* are large. We call the distance in this subspace the self induced distance: $O = V^* V^{*T}$.

To illustrate the usefulness of the *self induced distance measure*, we will apply it to the problem of texture similarity measurement and segmentation by setting up a relational graph on the texture feature space. The nodes in the graph are the pixels in the image, and the attributes on each graph edge are the correlations between the local filter outputs. We will show in the next two sections the detail of how such a relational graph can be set up, and how the self induced relational distance can be used to solve the segmentation problem.

3 Texture Measurements

First we will describe the local texture descriptors. The texture measurements used in the paper is based on the image response to a set of filter banks. As shown in the work of [12, 11, 13], the filter responses contain sufficient information for discriminating different texture patterns. The set of filters that we will use consists of even symmetric elongated difference of Gaussian(DOOG) filters as used in[12]. There are total of 6 orientations repeated over 3 different scales. We will denote by $F_{\sigma,\theta,\alpha}$ an elongated DOOG filter of orientation θ, scale σ, and elongation ratio α. Furthermore, to reduce any unwanted bias, all the filters are made zero mean and are normalized so that the L_1 norms equal 1. Let $I_{\sigma,\theta,\alpha}$ denote the filter responses:

$$I_{\sigma,\theta,\alpha} = I * F_{\sigma,\theta,\alpha} \tag{3}$$

For the remainder of the paper, we will fix the elongation factor $\alpha = 3$, and drop the subscript α. For convenience, we will treat the image I itself as the filter response to an impulse function, or $I = I_{0,0,0}$.

Because the filter responses only characterize the intensity variation at a single point in the image, and in describing a texture pattern one would like to integrate information over a spatial local neighborhood; a histogram representation of the filter responses has emerged as an attractive alternative. Theoretical as well as practical benefits of using this histogram representation has been illustrated in the work of [10, 25, 15].

We will use a similar representation which is a *soft* histogram defined over the bins, $\boldsymbol{b}_{\sigma,\alpha} = (b_{\sigma,\alpha}^{min}, ..., b_{\sigma,\alpha}^{max})$ of length K:

$$H_{\theta,\sigma,s}^i(k) = \sum_{j \in N_s(i)} h_{\theta,\sigma}^j(k), \tag{4}$$

where

$$h_{\theta,\sigma}^j(k) = \frac{1}{2\pi} \int_{\boldsymbol{b}(k)}^{\boldsymbol{b}(k+1)} e^{-(I_{\theta,\sigma}^i - x)/\sigma_t^2} dx. \tag{5}$$

The σ_t is related to the degree of uncertainty tolerated in the filter response, and s denotes the spatial radius of the neighborhood centered at i. This definition of the histogram softens the effect of binning and the uncertainties in the measurement. Since we also don't know a priori the size of the neighborhood in which texture pattern exists, we will compute this soft histogram over several different neighborhood sizes. Note also that the L_1 norm of $H_{\theta,\sigma,s}^i = |N_s(i)|$ the number of nodes in that neighborhood.

4 Relational Brightness-Texture Distance

Given a brightness-texture image, an attributed relational graph can be constructed by taking each pixel as a node, and defining a set of attributes on each graph edge connecting two nodes based on the correlation between their local soft histograms. Although we can take the inner product of the histograms as their correlation, this definition has a bias since the L_2 norm of the histograms, $\|H_{\theta,\sigma,s}^i\|$, varies depending on the distributions in the histogram. To correct for this bias, we let $G_{\theta,\sigma,s}^i(k) = H_{\theta,\sigma,s}^i(k)^{\frac{1}{2}}$, and define the attributes on the graph edge (v_i, v_j) as:

$$\boldsymbol{A}_{\theta,\sigma,s}(i,j) = \frac{1}{|N_s i||N_s j|} G_{\theta,\sigma,s}^i{}^T \cdot G_{\theta,\sigma,s}^j, \tag{6}$$

for each set of parameters θ, σ, and s.

As mentioned in section (2.2), for the purpose of computing the *self induced relational distance*, we can get an approximation with a scalar attribute graph where the attribute on graph edge (v_i, v_j) is

$$\boldsymbol{A}^*(i,j) = \left(\sum_{\theta,\sigma,s} \boldsymbol{A}_{\theta,\sigma,s}^2(i,j) \right)^{1/2}. \tag{7}$$

(a)

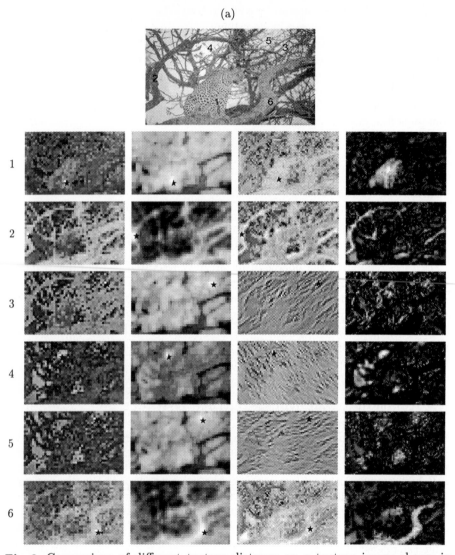

Fig. 6. Comparison of different texture distance on a texture image shown in (a). The ith row shows the texture similarity between pixel i(star) labelled in (a) to all other pixels in the image according to (1) χ^2 difference on the local histogram with neighborhood size of 3×3 pixels (column 1), (2) χ^2 difference with neighborhood size of 11×11(column 2), (3) L^∞ norm in filter responses computed with neighborhood size of 5×5 (column 3), and (4) self induced distance(column 4). Note that picking the right neighborhood size could be a hard problem with χ^2 distance– with too small neighborhood size connections in the texture image are sparse and weak, with too large a neighborhood size object boundaries are blurred. Similarly L^∞ could cause over-fragmentation in areas such as the tree branches. With the self-induced texture distance, relational coherence in texture feature space is enhanced, without sacrificing the sharpness of the texture boundaries.

Given this relational graph, we can compute the self induced relational distance as described in section 2.1. Experimental tests on brightness-texture images such as the one illustrated in figure (1a) are shown in figure(6). The self induced relational distance clearly depends on the number of eigenvectors of the attribute graph taken in equation (2). In all of our experiments, we set the threshold of the minimum *gap* value to be $\delta_{gap} = 8 \times 10^{-4} \times \lambda_1$, where λ_1 is the largest eigenvalue of $\boldsymbol{A}_G$. This threshold of δ_{gap} determines the number of eigenvectors to be used. Figure (7) shows the effect of using different numbers of eigenvectors in computing the self induced relational distance for the scene shown in figure (7a).

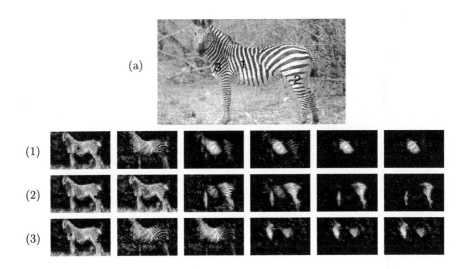

Fig. 7. Row i shows the effect of using different number of eigenvectors in computing the self induced relational distance $O(i, j)$ between pixel i labelled in (a) and all other pixels j in the image. Each of the columns correspond to distances computed with 2,3,4,6,9,12 eigenvectors from left to right, respectively. With our setting of δ_{gap}, the first 9 eigenvectors will be used in computing the self induced relational distance.

4.1 Normalized Cuts

Using the newly defined texture similarity measure, we can produce a segmentation of a scene using the *normalized cut* algorithm [20]. In the normalized cuts scheme, the image segmentation problem is reduced to a hierarchical graph partitioning problem. In this case, the nodes in the graph are the pixels in the image, and the weights on graph edge connecting two nodes are the self induced relational similarity measures. We then seek a sub-partitioning of the graph, such that the similarities within subgraphs are high and similarities between the subgroups are low.

Let $\mathbf{G} = (\mathbf{V}, \mathbf{E})$ be a weighted graph, with adjacency graph weight matrix $\mathbf{W}$. $\mathbf{W}(u, v)$ is the weight on the graph edge connecting nodes u and v reflecting the similarity between the two nodes. We can break $\mathbf{G}$ into two disjoint sets, $A, B, A \cup B = \mathbf{V}, A \cap B = \emptyset$, by simply removing edges connecting the two parts. Following our previous work[20], we will use the *normalized cut* as a measure of dissimilarity between the two groups:

$$Ncut(A, B) = \frac{cut(A, B)}{asso(A, V)} + \frac{cut(A, B)}{asso(B, V)}, \tag{8}$$

where $cut(A, B) = \sum_{u \in A, v \in B} W(u, v)$ is the connection between A and B, $asso(A, V) = \sum_{u \in A, t \in V} w(u, t)$ is the total connection from nodes in A to all nodes in the graph, and $asso(B, V)$ is similarly defined. Let $\mathbf{W}$ be the graph weight matrix, and $\mathbf{D}$ be the diagonal matrix with $\mathbf{D}(i, i) = \sum_j \mathbf{W}(i, j)$. In [20], we showed that minimizing $Ncut$ can be reduced to minimizing a Rayleigh quotient:

$$min. \ Ncut = min_y \frac{y^T(D - W)y}{y^T Dy}, \tag{9}$$

with the condition $y_i \in \{1, -b\}$ and $y^T D1 = 0$. By relaxing y to take on real values, we can minimize equation (9) with its constraint by solving for the generalized eigenvector corresponding to second smallest eigenvalue of the system,

$$(\mathbf{D} - \mathbf{W})y = \lambda \mathbf{D}y. \tag{10}$$

The vector y can be thought of an indicator vector for the partition. Furthermore, the subsequent eigenvectors are the real valued solutions that form the optimal sub-partitions. From those vectors a discrete partition can be obtained as shown in [20].

4.2 Overall Procedure and Texture Segmentation Result

In summary our texture segmentation algorithm can be described as:
1. Compute filter outputs $I_{\theta, \sigma}$ from an input image I,
2. Construct soft histogram at each pixel i, $H^i_{\theta, \sigma, s}$, over a neighborhood of radius $s = [1, 3, 5, 9, 15, 26]$ pixels,
3. Set up attributes $A_{\theta, \sigma, s}$ and A^* from $H^i_{\theta, \sigma, s}$,
4. Compute the distance measure $O = |U_A^* U_A^{*T}|$, where $A^* = U_A \Sigma_A U_A^T$, $U_A^* = U_A(:, 1 : k)$ such that $\forall (j > k) \ gap_j < \delta_{gap}$,
5. Produce image segmentation using normalized cut algorithm[20].

The segmentation result using normalized cuts on the self induced relational texture distance are shown in figures (8) and (9). Unlike our previous work, the spatial proximity factor is not used in the segmentation algorithm, hence we obtain somewhat less spatially coherent groups. This is done on purpose to emphasize the texture similarity in our new relational distance measure. Adding spatial proximity factor in our framework is very easy. Note also our segmentation procedure produces a hierarchical partitioning of the scene, some of the under-segmented regions can be sub-divided into smaller parts.

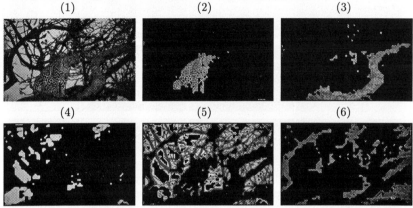

(1)   (2)   (3)

(4)   (5)   (6)

Fig. 8. Segmentation results on the image in (a) with the newly defined relational distance. The relational graph is built by taking pixels from every $5th$ row and column as graph nodes. These are also the nodes used in normalized cuts. The full image size is 220×350. Note both the cheetah in (2) and the random tree branches in (5) come out as single coherent groups. The tree trunks in (3) and (6) are in two different groups because of the difference in intensity value.

5 Conclusion

In this paper, we have shown how a self induced feature distance can be derived by analyzing its relational graph. In particular, the process of finding a stable matching of the relational graph produces as a by-product a distance measure which captures the relative importance of the feature relationships. By applying it to the problem of image segmentation in the brightness-texture feature space, very good results are obtained on difficult images of natural scenes.

6 Acknowledgment

This research is supported by (ARO)DAAH04-96-1-0341, and an NSF Graduate Fellowship to J. Shi. We would like to thank Thomas Leung and Serge Belongie for useful discussions.

References

1. H.G. Barrow and R.M. Burstall. Subgraph isomorphism, matching relational structures and maximal cliques. *Information Processing Letters*, 4:83–84, 1976.
2. H.G. Barrow and R.J. Popplestone. Relational descriptions in picture processing. *Machine Intelligence*, 6:377–396, 1971.

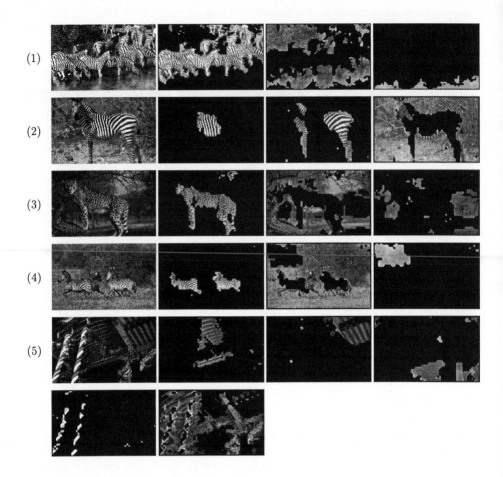

Fig. 9. Segmentation results on a set of brightness-texture images. The relational graph is built by taking pixels in every 5*th* row and column as nodes in (1) and every 7*th* row and column as nodes in (2) to (5). The full image size is 220 × 350. In all examples, images are broken into visually similar texture, brightness patches. Note in (2), the stripes of the zebra are broken into two parts because in this image, the "stripe-ness" feature and the orientations of the stripe are of equal prominence.

3. K. Boyer and A. Kak. Structural stereopsis for 3d vision. *IEEE Trans. Pattern Anal. Mach. Intell.*, 10:144–166, 1988.

4. R.W. Brockett. Least squares matching problems. *Linear Algebra and its applications*, pages 761–777, 1989.

5. R.W. Brockett. Dynamical systems that sorts lists, diagonalize matrices, and solve linear programming problem. *Linear Algebra and its applications*, pages 79–91, 1991.

6. W. Christmas, J. Kittle, and M. Petrou. Probabilistic feature labeling schemes – modeling compatibility coefficient distribution. *Image and Vision Computing*, 14:617–625, 1996.

7. C.E. Cormen, R.L. Leiserson, and L. Rivest. *Introduction to Algorithms*. McGraw-Hill, 1990.

8. O.D. Faugeras and K.E. Price. Semantic labeling of aerial images using stochastic relaxation. *IEEE Trans. Pattern Anal. Mach. Intell.*, 3:633–642, 1981.

9. S. Gold and A. Rangarajan. A graduated assignment algorithm for graph matching. *IEEE Trans. Pattern Anal. Mach. Intell.*, 18:377–388, 1996.

10. D.J. Heeger and J.R. Bergen. Pyramid-based texture analysis/synthesis. In *SIGGRAPH 95*, pages 229–238, 1995.

11. A.K. Jain and F. Farrokhnia. Unsupervised texture segmentation using gabor filters. *IEEE Trans. Pattern Anal. Mach. Intell.*, 24(12):1167–1186, 1991.

12. J. Malik and P. Perona. Preattentive texture discrimination with early vision mechanisms. *J. Opt. Soc. Am. A*, 7(5):923–932, 1990.

13. B.S. Manjunath and W.Y. Ma. Texture features for browsing and retrieval of image data. *IEEE Trans. Pattern Anal. Mach. Intell.*, 18(8):837–842, 1996.

14. C.H. Papadimitriou. *Computational Complexity*. Addison-Wesley Publishing Company, 1994.

15. J. Puzicha, T. Hofmann, and J.M. Buhmann. Non-parametric similarity measures for unsupervised texture segmentation and image retrieval. In *Proc. IEEE Conf. Computer Vision and Pattern Recognition*, pages 267–272, 1997.

16. A. Rosenfeld, R. Hummel, and S. Zucker. Scene labeling by relaxation operations. *IEEE SMC*, 6:420–433, 1976.

17. A. Sanfeliu and K.S. Fu. A distance measure between attributed relational graph. *IEEE SMC*, 13:353–362, 1983.

18. G.L. Scott and H.C. Longuet-Higgins. An algorithm for associating the features of two images. In *Proc. R. Soc. Lond. B.*, pages 21–26, 1991.

19. L. Shapiro and R.M. Haralick. A metric for comparing relational descriptions. *IEEE Trans. Pattern Anal. Mach. Intell.*, 7:90–94, 1985.

20. J. Shi and J. Malik. Normalized cuts and image segmentation. In *Proc. IEEE Conf. Computer Vision and Pattern Recognition*, pages 731–737, 1997.

21. S. Umeyama. An eigendecomposition approach to weighted graph matching problems. *IEEE Trans. Pattern Anal. Mach. Intell.*, 10(5):695–703, 1988.

22. J. von Neumann. Some matrix-inequalities and metrization of matric-spaces. *Tomsk Univ. Rev.*, 1:286–300, 1937. also in John von Neumann: Collected Works,(A.H. Taub, Ed.) Vol. IV, Pergamon, New York, 1962, pp 205-218.

23. G. Vosselman. *Relational Matching*. Springer-Verlag, 1992. Lectures in Computer Science, number 628.

24. R.C. Wilson and E.R. Hancock. Structual matching by discrete relaxation. *IEEE Trans. Pattern Anal. Mach. Intell.*, 19:1–2, 1997.

25. S.C. Zhu, Y. Wu, and D. Mumford. Frame: Filters, random fields, and minimax entropy. In *Proc. IEEE Conf. Computer Vision and Pattern Recognition*, pages 686–693, 1996.

Contour Continuity in Region Based Image Segmentation

Thomas Leung and Jitendra Malik

Department of Electrical Engineering and Computer Sciences
University of California at Berkeley, Berkeley, CA 94720, USA
{leungt,malik}@cs.berkeley.edu

Abstract. Region-based image segmentation techniques make use of similarity in intensity, color and texture to determine the partitioning of an image. The powerful cue of contour continuity is not exploited at all. In this paper, we provide a way of incorporating curvilinear grouping into region-based image segmentation. Soft contour information is obtained through orientation energy. Weak contrast gaps and subjective contours are completed by contour propagation. The normalized cut approach proposed by Shi and Malik is used for the segmentation. Results on a large variety of images are shown.

1 Introduction

Grouping is a very important problem in visual perception. To humans, an image is not just a random collection of pixels; it is a meaningful arrangment of regions and objects. Figure 1 shows a variety of images — (a) an artificial image showing strong subjective contours in the Kanizsa triangle; (b) a painting which combines line and paint and; (c) a natural photograph. Despite the large variations of these images, humans have no problem interpreting them. We can agree about the different regions in the images and recognize the different objects.

Human visual grouping was studied extensively by the Gestalt psychologists in the early part of the century [28]. They identified several factors that lead to human perceptual grouping: similarity, proximity, continuity, symmetry, parallelism, closure and familiarity. In computer vision, these factors have been used as guidelines for many grouping algorithms. The most studied version of grouping in computer vision is image segmentation. Image segmentation techniques can be classified into two broad families–(1) region-based, and (2) contour-based approaches. Each of these has characteristic advantages and disadvantages.

Region-based approaches try to find partitions of the image pixels into sets corresponding to coherent image properties such as brightness, color and texture. This gives rise to proto-surfaces. This is important for a number of reasons: (1) surfaces are the natural units of perception [19]; (2) one can compute texture/color descriptors for each region, which is necessary for applications such as content-based image querying.

Region-based techniques usually involve defining a global objective function (for example, Markov random fields [7] or other variational formulations [18]).

Fig. 1. Some challenging images for a segmentation algorithm. The left image is the Kanizsa triangle. Subjective contours induced in this image lead us to interpret it as a triangle occluding 3 circles instead of 3 "pacman" figures. The middle image is a combination of line drawing and paint. The right image is a photograph with several low contrast edges, e.g. between the man's jacket and the woman's blouse. Our goal is to develop a single grouping procedure which can deal with all these types of images.

The advantage of having a global objective function is that hard decisions are made only when information from the whole image is taken into account at the same time. The major drawback of region techniques is that curvilinear continuity, a very powerful constraint, is not exploited.

Contour-based approaches usually start with a first stage of edge detection, followed by a linking process that seeks to exploit curvilinear continuity. Examples include dynamic programming [14], relaxation approaches [21] and saliency networks [23]. The major advantage of contour-based approaches is that the grouping factor of curvilinear continuity can be treated very naturally. The disadvantages are: (1) contour-based techniques do not give us closed connected regions; so the grouping problem of finding closed connected surfaces is not really solved. As mentioned earlier, surfaces are desirable entities. Thus a post-processing step remains. This may take the form of explicitly enforcing closure of contours as in [4, 11]. (2) Contour-based techniques cannot deal with textured regions easily. Basically, for textured regions, we have to find feature vectors and look for differences — that is more natural in region approaches. (3) Hard decisions are made locally and prematurely. To detect an extended contour of very low contrast, a very low threshold has to be set for the edge detector. This will cause random edge segments being found everywhere in the image. The linking process then has to deal with all the spurious edge segments everywhere. In other words, there is no recognition of the fact that extended contours, though with low contrast, are perceptually more significant than short random edges in the image.

Our goal in this paper is to incorporate curvilinear grouping in a region-based setting. In all region approaches, one needs to define a distance function

— a measure of dissimilarity between pairs of pixels. Then, some procedure is needed to find regions where similarity between pixels in a given region is high and similarity between pixels in different regions is low. We propose a distance function which takes contours into account softly through orientation energy. Similarity is low if the orientation energy between two pixels is high, hinting at the possible presence of a contour between them. Low contrast gaps along a contour are completed by the propagation of orientation energy. We would like to emphasize that subjective contours, those enabling us to perceive the Kanizsa triangle in Figure 1(a), are simply the extreme case of low contrast contours (contrast is zero). Thus, any algorithm exploiting curvilinear continuity should be able to deal with subjective contours naturally. With the distance function defined, the normalized cut procedure proposed by Shi and Malik in [25] is employed to produce the segmentation.

The outline of the paper is as follows. In Section 2, previous work in curvilinear grouping will be reviewed. How we exploit curvilinear continuity in defining pixel similarity is described in Section 3. The overall image segmentation algorithm is presented in Section 4. A review of the normalized cuts approach for image segmentation will be given in Section 4.1. In Section 5, we will show results on various kinds of images like those shown in Figure 1. We conclude in Section 6.

2 Previous Work on Curvilinear Grouping

Psychophysical studies on curvilinear grouping date back to the early part of the century. Wertheimer pointed out the factor of good continuation in perceptual grouping in [28]. Subjective contours, first discovered by Schumann [22], were studied extensively by Kanizsa [12]. Kanizsa was the first to point out that subjective contours are simply gradientless edges — the extreme case of low contrast edges. More recently, Kellman and Shipley [13] and Field et al [5] studied the formation of curvilinear groups psychophysically.

In computer vision, the problem of contour completion has been approached in many different ways. Most techniques employ some form of edge detection followed by a linking process. The linking process can take the form of: dynamic programming [14], relaxation [21], saliency networks [23], voting [8] or sequential tracking in a Bayesian framework [2]. In general, these methods can bridge small gaps along an edge to produce an extended contour.

Another direction of work is the computation of subjective contours. Most methods involve first the computation of key-points, such as junctions, corners and line ends. Different models of subjective contour completion from these key-points are proposed: variational models [6, 20], random walk [29] or a grouping field [9]. Occlusion reasoning is also studied in [9, 20]. Most of these approaches have only been applied to artificial images, while some have been tested on very simple real images. Since subjective contours are just the extreme case of low contrast contours, a useful model should be able to work on realistic photographs.

We believe the inadequacy of previous work is partly due to the dependence on key point detection, which is rather unreliable in realistic images.

3 Curvilinear Continuity

The main idea of region-based segmentation is to compute local similarity and then optimize the segmentation over the whole image through a global criterion. For segmentation using intensity alone, local similarity is invariably some measure of how much the intensities of two pixels are alike. In this section, we describe how information about curvilinear continuity can be incorporated into the similarity measure between two pixels.

3.1 Soft Contour Information

Most previous curve detection methods rely on a first step of edge detection, followed by edge linking. Edge detection is a local process. This has the important drawback that hard decisions are made prematurely. We propose that contour information be computed "softly" and hard decisions be made only when the image is considered as a whole. Information about the strength of a contour can be obtained through *orientation energies* [15, 16]. Let $\mathcal{F}_1(x, y)$ be the second derivative of an elongated gaussian kernel and $\mathcal{F}_2(x, y)$ be the Hilbert transform of $\mathcal{F}_1(x, y)$. More precisely:

$$\mathcal{F}_1(x, y) = \frac{d^2}{dy^2}(\frac{1}{C}\exp(\frac{y^2}{\sigma^2})\exp(\frac{x^2}{\lambda^2\sigma^2}))$$
$$\mathcal{F}_2(x, y) = Hilbert(\mathcal{F}_1(x, y))$$

where σ is the scale and λ is the elongation of the filter. C is a constant. The orientation energy at angle $0°$ is defined as:

$$OE_{0°} = (I * \mathcal{F}_1)^2 + (I * \mathcal{F}_2)^2$$

$OE_{0°}$ has maximum response for horizontal contours. Rotated copies of the two filter kernels will be able to pick up edge contrast at various orientations. These kernels are shown in Figure 2. At each pixel, we can define the orientation energy and the orientation as:

$$OE_{con}(x, y) = \max_{\phi} OE_\phi(x, y) \tag{1}$$
$$\phi(x, y) = \arg\max_{\phi} OE_\phi(x, y)$$

The orientation energy defined in Equation 1 has the following nice properties: (1) the second derivative of the gaussian and the Hilbert transform of it are a quadrature pair [15, 16]. Quadrature pairs are phase independent and they are not affected by exact localization of the edges. (2) The filters are insensitive to linear intensity variations, which are usually caused by smooth shading,

Fig. 2. Top: rotated copies of the second derivative of an elongated gaussian kernel. $\sigma = 1.0$ and the elongation ratio is 4. Bottom: rotated copies of the Hilbert transform of the second derivative kernel. In our implementation, we use 12 orientations uniformly sampled in the range from $0°$ to $180°$. This quadrature pair is chosen because both filters are insensitive to linear variations of intensity, which are usually caused by smooth shading, rather than object boundaries. The orientation energy resulting from the quadrature pair is phase independent and is not affected by the precise localization of the contour.

rather than object boundaries. (3) The filters are elongated, thus information is integrated along the edge. Long contours will produce stronger responses than shorter ones. Extended low contrast contours will also have significant response because of the integration. (4) Our filters do not respond well to high curvature contours. This property agrees with human perception that curvilinear grouping does not occur over high curvature contours.

From the orientation energy, we can compute the dissimilarity between two pixels due to the factor of curvilinear continuity. Intuitively, two pixels belong to two different groups if there is a contour separating them. The dissimilarity is stronger if the contour separating them is extended. Figure 3 is a good illustration of this intuition. On the left is the image. The middle figure shows a magnified part of the original image. On the right is the orientation energy. Pixels p_1, p_2 and p_3 all have similar intensity values. Based purely on intensity (normally the only cue for region based segmentation), all three locations will have strong similarities. However, there is an extended contour separating p_3 from p_1 and p_2. Thus, we expect p_1 to be much more strongly related to p_2 than p_3. This intuition carries over in our definition of dissimilarity between two pixels: if the orientation energy along the line between two pixels is strong, the dissimilarity between these pixels should be high. Formally, we define the dissimilarity, $d_{edg}(p_1, p_2)$, between two pixels as follows:

$$d_{edg}(p_1, p_2) = OE_{con}(\hat{x}) - \text{avg}(OE_{con}(p_1), OE_{con}(p_2); \hat{x}) \qquad (2)$$

where

$$\hat{x} = \arg\max_{x \in l} OE_{con}(x)$$

 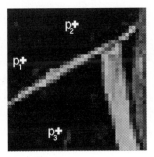 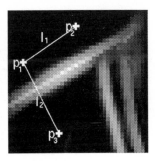

Fig. 3. Left: the original image. Middle: part of the image marked by the box. The intensity values at pixels p_1, p_2 and p_3 are similar. However, there is an edge in the middle, which suggests that p_1 and p_2 belong to one group while p_3 belongs to another. Just comparing intensity values at these three locations will mistakenly suggest that they belong to the same group. Right: orientation energy. The orientation energy somewhere on l_2 is strong which correctly proposes that p_1 and p_3 belong to two different partitions, while orientation energy along l_1 is weak throughout, which will maintain the hypothesis that p_1 and p_2 belong to the same group.

$$\text{avg}(OE_{con}(p_1), OE_{con}(p_2); \hat{x}) = \frac{|p_2 - \hat{x}|}{|p_1 - p_2|} OE_{con}(p_1) + \frac{|\hat{x} - p_1|}{|p_1 - p_2|} OE_{con}(p_2) \quad (3)$$

l is the straight line between p_1 and p_2; $\hat{x}$ is the location where the orientation energy is maximum on l; and $\text{avg}(OE_{con}(p_1), OE_{con}(p_2); \hat{x})$ is the weighted average orientation energy of p_1 and p_2. It is worth noting that in our definition, we considered the *relative* difference in orientation energy. When images are noisy, orientation energy along the path may be high merely due to noise. In this case, orientation energies at p_1 and p_2 will be high as well. Thus, the relative difference is a better indicator of the presence of a contour.

3.2 Contour Propagation

The orientation energy defined in the previous section will be high at a sharp contour. When there are gaps along a contour where contrast is low (or even absent in the case of subjective contours), the orientation energy will not do a very good job. However, it is worth pointing out that due to the integration of the filter kernels along a contour, orientation energy will still be reasonable when the gaps are small. It will fail when gaps are large. In this section, we provide a more explicit way of enhancing the orientation energy at low contrast gaps by propagation from neighboring pixels along an extended contour. Before we proceed, let us repeat that subjective contours are just the extreme case of a low contrast contour (the contrast is zero). Thus, our treatment here will be able to capture subjective contours in the same way as we enhance the orientation energy at low contrast gaps.

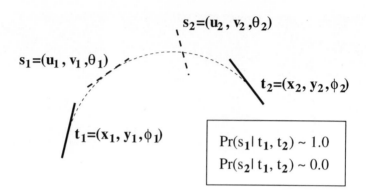

Fig. 4. Consider pixel location (u_i, v_i). We are interested in the probability $P_{cp}(s_i|t_1, t_2)$ that there is an image curve originating from t_1 and terminating in t_2 which passes through s_i. This probability can be related to the minimum energy of all curves passing through the three points. Notice that this probability will depend heavily on the orientation θ_i. In this case, $P_{cp}(s_1|t_1, t_2)$ will be high while $P_{cp}(s_2|t_1, t_2)$ will be close to 0.

Consider the oriented element (u_1, v_1, θ_1) where (u_1, v_1) are the coordinates and θ_1 is the orientation. What is the probability that there is an image contour originating at (x_1, y_1, ϕ_1), passing through (u_1, v_1, θ_1) and ending up at (x_2, y_2, ϕ_2)? There are infinitely many curves that satisfy our requirement. One popular choice is the curve that minimizes the *elastica* functional, ie. the image curve with the minimum energy. [1] The elastica was already introduced in Euler's time. Ullman [27] and Horn [10] are among the first to apply it to contour completion. For a discussion of the application of the elastica to computer vision, readers are referred to [17]. Using the elastica, the probability in which we are interested can be related to the energy of the minimizing curve: $P_{cp}(s_1|t_1, t_2) = \exp(-E_{elastica})$, where $s_i = (u_i, v_i, \theta_i)$, $t_i = (x_i, y_i, \phi_i)$ and $E_{elastica}$ is the minimum energy. Likewise, the probability that there is no image curve passing through (u_1, v_1, θ_1) is simply $1 - P_{cp}(s_1|t_1, t_2)$. First notice that $P_{cp}(s_1|t_1, t_2)$ should depend heavily on θ_1: in Figure 4, $P_{cp}(s_1|t_1, t_2)$ should be close to 1, while $P_{cp}(s_2|t_1, t_2)$ will be close to 0.

Computing the elastica energy exactly is not necessary and not computationally advisable. Sharon et al [24] showed that we can have a simple approximation by assuming that $P_{cp}(s_i|t_1, t_2)$ can be factored into two terms: $P_{cp}(s_i|t_1, t_2) = f(s_i, t_1)f(s_i, t_2)$ with $f(\cdot)$ as:

$$f(s_i, t_i) = \exp(-\frac{R}{\sigma_R} - \frac{D_\beta}{\sigma_\beta}) \tag{4}$$

$$D_\beta = \beta_1^2 + \beta_2^2 - \beta_1\beta_2$$

---

[1] Energy is defined as the integral of the square of the curvature along the curve.

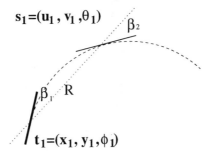

Fig. 5. Two oriented elements t_1 and s_1 separated by a distance R. β_1 is the angle between the orientation at t_1 and the line joining the two pixels. Similarly, β_2 is the angle between the orientation at s_1 and the line joining the two pixels.

where β_1, β_2 and R are defined in Figure 5. σ_R and σ_β specify the amount of variations allowed in the distance and the agreement of the angles.

Using, $P_{cp}(s_1|t_1, t_2)$, the propagation of orientation energy can be defined as:

$$OE_{cp}(u, v) = \max_\theta \max_{(x_1, y_1), (x_2, y_2) \in \mathcal{N}} P_{cp}((u, v, \theta)|t_1, t_2) \cdot \overline{OE_{con}}$$

where $\overline{OE_{con}} = \frac{1}{2}(OE_{con}(x_1, y_1) + OE_{con}(x_2, y_2))$ and $\mathcal{N}$ is a local neighborhood of (u, v). Notice that this definition maintains the intuitive requirement that the propagated orientation energy is never larger than the average energy of the propagating sites. Moreover, the propagation is biased towards extended low curvature contours. Combining orientation energy due to contour contrast (OE_{con}) and contour propagation (OE_{cp}), we have, at each pixel:

$$OE_{tot}(x, y) = \max(OE_{con}(x, y), OE_{cp}(x, y))$$

Let us discuss what the above equation implies. If the orientation energy due to contour contrast at (u, v) is high (OE_{con} is large), we do not change anything. However, when the energy is low, caused by low contrast, we are enhancing the energy through the propagation from neighboring elements. In the case when energy at (u, v) is zero (subjective contours), we can complete the curve by propagating from neighboring contours.

With the combined orientation energy, we can update our dissimilarity measure (Equation 2) as:

$$d_{edg}(p_1, p_2) = OE_{tot}(\hat{x}) - \text{avg}(OE_{tot}(p_1), OE_{tot}(p_2); \hat{x}) \tag{5}$$

with $\hat{x} = \arg\max_{x \in l} OE_{tot}(x)$ and $\text{avg}(\cdot, \cdot; \cdot)$ defined in Equation 3.

4   Partitioning Images

All region-based image segmentation techniques start with local measurements of similarity. Local information is combined over the image through a global criterion. The "correct" segmentation is the one that maximizes this global criterion. Equation 5 tells us the dissimilarity between two pixels based on contour information alone. We combine contour information with intensity and/or color to produce the overall similarity measure between pixels p_i and p_j as follows:

$$W_{ij} = \exp(-\alpha_{edg}d_{edg}(p_i, p_j) - \alpha_{int}d_{int}(p_i, p_j) - \alpha_{col}d_{col}(p_i, p_j)) \tag{6}$$

$d_{int}(p_1, p_2) = |I_1 - I_2|$ and $d_{col}(p_1, p_2) = |H_1 - H_2| + |S_1 - S_2|$ where I_i, H_i, S_i are the intensity, hue and saturation at pixel i. The α's are weighting coefficients for the different factors. One can think of the α's as prior knowledge relating to the relative importance of the different factors. In this paper, we provide a way of adjusting these parameters for each image. This will be discussed in section 4.2. First, we will review the normalized cuts algorithm [25] which we used to segment the image based on the similarity measure in Equation 6.

4.1   Image Segmentation using Normalized Cuts

Let $W \in \mathbb{R}^{N \times N}$ be the association matrix, i.e. W_{ij} is the weight between pixels i and j (Equation 6). We proceed to apply the normalized cut criterion proposed by Shi and Malik in [25]to partition the image. Shi and Malik formulate visual grouping as a graph partitioning problem. The nodes of the graph are the entities that we want to partition, for example, in image segmentation, they will be the pixels. The edges between two nodes correspond to the *strength* that these two nodes belong to one group, again in image segmentation, the edges of the graph will correspond to how much two pixels agree in intensity, color, etc. Intuitively, the criterion for partitioning the graph will be to minimize the sum of weights of connections *across* the groups and maximize the sum of weights of connections *within* the groups.

Let $G = \{V, E\}$ be a weighted undirected graph, where V are the nodes and E are the edges. Let A, B be a partition of the graph: $A \cup B = V, A \cap B = \emptyset$. In graph theoretic language, the similarity between these two groups is called the *cut*:

$$cut(A, B) = \sum_{u \in A, v \in B} w(u, v)$$

where $w(u, v)$ is the weight on the edge between nodes u and v. Shi and Malik proposed to use a *normalized* similarity criterion to evaluate a partition. They call it the *normalized cut*:

$$Ncut(A, B) = \frac{cut(A, B)}{assoc(A, V)} + \frac{cut(B, A)}{assoc(B, V)} \tag{7}$$

where $assoc(A, V) = \sum_{u \in A, t \in V} w(u, t)$ is the total connection from nodes in A to all the nodes in the graph. For discussions on this criterion, please refer to [25].

One key advantage of using the normalized cut is that a good approximation to the optimal partition can be computed very efficiently. [2] Let W be the association matrix, i.e. W_{ij} is the weight between nodes i and j in the graph. Let D be the diagonal matrix such that $D_{ii} = \sum_j W_{ij}$, i.e. D_{ii} is the sum of the weights of all the connections to node i. Shi and Malik showed that the optimal partition can be found by computing:

$$y = \arg\min Ncut$$
$$= \arg\min_y \frac{y^T(D - W)y}{y^T D y} \tag{8}$$

where $y = \{a, b\}^N$ is a binary indicator vector specifying the group identity for each pixel, ie. $y_i = a$ if pixel i belongs to group A and $y_j = b$ if pixel j belongs to B. N is the number of pixels. Notice that the above expression is a Rayleigh quotient. If we relax y to take on real values (instead of two discrete values), we can optimize Equation 8 by solving a generalized eigenvalue system. Efficient algorithms with polynomial running time are well-known for solving such problems. For details of the derivation of Equation 8, please refer to [25].

Transforming the vector y to a discrete bipartition $\hat{x}$ can simply be done by finding the threshold τ such that if we let $\hat{x}_i = 1$ when $y_i > \tau$ and $\hat{x}_i = -1$ otherwise, the normalized cut value in Equation 7 is minimized. In our implementation, we try τ at 10 values uniformly distributed between the maximum and minimum of y. Given a bipartition of the image, we recursively bipartition each segment until either a pre-defined number of steps is reached, or when the normalized cut value resulting from the bi-partitioning is too large. When normalized cut value is too large, it means there is no more segmentation necessary for this group.

4.2   Parameter Estimation

One natural question to ask is that now we have the various factors combined at the same time, how do we evaluate the importance of each of the them in an image. In other words how do we determine the α's in Equation 6? One may look at this problem as finding prior weights for the various factors. However, we argue that these weights should change from image to image. For example, in a line drawing, all information comes from the contours. Intensity and color should be de-emphasized. Thus, α_{edg} should be much larger than α_{int} and α_{col}. On the other hand, in an image with regions of distinctly different colors, but similar intensities, α_{col} should dominate.

Since the goodness of each partition is given by the normalized cut value (the smaller the better), we can simply use gradient descent on the parameters to minimize this value. The gradient of $Ncut$ with respect to α_i is:

$$\frac{\partial Ncut}{\partial \alpha_i} = \frac{Ncut(\alpha_i + \delta_i) - Ncut(\alpha_i)}{\delta_i}$$

---

[2] Finding the true optimal partition is an NP-complete problem.

We update the parameters by moving them in the negative gradient direction of $Ncut$. Notice that computing $Ncut(\alpha_i + \delta_i)$ is very efficient. When δ_i is small, the partition for $Ncut(\alpha_i + \delta_i)$ is similar to the one already found for $Ncut(\alpha_i)$. Therefore, we can use the optimal partition for $Ncut(\alpha_i)$ as an initial estimate for solving the generalized eigenvalue system in Equation 8 with the new parameters. This can save at least an order of magnitude in computation time.

5   Results

In this section, we will demonstrate some of the results on various kinds of images: (1) images with strong subjective contours; (2) line-drawings; (3) paintings which combine both line-drawing and paint; and (4) gray-level images. In all the examples shown in this paper, there was no manual tuning of thresholds or parameters. The large variety of images presented in this paper illustrate the wide applicability of our algorithm.

Since subjective contours are just the extreme case of low contrast contours, all curvilinear grouping algorithms should be general enough to deal with this special case. The Kanizsa triangle and the Kanizsa "2-fish" images [12] shown in Figures 6 and 7 are good examples to demonstrate how our algorithm performs in the presense of subjective contours. Orientation energies due to contours alone (OE_{con}) and after contour propagation (OE_{tot}) are also shown. Notice the spurious completion in the orientation energy after contour propagation, OE_{tot}. These are the results of propagation between points in the middle of two different contours. In some previous work, this problem is avoided by detecting key-points (junctions, corners and line ends) and then performing subjective contour completion only from the key-points. However, we argue that detecting these features in real images is a problem in itself. We believe that such features cannot be reliably detected purely from local information. In other words, in realistic images, we have to live with such artifacts and rely on a global criterion to sort out what is significant and what is not. The segmentations of the Kanizsa figures are also shown in Figures 6 and 7. Notice that the results agree with our percepts.

The result on a 3D line drawing is shown in Figure 8. Region-based segmentation usually has problems dealing with these line-drawings because the intensity values in the different regions are the same. The only information comes from the contours. Results of the segmentation on graylevel images are shown in Figure 9. The original image is shown on the left; the segmentations are shown in the middle. The right column shows the edges of the segmentation. The edges are shown just because the contrast between two different segments in the middle figure may not be high enough to be seen. As we have argued earlier, regions are more useful than just edges. The reader is urged to check the edge image while examining the segmentation. Notice the extended weak contrast edges in the images: (1) between the bodies of the penguins and the snow; (2) between the suit and the pants in the third image; (3) between the man's jacket and the woman's blouse in the fourth image. Our algorithm is able to pick them up

Fig. 6. Top left: the Kanizsa triangle. While we perceive a triangle occluding 3 circles, any region segmentation technique based just on intensity will invariably find 3 "pacman" figures. Middle: the orientation energy from contours (OE_{con}). Right: orientation energy after contour propagation (OE_{tot}). Notice that contour propagation also produces spurious extensions around the figure. We argue that they are unavoidable and the only way to resolve the problem is through a global criterion. Bottom: The sequence of segmentation as obtained from our recursive partitioning. Notice that the spurious contour propagation does not affect our segmentation. The reason is that the global criterion is able to gather information from the whole image and realize that the spurious contour propagation is not significant.

without producing lots of random edgels everywhere, as would be expected from an edge detector. The fifth image demonstrates a combination of line drawing and paint, which is segmented by our algorithm as well. Notice once again that the same parameter settings were used for all segmentation results shown in Figures 6 to 9. Running times of the algorithm are on the order of 3-5 minutes for 200×200 images on a Pentium II.

6 Discussions

In our study, we have not investigated the issue of occlusion. Previous work on subjective contours has tried to reason about occlusions through junctions, corners and line ends at the same time contours are formed. However, we believe that local detection of key-points is unreliable. Instead, once a reliable segmentation is produced, junctions can be easily detected as the intersection of regions. Moreover, junctions in the image does not always correspond to occlusion events. For example, any objects with surface markings will produce lots of "junctions"

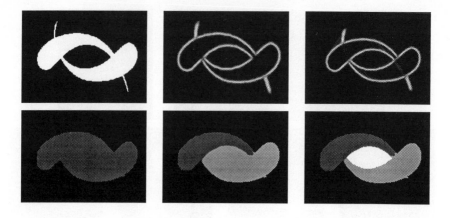

Fig. 7. Top left: the Kanizsa "2-fish" image — two mutually occluding fishes with the bodies of each overlapping the tails of the other. Middle and Right: orientation energy due to contours (OE_{con}) and after propagation (OE_{cp}). Notice the spurious completion around the figure. Bottom: the sequence of recursive partitioning. The "tails" are missed because they are too small.

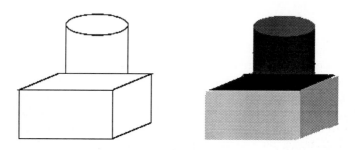

Fig. 8. A linedrawing and its segmentation into regions found by our algorithm. Traditional region-based segmentation techniques would be completely useless on this image because the intensity or color in the different regions are identical.

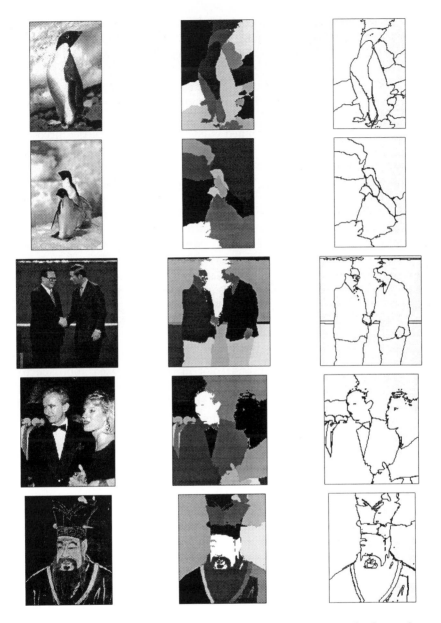

Fig. 9. The segmentation of gray-level images. Original image in the first column, segmentation in the middle, and the edges of the segments in the third. The edges are shown to indicate the boundaries between the segments in cases where the contrast in the middle figure may not be high enough to be seen. Notice the weak contrast edges in the images and our segmentation result. The same parameter settings were used for all the results shown in Figures 6 to 9.

in the image. We believe the problem of occlusion, or more generally figure-ground segregation is best tackled when contour belongingness and junctions are considered at the same time. For example, the Gestalt grouping factor of symmetry is a useful cue for figure-ground determination. A pair of symmetry contours suggest that the contours and the space in between are likely to belong to the same object, thus the "figure". Contours, together with junctions, can provide better figure ground segregation.

In our work, we have only studied curvilinear grouping in the direction parallel to the curve. However, Heitger and von der Heydt [9] showed that contour completion also occurs at line ends, inducing subjective contours orthogonal to the direction of the line ends. Our algorithm can be easily extended to take this into account. Together with orientation energy, we can compute *end-stop energy*. Contour propagation will then occur from locations of high end-stop energy perpendicular to the orientation of the line ends.

Note that in this paper, we have only considered gray-level and color images. However, real images will also have texture. The normalized cuts framework can incorporate texture information very naturally. Techniques for doing texture segmentation in the normalized cuts framework are studied in [1, 26]. However, the effect of contour continuation in textured regions may have to be treated in a more subtle fashion, depending on the class of texture [3]. We are exploring this in ongoing work.

To conclude, we have presented a technique of combining information about curvilinear continuity, intensity and color in a region-based approach to perform image segmentation. Contour information is obtained through orientation energy. Low contrast gaps or subjective contours are completed by the propagation of orientation energy. Segmentation results for a large varieties of images are demonstrated.

Acknowledgement

The authors would like to thank Serge Belongie and Jianbo Shi for valuable discussions related to this work. This research was supported by (ARO) DAAH04-96-1-0341, the Digital Library Grant IRI-9411334, and a Berkeley Fellowship.

References

1. S. Belongie and J. Malik. Finding boundaries in natural images: A new method using point descriptors and area completion. In *Proc. 5th Euro. Conf. Comp. Vision*, Freiburg, Germany, June 1998.

2. I.J. Cox, J.M. Regh, and S. Hingorani. A bayesian multiple-hypothesis approach to edge grouping and contour segmentation. *Int. J. of Comp. Vision*, 11(1), 1993.

3. B. Dubuc and S.W. Zucker. Indexing visual representations through the complexity map. In *Proc. 5th Int. Conf. Computer Vision*, Cambridge,MA,U.S.A., June 1995.

4. J.H. Elder and S.W. Zucker. Computing contour closures. In *Proc. Euro. Conf. Computer Vision*, volume I, Cambridge, England, Apr 1996.

5. D.J. Field, A. Hayes, and R.F. Hess. Contour integration by the human visual system: evidence for a local "association field". *Vision Research*, 33(2), 1993.

6. D. Geiger and K. Kumaran. Visual organization of illusory surfaces. In *Proc. Euro. Conf. Computer Vision*, volume I, Cambridge, England, Apr 1996.

7. S. Geman and D. Geman. Stochastic relaxation, gibbs distribution, and the bayesian retoration of images. *IEEE Trans. PAMI.*, 6, Nov. 1984.

8. G. Guy and G. Medioni. Inferring global perceptual contours from local features. *Int. J. of Computer Vision*, 20(1-2), Oct. 1996.

9. F. Heitger and R. von der Heydt. A computational model of neural contour processing. In *Proc. Int. Conf. Computer Vision*, Berlin, Germany, May 1993.

10. B.K.P. Horn. The curve of least energy. *ACM Trans. on Math. Soft.*, 9(4), 1983.

11. D. Jacobs. Robust and efficient detection of salient convex groups. *IEEE Trans. Pattern Anal. Mach. Intell.*, 18(1), Jan. 1996.

12. G. Kanizsa. *Organization in vision: essays on gestalt perception.* Praeger, 1979.

13. P.J. Kellman and T.F. Shipley. A theory of visual interpolation in object perception. *Cognitive Psychology*, 23, 1991.

14. U. Montanari. On the optimal detection of curves in noisy pictures. *Comm. Ass. Comput.*, 14, 1971.

15. M.C. Morrone and D.C. Burr. Feature detection in human vision: a phase dependent energy model. *Proc. R. Soc. Lond. B*, 235, 1988.

16. M.C. Morrone and R.A. Owens. Feature detection from local energy. *Pattern Recognition Letters*, 6, 1987.

17. D. Mumford. Elastica and computer vision. In Chandrajit Bajaj, editor, *Algebraic Geometry and Its Applications.* Springer Verlag, 1994.

18. D. Mumford and J. Shah. Optimal approximations by piecewise smooth functions, and associated variational problems. *Comm. Pure Math.*, 1989.

19. K. Nakayama and S. Shimojo. Experiencing and perceiving visual surfaces. *Science*, 257, Sept 1992.

20. M. Nitzberg, D. Mumford, and T. Shiota. *Filtering, Segmentation and Depth.* Springer-Verlag, 1993.

21. P. Parent and S.W. Zucker. Trace inference, curvature consistency, and curve detection. *IEEE Trans. Pattern Anal. Mach. Intell.*, 11(8), Aug. 1989.

22. F. Schumann. Contriutions to the analysis of visual perception — first paper: some observations on the combination of visual impressions into units (a. hogg, trans.). In S. Petry and G. Meyer, editors, *The perception of illusory contours.* Springer-Verlag, 1987. (original work published 1900).

23. A. Sha'ashua and S. Ullman. Structural saliency: the detection of globally salient structures using a locally connected network. In *Proc. 2nd Int. Conf. Computer Vision*, Tampa, Fl., U.S.A., 1988.

24. E. Sharon, A. Brandt, and R. Basri. Completion energies and scale. In *Proc. IEEE Conf. Comp. Vision and Pat. Rec.*, San Juan, Puerto Rico, June 1997.

25. J. Shi and J. Malik. Normalized cuts and image segmentation. In *Proc. IEEE Conf. Computer Vision and Pattern Recognition*, San Juan, Puerto Rico, June 1997.

26. J. Shi and J. Malik. Self inducing relational distance and its application to image segmentation. In *Proc. 5th Euro. Conf. Comp. Vis.*, Freiburg, Germany, June 1998.

27. S. Ullman. Filling-in the gaps: the shape of subjective contours and a model for their generation. *Biological Cybernetics*, 25, 1976.

28. M. Wertheimer. Laws of organization in perceptual forms (partial translation). In W.B. Ellis, editor, *A sourcebook of Gestalt Psychology.* Harcourt Brace and Company, 1938.

29. L.R. Williams and D.W. Jacobs. Local parallel computation of stochastic completion fields. *Neural Computation*, 9(4), May 1997.

Colour and Indexing
Grouping and Segmentation
Tracking

On Spatial Quantization of Color Images*

Jens Ketterer, Jan Puzicha, Marcus Held,
Martin Fischer, Joachim M. Buhmann, and Dieter Fellner

Institut für Informatik III,
Rheinische Friedrich–Wilhelms–Universität
Römerstraße 164, D-53117 Bonn, Germany
email:{ketterer,jan,held,jb,dieter}@cs.uni-bonn.de
WWW:http://www-dbv.cs.uni-bonn.de

Abstract. Image quantization and dithering are fundamental image
processing problems in computer vision and graphics. Both steps are
generally performed sequentially and, in most cases, independent of each
other. Color quantization with a pixel-wise defined distortion measure
and the dithering process with its local neighborhood typically optimize
different quality criteria or, frequently, follow a heuristic approach without reference to any quality measure.
In this paper we propose a new model to *simultaneously* quantize and
dither color images. The method is based on a rigorous cost–function
approach which optimizes a quality criterion derived from a simplified
model of human perception. Optimizations are performed by an efficient
multiscale procedure which substantially alleviates the computational
burden.
The quality criterion and the optimization algorithms are evaluated on
a representative set of artificial and real–world images thereby showing
a significant image quality improvement over standard color reduction
approaches.

1 Introduction

True color images typically contain up to 16 million different colors. One of the
basic tasks of low level image processing consists of reducing the number of colors with minimal visual distortion. Such a coarse graining of colors is important
for fast image manipulation on a reduced *color palette*, for computational efficiency in subsequent image processing and computer vision applications, and for
image coding and transmission. Furthermore, many image display and printing
devices provide only a limited number of colors. The representation problem for
colors aggravates when many images are displayed simultaneously resulting in
a palette size of 256 or even substantially less colors assigned to each image.
Several techniques have been proposed for color reduction, most of which obey
a two–step scheme:

* A more detailed report is found in [16]. This work has been supported by the German
Research Foundation (DFG) under grant #BU 914/3–1, by the German Israel Foundation for Science and Research Development (GIF) under grant #1-0403-001.06/95
and by the Federal Ministry for Education, Science and Technology (BMBF #01 M
3021 A/4).

Fig. 1. Pointillism artwork: Paul Baum (1859–1928): Place à St. Anna, Hollande, 1905.

1. Initially, a color set is selected by minimizing a proper *pixel distortion* error. Examples are the popular median–cut quantizer [1] and the application of a variety of clustering methods like LBG [2] or agglomerative clustering [3]. In fact, any suitable clustering approach could be used, see [4] for an overview. It is a characteristic fact for all clustering approaches, that they neglect spatial, i. e. contextual, information.

2. Several types of degradation appear in the quantized image due to the limited number of colors. The most severe is the appearance of contouring artifacts in uniform regions. *Dithering* methods as a subsequent processing step provide a way to address this problem by exploiting a property of the human visual system. Human beings perceive high frequency spatial variations in color without preferred direction as a *uniform* color, which can be understood as an averaging superposition. Impressionistic painters from the French school of pointillism have exploited this effect in a spectacular way as illustrated in Fig. 1. Therefore, additional illusionary colors can be created by spatial mixing. In a common dithering technique called *error diffusion* the quantization error is spread to neighboring pixels, i.e. the distortion at neighboring pixels is biased in opposite direction. Several error diffusion filters have been proposed [5, 6].

Quantization and dithering are generally performed sequentially. Therefore, quantization and dithering usually optimize different quality criteria. While clustering distortion measures like the well–known K–means cost function are exclusively pixel–based, dithering techniques rely on spatial information and distribute the distortion error among neighboring pixels. Joint quantization and dithering approaches have been considered only occasionally on a heuristic ad–hoc basis [7].

In this paper we propose a rigorous cost–function based approach, which simultaneously performs quantization and dithering of color images in a joint error minimizing algorithmic step, which we refer to as *spatial quantization*. The presented cost function extends the K–means criterion to a spatially weighted distortion measure. It, thereby, incorporates dithering techniques into the quantization cost–function. The strengths of both, quantization and dithering, are combined in a rigorous fashion leading to a significant improvement in image display quality.

From our point of view a successful optimization approach consists of two conceptually well–separated parts:

1. A good quality criterion, which appropriately *models* the information processing task: For color reduction the global minima of the cost function should correspond to psychophysically pleasing image reproductions.
2. An efficient optimization algorithm to minimize the proposed cost function.

We develop two closely related optimization algorithms for the spatial clustering criterion, (i) an extension of the Iterative Conditional Mode (ICM) algorithm, which is similar in spirit to K–means clustering and (ii) a *deterministic annealing* variant along the lines of the maximum entropy quantization [8].

While ICM is fast, it is a purely local optimization procedure. Deterministic Annealing (DA) as a homotopy method inspired by statistical physics is closely related to simulated annealing and has been empirically shown to be fast, yet to possess global optimization properties in the sense, that optimal or near optimal solutions are found and bad local minima are avoided. We extend the convergence proof for assignment problems given in [9] to the case of additional continuous parameters and derive efficient mean-field equations for spatial clustering.

Both ICM and DA are significantly accelerated by applying *multiscale optimization* techniques [10]. Multiscale optimization can be understood as the minimization of the original cost function over a properly reduced search space and has been shown to substantially accelerate the algorithms for other clustering cost functions [11]. For spatial quantization the corresponding cost functions on coarse image grids are derived.

In Sect. 2 we discuss color spaces and present the novel dithered color quantization cost function. Sect. 3 is dedicated to optimization methods. Multiscale expressions are derived and both DA and ICM are discussed in detail. Results are presented in Sect. 4 followed by a short conclusion.

2 Combining Quantization and Error Diffusion

2.1 Perception model

The spatial frequency response of the human vision system performs poorly at high frequencies due to the finite resolution of the human eye and the physical limitations of display devices. Thus, additional imaginary colors can be generated by *digital half-toning*. To simplify the model of imaginary colors the chosen color space should represent perceived superposition of colors as linear superpositions. A color space with this property is called a *uniform* or *linear color space*. The commonly used RGB color space and its linear derivates do not define linear color spaces. In contrast, the CIE Lab color space [12] represents differences in color by the Euclidean metric in a psychophysically meaningful way, although it is well known to suffer from some minor defects [13]. To overcome this shortness, new non-Euclidean metrics were proposed. Despite these facts, in this paper RGB and CIE Lab color spaces with the Euclidean metric are used for computational simplicity and to provide a general interface for other color spaces.

Having defined a linear color space U, we propose to model human perception as a blurring operation, i.e. a convolution of the image with a Gaussian kernel to ensure locality. To obtain a formulation for a discrete image grid we introduce a neighborhood system $\mathcal{N}_i$ defined as the spatial support for a Gaussian kernel with standard deviation σ centered at pixel i. We define the weights w_{ij} for neighborhood pixels as

$$w_{ij} \sim \exp\left(-\frac{(i-j)^2}{\sigma^2}\right), \quad \sum_{j \in \mathcal{N}_i} w_{ij} = 1 \ . \tag{1}$$

The perceived color $c_i \in U$ at location i for a given image is modeled as

$$c_i(x) = \sum_{j \in \mathcal{N}_i} w_{ij} x_j \ , \tag{2}$$

where $x_j \in U$ denotes the pixel value at location j.

2.2   Spatial Quantization Cost Function

To define the spatial quantization cost function we first introduce a set or palette of colors, which are denoted by a vector of prototype variables $Y = (y_\nu^t)_{\nu=1,\dots,K}$, $y_\nu \in U \subset \mathbb{R}^3$, where U is again the linear color space defined above and the superscript t denotes the transpose of a vector. A quantization is then defined as an assignment of pixel colors x_i to prototypical colors y_ν, which is formalized by Boolean assignment variables $M_{i\nu} \in \{0,1\}$. $M_{i\nu} = 1(0)$ denotes that the image site x_i is (is not) quantized to color y_ν. All assignments are summarized in terms of a Boolean assignment matrix $M \in \mathcal{M}$, where

$$\mathcal{M} = \left\{ M \in \{0,1\}^{N \times K} : \sum_{\nu=1}^{K} M_{i\nu} = 1, \ 1 \leq i \leq N \right\} \ . \tag{3}$$

As a cost function for faithful color reproduction we employ the pixel-wise distance between the perceived image before and after quantization. For a linear color space the Euclidean norm is the natural choice yielding costs[1]

$$\mathcal{H}(M,Y) = \sum_{i=1}^{N} \left\| \left(\sum_{j \in \mathcal{N}_i} w_{ij} x_j \right) - \left(\sum_{j \in \mathcal{N}_i} \sum_{\nu=1}^{K} M_{j\nu} w_{ij} y_\nu \right) \right\|^2 \ . \tag{4}$$

---

[1] The classical K–means cost function is obtained for $w_{ij} = \delta_{ij}$ and can be understood as the special case of our model with a blur free perception model.

The task of spatial quantization is then defined as a search for a parameter set $(\boldsymbol{M}, \boldsymbol{Y})$ which minimizes (4) [2]. In contrast to the K-means cost function, which is linear with respect to discrete and continuous parameter set, (4) is quadratic. Standard quantization techniques are computationally efficient, whereas our color quantization approach achieves substantially better modeling quality at higher computational costs. The reader should be aware at this point that changes in the model of human perception only result in a different cost function, when the perception model is no longer linear w.r.t. the input image. Thus (4) covers a broad range of possible perception models.

The cost function (4) can be rewritten as a quadratic form in the assignment variables and in the continuous variables $\boldsymbol{Y}$. For this purpose, we introduce a new, enlarged neighborhood

$$\tilde{\mathcal{N}}_i = \{k : \exists j : j \in \mathcal{N}_i \wedge j \in \mathcal{N}_k\} \ . \tag{5}$$

Abbreviate

$$b_{ij} = \sum_{\substack{k \in \mathcal{N}_i \\ \wedge k \in \mathcal{N}_j}} w_{ik} w_{jk}, \ \ j \in \tilde{\mathcal{N}}_i, \quad a_i = -2 \sum_{j \in \tilde{\mathcal{N}}_i} b_{ij} x_j \tag{6}$$

and note that b_{ij} is translation and rotation invariant and depends only on $|i - j|$ for our specific perception model (1). An equivalent expression for (4) is given by

$$\mathcal{H}(\boldsymbol{M}, \boldsymbol{Y}) = \sum_{i=1}^{N} \sum_{j \in \tilde{\mathcal{N}}_i} \sum_{\nu=1}^{K} \sum_{\alpha=1}^{K} b_{ij} M_{j\nu} M_{i\alpha} \boldsymbol{y}_{\nu}^t \boldsymbol{y}_{\alpha} + \sum_{i=1}^{N} \sum_{\nu=1}^{K} M_{i\nu} \boldsymbol{a}_i^t \boldsymbol{y}_{\nu} \ , \tag{7}$$

which makes the quadratic nature of $\mathcal{H}$ explicit. Constant terms without influence on either the assignments or the prototypes have been discarded.

3 Optimization for Spatial Quantization

3.1 Multiscale Optimization

The statistics of natural images support the assumption that colors are distributed homogeneously in images, i. e. pixels adjacent to each other contain with high probability similar colors. This fact can be exploited to significantly accelerate the optimization process by minimizing the criterion over a suitable nested sequence of subspaces in a coarse to fine manner. Each of these subspaces is spanned by a greatly reduced number of optimization variables. In contrast to most multi-resolution optimization schemes the identical cost function is optimized at all grids, solely the variable configuration space is reduced.

---

[2] It is also possible to (partially) fix a set of prototypes, e.g. a set of available colors, and to optimize the assignments of pixels to colors alone. Therefore, this cost function provides also a new method for dithering an image given a fixed color table.

This strategy is formalized by the concept of *multiscale optimization* [10] and it leads in essence to cost functions redefined on a coarsened version of the original image. Formally, we denote by $\mathcal{S}^0 = \mathcal{S}$ the original set of sites and we assume that a set of grid sites $\mathcal{S}^l = \{1, \ldots, N^l\}$ is given for each coarse grid level l. Throughout this section coarse/fine grid entities are denoted by upper/lower case letters. Define a coarsening map C_l on the sets of indices:

$$C_l : \mathcal{S}^l \to \mathcal{S}^{l+1}, \qquad i \mapsto I = C_l(i) , \tag{8}$$

where each fine grid point is linked to a single coarse grid point. Typically $\mathcal{S}^0 = \mathcal{S}$ corresponds to the set of pixel sites and $\mathcal{S}^{l+1}$ is obtained by sub-sampling $\mathcal{S}^l$ by a factor of 2 in each direction, i. e. 4 sites are combined into a single coarse site by the two–dimensional index operation $(I, J) = (\lfloor i/2 \rfloor, \lfloor j/2 \rfloor)$. Since this operation is a many-to-one map the inverse C_l^{-1} is a subset of the fine grid sites, $C_l^{-1}(I) \subset \mathcal{S}_l$. Multiscale optimization proceeds not by coarsening the image, but by *coarsening the variable space*. Each coarse grid is associated with a reduced set of optimization variables $\boldsymbol{M}^l \in \mathcal{M}^l$,

$$\mathcal{M}^l = \left\{ \left(M_{I\nu}^l \right)_{\substack{I=1,\ldots,N^l \\ \nu=1,\ldots,K}} : M_{I\nu}^l \in \{0,1\} \right\} . \tag{9}$$

Thus K Boolean variables $M_{I\nu}^l$ are attached to each grid point I denoting whether the set of respective pixels is assigned to color $\boldsymbol{y}_\nu$. Coarsened cost functions at level $l+1$ are defined recursively by proper restriction of the optimization space at level l:

$$\mathcal{H}^{l+1}(\boldsymbol{M}^{l+1} \in \mathcal{M}^{l+1}, \boldsymbol{Y}) := \mathcal{H}^l(\boldsymbol{M}^l \in \tilde{\mathcal{M}}^l : M_{i\nu}^l = M_{C_l(i)\nu}^{l+1}, \boldsymbol{Y}) , \tag{10}$$

where

$$\tilde{\mathcal{M}}^l = \left\{ \boldsymbol{M}^l \in \mathcal{M}^l : M_{i\nu}^l = M_{j\nu}^l \text{ for } C_l(i) = C_l(j) \right\} \tag{11}$$

denotes the subspace $\tilde{\mathcal{M}}^l \subset \mathcal{M}^l$ with identical assignments for sites with the same coarse grid point. Now introduce a coarse grid neighborhood by

$$\tilde{\mathcal{N}}_I^{l+1} = \left\{ J : \exists i \in C_l^{-1}(I), j \in C_l^{-1}(J) : j \in \tilde{\mathcal{N}}_i^l \right\} . \tag{12}$$

We recursively define

$$b_{IJ}^{l+1} = \sum_{i \in C_l^{-1}(I)} \sum_{\substack{j \in C_l^{-1}(J) \\ \wedge j \in \tilde{\mathcal{N}}_i}} b_{ij}^l, \qquad a_I^{l+1} = \sum_{i \in C_l^{-1}(I)} a_i^l . \tag{13}$$

For the spatial quantization cost function (7) the following coarse grid cost functions are obtained applying definition (10):

$$\mathcal{H}^l(\boldsymbol{M}^l, \boldsymbol{Y}) = \sum_{I=1}^{N^l} \sum_{J \in \tilde{\mathcal{N}}_I^l} \sum_{\nu=1}^K \sum_{\alpha=1}^K b_{IJ}^l M_{I\nu}^l M_{J\alpha}^l \boldsymbol{y}_\nu^t \boldsymbol{y}_\alpha + \sum_{I=1}^{N^l} \sum_{\nu=1}^K M_{I\nu}^l \left(a_I^l \right)^t \boldsymbol{y}_\nu . \tag{14}$$

Note, that $\mathcal{H}^l$ has the same functional form as $\mathcal{H}^0 = \mathcal{H}$ and, therefore, an optimization algorithm developed for $\mathcal{H}$ is applicable to any coarse grid cost function $\mathcal{H}^l$ without change.

3.2 Deterministic Annealing

A common way to optimize mixed combinatorial optimization problems such as $\mathcal{H}(\boldsymbol{M}, \boldsymbol{Y})$ is by an alternating minimization scheme, i.e. to optimize with respect to the discrete parameters keeping the continuous parameters fixed and then to optimize the continuous parameters for a fixed discrete set. This twofold optimization is iterated until a predefined convergence criterion is fulfilled.

For fixed $\boldsymbol{Y}$ the cost function $\mathcal{H}(\boldsymbol{M}, \boldsymbol{Y}) = \mathcal{H}(\boldsymbol{M})$ expresses a purely combinatorial problem, which can be efficiently tackled by the class of *annealing methods*. The basic idea of annealing methods is to treat the unknown Boolean variables as random variables, to introduce a scale parameter T, often called the computational temperature, and to calculate equilibrium Gibbs averages of assignments $M_{i\nu}$. This estimate can be achieved either by Monte Carlo sampling or (at least approximately) by analytical methods. The temperature T is gradually lowered and for $T \to 0$ a solution of the combinatorial optimization problem is obtained. In Deterministic Annealing (DA) approaches [8, 14] the stochasticity is incorporated in a *probabilistic formulation* of the optimization problem and a *deterministic optimization* is performed over a *probabilistic state space* $\mathcal{Q}(\mathcal{M})$. The minimization is carried out over the space of factorial distributions

$$\mathcal{Q} = \left\{ Q(\boldsymbol{M}) := \prod_{i=1}^{N} \sum_{\nu=1}^{K} M_{i\nu} m_{i\nu}, \; \forall \boldsymbol{M} \in \mathcal{M} \right\} \tag{15}$$

to guarantee computational tractability and efficiency. For factorial distributions random variables at different sites are independent, i.e. $\langle M_{i\nu} M_{j\alpha} \rangle_Q = \langle M_{i\nu} \rangle_Q \langle M_{j\alpha} \rangle_Q$ is valid for $i \neq j$. Furthermore, the distribution parameters $m_{i\nu}$ equal the variable expectations, $m_{i\nu} = \langle M_{i\nu} \rangle_Q$. The original cost function $\mathcal{H}$ over $\mathcal{M}$ is embedded in the family of smoothed cost functions over $\mathcal{Q}$

$$\mathcal{F}_T(Q) = \langle \mathcal{H} \rangle_Q - T S(Q) \;, \tag{16}$$

where S denotes the entropy. $\mathcal{F}_T$ is called *generalized free energy* referring to its usage in statistical physics and it is convex over $\mathcal{Q}$ for sufficiently large T. Thus $\mathcal{F}_T$ can be understood as a *coarse* version of $\mathcal{H}$ while T takes the role of a *scale parameter* in optimization space. Denote by $Q^{i\alpha}$ the matrix obtained by replacing the i-th row of $Q = (m_{i\nu})$ with the unit vector $\boldsymbol{e}_\alpha$. The fundamental relationship [9]

$$m_{i\nu} = \frac{\exp\left(-\langle \mathcal{H} \rangle_{Q^{i\nu}} / T\right)}{\sum_{\alpha=1}^{K} \exp\left(-\langle \mathcal{H} \rangle_{Q^{i\alpha}} / T\right)} \tag{17}$$

is valid for distributions Q minimizing (16). A transcendental system of equations is obtained for the $m_{i\nu}$ from (17), which is solved by an asynchronous, iterative and convergent fixed-point relaxation. DA can be understood as a continuation method [14], since the (unique) minimum at high temperature is tracked while gradually lowering ('annealing') T. The local ICM–algorithm is obtained in the $T = 0$ limit, where $m_{i\nu} \in \{0, 1\}$ and $m_{i\nu} = M_{i\nu} = 1$, iff $\nu = \arg\max_\alpha \langle\mathcal{H}\rangle_{Q^{i\alpha}}$.

We now turn to the derivation of mean-field equations for the general spatial clustering cost function. Both ICM and DA are implemented using an efficient bookkeeping scheme. The so–called meanfields $\langle\mathcal{H}\rangle_{Q^{i\nu}}$ are given by

$$\langle\mathcal{H}\rangle_{Q^{i\nu}} = y_\nu^t \left(p_i + b_{ii} y_\nu\right) \tag{18}$$

with the bookkeeping entities

$$p_i = 2 \sum_{\substack{j \in \tilde{\mathcal{N}}_i \\ j \neq i}} b_{ij} \sum_{\alpha=1}^{K} m_{j\alpha} y_\alpha + a_i \ . \tag{19}$$

For fixed Boolean variables M the optimization of $\mathcal{H}(M, Y) = \mathcal{H}(Y)$ yields a simple matrix equation. Let $S = (s_{\nu\alpha}) \in \mathbb{R}^K \times \mathbb{R}^K$ and $R = (r_\nu^t) \in \mathbb{R}^K \times \mathbb{R}^3$, where

$$s_{\nu\alpha} = \sum_{i=1}^{N} \sum_{j \in \tilde{\mathcal{N}}_i} b_{ij} m_{i\nu} m_{j\alpha}, \qquad r_\nu = \sum_{i=1}^{N} m_{i\nu} a_i \ , \tag{20}$$

then the generalized free energy (16) is equivalent to the quadratic form

$$\mathcal{F}_T(Q) \equiv \langle\mathcal{H}(Y)\rangle_Q = \sum_{\nu=1}^{K} \sum_{\alpha=1}^{K} s_{\nu\alpha} y_\alpha^t y_\nu + \sum_{\nu=1}^{K} r_\nu^t y_\nu \ . \tag{21}$$

Therefore the optimal Y is given by

$$Y = -(2S)^{-1} R \ . \tag{22}$$

For fixed T the overall alternating minimization scheme can be proven to converge to a local minimum of (16). In the proof given in [15] for arbitrary assignment problems the free energy (16) plays the role of a Lyapunov function. Extending this proof to mixed combinatorial problems it is straight forward to show that (22) also decreases the free energy in each step, see [16] for details. For large T the inverse of S becomes singular and the system of linear equations is solved e.g. by a conjugate gradient method or the Moore–Penrose inverse to avoid numerical instabilities.

3.3 Multiscale Annealing

Algorithms like K–means or LBG efficiently minimize $\mathcal{H}$ by *splitting techniques* to obtain successive solutions for a growing number of clusters. For ICM we adopt an idea from K–means clustering by splitting clusters with high distortion. One of the key advantages of the DA approach is the *inherent splitting strategy.* Clusters degenerate at high temperature and they successively split at *bifurcations* or *phase transitions* when T is lowered [8]. Therefore, at a specific temperature scale an easily measurable *effective number* K_T of clusters is visible. Since the number of effective data points available drastically reduces at coarser resolution levels, splitting strategy and coarse–to–fine optimization should be interleaved. Thus for a given resolution level l we anneal until K_T exceeds a certain maximal number of clusters $K_{\max}^l$ for some temperature T^*. After prolongation to level $(l-1)$ the DA optimization is continued at temperature T^*. This scheme has been introduced as *multiscale annealing* in [11], where also the question of choosing the maximal number of clusters for a given resolution has been addressed in a statistical learning theory context. We adopt this approach by choosing $K_{\max}^l \sim N^l/\log N^l$ and by determining the proportionality factor on an empirical basis. The complete algorithm is summarized in Algorithm I.

Algorithm I

```
INPUT wij, xi, K
INITIALIZE m_{iν}^{lmax} randomly, temperature T = Tstart, l = lmax;
COMPUTE ai, bij according to (6), a_I^l, b_{IJ}^l according to (13).
WHILE (T > TFINAL) and (l ≥ 0) (multiscale annealing)
    REPEAT
        REPEAT
            generate a permutation π ∈ SN
            FOR i = 1, ... , N^l
                update all m_{π(i)ν}^l according to (17)
        UNTIL converged
        UPDATE Y according to (22)
    UNTIL converged
    IF K_T > K_{max}^l PROPAGATE m_{Iν}^l to m_{iν}^{l-1}, SET l = l - 1
    ELSE SET T = η · T, 0 < η < 1
SET M_{Iν}^l = δ_{ν,arg max_α m_{Iα}} (winner-takes-all rule)
WHILE (l ≥ 0) (T = 0 ICM-optimization)
    PROPAGATE M_{Iν}^l to M_{iν}^{l-1}, SET l = l - 1
    REPEAT
        UPDATE M_{iν}^l by ICM until converged
        UPDATE Y according to (22)
    UNTIL converged
```

4 Results

The proposed spatial quantization algorithms are compared with several standard color image quantization methods, which all employ both quantization and dithering. As median cut quantizer [1] in conjunction with the Floyd–Steinberg (FS) dithering algorithm ppmquant found in the PPM tools by Jef Poskanzer is used. The octree quantization [17] implementation is based upon C code published in Dr. Dobbs Journal. As the most simple alternative we have applied a

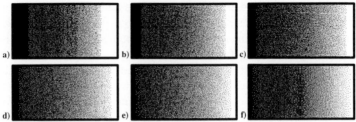

Fig. 2. Image quantization on a smooth transition of grey levels (256 different grey values): (a) to (e) spatial quantization with neighborhood sizes from 3×3 to 11×11 (from left to right), (f) Floyd–Steinberg (FS) dithering.

	Pool	Tea Pot	Mandrill	Rose	Golden Gate
Spatial quantization	0.29 (0.81) 72 s	0.39 (1.04) 115 s	1.54 (5.33) 213 s	0.97 (2.89) 19 s	0.92 (2.74) 174 s
median cut + FS	1.36 (1.95) 2 s	0.73 (1.27) 4 s	2.24 (4.36) 5 s	1.59 (2.95) 1 s	1.45 (2.66) 6 s
octree + FS	1.37 (2.36) 3 s	1.00 (1.86) 5 s	6.00 (8.76) 4 s	4.95 (6.67) <1 s	3.77 (5.13) 5 s
bit–cut + FS	9.79 (25.25) 1 s	18.98 (39.05) 1 s	27.1 (48.05) 1 s	22.02 (42.63) <1 s	28.45 (46.61) 1 s

Table 1. Comparison of different color image quantization methods for quantization to 64 colors. First row: Quality measured in terms of (4) on a scale $[0, 100]$ (average deviation). In brackets the quality measured by pixel–wise squared difference (K–means) is given. Second row: run–time in seconds (Pentium Pro 200MHz). ICM has been used for optimization in spatial quantization. Every quantization is performed in the RGB color space. The neighborhood size for our approach has been set to 5×5.

simple bit–cutting for quantization followed again by a Floyd–Steinberg dithering procedure [6]. A representative set of images has been chosen for comparison and evaluation, which are depicted in Fig. 4.

To examine the dithering properties of the novel cost function independently from the built–in quantization several runs on an artificial image with smooth transition of grey values as depicted in Fig. 2 have been carried out. To identify the role of the neighborhood size for the quality of our dithering approach is the main purpose of this experiment. The available two colors were fixed as black & white and only the assignments of pixels to the given color values were optimized.

It has to be noticed that the (subjective) dithering quality grows with neighborhood size. Starting with a neighborhood size of 5×5 a smooth transition between grey values is obtained, while the smaller neighborhood of 3×3 suffers from its limited variability to distribute black and white pixels and generates artificial 'edge' structures. In contrast, the Floyd–Steinberg algorithm introduces significant visual distortions by edge effects and over–regular patterns and it is not capable to generate a smooth transition of grey values. In Fig. 5 the full spatial quantization approach is compared to median cut / Floyd–Steinberg with respect to quality for different number of colors. The "Pool" image was selected for its large range of colors. Especially the billiard balls exhibit a smooth

	Pool	Tea Pot	Mandrill	Rose	Golden Gate
Multiscale optimization	0.62	0.83	2.38	1.71	1.64
	119 s	180 s	225 s	20 s	242 s
Single scale optimization	1.02	0.95	2.75	1.87	1.82
	259 s	373 s	666 s	65 s	429 s

Table 2. Comparison of multiscale and single scale methods. First row: Quality measured in terms of (4). Second row: run–time in seconds measured on a Pentium Pro 200MHz. The images were quantized to 16 colors with a neighborhood size of 7×7.

transition from dark to bright primary colors. It can be seen that the proposed algorithm is able to distribute the small number of available colors in a more efficient way than ppmquant. Notice especially the lack of any yellow color in the image quantized by ppmquant. This unsatisfactory behavior is caused by the large size of the green area in the original image. The median cut quantizer assigns too much resources, i. e. color prototypes, to green color values. This behavior is basically caused by the fact that median cut creates clusters with approximately equal size instead of rigorously optimizing a distortion measure. Depending on the number of desired colors only four to one prototypes are left for all other colors in the image. To represent the large range of leftover colors the center color was taken which is some greyish color[3].

In Fig. 6 the "Mandrill" image quantized to 8 colors is depicted. It is possible to reduce the number of colors from 171877 with only minor perceptive defects, since many illusionary colors are created by dithering. This result is illustrated by the magnification of the monkey's eye in Fig. 6 (b) and (c), which demonstrates that very different colors can be used to create a highly similar visual perception.

Fig. 7 studies the role of the chosen color space, in which the spatial quantization is performed. Quantization in CIE Lab space improves the rendering of bright colors by reducing the number of darker colors. At low luminance the human vision system looses its ability to distinguish chromaticity. For the "Tea Pot" image, reduced to 16 colors, just two (the RGB image reserves four) dark colors were needed to render the shadows, all other dark colors are imaginary. Instead more yellowish colors were allocated to reproduce all reflections and highlights correctly.

The quality and performance results for all images are summarized in Tab. 1. In absence of a better, psychophysically defined distortion measure the quality according to the K–means criterion and the novel spatial quantization cost function (4) are reported, although we are convinced that (4) better reflects visual distortion. As expected, according to its own cost function spatial quantization outperforms all other methods significantly. But even according to the K–means criterion it produces better results, which can be explained by the fact that the heuristic dithering procedures tend to increase the K–means distortion costs drastically.

The quality of spatial clustering is improved by better optimization techniques. In Fig. 3 quantization results of the image "Rose" to 4 colors are de-

---

[3] A more complete comparison with other color reduction schemes is found in [16].

picted. The costs obtained according to (4) by the deterministic annealing (DA) algorithm are lower than the cost of the ICM solution. The resulting images clearly indicate that better minimization techniques can result in an improved perception quality of the color reduced image. In the ICM solution some smaller details (especially in the lower right corner) vanish. For a more detailed discussion of the deterministic annealing approach for color quantization see [16].

Fig. 3 also indicates that color reduction down to 4 colors still results in recognizable images, which might be of interest for generating iconized images in multimedia applications. Also, some widespread operating systems restrict icons to resolutions of 32×32 with a maximum of 12 colors.

On the other hand it has to be stressed that the computational complexity of spatial quantization increases significantly in comparison to the other methods, see again Tab. 1. It is therefore of particular importance to design efficient optimization algorithms such as the multiscale approach. As seen in Tab. 2 multiscale optimization accelerates the optimization by a factor 2–5. Fig. 8 illustrates the typical progress in multiscale optimization. According to (13) colors in coarse images are replaced by local averaging, thus coarse grid colors correspond to perceived colors. At the same time the neighborhood smoothing kernel sharpens according to (13). Therefore, spatial optimization on coarser grids has a tendency to suppress dithering of colors. Thus a bias towards local minima with homogeneous colors is introduced. On the other hand it is well–known that multiscale coarsening leads to an *implicit smoothing* of the energy landscape [10] and therefore avoids bad local minima. This effect is confirmed by the results in Tab. 2.

 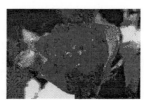 

Fig. 3. Original image "Rose" (left), spatial quantization with ICM using 4 colors (center), spatial quantization with DA using 4 colors (right).

5 Conclusion

We have presented a novel approach to simultaneous color image quantization and dithering on the basis of a novel quality measure. This criterion incorporates error diffusion in the clustering cost function and it is motivated by a model of the human visual system. An efficient deterministic annealing algorithm has been developed and an extension to multiscale optimization has been derived to accelerate the algorithmic process.

Using a rigorous cost function approach it is possible to evaluate the modeling quality independently of the optimization procedure. The algorithm has been shown to yield a significant improvement in quality compared to alternative approaches on a large set of images. The results are especially impressive for small color palettes, where standard quantization schemes completely fail. Moreover, it is possible to incorporate a (partially) predefined color palette in the optimization process.

In the derivation of the cost function a simplified model of human perception has been used. More elaborated models with emphasis on color constancy and feature preservation will be discussed elsewhere.

References

1. P. Heckbert, "Color image quantization for frame buffer displays," *Computer Graphics*, vol. 16, no. 3, pp. 297–307, 1982.
2. G. Braudaway, "A procedure for optimum choice of a small number of colors from a large palette for color imaging," in *Electron Imaging'87*, 1987.
3. Z. Xiang and G. Joy, "Color image quantization by agglomerative clustering," *IEEE Computer Graphics and Applications*, vol. 14, no. 3, pp. 44–48, 1994.
4. A. Jain and R. Dubes, *Algorithms for Clustering Data*. Prentice Hall, 1988.
5. R. Ulichney, "Dithering with blue noise," *Proceedings of the IEEE*, vol. 76, pp. 56–79, 1988.
6. R. Floyd and L. Steinberg, "An adaptive algorithm for spatial greyscale," in *Proc. SID, Vol. 17, No. 2*, Wiley, 1976.
7. L. Akarûn, D. Özdemir, and Ö. Yalcun, "Joint quantization and dithering of color images," in *Proceedings of the International Conference on Image Processing (ICIP'96)*, pp. 557–560, 1996.
8. K. Rose, E. Gurewitz, and G. Fox, "A deterministic annealing approach to clustering," *Pattern Recognition Letters*, vol. 11, pp. 589–594, 1990.
9. T. Hofmann, J. Puzicha, and J. Buhmann, "Deterministic annealing for unsupervised texture segmentation," in *Proc. of the EMMCVPR'97*, LNCS 1223, pp. 213–228, 1997.
10. F. Heitz, P. Perez, and P. Bouthemy, "Multiscale minimization of global energy functions in some visual recovery problems," *CVGIP: Image Understanding*, vol. 59, no. 1, pp. 125–134, 1994.
11. J. Puzicha and J. Buhmann, "Multiscale annealing for real–time unsupervised texture segmentation," Tech. Rep. IAI–97–4, Institut für Informatik III (a short version appeared in: Proc. ICCV'98, pp. 267–273), 1997.
12. C. I. de L'Eclairage, "Colorimetry." CIE Pub. 15.2 2nd ed., 1986.
13. D. Alman, "Industrial color difference evaluation," *Color Res. Appl. 18 137-139*, 1993.
14. G. Bilbro, W. Snyder, S. Garnier, and J. Gault, "Mean field annealing: A formalism for constructing GNC–like algorithms," *IEEE Transactions on Neural Networks*, vol. 3, no. 1, 1992.
15. T. Hofmann, J. Puzicha, and J. Buhmann, "A deterministic annealing framework for textured image segmentation," Tech. Rep. IAI-TR-96-2, Institut für Informatik III, 1996.
16. J. Puzicha, M. Held, J. Ketterer, J. Buhmann, and D. Fellner, "On spatial quantization of color images," Tech. Rep. IAI–TR–98–1, Department for Computer Science III, University Bonn, 1998.
17. M. Gervauz and W. Purgathofer, "A simple method for color quantization: Octree quantization," in *Graphic Gems*, pp. 287–293, Academic Press, New York, 1990.

Fig. 4. Original images used for the different experiments: (a) "Pool", (b) "Golden Gate", (c) "Mandrill", (d) "Tea Pot" and (e) grey wedge.

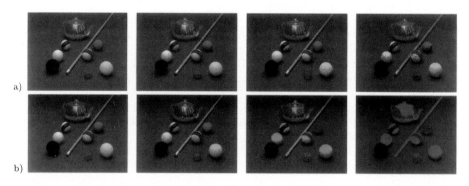

Fig. 5. Image quantization with different numbers of colors (from left to right: 256, 64, 32 and 16 colors): (a) spatial image quantization, (b) median cut quantization and Floyd–Steinberg (FS) dithering.

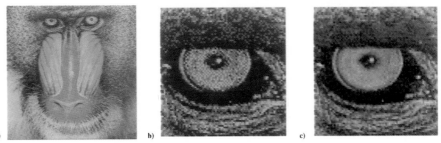

Fig. 6. Spatial quantization of the image "Mandrill": (a) Image with 8 colors, (b) detail of 8 color image and (c) same sub image from the original image with 171877 colors.

Fig. 7. Spatial image quantization using 16 colors in different color spaces ("Tea Pot" image): (a) RGB color space and (b) CIE Lab color space.

Fig. 8. Multi-scale optimization of the "Golden Gate". (a) to (d) intermediate coarse scale results ((a) 16 colors and (b) to (d) 32 colors), (e) resulting image (32 colors).

Using Ifs and Moments to Build a Quasi Invariant Image Index

Jean Michel Marie-Julie, Hassane Essafi

LETI(CEA-Technologies Avancées) DEIN/SLA - CEA Saclay
F91191 Gif sur Yvette Cedex France
jmmjulie@gaap.saclay.cea.fr
hessafi@gaap.saclay.cea.fr

Abstract. Automatic indexing or registration is an essential task for image databases. It allows to archive, organise and retrieve a large amount of images by using inner properties. In this paper, we propose an indexing technique which allows to solve indexing problems due to geometric or photometric transformations, inferred by the different image acquisitions. This approach is based on an invariant partition of the image thanks to the use of interest points (or keypoints) and a characterisation with Ifs parameters or barycentric moments. The research process is based on a similarity measure taking in account a numerical distance and a localisation criterion. This work is based on a local characterisation of the image, we use the interest points to build a triangular partition or a set of triangles. We associate to each polygon a vector containing its photometric properties. In other approaches the keypoints are directly characterised by local invariants. The use of the Ifs parameters to index the image has been studied in early publications, the improvement (robustness against rotations and scaling) comes from the use of the invariant partition and the barycentric coordinates. The research process is particularly important, it uses traditional spatial relations and integrate them with a numerical distance to calculate a score associated to each image.

1. Introduction

Automatic indexing or registration is an important task in all applications dealing with huge amount of images [1] [2] [3] [9]. It allows to associate to each image a numerical or symbolic representation which can be used for retrieval, model matching or recognition tasks. These representations have to integrate the need of the application in terms of robustness against image variations or transformations.

Lots of fields have real needs in image registration as for instance, medical imaging, satellite monitoring, multimedia industry production, and document processing. Some application examples could be the alignment of images from different medical modalities for diagnostic, or the monitoring of global land by using satellite images.

The first major tasks of the indexing or the registration is to find an image representation which is well suited to the application and close enough to an human visual perception. The second task is to synthesise a similarity measure as significant as possible for an human being, in other words close to his own conception of similarity.

The indexing must integrate some invariance properties in regard of image geometric (rotation, scaling, warping, perspective projection,...) and valuemetric (lightning variation, noise addition,...) transformations due to differences between several acquisitions (different time, different point of view,...). In some applications, these variations are well known and modelled, so the images can be corrected and realigned. But in major cases, the variations cannot been predicted, the indexing has to deal with. The ideal case is to obtain the same index for an image and the same image affected by some variations.

The image signature is represented as a set of numerical or symbolic features, commonly, this is a set of numerical vectors associated to geometric properties of image primitives (edges, regions, curves, interest points,...).

The main concept for defining a registration are :
— the feature space, the space where the numerical properties or symbolic information are expressed ;
— the similarity measure, the way to express the similarity between images
— the search space, the set of transformations, or hypothesis applied to the image request to aligned it with the images ;
— the search strategy, method to evaluate and validate the hypothesis inferred in the search space.

Different types of requests can be envisaged. For instance, the system can be asked to find all the images containing a fragment or similar to a given image or close to a sketch drawn by the user.

Two families of indexing methods can be found, the first one is based on the analysis of graphic primitives (as edges, lines, ellipses), the second one uses the photometric information of the image (e.g. the pixel values).

The analysis of graphic primitives consists in calculating local properties to construct a model [4] [14] [18]. Then, the research process involves a matching between the model and the image to recognise. This matching could be an expensive operation because of the number of models in the database.

These kinds of approach own some problems due to the difficulties to extract easily interesting primitives (compute a meaningful semantic segmentation of the image) especially with complex objects. Furthermore, the extraction which is a low-level process, has to be robust against variations generated by different acquisitions of the scene, it is very hard to fulfil this requirement. Another problem is that it is difficult to discriminate efficiently objects, because of the symbolic nature of the primitives.

The photometric analysis offers better discrimination properties and is less sensitive to local variation in the image. For instance the colour and some robust representations against the variations of the luminance [15] has been used. The Principal Component Analysis, *PCA* [16] for face recognition or in general case [9] [17] has been studied. The wavelet analysis allows a spectral and spatial analysis and an optimisation of the correlation approach [11].

But in major cases, they are global and non relevant to some requests (research of image fragments) or dedicated to specific images or realigned images.

At least, some local approaches consist in characterising keypoints (or interest points) by calculating invariant properties of the neighbourhood of the keypoints [12].

We adopt a local approach with a photometric analysis of small images regions. The feature space is a set of numerical photometric properties of the image regions. The basis framework is to segment the image in a set of polygonal regions and then to characterise each region by calculating photometric properties. The characterisations presented in this paper are the Ifs parameters and the moments of the image regions.

In this method, the invariance properties are introduced into the generation of the polygonal regions. These regions engender a partition or are simply a set of polygons.

We just present here two kinds of region characterisations, but others can be computed and we plan to study, for instance, some spectral/spatial or fractal representations.

We obtain interesting invariance (rotation, scaling and occlusion) and performances, in term of processing time.

This paper will present initially the indexing method. In this first part, we shall explain how the invariant partition or invariant set of polygons is built by using the interest points and we shall present two characterisations of the polygons (Ifs parameters and barycentric coordinates moments). Afterwards, the search strategy is presented. At last, we shall finish with some results and performances.

2. Indexing

The indexing is based on a invariant partition or polygons set of the image. The major interest of this method is to integrate a part of the invariant requirements in the partition. This index can be used to process different types of requests.

Then each polygon of the partition is characterised by using its inner properties. We shall present two characterisations, the first one uses the p-Ifs parameters and the second one the barycentric moments.

In the following parts, the major points of the method are described.

2.1 Image partitioning

The image partitioning is a fundamental element of the technique, because it includes an important part of the invariance properties.

Generalities. Current image partitioning methods do not offer invariant (in terms of rotation and scaling) partition (quadtrees, HV-trees,...). The reason is that the partitioning methods use the image content only during the split and merge process, but the sites or germs are selected without considering it. For instance, if we consider the partition P_1 of an image and the partition P_2 of the same image rotated. We observe that partitions P_2 is different to P_1 rotated, some important artefacts appear. And we can observe the same problem with other geometric transformations such as scaling, warping or projection.

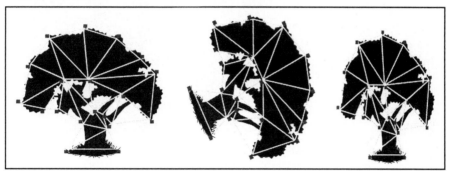

Fig. 1. Single object partition. Several transformations are applied to the object, the partition follows it. In fact, the object tracking is done by the germs of the partition. A part of the invariance is transferred to the germs generation algorithm.

The basic idea is to modify the germs generation in order to have an algorithm which generates invariant germs (see Fig. 1). We choose to use an interest points detector, IPD. The detection of interest point is a very active field of image processing, because it is the basis of lots of computer vision application frameworks.

There are two classes of IPDs, the first class of IPDs consists in working on the edges of image and then extracting points by calculating some maxima of curvature or by approximating them by polygons to extract intersection or inflexion points. The second class of IPDs considers directly the image signal ; the detector calculates for each point of the image, a measure depending of the neighbourhood, based on various orders of derivatives of the signal in both directions [12] [13] [19]. This measure indicates where the probability of presence of an interest point, here a corner, is important.

Some IPDs have demonstrated their capabilities to be invariant to some transformations as translations, rotations, and in certain cases to scaling and warping. We choose the Stephens-Harris IPD [13].

C. Schmid [12] proposes to use the derivatives of the Gaussian to derive the image and then to increase the robustness of the Stephen-Harris IPD. This improvement of the Stephen-Harris IPD allows to increase the repeatability[1] of the algorithm. Furthermore, we use a multi resolution approach to select « good » interest points. This consists in detecting the interest points at different resolutions by using the

---

[1] The repeatability measures the ability of the IPD to detect the interest points at the same relative position even if the image is transformed.

parameter sigma (σ) of the Gaussian function used to derive the signal, then points appearing in most resolutions are selected and create the final interest points map. The keypoints detected in textured areas, are deleted.

Fig. 2. At left, the illustration of the Stephen-Harris IPD on an image. The interest points are the small black and white boxes. At right, the Delaunay triangulation of a part of the image.

Building of the partition. The partition is built by using the interest points as germs. We choose the Delaunay triangulation to construct a triangular partition of the image (see Fig. 2).

This partition is refined by using a split and merge algorithm as described in [8]. A triangle is divided in several triangles, if its content is non homogeneous according to a given measure (the standard deviation for instance).

The merge algorithm is difficult to apply in this case, because it could destroy some interest points by merging two triangles. To alleviate this drawback, we propose to keep locally in the partition structure two configurations (represented as layers), one with the non-merged triangles and another with the merged triangle.

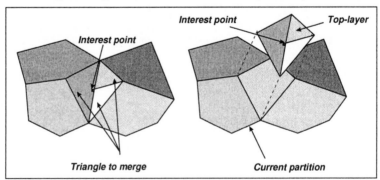

Fig. 3. One edge of the triangles to merge is an interest point. In order not to make it disappear, we build locally two layers, one with the merged triangle and one with the separated triangles.

The partition obtained could be seen as a meaningful partition because the contents of the triangles are homogenous, if we do not consider the top layer. This is important if other characterisations are applied, or to match the images of the database with an user sketch.

Building of a set of polygons with a locally exhaustive set of polygons. For some applications, the repeatability of the IPD is too low, because of very textured images (high frequencies textures). So, an invariant partition is very difficult to obtain. In this case, instead of building a partition, we built a set of triangles. The generation of this set is simple ; for each point and its neighbourhood, a triangle is built (see Fig. 4).

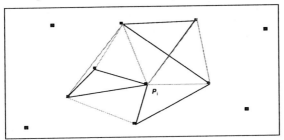

Fig. 4. Triangles generated by a point P_1 and with the neighbour points.

This approach is well suited for difficult images (highly textured or very noisy) when the performances of the IPD are low. The merge process is impossible because some triangles could overlap each others. The split process can be applied without any difficulties.

2.2 Partition element Signatures

The second step consists in calculating for each element of the polygonal partition or the polygons set, a collection of measures based on the photometric content of the polygon. These measures can be seen as local signatures.

The elements of the partition can be seen as homogeneous image regions - because of the split process - so we can use traditional characterisations of image regions.

Lots of signatures could be used to characterise a region. We can use the derivatives of the signal (local jet), a spectral description by using wavelets, moments (orthogonal moments, Zernike moments) or fractal properties. The signature must conserve the invariance introduced in the partition or the set of polygons.

We choose to evaluate our approach with two characterisations, the p-Ifs parameters and the barycentric moments.

The P-Ifs (Partitioned Iterated Function System) is a tool allowing to describe a complex n-dimensional signal with a set of simple functions. These functions could be linear, as it is used in fractal image compression. The advantages are that the number of parameters to define a linear Ifs is low (here we use 15 coefficients) and this description is intrinsically scale invariant. A P-Ifs defines an entire partitioned image, and we note p-Ifs as an element of an P-Ifs. In our case, a p-Ifs is a linear function and is expressed for each triangle in its barycentric coordinates space.

The second characterisation is the measure moments expressed on barycentric or trilinear coordinates, for each triangle.

We use the barycentric coordinates to represent a triangle in order to keep the invariance and to avoid the anisotropy of the cartesian mesh. Both characterisations are independent.

P-Ifs representation of a partitioned image. The calculation of an P-Ifs associated to a partitioned image is an inverse problem. For each polygon of the partition, the p-Ifs computation uses one or more other polygons of the image. The p-Ifs is a map between a part of the image and another. In the following paragraph, we define and explain the p-Ifs calculation precisely.

P-Ifs coding of an image - Fractal image compression. The P-Ifs coding is currently used for the Fractal image compression in the decorrelation step of the compression process.

The basic idea of the fractal compression [5] [6] [7] is that the image is the attractor of a contractive map. This map is an P-Ifs and can be described by its parameters set. The aim of compression is to determine these parameters and therefore the P-Ifs map.

First, we consider the image f as a function defined on $[0,1]\times[0,1]=I^2$ such as:

$$f:I^2 \to I \qquad (1)$$
$$(x,y) \mapsto z = f(x,y)$$

The image f is the attractor of a map W, W is a P-Ifs:

$$f \equiv |W| = \lim_{n \to \infty} W^{\circ n} = WoWoWo...oW \qquad (2)$$

W is a set of n p-Ifs maps w_i, each w_i works on a compact part of the image, called *domain block* $D^i_{x,y}$ and transforms it into another compact part, called *range block* $R^i_{x,y}$ (element of the image partition) such as :

$$w_i\left(D^j_{x,y}\right) = \widetilde{R}^i_{x,y} \text{ with } \widetilde{R}^i_{x,y} \text{ close to } R^i_{x,y} \qquad (3)$$

w_i can be written at order 0 as:

$$\widetilde{R}^i_{x,y} = w_i\left(D^j_{x,y}\right) = s\varphi\left(D^j_{x,y}\right) + t \qquad (4)$$

with φ an isometrie.

w_i contains a geometric part (isometrie and scaling) and a massic part applied to image pixels. s and t are respectively the contrast scaling and luminosity offset parameters.

We can write w_i at order 1 as :

$$\widetilde{R}^i_{x,y} = a_1^{(i)}x + b_1^{(i)}y + s^{(i)}\varphi\left(D^j_{x,y}\right) + t^{(i)} \tag{5}$$

At order 2, we have :

$$\widetilde{R}^i_{x,y} = a_1^{(i)}x + a_2^{(i)}x^2 + b_1^{(i)}y + b_2^{(i)}y^2 + s^{(i)}\varphi\left(D^j_{x,y}\right) + t^{(i)} \tag{6}$$

The contractivity of W assumes the uniqueness of the fixed point, here the image f. To encode an image f, we need to find the transformation set $w_1, w_2, ..., w_N$ with :

$$W = \bigcup_{i=1}^{N} w_i \tag{7}$$

and $f=|W|$. In other words, f is the fixed point of W:

$$f = W(f) = w_1(f) \cup w_2(f) \cup ... \cup w_N(f) \tag{8}$$

In reality we are looking for:

$$f \approx f' = W(f') \approx W(f) = w_0(f) \cup ... \cup w_N(f) \tag{9}$$

To determine the w_i transformations, we search for each range $R^i_{x,y}$, the domain $D^j_{x,y}$ which is the most similar after applying the p-Ifs w_i with the optimal parameters.

The p-Ifs parameters are calculated by using a least squares regression to minimise the root mean square r.

$$r = \sum_{x,y} (w_i\left(D^j_{x,y}\right) - R^i_{x,y})^2 \tag{10}$$

Application of the p-Ifs for partition element characterisation. As described in the preceding part, the P-Ifs calculation consists in computing a p-Ifs for each element of the image partition (range block). This process uses for each range block one domain block and expresses the mapping of the domain block to the range block. We shall explain how to apply the calculation of the P-Ifs to the partition described previously.

In the paragraph 1.1 (*Image partitioning*), we expose our image partition method. The resulting partition is considered as the *domain* partition, we subdivide it by placing a germ in the centre of each triangle and then we use these new germs to generate the new triangles. The new partition is the *range* partition.

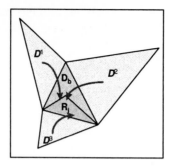

Fig. 5. The *range* R_i is encoded by an Ifs element by considering the adjacent polygons of D_b, *domain* containing R_i.

The use of cartesian coordinates to describe the *range* or *domain blocks* is not relevant, because it is not invariant in case of geometric transformations (rotations for instance). We suggest to use the barycentric or trilinear coordinates which are locally defined for each polygon.

In the case of triangles, the barycentric coordinates are the real numbers α, β, γ such as a point p in the cartesian space is :

$$p = \alpha \cdot A + \beta \cdot B + \gamma \cdot C \qquad (11)$$

with

$$\alpha + \beta + \gamma = 1, \ \alpha, \beta, \gamma \in [0;1] \qquad (12)$$

The p-Ifs w_i expressed with the barycentric coordinates is :

$$w_i\left(D_{\alpha,\beta,\gamma}^j\right) = \tilde{R}_{\alpha,\beta,\gamma}^i = a_1^i \alpha + b_1^i \beta + c_1^i \gamma + s_i D_{\alpha,\beta,\gamma}^j + t_i \qquad (13)$$

Another adaptation is directly related to the indexing, in the traditional compression scheme, the *domain block* $D_{\alpha,\beta,\gamma}^j$ associated to the *range block* $R_{\alpha,\beta,\gamma}^i$ is searched in all the image. This characteristic represents an important limitation for the indexing for two reasons :

– The domain $D_{\alpha,\beta,\gamma}^j$ selected during the calculation of the p-Ifs, is the most similar to $R_{\alpha,\beta,\gamma}^i$ after applying the p-Ifs w_i. If a perturbation is applied to $D_{\alpha,\beta,\gamma}^i$, it cannot be chosen to encode $R_{\alpha,\beta,\gamma}^i$, so another *domain block* is preferred ;

– The image fragment specified during the request could have a different coding because of the lack of some *domain blocks* [10].

To alleviate this drawback, we propose to express the p-Ifs by considering all the *domain blocks* in immediate neighbourhood (adjacent) of the *domain block* containing the *range block* (see Fig. 5).

At last, we use a p-Ifs of order 1 to encode the *range blocks* expressed with the barycentric coordinates :

$$w_i\left(D_{\alpha,\beta,\gamma} \text{ adjacents}\right) = \tilde{R}^i_{\alpha,\beta,\gamma} = \sum_{D_k \text{ adjacents}} a^i_{1,k}\alpha + b^i_{1,k}\beta + c^i_{1,k}\gamma + s^i_k D^k_{\alpha,\beta,\gamma} + t^i_k \tag{14}$$

We obtain a vector V_i characterising the *range block* $R^i_{\alpha,\beta,\gamma}$:

$$V_i = \left[\left(a_k\right),\left(b_k\right),\left(c_k\right),\left(s_k\right)\right] \tag{15}$$

We do not use the t_k parameters to be robust against the luminance variations.

Moments on barycentric coordinates. The second characterisation is based on the moments of the distribution of pixel values. For each element of the polygons set built as described in 1.1 (Image partitioning), different moments are calculated. Here, we consider that the partition is a triangular partition.

This characterisation can be used with a partition or a set of triangles.

The moments are calculated by using the barycentric coordinates, we note m^n_α, m^n_β, m^n_γ as the barycentric moments at the order n of the triangle $D_{\alpha,\beta,\gamma}$:

$$m^n_\alpha = \lambda \iiint_{\alpha+\beta+\gamma=1} \alpha^n \cdot \left(D_{\alpha,\beta,\gamma} - \overline{D}\right) d\alpha d\beta d\gamma \tag{16}$$

$$m^n_\beta = \lambda \iiint_{\alpha+\beta+\gamma=1} \beta^n \cdot \left(D_{\alpha,\beta,\gamma} - \overline{D}\right) d\alpha d\beta d\gamma$$

$$m^n_\gamma = \lambda \iiint_{\alpha+\beta+\gamma=1} \gamma^n \cdot \left(D_{\alpha,\beta,\gamma} - \overline{D}\right) d\alpha d\beta d\gamma$$

$\overline{D}$ is the average of $D_{\alpha,\beta,\gamma}$. The use of the average and the normalisation coefficient λ allows to introduce some invariances against the luminance variations.

The moments are stored in a vector V :

$$V = \left[\left(m^i_\alpha\right),\left(m^i_\beta\right),\left(m^i_\gamma\right)\right]_{i\in[0...n]} \tag{17}$$

with i denoting the moment order.

We use a discrete notation :

$$\alpha = k_\alpha \Delta \tag{18}$$
$$\beta = k_\beta \Delta$$
$$\gamma = k_\gamma \Delta$$

with Δ an constant increment for α, β, γ, the expression of the moment for α becomes :

$$m_\alpha^n = \lambda \sum_{k_\alpha} \sum_{k_\beta} \sum_{k_\gamma} 1_{\left(k_\alpha + k_\beta + k_\gamma = 1\right)} \cdot \left(k_\alpha \Delta\right)^n \left(D_{k_\alpha \Delta, k_\beta \Delta, k_\gamma \Delta} - \overline{D}\right) \qquad (19)$$

To enhance the robustness of the moment characterisation against the error on the position of the triangle edges, we use a Gaussian function. The expressions become :

$$m_\alpha'' = \lambda \iiint_{\alpha+\beta+\gamma=1} \alpha'' \cdot \left(D_{\alpha,\beta,\gamma} \cdot G(\alpha,\beta,\gamma) - \overline{D}\right) d\alpha d\beta d\gamma \qquad (20)$$

$$m_\beta'' = \lambda \iiint_{\alpha+\beta+\gamma=1} \beta'' \cdot \left(D_{\alpha,\beta,\gamma} \cdot G(\alpha,\beta,\gamma) - \overline{D}\right) d\alpha d\beta d\gamma$$

$$m_\gamma'' = \lambda \iiint_{\alpha+\beta+\gamma=1} \gamma'' \cdot \left(D_{\alpha,\beta,\gamma} \cdot G(\alpha,\beta,\gamma) - \overline{D}\right) d\alpha d\beta d\gamma$$

with $G()$ the Gaussian function.

These moments are invariant against some rotations or the scale variations, if the content of the triangle stay identical.

3. Research strategy

3.1 Generalities

The indexing step generates a vector set for each image. All these vectors are stored in an index. We get an important number of vectors with a given dimension (3 for the graylevel barycentric moments, 9 for the colour barycentric moments and 15 the p-Ifs parameters). The index structure must be good suited to obtain the best performances.

We use the algorithm of A. Nene and S. K. Nayar [20] but other techniques are applicable as kd-trees, for instance.

The search process consists in finding the nearest vectors in the database to the request vectors. A first, distance score is computed taking in account the average distance between the selected vectors of the database and the vectors of the request. Then a localisation score is computed by using the spatial relations in selected images and comparing them to those calculated in the request.

At last, each image of the database has a distance score and a localisation score.

3.2 Similarity evaluation and spatial localisation

The basis of the principle is to search for all vectors of the request, the list of the closer vectors, then we compute a distance score and a spatial localisation score.

We note as Γ, the application which transforms an image I_j in a set V_j, each element of V_j is a numerical characterisation of one polygon :

$$V_j = \Gamma\left(I_j\right) \tag{21}$$

The set V_j is in fact a list of tupple (v_k, j) :

$$V_j = \left\{ \left(v_k, j\right) \middle| v_k \in \Re^d \right\} \tag{22}$$

The image database DB is:

$$DB = \bigcup_j V_j \tag{23}$$

The image I_r of the request is transformed as a set V_r of tupples (v_i, r) with the transformation Γ:

$$V_r = \Gamma\left(I_r\right) \tag{24}$$

For each tupple (v_i, r) of V_r, we compute the set W_i containing the vectors of DB which are "close" to v_i :

$$W_i = \left\{ \left(v_k, i, j\right) \middle| d\left(v_i, v_k\right) < \varepsilon, \left(v_k, j\right) \in V_j \right\} \tag{25}$$

with d a distance and ε a real number.

The Euclidean distance can be used because the vector are normalised. However ε could be different for each component, instead of using a scalar ε, it is preferable to use a vector.

Now, the resulting tupples (v_k, i, j) in the set $\bigcup_i W_i$ are dispatched according their image identifier:

$$\Pi_j = \left\{ \left(v_k, i\right) \middle| \left(v_k, i, j\right) \in W_i \right\} \tag{26}$$

Calculation of the distance score. A first score $S_{dist}(I_j)$ can be associated to each image I_j. This score represents the distance between the request and the image.

$$S_{dist}\left(I_j\right) = 1 - \sum_{v_i \in V_r} \min_{\left(v_k,i\right) \in \Pi_j} \left\{d\left(v_i, v_k\right)\right\}$$ (27)

S_{dist} is maximal ($S_{dist}=1$) when the request is very close from the image and null if completely different.

Calculation of the localisation score. For each image I_j, we have the vectors corresponding to the request, we can select the candidates images at this step by computing the cardinal of the sets Π_j and setting a threshold t. An image I_i is selected if:

$$\frac{card\left(\Pi_j\right)}{card\left(V_r\right)} > t$$ (28)

We can choose $t=0.5$.

For the selected images, the localisation coefficients of the selected vectors are evaluated by computing the spatial relations. The spatial relations are modelled with a function R_s.

$$R_s : \Re^d \times \Re^d \to \Re^2$$ (29)

$$\left(v, v'\right) \mapsto \left(\tau_{v,v'}, d_{v,v'}\right)$$

$\tau_{v,v'}$ and $d_{v,v'}$ are respectively, the angle and the distance between the centroids of the triangles characterised by the vectors v and v' (see Fig. 6).

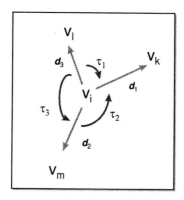

Fig. 6. Spatial relations defined from the vector v_i. The relations are valuated with the angles τ_i and distances d_i.

The spatial relations are computed between each vector v_i of the request and its neighbourhood. The relations are stored in a set R_s^i:

$$R_s^i = \left\{ R_s\left(v_i, v_{ii}\right) \middle\| \left\| v_{ii} - v_i \right\| < d_{neighbourhood} \right\} \tag{30}$$

In each image, each tupple (v_j, i) of the set Π_j is evaluated by verifying that all spatial relations $R_s(v_i, v_{ii})$ present in the request are verified in the set Π_j. A score is associated to each tupple (v_k, i) of Π_j:
- If we consider $(v_k, i) \in \Pi_j$ and $(v_{kk}, ii) \in \Pi_j$
- The spatial relation between (v_k, i) and (v_{kk}, ii) must be similar to the relation between v_i and v_{ii}:

$$R_s\left(v_k, v_{kk}\right) \cong R_s\left(v_i, v_{ii}\right) \tag{31}$$

- If it is true, the score of v_k is increased. The scores are stored in a table $S_j(v_k)$.

Then we compute the ratio between the number of spatial relations verified for one tupple (v_k, i) of Π_j $S_j(v_k)$ and the number of relations of the vector v_i, $card(R_s^i)$. The vector is validated if this ratio is bigger than a given threshold:

$$\frac{card\left(R_s^i\right)}{S_j\left(v_k\right)} > t_s \tag{32}$$

For each tupple (v_k, i) of Π_j validated, the spatial score of the image I_j, $S_{spatial}(I_j)$ is incremented by one :

$$S_{localisation}\left(I_j\right) = 1 - card\left\{ \left(v_k, i\right) \frac{card\left(R_s^i\right)}{S_j\left(v_k\right)} > t_s \text{ with } i \in \left[0 \ldots card\left(V_r\right)\right] \right\} \tag{33}$$

The localisation score $S_{localisation}(I_j)$ is maximal when the request is close from the image I_j in terms of numerical distance (the vectors involved in the localisation calculation are close to the request in terms of the Euclidean distance) and spatial relations.

4. Results and performances

The following figures illustrate the results and performances obtained with our system. The Fig. 7 and Fig. 8 show some fragments extracted from the database (100 images). We submit three requests to the system with each fragment. The Table 1 and Table 2 give the results obtained with the first fragment and for the two types of characterisations (p-Ifs parameters and barycentric moments). We obtain very similar result with the two other fragments.

We test the system with a 100 images database of current images and a 90 images database of painting. The results obtained for both databases are close. With entire images or for fragments with a rotation, the recognition rate is close to 100%. The scale variations engender lower results, the recognition rate is close to 90% if the scaling factor is less than 1.3 and bigger than .7.

The experiment with the paintings database (100 images) allows to show that the characterisation (with barycentric moments or p-Ifs parameters) is discriminating and can be used for large databases.

In these tables, we only gives the best scores (localisation and distance), the others are very low (inferior to .01 for the localisation and .3 for the distance).

The localisation score is more discriminating than the distance score. In fact, the distance evaluation is included in the localisation score.

The processing times are very low (typically 0.01 seconds for a request on a 100 images database).

5. Conclusion

The approach explained in this paper presents some interesting solutions to invariance problems in image indexing by using an invariant partition and two possible characterisations (p-Ifs parameters or barycentric coordinates). The photometric properties of the partition elements are stored in a list of vectors. The search strategy is based on a vector distance calculation (nearest neighbour search) - between the request and the images of the database - and the checking of the spatial relations of founded vectors. During this process, each image is marked by a score.

The indexing step is highly dependant to the interest points robustness, we propose to use a list of polygons instead of a partition when the images are too textured or noisy. We plan to study other characterisations as the analysis of the spectral/spatial properties of the partition regions or other kinds of moments.

Fig. 7. Three requests (respectively fragments of image *gondole, gondole10, gondole20*) returning the three images *gondole, gondole10,* or *gondole20*. The Table 1 gives the scores for the request based on the first fragment.

Image	Barycentric moments			p-Ifs parameters		
	Localisation score	Distance score	Vector number	Localisation score	Distance score	Vector number
Gondole10	0.894	0.0176	48	0.820	0.0095	45
Gondole	0.944	0.986	54	0.937	0.965	54
Gondole20	0.849	0.087	47	0.760	0.127	44

Table 1. Scores for the request containing the fragment gondole #1 by using the barycentric moments or p-Ifs parameters (see Fig. 7). The database contains three images representing the gondole with various rotations (10° et 20°), the fragment gondole #1 is extracted from the image gondole. The research system returns the three images with the results shown in this table.

Fig. 8. Three fragments of the *house* images with various orientations. The first fragment is used as a request the results are written in the **Table 2**.

Image	Barycentric moments			p-Ifs parameters		
	Localisation score	Distance score	Vector number	Localisation score	Distance score	Vector number
House	1	0.994	71	0.963	0.952	71
House1	0.995	0.919	69	0.823	0.813	63
House2	0.973	0.832	66	0.805	0.795	58

Table 2. Results of the search of the house fragment #1 extracted from the image *house* (see Fig. 8). The different images are rotated.

References

[1]   P. Aigrain, H. Zhang, D. Petkovic. "Content-based Representation and Retrieval of Visual Media: A State-of-the-Art Review", *Multimedia Tools and Applications special issue on Representation and Retrieval of Visual Media*

[2]   L. Gottesfeld Brown. « A survey of Image Registration Techniques », ACM Computing Surveys, Vol. 24, No. 4, December 1992

[3]   W. Niblack, R. Barber, W. Equitz, M.D. Flickner, E. H. Glasman, D. Petkovic, P. Yanker, C. Faloutsos, G. Taubin. "QBIC Project: querying images by content, using color, texture, and shape", Storage and Retrieval for Image and Video Databases

[4]   B. Scassellati, S. Alexopoulos, M.D. Flickner. "Retrieving images by 2D shape: a comparison of computation methods with human perceptual judgments", Storage and Retrieval for Image and Video Databases

[5]   Y. Fisher. "Fractal Compression: Theory and Application to Digital Images", Springer Verlag, New York 1994.

[6]   A. Jacquin. "Image Coding Based on a Fractal Theory of Iterated Contractive Image Transformation", IEEE Transaction on Image Processing, 1992, Vol 1

[7]   D. M. Monro, F. Dudbridge. « Fractal approximation functions for image and signal coding », 3rd IMA Conference on Mathematics in Signal Processing, University of Warwick, 1992

[8]   F. Davoine, J.-M. Chassery. « Adaptative Delaunay Triangulation for Attractor Image Coding » 12th International Conference on Pattern Recognition, Oct. 1994.

[9]   A. Pentland, R.W. Picard, S. Sclaroff. "Photobook: Content-Based Manipulation of Image Databases", International Journal of Computer Vision, Fall 1995.

[10]   J. M. Marie-Julie, H. Essafi « Image Database Indexing and Retrieval using the Fractal Transform », ECMAST'97, Milan.

[11]   J.M. Marie-Julie - H. Essafi. "Fast parallel multimedia data base access based on wavelet multiresolution pyramidal decomposition", MVA'96, IAPR Workshop on Machine Vision Applications.

[12]   C. Schmid, R. Mohr. « Combining greyvalue invariants with local constraints for object recognition », Pattern Analysis and Machine Intelligence, 1997.

[13]   C. Harris, M. Stephens. « A combined corner and edge detector », Plessey Research Roke Manor, United Kingdom

[14]   C.A. RothWell, A. Zisserman, D.A. Forsyth, J.L. Lundy. « Canonical frames for planar object recognition » 2nd European Conference on Computer Vision, 1992

[15]   B. Funt, G. Finlayson « Color constant indexing ». IEEE Transactions on Pattern and Machine Intelligence, 13 (9), 1991

[16]   M.A. Turk, A.P. Pentland. « Face recognition using eigenfaces ». Conference on Computer Vision and Pattern Recognition, 1991

[17]   H. Murase, S.K. Nayar, « Visual learning and recognition of 3D objects from appearance », International Journal of Computer Vision, 14, 1995

[18]   R. Mehrotra, J.E. Gary. "Similar-Shape Retrieval In Shape Data Management", Computer September 1995

[19]   H. Moravec. « Visual mapping by a robot rover », 6th International Joint Conference on Artificial Intelligence, 1979

[20]   A. Nene, S. K. Nayar. « A simple algorithm for nearest neighbour search in high dimension », Dept. of Computer Science Columbia University, New York, Technical report No. CUCS-030-95

Determining a Structured Spatio-temporal Representation of Video Content for Efficient Visualization and Indexing

Marc Gelgon and Patrick Bouthemy

IRISA/INRIA
Campus universitaire de Beaulieu
35042 Rennes cedex, France
e-mail : mgelgon@irisa.fr, bouthemy@irisa.fr
Tel : 33-2.99.84.74.32 Fax : 33-.2.99.84.71.71

Abstract. Efficient access to information contained in video databases implies that a structured representation of the content of the video is built beforehand. This paper describes an approach in this direction, targeted at video indexing and browsing. Exploiting a 2D motion model estimator, we partition the video into shots, characterize camera motion, extract and track mobile objects. These steps rely on robust motion estimation, statistical tests and contextual statistical labeling. The content of each shot can then be viewed on a synoptic frame composed of a mosaic image of the background scene, on which trajectories of mobile objects are superimposed. The proposed method also provides instantaneous and long-term, qualitative and quantitative object motion cues for content-based indexing. Its different steps and the system they form are designed to keep computational cost low, while being able to cope with general video content was aimed at. We provide experimental results on real-world sequences. The structured output opens important possible extensions, for instance in the direction of higher-level interpretation. [1]

1   Introduction and related work

Fast, reliable and convenient access to visual information in still image and video databases is of growing importance in tasks concerning professionals in a variety of fields, as well as emerging services targeted at the general public.

Broadly, still image and video have led to their own direction in the research carried out for accessing content-based information. The major issues and cues have been reviewed in [2, 9, 14]. In the former field, prototypes such as QBIC

---

[1] This work was supported in part by DGA (Délégation Générale pour l'Armement - French Ministry of Defense) and AFIRST (French-Israeli Scientific and Technical Research Agency).

[11] are now available, but recent work such as [22], should contribute to largely improving the performance of still image retrieval applications.

This paper is concerned with access to information contained in image sequences. Ideally, a retrieval system should allow two types of accesses. The first one consists in expressing a query to the system, which returns matching entries. The second one consist in viewing the documents, leaving the user to find the relevant information. Indeed, if the query cannot be precisely defined in the terms offered by the interface, or if relevant information has not been correctly indexed, it is necessary to be able to browse in an efficient way through the video. Hence, it is desirable to represent the videos in two ways, an indexed version of video used by a query-type interface, and a version for browsing through an appropriate interface.

Content-based video indexing and efficient content visualization share the necessity for a phase of video structuring. Three levels of analysis can be distinguished. A fundamental and early task is the partitioning of the video into shots, which is mainly done by detecting shot changes. Current systems generally rely on comparison of grey-level or color histograms, computed on successive frames [1, 17, 26]. Thresholding on the sum of histogram bin differences, or a χ^2 test have been proposed. In [17], a set of histograms are computed on a partition of the image into blocks, and the eight largest differences are discarded, so as to reduce the perturbation causes by camera motion and mobile objects. An experimental comparison of these approaches is presented in [5]. Direct processing of the MPEG bit-stream has been proposed for instance in [19], by computing histograms using the DC components of the DCT related to I-frames. The main issues that arise in this task are the presence of progressive transitions, such as dissolve or wipe effects, strong camera motion, and the presence of mobile objects. The first problem is tackled in [1] and [26] by using different tests for cuts and progressive transitions. Coping simultaneously with all three problems generally involves the use of several dedicated techniques, and then implies tuning of multiple and sensitive parameter values. We exploit here an approach addressing these problems jointly, which we proposed in [6].

Shot content is often characterized by the estimated type of camera motion during the shot, and by one or several key-frames. Displaying the sequence of these key-frames is a simple way of visualizing the video. Shot content indexing has been proposed in [27], consisting in mapping the shot content on its key-frames, and applying to them still image indexing techniques.

Starting from a partition of a video into shots, some studies aim at summarizing the video even more, doing so-called video skimming, as for instance in [23]. In order to build shot summaries which are more informative than basic key-frames, analysis of the spatio-temporal contents of the shots can be performed. Doing so allows content-based indexing using the determined spatio-temporal structure. In [3], the structured representation of a sequence takes the form of a set of layers, after a joint estimation of the motion models and of their support, considered as a mixture model problem, and the number of models is determined through a MDL criterion. This approach has shown efficient, though a shortcoming of mixture-based approaches is the difficulty to update the number of models along the image sequence. Top-down methods consist in iteratively computing successive dominant motions and assigning their support a single label [16]. Another category of techniques adresses the segmentation issue in a Markovian framework, as a contextual labeling problem [24]. Finally, clustering approaches such as [25], in contrast, start from elementary regions and group them to form the desired regions. The approach we use in the work presented belongs to the Markovian-Bayesian methods, although working also upon a layer of elementary regions.

Mosaic images have been used to represent conveniently the scene background [3, 15], and mobile objects can for instance be superimposed on the mosaic image at several of their positions during the sequence so as to suggest their trajectories.

Research has also been carried out at the higher level of scene interpretation. This step is important, because scene understanding provides a high level video structuring which is very relevant to content-based indexing and retrieval. The spatio-temporal content, supplied as motion-based segmentation maps by the previous phase, can be represented in a symbolic manner in terms of events and spatio-temporal organization of the scene. In [8], mobile objects in a static scene are detected and tracked. The scene is then indexed in terms of e.g. appearance, disappearance or removal of an object. In [10], the 3D scene is played by the user with an appropriate interface, and translated into a spatio-temporal logic formulation so as to characterize the scenario in the database. The formalism of Petri nets has been proposed in [7] for scenario description. In [10] and [7], the location and temporal tracking of objects of interest were assumed. In a complete scheme, however, this high-level analysis relies strongly on the efficiency of the earlier phases.

The work presented in this paper first, proposes an approach for the earlier phases, that is shot change detection and motion-based segmentation, and then derives a set a object and camera motion descriptors and a compact representation of the dynamic content of a sequence. The method is summarized on Figure 1. We first partition the image sequence into shots, using a technique which handles both cuts and progressive transitions with the same test, and copes with the presence of camera motion and mobile objects. Then, for each shot, we extract and track mobile entities along the shot. The method provides, for each shot, a synoptic view consisting of a mosaic image of the background scene, on which trajectories of mobile objects are represented. Besides, qualitative and quantitative camera and object motion descriptors are obtained. The scheme proposed here is unified around a low-cost robust 2D motion model estimator; the various steps of the method exploit its robustness. In comparison with [8] which is targeted at particular scenes (assuming a static camera and disconnected mobile objects), we aim at general sequences by performing a motion-based segmentation. In contrast with [15], we have an explicit segmentation and trajectory of mobile objects, which can be used for further analysis and elaboration of object descriptors. The paper is organized as follows. Section 2 outlines the robust motion model estimator, while Section 3 recalls the method for partitioning a video into shots. Section 4 explains how objects are extracted within these shots. Section 5 describes how a synoptic view of the shots content is derived. Section 6 deals with motion descriptors. Section 7 provides experimental results, and Section 8 contains concluding remarks.

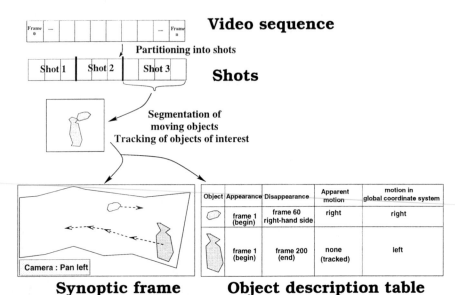

Fig. 1. *An overview of the video structuring and representation method : partitioning into shots, locating and tracking mobile objects, and building a still image summary of the shot content showing the trajectories of objects. For indexing or understanding purposes, a table describing each mobile object is also produced, and camera motion is annotated.*

2   Dominant motion estimation

In this work, we manipulate motion information, which support can be either the whole image, or a region in the image. In both cases, motion is represented by 2D affine motion model. The motion model parameters are estimated on the relevant support (a region, or the whole frame) using a motion estimator called $RMRmod$ presented in [18]. Since a robust estimator is exploited, only the model accounting for the dominant motion between a pair of successive frames within the considered support is estimated.

Between two successive frames, we first estimate the global dominant motion over the whole image. This measurement is then exploited in the successive phases of the scheme : partitioning of the video into shots, characterization of camera motion, construction of a mosaic image by image warping, and determination of trajectories and object motions in a coordinate system, called synoptic frame in the subsequent, where estimated camera motion is compensated for. Motion model estimation on region supports is used for the motion-based segmentation and tracking phases, and for the derivation of object motion descriptors.

We briefly recall here the general case where the estimation support is denoted by R, which gravity center is denoted $g = (x_g, y_g)$. R can be the whole image or a given region in the image. The displacement vector $\boldsymbol{w}_\Theta$ at pixel $p(x, y)$ between two successive frames I_t and I_{t+1} is expressed as :

$$\boldsymbol{w}_\Theta(p) = \begin{pmatrix} a_1 + a_2(x - x_g) + a_3(y - y_g) \\ a_4 + a_5(x - x_g) + a_6(y - y_g) \end{pmatrix} \tag{1}$$

where $\Theta = (a_1, a_2, a_3, a_4, a_5, a_6)$ represents the parameters of the 2D affine motion model. To estimate Θ, an incremental approach is adopted in a multiresolution framework to handle large displacements. Given the current estimate $\widehat{\Theta}^k$, at step k, of the motion parameter vector, we calculate the increment $\widehat{\Delta\Theta^k}$ as :

$$\widehat{\Delta\Theta^k} = \arg\min_{\Delta\Theta^k} \sum_{p_i \in R} \rho(r_i) \tag{2}$$

where the residual r_i is computed using the spatial intensity gradient ∇I and the current motion model estimate $\widehat{\Theta}^k$ as follows :

$$r_i = I(p_i + \boldsymbol{w}_{\widehat{\Theta}^k}(p_i), t + 1) - I(p_i, t) + \nabla I(p_i + \boldsymbol{w}_{\widehat{\Theta}^k}(p_i), t + 1).\boldsymbol{w}_{\Delta\Theta^k}(p_i) \tag{3}$$

$\rho(x)$ is a hard-redescending M-estimator. Here, we consider Tukey's biweight function. We can then update the estimate $\widehat{\Theta}^k$: $\widehat{\Theta^{k+1}} = \widehat{\Theta^k} + \widehat{\Delta\Theta^k}$. This incremental process is iterated until a stopping criterion is met. This estimator allows us to get an accurate computation of the dominant motion on the support at hand, even if other motions are present.

3 Video partitioning into shots

The method we employ for this early step in structuring an image sequence uses motion models accounting for the global dominant image motion between successive images [6]. The evolution of the size of the associated estimation support enables the detection of both cuts and progressive transitions. More precisely, we consider the variable $\zeta_t = n_d/n_0$, where n_d is the measured size of the estimation support. n_d is provided by the motion estimation phase, as the set of pixels conforming to the global dominant motion. n_0 is the maximum expected support area, and is computed geometrically as the size of the part of $I(t)$ which is likely to be also in $I(t + 1)$. This is derived from the dominant motion, supposed to correspond to the camera motion and estimated between t and $t+1$. Observations of the evolution of this variable along the sequence are as follows. Within a shot, ζ_t is close to 1. Between two images of different shots, i.e. at a cut instant, no consistent motion can be estimated, and ζ_t suddenly drops close to 0. In the case of progressive transitions, we observe a less pronounced decrease of ζ_t, but which still enables a correct detection. Significant jumps in ζ_t are detected using the statistical cumulative Hinkley's test [4], involving very little computation, and providing also the temporal bounds of the detected transition.

The key point of this technique is its generality of use in terms of kind of transitions and scene content. First, in contrast with most approaches which perform different tests for cuts and gradual changes, the proposed approach copes with these different kinds of transitions with the same test involving a single threshold which is kept constant [6]. Secondly, the scheme can cope with scenes including mobile objects, even of important size, and important camera motion. The scheme has also been validated on MPEG-1 and -2 reconstructed image sequences.

4 Segmentation-Tracking

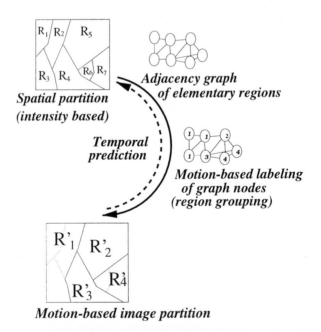

Fig. 2. *Overview of the segmentation and tracking method. A spatial partition of the image is tracked along the sequence, along with a region-level motion-based partition built upon this spatial partition.*

Once partitioned into shots, we apply to the content of each shot a hierarchical motion-based segmentation method we more extensively describe in [13]. An overview diagram is provided in Figure 2. An intensity-based partition of the image is first built. Affine motion models are robustly estimated on each of these regions, using the approach described in Section 2. This first stage leads to deliberately over-segmented partition, relatively to a meaningful partition in terms of moving objects of interest. Its purpose is to retrieve all relevant boundaries. In a second stage, the elementary regions are grouped on a more meaningful motion-based criterion. The adjacency graph defined on the regions of the elementary partition is considered. The goal is then to assign labels to the nodes of this graph in such a way that regions undergoing similar (resp. different) motions are attributed the same (resp. different) labels. An optimal label configuration is sought for as a statistical contextual labeling problem. An energy function $U(e, o)$ is defined, associated to a graph-level Markovian model, and composed of the sum os local potentials V_1 and V_2 defined on pairs of neighbouring nodes as follows :

$$U(e, o) = \sum_{\gamma_j \in \Gamma} V_1(e(\gamma_j), o(\gamma_j)) + \sum_{\gamma_j \in \Gamma} V_2(e(\gamma_j)) \qquad (4)$$

where $e(\gamma_j)$, $o(\gamma_j)$ respectively denote the local label configuration and the observations assigned to a pair of neighbouring nodes γ_j. Γ is the set of all such pairs on the graph. The two potentials relate assignment of labels to motion and geometrical measurements made on the regions. V_1 is defined so as to favour identical label of neighbouring nodes, if the two motion fields estimated on each of the two corresponding regions form a coherent motion field [13]. V_2 is defined so as to favour identical label of neighbouring nodes, also taking into account the degree of geometrical adjacency of the region pair. An HCF procedure is used to perform the minimization of $U(e, o)$. The motion-based regions are derived from the label configuration at convergence. A motion model is then estimated over each motion-based region group, thus characterizing the motion of mobile objects, or of the background region. A temporal prediction-updating technique, both of the spatial partition and of the region-level label configuration, enables a correct updating of spatial and motion boundaries along the sequence, as well as emergence of new motion-based regions, as appropriate.

The advantages of this technique are that, in contrast with merging-only, split-and-merge or clustering methods, and because the topology of the graph is kept unchanged throughout the labeling of its nodes, groups of elementary regions can be re-arranged in a flexible and well-controlled manner during the grouping step and from one frame to the next. Besides, contextual information can easily be incorporated in such a formalism.

5   Camera and object motion description

Section 3 and 4 have described the steps leading to a structured representation of the image sequence content. In this section, we describe how motion descriptors can be obtained for the entities that have been extracted, namely for shots and mobile objects.

First, a qualitative descriptor of camera motion for each pair of successive frames can be provided. To this purpose, the spatial support associated to the global dominant motion model, that has been computed in the shot change detection step, can be again exploited. The parameters of the affine motion model as here expressed in the following basis, corresponding to basic translational, divergence, curl and hyperbolic models, so as to be physically more meaningful:

$$\Theta = (t_1, t_2, div, rot, hyp_1, hyp_2) \qquad \text{with :} \qquad (5)$$

$$t_1 = a_1 \qquad\qquad t_2 = a_4$$
$$div = \tfrac{1}{2}(a_2 + a_6) \; rot = \tfrac{1}{2}(a_5 - a_3) \; hyp_1 = \tfrac{1}{2}(a_2 - a_6) \; hyp_2 = \tfrac{1}{2}(a_3 + a_5)$$

For the various basic types of camera shooting situations, such as zooming, panning, static camera, only a subset of the six parameters as expressed in this basis should be non zero. In the case of pure horizontal panning, for instance, only parameter t_1 should be non zero. If camera is pure zooming, only the divergence term will be non-zero. In practice, the presence of noise and estimation errors has to be accounted for, and one must shift from an idea of "non-zero" to "significant value".

As regards the problem of determining which motion parameters are significant, we have shown in [12] that likelihood ratio tests tackled this issue in an efficient way, not requiring unstable parameter tuning. We resort to this approach, consisting in testing, for each parameter in Θ, the hypothesis that it is significant, against the hypothesis that it is equal to zero. This is carried out by re-estimating the motion model on the support associated to the dominant motion, while applying the constraint that the considered parameter is equal to zero, and evaluating whether this constrained model explains the data almost as well as the full-affine model. The degree of fitness of the two models to the data are compared using a statistical log-likelihood ratio test. The support on which motion estimation is performed makes the motion characterization technique resilient to mobile objects, even of significant size. Using this test, measurement noise and inadequacy of the model to explain the data can be implicitly taken into account [12].

The application of this significance test to each of the six parameters supplies a binary symbolic parameter vector, which can be mapped onto a set of qualitative motion labels, such as static camera, pan, zoom or sideways, forward or backward traveling. The sign of the significant parameters can also be exploited. It indicates, for instance, the direction of panning (left, right, up, down), whether a zoom or traveling is forward or backward, or the direction of a possible rotation around the optical axis.

The method for qualitative motion labeling, applied to the whole frame when dealing with camera motion, can in the same way be applied to the regions corresponding to the mobile objects extracted by the segmentation and tracking steps. By this means, we obtain, for each mobile object in each frame, a characterization of its motion. The motion-based segmentation step involves the robust estimation of a motion model on every region, and thus of the associated estimation support. We advocated that on the whole frame, utilizing the support of the dominant motion model made the motion characterization technique robust to other mobile objects. In the same way, at region level, we benefit from the respective dominant motion model supports by increasing resilience to minor errors in the determination of region boundaries.

Qualitative description of motion, whether of the camera or of mobile entities in the scene, is well suited for indexing. Indeed, the user may want to retrieve objects on a motion criterion, such as an object going leftwards, or coming towards the camera. However, it is likely the user will express his query in terms of perceived object motion, regardless of the camera motion in the scene. For instance, if he asks for an object going right, it is likely he may be interested in objects going rightwards in a fixed coordinate systen, and consequently also in objects being tracked rightwards by the camera. In many cases, an object motion descriptor obtained after having compensated for camera motion should fulfill better the goal of motion cues for indexing. We thus operate as follows.

Given two successive frames I_t and I_{t+1}, let us denote the estimated global dominant motion parameter vector $\widehat{\Theta_{t+1}^t}$ between these frames, to indicate clearly the temporal aspect of the problem. We built the image $\tilde{I}_{t+1}$ using a back-warping technique and exploiting $\widehat{\Theta_{t+1}^t}$, so as to compensate for camera motion. Assuming the scene is approximately planar and that this plane is not too much slanted, only the projected motion of mobile objects remains between I_t and $\tilde{I}_{t+1}$. The technique described above, applied between I_t and $\tilde{I}_{t+1}$, for each of the relevant regions, provides qualitative "scene related" motion descriptors of significant interest to an indexing system. We also indicate frame appearance and disappearance number, whether a mobile object emerges or disappears within the image, or from an image side, and in this case, from which side. Objects with no apparent translation, while camera translation is significant, are labeled as "tracked by the camera". This information can identify them to indexing or higher-level analysis systems as objects of interest. The part of the image corresponding to the object in a given image frame, can be stored in the database (Figure 1), enabling the use of region-based still image cues.

6   Synoptic views of the dynamic content of a shot

We describe here how, for each shot, a still image can be built that aims at summarizing its content, using the structured spatio-temporal representation and the motion descriptors found.

First, the background scene is represented by a mosaic image. Because we wish to build a view for quick visualization, in a context where a user searches for the part of interest in a video, we do not require a mosaic image displaying very low distortion. Such advances have however been recently proposed for instance in [20, 21]. Hence, we use an elementary technique consisting in considering a reference frame I_{t_0}, the first one in the shot, and back-warping all the frames towards a coordinate system related to this first frame, using the global dominant motion model $\widehat{\Theta_{t_0}^t}$, computed by composing $\widehat{\Theta_{t_0}^{t_1}} \ldots \widehat{\Theta_{t-1}^t}$. The parts of the image corresponding to mobile objects are withdrawn beforehand. The processing is fast, since the dominant motion model between successive frames is readily available.

We then superimpose on this mosaic the trajectories of mobile objects during the shot. The trajectory of an object is represented as the sequence of position measurements of its gravity center along the shot, also back-warped in the reference frame, so as to coincide with the mosaic image. For objects that are detected to be either partially appearing or disappearing from one side of the image, the gravity center does not approximately correspond to a single physical point along the sequence. For such objects, only the first gravity center measurement is used, the trajectory is built from there on using motion estimates. The mosaic image with the superimposed trajectories suggest in a simple way, yet effective, the contents of the shot. Rotation of objects around their center and objects coming towards or moving away from the camera are annotated with appropriate icons.

7 Results

The method was validated on several real video sequences. The experimental results presented here show the application of the different steps of the method for different sequences, so as to illustrate better their performance.

We report here results for the partitioning into shots and camera motion characterization on a real documentary, that includes various types of camera motions, cuts, dissolves and a special video effect. It also include a mobile person occupying a significant part of the image. The summary created for that sequence is shown on Figure 3, and corresponds to the correct partitioning, with an accurate temporal location of shots. A key-frame per shot is shown, and for any user-selected shot, the synoptic frame is displayed, along with qualitative camera motion estimated during the shot. Results obtained on various MPEG-reconstructed versions of the same sequence at various compression rates showed almost no difference with regard to the original sequence. Unoptimized code leads to a computation time per frame pair of about 30s (image size 360x288) on an Sun UltraSparc workstation. The time-consuming operations are mainly the spatial segmentation updating phase and motion model estimations (one per spatial region and seven per motion-based region). As far as interesting configuration in terms of mobile objects is concerned, we show how a shot content can be structured and represented on a 125 frame sequence called *Mobi*. In this sequence, the camera is panning leftwards and tracking a train, which is pushing a rolling ball. This ball stops rolling from frame 35 to frame 47. On the right, a calendar is being pulled upwards, it stops, and then goes downwards. On the left is a rapidly swinging gyroscope. These mobile objects cause shadow effects. The extracted motion boundaries for frames 1, 60 and 120 are shown in Figure 4. The calendar and the train are correctly separated from the background tapestry. The rolling ball is identified, but its boundaries are unstable over time. It disappears from

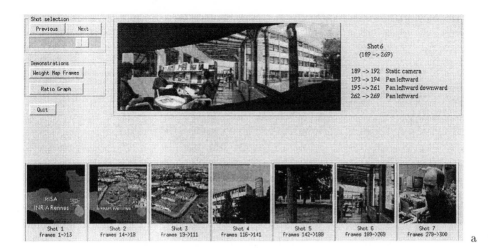

a

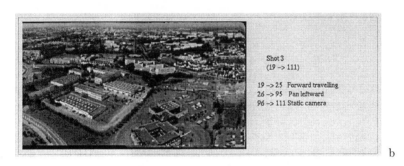

b

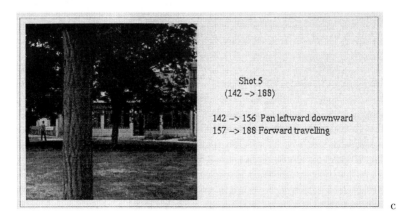

c

Fig. 3. *Visualization of the video summary (a). A key-frame per detected shot is displayed (bottom row), and, for a user-selected shot, more information about its contents is supplied (mosaic image and sequence of camera motion types). Examples shown correspond to (a) shot 6, (b) shot 3 and (c) shot 5. The first frame and last frame numbers for each shot account for having suppressed frames within progressive transitions.*

frames 37 to 47, and reappears as a new object, because no long-term trajectory association technique is included. The same issue arises for the calendar. A low-cost extension to alleviate these problems for simple cases, considering each object in the scene is to be indexed by still image cues anyway, would consist in matching objects using these cues. Figure 5 shows the created synoptic view. Camera motion is correctly globally characterized as "left panning". The trajectories of the train and the calendar, and the piece-wise trajectory of the rolling ball are drawn as described in Section 6. Because they are temporarily motionless, two distinct objects are considered, both in the case of the ball and the calendar, hence the trajectories on the synoptic view. Descriptors assigned to meaningful objects have been summarized in Figure 6, and describe correctly their behaviour. Though Figure 6 only includes qualitative measurements, the trajectory could also be used for indexing, and retrieval on this cue could be done by a sketch. A few spurious regions are extracted and are not included in the table. They slightly perturbate the clarity of the synoptic view, but, with a view to indexing, the effect on memory occupation in the database is minor, and besides, they do not severely disturb the features found for the meaningful objects.

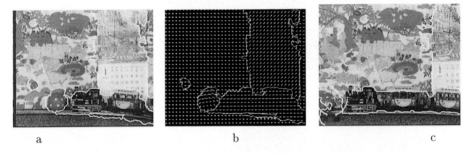

a   b   c

Fig. 4. Mobi sequence : extracted motion segmentation boundaries for frame 4(a) and associated estimated motion(b), motion boundaries for frame 120(c)

8 Conclusion

We have described a method for structuring the content of a video in several steps, namely video partitioning into shots, motion-based segmentation of each shot, and tracking of mobile objects. From this structure, we infer a technique for indexing and quick-viewing of the dynamic content. The method supplies ample descriptions of object and camera motions, that are relevant and useful for indexing. They are both of instantaneous and long-term, qualitative and quantitative nature, by exploiting the extracted motion information and trajectories. The various steps of the scheme exploit an efficient robust 2D motion

Fig. 5. Mobi sequence : Synoptic summary of the dynamic content of the shot. The background scene is discarded, mobile objects are displayed at their first position in the sequence, and their trajectories are drawn in the global coordinate system. The rotation of the ball is annotated by a curved arrow.

Name	Calendar 1	Calendar 2	Train	Ball 1	Ball 2
Icon					
Appearance frame	1	66	1	1	47
Disappearance frame	56	125	125	33	125
Apparent motion	up-left (1-56)	down-left (60-125)	none (tracked)	clockwise rotation (tracked)	clockwise rotation (tracked)
Global view motion	up (1-56)	down (60-125)	left	left clockwise rotation	left clockwise rotation

Fig. 6. Object motion descriptors

estimator, applied as appropriate on the whole image or on regions. So doing, the same motion measurements have multiple purposes in the structuring and description phases. Overall, the system is designed with a view to providing rich spatio-temporal information, coping with a broad range of scene contents, while keeping computational cost low.

Possible extensions are numerous. First, since objects are delimited, the cues used in still image indexing, such as shape, color, that are usually measured either globally, or on somewhat arbitrary regions, can then be computed on meaningful regions. In another direction, we are currently experimenting a long-term multi-trajectory approach to region tracking. This would enable additional description of spatio-temporal relations between mobile objects, such as occlusions and crossings, which are interesting from the semantic point of view, and improve the quality of long-term motion description in the case of piece-wise trajectories, or in cases as shown for the *Mobi* sequence.

References

1. P. Aigrain and P. Joly. – The automatic real-time analysis of film editing and transition effects and its applications. – *Computer & Graphics*, 18(1):93–103, 1994.
2. P. Aigrain, H.J. Zhang, and D. Petkovic. – Content-based representation and retrieval of visual media : a state-of-the-art review. – *Multimedia Tools and Applications*, 3(3):179–202, November 1996.
3. S. Ayer and H.S Sawhney. – Compact representations of videos through dominant and multiple motion estimation. – *IEEE Trans. on Pattern Analysis and Machine Intelligence*, 18(8):814–830, August 1996.
4. M. Basseville. – Detecting changes in signals and systems - a survey. – *Automatica*, 24(3):309–326, 1988.
5. J.S. Boreczky and L.A. Rowe. – Comparison of video shot boundary detection techniques. – In *In I.K. Sethi and R.C. Jain, editors, Proceedings of IS-T/SPIE Conference on Storage and Retrieval for Image and Video Databases IV, Vol. SPIE 2670*, pages 170–179, 1996.
6. P. Bouthemy and F. Ganansia. – Video partitioning and camera motion characterization for content-based video indexing. – In *Proc. of 3rd IEEE Int. Conf. on Image Processing*, volume I, pages 905–909, Lausanne, Sept 1996.
7. C. Castel, L. Chaudron, and C. Tessier. – What is going on ? A high level interpretation of sequences of images. – In *4th European Conf. on Computer Vision,*, Cambridge UK, April 1996. – LNCS 1065.
8. J.D. Courtney. – Automatic video indexing via object motion analysis. – *Pattern Recognition*, 30(4):607–625, April 1997.
9. M. De Marsico, L. Cinque, and S Levialdi. – Indexing pictorial documents by their content : a survey of current techniques. – *Image and Vision Computing*, (15):119–141, 1997.
10. A. Del Bimbo, E. Vicario, and D. Zingoni. – Symbolic description and visual querying of image sequences using spatio-temporal logic. – *IEEE Trans. on Knowledge and Data Engineering*, 7(4):609–621, August 1995.
11. M. Flickner et al. – Query by image and video content : the QBIC system. – *IEEE Computer*, pages 23–32, Sept. 1995.

12. E. François and P. Bouthemy. – Derivation of qualitative information in motion analysis. – *Image and Vision Computing*, 8(4):279–287, Nov. 1990.

13. M. Gelgon and P. Bouthemy. – A region-level graph labeling approach to motion-based segmentation. – In *Proc. of Conf. on Computer Vision and Pattern Recognition*, pages 514–519, Puerto-Rico, June 1997.

14. F. Idris and S. Panchanathan. – Review of image and video indexing techniques. – *Jal of Visual Communication and Image Representation*, 8(2):146–166, June 1997.

15. M. Irani, P. Anandan, J. Bergen, R. Kumar, and S. Hsu. – Efficient representations of video sequences and their applications. – *Signal Processing : Image Communication*, (8):327–351, 1996.

16. M. Irani, B. Rousso, and S. Peleg. – Detecting and tracking multiple moving objects using temporal integration. – In *Proc. of Second European Conference on Computer Vision*, pages 282–287, Santa Margherita Ligure, Italy, May 1992.

17. A. Nagasaka and Y. Tanaka. – Automatic video indexing and full-video search for objects appearances. – *Visual Database Systems II*, pages 113–127, 1992. – E. Knuth and L.M. Wegner (eds.), Elsevier Science Publ.

18. J.M Odobez and P. Bouthemy. – Robust multiresolution estimation of parametric motion models. – *Jal of Visual Communication and Image Representation*, 6(4):348–365, December 1995.

19. N.V. Patel and I.K. Sethi. – Video shot detection and characterization for video databases. – *Pattern Recognition*, 30(4):607–625, April 1997.

20. B. Rousso, S. Peleg, I. Finci, and A. Rav-Acha. – Universal mosaicing using pipe projection. – In *Proc. of IEEE International Conf. on Computer Vision (ICCV'98)*, pages 945–952, Bombay,India, January 1999.

21. H. Sawhney and R. Kumar. – True multi image alignment and its application to mosaicing and lens distorsion correction. – In *Proc. of Conf. on Computer Vision and Pattern Recognition*, pages 450–456, Puerto-Rico, June 1997.

22. C. Schmid and R. Mohr. – Combining greyvalue invariants with local constraints for object recognition. – In *Proc. of Conf. on Computer Vision and Pattern Recognition*, pages 872–877, San Francisco, USA., June 1996.

23. M.A Smith and T. Kanade. – Video skimming and characterization through the combination of image and language understanding techniques. – In *Proc. of Conf. on Computer Vision and Pattern Recognition*, pages 775–781, Puerto-Rico, June 1997.

24. C. Stiller. – Object-oriented estimation of dense motion fields. – *IEEE Trans. on Image Processing*, 6(2), February 1997.

25. J.Y.A Wang and E.H Adelson. – Representing moving images with layers. – *IEEE Trans. on Image Processing*, 3(5):625–638, September 1994.

26. H.J Zhang, A. Kankanhalli, and S.W. Smoliar. – Automatic partitioning of full-motion video. – *Multimedia Systems*, 1:10–28, 1993.

27. H.J Zhang, J. Wu, D. Zhong, and S.W. Smoliar. – An integrated system for content-based video retrieval and browsing. – *Pattern Recognition*, 30(4):643–658, April 1997.

Demosaicing:
Image Reconstruction from Color CCD Samples

Ron Kimmel[1*]

Computer Science Department, Technion, Haifa 32000, Israel

Abstract. A simplified color image formation model is used to construct an algorithm for image reconstruction from CCD sensors samples. The proposed method involves two successive steps. The first is motivated by Cok's [1] template matching technique, while the second step uses steerable inverse diffusion in color. Classical linear signal processing techniques tend to over smooth the image and result in noticeable color artifacts along edges and sharp features. The question is how should the different color channels support each other to form the best possible reconstruction. Our answer is to let the edges support the color information, and the color channels support the edges, and thereby achieve better perceptual results than those that are bounded by the sampling theoretical limit.

Keywords: *Color enhancement, Multi channel image reconstruction, Steerable inverse diffusion, Non linear image processing.*

1   Introduction

In recent years, digital cameras for still images and movies became popular. There are many obvious advantages to digital images comparing to classical film based cameras, yet there are limitations as well. For example, the spatial resolution is limited due to the physical structure of the sensors. 'Super resolution' beyond the sensors resolution can be achieved by considering a sequence of images.

In this note we deal with the reconstruction of a single color digital image from its color CCD sensors' information. We limit our discussion to Bayer color filter array (CFA) pattern as presented in Figure 1. We will start with a simple color image formation model and explore the relation between the different color channels such that the channels support the edges, and the edges support the colors. This relation with a simple color image formation model enables a reconstruction beyond the linear optimal signal processing approach that is limited by the Nyquist sampling rate.

---

* Part of this work was done while the author was a postdoctoral fellow at LBNL, and Math Dept. UC Berkeley, and supported in part by the OER Applied Mathematics Subprogram under DE-AC03-76SFOOO98, and ONR grant under NOOO14-96-1-0381.

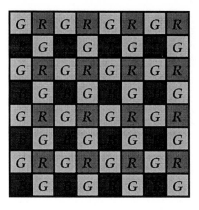

Fig. 1. Bayer CFA (color filter array) pattern (US Patent 3,971,065, 1976). [This is a color figure]

We follow Cok's [1] exposition for constructing the first step of the algorithm: The reconstruction stage. The Green component is reconstructed first with the help of the Red and Blue gradients. Then the Red and Blue are reconstructed using the Green values, edge approximations, and a simple color ratio rule: Within a given 'object' the ratio $Red/Green$ is locally constant (the same is true for $Blue/Green$). This rule falls apart across edges where the color gradients are high, which are the interesting and problematic locations from our reconstruction point of view.

Next the Green, Red, and Blue pixels are adjusted to fit the color cross ratio equivalence. The interpolation and the adjustment are weighted by a function of the directional derivatives to reduce the influence of ratios across edges. This is the main difference from Cok's [1] method, who try to match templates that predict the local structure of the image for a bilinear interpolation.

The second step, the enhancement stage, involves an anisotropic inverse diffusion flow in color space, which is an extension of Gabor's geometric filter [6], and is based on the geometric framework for color introduced in [11, 8]. It is also related to Weickert's texture enhancement method [12], and to the recent results of Sapiro and Ringach [10], and Cottet and El Ayyadi [2]. The idea is to consider the color image as a two dimensional surface in 5D (x, y, R, G, B) space, extract its induced metric and smooth the metric in order to sense the structure of the image surface beyond the local noise. Then diffuse the different channels along the edges and simultaneously enhance the image by applying an 'inverse heat' operator across the edges.

The structure of this note is as follows: Section 2 introduces a simple model for color images. Next, Section 3 uses this model for the reconstruction of a 1D image. Section 4 presents the first step of the algorithm, the reconstruction stage, that involves weighted interpolation subject to constant cross ratio of the spectral channels. Section 5 presents the second step of the algorithm. It is a non linear enhancement filter based on steerable anisotropic inverse diffusion flow in color space. Section 5 concludes with experimental results on a set of benchmark images. Some of the techniques we present were developed as a result of discussions with Prof. J.A. Sethian from UC Berkeley, and with Dr. Y. Hel-Or from HP Labs Israel.

2   A Simple Color Image Formation Model

A simplified model for color images is a result of viewing Lambertian non flat surface patches. Such a scene is a generalization of what is known as a 'Mondriaan world'. According to the model, each channel may be considered as the projection of the real 3D world surface normal $\hat{\mathbf{N}}(\mathbf{x})$ onto the light source direction $\mathbf{l}$, multiplied by the albedo $\rho(x, y)$. The albedo captures the characteristics of the 3D object's material, and is different for each of the spectral channels. That is, the 3 color channels may be written as

$$
\begin{aligned}
I^R(\mathbf{x}) &= \rho_R(\mathbf{x})\hat{\mathbf{N}}(\mathbf{x}) \cdot \mathbf{l} \\
I^G(\mathbf{x}) &= \rho_G(\mathbf{x})\hat{\mathbf{N}}(\mathbf{x}) \cdot \mathbf{l} \\
I^B(\mathbf{x}) &= \rho_B(\mathbf{x})\hat{\mathbf{N}}(\mathbf{x}) \cdot \mathbf{l}.
\end{aligned}
\tag{1}
$$

This means that the different colors capture the change in material via ρ_i (where i stands for R, G, B) that multiplies the normalized shading image $\tilde{I}(\mathbf{x}) = \hat{\mathbf{N}}(\mathbf{x}) \cdot \mathbf{l}$. The Mondriaan color image formation model [4] was used for color based segmentation [7] and shading extraction from color images [5]. Let us follow the above generalization of this model and assume that the material, and therefore the albedo, are the same within a given object in the image, e.g. $\rho_i(\mathbf{x}) = c_i$, where c_i is a given constant. Thus, within the interior of a given object the following constant ratio holds:

$$
\frac{I^i(\mathbf{x})}{I^j(\mathbf{x})} = \frac{\rho_i(\mathbf{x})\tilde{I}(\mathbf{x})}{\rho_j(\mathbf{x})\tilde{I}(\mathbf{x})} = \frac{\rho_i(\mathbf{x})}{\rho_j(\mathbf{x})} = \frac{c_i}{c_j} = \text{constant}.
\tag{2}
$$

That is, the color ratio within a given object is constant. We note, that this is an oversimplified assumption for general analysis of color images. However, its local nature makes it valid and useful for our technological purpose.

3   The 1D Case

Let us start with a simple 1D example with two colors, see Fig. 2. Our assumption is that the colors are smooth within a given object and go through a sudden jump at the boundaries. Define the central difference approximation to be $D_x I_i \equiv \frac{I_{i+1} - I_{i-1}}{\Delta x}$, where $I_i \equiv I(i\Delta x)$ is the value of the function $I(x)$ at the point $x = i\Delta x$, and Δx is the spatial discretization interval.

Given the samples (odd points for the Red and even points for the Green) we use the gradient to construct an edge indicator for the interpolation. Let the

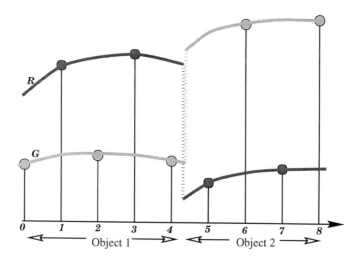

Fig. 2. The Red and Green components of a 1D image.

edge indicator be $e_i^g = f(D_x G_i)$, where $f(\circ)$ is a decreasing function, e.g. $e_i^g = (1 + (D_x G_i)^2)^{-1/2}$, and respectively e_i^r. One simple reconstruction procedure is as follows:

– <u>Init:</u> Interpolate for the Green at the missing points

$$G_i = \frac{e_{i-1}^r G_{i-1} + e_{i+1}^r G_{i+1}}{e_{i-1}^r + e_{i+1}^r}.$$

– <u>Repeat for 3 times:</u>
– Interpolate the Red values via the ratio rule weighted by the edge indicator

$$R_i = G_i \frac{e_{i-1}^g \frac{R_{i-1}}{G_{i-1}} + e_{i+1}^g \frac{R_{i+1}}{G_{i+1}}}{e_{i-1}^g + e_{i+1}^g}.$$

– Correct the Green values to fit the ratio rule

$$G_i = R_i \frac{e_{i-1}^r \frac{G_{i-1}}{R_{i-1}} + e_{i+1}^r \frac{G_{i+1}}{R_{i+1}}}{e_{i-1}^r + e_{i+1}^r}.$$

– <u>End of loop.</u>

Note that this is a numerically consistent procedure for the proposed color image formation model. It means that as the sampling grid is refined, the result converges to the continuous solution.

Here, again we recognize the importance of segmentation in computer vision. An accurate segmentation procedure, that gives the exact locations of the objects boundaries, would have allowed an image reconstruction far beyond the sampling limit (under the assumption that within a given object there are no high spatial frequencies).

4 First Step: Reconstruction

For real 2D images with three color channels the reconstruction is less trivial. Edges now become curves rather than points, and in many cases one needs to interpolate missing points along the edges. We would still like to avoid interpolating across edges.

Based on the simplified color image formation model, the three channels go through a sudden jump across the edges. Thus, the gradient magnitude can be used as an edge indicator, and its direction can approximate the edge direction (it is easy to verify that the gradient ∇G is normal to the level set curves of $G(\mathbf{x})$, i.e. $G(\mathbf{x}) = const.$)

The directional derivatives are approximated at each point based on its 8 nearest neighbors on the grid. Define the finite difference approximation for the directional derivatives, central D, forward D^+, and backwards D^-, as follows:

$$
\left\{
\begin{array}{ll}
D_x G_{i,j} = \frac{G_{i+1,j} - G_{i-1,j}}{2\Delta x} & D_y G_{i,j} = \frac{G_{i,j+1} - G_{i,j-1}}{2\Delta y} \\[2ex]
D_{x'} G_{i,j} = \frac{G_{i+1,j+1} - G_{i-1,j-1}}{2\sqrt{\Delta x^2 + \Delta y^2}} & D_{y'} G_{i,j} = \frac{G_{i-1,j+1} - G_{i+1,j-1}}{2\sqrt{\Delta x^2 + \Delta y^2}} \\[2ex]
D_{x'}^+ G_{i,j} = \frac{G_{i+1,j+1} - G_{i,j}}{\sqrt{\Delta x^2 + \Delta y^2}} & D_{x'}^- G_{i,j} = \frac{G_{i+1,j+1} - G_{i,j}}{\sqrt{\Delta x^2 + \Delta y^2}} \\[2ex]
D_{y'}^+ G_{i,j} = \frac{G_{i-1,j+1} - G_{i,j}}{\sqrt{\Delta x^2 + \Delta y^2}} & D_{y'}^- G_{i,j} = \frac{G_{i,j} - G_{i+1,j-1}}{\sqrt{\Delta x^2 + \Delta y^2}}
\end{array}
\right. \tag{3}
$$

At the Green points use $\max\{|D_{x'}^+ G_{i,j}|, |D_{x'}^- G_{i,j}|\}$ for the magnitude of the directional derivative along the x' direction (and similarly for y'). For the rest of the points and the x and y directions use central differences. We thereby construct an approximation for the directional derivatives at each and every point. Denote these approximations as $Dx_{ij}, Dy_{ij}, Dx'_{ij}$, and Dy'_{ij}, respectively.

Next, we generalize an edge indicator function. When a point at location $((i+1)\Delta x, j\Delta y)$ is taking part in the interpolation at the $(i\Delta x, j\Delta y)$ location, we use the following weight as an edge indicator: $e_{ij}^{i+1,j} = (1 + Dx_{ij}^2 + Dx_{i+1,j}'^2)^{-1/2}$

Based on the edge indicators as weights for the interpolation we follow similar steps as for the 1D case to reconstruct the 2D image:

– Init: Interpolate for the Green at the missing points

$$
G_{ij} = \frac{e_{ij}^{i-1,j} G_{i-1,j} + e_{ij}^{i+1,j} G_{i+1,j} + e_{ij}^{i,j-1} G_{i,j-1} + e_{ij}^{i,j+1} G_{i,j+1}}{e_{ij}^{i-1,j} + e_{ij}^{i+1,j} + e_{ij}^{i,j-1} + e_{ij}^{i,j+1}}.
$$

Interpolate for the Blue and Red in two steps.
Step 1 (interpolate missing Blue at Red locations) :

$$B_{ij} = G_{ij} \frac{e_{ij}^{i+1,j+1} \frac{B_{i+1,j+1}}{G_{i+1,j+1}} + e_{ij}^{i-1,j-1} \frac{B_{i-1,j-1}}{G_{i-1,j-1}} + e_{ij}^{i-1,j+1} \frac{B_{i-1,j+1}}{G_{i-1,j+1}} + e_{ij}^{i+1,j-1} \frac{B_{i+1,j-1}}{G_{i+1,j-1}}}{e_{ij}^{i+1,j+1} + e_{ij}^{i-1,j-1} + e_{ij}^{i-1,j+1} + e_{ij}^{i+1,j-1}}.$$

Step 2 (interpolate at the rest of the missing Blue points):

$$B_{ij} = G_{ij} \frac{e_{ij}^{i+1,j} \frac{B_{i+1,j}}{G_{i+1,j}} + e_{ij}^{i-1,j} \frac{B_{i-1,j}}{G_{i-1,j}} + e_{ij}^{i,j+1} \frac{B_{i,j+1}}{G_{i,j+1}} + e_{ij}^{i,j-1} \frac{B_{i,j-1}}{G_{i,j-1}}}{e_{ij}^{i+1,j} + e_{ij}^{i-1,j} + e_{ij}^{i,j+1} + e_{ij}^{i,j-1}}.$$

Interpolate the Red with two similar steps.
− Repeat for 3 times:
− Correct the Green values to fit the ratio rule

$$G_{ij}^B = B_{ij}(e_{ij}^{i+1,j} \frac{G_{i+1,j}}{B_{i+1,j}} + e_{ij}^{i-1,j} \frac{G_{i-1,j}}{B_{i-1,j}} + e_{ij}^{i,j+1} \frac{G_{i,j+1}}{B_{i,j+1}} + e_{ij}^{i,j-1} \frac{G_{i,j-1}}{B_{i,j-1}}$$
$$+e_{ij}^{i+1,j+1} \frac{G_{i+1,j+1}}{B_{i+1,j+1}} + e_{ij}^{i-1,j-1} \frac{G_{i-1,j-1}}{B_{i-1,j-1}} + e_{ij}^{i-1,j+1} \frac{G_{i-1,j+1}}{B_{i-1,j+1}} + e_{ij}^{i+1,j-1} \frac{G_{i+1,j-1}}{B_{i+1,j-1}})/$$
$$(e_{ij}^{i+1,j} + e_{ij}^{i-1,j} + e_{ij}^{i,j+1} + e_{ij}^{i,j-1} + e_{ij}^{i+1,j+1} + e_{ij}^{i-1,j-1} + e_{ij}^{i-1,j+1} + e_{ij}^{i+1,j-1}).$$

$$(4)$$

and average between the Blue and Red interpolation results

$$G_{ij} = \frac{G_{ij}^B + G_{ij}^R}{2}.$$

− Correct the Blue and Red values via the ratio rule weighted by the edge indicator

$$B_{ij} = G_{ij}(e_{ij}^{i+1,j} \frac{B_{i+1,j}}{G_{i+1,j}} + e_{ij}^{i-1,j} \frac{B_{i-1,j}}{G_{i-1,j}} + e_{ij}^{i,j+1} \frac{B_{i,j+1}}{G_{i,j+1}} + e_{ij}^{i,j-1} \frac{B_{i,j-1}}{G_{i,j-1}}$$
$$+e_{ij}^{i+1,j+1} \frac{B_{i+1,j+1}}{G_{i+1,j+1}} + e_{ij}^{i-1,j-1} \frac{B_{i-1,j-1}}{G_{i-1,j-1}} + e_{ij}^{i-1,j+1} \frac{B_{i-1,j+1}}{G_{i-1,j+1}} + e_{ij}^{i+1,j-1} \frac{B_{i+1,j-1}}{G_{i+1,j-1}})/$$
$$(e_{ij}^{i+1,j} + e_{ij}^{i-1,j} + e_{ij}^{i,j+1} + e_{ij}^{i,j-1} + e_{ij}^{i+1,j+1} + e_{ij}^{i-1,j-1} + e_{ij}^{i-1,j+1} + e_{ij}^{i+1,j-1}).$$

$$(5)$$

− End of loop.

Up to this point, the original values given as samples were not modified. We have interpolated the missing points weighted by edge indicator functions subject to the constant cross ratio. Next, we apply inverse diffusion in color to the whole image as an enhancement filter.

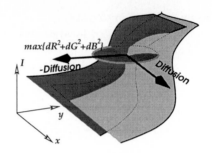

Fig. 3. The Red and Green components painted as surfaces in x, y, I with the inverse diffusion (across the edge) and diffusion (along the edge) directions.

5 Second Step: Enhancement

This section is a brief description of one of the non linear filters introduced in [8] that we apply as a second step for enhancing the color image.

In [6], Gabor considered an image enhancement procedure based on an anisotropic flow via the <u>inverse</u> second directional derivative in the 'edge' direction and the geometric heat equation as a diffusion along the edge, see also [9]. Cottet and Germain [3] used a smoothed version of the image to direct the diffusion. Weickert [12] smoothed the 'structure tensor' $\nabla I \nabla I^T$ and then manipulated its eigenvalues to steer the smoothing direction, while Sapiro and Ringach [10] eliminated one eigenvalue from the structure tensor in color space without smoothing its coefficients.

Motivated by all of these results, a new color enhancement filter was introduced in [8]. The inverse diffusion and diffusion directions are deduced from the smoothed metric coefficients $g_{\mu\nu}$ of the image surface. The color image is considered as a 2D surface in the 5D (x, y, R, G, B) space, as suggested in [11]. The induced metric coefficients are extracted for the image surface and used as a natural structure tensor for the color case.

The induced metric $(g_{\mu\nu})$ is a symmetric matrix that captures the geometry of the image surface. Let λ_1 and λ_2 be the largest and the smallest eigenvalues of $(g_{\mu\nu})$, respectively. Since $(g_{\mu\nu})$ is a symmetric positive matrix its corresponding eigenvectors u_1 and u_2 can be chosen orthonormal. Let $U \equiv (u_1|u_2)$, and $\Lambda \equiv \begin{pmatrix} \lambda_1 & 0 \\ 0 & \lambda_2 \end{pmatrix}$, then we readily have the equality

$$(g_{\mu\nu}) = U \Lambda U^T. \tag{6}$$

Note also that

$$(g^{\mu\nu}) \equiv (g_{\mu\nu})^{-1} = U \Lambda^{-1} U^T = U \begin{pmatrix} 1/\lambda_1 & 0 \\ 0 & 1/\lambda_2 \end{pmatrix} U^T, \tag{7}$$

and that

$$g \equiv \det(g_{\mu\nu}) = \lambda_1 \lambda_2. \tag{8}$$

Let us use the image metric as a structure tensor. We extract the structure from the metric $(g_{\mu\nu})$ and then modify it to be a non-singular symmetric matrix with one positive and one negative eigenvalues. That is, instead of diffusion we introduce an inverse diffusion in the edge direction. This is an extension of Gabor's idea [6] of inverting the diffusion along the gradient direction, see Fig. 3.

The proposed inverse diffusion enhancement for color images is then given as follows:

1. Compute the metric coefficients $g_{\mu\nu}$.

$$g_{\mu\nu} = \delta_{\mu\nu} + \sum_{k=\{R,G,B\}} I_\mu^k I_\nu^k. \tag{9}$$

or explicitly

$$(g_{\mu\nu}) = \begin{pmatrix} 1 + R_x^2 + G_x^2 + B_x^2 & R_x R_y + G_x G_y + B_x B_y \\ R_x R_y + G_x G_y + B_x B_y & 1 + R_y^2 + G_y^2 + B_y^2 \end{pmatrix} \tag{10}$$

2. Diffuse the $g_{\mu\nu}$ coefficients by convolving with a Gaussian of variance ρ, thereby

$$\tilde{g}_{\mu\nu} = G_\rho * g_{\mu\nu}. \tag{11}$$

Where $G_\rho = e^{-(x^2+y^2)/\rho^2}$.

3. Change the eigenvalues of $(\tilde{g}_{\mu\nu})$ such that the largest eigenvalue λ_1 is now $\lambda_1 = -\alpha^{-1}$ and $\lambda_2 = \alpha$, for some given positive scalar $\alpha < 1$. This yields a new matrix $\hat{g}_{\mu\nu}$ that is given by:

$$(\hat{g}_{\mu\nu}) = \tilde{U} \begin{pmatrix} -\alpha^{-1} & 0 \\ 0 & \alpha \end{pmatrix} \tilde{U}^T = \tilde{U} \Lambda_\alpha \tilde{U}^T. \tag{12}$$

A single scalar α is chosen for simplicity of the presentation. Different eigenvalues can be chosen, like eigenvalues that depend on the original ones. The important idea is to set the original largest eigenvalue to a negative value. This operation inverts the diffusion direction across the color edge and thereby enhance it.

4. Evolve the k-th channel via the flow:

$$\begin{aligned} I_t^k &= \partial_\mu \hat{g}^{\mu\nu} \partial_\nu I^k \\ &= \operatorname{div}\left(\tilde{U} \begin{pmatrix} -\alpha & 0 \\ 0 & \alpha^{-1} \end{pmatrix} \tilde{U}^T \nabla I^k \right). \end{aligned} \tag{13}$$

Inverting the heat equation is an inherently unstable process. However, if we keep smoothing the metric coefficients, and apply the diffusion along the edge (given the positive eigenvalue), we get a coherence-enhancing flow that yields sharper edges and is stable for a short duration of time.

Experimental Results

We tested the proposed method on four benchmark images that were sampled with Bayer color filter array pattern. The following examples demonstare the reconstruction and enhancement results for four benchmark images: Statue, Sails, Window, and Lighthouse. For each case, the top left is the original image. As a reference we present the result of a bilinear interpolation for the missing points for each channel separately at the top right. The bottom left is the result of the first reconstruction by weighted interpolation step, and the bottom right is the second step enhancement result. These are color images, and for a better color view we refer to www.lbl.gov/~ron. The same parameters were used for the reconstruction in all the examples, i.e. case dependent tuning was not used for the different images.

Acknowledgments
I am grateful to Prof. James Sethian for the helpful discussions, and to Dr. Yacov Hel-Or for introducing the problem, the helpful discussions that followed, and supplying the color benchmark images.

References

1. D R Cok. Reconstruction of CCD images using template matching. In *Proc. of IS&T's Annual Conference/ICPS*, pages 380–385, 1994.
2. G H Cottet and M El Ayyadi. A Volterra type model for image processing. *IEEE Trans. on IP*, to appear, 1997.
3. G H Cottet and L Germain. Image processing through reaction combined with nonlinear diffusion. *Math. Comp.*, 61:659–673, 1993.
4. P T Eliason, L A Soderblom, and P S Chavez. Extraction of topographic and spectral albedo information from multi spectral images. *Photogrommetric Engineering and Remote Sensing*, 48:1571–1579, 1981.
5. B V Funt, M S Drew, and M Brockington. Recovering shading from color images. In G Sandini, editor, *Lecture Notes in Computer Science, 588, Computer Vision: ECCV'92*, pages 124–132. Springer-Verlag, 1992.
6. D Gabor. Information theory in electron microscopy. *Laboratory Investigation*, 14(6):801–807, 1965.
7. G Healey. Using color for geometry-insensitive segmentation. *J. Opt. Soc. Am. A*, 6:920–937, 1989.
8. R Kimmel, R Malladi, and N Sochen. Image processing via the beltrami operator. In *Proc. of 3-rd Asian Conf. on Computer Vision*, Hong Kong, January 1998.
9. M Lindenbaum, M Fischer, and A M Bruckstein. On Gabor's contribution to image enhancement. *Pattern Recognition*, 27(1):1–8, 1994.
10. G Sapiro and D L Ringach. Anisotropic diffusion of multivalued images with applications to color filtering. *IEEE Trans. Image Proc.*, 5:1582–1586, 1996.
11. N Sochen, R Kimmel, and R Malladi. A general framework for low level vision. *IEEE Trans. on Image Processing*, to appear, 1997.
12. J Weickert. *Anisotropic diffusion in image processing*. Ph.D. thesis, Kaiserslautern Univ., Kaiserslautern, Germany, November 1995.

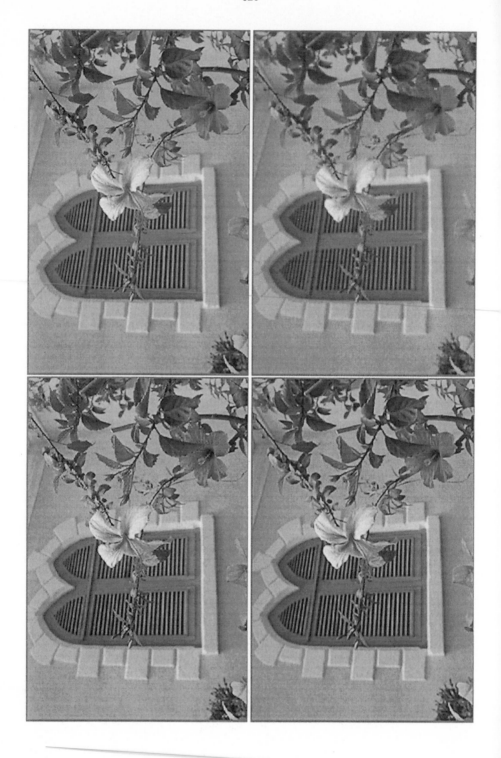

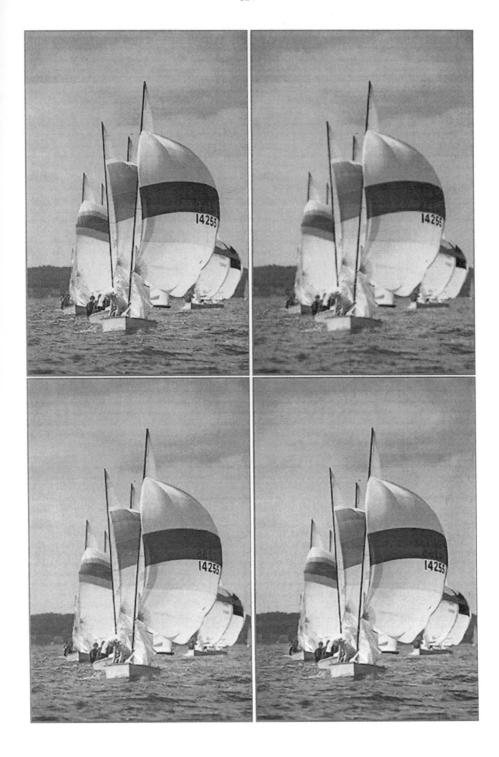

Perceptual Smoothing and Segmentation of Colour Textures

M. Petrou, M. Mirmehdi, and M. Coors

Centre for Vision, Speech and Signal Processing,
Surrey University, Guildford GU2 5XH, England
{M.Petrou,M.Mirmehdi}@ee.surrey.ac.uk

Abstract. An approach for perceptual segmentation of colour image textures is described. A multiscale representation of the texture image, generated by a multiband smoothing algorithm based on human psychophysical measurements of colour appearance is used as the input. Initial segmentation is achieved by applying a clustering algorithm to the image at the coarsest level of smoothing. Using these isolated *core clusters* 3D colour histograms are formed and used for probabilistic assignment of all other pixels to the core clusters to form larger clusters and categorise the rest of the image. The process of setting up colour histograms and probabilistic reassignment of the pixels is then propagated through finer levels of smoothing until a full segmentation is achieved at the highest level of resolution.

1   Introduction

The topics of texture segmentation and colour segmentation have attracted the attention of many researchers. At first sight it might seem trivial to solve the problem of colour texture segmentation, as it may appear that the obvious route would be to combine the knowledge gained from the research in the texture area with that gained in the colour area. However, there is a fundamental property which characterises colour texture and which has just emerged from the research in psychophysics [1]: Human perception of colour depends on the spatial frequency of the colour component. In other words, the perceptual response of the human visual system to a certain part of the electromagnetic spectrum depends on the frequency with which this stimulus is spatially distributed. Thus, colours that appear in a multicolour pattern are perceived differently from colours that form uniform areas (e.g. it has been shown [2] that any coloured pattern with frequency higher than 8 cycles per 1° of visual angle is seen as black). Zhang and Wandell [1] actually proposed a new colour system, called SCIE-Lab, which takes into consideration exactly this property of the visual system.

At least two issues seem relevant here. Firstly, the human vision system is able to extract colour textures as single entities without difficulties, with colour being a segmentation cue that is an integral part of pre-attentive vision. Secondly, image features which characterise a texture at a certain resolution may be entirely different from image features that characterise the same texture at another resolution. Another important characteristic of the human vision system is that it works as a process, with the analysis of a frame relying on a previous grosser analysis. This is achieved either with the help of peripheral vision followed by foveation to the area of interest, or by increasing the physical proximity of the viewed object. The former approach relies on the mechanism of switching sensors (going from the information obtained by the rods to that obtained by the cones). The latter approach, however, relies on using the same sensor but changing the number of degrees of visual angle it occupies in the field of view, in other words changing the spatial frequency a pattern extents to the eye. Both approaches are characterised by causality: the information flows from the coarse level to the finer level of resolution as the coarser analysis precedes the one performed at the finer level.

The reason we are concerned with the human colour perception is because the criteria by which we judge a segmentation to be good or not are subjective. In the absence of specific application requirement, we expect the segmentation of an image to agree with that performed by our own vision system. Thus, our interest in colour texture perception here concerns the way different textures can be perceived as separate homogeneous regions in the preattentive stage of vision.

Inspired by the above observations, in this paper we are proposing a mechanism of segmenting colour textures, by constructing a *causal*, multiscale *tower* of image versions based on perceptual considerations. The reason we call it "tower" and not a "pyramid" is because we do not perform subsampling and thus we preserve the same number of pixels at all levels. The levels of the tower are constructed with the help of blurring masks put forward by Zhang and Wandell [1], by assuming that the same colour-textured object is seen at 1,2,3,... meters distance. Hence, each coarser version of the image imitates the blurred version the human vision system would have "seen" at the corresponding distance. The analysis of the image starts at the coarsest level and proceeds towards the finest level, just like it would have happened if a person was slowly approaching a distant object. The mechanism with which information is transfered from a coarse to a finer level is probability theory that makes use of causality. We do not advocate that this is actually the mechanism deployed by humans; we use this approach because it is a sound mathematical tool that allows the incorporation of both features and preliminary conclusions that refer to many different levels of analysis.

The originality of the work presented is twofold: While multiresolution pyramids have been proposed and successfully utilised for several tasks, including texture segmentation [3–6], it is the first time that a multiscale/multilevel representation of the image which emulates the human colour perception, and which most significantly, takes into consideration the change in spatial frequency of the perceived pattern, is used for segmentation. Secondly, although the issue of transfer of information from one level of resolution to the next has been tackled by several researchers, and probabilistic relaxation has been used in multiresolution pyramid representations of data [7–10], it is the first time that a probabilistic relaxation theory, appropriate for operating *across* different levels of scale and exploiting a dictionary of permissible label configurations appropriate for *region labelling*, as opposed to edge or line labelling [10], is developed.

In the next section we shall give a brief literature review of the relevant issues. We must stress that there is very little work that is directly concerned with colour textures. In Section 3 we shall describe the method by which the perceptual tower of images is created. In Section 4, we shall present our probabilistic framework of propagating information in the causal direction across the levels of the tower, and in Section 5, the application of the probabilistic framework to colour texture images will be described. In Section 6, we shall present results of our approach when used to segment several colour texture images. We shall compare them with the results obtained by the recently proposed method in [11]. Our conclusions are presented in Section 7.

2 Literature Survey

The main consideration of *texture perception* in the Computer Vision literature has been with the derivation of descriptive features of the underlying texture. For example, Julesz and Bergen [12] used descriptions such as colour, widths, lengths, and orientations of local features, namely *textons*, to explain differences in artificially generated images. Also, Malik and Perona [13] provided a comparison of their computational model of human texture perception with psychophysical data obtained in texture discrimination experiments, while Tamura et al. [14] approximated computationally some basic textural features such as coarseness, directionality, line-likeness, contrast, roughness and regularity, which correspond to human visual perception. Most of these studies did not consider colour information, and moreover, their features are useful when viewing a scene from a fixed distance only.

Segmentation of texture images is a major field of research in Computer Vision. Textures may be regular or randomly structured, and various structural, statistical and spectral approaches have been proposed towards segmenting them [15–17]. One example of a recent technique is by Jain and Farrokhnia [18] who presented a texture segmentation algorithm focussed on a multi-channel Gabor filtering approach which is believed to characterise the processing of visual information in the early stages of the human visual system. Multi-scale approaches for texture analysis are few and far in-between. Unser and Eden[19] extracted texture energy measures form the image and smoothed the output of the extraction filter bank using Gaussian smoothing at different scales. The features in these multiscale planes are reduced, by diagonalising scatter matrices evaluated at two different spatial resolutions, and thresholded to yield texture segmentation. Matalas et al.[20], used a B-spline transform in order to obtain images at several smoothing levels to calculate vector dispersion and gradient orientation at different scales. A small disparity function is then applied to segment textures. Roan et al. [21] describe a method for classification of textured surfaces viewed at different resolutions, i.e. viewed at different scales or distances, while the image size remains constant. They used greylevel cooccurrence matrices and the Fourier power spectrum of an unknown texture image, taken at one of any several resolutions, to classify it as one of six known textures.

None of the above approaches is concerned with colour textures. On the other hand, there is a vast forum of work on *colour image segmentation* e.g. [22–27, 11]. In general, most colour texture representation schemes either use a combination of gray level texture features together with pure colour features, or they derive texture features computed separately in each of the three colour spectral channels. For example, Coleman and Andrews [28] used K-means clustering in each colour band and maximised a cluster fidelity parameter for a more psychovisually acceptable segmented image. Tan and Kittler [29] used eight DCT texture features computed from the intensity image and six colour features derived from the colour histogram of a textured image for classification. Panjwani and Healey[30] presented an unsupervised segmentation technique based on Markov Random Fields which clustered a colour image in the RGB space. Their Markov Random Fields approach made use of the spatial interaction of RGB pixels within each colour plane and the interaction between different colour planes. Matas and Kittler [11] grouped colour pixels by taking into account simultaneously both their feature space similarity and spatial coherence.

None of the above approaches or any other colour segmentation work known to the authors have taken into consideration the interaction between colour and spatial frequency of patterns.

3   Building the Perceptual Tower

The resolution of an image signifies the area in physical units a pixel corresponds to. For example, 1 pixel $= 3 \times 3 mm^2$ in the scene. When the same physical object is seen at a different distance, the resolution of the image changes, for example, 1 pixel $= 3 \times 3 cm^2$. At the same time, the number of "pixels" the image of the object occupies in the retina reduces. Each pixel now carries the (blurred) information from several other pixels in the finer resolution version. Thus, when one blurs the image to imitate human vision, one should subsequently subsample the image as well. This way, a pyramid of image resolutions is created. We chose not to perform this subsampling, hence we create a tower of images instead of a pyramid. The reason is dual: (1) we like to keep the redundant information in the coarse levels to increase the robustness of the system, (2) we maintain a direct correspondence between the pixels across the resolution/scale levels. As we do not perform subsampling, the sizes of the blurring masks we use become larger and larger in number of pixels as we proceed to compute the coarser levels of the tower. Seen in this way, our approach is multiscale as filters of various scale sizes are employed. Therefore, throughout this paper, we do not distinguish between the terms multiresolution and multiscale.

The response characteristics of the human visual mechanism are functions of not only the spectral properties of the stimuli, but also of the temporal and spatial variations of these stimuli. When an observer deals with multi-coloured objects, with fine textures, their colour matching behaviour is affected by the spatial properties of the observed pattern. Furthermore, the human visual system will experience loss of detail at increasing distances away from the object. It perceives coloured textures at a large distance as areas of fairly uniform colour, whereas variations in luminance, e.g. at the borders between two textured areas, are still perceived. Therefore it is necessary to introduce a multiscale smoothing algorithm that smooths an image according to human perception. Zhang and Wandell [1] studied recently systematically the colour perception of human subjects for different frequencies of spatial colour variation. They proposed an algorithm for perceptual smoothing appropriate for evaluating image coding schemes. It is based on measurements in psychophysical studies which showed that discrimination and appearance of small-field or fine patterned colours differ from similar measurements made using large uniform fields. The human eye perceives high spatial frequencies of colour as a uniform colour instead of being able to separate these colours. An algorithm, which takes this into account must smooth the image in luminance and chrominance colour planes separately with different filter matrices for the planes. Zhang and Wandell[1] advocated the use of the opponent colour space, which consists of three different colour planes, O_1, O_2, O_3, representing the luminance, the red-green and the blue-yellow planes respectively. In the $O_1O_2O_3$ colour space, each of the planes is smoothed separately with two-dimensional spatial kernels, defined as sums of Gaussian functions with different values of σ. The result of this operation is that the luminance plane is blurred lightly, whereas the red-green and the blue-yellow planes are blurred more strongly. This spatial processing technique is pattern-colour separable. Zhang and Wandell's filtered representation was then transformed back to CIE-XYZ and then to CIE-Lab resulting in their Spatial CIE-Lab space, namely SCIE-Lab.

In this application, we set up three convolution matrices for the colour planes for each separate viewing distance. In any particular set, each of the three matrices consists of a weighted sum of Gaussian kernels. The matrices are computed according to[1]:

$$\frac{1}{m} \sum_i \frac{w_i}{n_i} e^{-\frac{x^2+y^2}{\sigma_i^2}} \tag{1}$$

The values for (w_i, σ_i) which have been determined from psychological measurements of colour appearance on human subjects are given in [1] for a distance of 18 inches from the screen. We have derived new values for various distances by appropriate scaling. Divisor n_i in equation 1 is introduced to normalise the sum of the matrix elements of each individual Gaussian kernel before the weighted sum is applied. Divisor m normalises the sum of the final matrix to 1. These kernels are scaled, so that they each sum up to one.

Once the kernels are applied to the image in the opponent colour space, we transform the image data from the $O_1O_2O_3$ to the CIE-Luv space and use it as input in the ensuing steps of the algorithm. This step is performed because the CIE-Luv space is a perceptually uniform space and therefore more suitable

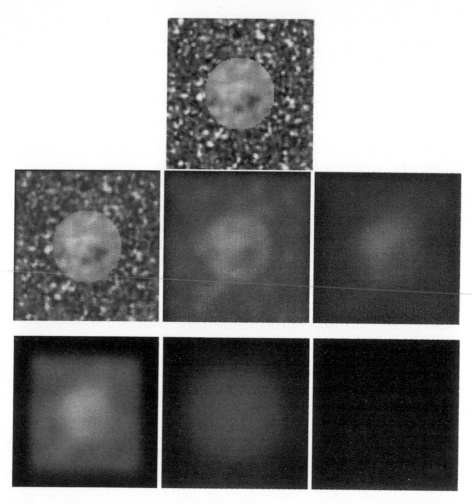

Fig. 1. (Row 1) Real texture collage image (Row 2) perceptual and (Row 3) Gaussian smoothed transformations corresponding to viewing distances of 1, 5, and 10 meters respectively.

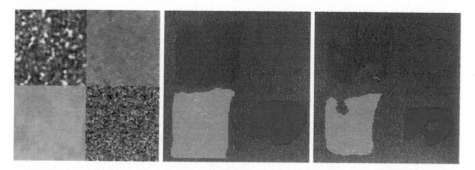

Fig. 2. Real texture collage image with initial clusters and derived core clusters.

for carrying out colour measurements. Figure 1 shows a real texture collage and its associated smoothed images at varying distances for both perceptual and Gaussian smoothing. Clearly, the perceptually smoothed images provide a more realistic representation and blurring of an "object" viewed at varying distances. Most particularly, the Gaussian has vastly mixed and smoothed the colour values when convolved with each of the three colour channels.

4 Multiscale Probabilistic Relaxation

The problem of multiscale probabilistic labelling of the input image using a set of perceptually blurred versions of the image can be stated as follows. Let l indicate the levels of coarsening with $l = 1, ..., L$, representing the levels from full resolution to the coarsest level. Let $i, i = 1, ..., N$ be a pixel and $\mathbf{x}_i^l$, the associated measurement vector for that pixel at resolution level l. We define a label set Ω, $\Omega = \{\omega_1, \omega_2, ..., \omega_m\}$, which contains all possible labels of the image for m possible perceptual categories. Thus, each pixel i has label θ_i that can take on values from Ω.

We wish to choose for pixel i the most probable label θ_i given all the available information. In other words we wish to set:

$$\theta_i = arg\{\max_k P(\theta_i = \omega_k \mid \mathbf{x}_j^l, \forall j, \forall l)\} \tag{2}$$

For simplicity and clarity of exposition we shall restrict ourselves in considering only two successive levels of resolution l and $l+1$. Then, using Bayes's rule we have:

$$P(\theta_i = \omega_k \mid \mathbf{x}_j^l, \mathbf{x}_j^{l+1}, \forall j) = \frac{P(\theta_i = \omega_k, \mathbf{x}_j^l, \mathbf{x}_j^{l+1}, \forall j)}{P(\mathbf{x}_j^l, \mathbf{x}_j^{l+1}, \forall j)} \tag{3}$$

We can expand the terms in the numerator and the denominator by applying the theorem of total probability:

$$P(\theta_i = \omega_k \mid \mathbf{x}_j^l, \mathbf{x}_j^{l+1}, \forall j) =$$

$$\frac{\sum_{\omega_{\theta_1}} \cdot \cdot \sum_{\omega_{\theta_{i-1}}} \sum_{\omega_{\theta_{i+1}}} \cdot \cdot \sum_{\omega_{\theta_N}} P(\theta_1 = \omega_{\theta_1}, .., \theta_i = \omega_k, .., \theta_N = \omega_{\theta_N}, \mathbf{x}_j^l, \mathbf{x}_j^{l+1}, \forall j)}{\sum_{\omega_{\theta_1}} \cdot \cdot \sum_{\omega_{\theta_i}} \cdot \cdot \sum_{\omega_{\theta_N}} P(\theta_1 = \omega_{\theta_1}, .., \theta_i = \omega_{\theta_i}, .., \theta_N = \omega_{\theta_N}, \mathbf{x}_j^l, \mathbf{x}_j^{l+1}, \forall j)} \tag{4}$$

The joint probability that appears in equation 4 can be factorised as follows:

$$P(\theta_1 = \omega_{\theta_1}, ..., \theta_N = \omega_{\theta_N}, \mathbf{x}_j^l, \mathbf{x}_j^{l+1}, \forall j) =$$
$$P(\mathbf{x}_1^{l+1}, ..., \mathbf{x}_N^{l+1} \mid \theta_1 = \omega_{\theta_1}, ..., \theta_N = \omega_{\theta_N}, \mathbf{x}_1^l, ..., \mathbf{x}_N^l) \times$$
$$P(\theta_1 = \omega_{\theta_1}, ..., \theta_N = \omega_{\theta_N}, \mathbf{x}_1^l, ..., \mathbf{x}_N^l) \tag{5}$$

As we try to emulate here perceptual segmentation, we can imagine that due to causality, measurements obtained at level $l + 1$ (the coarser level) can not possibly depend on measurements obtained at level l. Thus, the first factor on the right hand side of equation 5 can be simplified as follows:

$$P(\mathbf{x}_1^{l+1}, ..., \mathbf{x}_N^{l+1} \mid \theta_1 = \omega_{\theta_1}, ..., \theta_N = \omega_{\theta_N}, \mathbf{x}_1^l, ..., \mathbf{x}_N^l) =$$
$$P(\mathbf{x}_1^{l+1}, ..., \mathbf{x}_N^{l+1} \mid \theta_1 = \omega_{\theta_1}, ..., \theta_N = \omega_{\theta_N}) \qquad (6)$$

We also expect that the measurement concerning a certain pixel depends on the identity of that pixel alone and on nothing else. Therefore, we can further write:

$$P(\mathbf{x}_1^{l+1}, ..., \mathbf{x}_N^{l+1} \mid \theta_1 = \omega_{\theta_1}, ..., \theta_N = \omega_{\theta_N}) =$$
$$\prod_j P(\mathbf{x}_j^{l+1} \mid \theta_j = \omega_{\theta_j}) = \prod_j \frac{P(\theta_j = \omega_{\theta_j} \mid \mathbf{x}_j^{l+1})}{\hat{p}(\theta_j = \omega_{\theta_j})} \, \hat{p}(\mathbf{x}_j^{l+1}) \qquad (7)$$

where $\hat{p}(\mathbf{x}_j^{l+1})$ is the prior probability of measurements $\mathbf{x}_j^{l+1}$ to arise, and $\hat{p}(\theta_j = \omega_{\theta_j})$ is the prior probability of label ω_{θ_j}. Now consider the second factor on the right hand side of equation 5:

$$P(\theta_1 = \omega_{\theta_1}, ..., \theta_N = \omega_{\theta_N}, \mathbf{x}_1^l, ..., \mathbf{x}_N^l) =$$
$$P(\mathbf{x}_1^l \mid \theta_1 = \omega_{\theta_1}, ..., \theta_N = \omega_{\theta_N}, \mathbf{x}_2^l, ..., \mathbf{x}_N^l) \times$$
$$P(\theta_1 = \omega_{\theta_1}, ..., \theta_N = \omega_{\theta_N}, \mathbf{x}_2^l, ..., \mathbf{x}_N^l) \qquad (8)$$

We can further expand the second term on the right hand side of equation 8 to write:

$$P(\theta_1 = \omega_{\theta_1}, ..., \theta_N = \omega_{\theta_N}, \mathbf{x}_1^l, ..., \mathbf{x}_N^l) =$$
$$P(\mathbf{x}_1^l \mid \theta_1 = \omega_{\theta_1}, ..., \theta_N = \omega_{\theta_N}, \mathbf{x}_2^l, ..., \mathbf{x}_N^l) \times$$
$$P(\mathbf{x}_2^l \mid \theta_1 = \omega_{\theta_1}, ..., \theta_N = \omega_{\theta_N}, \mathbf{x}_3^l, ..., \mathbf{x}_N^l) \times .... \times$$
$$P(\mathbf{x}_N^l \mid \theta_1 = \omega_{\theta_1}, ..., \theta_N = \omega_{\theta_N}) \times$$
$$P(\theta_1 = \omega_{\theta_1}, ..., \theta_N = \omega_{\theta_N}) \qquad (9)$$

For the same reasons explained earlier, we expect that the measurement obtained for a particular object depends on the identity of the object itself and on nothing else. Thus, all factors on the right hand side of equation 9, except the last one, can be simplified to express dependence only on the identity of the object they refer to. The last factor is the joint probability of a certain label assignment to arise. So we have:

$$P(\theta_1 = \omega_{\theta_1}, ..., \theta_N = \omega_{\theta_N}, \mathbf{x}_1^l, ..., \mathbf{x}_N^l) =$$
$$\prod_j P(\mathbf{x}_j^l \mid \theta_j = \omega_{\theta_j}) \times P(\theta_1 = \omega_{\theta_1}, ..., \theta_N = \omega_{\theta_N}) \qquad (10)$$

Now by substituting from equations 7 and 10 in equation 5 we obtain:

$$P(\theta_1 = \omega_{\theta_1}, ..., \theta_N = \omega_{\theta_N}, \mathbf{x}_j^l, \mathbf{x}_j^{l+1}, \forall j) =$$

$$\prod_j \frac{1}{\hat{p}(\theta_j = \omega_{\theta_j})} \, P(\theta_j = \omega_{\theta_j} \mid \mathbf{x}_j^{l+1}) \, \hat{p}(\mathbf{x}_j^{l+1}) \, P(\mathbf{x}_j^l \mid \theta_j = \omega_{\theta_j}) \times$$

$$P(\theta_1 = \omega_{\theta_1}, ..., \theta_N = \omega_{\theta_N}) \tag{11}$$

Then, upon substitution in equation 4:

$$P(\theta_i = \omega_k \mid \mathbf{x}_j^l, \mathbf{x}_j^{l+1}, \forall j) =$$

$$\frac{P(\mathbf{x}_i^l \mid \theta_i = \omega_k) \, P(\theta_i = \omega_k \mid \mathbf{x}_i^{l+1}) \, \hat{p}(\mathbf{x}_i^{l+1}) \, \prod_j \hat{p}(\mathbf{x}_j^{l+1}) \, Q(\theta_i = \omega_k)}{\sum_{\omega_{\theta_i}} P(\mathbf{x}_i^l \mid \theta_i = \omega_{\theta_i}) \, P(\theta_i = \omega_{\theta_i} \mid \mathbf{x}_i^{l+1}) \, \hat{p}(\mathbf{x}_i^{l+1}) \, \prod_j \hat{p}(\mathbf{x}_j^{l+1}) \, Q(\theta_i = \omega_{\theta_i})} \tag{12}$$

where

$$Q(\theta_i = \omega_{\theta_i}) =$$

$$\frac{1}{\hat{p}(\theta_i = \omega_{\theta_i})} \sum_{\omega_{\theta_1}} \cdots \sum_{\omega_{\theta_{i-1}}} \sum_{\omega_{\theta_{i+1}}} \cdots \sum_{\omega_{\theta_N}} \prod_j \frac{P(\mathbf{x}_j^l \mid \theta_j = \omega_{\theta_j}) P(\theta_j = \omega_{\theta_j} \mid \mathbf{x}_j^{l+1})}{\hat{p}(\theta_j = \omega_{\theta_j})} \times$$

$$P(\theta_1 = \omega_{\theta_1}, ..., \theta_N = \omega_{\theta_N}) \tag{13}$$

In the above expression $\hat{p}(\mathbf{x}_i^{l+1})$ is independent of the summation indices and cancels in the numerator and denominator. Therefore, equation 12 further simplifies to:

$$P(\theta_i = \omega_k \mid \mathbf{x}_j^l, \mathbf{x}_j^{l+1}, \forall j) = \frac{P(\mathbf{x}_i^l \mid \theta_i = \omega_k) \, P(\theta_i = \omega_k \mid \mathbf{x}_i^{l+1}) \, Q(\theta_i = \omega_k)}{\sum_{\omega_{\theta_i}} P(\mathbf{x}_i^l \mid \theta_i = \omega_{\theta_i}) \, P(\theta_i = \omega_{\theta_i} \mid \mathbf{x}_i^{l+1}) \, Q(\theta_i = \omega_{\theta_i})} \tag{14}$$

At the finest resolution equations 2 and 14 give the final labelling result.

5 Application to Colour Texture Segments

In the previous two sections we presented the basic ingredients of our algorithm. The core of the multilevel probabilistic relaxation lies in the implementation of equations 13 and 14 and the estimation of the quantities that appear in them. The method works in a bootstrapping manner to estimate the various quantities needed. Thus, it is almost wholly unsupervised, with the possible exception of specifying the initial number of clusters in the coarsest level, if the K-means clustering method is used. It is possible to eliminate totally even this requirement by using a self-organising initial segmentation algorithm, like for example a watershed approach, or the method presented in [11], but we consider this as a point of secondary importance at present. In what follows we shall describe how each quantity that appears in 13 and 14 is estimated.

5.1 Core Clusters

The core clusters describe groups of pixels which can be confidently associated with the same region of texture in the image. The core clusters form the basis for setting up the colour histograms at different levels. To derive core clusters from the initial clusters, we need to fuzzify the segmentation/classification result obtained at the coarsest initialisation level. As this is only a step to help start the iteration process, we are adopting a rather simplistic approach: we first calculate the standard deviation σ_c of each cluster $c, c = 1, .., C$ where C is the total number of clusters. Then, we associate with every pixel a confidence, $\hat{p}_c^i$, with which it may be associated with each cluster:

$$\hat{p}_c^i \equiv \frac{\frac{\sigma_c^2}{d_c^{i2} + \sigma_c^2}}{\frac{\sigma_1^2}{d_1^{i2} + \sigma_1^2} + \frac{\sigma_2^2}{d_2^{i2} + \sigma_2^2} + ... + \frac{\sigma_C^2}{d_C^{i2} + \sigma_C^2}} \qquad \forall i, \forall c \qquad (15)$$

where d_c^{i2} is the squared distance of pixel i from the mean of cluster c. Note that this formula has the property of giving a confidence higher than 50% to pixels that are closer than 1σ from the mean of the cluster to belong to that cluster. Each core cluster is formed from the pixels that can be associated with it with a confidence of at least 80%. Figure 2 shows an example image with both its initial clusters and the subsequently derived core clusters.

Quantities $\hat{p}_c^i$ are also used to initialise the values of $P(\theta_i = \omega_{\theta_i} \mid \mathbf{x}_i^{l+1})$ which appear in 13 and 14. Thus, we set:

$$P(\theta_i = \omega_c \mid \mathbf{x}_i^L) = \hat{p}_c^i \qquad \forall i, \forall c. \qquad (16)$$

At all other levels $l < L$ these quantities are the probability label assignments computed for each pixel at level $l + 1$.

5.2   Prior Probabilities

The relative sizes of the core clusters are used as measures of the prior probabilities of the cluster labels, i.e. quantity $\hat{p}(\theta_j = \omega_{\theta_j})$ appearing in equation 13.

This is based on the observation that the larger clusters will appear most dominant when a texture mosaic is viewed from a large distance, and at the same time the prior probability of a pixel to belong to each cluster is proportional to the size of each cluster, in absence of any other information concerning the pixel.

5.3   3D Colour Histograms

The core clusters formed at resolution level $l+1$ are mapped back into the image at resolution l and using the colour pixel values in those regions, a three dimensional colour histogram is set up (dynamically) for each region. This provides a statistical characterisation for each different texture at each resolution. From these colour histograms, the likelihood of a pixel i at smoothing stage l to have label ω_k can be calculated using the colour of this pixel. This likelihood is represented by $P(\mathbf{x}_i^l \mid \theta_i = \omega_k)$. Note that this way the distribution of the features that characterise a texture at each resolution level can be derived.

5.4   The Q-Function Pattern Dictionary

Equation 13 involves a summation over all possible labels of all pixels other than the pixel under consideration. Clearly, such a summation is impossible due to the enormous number of combinations one would have to consider. We prune the number of possibilities by imposing a limit to the number of pixels we shall consider as influencing the labelling of the pixel under consideration. Thus, instead of examining all other $N - 1$ pixels, we handle only a subset of them constituting a local neighbourhood around the pixel. We restrict this to be a 3×3 neighbourhood. This allows us then to introduce a dictionary of permissible label configurations within each 3×3 patch. As junctions are rare events in images, in most cases we have only 1 or at most 2 regions present in any 3×3 patch. Hence, we restrict the entries of our dictionary to be of the form presented in Figure 3 where A and B stand for any pair of cluster labels present in the image. All entries of the dictionary are assigned equal probability, thus factor $P(\theta_1 = \omega_{\theta_1}, ..., \theta_N = \omega_{\theta_N})$ in 13 becomes a constant and therefore redundant. Label combinations that do not appear in the dictionary have zero probability to exist and so they do not enter the summation on the right hand side of 13. Thus, equation 13 simplifies to

$$Q(\theta_i = \omega_{\theta_i}) = \frac{1}{\hat{p}(\theta_i = \omega_{\theta_i})} \sum_{\Re} \sum_{\Im} \prod_{\aleph} \frac{P(\mathbf{x}_j^l \mid \theta_j = \omega_{\theta_j}) P(\theta_j = \omega_{\theta_j} \mid \mathbf{x}_j^{l+1})}{\hat{p}(\theta_j = \omega_{\theta_j})} \quad (17)$$

where $\Re$ is the set of all patterns in the dictionary, $\Im$ is the set containing all possible combinations of two labels where centre pixel has label ω_{θ_i}, and $\aleph$ is the set of 3×3 pixel neighbourhood entries in dictionary

An improvement of the Q-function is possible by expanding the pattern dictionary to patterns with more than two different labels. It is also possible to calculate the Q-function for a neighbourhood larger than 3×3 pixels.

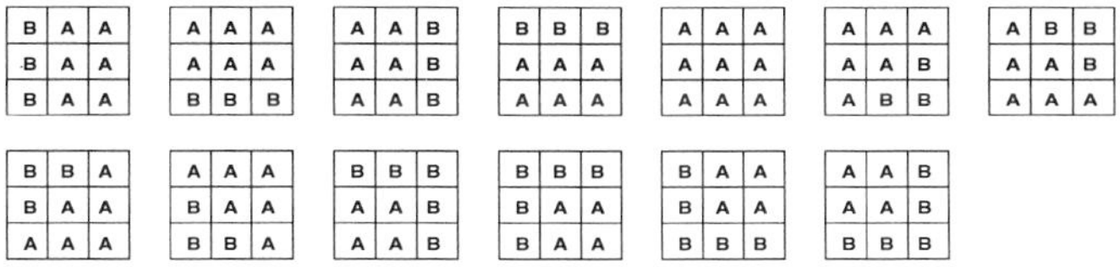

Fig. 3. Entries in pattern dictionary

6 Experimental Results

The results in this section are shown using arbitrarily selected colours to high-light different regions. All images tested were smoothed at different scales "or distances" (every meter up to $10m$) using the perceptual smoothing kernels. The processing commences from the distance at which the cluster histograms can be regarded as having separated modes. The results for the Gaussianly smoothed images were simply very wrong. To save space we do not report them here. Instead, we compare the results to an alternative approach (Matas and Kittler [11]) which is a more objective and comparable exercise.

The images shown on the left of Figure 4 are the original images of real texture collages put together from ceramic tile and granite stone textures. These textures are inherently random in nature. Our segmentation results are shown in the rightmost column while in the middle column the results from Matas and Kittler's [11] approach (hereafter referred to as MK) are demonstrated. MK exploit global and local image statistics simultaneously while also incorporating connectivity information. They discard the intensity information and form a 2D histogram of the chromaticity components. The image feature space is then partitioned by locating locally unimodal parts of the histogram. The spatial consistency of this segmentation is then examined and refined by incorporating neighbourhood connectivity. In the latter sense, our Q-function is also involving neighbourhood information. Moreover, we also consider more global contextual information by incorporating the prior label probabilities and the iterative re-finement of the initial segmentation. More poignantly, we encompass information from all three bands in our 3D histograms. Ignoring the intensity information can be useful if observing non-flat objects where the changes in intensity will deceive the observer's true colour perception. However, our purpose is to segment the scene as the observer views it, and not necessarily as the scene colours truly are. Therefore, considering the intensity band is very important.

As we have ground-truth information on these cases, the error measures for incorrectly classified pixels in both MK's and our perceptual segmentation are compared in Table 1. In every case we achieve a better segmentation. In the difficult test case T1, MK's technique finds a slightly smaller circle, therefore quite a number of pixels along the perimeter of the circle are misclassified. In test case T2, MK's technique has incorrectly combined the top-left and bottom-right patches as one class, while the latter is riddled with noisy segmentation; this is due to the non-unimodal representation of the guilty texture in MK's histograms, while it also is affected in a different way through its association with other types of texture in the image. In case T4, in which the image is a combination of real granite stone textures, the pixel values are quite spread out in the histogram, and there is little gradient there for MK's algorithm to work, while by perceptual segmentation the image can be correctly segmented (98.3%).

It is noteworthy that the perceptual segmentation algorithm has the ability to recover from incorrectly assigned pixels through the iterative relaxation process. Pixels already assigned to the wrong cluster, change their label again in future

Test Image	T1	T2	T3	T4
Matas & Kittler	2.2%	30%	1.3%	-
Perceptual	0.02%	1.2% %	0.04%	1.7%

Table 1. Error percentages of incorrectly classified pixels

steps thanks to the refinement in context, new neighbourhood information, and higher resolution information at consecutive levels.

The next set of results are more subjective and are expected to provide a more perception based representation of an image. Figures 5, 6, 7 respectively show the perceptual segmentation of a forest scene, the painting *La seine à argenteuil* by *Claude Monet*, and an aerial image. In all these cases, there are no nice straight edges that the Q-function could take advantage of to give an "accurate" segmentation. This is in fact the desired result as these images demonstrate the typical fuzzy segmentation of a scene that an observer may view from a distance.

Other important issues to note are that the histogram resolution in our experiments allows each bucket to cover an interval of 3.5 units in each direction in the Luv colour space. This is the resolution for the minimum perceivable colour distance for human vision. The clustering parameters are naturally very important since they determine the quality of the initial clusters on which our perceptual segmentation technique is based. However, we hope to use a parameter-free clustering approach in the future such as histogram watershed clustering[31].

The relaxation process can be iterated not only through the smoothed images, but also at each smoothed image for further incorporation and validation of image context. Naturally, this would add to the computational cost. At present, the smoothing stage demands a high computational cost due to the convolution filter sizes of Zhang and Wandell. However, the clustering and the relaxation process take approximately 60 seconds on a Silicon Graphics R10000 processor for a 128×128 image.

7 Discussions and Conclusions

Colour is an important parameter in the human visual experience. Most work in the past on texture analysis and segmentation has been concerned with deriving structural descriptors of texture, e.g. coarseness, regularity, blobiness, orientation etc., with the colour information perhaps used as an extra cue.

In this paper we treated the interplay of colours and their spatial distribution in an inseparable way as they are actually perceived during the pre-attentive stage of human colour vision. To do this we developed a tower of blurred versions of an image created by masks imitating the blurring the human vision sensors experience for scenes viewed at different distances, and allowed the information in this tower to flow in a causal direction, from the most blurred level to the most focussed. The creation of the tower made use of the latest results of psychophysics research, while the framework developed for the causal transfer of information is quite general and can be applied for image segmentation where the features used could be other than colour.

Finally, the probabilistic relaxation methodology developed works in the opposite sense than other probabilistic relaxation schemes where the flow of information starts from the immediate neighbours of a pixel and, as the iteration steps progress, the influence of more distant pixels is incorporated through the succession of immediate neighbour interactions. In our case, probabilistic relaxation works in the same sense as all other multiresolution/multiscale schemes where first the information of long-range interaction is absorbed, followed by the information from the shorter range interaction. As we do not perform subsampling when we create the levels of the multiscale tower and we keep only the same immediate neighbours as contextual neighbourhood of a pixel, it may appear that we lack the mechanism to incorporate information from distant pixels. This is not so, because through the increasing size of the blurring masks we use to create the multiscale tower, the information from larger and larger distances is "smeared" into the immediate neighbours of a pixel and through interaction with them is incorporated into it.

References

1. X. Zhang and B.A. Wandell. A spatial extension of CIELAB for digital color image reproduction. In *Society for Information Display Symposium, San Diego*, 1996. WWW address: ftp://white.stanford.edu/scielab/spie97.ps.gz.
2. B.A. Wandell and X. Zhang. SCIELAB: a metric to predict the discriminability of colored patterns. In *9th Workshop on Image and Multidimensional Signal Processing*, pages 11–12, 1996.
3. S. Peleg, J. Naor, R. Hartley, and D. Avnir. Multiple resolution texture analysis and classification. *IEEE Trans. Pattern Analysis and Machine Intelligence*, 6(4):518–523, 1984.
4. J.L. Crowley and A.C. Sanderson. Multiple resolution representation and probabilistic matching of 2-d gray-scale shape. *IEEE Trans. Pattern Analysis and Machine Intelligence*, 9:113–120, 1987.
5. C. Bouman and B. Liu. Multiple resolution segmentation of textured images. *IEEE Trans. Pattern Analysis and Machine Intelligence*, 13(2):99–113, 1991.
6. S. Lam and H. Ip. Structural texture segmentation using irregular pyramid. *Pattern Recognition Letters*, 15:691–698, 1994.
7. F. Glazer. Multilevel relaxation in low-level computer vision. In A. Rosenfeld, editor, *Multiresolution Image Processing and Analysis*, pages 312–330. Springer, 1984.
8. D. Terzopoulos. Image analysis using multigrid relaxation methods. *IEEE Trans. Pattern Analysis and Machine Intelligence*, 8(2):129–139, 1986.
9. D. Zhang, J. Liu, and F. Wan. Multiresolution relaxation: Experiments and evaluations. In *Proceedings of International Conference on Pattern Recognition*, pages 712–714, 1988.
10. E. R. Hancock, M. Haindl, and J. Kittler. Multiresolution edge labelling using hierarchical relaxation. In *Proceedings of International Conference on Pattern Recognition*, pages 140–144, 1992.

11. J. Matas and J. Kittler. Spatial and feature based clustering: Applications in image analysis. In *CAIP95*, pages 162–173, 1995.

12. B. Julesz and J.R. Bergen. Textons, the fundamental elements in preattentive vision and perception of textures. *Bell Systems Technical Journal*, 62(6):1619–1645, 1983.

13. J. Malik and P. Perona. A computational model of texture perception. Technical Report CSD-89-491, University of California Berkeley, CS, 1989.

14. H. Tamura, S. Mori, and T. Yamawaki. Textural features corresponding to visual perception. *SMC*, 8(6):460–473, June 1978.

15. R. M. Haralick. Statistical and structural approaches to texture. *Proceedings of the IEEE*, 67(5):786–804, 1979.

16. L. V. Gool, P. Dewaele, and A. Oosterlinck. Texture analysis anno 1983. *Computer Vision, Graphics and Image Processing*, 29:336–357, 1985.

17. T.R. Reed and J. du Buf. A review of recent texture segmentation and feature extraction techniques. *CVGIP: Image Understanding*, 57:359–372, 1993.

18. A.K. Jain and F. Farrokhnia. Unsupervised texture segmentation using gabor filters. *Pattern Recognition*, 24(12):1167–1186, 1991.

19. M. Unser and M. Eden. Multiresolution feature extraction and selection for texture segmentation. *IEEE Trans. Pattern Analysis and Machine Intelligence*, 11(7):717–728, July 1989.

20. I. Matalas, S. Roberts, and H. Hatzakis. A set of multiresolution texture features suitable for unsupervised image segmentation. In *Proceedings of Signal Processing VIII, Theories and Applications*, volume III, pages 1495–1498, 1996.

21. S.J. Roan, J.K. Aggarwal, and W.N. Martin. Multiple resolution imagery and texture analysis. *Pattern Recognition*, 20(1):17–31, 1987.

22. Y. Ohta, T. Kanade, and T. Sakai. Color information for region segmentation. *Computer Graphics and Image Processing*, 13:222–241, 1980.

23. G. Healey. Segmenting images using normalized color. *IEEE Trans. Systems, Man, and Cybernetics*, 22(1):64–73, 1992.

24. J. Liu and Y-H. Yang. Multiresolution color image segmentation. *IEEE Trans. Pattern Analysis and Machine Intelligence*, 16:689–700, July 1994.

25. W. Skarbek and A. Koschan. Colour image segmentation - a survey. Technical report, Technical University Berlin, 1994.

26. M.J. Swain. *Color Indexing*. PhD thesis, University of Rochester, 1990.

27. G. J. Klinker. *A Physical Approach to Color Image Understanding*. A K Peters, Wellesley, Massachusetss, 1993.

28. G. B. Coleman and H. C. Andrews. Image segmentation by clustering. *Proceedings of the IEEE*, 67(5):773–785, 1979.

29. S. C. Tan and J. Kittler. Colour texture classification using features from colour histogram. *Proceedings of the Eighth Scandinavian Conference on Image Processing*, 1993.

30. D.K. Panjwani and G. Healey. Unsupervised segmentation of textured color images using markov random field models. In *Conference on Computer Vision and Pattern Recognition*, pages 776–777, 1993.

31. L. Shafarenko, M. Petrou, and J. Kittler. Automatic watershed segmentation of randomly textured color images. *IEEE Transactions on Image Processing*, 6(11):1530–1544, November 1997.

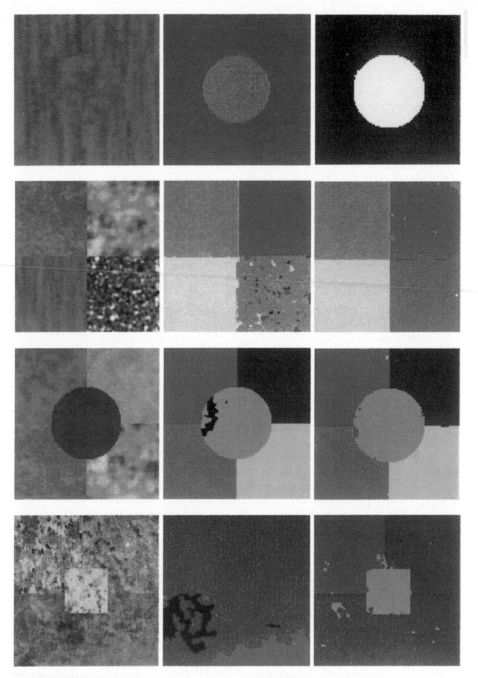

Fig. 4. Four test cases (T1-T4) and their segmentation by applying (mid-column) Matas & Kittler's approach and (right-column) perceptual segmentation.

Fig. 5. Forest image and its perceptual segmentation.

Fig. 6. Monet's painting and its perceptual segmentation.

Fig. 7. Land image and its perceptual segmentation.

Visual Recognition Using Local Appearance

Vincent Colin de Verdière and James L. Crowley

Project PRIMA - Lab. GRAVIR - IMAG
INRIA Rhône-Alpes
655, avenue de l'Europe
38330 - Montbonnot Saint Martin, France
{Vincent.Colin-de-Verdiere, Jim.Crowley}@imag.fr

Abstract. This paper presents a technique for visual recognition in which physical objects are represented by families of surfaces in a local appearance space. An orthogonal family of local appearance descriptors is obtained by applying principal components analysis to image neighborhoods. The principal components with the largest variance are used to define a space for describing local appearance. The projection of the set of all neighborhoods from an image gives a discrete sampling of a surface in this space. Projecting neighborhoods from images taken at different viewing positions gives a family of surfaces which represent the possible local appearances from those viewing directions.

Recognition is achieved by projecting windows from newly acquired images into the local appearance space and associating them to nearby surfaces. An efficient search tree data structure is used to associate projected points to surfaces. Our results show that in many common situations, a single window is sufficient to obtain the correct recognition. Robust recognition is easily obtained by reinforcing matching using multiple windows and their mutual spatial coherence.

1 Introduction

Visual recognition is the problem of determining the identity of a physical object from an arbitrary viewpoint under arbitrary lighting conditions. Changes in the appearance of the object under variations in lighting and viewpoint make this a very difficult problem in computer vision. The classic approach is based on the idea that the underlying 3D structure is invariant to viewpoint and lighting. Thus recovery of the 3D structure should permit the use of techniques such as back-projection and features matching [6] to match the observed structure to a data base of objects.

While such approaches can be made to work in a controlled laboratory environment, they are known to generate several problems in a real environment. For example, the detection of commonly used image features, such as key-points, edges and lines, tends to be unreliable. Photo-optic effects and image noise contribute to creating feature drop-outs and spurious features. Correcting or compensating for such errors leads to the use of ad-hoc techniques with high computational complexities. In addition, such techniques are generally fragile, and their failure conditions are difficult to predict.

An alternative to 3D reconstruction is to remain in the 2-D image space and to work with measurements of the object appearance. A variety of techniques are possible with this approach. A pure information theory model suggests making an inner product (or sum of squared difference) with the very large set of possible appearances masks for each object [12]. This approach can be studied formally and it can be shown to lead to the smallest possible probability of error. However, except for highly constrained problems, this approach is generally rejected as requiring an impossible number of correlation masks. Sirovitch and Kirby [21] showed that in the case of face recognition, principal components analysis (PCA) of the set of images could be used to generate an orthogonal space in which inner products could be reduced to a neighborhood search in a relatively small number of dimensions. Turk and Pentland [22] refined and popularized this approach for face recognition, greatly enhancing the acceptance of principal components analysis as a vision technique. Murase and Nayar [14] extended this idea by expressing the set of appearances of objects as a trajectory in a PCA space. Black and Jepson[2] demonstrated that the appearance of a hand making a gesture could also be expressed and matched as a trajectory in a PCA space.

All of the above techniques suffer from several important difficulties. It is often noted that projection to a PCA space is sensitive to partial occlusions, although recently, a new projection technique has been developed which operates under occlusion [1]. More fundamentally, the projection of an image to a PCA space depends on the precise position of the object in the image, on the intensity and shape of back-ground regions, and on the intensity and color of illumination. Thus, these techniques require that the object be detected, segmented and normalized in intensity, size and position. Such segmentation and normalization is a very difficult problem, and perhaps unsolvable in the general case.

The technique described in this paper began as a search for a method to describe and match the appearance of objects independent of illumination intensity, background, image position, and occlusions. Our approach is to minimize the effects of background and occlusion by working with as small a neighborhood as possible. Our approach overcomes the problem of image position by mapping the locally connected structures in the image space into surfaces in a space of local appearances. Robustness to changes in illumination intensity are obtained by energy normalization during the projection from image to the appearance space. The result is a technique which reliably produces object hypotheses from a large data base of objects when presented with a very small number of very local neighborhoods from a newly acquired image.

In a sense this technique trades memory for computational cost. Once the data base of appearances has been constructed by an off-line process, the identity of objects in a newly acquired image of a scene can be determined at a very small computational cost. Further more, the technique is composed of linear transformations and distance matching techniques, all of which are formally analyzable. Thus, no ad-hoc tricks are required. The operating conditions and probability of error can be analyzed and predicted.

This approach is similar in spirit to the work of Rao and Ballard [17] who used very large vectors of local measurements as features for pattern recognition. We have taken inspiration from Schiele [19] who recognizes objects in scenes using multi-dimensional statistics of local operators and from Schmid and Mohr [20] who uses a local jet of viewpoint invariant descriptors to detect and match key-points in a view-invariant manner. Another close approach to this problem is the system SEEMORE [13] developed by B.W. Mel which efficiently recognized objects by using a large set of image features.

With our approach, local appearance is described using the appearance of small (9 by 9) neighborhoods. This size was selected for our initial experiments as the smallest size for which the local spatial frequency is not perturbed by the sinc function which is inherent in neighborhood selection. The set of all possible 9 by 9 neighborhoods have an 81 by 81 covariance matrix with 81 principal components. Any (9 by 9) neighborhood can be exactly represented by a projection into this 81 dimensional space. For real images, the variance (principal values) for most of these dimensions is extremely small. Thus it has proved possible to use a much smaller number of principal components to define an orthogonal subspace for expressing local appearance.

The experiments described below use an orthogonal space defined by the first principal components (10) from a very large collection of 9 by 9 neighborhoods. An image is modeled in this space as a surface. A collection of images from different viewpoints and different lighting conditions is represented as a discrete sampling of a manifold in this 10 dimensional space. The number of dimensions of the manifold structure is determined by the number of dimensions variation of appearance.

The recognition criterion for local appearance is the distance between an observed window and the surface points of the manifold. Thus such a data-base structure can potentially be searched by table lookup. In reality, the appearance space in which the manifolds are expressed is both very large and very sparse. Thus for a fixed memory cost, a very large gain in the number of objects (manifolds) and in the variations of appearance (dimensions in the manifold structure) can be obtained by using an appropriate search algorithm.

In many of our experiments, a single 9 by 9 neighborhood proves sufficient to recall the correct objects, the correct viewpoint and the correct position on the objects surface. However, many ambiguous neighborhoods, such as uniform regions and high-contrast also exist. Thus we obtain a high robustness by using spatial coherence criteria between the windows.

The problem of recognition with local features may be divided into three independent sub-problems. The first sub-problem consists in choosing a set of local descriptors. The experiments described here are based on PCA of small neighborhoods, but we believe that other orthogonal families of neighborhood descriptors such as Gabor filters could also be used. The second sub-problem is to define where to apply the descriptors: on selected interest points or on a predefined grid. The third sub-problem is to define a data structure to store and search these descriptors. The following sections address each of these sub-problems.

2 Local Eigenspaces of Appearance

The first part in recognition is to choose which local descriptors of images are to be used. A local descriptor is a scalar value computed from a small region around a point in an image: a window. A window can be characterized by a vector of N local descriptors. These descriptors should have some certain required properties such as stability to change of viewpoint and illumination, stability under partial occlusion. It is also desirable that the descriptors be highly discriminate for the patterns to be distinguished and that they be inexpensive to compute.

Formally, the computation of a vector of descriptors can be modeled as a projection from the image pixel space to a new space more suitable for recognition. In our technique, this descriptor space is composed of N orthogonal filters (in the experiments below, N equals 10). This space provides the desirable property that an image window which is a vector in a $M \times M$ space is represented by a single vector in the descriptor space with $N \ll M$. Recognition is obtained by using the property that close points in the projection space correspond to similar image windows. The confidence in the recognition is given by the value of the distance between points.

The first paragraph of this section presents the computation of the descriptor space using a Principal Components Analysis on image windows. Then, in the next paragraphs, the values of the different parameters of the technique (window size, number N of dimensions and quantification of descriptors) are discussed.

Computing the projection space: In our approach, we chose to use a Principal Components Analysis to compute the descriptors space (P). We wish to stress that the use of PCA is not intrinsic to our approach. Other families of orthogonal operators can be used for such a technique. For example, Rao [17] used Gaussian derivatives as local descriptors. Schiele [18] uses Gabor filters and Gaussian derivatives. These analytic descriptors present an important property: it is possible de compute them at any scale or orientation [7]. Their drawback is that they are chosen arbitrary.

PCA has certain properties which make it convenient to use as a starting point. The main advantage of these vectors is that are derived directly from the image database. The PCA descriptors provide a basis for which the image data will project with a maximum variance for a minimum number of dimensions. Selecting the first eigenvectors is optimal in the least-square-error sense for representing the data. However this does not mean that this choice is also optimal for recognition.

Using the Karhunen-Loève or PCA [8], it is possible to compute an orthogonal space from a list of data vectors. This space is composed of as many dimensions as the original data, but it is easy to derive from it an optimal subspace on the reconstruction viewpoint. In this new space, distances have the same meaning as in the image space. This leads to the fact that two points close in PCA space correspond to close windows in the original space. Distances in the subspace provide an accurate approximation of distances in the original space. In our case, vectors are $M \times M$ image windows.

A physical object is represented by images from its different appearances. Thetraining set is composed by all overlapping windows from all images of the objetcs toe recognized. The application of PCA on this set provides M^2 eigenvectors e_i with their associated eigenvalues λ_i. The eigenvectors e_i form an orthogonal set. For a complete and accurate representation of the training set, all M^2 eigenvectors should be maintained. However, the amount of information (defined as the ability to discriminate) captured by the projection onto an eigenvector is related to the variance (the eigenvalue) of the projection of all neighborhoods on that eigenvector. Thus it is possible to use the eigenvalues to sort and select the dominant eigenvectors to compose the descriptors space P.

Distances in P are an approximation of correlations in the image space. Correlation techniques [12] are efficient for recognition of a small number of features, such as in the case of tracking an object. The projection into the eigenspace an association between an observed window and a prelearned window to be determined by direct addressing. In a sense, this is correlation without search. This the approach is easily adapted to real time.

As an example, a 400 image database extracted from the Columbia database [15] provides a space P for windows of size 9×9. The first 10 eigenvectors were selected to define this projection space P. Figure 1 presents the 10 first eigenvectors and their associated eigenvalues.

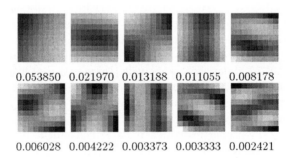

0.053850 0.021970 0.013188 0.011055 0.008178

0.006028 0.004222 0.003373 0.003333 0.002421

Fig. 1. Descriptors space and eigenvalues

In the space P, an image window W is associated to a single point A and close windows are associated to close points. A is obtained by projecting W into P, i.e. by computing a dot product between the window W and each eigenvectors e_i. In order to increase the stability to luminosity changes, a normalized dot product is used:

$$A_i = \; <W, e_i> \; = \frac{\sum_{j=1}^{M^2} W_j . e_{i,j}}{\sqrt{\sum_{i=j}^{M^2} W_j^2} \sqrt{\sum_{i=j}^{M^2} e_j^2}}$$

Division by the energy of windows provides stability of A against the changes of the intensity of the light. The choice of this energy normalization rather then a mean and variance normalization or a max-min normalization [3] is motivated by Schiele's study [18]. A better invariance against light change can also be obtained by the use of color as in [9,4].

Parameters of our approach. The computation of the descriptor space depends on 3 main parameters: the image window size, the number of dimensions and the quantification in each dimension.

- Image Window Size: The objective is to use very small windows so as to be robust to changes in background and occlusion. Previous work shows that 9×9 is the minimum size size stable enough to image noise. Good recognition results have confirmed the validity of this windows size. Systematic exploration of possible window sizes remains to be done. We note that 9 by 9 neighborhoods extracted from a pyramid can be used to capture the multi-scale structure of appearance.
- Number of dimensions: The higher the number of dimensions, the greater the discriminatory power the descriptor vector will have. However, memory requirements are expressed as the number of quanta in each dimension to the power of the number of dimensions. Thus increasing the number of dimensions dramatically increases the amount of memory required. This fact leads to a trade-off between the number of dimensions and the discriminatory power between object classes and appearance variations.
  Using one dimension, it is possible to separate at best k different vectors. The parameter k depends on the stability of the descriptors to small changes in the images. Experimentally, it is possible to evaluate a distance threshold th which define the maximum distance between two vectors corresponding to the same window. Vectors values are in the interval $[0; 1]$, so we have $k = \frac{1}{th}$. For N dimensions and L_∞ distance, the maximum number of different descriptors vectors is $k_N = k^N = \frac{1}{th^N}$. For $th = 0.1$ and $N = 10$, it leads to $k_N = 10$ billions which is a lot more than the number currently stored cells. This calculus gives an idea of the storage capacity of the data structure. However, in the data itself, all the possible values are not used: the distribution of the data on the vectors is not regular (see Fig.2 on the distribution of vectors on the 3 first dimensions). The irregular repartition encourages to increase the number of dimensions. However, memory requirements limits this number and leads to a trade-off.
- Quantification of dimensions: The quantification of dimensions results create imprecision in distance. Specifically, signal processing theory shows that

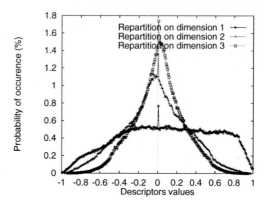

Fig. 2. Histograms of distribution of descriptors on the 3 first dimensions

quantification acts as Gaussianly distributed random noise. The variance of this noise is related to the logarithm of the number of bits.

It is not relevant to use a quantification which is more accurate than the data noise itself. The descriptors have a certain stability to small changes and the separability of different descriptors should be maintained by the quantification.

3   The Local Appearance Grid

After the choice of local descriptors, the next question is where to apply the discriptors to images. Two main approaches are possible: selecting the windows according to a criteria or selecting windows from a predefined grid.

The first approach is equivalent to a detector for interest points (or keyponts). Schmid and Mohr [20] employ the Harris Detector [10] to select interest points for indexing. Ohba and Ikeuchi [16] select windows with a local measure of trackability and a global measure of similarity. Rao and Ballard [17] used both approaches: selecting discriminant windows and selecting windows on an object centered circular grid.

Techniques based on detectors provided good results, but there is a major drawback on the stability of the detectors. This stability is hard to guarantee when the viewpoint or the luminosity changes. Therefore, our approach consists of first selecting and storing all possible windows. Subsequently, windows which are not discriminant are removed from the training test. Discriminability is determined by the number of nearby projections in the descriptor space.

Appearance Grid. In our technique, the training set is composed of all the windows from all the images. A window is projected into a point of the space P. Images are divided into a grid of 9×9 windows.

Figure 3 presents an image decomposed in non overlapping windows and the corresponding surface in a 3 dimensional subspace of P. In practice, the images

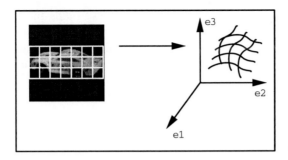

Fig. 3. Representation of an image as a surface in a 3D subspace of P (not real data)

are decomposed in overlapping windows with a shift of one pixel between two neighboring windows. Then, an image is represented by a surface in the space P. This surface is stored as a discrete grid. As the overlap between two successive windows is very large (89%), except in rare cases, two neighboring windows in an image generally have close projections in P. Therefore, a continuity property can be defined which holds between most points of the grid which represents a surface on P. A physical object is represented by a set of images and therefore, in the database, by a set of surfaces.

Recognition can be obtained by using this image representation. An unknown window is projected onto the space P into a vector v. Recognition is achieved by searching vectors in P which are close to v. Formally, the goal is to find the set S of all vectors w from the training set which are inside a ball of radius R: $S_{solutions} = \{w/dist(w, v) < R\}$. R is a threshold defining the maximum distance between two similar vectors and then image windows.

Grid constraints for filtering hypotheses. A search for vectors within a ball centered on a vector v projected from a window W usually gives several possible matches. Several techniques are possible to select the correct match. The first idea is to sort the set of solutions with the distance to v. Then, the first element x of this set correspond to the window X the closest to V. Nevertheless, the set of solutions is often too large to be completely relevant and needs some treatment. The first problem is very large sets of solutions from some very low discriminancy windows: for example, a window of constant gray value. Two approaches are possible to solve this problem:

- During the learning of the training data, it is possible to detect that some projections occurs very often and should be suppressed from the database as they will nether produce a correct recognition. This can also be done during the search phase: if a search has given too many results, the database can be updated by suppressing these irrelevant vectors.
- If the refinement of the database has not been done during the construction, it is also possible to abort a search when too many possible answers are detected.

Another problem is that neighboring windows usually project into neighboring points in P. Therefore, if a window w_i is recognized, its neighboring window w_{i+1} is likely to be recognized as well. For example, on Fig.4, on a two dimensional subspace of P, the points A, B, C and D are inside the X centered ball but corresponds to neighboring image windows. So, only the closest C should be selected as an answer.

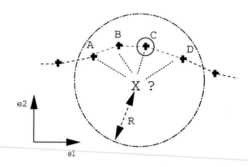

Fig. 4. redundancy of solutions in a 2D subspace of P

In this case, there are two solutions also:

- It is possible to remove some redundancy from the database during the learning phase. After adding all the windows from an image, it is possible to reproject and search all the windows with a low distance threshold. When a neighbor window is recognized, the searched window can be suppressed. The redundant window is marked so as not to be also suppressed from the database.
- It is also possible after the search to detect which projections are similar and to select the best one as the answer.

The latter technique is implemented and gives acceptable results. The drawback is some computation time for the search. The first solution should improve the technique. This logical representation needs some data structure to be usable for searching.

4   Recognizing and Searching descriptors

As shown in the previous sections, our recogntion technique needs to store and search N dimensional descriptor vectors. A naive structure would be a 2D array storing each vectors according to their positions on images. This structure provides easy access to proximity criteria during a search but requires an impossible exhaustive search. Therefore, a tree search structure is necessary.

Hierarchical search tree. The data structure used for our technique is a search tree. Each 10 dimensions are decomposed into 4 parts successively. During the database training, new dimensions are divided according to the need to separate the data. On the example of Fig.5, L_i represents short lists of stored vectors.

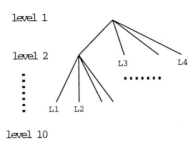

Fig. 5. Indexation Storage Tree

L_1 and L_2 have been classified up to the 3rd level of the tree while, for L_3 and L_4, the 2nd level was sufficient. This structure provides a very easy addition of elements: just find the right leaf and add the new vector to the list. If the list length is larger than a predefined threshold, the list is separated into 4 new lists of the next level. Large lists on the last level of the structure are likely to happen for very frequent and low discriminancy windows. But, these lists are useless to store as they will not provide recognition and therefore can be suppressed. A very nice property of this structure is, that, it is very easy to detect when adding a new vector that this vector is redundant or not discriminant. So, suppressing irrelevant vectors can be done very easily. In fact, a substitution of vector lists by their length converts the structure into a tree of the probability of each vectors.

Searching the tree. During the search phase, it is necessary to find all vectors w in the tree which are inside a sphere centered on the searched vector v. The radius R depends on the stability of the descriptors (see Sect.2). A classic technique would be to just look for the vectors in the leaf of the tree corresponding to v. This technique would miss some solutions. There is no guarantee that the search ball is included in a leaf. As a result, the search needs to explore some neighboring branches of the tree depending on the radius R. At each level of the tree, it is possible to compute the minimum distance between the searched vector and each branches of the tree. Branches with distances higher than the search threshold can be removed from the current search.

As an example, our descriptor space is constituted of 10 dimensions which values are between 0 and 255. A high number of vectors need to be stored (more than 300.000 currently in our database). Each dimension is divided into 4 branches: 0-63, 64-127, 128-191 and 192-255. The radius R is 30 which is lower that half the width of a tree cell. This leads to, in the worst case, in a full tree,

1024 cells will need to be evaluated out of a one million cells tree. Experimentally, the numbers of cells is nether over 200 and its mean is around 30 cells.

Overall, 70 to 80 % of images windows provides a direct recognition of the object. This result was achieved without any selections of the windows in the unknown images (images not used in the construction of the database).

5 Searching multiple vectors

The previous sections described the search of a single window within the data-base. A single window cannot guarantee a good recognition especially if randomly selected. Another approach to the recognition problem is to search multiple vectors. A classic technique is to use a voting algorithm based on the idea of k-Nearest-Neighbor rule [5]. Each search provides a list of object hypotheses. An hypothesis generates a vote for an object. The object that obtains the maximum number of votes is recognized. The first paragraph presents another approach which focused on spatial constraints between hypotheses of the same object.

Another aspect is that as the descriptors are not invariant to scale or rotation, a multiscale and multirotation search is required.

Spatial Constraints. If two different windows from an image are searched in the database, there relative position is well known. So, the results of such search are only coherent if they have an equivalent relative position. This spatial criteria can be used to reject many false recognition. More precisely, in the simple case where no 2D rotation or scale change are accepted, two windows w_1 and w_2 from an image are searched. $\delta_p = w_2 - w_1$ is the displacement vector between the two windows. Two solutions s_1 and s_2 are compatible with δ_p if $dist((s_2-s_1), \delta_p) < th$ with th a predefined threshold. This constraint allow to select the right solution in a smarter way than the basic voting technique.

The technique consists in defining an hypothesis as being an object and its position in the image. A new hypothesis for an object generates a vote for a previous hypothesis only it is coherent. At the end, only the coherence sets of hypotheses remained. The larger one gives the recognition. In this case, two in-coherent hypotheses of the same object won't disturb the recognition algorithm.

Generalization over scale and 2D orientation. The descriptors which have been chosen for the recognition are not invariant to rotation or scale. Recognizing robustly in case of scale or rotation depends on the stability of the descriptors to these images transformations. Recognition beyond scale change may be obtain by two approaches. The first approach is a multiscale technique: images of object at different scale are learned by the search database. A searched image will have a sufficiently close scale to one of the images used to create the database and thus will be recognized. The other approach consists in storing a single scale into the database but to compute the descriptors at several scales. One of the computed scale will match the database scale. Using simultaneously both techniques is also possible. For orientation, the same two approaches can be used.

If multiple objects are in the image, the first answers will hopefully correspond to the objects.

All theses approaches are linked to the possibility of computing the descriptors from different scales and orientations. Our descriptors based on the PCA need to compute the transformation on the image and then project into the descriptor space whereas other analytic descriptors can be computed directly at different scales or orientations. As a conclusion, robustness to scale and orientation is accessible but requires a additional computational or memory consumption.

6 Recognition Experiments

The technique presented in the previous sections have been evaluated in preliminary recognition experiments. The first experimental database is extracted from the Colombia database [15]. Four images of 49 first objects are used in our search database. Each image is selected with a 20 degrees shift in viewing position (angle 0, 20, 40 and 60). The test images are all the remaining images between the 5 and 65 degree viewpoints.

A 20 degree change in viewing angle is an arbitrary choice which provides good recognition results. To improve the technique, the image viewpoints should be selected for their appearance rather than for any arbitrary rule. Some objects are very stable along some viewpoints change.

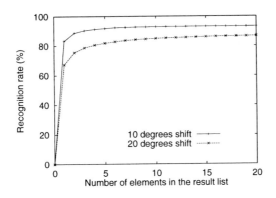

Fig. 6. Recognition Rate by a Single Random Window

A first experiment study the recognition on the Columbia database with a single random window of the test images. Two subsets of the Columbia database were tested (Fig.6). In the first case, there is a 10 degrees shift between viewpoints of objects. The second one uses a 20 degrees shift. The recognition process returns a sorted list of the k best objects. k is represented on the abscissa axis. $k = 2$ means the correct object is recognized in first or second position of the result list. Recognition does not achieve 100% with a single window because some windows are not discriminant at all (for example, window with a constant gray level). A better interpretation of this result is to say that 70% of image windows are usable for direct recognition and 90% for multiple windows recognition.

To increase the recognition rate, our technique requires the use of multiple windows. An experiment (Fig.7) studies the recognition using two random windows separated from 5 and 10 pixels. The first graph (already shown on the previous figure) is reproduced for comparison. Spatial coherence criteria are used to join searches from the two windows. Recognition does not achieve 100% because no window selection was made and some non discriminant windows were searched. It is possible to increase the recognition by increasing the number of searched windows. The spatial coherence criteria guarantee that the more window are used, the more likely the right window is recognized. Recognizing from a few windows can be considered as an initial stage, to be followed, if necessary, by recognition from a region or an entire image.

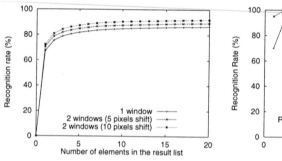

Fig.7. Recognition Rate by a Two Random Window.

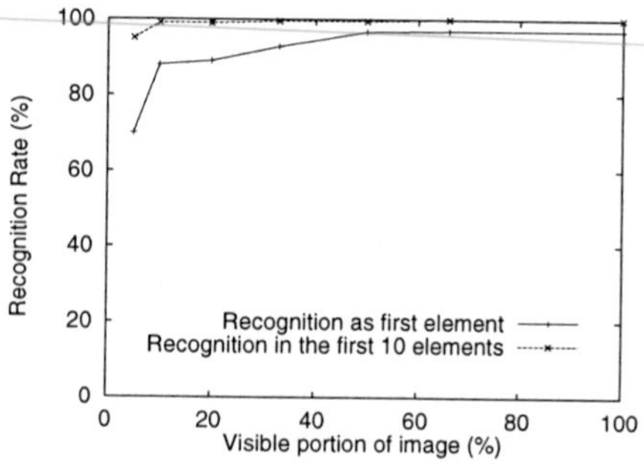

Fig.8. Recognition Rate depending on objects occlusion.

The next experiment evaluates recognition from an image region. This means that part of images are occluded to the recognition process. The test images were occluded for 95% to 0%. Figure 8 shows that recognition is very high as a first element and perfect in the first 10 results.

In the previous experiments, scale was supposed to be stable, but in the real world, object size will change depending on the distance with the camera. It is possible to generate a multiscale database by using images of different scales. An object database of five objects with scale shift of 20% between two images has been computed to test this idea. Test images of different scales (every 5%) were successfully used for recognition. 80% of windows provide a correct recognition. Other windows correspond to non discriminant windows or non scale stable windows.

Overall, experiments show that this technique provides reliable recognition of objects. Robustness to scale and orientation variations is accessible by using multiple images of objects. The memory storage requirements is nevertheless increased and the suppression of non discriminant windows becomes necessary.

7 Conclusions

Recognition of objects using the projection of an entire image to an orthogonal feature space poses serious problems. The point in a feature space to which the entire image is projected is perturbed by changes in background, in illumination, in the image position of objects and occlusions. It is possible to overcome these problems by applying such a method to local neighborhoods together with proper normalization. In this case, an image projects to a surface in a local appearance space. Changes in viewpoint and lighting deform this surface in a continuous manner, creating a family of surfaces which represent the family of appearances of the object. If the basis functions and number of dimensions of this feature space are appropriately chosen, the space will be sufficiently sparse so as permit discrimination of a large number of families of surfaces.

The experiments presented here demonstrate that an object can be recognized using a representation in which appearances are represented by surfaces in a local appearance space. This approach has been tested using 9 by 9 image neighborhoods, and a 10 dimensional space using images from the Colombia image data base.

The association of a small neighborhood of an image with a point on a surface of local appearances can be structured as an addressing operation (a table lookup). However, when the space is very large (and very sparse) it is more convenient to use a tree-structure scheme for addressing. In either case, the recognition of an object is possible in a large variety of viewing conditions, provided that those conditions (or similar conditions) have been represented in the space.

The technique is based on the storage a huge number of descriptors vectors in a search tree. An extension to this technique is to reduce effectively the number of vectors by suppressing redundant or non-discriminating vectors. It also appears possible to use filters such as Gaussian derivatives or Gabor functions to provide robustness to orientation and scale. However, this robustness has an effective cost in discrimination: many windows will project to the same point and therefore more dimensions become necessary. Our initial experiments indicate that this method provides a robust and computationally efficient for recognizing physical objects under varying conditions of viewpoint and illumination.

References

1. H. Bischof A. Leonardis and R. Ebensberger. Robust recognition using eigimages. Technical Report PRIP-TR-47, Pattern Recogntion and Image Processing group - Vienna University of Technology, june 1997.
2. M.J. Black and A.D. Jepson. Eigentracking: Robust matching and tracking of articulated objects using a view-based representation". In Springer Verlag, editor, *ECCV'96, Fourth European Conference on Computer Vision*, pages 329–342, 1996.
3. P. Bobet. *Tête stéréoscopique, Réflexes oculaires et Vision*. PhD thesis, INPG France, 1995.

4. V. Colin de Verdière. Reconnaissance d'objets par leurs statistiques de couleurs. Master's thesis, projet PRIMA, I.N.P. Grenoble, France, June 1996. only in french (available at http://pandora.imag.fr/~colin/projetDEA.html).

5. R.O. Duda and P.E. Hart. *Pattern Classification and Scene Analysis*, chapter 4. J. Wiley and sons, 1973.

6. O. Faugeras. *Three-Dimensional Computer Vision : A Geometric Viewpoint*. The MIT Press, 1993.

7. W.T. Freeman and E.H. Adelson. The design and use of steerable filters. *IEEE Transactions on Pattern Recognition and Machine Intelligence*, 13(9):891–906, september 1991.

8. K. Fukunaga. *Statistical Pattern Recognition*, chapter Feature Extraction and Linear Mapping for Signal Representation. Academic Press, School of Electrical Engineering, West Lafayette, Indiana, 1990.

9. B. V. Funt and G. D. Finlayson. Color constant color indexing. *IEEE Transactions on Pattern Recognition and Machine Intelligence*, 17(5):522–529, 1995.

10. C. Harris and M. Stephens. A combined corner and edge detector. In *Proc. 4th Alvey Vision Conference*, 1988.

11. A. Lux and B. Zoppis. An Experimental Multi-language Environment for the Development of Intelligent Robot Systems. In *5th International Symposium on Intelligent Robotic Systems, SIRS'97*, pages 169–174, 1997. more informations at http://pandora.imag.fr/Prima/Ravi/.

12. J. Martin and J.L. Crowley. Comparison of correlation techniques. In U. Rembold et al., editor, *Intelligent Autonomous Systems – IAS-4*, pages 86–93, Karlsruhe, Germany, March 27–30 1995.

13. B.W. Mel. Seemore: A view-based approach to 3-d object recognition using multiple visual cues. *Advances in neural information processing systems*, 8:865–871, 1996.

14. H. Murase and S. K. Nayar. Visual learning and recognition of 3d objects from appearance. *International Journal of Computer Vision*, 14:5–24, 1995.

15. S. A. Nene, S. K. Nayar, and H. Murase. Columbia object image library (coil-100). Technical report, Columbia University, New York, february 1996.

16. K. Ohba and K. Ikeuchi. Recognition of the multi specularity objects for bin-picking task. *IROS 96*, 3:1440–1448, 1996.

17. R. P. N. Rao and D. H. Ballard. Object indexing using an iconic sparse distributed memory. In *ICCV'95 Fifth International Conference on Computer Vision*, pages 24–31, 1995.

18. B. Schiele. *Object Recognition using Multidimensional Receptive Field Histograms*. PhD thesis, I.N.P. Grenoble, France, 1997. English translation.

19. B. Schiele and J. L. Crowley. Object recognition using multidimensional receptive field histograms. In *ECCV'96, Fourth European Conference on Computer Vision, Volume I*, pages 610–619, 14–16 April 1996.

20. C. Schmid and R. Mohr. Combining grayvalue invariants with local constraints for object recognition. In *International Conference on Computer Vision and Pattern Recognition*, 1996.

21. I. Sirovich and M. Kirby. Low-dimensional procedure for the caracterization of human faces. *J. Opt. Soc Am. A*, 4(3):519–524, March 1987.

22. M. Turk and A. Pentland. Eigenfaces for recognition. *Journal of Cognitive Neuroscience*, 3(1):71–86, 1991.

Experiments presented in this article were programmed using the RAVI multi-language environment [11].

A Factorization Approach to Grouping

P. Perona[12] and W. Freeman[3]

[1] California Institute of Technology MS 136-93, Pasadena CA 91125, USA
[2] Università di Padova, Italy
[3] Mitsubishi Electric Research Lab., 201 Broadway, Cambridge MA 02139

Abstract. The foreground group in a scene may be 'discovered' and computed as a factorized approximation to the pairwise affinity of the elements in the scene. A pointwise approximation of the pairwise affinity information may in fact be interpreted as a 'saliency' index, and the foreground of the scene may be obtained by thresholding it. An algorithm called 'affinity factorization' is thus obtained which may be used for grouping.
The affinity factorization algorithm is demonstrated on displays composed of points, of lines and of brightness values. Its relationship to the Shi-Malik normalized cuts algorithms is explored both analytically and experimentally. The affinity factorization algorithm is shown to be computationally efficient (O(n) floating-point operations for a scene composed of n elements) and to perform well on displays where the background is unstructured. Generalizations to solve more complex problems are also discussed.

1 Introduction

Fig. 1 shows a distribution of points in the plane. Taken one by one the points are identical to each other. However, it is quite apparent that their mutual positions in the plane contain some 'global' information. While it is somewhat unclear how to define this global information, it is natural to consider a local property: the 'pairwise similarity' of these points: two points that are close by are 'similar' and two points that are far apart are 'different'.

This is a common situation in vision: we extract tokens from an image using some early visual process, and the notion of 'closeness' between pairs of tokens is natural and well defined. The tokens may be anything: from pixels to points, to edgels, to textured patches. While it is unclear how to extract, and even how to define, the global high-level properties of the scene, it is easy and natural to define the pairwise affinity of any two tokens. This idea comes to us from the work by Shi and Malik on grouping using normalized-cuts (see [8] and references therein). In this paper we explore a weaker approach than that of Shi and Malik: rather than formulating a grouping problem explicitly, we notice that a useful global property of the scene, the foreground set, may be both 'discovered' and estimated starting from the notion of pairwise closeness, or pairwise affinity, of individual elements. We develop a simple algorithm which factorizes the matrix of pairwise element affinities, and compare it with the algorithm of Shi and Malik.

2 The affinity function

Given two elements (i, j) in the scene S, let's suppose that it is possible to assign a number $A_{i,j}$ that tells us how 'similar' the two objects are. When the two objects are very similar then $A_{i,j}$ has a high value and when they are not similar at all then $A_{i,j} \approx 0$. We will suppose that this affinity function has the following properties:

$$\forall i, j \in S: \quad A_{i,j} \in [0, 1], \quad A_{i,i} = 1, \quad A_{i,j} = A_{j,i}$$

The first and second properties impose a normalization on A. The third property is a symmetry requirement.

Fig. 1. A set of points on the plane

As an example, two points in Fig. 1 are 'similar' if they are close-by. One could define $A_{i,j}$ as:

$$A_{i,j} = e^{-d^2(i,j)} \tag{1}$$

$$d^2(i,j) \doteq \frac{\|x_i - x_j\|^2}{d_o^2}$$

where d_o is a reference distance below which two points are thought to be similar and beyond which two points are thought to be dissimilar, and x_i is the vector of coordinates of point i. There is nothing magical about this particular definition of affinity: depending on the situation another definition may be more natural and appropriate. Affinity functions for line segments and other objects will be discussed later.

3 $O(n)$ approximation of the affinity matrix

Notice that if the scene contains N objects we need $(N - 1)N/2 = O(N^2)$ numbers in order to describe its affinity properties. If the image is composed of tens of thousands of objects (points, lines, pixels), as it is the case in vision, this means hundreds of millions of numbers. It makes sense to wonder whether we could describe some fundamental aspects of the scene in a cheaper way: rather than by a function A_{ij} of object pairs (i, j), by a pointwise function p_i of objects i taken one by one. This way the complexity of our description will drop to $O(N)$ (bits, as it will turn out).

We propose, as a possible approach, to approximate A by products of p's: $A_{i,j} = p_i p_j$. We are trading off some accuracy in representing A with a great improvement in storage costs. What is the best p that we could use? This depends on our definition of approximation error. We will start by using the L^2 norm in order to define a distance between two matrices:

$$p = \arg\min_{\hat{p}} \sum_{i,j=1}^{N} (A_{i,j} - \hat{p}_i \hat{p}_j)^2 \qquad (2)$$

the L^2 norm is not necessary (see the discussion section at the end).

Notice that we are approximating A with the rank-one matrix pp^T. The best solution to this problem (in the sense that it minimizes the Frobenius, or L^2, norm of the approximation error) is well known:

Proposition 1 The best order-one L^2 approximation of a matrix A is the first singular vector of the matrix A multiplied by the square root of the corresponding singular value. Calling (U, S, V) the singular value decomposition of A, and U^i the columns of U and $\sigma_i^2 = S_{i,i}$ the singular values of A we have:

$$p = \sigma_1 U^1 \qquad (3)$$

Proof : See [6].

Notice that $A = A^T$ and therefore $U = V$. Also: since $A = A^T$ p is also equal to the eigenvector v_1 of A with largest eigenvalue λ_i: $p = \lambda_1^{1/2} v_1$.

Let's take a look at Fig. 2 where the function p that we obtain for the example of Fig. 1 is shown. We may notice that p takes values between 0 and 1, and that for some indices i the value of p is exactly equal to 0. In Fig. 2(right) the function p is shown together with the position of the points. We may notice that the points for which p is different from zero are in the same region of the picture, with higher values of p for points in the middle of that region. For reasons that will become apparent later let's call 'foreground' that region, and 'background' the rest of the points.

How well does pp^T approximate A? One may take a look at the error in approximation of the entries of A (Fig. 3, left group, right matrix), however, this does not give much insight. If we permute the entries of A using the permutation of indices that sorts the values of p in ascending order (see Fig. 3, right group), then the picture becomes clearer. Notice that the approximation is poor when both i and j belong to the background group, while it is better for both the foreground group and the mixed terms $A_{i,j}$ with i belonging to the foreground and j belonging to the background.

Let's summarize our observations so far:

1. The function p takes values between 0 and 1.

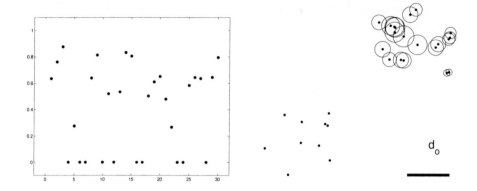

Fig. 2. (left)The approximant p for the distribution of points shown in Fig. 1. The affinity function defined in Eq. 1. The reference distance d_0 is shown in the display on the right. (Right) Pictorial representation of p: a dot indicates each point's position; the radius of the circle around each dot is proportional to the magnitude of the corresponding value of p. Points for which $p = 0$ do not have a visible surrounding circle. The reference distance d_0 is shown in the lower right corner.

Fig. 3. (Left group of 3) The approximation of the affinity matrix obtained using p. Brighter pixels indicate values that are larger. (Left) The affinity matrix. (Center) The approximation of A provided by $p * p^T$. (Right) The difference between the two matrices. In the right group of three the same matrices are shown – the indices were permuted so that the vector p is sorted in ascending order.

2. For some i's p_i is exactly equal to zero.
3. The points for which $p > 0$ tend to cluster in one 'foreground' group.
4. The approximation of A appears to be good when at least one of the points involved belongs to the foreground. It is bad otherwise.

We may conclude with the key observation of this paper:
By calculating the pointwise approximation p_i of the pairwise affinity A_{ij} of the elements in the scene we have discovered a new global property: the partition of a scene into two groups, which we call 'foreground' and 'background'. We may see p as a 'saliency' function of the points.

After discovering the concept of foreground group we may specify an algorithm for calculating the foreground group. We call it the 'affinity factorization' algorithm:

1. Form a matrix A_{ij} containing the pairwise affinity of each pair of elements in the scene.
2. Call p the eigenvector of A that is associated to its largest eigenvalue.
3. Define the foreground F as the set of objects i whose corresponding p_i is not equal to zero (more practically, $p > \epsilon > 0$).

4   Approximation properties

Why does the first eigenvector of the affinity matrix A behave in the way we observed? We give here an explanation.

Lemma 1 Consider a symmetric nonnegative matrix B: $B_{ij} = B_{ji} \geq 0, \forall i, j$. Then the eigenvector v_1^B of B that is associated to its largest eigenvalue is nonnegative: $v_1^B \geq 0$.

Proof It is well known that the iteration $v^{t+1} = Bv^t$ converges to v_1^B for almost all initial conditions v^0. Without loss of generality we initialize the computation with $v^0 > 0$. Since, by hyp., all entries of B are non-negative, then v^1 and therefore any v^k is also non-negative.

Lemma 2 Consider a symmetric block-diagonal $n \times n$ matrix C, whose b diagonal blocks B_i are nonnegative. Call $\lambda_j^{B_i}$ the eigenvalues of B_i and call $v_j^{B_i}$ the corresponding eigenvectors. Suppose that all such eigenvalues are distinct. Call $w_j^{B_i}$'s the n-vectors obtained by padding the $v_j^{B_i}$'s by zeros so that the nonzero entries correspond to the position taken by B_i within A.
Then the $w_j^{B_i}$'s are the eigenvectors of C and the $\lambda_j^{B_i}$ are the corresponding eigenvalues.

Proof By inspection.

Lemma 3 Consider C as above and call v_1 its eigenvector associated to its largest eigenvalue.
Then the entries of v_1 are zero corresponding to $b - 1$ of the blocks and are nonnegative corresponding to the remaining block.

Proof The largest eigenvalue of C is equal to the largest eigenvalue of one of the blocks B_i. The corresponding eigenvector therefore is nonnegative corresponding to that block and it zero elsewhere.

Proposition 2 Consider an affinity matrix A constructed on a scene where the affinity between elements of distinct groups is exactly zero. Then the first eigenvector of A is zero corresponding to elements in all groups minus one, and nonnegative corresponding to elements of that group.

Proof A is symmetric and nonnegative. By permutation $C = P^T A P$ it may be transformed into a block-diagonal matrix with nonnegative blocks, each block corresponding to a group in the scene. Its largest eigenvector may be obtained from the largest eigenvector of C by using the same permutation P.

Proposition 3 Consider the affinity matrix A of a scene where the affinity between elements of distinct groups has size of order ϵ.
Then the elements of the first eigenvector of A are nonnegative for one group and are of order ϵ for all other groups.

Proof Call v_i, λ_i the eigenvectors and eigenvalues of A. Write $A = A' + \epsilon N$ where N is a 'noise' matrix whose entries are distributed between zero and 1, and A' is block-diagonal. Write $v = v' + \delta v$ and $\lambda = \lambda' + \delta \lambda$, where v', λ' are the eigenvalues and eigenvectors of A'. Then $A v_1 = \lambda_1 v_1$. Multiply on the left by v_i, $i > 1$: $v_i^T A v_1 = \lambda_1 v_i^T v_1$. Expand A and v_1 and simplify using $A' v_1' = \lambda_1' v_1'$ obtaining:

$$v_i^t \delta v_1 = \frac{\epsilon}{\lambda_1 - \lambda_i} v_i^T N v_1 \tag{4}$$

i.e. the projection of the variation of v_1 due to the ϵ-sized noise in the direction of v_i is proportional to ϵ.

A comment stemming from the proof of proposition 3: when the magnitude of the 2nd eigenvalue of A approaches the magnitude of the first we expect the eigenvector corresponding to the largest eigenvalue to lose the attractive property of having zero entries corresponding to the background items.

5   Relationship with normalized-cuts grouping

5.1   Normalized cuts

Shi and Malik [8] have proposed to perform grouping using normalized cuts. They see the tokens that one wishes to group as the nodes of a graph, whose arcs carry the affinity between pairs of nodes. The cost of a cut $C(G_1, G_2)$ of the graph into two subgraphs is defined as the sum of the affinities associated with the arcs that are being cut. The affinity $V(G_1, G)$ between a subset G_1 of the graph and the rest of the graph G is the sum of all the arcs that connect the nodes in G_1 to every other node. They propose to minimize the normalized cut cost $N(G_1, G_2)$:

$$C(G_1, G_2) = \sum_{i \in G_1, j \in G_2} A_{i,j}, \quad V(G_k, G) = \sum_{i \in G_k, j \in G} A_{i,j}$$

$$N(G_1, G_2) = \frac{C(G_1, G_2)}{V(G_1, G)} + \frac{C(G_1, G_2)}{V(G_2, G)}, \quad G_1, G_2 = \arg \min_{G_1, G_2} N(G_1, G_2)$$

Shi and Malik develop a heuristic for calculating efficiently an approximation of the optimal partition. They solve the generalized eigenvector problem: $(A - D)x = \lambda D x$, where A is the affinity matrix, x is an unknown vector, and D is a diagonal matrix with $D_{i,i} = \sum_j A_{i,j}$. The second-to-last eigenvector x turns out to be an indicator vector for the two sets G_1 and G_2: $i \in G_1 \iff x_i \geq \alpha$. Where α is a constant that is determined by solving a related optimization.

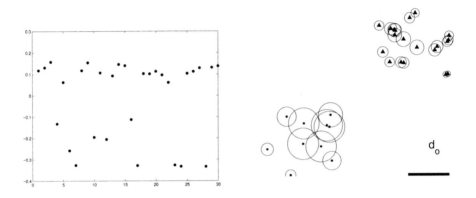

Fig. 4. The Normalized-Cut algorithm on the dataset shown in Fig. 1. On the left the value of the indicator eigenvector is shown (see text). The plot to the right, analog to the one in Fig. (2), shows the corresponding grouping – triangles indicate positive values of the eigenvector, dots indicate negative values, the diameter of the circles surrounding each marker indicates the magnitude.

5.2 Foreground cut

Consider an asymmetric variation of Shi and Malik's cost function. Define one of the two subsets of G to be a foreground F, and its complement $B = G \setminus F$ to be the background, and minimize:

$$N(F) = \frac{C(F, B)}{C(F, F)} \tag{5}$$

The problem may be solved along the lines of Shi and Malik. Define a vector x of zeros and ones, with the 1's being the foreground indices ($x_i = 1 \iff i \in F$).

Define a vector **1** as a vector of ones. Call B the background, complement of F: $B = G \setminus F$. Then:

$$N(F) = \frac{\sum_{i \in F, j \in B} A_{i,j}}{\sum_{i \in F, j \in F} A_{i,j}} \tag{6}$$

$$= \frac{x^T A(\mathbf{1} - x)}{x^T A x} = \frac{x^T A \mathbf{1}}{x^T A x} - 1 \tag{7}$$

Note that minimizing $N(F)$ is equivalent to minimizing $N(F) + 1 = \frac{x^T A \mathbf{1}}{x^T A x}$.

Now call (U, S, V) the SVD of A and notice that $U = V$ since A is symmetric. Define $z \doteq S^{\frac{1}{2}} U^T x$, and rewrite the cost function as:

$$N(F) + 1 = \frac{z^T S^{\frac{1}{2}} U^T \mathbf{1}}{\|z\|^2} = \frac{z^T u}{\|z\|^2} \tag{8}$$

$$\text{with} \quad u_i \doteq S^{\frac{1}{2}}(i,i) \sum_j U_{j,i} \tag{9}$$

Remember that we are trying to find a minimum of N subject to the constraint that x is composed of zeros and ones. It is not clear how to perform this optimization efficiently. We may proceed heuristically as in Shi and Malik by letting x take analog values, and imposing a constraint on its norm. The easiest such constraint, here, is to impose that $\|z\| = \|x\|_A = 1$. In this case we just need to minimize the numerator of our cost function. This is easily done by discovering the largest (in absolute value) entry of u, and picking $z^T = \pm[0, \ldots, 0, 1, 0, \ldots, 0]$ with 1 in the corresponding position k. The sign of z has to be chosen so that it is opposite to the sign of the maximum entry of u. Now remember that $x = S^{-\frac{1}{2}} U z$ – this means that the minimizing x is the k-th column of U appropriately scaled.

As a result we derive the following 'foreground cut' algorithm:

1. Calculate the SVD of A: $A = USV$.
2. Calculate the vector $u = SU\mathbf{1}$.
3. Determine the index k of the maximum entry of u.
4. Define the foreground vector x as the k-th column of U.
5. Threshold x, the foreground F correspond to the non-zero entries of x.

It turns out that the largest entry of u is typically the first, since, as previously discussed, if A is block-diagonal, then the 1st singular vector will have non-negative entries (it is the first eigenvector), while the other eigenvectors tend to have zero-mean; moreover, the sums of the columns of U enter in u weighted by the singular values in S, which imposed an additional bias in favor of low-index entries. Therefore, apart for rare cases, the 'foreground cut' algorithm gives identical results as the 'affinity factorization' algorithm.

6 Line affinity

The fact that line segments tend to group into longer line-like structures when they are roughly aligned in the image was noticed in the '30s by the Gestalt psychologists. Computer vision researchers have worked on the problem at least since the early 80s [3], with methods reaching a considerable level of sophistication by the end of the 80s [7, 5].

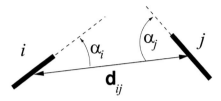

Fig. 5. Variables involved in the computation of the affinity of two edgels i and j.

A reasonable form for the affinity of line segments (or edgels), suggested by the observations of the Gestalt psychologists and supported by psychophysical measurements of Sagi, Kovacs, Braun and collaborators [2, 4, 1], assumes that that two lines are 'similar' when they are close by, when they are aligned and, failing that, when they are co-circular, i.e. tangent to the same circle. A possible implementation of these intuitions is (see also Fig. 5):

$$A_{i,j} = e^{-\frac{d_{ij}^2}{d_0^2} - \frac{2-\cos(2\alpha_i)-\cos(2\alpha_j)}{1-\cos(2\theta_0)} - \frac{1-\cos(2\alpha_i-2\alpha_j)}{1-\cos(2\delta\theta_0)}} \qquad (10)$$

where the first term in the exponential is a distance-related affinity, the second term penalizes the average deviation of the line segments from being collinear, and the third term penalizes the non-cocircularity of the two line segments. The scaling constants $d_0, \theta_0, \delta\theta_0$ are somewhat arbitrary. Good values for d_0 range between the spacing of the elements and five times that value. Good values for θ_0 typically range from $\pi/2$ to $\pi/10$, while $\delta\theta_0$ typically should be half to one-fourth as large as θ_0 (see the experiments).

7 Computational complexity

The affinity factorization algorithm may be implemented efficiently. The cost function of Eq. 2 may be minimized, rather than computing the SVD of the matrix A, by gradient descent $p^{t+1} = (1 - \lambda)p^t + \frac{\lambda}{\|p^t\|^2}Ap$, which for $\lambda = 1$ is:

$$p^0 = 1, \qquad p^{t+1} = \frac{1}{\|p^t\|^2}Ap \qquad (11)$$

Typically 10-40 iterations of (11) achieve a stable result. If the computations are implemented using sparse matrices the total complexity is linked linearly to the number of neighbors of each element (this may be verified by inspecting (11)). Let N be the average number of neighbors of each element, and let E

be the number of elements in the set to be grouped, then the computational cost is $C \approx < 100 \times N \times E$ floating point operations for the minimization. This cost has the same order as that of the Shi-Malik algorithm with a multiplicative constant that is roughly half as large. The computation of the matrix A may also be reduced to a linear cost by using quad-trees for referencing the data points (we have not implemented this). This appears to be faster than both Shashua and Ullman [7] and Parent and Zucker [5], although we have not yet implemented their algorithms and we were unable to find a precise assessment of computational complexity in their papers.

8 Experiments

We explore some of the characteristics of the affinity factorization (or, equivalently the foreground cut) and the normalized cuts algorithms. In our experiments we have picked thresholds by hand – the problem of automatic threshold selection is discussed in [8]; in some experiments, where we thought that this may be illuminating, we used multiple thresholds. Another issue that we do not discuss here is the extraction of multiple groups from the image. This is also discussed in [8]. Here we will restrict ourselves to showing the most salient group found by the affinity factorization algorithm, and the most salient cut found by the normalized cuts algorithm.

The method we used for calculating p in the affinity factorization algorithm is specified in Eq. (11); the calculation of x in the normalized-cuts algorithm was performed using Matlab's SVD function. The constants used in the experiments are specified in the figures.

8.1 Experiment 1: Point Clusters

A first experiment is shown in Figures 1, 2, 3, 4. A second experiment using data from [8] is shown in Fig. 6. Both algorithms achieve good grouping.

8.2 Experiment 2: Foreground-background

A second experiment compares the algorithms on a foreground-background display shown in Fig 7, left. See Figures 8, 9. The normalized cuts algorithm does not achieve grouping for any value of p, probably due to it's symmetric formulation, where both sets in which the scene is grouped are supposed to be 'meaningful'. The affinity factorization algorithm does achieve grouping instead.

8.3 Line grouping

We used the affinity function reported in Sec. 6 to group lines in the line figure shown in Fig 7, right. The affinity factorization algorithm achieves good grouping, while the normalized-cuts algorithm does not, probably due to the foreground-background problem mentioned above.

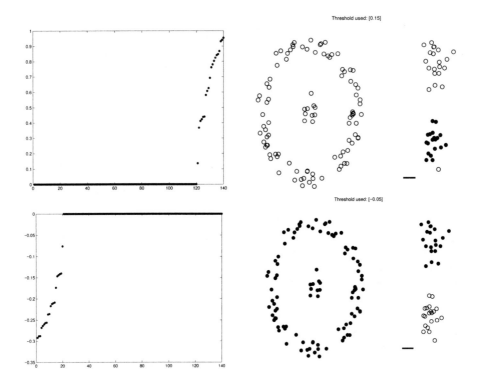

Fig. 6. (Top) Grouping using the affinity factorization algorithm. (Bottom) Using Shi-Malik's normalized cuts.

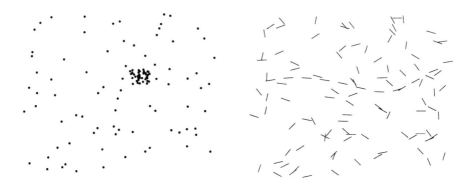

Fig. 7. (Left) Foreground/background point figure. (Right) Line segments on a plane forming an 'emergent line'.

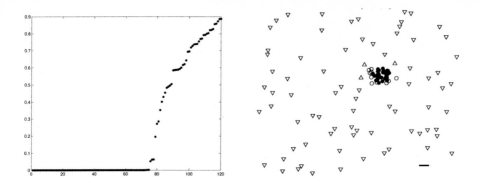

Fig. 8. The 'groupiness' vector p (left) and the groups (right) obtained for a foreground-background dot figure using the affinity factorization algorithm. The short bar at the bottom right indicates the length of the critical distance d_0. Capsized triangles indicate points for which $p < 0.01$; upright triangles indicate points for which $p \in (0.01, 0.1)$; open circles indicate dots for which $p \in (0.1, 0.5)$; closed circles are associated to $p > 0.1$. Notice that the circles indicate the foreground group, with open circles at its periphery and 3 upright triangles at the extreme periphery.

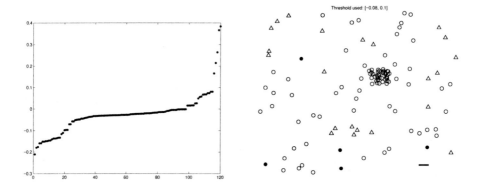

Fig. 9. Performance of the normalized cuts algorithm on same data as in Fig. 8. The indicator eigenvector x of A is shown in the plot on the left. Unlike the vector p of the affinity factorization algorithm, x takes both positive and negative values. The grouping is shown on the right, with triangles indicating $x < -0.08$, open circles indicating $x \in (-0.08, 0.1)$ and closed circles $x > 0.1$. The symbols are mixed and therefore no good groups emerge.

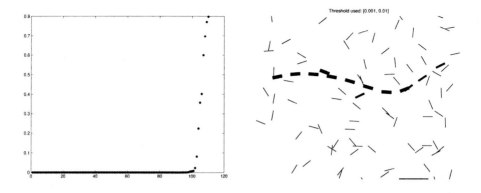

Fig. 10. Grouping performed by the affinity factorization algorithm.The thickest line segments correspond to $p > 0.01$, the medium-thick segments correspond to $p \in (0.0001, 0.01)$, while the thin segments correspond to $p < 0.0001$. The long line at the bottom right indicates the critical distance d_0. The constants used in (10) were $\theta_0 = \pi/8$ and $\delta\theta_0 = \pi/16$.

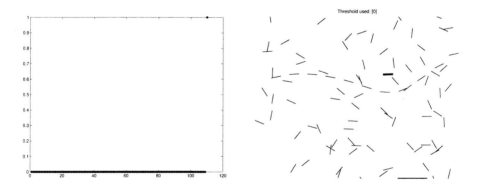

Fig. 11. Grouping performed by normalized cut algorithm. The same affinity matrix as in (10) was used (i.e., same affinity function and same constants). The vector x only has one non-zero value (corresponding to the short bold line, roughly at the center of the display).

8.4   2D images

We explored the behavior of the algorithms on the synthetic brightness images shown in Fig. 12. The images are identical apart from the background (relatively noisy or 'unstructured' in the right image).

Fig. 12. Two brightness 'Mondrians' used in our experiments. The brightness values are uniformly distributed between 0 and 0.1 for the background of the left image and between 0 and 10 for the background of the right image. The rectangles are identical in the two images, with brightness uniformly distributed between 2 and 2.1 for the larger one and between 3 and 3.3 for the smaller one. The units of brightness are arbitrary. The images are shown with different colormaps.

An exponential affinity function was used (i and j are pixel indices):

$$A_{ij} = \exp^{-\frac{d^2(i,j)}{d_0^2} - \frac{(I(i)-I(j))^2}{dI_0}} \tag{12}$$

with I indicating brightness values and constant values $d_o = 3$ and $dI_o = 1$.

In Fig. 13 the results of the experiment are shown. Both algorithms work well on the first Mondrian (Fig. 13, first row), with the normalized cuts algorithm showing a more uniform value than the factorization algorithm (although, as shown in the middle column, the log of the first singular vector shows equivalently sharp boundaries). In the Mondrian with unstructured background (Fig. 13, second row) the normalized cuts algorithms groups a small cluster of pixels rather than one of the two large rectangles.

9   Discussion and Conclusions

We have shown that concepts such as 'grouping' and 'foreground' may be obtained from an intuitive concept of 'pairwise similarity' or 'pairwise consistency' between elements of the scene. The derivation consists in choosing to approximate the pairwise relationships between all elements with a pointwise property

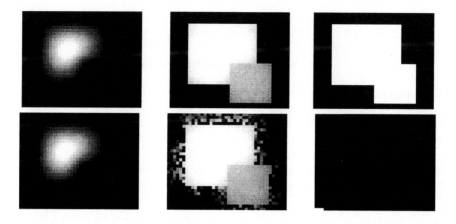

Fig. 13. First eigenvector of the affinity matrix (left), log of the same (center) and normalized cuts (right). The first row shows the results on the first Mondrian, the second on the second.

of each element. It turns out that the pointwise property that best approximates pairwise similarity may be interpreted as a 'saliency' measure, and one may obtain the foreground group in the scene by thresholding this saliency measure. Propositions 2 and 3 give an explanation, based on the properties of the eigenvectors of (noisy) block-diagonal matrices, of why this is the case.

Our derivation suggests an algorithm for grouping which we call 'affinity factorization algorithm'. We derive a second grouping algorithm which we call 'foreground cuts' by modifying the 'normalized cuts' formulation of Shi and Malik [8], and we show that 'foreground cuts' and 'affinity factorization' are essentially the same algorithm, although they are derived from a different starting point.

We compare affinity factorization and normalized cuts on a number of test sets of points and lines and brightness images. The experiments demonstrate the good grouping performance of affinity factorization even on data sets where the background is unstructured, which the normalized cuts algorithm is not constructed to handle. Malik and collaborators approach this problem by defining more sophisticated affinity measures, including texture and brightness histograms, for which the class of unstructured image patches is smaller (see their papers in the present proceedings and of ICCV 1998).

The experiment on brightness Mondrians shows that value of the saliency vector p of the affinity factorization algorithm drops near the boundaries of the foreground region (compare with the very desirable piecewise constant behavior of the normalized cuts vector). However, its logarithm shows sharp boundary discontinuities (it is natural to consider the log. since we are guaranteed that p is non-negative). This suggests that maybe the log of the largest eigenvector of the affinity matrix should be considered as the proper definition of the affinity function.

The implementation of the affinity factorization algorithm that we propose is efficient, in that it executes in $O(n)$ operations, where n is the number of elements in the display.

Directions for further research and experimentation include:

1. Generalization to the situation in which, rather than pairwise affinities between elements, we have three-way or n-way relationships. In that case we may start from the affinity tensor A_{ijk} and approximate it with $p_i p_j p_k$.
2. Generalization to the situation where the affinity is non-symmetric (think of the line-elements forming a T junction). In that case we may approximate A with $p_i q_j$ and use both p and q to select the foreground set.
3. Study other norms than L^2. The L^1 norm, for example, may be more appropriate. Eq. (11) may be suitably modified for this purpose.
4. Incorporate 'top-down attention' by imposing that the solution contains a certain subset of elements. This may be done by introducing a bias term in Eq. (11).

Acknowledgements

Conversations with Allen Tannenbaum, Xiaolin Feng, Max Welling, Sandro Zampieri, Jitendra Malik, Janbo Shi, Serge Belongie, Thomas Leung and Josh Tannenbaum are gratefully acknowledged. This research was in part supported by the NSF Engineering Research Center in Neuromorphic Systems Engineering at Caltech.

References

1. Y Adini, D Sagi, and M Tsodyks. Excitatory-inhibitory network in the visual cortex: psychophysical evidence. *Proc. Natl Academy Sci.*, 94(19):10426–10431, September 1997.
2. J. Braun and E. Niebur. Perceptual contour completion: a model based on local anisotropic, fast-adapting interactions between oriented filters. *Soc. Neurosci. Abstract*, 20(1665), 1994.
3. M. Hedlund, G. H. Granlund, and H. Knutsson. A consistency operation for line and curve enhancement. In *Proc. IEEE Comp. Soc. Conf. on Pattern Recognition and Image Processing*, pages 93–96, 1982.
4. I Kovacs. Gestalten of today: early processing of visual contours and surfaces. *Behavioural brain research*, 82:1–11, 1996.
5. P. Parent and S. Zucker. Trace inference, curvature consistency, and curve detection. *IEEE Trans. Pattern Anal. Mach. Intell.*, 11(8):823–839, 1989.
6. A. Pinkus. *n-Widths in Approximation Theory*. Springer Verlag, 1985.
7. A. Shashua and S. Ullman. Structural saliency: the detection of globally salient structures using a locally connected network. In *2nd International Conference on Computer Vision (ICCV)*, pages 321–327, December 1988.
8. J. Shi and J. Malik. Normalized cuts and image segmentation. In *Proc. IEEE Comput. Soc. Conf. Comput. Vision and Pattern Recogn.*, Puerto Rico, June 1997.

Faithful Least-Squares Fitting of Spheres, Cylinders, Cones and Tori for Reliable Segmentation

Gabor Lukács[1,2], Ralph Martin[2], and Dave Marshall[2]

[1] Computer and Automation Research Institute, Hungarian Academy of Sciences,
H-1518 Budapest, POB 63, Hungary
lukacs@sztaki.hu

[2] Dept of Computer Science, Cardiff University, PO Box 916, Cardiff, UK, CF2 3XF
ralph@cs.cf.ac.uk, dave@cs.cf.ac.uk

Abstract. This paper addresses a problem arising in the reverse engineering of solid models from depth-maps. We wish to identify and fit surfaces of known type wherever these are a good fit. This paper presents a set of methods for the least-squares fitting of spheres, cylinders, cones and tori to three-dimensional point data. Least-squares fitting of surfaces other planes, even of simple geometric type, has been little studied.

Our method has the particular advantage of being robust in the sense that as the principal curvatures of the surfaces being fitted decrease (or become more equal), the results which are returned naturally become closer and closer to those surfaces of 'simpler type', *i.e.* planes, cylinders, cones, or spheres which best describe the data, unlike other methods which may diverge as various parameters or their combination become infinite.

1   Introduction

The motivation for this paper lies in reverse engineering of the geometric shape of simple mechanical components. A laser scanner is used to capture three-dimensional point data from the surface of an object. From this we wish to construct a boundary representation solid model of the object's shape. In particular, we wish to identify and fit particular simple surfaces to portions of the boundary wherever these are in good agreement with the point data. The problem can be decomposed into two logical steps: *segmentation*, where the data points are grouped into sets each belonging to a different surface, and *fitting*, where the best surface of an appropriate type is fitted to each set of points. The new results in this paper concern the latter problem, but we first outline the segmentation method used, as it has a significant effect on the final model created. We present new results on the fitting of spheres, cylinders, cones and tori, after giving a review of previous approaches. Detailed analysis and explicit formulae for the partial derivatives used in the non-linear least-squares optimisation can be found in [16].

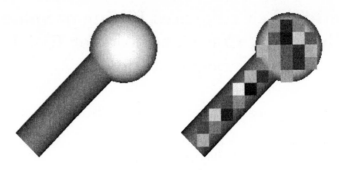

Fig. 1. Initial 3D data; seed placement

2 Segmentation

Segmentation is the problem of grouping the points in the original dataset into subsets each of which logically belongs to a single primitive surface. Various approaches exist for segmenting simple surfaces from three-dimensional data [1–3, 5, 7, 10, 15]. Most commonly, segmentation is treated as a local-to-global aggregation problem with similarity constraints employed to control the process. Often several stages are required, mostly applied in a sequential fashion, ranging from the estimation of local surface properties such as curvature, to more complex feature clustering such as symmetry seeking. Typically, small initial seed regions are chosen at random positions. These are then grown and homogeneous regions are merged together. However, such approaches tend to isolate the segmentation stage from the representation stage with the result that the data partitioning may not agree well with the given primitive types. In addition, the sensitivity of these methods to noise in the data (especially outliers) may also lead to misclassification and, hence, poor results [12]. An efficient and reliable segmentation process thus depends on employing geometric knowledge of the primitive types, firstly, to guide the detection and grouping processes, and secondly, to assure the coherence and consistency of models throughout the whole segmentation process [1].

The approach used for segmentation in our reverse engineering project is the *recover and select* paradigm of Leonardis et al.[11, 13, 12, 14]. Here an iterative process recovers and selects specific instances of the required geometric primitives (planes, spheres, cylinders, cones and tori). The basic approach partitions the data according to primitives by choosing the models such that the description is *best* in terms of global shape and error of fit. Initially seed regions are placed at arbitrary locations in the data and models of each primitive approximated (Fig. 1). Grossly mismatching models may be rejected at this stage. An iterative grow and select phase is then operated. All valid models are grown for an equal number of steps (see left of Fig. 2); note that the models are allowed to overlap. The resulting models are then inspected and some are selected for

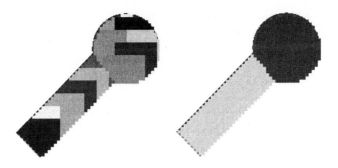

Fig. 2. Grown and selected regions at an intermediate stage; final segmentation

further growing. Optimal models from the overlapping sets are selected on the basis of the following criteria:

Area — the number of image elements contained in the model
Error of Fit — the maximum or average distance to the model
Quality of Fit — the number of parameters used to describe the model
Surface Type — the class of surface of the model

When different models have similar goodness of fit, some types of model may be preferred to others, and the **Surface Type** is used to impose an ordering of selection in the way suggested by Besl and Jain [2, 3]. This is, typically, done in terms of increasing surface type complexity (*i.e.* plane, sphere, cylinder, cone, torus), where the simpler surface would be chosen first. A weighted sum of the above criteria is used as a cost-benefit measure to select the optimal model or models.

Models that simply have a poor error of fit (even if not overlapping other models) are also rejected at the selection stage.

The rest of this paper discusses novel fitting methods for spheres, cylinders, cones and tori which are used in this segmentation framework.

3 Surface Fit and General Nonlinear Least-Squares

Initially, we outline some basic concepts for least-squares fitting of simple geometric surfaces, and then review previous approaches to this problem.

Let us assume that each of the three-dimensional points $\mathbf{p}_i$ for $i = 1, \ldots, m$ lies close to the same member of a family of surfaces which can be parameterized by $\mathbf{s} \in G \subseteq \mathbb{R}^s$ where G is an open set. Let d be a function which is defined as the distance of the point $\mathbf{p}_i \in \mathbb{R}^3$ from that surface in the family identified by $\mathbf{s}$. Throughout, d will be called the 'true' distance function of the surface (fitting methods generally rely on approximations to this distance as will be explained later).

A surface which goes through all the points can be viewed as that member of the family which corresponds to the solution of the simultaneous system of m equations:

$$d(\mathbf{s}, \mathbf{p}_i) = 0, \qquad \text{for } i = 1, \ldots, m. \tag{1}$$

Since the number of points m is usually much greater than the number of degrees of freedom s, this system of equations is overdetermined and in general cannot be solved. However it is possible to solve it in the least-squares sense, *i.e.* to find that surface which is the best fit to the points 'on the average', minimising

$$\sum_{i=1}^{m} d(\mathbf{s}, \mathbf{p}_i)^2 \tag{2}$$

Sometimes we may have additional non-linear constraints expressed as

$$H(\mathbf{s}) = \mathbf{0} \in \mathbb{R}^t \tag{3}$$

for $t < s$. For example, the surface form in use might describe a general quadric, but we may wish to impose that the surface found is a cylinder, which can by done by imposing constraints on $\mathbf{s}$. Using the principle of Lagrangian multipliers to include these constraints, a non-linear generalised eigenvalue problem results, which is not easy to solve. A simpler approach is to use Eqn. 3 to eliminate t unknowns, to reduce the problem to an unconstrained optimisation problem in a lower dimensional space. This is the method we use.

Usually the family of surfaces is defined as points satisfying an implicit equation:

$$f(\mathbf{s}, \mathbf{x}) = 0, \qquad \text{for } \mathbf{x} \in \mathbb{R}^3, \tag{4}$$

where $\mathbf{s}$ is the family parameter. Although if we fix $\mathbf{s}$, f and d have the same roots in space, they may behave quite differently for points which do not lie on the surface. Thus, if instead of Expression 2, one minimises $\sum f^2$ this may give quite different results. However, this approach can be justified if *both* the function f and the constraint H in Eqn. 3 are of particularly simple form. If f is linear and H is quadratic in terms of the parameters then linear generalised eigenvalue techniques work (*e.g.* see [8]). If f is non-linear but H is still quadratic then one can try Taubin's generalised eigenvector fit [21]. Nevertheless, the choice of form for f influences the behaviour of the non-linear fitting algorithm, and consequently the quality of the solution. For fitting ellipses, Rosin [20] shows that choosing f carelessly can lead to severely biassed estimates for $\mathbf{s}$. Below we give 'fairly good' f functions (*i.e.* for which f behaves much like d near the surface) which are highly non-linear, and which have no additional constraints on the parameters $\mathbf{s}$.

4 Approximating the True Distance

As far as possible one has to avoid singularities of $d(\mathbf{s}, \mathbf{p}_i)$ in the range where solutions may lie. These may be places where some denominator in $d(\mathbf{s}, \mathbf{p}_i)$

vanishes, or where the distance function is not differentiable. Using Euclidean metrics such singularities arise frequently since the Euclidean distance from a given fixed point is *itself* singular in this sense. Nevertheless, most of these nonlinear singularities are only *computational*, *i.e.* inessential discontinuities in the mathematical sense, meaning that a limiting value of the distance function can still be found for the critical parameter value. Even so, the computation of the distance function (or its derivatives) can be unstable at such points, since it may require the subtraction of similar quantities *etc.*

Avoiding the effects of singularities uses various techniques. Firstly, one uses a suitable parameterization where the critical values do not lie on the border of G. Secondly, one changes the definition of $d(\mathbf{s}, \mathbf{p}_i)$ slightly in order to get rid of singularities. We shall say that this modified definition is *faithful* to the true Euclidean distance function if, firstly, the function is 0 where the true distance is 0, and, secondly, at these points, the derivatives with respect to the parameters are the same for the true distance and the modified definition.

Faithful distance functions can be obtained if one approximates square roots within $d(\mathbf{s}, \mathbf{p}_i)$ in the following way. Suppose that the distance function is of the following form:

$$d(\mathbf{s}, \mathbf{p}_i) = \sqrt{g} - h, \tag{5}$$

where both g and h may depend on the parameter vector $\mathbf{s}$ and on the point $\mathbf{p}_i$ in three space. In order to get rid of the square root we might try to minimise $\sum (g - h^2)^2$ instead of Eqn. 2 since $d = 0$ when $g = h^2$. Unfortunately, the effect is now that we are searching for the surface which fits best in terms of the *square* of the distance instead of the distance. This transformation undesirably amplifies the importance of the further points, and flattens the goal function in the neighbourhood of the solution. Instead, let us put

$$\tilde{d} = \frac{g - h^2}{2h} = d + \frac{d^2}{2h}. \tag{6}$$

and let us minimise

$$\sum \tilde{d}^2(\mathbf{s}, \mathbf{p}_i) = \sum \frac{\left(g(\mathbf{s}, \mathbf{p}_i) - h^2(\mathbf{s}, \mathbf{p}_i)\right)^2}{4h^2(\mathbf{s}, \mathbf{p}_i)}. \tag{7}$$

Under very general assumptions (see [16]), this function is faithful to the Euclidean distance.

In summary, in our approach we start with an exact expression for the distance d. This is replaced by a simplification which is easier to compute, but which still has the same zero set and derivatives at the zero set. In contrast, similar work by Taubin [21] starts from a parameterized family of implicit functions $f = 0$. He notes that while f itself is not a good approximation to d, $f/|\nabla f|$ is much better, *i.e.* he replaces the original implicit function with a new one whose value is a better approximation to d. Although Taubin does not state so explicitly, it is clear that it is better because the derivatives with respect to spatial parameters of this function are the same as those of the distance function. In practice Taubin's approach can be used only if f is linear with respect to the parameters, and the system to be solved then includes a quadratic constraint. Another difference is that our approach is better behaved with respect to singularities.

5 Fitting Spheres, Cylinders, Cones and Tori

The linear least-squares fitting of second order curves and surfaces has been considered by several authors recently (see [18], [19], [9], [8]). However, specific linear methods still do not exist for right cylinders and cones—the reason is that the equations expressing the conditions for a quadric to be a right cylinder or a cone are not quadratic. If general linear methods are used for algebraic second order surfaces the solutions found are usually not right cylinders or cones and may even be very different from the optimum surfaces of such type. In this sense, algebraic techniques which use the value of the implicit quadratic form as the 'distance' from the surface approximate the true geometric distance in an unfaithful way.

The situation is much simpler for spheres since straightforward algebraic methods work in this case: under a suitable normalisation the minimised algebraic distance will reflect the geometric distance as well. For example, the method in [18] minimises

$$\sum_i \left(A(x_i^2 + y_i^2 + z_i^2) + Dx_i + Ey_i + Fz_i + G \right)^2 \tag{8}$$

under the condition

$$D^2 + E^2 + F^2 - 4AG = 1 \tag{9}$$

which is basically equivalent to our minimisation in Eqn. 7. (Note that the simple constraint $A = 1$ may give quite unfaithful results as shown in [18].) Nevertheless, we give our non-linear method for spheres in the next section as an illustration of our method, as it has certain advantages.

Nonlinear methods which take into account the true geometric distance match well with the requirements of our reverse engineering method. Those points belonging to the same surface are selected by means of a segmentation technique which usually provides an initial approximation for the parameters of each surface. Starting from these, at the expense of some computing time, one can obtain a more accurate fit. Our nonlinear methods also work well in other applications where an initial approximate fit for the surface is known.

Earlier nonlinear estimation approaches usually worked with cylinders and spheres. As a rule the equations contain positional parameters of centres or axes and so they become ill-conditioned in limiting situations (see e.g. [4]), which is unacceptable if automatic segmentation is the objective. Our nonlinear methods have been carefully designed to overcome this problem.

5.1 Sphere Fitting

For non-linear least-squares fit the parameterization of the sphere will be the following. Suppose that the *closest* point of the sphere (*not* its centre) to the origin is $\varrho\mathbf{n}$, where $|\mathbf{n}| = 1$ and the radius of the sphere is $1/k$. Then if $\mathbf{p}$ is an arbitrary point in space, the distance of this point from the surface of the sphere is:

$$d(\mathbf{s}, \mathbf{p}) = \left|\mathbf{p} - (\varrho + \frac{1}{k})\mathbf{n}\right| - \frac{1}{k} = \sqrt{\langle\mathbf{p} - (\varrho + \frac{1}{k})\mathbf{n}, \mathbf{p} - (\varrho + \frac{1}{k})\mathbf{n}\rangle} - \frac{1}{k} \quad (10)$$

Since this function is of the form Eqn. 5 we can apply Approximation 6 to give

$$\tilde{d}(\mathbf{s}, \mathbf{p}) = \frac{k}{2}\left(|\mathbf{p}|^2 - 2\varrho\langle\mathbf{p}, \mathbf{n}\rangle + \varrho^2\right) + \varrho - \langle\mathbf{p}, \mathbf{n}\rangle, \quad (11)$$

or if one introduces the notation

$$\hat{\mathbf{p}} = \mathbf{p} - \varrho\mathbf{n}, \quad (12)$$

one obtains

$$\tilde{d}(\mathbf{s}, \mathbf{p}) = \frac{k}{2}|\hat{\mathbf{p}}|^2 - \langle\hat{\mathbf{p}}, \mathbf{n}\rangle. \quad (13)$$

Note that here $\hat{\mathbf{p}}$ is the expression of $\mathbf{p}$ with respect to an origin at $\varrho\mathbf{n}$. Now let us parameterize $\mathbf{n}$ using polar coordinates, so in the usual way

$$\mathbf{n} = (\cos\varphi\sin\vartheta, \sin\varphi\sin\vartheta, \cos\vartheta), \quad (14)$$

where ϑ is the angle between $\mathbf{n}$ and the z axis and φ is the angle between the projection of $\mathbf{n}$ onto the plane $z = 0$ and the x axis. Differentiating $\mathbf{n}$ with respect to φ and ϑ one obtains two partial derivative vectors which are orthogonal to each other and to $\mathbf{n}$ (superscripts denote derivatives); these will be used later:

$$\mathbf{n}^\varphi = (-\sin\varphi\sin\vartheta, \cos\varphi\sin\vartheta, 0) \quad (15)$$
$$\mathbf{n}^\vartheta = (\cos\varphi\cos\vartheta, \sin\varphi\cos\vartheta, -\sin\vartheta). \quad (16)$$

Thus $\mathbf{n}$ and hence $\tilde{d}$ can be parameterized without constraints by $\mathbf{s} = (\varrho, \varphi, \vartheta, k)$.

Note that unlike Expression 8, Eqn. 11 is nonlinear but it behaves well as the curvature of the sphere decreases, as in that case, $k \to 0$, all the terms are bounded, and Eqn. 11 reduces to the expression that would be used for least-squares plane fitting. In contrast, observe that some of the terms will tend to infinity both in the objective function given in Eqn. 8and in the constraint given in Eqn. 9.

5.2 Right Circular Cylinder Fitting

The parameterization used for the cylinder is similar to that for the sphere. The closest point of the cylinder to the origin is $\varrho\mathbf{n}$, where $|\mathbf{n}| = 1$. Assume that

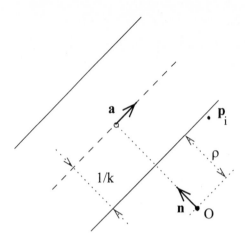

Fig. 3. Parameterization of the cylinder

the direction of the axis of the cylinder is $\mathbf{a}$ with $|\mathbf{a}| = 1$, and the radius of the cylinder is $1/k$. Note that $\langle \mathbf{n}, \mathbf{a} \rangle = 0$. Now let us suppose that $\mathbf{p}$ is an arbitrary point in space whose distance from the surface of the cylinder is to be found. This is done by finding its distance from the symmetry axis and from that subtracting the radius of the cylinder (see Fig. 3):

$$d(\mathbf{s}, \mathbf{p}) = \left| (\mathbf{p} - (\varrho + \frac{1}{k})\mathbf{n}) \times \mathbf{a} \right| - \frac{1}{k}$$

$$= \sqrt{|\mathbf{p} - (\varrho + \frac{1}{k})\mathbf{n}|^2 - \langle \mathbf{p} - (\varrho + \frac{1}{k})\mathbf{n}, \mathbf{a} \rangle^2} - \frac{1}{k} \qquad (17)$$

Since this function is of the form in Eqn. 5 we can apply Approximation 6 to obtain

$$\tilde{d}(\mathbf{s}, \mathbf{p}) = \frac{k}{2} \left(|\mathbf{p}|^2 - 2\varrho\langle \mathbf{p}, \mathbf{n} \rangle - \langle \mathbf{p}, \mathbf{a} \rangle^2 + \varrho^2 \right) + \varrho - \langle \mathbf{p}, \mathbf{n} \rangle = \frac{k}{2}|\hat{\mathbf{p}} \times \mathbf{a}|^2 - \langle \hat{\mathbf{p}}, \mathbf{n} \rangle,$$

$$(18)$$

where $\hat{\mathbf{p}} = \mathbf{p} - \varrho\mathbf{n}$ as in Eqn. 12. Using appropriate parameterizations for $\mathbf{n}$ and $\mathbf{a}$ we wish to minimise the function

$$\sum_i \tilde{d}^2(\mathbf{s}, \mathbf{p}_i).$$

Let us make some observations about the right hand side of Eqn. 18. Firstly, it is linear in the curvature k if all other parameters are fixed, which results in a *separable* non-linear least squares problem (see *e.g.* [6]). Such problems can be easier to solve than the fully non-linear case. Clearly, an initial estimate for k is not needed if we have estimates for the other parameters, as an initial value for k can be found by solving a linear least-squares problem in which all other parameters are fixed. Note that Eqn. 18 behaves well as k gets smaller (ϱ is bounded within sensible limits by the geometric configuration of the scanner); compare Eqn. 17 which subtracts two large quantities as k becomes small. In the limit as $k \to 0$ we get $\tilde{d} = \varrho - \langle \mathbf{p}, \mathbf{n} \rangle$, and as before the problem reduces to linear least-squares fitting of a plane.

Again, we wish to parameterize $\mathbf{n}$ and $\mathbf{a}$ to satisfy the constraints

$$|\mathbf{n}| = |\mathbf{a}| = 1, \quad \langle \mathbf{n}, \mathbf{a} \rangle = 0;$$

again we use polar coordinates. The parameterization for $\mathbf{n}$ was introduced in Eqn. 14, and Eqns. 15 and 16 are the partial derivatives of $\mathbf{n}$. Thus if we put

$$\overline{\mathbf{n}^\varphi} = (-\sin\varphi, \cos\varphi, 0) = \frac{\mathbf{n}^\varphi}{\sin\vartheta}, \tag{19}$$

then $\mathbf{n}^\vartheta$, $\overline{\mathbf{n}^\varphi}$ and $\mathbf{n}$ form an orthonormal basis. Thus we can parameterize $\mathbf{a}$ as follows:

$$\mathbf{a} = \mathbf{n}^\vartheta \cos\alpha + \overline{\mathbf{n}^\varphi} \sin\alpha, \tag{20}$$

where α is the angle between $\mathbf{a}$ and $\mathbf{n}^\vartheta$. Thus, $\mathbf{n}$ and $\mathbf{a}$ are parameterized through φ, ϑ and α by means of Eqns. 14, 16, 19 and 20.

5.3 Right Circular Cone Fitting

The parameterization used for the cone is similar to that for the cylinder. Let $\varrho\mathbf{n}$ with $|\mathbf{n}| = 1$ be that point on the cone surface for which a line in the direction of the surface normal passes through the origin. (Hence $\mathbf{n}$ is a normal to the cone.) Let the non-zero principal curvature of the cone at the point $\varrho\mathbf{n}$ be k. Let us denote the unit direction of the axis of the cone by $\mathbf{a}$. $\mathbf{n}$ is parameterized by φ and ϑ as in Eqn. 14. Since $\mathbf{n}$ and $\mathbf{a}$ are not in this case perpendicular, $\mathbf{a}$ can be parameterized freely by two polar coordinate angles, σ and τ

$$\mathbf{a} = (\cos\sigma\sin\tau, \sin\sigma\sin\tau, \cos\tau), \tag{21}$$

where τ is the angle between $\mathbf{a}$ and the z axis and σ is the angle between the projection of $\mathbf{a}$ onto the plane $z = 0$ and the x axis. The six parameters $(\varrho, \varphi, \vartheta, k, \sigma, \tau)$ characterise the right circular cone surface.

In order to understand how this works, let the half angle of the cone be ψ (see Fig. 4), and the position of the apex of the cone be $\mathbf{c}$; we shall express ψ and $\mathbf{c}$ using the above parameters later. Let the angle between the axis of the cone and $\mathbf{p} - \mathbf{c}$ be ω. Using these, the distance of $\mathbf{p}$, an arbitrary point, from the cone surface is given by (note that $\mathbf{p}$ may not lie in the plane of $\mathbf{n}$ and $\mathbf{a}$)

$$d(\mathbf{s}, \mathbf{p}) = |\mathbf{p} - \mathbf{c}| \sin(\omega - \psi) = |\mathbf{p} - \mathbf{c}| \sin\omega \cos\psi - |\mathbf{p} - \mathbf{c}| \cos\omega \sin\psi.$$

Without loss of generality we can suppose that both ψ and ω are acute angles. Since the direction of the axis, $\mathbf{a}$ is a unit vector we have:

$$d(\mathbf{s}, \mathbf{p}) = |(\mathbf{p} - \mathbf{c}) \times \mathbf{a}| \cos\psi - |\langle \mathbf{p} - \mathbf{c}, \mathbf{a} \rangle| \sin\psi. \tag{22}$$

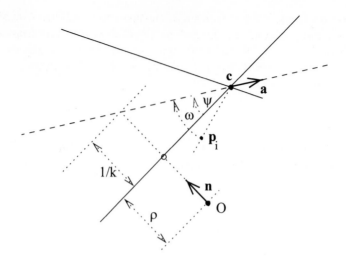

Fig. 4. Parameterization of the cone

Moreover since the angle between $\mathbf{n}$ and $\mathbf{a}$ is the complementary angle to ψ we have:

$$\cos\psi = |\mathbf{n} \times \mathbf{a}| \qquad \sin\psi = |\langle\mathbf{n}, \mathbf{a}\rangle|. \tag{23}$$

Thus from Eqn. 22 one obtains:

$$d(\mathbf{s}, \mathbf{p}) = |(\mathbf{p} - \mathbf{c}) \times \mathbf{a}| \, |\mathbf{n} \times \mathbf{a}| - |\langle\mathbf{p} - \mathbf{c}, \mathbf{a}\rangle\langle\mathbf{n}, \mathbf{a}\rangle|$$
$$= |\mathbf{n} \times \mathbf{a}|\sqrt{|\mathbf{p} - \mathbf{c}|^2 - \langle\mathbf{p} - \mathbf{c}, \mathbf{a}\rangle^2} - |\langle\mathbf{n}, \mathbf{a}\rangle\langle\mathbf{p} - \mathbf{c}, \mathbf{a}\rangle|. \tag{24}$$

Again this function is of the form given in Eqn. 5, and using Approximation 6 gives

$$\tilde{d}(\mathbf{s}, \mathbf{p}) = \frac{|\mathbf{p} - \mathbf{c}|^2 \cos^2\psi - \langle\mathbf{p} - \mathbf{c}, \mathbf{a}\rangle^2}{2\langle\mathbf{p} - \mathbf{c}, \mathbf{a}\rangle\sin\psi} = \frac{|\mathbf{p} - \mathbf{c}|^2 |\mathbf{n} \times \mathbf{a}|^2 - \langle\mathbf{p} - \mathbf{c}, \mathbf{a}\rangle^2}{2\langle\mathbf{p} - \mathbf{c}, \mathbf{a}\rangle\langle\mathbf{n}, \mathbf{a}\rangle}. \tag{25}$$

We now express the position of the apex $\mathbf{c}$ in terms of the normal vector $\mathbf{n}(\varphi, \vartheta)$, the distance ϱ, the curvature k and the axis of the cone $\mathbf{a}(\sigma, \tau)$:

$$\mathbf{c} = (\varrho + \frac{1}{k})\mathbf{n} + \gamma\mathbf{a}.$$

Now $\langle\mathbf{c}, \mathbf{n}\rangle = \varrho$, so $\gamma = -1/(k\langle\mathbf{n}, \mathbf{a}\rangle)$, and thus

$$\mathbf{c} = (\varrho + \frac{1}{k})\mathbf{n} - \frac{\mathbf{a}}{k\langle\mathbf{n}, \mathbf{a}\rangle}. \tag{26}$$

Substituting this into Eqn. 25 one obtains (again $\widehat{\mathbf{p}} = \mathbf{p} - \varrho\mathbf{n}$)

$$\tilde{d} = \frac{|\mathbf{n} \times \mathbf{a}|^2 \left(|\widehat{\mathbf{p}} - \mathbf{n}/k|^2 - \langle\widehat{\mathbf{p}} - \mathbf{n}/k, \mathbf{a}\rangle^2\right) - \left(\langle\widehat{\mathbf{p}} - \mathbf{n}/k, \mathbf{a}\rangle\langle\mathbf{n}, \mathbf{a}\rangle + 1/k\right)^2}{2\left(\langle\widehat{\mathbf{p}} - \mathbf{n}/k, \mathbf{a}\rangle\langle\mathbf{n}, \mathbf{a}\rangle + 1/k\right)},$$

Using Pythagoras' theorem it is easy to see that the coefficient of $1/k^2$ in the numerator is zero. Multiplying both the numerator and the denominator by k we arrive at

$$\tilde{d}(\mathbf{s}, \mathbf{p}) = \frac{\frac{k}{2}(|\mathbf{n} \times \mathbf{a}|^2|\widehat{\mathbf{p}}|^2 - \langle \widehat{\mathbf{p}}, \mathbf{a}\rangle^2) - \langle \widehat{\mathbf{p}}, \mathbf{n}\rangle|\mathbf{n} \times \mathbf{a}|^2}{k\langle \widehat{\mathbf{p}}, \mathbf{a}\rangle\langle \mathbf{n}, \mathbf{a}\rangle + |\mathbf{n} \times \mathbf{a}|^2}. \tag{27}$$

5.4 Torus Fitting

Our approach for tori is again similar. A torus can be parameterized through seven unconstrained parameters. A torus can be obtained as a surface swept by a circular disc rotated around an axis in the plane of the circle. We call the radius of the disc the 'minor radius' and the distance of the centre of the disc from the axis 'major radius' of the torus. Tori whose major radius is *smaller* then the minor one can also be considered. In this case the resulting surface is self-intersecting, and it is necessary to distinguish the different parts in the following. The smaller arcs sweep a 'lemon-torus' (*i.e.* the inner part of the torus surface), while the larger arcs sweep an 'apple-torus' (*i.e.* the outer part of the torus surface); we will also refer to a non-self-intersecting torus as 'apple-shaped'. In special cases the torus may degenerate into a sphere, as the major radius vanishes, or or into a cone, as the minor radius tends to infinity. Our equations appropriately reduce to those for sphere or cone fitting. (If the major radius tends to infinity the torus becomes a cylinder. This case will be singular, but mathematically will be close to the cylinder fit.) The parameterization used for the torus is the following. As before, the point on the torus where a line through the surface normal passes through the origin is $\varrho\mathbf{n}$, where $|\mathbf{n}| = 1$. The principal curvature of the torus corresponding to the minor radius at the point $\varrho\mathbf{n}$ is k (*i.e.* the radius of the disk is $1/k$). The other principal curvature is s, and the corresponding centre of curvature lies on the axis of the torus. Let the unit direction vector of the torus axis be $\mathbf{a}$. (See Fig. 5.) We parameterize $\mathbf{n}$ by φ and ϑ as in Eqn. 14 and the unit vector $\mathbf{a}$ as in Eqn. 21:

$$\mathbf{a} = (\cos \sigma \sin \tau, \sin \sigma \sin \tau, \cos \tau).$$

The unconstrained parameters $(\varrho, \varphi, \vartheta, k, s, \sigma, \tau)$ entirely characterise the torus surface.

We may now state (the proof may be found in [16]) that a non-linear distance function for tori which is faithful up to the first derivative is

$$\tilde{d}(\mathbf{s}, \mathbf{p}) = \tilde{d}_0(\varrho, \varphi, \vartheta, k, \mathbf{p}) - \delta_\epsilon(\varrho, \varphi, \vartheta, k, s, \sigma, \tau, \mathbf{p}) \tag{28}$$

where $\tilde{d}_0$ is the approximate distance function for the sphere given in Eqn. 11:

$$\tilde{d}_0 = \frac{k}{2}\left(|\mathbf{p}|^2 - 2\varrho\langle \mathbf{p}, \mathbf{n}\rangle + \varrho^2\right) + \varrho - \langle \mathbf{p}, \mathbf{n}\rangle = \frac{k}{2}|\widehat{\mathbf{p}}|^2 - \langle \widehat{\mathbf{p}}, \mathbf{n}\rangle,$$

while

$$\delta_\epsilon = (\frac{k}{s} - 1)\left[\epsilon \cdot \text{sign}(\frac{k^2}{s} - k)|(\widehat{\mathbf{p}} - \mathbf{n}/s) \times \mathbf{a}||\mathbf{n} \times \mathbf{a}| + \langle(\widehat{\mathbf{p}} - \mathbf{n}/s) \times \mathbf{a}, \mathbf{n} \times \mathbf{a}\rangle,\right] \tag{29}$$

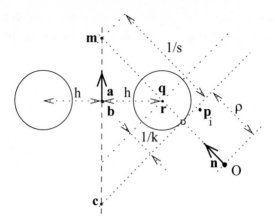

Fig. 5. Parameterization of the torus

where $\epsilon = +1$ for an apple torus surface and $\epsilon = -1$ for a lemon torus surface.

This function behaves well in limiting situations. If $k = s$ then from Eqn. 29 we simply get the distance expression for a sphere given in Eqn. 13. If $k \to 0$ and s is bounded from below then either for $\epsilon = -1$ or for $\epsilon = +1$ we get the distance expression for a cone given in Eqn. 24. If $s \to 0$ then Eqn. 28 degenerates to the distance function of a cylinder given in Eqn. 18 with axis direction $\mathbf{n} \times \mathbf{a}$. (See [16].)

6   Initial Estimates

To find the solution of any of the above nonlinear least-squares problems, an iterative technique is used; in practice we use the Levenberg-Marquardt method (see [6]). Any such algorithm requires some good initial estimate of the solution which is then refined. Here we give one method of finding such initial estimates.

The first step of this process is to find an estimate of the rotational axis (except for sphere fitting). A method is given to do this in [16] which is based only on estimates of the surface normal vector. It computes the axis from a number of four-tuples of normals. An alternative approach which finds the best (least-squares) rotational axis has recently been suggested by Pottmann [17].

We then pick a surface point at which we have a normal vector estimate and locate the origin at this point, which we call the 'base point'. Thus we have an estimate for $\mathbf{n}$ and hence φ, ϑ; the initial estimate for ϱ is 0. (Note that the solution surface need not pass through the base point, since ϱ can change.)

For sphere fitting, these values alone are sufficient, and an estimate for k can now be found by solving a linear least-squares problem as mentioned earlier.

For cylinder fitting, we adjust the normal to be perpendicular to the axis. We then compute α as the angle between $\mathbf{a}$ and $\mathbf{n}^\vartheta$ and compute the distance of the base point from the axis, which is $1/k$ signed with the direction of $\mathbf{n}$.

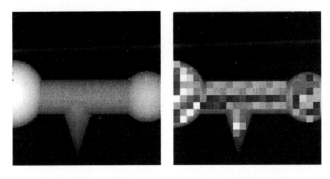

Fig. 6. Simulated part depth-map; seed placement

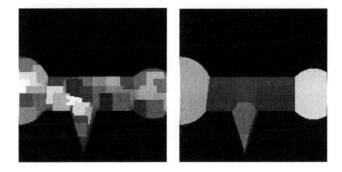

Fig. 7. Simulated part intermediate grown regions; final segmentation

In the case of cone fitting, after estimating the rotational axis **a** we compute the distance of the base point from the axis *along* the estimated normal line in order to obtain $1/k$.

In the torus case, for better conditioning one has to pick a base point at which the normal subtends as large an angle as possible with the estimated axis. We get $1/s$ as the distance along the normal between the base point and the estimated axis. For simplicity, we can put $k = 0$ (*i.e.* start from a cone) and try fitting both $\epsilon = +1$ (apple-torus) and $\epsilon = -1$ (lemon-torus). More robustly, one can opt to estimate principal curvatures of the surface at the base point. As s is one of the principal curvatures we can compute the other, k, even if we only estimate the Gaussian curvature. We can then determine ϵ by noting on which sheet of the torus the base point lies. Thus $\epsilon = +1$ if $|k| > |s|$ or $ks < 0$ and $\epsilon = -1$ otherwise (the decision should be clear provided we have chosen a well placed base point as described above). We assume here that the point set being fitted does not contain points belonging to both the apple and lemon sheets of the same torus simultaneously. This is very unlikely to happen in practice, but if it is considered to be a possibility, before fitting we should separate the points into two sets, one for each sheet, using curvature estimates and the given criterion.

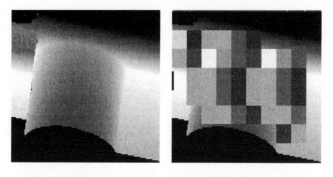

Fig. 8. Heriot-Watt part depth-map; seed placement

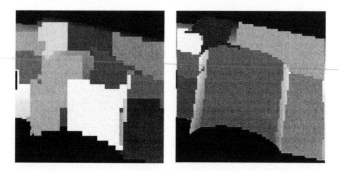

Fig. 9. Heriot-Watt part intermediate grown regions; final segmentation

7 Results and Conclusion

The fitting routines described in this paper have been tested using the segmentation approach outlined earlier. In the case of simulated 3D point data, which was accurate to five significant digits, in all cases the models recovered fitted the data to an accuracy of at least four significant digits, and segmentations consistent with the underlying geometric primitives were obtained. An example of the final segmentation obtained for the peg composed of a cylinder and sphere shown in Fig. 1 is given in Fig. 2. A further example containing a cone, a cylinder and two spheres is shown in Figs. 6 and 7.

Our fitting methods also work well in practice with real scanner data, which is somewhat less accurate than the simulated data. The segmentation process for a depth-map of the well-known 'Heriot-Watt' test part captured using a 3D Scanners *Replica* device is illustrated in Figs. 8 and 9. The segmentation results here are not as clean as for the simulated parts, but are adequate for input to the further model building processes of our reverse engineering system.

Whilst our motivation is the reverse engineering of boundary representation solid models from three-dimensional depth-maps of scanned objects, we believe that the fitting methods described in this paper are of interest to the computer vision and CAD communities in general.

In summary, we have described novel methods for the least-squares fitting of spheres, cylinders, cones and tori to point data. We have outlined how they can be used in a segmentation strategy that is capable of extracting these surfaces from three-dimensional data. Initial results show that the accuracy achieved by these methods is good, although space limitations preclude a full presentation here. Our fitting methods have the major advantage of being robust in the sense that as the principal curvatures of the surfaces being fitted decrease (or as they become more equal), the results which are returned naturally become closer and closer to surfaces of 'simpler type', *i.e.* planes, cylinders, or cones (or spheres, in the case of equal curvatures) which best describe the data. Furthermore, our methods inherently avoid all singularities (except in the case of the torus, for which the problem can readily be overcome by choosing the origin appropriately).

References

1. R. Bajcsy, F. Solina, and A. Gupta, *Segmentation versus object representation— are they separable?*, In Analysis and Interpretation of Range Images, Eds. R. Jain and A. K. Jain, Springer-Verlag, New York, 1990.

2. P. J. Besl, *Surfaces in Range Image Understanding*, Springer-Verlag, New York, USA, 1988.

3. P. J. Besl and R. K. Jain, *Segmentation Through Variable-Order Surface Fitting*, IEEE Transactions on Pattern Analysis and Machine Intelligence, **10** (2), 167–192, 1988.

4. R. M. Bolle and D. B. Cooper, *On optimally combining pieces of information, with application to estimating 3-D complex-object position from range data*, IEEE Transactions on Pattern Analysis and Machine Intelligence **8**, 5, 619–638, 1986.

5. R. M. Bolle and B. C. Vemuri, *On Three-Dimensional Surface Reconstruction Methods*, IEEE Transactions on Pattern Analysis and Machine Intelligence, **13** (1), 1–13, 1991.

6. Å. Björk, *Numerical methods for least squares problems*, SIAM. Society for Industrial and Applied Mathematics, Philadelphia, 1996.

7. O. D. Faugeras, M. Hebert, and E. Pauchon, *Segmentation of Range Data into Planar and Quadric Patches*, Proceedings of Third Computer Vision and Pattern Recognition Conference, Arlington, VA, 8–13, 1983.

8. A.W. Fitzgibbon, M. Pilu, and R.B. Fisher, *Direct least-square fitting of ellipses*, 13th International Conference on Pattern Recognition (Washington, Brussels, Tokyo), IAPR, IEEE Computer Society Press, June 1996, Proceedings of the 13th ICPR Conference, Vienna Austria, August 1996.

9. W. Gander, G.H. Golub, and R. Strebel, *Least-squares fitting of circles and ellipses*, BIT **34**, 558–578, 1994.

10. M. Hebert and J. Ponce, *A new method for segmenting 3-D scenes into primitives*, 6th International Conference on Pattern Recognition (Munich), 836–838, IAPR DAGM, IEEE Computer Society Press, October 1982, Proceedings of the 6th ICPR Conference, Munich Germany, Oct. 19–22, 1982.

11. A. Jaklic, A. Leonardis, and F. Solina. *Segmentor: An object-oriented framework for image segmentation.* Technical Report LRV-96-2, Computer Vision Laboratory, University of Ljubljana, Faculty of Computer and Information Science, 1996.

12. A. Leonardis. *Image analysis using parametric models: model-recovery and model-selection paradigm*, PhD dissertation,University of Ljubljana, Faculty of Electrical Engineering and Computer Science, May 1993.

13. A. Leonardis, A. Gupta, and R. Bajcsy. *Segmentation as the search for the best description of the image in terms of primitives.* Proceedings of the Third International Conference of Computer Vision, Osaka, Japan, 1990.

14. A. Leonardis, A. Gupta, and R. Bajcsy. *Segmentation of range images as the search for geometric parametric models.* International Journal of Computer Vision, **14**, 253–277, 1995.

15. P. Liong, and J. S. Todhunter, *Representation and recognition of surface shapes in range images: a differential geometry approach,* Computer Vision, Graphics and Image Processing, **52**, 1, 78–109, 1990.

16. G. Lukács, A. D. Marshall, and R. R. Martin, *Geometric least-squares fitting of spheres, cylinders, cones and tori,* RECCAD, Deliverable Document 2 and 3, COPERNICUS project, No 1068 (Budapest) (R. R. Martin and T. Várady, eds.), Geometric Modelling Laboratory Studies/1997/5, Computer and Automation Research Institute, Budapest, July 1997.

17. H. Pottmann and T. Randrup, *Rotational and helical surface approximation for reverse engineering,* Tech. Report 43, Institut für Geometrie, Technische Universität Wien, A-1040 Wien, Wiedner Hauptstraße 8–10, Austria, June 1997, Submitted to Computing.

18. V. Pratt, *Direct least-squares fitting of algebraic surfaces,* COMPUTER GRAPHICS Proceedings, vol. 21, Annual Conference Series, no. 4, ACM, Addison Wesley, July 1987, Proceedings of the SIGGRAPH 87 Conference, 145–152, Anaheim, California, 27-31 July 1987.

19. P. L. Rosin, *A note on the least squares fitting of ellipses,* Pattern Recognition Letters **14**, 799–808, 1993.

20. P. L. Rosin, *Analysing error of fit functions for ellipses,* Pattern Recognition Letters **17**, 1461–1470, 1996.

21. G. Taubin, *Estimation of planar curves, surfaces, and nonplanar space curves defined by implicit equations with applications to edge and range image segmentation,* IEEE Transactions on Pattern Analysis and Machine Intelligence **13** (11), 1115–1138, 1991.

Multi-step Procedures for the Localization of 2D and 3D Point Landmarks and Automatic ROI Size Selection

Sönke Frantz, Karl Rohr, and H. Siegfried Stiehl

Universität Hamburg, Fachbereich Informatik
Arbeitsbereich Kognitive Systeme, D-22527 Hamburg, Germany
frantz@informatik.uni-hamburg.de

Abstract. In this contribution, we are concerned with the detection and refined localization of 3D point landmarks. We propose multi-step differential procedures for subvoxel localization of 3D point landmarks. Moreover, we address the problem of choosing an optimal size for a region-of-interest (ROI) around point landmarks. That is, to reliably localize the landmark position, on the one hand, as much as possible image information about the landmark should be incorporated. On the other hand, the ROI should be restricted such that other structures do not interfere. The multi-step procedures are generalizations of an existing two-step procedure for subpixel localization of 2D point landmarks. This two-step procedure combines landmark detection by applying a differential operator with refined localization through a differential edge intersection approach. In this paper, we investigate the localization performance of this two-step procedure for an analytical model of a Gaussian blurred L-corner. The results motivate the use of an analogous procedure for 3D point landmark localization. We generalize the edge intersection approach to 3D and combine it with 3D detection operators to obtain multi-step procedures for subvoxel localization of 3D point landmarks. The multi-step procedures are experimentally tested for 3D synthetic images and 3D MR images of the human head. We also propose an approach to automatically select an optimal ROI size. This approach exploits the uncertainty of the position estimate resulting from the edge intersection approach. We present first promising results for a real 2D image with different types of corners as well as for anatomical brain landmarks in 2D slices of a 3D MR image.

1 Introduction

The registration of medical images of the human head such as MR (Magnetic Resonance) and CT (X-Ray Computed Tomography) images is important, e.g., for the planning of neurosurgical interventions, radiotherapy, and therapy evaluation. One possibility to register two images is a point-based approach. In this case, prominent points, denoted also as point landmarks, have to be extracted from images. In general, the registration result heavily depends on the accurate localization of suitable point landmarks. Potential point landmarks of the human head are salient tips, which can be found, for instance, on the ventricular system, the skull base, as well as on other anatomical structures. Usually, such 3D point landmarks are manually selected—a task which is difficult, time-consuming, and which often lacks accuracy. An alternative to manual selection is a semi-automatic approach to landmark localization. The advantage of such an approach is that the user has the possibility to interactively control the results, which is important in clinical applications. For example, first, an approximate position of a specific landmark is manually determined. Second, to extract potential landmark candidates, a computational approach is applied within a region-of-interest (ROI) around the approximate position. Third, the user selects the most promising candidate. The computational approach has to reliably and robustly detect as well as to accurately localize prominent points. Recently, 3D differential operators have been introduced [15, 14, 2] which are, however, only designed for the detection of 3D point landmarks. Since reliable and robust landmark detection generally requires operators with large size, the accuracy of the detected points often is not satisfactory and additional steps are necessary to obtain better position estimates.

In the first part of this paper, we propose differential-based multi-step procedures for refined localization of 3D point landmarks. Our multi-step procedures are based on a two-step procedure for localizing point landmarks in 2D images [5]. This two-step procedure combines landmark detection by applying a 2D differential operator with refined localization through a 2D differential edge intersection approach. This two-step procedure only employs first-order partial derivatives of the image function and therefore does not suffer from potential instabilities of computing high-order partial derivatives. In this contribution, first, we investigate the localization performance of the two-step procedure for a 2D analytical model of a Gaussian blurred L-corner. We then generalize the 2D edge intersection approach to 3D. By combining the 3D edge intersection approach with 3D differential operators for landmark detection we propose multi-step procedures for refined localization of 3D point landmarks. We present experimental results for 3D synthetic images as well as 3D MR images of the human head.

In the second part of the paper, we address the problem of choosing an optimal size of the ROI. Obviously, the chosen ROI should be adapted to the scale of a landmark. On the one hand, it is reasonable to use as much as possible information about the structure containing the landmark to reliably localize the position of the landmark. On the other hand, it is clear that the ROI should not include other structures. In this paper, we introduce a new approach to automatically select the optimal size of a ROI. Our approach is based on the uncertainty of the position estimate resulting from the edge intersection approach. A comparable approach has been proposed in [7]. However, there a different detection operator has been used and also the criterion for ROI size selection is different. We show for a real 2D image that our approach allows the extraction of ROIs with optimal size for various image structures such as L-, Y-, and Arrow-corners. Results for a number of anatomical landmarks in 2D slices of a 3D MR image also demonstrate the suitability of our approach for medical images.

2 Multi-Step Procedures for Point Landmark Localization Using an Edge Intersection Approach

2.1 Two-step procedure for localizing 2D point landmarks

Förstner and Gülch [5] proposed a two-step procedure for localizing 2D point landmarks (corners) which combines landmark detection by applying a 2D differential operator with refined localization through a differential edge intersection approach.

Landmark detection The used differential operator [4, 8] exploits the matrix

$$\mathbf{N} = \begin{pmatrix} \sum_i g_{x_i}^2 & \sum_i g_{x_i} g_{y_i} \\ \sum_i g_{x_i} g_{y_i} & \sum_i g_{y_i}^2 \end{pmatrix}.$$

This matrix represents (up to a factor) the averaged dyadic product of the intensity gradient. The subscripts x and y of the intensity function $g(x, y)$ stand for the partial derivatives in the respective spatial direction and the sum index i denotes the spatial location. The detection operator reads

$$F(\mathbf{x}) = \frac{det(\mathbf{N})}{tr(\mathbf{N})}, \qquad (1)$$

where $det(\cdot)$ denotes the determinant and $tr(\cdot)$ the trace of a matrix. Each point $\mathbf{x} = (x, y)$ in the image is being assigned the measure in (1), where $\mathbf{N}$ is usually computed in a symmetric and quadratic window of certain size around that point. Point landmarks are detected by searching for local maxima of $F(\mathbf{x})$.

Refined localization We consider the neighborhood around a detected point. Suppose an L-corner has been detected and the observation window captures sufficient edge information of the structure. For simplicity, a local coordinate system with the detected point as origin is chosen. For each edge point in the observation window we define a tangent locally approximating the edge direction. For this, the intensity gradients are taken as normals to the tangents. The tangents are represented in the Hessian normal form, that is, for a point $\mathbf{x}_i$ with intensity gradient ∇g_i we have $< \nabla g_i, \mathbf{x} > = < \nabla g_i, \mathbf{x}_i >$, where $< \cdot, \cdot >$ denotes the inner product. Rewriting this as $\varepsilon_i(\mathbf{x}) = < \nabla g_i, \mathbf{x} - \mathbf{x}_i >$ yields the perpendicular distance from $\mathbf{x}$ to the tangent at $\mathbf{x}_i$. Note that the distance is implicitly multiplied with the gradient magnitude since ∇g_i generally is not a unit vector. The position of the tip can be estimated through intersection of all tangents using the least-squares method, that is, through minimization of the residual error function

$$E(\mathbf{x}) = \sum_i \varepsilon_i(\mathbf{x})^2. \qquad (2)$$

So far, solely edge points have been considered. However, due to implicitly weighting the residual errors with the gradient magnitude, it is possible to give up this restriction and to include in the sum in (2) all points within the observation window. Points in rather homogeneous regions with low gradient magnitude should hardly contribute to the sum anyway. On the other hand, edge points with generally high gradient magnitude should actually force a small distance from the position estimate to their corresponding tangent. Finally, the condition $\nabla E(\mathbf{x}) = \mathbf{0}$ yields the system of normal equations

$$\mathbf{N}\mathbf{x}^* = \mathbf{y}, \tag{3}$$

where $\mathbf{x}^*$ denotes the position of the tip w.r.t. the local coordinate system, $\mathbf{N}$ is the matrix from above, and

$$\mathbf{y} = \begin{pmatrix} \sum_i g_{x_i}^2 x_i + \sum_i g_{x_i} g_{y_i} y_i \\ \sum_i g_{x_i} g_{y_i} x_i + \sum_i g_{y_i}^2 y_i. \end{pmatrix}.$$

2.2 Analytical study for an L-corner

It is known that for an L-corner the detection operator in (1) yields systematic localization errors w.r.t. the correct corner position. The error generally depends on the blur, the aperture angle of the structure, and the size of the operator (see [13] for an analytical study). Hence, in general, additional steps are necessary to improve the localization accuracy. In the following, we analyze the localization performance of the two-step procedure for an analytical model of a Gaussian blurred L-corner [11] and compare the achieved accuracy with that resulting from the detection operator alone.

In [13], the positions for the detection operator alone have been determined. We have centered the observation window for the edge intersection approach at the position determined with the detection operator. Then, we have computed the matrix $\mathbf{N}$ and the vector $\mathbf{y}$ and have solved the system of normal equations in (3) to obtain the position estimate.

In Fig. 1a, the distances e from the localized positions to the correct corner position are depicted in dependence on the aperture angle β. The standard deviation of the Gaussian blur function has been set to $\sigma = 1$. The solid line results from the detection operator alone and the dashed line results from the two-step procedure using the edge intersection approach. The size of the observation window for the edge intersection approach has been the same as that for the detection operator, that is, 3×3 pixels. It can be seen that the edge intersection approach yields an improvement of about $1 pix$ (pix denotes spatial unity) for a large range of aperture angles. Moreover, we can obtain even better position estimates if we further enlarge the observation window for the edge intersection approach. The result for a window size of 15×15 pixels is shown in Fig. 1b. The localization error is thus reduced to nearly zero. We conclude that a reasonable strategy for improving the localization accuracy is to capture with the observation window as much as possible information of the intensity structure. On the other hand, it should be guaranteed that no other structures interfere. As a second main topic of this paper, we will report on optimal size selection for a region-of-interest (ROI) around point landmarks in Section 3.

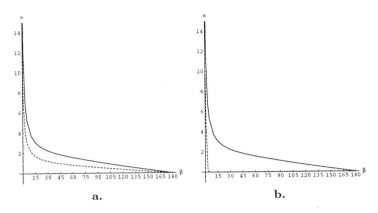

Fig. 1a and b. Localization accuracy for a Gaussian blurred L-corner with $\sigma = 1$. The distances e from the localized positions to the correct corner position are depicted in dependence on the aperture angle β. The solid lines result from the detection operator alone and the dashed lines result from the two-step procedure. Observation windows of sizes 3×3 pixels (a) and 15×15 pixels (b) have been used.

2.3 Extension of the edge intersection approach to 3D

In the 2D case, we have dealt with an L-corner to motivate the edge intersection approach. A 3D generalization of an L-corner is a tetrahedron. Suppose we have obtained an approximate position of the tip, for instance, by applying a 3D detection operator, and have placed there an observation window capturing sufficient image information. The position of the tip of the tetrahedron is the intersection point of three plane surfaces which correspond to 3D edges. Analogously to the 2D case, we locally approximate the surfaces of a landmark through tangent planes. The intensity gradients are taken as normals to the tangent planes. The Hessian normal form of the tangent plane at a point $\mathbf{x}_i$ reads $< \nabla g_i, \mathbf{x} >=< \nabla g_i, \mathbf{x}_i >$. The position of the tip can be estimated through intersection of all tangent planes using the least-squares method, that is, through minimization of a residual error function which formally agrees with that in (2) of the 2D edge intersection approach. Note that also here the gradient magnitudes implicitly weight the residual error function. We thus obtain a system of normal equations

$$\mathbf{N}\mathbf{x}^* = \mathbf{y}, \tag{4}$$

where $\mathbf{x}^*$ denotes the estimated subvoxel position of the tip and

$$\mathbf{N} = \begin{pmatrix} \sum_i g_{x_i}^2 & \sum_i g_{x_i} g_{y_i} & \sum_i g_{x_i} g_{z_i} \\ \sum_i g_{x_i} g_{y_i} & \sum_i g_{y_i}^2 & \sum_i g_{y_i} g_{z_i} \\ \sum_i g_{x_i} g_{z_i} & \sum_i g_{y_i} g_{z_i} & \sum_i g_{z_i}^2 \end{pmatrix}$$

and

$$\mathbf{y} = \begin{pmatrix} \sum_i g_{x_i}^2 x_i + \sum_i g_{x_i} g_{y_i} y_i + \sum_i g_{x_i} g_{z_i} z_i \\ \sum_i g_{x_i} g_{y_i} x_i + \sum_i g_{y_i}^2 y_i + \sum_i g_{y_i} g_{z_i} z_i \\ \sum_i g_{x_i} g_{z_i} x_i + \sum_i g_{y_i} g_{z_i} y_i + \sum_i g_{z_i}^2 z_i \end{pmatrix}.$$

2.4 Multi-step procedures for localizing 3D point landmarks using the 3D edge intersection approach

In [14], 3D differential operators for detecting point landmarks have been proposed. The operators exploit the matrix $\mathbf{N}$ in (4) (up to a factor) and read $Op3(\mathbf{x}) = det(\mathbf{N})/tr(\mathbf{N})$, $Op3'(\mathbf{x}) = 1/tr(\mathbf{N}^{-1})$, and $Op4(\mathbf{x}) = det(\mathbf{N})$. The operators are 3D extensions of existing 2D corner detectors in [4, 8, 10, 11]. In this contribution, we propose three multi-step procedures for refined point landmark localization in 3D images, combining the 3D detection operators with the 3D edge intersection approach.

i) **Two-step procedure**

First, points are detected with either $Op3$, $Op3'$, or $Op4$, where a large operator size is chosen for reasons of robustness w.r.t. noise in images. Second, to refine the positions, a small operator size is chosen and the respective differential operator is applied within a small neighborhood around the detected points. A similar procedure for 2D point landmark localization was proposed earlier [3, 10].

ii) **Two-step procedure with subvoxel localization**

First, points are detected with either $Op3$, $Op3'$, or $Op4$. Second, the positions are refined through the 3D edge intersection approach. This scheme essentially is the 3D extension of the two-step procedure of Förstner and Gülch [5].

iii) **Three-step procedure with subvoxel localization**

This procedure is a combination of the procedures i) and ii) and is therefore a three-step procedure. The first two steps correspond to the two-step procedure i). In the third step, the position estimates resulting from i) are further refined through the 3D edge intersection approach.

2.5 Experimental results

We report on experiments for 3D synthetic images as well as 3D MR images of the human head. The partial derivatives have been estimated with 3D extensions of the 2D filters of Beaudet [1]. For the detection step we have used a filter size of $5 \times 5 \times 5$ voxels. For the refinement steps of the procedures i) and iii) filters of size $3 \times 3 \times 3$ voxels have been used. The components of the matrix $\mathbf{N}$ and the vector $\mathbf{y}$ in (4) are the averaged values of products of the partial derivatives within an observation window. To study the localization accuracy of the different procedures in dependence on the width w of the observation window, we have investigated various window widths, starting with $w = 3$ voxels. The size of the observation window for the 3D edge intersection approach has been the same as that for the detection operator. Maxima of the detection operator responses have been determined by local maximum search in neighborhoods of $3 \times 3 \times 3$ voxels. In the case of several maxima within the chosen ROI of the image, we have selected the candidate with the largest operator response. To alleviate subjectivity in our experiments we have not used any thresholds on the operator responses. However, a few cases in the experiments on medical images have required special attention.

3D synthetic images We have investigated the localization accuracy of the procedures i), ii), and iii) for the tip of a 3D tetrahedron. This structure is a 3D generalization of an L-corner with aperture angle β. For the construction of the
3D object in Fig. 2a, where the tip is marked through a black dot, the symmetric axis of the L-corner has been spread into the direction of the z-axis such
that it also encloses the angle β with the x-axis. The shape of the so constructed
tetrahedron is determined by the aperture angle β.

In Fig. 2b, for a tetrahedron with $\beta = 90°$ the Euclidean distances e from the
localized positions to the position of the tip are depicted in dependence on the
width w (in voxels) of the observation window. DET denotes the detection operator $Op3'$. We see that applying the detection operator alone yields the worst
results. Procedure i) is only for $w = 5$ better than DET. The position estimates
resulting from the procedures ii) and iii) are significantly more accurate than
those resulting from DET and procedure i). The accuracy gets worse for DET
and procedure i) if w increases. By contrast, the accuracy for the procedures
ii) and iii) gets better if w increases. In Fig. 2c, the results for a much more
tapered tetrahedron with $\beta = 45°$ are shown. The results are comparable with
those for the tetrahdron with $\beta = 90°$. However, for the procedures ii) and iii)
the localization error slightly increases for $w \geq 11$ and $w \geq 7$, resp. We suspect
that discretization errors give rise to this effect.

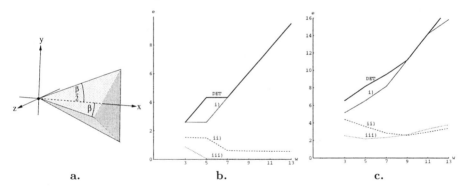

a.　　　　　　　b.　　　　　　　c.

Fig. 2a. Tetrahedron with aperture angle β. **b and c.** Localization accuracy for tetra-
hedrons with $\beta = 90°$ and $\beta = 45°$, resp. The Euclidean distances e from the localized
positions to the position of the tip are depicted in dependence on the width w of the
observation window.

3D MR images Here, we present results for three 3D MR images of the human
head. We consider as anatomical landmarks the tips of the frontal, occipital, and
temporal horns of the ventricular system, abbreviated by MC6, MC7, and MC13,
resp. The tips are indicated in Fig. 3a through black dots within dashed circles.
The letters 'l' and 'r' denote the respective hemispheric part. We have manually
specified the positions of these landmarks in the investigated data sets and have
taken them as 'ground truth' positions, although we know that manual localization of 3D landmarks generally is difficult and may be prone to error. Note

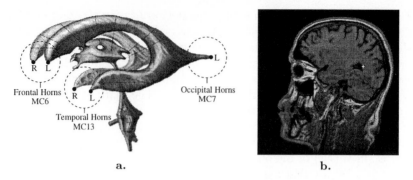

a.   b.

Fig. 3a. Anatomical preparate of the ventricular system of the human head (adapted from Sobotta, 1988) **b.** Off-sagittal slice of MR image 1. The manually specified position of the tip of the left occipital horn is marked through a white cross.

also that manually we have only determined voxel positions, while the multi-step procedures ii) and iii) use the 3D edge intersection approach and hence yield subvoxel positions. We have respectively chosen a region-of-interest (ROI) around the 'ground truth' positions and then have applied the computational approaches described above. For landmark detection and the refinement steps of the procedures i) and iii) we here have used the operator $Op3$. We have used the same filter widths to estimate the partial derivatives as in the experiments for the 3D synthetic images. The size of the observation window for the 3D edge intersection approach has been the same as that for the detection operator. To alleviate subjectivity, we have not used any thresholds on the detection operator responses. In the case of several detected points within the ROI, we have selected that point with the largest operator response. The thus selected candidates have been visually inspected for validity, according to the semi-automatic approach described in Section 1.

In Figs. 4a and b, the mean values $\bar{e}$ for both $w = 3$ and $w = 5$ of the Euclidean distances from the localized positions to the manually specified positions are depicted according to each landmark and according to each MR image, resp. In general, the procedures ii) and iii) yield the most accurate positions. Also procedure i) generally yields better positions than the detection operator alone, although not as good as ii) and iii)). Basically, we have selected the candidates with the largest operator responses. The visual inspection of the detected candidates for the left and right temporal horns MC13l,r in MR image 2 and the left temporal horn in MR image 3 has been very difficult since in these images the temporal horns are extremely poorly pronounced. Also, the positions of these landmarks resulting from manual localization are rather uncertain. Therefore, for these images the respective landmarks have not been considered. For the right temporal horn MC13r in MR image 3 two points with extremely high operator responses have been detected. Visual inspection has revealed that the respective candidates with the highest operator responses are false detections and has caused us instead to select the candidates with the second-highest operator responses.

All in all, for the detection operator alone the mean of the Euclidean dis-

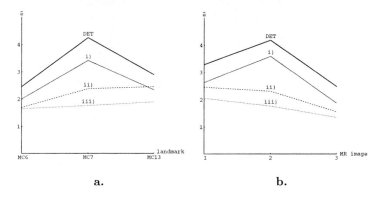

Fig. 4a and b. Localization accuracy of the detection operator alone (DET) and the multi-step procedures i), ii), and iii) for the ventricle landmarks in the investigated three MR images. The mean values $\bar{e}$ for both $w = 3$ and $w = 5$ of the Euclidean distances from the localized positions to the manually specified positions are depicted according to each landmark (a) and according to each MR image (b).

tances from the localized positions to the manually specified positions amounts to $3.27vox$ (vox denotes spatial unity). The two-step procedure i) improves the accuracy w.r.t. DET by $0.59vox$. Additionally using the 3D edge intersection approach further improves the accuracy w.r.t. i) by $0.93vox$. Thus, the three-step procedure iii) improves the accuracy w.r.t. DET by $1.52vox$. The two-step procedure ii) improves the accuracy w.r.t. DET by $1.14vox$.

To give a visual impression of the localization capabilities of the different procedures, we also show in Fig. 5 orthogonal image cuts at the respectively localized positions for the tip of the left occipital horn in MR image 1 ($w = 5$). The location of the landmark within the human head is marked through a white cross in a sagittal view in Fig. 3b. Note that, due to technical reasons, the subvoxel coordinates resulting from the multi-step procedures ii) and iii) have been rounded to voxel coordinates. Nevertheless, it can be seen that the multi-step procedures ii) and iii) yield the best results.

3   Automatic ROI Size Selection for Point Landmarks

The performance of the semi-automatic approach for landmark localization described in Section 1 substantially depends on the size of the region-of-interest which generally should be adapted to the scale of a specific landmark. On the one hand, the ROI should capture as much as possible information about the landmark. On the other hand, the ROI should not include neighboring structures. In the following, we introduce a novel approach for automatically determining an optimal size for the ROI. The approach is based on the uncertainty of the position estimate resulting from the edge intersection approach.

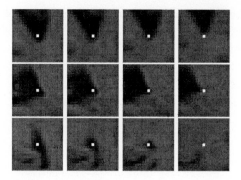

Fig. 5. Localized positions at the tip of the left occipital horn in MR image 1 ($w = 5$) for the detection operator alone and the multi-step procedures i), ii), and iii) (from left to right) in axial, sagittal, and coronal views (from top to bottom).

3.1 Localization uncertainty of the edge intersection position estimate

The covariance matrix of the position estimate $\mathbf{x}^*$ in (3) (resp. (4) in the 3D case) is given by

$$\boldsymbol{\Sigma} = \sigma_\varepsilon^2 \mathbf{N}^{-1}, \tag{5}$$

under the assumption that the residuals ε_i are independently and normally distributed random errors with zero mean and variance σ_ε^2. We estimate the variance through $\sigma_\varepsilon^2 = \mathrm{E}(\mathbf{x}^*)/(n-2)$ (2D) and $\sigma_\varepsilon^2 = \mathrm{E}(\mathbf{x}^*)/(n-3)$ (3D), where $\mathrm{E}(\cdot)$ is the respective residual error function and n stands for the number of points in the chosen observation window (see also [5]). In the 2D case, the localization uncertainty of the position estimate is represented by the covariance ellipse (covariance ellipsoid in the 3D case). Evidently, the size of the covariance ellipse (ellipsoid) should be small, indicating low localization uncertainty of the position estimate. In the 2D case, the Eigenvalues of the covariance matrix, λ_1 and λ_2, are the squared lengths of the the semi-axes of the covariance ellipse. A scalar measure for the localization uncertainty of the position estimate is the product of the Eigenvalues $U = \lambda_1 \lambda_2$, which is actually the squared area of the covariance ellipse. Analogously, a scalar measure for the localization uncertainty in 3D is $U = \lambda_1 \lambda_2 \lambda_3$, where λ_i denote the Eigenvalues of the 3D covariance matrix and represent the squared lengths of the semi-axes of the ellipsoid. That is, in the 3D case, U is the squared volume of the covariance ellipsoid. Equivalently, when using the determinant of the covariance matrix, we can write in both cases

$$U = det(\sigma_\varepsilon^2 \mathbf{N}^{-1}). \tag{6}$$

3.2 Localization uncertainty in dependence on the ROI size

Suppose we have an initial position for a landmark around which we place a symmetric observation window. Let us define an uncertainty function $U(w)$ depending on the width w of the ROI. Then, for example, $U(5)$ gives the localization uncertainty of the position estimate for an observation window of size

5×5 pixels ($5 \times 5 \times 5$ voxels in the 3D case). Assume that further enlarging the observation window gives us more edge information about the landmark but other structures are still excluded. In this case, we do not expect a significant signal change in $U(w)$. On the other hand, additionally capturing other structures by the ROI gives rise to a more or less strong increase of $U(w)$ which tells us that further enlargement of the ROI is not useful. The respective value of w then gives us the width of a suitable ROI.

Let us now see how this works in practice for the 2D case. We consider an L- and a Y-corner in a real image containing a polyhedral object as shown in Fig. 6. In accordance to the semi-approach procedure for landmark localization, we have manually determined the corner positions. The manually selected corner positions are marked by a small square for the L-corner in Fig. 6a and the Y-corner in Fig. 6b. We have placed symmetric observation windows of width $w = 5$ pixels around that points. The widths of the windows have been successively enlarged by 2 pixels, that is, 1 pixel on each side. In Fig. 7a, for the L-corner the localization uncertainty in (6) in dependence on the width of the ROI is depicted. In Fig. 7b, for the Y-corner the uncertainty measure in dependence on the width of the ROI is depicted (please ignore for a moment the vertical lines which have been added to the graphs). We see that for the L-corner the uncertainty function

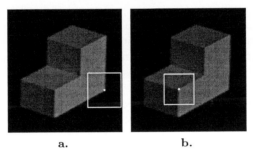

a.   b.

Fig. 6a and b. ROI size selection for two differently complex structures in a real image of a polyhedral object. The, based on the uncertainty measure U, manually selected optimal ROIs are drawn for an L-corner and a Y-corner, resp. The also manually specified corner positions (centers of the ROIs) are marked by small squares (see text).

continuously decreases with increasing width of the ROI which is what we expect. Other structures do not interfere. In such a case, it is reasonable to choose the ROI as large as possible. The width is only restricted due to the image size. The thus manually determined ROI ($w = 71$) is drawn in Fig. 6a. For the Y-corner we note interferences of other edges when the observation window exceeds a certain size. This is reflected through a strong increase of the uncertainty function, beginning at $w = 63$. Therefore, a maximal ROI with $w = 63$ seems suitable. An observation window of this size is drawn in Fig. 6b.

3.3 Determining ROIs with optimal size

According to the above discussion, there are two principal optimality criteria w.r.t. the size of the ROI. We speak of 'criterion A' if we mean optimality of the ROI w.r.t. minimal localization uncertainty. We refer with 'criterion B' to optimality w.r.t. maximal size of the ROI. Thus, depending on the need of the user, we suggest the following procedure to select a ROI with optimal size: First, determine a ROI with maximal size (criterion B). Then, if desired, reduce the ROI by selecting the corresponding width of the minimal value of $U(w)$ (criterion A).

We have to detect a strong increase of the uncertainty function (criterion B). Signal changes in $U(w)$ are generally accompanied by a variation of the position estimate resulting from the edge intersection approach. We have found that the variation of the position estimate is a strong criterion to decide whether other structures interfere due to enlargement of the observation window. In our case, we compute the distance between the position estimates $\mathbf{x}_w^*$ (for the observation window width w) and $\mathbf{x}_{w-2}^*$ (for the observation window width $w-2$) and define a function

$$D(w) = |\mathbf{x}_w^* - \mathbf{x}_{w-2}^*| \tag{7}$$

which is compared with a threshold t_D prescribing to what extent variations of the position estimate are allowed. Additionally, we use a second criterion which measures the increase of uncertainty. In our case, we simply compare successive values of $U(w)$ which has given good results. Alternative measures are the 'derivative' or the 'curvature' of $U(w)$. Altogether, we propose to abort ROI enlargement if a) $U(w+2) > U(w)$ (increase of uncertainty) and b) $D(w+2) \geq t_D$. If these conditions are both fulfilled, then the value of w gives us the optimal size of the ROI according to criterion B.

3.4 Resulting algorithm for automatic ROI size selection

To sum up, our algorithm for ROI size selection consists of the following four steps:

1. Determine an initial position for the searched landmark. Place a symmetric and quadratic observation window of width $w = w_{min}$ around that point, for example, $w_{min} = 5$ pixels. Note that w_{min} determines the minimal width of the ROI. Compute the uncertainty measure $U(w)$ in (6) for the position estimate.

2. If further enlargement of the observation window is not possible, for instance, due to user restriction or image size, then either stop (criterion B with optimal width $w_{opt} = w$) or go to step 4 (criterion A, then let $w_B = w$ denote the maximal width of the ROI). Otherwise enlarge the observation window: $w = w + 2$.

3. Compute $U(w)$ and the variation of the position estimate $D(w)$ in (7). If a) $U(w) > U(w-2)$ and b) $D(w) \geq t_D$, then either stop (criterion B,

$w_{opt} = w - 2$) or goto step 4 (criterion A, then let $w_B = w - 2$ denote the maximal width of the ROI). Otherwise continue with step 2.

4. Select the corresponding width ($w_{min} \leq w \leq w_B$) for which $U(w)$ attains its minimum, that is, minimal localization uncertainty for the position estimate resulting from the edge intersection approach. Set $w_{opt} = w$.

3.5 Experimental results

We present results for real 2D images. In our experiments, we have used Gaussian filters for derivative estimation. If not stated otherwise, then the standard deviation $\sigma = 1.0$ has been chosen. The minimal width of the ROI has always been set to $w_{min} = 5$. The initial positions (ROI centers) have been selected manually. In all experiments the threshold for the variation of the position estimate has been fixed to $t_D = 0.5pix$.

First, we have applied the algorithm on the image containing a polyhedral object. In Fig. 7, the uncertainty measure U in dependence on the width of the observation window is depicted for an L-corner (a), Y-corner (b), and Arrow-corner (c). In these graphs, the automatically determined optimal ROI widths are marked by a solid line for criterion A (minimal localization uncertainty of the position estimate) and by a dashed line for criterion B (maximal size of the ROI). The automatically determined ROIs are shown in Fig. 8a for criterion A and in Fig. 8b for criterion B. The loci of the position estimates resulting from the edge intersection approach are indicated through white crosses, although, due to technical reasons, the coordinates have been rounded to pixel coordinates. We see that for citerion B we obtain ROIs with more or less maximal size.

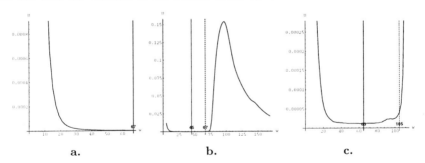

a.   b.   c.

Fig. 7. Uncertainty measure U in dependence on the window width w for the L-corner (a), Y-corner (b), and Arrow-corner (c). The automatically selected ROI widths are marked by a solid vertical line for criterion A and by a dashed vertical line for criterion B (see text).

The ROIs capture no other structures. The algorithm stops nearby the obvious strong increases of $U(w)$ ($w_{opt} = 105$ for the Arrow-corner and $w_{opt} = 67$ for the Y-corner). However, for the L-corner no other edges interfere if the observation window is enlarged. Thus for the L-corner in both cases we have $w_{opt} = 67$. However, for criterion A we obtain for both the Arrow- and the Y-corner a significantly smaller ROI.

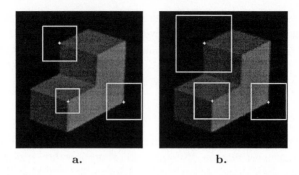

a.   b.

Fig. 8. Automatically determined ROIs for criterion A (a) and and criterion B (b). The position estimates resulting from the edge intersection approach are marked by white crosses (see text).

To analyze the localization accuracy of the position estimates resulting from the edge intersection approach in more detail, we have compared the here calculated positions with those obtained by fitting a parametric corner model to the data [12]. Using this 'ground truth' we have computed the respective distances to the position estimates. We have varied the scale σ of the Gaussian filters for estimating the partial derivatives to study the localization error in dependence on the scale. The distances in dependence on σ are listed for criterion A in Tab. 1a and for criterion B in Tab. 1b. To show the relation between the localization error and the size of the observation window, we have also listed the respective value w_{opt} (in parentheses) for each scale σ. From Tabs. 1a and b we see that the

σ	Arrow	L	Y
0.5	0.12 (31)	0.33 (61)	0.27 (33)
1.0	0.11 (65)	0.16 (67)	0.28 (45)
1.5	0.25 (79)	0.13 (65)	0.32 (51)

a.

σ	Arrow	L	Y
0.5	0.96 (105)	0.39 (71)	0.49 (67)
1.0	0.99 (105)	0.16 (67)	0.52 (67)
1.5	1.26 (105)	0.13 (65)	0.46 (67)

b.

Table 1. Localization error (in *pix*) of the position estimates resulting from the edge intersection approach for the Arrow-, L-, and Y-corner for criterion A (a) and criterion B (b). The values in parentheses denote the width of the determined ROI and σ denotes the respective scale of the Gaussian filters for estimating the partial derivatives (see text).

accuracy of the positions for criterion A is always better than or equal to that for criterion B. On the other hand, the selected ROIs are, with except for the L-corner, significantly smaller. A general statement concerning the best suited filter scale σ is not possible. However, we note that for criterion A we generally obtain a larger ROI with increasing scale. On the other hand, with increasing scale, for the Arrow- (criteria A and B) and Y-corner (criterion A), the localization error increases, whereas that for the L-corner decreases. We assume that the more complex structure of the Arrow- and Y-corner is the reason for this effect.

As a second example, we have investigated 2D slices of a 3D MR image of the human brain. In Fig. 9a, for criterion A the automatically determined ROIs for several anatomical landmarks, namely the genu of corpus callosum (most left), top of pons (middle), and the tip of fourth ventricle (most right) are shown. In Fig. 9b, for criterion A the ROIs for the tip of the frontal horn (most left) and the tip of a gyrus (top) are shown. In Figs. 9c and d, for criterion B the ROIs are shown. The position estimates resulting from the edge intersection approach are marked by white crosses. The determined ROIs have nearly the same sizes for

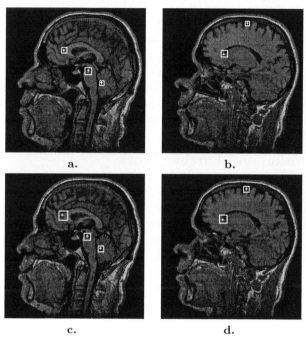

a.   b.

c.   d.

Fig. 9. Automatically selected ROIs for different anatomical landmarks in a 3D MR data set. For criterion A (a and b) and criterion B (c and d). The respective position estimates are marked by white crosses (see text).

criteria A and B, except for the genu of corpus callosum, where the widths are $w_{opt} = 11$ and $w_{opt} = 17$, resp. For this landmark, it appears that the accuracy of the position estimate for criterion B is much worse, possibly due to interfering brain convolutions in the neighborhood. One could expect that the maximal ROI for the frontal horn could be larger. However, note that there are several brain structures in the area below (see the lower border of the ROI) which causes our algorithm to stop with the selected width. All in all, it seems that the selected observation windows for both optimality criteria actually cover representative regions around all considered landmarks.

3.6 Related Work

Related work on the selection of suitable windows has been done in the context of matching stereo images by Okutomi and Kanade [9] and for junction localization by Lindeberg [7]. Lindeberg presented an approach for junction localization with automatic scale selection. This approach differs in various aspects from our approach. First of all, he selects so-called scale-space maxima of the operator by Kitchen and Rosenfeld [6]. The respective scale at which a certain junction is detected is assumed to be an appropriate scale for an observation window around the structure. Note, however, that the used operator for structures of more complex form than an L-corner (e.g., Y- and Arrow-corners) lacks for a well-founded geometric interpretation. Also, it is not clear whether such a selected ROI is optimal w.r.t. localization uncertainty. That is, his criterion for selecting the size of the ROI differs from ours. Second, he defines an error function based on the residuals of the edge intersection approach. This error function is minimized by varying the scale of the filters for partial derivative estimation. The scale of the obtained minimum is taken as optimal scale for derivative estimation. However, with this approach the residual error is minimized, whereas we have considered the uncertainty of the position estimate which is generally not the same.

4 Conclusion and Further Work

We have investigated multi-step differential procedures for the refined localization of 3D point landmarks. The promising results due to our analytical study of the 2D edge intersection approach motivated a generalization to 3D. Based on this 3D extension, we have proposed two two-step and one three-step procedures for the localization of 3D point landmarks, combining the detection of points with refined localization through 3D edge intersection. We have experimentally studied these approaches for 3D synthetic images as well as for 3D MR images of the human head. For synthetic data, the combination of a two-step procedure of large-scale and small-scale 3D differential operators followed by the 3D edge intersection approach, that is, the three-step procedure, has yielded the most accurate results. For the MR images, the two-step and three-step procedures, both including 3D edge intersection, have yielded the best results. In comparison to applying a 3D detection operator alone, the localization accuracy has been significantly improved. We have also proposed a novel approach for automatically determining an optimal size for the ROI given a considered landmark. Our approach is based on the uncertainty of the position estimate resulting from the edge intersection approach. We have presented results for a real 2D image containing a polyhedral object as well as for 2D slices of a 3D MR image demonstrating the applicability of our approach.

Further experiments on medical images will be performed taking also other types of point landmarks into account. Our approach for ROI size selection has been formulated for use in 2D as well as 3D but so far has only been applied to 2D images. Thus, we will also study the performance for 3D images. Future work will also concern the registration of 3D medical images using the semi-automatically localized point landmarks.

Acknowledgement

Support of Philips Research Laboratories Hamburg, project IMAGINE (IMage-
and Atlas-Guided Interventions in NEurosurgery), is gratefully acknowledged.
The MR images have been provided by the Philips Research Laboratories Hamburg, the IMDM at the University Hospital Hamburg-Eppendorf, as well as the
AIM project COVIRA (COmputer VIsion in RAdiology).

References

1. P.R. Beaudet. Rotationally invariant image operators. In *Proc. International Conference on Pattern Recognition*, pages 579–583, Kyoto,Japan, 1978.
2. W. Beil, K. Rohr, and H.S. Stiehl. Investigation of Approaches for the Localization of Anatomical Landmarks in 3D Medical Images. In H.U. Lemke, M.W. Vannier, and K. Inamura, editors, *Proc. Computer Assisted Radiology and Surgery*, pages 265–270, Berlin,Germany, 1997. Elsevier Amsterdam Lausanne.
3. L. Dreschler. *Ermittlung markanter Punkte auf den Bildern bewegter Objekte und Berechnung einer 3D-Beschreibung auf dieser Grundlage*. Dissertation, FB Informatik, Universität Hamburg, 1981.
4. W. Förstner. A feature based algorithm for image matching. *International Archives of Photogrammetry and Remote Sensing*, 26(3):150–166, 1986.
5. W. Förstner and E. Gülch. A Fast Operator for Detection and Precise Location of Distinct Points, Corners and Centres of Circular Features. In *Proc. Intercommission Conference on Fast Processing on Photogrammetric Data*, pages 281–305, Interlaken,Switzerland, 1987.
6. L. Kitchen and A. Rosenfeld. Gray-level corner detection. *Pattern Recognition Letters*, 1(2):95–102, 1982.
7. T. Lindeberg. Junction Detection with Automatic Selection of Detection Scales and Localization Scales. In *Proc. First International Conference on Image Processing*, volume 1, pages 924–928, Austin,TX,USA, 1994.
8. J.A. Noble. Finding corners. In *Proc. Third Alvey Vision Conference*, pages 267–274, Cambridge,UK, 1987.
9. M. Okutomi and T. Kanade. A Locally Adaptive Window for Signal Matching. *International Journal of Computer Vision*, 7(2):143–162, 1992.
10. K. Rohr. *Untersuchung von grauwertabhängigen Transformationen zur Ermittlung des optischen Flusses in Bildfolgen*. Diplomarbeit, Institut für Nachrichtentechnik, Universität Karlsruhe, 1987.
11. K. Rohr. Modelling and identification of characteristic intensity variations. *Image and Vision Computing*, 10(3):66–76, 1992.
12. K. Rohr. Recognizing Corners by Fitting Parametric Models. *International Journal of Computer Vision*, 9(3):213–230, 1992.
13. K. Rohr. Localization Properties of Direct Corner Detectors. *Journal of Mathematical Imaging and Vision*, 4(2):139–150, 1994.
14. K. Rohr. On 3D differential operators for detecting point landmarks. *Image and Vision Computing*, 15(3):219–233, 1997.
15. J.-P. Thirion. Extremal Points: Definition and Application to 3D Image Registration. In *Proc. IEEE Conference on Computer Vision and Pattern Recognition*, pages 587–592, Seattle,WA,USA, 1994.

Object Oriented Motion Estimation in Color Image Sequences

Volker Rehrmann

University of Koblenz–Landau
Image Recognition Lab
Rheinau 1, D-56075 Koblenz
volker@uni-koblenz.de

Abstract. This paper describes a color region-based approach to motion estimation in color image sequences. The system is intended for robotic and vehicle guidance applications where the task is to detect and track moving objects in the scene. It belongs to the class of feature-based matching techniques and uses color regions, resulting from a prior color segmentation, as the matching primitives. In contrast to other region-based approaches it takes into account the unavoidable variations in the segmentation by the extension of the matching model to multi matches. In order to provide extended trajectories, color regions that could not be matched on the feature level are matched on the pixel level by the integration of a correlation-based mechanism. The usage of color information and the combination of feature-based and correlation-based matching leads to robust and efficient algorithms. The system was applied to a motion segmentation task in vehicle guidance. Experiments on more than 1000 natural color outdoor images, taken from a moving car, show promising results.

Keywords: Motion estimation, motion segmentation, color vision, feature matching

1 Introduction

Motion estimation has long been a field of extensive research (s. [8] for an overview). However, motion estimation in color image sequences has rarely been studied due to different reasons. The devices to store high quality color image sequences at high sampling rates have been very expensive. The computational complexity of motion estimation algorithms in gray value images was already high enough. The classical differential approach gained little when transferred to RGB images. The three color channels are highly correlated, such that the improvements did not justify the increased complexity. Nevertheless, experiences from image segmentation have shown that color is a rich source of information that can significantly improve the robustness of vision algorithms. Our intention is the development of a system for the analysis of color image sequences that is accurate, robust and efficient. In [7] it was stated that most of the existing motion algorithms are either very fast or very accurate. What is needed in real world applications is a good trade–off between accuracy and efficiency. In this paper we present our OOMECS (Object Oriented Motion Estimation in Color Image Sequences) system that tries to fill this gap and is intended to provide fast and reliable results. Our system belongs to the class of feature-based matching techniques which are known to be more robust than the differential techniques, at least in natural scenes. In contrast to the common corner or edge matching techniques that provide only sparse displacement fields we use complete color regions as matching primitives. Thus, prior to the matching phase each image is independently segmented using a fast and robust color segmentation algorithm. Region-based approaches for motion estimation have been applied in gray value images in [2] and [6]. The image is segmented using various approaches and the correspondence of regions is based on features. The displacement among centroids determines the displacement between regions. In [3] a complex texture-based segmentation of a gray value image is used to get the initial partition into regions. Then affine motion parameters are computed for each region using a robust multi-resolution estimator. Price ([10]) was the first to explore a region-based change detection in color images. In his algorithm the images are segmented using the well-known recursive histogram splitting technique. The resulting regions are described by features and the feature-based descriptions of two images are compared to determine the corresponding regions. In [4] a similar approach was used to track color regions, generated by simple color space clustering, over long image sequences. In [1] the segmentation and motion estimation is simultaneously performed by a clustering process based on color, motion and pixel position.

The simple region-based approaches trying to match one region in an image with exactly one corresponding region in the successive image are successful in simple scenes, where enough contrast exists between regions to stably segment them from frame to frame. However, in natural scenes even the best segmentation algorithm usually can not guarantee that regions will be uniformly stable segmented. More elaborate approaches based on statistical regularization provide accurate results but are far away from fast processing. In our OOMECS system we combine a very efficient feature-based matching algorithm with an accurate correlation-based matching algorithm. As much regions as possible are matched on the feature level. To account for the unavoidable variations in the segmentation we extended our matching model from simple $1:1$ matches to the general case of $n:m$ matches, where sets of color regions are matched. In order to provide extended trajectories, color regions that could not be matched on the feature level are matched on the pixel level using a correlation-based mechanism. The object-oriented correlation provides very accurate results but requires elaborate processing. The combination of both techniques assures that the main design goals, robustness and efficiency, are achieved. The system is intended for robotic and vehicle guidance applications where the task is to detect and track moving objects in the scene. It is not intended for high accuracy measurements like structure from motion, although further algorithms may be based on its results. In the next section we present the color region based motion estimation algorithm combining matching on feature and pixel level. In section 3 we present results of our experiments with more than 1000 color outdoor scenes from the field of vehicle guidance. The system was applied to the problem of segmenting moving objects from color image sequences. The results show the effectiveness of this approach in such difficult real-world problems. The speed of the algorithm allows for a fast processing rate.

2   Color Region Matching

We assume color image sequences of natural color outdoor scenes with an arbitrary number of moving objects especially due to a moving camera. As our system is based on matching color regions, in a first step each color image is independently segmented. We use the *CSC* (Color Structure Code) as our segmentation tool (s. [11]). The CSC has proven to be an efficient and reliable scene segmenter in a variety of real-world applications. Figure 7 shows an example of the segmentation results of two consecutive images. However, any other color segmentation tool can be used. The matching quality, of course, increases with the stability of the segmentation results in successive images. The input to the color region matching algorithm is therefore a partition of each image in the sequence into a set of color regions. The goal of the color region matching is to find a definite correspondence between color regions of two consecutive images. We explicitly allow for the fact that a segmented region in one image may split or merge into several regions in the next image. We therefore extended our matching model from simple $1:1$ matches to the general case of $n:m$ matches. A $1:1$ match, where one color region corresponds to exactly one color region (s. Fig. 1 (a)), is the most simple case and the only kind of match accounted for in the previously published papers on region matching. Often a color region splits into two or more regions in the segmentation of the next image. This is a typical $1:n$ match (s. Fig. 1 (b)). The analogous case is the $n:1$ match (s. Fig. 1 (c)). The most general case is the $n:m$ match (s. Fig. 1 (d)): a set of n color regions corresponds to a set of m color regions. Our systems accounts for this general model of $n:m$ matching and is thus more robust against unavoidable variations in the segmentation. Slightly over-segmented images are favorable because objects split into several regions can be composed again in the $n:m$ matching algorithm, whereas differently moving objects merged together into one color region need some special consideration. In this paper we assume that motion boundaries coincide with spatial boundaries. The next version of our system will not be based on this assumption.

The matching phase is divided into two main steps. In a first step we try to match regions solely based on their region attributes. This feature-based matching is very efficient and is best explained in terms of graph algorithms. Color regions that could not be matched on feature level are matched on pixel level in the *iconic color region matching* step. Here color regions are matched using a correlation-based mechanism delivering very accurate results at the expense of higher computational complexity. The combination of both techniques leads to

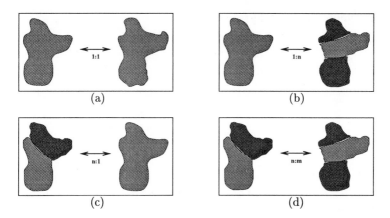

Fig. 1. Four different cases of region matching, from simple 1 : 1 matches (a) to complex $n : m$ matches (d).

reliable and robust results while being very efficient. The limits of the system are obviously reached when no homogeneous color regions appear in the image.

2.1 Feature-Based Color Region Matching

The feature-based color region matching relies on the computation of the similarity of two color regions from consecutive images solely based on their features. In order to efficiently handle the complex $n : m$ matches the algorithm operates in four phases, which are described in the following.

Similarity function. In this section we define the similarity function used to compare two color regions. We use the following features for the feature-based matching of color regions: color, area, position (centre of gravity), proportion (of the equivalent ellipse, calculated from the second central moments), orientation (of the equivalent ellipse), minimum bounding rectangle.

In order to reduce the computational complexity of the matching phase we only analyze regions with a minimum size of 40 pixels. The overall similarity EQ between two regions is calculated as the weighted sum of the single features similarity values:

$$EQ = \omega_{color} \cdot EQ_{color} + \omega_{area} \cdot EQ_{area} + \omega_{centre} \cdot EQ_{centre} + \omega_{prop} \cdot EQ_{prop} + \\ + \omega_{ori} \cdot EQ_{ori} + \omega_{mbr} \cdot EQ_{mbr}$$

All single similarity values are normalized to lie in the range [0..1] and are calculated as follows:

$$EQ_{area} = \frac{|A_0 - A_1|}{A_0 + A_1} ,$$

where A_i denotes the area of region i.

$$EQ_{prop} = \frac{1}{2} \cdot \left(\frac{|m_0 - m_1|}{m_0 + m_1} + \frac{|s_0 - s_1|}{s_0 + s_1} \right) ,$$

where m_i denotes the major axis and s_i the minor axis of the equivalent ellipse.

$$EQ_{ori} = \left(1 - \frac{1}{e^{4 \cdot (\Pi - 1)}} \right) \cdot \frac{| \lfloor \frac{\Delta\Theta + 90}{180} \rfloor \cdot 180 - \Delta\Theta |}{90} ,$$

with $\Delta\Theta = |\Theta_0 - \Theta_1|$, $\Pi = min(\frac{m_0}{s_0}, \frac{m_1}{s_1})$. Θ_i denotes the angle of orientation of the equivalent ellipse of region i.

$$EQ_{mbr} = \frac{1}{2} \cdot \left(\frac{|w_0 - w_1|}{w_0 + w_1} + \frac{|h_0 - h_1|}{h_0 + h_1} \right) ,$$

where w_i denotes the width and h_i the height of the bounding rectangle.

EQ_{color} and EQ_{centre} are calculated as normalized Euclidean distances between color vectors in the CIE-Lab color space respectively position vectors. The complex equation for EQ_{ori} computes the simple difference between two angles without considering the different quadrants. It is additionally weighted depending on the proportions of the involved regions, as the reliability of the orientation decreases with decreasing proportion (a circle with proportion 1 has no orientation). The weights ω in the overall similarity equation for EQ can be set specific to the application. We use a high weight for color and position and a small weight for the other features in our applications.

This similarity function is also applied to compare two sets of color regions ($n : m$ match). The composition of several color regions implies the calculation of the new composed feature set from the features of all involved single color regions. This computation is very efficient because it can be computed directly from the feature values of the involved regions without referring to their single pixels. Thus, we use the same similarity function, no matter if comparing single color regions or composed color regions.

Four Phase Matching. Phase 1 In the first phase a graph is built, connecting all regions in image I_t at time t with all regions in image I_{t+1} at time $t + 1$ that are possible candidates for a match. Let $G_{inter} = (V, E)$ be an undirected graph with vertex set V and edge set E. The vertices of G are the color regions in I_t and I_{t+1}. Color regions r_1 from image I_t and r_2 from image I_{t+1} are connected by an edge, if:

1. $EQ_{color}(r_1, r_2) < $ max_color.
2. $EQ_{centre}(r_1, r_2) < $ max_dist.

The graph G_{inter} (s. Fig. 2) is solely based on the two main features color and position. Only regions connected by an edge in G_{inter} can be matched in one of the following phases. A connection in G_{inter} is therefore a necessary condition

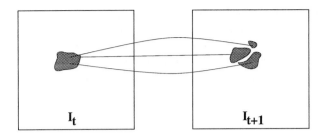

Fig. 2. An example for a subgraph of G_{inter}. A color region in image I_t is connected with three color regions in image I_{t+1}

for a match. The purpose of this graph is mainly the reduction of complexity. It can be viewed as a first check in a hierarchical decision tree. Regions not connected by an edge in G_{inter} are excluded from the subsequent analysis.

Phase 2 The goal of phase 2 is to find all single color regions that perfectly match with each other. Two regions r_1 from image I_t and r_2 from image I_{t+1} perfectly match, if:

1. r_1 and r_2 are connected by an edge in G_{inter}.
2. $EQ(r_1, r_2) < T \ \wedge \ \forall s \in I_t : EQ(r_1, r_2) \leq EQ(s, r_2) \ \wedge$
   $\forall t \in I_{t+1} : EQ(r_1, r_2) \leq EQ(r_1, t)$

where T is an application specific threshold depending on the chosen feature weights. Again, the purpose of this phase is mainly a reduction of complexity. Perfectly matched regions are deleted from G_{inter} and are no longer candidates for a $n : m$ match. The perfect matches are the simple $1 : 1$ matches. Homogeneous regions with distinct contrast to the background can often be perfectly matched. However, in natural scenes this is not always the case.

Phase 3 In this phase those color regions are further analysed that could not be perfectly matched in phase 2. These regions are the candidates for an $n : m$ match. The goal of $n : m$ matching is to determine those *subsets* from two sets of color regions that are best corresponding to each other. As the number of all possible subsets from a set with n elements is 2^n, it is impossible to exhaustively search for the optimal correspondence (usually there are about 100 regions in an image). However, it is possible to decrease the complexity by using the regions color and topological relations. Not all possible subsets of regions are evaluated, but only those subsets where the regions are topologically neighbored and similar in color. Only these regions may merge one with another in the segmentation of the successive image.

In this phase so called clusters of regions are determined independently for each image I. We define the graph G_{intra} as follows:

$G_{intra} = (V, E)$ is an undirected graph with V = {regions in image I}, $E \subseteq V x V$ with $(u, v) \in E :\Leftrightarrow$

1. u and v are similar in color.
2. u and v are topologically neighbored, e.g. $\min_{x \in u, x' \in v} \|x - x'\| <$ top_thresh.
3. u and v move in a similar way (initially always true).

Similarity in color should here be specified analogous to the color similarity measure used in the segmentation phase (but with a higher tolerance). The decision about the similarity of trajectories depends on an appropriate motion model. We use the predicate defined in 3.1. Regions with different trajectories can not belong to one object and are no candidates for a $n : m$ match.

As in phase 1 regions are connected that are topologically neighbored and similar in color. The difference is that in phase 1 a graph is built between the regions of two consecutive images and here a graph is built between the regions within the same image. G_{intra} is usually not connected (s. Fig. 3). A cluster of regions is defined as a maximally connected subgraph of G_{intra}. Candidates for an $n : m$ match are now only the subsets of a cluster. But it makes no sense to consider every subset of a cluster as a possible candidate for an $n : m$ match. Only connected subgraphs of a cluster are permissible candidates as only topologically neighbored regions with similar colors can merge in the segmentation of the next image of a sequence. In order to compute all connected subgraphs of a graph we use an efficient algorithm based on dynamic programming. At first all connected subgraphs with only one vertex are determined; this is exactly the set of all single vertices of the graph. All larger connected subgraphs are determined iteratively using the same algorithm: To get all connected subgraphs with n vertices consider all connected subgraphs with $n - 1$ vertices and expand them by exactly one vertex v, if there exists a direct edge from any of the $n - 1$ vertices of the subgraph to v.

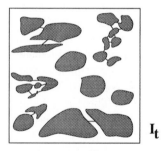

Fig. 3. An example for a graph G_{intra}. There are eight clusters contained in image I_t.

Phase 4 In the last phase all possible $n : m$ matches are computed using the graphs G_{inter} and G_{intra} of the preceding phases. In order to find the optimal $n : m$ matches all connected subgraphs of one cluster C_t in image I_t are compared with **all** connected subgraphs of a corresponding cluster C_{t+1} in image I_{t+1}. Clusters in consecutive images are corresponding if there exists at least one edge in G_{inter} connecting the clusters. This means that there is at least one region in cluster C_t connected with a region in cluster C_{t+1}. For each pair of composed color regions, computed in this way, the similarity function value EQ is calculated.

Note that this algorithm always finds the optimal matches (in the sense of similarity value EQ) between two sets of color regions, as it compares all allowed subsets within each cluster with each other. Several $n : m$ matches between two corresponding clusters are possible as we delete successfully matched regions from the clusters and again check the remaining regions in the clusters for possible further matches. The key to improved efficiency is holding the clusters small. This is achieved by considering only neighbored regions similar in color. If a cluster consists of many segments we additionally apply the heuristic that usually not more than k (4 to 5 in our applications) regions are involved in one $n : m$ match. Thus, we only evaluate subgraphs with a maximum of k elements avoiding combinatorial explosion. Figure 8 shows some examples of $n : m$ matches from natural scenes found in this way.

Displacement estimation for feature-based region matching. After having established the corresponding color regions based on the similarity of their features the motion parameters for the matched sets of color regions are calculated. We only compute the planar motion which in practice is sufficient assuming a high sampling rate. However, more sophisticated motion models like the affine motion model can directly be applied to region matching approaches (s. [5]).

First of all the displacement vector $\Delta[d]$ between two matched regions r_1 and r_2 is approximated by the displacement of the objects centres of gravity. When regarding $n : m$ matches the centre of gravity refers to the composed color region. The displacement of the centres of gravity is sometimes inaccurate due to small variations in the segmentation of an object in consecutive images. We therefore additionally apply a boundary correlation method as in [9]. The boundary of a region is taken as a template and cross–correlated with the boundary of the corresponding matched region. This boundary correlation is very efficient to compute because it is only a bit-type correlation, only the boundary has to be correlated (not the entire region) and the search width can be restricted to a small size, because $\Delta[d]$ constitutes a good starting point. Using this boundary correlation the displacement vector can be determined rather accurate even if small parts of the object are missing.

2.2 Iconic Color Region Matching

The introduction of the general $n : m$ type matches significantly increased the quality of the matching results. However, there are still some color regions left that could not be matched on the feature level. They belong to one of the following classes (in decreasing order of frequency):

- Small regions, where small variations lead to significant changes of the shape parameters.
- Regions near the image borders, whose size and shape varies significantly because parts of them leave the image in the next frame.

- Occlusions of one segment by another.
- Significant variations of the regions due to changes in segmentation.

In order to match these regions we use an iconic matching technique on pixel level. Iconic matching operates similar to the well-known block-matching techniques. The idea of block-matching is to partition an image I_t at time t into equally sized blocks and to search for each of the blocks the corresponding block in the successive image I_{t+1} at time $t+1$. The similarity function often used in color images is the simple displaced frame difference

$$DFD(u,v) = \sum_{x,y \in B} |R(x,y,t) - R(x+u,y+v,t+1)| + \\ |G(x,y,t) - G(x+u,y+v,t+1)| + \\ |B(x,y,t) - B(x+u,y+v,t+1)|$$

The advantage of the common block-matching method is its simplicity and the supply of dense displacement vectors. Its main drawbacks are a high computational complexity, the fixed choice of block size and shape, the missing of a clear minimum of the similarity function within homogeneous regions and the aperture problem due to a pure local view. In contrast to the block-matching technique we do not use fixed block sizes and shapes, but block sizes and shapes that are adjusted to the object boundaries. The color regions resulting from the segmentation phase simply form the blocks. This content-based displacement estimation explicitly accounts for the discontinuities of the displacement vector field occurring at the boundaries of contrary moving objects. Three of the above mentioned block-matching drawbacks no longer hold with iconic color region matching. The displacement vectors are very accurate due to the blocks adjusted to the object shape. The remaining drawback, the high computational complexity, is also strongly weakened when using the iconic region matching in a hybrid manner in the entire system. The iconic color region matching is only applied to those regions that could not be matched on the feature level. This is often only a small part of the image. Especially the large regions in natural scenes (sky, road, meadows) can well be matched on the feature level. Due to the distinct minima of the similarity function all the well-known efficient search techniques for block-matching methods can excellently be applied here. If for example a color region is large we use the hierarchical search technique. Of course, the search width can be restricted if the position of a color region in the successive image can well be predicted based on the trajectory computed so far. We use a simplified Kalman-filter to predict the position of a color regions centre of gravity.

In order to track color regions over several frames and thus yield extended trajectories, the displacement vectors found by iconic region matching are not sufficient. A displacement vector found in this way describes the displacement of a color region from an image I_t to the consecutive image I_{t+1}. This information has to be transmitted to the corresponding color region or regions in image I_{t+1}. The entire system is based on the fact that a color region from frame to frame transfers its motion history to the corresponding color regions in the consecutive image. Only in this way a maximum of the information contained in a sequence of images can be used for consecutive analysis phases like motion segmentation.

Therefore, let A' denote a color region in image I_t at time t and $d_{A'} = (x_{A'}, y_{A'})$ the displacement vector of A' found by iconic color region matching. Let A be the color region displaced by $d_{A'}$, $A = \{(x + x_{A'}, y + y_{A'}) \mid (x, y) \in A'\}$, projected into the successive image I_{t+1} (s. Fig. 4). Let $F \in CR(I_{t+1}) = \{$color regions in image $I_{t+1}\}$. In $(F \cap A)$ are all those pixels of I_{t+1} that as well belong to the color region F as are covered by A. Let B be the color region of I_{t+1} which covers the maximum part of A (s. Fig. 4), that is

$$area(B \cap A) > area(F \cap A) \; \forall F \in CR(I_{t+1})$$

where $area(F)$ denotes the number of pixels of a color region F.

We distinguish the following 4 cases:

1. $\frac{area(A \cap B)}{area(A)} \approx 1$ and $\frac{area(A \cap B)}{area(B)} \approx 1 \Longrightarrow$ match A with B (s. Fig. 5 (a)).
2. $\frac{area(A \cap B)}{area(A)} \approx 1$ and $\frac{area(A \cap B)}{area(B)} \ll 1 \Longrightarrow$ match A with B.
   If B is already matched $\longrightarrow$ multi match (s. Fig. 5 (b))
3. $\frac{area(A \cap B)}{area(A)} \ll 1$ and $\frac{area(A \cap B)}{area(B)} \approx 1 \Longrightarrow$ match A with B.
   If B is already matched, delete match.
   If A is already matched $\longrightarrow$ multi match (s. Fig. 5 (c)).
4. $\frac{area(A \cap B)}{area(A)} \ll 1$ and $\frac{area(A \cap B)}{area(B)} \ll 1 \Longrightarrow$ no match (s. Fig. 5 (d)).

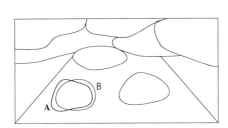

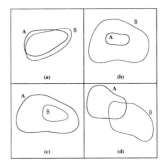

Fig. 4. The displaced color region A of image I_t projected into image I_{t+1}.

Fig. 5. Four possible cases, how A and B may overlap.

Hence, the results of the iconic color region matching are integrated in the entire system in the same way as the results of the feature-based color region matching. The matching results are represented in a graph data structure describing the correspondence of color regions from frame to frame. In addition to the classical region attributes like color, area, etc. each color region possesses a motion trajectory resulting from the matching phase. This motion trajectory clearly describes the path a color region has taken through time (s. Fig. 9).

3 Results

Our system has been applied to real world scenes, especially to a typical situation in vehicle guidance. The images were taken from a vehicle travelling along a highway with a 3-CCD color camera and recorded on a digital video recorder (Y:U:V=4:2:2, 720x560 pixels, 25 frames/sec). Due to the interlaced mode we only used half resolution images in our experiments. The color image sequences were kindly provided by the Daimler-Benz Research Institute in Ulm. The following statistics refer to eight sequences with altogether 1000 images. 85 color regions appeared on average in each image. About 89 % of them successfully were matched. The area covered by the successfully matched color regions is about 99 % of the whole image area. This implies that mainly very small regions were not matched. Visual judgement by human observers showed that nearly all of the matches are correct, which is explained by the usage of strict thresholds for allowable matches. About 35 % of the color regions are involved in $n : m$ matches. The expansion to $n : m$ matches has therefore led to a significant increase in performance. Described in percentage of the whole image area, only 11 % of the whole image area were matched using iconic region matching. This small amount is important for the efficiency of the entire system. The successful matching rate led to extended motion trajectories, which are very useful for subsequent tasks like motion segmentation. The trajectories are accurate due to the boundary and region correlation used to estimate the displacement.

The average processing time was 800 msec per image on a SUN ULTRA SPARC I (166 MHz). Thus, even today it is possible to operate at rates of 10 frames/sec using the latest processor technology on symmetric multiprocessor architectures. The share of color segmentation and feature extraction is about 55 % of the total processing time. The feature-based matching part requires 22 % and the iconic region matching part 23 % on average (search width 10 pixels). The time required for color segmentation is nearly constant, whereas the required time of the matching phase depends on the complexity of the scene, e.g. the number of regions, the size of the clusters and the number of regions matched using iconic region matching.

3.1 Motion segmentation

In order to demonstrate the effectiveness of our approach we applied the system to partition each image of a sequence into regions having different motion characteristics. We developed a simple algorithm to compute the motion segments based on the motion trajectories determined in the matching phase. All color regions that are topologically neighbored and possess similar motion trajectories are combined to one motion segment (s. Fig. 9). To decide about the similarity of motion trajectories, a proper motion model is necessary. Here we restrict ourselves to the case of simple 2D-motion, which already leads to promising results in our application. In order to tolerate local faults, the trajectories are split into overlapping, piecewise linear approximations (s. Fig. 6).

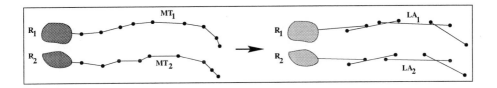

Fig. 6. Two regions R_1 and R_2 with their motion trajectories MT_1 and MT_2 and their corresponding linear approximations LA_1 and LA_2.

A trajectory is divided into sections of three contiguous displacement vectors. Two trajectories are now called similar, if their corresponding linear approximations are similar. We only use the last 12 images for the comparison, which means we use not more than the last five sections of the linear approximation. Let $LA_i = (v_{i1}, v_{i2}, v_{i3}, v_{i4}, v_{i5})$ for $i = 1, 2$ be the linear approximations of two motion trajectories t_1 and t_2. The similarity d of two trajectories t_1 and t_2 is defined by the predicate:

$$d(t_1, t_2) = d(v_{11}, v_{21}) \land d(v_{12}, v_{22}) \land d(v_{13}, v_{23}) \land d(v_{14}, v_{24}) \land d(v_{15}, v_{25}) \text{ with}$$
$$d(v_{1j}, v_{2j}) = (|vect\_length(v_{1j}) - vect\_length(v_{2j})| < LENGTH\_THRESH) \land$$
$$(vect\_angle(v_{1j}, v_{2j}) < 30°)$$

where $vect\_length$ denotes the length of a vector and $vect\_angle$ the angle between two vectors. The threshold $LENGTH\_THRESH$ is dynamically defined as a linear function depending on the velocity of the slower color region. Figures 10 to 13 show some examples of the motion segmentation application. A fast approximation of the convex hull of a motion segment (a regular polygon with 24 edges) is plotted in green (s. Fig. 9). The trajectory of a motion segment is drawn in yellow. There are several more motion segments than the one plotted in the example. To better visualize the results, only one manually chosen motion segment is shown per image. Of course, not all motion segments in all sequences are as accurate as in the shown examples. But the quality is comparable to them. Problems occur sometimes with parts of the road that merge into the motion segment due to a *pseudo* motion of the part. This has to be solved using knowledge about the specific application. Note that no model of the scene or application has been used. The computed motion segments are accurate and stable even e.g. in Figure 12 where the car is entering the shadow of the van. The above simple similarity measure works well because the extended trajectories resulting from the robust matching allow for a clear discrimination of the independent motions in the scene.

4   Conclusions

In this paper we introduced an original approach to motion estimation in color image sequences based on color region matching. The main design criteria of the system have been efficiency and robustness. The robustness was achieved by using a region-based approach, exploiting color information and extending the matching model to $n : m$ matches. The combination of the feature-based color region matching and the iconic color region matching contributes to the robustness and provides the basis for the efficiency of the approach. With feature-based region matching, extended to $n : m$ matches, nearly 90 % of the image area can be matched in an efficient and accurate way. The iconic region matching, which requires more elaborate processing, is thus only applied to a small fraction of the image area. It yields very accurate displacement vectors and most of the time finds the corresponding color regions. The combined approach delivers therefore dense displacement fields and extended trajectories. The experiments on natural color images proved the suitability of this approach to difficult tasks like motion segmentation in the field of vehicle guidance. Future work lies in the improvement of the motion segmentation based on the matched extended trajectories and the extension of the system to more sophisticated motion models.

References

1. M. Etoh and Y. Shirai. Segmentation and 2d motion estimation by region fragments. In *Proc. of IEEE Int. Conf. on Computer Vision*, pages 192–199, 1993.
2. C.-S. Fuh and P. Maragos. Region-based optical flow estimation. In *Proc. of the IEEE Conf. on Computer Vision and Pattern Recognition*, pp. 130–135. IEEE, 1989.
3. M. Gelgon and P. Bouthemy. A region-level graph labeling approach to motion-based segmentation. Research report 3054, INRIA, http://www.inria.fr/RRRT/RR-3054.html, 1996.
4. B. Heisele and W. Ritter. Obstacle Detection based on Color Blob Flow. In *Proc. of the Intelligent Vehicles Symposium*, pp. 282–286. IEEE, 1995.
5. D.S. Kalivas and A.A. Sawchuk. A Region Matching Motion Estimation Algorithm. *Computer Vision, Graphics, and Image Processing*, 54(2):275–288, 1991.
6. D.P. Kottke and Y. Sun. Motion estimation via cluster matching. *IEEE Transactions on Pattern Analysis and Machine Intelligence*, 16(11):1128–1132, 1994.
7. H. Liu, T.-H. Hong, M. Herman, and R. Chellappa. Accuracy vs. Efficiency Tradeoffs in Optical Flow. In B. Buxton and R. Cipolla, editors, *Proc. 4th European Conference on Computer Vision*, pages 174–183. Springer Verlag, 1996.
8. A. Mitiche and P. Bouthemy. Computation and analysis of image motion: A synopsis of current problems and methods. *International Journal of Computer Vision*, 19:29–55, 1996.
9. H.-H. Nagel. Formation of an object concept by analysis of systematic time variations in the optically perceptible environment. *Computer Graphics and Image Processing*, 7:149–194, 1978.
10. K. Price. *Change Detection and Analysis in Multi-Spectral Images*. PhD thesis, Carnegie Mellon University, Pittsburgh, Pennsylvania, 1976.
11. V. Rehrmann and L. Priese. Fast and Robust Segmentation of Natural Color Scenes. In *Proc. of the 3rd Asian Conf. on Computer Vision, Special Session on Advances in Color Vision*, Vol. I, pp. 598-606. Springer Verlag, 1998.
12. V. Rehrmann. Object Oriented Motion Estimation in Color Image Sequences. http://www.uni-koblenz.de/~lb/lb_publications.e.html, 1998.

Fig. 7. An example for the color segmentation of two successive images. See [12] for the original color image.

Fig. 8. Three examples for $n : m$ matches. Left: 1 : 3 match. Middle: 2 : 1 match. Right: 2 : 3 match. See [12] for the original color image.

Fig. 9. Left: Original scene. Middle: 9 color regions with similar trajectories. Right: The resulting motion segment, drawn in green the approximation of the convex hull. See [12] for the original color image.

Fig. 10. Example of the color region based motion segmentation. See [12] for the original color image.

Fig. 11. Example of the color region based motion segmentation. See [12] for the original color image.

Fig. 12. Example of the color region based motion segmentation. See [12] for the original color image.

Fig. 13. Example of the color region based motion segmentation. See [12] for the original color image.

Multi-scale and Snakes for Automatic Road Extraction

Helmut Mayer, Ivan Laptev, Albert Baumgartner

Chair for Photogrammetry and Remote Sensing
Technische Universität München
D-80290 München, Germany
Phone: +49-89-2892-2688, Fax: +49-89-2809573
E-Mail: {helmut|ivan|albert}@photo.verm.tu-muenchen.de

Abstract. This paper proposes an approach for automatic road extraction in aerial imagery which exploits the scale-space behavior of roads in combination with geometric constrained snake-based edge extraction. The approach not only has few parameters to be adjusted, but for the first time allows for a bridging of shadows and partially occluded areas using the heavily disturbed evidence in the image. The road network is constructed after extracting crossings of various shape and topology. Reasonable results are obtained which are evaluated based on ground truth.

1 Introduction

Aerial imagery is one of the standard data sources to extract topographic objects like roads or buildings for geographic information systems (GIS). Road data in GIS are of major importance for applications like car navigation or guidance systems for police, fire service or forwarding agencies. As their extraction is time consuming, their is a need for automation.

For practical applications there will be, at least for some time, human interaction needed which leads to semi-automatic approaches. Approaches relying strongly on this interaction are for instance based on road tracking [15, 23] starting from a given point and a given direction after extracting parallel edges or by extrapolation and matching of profiles in high resolution images. Other semi-automatic approaches are based on finding an optimal path between a few given points using for instance dynamic programming [9, 16] or the F*-algorithm [6] after detecting lines from low-resolution. When more than one image is available, it is possible to track the line in 3D which constrains the path of the road and makes it possible to handle occlusions using robust optimization [9]. So-called "ziplock snakes" [17] are another means to connect given points in the presence of obstacles. In [7] the model-based optimization of ribbon snakes networks is proposed to improve coarsely digitized road networks.

Another way to tackle the problem is to start with fully automatic extraction and manually edit the result only afterwards. This is the way taken in this paper and by many others. [24] extends [15] to fully automatic extraction by finding starting points. [5] and [3] concentrate on how to improve road extraction using given GIS-data. One of the recent approaches which are similar to the one proposed here is [1]. It complements a low-level Markov-Random-Field model for the extraction of road seeds and the tracking of roads with a simple clutter and occlusion model and a Kalman filter. Another recent approach improves road extraction by modeling the context, i.e., other objects like shadow, car or tree hindering or supporting the extraction of the road [18, 19]. A division of the context into spatially more global and more local parts is presented in [2]. In [18, 19] roads in urban areas are extracted by detecting and grouping of cars. [2, 22] utilize the scale-space behavior of the roads, the road network is globally optimized, intersections are modeled, and markings are used to verify the existence of the road.

This paper is an extension of [12]. Its main idea is to take advantage of the scale-space behavior of roads in combination with geometric constrained edge extraction by means of snakes. From the scale-space behavior of roads it is inferred to start with extracting lines in coarse scale which are less precise but also less disturbed by cars, shadows, etc., than features in fine scale. The lines initialize ribbon snakes in fine scale which describe the roads as bright, more or less homogeneous elongated areas. Ribbons with constant width are accepted as *salient* roads. The connections between adjacent ends of *salient* roads are checked if they correspond to *non-salient* roads. As those are disturbed, the evidence for the road in the image can only be exploited when additional constraints and a special strategy focus the extraction. The constraints are low curvature and constant width of roads as well as the connectivity of the road network, i.e., start and end point are given. The strategy is to optimize the width only after optimizing the center of the snake with the "ziplock" method.

The paper is organized as follows: In Section 2 model and inherent strategy essentially based on the scale-space behavior of roads and ribbon snakes are introduced and the terms *salient* road, *non-salient* road, and crossing are defined. While Section 3 gives basic theory for ribbon snakes Section 4 comprises the main part of the paper. The extraction of *salient* roads supplies the information needed to extract the *non-salient* roads. *Salient* as well as *non-salient* roads are linked by crossings of various shape and topology. Section 5 shows that the approach gives reasonable results for which the performance was evaluated based on ground truth. The paper is concluded with a summary in Section 6.

2 Model and Strategy

The appearance of roads in digital imagery depends on the sensor's spectral sensitivity and its resolution, i.e., scale in object space. The remainder of this paper is restricted to grey-scale images, and only scale dependencies are considered. Images with various scale exhibit different characteristics of roads. In images with coarse scale, i.e., more than 2 m per pixel, roads mainly appear as lines establishing a more or less dense network. Opposed to this, in images with a finer scale, i.e., less than 0.50 m, roads are depicted as bright, more or less homogeneous elongated areas with almost constant width and bounded curvature.

In this paper results from [14] are taken advantage of. There it is shown, that in a smoothed image (here a Gaussian scale-space [13] was used), i.e., a coarser scale, lines as defined in [21] representing road axes can be extracted in a stable manner even in the presence of background objects like tree, building, or car. Here the "scale" in object space resulting from smoothing is of first importance, as the goal is to extract objects in the real world which have specific sizes. This scale depends on the resolution of the image, the scale-space and the scale-parameter. Seen from a symbolical point of view, in the finer scale substructure of the road, i.e., a car on the road or also markings, as well as disturbances like shadows or partial occlusion are eliminated. This can be interpreted as an *abstraction*, i.e., an increase of the level of simplification and emphasis of the road. Abstraction is achieved simply by changing the scale of the image. Whereas coarse scale gives global information which is especially suited for initial detection of the road, the fine scale adds detailed information which can be used to verify and complete the road network. If the information of both levels is fused, wrong hypotheses for roads are eliminated by using the abstract coarse scale information, while integrating details from the fine scale, like the correct width of the roads. With this, the advantages of both scales are merged.

For line extraction in coarse scale [21] is a good choice, because it is formally well defined, its scale-space behavior was analyzed for roads (see above). In [2] it was combined with the following idea: The elongated areas of constant width describing roads in fine scale are extracted as parallel edges in the image using a local edge detector such as [4] in combination with grouping [20]. This has the following problems: The quality of edges varies due to noise, changes in radiometry of the road surface and its background, occlusions, etc. [8]. Therefore, the extraction of edges based on purely local photometric criteria often results in an incomplete detection of few significant edges or in the detection of many irrelevant edges. When these edges are grouped into parallelograms, they tend to be fragmented, even when lines from coarse scale are used in the grouping process and help to eliminate many wrong hypotheses. When parallel edges are linked based on purely geometric criteria, the precision is poor and wrong hypotheses are common [2].

Opposed to this, the framework of snakes introduced in [11] gives the possibility to focus the extraction of edges by their priori known geometric properties. Here this is done by linking two edges into a "ribbon" defined by its center and its width. The ribbon is optimized using the idea of "snakes" [11] which leads to the so-called "ribbon snakes". Based on the scale-space behavior and the ribbon snakes, the model and the inherent "hypothesize and verify" strategy for the extraction of the road network are as follows:

- *Salient* **roads** have a distinctive appearance in the image. A line from coarse scale initializes the center of a ribbon snake in fine scale. Criteria for the verification of a *salient* road are the constancy of the width and the homogeneity of the corresponding image region. Since man-made objects such as houses have similar properties, the extraction of *salient* roads is restricted to rural areas, given by a GIS or segmented by means of texture features. This is similar to [2], where the "context regions" *suburb_urban*, *forest*, and *open_rural* are introduced and the extraction of roads is restricted to the latter ones.

- **Non-salient** roads correspond to parts of the road network which are in the image more or less disturbed by shadows or partial occlusions. They can only be extracted top-down, when a start and an end point are available. This exploits the fact that all roads are connected into a global network. Taking adjacent ends of *salient* roads as start and end point, these points are connected by a ribbon snake with fixed width using the "ziplock" method. After a subsequent optimization of the width, its constancy is used for the verification of the *non-salient* roads.

- **Crossings** link the road network together. In coarse scale they correspond to the junctions from line extraction [21]. These hypotheses for crossings are verified in fine scale by expanding a closed snake around each junction and checking the connections between the crossings' outline and adjacent roads.

3   Ribbon Snakes

The original snakes introduced in [11] are curves with a parametric representation whose position is optimized under a number of constraints. On the one hand, the photometric constraints evoke the *image* forces which "pull" the snake to features in the image. On the other hand, the geometric constraints give rise to the *internal* forces which control the shape of the snake ensuring its piecewise smoothness. During optimization the snake evolves from its initial position to a position where the forces compensate each other and the energy of the snake is minimized. This state implies that the snake is located at the image features which best of all satisfy the desired properties.

For road extraction the original snakes are extended with a width component [7] leading to a ribbon snake defined as:

$$v(s,t) = (x(s,t), y(s,t), w(s,t)), \qquad (0 \leq s \leq 1), \tag{1}$$

where s is proportional to the ribbon's length, t is the current time, x and y are the coordinates of the ribbon's centerline, and w is the ribbon's half width. As shown in Figure 1(a) the centerline $(x(s,t), y(s,t))$ and its width $w(s,t)$ define the sides of the ribbon $v_L(s,t)$ and $v_R(s,t)$. Using this representation, the original expression for the snake's *internal* energy still holds and the width is constrained by the same "tension" and "rigidity" forces as the two coordinate components. Differently from snakes, the image forces for ribbon snakes are considered along the sides. When optimizing a ribbon to a bright road on a dark background the image function P can be redefined as the sum of the magnitudes of the image gradient along the curves $v_L(s,t)$ and $v_R(s,t)$. An even better way is to use the projections of the image gradient onto the ribbon's normal $n(s,t)$ constraining them to be positive at the ribbon's left side and negative at its right

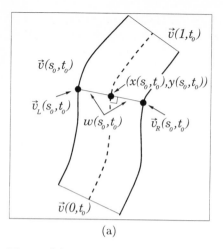 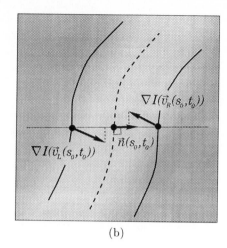

(a)   (b)

Fig. 1. (a) Parametric representation of the ribbon snake. Each slice of the ribbon $v(s_0, t_0)$ is characterized by its center $(x(s_0, t_0), y(s_0, t_0))$ and width $w(s_0, t_0)$. Center and width define points $v_L(s_0, t_0)$ and $v_R(s_0, t_0)$ corresponding to the left and right side of the ribbon. (b) Image gradients for the left and the right side and their projection to the ribbon's unit normal vector $n(s_0, t_0)$.

side (cf. Figure 1(b)). By this means the correspondence between the road sides and the sides of the ribbon is obtained. Using

$$P(v(s,t)) = (\nabla I(v_L(s,t)) - \nabla I(v_R(s,t))) \cdot n(s,t) \qquad (2)$$

for the image function, the expression for the total energy of the ribbon snakes remains identical with the correspondent formula for the energy of the original snake:

$$E(v) = - \int_0^1 P(v(s,t))ds + \frac{1}{2} \int_0^1 \alpha(s) \left| \frac{\partial v(s,t)}{\partial s} \right|^2 + \beta(s) \left| \frac{\partial^2 v(s,t)}{\partial s^2} \right|^2 ds. \qquad (3)$$

The first term of equation (3) represents the *image* energy and the second corresponds to the *internal* energy. $\alpha(s)$ and $\beta(s)$ are arbitrary functions which determine the influence of the geometric constraints on the optimization.

The application of the ribbon snakes to fully-automatic extraction requires that the balance between their *image* and *internal* energies has to be achieved automatically. Assuming the initial estimate of the ribbon to be close to the final solution, this can be enforced by substituting the functions $\alpha(s)$ and $\beta(s)$ in (3) with a factor λ [8]:

$$\lambda = \frac{|\delta E_{img}(v)|}{|\delta E_{int}(v)|}, \qquad (4)$$

where δ is the variational operator. This simplification avoids the manual adjustment of $\alpha(s)$ and $\beta(s)$. What is also important for the extraction is the ability to restrict and control the ribbon's motion during optimization. For this reason it is a good idea to "embed" the ribbon in a viscous medium and obtain the solution by minimizing the term $\int E(\boldsymbol{v}) + D(\boldsymbol{v})dt$, where D is the dissipation functional $D(\boldsymbol{v}) = \frac{1}{2}\int_0^1 \gamma(s)|\boldsymbol{v}_t|^2 ds$ with the damping coefficient γ. As shown in [8] the derivation of γ from

$$\gamma = \frac{\sqrt{2n}}{\Delta}\left|\frac{\partial E(\boldsymbol{v})}{\partial \boldsymbol{v}}\right| \tag{5}$$

ensures that the displacement of each vertex of the ribbon during one optimization step is on average of magnitude Δ. This property has shown to be very useful for automatic road extraction since changing the Δ, the search space for the hypothetical road sides can be directly controlled by a higher level program.

4 Road Extraction

4.1 Extraction of *Salient* Roads

According to model and strategy in Section 2, the first step is the extraction of lines in coarse scale [21]. However, as shown in Figure 2(a), there can be many other features with properties similar to roads which will be extracted as well. In order to separate them from the roads, i.e., to verify the roads, more evidence is required. In fine scale it is possible to determine the precise width of the structure corresponding to the line in coarse scale. Thresholding the variation of width along each hypothesis, irrelevant structures can mostly be eliminated since their width is much more unstable than the width of roads.

Following this idea the boundaries of the structures corresponding to the lines in coarse scale are extracted with ribbon snakes. For each detected line a ribbon is optimized. The initial position of the ribbons' centerlines coincide with the lines and the width is set to 0. In order to obtain a rough approximation of the searched boundaries the ribbons are firstly optimized in the images of coarse scale. Later, re-optimization in fine scale is performed to delineate the details of the boundaries. During optimization the width of the ribbons is expanded to ensure, that the sides of wide objects will be extracted as well.

As can be seen in Figure 2(b) the optimized ribbons which correspond to wrong road hypotheses have a stronger variation of width than the ribbons optimized at *salient* roads. Thus, thresholding the standard deviation of width for the short pieces of ribbons enables selection of ribbon's parts which correspond to roads with high probability (cf. Figure 2(c)).

4.2 Extraction of *Non-Salient* Roads

Typical reasons for gaps between *salient* roads are shadows or partial occlusions (cf. Section 2). To bridge the gaps, two adjacent ends of *salient* roads are connected with a road hypothesis which is then verified based on homogeneity and

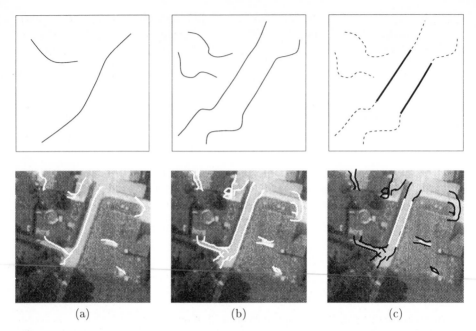

Fig. 2. Extraction of *salient* roads. (a) Extraction of lines (b) Optimization of ribbons' boundaries (c) Selection of ribbons' parts with constant width. Only the white ribbon is accepted as a correct hypothesis for a *salient* road.

the constancy of width (cf. Figure 3). The regions corresponding to the gaps show in many cases at least one traceable road side, although they may contain many other irrelevant edges which potentially disturb road extraction. However, as shown in Figure 3(a), the curvature of these edges is mostly much higher then the curvature of the road sides.

For each hypothesis a ribbon snake is initialized with its position, direction and width at its ends corresponding to the position, direction, and width at the end points of the adjacent *salient* roads (cf. Figure 4(a)). Since the initial approximation of the ribbon's centerline can be far away from the road's correct centerline, the optimization uses the "ziplock" method [17]. "Ziplock" method means that the information is gradually propagated from the ribbon's ends toward its center by optimizing only parts of the snake at a time while approaching the center. The curvature of the ribbon is constrained to be low. By this means, the "active" parts of the ribbon remain close to the road sides during the whole optimization (cf. Figure 4). At this point only the centerline of the ribbon is optimized and the width is fixed and equal to the average width of the *salient* roads at the ribbon's ends. Note, that due to the choice of the image function P in equation (2), the ribbon is insensitive to edges which cross perpendicular to its direction. This property is important because shadows and occlusions often

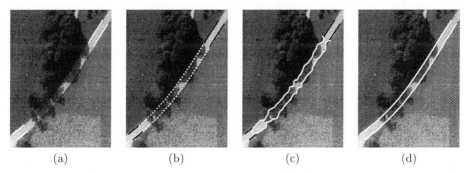

(a)   (b)   (c)   (d)

Fig. 3. Extraction of *non-salient* roads. (a) Selection of initial hypothesis (b) Extraction of optimal path; (c) Verification by optimization of width (d) Selection of hypothesis with constant width

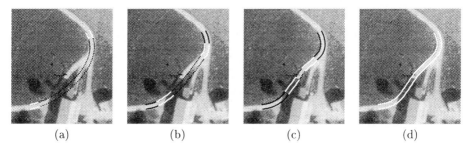

(a)   (b)   (c)   (d)

Fig. 4. Steps of the optimization of a "ziplock" ribbon. (a)-(c) Dotted lines indicate the passive part of the ribbon. White parts are currently optimized. Black ends indicate the result of the optimization so far. (d) Final result

result in this kind of edges. At the same time even weak contrast of road sides attracts the ribbon and supports correct road extraction.

Because it is not clear at this point which connections of adjacent ends of *salient* roads correspond to roads, there will always be wrong hypotheses. This implies that the result obtained in Figure 4(d) has to be verified. The verification is performed in two steps. Firstly, the homogeneity of the region in the image which corresponds to the ribbon is checked and ribbons with low variation of the image intensity are accepted as *non-salient* roads. This, however, will reject most of the shadowed and occluded roads and therefore a second step is taken: The centerlines of the ribbons are fixed and only the width is expanded and optimized. As shown in Figures 5(a,b), given a correctly located road hypothesis, the fixed centerline together with the contrast on one road side stops the expansion of the width at the right place. However, random features localized close to wrong hypotheses will in most cases result in a large variation of the width (cf. Figure 5(c,d)). This implies that wrong hypotheses can be rejected based on their high variation of the width.

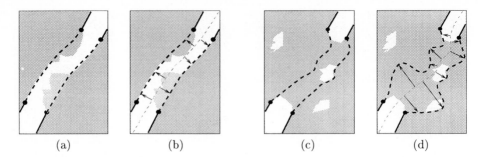

Fig. 5. Verification of hypotheses by expanding the width (a),(b) Verification of correct hypothesis. Since the ribbon's centerline in (b) is fixed, the contrast at only one side is enough to stop the expansion (c),(d) Verification of wrong hypothesis. Random features result in a big variation of the width (d).

4.3   Extraction of Crossings

The extraction of crossings is complicated since the variability of their shape makes it difficult to distinguish them from other objects. However, as shown below, the *salient* and *non-salient* roads greatly help to reduce the search-space.

In order to generate initial hypotheses for crossings, two observations are taken advantage of:

- During the extraction of *non-salient* roads most of the gaps in *salient* roads caused by crossings will be bridged (cf. Figure 4(d) and 6(a)).
- As exemplified in Figures 2(a) and 8(a), line extraction often results in junctions inside crossings. However, a big number of such junctions corresponds to irrelevant features.

Combining these two observations, crossings are hypothesized at junctions which are adjacent to previously extracted roads (cf. Figure 6(a)). Next, the outline of the crossing is approximated. A closed snake is initialized around the junction, its contour is expanded and optimized (cf. Figures 7(a)-(c), 6(b)). Based on this, as shown in Figure 6(c), the connections between the crossing and adjacent ends of roads are established and verified using the method of the previous Section. Finally, the crossing is accepted if at least one of the adjacent roads can be connected to it (cf. Figures 6(d), 7(d)).

The advantage of the chosen strategy is that it does not make restricting assumptions about the shape and the topology of the crossings. Therefore, crossings with different size connecting a varying number of roads can be extracted.

5   Results and Their Evaluation

Although the approach was developed for rural areas, a successful recognition is in some cases possible also in built-up areas (cf. Figure 8). As presented in

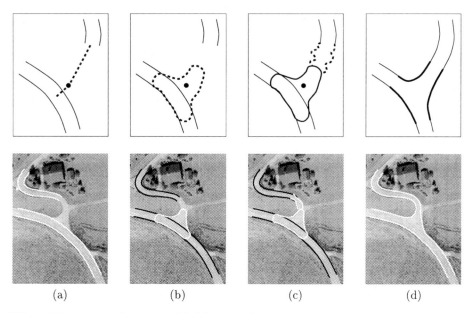

(a)   (b)   (c)   (d)

Fig. 6. Extraction of crossings (a) Selection of initial hypothesis (b) Approximation of the crossing's outline (c) Verification of connections to adjacent roads (d) Construction and connection of the crossing

Figure 8(a), line extraction alone will in most cases not detect all roads and can result in more wrong hypotheses than correct ones. However, using the proposed approach, all wrong hypotheses are eliminated and additionally gaps caused by shadows are bridged (cf. Figure 8(b)). Figure 9 shows the result for a larger scene. As can be seen, most of the roads are correctly delineated and connected into a network by the crossings. An evaluation of the results according to [10] is shown in Table 1 for the previous and two other images. The evaluation is based on the comparison of the extracted road centerlines to ground truth, i.e., manually plotted road axes used as reference. Figure 9 is a part of the image "Erquy", which can be described as "flat, agricultural, difficult", whereas the image "Marchetsreut" is "flat, agricultural, easy".

The "correctness" in Table 1 represents the ratio of the length of correctly extracted roads to the length of all extracted roads. The values prove that only a small number of false roads is extracted. "Completeness" corresponds to the ratio of the length of the correctly extracted roads and the length of the reference roads. Though the values for completeness are quite high for an automatic approach, they could have been even higher if forest and urban areas, where contrast on both road sides is weak, had been excluded from evaluation. The RMS values show that the precision is high and, most important, much better than demanded in most standards for topographic objects in GIS. For all three examples they are better than one pixel and close to the value which arises from

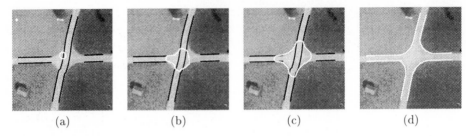

| | (a) | | (b) | | (c) | | (d) |

Fig. 7. Steps of the optimization of a crossing's outline (a) Initial state of the closed snake (b),(c) 10th and 20th step (d) Final result.

	Figure 9	Erquy	Marchetsreut
Correctness	0.97	0.95	0.99
Completeness	0.83	0.72	0.84
RMS [m]	0.46	0.46	0.37
Image size [pixel]	1800 · 1600	4500^2	2000^2
Time [min]	18	80	15

Table 1. Evaluation of results obtained by snake-based road extraction in images with a resolution of $0.5m$

the fuzzy definition of the road sides. The time for the extraction (Sun Sparc 20) is reasonable. It is mostly proportional to the size of the image. However, it also depends on the scene and the number of roads, or more specifically, lines in it. The more gaps there are due to shadows and other disturbances in the *salient* roads, the more time it takes to verify all probable connections during the extraction of the *non-salient* roads.

6 Outlook

This paper shows how by using snakes it is possible to take advantage of the little evidence in shadowed parts of the road or when one side of the road is occluded. This overcomes some of the problems of the recent approaches for road extraction. Nevertheless, the proposed approach is mostly restricted to rural areas. Therefore, the best idea would be to combine it with the assets of other approaches. These are particularly the modeling of the context in [2] or [18], the extraction of groups of cars to extract roads in urban areas of [19] and the use of GIS information in [3].

Acknowledgments

We would like to thank Wolfgang Eckstein, Tony Lindeberg, Carsten Steger, and Christian Wiedemann for many fruitful discussions.

 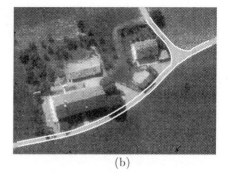

(a)   (b)

Fig. 8. Road extraction for a complicated scene (a) Line extraction (b) Final result

References

1. M. Barzohar, M. Cohen, I. Ziskind, and D.B. Cooper. Fast Robust Tracking of Curvy Partially Occluded Roads in Clutter in Aerial Images. In *Automatic Extraction of Man-Made Objects from Aerial and Space Images (II)*, pages 277–286, Basel, Switzerland, 1997. Birkhäuser Verlag.
2. A. Baumgartner, C. Steger, H. Mayer, and W. Eckstein. Multi-Resolution, Semantic Objects, and Context for Road Extraction. In *Semantic Modeling for the Acquisition of Topographic Information from Images and Maps*, pages 140–156, Basel, Switzerland, 1997. Birkhäuser Verlag.
3. G. Bordes, G. Giraudon, and O. Jamet. Road Modeling Based on a Cartographic Database for Aerial Image Interpretation. In *Semantic Modeling for the Acquisition of Topographic Information from Images and Maps*, pages 123–139, Basel, Switzerland, 1997. Birkhäuser Verlag.
4. J. Canny. A Computational Approach to Edge Detection. *IEEE Transactions on Pattern Analysis and Machine Intelligence*, 8(6):679–698, 1986.
5. M. de Gunst and G. Vosselman. A Semantic Road Model for Aerial Image Interpretation. In *Semantic Modeling for the Acquisition of Topographic Information from Images and Maps*, pages 107–122, Basel, Switzerland, 1997. Birkhäuser Verlag.
6. M.A. Fischler, J.M. Tenenbaum, and H.C. Wolf. Detection of Roads and Linear Structures in Low-Resolution Aerial Imagery Using a Multisource Knowledge Integration Technique. *Computer Graphics and Image Processing*, 15:201–223, 1981.
7. P. Fua. Model-Based Optimization: Accurate and Consistent Site Modeling. In *International Archives of Photogrammetry and Remote Sensing*, volume (31) B3/III, pages 222–233, 1996.
8. P. Fua and Y.G. Leclerc. Model Driven Edge Detection. *Machine Vision and Applications*, 3:45–56, 1990.
9. A. Grün and H. Li. Linear Feature Extraction with 3-D LSB-Snakes. In *Automatic Extraction of Man-Made Objects from Aerial and Space Images (II)*, pages 287–298, Basel, Switzerland, 1997. Birkhäuser Verlag.
10. C. Heipke, H. Mayer, C. Wiedemann, and O. Jamet. Evaluation of Automatic Road Extraction. In *International Archives of Photogrammetry and Remote Sensing*, volume (32) 3-2W3, pages 47–56, 1997.
11. M. Kass, A. Witkin, and D. Terzopoulos. Snakes: Active Contour Models. *International Journal of Computer Vision*, 1(4):321–331, 1987.

Fig. 9. Road extraction in larger image

12. I. Laptev. Road Extraction Based on Snakes and Sophisticated Line Extraction. Master thesis, Computational Vision and Active Perception Lab (CVAP), Royal Institute of Technology, Stockholm, Sweden, 1997.

13. T. Lindeberg. *Scale-Space Theory in Computer Vision.* Kluwer Academic Publishers, Boston, USA, 1994.

14. H. Mayer and C. Steger. Scale-Space Events and Their Link to Abstraction for Road Extraction. *ISPRS Journal of Photogrammetry and Remote Sensing*, 53:62–75, 1998.

15. D.M. McKeown and J.L. Denlinger. Cooperative Methods For Road Tracking In Aerial Imagery. In *Computer Vision and Pattern Recognition*, pages 662–672, 1988.

16. N. Merlet and J. Zerubia. New Prospects in Line Detection by Dynamic Programming. *IEEE Transactions on Pattern Analysis and Machine Intelligence*, 18(4):426–431, 1996.

17. W. Neuenschwander, P. Fua, G. Székely, and O. Kübler. From Ziplock Snakes to Velcro^{TM} Surfaces. In *Automatic Extraction of Man-Made Objects from Aerial and Space Images*, pages 105–114, Basel, Switzerland, 1995. Birkhäuser Verlag.

18. R. Ruskoné and S. Airault. Toward an Automatic Extraction of the Road Network by Local Interpretation of the Scene. In *Photogrammetric Week*, pages 147–157, Heidelberg, Germany, 1997. Wichmann Verlag.

19. R. Ruskoné, L Guigues, S. Airault, and O. Jamet. Vehicle Detection on Aerial Images: A Structural Approach. In *13th International Conference on Pattern Recognition*, volume III, pages 900–903, 1996.

20. S. Sarkar and K.L. Boyer. Integration, Inference, and Management of Spatial Information Using Bayesian Networks: Perceptual Organization. *IEEE Transactions on Pattern Analysis and Machine Intelligence*, 15(3):256–274, 1993.

21. C. Steger. An Unbiased Detector of Curvilinear Structures. *IEEE Transactions on Pattern Analysis and Machine Intelligence*, 20(2):113–125, 1998.

22. C. Steger, H. Mayer, and B. Radig. The Role of Grouping for Road Extraction. In *Automatic Extraction of Man-Made Objects from Aerial and Space Images (II)*, pages 245–256, Basel, Switzerland, 1997. Birkhäuser Verlag.

23. G. Vosselman and J. de Knecht. Road Tracing by Profile Matching and Kalman Filtering. In *Automatic Extraction of Man-Made Objects from Aerial and Space Images*, pages 265–274, Basel, Switzerland, 1995. Birkhäuser Verlag.

24. A. Zlotnick and P.D. Carnine. Finding Road Seeds in Aerial Images. *Computer Vision, Graphics, and Image Processing: Image Understanding*, 57:243–260, 1993.

A Model-Free Voting Approach for Integrating Multiple Cues

Carsten G. Bräutigam, Jan-Olof Eklundh and Henrik I Christensen

Computational Vision and Active Perception
Kungliga Tekniska Högskolan
S-100 44 Stockholm, Sweden
{carsten, joe, hic}@nada.kth.se

Abstract Computer vision systems, such as "seeing" robots, aimed at functioning robustly in a natural environment rich on information benefit from relying on multiple cues. Then the problem of integrating these become central. Existing approaches to cue integration have typically been based on physical and mathematical models for each cue and used estimation and optimization methods to fuse the parameterizations of these models.

In this paper we consider an approach for fusion that does not rely on the underlying models for each cue. It is based on a simple binary voting scheme. A particular feature of such a scheme is that also incommensurable cues, such as intensity and surface orientation, can be fused in a direct way. Other features are that uncertainties and the normalization of them is avoided. Instead, consensus of several cues is considered as non-accidental and used as support for hypotheses of whatever structure is sought for. It is shown that only a small set of cues need to agree to obtain a reliable output.

We apply the proposed technique to finding instances of planar surfaces in binocular images, without resorting to scene reconstruction or segmentation. The results are of course not comparable to the best results that can be obtained by complete scene reconstruction. However, they provide the most obvious instances of planes also with rather crude assumptions and coarse algorithms. Even though the precise extent of the planar patches is not derived good overall hypotheses are obtained.

Our work applies voting schemes beyond earlier attempts, and also approaches the cue integration problem in a novel manner. Although further research is needed to establish the full applicability of our technique our results so far seem quite useful.

Keywords: cue integration, grouping and segmentation, consensus voting, model-free.

1 Introduction

Our understanding of the fundamental principles of computer vision has increased considerably in recent years. Techniques incorporating sophisticated mathematical, physical and perceptual models provide an emerging theory of computational vision. Despite this, it is well-known that progress is slow when it comes to the development of robust *vision systems*, such as robots using vision to guide their actions, or other systems that use machine vision in real world situations. This has among other things lead to research in performance characterization, but such research does not address the problem of robustly functioning vision systems per se.

In formulating the goals for computer vision we often resort to the capabilities of biological vision systems, especially the human visual system: since *we* are capable of performing certain visual tasks in unstructured or unknown environments we expect machine vision systems to perform in a similar way. What is often not explicitly noted, though, is that the human system is able to capitalize on available information in an efficient way, since it runs a number of different processes in parallel. Hence, it can use information from e.g. luminance, color, shape, motion and stereopsis depending on what can be observed. The use, integration and selection of multiple cues is therefore an important problem to study in the context of computer vision systems.

It is characteristic that almost all of the research on cue integration has been model-based in the sense that a mathematical model for each of the cues is developed and a parametric approach is used for combination of the cues. Many of the fusion methods are based on underlying physical models or optimization theory, see for example Clark and Yuille (1990), and Bülthoff and Mallot (1987). Through application of mathematically well-defined models it becomes possible to apply standard mathematical techniques from estimation or optimization theory. Unfortunately it is often difficult if not impossible to verify or estimate the validity of the underlying mathematical/physical models. Moreover, such approaches assume that the estimated information measures are of commensurable types. Typically such methods have been used for surface reconstruction, fusing estimates of depth and surface orientation pointwise.

In this paper we investigate to what extent it is possible to use a model-free approach to cue integration. In a model free cue integration framework the cues are integrated without use of any mathematical model that relies on the underlying physical phenomena. This does not imply that each cue to be integrated cannot rely on a model. Actually it is difficult to imagine a cue estimator that does not utilize a model. However, the fusion of the different cues relies on simple combination of the different cues. The hypothesis is that such a technique allows reliable estimation of features given that a large number of estimates are available. The consensus among the estimates is considered to be more likely than the accidental co-occurrence of incorrect estimates. To verify this hypothesis voting techniques are used for fusion of different cues.

The paper is organized as follows. Initially the methodology of voting based fusion is outlined. It is then described how these voting techniques can be used for classification and cue estimation. Having presented the overall framework it is described how the methodology can be used for estimation of planar surfaces. A set of different cue estimators, available from our own work and in the literature is outlined and a simple integration technique is presented. It is demonstrated how improved performance is achieved for a number of different (complex) scenes. Finally the contributions are summarized and several issues for future research are outlined.

2   Voting Methods

Many different methods for integration of information have been suggested in the literature, as for example described in (Bloch, 1996) and (Lam and Suen, 1997). These method have primarily been used for pattern recognition. Voting methods has been used as a model-free approach to recognition. Within the domain of voting several possible approaches are outlined in (Parhami, 1994).

For integration of information there is a need for a common estimation/classification space Θ. One can then think of each cue estimator c as a mapping:

$$c : \Theta \rightarrow [0,1]. \tag{1}$$

The estimation space may for example be 3-space or the image plane. I.e., we can estimate the presence of a particular feature at a given location in the image, which for example is the approach used in many image segmentation methods.

In terms of voting there are several possible methods that can be used. If each, of the n, cue estimators (v_i) produce a binary vote for a single class (i.e. present or not present) a set of thresholding schemes can be used:

Unanimity: $\sum v_i(\theta) = n$
Byzantine: $\sum v_i(\theta) > \frac{2}{3}n$
Majority: $\sum v_i(\theta) > \frac{n}{2}$

If each cue estimator is allowed to vote for multiple classes, and the maximum vote is used to designate the final classification, the voting scheme is denoted consensus voting. I.e., the class θ' is chosen according to:

$$\delta(\theta') = \max\{\delta(\theta)|\theta \in \Theta\}. \tag{2}$$

Where δ is the combination method, which for example could be simple addition of the votes.

A general class of voting schemes, known as *weighted consensus voting*, is defined by

Definition 1 (m-out-of-n voting)
A m-out-of-n voting scheme, $V : \Theta \rightarrow [0,1]$, where n is the number of cue estimators, is defined in the following way:

$$V(\theta) = \begin{cases} \Lambda(c_1(\theta),...,c_n(\theta)) & \text{if } \sum_{i=1}^{n} v_i(\theta) \geq m; \\ 0 & \text{otherwise} \end{cases} \tag{3}$$

where

$$v_i(\theta) = \begin{cases} 1 \text{ if } c_i(\theta) > 0; \\ 0 \text{ otherwise} \end{cases} \quad \text{for } i = 1,...,n. \tag{4}$$

is the voting function and $\Lambda : [0,1]^n \rightarrow [0,1]$ is a function for combining the confidence for each estimator. □

A cue estimator can here give a vote for a given class, θ, if the output of the estimator is > 0. If m or more cues vote for a given class θ the value is estimated using the fusion method Λ. As an example multiple cues may be used for estimation of planarity. If more than m cues suggest the presence of a planar structure the orientation is estimated using Λ. The motivation for not using simple averaging is that the different cues might have different levels of uncertainty associated, these can be taken into account by the fusion operator Λ.

3   Cue Integration Using Fusion

In its most basic form cue integration can be carried out through simple majority or m-out-of-n voting. To accommodate this a common voting space must be set up. For image based cue integration it is convenient to use the image space. I.e., for each pixel the different estimators vote for a particular characteristic. In addition to spatial coordinates the space must also include dimensions corresponding to the possible outcomes. It is here important to note that cues can be divided into two categories.

Qualitative classes
Quantitative descriptors

For the qualitative cues the voting space is augmented by a dimension corresponding to the possible classes. For figure-ground segmentation the axes would be $(x, y, \{$figure, background$\})$. As different cues might provide different types of output it is here necessary to chose the lowest common denominator as the basis for the voting space. Each cue will then provide a binary vote specifying class membership. Subsequently the voting space is thresholded and the class membership is determined. For the quantitative estimators the voting space is augmented by dimensions corresponding to the cardinality of the parameter space.

One problem that must be observed is that it is not sufficient to use point based votes. Hence a cue estimator should provide a vote for the entire region that was used for computation of a cue as different cues otherwise migth vote at different locations in voting space which in the end might lead to non-robust output. In some situations it is further of interest to vote in a neighborhood of the determined cue position to ensure robustness. This is illustrated in Figure 1. If an estimate of the reliability of different cues is available, for example from empirical evaluation, it is possible to estimate the reliability of the integrated representation. For binary cue estimators each cue can be modeled as Bernoulli random variable. The combination of different cues can then be estimated by the combination

$$\sum_{i \geq m} \sum_{\Omega} P(V(v_1, v_2, \ldots) = i) \tag{5}$$

where Ω denotes possible combination of cues to achieve i-out-of-m votes. P denotes the corresponding probability. If the cues can be considered as independent and of equal reliability the sum turn into a cumulative binomial. The formula above can be used to demonstrate that voting based cue integration can improve reliability considerably even if a small number of cues are in agreement. The relationship between m-out-of-5

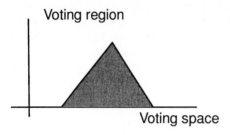
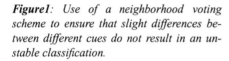

Voting region

Voting space

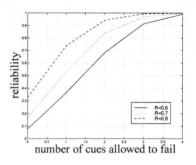

number of cues allowed to fail

Figure1: *Use of a neighborhood voting scheme to ensure that slight differences between different cues do not result in an unstable classification.*

Figure2: *Reliability as a function of the number of cue estimators that are allowed to fail. The reliability is plotted for the values 0.6, 0.7 and 0.8, respectively.*

voting and cue reliability is shown in Figure 2 It is here immediately obvious that good realiability can be achieved if only 2 out of 5 cues are in agreement, even if they on the average fail 60% of the time.

One disadvantage of the above approach is that the voting is carried out in a space that is common to all cue estimators. This implies that extra information that might be available from some of the estimators is discarded.

This problem can be circumvented by using a hierarchical approach. The voting space is now the super-set of the output from all estimators. Each estimator then carries out voting is a sub-set of the full voting space. An initial segmentation/classification is then again carried out in the common voting space, as outlined above. Once a classification has been performed the actual fusion is then carried out in the full space. The combination of different cues is here performed using the fusion operator Λ mentioned in Section 2.

Such an approach can for example be used for in motion estimation. Some of the cue estimators might only specify motion/stationary for different regions in the image, while others like optical flow might specify the perpendicular or full optical flow. Finally feature based approaches might indicate motion for particular features. All of these cue estimators will vote for motion/no-motion, but some of them will in addition vote for a particular velocity and direction of motion for each pixel/region. The initial classification is then performed to locate regions that might have moving objects. Subsequently the parametric information is fused using the fusion operator. The fusion might either be simple averaging. If confidence information is available for each of the cue estimators this might even be taken into account.

A third approach is to use (simple) binary cues for hypothesis generation. Once regions of interest have been hypothesized the richer cues can be used for a more detailed/accurate estimation.

4 Estimation of Planar Surfaces

The demonstration task that we have chose for the fusion process is to find planar surface regions in the image. This is by itself an important task especially in robot vision. By examining local depth and surface orientation cues in the images, the strength of the support from these local cues, the number of image points supporting it, and, above all, the number of different cues that support planarity, we rapidly generate hypotheses about planarity without actually reconstructing the surface or segmenting any image or surface.

In the present implementation we are using point based disparities in a multi-point matching framework, perspective distortion of texture pattern assuming weak isotropy, algebraic invariants of five matched points, grey level homogeneity, and monocular junction angles. We will now briefly describe these techniques.

4.1 Cue Estimation Methods

Junction estimation Line and junction finding is based on an edge detection algorithm with sub-pixel accuracy derived from an improved version of Canny's algorithm (Canny, 1986). The edges are post-processed by a polygonal approximation scheme (Bengtsson and Eklundh, 1991), and these polygons are then examined and junctions are extracted. Junctions are defined as intersections of (possibly extended) straight edge elements. Each junction is represented by two line segments and their intersection point. In cases where more than two edge elements meet at the same point, each edge pair is represented by one junction. Hence, in terms of the junction classification schemes proposed for instance by Sugihara (1986) and Malik (1987), our junctions are L-junctions. T-junctions and Y-junctions are represented by two and three L-junctions respectively.

Perspective distortion of texture patterns The basic principle of shape-from-texture is to use the observed perspective distortion of the texture pattern to estimate the parameters of the distorting transformation. We are using a two-dimensional *second moment matrix* for estimating local linear[1] distortion evaluating orientational disparities of local brightness patterns in the surface and its image, as defined in Lindeberg and Gårding (1993):

$$\mu_L(q) = \begin{pmatrix} \mu_{11} & \mu_{12} \\ \mu_{21} & \mu_{22} \end{pmatrix} = E_q \begin{pmatrix} L_x^2 & L_x L_y \\ L_x L_y & L_y^2 \end{pmatrix} = E_q((\nabla L)(\nabla L)^T)$$

where $L : \mathbb{R}^2 \to \mathbb{R}$ be the brightness image, $\nabla L = (L_x, L_y)^T$ and E_q denotes an averaging operator centered at $q = (x,y)^T \in \mathbb{R}^2$. E_q is defined as the local weighted mean using a Gaussian as a symmetric and normalized window function. We assume weak isotropy, i.e. that there is no single preferred direction in the surface texture, see Gårding (1993).

---

[1] As Gårding and Lindeberg (1996) showed, it is sufficient to consider the linear part of the perspective distortion to reconstruct properties of the surface and/or viewing geometry.

Homogeneous Intensity Distribution Barring shadows and specularities a planar uni-colored surface generally gives rise to a region in the image in which the intensity varies at most linearly along cross sections of the region. This is of course a rather crude indication of planarity but since it does provide the correct information in some cases it can be used as a weak cue in the spirit of our framework. To apply it we need a way to establish linear variation.

Using least squares to fit n data points $(x_i, y_i), i = 1..n$ to a model $y(x) = y(x, a_1...a_m)$ that has m adjustable parameters $a_j, j = 1..m$, means to

$$\text{minimize over } a_1..a_m: \qquad \sum_{i=1}^{n}(y_i - y(x_i; a_1..a_m))^2.$$

Supposing that each data point y_i has a measurement error that is independently random and distributed as a normal distribution around the "true" model of $y(x)$, and supposing that the standard deviations σ of these normal distributions are the same for all points, means that the least-square fitting is a maximum likelihood estimation of the fitted parameter. The maximum likelihood estimate of the model parameters is obtained by minimizing the quantity

$$\chi^2 = \frac{1}{\sigma^2} \sum_{i=1}^{n} y_i - y(x_i; a_1...a_m)^2.$$

In cases, where the uncertainties associated with the set of measurements are not known in advance, considerations related to χ^2 fitting may be used to derive a value for σ. Using the same assumptions, we can proceed by first assigning an arbitrary constant σ to all points, fitting the model parameters by minimizing χ^2 and finally recomputing

$$\sigma^2 = \frac{1}{n-m} \sum_{i=1}^{n}(y_i - y(x_i))^2. \tag{6}$$

Obviously, this approach prohibits an independent assessment of goodness-of-fit, however, at least some kind of measurement error can be assigned to the points.

In principle one could use analogous simple tests to find support for a regular textured planar patch. Such information exists in some of our experiments, but have not been used so far.

5-point invariant In the case that a set of 3D points, X_i i=1..n, lie on a plane, then without loss of generality, the z coordinate of X_i can be chosen as zero. The general projection between world and image then reduces to a 3x3 matrix, a *plane projective transformation*.

Eight parameters are required to define this 2D projective transformation matrix up to an arbitrary scale factor.

There are a number of algebraic invariants to plane projective transformations, like the cross-ratio of four points on a line, on five points, a conic and two points, or two conics (see Weiss (1988); Mundy and Zisserman (1992)). We are using five points to calculate algebraic invariants. Two functionally independent invariants can be constructed for five points X_i, i=1..n, in a plane, of which no three are co-linear

$$I_1 = \frac{|S_{134}||S_{125}|}{|S_{124}||S_{135}|}, I_2 = \frac{|S_{124}||S_{235}|}{|S_{234}||S_{125}|}$$

where $S_{ijk} = (X_i, X_j, X_k)$ with $X_i = (x_i, y_i, 1)^T$ and $|S|$ the determinant of S. These invariants are ratios of ratios of areas.

Disparity The disparity gradient depends on the viewing geometry and the local surface orientation. A reasonably accurate approximation of the disparity field depends on the shape of the surface. Introducing the small baseline approximation[2] the scene structure can be determined without knowing the viewing geometry up to a relief transformation. As the relief transformations preserves depth ordering, shape judgments such as planar–curved or convex–concave can be performed without resolving the relief ambiguity.

Planar patches in the world often have polygonal shapes, or partly polygonal boundaries. Hence they contain sets of L-junctions and these sometimes form right angles. This can be used as a cue in stereopsis in the following way. A corresponding pair of junctions defines one positional disparity (between the intersection points) and two orientation disparities (between the edge elements). In combination with partial information about the viewing geometry, this information is sufficient for computing the local surface orientation (see Wildes, 1991; Jones and Malik, 1992; Gårding and Lindeberg, 1994).

To solve the correspondence problem, i.e. to match the junctions in the left and right images, we use Pollard et al.'s (1985) PMF algorithm. This algorithm evaluates match candidates based on the support from neighboring match candidates that satisfy the *disparity gradient limit* constraint, which is motivated both by computational considerations and psychophysical findings about human binocular vision (see Burt and Julesz, 1980; Tyler, 1973).

We are using multi-point matching described in (Li, 1989) for matching single image points. Multi-point matching matches a group of points from one image to the other of a stereo pair at the same time. This group of points usually forms a regular grid in one image and most likely irregularly distributed corresponding points in the other image. These grid points are connected to each other by the finite element method via bilinear functions.

Using ML estimators for texture estimation When applying a shape-from-texture algorithms or any disparity-based method for calculation on the imaged scene structure, we assume that there is enough texture in the image (to find corresponding points etc.). If this is not the case, the calculations give none or *any arbitrary* result.

This can of course be determined by evaluating certainties of various sorts. A simple approach is to apply χ^2 fitting to detect the cases when there is no reasonable texture at a specific location in an image. We try to fit a plane to a set of points in the image and test the goodness-of-fit of the found plane parameters. The "measurement errors" given

---

[2] see Gårding and Lindeberg (1994)

by σ^2 (formula (6)) will give a direct indication how good the intensities really fit to the plane. If σ is small (approximately less than 6-8 pixels in our cases), it means that the intensity level changes linearly in a neighborhood and that there is no (or hardly any) texture in the image. This gives rise to the assumption that there is a uniformly colored planar surface in this region.

As a first step, we check the image points only along a line and try to fit a line to the image intensities. The goodness-of-fit is calculated using formula (6) with $M = 2$ and $y_i(x_i; a_1, a_2) = a_1 x_i + a_2$. Figure 3 shows examples.

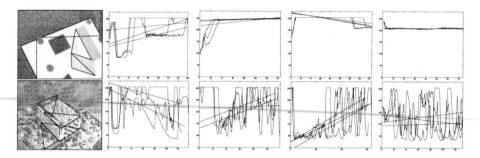

Figure3: *In these images shown to the left, 4 junctions have been selected and in their inside area checked for linear intensity changes. Each diagram shows the gray levels along the half-angle and a neighboring line to the left and right, as well as the least-square approximation of the intensities to a straight line. The linear approximation to the intensities result in very small errors in the first image, while the approximations are highly erroneous in the second image with its highly textured surfaces.*

4.2   Cue Integration

The general idea is a hypothesis-and-test approach which uses a quick and simple to compute cue exploiting local image data to get an idea whether a planar surface is seen in the image and at what location this surface is situated. Having found an indication, other cues will be used to support or reject the hypothesis. The results of the different cues are then combined. While coinciding results from different cues give strong support for the existence of a planar surface in the image, contradicting results are not that easy to interpret. Because each cue might give wrong results due to singularities, inconvenient input data or outliers, the cue selection and the subsequent combination of the results from different cues are essential.

We are using junctions for generating the hypothesis. Junctions in an image are in general good hints for planar surfaces in the vicinity, although they don't provide direct information about their location. The longer the legs of the junctions are, the more likely it is, that there is a planar surface adjacent to them due to the increased support for linearity and decreased support for an accidental view. The planar surface can be expected to lie between the two edges of a junction (i.e. enclosed by the smaller angle formed by the two legs), but it does not have to. Figure (4) shows where planar surfaces can be expected in the vicinity of a junction.

This way of generating hypotheses seems to be non-robust in the sense that it does only provide hypotheses when clear junctions are visible in the image. This is of course not valid for general images, but it proved to be sufficiently good for indoor scenes, where planes and objects are having clear straight boundaries typical for man-madde environments. Nevertheless, other hypothesis generation methods should be investigated in the future.

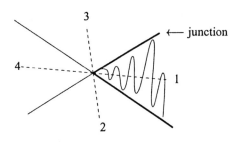

Figure4: *There are four convex regions in the vicinity of a junction where to look for planar surfaces (around the four dashed lines).*

Having the hypothesis, we examine local surface orientation cues in the image region of the hypothesis and classify the shape of the image region on the basis of the output of the cues. Like most other visual processes for computing shape, our cues are dependent on the availability of texture or visible surface markings. Neither multi-point matching (MPM) nor shape-from-texture (WSM) or algebraic invariants (5PT) can be computed reliably if there is no such information is available in the investigated region. Even though MPM and and WSM always give a surface orientation output, the results are unreliable if no texture information is available.

Therefore we first test in a rather crude way whether there may be texture information available in the investigated image or not. We use a maximum likelihood estimator as described in Section 4.1 to test the homogeneity of the intensity distribution in the image region. Having found that the least-square fit of a linear approximation of the intensities results in very small errors it is assumed that the intensity distribution in the investigated region is quite homogeneous and thus not enough texture information is available to reliably calculate other cues. In this case we do not calculated any further cue and have thus no further information about the shape of the image region.

The output of the different cues Each of the described cues gives an estimate of the planarity if the investigated image region. The estimation space is $\Theta = \{'yes - planar','no - not planar'\}$.

The investigated image region is then divided into several sub-patches. Multi-point matching is applied on each of these sub-patches and the resulting orientation estimates are compared. If they are clustering to one orientation the region is estimated as being planar else the hypothesis is rejected. The same approach is applied for the monocular shape-from-texture cue.

If junction pairs are available which appear to be right angles, the orientation is estimated for these pairs. If they are clustering to one orientation the region is estimated as being *planar*, else as *not planar*.

If there are five or more matched image points in the hypothesis region of which no three are linear dependent of each other, the algebraic five-point invariant of these points is calculated. The cue is voting for planarity if the two invariants are the same in the left and right image, else it is voting against planarity. If more than five points are available, at most n_{max} invariant pairs are tested on randomly chosen 5-tuples. The cue votes for planarity if at least one 5-tuple is found which invariants are equal in the right and left image, else it votes against planarity.

The ML texture estimator gives its output dependent on the "measurement error" σ (see formula 6) of a linear approximation of the intensities in the image region. Reasonable thresholds for σ dividing *reasonable texture available* from *not enough texture available* are lying in our examples between 8 and 15. In our experiments, we have set the threshold to 15, thus having $\sigma \geq 15$ results in a positive answer while $\sigma < 15$ results in *not enough texture available for further processing*.

The m-out-of-n voting scheme: For combining the visual cues, we were investigating several voting methods. The most simple method checked for rejections of the hypotheses only: if no cue rejects the hypothesis of a planar surface patch in the investigated region, the outcome of the voting scheme is in favor of the hypothesis. Figure 5a shows the result of this method testing 15 images with 63 generated hypotheses. Alltogether 69% of all hypotheses were classified correctly, but also 14% false alarms occured, where non-planar surface patches were classified as planar. Nevertheless the performance of this non-rejection method was better than the simple m-out-of-n voting scheme. The results of simple m-out-of-n voting method is shown in Figure 5b. At best we got 65% correct classifications with 19% false alarms. First with introducing the ML texture estimator and the assumption that no texture informtion is due to uniformly colored planar surfaces, the success rate went up to 80%. The results of these test are shown in Figure 5c.

Choosing a voting strategy is a trade-off, between high success rate and low false alarm rate. We chose the 2-out-of-4 voting with slightly less success rate (78%) but significantly lower false alarm rate (12%) than the 1-out-of-4 voting (success rate: 80%, false alarm rate: 19%).

5   Experimental Evaluation

Having collected the outcome of the different cues, we apply an m-out-of-n voting scheme as described in Section 2. The properties of this m-out-of-n voting scheme will be illustrated using several natural images of indoor scenes. We apply in all cases the voting scheme as described above with $n = 4$ cues and $m = 2$, i.e. we demand at leaast 2 out of four cues voting for planarity in order to reach a positive consent. The cue for initialising the hypothesis is not counted in this voting scheme.

The result of the first experiment is shown in Figure 6. The images (a) and (b) show the left an right images respectively. The extracted junctions can be seen in the images (c) and (d). Junctions with a length of less than 10 pixels are discarded in the calculations and are not seen in the images. Image (e) shows than the ten largest junctions (in area) found in the images. The regions described by these junctions are used as hypotheses for planar surface patches.

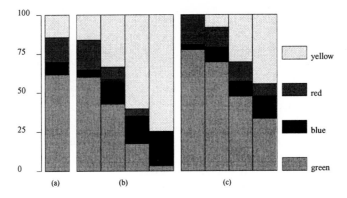

Figure5: *Different voting methods have been tested on 15 images with 63 generated hypotheses: Green and blue are the hypotheses, which are classified correctly as planar and not planar respectively, red and yellow are the hypotheses classified wrongly as planar and not planar respectively. Image (a) shows the results of the simplest 'no rejection' test. As soon as no cue votes against planarity of the hypothesis region, the voting mechanism outputs planarity. Image (b) shows the results of n-out-of 4 voting (for n = 1..4) and image (c) applies n-out-of-4 voting scheme under the consideration of the assumption that 'no texture is due to a uniformly colored planar surface'.*

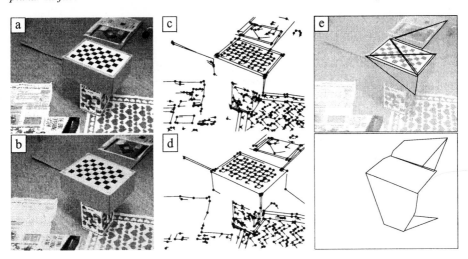

Figure6: *mxli/plan3: The images (a) and (b) show the left an right images respectively. The extracted junctions can be seen in the images (c) and (d). Image (e) shows than the ten largest junctions (in area) found in the images. The regions described by these junctions are used as hypotheses for planar surface patches. Image (f) is the result of combining the tested hypotheses: 3 different planar surface have been found.*

It is clearly visible that the most obvious planar surface are found by the hypothesis generation. The Table 1 shows that in all cases except one at least two cues supported

	mxli/plan3	
No.	the cues	voting
1	1011	1
2	1110	1
3	1011	1
4	1011	1
5	1011	1
6	1101	1
7	1001	1
8	0011	1
9	1000	0
10	1101	1

	TableSTV	
No	The cues	voting
1	0100	0
2	xxxx	x
3	xxxx	x

Table1: *mxli/plane3: The m-out-of-n voting scheme succeeds for all ten hypotheses. Hypothesis number 9, describing the front surface of the box, does not contain any textured pattern. The cues fail to give reliable results, but the ML texture estimator detects this case correctly.*

Table2: *TableSTV: The majority of cues votes against planarity in the first region and thus is the result of the voting process. In region 2 and 3 no voting takes place as the ML estimator indicates that there is not sufficient texture information available.*

the hypothesis and thus the voting gives a positive result. The case where the voting does not come to the conclusion of investigating a planar surface (junction number 9) is the junction describing the front surface of the box. This surface does not contain any textured pattern. This case is detected by the ML texture estimator and thus rejected from the voting procedure from the beginning. The assumption that no texture information indicates "most probably" a uniformly colored planar surface is true in this case.

The second experiment is an example where planar surfaces do not provide any texture information. The ML texture estimator classifies them correctly. In the plot below each region of Figure 7 you see the gray values along a cut through the region and it's approximation by a linear function. The goodness-of-fit of the linear approximation is expressed by the error σ^2 (see formula 6). Because regions (b) and (c) do not contain sufficient texture information, we do not proceed with further cues. They would not give reliable results due to this lack of information. We assume that no texture means uniformly colored planar surface. The voting on the outcome of the cues is the first region result in a correct negative answer, as shown in Table 2. This shows that we can detect whether there is sufficient intensity variation in the investigated image region and thus whether the applied cues can provide reasonable results. The voting scheme succeeds accordingly.

The assumption that missing texture information is due to a uniformly colored planar region is not generally true. The image in Figure 8 shows a counter example, where this assumption fails. We applied this assumption because in our experiments in man-made environments this was almost always true (the only exceptions were especially designed to fail here).

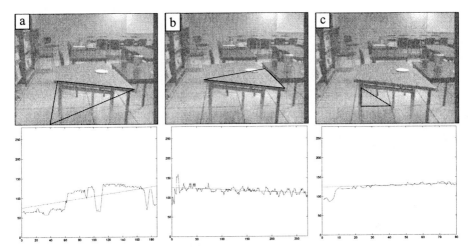

Figure7: *TableSTV: Three hypotheses for planar surfaces. The region in (a) is a coincidence junction from shadows, while the regions in (b) and (c) are part of planar surfaces. Looking at the texture information available in the regions, we see a remarkable difference: while the first region does contain intensity variations in the grey values, the second and third region do almost not.*

When investigating image regions which contain more than one planar surface, as for example in Image 9c, the results of the voting scheme get less reliable. The hypothesis in image 9c comprises two distinct but well established planar surfaces. The five-point invariant is point-based and is only testing for a pla-

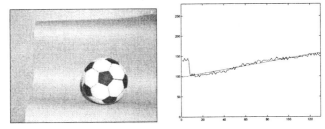

Figure8: *Baballe: An example where there is no texture information available in the image but the assumption is wrong, that this is due to a uniformly colored planar region.*

narity. If there are five points lying on one of the two visible planes, the cue will vote for planarity. The result of the m-out-of-n voting scheme is also in favor of the planar surface, even though it is wrong. Multi-point matching and shape-from-texture are testing for a common set of surface orientations in the image regions. The threshold for their majority based decision is in our experiments set to 2/3 (Byzantine majority); they should therefore vote against a single planar surface in most cases of multiple planar surfaces in a region. Tests on a series of images (see Figure 9 where together

13 hypothesis regions contained more than one planar surface resulted in four wrong classifications, i.e. the voting scheme voted four times wrongly for planarity.

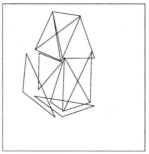

Figure9: *Image (b) shows the generated hypotheses for image (a). The hypothesis in (c) comprises two distinct planar surfaces.*

6 Summary and discussion

In this paper we have considered a model-free voting based approach to cue integration. It is motivated by the intent to develop vision systems, such as "seeing" robots, that are capable of functioning robustly in an unknown environment rich on information. In such a case the consensus between different sources of information tend to give reliable output, even if each source is based on crude assumptions and rather coarse algorithms.

Notably, it is quite common that visually observable structure or objects stand out from their environment in several ways, such as with regard to depth, surface orientation, speed, motion direction, color and luminance. For instance, depth or motion discontinuities often co-occur with reflectance, illumination and orientation discontinuities An approach like the one we use is well suited to such cases. It can in particular be applied when we want to recognize a certain type of structure, such as planar surfaces or prespecified motion patterns.

An approach of this type will of course never be as precise and powerful as more sophisticated methods for scene reconstruction and segmentation, e.g. using uncertainties. However, it can provide results when cues are incommensurable and it also avoids problems with normalizing the uncertainties obtained with different processes. This is of particular importance when there is no information at all about the cue. Moreover, the most obvious occurrences of the desired structure generally pop out, which is not always the case in conventional segmentation methods. Hence, an approach like this can be used to initialize other methods as well.

A number of problems remain to be studied in more depth. One is the use of probability maps, which would allow voting over the entire images. Calculations of surface orientation and depth can provide uncertainty measures that can be used for that. However, to derive probabilities for the more crude models we need to investigate the statistics of these cues in more detail.

Figure10: This image mask shows the result of segmenting out (in white) the main planar surface from Image 6 by using stereo disparities for hypothesis generation and calculating the plane projectivity between the calibrated left and right image for verification. For reference see Bräutigam et al. (1996)

Another problem concerns the initialization step: we have in this case used rather simple cues to form the first hypothesis. In an earlier paper (Bräutigam et al. (1996)) we relied on a stereo cue to form the first hypothesis (actually also with calibration). Stereo provides a much stronger hypothesis. As is shown in our experiments our simplistic initialization sometimes give comparable results, although with a worse segmentation (compare Figure 6 to the results of applying stereo disparities for hypothesis generation and calculating the plane projectivity between the calibrated left and right image for verification as seen in Figure 10). Further work will investigate the the relation between a weak and a strong initialization technique.

In summary, our results indicate that a voting scheme of the type we have used is effective provided that there is a reasonable number of cues that provide the needed information and that the underlying problem can be formulated in analogy to the plane finding problem. We have applied a number of seemingly complex algorithms, that were available to us. Hence the computations here are sometimes considerable. However, most of these algorithms can be replaced by methods based on the notion of a visual front-end (see Lindeberg (1995)) and therefore in fact also be made very fast.

Acknowledgment: The work by Carsten Bräutigam and Jan-Olof Eklundh has been supported by a grant from the Swedish Research Council for Engineering Science. The work by Henrik Christensen has been performed within the Center of Autonomous Systems, supported by the Swedish Foundation for Strategic Research. This support is gratefully acknowledged. We also like to thank INRIA-Syntim, and Roger Mohr for providing images used in this work.

References

Bengtsson, A. and Eklundh, J.-O. (1991). Shape representation by multiscale contour approximation, *IEEE Trans. Pattern Analysis and Machine Intell.* **13**: 85–94.

Bloch, I. (1996). Information combination operators for data fusion: A comparative review with classification, *IEEE transactions on Systems, Man, And Cybernetics, Part A: systems and humans* **26**(1): 42–52.

Bräutigam, C., Gårding, J. and Eklundh, J.-O. (1996). Seeing the obvious, *Proc. 13th International Conference on Pattern Recognition*, Vol. I, IEEE Computer Society Press, Vienna, Austria, pp. 67–72.

Bülthoff, H. and Mallot, H. (1987). Interaction of different modules in depth perception, *Proceedings of the First International Conference on Computer Vision*, pp. 295–305.

Burt, P. and Julesz, B. (1980). Modifications of the classical notion of panum's fusional area, *Perception* **9**: 671–682.

Canny, J. (1986). A computational approach to edge detection, *IEEE Transactions on Pattern Analysis and Machine Intelligence* **PAMI-8**(6): 679–698.

Clark, J. and Yuille, A. (1990). *Data fusion for sensory information processing systems*, Kluwer, Boston, Mass.

Gårding, J. (1993). Shape from texture and contour by weak isotropy, *J. of Artificial Intelligence* **64**(2): 243–297. Also ISRN KTH/NA/P--90/12--SE. Shortened version in Proc. 10th International Conference on Pattern Recognition.

Gårding, J. and Lindeberg, T. (1994). Direct estimation of local surface shape in a fixating binocular vision system, *in* J.-O. Eklundh (ed.), *Proc. 3rd European Conference on Computer Vision*, Vol. 800 of *Lecture Notes in Computer Science*, Springer Verlag, Berlin, Stockholm, Sweden, pp. 365–376.

Gårding, J. and Lindeberg, T. (1996). Direct computation of shape cues using scale-adapted spatial derivative operators, *International Journal of Computer Vision* **17**(2): 163–191.

INRIA-Syntim (1994, 1995, 1996). Stereo images.
    *http://www-syntim.inria.fr/syntim/analyse/paires-eng.html

Jones, D. and Malik, J. (1992). Determining three-dimensional shape from orientation and spatial frequency disparities, *in* G. Sandini (ed.), *Proc. 2nd European Conference on Computer Vision*, Vol. 588 of *Lecture Notes in Computer Science*, Springer Verlag, Berlin, pp. 661–669.

Lam, L. and Suen, C. Y. (1997). Application of majority voting to pattern recognition: An analysis of its behaviour and performance, *IEEE Trans. on Systems, Man And Cybernetics, Part A: Systems and Humans* **27**(5): 553–568.

Li, M. (1989). *Hierarchical Multi-point Matching with Simultaneous Detection and Location of Breaklines*, PhD thesis, Royal Institute of Technology, Department of Photogrammetry, S-100 44 Stockholm, Sweden.

Lindeberg, T. (1995). Direct estimation of affine deformations of brightness patterns using visual front-end operators with automatic scale selection, *Proc. 5th International Conference on Computer Vision*, Cambridge, MA, pp. 134–141.

Lindeberg, T. and Gårding, J. (1993). Shape from texture from a multi-scale perspective, *Proc. 4th International Conference on Computer Vision*, IEEE Computer Society Press, Berlin, Germany, pp. 683–691.

Malik, J. (1987). Interpreting line drawings of curved objects, *International Journal of Computer Vision* pp. 73–104.

Mundy, J. and Zisserman, A. (1992). *Geometric Invariance in Computer Vision*, MIT Press, Boston, MA.

Parhami, B. (1994). Voting algorithms, *IEEE Transactions on reliability* **43**(4): 617–629.

Pollard, S., Mayhew, J. and Frisby, J. (1985). PMF: A stereo correspondence algorithm using a disparity gradient limit, *Perception* **14**: 449–470.

Shakunaga, T. and Kaneko, H. (1988). Shape from angles under perspective projection, *Proc. 2nd International Conference on Computer Vision*.

Sugihara, K. (1986). *Machine Interpretation of Line Drawings*, MIT Press, Cambridge, MA.

Tyler, C. (1973). Stereoscopic vision: cortical limitations and a disparity scaling effect, *Science* **181**: 276–278.

Weiss, I. (1988). Projective invariants of shape, *Proc. IEEE Conf. Computer Vision and Pattern Recognition*, Vol. CVPR88, Ann Arbor, Michigan, June5-9, pp. 291–297.

Wildes, R. (1991). Direct recovery of three-dimensional scene geometry from binocular stereo disparity, *IEEE Trans. Pattern Analysis and Machine Intell.* **13**(8): 761–774.

Finding Boundaries in Natural Images:
A New Method Using Point Descriptors and
Area Completion

Serge Belongie and Jitendra Malik

Department of Electrical Engineering and Computer Sciences
University of California at Berkeley, Berkeley, CA 94720, USA
{sjb,malik}@cs.berkeley.edu

Abstract. We develop an approach to image segmentation for natural
scenes containing image texture. One general methodology which shows
promise for solving this problem is to characterize textured regions via
their responses to a set of filters. However, this approach brings with it
many open questions, including how to combine texture and intensity
information into a common descriptor and how to deal with the fact
that filter responses inside textured regions are generally spatially inhomogeneous. Our goal in this paper is to introduce two new ideas which
address these open questions and to demonstrate the application of these
ideas to the segmentation of natural images. The first idea consists of
a novel means of describing points in natural images and an associated
distance function for comparing these descriptors. This distance function
is aided in textured regions by the use of the second idea, a new process
introduced here which we have termed *area completion*. Experimental
segmentation results which incorporate our proposed approach into the
Normalized Cut framework of Shi and Malik are provided for a variety
of natural images.

1 Introduction

In this paper we study image segmentation, defined to be the process of partitioning the image into regions of coherent color, brightness, and texture. In
each region there may be smooth variation in the attributes due to shading and
texture gradients; segmentation should be tolerant to such variation.

There are several reasons why a satisfactory solution to image segmentation
for natural scenes has remained elusive. Perhaps the foremost of these is image
texture. Edge detection applied to natural images usually results in a tangled
web of edges, leaving the grouping problem to be addressed by processes that
might operate on such a representation. Approaches based on finding texture
boundaries will be reviewed in more detail later, but it is fair to say that such
algorithms have been demonstrated largely on synthetic collages of Brodatz texture patches.

The boundaries that we wish to find are those that separate coherent regions
from one another. These are, in general, different from the boundaries that separate an object from its background, or from another object, since objects are

often made up of several coherent regions. To find an object boundary, one must make use of a fairly specific model which encodes the knowledge of what components, coherent or not, constitute the object.

By no means does this imply, however, that boundaries of coherent regions are easy to find. The difficulties in this task principally arise from the need to quantify the notion of perceptual coherence for image texture. One general methodology which shows promise for solving this problem is to characterize textured regions via their responses to a set of filters. However, as discussed in the next section, this approach brings with it many open questions, including how to combine texture and intensity information into a common descriptor, and how to deal with the fact that filter responses inside textured regions are generally spatially inhomogeneous. Our goal in this paper is to introduce two new ideas. The first idea consists of a method of describing texture via the filter outputs computed at a "point" and a means of including intensity and/or color information in the same point descriptor. The second idea addresses the problem of inhomogeneity of the filter responses in textured regions through the use of *area completion*, which is analogous to contour completion.

The organization of this paper is as follows. In section 2 we discuss other relevant work in the area of texture segmentation in relation to our approach. In section 3 we introduce a novel means of describing "points" in natural images and an associated distance function for comparing these descriptors. The process of area completion is then discussed in section 4. In order to apply this new distance function to the problem of finding boundaries, we need a grouping criterion. For this purpose we appeal to the *Normalized Cut* approach of Shi and Malik [25], discussed in 5. Experimental results using Normalized Cuts for region segmentation and edge detection are presented in Sections 5.1 and 5.2. We conclude and discuss future work in section 6.

2   Related Work

Since the early 1980s, many approaches have been proposed in the literature which employ *filter-based* descriptions of texture [17, 26, 15, 21, 22, 4, 3]. By the term *filter-based* we mean that the fundamental representation for a pixel in an image includes not only its intensity or color information, but also the inner product of the neighborhood centered on that pixel with a set of filters tuned to various orientations and spatial frequencies.

As discussed for example in [16, 19], vectors of filter responses have many appealing properties, including relationships to physiological findings in the primate visual system [8] and to the basic mathematical notion of a Taylor series expansion.

As rich as the information provided by these filter response vectors may be, a number of complications arise when one tries to use them for segmenting regions in natural images. Unlike intensity and color descriptors for a smooth image region, filter response vectors in a patch of coherent texture cannot be expected to simply pool together into a tight cluster in feature space, where the only variance is due to noise and measurement error. Rather, such a pool of feature vectors is bound to contain representatives from many different distinctive points throughout what may be called an "element" of the texture, or "texel." For example, assuming the filtering scale is not excessively large, filter responses computed at the center of a polka dot are quite different from those computed at the edge of a polka dot. (This is illustrated in Figure 2.)

Another way of saying this is that it is intrinsic to the nature of filter-based approaches that the filter responses will vary from one point to the next inside a region of coherent texture. The responses will of course vary from one point to the next inside incoherent regions, as well; what makes these two situations different, of course, is whether or not the variation exhibits a certain regularity.

Pervasive throughout the literature has been the use of profuse spatial averaging, which serves in one way or another to beat down the feature vectors until they become homogeneous [15, 21, 6]. Although the use of quadrature filter pairs [17, 11] allows for certain kinds of spatial texture variation to appear as a phase factor, this component is often discarded in favor of the quadrature energy [17, 3, 12] . Other approaches [20] seek to select a local scale at each pixel as a preprocessing step, so as to disallow the very extraction of any feature vectors which may be spatially inhomogeneous.

The price paid for these averaging approaches is that the richness of the descriptors is lost. Less damaging in this sense is the use of histogramming inside local patches [13, 28, 23] which does a much better job of preserving the local empirical feature distribution, though local spatial information is discarded for the sake of obtaining spatial homogeneity. Whether histogramming or simply averaging, however, all of these methods rely on the use of local windows or *patches*, which are naturally quite problematic around region boundaries.

It is worth noting that the ill effects of the use of patches are unlikely to arise in segmentation experiments on Brodatz mosaics [3, 23, 15]. The piecewise-coherent nature of such images can artificially induce clustering behavior in the feature space since, due to a lack of shading and perspective effects, there is not enough real-world variation present to challenge the cluster decision regions. This is particularly true when the texture cut-outs in the mosaic are squarish, lacking narrow or irregular regions, especially when the pixel coordinates are thrown into the clustering machinery.

One of the points we wish to put forward in this work is that profuse averaging of texture descriptors is both damaging and unnecessary. It is our view that a filter-based approach can succeed without appealing to unduly large scales if one properly exploits the behavior of feature response vectors in regions of coherent texture. We feel that the proper domain for a filter-based approach is that of describing *points*. Here we use the term *point* in the sense used by Koenderink and Van Doorn in [18] and [19], i.e., a small Gaussian point spread, at a sub-texel scale. The concept of *area completion* introduced in this paper is a step toward what we believe to be a proper treatment of point descriptors and thereby of filter-based texture segmentation in general.

A challenge which is met along the way is the problem of how to encode intensity alongside the filter responses. In the following section, we argue against appending intensity onto the filter response vector as a single scalar value; though it may seem intuitive since intensity is captured by the "zero-frequency" filter, it is in fact on a completely different scale from tuned texture filters. In order to be placed on equal footing with the texture filters, it must be represented in a compatible way. In section 3.2 we present one such solution.

3 Representing Texture and Intensity in the Same Feature Vector

In this section, we introduce a new method for describing and comparing points in an image. As discussed in the preceding section, we use the term "point" to refer to a small local neighborhood. Our approach is motivated by what one is likely to find at a randomly selected point in a natural image. The filter set described below allows us to characterize oriented edge or bar fragments, small spots, and some simple junction types; this accounts for a large share of the local structure one can expect to find in natural images. When such structure is absent, however, the best descriptor for a point is simply its color, or for grayscale images, its intensity.

Since there exists a continuum across these different point types, it is important that the *point descriptor* gracefully adapt to whichever form of description is most appropriate. The intensity encoding we propose in section 3.2, together with the normalization step described in the following section, represents one means of obtaining a point descriptor with this desirable property. We will also see that the format of the point descriptor described here admits the definition of a simple distance measure, described in 3.4, which allows us to measure similarity in a consistent manner for both textured and non-textured points.

3.1 Linear Filters for Texture Description

The filter set used in our experiments, depicted in Figure 1, is composed of zero-mean difference of Gaussian (DOG) and difference of offset Gaussian (DOOG) kernels. This choice of filters is similar to those used in [21], except that we use only one scale and we include odd-symmetric (edge-sensitive) oriented kernels. Each filter is divided by its L_1 norm in order to equalize the dynamic range across the filter set.

The vector of filter responses to an image I is defined as

$$\mathbf{u}_{tex} = (f_1 * I, f_2 * I, \ldots, f_{N_F} * I)^T$$

where in our case $N_F = 14$. Note that relative to the dimensions of our test images, which are 128×192, all of the filters reside at a fine scale.

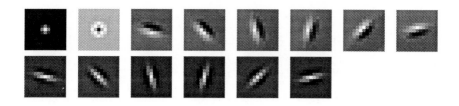

Fig. 1. Impulse responses of the filters f_1 through f_{14}, numbered left to right, top to bottom. Each kernel, which is of size 13×13, has been divided by its L_1 norm. f_1 are f_2 are DOG2 and DOG1 filters, respectively; f_3 through f_8 are DOOG1 filters; f_9 through f_{14} are DOOG2 filters. The oriented kernels are spaced at $30°$ increments, and have been offset by $15°$ to make quantization error more evenly distributed across the different orientations.

3.2 Intensity Value Encoding

In order to represent intensity alongside the components of the filter response vector, we make use of a "soft binning" of the intensity axis. Specifically, we encode the intensity I by the values taken on by N_I equally spaced Gaussians $g_k(I)$ on the interval $[0, 1]$.

The functions $g_k(I)$ are given by

$$g_k(I) = Ce^{-(I-\mu_k)^2/2\alpha^2}, \qquad k = 1, \ldots, N_I$$

where

$$\mu_k = \frac{k-1}{N_I - 1}, \qquad \alpha^2 = \frac{1}{2N_I^2}$$

The variance is chosen so as to make the sum of the N_I Gaussians approximately uniform on $[0, 1]$. The constant C is set to 0.1 so as to approximately match the dynamic range of the texture components.

The intensity feature vector is defined as

$$\mathbf{u}_{int} = (g_1(I), g_2(I), \ldots, g_{N_I}(I))^T$$

In our experiments we use $N_I = 10$. Thus, for a value of $I = 0.5$, the $k = 5$ and $k = 6$ components will "fire" strongly while the rest of the components will be quite small.

This representation is an example of a *value encoding*, as opposed to a *variable encoding*, in the sense discussed in [2]. In this manner, an intensity of 0.1 is held in as high a regard as an intensity of 0.9; each has its own place on the number line, and the former should not be viewed as a weak or low-magnitude version of the latter. Value encodings in this sense have been widely accepted in the context of filter orientation and scale, with various filters occupying different points on the frequency plane. It is natural therefore that a similar encoding be used for points on the intensity axis. An immediate benefit of this "equal-footing" representation is the appealing interpretation it lends to the normalization of the combined texture/intensity feature vector; this is discussed next.

3.3 Normalization

The complete feature vector at pixel i and the normalized feature vector are defined as

$$\mathbf{u}_i = (\mathbf{u}_{tex,i}^T, \mathbf{u}_{int,i}^T)^T, \qquad \hat{\mathbf{u}}_i = \frac{\mathbf{u}_i}{\|\mathbf{u}_i\|_2}$$

respectively. Since the L_2 norm of $\mathbf{u}_{int}$ is approximately equal to a constant, which we will refer to as β, we can also express $\hat{\mathbf{u}}_i$ as

$$\hat{\mathbf{u}}_i = \frac{\mathbf{u}_i}{\sqrt{\|\mathbf{u}_{tex,i}\|_2^2 + \beta}}$$

Thus we may think of the normalization step as a form of gain control, which diminishes the contribution of the intensity components when there is a lot of activity in the texture components. This can be related to the model of local gain control in primary visual cortex simple cells discussed in [5].

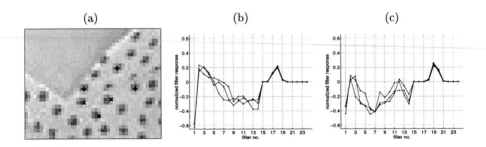

Fig. 2. Examples of normalized feature vectors for selected points in (a). Feature vectors from spot centers, marked by +'s, and spot edges, marked by x's, are plotted in (b) and (c), respectively. Components 1-14 correspond to the texture filter responses, where the numbering is consistent with that in Figure 1. The remaining 10 components correspond to the intensity value encoding.

3.4 Distance Measure

We define the distance between two normalized feature vectors $\hat{\mathbf{u}}_i$ and $\hat{\mathbf{u}}_j$ as

$$d^2(\hat{\mathbf{u}}_i, \hat{\mathbf{u}}_j) = (\hat{\mathbf{u}}_i - \hat{\mathbf{u}}_j)^T \Sigma^{-1} (\hat{\mathbf{u}}_i - \hat{\mathbf{u}}_j) \tag{1}$$

where the covariance matrix is given by

$$\Sigma = \mathrm{diag}(\underbrace{1, \ldots, 1}_{N_F}, \underbrace{\sigma_I^2, \ldots, \sigma_I^2}_{N_I})$$

The value of σ_I^2 represents the tolerance allowed on differences in the intensity components relative to those in the texture components. Its value was chosen empirically according to the following heuristic: distances inside regions possessing perceptually equivalent coherence should be as similar as possible, whether those regions be uniformly gray or uniformly textured. By observing distances within uniform regions of "clear sky" and "zebra stripes," to name two examples, we arrived at the value $\sigma_I^2 = 0.01$.

4 Area Completion

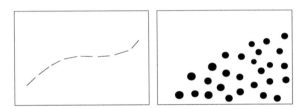

Fig. 3. Comparison of contour completion and area completion. Shown on the left is a set of disconnected contour fragments. These are readily grouped into a single smooth contour. In this process, the gaps, which locally bear no resemblance to the fragments, are assimilated into the final grouping when the "sum of the parts" is brought to bear. With area completion, the basic idea is the same. This is illustrated using the stylized polka dot texture boundary shown on the right. The grouping bridges the gaps between the dots and the area is completed.

The basic motivation behind area completion comes from the related process of contour completion. The latter problem is illustrated in Figure 3, left, by a set of disconnected contour fragments. We readily group the fragments together into a single contour [27]. In this grouping process, one implicitly absorbs the gaps between the fragments into the final smooth, continuous contour: the contour is completed. Conversely, we might conceive that the grouping takes place among the gaps, which then assimilate the fragments into the final contour. Of course the former interpretation is more readily apparent, but the latter highlights an important fact. This fact is that two kinds of elements, which locally bear negligible similarity, can become members of the same group, and thereby similar to one another, when the "sum of the parts" is taken into account.

The process of area completion logically extends this idea to 2D patterns, or in our context, to textures. The idea is the same: if two points are highly similar in terms of proximity and similarity, then they and that which is between them most likely belong together, as well. Figure 3, right, illustrates this idea with a stylized polka dot texture boundary.

Both contour completion and area completion rely on the statistics of the real world. In the case of contour completion, the relevant statistics pertain to the fact that object *boundaries* tend to be smooth and continuous. In the case of area completion, we appeal to the tendency for object *surfaces* to be smooth and continuous.

We shall operationalize this idea shortly. We wish to emphasize that the approach described here represents a departure from the practice of studying texture via large patches centered on pixels. Rather, we advocate an approach based on local computation of similarity, and the judicious propagation of this similarity along lines between matching points according to the process of area completion.

4.1 Explanation of Algorithm

The area completion algorithm begins with the computation of connection weights between pixel pairs in the $M \times N$ image I. A "weight" in this context refers to a monotonically decreasing function of $d(\hat{u}_i, \hat{u}_j)$, such as a Gaussian. (A specific choice of weighting function is given in Equation (3).)

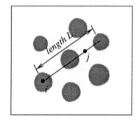
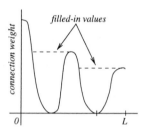

Fig. 4. Illustration of area completion. On the left, two pixels i and j in a textured image patch are depicted along with a line segment of length L starting at pixel i and passing through pixel j. A profile of hypothetical connection weights between pixel i and the pixels along this line segment is plotted on the right. The position of pixel j is indicated by a tick mark on the abscissa. Initially, the connection weight from pixel j to pixel i is zero. After area completion, this weight is updated to the maximum weight found along the line segment between j and the point at L. As indicated by the dashed lines, this procedure is equivalent to a "flood fill" operation on the original solid curve.

The area completion step is illustrated in Figure 4. Consider a line segment of length L extending from pixel i through pixel j. The solid curve in the plot on the right illustrates a hypothetical profile of connection weights for pixels along the line segment to pixel i. As indicated in the plot, the original connection weight from pixel j to pixel i is zero.

The connection weight from pixel j to pixel i after area completion is shown by the dashed curve: it is equal to the maximum over the weights between pixel j and the pixel at the far end of the line segment. This process is illustrated for a patch of real texture in Figure 5.

Let the matrix $\tilde{\mathbf{W}}$ denote the set of connection weights over all i and j after the area completion step. In general, $\tilde{\mathbf{W}}$ will be asymmetric. This arises from the fact that different points within a texture have varying amounts of distinctiveness. For example, the connection weight from one spot center to another spot center in Figure 4 is likely to be greater than the weights between pixels located elsewhere.

$\tilde{\mathbf{W}}$ can be made symmetric in a number of ways, including reassigning it as the maximum or minimum of $\tilde{\mathbf{W}}$ and $\tilde{\mathbf{W}}^T$, computed component-wise. In general, it is most appropriate to use the maximum since this choice automatically favors the weights contributed by the most distinctive elements.

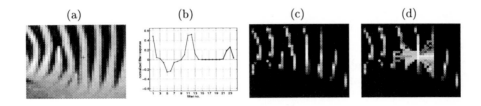

Fig. 5. Illustration of the area completion step applied to a patch of zebra texture. The point descriptor (feature vector) for the pixel marked in (a) is plotted in (b). Components 1-14 correspond to the texture filter responses, where the numbering is consistent with that in Figure 1. The remaining 10 components correspond to the intensity value encoding. The raw connection weights from each pixel in the image to the pixel marked in (a) are shown in (c), where the pixel intensity is proportional to the weight strength. The point descriptor for the marked pixel is highly similar to those found along other vertical white stripes, but is highly dissimilar to those found elsewhere. The connection weights to the marked pixel after area completion (out to a radius of $L = 10$) are shown in (d).

5 Normalized Cuts

The normalized cut approach frames the task of image segmentation as a graph partitioning problem, wherein each vertex represents a pixel and each edge represents a connection weight between two pixels. The term *normalized cut* actually refers to a criterion for measuring the goodness of a putative graph partition. This criterion, abbreviated as $NCut$, is related to the graph-theoretic notion of a *cut*. It is shown in [25] that, in the context of perceptual grouping, the minimum-$NCut$ criterion leads to partitions which are preferable to those offered by the standard minimum-*cut* criterion.

Consider the graph $\mathbf{G} = (V, E)$ with vertices V, edges E, and weighted adjacency matrix $\mathbf{W}$. We may think of the weights W_{ij} which comprise $\mathbf{W}$ as a measure of similarity between pixels (i.e. vertices) i and j. Since the weights are symmetric, we say that $\mathbf{G}$ is an *undirected graph*. Let A and B represent two disjoint sets on $\mathbf{G}$, $A \cup B = V$, $A \cap B = \emptyset$, obtained by removing the edges connecting the two sets. These sets may represent, for example, pixels on the tiger skin and pixels on the pond background, respectively, in the tiger image in Figure 8. The normalized cut for (A, B) is a function of the *cut* between A and B and the *association* between A and B, as given by the expression

$$NCut(A, B) = \frac{cut(A, B)}{assoc(A, V)} + \frac{cut(A, B)}{assoc(B, V)}$$

where

$$cut(A, B) = \sum_{i \in A, j \in B} W_{ij}$$

and

$$assoc(A, V) = \sum_{i \in A, j \in V} W_{ij}, \qquad assoc(B, V) = \sum_{i \in B, j \in V} W_{ij}$$

As shown in [25], an approximation to the partition that minimizes the normalized cut criterion can be found by solving

$$(\mathbf{D} - \mathbf{W})\mathbf{v}_k = \lambda_k \mathbf{D} \mathbf{v}_k \tag{2}$$

for $\mathbf{v}_2$, the generalized eigenvector corresponding to the second smallest eigenvalue λ_2, where $\mathbf{D}$ is the diagonal matrix of total connection weights given by $D_{ii} = \sum_j W_{ij}$.

Since $\mathbf{v}_2$ is real-valued, it represents a soft assignment of pixels to the sets A and B. Similarly, successive eigenvectors suggest further partitioning of A and B into smaller groups. To transform this soft information into a more final result, one can proceed in two general directions: that of recursive thresholding to produce regions, and that of combining information from across the eigenvectors to produce edges.

5.1 Region Segmentation

The recursive thresholding procedure used in [25] proceeds as follows. First, 10 equally spaced values are considered between the maximum and minimum values in $\mathbf{v}_2$. Next, $\mathbf{v}_2$ is split into two groups using each threshold, thus resulting in 10 different choices for the sets A and B. The winner is then declared as the one for which $NCut(A, B)$ is a minimum. If K eigenvectors are found, then the above thresholding procedure can be run recursively within each partition until the $NCut$ value exceeds a threshold.[1]

In our implementation of the above described algorithm, we have used the following Gaussian weighting function,

$$W_{ij} = \begin{cases} e^{-d^2(\hat{u}_i, \hat{u}_j)/2} & \text{if } \|\mathbf{x}_i - \mathbf{x}_j\| < R \\ 0 & \text{otherwise} \end{cases} \tag{3}$$

---

[1] Note that the maximum $NCut$ value is 2, since in Equation (5), *cut* is always less than or equal to *assoc*.

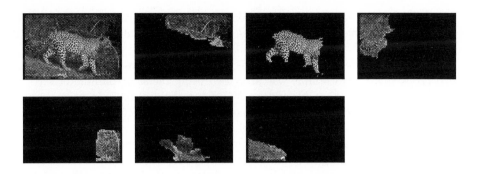

Fig. 6. Segmentation of leopard scene. Please refer to text for parameter settings.

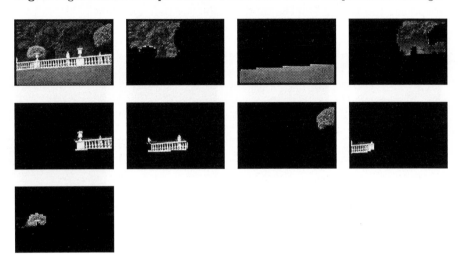

Fig. 7. Segmentation of landscape, with parameter settings as in Figure 6.

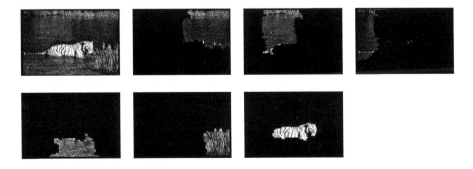

Fig. 8. Segmentation of tiger scene, with parameter settings as in Figure 6.

where $d^2(\hat{\mathbf{u}}_i, \hat{\mathbf{u}}_j)$ is as given in Equation (1), and $\mathbf{x}_k$ represents the coordinates of pixel k. Note that $\mathbf{W}$ will be sparse as a result of the distance threshold at radius R.

Our results are shown in Figures 6–10. The test images are all grayscale, of size 128×192. Each example was processed using the same parameter settings of $L = 10$, $R = 16$, $K = 14$, and an $NCut$ threshold of 0.07. In order to save memory, the connection weights were subsampled by a factor of 3 with respect to each dimension of the original image.

We used the Matlab function eigs.m to solve the eigenvalue problem using the area-completed weights $\tilde{\mathbf{W}}$ in place of $\mathbf{W}$ in Equation (2).[2]

In each figure, the original image is shown at the top left, followed by a set of masked-out partitions found using the technique described above. The segmented regions are sorted in descending order according to area; segments comprising less than 2% of the total possible area are not shown.

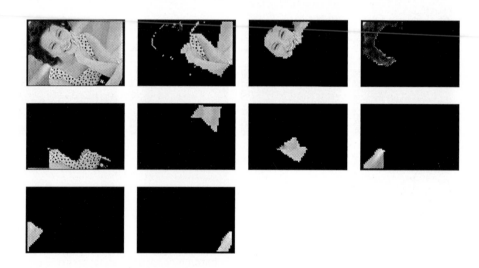

Fig. 9. Segmentation of person with parameter settings as in Figure 6.

5.2 Combined Brightness/Texture Edge Detection Using the Inter-Group Distance

As discussed in the introduction to this section, the Normalized Cut algorithm requires the solution of a generalized eigensystem involving the weighted adjacency matrix. In this section, we consider a physical interpretation of this

---

[2] eigs.m uses Arnoldi iteration, which reduces to Lanczos iteration since $\tilde{\mathbf{W}}$ is symmetric. The processing time for this operation is approximately 2 minutes on an HP J200/9000 using a convergence tolerance of 1e-10.

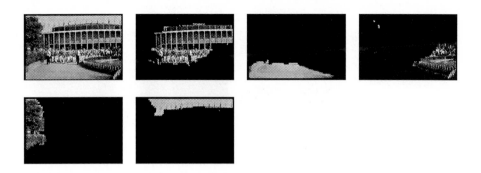

Fig. 10. Segmentation of building scene with parameter settings as in Figure 6.

eigensystem which leads to a new measure of "edginess" that we call *inter-group distance*.

The inter-group distance idea arises from the connection between generalized eigensystems and the analysis of mechanical vibrations in mass-spring systems[7, 10]. One can readily verify that the symmetric positive semidefinite matrix $(\mathbf{D} - \mathbf{W})$, known in graph theory as the *Laplacian* of the graph $\mathbf{G}$, corresponds to the *stiffness matrix* while the diagonal positive semidefinite matrix $\mathbf{D}$ represents a *mass matrix*. These matrices are typically denoted by $\mathbf{K}$ and $\mathbf{M}$, respectively, and appear in the equations of motion as

$$\mathbf{M}\ddot{\mathbf{x}}(t) = -\mathbf{K}\mathbf{x}(t)$$

If we assume a solution of the form $\mathbf{x}(t) = \mathbf{v}_k \cos(\omega_k t + \phi)$, we obtain the following generalized eigenvalue problem for the time-independent part,

$$\mathbf{K}\mathbf{v}_k = \omega_k^2 \mathbf{M}\mathbf{v}_k$$

in analogy to Equation (2).

The intuition is that each pixel represents a mass and each connection weight represents a Hooke spring constant. If the system is shaken, tightly connected groups of pixels will tend to shake together.

In light of this connection, the generalized eigenvectors in Equation (2) represent normal modes of vibration of an equivalent mass-spring system based on the pairwise pixel similarities.[3] When the system is excited, the resulting motion may be expressed as a superposition of the modes, with each mode weighted by a sinusoidal time-dependent term times some constant,

$$\mathbf{x}(t) = \sum_k \alpha_k \mathbf{v}_k \cos(\omega_k t + \phi)$$

where ω_k is equal to $\sqrt{\lambda_k}$ in Equation (2). A few eigenvectors for the test image of Figure 7 are shown in Figure 11, together with a snapshot of $\mathbf{x}(t)$.

---

[3] Note that since we assume free boundary conditions around the edges of the image, we ignore the first mode since it corresponds to uniform translation.

(a) (b) (c) (d)

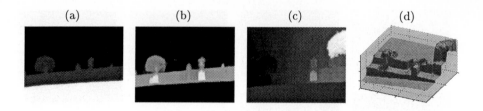

Fig. 11. Three generalized eigenvectors ($\mathbf{v}_2$, $\mathbf{v}_3$ and $\mathbf{v}_4$) for the landscape test image are shown in (a)-(c), reshaped as images. As an illustration of the connection between Normalized Cuts and the analysis of mass-spring systems, a superposition of the modes at an arbitrary time instant is shown in (d) as a surface plot.

The inter-group distance emerges when one considers the maximum extension of a spring over all time. In order to quantify this, we must specify a value for the α_k's that are used to combine the modes. For this purpose, we appeal to the *equipartition theorem* [24] which states that if a system described by classical statistical mechanics is in equilibrium, then it has equal energy in each mode. Since the energy of the kth mode [10] is given by

$$E_k = \frac{1}{2}\alpha_k^2\omega_k^2$$

we set α_k equal to $1/\omega_k$ for $k = 2, \ldots, K$.

Given this choice of α_k, we may define the inter-group distance between two pixels i and j as

$$d_{IG}(i,j) = \sum_{k=2}^{K} \frac{1}{\sqrt{\lambda_k}}|\mathbf{v}_k^i - \mathbf{v}_k^j| \tag{4}$$

As a simple illustration of the inter-group distance, we have shown in Figure 12 the average inter-group distance from each pixel to its closest four neighbors for the test images of the preceding section. Noting the similarity to conventional edge gradient images, one may employ contour closure techniques such as [9, 14, 1] to cut salient regions out of such a representation.

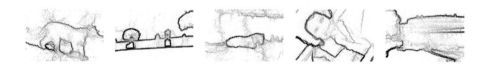

Fig. 12. Illustration of the inter-group distance from each pixel to its closest four neighbors.

6 Conclusion

In this work we have presented two new ideas which allow one to compute meaningful distances in feature space between points in natural images. The first idea consists of a new point descriptor which represents texture and intensity information in a compatible manner. The second idea is a process which is analogous to contour completion for textured regions which we have termed *area completion*. In order to demonstrate the effectiveness of these ideas, we performed several experiments using our new feature distance in the Normalized Cut framework.

In developing our proposed technique, we never appeal to the use of large amounts of spatial averaging to eliminate the inhomogeneities that occur in textured regions. As our method is based on the use of highly local point descriptors, the problem of patches straddling texture boundaries does not arise.

It is important to note that our experiments have been performed on natural images, rather than synthetic mosaics, and that the parameter settings are the same from image to image. Our plans for future work include further investigation of uses of the inter-group distance and the incorporation of color information into the point descriptor.

Acknowledgements

We would like to thank Thomas Leung and Jianbo Shi for their valuable input related to this work. We also wish to thank W. Kahan for numerous helpful discussions on the material discussed in Section 5.2. This work was supported by an NSF Digital Library Grant (IRI 94-11334), (ARO) DAAH04-96-1-0341, and an NSF Graduate Fellowship and U.C. Berkeley Chancellor's Opportunity Predoctoral Fellowship for Serge Belongie.

References

1. T.D. Alter. *The Role of Saliency and Error Propagation in Visual Object Recognition.* PhD Thesis, MIT, 1995.
2. D.H. Ballard. Cortical connections and parallel processing: Structure and function. *The Behavioral and Brain Sciences*, 9:67–120, 1986.
3. J. Bigün and J.M. Hans du Buf. N-folded symmetries by complex moments in gabor space and their application to unsupervised texture segmentation. *IEEE Trans. Pattern Anal. Mach. Intell.*, 16(1):80–87, 1994.
4. A. Bovik, M. Clark, and W.S. Geisler. Multichannel texture analysis using localized spatial filters. *IEEE Trans. Pattern Anal. Mach. Intell.*, 12(1):55–73, 1990.
5. M. Carandini and D.J. Heeger. Summation and division by neurons in primate visual cortex. *Science*, 264:1333–1336, 1994.
6. S. Casadei, S. Mitter, and P. Perona. Boundary detection in piecewise homogeneous images. In *Proc. 2nd Europ. Conf. Comput. Vision, G. Sandini (Ed.), LNCS-Series Vol. 588, Springer-Verlag*, pages 174–183, 1992.
7. J.W. Demmel. *Applied Numerical Linear Algebra.* SIAM, 1997.
8. R. DeValois and K. DeValois. *Spatial Vision.* Oxford University Press, 1988.

9. J.H. Elder and S.W. Zucker. Computing Contour Closure. *Fourth European Conf. Computer Vision*, 1996, Cambridge, England.

10. J.N. Franklin. *Matrix Theory*. Prentice-Hall, 1968.

11. W. Freeman and E. Adelson. The design and use of steerable filters. *IEEE Trans. Pattern Anal. Mach. Intell.*, 13:891–906, 1991.

12. H. Greenspan, S. Belongie, P. Perona, and R. Goodman. Rotation-Invariant Texture Recognition Using a Steerable Pyramid. *12th Int. Conf. Patt. Rec.*, 1994.

13. D.J. Heeger and J.R. Bergen. Pyramid-based texture analysis/synthesis. *Computer Graphics: SIGGRAPH*, pages 229–238, 1995.

14. D.W. Jacobs. Finding Salient Convex Groups. In I.J. Cox, P. Hansen, and B Julesz, eds., *Partitioning Data Sets*, vol. 19 of *DIMACS (Series in Discrete Mathematics and Theoretical Computer Science)*. 1995.

15. A.K. Jain and F. Farrokhnia. Unsupervised texture segmentation using gabor filters. *Pattern Recognition*, 24(12):1167–1186, 1991.

16. D. Jones and J. Malik. Computational framework for determining stereo correspondence from a set of linear spatial filters. *Image and Vision Computing*, 10(10), 1992.

17. H. Knutsson and G.H. Granlund. Texture analysis using two-dimensional quadrature filters. In *Workshop on Computer Architecture for Pattern Analysis and Image Database Management*, pages 206–213. IEEE Computer Society, 1983.

18. J.J. Koenderink. Operational significance of receptive field assemblies. *Biol. Cybern.*, 58:163–171, 1988.

19. J.J. Koenderink and A.J. van Doorn. Representation of local geometry in the visual system. *Biol. Cybern.*, 55:367–375, 1987.

20. T. Lindeberg. *Scale-Space Theory in Computer Vision*. Kluwer, 1994.

21. J. Malik and P. Perona. Preattentive texture discrimination with early vision mechanisms. *J. Opt. Soc. Am. A*, 7(5):923–932, 1990.

22. B.S. Manjunath and W.Y. Ma. Texture features for browsing and retrieval of image data. *IEEE Trans. Pattern Anal. Mach. Intell.*, 18(8):837–842, 1996.

23. J. Puzicha, T. Hofmann, and J.M. Buhmann. Non-parametric similarity measures for unsupervised texture segmentation and image retrieval. In *Proc. IEEE Conf. Computer Vision and Pattern Recognition*, pages 267–272, 1997.

24. F. Reif. *Statistical Physics*. McGraw-Hill, 1965.

25. J. Shi and J. Malik. Normalized cuts and image segmentation. In *Proc. IEEE Conf. Computer Vision and Pattern Recognition*, pages 731–737, 1997.

26. M.R. Turner. Texture discrimination by gabor functions. *Biol. Cybern.*, 55:71–82, 1986.

27. M. Wertheimer. Laws of organization in perceptual forms(partial translation). In W.B. Ellis, editor, *A Sourcebook of Gestalt Psycychology*, pages 71–88. Harcourt, Brace and Company, 1938.

28. S.C. Zhu, Y. Wu, and D. Mumford. Frame: Filters, random fields, and minimax entropy. In *Proc. IEEE Conf. Computer Vision and Pattern Recognition*, pages 686–693, 1996.

A Smoothing Filter for CONDENSATION

Michael Isard and Andrew Blake

Department of Engineering Science,
University of Oxford, Oxford OX1 3PJ, UK,
misard,ab@robots.ox.ac.uk,
WWW home page: http://robots.ox.ac.uk/~ab

Abstract. CONDENSATION, recently introduced in the computer vision literature, is a particle filtering algorithm which represents a tracked object's state using an entire probability distribution. Clutter can cause the distribution to split temporarily into multiple peaks, each representing a different hypothesis about the object configuration. When measurements become unambiguous again, all but one peak, corresponding to the true object position, die out. While several peaks persist estimating the object position is problematic. "Smoothing" in this context is the statistical technique of conditioning the state distribution on both past and future measurements once tracking is complete. After smoothing, peaks corresponding to clutter are reduced, since their trajectories eventually die out. The result can be a much improved state-estimate during ambiguous time-steps. This paper implements two algorithms to smooth the output of a CONDENSATION filter. The techniques are derived from the work of Kitagawa, reinterpreted in the CONDENSATION framework, and considerably simplified.

1 Introduction

The CONDENSATION algorithm was recently introduced in the context of computer vision, originally to allow contour-tracking through heavy clutter [5], and more recently as the engine for exploring more complex non-linear dynamical models than have been traditionally used in vision [6, 4]. The algorithm is attractive because it is both simple and very general, and thus has potential application to a wide range of estimation problems beyond those contour-based tracking applications for which is has so far been used in computer vision. In fact, the CONDENSATION algorithm is functionally identical to algorithms developed in the target-tracking [2] and statistical literature [7]. In his formulation of the algorithm, Kitagawa [7] also presented two smoothing algorithms which allow the state at time t to be estimated in the light of all of the measurement data in a sequence, rather than just the data up until time t. Note that in this paper "smoothing" refers to the statistical technique of conditioning the state density on both past and future measurements. It has nothing to do with the standard computer vision definition involving convolution with a smoothing kernel, either spatially or temporally.

This paper implements Kitagawa's smoothing algorithms in the CONDENSATION framework, and in doing so incorporates a significant simplification of one of them which extends its use to a wider class of dynamical model. Smoothing highlights an aspect of CONDENSATION which has not so far been much studied. One of the distinguishing characteristics of the CONDENSATION algorithm is that it represents multiple hypotheses about object state in the form of a multi-modal state density. All of the known information about the object is contained in the state density, and this information must be processed in some way if a single estimated object position is required at each time-step. Existing implementations calculate simple moments of the state density, for example the mean, for display purposes. This approach breaks down when the density has several peaks, and one advantage of a smoothing filter is that it tends to eliminate hypotheses which become unlikely with hindsight. The result is that the smoothed density better approximates a uni-modal density, and simple mean-estimation produces a more accurate representation of the density. The next section briefly describes the CONDENSATION algorithm, and smoothing extensions are presented in following sections.

2 The CONDENSATION algorithm

The CONDENSATION algorithm [5, 6] was developed to address the problem of tracking contour outlines through heavy image clutter. The filter's output at a given time-step, rather than being a single estimate of position and covariance as in a Kalman filter, is an approximation of an entire probability distribution of likely object positions. This allows the filter to maintain multiple hypotheses and thus be robust to distracting clutter.

The object's position, shape and velocity are encoded in a state vector $\mathbf{X} \in \mathbb{R}^{N_x}$ (which may, for example, represent the outline of a curve using a low-dimensional parameterisation), and the observed image at time t is denoted $\mathbf{Z}_t$, with measurement history $\mathcal{Z}_t = (\mathbf{Z}_1, \ldots, \mathbf{Z}_t)$. The representation used for probability distributions is derived from factored sampling [3, 9], where it was applied to static images. Factored sampling is a Bayesian technique to approximate a distribution $p(\mathbf{X}|\mathbf{Z})$ which applies when $p(\mathbf{X}|\mathbf{Z})$ is too complicated to sample directly, but when the prior $p(\mathbf{X})$ can be sampled, and the measurement density $p(\mathbf{Z}|\mathbf{X})$ can be evaluated. The algorithm proceeds by generating a set of N samples $\{\mathbf{s}^{(n)}\}$ from the prior $p(\mathbf{X})$ and then assigning to each sample a weight $\pi^{(n)} = p(\mathbf{Z}|\mathbf{X} = \mathbf{s}^{(n)})$ corresponding to the measurement density. The $\pi^{(n)}$ are normalised to sum to 1 and then the weighted set $\{(\mathbf{s}^{(n)}, \pi^{(n)})\}$ is an approximation $\tilde{p}(\mathbf{X}|\mathbf{Z})$ to the desired posterior $p(\mathbf{X}|\mathbf{Z})$, where a sample is drawn from $\tilde{p}(\mathbf{X}|\mathbf{Z})$ by choosing one of the $\mathbf{s}^{(n)}$ with probability $\pi^{(n)}$. As $N \to \infty$ samples from $\tilde{p}(\mathbf{X}|\mathbf{Z})$ arbitrarily closely approximate fair samples from $p(\mathbf{X}|\mathbf{Z})$. Moments of the posterior can also be estimated as

$$\mathcal{E}[\phi(\mathbf{X})] \approx \sum_{n=1}^{N} \pi^{(n)} \phi\left(\mathbf{s}^{(n)}\right).$$

The CONDENSATION algorithm is a generalisation of factored sampling to temporal sequences, where the conditional state density $p(\mathbf{X}_t|\mathcal{Z}_t)$ at time t is approximated by a weighted, time-stamped sample set $\{(\mathbf{s}_t^{(n)}, \pi_t^{(n)})\}$. Each iteration of the algorithm is a self-contained application of factored sampling in which the prior $p(\mathbf{X}_t)$ is replaced by a prediction density $p(\mathbf{X}_t|\mathcal{Z}_{t-1})$. This density is approximated by taking the sample set $\{(\mathbf{s}_{t-1}^{(n)}, \pi_{t-1}^{(n)})\}$ from the previous time-step and applying a prediction from a dynamical model. The iterative process applied to the sample-sets is depicted in figure 1. At the top of the diagram, the output

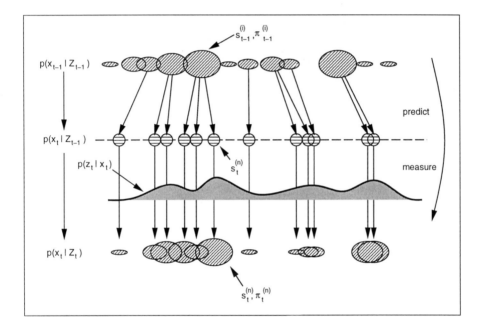

Fig. 1. One time-step in the CONDENSATION algorithm. *Blob centres represent sample values and sizes depict sample weights.*

from time-step $t-1$ is the weighted sample-set $\{(\mathbf{s}_{t-1}^{(n)}, \pi_{t-1}^{(n)}), n = 1, \ldots, N\}$. The aim is to maintain, at successive time-steps, sample sets of fixed size N, so that the algorithm can be guaranteed to run within a given computational resource.

The procedure for a single time-step consists of N iterations to generate the N elements of the new sample set. The first operation of iteration n is to choose a "base sample" $\mathbf{s}_{t-1}^{(i)}$ from the sample-set at time $t-1$. This is done by sampling (with replacement), choosing a given element $\mathbf{s}_{t-1}^{(i)}$ with probability $\pi_{t-1}^{(i)}$. Some elements, especially those with high weights, may be chosen several times as n goes from 1 to N, while others with relatively low weights may not be chosen at all. The second step is to subject the chosen element to a prediction corresponding to the dynamical model. This is a stochastic model, and the prediction of a new sample $\mathbf{s}_t^{(n)}$ from a base sample $\mathbf{s}_{t-1}^{(i)}$ corresponds to sampling from the process density $p(\mathbf{X}_t|\mathbf{X}_{t-1} = \mathbf{s}_{t-1}^{(i)})$, so the predictions from identical base samples will in general be different. Any dynamical model can be used efficiently within the algorithm provided that it is straightforward to sample from this process density. At this point the $\mathbf{s}_t^{(n)}$ are approximately a fair sample from the distribution $p(\mathbf{X}_t|\mathcal{Z}_{t-1})$. Finally, the observation step is applied, calculating a weight $\pi_t^{(n)}$ for $\mathbf{s}_t^{(n)}$ by evaluating the observation density $p(\mathbf{Z}_t|\mathbf{X}_t = \mathbf{s}_t^{(n)})$. After iterating over n the $\pi_t^{(n)}$ are normalised and the sample-set representation $\{(\mathbf{s}_t^{(n)}, \pi_t^{(n)})\}$ of the state-density for time t, an approximation to $p(\mathbf{X}_t|\mathcal{Z}_t)$, has been obtained. As with factored sampling, at any time-step it is possible to "report" on the current state, for example by evaluating some moment of the state density as

$$\mathcal{E}[\phi(\mathbf{X}_t)|\mathcal{Z}_t] \approx \sum_{n=1}^{N} \pi_t^{(n)} \phi\left(\mathbf{s}_t^{(n)}\right), \tag{1}$$

where typically $\phi(\mathbf{X}) = \mathbf{X}$ is used to estimate the mean of the distribution.

3 Smoothing the output of CONDENSATION

The conditional state density $p(\mathbf{X}_t|\mathcal{Z}_t)$ encodes all of the known information about the object state given the current measurement history $\mathcal{Z}_t \equiv (\mathbf{Z}_1, \ldots, \mathbf{Z}_t)$. Once tracking has completed it may be desirable to return, in batch-mode, to calculate $p(\mathbf{X}_t|\mathcal{Z}_T)$, the state density for each time-step given the *entire* measurement history. This is particularly valuable in the case of temporary distraction, when the state density splits for a few time-steps into several distinct trajectories. During real-time[1] tracking, it is impossible to reliably determine which of these competing hypotheses corresponds to the true object trajectory, however all but one of the trajectories will "die out" eventually when it becomes apparent that they correspond to clutter, distractions or mis-estimation.

Kitagawa [7] presents two algorithms to smooth a time-series of sample-set state estimates, which we reproduce here in the CONDENSATION framework. The first is very straightforward. Rather than storing the set $\{(\mathbf{s}_t^{(n)}, \pi_t^{(n)})\}$ at each time t, the sample position $\mathbf{s}_t^{(n)}$ is replaced by an entire trajectory $\mathcal{S}_t^{(n)} = (\mathbf{s}_t^{(n,1)}, \ldots, \mathbf{s}_t^{(n,t)})$. The history $(\mathbf{s}_t^{(n,1)}, \ldots, \mathbf{s}_t^{(n,t-1)})$ is taken to be the trajectory of the base sample which is chosen in the first step of the CONDENSATION algorithm, and the moments of the smoothed density $p(\mathbf{X}_\tau|\mathcal{Z}_t)$ can be

---

[1] Real time is used here to distinguish the standard CONDENSATION tracking algorithm from any batch-mode post-processing. It does not imply the standard computer vision meaning, that tracking is effected in the time between acquisition of consecutive images.

estimated for $1 \leq \tau \leq t$ by computing the expectation

$$\mathcal{E}[\phi(\mathbf{X}_\tau)|\mathcal{Z}_t] \approx \sum_{n=1}^{N} \pi_t^{(n)} \phi\left(\mathbf{s}_t^{(n,\tau)}\right).$$

The sequence-based smoothing algorithm is shown in figure 2. Note that it is reminiscent of the Viterbi dynamic programming algorithm used, for example, to estimate the most likely path through a Hidden Markov Model (HMM) [8]. This algorithm has the disadvantage that in practice, the variance of the samples

---

Iterate

From the "old" sample-sequence set $\{(\mathcal{S}_{t-1}^{(n)}, \pi_{t-1}^{(n)}),\ n = 1,\dots,N\}$ at time-step $t-1$, construct a "new" sample-sequence set $\{(\mathcal{S}_t^{(n)}, \pi_t^{(n)}),\ n = 1,\dots,N\}$ for time t, where $\mathcal{S}_t^{(n)} = (\mathbf{s}_t^{(n,1)},\dots,\mathbf{s}_t^{(n,t)})$.

Construct the nth of N new samples as follows:

1. **Select** a base sequence $\mathcal{S}_{t-1}^{(i)} = (\mathbf{s}_{t-1}^{(i,1)},\dots,\mathbf{s}_{t-1}^{(i,t-1)})$ by sampling with probability $\pi_{t-1}^{(i)}$. This can be done efficiently, for example using cumulative probabilities.
2. **Predict** by sampling from $p(\mathbf{X}_t|\mathbf{X}_{t-1} = \mathbf{s}_{t-1}^{(i,t-1)})$ to choose $\mathbf{s}_t^{(n,t)}$.
3. **Measure** and weight the new position in terms of the image data $\mathbf{Z}_t$, setting $\pi_t^{(n)} = p(\mathbf{Z}_t|\mathbf{X}_t = \mathbf{s}_t^{(n,t)})$, then set $\mathcal{S}_t^{(n)} = \mathcal{S}_{t-1}^{(i)} \cup \mathbf{s}_t^{(n,t)}$.

Finally normalise so that $\sum_n \pi_t^{(n)} = 1$ to find the new sample-sequence set $(\mathcal{S}_t^{(n)}, \pi_t^{(n)})$. Moments ϕ of the smoothed density $p(\mathbf{X}_\tau|\mathcal{Z}_t)$ for $1 \leq \tau \leq t$ can be found from

$$\mathcal{E}[\phi(\mathbf{X}_\tau)|\mathcal{Z}_t] \approx \sum_{n=1}^{N} \pi_t^{(n)} \phi\left(\mathbf{s}_t^{(n,\tau)}\right)$$

Fig. 2. The sequence-based smoothing algorithm for CONDENSATION. *The algorithm is identical to standard* CONDENSATION *filtering, except that entire trajectories $\mathcal{S}_t^{(n)}$ are stored instead of sample positions $\mathbf{s}_t^{(n)}$.*

$\{\mathbf{s}_t^{(n,\tau)}\}$ for $\tau \ll t$ is very small. In fact, for large $t - \tau$ it is typical to find that all of the $\{\mathbf{s}_t^{(n,\tau)},\ 1\dots N\}$ are identical, meaning that all of the sample-sequences share a common ancestor trajectory. (In later results this is typically true for $t - \tau > 10$.) This may be acceptable if the only required output is a single estimated position for each time-step, but in some circumstances it is preferable to maintain more detailed information as long as possible, and so a more complex algorithm follows. Note that the collapse of the trajectories $\mathcal{S}_t^{(n)}$ into common histories permits pruning, thus allowing a significant economy of storage, which is otherwise $O(Nt)$.

The second smoothing algorithm presented in [7] is a forward–backward algorithm, analogous to the smoothing algorithm for Gaussians [1] which is a two-pass extension of the Kalman filter, and also related to the Baum-Welch forward–backward algorithm for HMMs [8]. The forward pass consists of a standard application of the CONDENSATION tracker, during which all the sets $\{(s_t^{(n)}, \pi_t^{(n)})\}$ for $t = 1 \ldots T$ are stored. Now smoothing is done purely by reweighting the $\pi_t^{(n)}$ — all of the $s_t^{(n)}$ remain fixed. The algorithm presented in [7] contains a backward filtering step which requires access to the measurements $\mathbf{Z}_t$ during the second pass, and also means that the density $p(\mathbf{X}_{t-1}|\mathbf{X}_t)$ must be available for sampling, a condition which is not true for the standard CONDENSATION algorithm. We believe this backward filtering step is unnecessary and so do not include it, however the mathematical treatment and the basic structure of our algorithm are both derived from [7]. Note that our algorithm, like that in [7], does require the evaluation of $p(\mathbf{X}_t|\mathbf{X}_{t-1})$ which imposes some restriction on the form of dynamical model used.

Defining $\mathcal{Z}_t^T = (\mathcal{Z}_t, \ldots, \mathcal{Z}_T)$ we have $\mathcal{Z}_T = \mathcal{Z}_{t-1} \cup \mathcal{Z}_t^T$. Therefore,

$$p(\mathbf{X}_t|\mathcal{Z}_T) = p(\mathbf{X}_t|\mathcal{Z}_{t-1}, \mathcal{Z}_t^T)$$
$$\propto p(\mathbf{X}_t, \mathcal{Z}_t^T|\mathcal{Z}_{t-1})$$
$$= p(\mathcal{Z}_t^T|\mathbf{X}_t)p(\mathbf{X}_t|\mathcal{Z}_{t-1}) \text{ by the independence of the } \mathbf{Z}_t.$$

It is this rearrangement which allows the sample positions $s_t^{(n)}$ to remain fixed after the smoothing step. Recall that the set $\{s_t^{(n)}\}$ is approximately a fair sample from $p(\mathbf{X}_t|\mathcal{Z}_{t-1})$, so by replacing the original $\pi_t^{(n)}$ by smoothing weights

$$\psi_t^{(n)} = p(\mathcal{Z}_t^T|\mathbf{X}_t = s_t^{(n)}),$$

the set $\{(s_t^{(n)}, \psi_t^{(n)})\}$, when normalised, will approximate $p(\mathbf{X}_t|\mathcal{Z}_T)$ as required. It is therefore the weights $\psi_t^{(n)}$ which the backward smoothing pass will calculate.

A recursive algorithm to calculate the densities $p(\mathcal{Z}_t^T|\mathbf{X}_t)$ can be specified mathematically as follows:

$$p(\mathcal{Z}_T^T|\mathbf{X}_T) = p(\mathbf{Z}_T|\mathbf{X}_T)$$
$$p(\mathcal{Z}_{t+1}^T|\mathbf{X}_t) = \int p(\mathcal{Z}_{t+1}^T|\mathbf{X}_{t+1})p(\mathbf{X}_{t+1}|\mathbf{X}_t) \, d\mathbf{X}_{t+1}$$
$$p(\mathcal{Z}_t^T|\mathbf{X}_t) = p(\mathbf{Z}_t|\mathbf{X}_t)p(\mathcal{Z}_{t+1}^T|\mathbf{X}_t)$$

A concrete implementation requires the derivation of an approximation $\delta_t^{(n)}$ to $p(\mathcal{Z}_{t+1}^T|\mathbf{X}_t = s_t^{(n)})$. The integral is approximated as a sum:

$$p(\mathcal{Z}_{t+1}^T|\mathbf{X}_t = s_t^{(n)}) \approx \delta_t^{(n)} = \sum_{m=1}^{N} p(\mathcal{Z}_{t+1}^T|\mathbf{X}_{t+1} = s_{t+1}^{(m)}) \frac{p(\mathbf{X}_{t+1} = s_{t+1}^{(m)}|\mathbf{X}_t = s_t^{(n)})}{p(\mathbf{X}_{t+1} = s_{t+1}^{(m)}|\mathcal{Z}_t)}$$

where the correction

$$p(\mathbf{X}_{t+1} = \mathbf{s}_{t+1}^{(m)}|\mathcal{Z}_t) = \gamma_t^{(m)} = \sum_{k=1}^{N} \pi_t^{(k)} p(\mathbf{X}_{t+1} = \mathbf{s}_{t+1}^{(m)}|\mathbf{X}_t = \mathbf{s}_t^{(k)}).$$

It is introduced because the $\mathbf{s}_{t+1}^{(m)}$ are not distributed uniformly but are a sam-

---

At this stage a forward pass of standard CONDENSATION has been performed, storing a weighted sample-set $\{(\mathbf{s}_t^{(n)}, \pi_t^{(n)})\}$ for each $t = 1 \ldots T$.

1. **Initialise** smoothing weights $\psi_T^{(n)}$:

$$\psi_T^{(n)} = \pi_T^{(n)} \quad \text{for } n = 1 \ldots N.$$

2. **Iterate** backwards over the sequence for $t = T - 1 \ldots 1$:

   (a) **Calculate** prediction probabilities:

   $$\alpha_t^{(m,n)} = p(\mathbf{X}_{t+1} = \mathbf{s}_{t+1}^{(m)}|\mathbf{X}_t = \mathbf{s}_t^{(n)}) \quad \text{for } m, n = 1 \ldots N.$$

   (b) **Calculate** correction factors:

   $$\gamma_t^{(m)} = \sum_{k=1}^{N} \pi_t^{(k)} \alpha_t^{(m,k)} \quad \text{for } m = 1 \ldots N.$$

   (c) **Approximate** backward variables:

   $$\delta_t^{(n)} = \sum_{m=1}^{N} \psi_{t+1}^{(m)} \frac{\alpha_t^{(m,n)}}{\gamma_t^{(m)}} \quad \text{for } n = 1 \ldots N.$$

   (d) **Evaluate** smoothing weights

   $$\psi_t^{(n)} = \pi_t^{(n)} \delta_t^{(n)} \quad \text{for } n = 1 \ldots N$$

   then normalise multiplicatively so $\sum \psi_t^{(n)} = 1$, and store with sample positions as

   $$\{(\mathbf{s}_t^{(n)}, \psi_t^{(n)}), \; n = 1 \ldots N\}$$

Fig. 3. The backward stage of the two-pass smoothing algorithm for CON-DENSATION.

ple from $p(\mathbf{X}_{t+1}|\mathcal{Z}_t)$, and without the correction this could bias the sum. This method of correcting the estimate of an integral over sample-sets is borrowed from the technique of importance sampling [9]. The backward pass of the two-pass smoothing algorithm is shown in figure 3. Note that the complexity of the

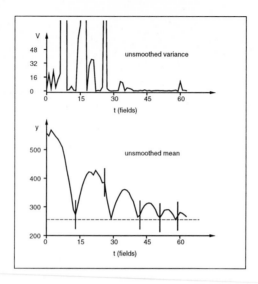

Fig. 4. The unsmoothed output of a mixed-state CONDENSATION algorithm contains estimation errors. *The mean of the y coordinate of the distribution is shown in pixels, along with the mean-square variance around the curve in pixels². Vertical bars correspond to time-steps which are estimated to contain bounce events. The variance is high when several hypotheses have high probabilities (see figure 5).*

algorithm is $O(TN^2)$ and that $O(TN)$ storage is required for the sample-sets, and $O(N^2)$ for the $\alpha_t^{(m,n)}$. This latter storage requirement can be avoided by eliminating the $\alpha_t^{(m,n)}$ from the algorithm and instead calculating each of the $p(\mathbf{X}_{t+1} = \mathbf{s}_{t+1}^{(m)} | \mathbf{X}_t = \mathbf{s}_t^{(n)})$ twice. Since this calculation is typically the most computationally expensive step of the algorithm, this tradeoff must be carefully considered.

4   Applying the smoothing algorithms

First, the sequence-based smoothing algorithm was applied to a test sequence from [6] which shows a ball bouncing against a backdrop of heavy clutter. The ball moves under the action of a two-mode motion model, where the first mode is constant acceleration due to gravity and the second mode corresponds to an instantaneous bounce event during which the ball's vertical velocity is reversed. The state vector $\mathbf{X}_t$ now includes a discrete variable labelling which of the two transition modes the model has just executed. The unsmoothed output of a mixed-state CONDENSATION tracker is depicted in figure 4. At each time-step, an MAP estimate is computed to determine which of the two modes the tracker has executed, and the mean and variance of the y translation coordinate within that mode are shown, along with an indication of which time-steps were estimated to contain bounce events. The unsmoothed output is rather jittery due

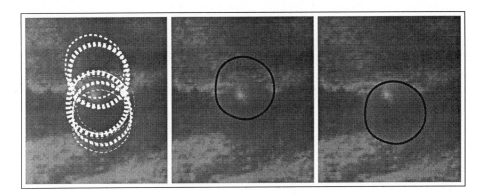

Fig. 5. Smoothing eliminates false hypotheses. *Before smoothing, multiple hypotheses can increase the variance of the distribution (top left) and shift the mean away from the object position (top right). After running the sequence-based smoothing algorithm the estimated variance has dropped to zero (see text) but the mean is now correctly positioned (bottom). Detail from field 26 of the sequence is shown (see figures 4 and 6). The solid black line is the distribution mean, and the dotted white lines are high-scoring samples, where the width of the sample outline is proportional to its sample weight. A ball is being tracked against heavy clutter, and it is difficult to distinguish in a single still image. The ball is located under the contour in the right-hand image.*

to the clutter, and the bounce events are not always accurately found. Figure 5 demonstrates the mis-estimation problem; the distribution has split into several peaks, and although one peak is present at the true ball position, the other peaks pull the distribution mean away from the desired value. After running the sequence-based smoothing algorithm (figure 6) most of the jitter has been eliminated and the trajectory shows smooth parabolas between bounces. One field has still been incorrectly estimated to contain a bounce. As discussed in the previous section, the variance is estimated to be zero except over the last few time-steps, since all the samples in the final distribution share the same history until $t = 60$ fields. Of course, this must be an under-estimate. Figure 5 shows detail from field 26 of the sequence before and after smoothing.

The two-pass algorithm also successfully smooths the raw tracked output (figure 7), and now correctly determines the bounce events. Variance information is also preserved by the two-pass filter, and a small spread of samples in the distribution can be seen in figure 8. Note that neither smoothing algorithm incorporates any separate machinery to estimate the mixed-state transitions. These transition labels, forming part of the state-vector $\mathbf{X}_t$, are automatically estimated along with the continuous state variables. Of course, the values of the transition labels of $\mathbf{s}_t^{(n)}$ and $\mathbf{s}_{t-1}^{(m)}$ play a large part in determining the density $p(\mathbf{X}_{t+1} = \mathbf{s}_{t+1}^{(n)} | \mathbf{X}_t = \mathbf{s}_t^{(m)})$ for the two-pass algorithm.

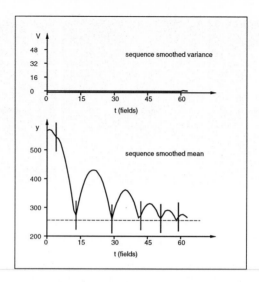

Fig. 6. The sequence-based algorithm smooths away jitter. *The mean of the y coordinate of the distribution is shown in pixels, along with the mean-square variance around the curve in pixels². Vertical bars correspond to time-steps which are estimated to contain bounce events, and a bounce is incorrectly estimated at field 4. The sequence-based smoothing algorithm collapses the variance to zero for all but the last few time-steps (see text).*

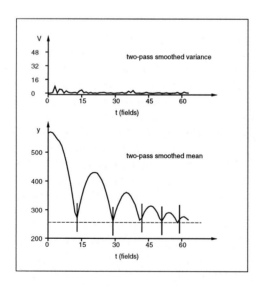

Fig. 7. The two-pass algorithm preserves sample variance while smoothing. *The mean of the y coordinate of the distribution is shown in pixels, along with the mean-square variance around the curve in pixels². Vertical bars correspond to modes which are estimated to contain bounce events. The bounce events are correctly identified.*

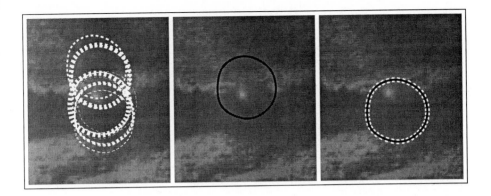

Fig. 8. Smoothing eliminates false hypotheses. *The two-pass smoothing algorithm collapses the distribution down to a single peak (bottom), since the other peaks in the raw data (top left) which cause a mis-estimation of the object position (top right), die out in subsequent time-steps due to lack of support. Within the peak, however, variance information is preserved, and so a small spread of samples is present around the mean (figure 7 indicates that the estimated mean-square variance around the curve is only a few pixels). Detail from field 26 of the sequence is shown. The solid black line is the distribution mean, and the dotted white lines are high-scoring samples, where the width of the sample outline is proportional to its sample weight. A ball is being tracked against heavy clutter, and it is difficult to distinguish in a single still image. The ball is located under the contour in the right-hand image.*

Finally, the algorithms were applied to another test sequence showing a hand moving over a cluttered desk. The hand translates and deforms in a 12-dimensional linear shape-space. After approximately 30 fields, the distribution splits into two peaks (figure 9), one of which is caused by clutter. The clutter peak dominates for 10 fields, causing a serious error in the estimated state, although the true position is maintained as a smaller peak in the distribution throughout, and the tracker recovers eventually. Figure 10 shows a graphs of the y coordinate of the estimated mean of the distribution along with the variance of the sample-set. The hand moves up smoothly from field 20 to field 40, but the unsmoothed estimate is distracted between fields 30–40, before rapidly regaining the correct position at field 42. Note the very high variances, especially just before the tracker recovers.

Figure 11 shows the result of applying the two-pass smoothing algorithm to the hand sequence (the sequence-based algorithm provides similar state estimates and lower variance as before). When the entire sequence is taken into account, it is apparent that the lower peak in figure 9 corresponds to clutter, and so only the trajectory corresponding to the actual hand position survives. Figure 12 graphs the estimated y coordinate and the mean-square curve variances for the output of the two-pass smoother. As in the case of the ball, the jitter on the state estimates is reduced, and the hand position is significantly more accurately determined compared with the raw CONDENSATION algorithm. The

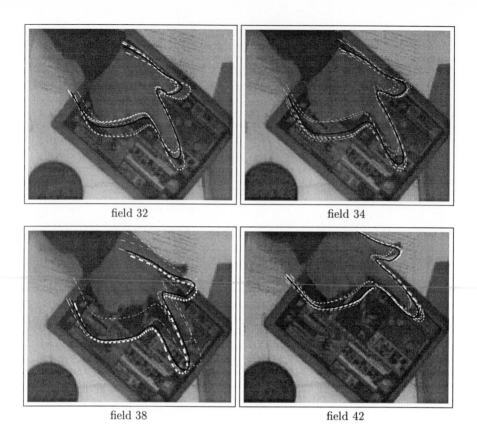

field 32 field 34

field 38 field 42

Fig. 9. Clutter causes temporary mis-estimation from unsmoothed data. *The unsmoothed state distribution has begun to diverge in field 32, and by field 34 the clutter peak dominates. The multi-modality persists until field 38, after which the clutter peak rapidly dies away, leaving a single peak around the object again by field 42. The solid line is the distribution mean, and the dotted lines are high-scoring samples, where the width of the sample outline is proportional to its sample weight.*

variance of the sample-sets is also much reduced, although clearly towards the end of the sequence the variance must increase to match that of the raw data.

5 Conclusions and future work

Both of the smoothing algorithms presented here significantly aid the interpretation of the output of a CONDENSATION tracker. One of the major benefits of the CONDENSATION algorithm is that it allows the state density to split into several peaks to transiently represent multiple hypotheses about object configuration. This facility enables the tracker to follow the object while measurements are ambiguous, keeping track of several possible trajectories until the true ob-

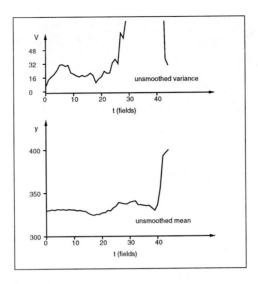

Fig. 10. The unsmoothed hand data leads to estimation errors. *The mean of the y coordinate of the distribution is shown in pixels, along with the mean-square variance around the curve in pixels^2. Figure 9 shows the distribution splitting into two peaks between fields 32–34, and this is apparent from the variances. The clutter peak is stronger, and causes the position to be mis-estimated by shifting the distribution mean. Although the hand moves up steadily during fields 30–40, the estimated position moves down before suddenly recovering at field 42.*

ject position can once more be confidently established. During the period that the distribution contains multiple peaks, however, existing implementations of CONDENSATION may report grossly misleading state estimates even though they ultimately recover. This is because the state estimates are based on the mean of the distribution, and thus implicitly assume a single peak. The application of a smoothing algorithm concentrates the distribution into those areas which are most likely given the entire tracking sequence, and the result is that peaks caused by temporary clutter distractions tend to be greatly reduced in size. The distribution is then more approximately uni-modal, and its mean is a good estimator for the object configuration. The forward–backward algorithm may also prove very useful for learning mixed-state motion models. The algorithm can be used as the basis of an E–M procedure analagous to the Baum-Welch algorithm for learning Hidden Markov Model coefficients, and this is the subject of current research.

The two algorithms were tested on sequences where the state distribution periodically diverges to form several hypotheses and all but one of these competing hypotheses ultimately dies out. Both algorithms successfully smoothed the test sequences, with slightly improved accuracy from the two-pass algorithm, and this suggests that for tasks of this kind the sequence-based algorithm should be used, given its greater conceptual and computational simplicity. It is anticipated

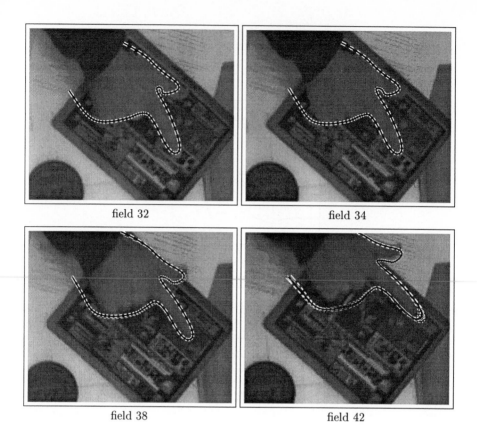

field 32

field 34

field 38

field 42

Fig. 11. The smoothing algorithm correctly follows the hand. *Compare with figure 9; after smoothing using the two-pass algorithm, all of the visible distribution is concentrated on the correct peak. The solid line is the distribution mean after smoothing, and the dotted lines are high-scoring samples, where the width of the sample outline is proportional to its weight.*

that the two-pass algorithm will come into its own as more complex distributions come to be used while tracking, and more complex state estimates are required than a single configuration at each time-step. A situation could arise where the state density repeatedly split into competing hypotheses and then merged again, for example if two similar objects were moving in front of one another. The sequence-based algorithm would be very unlikely to preserve the structure of the trajectories; instead it would tend to choose the most likely single path. The two-pass algorithm, on the other hand, by computing a richer representation of the past history, is more likely to keep all the likely hypotheses and only reject genuine clutter. It may also be desirable to estimate sample-set variances to detect periods of uncertainty, for example due to partial occlusion of an object, and the two-pass algorithm is much better suited to this task.

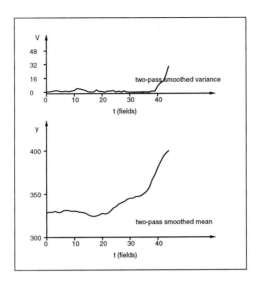

Fig. 12. The two-pass smoothing algorithm corrects estimation errors. *Figure 11 shows that the two-pass algorithm eliminates the clutter peak which distracted the standard tracker. Now the estimated state corresponds to the true hand position as it moves steadily up the image from field 20 (compare with figure 10). The variance of the sample-set is also greatly reduced, although clearly at the end of the sequence the variance increases to match that of the raw output. The mean of the y coordinate of the distribution is shown in pixels, along with the mean-square variance around the curve in pixels^2.*

References

1. A. Gelb, editor. *Applied Optimal Estimation*. MIT Press, Cambridge, MA, 1974.
2. N. Gordon, D. Salmond, and A.F.M. Smith. Novel approach to nonlinear/non-Gaussian Bayesian state estimation. *IEE Proc. F*, 140(2):107–113, 1993.
3. U. Grenander, Y. Chow, and D.M. Keenan. *HANDS. A Pattern Theoretical Study of Biological Shapes*. Springer-Verlag. New York, 1991.
4. T. Heap and D. Hogg. Wormholes in shape space: Tracking through discontinuous changes in shape. In *Proc. 6th Int. Conf. on Computer Vision*, 1998.
5. M.A. Isard and A. Blake. Visual tracking by stochastic propagation of conditional density. In *Proc. 4th European Conf. Computer Vision*, 343–356, Cambridge, England, Apr 1996.
6. M.A. Isard and A. Blake. A mixed-state Condensation tracker with automatic model switching. In *Proc. 6th Int. Conf. on Computer Vision*, 107–112, 1998.
7. G. Kitagawa. Monte Carlo filter and smoother for non-Gaussian nonlinear state space models. *Journal of Computational and Graphical Statistics*, 5(1):1–25, 1996.
8. L. Rabiner and J. Bing-Hwang. *Fundamentals of speech recognition*. Prentice-Hall, 1993.
9. B.D. Ripley. *Stochastic simulation*. New York: Wiley, 1987.

Camera-Based ID Verification
by Signature Tracking

Mario E. Munich[1] and Pietro Perona[1,2]

[1] California Institute of Technology 136-93
Pasadena, CA 91125
{mariomu,perona}@vision.caltech.edu
[2] Università di Padova, Italia

Abstract. A number of vision-based biometric techniques have been proposed in the past for personal identification. We present a novel one based on visual capturing of signatures. This paper describes a system based on correlation and recursive prediction methods that can track the tip of the pen in real time, with sufficient spatio-temporal resolution and accuracy to enable signature verification. Several examples and the performance of the system are shown.

1 Introduction and Motivation

A number of biometric techniques have been proposed for personal identification in the past. Among the vision-based ones, we can mention face recognition [21], [22], [23], fingerprint recognition [6], iris scanning [4] and retina scanning. Voice recognition or signature verification are the most widely known among the non-vision based ones. Signature verification requires the use of electronic tablets or digitizers for on-line capturing and optical scanners for off-line conversion [20]. These interfaces have the drawback that they are bulky and complicated to use, increasing the complexity of the whole identification system. Cameras, on the other hand, are much smaller and simple to handle, and are becoming ubiquitous in the current computer environment. This paper presents a visual interface that can be built using video technology and computer vision techniques in order to capture signatures to be used for personal identification. This vision-based personal identification system could be integrated as a component of a complete visual pen-based computer environment. Some related work can be found in [3], [11].

Handwriting recognition is still an open problem, even though it has been extensively studied for many years. Signature verification is a reduced problem that still poses a real challenge for researchers. The literature on signature verification is quite extensive (see [1], [9], [16] for very comprehensive surveys) and shows two main areas of research, off-line and on-line systems. Off-line systems deal with a static image of the signature, i.e. the result of the action of signing while on-line systems work on the dynamic process of generating the signature, i.e. the action of signing itself. The system proposed in this paper falls within the category of on-line systems since the visual tracker of handwriting captures the timing information in the generation of the signature.

Section 2 describes the system. Section 3 presents the experimental setup and the results of experiments. The final section summarizes the results and discusses future work.

2 Overview of the System

Figure 1 shows a basic block diagram of the system and the experimental setup. The preprocessing stage performs the initialization of the algorithm, i.e. it finds the position of the pen on the first frame of the sequence and selects the template corresponding to the pen tip to be tracked. In subsequent frames, the preprocessing stage performs one function only: it cuts a piece of image around the predicted position of the pen tip and feeds it into the next block. The pen tip tracker has the task of finding the position of the pen tip on each frame of the sequence. A Kalman filter predicts the position of the tip in the next frame based on an estimate of the current position, velocity and acceleration of the pen. Finally, the last block of our system performs signature verification. Section 2.1 describes in more detail the handwriting acquisition component of our system and section 2.2 describes the algorithm used for signature verification.

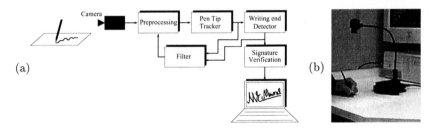

Fig. 1. (a) Block Diagram of the system. The camera feeds a sequence of images to the preprocessing stage. This block initializes the algorithm and selects the template to perform the tracking of the pen tip. The tip tracker obtains the position of the pen tip in each image of the sequence. The filter predicts the position of the pen tip in the next image. Finally, the last block of our system performs signature verification. (b) Experimental setup. The camera is looking at a person signing on a piece of paper.

2.1 Handwriting Acquisition

Initialization. The first problem to solve is locating the position of the pen tip in the first image of the sequence and selecting the kernel to be tracked. There are three possible scenarios: 1) In a batch analysis the tracker is initialized manually by mouse-clicking on the pen tip in the first frame. 2) The user writes with a pen that is familiar to the system. 3) An unknown pen is used.

The familiar-pen case is easy to handle: the system may use a previously stored template representing the pen tip and detect its position in the image by correlation. There are a number of methods to initialize the system when the pen is unknown [11].

Tracking the Pen. The second block of the system has the task of finding the position of the pen tip in the current frame of the sequence. The solution of this task is well known in the optimal signal detection literature. The optimal detector is a filter matched to the signal (in our case a segment of the image) and the most likely position of the pen is given by the best match between the signal and the optimal detector.

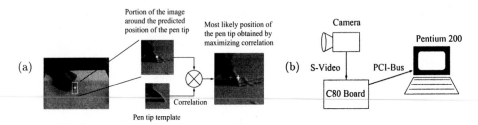

Fig. 2. (a) Given the predicted location of the pen tip in the current frame, the most likely position of the pen is obtained by finding the place that has maximum correlation with the previously stored template of the pen tip. (b) System configuration: The hardware architecture comprises a commercial camera, a video board, and a Pentium 200.

Assuming that the changes in size and orientation of the pen tip during the sequence are small, the most likely position of the pen tip in each frame is given by the location of the maximum of the correlation between the kernel and the image neighborhood, as shown in figure 2(a).

Filtering. Using the output of the correlation-based tracker, the filter predicts the position of the pen tip in the next frame based on an estimate of the position, velocity and acceleration of the pen tip in the current frame. This filter improves the performance of the system since it allows us to reduce the size of the neighborhood used to calculate correlation. The measurements are acquired faster and the measured trajectory is smoother due to the noise rejection of the filter. A Kalman Filter [2], [7], [8] is a suitable recursive estimation scheme for this problem. We assumed a simple random walk model for the acceleration of the pen tip on the image plane. The model is given by

$$\begin{cases} \dot{\mathbf{x}}(t) = \mathbf{v}(t) \\ \dot{\mathbf{v}}(t) = \mathbf{a}(t) \\ \dot{\mathbf{a}}(t) = \mathbf{n}_a(t) \\ \mathbf{y}(t) = \mathbf{x}(t) + \mathbf{n}_y(t) \end{cases} \tag{1}$$

where $\mathbf{x}(t)$, $\mathbf{v}(t)$ and $\mathbf{a}(t)$ are the two dimensional-components of the position, velocity and acceleration of the tracked point, and $\mathbf{n}_a(t)$ is additive zero-mean,

Gaussian, white noise. The state of the filter $\mathbf{X}(t)$ includes three 2-dimensional variables, $\mathbf{x}(t)$, $\mathbf{v}(t)$ and $\mathbf{a}(t)$. This second order model is appropriate to describe the dynamics of a point object moving on a plane. The output of the model $\mathbf{y}(t)$ is the estimated position of the pen tip.

Real-time Implementation. Figure 2(b) shows a block diagram of the implementation hardware, which consists of a video camera, a video processing board, and a Pentium 200 PC. The camera is a commercial Flexcam ID, manufactured by Videolabs, equipped with manual gain control. It has a resolution of 480x640 pixels per interlaced image. A TI TMS3020C80 based signal and image processing board was used to perform the image capturing. The input camera image is digitized by the board and the even and odd fields of the image are separated for future processing. The even field of the image is transferred via DMA to the memory of the host PC. All further computations are performed with the Pentium 200. We achieved a total processing time of 31ms per frame.

2.2 Signature Verification

Preliminaries. We consider the algorithms presented in references [1], [9], [16] as well as in the work of V. Nalwa [12] in order to choose one of them to be implemented and included in our system. We decided to explore the performance of Dynamic Time Warping (DTW) applied to this problem. This algorithm was initially proposed in the field of Speech Recognition by Sakoe and Chiba [18] and it is described in full extent in the book of Rabiner and Juang [17]. In the area of signature verification, Sato and Kogure [19] used DTW to align signature shapes, Parizeau and Plamondon [13] compared the performance of DTW with regional correlation and skeletal tree matching for signature verification, Huang and Yan [5] applied DTW to align signature strokes and Nalwa [12] employed a similar dynamic programming technique to align different characteristic functions of the signature parameterized along its arc length.

Sato and Kogure [19] proposed to use DTW in order to align the shape of signatures, consisting only of pen down strokes, after having normalized the data with respect to translation, rotation, trend and scale. They further used the result of DTW in order to compute the alignment of the pressure function and a measure of the difference in writing motion. Finally, they perform the classification based on the residual distance between shapes after time alignment, the residual distance between pressure functions and the distance between writing motions.

Parizeau and Plamondon [13] evaluated the use of DTW for signature verification by aligning either $x(t)$, $y(t)$, $v_x(t)$, $v_y(t)$, $a_x(t)$ or $a_y(t)$. In their work, they used the complete signing trajectories, i.e., pen down and pen up strokes.

Huang and Yan [5] presented the use of DTW for matching signature strokes by finding a warp path that minimizes the cost of aligning the shape, velocities and accelerations of the individual strokes at the same time. Pen up strokes are considered in the preprocessing phase of their algorithm, in order to be merged with the pen down strokes.

Nalwa [12] parameterized the pen down strokes of the signature along its arc length and then compute a number of characteristic functions such as co-ordinates of the center of mass, torque, and moments of inertia using a sliding computational window and a moving coordinate frame. He performed a simul-taneously dynamic warping over arc length of all these characteristic functions for the two signatures under comparison. A measure of the similarity of the signatures is used for classification.

Our implementation of DTW for signature verification attempts to perform the best time alignment of the 2D shape of the signatures, i.e., we find the time warping function that has the minimum cost of aligning the planar curves that represent signatures. The visual tracker does not have the capability of detecting the positions in which the pen is up and not writing, so we used the full signing trajectory in our experiments. We note that the pen up strokes drawn by each subject were as consistent as the pen down strokes. This observation agrees with the belief [1] that signatures are produced as a ballistic or reflex action, without any visual feedback involved. We do not perform any type of normalization on the signatures since we consider that users are very consistent on their style of signing, they write their signatures with a similar slant, in a similar amount of time, with similar dimensions and with a similar motion. As presented, our DTW algorithm for signature verification is different from all the mentioned previous work although it shares with them some characteristics.

Figure 3 shows an example of dynamic time warping applied to align the 2D shape of two signatures. The first column shows $x(t)$ before and after time warping and the second column shows $y(t)$ before and after alignment. The upper plot of the third column shows the two signatures under comparison and the lower plot of the third column shows the alignment path. We note that the alignment is quite good regardless of the differences in the shapes of $x(t)$ and $y(t)$. The remaining mismatch between these signals accounts for the differences in shape of the signatures.

Description of the Algorithm. Dynamic time warping is a dynamic program-ming technique that performs alignment of two different examples of a signal. Given the two examples $X = (\mathbf{x}(1), \mathbf{x}(2), \cdots \mathbf{x}(T_x))$ and $Y = (\mathbf{y}(1), \mathbf{y}(2), \cdots \mathbf{y}(T_y))$, and a distance function $d(\mathbf{x}(t_x), \mathbf{y}(t_y))$, we can define the total dissimilarity be-tween X and Y as follows

$$\mathbf{D}(X, Y) = \sum_{t=1}^{T} d(\mathbf{x}(t), \mathbf{y}(t)) \qquad (2)$$

where the above summation is performed over a common time axis. In the sim-plest case of time alignment, i.e., linear time alignment, the above summation would be computed over one of the individual time axis t_x or t_y that would be related to each other by $t_x = \frac{T_x}{T_y} t_y$.

Linear time alignment assumes that the rates of production of the signals are constant and proportional to the duration of the signals. It corresponds to

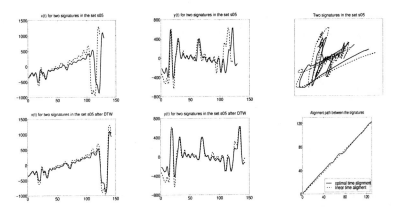

Fig. 3. Example of dynamic time warping applied to align the 2D shape of two realizations of the same signature. The first column shows $x(t)$ before and after time warping, the second column shows $y(t)$ before and after alignment. The upper plot of the third column shows the two examples of the signature. The lower plot of the third column shows the optimal time alignment path compared with a linear time alignment path.

the diagonal straight line showed in the (t_x, t_y) plane of figure 4(a). In the general setting, signatures are generated at a variable rate showing local motion changes. Therefore, we need to obtain two warping functions ϕ_x and ϕ_y that relate the time indices of the examples with a common time axis. The accumulated distortion between X and Y in this case is

$$\mathbf{D}_\phi(X, Y) = \sum_{t=1}^{T} d(\mathbf{x}(\phi_x(t)), \mathbf{y}(\phi_y(t))) \tag{3}$$

with $\phi = (\phi_x, \phi_y)$. These warping functions define a warping path in the (t_x, t_y) plane of figure 4(a) (solid line). Of all the possible warping functions that could be chosen, we would look for the one that minimize the distortion between X and Y:

$$\mathbf{D}(X, Y) = \min_\phi \sum_{t=1}^{T} d(\mathbf{x}(\phi_x(t)), \mathbf{y}(\phi_y(t))) \tag{4}$$

The solution to this problem is obtained with a dynamic programming algorithm that relies on the following recursion:

$$\mathbf{D}(t_x, t_y) = \min_{(t'_x, t'_y)} \{\mathbf{D}(t'_x, t'_y) + c((t'_x, t'_y), (t_x, t_y))\} \tag{5}$$

where $\mathbf{D}(t'_x, t'_y)$ is the cumulated cost of the best path ending at node (t'_x, t'_y), and $c((t'_x, t'_y), (t_x, t_y))$ is the elementary cost of the arc joining nodes (t'_x, t'_y) and (t_x, t_y) in the warping plane.

From the above recursion equation, we can see that a simple algorithm yields the optimal path: for each node on the discrete plane (t_x, t_y), the minimum cumulated cost is computed with equation (5). The node that provides the minimum cost is stored in memory. The cumulative cost is computed serially starting from

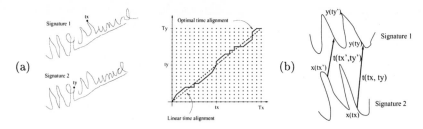

Fig. 4. (a) Two different realizations of the same signature and the discrete (t_x, t_y) plane in which the time alignment is performed. The warping path in dashed line corresponds to linear time alignment while the warping path in solid line corresponds to a possible solution for the optimal time alignment. (b) Translation vectors between two pairs of points in each signature.

the first column until the last column in the discrete plane (t_x, t_y). Finally, the last column is searched for the node with minimum cost and then the optimum warping path is found by backtracking the stored nodes.

For the time alignment process to be meaningful in terms of time normalization for different realizations of a signature, some constraints on the warping functions are necessary. Unconstrained minimization in equation (5) may conceivably result in a near-perfect match between two different signatures, thus making the comparison meaningless for recognition purposes. Typical time warping constraints that are considered reasonable for time alignment include endpoint constraints, monotonicity conditions, local continuity constraints, global path constraints and slope weighting (see [17] for a more extensive treatment of the subject).

We enforce only a few simple constraints. First, we only allow monotonic paths to be explored, so if point t_x is matched with point t_y, then point $t_x + 1$ can only be matched with a point after point t_y. Second, we only allow point (t_x, t_y) to be reached from points $(t_x - 1, t_y)$, $(t_x - 1, t_y - 1)$ and $(t_x, t_y - 1)$. Third, we require that the warping path start at point $(0, 0)$ and end at point (T_x, T_y). Finally, we constrain the number of points t_y that can be explored for each point t_x in minimizing equation (5). With all these constraints, the algorithm can be summarized as follows:

1. Initialization: $\mathbf{D}(0, 0) = 0$
2. Recursion: for $1 \le t_x \le T_x$, $1 \le t_y \le T_y$, such that t_x and t_y stay within the allowed grid, compute:

$$\mathbf{D}(t_x, t_y) = \min \begin{cases} \mathbf{D}(t_x - 1, t_y) + c((t_x - 1, t_y), (t_x, t_y)) \\ \mathbf{D}(t_x - 1, t_y - 1) + c((t_x - 1, t_y - 1), (t_x, t_y)) \\ \mathbf{D}(t_x, t_y - 1) + c((t_x, t_y - 1), (t_x, t_y)) \end{cases} \quad (6)$$

3. Termination: $\mathbf{D}(X, Y) = \mathbf{D}(T_x, T_y)$

The only missing element in the algorithm is the specification of the elementary cost of the arc joining nodes (t'_x, t'_y) and (t_x, t_y), $c((t'_x, t'_y), (t_x, t_y))$. Assume that the point $\mathbf{x}(t'_x)$ in the first signature is matched with point $\mathbf{y}(t'_y)$ in the second signature, and that point $\mathbf{x}(t_x)$ in the first signature is matched with point $\mathbf{y}(t_y)$ in the second signature. The translation vectors associated with each match are $\mathbf{t}(t'_x, t'_y) = \mathbf{x}(t'_x) - \mathbf{y}(t'_y)$ and $\mathbf{t}(t_x, t_y) = \mathbf{x}(t_x) - \mathbf{y}(t_y)$. The error between matches is $d((t'_x, t'_y), (t_x, t_y)) = \mathbf{t}(t_x, t_y) - \mathbf{t}(t'_x, t'_y)$. We choose the elementary cost to be the Euclidean norm of the error between matches: $c((t'_x, t'_y), (t_x, t_y)) = \|d((t'_x, t'_y), (t_x, t_y))\|^2$, as shown in figure 4(b). This cost function tends to give minimum elementary cost to pair of places in the warping plane that corresponds to pairs of points in the signatures that have the same displacement vectors, providing zero cost in the case in which one signature is a translated version of the other.

3   Experiments

The performance of our tracking system has been presented in references [10], [11]. In this paper, we focus our experiments on the results of the automatic personal identification. In section 3.1 we present the performance of the time warping algorithm tested on a database of signatures collected with a tablet digitizer. In section 3.2 we show the results of the visual identification system.

3.1   Performance of the Signature Verification Algorithm

We collected signatures from 38 subjects. Each of them was asked to provide 20 signatures, 10 of them to be used as the training set and the other 10 to be used as the test set. The test set allows us to evaluate the Type I error (or False Rejection Rate (FRR)). We did not collect any real forgery so we used all the signatures from the other subjects as *random forgeries* in order to obtain the Type II error (or False Acceptance Rate (FAR)). The tablet is a WACOM Digitizer, Active area: 153.6x204.8 mm, Resolution: 50 lpmm, Accuracy: $\pm$ 0.25 mm and Maximum report rate: 205 points/second. In our experiments we used the full signing trajectory, in order to be consistent with the experiments that we will perform with the real-time system.

Training. During training the system must *learn* a representation of the training set that will yield minimum generalization error. The dynamic time warping algorithm provides the optimal alignment of two signatures, so we could compute the mean signature of these two along the warping path. This mean signature would provide a more robust representative for the class since the inherent noise in capturing the signatures will be averaged. In the case in which there are more than two examples in the training set, there is no clear way of defining the mean signature. In principle, one could think of performing the simultaneous alignment of all the examples at the same time, working on an N-dimensional tensor instead of a matrix. The disadvantage of this approach is that there is no clear way of defining the elementary cost of the arc joining two nodes of this tensor. We propose a sub-optimal training procedure. We perform only pairwise alignment in order to find all the pairwise mean signatures out of all the possible pairs of elements in the training set. The mean signature that yields minimum alignment cost with all the remaining signatures in the training set is the one that represents the training set. The individual costs of aligning each of the signatures in the training set with this reference signature are collected in order to estimate the statistics of the alignment process. This statistics are subsequently used for classification. In figure 5 we show several examples of signatures collected for our database and their corresponding training reference.

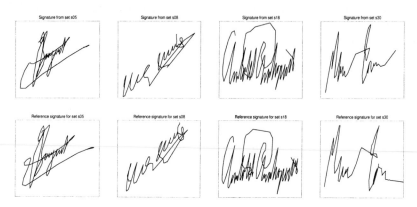

Fig. 5. Several examples of signatures in our database. In the first row we display signatures captured with the tablet while in the second row we show the corresponding reference signature of the training set.

We evaluated several possible alignment schemes in our experiments. Lorette and Plamondon [1] show evidence that the best representation space for a 2D signature verification system is the velocity domain, in concordance with the kinematic theory of rapid human movements developed by Plamondon [14], [15]. Therefore, one of the schemes that we tested was time alignment of the 2D velocity shape of the signatures. The x and y velocities were computed using first-order central finite differences. We examined two more schemes in which we perform time alignment of the 2D shape of the signature. In one of them, we align the raw data acquired with the tablet and in the other, we align the signatures after having rotated them so that their main axis coincide with the horizontal axis.

Testing. As we stated before, we used a test set of 10 signatures for computing the FRR and all the 740 signatures from other subjects for computing the FAR, both of them as a function of the classification threshold. Clearly, we can trade off one type of error for the other type of error. As an extreme example, if we accept every signature, we will have a 0% of FRR and a 100% of FAR, and if we reject every signature,we will have a 100% of FRR and a 0% of FAR. The simplest characterization of the FAR-FRR tradeoff is given by the *equal error rate*, i.e., the error rate at which the percentage of false accepts equal the percentage of false rejects. This equal error rate provides an estimate of the statistical performance of the algorithm, i.e., it provides an estimate of its generalization error. We calculate the value of the equal error rate by intersecting the FAR and FRR curves that we computed, considering them to be piecewise linear.

In figure 6 we plot the value of the equal error rate for the 38 signers, for each of the three schemes under test. We observe that the alignment of 2D shapes of the signatures using the raw data gives the best performance of the three. We note that, for this case of best performance, there are three signatures for which the equal error rate is 10% and one for which the equal error rate is 20%, that, in our present experimental setting, accounts for having one or two signatures being falsely rejected. In figure 7 we show one of the original signatures, the reference signature, the signature that is falsely rejected and one of the falsely accepted signatures for each of these worst performance cases.

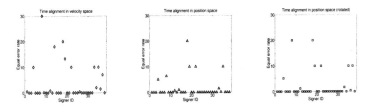

Fig. 6. Value of the equal error rate for each of the 38 subjects. The first plot corresponds to time alignment in velocity space, the second plot corresponds to time alignment of the 2D shape of the signatures and the third plot corresponds to time alignment of the 2D shape of the signatures, having previously aligned their main axis with the horizontal axis.

Table 3.1 summarizes the results shown in figure 6 for the best case, i.e., the one corresponding to the alignment of the 2D shape of the signatures. There is a noticeable difference between the numbers on table 3.1 and the values plotted on figure 6. The difference is due to the fact that in figure 6 we plot the value of equal error rate, that was computed as the intersection of the FAR and FRR curves and corresponds to an estimate of the performance of the algorithm in average, while in table 3.1 we show the values of FAR and FRR that correspond to a particular realization of the performance of the algorithm given by our test set. In the first four columns of the table, we show the number of signatures falsely rejected and falsely accepted, as well as the FRR and FAR for the condition of equal error rate. In the last four columns of the table, we present the number of signatures falsely rejected and falsely accepted, as well as the FRR and FAR for the condition of FAR < 1%. We note the mentioned trade off between FRR and FAR comparing the results obtained under these two conditions. In a verification system used for credit card transactions, it is very reasonable to operate with FAR < 1% since accepting a false signature could cause a substantial financial loss while rejecting a true signature could produce a little annoyance in the customer that would have to repeat the signature. For this case, the algorithm has an average FRR of 4 %. We should note that the overall performance of the

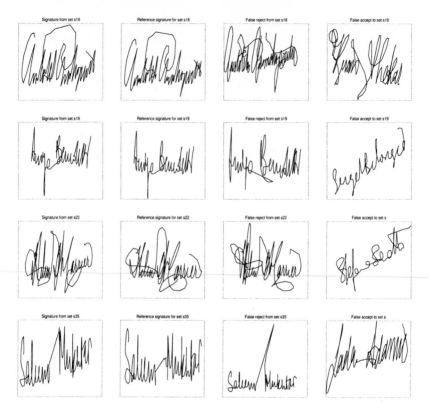

Fig. 7. The 4 cases in which the algorithm has biggest error. The first column shows signatures in the training set, the second column shows the reference signatures, the third column shows the signatures that were falsely rejected and, the last column shows signatures that were falsely accepted.

algorithm is quite good, with error rates comparable to the best presented in the literature [5], [12], [13], [19] under similar conditions.

3.2 Performance of Visual Signature Verification System

We collected signatures from 15 subjects. They were asked to train the system with 5 signatures and test it with at least 2 genuine signatures and 2 quasi-random forgeries (some piece of handwriting that has similar writing pattern as the genuine signature and it is written by the same subject).

Given the results showed in the previous section, we only implemented the 2D signature shape alignment in our real time system. The training is performed in the same way as it was described in section 3.1, right after the signatures have been captured. The training time is variable, depending on the duration of the signatures, experimentally we observe a maximum training time of 5 seconds. We should point out that our visual tracker is working in real-time at 30Hz. As shown in our previous work [10], we are able to track the pen tip in conditions of normal cursive or printed handwriting and drawings. However, in the case of

Table 1. Performance of the algorithm tested on the database of signatures collected with the tablet.

Signer ID	Equal error condition				FAR<1% condition			
	# FRs	# FAs	FRR (%)	FAR (%)	# FRs	# FAs	FRR (%)	FAR (%)
1	0	0	0	0	0	0	0	0
2	0	0	0	0	0	0	0	0
3	0	0	0	0	0	0	0	0
4	1	42	10	5.6757	1	7	10	0.9459
5	0	0	0	0	0	0	0	0
6	0	0	0	0	0	0	0	0
7	0	0	0	0	0	0	0	0
8	1	55	10	7.4324	2	3	20	0.4054
9	0	0	0	0	0	0	0	0
10	0	0	0	0	0	0	0	0
11	0	0	0	0	0	0	0	0
12	1	5	10	0.6757	0	5	0	0.6757
13	0	0	0	0	0	0	0	0
14	1	8	10	1.0811	1	2	10	0.2703
15	0	0	0	0	0	0	0	0
16	0	0	0	0	0	0	0	0
17	0	0	0	0	0	0	0	0
18	2	153	20	20.6757	3	2	30	0.2703
19	1	77	10	10.4054	4	2	40	0.2703
20	0	0	0	0	0	0	0	0
21	0	0	0	0	0	0	0	0
22	1	77	10	10.4054	1	2	10	0.2703
23	0	0	0	0	0	0	0	0
24	0	0	0	0	0	0	0	0
25	0	0	0	0	0	0	0	0
26	0	0	0	0	0	0	0	0
27	0	0	0	0	0	0	0	0
28	0	0	0	0	0	0	0	0
29	0	0	0	0	0	0	0	0
30	0	0	0	0	0	0	0	0
31	0	0	0	0	0	0	0	0
32	0	0	0	0	0	0	0	0
33	1	11	10	1.4865	1	7	10	0.9459
34	1	1	10	0.1351	0	6	0	0.8108
35	1	83	10	11.2162	1	1	10	0.1351
36	0	0	0	0	0	0	0	0
37	0	0	0	0	0	0	0	0
38	0	0	0	0	0	0	0	0
Total	11	512	2.8947	1.8208	14	37	3.6842	0.1316

signatures, we observe that the system occasionally loses track of the pen tip when the subject produces an extremely fast stroke. This problem of losing track of the pen tip could be solved in the future by using a more powerful machine or dedicated hardware. However, after a few trials, the user learns how to utilize the system without driving it to its limits.

The results of our tests were very encouraging and they are summarized in table 3.2. After the training, we obtain the individual costs of aligning each signature in the training set with the reference signature. We compute the mean and the standard deviation of these individual costs in order to use them for classification. When a new signature is captured for testing the system, the cost of aligning this signature with the reference signature is computed. The signature will be classified as genuine if this cost is smaller than a threshold and classified as forgery otherwise. In all our experiments, the threshold was taken to be the mean plus twice the standard deviation of the training costs.

We observe that the performance of subject 6 is not very good. Figure 8 shows signatures corresponding to this subject. We believe that this low performance is due to the fact that he was writing Greek letters with a big change in the inter-letter hesitation, generating in this way a series of sequences that are not very consistent time-wise when we compare them with signatures. We should point out that these results from the visual system need to be verified

Table 2. Results obtained by testing the algorithm in real time.

Signer ID	False Rejects	False Accepts	FRR(%)	FAR (%)
1	0	0	0	0
2	0	0	0	0
3	1	0	33	0
4	0	0	0	0
5	0	0	0	0
6	4	0	80	0
7	0	0	0	0
8	0	0	0	0
9	0	0	0	0
10	0	0	0	0
11	0	0	0	0
12	0	0	0	0
13	0	0	0	0
14	0	0	0	0
15	0	0	0	0
Total	5	0	7.5	0

by doing a bigger set of experiments, in order to fully characterize the performance of the algorithm. Nevertheless, we note that these results correspond to the most pessimistic scenario since the subjects were writing their signatures without any feedback from the system on the consistency of their signatures. In a more realistic scenario in which the subjects receive feedback from the system, one could expect that they would adapt, learning to sign in a way that would be considered consistent for the system.

Fig. 8. Signature from subject 6, reference signature and false rejected signature.

In figure 9 we show some original signatures, the corresponding reference signature and one of the random forgeries provided by the same subject.

The last part of our experiment was to compute the the FAR and FRR in the same way as we calculated it in section 3.1, i.e., the FRR was obtained by using the 2 signatures that we had for testing and the FAR was obtained by using all the other signatures provided by the other signers and all the forgeries. The result provided by the algorithm were perfect with 0% of FAR and FRR, probably due to the fact that our test set was very small. Nevertheless, these results are very encouraging in order to further pursue the development of a visual password verification system.

4 Conclusions and Further Work

We have presented a novel vision-based technique for personal identification. The system does not require any special hardware, unlike fingerprint verification, iris or retina scanning systems. It is comparable to face recognition systems in terms of hardware since it uses a camera for tracking the signature. We demonstrated

Fig. 9. Sequences acquired with the visual tracker. The first row shows signatures in the training set, the second row shows the reference signatures and the third row shows the quasi-random forgeries provided by the subjects.

the feasibility of having such a system working in real time with a high degree of accuracy in verifying signatures.

We consider it important to increase the robustness of the signature verification algorithm by adding some global parameterization of the signatures that will allow the system to discard coarse forgeries. The dynamic time warping algorithm could be improved by using different constraints or even using continuous time warping. We would also like to explore ways of training the system by aligning all the signatures at the same time, so that the resulting mean signature will be a more robust representative of its class. More extensive testing of the algorithm is required in order to understand its week points and correct them. In particular, we should include more actual forgeries in our database.

We note that the user would need some minimal training in order to master the system. When the signatures have extremely fast strokes, the system loses track of the pen tip. We asked the users to slow down a bit the motion of these strokes so that the tracker could acquire the signature. We believe that the use of a more powerful machine or the implementation of our tracking algorithm in hardware using FPGA's will eliminate this problem, allowing users to sign at normal speed.

References

1. Dynamic approaches to handwritten signature verification. G. lorette and r. plamondon. *Computer Processing of Handwriting*, pages 21–47, 1990.
2. R.S. Bucy. Non-linear filtering theory. *IEEE Trans. A.C. AC-10, 198*, 1965.

3. J.L. Crowley, F. Bernard, and J. Coutaz. Finger tracking as an input device for augmented reality. *Int. Work. on Face and Gecture Recog.*, pages 195–200, 1995.

4. J.G. Daugman. High confidence visual recognition of persons by a test of a statistical independence. *IEEE Trans. Pattern Analysis and Machine Intelligence*, 15(11):1148–1161, 1993.

5. K. Huang and H. Yan. On-line signatuer verification based on dynamic segmentation and global and local matching. *Optical Engineering*, 34(12):3480–3487, 1995.

6. A.K. Jain, L. Hong, S. Pankanti, and E. Bolle. An identity-authentication system using fingerprints. *Proceedings of the IEEE*, 85(9):1365–1388, 1997.

7. A.H. Jazwinski. *Stochastic Processes and Filtering Theory.* Academic Press, 1970.

8. R.E. Kalman. A new approach to linear filtering and prediction problems. *Trans. of the ASME-Journal of basic engineering.*, 35-45, 1960.

9. F. Leclerc and R. Plamondon. Automatic signature verificationand. *International Journal of Pattern Recognition and Artificial Intelligence*, 8(3):643–660, 1994.

10. M. Munich and P. Perona. Visual input for pen-based computers. In *Proc. 13th Int. Conf. Pattern Recognition*, 1996.

11. M.E. Munich and P.Perona. Visual input for pen based computers. *CNS Technical Report CNS-TR-95-01, California Institute of Technology*, 1995.

12. Vishvjit S. Nalwa. Automatic on-line signature verification. *Proceedings of the IEEE*, 85(2):215–239, 1997.

13. M. Parizeau and R. Plamondon. A comparative analysis of regional correlation, dynamical time warping and skeletal tree matching for signature verification. *IEEE Trans. Pattern Analysis and Machine Intelligence*, 12(7):710–717, 1990.

14. R. Plamondon. A kinematic theory of rapid movements. part i: Movement representation and generation. *Biological Cybernetics*, 72:295–307, 1995.

15. R. Plamondon. A kinematic theory of rapid movements. part ii: Movement time and control. *Biological Cybernetics*, 72:309–320, 1995.

16. R. Plamondon and G. Lorette. Automatic signature verification and writer identification, the state of the art. *Pattern Recognition*, 22(2):107–131, 1989.

17. L. Rabiner and B. Juang. *Fundamentals of Speech Recognition.* Prentice Hall, Inc., 1993.

18. H. Sakoe and S. Chiba. Dynamic programming algorithm optimization for spoken word recognition. *IEEE Trans. Acoustics, Speech, Signal Processing*, 26(1):43–49, 1978.

19. Y. Sato and K. Kogure. On-line signature verification based on shape, motion and writng pressure. *Proc. 6th Int. Conf. on Patt. Recognition*, pages 823–826, 1982.

20. C.C. Tappert, C.Y. Suen, and T. Wakahara. The state of the art in on-line handwriting recognition. *IEEE Trans. Pattern Analysis and Machine Intelligence*, 12:787–808, 1990.

21. C.J. Taylor, T.F. Cootes, A. Lanitis, G. Edwards, and P. Smyth et al. Model-based interpretation of complex and variables images. *Philosophical transactions of the Royal Society of London*, 352(1358):1267–1274, 1997.

22. M. Turk and A. Pentland. Eigenfaces for recognition. *J. of Cognitive Neurosci.*, 3(1):71–86, 1991.

23. L. Wiskott, J.M. Fellous, N. Kruger, and C. Von der Malsburg. Face recogniton by elastic bunch graph matching. *IEEE Trans. Pattern Analysis and Machine Intelligence*, 19(7):775–779, 1997.

Model Based Tracking for Navigation and Segmentation

B Southall[1,2], J A Marchant[1], T Hague[1], and B F Buxton[2]

[1] Silsoe Research Institute, Wrest Park, Silsoe,
Bedfordshire, MK45 4HS, UK

[2] Department of Computer Science, University College London, Gower Street,
London, WC1E 6BT, UK
B.Southall@cs.ucl.ac.uk

Abstract. An autonomous vehicle has been developed for precision application of treatment on outdoor crops. This document details a new vision algorithm to aid navigation and crop/weed discrimination being developed for this machine. The algorithm tracks a model of the crop planting pattern through an image sequence using an extended Kalman filter. A parallel update scheme is used to provide not only navigation information for the vehicle controller but also estimates of plant position for the treatment system. The algorithm supersedes a previous Hough transform tracking technique currently used on the vehicle which provides navigation information alone, from the rows of plants. The crop planting model is introduced and the tracking system developed, along with a method for automatically starting the algorithm. In applications such as this, where the vehicle traverses unsurfaced outdoor terrain, "ground truth" data for the path taken by the vehicle is unavailable; lacking this veridical information, the algorithm's performance is evaluated with respect to human assessment and the previous row-only tracking algorithm, and found to offer improvements over the previous technique.

1 Introduction

An autonomous agricultural vehicle [2] has been developed at the Silsoe Research Institute to perform the task of *plant scale husbandry*, which aims, for example, to reduce the use of chemicals in crop protection by treating individual plants and weeds separately, with little waste chemical sprayed onto the bare earth. Such a level of treatment provides obvious environmental and economic advantages over more traditional field spraying techniques. It is important in such applications both to be able to steer the vehicle accurately along rows of plants and to be able to identify where individual plants are.

The algorithm described here uses perspective images captured from a camera mounted on the front of the vehicle to provide estimates of the position of both the structure of the crop row planting pattern and the position of individual plants within that structure. At the heart of the algorithm is a Kalman filter with a non-linear measurement model (to correct for the perspective distortion of the images), which is used to track a model of the crop planting pattern through the image sequence generated as the vehicle traverses the field. The crop row structure is a cue used by the vehicle, in combination with non-vision sensors [3], to navigate along the rows. A Hough transform algorithm for tracking the plant rows has been previously reported [7] [8] and is currently part of the system. The existing algorithm extracts only the direction and offset of the rows of plants whereas the new algorithm also provides an estimate of individual plant positions which can then be used to target treatment by the spray system. A second advantage of the new algorithm is that the Kalman filter provides a covariance matrix for the state estimate which can be given to the vehicle controller; the Hough transform does not produce these covariances.

The use of a rigid model in tracking systems is well established, notably [4] where the rigid model in question consisted of control points on straight edge segments, thus suitable mainly for man-made *objects*. The problem here is extracting man-made *structure* imposed on a natural world. The rigid model gives a perfect version of the relationship expected between the plant centres on the ground plane, and the non-ideal nature of the real world must be catered for. However, how to model the effects of the noise of individual plant locations on the estimation of the crop planting pattern position is unclear; for the purposes of this paper the simplifying step of accommodating plant position noise as uncertainty in the observation model has been taken.

Other vision work within the scope of this project [10][11] (neither of which have been implemented on the vehicle) has addressed tracking individual plants rather than the planting pattern as a whole as approached in this paper; by tracking the whole pattern it is believed a more robust system will be realised. The two methods mentioned make use of plant models (in [11] a cluster of chain-coded areas, in [10] a more complex shape model) both of which could potentially be distracted by large clusters of weed material. By using the information available on the planting pattern, the search for plant material is constrained, and weed patches away from the crop structure will be ignored.

This paper describes the model of the planting structure, the extended Kalman filter used to track the model through the image sequence, and a method for automatically boot-strapping the algorithm. Finally, results are presented from experiments with real images (in the examples given, the crop is cauliflower) and conclusions drawn on the performance of the technique.

2　The Crop Planting Model

2.1　Model Parameters

Figure 1 shows a schematic view of a patch of crop, with the plants being represented by black circles. There are two sets of axes in the figure, (x_w, y_w) and (x_c, y_c, z_c) which represent the world and camera co-ordinate systems respectively, with the world z_w axis projecting out of the page, and camera axis z_c projecting into the page. It can be seen that the world y axis is coincident with the middle plant row. The model of the crop consists of the four measurements; r, the spacing between the rows, l the space between plants in the row, D_{-1}, which is a measure of the offset between the left-hand row of plants and the central row of plants and finally D_1, which is the corresponding quantity for the right-hand row. The model makes the assumption that the crop is planted in perfect position, although in reality there is error in the planting positions, and some plants are missing – both of these problems are tackled by the Kalman filter.

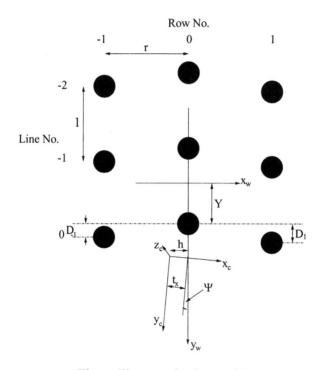

Fig. 1. The crop planting model

Three parameters (t_x, Y and Ψ), specify the position of the model relative to the camera as shown in the diagram, and these will later be seen as the state vector $\mathbf{x} = [t_x, Y, \Psi]^T$ estimated by the Kalman filter. The measurement Y is the offset in world co-ordinates from the world origin of the plant in the central row at the bottom of the image. The offset of the camera y_c axis from the world origin t_x is approximately equal to the distance h when angle Ψ is small. It can be seen then that the t_x and Ψ parameters may be used to provide navigation information in terms of a heading angle and offset of the camera (and hence the vehicle) relative to the rows, and the parameter Y, in conjunction with model parameters D_{-1} and D_1 can yield the position of individual plants via equations 1 and 2 (extended from those presented in [8]) below.

$$x_w = nr \qquad (1)$$

$$y_w = ml + Y + D_n \qquad (2)$$

The quantities $n \in \{-1, 0, 1\}$ and $m \in \{0, -1, -2, \ldots, -(m_{max} - 1)\}$ index into the $3 \times m_{max}$ grid formed by the planting pattern. The term D_0 is the offset of the central row; by definition $D_0 = 0$. It should be noted that the plant centres are assumed to be on the ground plane ($z_w = 0$). It is stressed that the model describes the grid on which individual plants should lie, rather than the actual location of the individual plants.

The origin of the world axes (x_w, y_w, z_w) is not fixed on the ground plane, but is local to the vehicle (and therefore moves along with the vehicle); as stated above the y_w axis is always coincident with the middle crop row, whilst the x_w axis passes through the point where the camera's optical axis z_c intersects the ground plane.

2.2 Observation of the Model in the Image

Having specified a model for the planting pattern, attention must now be turned to how this model will appear in the image. Owing to the angle at which the camera is mounted on the vehicle, features on the ground plane are viewed on the image plane under a perspective projection. Marchant and Brivot [8] arrive at the following expressions for the 2D image plane co-ordinates (x_u, y_u) of 3D world points $(x_w, y_w, 0)$ (t_y, t_z and ϕ are explained below):

$$x_u = f \frac{(x_w \cos \Psi + y_w \sin \Psi + t_x)}{x_w \sin \Psi \sin \phi - y_w \cos \Psi \sin \phi + t_z} \qquad (3)$$

$$y_u = f \frac{(-x_w \sin \Psi \cos \phi + y_w \cos \Psi \cos \phi + t_y)}{x_w \sin \Psi \sin \phi - y_w \cos \Psi \sin \phi + t_z} \qquad (4)$$

Equations 3 and 4 are derived from those given by Tsai [12], with the added assumption that the camera does not pitch or roll (i.e that the camera axes (x_c, y_c, z_c) of figure 1 do not rotate about the world axes x_w or y_w). This assumption has been made on the basis of observation of long image sequences and also because the vehicle is running on well tended tilled fields. The angle ϕ is that of the camera's optical axis (z_c) to the world z_w axis, and Ψ is that shown in figure 1. The quantity t_z is distance along the optic axis between the camera optical centre and the intersection with the ground plane, and t_y gives the offset (in camera co-ordinates) of the point where the optical axis intersects the world x_w axis and, as in [8], this can be set to zero. One further assumption is that the angle Ψ is small enough for the approximations $\cos \Psi \approx 1$ and $\sin \Psi \approx \Psi$ to hold.

From the above, it is possible to generate image pixel co-ordinates (x_f, y_f) for each plant centre (m, n) by combining equations 1 and 2 with 3 and 4, and inserting a suitable estimate of the parameters t_x, Y and Ψ

$$x_f(x, Y, \Psi, m, n) = \frac{f}{dx} \frac{nr + \Psi(ml + Y + D_n) + t_x}{nr\Psi \sin\phi - (ml + Y + D_n)\sin\phi + t_z} + C_x \quad (5)$$

$$y_f(x, Y, \Psi, m, n) = \frac{f}{dy} \frac{(ml + Y + D_n - \Psi nr)\cos\phi}{nr\Psi \sin\phi - (ml + Y + D_n)\sin\phi + t_z} + C_y \quad (6)$$

The values of dx and dy give the horizontal and vertical side length of the camera pixels respectively, and (C_x, C_y) is the co-ordinate (in pixels) of the centre of the imaging surface. In practice it has been found that the maximum number of plants seen in a single image is 15, so $m_{max} = 5$ generates a suitable number of predictions (if there are less than 15 plants in the image, then some predictions will lie outside the bounds of the image; such predictions are ignored).

3 Tracking the Pattern

The Kalman filter [5] is used to provide a means of tracking the plant model through the image sequence by *predicting* the crop structure position (and hence the individual plant positions) and using observations of plants taken from the image to *correct* this prediction. The filter estimates not only the state of a system $\mathbf{x}$, but also provides a covariance for the estimates, $\mathbf{P}$.

3.1 The System Model

The prediction is made by means of a (linear) state transition model which describes the evolution of the state $\mathbf{x} = [t_x, Y, \Psi]$ as the vehicle moves between between image k and $k + 1$:

$$\mathbf{x}(k + 1) = \mathbf{A}\mathbf{x}(k) + \mathbf{U}(k) + \mathbf{n}(k), \quad (7)$$

where $\mathbf{A}$ is the 3×3 state transition matrix and $\mathbf{U}$ the 3×1 control input, i.e. the vehicle motion between image k and $k+1$. By treating $\mathbf{U}$ as an external variable, rather than a state to be estimated, the kinematic model of the vehicle is hidden from the algorithm (therefore providing an estimate that is independent of a kinematic model which will be violated in certain circumstances, e.g. when the vehicle's wheels slip); the problem of integrating the vision system Kalman filter given here with the vehicle control system filter (where the vehicle kinematics are used to estimate $\mathbf{U}$) will be addressed in the future. There is also an additive zero-mean Gaussian noise term $\mathbf{n}$ which has (3×3) covariance matrix $\mathbf{Q}(k)$, and quantifies the uncertainty in the vehicle motion estimates. Because the planting pattern is assumed to be of fixed size and shape, $\mathbf{A}$ is taken to be the identity matrix.

The observation of the crop planting model in the image has already been discussed in section 2.2, and this can also be more formally stated in state-space terms:

$$\mathbf{z}(k, m, n) = \mathbf{h}[k, \mathbf{x}(k), m, n, \mathbf{w}(k)] = \begin{bmatrix} x_f(\mathbf{x}(k), m, n) \\ y_f(\mathbf{x}(k), m, n) \end{bmatrix} + \mathbf{w}(k) \quad (8)$$

The vector $\mathbf{w}(k)$ is zero-mean Gaussian noise described by (2×2) covariance matrix $\mathbf{R}(k, m, n)$. Here, the matrix $\mathbf{R}$ reflects the fact that the cauliflowers are not planted on a perfect grid, but deviate from the ideal positions predicted by the model. Note that the observation model $\mathbf{h}$ is both a function of the state $\mathbf{x}(k)$, and m and n, the integer variables which index the crop grid – so one state estimate generates $3 \times m_{max}$ observations. The observation model is also non-linear, so an extended Kalman filter [1] is required.

3.2   The Extended Kalman Filter

The extended Kalman filter allows a linearisation of the observation model about the state prediction point, and although it offers a sub-optimal solution to the estimation problem, and can converge to local minima (and therefore lose track) if poorly initialised, it offers a practical solution to the non-linear tracking problem. The filter predict-correct cycle is outlined here, with initialisation of the state prediction $\hat{\mathbf{x}}$ and its covariance $\mathbf{P}$ covered in section 4.

Owing to the fact that each state prediction produces several observations which must be incorporated into the filter to yield the corrected estimate, the predict-correct cycle takes a slightly unusual form. The "prior" prediction for each image is given by equations 9 and 10.

$$\hat{\mathbf{x}}(k + 1|k) = \hat{\mathbf{x}}(k|k) + \mathbf{U}(k) \tag{9}$$

$$\mathbf{P}(k + 1|k) = \mathbf{P}(k|k) + \mathbf{Q}(k) \tag{10}$$

From this single state prediction, equation 8 shows that a set of predicted observations is produced

$$\hat{\mathbf{z}}(k + 1|k, m, n) = \begin{bmatrix} x_f(\hat{\mathbf{x}}(k + 1|k), m, n) \\ y_f(\hat{\mathbf{x}}(k + 1|k), m, n) \end{bmatrix} \tag{11}$$

Each of these predicted observations $\hat{\mathbf{z}}(k + 1|k, m, n)$ must be matched to an observed image feature $\mathbf{z}(k + 1, m, n)$ and incorporated into the state estimate. Feature matching is achieved using the nearest-neighbour data association procedure [9], with each associated feature being validated prior to incorporation (see below). The incorporation itself is performed using a batch update method as used in [6] (originally appearing in [13]) as opposed to the more traditional recursive estimation procedure. The batch update is preferred because a single state update leads to the prediction of several $(3 \times m_{max})$ feature locations, and when a validation procedure is used, the order of incorporation would become important if a recursive update scheme were in place – if a "poor" feature-prediction pair were incorporated first, it could bias successive predictions in such a way that "good" features would fail the validation test, leading to inaccurate tracking performance.

Armed with the predictions from equation 11, the associated image features (see section 3.3) $\mathbf{z}(k + 1, m, n)$ may each be subjected to a validation test. This validation procedure allows a plant to be missing from the grid structure (without validation, if a plant were missing then the nearest-neighbour algorithm would associate a neighbouring plant with the prediction). If

$$v(k + 1, m, n) = z(k + 1, m, n) - \hat{z}(k + 1|k, m, n) \tag{12}$$

is the *innovation*, then feature $z(k + 1, m, n)$ is valid if

$$v^T(k + 1, m, n)S^{-1}(k + 1, m, n)v(k + 1, m, n) \le \chi^2 \tag{13}$$

where χ^2 is a chi-square figure of merit, corresponding to a desired confidence level, and $S(k+1, m, n)$ is the innovation covariance for observation (m, n), given by

$$S(k+1, m, n) = h_x(k+1, m, n)P(k+1|k)h_x{}^T(k+1, m, n) + R(k+1, m, n). \tag{14}$$

The Jacobian $h_x(k + 1, m, n)$ is that of the observation equations 8, which linearises (to the first order) the observation equation about the prediction point, thus enabling a projection of the state estimate covariance $P(k + 1|k)$ into the image plane. Its definition is

$$h_x(k+1, m, n) = \begin{bmatrix} \frac{\partial x_f}{\partial t_x}\Big|_{\hat{x}(k+1|k), m, n} & \frac{\partial x_f}{\partial Y}\Big|_{\hat{x}(k+1|k), m, n} & \frac{\partial x_f}{\partial \psi}\Big|_{\hat{x}(k+1|k), m, n} \\ \frac{\partial y_f}{\partial t_x}\Big|_{\hat{x}(k+1|k), m, n} & \frac{\partial y_f}{\partial Y}\Big|_{\hat{x}(k+1|k), m, n} & \frac{\partial y_f}{\partial \psi}\Big|_{\hat{x}(k+1|k), m, n} \end{bmatrix}. \tag{15}$$

Each observation passing the validation test (equation 13) is then used in the batch update of the state estimate and state covariance matrix. For each valid observation, the three quantities $h_x(k+1, m, n)$, $R(k+1, m, n)$ and $v(k+1, m, n)$ are stored. A batch innovation vector $v(k+1)$ is constructed by stacking each of the validated innovations $v(k + 1, m, n)$, and similarly a batch observation Jacobian $h_x(k + 1)$ is created by stacking the $h_x(k + 1, m, n)$ corresponding to the valid observations. Finally, a batch observation matrix $R(k + 1)$ is constructed which has block diagonal form, where the matrices on the diagonal are the validated $R(k + 1, m, n)$. The standard Kalman filter equations are then applied to these batch quantities to update the state estimate and state covariance matrix:

$$\hat{x}(k + 1|k + 1) = \hat{x}(k + 1|k) + W(k + 1)v(k + 1) \tag{16}$$

$$P(k + 1|k + 1) = P(k + 1|k) - W(k + 1)S(k + 1)W^T(k + 1), \tag{17}$$

with the covariance matrix of the stacked innovation

$$S(k + 1) = h_x(k + 1)P(k + 1|k)h_x{}^T(k + 1) + R(k + 1) \tag{18}$$

and Kalman gain

$$W(k + 1) = P(k + 1|k)h_x{}^T(k + 1)S^{-1}(k + 1). \tag{19}$$

The off-diagonal terms in the innovation covariance matrix $S(k+1)$ (equation 18) describe the correlations between successive observations made from the single state prediction.

3.3 Feature Extraction, Association and Validation

Although the state estimation framework has been described, there are still some matters to be discussed, one of which is the method of extracting the observations $\mathbf{z}(k+1, m, n)$ from the images. The images are of real crop planted and raised in accordance with standard agricultural practice and are collected outdoors under natural illumination. The sequences thus contain both crop and weeds, with some plants missing from the row structure. The images are collected using a camera sensitive to near infra-red wavelengths where contrast between plant and soil matter is enhanced [8] (the camera has a visible light blocking filter). Two methods have been used to extract plant positions from the images; an automatic method described below, and manual selection of features by a human, which is used to evaluate the performance of the tracker independently of the feature extraction mechanism.

The automatic feature extraction method is that used in [8], which chain-codes areas of the infra-red image exceeding a grey-level threshold (currently, the vehicle uses dedicated hardware to perform this function). The centre of each chain code is calculated and used as a candidate feature to be matched to a prediction generated by the Kalman filter. It has been observed that weed features in the image tend to be smaller than the plants, and a simple threshold on chain code area is also imposed in order to reject the smallest weeds from the matching process.

Owing to the simplicity of the differentiation between plant and non-plant pixels (by use of a threshold) the chain-coder does not always produce perfect plant outlines; parts of leaves may be missed out because of shadows, or a plant made of separate leaves may be fractured into several objects because the regions between leaves are dark. The result of these shortcomings is that the "centres" produced by the chain coder do not necessarily correspond to the real centres of plants. Improved feature detection will feature largely in further research, although results show that this relatively crude method produces satisfactory results.

3.4 Covariance Matrices

Three covariance matrices are required to run the filter; a measure of process noise $\mathbf{Q}(k)$, which may be obtained from the Kalman filter used to estimate the vehicle motion parameters [3], an observation noise matrix $\mathbf{R}(k, m, n)$, which will be discussed here, and an initial value of the estimate covariance $\mathbf{P}(0|0)$, which will be provided in section 4.

The observation covariance $\mathbf{R}(k+1, m, n)$ quantifies the noise associated with the predicted observation $\hat{\mathbf{z}}(k+1|k)$ of plant centre (m, n) – the Kalman filter framework implicitly assumes that the plant centres are being extracted from the image, and although, as seen above, this is not the case, results on real images bear out the fact that this is an acceptable working assumption. Additional noise arises because the plant centres are not placed ideally on the grid specified by the model, but are found on the ground plane in perturbed positions which may be modelled by a two dimensional (x_w, y_w) Gaussian distribution whose mean is the ideal plant position. This covariance in the world-frame is given by the matrix $\mathbf{R_w} = \mathrm{diag}[\sigma^2_{x_w}, \sigma^2_{y_w}]$, and can be projected into the image frame using standard first order error propagation via equations 3 and 4, giving

$$\mathbf{R}(k+1, m, n) = \mathbf{F_{\hat{x}}}(k+1, m, n)\mathbf{R_w}\mathbf{F_{\hat{x}}}^T(k+1, m, n) \tag{20}$$

Where the Jacobian $\mathbf{F_{\hat{x}}}(k+1, m, n)$ is defined as

$$\mathbf{F_{\hat{x}}}(k+1, m, n) = \begin{bmatrix} \left.\dfrac{\partial x_u}{\partial x_w}\right|_{\hat{x}(k+1|k),m,n} & \left.\dfrac{\partial x_u}{\partial y_w}\right|_{\hat{x}(k+1|k),m,n} \\[2ex] \left.\dfrac{\partial y_u}{\partial x_w}\right|_{\hat{x}(k+1|k),m,n} & \left.\dfrac{\partial y_u}{\partial x_w}\right|_{\hat{x}(k+1|k),m,n} \end{bmatrix} \tag{21}$$

x_w, y_w for the plant centres are defined in equations 1 and 2. As noted in the introduction, this noise source should manifest itself in the system noise model, but as yet it is unclear how this should be done; the method given here provides a working alternative.

4 Starting the Algorithm

To start the tracking process, an initial estimate of the crop pattern position $\mathbf{x}$ is acquired in two stages; the initial estimates of t_x and Ψ are obtained by a global search of the Hough space which is formed using the methods of [8]. The model position Y and row offsets D_{-1} and D_1 are then obtained from Fourier analysis of 1D image samples taken along the extracted rows. By sampling along the line of the rows in the image a profile of the grey-levels along the row is obtained. Figure 2 shows an idealised binary image with a row marked and its corresponding sample. The sampling is performed in world frame co-ordinates, which accounts for the regular spacing of the sample peaks in the figure, despite the perspective foreshortening in the image. To allow for non-ideal positioning of the row, and the fact that plants are two dimensional objects in the image rather than one dimensional, the sample analysed is constructed by taking the mean (at each sample point) of a set of 5 samples taken 5 mm apart on the ground plane around the row specified by the Hough transform method.

The procedure for obtaining offset values from these samples is as follows; form the discrete Fourier transform $F(j\omega)$ of the (1D) grey-level profile (ω is the angular spatial frequency in radians per metre) and calculate the phase θ of the coefficients corresponding to the frequency $2\pi/l$, the expected frequency of plant spacing l from the crop model. θ can be converted into spatial offset along the row using the following formula

$$\mathrm{Offset} = \frac{\theta l}{2\pi}. \tag{22}$$

Using this method, model position Y can be calculated from the central row, and D_{-1}, D_1 found subsequently from the outer rows.

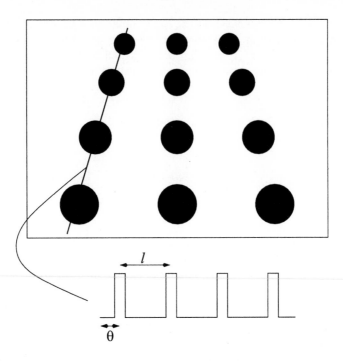

Fig. 2. Sampling along a row: the phase θ of the sample provides the offset of the planting pattern

Once initial values for t_x, Y and Ψ have been obtained, the state estimate $\hat{\mathbf{x}}(0|0)$ may be formed, leaving only the initial state covariance $\mathbf{P}(0|0)$ undetermined. From [8], an estimate of root mean square error has been obtained on the accuracy of the Hough transform algorithm, giving r.m.s error of 12.5 mm on t_x and 1° on Ψ. As noted in [1], in the extended Kalman filter the matrix $\mathbf{P}$ is not strictly a covariance, but a measure of mean square error on the estimate $\hat{\mathbf{x}}$, so these values of offset and angular error may be used directly. To obtain a measure of mean square error for the estimate of row offset, the method of [8] was used; the row offset algorithm was applied to 40 images, and estimates of the central row offset were acquired. A human operator was then asked to align a template of plant centres with the crop in each image, the position of the template giving the offset; the initial alignment of the template with the row structure was carried out using the Hough transform method, so that only the Fourier transform part of the algorithm was under test. A scatter plot of the human *vs* automatic measurements of offset is shown in figure 3. A regression line was then fitted through this set of points, and the r.m.s. error calculated, with the resulting error being 24.5 mm. It should be noted that this method implicitly assumes that all the errors arise from the algorithm (i.e. that the human assessment is perfect), so is far from ideal. However, with a lack of veridical data,

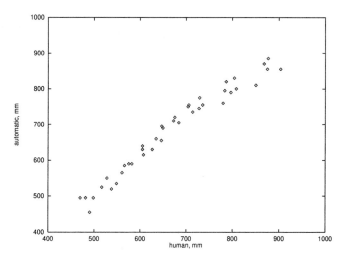

Fig. 3. Comparison of human and automatic assessment of row offset

this kind of comparison with subjective human judgement provides a pragmatic solution to the problem of estimating the initial state covariance.

Experiments in which the initial covariance was increased by up to a factor of 10, or decreased to zero showed that this only affected the initial response of the filter, with convergence to the same track after two or three images into the sequence.

5   Results and Discussion

Two sets of 20 near infra-red images have been digitised from video stock collected from the experimental vehicle during the Summer of 1997. In both sequences, the vehicle was instructed to follow the crop rows at a constant velocity. The image sequences were analysed using the following methods:

1. The fully automatic algorithm described in this paper (AUTO).
2. The Kalman filter using the human selected input features (SEMI).
3. Human assessment of the model position; a mouse-driven program has been designed to allow the user to place the crop pattern on each image in the sequence. Data from three different people has been collected (HUMAN 1–3).
4. The method of [8], which produces estimates of t_x and Ψ alone (HOUGH).

Figure 4 shows state trajectories from the first image sequence. The left-hand column plots the three human responses, whilst the right hand column shows the equivalent automatic results (note that there is no Y estimate available from the Hough transform algorithm).

As noted above, when ground truth trajectories are unavailable, as in this case, quantitative analysis of the accuracy of a tracking system is difficult to perform

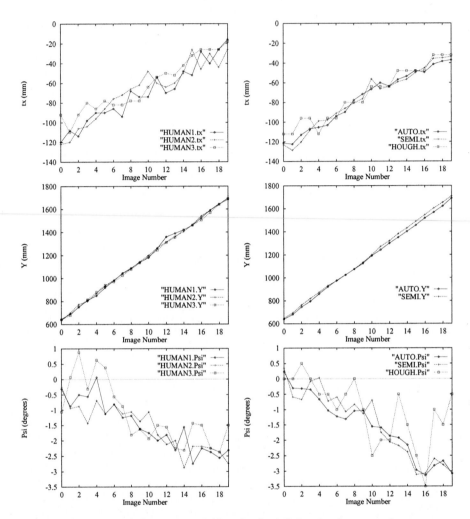

Fig. 4. Trajectories of the state variables. In the left-hand column are human assessments, and in the right the algorithm output (note that HOUGH does not produce a Y output). The negative values of t_x indicate that the vehicle was to the left of the planting pattern, but moving toward it. The Y estimates have been plotted with respect to a static global origin (as opposed to the moving co-ordinate system described in section 2) to illustrate clearly the vehicle's approximately constant velocity.

because it is not known how the errors are distributed between the automatic methods and human assessment. To provide some measure of performance, an approach has been taken which assumes errors are equally distributed between the automatic and human approach. By taking each set of results for t_x, Y and Ψ from the experiments conducted and pairing of corresponding data sets, scatter plots like figure 3 can be constructed. If a pair of algorithms agree exactly, then the points in the scatter diagram will lie on the line $x = y$. Taking this as the ideal response, a measure of how far a pair of algorithms depart from the ideal may be found by taking the root mean-square differences between feature points in the scatter plot and the nearest (in Euclidean terms) point on the line $x = y$. These values are tabulated for each of the state variables and algorithm pairs in tables 1 – 3. It should be stressed that the $x = y$ "ideal" does not mean that a pairing is correct, but that the two sets are consistent, so the larger this measure, the greater the inconsistency between them.

From the tabulated figures and perusal of the trajectory plots, three main conclusions may be drawn;

1. Human assessments are not wholly consistent. The table elements referring to the similarity between HUMAN data set pairs contain figures that are not zero; so, unsurprisingly, different people make differing assessments of the model position.
2. The various algorithm estimates are as consistent with the human results as the human results are with each other. In some cases, notably the t_x estimate of HUMAN 2, the human observation is more consistent with the automatic and semi-automatic methods than with the other humans. Importantly, the new method (AUTO) has similar r.m.s. measures of consistency to the HOUGH method, which has operated successfully on the vehicle. For the measurement of Ψ, the AUTO method is more consistent with human assessment than HOUGH; this is reflected in the plots of figure 4.
3. The fully automatic algorithm performs comparably with the semi-automatic algorithm. The similarity measure between the two is given in the table; in the case of t_x and Ψ, the differences are a fraction of the quantisation interval used in the Hough transform method, so it may be assumed that errors in the automatic method would make no operational difference, and the mean difference of 14 mm on a measurement of Y ranging from 600 – 1700 mm is also very small. It can be seen that when compared to the human assessments, the two differ even less.

6   Conclusions

A self-starting algorithm has been demonstrated which allows the extraction of crop planting patterns from a sequence of images, giving information for both vehicle navigation and plant treatment system control. The new method produces estimates of offset t_x and heading angle Ψ which compare favourably with those produced by the Hough transform algorithm, and furthermore yields both

	HUMAN 1	HUMAN 2	HUMAN 3	HOUGH	AUTO	SEMI
HUMAN 1	0	–	–	–	–	–
HUMAN 2	8.02	0	–	–	–	–
HUMAN 3	7.54	7.96	0	–	–	–
HOUGH	8.20	7.70	7.85	0	–	–
AUTO	6.63	6.41	8.89	5.06	0	–
SEMI	6.76	6.17	8.85	5.86	2.82	0

Table 1. Root-mean square differences on the t_x estimate, mm. '-' indicates that the value can be found in the lower half of table.

	HUMAN 1	HUMAN 2	HUMAN 3	HOUGH	AUTO	SEMI
HUMAN 1	0	–	–	n/a	–	–
HUMAN 2	14.20	0	–	n/a	–	–
HUMAN 3	13.72	13.84	0	n/a	–	–
HOUGH	n/a	n/a	n/a	n/a	n/a	n/a
AUTO	13.18	17.19	10.16	n/a	0	–
SEMI	12.55	10.82	12.50	n/a	14.11	0

Table 2. Root-mean square differences on the Y estimate, mm. 'n/a' indicates Y is not estimated by algorithm HOUGH.

	HUMAN 1	HUMAN 2	HUMAN 3	HOUGH	AUTO	SEMI
HUMAN 1	0	–	–	–	–	–
HUMAN 2	0.408	0	–	–	–	–
HUMAN 3	0.510	0.540	0	–	–	–
HOUGH	0.750	0.808	0.698	0	–	–
AUTO	0.363	0.365	0.510	0.666	0	–
SEMI	0.426	0.323	0.532	0.742	0.253	0

Table 3. Root-mean square differences on the Ψ estimate, degrees. The figures indicate that the set least consistent with the other data is from algorithm HOUGH, and this is reflected in the plots of figure 4.

an estimate of the Y measurement which is used to locate individual plants for treatment, and a measure of uncertainty **P** which will be utilised by the control system Kalman filter in the fusion of vision information with odometric measurements.

It is hoped to implement the algorithm to run in real time (which should be feasible due to the computational simplicity of the method) and to test it on longer image sequences. Incorporation of this method into the vehicle control system will also be addressed. A method of on-line model parameter adjustment is to be added in order to correct for any calibration errors, and to compensate for any gradual change in crop spacing which may occur during planting. It is also believed that more sophisticated feature extraction techniques may improve performance, particularly robustness to the changing lighting conditions often experienced in outdoor environments.

Acknowledgements

Thanks to Robin Tillett and Dickson Chan for their patience in producing the HUMAN 2 and HUMAN 3 data sets respectively. This work was funded by the BBSRC.

References

1. Y Bar-Shalom and T Fortmann. *Tracking and Data Association*. Academic Press, New York, 1988.
2. T Hague, J A Marchant, and N D Tillett. Autonomous robot navigation for precision horticulture. In *IEEE International Conference on Robotics and Automation*. Albuquerque, 1997.
3. T Hague and N D Tillett. Navigation and control of an autonomous horticultural robot. *Mechatronics*, 6(2):165–180, 1996.
4. C Harris. Tracking with rigid models. In A Blake and A Yuille, editors, *Active Vision*, chapter 4. MIT Press, 1992.
5. R E Kalman. A new approach to linear filtering and prediction problems. *Transactions of the ASME Journal of Basic Engineering*, 1960.
6. J J Leonard and H F Durrant-Whyte. Mobile robot localization by tracking geometric beacons. *IEEE Trans. Robotics and Automation*, 7(3):376–382, June 1991.
7. J A Marchant. Tracking of row structure in three crops using image analysis. *Computers and electronics in agriculture*, 15(9):161–179, 1996.
8. J A Marchant and R Brivot. Real time tracking of plant rows using a hough transform. *Real Time Imaging*, 1:363–371, 1995.
9. B Rao. Data association methods for tracking systems. In A Blake and A Yuille, editors, *Active Vision*, chapter 6. MIT Press, 1992.
10. D Reynard, A Wildenberg, A Blake, and J A Marchant. Learning dynamics of complex motions from image sequences. In B Buxton and R Cipolla, editors, *Computer Vision – ECCV '96*, Lecture Notes in Computer Science. Springer, April 1996.
11. J M Sanchiz, F Pla, J A Marchant, and R Brivot. Structure from motion techniques applied to crop field mapping. *Image and Vision Computing*, 14:353–363, 1996.
12. R Y Tsai. An efficient and accurate camera calibration technique for 3d machine vision. In *Proc. IEEE Computer Soc. Conf. Comp Vis Patt Recog*, Miami Beach, June 1986.
13. D Willner, C B Chang, and K P Dunn. Kalman filter algorithms for a multi-sensor system. In *Proc. IEEE Int. Conf. Decision and Control*, pages 570–574, 1976.

Beginning a Transition from a Local to a More Global Point of View in Model–Based Vehicle Tracking

Michael Haag[1] and Hans–Hellmut Nagel[1,2]

[1] Institut für Algorithmen und Kognitive Systeme, Fakultät für Informatik der Universität Karlsruhe (TH), Postfach 6980, D–76128 Karlsruhe, Germany
[2] Fraunhofer–Institut für Informations– und Datenverarbeitung (IITB), Fraunhoferstr. 1, D–76131 Karlsruhe, Germany

Abstract. This contribution attempts to move beyond the status where single moving objects in video image sequences are tracked separately in the scene domain, based on individually adapted approaches and parameters. Instead, we investigate which performance can be achieved by a combination of approaches based on edge element orientation and on optical flow, applied to a variety of image sequences and vehicles. Five different image sequences of traffic scenes recorded under different conditions have been evaluated. Quantitative statements are provided about the success rates of the approach after evaluating over 5.500 full video–frames, i. e. more than $3\frac{1}{2}$ minutes of real–world video, using *one single approach and a single parameter set*. Remaining tracking failures are analyzed and classified.

1 Introduction and Related Work

Surveillance of traffic scenes by means of video cameras potentially can have a variety of applications, including extraction of traffic statistics or the realization of intelligent control of traffic lights. Such applications require a robust system which is able to track vehicles and to characterize their maneuvers even under difficult conditions. Image sequences of road traffic recorded by a stationary standard S–VHS video camera are characterized by small vehicle images, shadows, changing illumination conditions, low contrast object images, uncertain camera calibration, and occluded scene objects. Since it is sometimes even impossible for a human observer to identify the low contrast image of a vehicle in a single grey value image, we combine purely spatial image features with motion analysis. Consequent exploitation of knowledge about the 3D–structure of the scene helps us to deal with significant occlusions between objects and with changing illumination conditions (for example objects moving from a bright region into a shadow).

This contribution does not address the problem of optimizing a tracking approach and its parameters for a particular moving object. Instead, we want to apply one and the *same approach* with the *same parameter* set in order to track as many objects as possible in different image sequences, well knowing that we may be able to track single objects better if we adapt the approach or the parameters to the specific circumstances. A summary after evaluation of over 5.500 frames and more than 50 tracking experiments should help to identify problems which have to be solved in order to meet the requirements of traffic surveillance systems as outlined above. With this contribution, we are leaving the status where basic research addressed tracking single vehicles under particular circumstances, for example low contrast images or occlusion. Instead, we shift the discussion from specific model–based techniques to an engineering–like process by systematically identifying and subsequently solving the most pressing among the remaining problems.

Surveys of the literature up to 1995 concerning image motion interpretation and visual surveillance can be found in [2, 1].

The majority of published approaches track vehicles in the 2D *picture domain*. [1] describe experiments regarding aspects of an integrated visual traffic surveillance system. Vehicles are tracked by extracting optical flow vectors and correlating them with causal constraints in a Bayesian Belief Network (BBN). [10] use these geometric results in order to identify 'overtaking' or 'give–way' situations in traffic sequences. [16] have to cope with particularly small object images since the vehicles are usually moving far away from the recording camera. Objects are tracked by computing differences between frames and by updating a background model in order to deal with image changes not originating from object motion. By careful combination of spatial 2D image features (the vehicle's contour and its 2D grey value pattern), [6, 7] track vehicles in the picture domain. [3] perform high level traffic scene interpretation. At the image evaluation level, only simple methods — like background subtraction and pattern matching — are employed in order to roughly characterize object movements based on a few frames.

Some recently published approaches can track vehicles in the 3D *scene domain*. [4] interactively track vehicles in image sequences recorded by hand–held, uncalibrated cameras exploiting physics–based models. Different image sequences showing traffic intersections are evaluated by [12] using a single approach and a single parameter set. They exploit the grey value gradient magnitude, but no motion information is used (except for the initialization step). [11] introduce optical flow matching during tracking in order to cope with low contrast vehicle images and occlusions. Tracking without exploitation of optical flow, but by taking explicitly modelled occlusions into account, has been reported by [8]. [13, 14] provide a motion model including the steering angle of vehicles and a stochastic model for the driving behaviour. Directed edges serve as image measurements. A function assessing the current vehicle pose estimation is maximized by means of a simplex search method. A new *covariance update filter* should capture fast changes in state variables which are not explicitly included in the motion model.

The investigations reported in this literature address specific technical problems and solution approaches. A transition phase from such methodologically oriented research towards approaches to design and evaluate practically applicable systems has not yet become recognizable.

2 Approach

2.1 Model Based Vehicle Tracking

Tracking of vehicles is initialized in our system by choosing a suitable start frame and computing its optical flow field. Neighboring similar optical flow vectors, which are assumed to correspond to the same moving object, are clustered in the image plane and are then back–projected onto a plane parallel to the road plane by means of the known camera calibration. Exploitation of the mean position, orientation, and magnitude of the back–projected flow vectors results in an initial estimate $\hat{\mathbf{x}}_0^-$ for the vehicle position, orientation, and speed *in the scene domain*. For each object candidate detected in this manner, we have to interactively select an appropriate polyhedral vehicle model. This vehicle model is subsequently projected into the image plane using the initial state estimate $\hat{\mathbf{x}}_0^-$. This state estimate is then updated by matching image features to the projected model as described in the following two subsections. The resulting updated state vector $\hat{\mathbf{x}}_0^+$ forms the basis for predicting the a priori state $\hat{\mathbf{x}}_1^-$ in the next half–frame using a model of circular motion with constant radius. Discrepancies between this motion model and reality are attributed to Gaussian system noise $\mathbf{w} \sim N(\mathbf{0}, Q)$ [5]: $\hat{\mathbf{x}}_{k+1}^- = \mathbf{f}(\hat{\mathbf{x}}_k^+) + \mathbf{w}$, where $\mathbf{f}$ is the system transition function and Q denotes the covariance matrix for the system noise.

In order to obtain spatio–temporal grey value gradients needed for edge element and optical flow extraction, we employ filter kernels especially adapted to *interlaced* video images, enabling us to evaluate both fields of a frame with full frame resolution. Thus, state vector estimation is performed for 50 *half–frames* in each second.

2.2 Matching Based on Edge Elements

One part of the update step of the state estimation is carried out by matching edge elements to model edge segments similar to [17], but adopted to image sequences with particularly small vehicle images. Edge elements $\mathbf{e} = (u, v, \phi)^T$ are defined as grey value transitions at image location $(u, v)^T$ whose gradient magnitude exceeds a threshold and which has a local maximum of the gradient magnitude in gradient direction ϕ. Edge segments of a polyhedral vehicle model are projected into the image plane exploiting the known camera model and employing a hiddenline algorithm. Visible projected model edge segments $\mathbf{m} = (u_m, v_m, \theta, l)^T$ are characterized by the image coordinates $(u_m, v_m)^T$ of the center of the edge segment, its orientation θ, and its length l. Matching of extracted edge elements to projected model edge segments is performed in two steps: (1) associate appropriate edge elements to model edge segments and (2) update the a–priori state estimation by minimizing a distance measure on this association.

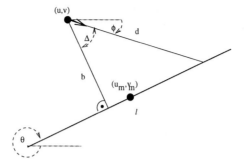

Fig. 1. Distance measure between an edge element $\mathbf{e} = (u, v, \phi)^T$ and a projected model edge segment $\mathbf{m} = (u_m, v_m, \theta, l)^T$ [9, 17]. Angles are measured against the horizontal. l denotes the length of the model segment projected into the image plane whereas (u_m, v_m) denote its centerpoint coordinates.

Data Association. The Euclidean distance b between an edge element and a model edge segment (see Fig. 1) induces a Mahalanobis distance where b is assumed to be Gauss–distributed with covariance σ_b^2:

$$\sigma_b^2 = \frac{\partial b(\mathbf{e}, \hat{\mathbf{x}}^-)}{\partial(\mathbf{e}, \mathbf{x})} \cdot \begin{pmatrix} \Sigma_e & 0_{3 \times 5} \\ 0_{5 \times 3} & P^- \end{pmatrix} \cdot \left(\frac{\partial b(\mathbf{e}, \hat{\mathbf{x}}^-)}{\partial(\mathbf{e}, \mathbf{x})} \right)^T \quad . \tag{1}$$

$\Sigma_e = \text{diag}(\sigma_u^2, \sigma_v^2, \sigma_\phi^2)$ denotes the measurement noise for edge elements and P^- represents the a priori state uncertainty about $\hat{\mathbf{x}}^-$. Edge elements are rejected if their Mahalanobis distance $b(\mathbf{e}, \hat{\mathbf{x}}^-) \frac{1}{\sigma_b^2} b(\mathbf{e}, \hat{\mathbf{x}}^-)$ exceeds the threshold of the $(1 - \alpha)$–quantile of the χ^2–distribution. Since the Mahalanobis distance depends on the current state estimation uncertainty P^-, the acceptance area for edge elements in the image plane is larger at the initialization time point than at subsequent time points due to relatively high initial state uncertainties, compared to smaller uncertainties at later time points. In order not to obtain too large acceptance areas incorporating edge elements which do not belong to the actual vehicle image, only certain maximal distances for b are allowed. These limits depend on the length of the corresponding model edge segments: for long model segments, larger Euclidean distances of edge elements are allowed since for long model segments larger distances to edge elements can occur when the model segments do not exactly overlap the edge elements to be associated.

State Estimation Update. In order to incorporate evidence about the *orientation* of edge elements into an assessment of their association with model segments obtained according to the preceding subsection, we employ the following distance measure d between edge elements $(u, v, \phi)^T$ and the corresponding projected model edge segment $(u_m, v_m, \theta, l)^T$ (see Fig. 1):

$$d(\mathbf{e}, \mathbf{x}) = \frac{b}{\cos \Delta} = \frac{- \sin \theta \cdot (u - u_m) + \cos \theta \cdot (v - v_m)}{\cos(\phi - (\theta + \frac{\pi}{2}))} \quad , \tag{2}$$

where $(u_m, v_m, \theta, l)^T$ denotes the projected model edge segment with smallest Mahalanobis distance to $\mathbf{e}$.

In order to update the state vector, a MAP–estimation is performed: given a Gauss–distributed state variable $\mathbf{x}_k$, the a–posteriori distribution at time point k conditioned on the measurements $\mathcal{Z}_k$ up to and including time point k is:

$$p(\mathbf{x}_k|\mathcal{Z}_k) = \frac{1}{p(\mathbf{z}_k|\mathcal{Z}^{k-1})} e^{-\Gamma(\mathbf{x}_k)} \quad . \tag{3}$$

The cost function $\Gamma(\mathbf{x}_k)$ is composed as follows:

$$\Gamma(\mathbf{x}_k) = \underbrace{\frac{1}{2}\sum_{\mathbf{e}} d(\mathbf{e},\mathbf{x}_k)^T \frac{1}{s} d(\mathbf{e},\mathbf{x}_k)}_{=:\Gamma_e} + \underbrace{\frac{1}{2}(\mathbf{x}_k - \hat{\mathbf{x}}_k^-)^T (P^-)^{-1}(\mathbf{x}_k - \hat{\mathbf{x}}_k^-)}_{=:\Gamma_s} \quad , \tag{4}$$

using the distance d of (2) and

$$s := \frac{\partial d(\mathbf{e}, \hat{\mathbf{x}}^-)}{\partial \mathbf{e}} \cdot \Sigma_e'(\mathbf{e}) \cdot \left(\frac{\partial d(\mathbf{e}, \hat{\mathbf{x}}^-)}{\partial \mathbf{e}}\right)^T \quad .$$

$\Sigma_e'(\mathbf{e})$ denotes the measurement noise Σ_e — see (1) — of edge element extraction, weighted with the gradient magnitude of the edge element $\mathbf{e}$:

$$\Sigma_e'(\mathbf{e}) = \left(\frac{\|\nabla g(\mathbf{e})\|}{\sum_{\mathbf{e}} \|\nabla g(\mathbf{e})\|}\right)^{-\frac{1}{2}} \cdot \Sigma_e \cdot \left(\frac{\|\nabla g(\mathbf{e})\|}{\sum_{\mathbf{e}} \|\nabla g(\mathbf{e})\|}\right)^{-\frac{1}{2}} \quad . \tag{5}$$

The measurement noise $\Sigma_e'(\mathbf{e})$ is thus large for edge elements with low gradient magnitude.

Search for the state vector $\mathbf{x}$ which maximizes the a–posteriori probability $p(\mathbf{x}_k|\mathcal{Z}_k)$ in (3) implies minimizing the cost function Γ in (4) with respect to $\mathbf{x}$. This results in an update step of an Iterated Extended Kalman Filter (IEKF).

2.3 Matching Based on Optical Flow

Optical flow matching is particularly valuable for tracking objects with low contrast images. Sometimes even a human observer can hardly recognize an object in a single frame, but notices it in a *sequence* of frames. We perform optical flow matching according to [11] with some modifications. For each image location $\boldsymbol{\xi}$, the corresponding scene point $\mathbf{x}_w(\mathbf{x})$ on the surface of the instantiated vehicle model is determined. The expected displacement rate $\dot{\boldsymbol{\xi}}$ at this image location is computed according to:

$$\dot{\boldsymbol{\xi}} = \frac{\partial \boldsymbol{\xi}}{\partial t} = \frac{\partial \boldsymbol{\xi}}{\partial \mathbf{x}_c} \frac{\partial \mathbf{x}_c}{\partial \mathbf{x}_w} \frac{\partial \mathbf{x}_w(\mathbf{x})}{\partial t} \quad ,$$

where $\mathbf{x}_w$ denotes the world coordinates of a surface point, $\mathbf{x}_c$ its camera coordinates and $\boldsymbol{\xi}$ its image location. The scene displacement rate $\dot{\mathbf{x}}_w = \frac{\partial \mathbf{x}_w}{\partial t}$ of the object point $\mathbf{x}_w$ is determined by means of the estimated speed and angular velocity of the object.

Data Association Displacement rate vectors $\dot{\xi}$ are matched to optical flow vectors $\mathbf{u}(\xi)$ estimated at the same image location, if the optical flow vector has a minimal confidence value and if its orientation and magnitude does not significantly differ from orientation and magnitude of the corresponding displacement rate vector. The idea behind the latter test is that expected displacement rate vectors express the global state of the vehicle while optical flow vectors are computed based on local, noisy grey value distributions. We reject, therefore, optical flow vectors which are not compatible with our expectation. In addition, optical flow vectors are not matched, if the magnitude of the corresponding displacement rate vector becomes too small. In other words: if we expect the image motion to be small or vanish, we only rely on the edge element matching described in the previous subsection. This facilitates the tracking of stopping vehicles.

State Estimation Update Like in Subsection 2.2, the state vector $\mathbf{x}$ is updated by means of a MAP estimation step which results in the minimization of the following cost function — see (4) — where $\xi = \xi(\mathbf{x})$:

$$\Gamma(\mathbf{x}) = \underbrace{\frac{1}{2}\sum(\dot{\xi} - \mathbf{u})^T \left(\Sigma'_{of}(\xi)\right)^{-1}(\dot{\xi} - \mathbf{u})}_{=:\Gamma_{of}} + \Gamma_s \quad . \tag{6}$$

The overall cost function $\Gamma(\mathbf{x})$ which has to be minimized when combining edge element and optical flow matching is thus composed as:

$$\Gamma(\mathbf{x}) = \Gamma_e(\mathbf{x}) + \Gamma_{of}(\mathbf{x}) + \Gamma_s(\mathbf{x}) \quad . \tag{7}$$

$\Sigma'_{of}(\xi)$ in (6) denotes the measurement noise $\Sigma_{of} = \sigma^2_{of} \cdot I$ of optical flow estimation weighted by an image location specific confidence value $c(\xi)$ which is given as the minimal eigenvalue of the outer gradient product $(g_x, g_y)^T \cdot (g_x, g_y)$ averaged over a local area around ξ:

$$\Sigma'_{of}(\xi) = \left(\frac{c(\xi)}{\sum_{\xi} c(\xi)}\right)^{-\frac{1}{2}} \cdot \Sigma_{of} \cdot \left(\frac{c(\xi)}{\sum_{\xi} c(\xi)}\right)^{-\frac{1}{2}} \quad . \tag{8}$$

The confidence value is a measure for the grey value structure in a local area around the location where an optical flow has to be estimated. Thus, a larger measurement uncertainty will be associated to optical flow vectors with low confidence value.

3 Results

3.1 Sequence 'nb'

In the 'nb' traffic intersection image sequence, 20 object candidates have been detected automatically by the optical flow segmentation step in half–frame #105, see Fig. 2, top right. The object candidates 1, 2, and 6 were not worth tracking: the first two belong to the bright truck and trailer configuration with joints for which an articulated model would be needed. The object candidate 6 belongs to a shadow cast by a transporter. The remaining 17 object candidates have been tracked in parallel, see Fig. 3.

Fig. 2. Object candidates have been automatically extracted by segmenting optical flow fields obtained at a suitable start frame of the sequences 'dt_v' (top left), 'nb' (top right), 'kwbB' (bottom left), and 'gas station' (bottom right).

Objects 3, 4, and 16 have been badly initialized. Object 4 is partially occluded by a bright truck whose occluding effect has not been taken into account. Object 16 is occluded by the tank lorry and lost early due to the bad initial pose estimation. Objects 5, 11, and 15 are tracked until leaving the field of view at the bottom of the image, but their models lag significantly behind the corresponding vehicle images. Since these three objects can be tracked without any lag by only using edge element matching without optical flow, it seems that optical flow is not able to capture the strong acceleration of these objects. This problem can not be observed for the objects 7, 10, and 17 which, too, are accelerating. But in contradistinction to objects 5, 11, and 15, these objects produce darker images. Object 8, which is hardly visible in the dark shadows cast by the buildings in the center right part of the image, has been tracked successfully until it reaches the right margin of the image. Object 9 which turns right sharply in the upper right part of the image has been lost around the time point #360 when it is occluded by a post which has not been modelled so far. Objects 10, 17, 18 and 19 have been tracked successfully until they leave the field of view at the bottom of the image. The left turning object 12 has been tracked until it leaves the image on the right hand side. Object 13 turns right sharply in the upper right quadrant of the image and has been tracked until disappearing from the image at the top, albeit with a lateral and longitudinal lag. Although the left turning tank lorry (object 14) is an articulated object, it could be tracked with a rigid, single parallelepiped model without modelling the joint. Finally, object 20 which just approaches the intersection in the lower left of the image and then stops, has been tracked successfully.

In this sequence, the invisible buildings positioned near the lower right corner of the image have been modelled approximately in the scene domain in order to determine their shadows. Shadows cast by vehicles driving in this region are not considered, since there is no evidence for such shadow contours in the images.

3.2 Sequence 'dt_v'

The initialization step for half–frame time point #5 of the 'dt_v' sequence (see Fig. 2, top left) delivers 10 object candidates which have been tracked in parallel. Object 2 is not completely in the field of view at the initialization time point, and object 10 is not completely visible due to occlusions by the time stamp in the lower right part of the image. The initial pose estimation, therefore, is quite inaccurate for these two objects. Nevertheless, they are not lost during tracking, although object 10 is even occluded in the bottom right corner of the image by a tree which has not been modelled. Object 1 is moving through a very dark shadow region and can hardly be identified even by human observers in single images during this period. Due to the exploitation of optical flow, it could nevertheless be tracked successfully.

The resulting trajectories after 88 half–frame time points can be seen in Fig. 4.

3.3 Sequence 'kwbB'

Tracking in the 'kwbB' sequence has been initialized at half–frame #10 (objects 2 and 3, see Fig. 2, bottom left), #430 (object 6), #600 (object 12), #780 (objects 13 and 14), #851 (objects 5, 7, 8, and 10), and #2010 (object 1). The resulting trajectories are shown in Fig. 5. Objects 2 and 10 are initialized with a lateral lag. Object 2 is occluded *completely* for some time by a big traffic sign (see Fig. 6), but has been tracked nevertheless until leaving the field of view.

Fig. 3. Tracking results of the 'nb' sequence at half–frame time point #580 after automatic initialization in half–frame #105 (see Fig. 2, top right). The shadow edges of the objects 8, 12, and 14 are automatically excluded when entering the shadow regions of the buildings.

This success must be attributed to the use of optical flow measurements and pose predictions by the Kalman Filter. Object 7, too, is completely occluded by this traffic sign. But unlike object 2, this object stops just behind the traffic sign. The renewed start of object 7 when the traffic light switched to green could, therefore, not be tracked.

3.4 Gas Station

Regarding the gas station sequence depicted in Fig. 2 (bottom right), tracking has been initialized each time when a moving object enters the field of view. For the gas station scene, we had the possibility to measure the real–world coordinates of several static 3D scene components. These measurements of 3D scene points have been interactively associated to their corresponding image locations, resulting in a more robust camera calibration than in the case of the intersection scenes where only 2D maps were available. The gas station sequence is characterized by larger vehicle images compared to the intersection scenes, significant occlusions by static and moving scene components, changing illumination conditions during recording, low contrast vehicle images (especially when objects move under the canopy of the gas station building), and by more complex driving maneuvers (stopping, starting, overtaking, backing up).

Fig. 4. Tracking results after evaluation of 88 half–frames of the 'dt_v' sequence.

While there was no need to explicitly treat occlusions in the intersection sequences after incorporating optical flow into the measurements, this is not sufficient for the gas station sequence. Occlusions by static scene components, like posts, bushes, or petrol pumps, and by moving vehicles occur. Unlike in most of the intersection scenes investigated, partially occluded vehicles remain stationary for long time intervals so that optical flow information will not help in these cases. We, therefore, explicitly model occlusion in the 3D scene domain by providing a model of the gas station, similar to [8]. Occluding moving scene objects are tracked automatically in the scene domain and are considered when tracking the occluded objects. All image features belonging to (known) occluding scene components are excluded when vehicles have to be matched. In contradistinction to [8], the order in which the objects have to be tracked (occluding objects must be tracked prior to occluded objects) is determined automatically for each half–frame time point. There is no need anymore to precompute the trajectories of occluding scene components before tracking occluded objects. This facilitates to track all object candidates in an image sequence in parallel, nevertheless taking mutual occlusions into account.

Fig. 5. Estimated trajectories at half–frame time point #2820 of the 'kwbB' sequence.

Fig. 6. Temporary, but complete occlusion of object 2 at half–frame #90 due to a traffic sign. Optical Flow and the Kalman Filter pose prediction facilitate nevertheless to track this vehicle in its *continuous motion* even through the period of (practically complete) transitory occlusion.

Objects 1, 2, and 4 (see Fig. 7) as well as objects 5 and 11 (see Fig. 8), respectively, have been tracked in parallel, automatically considering their mutual occlusions and the occlusions by static scene components which have been modelled in the 3D scene domain. Objects 2 and 4 are tracked well, though heavy occlusions occur, especially during tracking of object 4 which overtakes the standing object 1 on the back lane. The model match for object 1 becomes worse when it backs up beginning with half–frame #1800 in order to evade object 4 on the back lane. Similar considerations hold for object 10 when it proceeds after filling up in order to evade object 4 at half–frame #3200. Object 5 is tracked successfully on its way to the rightmost petrol pump on the back lane. The match becomes worse when the vehicle backs up after remaining stationary for about 1200 half–frames and subsequently evades object 11 standing in front. But object 5 is not lost until leaving the field of view. Although object 11 has been badly initialized automatically, it could be tracked somewhat while overtaking the standing object 5 and while standing behind the left post. Beginning with half–frame #6000, object 11 backs up in order to park in front of object 5. In this phase, the vehicle image is not lost, but the model match becomes quite inaccurate. Object 11 is definitely lost while proceeding to the left exit of the gas station beginning with half–frame #7000. Object 6 has been successfully tracked while proceeding to the leftmost petrol pump on the front lane, standing, backing up to the center petrol pump, and standing once again. The match becomes worse only while object 6 subsequently proceeds to the left exit due to significant occlusions by bushes and the (not modelled) left tree.

4 Performance

Table 1 gives an overview of the results obtained by tracking 56 object candidates in five different image sequences. The results of the intersection image sequence 'et', comprising about 90 half–frames and 11 moving objects, have not been presented in a figure, due to space limitations.

In total, only five objects have been completely lost, mainly either due to inaccurate initial pose estimations provided by the segmented optical flow field and/or due to occlusions. 34 object candidates could be successfully tracked, while 17 object candidates could be tracked, but only with significant lateral and/or longitudinal lags between estimated and actual vehicle position.

The main problems regarding the unsatisfactory as well as the completely failed tracking results seem to be initialization and occlusion. In nearly all cases, inaccurate initializations can be attributed to occlusions or to cases where vehicles just enter the field of view and are not yet completely visible. Indeed, we are not yet using any occlusion information at the initialization step. But there are also several cases of a perfectly initialized tracking which later failed due to occlusions, especially in cases where significantly occluded vehicles remain stationary for a while.

Please note that Table 1 only provides a quite aggregated representation of the evaluation since it does not contain the *length* of each object's trajectory.

Fig. 7. Estimated trajectories of objects 1, 2, and 4 at half–frame time point #4905 of the gas station sequence.

Table 1. Tracking rates and failure reasons for the five video image sequences considered in this contribution.

Sequence	'et'	'nb'	'dt_v'	'kwbB'	gas station	total
# half-frames processed	88	600	88	3.100	8.000	11.876
# object candidates	11	17	10	11	7	56
# successfully tracked	8	9	8	7	2	34
# satisfactorily tracked	3	5	2	3	4	17
# completely lost		3		1	1	5
reason for failures (multiple reasons per object possible):						
# bad initialization	2	3	2	2	1	9
# low contrast image					4	4
# occlusion	1	4	2	1	4	11
# too strong acceleration		3				3
# too strong turning		1		1		2

Fig. 8. Estimated trajectories of objects 5, 6, 10, and 11 at half–frame time point #8450. Note that object 6 is leaving the gas station premise beginning with this time point. This is the reason why the front trajectory does not yet extend to the left side of the image frame shown here.

If we consider the state prediction and update step per object and per half–frame as one processing unit ('tracking step'), we obtain a total of over 34.000 single tracking steps. We are, however, humbly aware of the fact that we have to evaluate at least an order of magnitude more image sequences in order to obtain a more reliable assessment of our tracking approach.

Although we do not focus on real–time evaluation in our vehicle tracking system, we were forced to drastically (by a factor of 10) reduce computation times in order to facilitate the evaluation of several image sequences each containing up to 20 moving objects within reasonable time. This now results in tracking times from between 3 and 7 sec (depending on the object image size) per object and half–frame on a SUN ULTRA I 167 MHz workstation including all input and output operations, like loading grey value images over a network.

5 Conclusion

This contribution adapts an edge element matching approach, originally developed for real–time tracking of large object images, and combines it with optical flow matching as well as 3D occlusion modelling. Significant modifications of different original approach versions were necessary in order to achieve robust tracking results for small and low contrast vehicle images in different image sequences: (1) employment of an *Iterated* Extended Kalman Filter in order to deal with larger discrepancies between a–priori state estimations and the true state, (2) incorporating the gradient magnitude into the measurement noise for edge elements in order to become independent of critical thresholds for gradient magnitudes, (3) limiting the area of acceptance for edge elements depending on the length of projected model edge segments, (4) switching–off optical flow matching for all image locations where no motion is expected in order to track stopping objects, (5) using bias–corrected optical flow in order to avoid systematic underestimations of optical flow vector magnitudes affecting the speed estimation of moving objects, (6) tracking multiple objects in parallel and determine automatically the tracking order at each particular point in time (occluding objects have to be processed prior to occluded objects), (7) reducing drastically the computation times of optical flow matching in order to obtain reasonable tracking times even for long image sequences and multiple object configurations.

The results reported here have been obtained by an *experimental* system where we focus on tracking most of the moving objects in different image sequences with a single approach and one parameter set instead of perfectly tracking single objects by individually adjusting the parameters to each moving object. In the research reported here, attention is neither directed towards vehicle classification nor towards real time evaluation.

The extended evaluation performed in this contribution now shifts us to a position where we can identify remaining key problems which still prevent us from constructing a robust traffic surveillance application as stated in the introductory remarks. These problems can be classified into three categories: (1) structural tracking and modelling problems (lost objects due to occlusion and strong acceleration or turning maneuvers), (2) initialization problems (better initial pose estimations required, elimination of 'false alarm' object candidates like pedestrians, automatic selection of appropriate initialization time points, automatic selection of appropriate models), and (3) real–time evaluation restrictions. The results reported in this contribution suggest the following strategy: First, consider the tracking and modelling problems which are not caused by unsuitable initializations. After that, develop initialization approaches delivering better initial pose estimations so that a sufficient majority of moving objects can be tracked. Subsequently, a fully automatic initialization, including frame and model selection, has to be established. Only when the evaluation system will have reached this stage, we intend to focus on the real–time aspect.

References

1. H. Buxton, S. Gong: *Visual Surveillance in a Dynamic and Uncertain World.* Artificial Intelligence **78** (1995) 431–459.
2. C. Cédras, M. Shah: *Motion–Based Recognition: A Survey.* Image and Vision Computing **13**:2 (1995) 129–155.

3. S. Dance, T. Caelli, Z.-Q. Liu: *A Concurrent, Hierarchical Approach to Symbolic Scene Interpretation*. Pattern Recognition **29**:11 (1996) 1891–1903.

4. W.F. Gardner, D.T. Lawton: *Interactive Model–Based Vehicle Tracking*. IEEE Transactions on Pattern Analysis and Machine Intelligence **18**:11 (1996) 1115–1121.

5. A. Gelb: *Applied Optimal Estimation*. The MIT Press, Cambridge / MA, 1974.

6. S. Gil, R. Milanese, and T. Pun: *Combining Multiple Motion Estimates for Vehicle Tracking*. Proc. Fourth European Conference on Computer Vision 1996 (ECCV '96), 15–18 April 1996, Cambridge / UK; B. Buxton and R. Cipolla (Eds.), Lecture Notes in Computer Science **1065** (Vol. II), Springer–Verlag, Berlin, Heidelberg 1996, pp. 307–320.

7. S. Gil, R. Milanese, and T. Pun: *Comparing Features for Target Tracking in Traffic Scenes*. Pattern Recognition **29** (1996) 1285–1296.

8. M. Haag, Th. Frank, H. Kollnig, H.-H. Nagel: *Influence of an Explicitly Modelled 3D Scene on the Tracking of Partially Occluded Vehicles*. Computer Vision and Image Understanding **65**:2 (1997) 206–225.

9. F. Heimes, H.-H. Nagel, Th. Frank: *Model-Based Tracking of Complex Innercity Road Intersections*. Mathematical and Computer Modelling, 1998, *in press*.

10. R. Howarth, H. Buxton: *Visual Surveillance Monitoring and Watching*. Proc. Fourth European Conference on Computer Vision 1996 (ECCV '96), 15–18 April 1996, Cambridge / UK; B. Buxton and R. Cipolla (Eds.), Lecture Notes in Computer Science **1065** (Vol. II), Springer–Verlag, Berlin, Heidelberg 1996, pp. 321–334.

11. H. Kollnig, H.-H. Nagel: *Matching Objects to Segments from an Optical Flow Field*. Proc. Fourth European Conference on Computer Vision 1996 (ECCV '96), 15–18 April 1996, Cambridge / UK; B. Buxton and R. Cipolla (Eds.), Lecture Notes in Computer Science **1065** (Vol. II), Springer–Verlag, Berlin, Heidelberg 1996, pp. 388–399.

12. H. Kollnig, H.-H. Nagel: *3D Pose Estimation by Directly Matching Polyhedral Models to Gray Value Gradients*. International Journal of Computer Vision **23**:3 (1997) 283–302.

13. S.J. Maybank, A.D. Worrall, G.D. Sullivan: *A Filter for Visual Tracking Based on a Stochastic Model for Driver Behaviour*. Proc. Fourth European Conference on Computer Vision 1996 (ECCV '96), 15–18 April 1996, Cambridge / UK; B. Buxton and R. Cipolla (Eds.), Lecture Notes in Computer Science **1065** (Vol. II), Springer–Verlag, Berlin, Heidelberg 1996, pp. 540–549.

14. S.J. Maybank, A.D. Worrall, G.D. Sullivan: *Filter for Car Tracking Based on Acceleration and Steering Angle*. Proc. of the 7th British Machine Vision Conference (BMVC '96), 9–12 September 1996, Edinburgh, England, R. B. Fisher and E. Trucco (Eds.), Vol. 2, ISBN 0 9521898 5 2, 1996, pp. 615–624.

15. H.-H. Nagel, M. Haag: *Bias-Corrected Optical Flow Estimation for Road Vehicle Tracking*. International Conference on Computer Vision (ICCV '98), 4–7 January 1998, Bombay/India, Narosa Publishing House New Delhi a. o. 1998, pp. 1006–1011.

16. M.K. Teal, T.J. Ellis: *Spatial–Temporal Reasoning Based on Object Motion*. Proc. of the 7th British Machine Vision Conference (BMVC '96), 9–12 September 1996, Edinburgh, England, R. B. Fisher and E. Trucco (Eds.), Vol. **2**, ISBN 0 9521898 5 2, 1996, pp. 465–474.

17. M. Tonko, K. Schäfer, F. Heimes, H.-H. Nagel: *Towards Visually Servoed Manipulation of Car Engine Parts*. Proc. IEEE International Conference on Robotics and Automation, Albuquerque/NM, 20–25 April 1997, R. W. Harrigan (Ed.), IEEE Computer Society Press, Los Alamitos/CA, 1997, pp. 3166–3171.

View-Based Adaptive Affine Tracking

Fernando de la Torre[1], Shaogang Gong[2], and Stephen McKenna[3]

[1] Department of Signal Theory, Universitat Ramon Llull, Spain
ftorre@salleURL.edu
[2] Department of Computer Science, Queen Mary and Westfield College, England
sgg@dcs.qmw.ac.uk
[3] Department of Applied Computing, University of Dundee, Scotland
stephen@dcs.qmw.ac.uk

Abstract. We propose a model for view-based adaptive affine tracking of moving objects. We avoid the need for feature-based matching in establishing correspondences through learning landmarks. We use an effective bootstrapping process based on colour segmentation and selective attention. We recover affine parameters with dynamic updates to the eigenspace using most recent history and perform predictions in parameter space. Experimental results are given to illustrate our approach.

1 Introduction

Object recognition in dynamic scenes using view-based representation requires establishing image correspondences in successive frames of a moving object which may undergo both affine and viewpoint transformations [1]. However, to obtain consistent dense image correspondence is both problematic and expensive since changes in viewpoint result in self-occlusions which prohibit complete sets of image correspondences from being established. Practically, only sparse correspondence can be established quickly for a carefully chosen set of feature points [2]. To realise near real-time performance, however, an entirely different approach is preferable which does not depend on reliable feature detection and tracking. Holistic texture-only-templates can be used [3]. This assumes that the object of interest is approximately rigid and therefore permits a relatively simplistic parametric model to be used. Furthermore, if the model is also built based on data from a large set of viewpoints, it can in theory recover pose change as well. Likewise, if it is trained under different illuminations, it can perform in changing lighting conditions (e.g. [4]).

The EigenTracking approach proposed by Black [5] essentially attempted to establish such holistic, appearance-based correspondence of a moving rigid object by recovering a parameterised affine transformation in an eigenspace, constructed from object images of different views. However, due to its rigidity assumption and the use of texture-only-templates, EigenTracking fails to capture changes which are not sufficiently affine. In particular, it copes poorly with flexible objects such as human faces. Furthermore, to be able to establish image correspondence across different viewpoints, EigenTracking requires a training image set that spans the view sphere. This is impractical and computationally expensive.

In this work, we propose an integrated scheme for view alignment which takes the following into consideration: (a) the use of both shape and texture in eigenspace in a simple manner relaxes the rigidity assumption without introducing too much computational cost, (b) a process for effective bootstrapping, (c) parameter recovery with selective attention, (d) affine parameter estimation using a dynamically updated, viewpoint centred eigenspace, and (e) parameter prediction.

The rest of this paper is arranged as follows. We first introduce the shape augmented affine tracking model in Section 2. In Section 3, we describe a colour based bootstrapping process for the affine tracking. We then introduce the concept of view dependent model adaptation in affine tracking in Section 4. Section 5 presents model prediction before experiments and discussion are given in Sections 6 and 7.

2 Affine Tracking with Shape Constraints

A set of p images with N dimensions, forming an $N \times p$ matrix $\mathbf{A}$, can be represented by the eigenspace of their covariance matrix $\mathbf{C}$ where usually $p < N$. The image matrix $\mathbf{A}$ can be decomposed using Singular Value Decomposition (SVD) which gives

$$\mathbf{A} = \mathbf{U}\boldsymbol{\Lambda}\mathbf{V}^{\mathsf{T}}$$

where $\mathbf{U}$ is an orthogonal matrix of eigenvectors of $\mathbf{C}$ and $\boldsymbol{\Lambda}$ is a diagonal matrix of its eigenvalues. The matrix $\mathbf{V}$ defines the nullspace of $\mathbf{C}$ (since $p < N$). For view alignment, an image $\mathbf{I}$ is represented by projection onto eigenvectors $\mathbf{u}_j$, i.e.

$$\mathbf{I} \approx \sum_{j=1}^{k} c_j \mathbf{u}_j = \mathbf{U}\,\mathbf{c}$$

where $k < p$ is the number of eigenvectors actually used and $\mathbf{c}$ gives projection coefficients. Note that throughout this paper, we use $\mathbf{I}$ to represent an image vector rather than the Identity matrix. A pre-filtering process is often necessary if global illumination is unstable [3].

2.1 Template-Only Affine Tracking: EigenTracking

If image changes are approximately affine, correspondence for alignment can be achieved by treating an image $\mathbf{I}(\mathbf{f}(\mathbf{x}, \mathbf{a})) = [I(\mathbf{f}(\mathbf{x}_1, \mathbf{a})), I(\mathbf{f}(\mathbf{x}_2, \mathbf{a})) \ldots I(\mathbf{f}(\mathbf{x}_N, \mathbf{a}))]^{\mathsf{T}}$ as a function of an affine transformation given by parameters $\mathbf{a} = (a_0, a_1, a_2, a_3, a_4, a_5)^{\mathsf{T}}$, where

$$\mathbf{f}(\mathbf{x}, \mathbf{a}) = \begin{bmatrix} a_0 \\ a_3 \end{bmatrix} + \begin{bmatrix} a_1 & a_2 \\ a_4 & a_5 \end{bmatrix} \begin{bmatrix} x - x_c \\ y - y_c \end{bmatrix} \tag{1}$$

and $\mathbf{x}_c = (x_c, y_c)^{\mathrm{T}}$ is the centre position of the object template. Alignment can then be accomplished by recovering both the affine parameters $\mathbf{a}$ and the projection coefficients $\mathbf{c}$ by minimising a cost function $\min_{\mathbf{c},\mathbf{a}} \rho\left[(\mathbf{I}(\mathbf{f}(\mathbf{x}, \mathbf{a})) - \mathbf{U}\mathbf{c}), \sigma\right]$, where ρ is a robust error norm and σ is a scale factor that controls the convexity of the norm [5,6]. In our scheme, we use the Geman-McClure error norm [7] given by

$$\rho(x, \sigma) = \frac{x^2}{\sigma^2 + x^2}$$

Outliers will be considered values from the inflexion point of the norm, which are residuals with $x_i > \sigma/\sqrt{3}$. In general, the above cost function is non-convex and minimisation can result in local minima. A minimisation algorithm found to be effective in this case is gradient descent with the continuation method of graduated non-convexity [8]. It begins with a large value of σ where all the points are inliers. Then σ is successively lowered, reducing the influence of outliers. While it is not guaranteed to converge to a global minimum, the method is effective for visual tracking since continuity of motion provides good starting points.

A dramatic reduction in computational cost is achieved by avoiding image warping in every iteration. This is done by adopting the following linear approximation to the above cost function:

$$\min_{\mathbf{c},\mathbf{a}} \rho\left[\left(\nabla \mathbf{I}^{\mathrm{T}} \mathbf{f}(\mathbf{a}) + (\mathbf{I} - \mathbf{U}\mathbf{c})\right), \sigma\right] \tag{2}$$

where $\nabla \mathbf{I}$ is the image gradient $[I_x, I_y]^{\mathrm{T}}$ [5].

2.2 Encoding Landmarks

The difficulty in encoding shape is to be able to compute correspondences quickly and sufficiently robustly. To achieve such a purpose, we encode the coordinates of known landmarks in the training images which are used for constructing the eigenspace. Let $\mathbf{A} = [\mathbf{I}_1 \, \mathbf{I}_2 \, \ldots \, \mathbf{I}_p]$ be the matrix of training images and $\mathbf{X} = [\mathbf{x}_1 \, \mathbf{x}_2 \, \ldots \, \mathbf{x}_p]$ be the coordinates of the landmarks in these images. The landmarks are assumed to have been located by hand. The landmarks $\mathbf{X}$ in Fig. 1 are the positions of the eyes.

We first took the approach of constructing a concatenated matrix:

$$\mathbf{A}^* = [\{\mathbf{I}_1, \mathbf{x}_1\} \, \{\mathbf{I}_2, \mathbf{x}_2\} \, \ldots \, \{\mathbf{I}_p, \mathbf{x}_p\}]$$

The new matrix $\mathbf{A}^*$ is a modification of $\mathbf{A}$ with additional feature vectors concatenated to the tail of each training image vector. However, the large scale difference in variances of $\mathbf{A}$ and $\mathbf{X}$ causes numerical problems. To obtain comparable variance, we scale each shape vector $\mathbf{x}_i$ by the largest norm. A more considered approach to achieve comparable variance between the texture and shape

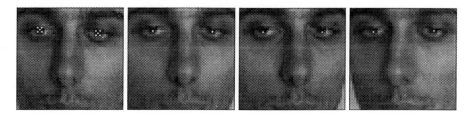

Fig. 1. Examples of landmarks used in the training images.

vectors in eigenspace can be adopted [9]. It is worth pointing out though that better results were actually achieved with modelling the texture and shape vectors in independent eigenspaces rather than with the concatenated eigenspace. This seems to re-confirm the evidence reported elsewhere [10].

Once the landmarks have been learned from the training set, we can recall the landmarks during the tracking process. If a new image is aligned with the eigenspace, the reconstruction from the coefficients in the eigenspace is given by $\mathbf{U}\mathbf{c}$. To recall the most likely landmark positions for the new image based on what has been learned in training, an inverse transformation between the eigenspace and the training set (related by the SVD) is performed on the shape components only:

$$\mathbf{x}_{new} = \mathbf{X}\left(\mathbf{V}\Sigma^{-1}\mathbf{c}\right) \qquad (3)$$

$\mathbf{V}\Sigma^{-1}\mathbf{c}$ are the coefficients which best reconstruct the new image in the least-square sense from the training data. Note that $\mathbf{V}\Sigma^{-1}$ can be pre-computed off-line in order to speed up the tracking process. Given sufficient training examples with known landmarks, incorporating shape with texture in eigenspace enables previously learned feature positions to be recalled during tracking, avoiding the need to perform on-line feature detection and correspondence which are computationally both expensive and problematic.

3 Initialisation

Colour-based segmentation can provide robust and very fast focus-of-attention for the initialization of the affine parameters [11]. Here we adopt multi-colour Gaussian mixture models to perform real-time object detection and focus of attention. The mixture models were estimated in two-dimensional hue-saturation colour space. Such representations are chosen to permit some level of robustness against brightness change. Probabilities are computed for pixels in an image search space and the size and position of the object are estimated from the resulting probability distribution in the image plane [11]. An example of colour-based, real-time, coarse segmentation using a mixture of four Gaussians can be seen in Fig. 2.

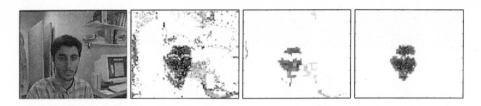

Fig. 2. From left to right: An image frame from a sequence; the object foreground colour probabilities in the image plane; results of segmentation with multi-resolution relaxation after 1 and 4 iterations.

3.1 Attentional Window

The most computationally expensive operation in recovering affine parameters is to recursively warp the image relative to its center in order to minimise the cost function of Equation (2). To address this problem, the affine transformation is only computed within an attentional window. The size of this window adapts to the size of the object (see Fig. 3). Affine transforms are performed relative to the center of the window which must coincide with the centroid of the object in order to minimize the errors in estimated rotation and scale parameters. The centre of the attentional window is estimated using prediction (see Section 5).

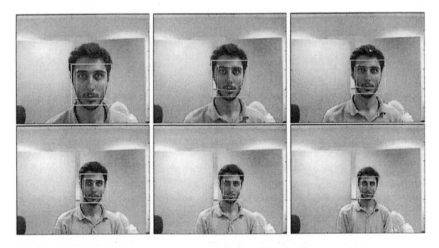

Fig. 3. Tracked face images with adaptive attentional windows shown by the larger bounding boxes. Affine transforms are applied only within these windows. The small bounding boxes give the tracked face with the recovered affine parameters.

3.2   Feature Extraction

Colour provides only a crude initial estimate for an attentional window. An improved estimate is obtained in a computationally efficient way by applying recursive, non-linear morphological operations at multiple resolutions. The method can be seen as a combination of relaxation and something similar in spirit to geodesic reconstruction in morphology [12]. This "geodesic relaxation" algorithm is as follows:

1. Compute log probabilities in a 1/4 sub-sampled image and normalise these probabilities to give a low resolution grey-scale "probability image" $\mathbf{I}^o_{N/16}$.
2. Apply grey-level morphological erosion to $\mathbf{I}^o_{N/16}$. This reduces noise and erroneous foreground and yields an image $\mathbf{I}^{er}_{N/16}$.
3. Let $\mathbf{I}^*_{N/16} = \mathbf{I}^{er}_{N/16}$, then apply the following operation for a fixed number of times:
   $\mathbf{I}^*_{N/16} = \frac{1}{2}(\mathbf{I}^*_{N/16} \otimes \texttt{low-pass-filter} + \mathbf{I}^o_{N/16})$, where $\otimes$ denotes convolution.

The resulting image $\mathbf{I}^*_{n/16}$ (see Fig. 2) is used to fit a bounding box which is then used as an initial attentional window. The iterative process is fast because good results are obtained in a few iterations using low resolution images. Morphological operators were also used to estimate the region within the initial attentional window occupied by the main facial features (see Fig. 4). The process was as follows:

1. Perform vertical erosion on the 1/2 sub-sampled attentional window $\mathbf{I}^{win}_{N/4}$ to give $\mathbf{I}^{er}_{N/4}$.
2. Perform geodesic reconstruction of $\mathbf{I}^{er}_{N/4}$ with $\mathbf{I}^{win}_{N/4}$ as the reference image to give $\mathbf{I}^{rec}_{N/4}$.
3. Compute $\mathbf{I}^{end}_{N/4} = \texttt{opening}(\mathbf{I}^{win}_{N/4} - \mathbf{I}^{rec}_{N/4})$

The extent of the estimated facial feature region was used to estimate initial affine scale parameters (a_1, a_5).

Fig. 4. Left: The attentional window estimated using colour cues. Right: The main facial feature region extracted using morphological operators.

3.3 Parameter Initialisation

Colour and morphological operators provide an initial attentional window and approximate estimates of translational and scale parameters. These initial parameter estimates are further refined by recursively applying Successive-Over-Relaxation [8] in order to minimize the cost function (2). Robust norms with a continuation method and a multi-resolution representation were used in order to avoid local minima. At first, only the translational parameters (a_0, a_3) were optimised in order to align the centre of the attentional window with the eigenspace. Subsequently, the scale parameters (a_1, a_5) were optimised. It was assumed that affine rotation was negligible in the initial frame. An example of this parameter initialisation process is shown in Fig. 5. In this example, the initial estimates provided by the colour model were unusually poor.

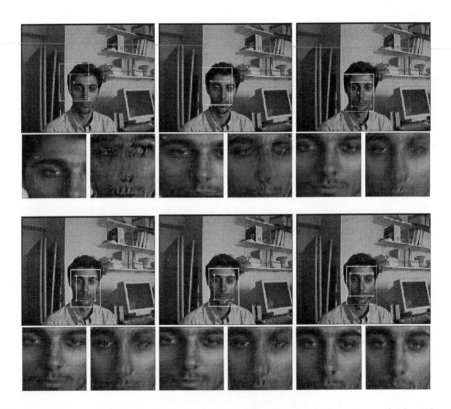

Fig. 5. Affine parameter initialisation: The attentional window is overlaid with a smaller box indicating estimated translation and scale parameters. Below each frame are the located region (left) and its reconstruction (right).

4 Model Adaptation

The EigenTracking method made use of a fixed, global eigenspace (GES) representation for reconstruction and tracking. This eigenspace was built by performing SVD on a relatively large, fixed training set. The alternative method described in this section yields faster and more accurate reconstruction. It involves the use of local eigenspace (LES) representations built using subsets of the original training set. In particular, at each time frame t, the k training images which are "closest" to the previous affine-normalised, tracked image $\mathbf{I}_{t-1}$, were selected. A new LES is then computed from these k images along with $\mathbf{I}_{t-1}$. The inclusion of $\mathbf{I}_{t-1}$ helps to compensate for temporary changes not represented in the original training set (e.g. unusual facial expressions).

The computation of a new LES in (potentially) every frame might seem prohibitively expensive. However, the iterative matching algorithm typically converges more quickly when reconstructions are performed using an LES. In practise, this faster convergence more than compensates for the expense of computing the LES. The overall result is faster and gives more robust tracking. The k selected training images are usually images with similar 3D pose and facial expression and can therefore be accurately represented using only a few eigenvectors. In order to achieve sufficiently good reconstruction, enough eigenvectors are retained to account for 95% of the variance in the training set.

In order to compute an LES, the k "closest" training images must be selected. An obvious way in which to perform this selection is to measure the Euclidean distance between $\mathbf{I}_{t-1}$ and each of the training images and to select the k nearest images. These distance measurements can be efficiently approximated using projections onto the precomputed GES [13]. Further efficiency can be obtained using a multi-resolution scheme in which $\mathbf{I}_{t-1}$ is sub-sampled and projected onto a precomputed GES of equally low resolution.

If an ordering can be imposed on the training set, however, an alternative scheme becomes possible. The closest match in the training set is then used to index into this ordered set and the k images for the LES are selected using the predetermined ordering. There are other strategies that have been suggested for performing such a nearest neighbour search. See [14] for a detailed discussion. In our case, if the training set consists of a sequence of a head rotating from left to right then time imposes a natural ordering. The nearest match then yields an estimation of head pose and the LES is computed from images of similar poses. Another way to derive the same matching could be done using the information of the projection coefficients and their relation with the training set. The p coefficients $\mathbf{y} = [y_1 \, y_2 \, \ldots \, y_p]^{\mathsf{T}}$ whose linear combination of the training set minimises the Euclidean distance, $\min_{\mathbf{y}} \| \mathbf{I}_{t-1} - \mathbf{A}\mathbf{y} \|^2$, are given by:

$$\mathbf{y} = \mathbf{V}\mathbf{\Sigma}^{-1}\mathbf{c}, \qquad \mathbf{y} = (\mathbf{A}^{\mathsf{T}}\mathbf{A})^{-1}\mathbf{A}^{\mathsf{T}}\mathbf{I} \qquad (4)$$

As we are working with normalized images, minimising the Euclidean distance is equivalent to maximising the dot product. Note that we can obtain the dot products if the coefficients in the eigenspace $\mathbf{c}$ are known, that is:

$$\mathbf{A}^T\mathbf{I} = (\mathbf{A}^T\mathbf{A})\mathbf{y} = \mathbf{V}\Sigma\mathbf{c} \tag{5}$$

The position of the maximum component of $\mathbf{A}^T\mathbf{I}$ corresponds to the "closest" image in the training set. It can be easily shown that this is computationally equivalent to [13]. However, our approach establishes correspondence between the eigen-coefficients and the training images directly and is less expensive for computing the GES. For example, computing $\mathbf{C} = \mathbf{c}_1\mathbf{c}_2...\mathbf{c}_p = \mathbf{U}^T\mathbf{A}$ requires kpN operations. With SVD of A, computing $\mathbf{C} = \Sigma\mathbf{V}^T$ needs just k^2p operations which is more efficient since $k \ll N$.

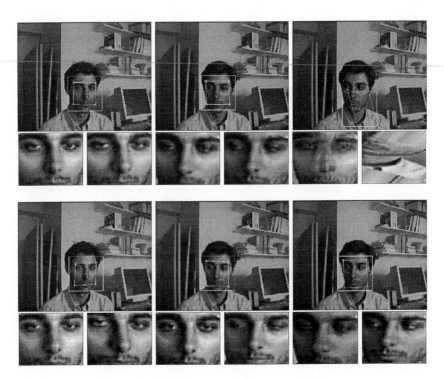

Fig. 6. Top row: EigenTracking without dynamic updating fails due to insufficient training views. Bottom row: The result from using the adaptive scheme.

5   Parameter Prediction

In order to cope with displacements of more than a few (2-3) pixels between frames, it was necessary to use prediction. In each frame, the affine parameters were predicted and these predictions were used to initialise the iterative optimisation algorithm. Each of the six affine parameters was predicted using a Kalman filter [15]:

$$\mathbf{x}_{k+1} = \mathbf{\Gamma}\mathbf{x}_k + \mathbf{B}\mathbf{n}_k, \tag{6}$$

$$\mathbf{z}_k = \mathbf{H}\mathbf{x}_k + \mathbf{r}_k \tag{7}$$

where $\mathbf{x}$ and $\mathbf{z}$ were 12-dimensional state and measurement vectors and $\mathbf{n}_k$ and $\mathbf{r}_k$ were zero-mean white noise with covariance matrices $\mathbf{Q}_k$ and $\mathbf{R}_k$. The dynamic system model used assumed constant velocity. This seemed to be reasonable due to the fact that pairwise plots of the affine parameter measurements typically revealed trajectories in the 6-dimensional affine parameter space which were approximately linear or piecewise linear (see Fig. 7). The elements of the vectors $\mathbf{x}$ and $\mathbf{z}$ corresponded to the affine parameters and their velocities.

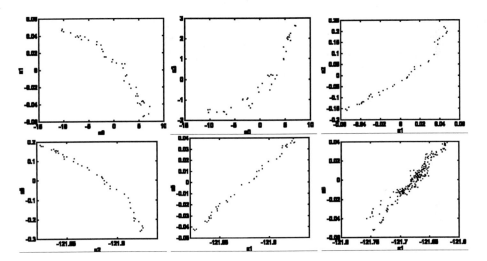

Fig. 7. Pairwise 2D affine parameter subspaces in our case are mostly linear. The example subspaces shown are a0-a1, a0-a3, a1-a2, a1-a4, a1-a5 and a1-a6, from top-left to bottom-right.

Appropriate noise covariance matrices were estimated using the EM algorithm with the following least-squares approximations of observation noise and state noise:

$$\mathbf{r}_k \approx \mathbf{z}_k - \mathbf{H}\mathbf{x}_k^-, \tag{8}$$

$$\mathbf{n}_k \approx (\mathbf{B}^{\mathsf{T}}\mathbf{B})^{-1}\mathbf{B}^{\mathsf{T}}(\mathbf{x}_{k+1}^+ - \mathbf{\Gamma}\mathbf{x}_k^+) \tag{9}$$

where $^+$ denotes *a posteriori* estimation and $^-$ denotes *a priori* estimation. The estimated covariance noise between the affine parameters was also verified visually by plotting pairwise parameter observations. An alternative approach is to derive an optimal estimate based on the Kalman filter's underlying cost function. Estimation of the state vector $\mathbf{x}_{k+1}$ based upon previous measurements is equivalent to minimising cost function:

$$E(\mathbf{x}_{k+1}^{+}) = \tfrac{1}{2}(\mathbf{x}_{k+1}^{+} - \mathbf{x}_{k-1}^{-})^{\mathrm{T}}(\mathbf{P}^{-1})(\mathbf{x}_{k+1}^{+} - \mathbf{x}_{k-1}^{-})$$
$$+ \tfrac{1}{2}(\mathbf{z}_k - \mathbf{H}\mathbf{x}_{k+1}^{+})^{\mathrm{T}}(\mathbf{R}^{-1})(\mathbf{z}_k - \mathbf{H}\mathbf{x}_{k+1}^{+})$$

The first term specifies the temporal constraint while the second expresses the data conservation, where all errors are measured using the Mahalanobis distance. We apply one robust norm to the second term in order to derive a robust Kalman filter. Efficient minimization of this function could be performed using a technique such as Iteratively Recursive Least Squares (IRLS) [16].

The human head will inevitably move in ways which are not predictable using these simple dynamic models. An effective way in which to detect this "unpredictability" is to run one iteration of the optimisation algorithm used for tracking. Only if the direction in affine parameter space from this iteration "agrees" with that of the Kalman prediction are the predictions utilised. This works well if not many outliers are present.

6 Experiments

The system was initially implemented in Matlab and takes an average of 14 sec/frame. In C, it could run at near 2 sec/frame on a standard 200MHz PC. Applying IRLS to the minimisation process can solve an approximation of the robust formulation in near real-time.

Fig. 8 shows the ability of the new adaptive scheme with shape encoded to align a face undergoing non-rigid expression change. Similar problems occur when the assumption of affine transformation is no longer valid. The adaptive scheme was shown to be able to overcome the problem when changes in pose were not sufficiently captured by the training data (see examples in Fig. 6).

Fig. 9 shows view alignment from a 260 frame sequence with both affine and pose variations. The training set had 100 images and 54 eigenvectors were used in a GES capturing 95% of the variance. However, with the adaptive scheme using LES, only 6 eigenvectors were needed to recover sufficiently accurate parameters for alignment.

Fig. 10 gives an indication of savings in computational cost when the adaptive scheme is applied. It shows the time taken in seconds to perform the minimisation (Equation (2)). The first plot shows the time required for each frame using GES with 54 eigenvectors. The second plot shows the time required for each frame with LES but without the previous history at $t-1$. The third plot shows the result from augmented LES using $t-1$ tracked data. The mean frame rate were: 29 sec/frame for GES, 15 sec/frame for LES and 12 sec/frame for $t-1$ augmented LES.

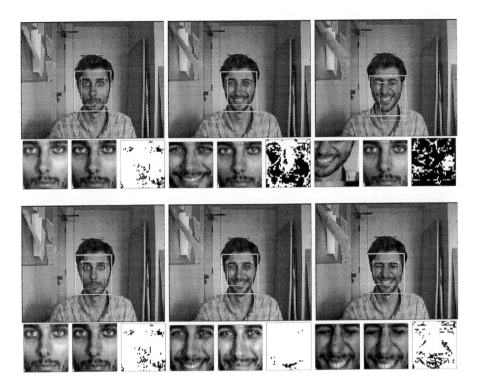

Fig. 8. This sequence demonstrates the advantage in using shape with non-rigid expression changes. The first two frames show the overlaid results from EigenTracking without shape. The corresponding three small images are, from left to right, the aligned object image, the reconstructed object image using the estimated affine parameters, and the outliers. The last two frames show the results on the same sequence from the adaptive scheme with shape encoded.

7   Conclusion

In this paper we presented an integrated scheme for view alignment. We exploited the transformation between the training set and the eigenspace in a computationally inexpensive manner in order to establish the correspondence between the landmarks in the training set and the image.

A dynamically adaptive scheme was adopted to compensate the small changes in illumination and the nonlinear transformations that cannot be recovered with global affine transformations. One advantage of our scheme is that the adaption does not change essentially the basis dataset of the eigenspace since the current tracked frame is only used once as an added bias in constructing the eigenspace at that time frame. It is not used to replace any initial sample images in the training set therefore the tracker is unlikely to eventually adapt and track the background.

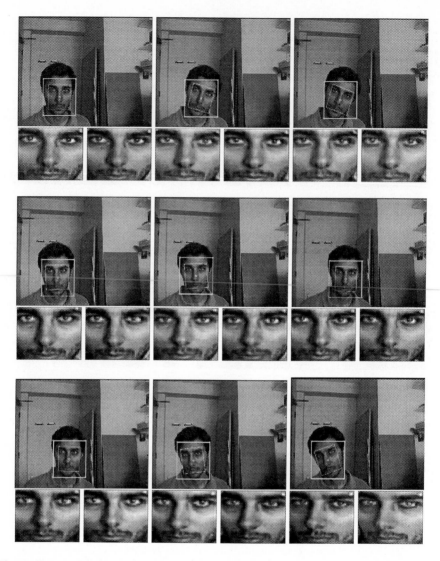

Fig. 9. Every 10th frame from a sequence with attentional windows and aligned face images overlaid. Below each frame are the located region (left) and its reconstruction (right). The affine parameters were recovered using LES.

Our current scheme did not include a pre-filtering process to address changes in global illumination. This can be addressed by estimating the illumination in the new image dynamically with homomorphic filtering. An alternative approach to resolve the problem is to use an additional basis to represent all the probable illumination situations [4]. Gabor wavelets representation can also be employed which gives a certain degree of invariance to global illumination change [2].

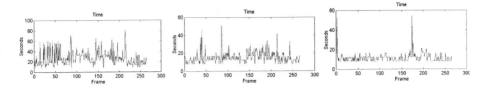

Fig. 10. Convergence times required by the minimisation process of different affine tracking schemes.

Currently, the parameters are only predicted independently. Prediction can therefore be rather under-constrained and allows for too much freedom. On the other hand, Fig. 7 indicates strongly that all the parameters should be tracked with a prediction model simultaneously since they are highly correlated and mostly linear in their correlations. This will enable the prediction and tracking much better constrained and consequently more robust and consistent.

Although the segmentation process in the initialisation stage utilises colour information, it still relies heavily upon morphological operations which can be relatively slow and inconsistent. Future work includes incorporating the adaptive affine tracking scheme developed here with a robust adaptive multi-colour model [17] in order to cope with changes in illumination over time.

References

1. D. Beymer and T. Poggio, "Image representations for visual learning," *Science*, vol. 272, pp. 1905–1909, June 1996.

2. S. McKenna, S. Gong, R. Wurtz, J. Tanner, and D. Banin, "Tracking facial feature points with gabor wavelets and shape models," in *IAPR International Conference on Audio-Video Based Biometric Person Authentication*, Crans-Montana, Switzerland, March 1997.

3. S. McKenna and S. Gong, "Real-time face pose estimation," *Real Time Imaging*, 1998, To appear in the Special Issue on Real-time Visual Monitoring and Inspection.

4. G. Hager and P. Belhumeur, "Real-time tracking of image region with changes in geometry and illumination," in *IEEE Conference on Computer Vision and Pattern Recognition*, 1996.

5. M. Black and Y.Yacoob, "Eigen tracking: Robust matching and tracking of articulated objects using a view-based representation," in *European Conference on Computer Vision*, Cambridge, England, April 1996.

6. P. Huber, *Robust statistics*, John Wiley and Sons, 1981.

7. S. Geman and D. McClure, "Statistical methods for tomographic image reconstruction," *Bull. Int. Statis. Inst.*, pp. 5–21, 1987.

8. M.J. Black and P. Anandan, "The robust estimation of multiple motions: Parametric and piecewise-smooth flow fields," *CVIU*, vol. 63, no. 1, pp. 75–104, 1996.

9. N. Sumpter, R. Boyle, and R. Tillett, "Modelling collective animal behaviour using extended point distribution models," in *British Machine Vision Conference*, Colchester, September 1997, pp. 242–251.

10. I. Craw, "A manifold model of face and object recognition," in *Cognitive and Computational Aspects of Face Recognition*, T. R. Valentine, Ed., pp. 183–203. Routledge, 1995.

11. Y. Raja, S. McKenna, and S. Gong, "Tracking and segmenting people in varying lighting conditions using colour," in *IEEE International Conference on Automatic Face and Gesture Recognition*, Nara, Japan, April 1998.

12. F. De la Torre, E. Martinez, E. Santamaria, and J.A Morin, "Moving object detection and tracking system: a real-time implementation," in *GRETSI*, Grenoble, 1997, pp. 375–378.

13. H. Murase and S. Nayar, "Detection of 3d objects in cluttered scenes using hierarchical eigenspace," *Pattern Recognition Letters*, vol. 18, pp. 375–384, 1997.

14. S. Nene and S. Nayar, "A simple algorithm for nearest neighbor search in high dimensions," *IEEE Transactions on Pattern Analysis and Machine Intelligence*, vol. 19, no. 9, 1997.

15. S. Kay, *Fundamentals of statistical signal processing: Estimation theory*, Prentice Hall, 1993.

16. Z. Zhang, "Parameter estimation techniques: A tutorial with application to conic fitting," *Image and Vision Computing*, 1996.

17. Y. Raja, S. McKenna, and S. Gong, "Colour model selection and adaptation in dynamic scenes," in *European Conference on Computer Vision*, Freiburg, Germany, June 1998.

An Efficient Combination of 2D and 3D Shape Descriptions for Contour Based Tracking of Moving Objects

J. Denzler, B. Heigl*, H. Niemann

Universität Erlangen–Nürnberg
Lehrstuhl für Mustererkennung (Informatik 5)
Martensstr. 3, D–91058 Erlangen
Tel.: +49–9131–85-7894, FAX: +49–9131–303811
email: denzler@informatik.uni-erlangen.de

Abstract Tracking the 2D contour of a moving object has widely been used in the past years. So called active contour models have been proven to be a promising approach to real–time tracking of deformable objects. Also tracking 2D contours, which are projections of rigid 3D objects, is reduced to tracking deformable 2D contours. There, the deformations of the contour are caused by the movement in 3D and the changing perspective to the camera.

In this paper a combination of 2D and 3D shape descriptions is presented, which can be applied to the prediction of changes in 2D contours, which are caused by movement in 3D. Only coarse 3D knowledge is provided, which is automatically acquired in a training step. Then, the reconstructed 3D model of the object is used to predict the shape of the 2D contour. Thus, limitations of the contour point search in the image is possible, which reduces the errors in the contour extraction caused by heterogenous background.

The experimental part shows, that the proposed combination of 2D and 3D shape descriptions is efficient and accurate with respect to real–time contour extraction and tracking.

1 Introduction

In the past years a new framework has been established for representing a deformable object by its contour. Active contours [11] and related models have been developed and have been widely used in computer vision, for example for medical imaging, vision aided speech recognition (lip reading), segmentation and tracking [3, 14, 16].

Although active contour models have been used for tracking moving objects, it is an open question how changes in the contour during tracking can be predicted. Using the data driven approach of active contours usually no a priori knowledge of the object is available. Only a few mechanisms have been included providing the possibility for predicting the deformation of the object's contour. For this, most researchers concentrate on the prediction of 2D changes without taking into account the motion of the object

---

* This work was partially funded by the German Research Foundation (DFG) under grant number SFB 182. Only the authors are responsible for the contents.

in 3D. [19] presents a Kalman–Snake combining the principles of active contours and prediction by a Kalman–Filter. In [1] the motion of the contour in the 2D image plane is predicted by computing the normal flow at the contour points. In the case of tracking rigid or elastic objects moving in a 2D plane parallel to the image plane some work have been presented which learn the possible deformations of the object and limit the contour point search on certain areas in the image [4, 12].

In the following, we focus on tracking the contours of rigid objects moving in 3D. Then, the deformation of the contour depends on the 3D shape of the object and is caused by the changing view to the camera. Without any prediction, problems arise, when the object moves in front of a heterogeneous background. Strong background edges often define local minima during the contour extraction process. As a result, the active contour is caught by the background and the moving object is lost.

One straightforward approach to handle these problems is to predict the motion of the contour in the 2D image plane. This works very well (see [19]) in the case of tracking a single patch of the object or tracking an object, whose visible patches do not change. In contrary, if the visible parts of the object change, new object edges appear near the object itself (see Figure 1, (a)). Without any coarse knowledge about the 3D shape of the object these new edges cannot be distinguished from appearing background edges which have been covered before by the object (Figure 1, (b)).

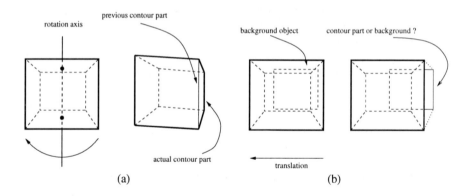

(a) (b)

Figure1. Problem of predicting new contour parts: how can an active contour distinguish between a new contour part and an appearing background edge? (a) rotation of object. (b) translation and appearing background object.

How can we get a solution for this problem? On the one hand we do not like to give up the data driven approach allowing a very fast and efficient tracking of moving objects even in real–time [5]. On the other hand, one needs to introduce knowledge about the moving object to increase robustness during tracking. Using knowledge can be a time consuming task which might prevent the use in real–time applications.

In our contribution we concentrate on this trade–off. We present an efficient combination of a 2D data driven contour extraction method and a 3D shape modelling technique. For 2D modelling of the contour as well as for 3D shape modelling a radial representation is used. Both representations can easily be mapped on each other, i.e. having several 2D views of the object the 3D representation can be built; having the 3D representation the corresponding 2D contour can be predicted. And with a 3D representation and a single 2D contour corresponding to a unique view of the object the position of the object in 3D can roughly be estimated. For both the 2D and 3D case, it is possible to dynamically adjust the accuracy of the representation to the available computation time. This is an important feature for real–time applications. Thus, possible applications for our method exist in the field of autonomous mobile systems, where in different situations different objects need to be tracked: from unknown objects (obstacles) which need to be identified quickly and tracked without knowledge up to known objects in visual grasping tasks, where more time can be spent. Finally, the 3D contour prediction method itself can also be integrated in arbitrary contour tracking algorithms.

In contrast to model based tracking algorithms [9, 10], we are not interested in an accurate 3D representation of the object. Active contours need only a coarse initialization near the contour which should be extracted. In our approach, the model of the object can also be constructed very quickly by presenting a sufficient number of 2D views and applying shape from contour methods. Finally, the experimental part will prove, that the 2D contour extraction, the 3D model construction as well as the prediction can be done in real–time on general purpose hardware.

The paper is structured as follows. In Section 2 we shortly summarize the principles of 2D contour extraction by active rays. Section 3 discusses the basic concepts of shape from contour which is the key idea for our automatic shape reconstruction step. We focus on a radial representation of the object's shape by rays in Section 4, and show how the accuracy of the shape description can be adjusted dynamically. In Section 5 the basic concepts of shape from contour, the 2D contour representation, and 3D shape models are merged together to automatically reconstruct a 3D model by single 2D views. We also show, how the resulting coarse 3D model can be used to predict the changes in the 2D contour. In Section 6, experiments show the improvement for tracking objects moving in 3D. The paper finishes with a discussion in Section 7.

2 A Radial Representation for Contour Extraction

In this section a new approach will be shortly summarized for 2D contour extraction. A detailed description can be found in [6]. Instead of modelling the elastic contour by a parametric function in the 2D image plane [11], a different strategy has been developed.

An initial reference point $m = (x_m, y_m)^T$ inside the contour, which should be extracted, has to be chosen. This is similar to a balloon model [3], where the initial balloon also needs to be inside the contour of the object. In the next step the 2D image $f(x, y)$ is sampled along straight lines — so called *rays* —

$$\varrho_m(\phi, \lambda) = f(x_m + \lambda \cos(\phi), y_m + \lambda \sin(\phi)), \tag{1}$$

from the reference point in certain directions. As a result for each ray we get 1D gray value signals which depend on the chosen reference point m. Usually, for ϕ the range from $[0, 2\pi[$ is sampled more or less dense, depending on the necessary accuracy of the extracted contour. For real–time applications, this can be controlled by the available computation time.

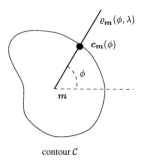

contour $\mathcal{C}$

Figure2. Representation of a contour point by active rays

Now, for contour extraction the rays $\varrho_m(\phi, \lambda)$ are taken. For each 1D gray value signal, features are computed to identify the position $\lambda^*(\phi) \geq 0$ of the object's boundary on the ray. One possible criterion, which we call external energy, is the gradient

$$\lambda^*(\phi) = \underset{\lambda}{\mathrm{argmin}} \left(-\left| \frac{\partial}{\partial \lambda} \varrho_m(\phi, \lambda) \right|^2 \right), \tag{2}$$

of the 1D gray value signal to identify contours by changes in the gray values. Also, more sophisticated energies have been used, for example changes in the variance of the gray values to extract textured regions.

Based on these features for direction ϕ the position $\lambda^*(\phi)$ is identified, which corresponds to the object boundary

$$c_m(\phi) = (x_m + \lambda^*(\phi)\cos(\phi), y_m + \lambda^*(\phi)\sin(\phi)), \tag{3}$$

in the 2D image plane, with $0 \leq \phi < 2\pi$. This works well for convex contours, because then each ray only hits the object contour once. Depending on the position of the reference point, this is also true for some concave contours. In the general case of concave contours, a mechanism has been provided, which allows more than one contour point on each 1D gray value signal. This case will not be discussed in this paper. A detailed description can be found [6]. In contrast to [18], where also a radial representation is proposed, but no energy description for the contour extraction, we force — similar to active contours — the smoothness of the 2D contour $c_m(\phi) \in \mathbb{R}^2$ by defining an internal energy E_i

$$E_i(c_m(\phi)) = \frac{\alpha(\phi)\left|\frac{d}{d\phi}\lambda(\phi)\right|^2 + \beta(\phi)\left|\frac{d^2}{d\phi^2}\lambda(\phi)\right|^2}{2}. \tag{4}$$

The internal energy is based on the distance of the contour point to the reference point. Since the derivative of the distance $\frac{d}{d\phi}\lambda(\phi)$ and the curvature $\frac{d^2}{d\phi^2}\lambda(\phi)$ describe the smoothness of the contour, this energy forces coherence of the contour in the image plane. Now, the contour extraction, i.e. searching for the function $\lambda^*(\phi)$ can be described as a minimization of the total energy E

$$\lambda^*(\phi) = \underset{\lambda}{\operatorname{argmin}} \int_0^{2\pi} \left[\frac{\alpha(\phi)|\frac{d}{d\phi}\lambda(\phi)|^2 + \beta(\phi)|\frac{d^2}{d\phi^2}\lambda(\phi)|^2}{2} - |\frac{d}{d\lambda}\varrho m(\phi,\lambda)|^2 \right] d\phi. \quad (5)$$

This algorithm has been successfully applied to real–time pedestrian tracking in natural scenes [8]. More details of the mathematical derivation can be found in [6]. In this paper we focus on the combination with a 3D prediction step. In the next two sections we summarize the mathematical preliminaries for 3D object modelling and shape from contour. In Section 5 we will show, that in a combination with a similar 3D representation the 2D radial representation has advantages. It is beyond the scope of this paper to make comparisons to other contour based tracking algorithms, especially active contours. Such a discussion can be found elsewhere.

3 Concept of 3D Reconstruction from 2D Contours

We are interested in tracking rigid objects moving in 3D. We focus on contour based methods (see Section 2). Thus, we need to describe formally, how 2D contours of 3D objects are generated. An important term in this context is the silhouette of an object. Since the next section describes how to build an object description out of segmented silhouettes, it is also important to define two further concepts, the visual and outer hull, which give approximations of 3D objects.

Let the object O be represented by a set of points $x \in \mathbb{R}^3$. The points $x_M \subset O$ are constant within the model coordinate system. In the following we assume, that the transformation of a point in model coordinates x_M to camera coordinates x_C is given by the relation $x_C = R_{MC}x_M + t_{MC}$. In the case of model reconstruction, the rotation matrix R_{MC} and the translation vector t_{MC} are assumed to be known, either by defining the viewing angle in a training stage or by estimating the pose of the object from 2D images.

3.1 Object Silhouettes

A descriptive illustration of an object silhouette is the shadow of an object produced on a plane by a single light spot. Following [13], a definition of a silhouette might be:

> The word *silhouette* indicates the region of a 2D image of an object O which contains the projections of the visible points of O.

The projection of object points to image points can be described by many different models. Generally, the projection function is denoted by $\mathcal{P} : \mathbb{R}^3 \rightarrow \mathbb{R}^2$. Here we only consider the cases of orthogonal and perspective projection, but other projections are adaptable to the later concepts without big efforts. The backprojection function $\mathcal{P}^{-1} : \mathbb{R}^2 \to \mathbb{R}^3$, concerning a specified projection $\mathcal{P}$, is defined by

$$\mathcal{P}^{-1} := \boldsymbol{x}_{\text{P}} \to \{\boldsymbol{x}_{\text{C}} \in \mathbb{R}^3 \,|\, \mathcal{P}(\boldsymbol{x}_{\text{C}}) = \boldsymbol{x}_{\text{P}}\}. \tag{6}$$

This mapping of image points $\boldsymbol{x}_{\text{P}}$ to points in $\boldsymbol{x}_{\text{C}}$ camera coordinates is not unique, because of $\mathcal{P}$ not being injective.

Using these definitions, the silhouette of an object O in the pose $(\boldsymbol{R}_{\text{MC}}, \boldsymbol{t}_{\text{MC}})$ created by projection $\mathcal{P}$ is formally denoted by

$$S_{\boldsymbol{R}_{\text{MC}}, \boldsymbol{t}_{\text{MC}}} = \{\mathcal{P}(\boldsymbol{R}_{\text{MC}}\boldsymbol{x}_{\text{M}} + \boldsymbol{t}_{\text{MC}}) \,|\, \boldsymbol{x}_{\text{M}} \in O\}. \tag{7}$$

It is assumed, that the silhoutte has no "hole", therefore it can be represented by its contour. As we know the contour of an object by tracking it using active rays, we have a representation of the object silhouette at any time of the trace.

3.2 Outer and Visual Hull

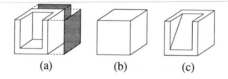

(a)   (b)   (c)

Figure3. Building two silhouettes of an object (a), the outer hull of these silhouettes (b) and the visual hull (c)

Now we examine the problem of reconstructing an object out of its silhouettes. Given n sequentially recorded silhouettes ${}^t S_{\boldsymbol{R}_{\text{MC}}(t), \boldsymbol{t}_{\text{MC}}(t)}, 1 \leq t \leq n$, we define the abbreviation $S(t) = {}^t S_{\boldsymbol{R}_{\text{MC}}(t), \boldsymbol{t}_{\text{MC}}(t)}$. The backprojection $C_{\text{M}}(t)$ of the Silhouette $S(t)$ is given by the union of the backprojections of all points $\boldsymbol{x}_{\text{P}} \in S(t)$. Written in model coordinates, we can calculate

$$C_{\text{M}}(t) = \boldsymbol{R}_{\text{MC}}^T(t) \cdot (\mathcal{P}^{-1}(S(t)) - \boldsymbol{t}_{\text{MC}}(t)), \tag{8}$$

where an operation $\circ$ between a set B and an element $\boldsymbol{b}$ is defined as the set of results of the operation between this vector and each element of B: $B \circ \boldsymbol{b} := \{\boldsymbol{x} \circ \boldsymbol{b} \,|\, \boldsymbol{x} \in B\}$.

Using equation 8, the concept of the outer hull A_{M} is defined in [17] as follows:

$$A_{\text{M}} := \bigcap_{t=t_1}^{t_2} C_{\text{M}}(t) \tag{9}$$

Figure 3 shows an example, comparing the principles of the outer and visual hull. Reconstructing objects by building the outer hull, is known in the literature as so called volume intersection algorithms or as shape from contour techniques. In [13] an overview

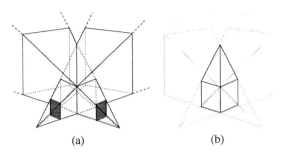

(a)   (b)

Figure4. Illustration of building the outer hull of two given rectangular silhouettes by intersecting their backprojections. (a): intersection, (b): outer hull

therefore is given. Figure 4 illustrates this concept. The outer hull is built out of two rectangular silhouettes. In the case of central perspective projection, the backprojections of rectangles are pyramids with infinite height. These pyramids are intersected, to build the outer hull.

Algorithm to calculate the outer hull of silhouettes
Parameters: $\qquad S(t), \boldsymbol{R}_{\text{MC}}(t), \boldsymbol{t}_{\text{MC}}(t), 1 \leq t \leq n$
Initialization: $\quad ^{0}A_{\text{M}} := \mathbb{R}^{3}$
FOR all t with $1 \leq t \leq n$
$\qquad$ Transformation into camera coordinates: $\qquad ^{t-1}A_{\text{C}} := \boldsymbol{R}_{\text{MC}}(t) \cdot \ ^{t-1}A_{\text{M}} + \boldsymbol{t}_{\text{MC}}(t)$
$\qquad$ Intersection with backprojection of silhouette: $\qquad ^{t}A_{\text{C}} := \ ^{t-1}A_{\text{C}} \cap \mathcal{P}^{-1}(S(t))$
$\qquad$ Transformation into model coordinates: $\qquad ^{t}A_{\text{M}} := \boldsymbol{R}_{\text{MC}}^{T}(t)(\ ^{t}A_{\text{C}} - \boldsymbol{t}_{\text{MC}}(t))$
Return: outer hull $\ ^{n}A_{\text{M}}$

Figure5. Algorithm for the iterative calculation of the outer hull

Joining all possible backprojections of an object, an upper limit for the outer hull is given by the concept called visual hull $H(O)$ of an Object O. It can be described in correspondence to [13] as the unity of all points, whose backprojection of any projection intersects the object O. The following relation holds: $O \subseteq H(O) \subseteq A_{\text{M}}$. We now use the outer hull A_{M} as an approximation of the true object O. As already mentioned, we can do this, because in the context of active contours, a coarse initialization of the contour around the true contour is sufficient.

The associative property of the uniting operation allows the construction of the outer hull as it is described in Figure 5. This algorithm has to be applied to the special 3D representation, which is used to model the point set, building the outer hull.

4 3D Radial Object Representation

The idea of representing contours with 2D rays is now extended to the third dimension.

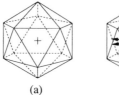

(a)   (b)

Figure6. Definition of ray directions as normal vectors on the boundary plains of regular polyhedrons; (a) icosahedron, (b) icosahedron with normal vectors

To avoid confusions, following notations are used to distinguish between the 2D and 3D case: the accent ˜ denotes, that the corresponding symbol belongs to 3D rays, the accent ˆ, that it belongs to the projection of a 3D ray, and without accent, that it belongs to a 2D ray. The 3D ray representation $\tilde{K}$ can then be written as a tuple:

$$\tilde{K} := (\tilde{W}, \ \tilde{m}, \ \tilde{\lambda} : \tilde{W} \to \mathbb{R} \cup \infty). \tag{10}$$

$\tilde{W}$ is the set of direction vectors n of the predefined 3D rays with $\|n\| = 1$. The vector $\tilde{m} \in \mathbb{R}^3$ denotes the reference point and the function $\tilde{\lambda}$ returns the length of the ray in direction n. The value ∞ means, that this ray length is undefined, yet.

Each ray represents a single point on the surface of the object. If we define the representation continuously, i.e. $\tilde{W} = \{x \in \mathbb{R}^3 \mid \|x\| = 1\}$, the represented point set is equal to $\{x \in \mathbb{R}^3 \mid x = \tilde{m} + kn, 0 \le k \le \tilde{\lambda}(n), n \in \tilde{W}\}$.

In the discrete case, the choice of the directions $\tilde{W}$ should be distributed regularly. Moreover the resolution should be changeable dynamically to achieve any-time behavior. If we define the regularity in the sense that neighboring directions shall enclose all the same angle, we are restricted to 20 directions, defined by the normal vectors of the icosahedron, being the regular polyhedron with the most plains (see Figure 6). This is equal to take the 20 corners of the dodecahedron, being the regular polyhedron with the most corners.

In [2] a method is described, to subdivide an icosahedron, so that the error in the regularity is minimized. Taking the 20 normals and the 12 corners of the icosahedron, 60 triangular plains can be defined.

This approximation can be refined by subdividing the triangles into subtriangles, defining three new points bisecting the three sides.

Using this representation, all convex and some concave objects can be described. Like in the 2D case concave objects exist, which cannot be represented. Also holes in the objects can better be approximated using different representations (for example octrees); since we are only interested in the contour and a efficient mapping from 3D to 2D rays and vice versa, this is not relevant for our approach.

5 Application to Contour Based Object Tracking

We have seen, how to build the outer hull of an object from its silhouettes (Section 3). Besides we have designed a 3D representation by 3D rays, similar to the 2D ray representation (Section 4). Using these concepts, it is shown how to create the 3D object model (Section 5.1) and to extract its contour in a given pose (Section 5.2). Section 5.3 describes how to use this model to predict contours during tracking objects.

5.1 3D Model Generation

Now we apply the algorithm described in Figure 5 to the 3D representation developed in Section 4. After each iteration step, the 3D ray model shall represent the outer hull, which is generated by intersecting the backprojections of the extracted silhouettes.

The goal is to represent the outer hull A_M by the 3D ray representation $\tilde{K}_M = (W_M, 0_3, \tilde{\lambda}_M)$. The reference point is set to 0_3 without any loss of generality.

According to Figure 5, ^0A_M has to be set to $\mathbb{R}^3$ at the beginning. This is done in $^0\tilde{K}_M$ by assigning $^0\tilde{\lambda}_M(n_M) = \infty$. In a second step, the set ^tA_M — using model coordinates — has to be transformed to camera coordinates. This is done by transforming $\tilde{K}_M$ to $\tilde{K}_C$ following:

$$^t\tilde{K}_C = (W_C, \tilde{m}_C, \tilde{\lambda}_C), \text{ with} \tag{11}$$
$$\tilde{W}_C = R_{MC}(t) \cdot \tilde{W}_M,$$
$$\tilde{m}_C = t_{MC}(t),$$
$$\tilde{\lambda}_C(n_C) = \tilde{\lambda}_M(n_M) \text{ where } n_C = R_{MC} \cdot n_M.$$

$^t\tilde{K}_C$ therefore represents the set ^tA_C.

Now, $^t\tilde{K}_C$ has to be intersected with the backprojection of the Silhouette $S(t)$, represented by the active contour ^tK. It is mathematically clear, that for an object O, a silhouette S and an arbitrary point $p \in \mathbb{R}^3$, the relation $\mathcal{P}(p) \notin \mathcal{P}(H(O))[= \mathcal{P}(O) = S] \Rightarrow p \notin H(O)$ holds. Besides we know $\mathcal{P}(p) \in S \Leftrightarrow p \in \mathcal{P}^{-1}(S)$. We see, that all points p with $\mathcal{P}(p) \notin S$ have to be removed. Applying this to the ray representation, only those rays are affected, whose projections are not totally contained in the silhouette. These rays have to be cut, so that the ends of their projections lie on the border of the silhouette. Figure 7 shows this operation and the notations used here.

Let us describe this cutting step formally, by first calculating the 2D projection of each of the 3D rays. The starting point of each ray, i.e the reference point $\tilde{m}_C$, is projected to $\mathcal{P}(\tilde{m}_C)$. For each 3D direction $n_C \in \tilde{W}_C$ the corresponding angle $\phi(n_C)$ and the length $\tilde{\lambda}(\phi(n_C))$ can be determined by applying the projection function $\mathcal{P}$.

These projected rays have to be intersected with the extracted contour ^tK. Therefore, we overlay ^tK with the projected rays. This is done by setting the reference point $m := \mathcal{P}(\tilde{m}_C)$, being possible, because m can be chosen arbitrarily.

According to the preliminaries, a unique intercept point of the backprojection of the contour point $c(\phi(n_C)) = m + \lambda(\phi(n_C)) \begin{pmatrix} \cos(\phi(n_C)) \\ \sin(\phi(n_C)) \end{pmatrix}$ with the ray in direction n_C exists. The intersection of a 3D ray with the backprojection of the silhouette S therefore

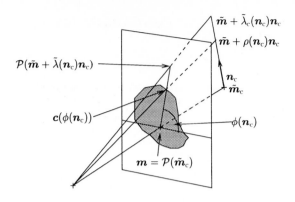

Figure7. Illustration of the cutting algorithm

is done by setting the ray length $\tilde{\lambda}_c(\boldsymbol{n}_c)$ to $\rho(\boldsymbol{n}_c)$, if the former ray length was larger. The value $\rho(\boldsymbol{n}_c)$ is defined by following relation: $\tilde{\boldsymbol{m}}_c + \rho(\boldsymbol{n}_c)\boldsymbol{n}_c \in \mathcal{P}^{-1}(\boldsymbol{c}(\phi(\boldsymbol{n}_c)))$. For the case of parallel or perspective projection, $\rho(\boldsymbol{n}_c)$ can be determined easily: $\rho(\boldsymbol{n}_c) = \frac{\tilde{\lambda}(\boldsymbol{n}_c)}{\hat{\lambda}(\phi(\boldsymbol{n}_c))} \cdot \lambda(\phi(\boldsymbol{n}_c))$. Formally, the intersection can be written as following:

$$\tilde{\lambda}_c(\boldsymbol{n}_c) := \begin{cases} \tilde{\lambda}_c(\boldsymbol{n}_c) & \text{if } \hat{\lambda}(\phi(\boldsymbol{n}_c)) \leq \lambda(\phi(\boldsymbol{n}_c)) \\ \rho(\boldsymbol{n}_c) & \text{if } \hat{\lambda}(\phi(\boldsymbol{n}_c)) > \lambda(\phi(\boldsymbol{n}_c)) \end{cases}. \tag{12}$$

By applying this cutting step to every single ray, ${}^t\tilde{K}$ represents the outer hull ${}^tA_M$, afterwards.

5.2 Model Based 2D Contour Computation

In the following, the method is shortly summarized to create the silhouette of the 3D ray model in a given pose $(\boldsymbol{R}_{MC}, \boldsymbol{t}_{MC})$. The resulting silhouette shall be represented by $K = (\boldsymbol{m}, \lambda)$. The reference point $\boldsymbol{m}$ is set to $\mathcal{P}(\tilde{\boldsymbol{m}}_c)$. It remains to determine the values $\lambda(\phi)$.

In the continuous case, for each value ϕ, a set of $B(\phi) \subset \tilde{W}$ of 3D rays can be found, defined by following relation: $\boldsymbol{n}_c \in B \Leftrightarrow \phi(\boldsymbol{n}_c) = \phi$, where the function ϕ is defined equal Section 5.1. For each direction $\boldsymbol{n}_c$ also the length $\hat{\lambda}(\phi(\boldsymbol{n}_c))$ can be determined. The value $\lambda(\phi)$ is now given by the following equation:

$$\lambda(\phi) = \max\{\hat{\lambda}(\phi(\boldsymbol{n}_c)) \mid \boldsymbol{n}_c \in B(\phi)\}. \tag{13}$$

In the discrete case, the set $B(\phi)$ is given by the relation $\boldsymbol{n}_c \in B \Leftrightarrow \phi - \Delta\phi \leq \phi(\boldsymbol{n}_c) < \phi + \Delta\phi$, where $\Delta\phi$ denotes the maximum 3D angle between two neighboring 3D rays. The value $\lambda(\phi)$ is then defined equal to the continuous case.

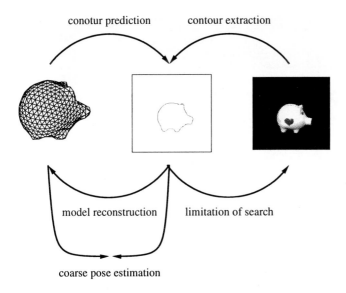

conotur prediction   contour extraction

model reconstruction   limitation of search

coarse pose estimation

Figure8. Data flow between 2D and 3D ray representations. A set of extracted 2D contours is used for 3D model generation. The model can then be used to predict a 2D contour for a given pose of the object.

5.3 System Integration

Now the 2D and 3D ray representations are tied together for contour based object tracking. In Figure 8 the connections between both representations and the system integration is clarified. The important aspect for object tracking is the possibility, that for each angle ϕ we get an interval $I(\phi) = [\lambda_s(\phi), \lambda_e(\phi)]$, which is used to limit the contour point search in the 2D image plane (compare Section 2). Thus equation (5) becomes

$$\lambda^*(\phi) = \underset{\lambda(\phi) \in I(\phi)}{\operatorname{argmin}} \int_0^{2\pi} \left[\frac{\alpha(\phi)|\frac{d}{d\phi}\lambda(\phi)|^2 + \beta(\phi)|\frac{d^2}{d\phi^2}\lambda(\phi)|^2}{2} - |\frac{d}{d\lambda}\varrho m(\phi, \lambda)|^2 \right] d\phi \quad (14)$$

Having both, the 2D contour and the 3D model, a coarse 3D pose estimation is possible, which is needed to perform a 3D motion estimation and prediction with a Kalman filter. For this, we have to define a distance function $\mathrm{dist}(v, v')$, which measures the similarity of two 2D contours v and v'. Then the 3D pose, defined by R^*_{MC} and t^*_{MC}, can be estimated by

$$\left(R^*_{\mathrm{MC}}, t^*_{\mathrm{MC}} \right)^T = \underset{R_{\mathrm{MC}}, t_{\mathrm{MC}}}{\operatorname{argmin}} \mathrm{dist}(v, v') \quad (15)$$

where v corresponds to the extracted 2D contour and v' is the 2D contour of the model under the transformation R_{MC} and t_{MC}.

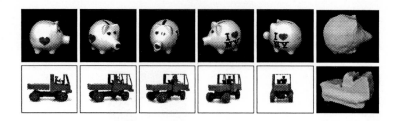

Figure9. Some images out of the sequence taken from [15] and one recorded by us, and reconstructed coarse models.

6 Experimental Evaluation

We have conducted several experiments, concerning the 3D reconstruction, 2D prediction and tracking. In Figure 9 some images of two sequences are shown with the models reconstructed models. The first sequence totally consits of 36, the second of 9 images. Several other objects (for example, see Figure 10, right) haven been reconstructed. We have tested convex objects as well as concave objects. Although the reconstructed 3D shape of concave objects does not look quite well, the model is accurate enough concerning the accuracy of the predicted 2D contour.

The computation time for model generation depending on the 2D and 3D ray resolution are summarized in Table 1. For the models in Figure 9 and 8 an amount of 960 3D rays and 36 2D rays have been chosen, which means, that also model generation can be done in real–time. This is important for an online model building during tracking in the future. Another example for model generation can be seen in Figure 10 showing a toy train, following an elliptic way. Although the real pose of the object was estimated very roughly by deviding the whole rotation angle by the number of images and assuming a vertical rotation axis, the reconstructed model nearly has the same side relations as the original one: 1 : 1.45 : 1.95 (model) and 1 : 1.37 : 1.63 (original object).

In Figure 10 three predicted contours and the corresponding extracted contours for the model from Figure 9 are shown, which proves the accuracy of contour prediction. The computation time for 2D contour prediction can be seen in Table 1. The mean error in the ray length is about 2% to 5% of the extracted ray length, varying in the different views.

Finally, in Figure 11 a result for tracking a moving toy train is shown. The extracted motion path is overlayed the image.

7 Discussion and Future Work

In this paper we have presented an efficient combination of a 2D contour representation and a 3D modelling technique. The motivation of the work has been to provide a mechanism for 2D contour prediction of rigid objects moving in 3D. This is an important aspect for contour based tracking algorithms in the case of natural scenes with heterogeneous background.

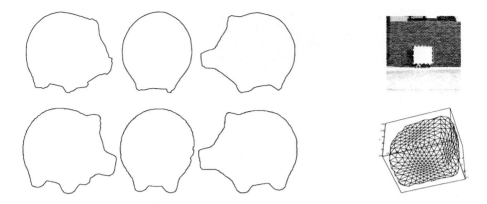

Figure10. Left: comparison between predicted 2D contour (first row) and extracted 2D contour (second row). The prediction is accurate enough to successfully limit the search space for 2D rays. Right: one image out of a sequence following a toy train (top) and the reconstructed coarse model (bottom).

	model generation			contour generation		
	number of 3D rays			number of 3D rays		
number of 2D rays	60	960	15360	60	960	15360
18	1	8	145	1	8	149
36	1	8	143	1	10	179
180	1	7	119	5	26	423
360	2	8	120	10	51	733

Table1. Computation time for processing one image during the process of model and contour generation, depending on the 2D and 3D ray resolution (in msec. with an SGI Onyx R10000)

A short introduction to a radial representation of 2D contours and an energy description for data driven contour extraction has been followed by a similar representation of 3D objects. The 3D model of an object can be built from a set of different 2D contours. Well known methods from shape from contour have been applied. The key idea has been, to make use of the similar representations, namely a radial representation for the 2D as well as for the 3D case, to achieve real–time performance. This has been proven in the experimental part.

It is worth noting, that we did not want to implement an accurate 3D model generation algorithm. In the context of active contours, a coarse 2D contour initialization is sufficient to extract the object's contour in the following energy minimization step. Thus, the 3D visual hull of the object is sufficient for modelling the contour changes during tracking. At present, we are integrating this approach in our real–time object tracking system. Preliminary results show, that the performance of the system can be

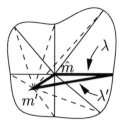

Figure11. Left: tracking result (3D path of the moving object overlayed the image) in the case of partial occlusions. Right: resampling of a 2D contour with a different reference point.

increased for partial occlusions of the moving object. Also, the 3D pose estimation over time can be used for qualitative 3D motion estimation (for example, the object is moving toward the camera) of the moving object, as it has been reported in [7].

In the near future we focus on the following. First, during 3D model generation, the 3D rays, which have been cut due to a segmentation error, cannot increase in length. This results in holes on the objects surface. Secondly, the initial 3D pose estimation of the object is a time consuming task, in the case that no a priori pose information is possible. Then, the complete parameter space R_{MC} and t_{MC} has to be searched. After the initialization, this can be done in real–time by assuming, that the pose of the object is changing slowly.

Appendix: Technical Details for the Contour Comparison

In our implementation of the system, we made the assumption of orthogonal projection. Then we are able to calculate the 2D translation t_{2D} between the extracted and the model contour: $t_{2D} = b - \hat{b}$, where b denotes the balance point of the extracted contour and $\hat{b}$ of the projection of the model silhouette.

To compare the two contours, we have to superimpose them and also their reference points must be equal. We set the projection of the reference point of the model to 0_2, so we only translate the extracted contour by subtracting the translation vector t_{2D} from the reference point m. Then we resample the extracted contour with the new reference point 0_2 by trigonometric calculations illustrated in Figure 11.

Afterwards for each new defined ray of the 2D representation, the corresponding ray length of the model projection can be determined by equation 13. To get the difference measure in equation (15) between the two contours, we integrate over the square difference of the accoring ray lengths.

References

1. M. Berger. Tracking rigid and non polyhedral objects in an image sequence. In *Scandinavian Conference on Image Analysis*, pages 945–952, Tromso (Norway), 1993.
2. R. Beß. Objekterkennung mit dem Extended Gaussian Image. Technical report, Diploma thesis, Lehrstuhl für Mustererkennung (Informatik 5), Universität Erlangen–Nürnberg, Erlangen, 1993.
3. L.D. Cohen and I. Cohen. Finite-element method for active contour models and balloons for 2–D and 3–D images. *IEEE Transactions on Pattern Analysis and Machine Intelligence*, 15(11):1131–1147, 1993.
4. T.F. Cootes, C.J. Taylor, D.H. Cooper, and J. Graham. Active shape models — their training and applications. *Computer Vision Graphics and Image Processing*, 61(1):38–59, 1995.
5. R. Curwen and A. Blake. Dynamic contours: Real–time active splines. In A. Blake and A. Yuille, editors, *Active Vision*, pages 39–58. MIT Press, Cambridge, 1992.
6. J. Denzler. *Active Vision for Real–Time Object Tracking*. Dissertation, Technische Fakultät, Universität Erlangen–Nürnberg, Erlangen, in preparation, 1997.
7. J. Denzler and H. Niemann. 3d data driven prediction for active contour models based on geometric bounding volumes. *Pattern Recogniton Letters*, 17(11):1171–1178, 1996.
8. J. Denzler and H. Niemann. Real–time pedestrian tracking in natural scenes. In G. Sommer, K. Daniliidis, and J. Pauli, editors, *Computer Analysis of Images and Patterns, CAIP'97, Kiel 1997*, pages 42–49, Berlin, 1997. Lecture Notes in Computer Science.
9. D.B. Gennery. Visual tracking of known 3d objects. *International Journal of Computer Vision*, 7(3):243–270, 1992.
10. C. Harris. Tracking with rigid models. In A. Blake and A. Yuille, editors, *Active Vision*, pages 59–74. MIT Press, Cambridge, 1992.
11. M. Kass, A. Wittkin, and D. Terzopoulos. Snakes: Active contour models. *International Journal of Computer Vision*, 2(3):321–331, 1988.
12. K.F. Lai and R.T. Chin. Deformable contours: Modelling and extraction. *IEEE Transactions on Pattern Analysis and Machine Intelligence*, 15(1):1–20, 1996.
13. A. Laurentini. How far 3d shapes can be understood from 2d silhouettes. *IEEE Transactions on Pattern Analysis and Machine Intelligence*, 17(2):188–195, 1995.
14. F. Leymarie and M.D. Levine. Tracking deformable objects in the plane using an active contour model. *IEEE Transactions on Pattern Analysis and Machine Intelligence*, 15(6):617–634, 1993.
15. S. A. Nene, S. K. Nayar, and H. Murase. Columbia object image library (coil-20), 1996. http://www.cs.columbia.edu/CAVE/coil-20.html.
16. R. Ronfard. Region-based strategies for active contour models. *International Journal of Computer Vision*, 13(2):229–251, 1994.
17. C.G. Small. Reconstructing convex bodies from random projected images. *The Canadian Journal of Statistics*, 19(4):341–347, 1991.
18. S.M. Smith and J.M. Brady. Asset-2: Real–time motion segmentation and shape tracking. *IEEE Transactions on Pattern Analysis and Machine Intelligence*, 17(8):814–820, 1995.
19. D. Terzopoulos and R. Szeliski. Tracking with Kalman snakes. In A. Blake and A. Yuille, editors, *Active Vision*, pages 3–20. MIT Press, Cambridge, 1992.

Tracking, CONDENSATION

2D-Object Tracking Based on Projection-Histograms

S. Huwer and H. Niemann

FORWISS - Knowledge-Processing Research Group,
Bavarian Research Center for Knowledge-Based Systems,
Am Weichselgarten 7,
D-91058 Erlangen,
{huwer,niemann}@forwiss.de

Abstract. Image-sequence analysis for real-time applications requires high quality and highly efficient algorithms for tracking as there is no time to do the costly object recognition each time a new image is captured. Tracking with projection histograms revealed amazing results compared with standard correlation methods. Trackers based on projection histograms performed 31% up to 211% better than the reference methods on a common test set. The new template-based method relying on projection histograms (RPH) is described and compared with two commonly known template based methods namely the normalized cross-correlation (NCC) and displaced-frame-distance (DFD) methods. The input to the system consists of live or recorded video data where filterbased preprocessing can be applied before tracking in order to enhance features such as edges, textures etc. A region of interest (ROI) is taken as a template for tracking. In subsequent images tracking exploits a Kalman-filtered local search in order to renew correspondence between the object template and the new object location. Comparative tests were performed with real-live image-sequences taken in underground stations. Tracking with projection histograms outperformed tracking by NCC and DFD on grey-level image-sequences as well as on edge-enhanced image-sequences. Even the worst chosen parameter set for tracking by the new RPH method resulted in better tracking as with the best ones for both NCC and DFD.
keywords: **template matching, 2D-tracking, real-time tracking**

1 Tracking in Realtime

As computers get faster, more and more complex problems in image analysis become practically solvable. Yet image-sequence analysis, especially in real-time environments, often stride the frontieres of feasibility. Visual surveillance systems are but one example of an emerging branch where hard time-constraints coupled with the desire for low-cost components still induce the need for sophisticated image-processing methods. In the newly founded research project "Intelligent Platform Station"[1] static cameras placed at various locations on the underground platform produce video streams in which the detection and tracking of passengers represents an important task on the way to an automatic dispatch of the underground-trains. Information on the motion of passengers is to be gathered and analyzed for a detailed security check of the platform. Obviously **real-time** analysis of the image sequence is necessary for the passengers safety. The subtask of passenger safety monitoring can be divided into the object localization and object tracking phases. The object tracking is responsible for producing reliable information on an object's movements in an image-sequence.

Problems arise from the changes of the object's appearence during the monitoring process, e.g. due to varying lighting conditions or movements of the object or of the camera itself.

With the projection-histogram method as presented in this paper, tracking of ROIs in the 2D image plane can be performed even in the presence of highly textured and changing background.

In the following section first the related research will be shortly described. The basic principles of 2D-template tracking are explained and semantically divided in a template matching phase and a tracking phase. Both are explained subsequently. The projection histogram templates are then explained in detail in an chapter of their own. Then the principles of the tracking mechanisms used for the comparative tests are explained and two important quality measures are derived. After describing the test image sequences, the results are given. It must be noted that for all of the tests that were performed, the same tracking methods were used and only the template-representation technique was changed. Anticipating just one result: The projection histograms performed in all test cases better than the reference methods. The computation time for two of the three tested projection histogram methods (differing in the number of histogram bins) were even superior to the reference methods.

2 Related Research

Tracking of objects in the 2D image plane can be carried out in a variety of possible ways. Modelbased trackers exploit previously stored explicit knowledge about interesting objects. [1] demonstrates a simple head-tracker that relies on the elliptical shape of human heads. [7] uses a 3D-volumetric model of persons in

---

[1] funded by "Free State of Bavaria"

order to track people in an industrial environment. Finding appropriate model parameters and the right modelling description for the objects is a challenging task, which must be repeated for each new class of objects to track.

The active contour approach utilizes physics in order to give model-shapes intrinsic properties such as stiffness or curviness [6]. An Image is then interpreted as a greylevel-landscape onto which the model-shapes are adapted by deforming them according to their model properties. A fast extension to "active contours" gives [3] with "active rays", where the active contours are replaced by rays of variable length radiating from the center of gravity of the object. The endpoints of the rays describe the contour of the object. Common to these energy-based methods is their neglect of object features inside the object. So occlusions of similar objects usually end up in merging both objects.

The above mentioned methods more or less make use of prior object knowledge which might not always be available. Another category of tracking methods is solely based on 2D image-regions (templates) and can thus be used to track without any object specific knowledge. Among these, both the cross-correlation (e.g. NCC) and the frame-distance methods (e.g. DFD) are most commonly used. [5] gives a comprehensive overview of correlation and frame-distance methods. It is pointed out that 2D-window tracking with small inter-frame displacements can be accomplished. Still tests revealed that the new tracking method based on projection histograms, which is described in the next section, can track templates significantly longer and with a higher accuracy according to the given quality measures.

3   Problems and Principles of Template Tracking

Template-based methods can be described according to the following common features (see also fig. 1):

1. **Initialization**:
   The initial template region must be localized previously to tracking by an object-localization method and an internal template representation is computed depending on the chosen template-matching method.
2. **Tracking**:
   (a) The template tracker searches in the next image for the best matching image-region, which defines the new position of the object.
   (b) The new object postion may be denoised by applying a smoothing filter, that takes the last measurements into account.
   (c) The last step of tracking may be the invocation of a motion-prediction method in order to predict the position of the object in the next image.

Problems in 2D-tracking arise when the tracked object changes its appearance as a result of:

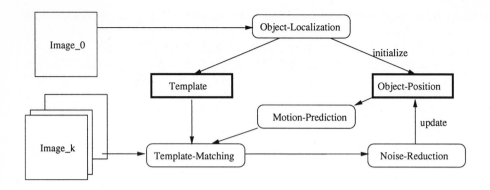

Fig. 1. Template-Tracking

- scaling or rotation
- a change of the object's 3D posture which results in a deformed object appearance in the 2D image-plane
- a large shift of the object in the image

Additional problems arise when lighting conditions or camera parameters change, such as lens-parameters or aperture.

Tracking with "Projection Histograms" (RPH) aims at solving the problem of changing object location with small changes in object appearance. So RPHs are compared with the two reference methods (NCC and DFD), which aim at solving the same task.

3.1 Notation

For an easier understanding of the following formal description a few definitions are given first:

- **Bounded sets of natural numbers:**

$$\mathcal{N}_{j,k} := \{j, j+1, ..., j+k-1\} \tag{1}$$
$$\mathcal{N}_k := \mathcal{N}_{0,k} \tag{2}$$

- **Sets :**
    - The cardinality of a set S is given as $|S|$.
    - 2^S denotes the powerset of S
- **Cartesian set product:** $\mathcal{N}^j := \underbrace{\mathcal{N} \times ... \times \mathcal{N}}_{j \text{ times}}$
- An **Image** f or **Template t** $f : \mathcal{N}_m \times \mathcal{N}_n \longrightarrow \mathcal{N}_g$, with m rows, n columns and g image values (grey values).
- The **size of the template** is given by its height h and its width w.
- A **region of interest** $\mathcal{R}_{h,w}$ positioned at $(u, v) \in \mathcal{N}_m \times \mathcal{N}_n$ of width w and height h has the domain $\mathcal{R}_{h,w}(u, v) := \mathcal{N}_{u,h} \times \mathcal{N}_{v,w}$

3.2 Template Matching by NCC and DFD

While NCC represents a measure of similarity which measures correlation, the DFD is a measure of distance between an image f and a given template t of the size h and w. Both can be motivated by simple distance measures on image regions.

The cross-correlation term CC can be deduced from the squared euclidean distance measure $\delta^{(2)}$:

$$\delta^{(2)}_{f,t}(u,v) = \sqrt{\sum_{(x,y)\in\mathcal{R}_{h,w}(u,v)} [f(x,y) - t(x-u, y-v)]^2} \tag{3}$$

Where (u, v) positions the ROI $\mathcal{R}_{h,w}(u, v)$.

Expanding this term leaves two squared summands and the negated doubled cross-correlation term:

$$CC_{f,t}(u,v) = \sum_{(x,y)\in\mathcal{R}_{h,w}(u,v)} f(x,y)t(x-u, y-v) \tag{4}$$

Since CC varies strongly with the image energy and the size of the template, it is normalized to:

$$NCC^\star_{f,t}(u,v) = \frac{CC_{f,t}(u,v)}{\sqrt{\sum_{(x,y)\in\mathcal{R}_{h,w}(u,v)} f^2(x,y)}\sqrt{\sum_{(x,y)\in\mathcal{R}_{h,w}(0,0)} t^2(x,y)}} \tag{5}$$

Geometrically $NCC^\star$ can be interpreted as the cosine of the angle between the vectorized template and the current image region. Thus $NCC^\star$ will be near 1 for very similiar vectors and smaller otherwise.

As we consider the template-matching in this article as a minimization problem on distance measures, $NCC^\star$ is transformed into a distance measure NCC by $NCC_{f,t}(u,v) := 1 - NCC^\star_{f,t}(u,v)$.

The second chosen reference method for measuring the distance between t and a given image-region located at (u, v) utilizes the simpler distance measure $\delta^{(1)}$, which is also known as city-block metric :

$$\delta^{(1)}_{f,t}(u,v) = \sum_{(x,y)\in\mathcal{R}_{h,w}(u,v)} |\, f(x,y) - t(x-u, y-v)\,| \tag{6}$$

This can be computed very quickly on as one saves the computation time for the squares and squareroots. In order to provide some independence of the template-size, the $\delta^{(1)}$ measure is normalized by the area $h * w$ of the template. This gives DFD:

$$DFD_{f,t}(u,v) = \frac{\delta^{(1)}_{f,t}(u,v)}{h * w} \tag{7}$$

The next section explains the new template matching technique based on projection histograms.

4   Projection 2D-Histogram-Matching

Both, the NCC and DFD do not use any special coding or transformation for template representation. A given ROI of an image immediately represents its own template. The projective histograms (PH) are based on a special coding of the template before measuring the distance between a template and a given ROI.

Computing the projective histogram of a ROI results in a vector containing all histograms of the columns and all histograms of the rows of the ROI. This vector is then used for matching either two given ROIs or a template with a ROI.

In order to correctly specify the computation of the histogram a **quantization-function** ϑ is needed which transforms the g image-values into b bins of the histogram:

$$\vartheta : \mathcal{N}_g \longrightarrow \mathcal{N}_b \tag{8}$$

Three different quantization functions were used for the tests:

1. Number of bins is equal to the number of greylevels: $\vartheta_I(i) := i$
2. Number of bins is 8: $\vartheta_8(i) := i \quad \text{div} \quad 8$
3. Number of bins is 2: $\vartheta_2(i) := \begin{cases} 0 & ; & i < 32 \\ 1 & ; & i \geq 32 \end{cases}$

4.1   Absolute Projection-Histograms

In order to get the projection-histogram of a given image-region the related histograms of all region columns and all region rows are computed. The combination of those row- and column histograms gives the projection histogram for the given region. Thus the **absolute projection-histogram** transformation $\overline{\Phi}_f$ applied to a region $\mathcal{R} := \mathcal{R}_{h,w}(u, v)$ of the image f can be defined as:

$$\overline{\Phi}_{f,\mathcal{R}} : \mathcal{N}_{h+w} \longrightarrow \mathcal{N}^b \text{ with } \overline{\Phi}_{f,\mathcal{R}}(i) := (\overline{\varphi}_{f,\mathcal{R},0}(i), ..., \overline{\varphi}_{f,\mathcal{R},b-1}(i)) \tag{9}$$

and

$$\overline{\varphi}_{f,\mathcal{R},k}(i) := \begin{cases} \overline{\alpha}_k(i) & ; & i < h \quad \text{``row-histogram-entry''} \\ \overline{\beta}_k(i-h) & ; & i \geq h \quad \text{``column-histogram-entry''} \end{cases} \tag{10}$$

Each entry $\overline{\varphi}_{f,\mathcal{R},k}(i)$ gives the corresponding row- or column histogram entry which is defined by $\overline{\alpha}$ for the rows and $\overline{\beta}$ for the columns.

Finally the basic transformations to get row-histograms $\overline{\alpha} : \mathcal{N}_b \longrightarrow \mathrm{I\!N}$ and column-histograms $\overline{\beta} : \mathcal{N}_b \longrightarrow \mathrm{I\!N}$ are specified:

$$\overline{\alpha}_k(i) := |\; \{(x, y) \in \mathcal{R} \mid \vartheta(f(x, y)) = k \wedge x = i\}\;| \tag{11}$$

$$\overline{\beta}_k(i) := |\; \{(x, y) \in \mathcal{R} \mid \vartheta(f(x, y)) = k \wedge y = i\}\;| \tag{12}$$

Thus $\overline{\alpha}_k(i)$ gives the number of pixels in row i whose pixel-values are mapped onto k by the quantization function ϑ. $\overline{\beta}_k(i)$ analogously counts the number of entries in column i whose pixel-values are mapped onto k via the quantization function ϑ.

So $\overline{\Phi}_{f,\mathcal{R}}$ can also be written as :

$$\overline{\Phi}_{f,\mathcal{R}} = (\overline{\alpha}(0), ..., \overline{\alpha}(h-1), \overline{\beta}(0), ..., \overline{\beta}(w-1)) \tag{13}$$

4.2 Relative Projection-Histograms

For a more scale-invariant version of the projection histograms, the **relative projection-histogram** transformation Φ is given with $\overline{\Phi}$ when exchanging all absolute $\overline{\alpha}$ and $\overline{\beta}$ with their relative correspondents $\alpha : \mathcal{N}_b \longrightarrow [0,1]$ and $\beta : \mathcal{N}_b \longrightarrow [0,1]$ respectively. α can thus be defined by dividing it by the length of a row. β is divided by the length of a column:

$$\alpha := \frac{\overline{\alpha}_k(i)}{w} \text{ and } \beta := \frac{\overline{\beta}_k(i)}{h} \tag{14}$$

The rest of the paper considers exclusively relative projection-histograms (RPH) instead of the absolute projection-histograms (PH).

In order to specify matching with (RPH) a distance measure is needed for optimizing on. This is given as a squared Euclidian measure $\delta_{\Phi}^{(2)}$ (same as in the derivation for the NCC-Matching see formula 3).

$$RPH_{f,t}(u,v) := \frac{1}{w+h} \sum_{i \in \mathcal{N}_{w+h}} \delta^{(2)}(\Phi_{f,\mathcal{R}_f}(i), \Phi_{t,\mathcal{R}_t}(i)) \tag{15}$$

$$\text{with } \delta^{(2)}(c,d) := \sqrt{\sum_{j \in \mathcal{N}_b} (c_j - d_j)^2} \tag{16}$$

$$\text{and } \mathcal{R}_f := \mathcal{R}_{h,w}(u,v) \tag{17}$$

$$\text{and } \mathcal{R}_t := \mathcal{R}_{h,w}(0,0) \tag{18}$$

There are three important properties of RPHs worth noting:

- The chosen number of bins of the histogram is crucial for the computation times and with a low number of bins a high data reduction is achieved. Thus Matchung can be done more efficiently.
- The RPH-transformation is a oneway transformation only. There is no inverse transformation for general RPHs.
- The complexity of RPH-transformation is linear with the area of the ROI $\mathcal{R}$, since each pixel of $\mathcal{R}$ must be looked at only once to set the right values for α and β.

Matching templates is but a first step towards tracking a template over a sequence of input images. The second step is the tracking method which is described in the following section.

5 Tracking 2D-Templates

Given an Image f_i at the time i and the position (u_i, v_i) of the template t in f_i: Once the position (u_0, v_0) is known as the position of the template t in the image f_i, the problem of tracking can be described as finding the correct position (u_{i+1}, v_{i+1}) for this template in the image f_{i+1}. Provided that some knowledge on the maximal disparity between two successive template positions exists, it is reasonable to limit the template matching to a specified region of about this size.

5.1 Local Search for the Best Match

The local search for the best template match in the next image is limited to a search region $S := S_{w_s, h_s}(u'_{i+1}, v'_{i+1})$ of width w_s and height h_s which is centered on the expected position (u'_{i+1}, v'_{i+1}) of the template. Given a template matching strategy Ψ, tracking with respect to Ψ can be described as a minimization problem, where one minimizes the template distance over the search region S.

Tracking a template can now be defined by a search function Γ that gives the point $(u_{i+1}, v_{i+1}) \in S$ with the smallest distance between image-region and the template:

$$\Gamma_{f,t,\Psi} \quad : \quad 2^{\mathcal{N}_m \times \mathcal{N}_n} \longrightarrow \mathcal{N}_m \times \mathcal{N}_n \tag{19}$$

$$\Gamma_{f,t,\Psi}(S) \quad := \quad (x, y) \tag{20}$$

$$\text{with } \Psi_{f,t}(x, y) = \min_{(x,y) \in S} \Psi_{f,t}(x, y) \tag{21}$$

$$\text{and } \Psi \in \{NCC, DFD, RPH\} \tag{22}$$

In cases where more than one (x, y) with the same minimal matching distance Ψ exist, such that a unique minimum cannot be identified, a **conflict resolution** strategy is needed. In this work the conflict resolution was chosen to depend on the distance between the new point (u_{i+1}, v_{i+1}) and the expected position (u'_{i+1}, v'_{i+1}). One expects this distance to be small, so in the case of a conflict we choose (u_{i+1}, v_{i+1}) not only to minimize Ψ but also to minimize the distance to (u'_{i+1}, v'_{i+1}). Other applications might need different heuristics to resolve this conflict.

5.2 Estimation of the Template-Position

There are various possibilities to estimate the expected position of a template:

- Use of the last position as the guess for the new position $(u'_{i+1}, v'_{i+1}) := (u_i, v_i)$. This approach can be used when no motion model of the object is available.
- Use of a modelling function π for the motion of a template $(u'_{i+1}, v'_{i+1}) := \pi((u_j, v_j) \mid j \leq i)$ (Note that the first case can be represented with a function π as well).

For the tracking tests performed in this paper the first method as well as the first-order Newtonian motion-model, which could also be interpreted as a linear extrapolation method for the positions, was applied.

But as the main focus of the research was at the difference between RPH, NCC and DFD a more detailed discussion of motion-estimation is not the scope of this article.

5.3 Noise-Filtering

In order to gain more independence of noise a Kalman-filtering system was applied. In this article the fundamental principles of linear Kalman-filtering for tracking are not explained, instead the reader is refered to study [2] or [4].

The first-order motion-model which was used for the filtering and motion-prediction tests is described in Kalman-filter terms:

$$s_{i+1} = A_i s_i + \xi_i \tag{23}$$
$$o_i = C_i s_i + \eta_i \tag{24}$$

with

- **Measurements** (Matched template positions) $o_i \in \mathcal{N}_m \times \mathcal{N}_n$ represents the sequence of observed template position.
- **Measurement-transformation** $C_i := \begin{pmatrix} 1 & 0 & 0 & 0 \\ 0 & 1 & 0 & 0 \end{pmatrix}$
- **Measurement-noise** η_i and **system-noise** ξ_i are considered zero-mean Gaussian white noise processes.
- **System-states** $s_i \in (\mathbb{R} \times \mathbb{R})^2$
- **System-transformation** (motion-modell) $A_i := \begin{pmatrix} 1 & 0 & \Delta_t & 0 \\ 0 & 1 & 0 & \Delta_t \\ 0 & 0 & 1 & 0 \\ 0 & 0 & 0 & 1 \end{pmatrix}$ with a fixed

Δ_t for equidistant o_i.

Usually one can use the Kalman-filter for both, noise-reduction and the motion-prediction.

The error covariance matrices were determined empirically with the following two matrices proven best:

- System error covariance matrix was set to:

$$\begin{pmatrix} 20 & 0 & 0 & 0 \\ 0 & 20 & 0 & 0 \\ 0 & 0 & 1 & 0 \\ 0 & 0 & 0 & 1 \end{pmatrix}$$

- Measurement error covariance matrix was set to:

$$\begin{pmatrix} 20 & 0 \\ 0 & 20 \end{pmatrix}$$

6 Quality Measures for Tracking

Good quality measures for tracking methods enable a quantitative comparison of approaches on a common test set. Thus the choice and definition of the quality measures is driven by two main requirements:

- The tracked templates should be as close as possible to the real object-region in the current image. This requirement defines a local property of the tracker which is represented by a local measure of quality. This was chosen as a measure of overlap between the correct template-region and the tracked template-region. Thus the measure is called the **local overlap** Λ_μ for a given reference track μ.
- A tracking method should also track the template as long as possible over the image-sequence. This defines a global property of the tracker as the fulfillment of this requirement can only be measured when considering the whole track of a template. A natural choice for a quality-measure that implements this requirement is given by the **tracking length** Θ_μ for a given reference track μ.

Both measures use template tracks, which are defined as mappings $\tau : \mathbb{N} \longrightarrow \mathcal{F} \times (\mathcal{N}_m \times \mathcal{N}_m)$, with $\mathcal{F}$ a set of images f and $\tau(i) := (f_i, u_i, v_i)$ producing the position of the template (u_i, v_i) in the image f_i. For clarity reasons the function $\tau_p : \mathbb{N} \longrightarrow \mathcal{N}_m \times \mathcal{N}_m$ gives only the position of the tracked template: $\tau_p(i) := (u_i, v_i)$ ($\mathcal{T}$ denotes the set of all possible tracks τ and $\mathcal{T}_m$ denotes the set of all manually labeled tracks).

The quality-measures **local overlap** and **tracking length** can now be specified in terms of our tracking notation. For the following description $\mu \in \mathcal{T}$ denotes a manually labeled reference track.

6.1 Local Overlap

The **local overlap** Λ_μ measures the size of the region that belongs to both, the correct manually determined template-region positioned at $\mu_p(i)$ and the automatically tracked region which is positioned at $\tau_p(i)$. Thus $\Lambda_\mu : \mathcal{T} \times \mathbb{N} \longrightarrow [0..1]$ is defined by:

$$\Lambda_\mu(\tau_p, i) := \frac{|\, \mathcal{R}_{h,w}(\mu_p(i)) \cap \mathcal{R}_{h,w}(\tau_p(i)) \,|}{|\, \mathcal{R}_{h,w}(\tau_p(i)) \,|} \tag{25}$$

This measure gives a value near 1 when the two given regions show a high overlap. If the compared regions are disjoint regions the **local overlap** measure is 0.

6.2 Tracking Length

The **tracking length** measure is defined by the number of steps for which the tracking method supplies a sufficiently good guess of the template position. Measuring the end of a track becomes the key-point for determining the tracking length. In this paper the end of a track was defined as tracking point when the local overlap is zero for the first time. Thus for a given manually labeled reference track μ the tracking length $\Theta_\mu : \mathcal{T} \longrightarrow \mathbb{N}$ can be defined as:

$$\Theta_\mu(\tau) := \min\{l \in \mathbb{N} \mid \Lambda_\mu(\tau, l) = 0\} \tag{26}$$

Both, the local overlap and the tracking length combined provide tracking method independent techniques for comparing different template trackers on a common test base.

In the result section of this article each of the test runs is described with 2 quality values. Those values are combinations of the basic measures Λ_μ and Θ_μ:

1. Mean tracking lengths: $\overline{\Theta}$
2. Mean local overlaps: $\overline{\Lambda}$
   The means local overlaps averages over all local overlap values for all the tracking steps smaller than the corresponding tracking length:

$$\overline{\Lambda} := \frac{\sum_{\mu \in \mathcal{T}_m} \sum_{i < \Theta_\mu(\tau_\mu)} \Lambda_\mu(\tau_\mu, i)}{\sum_{\mu \in \mathcal{T}_m} \Theta_\mu(\tau_\mu)} \tag{27}$$

with τ_μ corresponding automatic track for test track μ (28)

6.3 Computation Times

Another measure of quality for a given tracker is represented by the time which is consumed for each call to the tracking function. During the tests the exection time of the tracking function was an average of all performed tracking calls. The tracking time is measured in milliseconds and denoted as t.

7 Tests on Real-Live Video-Sequences

The comparison of the new tracking method based on projection histograms with the described standard methods of template matching was conducted on a video-sequence which was taken in an underground platform environment. The sequence consists of **1479** images in total which were taken at a frame-rate of around 18 frames per second. For the test a number of 30 different template tracks were manually labeled, all of them showing the motion-tracks of different persons heads (see fig. 2 for two example images):

- Mean length: 178.5, median length: 179 , min length: 33, max length: 419
- Standard deviation of length: 102.64

Fig. 2. 2 templates and related images

- Length of all manually segmented tracks: 5355

The tracking methods were tested by applying each method to all of the manually labeled template tracks in turn. Tracking the currently chosen track was stopped when the measured overlap quality became 0. The tracking test was then reinitialized with the template of the next track and tracking started over.

The following parameters were used for the tests on the real video-sequences:

- During the initialization of the tracker only the first manually labeled template region of each track is used to set up the template for tracking. Those initialization templates varied in size from around 15×20 to up to 40×50 pixel.
- During the tracking phase the manually labeled positions of the track were used only for calculating the tracking-quality measures.
- The search-region for the iteration of the template-matching was set to a rectangular region of size 20×20.
- The methods were tested on the grey-level sequence as well as on an edge-enhanced image-sequence which was used by applying a 3×3 Sobel-filter.
- The tests were carried out with both, the simple iteration of the template-matching approach on the one hand and the Kalman-filtering methods for noise-reduction and motion-prediction on the other hand.
- There were three different quantization functions ϑ used for the tests with projection-histograms $RPHs$.

The next section describes the results that were found for these tests.

8 Results

All the tests were performed on a SUN Ultra SPARC 2 station with two processors, each running at 200 MHz, still the function calls were not parallelized. The system had 256 MByte of RAM available and was driven by solaris2.5.

8.1 Results on Sobel-Filtered Images

The first test was run on the Sobel-filtered image sequence. All of the projection-based methods outperformed the standard template tracking methods in reference to the quality measures **overlaps** $\overline{\Lambda}$ and **tracking lengths** $\overline{\Theta}$ (see tab. 1). The following improvements of RPHs in contrast to the better reference method NCC can be observed:

- In case when simple position estimates were used RPHs performed by at least 31% to up to 89% better than NCC.
- When applying Kalman-filtering to the tracking methods, the RPHs even showed an improvement of 64 to 135% compared to NCC.

In all cases the RPH based methods performed better from a quality based point of view. Even when considering the execution times as the basis for comparing the different methods, the RPH method based on a threshold quantization of the template performs each call to the tracking function about 3[ms] faster than the reference methods.

Still for getting the best performance in tracking, about **20** more milliseconds must be spent for computing the NCC with ϑ_8 than for computing the NCC with ϑ_2. Similiar results were achieved for the tests on the grey-level image-sequences.

Methods	Simple Search		Kalman NR		Kalman Motion		Execution Times
	$\overline{\Theta}$	$\overline{\Lambda}$	$\overline{\Theta}$	$\overline{\Lambda}$	$\overline{\Theta}$	$\overline{\Lambda}$	t [ms]
RPH,ϑ_{256}	49.8	0.65	50.7	0.65	51.3	0.65	144 - 158
RPH,ϑ_8	**58.7**	**0.69**	**67.7**	**0.68**	**65.8**	**0.68**	36 - 37
RPH,ϑ_2	40.7	0.58	47.6	0.59	48.4	0.59	**15 - 16**
NCC	31.1	0.56	28.8	0.56	28.8	0.56	19 - 20
DFD	11.3	0.25	13.0	0.27	12.8	0.26	19 - 20

Table 1. Test results of tracking on Sobel filtered image sequences, with $\overline{\Theta}$ the mean tracking lengths, $\overline{\Lambda}$ the mean overlaps and the mean execution times t

8.2 Results on Grey-Level Images

The same tests were run on the grey-level images with even better results as with the Sobel-filtered image-sequence:

- RPHs again performed better than NCC and DFD by at least 69 to up to 211% better when considering the tracking-lengths.
- The execution times of the RPH based on a threshold quantization of the templates is faster than the NCC and DFD trackers by 1.5 to 3.4 [ms] for each call.

874

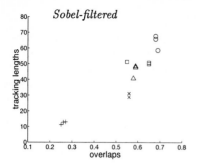
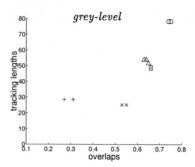

Fig. 3. Visualization of the Tracking Quality:The tracking lengths (Y-Axis) are plotted versus the overlaps (X-Axis). The left figure shows the results of the Sobel-filtered image-sequence. The results of the grey-level image-sequence are shown on the right. ($\square = RPH$ with ϑ_{256}, $\circ = RPH$ with ϑ_8, $\Delta = RPH$ with ϑ_2, $\times = NCC$ and $+ = DFD$)

Methods	Simple Search		Kalman NR		Kalman Motion		Execution Times
	$\overline{\Theta}$	$\overline{\Lambda}$	$\overline{\Theta}$	$\overline{\Lambda}$	$\overline{\Theta}$	$\overline{\Lambda}$	t [ms]
RPH,ϑ_{256}	49.3	0.66	49.3	0.66	48.3	0.66	144 - 151.4
RPH,ϑ_8	**78.4**	**0.74**	**78.4**	**0.75**	**78.4**	**0.75**	34 - 35
RPH,ϑ_2	54.0	0.63	54.0	0.64	51.6	0.65	**14 - 15**
NCC	25.2	0.53	25.2	0.55	25.2	0.55	18 - 19
DFD	28.6	0.27	28.6	0.31	28.6	0.31	17 - 18

Table 2. Test results of tracking on grey level image sequences, with $\overline{\Theta}$ the mean tracking lengths, $\overline{\Lambda}$ the mean overlaps and the mean execution times t

8.3 Different Thresholds for ϑ_2

Besides the quantization functions ϑ_{256} and ϑ_8, the quantization function ϑ_2 with a fixed threshold at 32 was chosen for the computation of the RPHs. This threshold value was not chosen with regard to the test-sequences, but instead can be chosen from a wide range of values as the figure 4 demonstrates. The figure shows the course of the achieved tracking-lengths on the test-sequences in relation to the chosen threshold value for ϑ_2. It can be observed that for a wide ranges of threshold values the tracking lengths are still better than the corresponding results for NCC and DFD Tracking. For the test-sequences of this paper the ranges were found as: thresholds with:

- $\{30, ..., 250\}$ for the Sobel-filtered image-sequences
- $\{30, ..., 170\}$ for the grey-level image-sequences

8.4 Different Quantizationsteps for ϑ_q

A similiar experiment was performed using different quantization steps $q \in \{2, 4, 8, 16, 32, 64, 128, 256\}$ for the quantization function ϑ. It was observed that for all possible quantization values the RPH tracker performed better than both, NCC and DFD on either test-sequences (see 4). Thus the choice of a special quantization values is not critically for the good performance of the tracker on these test sets.

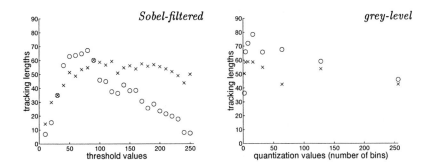

Fig. 4. Tracking-lengths in relation to different threshold values for ϑ_2 (left) or different quantization values for ϑ_q (right)
    o results on grey-level sequence
    × results on Sobel-filtered sequence

9 Conclusion

A new method for tracking two-dimensional image templates, based on projection histograms of the template-region, was presented. A comparison with the same tracking technique based on two standard template matching methods was performed and evaluated with previously defined quality measures. Both quality measures in combination give a means for rating different tracking techniques on the basis of a common test set.

Although the test-set included tracks of objects which changed their size over time, the method still does not incorporate a mechanism in order to account for significant changes in object size. Further work in this field of tracking objects with changing size has to be carried out in the future.

A significant superiority of all tested **projection-histogram** tracking methods was demonstrated, with improvements that ranged from 31% up to 211% in comparison with the reference methods .

The computation time depends on the chosen quantization function for the template coding with the projection histogram method. In the case of thresholded RPHs with a ϑ_2 the tracking methods also is the fastest methods of all tested techniques, with a computation time of 14.6 [ms] for one tracking step on a SPARC Ultra 2.

References

1. S. Birchfield. An elliptical head tracker. In *Asilomar Conference on Signals, Systems and Computers*, number 31. IEEE, November 1997.
2. C.K. Chui and G. Chen. *Kalman Filtering with Real-Time Applications*. Springer Series in Information Sciences. Springer, Berlin , Heidelberg, New York, 1987.
3. J. Denzler and H. Niemann. Active Rays: A New Approach to Contour Tracking. *International Journal of Computing and Information Technology*, 4(1):9–16, 1996.
4. R.E. Kalman. A new approach to linear filtering and prediction problems. *Trans., ASME, Basic Eng.*, 82:35–45, 1987.
5. J. Shi and C. Tomasi. Good features to track. In *CVPR*. IEEE, June 1994.
6. D. Terzopoulos and R. Szeliski. *Eds.: Blake, A. and Yuille, A. Active Vision*, chapter Tracking with Kalman Snakes, pages 3–20. Artificial Intelligence. MIT Press, Cambridge, Ma, 1992.
7. A. Tesei, G. L. Foresti, and C.S. Regazzoni. Human body modelling for people localization and tracking from real image sequences. In *Fifth International Conference on Image Processing and its Applications*, number 410 in 4, pages 806–809, Edinburgh, UK, July 1995. IEE.

W^4S: A Real-Time System for Detecting and Tracking People in $2\frac{1}{2}D$

Ismail Haritaoglu, David Harwood and Larry S. Davis
Computer Vision Laboratory
University of Maryland
College Park, MD 20742, USA

Abstract. W^4S is a real time visual surveillance system for detecting and tracking people and monitoring their activities in an outdoor environment by integrating realtime stereo computation into an intensity-based detection and tracking system. Unlike many systems for tracking people, W^4S makes no use of color cues. Instead, W^4S employs a combination of stereo, shape analysis and tracking to locate people and their parts (head, hands, feet, torso) and create models of people's appearance so that they can be tracked through interactions such as occlusions. W^4S is capable of simultaneously tracking multiple people even with occlusion. It runs at 5-20 Hz for 320x120 resolution images on a dual-pentium 200 PC.

1 Introduction

W^4S is a real time system for tracking people and their body parts in monochromatic stereo imagery. It constructs dynamic models of people's movements to answer questions about *What* they are doing, and *Where* and *When* they act. It constructs appearance models of the people it tracks in $2\frac{1}{2}D$ so that it can track people (*Who?*) through occlusion events in the imagery. W^4S represents the integration of a real-time stereo (SVM) system with a real-time person detection and tracking system (W^4[14]) to increase its reliability. SVM [12] is a compact, inexpensive realtime device for computing dense stereo range images which was recently developed by SRI. W^4 [14] is a real time visual surveillance system for detecting and tracking people in an outdoor environment using only monochromatic video.

In this paper we describe the computational models employed by W^4S to detect and track people. These models are designed to allow W^4S to determine types of interactions between people and objects, and to overcome the inevitable errors and ambiguities that arise in dynamic image analysis (such as instability in segmentation processes over time, splitting of objects due to coincidental alignment of objects parts with similarly colored background regions, etc.). W^4S employs a combination of shape analysis and robust techniques for tracking to detect people, and to locate and track their body parts using both intensity and stereo. W^4S builds "appearance" models of people so that they can be identified after occlusions or after interactions during which W^4S cannot track them individually. The incorporation of stereo has allowed us to overcome the difficulties that W^4 encountered with sudden illumination changes, shadows and occlusions. Even low resolution range maps allow us to continue to track people successfully, since stereo analysis is not significantly effected by sudden illumination changes and shadows, which make tracking much harder in intensity images. Stereo is also very helpful in analyzing occlusions and other interactions. W^4S has the capability to construct a $2\frac{1}{2}D$ model of the scene and its human inhabitants by combining a 2D cardboard model, which represents the relative positions and size of the body parts, and range as shown in figure 1.

Fig. 1. Examples of detection result: intensity image (left), detected people and their body parts form the intensity only (middle) and their placement in the $2\frac{1}{2}D$ scene by W^4S (right)

W^4S has been designed to work with only visible monochromatic video sources. While most previous work on detection and tracking of people has relied heavily on color cues, W^4S is designed for outdoor surveillance tasks, and particularly for low light level situations. In such cases, color will not be available, and people need to be detected and tracked based on weaker appearance, motion, and disparity cues. W^4S is a real time system. It currently is implemented on a dual processor Pentium PC and can process between 5-20 frames per second depending on the image resolution and the number of people in its field of view.

In the long run, W^4S will be extended with models to recognize the actions of the people it tracks. Specifically, we are interested in interactions between people and objects - e.g., people exchanging objects, leaving objects in the scene, taking objects from the scene. The descriptions of people - their global motions and the motions of their parts - developed by W^4S are designed to support such activity recognition.

W^4S currently operates on video taken from a stationary camera, and many of its image analysis algorithms would not generalize easily to images taken from a moving camera. Other ongoing research in our laboratory attempts to develop both appearance and motion cues from a moving sensor that might alert a system to the presence of people in its field of regard [10]. At this point, the surveillance

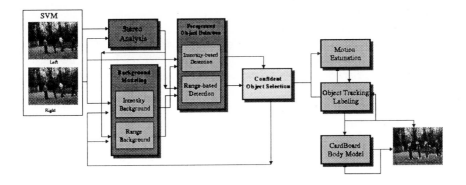

Fig. 2. Detection and Tracking System

system might stop and invoke a system like W^4S to verify the presence of people and recognize their actions.

The system diagram of W^4S is shown in Figure 2. Area-correlation based stereo is computed by SVM. Foreground regions in both the intensity image and the range image are detected in every frame using a combination of background analysis and simple low level processing of the resulting binary images. The background scene is modeled in the same way for the disparity and intensity images. The background scene for the disparity image is statistically modeled by the minimum and maximum disparity value and maximal temporal disparity derivative for each pixel recorded over some period. A similar statistical model is used to model the background scene for the intensity images using intensity values instead of disparity values. Both background models are updated periodically. These algorithms are described in Section 4. The foreground regions detected in the intensity and range images are combined into a unified set of foreground regions. Each foreground region is matched to the current set of objects using a combination of shape analysis and tracking. These include simple spatial occupancy overlap tests between the predicted locations of objects and the locations of detected foreground regions, and "dynamic" template matching algorithms that correlate evolving appearance models of objects with foreground regions. Second-order motion models, which combine robust techniques for region tracking and matching of silhouette edges with recursive least square estimation, are used to predict the locations of objects in future frames. These algorithms are described in Section 6. W^4S can detect and track multiple people in complicated scenes at 5-20 Hz speed at 320x120 resolution on a 200 MHz dual pentium PC.

2   Related Work

Pfinder [1] is a real-time system for tracking a person which uses a multi-class statistical model of color and shape to segment a person from a background scene. It finds and tracks people's head and hands under a wide range of viewing condition.

[6] is a general purpose system for moving object detection and event recognition where moving objects are detected using change detection and tracked using first-order prediction and nearest neighbor matching. Events are recognized by applying predicates to a graph formed by linking corresponding objects in successive frames.

KidRooms [3, 9] is a tracking system based on "closed-world regions". These are regions of space and time in which the specific context of what is in the regions is assumed to be known. These regions are tracked in real-time domains where object motions are not smooth or rigid, and where multiple objects are interacting.

Bregler uses many levels of representation based on mixture models, EM, and recursive Kalman and Markov estimation to learn and recognize human dynamics [5]. Deformable trackers that track small images of people are described in [7].

Realtime stereo systems have recently become available and applied to detection of people. Spfinder[2] is a recent extension of Pfinder in which a wide-baseline stereo camera is used to obtain 3-D models. Spfinder has been used in a smaller desk-area environment to capture accurate 3D movements of head and hands. Kanade [13] has implemented a Z-keying method, where a subject is placed in correct alignment with a virtual world. SRI has been developing a person detection system which segments the range image by first learning a background range image and then using statistical image compression methods to distinguish new objects [12], hypothesized to be people.

3   Stereo Analysis

W^4S computes stereo using area (sum of absolute difference) correlation after a Laplacian of Gaussian transform. The stereo algorithm considers sixteen disparity levels, perform postfiltering with an interest operator, and a left-right consistency check, and finally does $4x$ range interpolation. The stereo computation is done either in the SVM or on the host PC, the latter option providing us access to much better cameras than those used in the SVM. SVM is a hardware and software implementation of area correlation stereo which was implemented and developed by Kurt Konolige at SRI. The hardware consists of two CMOS $320x240$ grayscale imagers and lenses, low-power A/D converter, a digital signal processor and a small flash memory for program storage. A detailed description of the SVM can be found in [12]. SVM performs stereo at two resolutions (160x120 or 320X120) in the current implementation, with speed of up to 8 frames per second. The SVM uses CMOS imagers; these are an order of magnitude noisier and less sensitive than corresponding CCD's. Higher quality cameras can be

Fig. 3. Examples of the range images calculated by area correlation stereo

utilized by W^4S, with the stereo algorithm running on the host PC, to obtain better quality disparity images.

Figure 3 shows a typical disparity image produced by the SVM. Higher disparities (closer objects) are brighter. There are 64 possible levels of disparity and disparity 0 (black areas) are regions where the range data is rejected by the post-processor interest operator due to insufficient texture.

4 Background Scene Modeling and Foreground Region Detection

The background scene is modeled and the foreground regions are detected in both the intensity image and the disparity image simultaneously. Frame differencing in W^4S is based on a model of background variation obtained while the scene contains no people. The background scenes for the intensity images (the disparity images) are modeled by representing each pixel by three values; its minimum and maximum intensity (disparity) values and the maximum intensity (disparity) difference between consecutive frames observed during this training period. These values are estimated over several seconds of video and are updated periodically for those parts of the scene that W^4S determines to contain no foreground objects.

Foreground objects are segmented from the background in each frame of the video sequence by a four stage process: thresholding, noise cleaning, morphological filtering and object detection. This foreground object detection algorithm is simultaneously applied to both the intensity and disparity image. The objects detected in the intensity image and the disparity image are integrated to construct the set of objects that are included in the list of foreground objects, and subsequently tracked. The following detection method is explained only for the intensity images; it is the same for the disparity images.

Each pixel is first classified as either a background or a foreground pixel using the background model. Giving the minimum (M), maximum (N) and the largest interframe absolute difference (D) images that represent the background scene model, pixel x from image I is a foreground pixel if:

$$|M(x) - I(x)| > D(x) \quad \text{or} \quad |N(x) - I(x)| > D(x) \tag{1}$$

Thresholding alone, however, is not sufficient to obtain clear foreground regions; it results in a significant level of noise, for example, due to illumination changes. W^4S uses region-based noise cleaning to eliminate noise regions. After thresholding, one iteration of erosion is applied to foreground pixels to eliminate one-pixel thick noise. Then, a fast binary connected-component operator is applied to find the foreground regions, and small regions are eliminated. Since the remaining regions are smaller than the original ones, they should be restored to their original sizes by processes such as erosion and dilation. Generally, finding a satisfactory combination of erosion and dilation steps is quite difficult, and no fixed combination works well, in general, on our outdoor images. Instead, W^4S applies morphological operators to foreground pixels only after noise pixels are eliminated. So, W^4S reapplies background subtraction, followed by one iteration each of dilation and erosion, but only to those pixels inside the bounding boxes of the foreground regions that survived the size thresholding operation.

5   Foreground Region Selection

The foreground object detection algorithm is applied to both the disparity images and the intensity images for each frame in the video sequence. Generally, intensity-based detection works better than stereo-based detection when the illumination does not change suddenly or when there are no strong light sources that causes sharp shadows. The main advantage of the intensity-based analysis are that

- Range data may not available in background areas which do not have sufficient texture to measure disparity with high confidence. Changes in those areas will not be detected in the disparity image. However, the intensity-based algorithm can detect low textured areas when the brightness of the foreground regions differs significantly from the background.

Fig. 4. An example showing that how stereo-based detection eliminates shadows during object detection.

- Foreground regions detected by the intensity-based method have more accurate shape (silhouette) then the range-based method. The silhouette is very useful for tracking via motion estimation, and in constructing the appearance-based body model used to locate and track body parts.

However, there are three important situations where the stereo-based detection algorithm has an advantage over the intensity algorithm

- When there is a sudden change in the illumination, it is more likely that the intensity-based detection algorithm will detect background objects as foreground objects. However, the stereo-based detection algorithm is not effected by illumination changes over short periods of time as much as intensity-based detection.
- Shadows, which makes intensity detection and tracking harder, do not cause a problem in the disparity images as disparity does not change from the background model when a shadow is cast on the background. Figure 4 shows the foreground regions and their bounding boxes detected by the intensity based (left) and stereo-based detection (right) methods.
- The stereo-based method more often detects intact foreground objects than the intensity-based method. Intensity-based foreground detection often splits foreground objects into multiple regions due to coincidental alignment of the objects parts with similarly colored background regions.

After foreground objects are detected in both the intensity image and the disparity image, W^4S merges these objects into one set of objects. Objects are selected for tracking as follows:

A graph is constructed in which disparity region is linked to an intensity region that it significantly overlaps ($\geq$60%). The connected components of this graph are then considered as possible foreground objects. Generally, we find large disparity regions with poorly defined shapes that overlap a few intensity regions arising from fragmentation of a foreground object. When a connected component contains only one intensity and one disparity region that have very high overlap, then we represent the foreground object by their intersection.

A connected component is rejected if it contains a region only from the intensity image and disparity is available for that region (but does not differ from the background, since no disparity foreground region was detected). This is probably due to an illumination change or shadow. As the final step of foreground region detection, a binary connected component analysis is applied to the selected foreground regions to assign a unique label to each foreground object. W^4S generates a set of features for each detected foreground object, including its local label, centroid, median, median of the disparity, and bounding box.

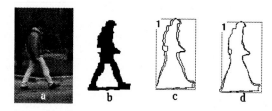

Fig. 5. Motion estimation of body using Silhouette Edge Matching between two successive frame a: input image; b: detected foreground regions; c: alignment of silhouette edges based on difference in median; d: final alignment after silhouette correlation

6 Object Tracking

The goals of the object tracking stage are to:

- determine when a new object enters the system's field of view, and initialize motion models for tracking that object.
- compute the correspondence between the foreground regions detected by the background subtraction and the objects currently being tracked by W^4S.
- employ tracking algorithms to estimate the position (of the torso) of each object, and update the motion model used for tracking. W^4S employs second order motion models (including a velocity and, possibly zero, acceleration terms) to model both the overall motion of a person and the motions of its parts.

W^4S has to continue to track objects even in the event that its low level detection algorithms fail to segment people as single foreground objects. This might occur because an object becomes temporarily occluded (by some fixed object in the scene), or an object splits into pieces (possibly due to a person depositing an object in the scene, or a person being partially occluded by a small object). Finally, separately tracked objects might merge into one because of interactions between people. Under these conditions, the global shape analysis and tracking algorithms generally employed by W^4S will fail, and the system, instead, relies on stereo to locate the objects and local correlation techniques to attempt to track parts of the interacting objects. Stereo is very helpful in analyzing occlusion and intersection. For example, in Figure 6 one can determine which person is closest to the camera when two or more people interact and one is occluded by the other. We can continue to track the people by segmenting the range data into spatially disjoint blobs until the interaction is complete. The range data gives helpful cues to determine "who is who" during and after the occlusion.

W^4S first matches objects to current foreground regions by finding overlap between the estimated (via the global motion model) bounding boxes of objects and the bounding boxes of foreground regions from the current frame. For each object, all current foreground regions whose bounding boxes overlap sufficiently are candidates for matching that object. Ideally, one to one matching (tracking) would be found while tracking one object. However, one to many (one tracked object splits into several foreground regions), many to one (two or more tracked objects merge into one foreground region), one to zero (disappearing) and zero to one (appearing) matchings occur frequently. W^4S tracks objects using different methods under each condition.

6.1 Appearing Objects

When a foreground region is detected whose bounding box does not sufficiently overlap any of the existing objects, it is not immediately evident whether it is a true object or a noise region. If the region can be tracked successfully through several frames, then it is added to the list of objects to be monitored and tracked.

6.2 Tracking

Here, we consider the situation that an object continues to be tracked as a single foreground region. W^4S employs a second order motion model for each object to estimate its location in subsequent frames. The prediction from this model is used to estimate a bounding box location for each object. These predicted bounding boxes are then compared to the actual bounding boxes of the detected foreground regions. Given that an object is matched to a single foreground region (and the sizes of those regions are roughly the same) W^4S has to determine the current position of the object to update its motion model. Even though the total motion of an object is relatively small between frames, the large changes in shape of the silhouette of a person in motion causes simple techniques, such as tracking the centroids of the foreground regions, to fail. Instead, W^4S uses a two stage matching strategy to update its global position estimate of an object. The

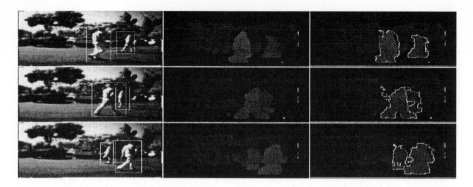

Fig. 6. An Example how range data is useful to track the people by segmenting the range data during occlusion

initial estimate of object displacement is computed as the motion of the **median** coordinate of the object. This median coordinate is a more robust estimate of object position, and is not effected by the large motions of the extremities (which tend to influence the centroid significantly). It allows us to quickly narrow the search space for the motion of the object. However, this estimate is not accurate enough for long term tracking. Therefore, after displacing the silhouette of the object from the previous frame by the median-based estimate, we perform a binary edge correlation between the current and previous silhouette edge profiles. This correlation is computed only over a 5x3 set of displacements. Typically, the correlation is dominated by the torso and head edges, whose shape changes slowly from frame to frame. This tracking process is illustrated in figure 5.

6.3 Region splitting

An object being tracked might split into several foreground regions, either due to partial occlusion or because a person deposits an object into the scene. In this case, one object will be matched to two or more current foreground regions. W^4S determines whether the split is a true-split or a false-split (due to noise transient) condition by monitoring subsequent frames, while tracking the split objects as individual objects. If W^4S can track the constituent objects over several frames, then it assumes that they are separate objects and begins to track them individually.

6.4 Region merging

When two people meet they are segmented as one foreground region by the background subtraction algorithm. W^4S recognizes that this occurs based on a simple analysis of the predicted bounding boxes of the tracked objects and the bounding box of the detected (merged) foreground region. The merged region

Fig. 7. W^4S uses range data to detect the people during occlusion and determine their relative location in $2\frac{1}{2}D$

is tracked until it splits back into its constituent objects. Since the silhouette of the merged regions tends to change shape quickly and unpredictably, W^4S uses a simple extrapolation method to construct its predictive motion model for the merged objects, and simple disparity segmentation method to predict the location of the objects during interactions. A segmentation is applied to the disparity data only inside the merged regions to locate the interacting objects. A hierarchical connected component algorithm [15] is used for segmentation. The disparity segmentation can successfully distinguish the objects when they are at different ranges as shown in figure 6. Intensity alone cannot determine whether or not the the people are in close proximity when their images merge into one foreground regions. Stereo helps W^4S to recover the relative distance among people when they are in the same foreground region. Figure 7 shows two examples of W^4S tracking people by illustrating their locations in $2\frac{1}{2}D$.

A problem that arises when the merged region splits, and the people "reappear", is determining the correspondence between the people that were tracked before the interaction and the people that emerge from the interaction. To accomplish this, W^4S uses two types of appearance models that it constructs while it is tracking an isolated person.

W^4S constructs a dynamic template -called a *temporal texture template* - while it is tracking an isolated object. The temporal texture template for an

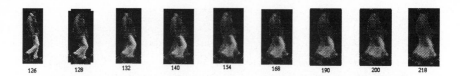

Fig. 8. An example of how temporal templates are updated over time

object is defined by:

$$\Psi^t(x,y) = \frac{I(x,y) + w^{t-1}(x,y) \times \Psi^{t-1}(x,y)}{w^{t-1}(x,y) + 1} \tag{2}$$

Here, I refers to the foreground region detected during tracking of the object, and all coordinates are represented relative to the **median** of the template or foreground region. The weights in (2) are the frequency that a pixel in Ψ is detected as a foreground pixel during tracking. The initial weights $w^t(x,y)$ of Ψ are zero and are incremented each time that the corresponding location (relative to the median template coordinate)is detected as a foreground pixel in the input image. An example of how the temporal texture template of a person evolves over time is shown in figure 8.

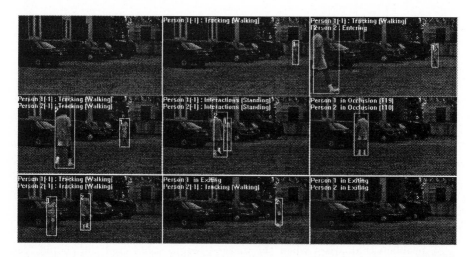

Fig. 9. An example for $W^4 S$ tracking; two people are entering, walking, meeting and leaving

After separation, each constituent object is matched with the separating objects by correlating their temporal templates. Since the temporal texture template is view-based, it could fail to match if there were a large change in the pose of the object during the occlusion event. Therefore, a non-view-based method, which uses a symbolic object representation, is also used to analyze the occlusion. For example, if the temporal texture templates fail to yield sufficiently high correlation values, then we match objects based on the average intensities in their upper, lower and middle parts, in an attempt to identify objects when they separates. Figure 9 illustrates W^4S tracking objects; W^4S detects people, assigns unique labels to them and tracks them through occlusion and interaction.

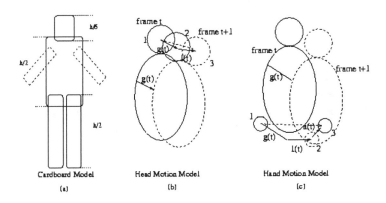

Fig. 10. Cardboard model used in W^4S (a), and motion models used for the head (b) and hands (c).

7 Tracking People's Parts

In addition to tracking the body as a whole, we want to locate body parts such as the head, hands, torso, legs and feet, and track them in order to understand actions. W^4S uses a combination of shape analysis and template matching to track these parts (when a person is occluded, and its shape is not easily predictable, then only template matching is used to track body parts). The shape model is implemented using a a *Cardboard Model* [11] which represents the relative positions and sizes of the body parts. Along with second order predictive motion models of the body and its parts, the Cardboard Model can be used to predict the positions of the individual body parts from frame to frame. Figure 10 illustrates the motion models used for the hands and head. These positions are verified (and refined) using dynamic template matching based on the temporal texture templates of the observed body parts.

The cardboard model represents a person who is in an upright standing pose, as shown in figure 10(a). It is used to predict the locations of the body parts (head, torso, feet, hands, legs). The height of the bounding box of an object

Fig. 11. An example of Cardboard Model to show How Head, Torso, Legs Hands and Feet are Located. Initial Bounding boxes are located on foreground regions (a); Cardboard model analysis locates the body part (b); illustration of body part location by ellipsis (c)

is taken as the height of the cardboard model. Then, fixed vertical scales are used to determine the initial approximate location (bounding box) of individual body parts, as shown in Figure 11. The lengths of the initial bounding boxes of the head, torso, and legs are calculated as 1/5, 1/2 and 1/2 of the length of bounding box of the object, respectively. The widths of the bounding boxes of the head, torso, and legs are calculated by finding the median width (horizontal line widths) inside their initial bounding boxes. In addition to finding sizes and locations, the moments of the foreground pixels inside the initial bounding boxes are calculated for estimating their principal axis. The principal axis provide information about the pose of the parts. The head is located first, followed by the torso and legs. The hands are located after the torso by finding extreme regions which are connected to the torso and are outside of the torso. The feet are located as extreme regions in the direction of the principal axes of the respective leg. Figure 11 show an example of how the cardboard model can be used to predict the locations of body parts in two stages (approximate initial location and final estimated location) and represent them as ellipsis.

After predicting the locations of the head and hands using the cardboard model, their positions are verified and refined using temporal texture templates. These temporal texture templates are then updated as described previously, unless they are located within the silhouette of the torso. In this case, the pixels corresponding to the head and hand are embedded in the larger component corresponding to the torso. This makes it difficult to accurately estimate the median position of the part, or to determine which pixels within the torso are actual part pixels. In these cases, the parts are tracked using correlation, but the templates are not updated.

The correlation results are monitored during tracking to determine if the correlation is good enough to track the parts correctly. Analyzing the changes in the correlation scores allows us to make predictions about whether a part is becoming occluded. For example, the graph in Figure 13 shows how the correlation (sum of absolute differences, SAD) results for the left hand of a person changes over time. Time intervals I,II,III and IV in the graph are the frame intervals in

Fig. 12. Examples of using the cardboard model to locate the body parts in different actions: four people meet and talk (first line), a person sits on a bench (second line), two people meet (third line).

which the left hand is occluded by the body, and they have significantly worse correlation scores (higher SAD).

8 Discussion

We described a real time visual surveillance system (W^4S) for detecting and tracking people and monitoring their activities in an outdoor environment by integrating realtime stereo computation into an intensity-based detection and tracking system. W^4S has been implemented in C++ and runs under the Windows NT operating system. Currently, for $320x120$ resolution images, W^4S runs at 20 Hz on a PC which has dual 200 Mhz pentium processor. It has the capa-

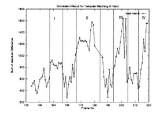

Fig. 13. An Example of hands and head tracking of a walking person and correlation results for the left hand of that person.

bility to track multiple people against complex background. Figure 12 illustrates some results of the W^4S system in scenes of parking lots and parkland.

There are several directions that we are pursuing to improve the performance of W^4S and to extend its capabilities. Firstly, the cardboard model used to predict body pose and position is restricted to upright people. We would like to be able to recognize and track people in other generic poses, such as crawling, climbing, etc. We believe this might be accomplished based on an analysis of convex hull-like representations of the silhouettes of people. Finally, our long term goal is to be able to recognize interactions between the people that W^4S is tracking. We are studying the use of temporal logic programs for the representation of actions, and to control the application of visual routines to peoples movements.

References

1. C. Wren, A. Azarbayejani, T. Darrell, A. Pentland "Pfinder: Real-Time Tracking of the Human Body", *In Proc. of the SPIE Conference on Integration Issues in Large Commercial Media Delivery Systems*, October 1995.
2. A. Azarbayejani, C. Wren and A. Pentland "Real-Time Tracking of The Human Body" *In Proc. IMAGE COM 96*, Bordeaux, France, May 1996
3. S. Intille, J. Davis, A. Bobick "Real-Time Closed-Word Tracking", *In Proc. of CVPR*, pp.697-703, June 1997
4. A. F. Bobick and J. Davis "Real-Time recognition of activity using TemporalTemplates" *In Proc. Third IEEE Workshop on Application of Computer Vision*,pp.1233-1251, December, 1996
5. C. Bregler "Learning and Recognizing Human Dynamics in Video Sequences" *In Proc. CVPR 97*, pp.569-574, June 1997
6. T. Olson, F. Brill "Moving Object Detection and Event Recognition algorithms for Smart Cameras" *In Proc. DARPA Image Understanding Workshop*, pp.159-176, May 1997.
7. R. Polona, R. Nelson "Low Level Recognition of Human Motion", *In Proc. Non Rigid Motion Workshop*, November 1994.
8. A. Pentland "Machine Understanding Human Actions" *In Proc. DARPA Image Understanding Workshop*,pp.757-764, 1996.
9. A. Bobick, J. Davis, S. Intille, F. Baird, L. Cambell, Y. Irinov, C. Pinhanez, A. Wilson "KidsRoom: Action Recognition In An Interactive Story environment" *M.I.T. TR No: 398*, December 1996
10. S. Fejes, L.S. Davis "Exploring Visual Motion Using Projections of Flow Fields" *In. Proc. of the DARPA Image Understanding Workshop*, pp.113-122 New Orleans, LA,1997
11. S. Ju, M. Black, Y. Yacoob, "Cardboard People: A Parameterized Model of Articulated Image Motion", *International Conference on Face and Gesture Analysis*, 1996
12. K. Konolige "Small Vision systems: Hardware and Implementation", *Eighth International Symposium on Robotics Research*, Hayama, Japan, November, 1997
13. T. Kanade, "A Stereo Machine For Video Rate Dense Depth Mapping and Its New Application", *In Proc. CVPR*, 1996.
14. ——, "W4: Who, When, Where, What: A Real Time System for Detecting and Tracking People" *Submitted to Face and Gesture Recognition Workshop, 1998*.
15. T. Westman, D. Harwood, T. Laitinen, M. Pietikainen "Color Segmentation by Hierarchical Connected Components Analysis With Image Enhancement by Symmetric Neighborhood Filters" *In Proc. CVPR*, pp:796-802, June, 1990

ICONDENSATION: Unifying Low-Level and High-Level Tracking in a Stochastic Framework

Michael Isard and Andrew Blake

Department of Engineering Science,
University of Oxford, Oxford OX1 3PJ, UK,
misard,ab@robots.ox.ac.uk,
WWW home page: http://robots.ox.ac.uk/~ab

Abstract. Tracking research has diverged into two camps; low-level approaches which are typically fast and robust but provide little fine-scale information, and high-level approaches which track complex deformations in high-dimensional spaces but must trade off speed against robustness. Real-time high-level systems perform poorly in clutter and initialisation for most high-level systems is either performed manually or by a separate module. This paper presents a new technique to combine low- and high-level information in a consistent probabilistic framework, using the statistical technique of importance sampling combined with the CONDENSATION algorithm. The general framework, which we term ICONDENSATION, is described, and a hand tracker is demonstrated which combines colour blob-tracking with a contour model. The resulting tracker is robust to rapid motion, heavy clutter and hand-coloured distractors, and re-initialises automatically. The system runs comfortably in real time on an entry-level desktop workstation.

1 Introduction

Current research into tracking has somewhat diverged into two camps — informally these can be distinguished as low-level vs. high-level. Low-level approaches include "blob trackers" [24, 17] and systems which track sets of point features [22, 6]. Blob trackers perform low-level processing, for example colour segmentation, usually on low-resolution images, and are fast and robust but convey little information other than object centroid. Rigid object deformations can be tracked by matching point correspondences frame-to-frame [21], but this relies on a rich set of point features on the object of interest, and segmenting the sets of points into coherent objects is challenging. An alternative is to use higher-level information, whether by modelling objects with specific grey-level templates [2] which may be allowed to deform [12], or with more abstract templates such as curved outlines [4, 5]. By including high-level motion models [4, 1] these trackers can follow complex deformations in high-dimensional spaces, but there tends to be a trade-off between speed and robustness. Kalman-filter based contour trackers which run in real time are very susceptible to distraction by clutter, and correlation-based systems are vulnerable to changes in object appearance and lighting, and rapidly slow down as the space of deformations increases in complexity. Contour trackers have been constructed which are highly robust to clutter [14, 18] but only by sacrificing real-time performance. The high-level approaches also tend to economise on processing time by searching only those regions of the image where the object is predicted to be. This diminishes robustness, and also precludes natural extensions of the trackers to perform initialisation when the object could be anywhere in the image. The difficulty of initialisation is compounded when the dimension of the tracking space increases, since it is rapidly impractical to perform an exhaustive search for the object.

This paper presents a framework, ICONDENSATION, to bridge the gap between low-level and high-level tracking approaches. An implementation is demonstrated which uses colour segmentation to find skin-coloured blobs in a subsampled image, and feeds this information to a contour tracker specialised for hands. The techniques used, however, apply to the general sensor fusion problem of augmenting a tracker operating with one measurement modality to use information from an auxiliary measurement source. Tracking is achieved using a CONDENSATION filter [14], extended to incorporate the statistical technique of "Importance Sampling." [20] Importance sampling offers a mathematically principled way of directing search, combining prediction information based on the previous object position and motion with any additional knowledge which may be available from auxiliary sensors. This *combination* confers robustness to temporary failures in one of the measurement processes, and allows the tracker to take advantage of the distinct qualities of different information sources. In the hand-tracking system presented here, for example, colour segmentation allows rapid initialisation and robust tracking of gross motions, while the contour tracker gives fine-scale position and shape information as well as maintaining lock on the object when colour blobs merge or momentarily disappear. Previous demonstrations of the CONDENSATION algorithm have been slower than real time, sometimes by a significant margin [14, 15]. The hand-tracker presented here operates comfortably in real time (30 or 60 Hz) on an entry-level desktop workstation (SGI O2 R5000 180SC). The speed improvement is due partly to a reduction in the required number of samples as a result of using importance sampling, and partly to a careful implementation which is discussed in section 4.

2   Shape representation and sample sets

Suppose that an object's position, shape and velocity are encoded in a state vector $\mathbf{X} \in \mathbb{R}^{N_x}$ (which may, for example, represent the outline of a curve using a low-dimensional parameterisation), and images observed at time t are denoted $\mathbf{Z}_t$, with measurement history $\mathcal{Z}_t = (\mathbf{Z}_1, \ldots, \mathbf{Z}_t)$. The Bayesian technique of factored sampling [20, 11] is a random-sampling method to approximate a distribution $p(\mathbf{X}|\mathbf{Z})$ which applies when $p(\mathbf{X}|\mathbf{Z})$ is too complicated to sample directly, but when the prior $p(\mathbf{X})$ can be sampled, and the measurement density $p(\mathbf{Z}|\mathbf{X})$ can be evaluated. Factored sampling proceeds by generating a set of N samples $\{\mathbf{s}^{(n)}\}$ from the prior $p(\mathbf{X})$ and then assigning to each sample a weight

$\pi^{(n)} = p(\mathbf{Z}|\mathbf{X} = \mathbf{s}^{(n)})$ corresponding to the measurement density. The $\pi^{(n)}$ are normalised to sum to 1 and then the weighted set $\{(\mathbf{s}^{(n)}, \pi^{(n)})\}$ represents an approximation $\tilde{p}(\mathbf{X}|\mathbf{Z})$ to the desired posterior $p(\mathbf{X}|\mathbf{Z})$, where a sample is drawn from $\tilde{p}(\mathbf{X}|\mathbf{Z})$ by choosing one of the $\mathbf{s}^{(n)}$ with probability $\pi^{(n)}$. As $N \to \infty$ samples from $\tilde{p}(\mathbf{X}|\mathbf{Z})$ arbitrarily closely approximate fair samples from $p(\mathbf{X}|\mathbf{Z})$. Moments of the posterior can also be estimated as

$$\mathcal{E}[\phi(\mathbf{X})] \approx \sum_{n=1}^{N} \pi^{(n)} \phi\left(\mathbf{s}^{(n)}\right). \tag{1}$$

Factored sampling has been generalised to deal with temporal sequences [14, 9, 16] under a variety of names. The CONDENSATION algorithm [14] was introduced in the context of computer vision, and it incorporates learned motion models to track deforming objects, represented by image-contours, through cluttered image sequences. This paper extends that work, however the importance sampling framework applies equally well to the algorithms of [9, 16]. In the case of temporal sequences, each time-step consists of an application of factored sampling, where the prior $p(\mathbf{X})$ is replaced by a prediction density $p(\mathbf{X}_t|\mathcal{Z}_{t-1})$ and the sample-set obtained is time-stamped and denoted $\{(\mathbf{s}_t^{(n)}, \pi_t^{(n)})\}$. The prediction density $p(\mathbf{X}_t|\mathcal{Z}_{t-1})$ is obtained by applying a dynamical model $p(\mathbf{X}_t|\mathbf{X}_{t-1})$ to the output $\{(\mathbf{s}_{t-1}^{(n)}, \pi_{t-1}^{(n)})\}$ of the previous time-step.

3 Importance sampling

In the standard formulation of the CONDENSATION algorithm, positions of samples $\mathbf{s}_t^{(n)}$ are fixed in the prediction stage using only the previous approximation to the state density $\{(\mathbf{s}_{t-1}^{(n)}, \pi_{t-1}^{(n)})\}$ and the motion model $p(\mathbf{X}_t|\mathbf{X}_{t-1})$. The portions of state-space (and thus the image $\mathbf{Z}_t$) which are to be examined in the measurement stage are therefore determined before any measurements are made. This is appropriate when the sample-set approximation to the state density is accurate. In principle, as the state density evolves over time, the random nature of the motion model induces some non-zero probability everywhere in state-space that the object is present at that point. With a sufficiently good sample-set approximation this would tend to cause all areas of state-space to lie near some samples, so even motions which were extremely unlikely given the model would be detected, and could therefore be tracked. In practice, however, the finite nature of the sample-set approximation means that all of the samples will be concentrated near the most likely object positions. There may be several such clusters corresponding to multiple hypotheses, but in general each cluster will be fairly localised, which in fact is precisely the behaviour which permits an efficient discrete representation of high-dimensional state spaces. The result is that large areas of state-space contain no samples at all. In order to robustly track sudden movements the process noise of the motion model must be artificially high, thus increasing the extent of each predicted cluster in state-space. To populate these larger clusters with enough samples to permit effective tracking, the sample-set size must be increased, and the algorithm therefore runs more slowly. Various techniques have been proposed to improve the efficiency of the representation in random sampling filters [9, 8] but to our knowledge none have been advanced which draw on information available from alternative sensors.

Importance sampling [20] is a technique developed to improve the efficiency of factored sampling. It applies when auxiliary knowledge is available in the form of an importance function $g(\mathbf{X})$ describing which areas of state-space contain most information about the posterior. The idea is then to concentrate samples in those areas of state-space by generating sample positions $\mathbf{s}^{(n)}$ from $g(\mathbf{X})$ rather than sampling from the prior $p(\mathbf{X})$. The desired effect is to avoid as far as possible generating any samples which have low weights, since they are "wasted" in the factored sampling representation as they provide a negligible contribution to the posterior. A correction term f/g must be added to the sample weights giving

$$\pi^{(n)} = \frac{f(\mathbf{s}^{(n)})}{g(\mathbf{s}^{(n)})} p(\mathbf{Z}|\mathbf{X} = \mathbf{s}^{(n)}) \quad \text{where} \quad f(\mathbf{s}^{(n)}) \equiv p(\mathbf{X} = \mathbf{s}^{(n)})$$

to compensate for the uneven distribution of sample positions. This correction term ensures that, for large N, importance sampling has *no effect* on the consistency of the approximation which $\tilde{p}(\mathbf{X}|\mathbf{Z})$ makes to the posterior. Any importance function could be chosen (subject to some weak constraints) and if N is sufficiently large then $\tilde{p}(\mathbf{X}|\mathbf{Z})$ will be a good approximation to $p(\mathbf{X}|\mathbf{Z})$. The purpose of importance sampling is to reduce the variance of the estimates for a given N and so improve the accuracy of $\tilde{p}(\mathbf{X}|\mathbf{Z})$ when N is small. Since samples are drawn from $g(\mathbf{X})$ it plays the part of a probability density, but note that it does not necessarily correspond to the distribution of any particular random variable.

A typical Bayesian approach to sensor fusion would be to combine measurements from the various sensors in the representation of $\mathbf{Z}_t$, weighted according to their inverse variances. This is only possible, however, when the statistical dependencies between the measurements are understood, and in practice it is often assumed that sensors produce independent measurements. This paper is concerned with combining measurements made with different modalities but from the same underlying image, so it is expected that such an independence assumption would be invalid. Instead of the traditional sensor fusion approach, therefore, importance sampling allows measurements to be combined in a Bayesian framework even when no knowledge at all is available about their dependence. The tradeoff is that the symmetry between sensors is broken, since the measurements used to define the importance function are not included in the overall model, and this may result in some genuine independent information being discarded.

Importance sampling can be applied in the context of CONDENSATION sampling, and we denote this extension ICONDENSATION. Now the importance function at time t is denoted $g_t(\mathbf{X}_t)$. In CONDENSATION, sample positions are drawn from the density

$$f_t(\mathbf{s}_t^{(n)}) \equiv \tilde{p}(\mathbf{X}_t = \mathbf{s}_t^{(n)} | \mathcal{Z}_{t-1})$$

$$= \sum_{j=1}^{N} \pi_{t-1}^{(j)} p(\mathbf{X}_t = \mathbf{s}_t^{(n)} | \mathbf{X}_{t-1} = \mathbf{s}_{t-1}^{(j)}). \tag{2}$$

Note that while the set $\{(\mathbf{s}_t^{(n)}, \pi_t^{(n)})\}$ provides a discrete point-representation of a distribution, the prediction density $\tilde{p}(\mathbf{X}_t | \mathcal{Z}_{t-1})$ is a mixture of continuous density kernels shaped by $p(\mathbf{X}_t | \mathbf{X}_{t-1})$, representing the dynamical model. Instead of sampling from $\tilde{p}(\mathbf{X}_t | \mathcal{Z}_{t-1})$, samples $\mathbf{s}_t^{(n)}$ can instead be drawn from some $g_t(\mathbf{X}_t)$ and then the weights need to be redefined as

$$\pi_t^{(n)} = \frac{f_t(\mathbf{s}_t^{(n)})}{g_t(\mathbf{s}_t^{(n)})} p(\mathbf{Z}_t | \mathbf{X}_t = \mathbf{s}_t^{(n)}). \tag{3}$$

The effect of the correction ratio is to preserve the information about motion coherence which is present in the dynamical model. Although the samples are positioned according to g_t, the distribution approximated by $\{(\mathbf{s}_t^{(n)}, \pi_t^{(n)})\}$ still generates $p(\mathbf{X}_t | \mathcal{Z}_t)$. Importance sampling is again intended to improve the efficiency of the sample-set representation, but does not change the probabilistic model. It should be noted that (2) imposes a restriction on the form of dynamical model which can be used; for CONDENSATION it is enough to be able to sample from $p(\mathbf{X}_t | \mathbf{X}_{t-1})$ but in the ICONDENSATION algorithm this density must also be evaluated. Existing implementations of CONDENSATION [14, 15, 13] use Gaussians or mixtures of Gaussians for this process density, and so evaluation is straightforward. The sum in (2) must be evaluated in (3) for each $n = 1, \ldots, N$, which changes the complexity of the algorithm from $O(N)^{\star}$ to $O(N^2)$. While this is a theoretical disadvantage, it has little effect in practice, since the time expended on the calculation of (2) in an efficient implementation, for practical values of N, is dwarfed by other stages of the computation.

In practice the importance function g_t will derive from an imperfect measurement process, so it may omit some likely peaks of $p(\mathbf{Z}_t | \mathbf{X}_t)$. It is therefore prudent to generate some samples using standard factored sampling and some by importance sampling using g_t. As long as $\tilde{p}(\mathbf{X}_t | \mathcal{Z}_{t-1})$ and g_t do not simultaneously fail to predict the object state, tracking will succeed.

It may also be advantageous to augment the dynamical model to include some probability q of reinitialisation — repositioning the object according to a prior which is independent of past history $\mathcal{Z}_t$. This allows a tracker to lock on to an object entering the scene, or rediscover an object which has been lost due to gross failures of measurements, perhaps because the object moved while it was entirely occluded. The amended model is of the form

$$\tilde{p}'(\mathbf{X}_t | \mathcal{Z}_{t-1}) = (1 - q)\tilde{p}(\mathbf{X}_t | \mathcal{Z}_{t-1}) + qp(\mathbf{X}_t)$$

---

* It was claimed in [14] that CONDENSATION was $O(N \log N)$, however by choosing base samples as described in section 4.4 of this paper the complexity is reduced to $O(N)$.

where $p(\mathbf{X}_t)$ is the required initialisation prior. This is an application of mixed-state CONDENSATION [15] with two discrete states, and in later sections the model will be augmented to include a further two states. A mixed-state model can be included in the factored sampling scheme by choosing with probability $1 - q$ to generate samples as before (using importance sampling with probability r and standard factored sampling with probability $1 - q - r$) and with probability q to generate $\mathbf{s}_t^{(n)}$ by sampling directly from $p(\mathbf{X}_t)$. In the absence of another initialisation prior, the importance function, suitably normalised, can be used, so $p(\mathbf{X}_t) \propto g_t$. A complete sampling algorithm is shown in figure 1.

Iterate

From the "old" sample set $\{(\mathbf{s}_{t-1}^{(n)}, \pi_{t-1}^{(n)}), \; n = 1, \ldots, N\}$ at time-step $t - 1$, construct a "new" sample set $\{(\mathbf{s}_t^{(n)}, \pi_t^{(n)}), \; n = 1, \ldots, N\}$ for time t. The importance function $g_t(\mathbf{X}_t)$ for time t is assumed to be known at this stage.

Construct the nth of N new samples as follows:

1. **Choose** the sampling method by generating a random number $\alpha \in [0, 1)$, uniformly distributed.
2. **Sample** from the prediction density $\tilde{p}'(\mathbf{X}_t | \mathcal{Z}_{t-1})$ as follows:
   (a) **If** $\alpha < q$ use the initialisation prior. Choose $\mathbf{s}_t^{(n)}$ by sampling from $g_t(\mathbf{X}_t)$ and set the importance correction factor $\lambda_t^{(n)} = 1$.
   (b) **If** $q \le \alpha < q + r$ use importance sampling. Choose $\mathbf{s}_t^{(n)}$ by sampling from $g_t(\mathbf{X}_t)$ and set $\lambda_t^{(n)} = f_t(\mathbf{s}_t^{(n)})/g_t(\mathbf{s}_t^{(n)})$, where

$$f_t(\mathbf{s}_t^{(n)}) = \sum_{j=1}^{N} \pi_{t-1}^{(j)} p(\mathbf{X}_t = \mathbf{s}_t^{(n)} | \mathbf{X}_{t-1} = \mathbf{s}_{t-1}^{(j)}).$$

   (c) **If** $\alpha \ge q + r$ use standard CONDENSATION sampling. Choose a base sample $\mathbf{s}_{t-1}^{(i)}$ with probability $\pi_{t-1}^{(i)}$, then choose $\mathbf{s}_t^{(n)}$ by sampling from $p(\mathbf{X}_t | \mathbf{X}_{t-1} = \mathbf{s}_{t-1}^{(i)})$ and set $\lambda_t^{(n)} = 1$.
3. **Measure** and weight the new position in terms of the image data $\mathbf{Z}_t$ and the importance sampling correction term:

$$\pi_t^{(n)} = \lambda_t^{(n)} p(\mathbf{Z}_t | \mathbf{X}_t = \mathbf{s}_t^{(n)})$$

then normalise multiplicatively so $\sum_n \pi_t^{(n)} = 1$ and store as $\{(\mathbf{s}_t^{(n)}, \pi_t^{(n)})\}$.

Fig. 1. ICONDENSATION: CONDENSATION **with importance sampling and reinitialisation.**

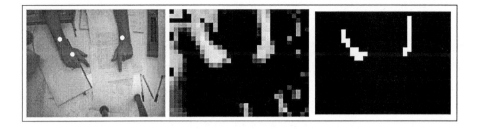

Fig. 2. Colour segmentation allows the detection of skin-coloured blobs.
Circles on the input frame (left) show the centres of blobs detected using colour-segmentation and a flood-fill. The output of the colour discriminant on a 32 × 24 pixel subsampled field of the original image is shown scaled (middle) so that white corresponds to a high probability of skin-colour. The output after convolution and blob-detection (right) shows white areas belonging to blobs.

4 Experiments with a real-time hand-tracker

The framework of ICONDENSATION applies to any parametric representation of objects and their motion, and any form of importance function g_t. The remainder of this paper presents a specific implementation of a real-time hand tracker, combining blob-tracking with a contour model. First, a crude colour-segmentation technique is described which is used to construct the importance function $g_t(\mathbf{X}_t)$.

4.1 Finding skin-coloured blobs

Previous researchers [17, 10] have noted that human skin can be effectively distinguished in a typical office scene using colour segmentation, and so this method is adopted here. Training images of hands are used to construct a colour discriminant based on a Gaussian prior in (r, g, b) space which expresses the probability that a given pixel is skin-coloured. The prior is clipped with an intensity threshold to ensure that very dark pixels are not classified as skin. Blob-detection is performed by taking the input image and subsampling to give 32 × 24 pixels per field, then evaluating the colour discriminant for each pixel. A 2 × 2 moving block average is applied to the image to reduce noise, and then pixels are grouped using a flood-fill with hysteresis [7]. An example image and the segmented output is shown in figure 2. The technique has been found to be very effective in separating skin colour from background, and works over the variation in lighting conditions from day to night in our office. Let B be the number of blobs detected, then the mean of each blob is computed as a coordinate $\mathbf{b}'_k$ in the original image, and a two-dimensional importance function $\tilde{g}_t$ is defined to be a mixture of Gaussians over $\mathbb{R}^2$

$$\tilde{g}_t(\mathbf{x}_{trans}) = \sum_{k=1}^{B} \delta_k N(\mathbf{b}_k, \Sigma_B)$$

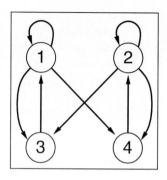

Fig. 3. The hand-tracker uses a four-state discrete/continuous motion model. *States 1 and 2 denote the left and right hand respectively, and states 3 and 4 correspond to initialising a sample with either the left or the right model.*

where $\mathbf{b}_k = \mathbf{b}'_k + \bar{\mathbf{x}}_B$, and $\bar{\mathbf{x}}_B$ and Σ_B are the mean and covariance respectively of the offset from the blob position to the centroid of the contour describing the hand. These are learned by following a user's hand using a contour tracker and comparing the output of the blob segmentation with the centroid of the tracked contour. The mixture weights δ_k will be discussed in the next section. A *hybrid* sampling scheme is now required since the importance function is defined only over translations, and this is outlined below.

4.2 A contour tracker for hands

A discrete-time second-order motion model is used to describe the hand, giving an augmented state-space

$$\mathbf{X}_t = \begin{pmatrix} \mathbf{x}_t \\ \mathbf{x}_{t-1} \end{pmatrix} \quad \text{where} \quad \mathbf{x}_t = (x_t, y_t, \theta_t, r_t, \chi_t)^T$$

and $\mathbf{x}_t$ is a non-linear representation of a Euclidean similarity transform applied to a template $\bar{\mathbf{x}}$. The extra parameter χ_t is a discrete label which determines whether the template is left- or right-handed — $\bar{\mathbf{x}}$ is reflected about the y-axis for the right hand. The left–right parameter χ_t is constant according to the motion model, and can only change as a result of a reinitialisation, and so the tracker effectively uses a four-state model (tracking or reinitialising either the left or the right hand) shown in figure 3. Note that the contour-based object representation allows accurate tracking of hand rotation and scaling as θ_t and r_t vary, which can be problematic for traditional correlation-based techniques. By the nature of the second-order representation, the lower half of $\mathbf{X}_t$ is found deterministically from $\mathbf{X}_{t-1}$, so we will refer interchangeably to $p(\mathbf{X}_t)$ and $p(\mathbf{x}_t)$ with slight abuse of notation.

The motion model is a second-order auto-regressive process (ARP) [3] where each of the four dimensions of the similarity is modelled by an independent one-dimensional oscillator. The oscillators are specified by parameters defining a damping constant β, a natural frequency f and a root-mean-square average displacement ρ. These parameters can be used to determine the ARP model in one dimension $x_t = a_2 x_{t-2} + a_1 x_{t-1} + b\omega_t$ where ω_t is Gaussian noise drawn from $N(0,1)$, a_1, a_2 and b are given by [3]

$$a_2 = -\exp(-2\beta\tau), \quad a_1 = 2\exp(-\beta\tau)\cos(2\pi f\tau)$$

$$b = \rho\sqrt{1 - a_2^2 - a_1^2 - 2\frac{a_2 a_1^2}{1 - a_2}}$$

and τ is the time-step length in seconds (so $\tau = 1/30\,s$ for NTSC frame-rate). Sensible default parameters for the oscillators are chosen by hand.

As explained in section 4.1, the importance function $\tilde{g}_t$ is defined only over the space of x–y translations, being the output of a crude blob-tracker. The state-space decomposes into a translation subspace $\mathbf{x}_t^{\mathcal{T}} = (x_t, y_t)^T$ and a deformation subspace $\mathbf{x}_t^{\mathcal{D}} = (\theta_t, r_t, \chi_t)^T$. Modifications to steps 2(a) and 2(b) of figure 1 can now be made to implement a hybrid sampling scheme. For initialisation in step 2(a), the translation component $\mathbf{s}_t^{(n)\mathcal{T}}$ is sampled from $\tilde{g}_t$ and the deformation component $\mathbf{s}_t^{(n)\mathcal{D}}$ is sampled from a fixed prior $p^{\mathcal{D}}(\mathbf{x}^{\mathcal{D}})$ which is taken to be Gaussian in θ_t and r_t and assigns equal probabilities for left and right to χ_t, then $\mathbf{s}_t^{(n)} = \mathbf{s}_t^{(n)\mathcal{T}} \oplus \mathbf{s}_t^{(n)\mathcal{D}}$. The hybrid importance sampling step 2(b) proceeds as follows. First generate a sample $\mathbf{s}_t'^{(n)} = \mathbf{s}_t'^{(n)\mathcal{T}} \oplus \mathbf{s}_t'^{(n)\mathcal{D}}$ using standard CONDENSATION sampling as in step 2(c). Then choose $\mathbf{s}_t^{(n)\mathcal{T}}$ by sampling from $\tilde{g}_t$ and set $\mathbf{s}_t^{(n)} = \mathbf{s}_t^{(n)\mathcal{T}} \oplus \mathbf{s}_t'^{(n)\mathcal{D}}$. Finally the importance correction factor $\lambda_t^{(n)}$ is replaced by $\lambda_t^{(n)\mathcal{T}} = f_t^{\mathcal{T}}(\mathbf{s}_t^{(n)})/\tilde{g}_t(\mathbf{s}_t^{(n)})$, where

$$f_t^{\mathcal{T}}(\mathbf{s}_t^{(n)}) = \sum_{j=1}^{N} \pi_{t-1}^{(j)} p(\mathbf{X}_t^{\mathcal{T}} = \mathbf{s}_t^{(n)\mathcal{T}} | \mathbf{X}_{t-1} = \mathbf{s}_{t-1}^{(j)}).$$

It remains to specify the mixture weights δ_k for g_t. One reasonable choice is to set $\delta_k = 1/B$, and apportion samples equally in the vicinity of each blob. Since the motivation for importance sampling is to avoid generating samples with low weights, it may be preferable to increase δ_k for blobs which are near to many predicted sample positions. This can be done approximately by setting $\delta_k \propto f_t(\mathbf{b}_k)$, and later results are produced using these weights.

The prior distribution over translation for reinitialisation is chosen to be the distribution obtained by sampling from g_t with $\delta_k = 1/B$ for all k. The parameters θ and r are chosen from a suitable Gaussian prior density, with parameters set by hand, and χ has an equal chance of being left- or right-handed. When $B = 0$ no importance or reinitialisation samples are generated, and all of the computing time is spent on standard CONDENSATION samples.

4.3 The measurement process

Having detailed the dynamical model it remains to specify the measurement density $p(\mathbf{Z}_t|\mathbf{X}_t)$. This is assumed to be constant over time and dependent only on the current configuration, so

$$p(\mathbf{Z}_t|\mathbf{X}_t) \equiv p(\mathbf{Z}|\mathbf{x}).$$

Recall that $\mathbf{x}$ specifies the outline in the image of a B-spline curve. The measurement density is approximated by examining a set of points $\mathbf{z}_m$ for $m = 1 \ldots M$ which lie on the curve outline, where the normal to the curve at $\mathbf{z}_m$ is $\mathbf{n}_m$. First of all, edge-operator convolutions are taken at $\mathbf{z}_m$ in the x and y directions, and the dot product of these is taken with the normal direction $\mathbf{n}_m$ to find a directed edge strength which is scaled and interpreted directly as a log probability p_m. When the edge strength is above a certain threshold an additional colour calculation is made to examine the pixels just inside the contour. This increases p_m when the area inside the curve scores highly according to the skin-colour discriminant, and decreases it when it scores poorly. Independence of the measurement points is assumed, so the density is given by

$$\log p(\mathbf{Z}|\mathbf{x}) = \text{const} + \sum_m p_m.$$

Constants are set manually, and the density is somewhat ad hoc; determining a more rigorous measurement density, possibly learned from training images, is deferred to future research.

4.4 Speed enhancements

Importance sampling has been presented as a mechanism to use complementary sources of visual information to choose an effective set of positions in state-space for a finite set of N samples. Given the constraint of real-time operation, a certain amount of care in the detailed implementation is necessary in order to maximise N. Much of this consists simply of standard code optimisation, but some parts of the algorithm can be redesigned for greater efficiency.

Base samples $\mathbf{s}_{t-1}^{(i)}$ are used both in standard CONDENSATION and for the hybrid importance sampling. These are chosen according to the $\pi_{t-1}^{(i)}$ and this selection can be done efficiently using cumulative probabilities $c_{t-1}^{(i)} = \sum_{j=1}^{i} \pi_{t-1}^{(i)}$. Quantising the cumulative probabilities

$$\tilde{c}_{t-1}^{(i)} = \lfloor c_{t-1}^{(i)} N \rfloor$$

suggests the following algorithm for generating samples which eliminates the $O(\log N)$ binary search stage in [14].

    initialise: $i = 1$. **for** $n = 1 \ldots N$
      while $(\tilde{c}_{t-1}^{(i)} < n)$ $i{+}{+}$
      generate $\mathbf{s}_t^{(n)}$ by sampling from $p(\mathbf{X}_t|\mathbf{X}_{t-1} = \mathbf{s}_{t-1}^{(i)})$.

Since predictions from a given base sample are made consecutively this also offers a saving in calculating the deterministic portion of the prediction, which need only be done once per base sample. Practical experience shows that this can lead to significant economy, since typically only 10% of samples may have high enough weight to be used as a base.

Software profiling shows that most of the tracker's computation is expended, as might be expected, on calculating the measurement density. It has been found that a significant speed improvement can be gained by presorting the measurement points in raster order before performing the convolution and colour-segmentation calculations of section 4.3. This has the advantage, as for the base samples, that identical measurement points are processed consecutively, which cuts down on the number of convolutions (typically the number of distinct measurement points is just over half of the total number of points). Clearly, performing the sort generates a large overhead, and in fact profiling reveals that typically 30% of time is spent sorting compared with about 50% making the measurements. This might seem to almost cancel the performance improvement from sorting, however the speedup on an SGI O2 is significantly greater than implied by these numbers, since the cache behaviour of evaluating points in raster order is much more benign than if the points are presented unsorted.

5 The tracker in operation

The hand-tracker has been implemented on an SGI O2 R5000 SC180 entry-level desktop workstation. The results shown were produced using $N = 400$ samples, which allows the tracker to run comfortably in real-time (30 Hz, using every other NTSC field). The number of samples can be increased to approximately $N = 575$ before any frames are dropped. Acceptable performance is obtained with $N = 150$ samples, and this runs comfortably at the field-rate of 60 Hz, although there is no noticeable benefit from using the additional fields. The main observed differences when using a smaller number of samples are a slight jitter when the hand is stationary and a longer time taken before the system reinitialises. As the number of samples is reduced below $N = 150$ the tracker begins to be distracted by clutter, although reinitialisation still functions to recover from these distractions.

The initialisation behaviour of the tracker is shown in figure 4. Initially the hand on the left is being tracked, and the spatial coherence inherent in the motion model means that the other blobs in the scene do not distract the tracker. When the thumb and forefinger are retracted, the shape no longer fits the template as accurately, and tracking reinitialises on the other hand within half a second. This behaviour corresponds to state transitions $2 \rightarrow 3 \rightarrow 1$ in figure 3. Figure 5 (a) demonstrates successful tracking at high speed, with interlace shown to indicate image velocities. Even if the hand makes a sudden movement which is not predicted by the motion model, the blob tracker will detect the new position, and importance samples will be generated in the vicinity of the hand allowing the motion to be tracked. Figure 5 (b) shows the advantage of using outline information as well as colour blob segmentation. The hands are adjacent, so their blobs merge, yet tracking continues to distinguish between the hands.

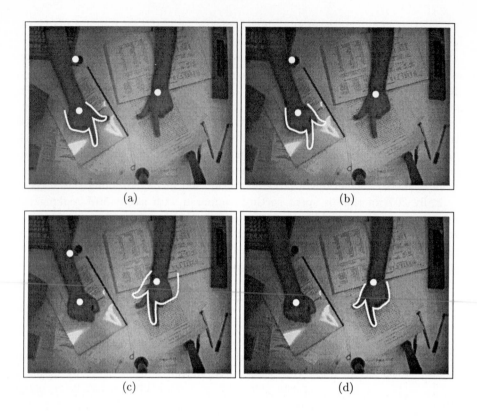

Fig. 4. **The tracker reinitialises when one hypothesis takes precedence over another.** *While the user's right hand fits the template well (a) the motion coherence in the dynamical model ensures that the tracker remains locked on (discrete state 2 in figure 3). When the shape no longer fits the template (b) the probability of reinitialising to another hypothesis increases. After 5 frames (1/6 s) the tracker has switched to the neighbourhood of the left hand, selecting the left-handed template (discrete state 3 followed by 1), and another 5 frames later, a total of 1/3 s from the time that the right hand no longer fit the template, the tracker has locked on to the user's left hand (discrete state 1). Detected blobs are shown as circles, and N=400 samples are used.*

6   Extending the tracker for multiple users

The hand tracker described so far is specialised to a single hand shape, encoded in the template $\bar{x}$. This requires the user's hand to be held fairly rigidly in the template pose, and necessarily means that some users' hands will fit the template better than others'. The main problem with an ill-fitting template is slow re-initialisation, but it also increases the chance of clutter distractions. It would be desirable, therefore, to allow some variation in $\bar{x}$. A shape-space of hand-deformations was therefore established by using Principal Components Analysis (PCA) on sequences of images collected from several subjects [4]. Each subject placed his or her left hand in a reference position and orientation, with

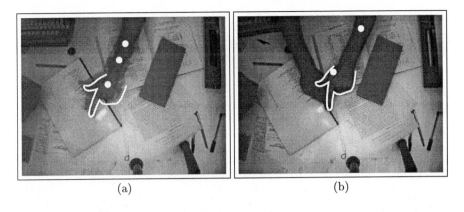

(a)   (b)

Fig. 5. Tracking is robust to high-speed motion and failures of colour segmentation. *Both fields of a frame are shown in (a) and interlacing artifacts demonstrate the rapid translation of the hand. When the hands move close to each other in (b), their colour-segmentation blobs merge, giving a mean value (circle) between the hands. The contour tracker continues to follow the left hand using motion coherence and edge information. The tracker is using N=400 samples.*

thumb and forefinger outstretched, and then made small movements to represent the variation of poses in which that user's hand will be presented to the system. These movements were recorded by a B-spline tracker, the spline positions from the separate sequences were concatenated, and PCA was used to find a six-dimensional space of deformations. In the interests of real-time tracking, it is not desirable to increase the dimension of x_t from 4 continuous Euclidean similarity parameters to 10 for rigid transformations plus deformation.

The solution adopted was to run two entirely separate trackers, one in the Euclidean similarity space as before, and one in a separate six-dimensional deformation space with N_D samples and parameter y_t, so that $\bar{x} = \bar{x}_0 + Wy_t$ where $\bar{x}_0$ and W were estimated by PCA. Since y_t is expected to vary slowly, only a small number of samples need be used in the deformation tracker, and good results are obtained using $N_D = 50$ samples. At each time-step, the trackers are run consecutively. First of all y_t is held fixed at $y_t = \hat{y}_{t-1}$ to establish $\bar{x}_t = \bar{x}_0 + W\hat{y}_{t-1}$. The Euclidean transformation tracker is then run, exactly as before, and an estimated Euclidean vector $\hat{x}_t$ is calculated from (1). Now the Euclidean transformation is held fixed at $x_t = \hat{x}_t$ and the deformation tracker is run to estimate the new sample-set distribution for y_t from which $\hat{y}_t$ can be estimated, again using (1). This procedure is not entirely satisfactory, since it prevents a meaningful probabilistic interpretation of the state densities. It would be preferable to combine the estimation of deformation and rigid motion in a consistent Bayesian framework while keeping the economy of computation, and this is discussed briefly in section 7. Despite this caveat, results using the two-tracker system are promising. The deformation-space tracker was run as a standard CONDENSATION tracker using dynamics learned from the hand-shape

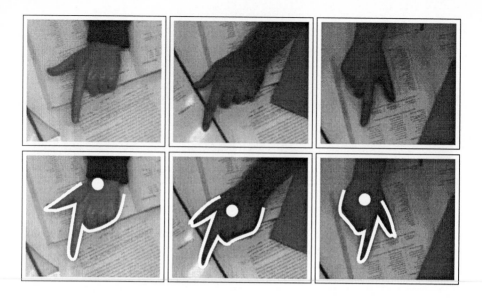

Fig. 6. The deformation tracker accommodates different hands. *Columns show different users. The lower images show tracked output approximately a second after the hand was introduced into the scene. The left-hand user was included in hand-shape training data, the other two were not. In this example N=400 for the Euclidean similarity tracker and N_D=50 for the deformation tracker.*

training sequences [4, 14]. The shape rapidly deforms to fit a hand as it enters the scene, and figure 6 shows that the tracker adapts to different hands as required.

7 Conclusions and future work

The hand-tracking system presented in this paper has proved to be extremely robust and agile over a wide range of desk clutter, for every test user who has so far tried it (about 10 people). Since it runs comfortably in real time, it offers the exciting possibility of being used as the user-interface back-end to drive some kind of interactive package. Perhaps as robust yet detailed trackers such as this are developed, the promise of the digital desk [23] will at last begin to be realised.

In the last few years real-time tracking has rapidly progressed, and expertise has been developed in exploiting a wide range of methodologies. ICONDENSA-TION offers a bridge between some competing approaches, and thus there exists considerable scope for building on the work presented here. Hand-tracking is a very specialised area since colour segmentation of skin is so accurate. It may be possible to build similar systems using other low-level approaches such as motion segmentation and image-differencing, opening the framework to other application domains. Within the hand-tracking system certain problems remain. Before

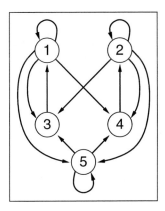

Fig. 7. A five-state model could encompass the possibility that no hand is present. *States 1 and 2 denote tracking the left and right hand, respectively, states 3 and 4 correspond to initialising a sample to start tracking with either the left or the right model, and state 5 is entered when no hand is present in the scene.*

the system can be used as an input device it will probably be necessary to devise a robust measure to determine whether or not the hand is in the scene, possibly using a contour discriminant [19]. The discrete model would then be expanded to include a fifth state (figure 7), denoting the event that no hand is present. A better method of accommodating deformations of the hand-template may also be possible. It is profligate to allow an entire 6-dimensional linear space to represent hand deformations, since most of the space consists of shapes which are very unlike a hand. It may be possible to collect a large number (perhaps 20–100) of template shapes, and include them as discrete states in the model, relying on each user's hand to be close to one of the example templates. Alternatively it may be possible to specify a non-linear parameterisation of the deformations which is efficient enough to allow the deformation space to be included directly with the Euclidean similarity parameters in the main tracker.

Finally it is worth noting that the combination of low-level and high-level approaches presented here may be applicable to problems which have been tackled using multi-resolution techniques. Importance sampling allows measurements to be combined even when no knowledge is available about their statistical dependence, and therefore may be applicable to other tasks where measurements are available at different granularities, but their dependence is poorly understood.

References

1. A. Baumberg and D. Hogg. Generating spatiotemporal models from examples. In *Proc. British Machine Vision Conf.*, volume 2, 413–422, 1995.
2. M.J. Black and A.D. Jepson. Eigentracking: robust matching and tracking of articulated objects using a view-based representation. In *Proc. 4th European Conf. Computer Vision*, 329–342, 1996.

3. A. Blake and M.A. Isard. *Active contours.* Springer, 1998.

4. A. Blake, M.A. Isard, and D. Reynard. Learning to track the visual motion of contours. *J. Artificial Intelligence*, 78:101–134, 1995.

5. T.F. Cootes, C.J. Taylor, A. Lanitis, D.H. Cooper, and J. Graham. Building and using flexible models incorporating grey-level information. In *Proc. 4th Int. Conf. on Computer Vision*, 242–246, 1993.

6. J. Costeira and T. Kanade. A multi-body factorization method for motion analysis. In *Proc. 5th Int. Conf. on Computer Vision*, 1071–1076, 1995.

7. J.D. Foley, A. van Dam, S.K. Feiner, and J.F. Hughes. *Computer Graphics: Principles and Practice*, chapter 13, 563–604. Addison-Wesley, 1990.

8. N. Gordon and D. Salmond. Bayesian state estimation for tracking and guidance using the bootstrap filter. *Journal of guidance, control and dynamics*, 18(6):1434–1443, November–December 1995.

9. N. Gordon, D. Salmond, and A.F.M. Smith. Novel approach to nonlinear/non-Gaussian Bayesian state estimation. *IEE Proc. F*, 140(2):107–113, 1993.

10. H.P. Graf, E. Cosatto, D. Gibbon, M. Kocheisen, and E. Petajan. Multi-modal system for locating heads and faces. In *Proc. 2nd Int. Conf. on Automatic Face and Gesture Recognition*, 88–93, 1996.

11. U. Grenander, Y. Chow, and D.M. Keenan. *HANDS. A Pattern Theoretical Study of Biological Shapes.* Springer-Verlag. New York, 1991.

12. G. Hager and K. Toyama. X vision: Combining image warping and geometric constraints for fast visual tracking. In *Proc. 4th European Conf. Computer Vision*, volume 2, 507–517, 1996.

13. T. Heap and D. Hogg. Wormholes in shape space: Tracking through discontinuous changes in shape. In *Proc. 6th Int. Conf. on Computer Vision*, 1998.

14. M.A. Isard and A. Blake. Visual tracking by stochastic propagation of conditional density. In *Proc. 4th European Conf. Computer Vision*, 343–356, Cambridge, England, Apr 1996.

15. M.A. Isard and A. Blake. A mixed-state Condensation tracker with automatic model switching. In *Proc. 6th Int. Conf. on Computer Vision*, 107–112, 1998.

16. G. Kitagawa. Monte Carlo filter and smoother for non-Gaussian nonlinear state space models. *Journal of Computational and Graphical Statistics*, 5(1):1–25, 1996.

17. R. Kjeldsen and J. Kender. Toward the use of gesture in traditional user interfaces. In *Proc. 2nd Int. Conf. on Automatic Face and Gesture Recognition*, 151–156, 1996.

18. D.G. Lowe. Robust model-based motion tracking through the integration of search and estimation. *Int. J. Computer Vision*, 8(2):113–122, 1992.

19. J. MacCormick and A. Blake. A probabilistic contour discriminant for object localisation. In *Proc. 6th Int. Conf. on Computer Vision*, 390–395, 1998.

20. B.D. Ripley. *Stochastic simulation.* New York: Wiley, 1987.

21. Torr P.H.S. An assessment of information criteria for motion model selection. In *Proc. Conf. Computer Vision and Pattern Recognition*, 1997.

22. Torr P.H.S. and Murray D.W. Stochastic motion clustering. In *Proc. 3rd European Conf. Computer Vision*, 328–337. Springer-Verlag, 1994.

23. P. Wellner. The Digital Desk calculator — tangible manipulation on a desk-top display. In *Proceedings of the ACM Symposium on User Interface Software and Technology*, Hilton Head, November 1991.

24. C. Wren, A. Azarbayejani, T. Darrell, and A. Pentland. Pfinder: Real-time tracking of the human body. In *Proc. 2nd Int. Conf. on Automatic Face and Gesture Recognition*, 51–56, 1996.

A Probabilistic Framework for Matching Temporal Trajectories: CONDENSATION-Based Recognition of Gestures and Expressions

Michael J. Black[1] and Allan D. Jepson[2]

[1] Xerox Palo Alto Research Center,
3333 Coyote Hill Road, Palo Alto, CA 94304 USA.
black@parc.xerox.com
[2] Department of Computer Science, University of Toronto,
Toronto, Ontario M5S 1A4 Canada.
jepson@vis.toronto.edu

Abstract. The recognition of human gestures and facial expressions in image sequences is an important and challenging problem that enables a host of human-computer interaction applications. This paper describes a framework for incremental recognition of human motion that extends the "CONDENSATION" algorithm proposed by Isard and Blake (ECCV'96). Human motions are modeled as *temporal trajectories* of some estimated parameters over time. The CONDENSATION algorithm uses random sampling techniques to incrementally match the trajectory models to the multi-variate input data. The recognition framework is demonstrated with two examples. The first example involves an augmented office whiteboard with which a user can make simple hand gestures to grab regions of the board, print them, save them, etc. The second example illustrates the recognition of human facial expressions using the estimated parameters of a learned model of mouth motion.

1 Introduction

Motion is intimately tied with our behavior; we move when we communicate through facial expressions and gestures. The estimation and explanation of this sort of human motion is a challenging problem with diverse applications in human-computer interaction, medicine, robotics, animation, video databases, and surveillance to name a few. In this paper we focus on the problem of recognizing human motion using a probabilistic framework that is based on random sampling techniques. We represent human motions as *temporal trajectories* and we match these to estimated trajectories in an on-line fashion. This framework applies the CONDENSATION algorithm [8,9] in a novel way to recognize complex human motions. We illustrate the method with examples of human gestures and human facial expressions.

Our focus here will be on recognition of gestures given some estimated representation of the human motion. For each pair of frames in a video sequence we compute a set of parameters that describe the motion. These might be simply horizontal and vertical velocity or the parameters of a more sophisticated parameterized model of optical flow [3]. Over time the estimated parameter vectors form *temporal trajectories* that characterize the gesture or expression. Given a number of examples of a gesture we construct a model of the temporal trajectory that encodes the mean trajectory and the expected variance along the trajectory. This model may be a single trajectory (discretely sampled or continuous) or a collection of such trajectories.

For a new image sequence, recognition is performed in an "on-line" fashion. As new parameter vectors are estimated, we incrementally match our trajectory models to the data. The input data is typically noisy and may deviate from the stored model in a variety of ways. When different subjects perform the same action, the recovered motion parameters will vary and the matching must account for this variability. Additionally, we do not know where activities begin or end so the algorithm must segment the input data automatically during recognition.

We have a variety of gestures or expressions that we wish to recognize and at a given instant in time the interpretation of the input data may be ambiguous. To accommodate this fact, our probabilistic framework maintains multiple hypotheses and automatically focuses more computational resources on the more likely hypotheses.

Our approach applies the CONDENSATION algorithm to the problem of recognizing temporal trajectories. The CONDENSATION (CONDitional dENSity propagATION) algorithm uses random sampling techniques to simply and elegantly search a multi-variate parameter space that is changing over time. The algorithm was proposed by Isard and Blake [8] for tracking objects in clutter and has recently been extended [9] to simple gesture-recognition tasks. Here we extend the method further to recognize more complex temporal activities. See also [11] for a related random sampling techinque used in dynamic probabilistic belief networks.

We define a "state" to be a set of parameters that align a trajectory model with the input data. A state includes parameters that control local stretching, scaling, and translation of the model with respect to the data. We define the probability of a state in terms of how well it matches the data. Then a set of states and their probabilities defines a discretely sampled probability distribution over the match parameters. This distribution evolves over time as the input data changes. The CONDENSATION algorithm uses stochastic dynamics and random sampling techniques to "track" this distribution as it evolves. We refer to the recognition framework as CONDENSATION-based Trajectory Recognition (CTR).

To illustrate the CTR framework we provide two examples. In the first we use gesture data gathered by a computer vision system that is observing an office whiteboard. We describe a vocabulary of gestures that a user can perform at the whiteboard to extend its functionality. The second example illustrates the recognition of facial motions from optical flow parameters.

The following section reviews related work on the CONDENSATION algorithm, and gesture recognition. Section 3 presents the algorithm in detail. Sections 4 and 5 present our two examples.

2 Previous Work

The recognition of temporal trajectories has received extensive study in the contexts of gesture, speech, and handwriting recognition. We do not attempt an exhaustive review here but rather highlight the relationships between the proposed framework and the most relevant related approaches. The two most common methods for recognizing temporal trajectories are Hidden Markov Models (HMM's) [14] and Dynamic Time Warping (DTW) [16]. There have been many applications of these basic techniques to the problem of gesture recognition in computer vision (e.g. [6, 18, 20]).

The proposed method can be seen as a generalization of HMM's in that it allows a discrete set of states with probabilistic transitions between states. With CTR, however, the recognition of the individual states involves the probabilistic matching of an entire temporal trajectory model that represents a portion of the gesture. In this way the CTR method uses the entire curve in a way similar to DTW but within a unified probabilistic framework. The temporal trajectories may be discrete or continuous and the method allows parameterized deformations of the trajectories (see also [21]). Computational resources are automatically applied to more fully explore the most probable matches.

The "EigenCurve" representation [22] has been proposed as an alternative to HMM's and DTW. The approach matches an input trajectory to an basisset representation of stored curves while allowing various global deformations. The CTR framework could be extended to represent temporal trajectories using this "eigen" basis representation. The advantages over [22] would include on-line recognition, automatic segmentation, and local curve deformations.

The most significant advantage of the CTR approach is that it allows the formulation of recognition and motion tracking in the same probabilistic framework. Isard and Blake [8] initially developed the CONDENSATION algorithm to deal with the difficult problem of tracking an object in a cluttered environment. In this case the algorithm is able to maintain a probability distribution over multiple tracking hypotheses which provides robustness while achieving near real-time performance.

In [9] they also show how this tracking ability can be combined with simple dynamical models of gestures to simultaneously perform tracking and recognition. They define a "mixed-state" representation that adds a discrete model parameter to the definition of a state. This allows the tracker to use multiple motion models corresponding to different gestures. The recognition in [9] is limited to fairly simple gestures (e.g. "scribbling" motion versus "smooth" motion).

In this paper we focus only the recognition part of the problem and by incorporating explicit, learned, temporal trajectories we extend the CONDENSATION method to more complex gestures. Our current research is focused on combining tracking and recognition thus allowing the temporal models to constrain the tracking problem (cf. [23]).

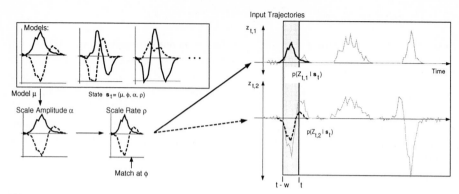

Fig. 1. Our goal is to incrementally match M, multiple-parameter, trajectory models to input data.

3 CONDENSATION Algorithm

Our goal is to take a set of M model trajectories $\{\mathbf{m}^{(\mu)}, \mu = 1, \ldots, M\}$ and match them against an N-dimensional input trajectory, given by $\mathbf{z}_t = (z_{t,1}, \ldots, z_{t,N})$ at time t (see Figure 1). The models are taken to be discretely sampled curves (though they may be continuous as well) with a phase parameter $\phi \in [0, \phi_{\max}]$ representing the current position in the model. The model values at position ϕ are a vector of N values $\mathbf{m}_\phi^{(\mu)} = (m_{\phi,1}^{(\mu)}, \ldots, m_{\phi,N}^{(\mu)})$ where the stored discrete curve is linearly interpolated at phase ϕ.

The parameters we need to estimate to match a model to the data are:

μ: an integer indicating the model type that is being matched,

ϕ: position (or phase) within the model that aligns it with the data at time t,

α: an amplitude parameter used to scale the model vertically to match the data, and

ρ: a rate parameter that is used to scale the model in the time dimension.

We define a state at time t to be a vector of parameters $\mathbf{s}_t = (\mu, \phi, \alpha, \rho)$.

We would like the find the state $\mathbf{s}_t$ that is most likely to have given rise to the observed data $Z_t = (\mathbf{z}_t, \mathbf{z}_{t-1}, \ldots)$. Let $Z_{t,i} = (z_{t,i}, z_{(t-1),i}, z_{(t-2),i}, \ldots)$ be the vector of observations for the ith coefficient over time. We define the likelihood of an observation $\mathbf{z}_t$ given the state $\mathbf{s}_t$ as

$$p(\mathbf{z}_t | \mathbf{s}_t) = \Pi_{i=1}^N p(Z_{t,i} | \mathbf{s}_t), \tag{1}$$

where

$$p(Z_{t,i} | \mathbf{s}_t) = \frac{1}{\sqrt{2\pi}\sigma_i} \exp \frac{-\sum_{j=0}^{w-1}(z_{(t-j),i} - \alpha m_{(\phi-\rho j),i}^{(\mu)})^2}{2\sigma_i^2(w-1)}$$

and where w is the size of a temporal window backwards in time over which we want the curves to match. The σ_i are estimates of the standard deviation for

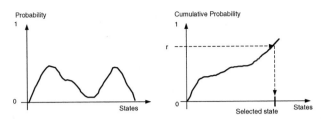

Fig. 2. We sample from the distribution over the states by constructing a cumulative probability distribution and sampling it uniformly. Choosing r from a uniform distribution over $[0, 1]$ gives us a corresponding state.

curve i. Also, $\alpha m^{(\mu)}_{(\phi - \rho j), i}$ is simply the value of the ith coefficient in the model μ interpolated at time $\phi - \rho j$ and scaled by α.

Given a definition for $p(\mathbf{z}_t | \mathbf{s}_t)$, we can construct a discrete representation of the entire probability distribution over the possible states. Initially, we sample uniformly for the state parameters

$$\mu \in [0, \mu_{\max}]$$
$$\phi = \frac{1 - \sqrt{y}}{\sqrt{y}}, \text{ where } y \in [0, 1]$$
$$\alpha \in [\alpha_{\min}, \alpha_{\max}]$$
$$\rho \in [\rho_{\min}, \rho_{\max}].$$

Note that the prediction for the initial phase ϕ is biased towards small values. We then compute the probability of the state $p(\mathbf{z}_t | \mathbf{s}_t)$. We can do this for S samples where we take S on the order of 1000. This gives us a set $\{\mathbf{s}_t^{(n)}, n = 1, \ldots, S\}$ of samples. We normalize these probabilities so that they sum to one, producing weights $\pi_t^{(n)}$

$$\pi_t^{(n)} = \frac{p(\mathbf{z}_t | \mathbf{s}_t^{(n)})}{\sum_{i=1}^{S} p(\mathbf{z}_t | \mathbf{s}_t^{(i)})} \tag{2}$$

The CONDENSATION algorithm [8, 9] uses this information (the sample states and their weights) to predict the entire probability distribution at the next time instant. Unlike traditional tracking methods (e.g. Kalman filtering) this approach can deal well with ambiguous data since multiple matches are propagated in time. The algorithm has three stages (selection, prediction, updating). Below we outline how to construct a new probability distribution with S samples at time t given the the distribution at time $t - 1$.

1. Selection: First we choose a state from time $t-1$ *according to the probability distribution* at time $t - 1$. That is, we use the current probability distribution over states to choose likely states to predict into the future.

This is done by constructing a cumulative probability distribution using the $\pi_{t-1}^{(n)}$ as illustrated in Figure 2. Let the cumulative probabilities be

$$c_{t-1}^{(0)} = 0$$
$$c_{t-1}^{(n)} = c_{t-1}^{(n-1)} + \pi_{t-1}^{(n)}.$$

We sample this distribution by uniformly choosing a value, r, between zero and one. We then find the smallest $c_{t-1}^{(n)}$ such that $c_{t-1}^{(n)} > r$. The state $s_{t-1}^{(n)}$ is then selected for propagation to the next time instant.

With this sampling method, states that are most probable will be selected with the highest frequency; this has been called the "survival of the fittest" algorithm [11]. To avoid getting trapped in local maxima and to deal with sudden changes in the input data, we randomly choose some fraction of the states to be replaced by random initial guesses (initialized as described above). We typically take these random guesses to be $5 - 10\%$ of the samples.

2. Prediction: Given a state $s_{t-1}^{(n)}$ we predict the parameters of the new state $s_t^{(n)}$ at time t to be

$$\mu_t = \mu_{t-1}$$
$$\phi_t = \phi_{t-1} + \rho_{t-1} + \mathcal{N}(\sigma_\phi)$$
$$\alpha_t = \alpha_{t-1} + \mathcal{N}(\sigma_\alpha)$$
$$\rho_t = \rho_{t-1} + \mathcal{N}(\sigma_\rho)$$

where $\mathcal{N}()$ is a normal distribution and the σ_* represent uncertainty in the prediction. Note that prediction can be viewed as sampling from the probability distribution $p(s_t^{(n)}|s_{t-1}^{(n)})$ [9]. For the time being, the model type μ does not change over time; we will extend the method below to allow transition probabilities to take μ to a new state.

During prediction, if $\phi_t > \phi_{max}$ then that model has been completed and the state is initialized as described above. For the other parameters, we draw samples from $\mathcal{N}$ until the predicted value of the parameter is within its allowed range.

It is interesting to note that the σ_* are used as a tool for locally searching the parameter space. They can be thought of as "diffusion" parameters that blur the probability distribution as it is predicted in time. They provide a way of performing a local search about a state. They also allow local deformations of the trajectories within the moving window of size w.

3. Updating: Given a new state we evaluate the probability, $p(z_t|s_t^{(n)})$, that it generated the data at time t using Equation (1). If the likelihood is zero (or below a threshold) then we return to Step 2 for a new prediction. We repeat this for a fixed number of tries. If no prediction from $s_{t-1}^{(n)}$ has sufficient probability then we generate a random initial sample.

After S new states have been generated, we compute the normalized weights, $\pi_t^{(n)}$, using Equation (2) and repeat the process for the next time instant.

Note that the CONDENSATION algorithm is a probabilistic hybrid of depth-first and breadth-first search. When no good match to the input data is found, the method resorts to uniform sampling (breadth-first). When the probability mass is centered around a set of parameters, more resources will automatically be spent to explore the neighborhood around these parameters (depth-first). Also, note that a "simulated annealing" method could be used in the search to start with high values of σ_i in Equation (1) and lower them over time.

3.1 Finite State Extension

We have also extended the method to allow compound models that are very like Hidden Markov Models in which each state in the HMM is one of our trajectory models (see also [9]). Let $\mathcal{M} = \{\mu_1, \mu_2, \ldots, \mu_i\}$ be a "parent state" which consists of a set of model types μ_i along with transition probabilities $p(\mu_t | \mathcal{M}, \mu_{t-1}, \phi_{t-1})$ between states. In the prediction step above, μ_t is chosen by sampling from the transition probabilities. When initializing a new random state, we first chose the parent type $\mathcal{M}$ from a uniform distribution. The initial model type μ_1 is defined by the parent. The remaining parameters are chosen as described above. Currently transition probabilities are set by hand; learning these probabilities is a topic of current research.

4 Gesture Models

To test the CONDENSATION-based trajectory recognition algorithm we consider the problem of recognizing a set of gestures in the context of an augmented whiteboard. A number of authors have looked at problem of scanning whiteboards at high resolution using mosaicing [19] and interacting with the board by making hand-drawn marks [17]. Here we look at the problem of recognizing dynamic gestures. Isard and Blake [9] used the CONDENSATION algorithm to recognize simple drawing gestures. Our extension to temporal trajectories allows more complex gestures to be recognized.

In our scenario, when the user wants to perform a command, they pick up a gesture "phicon" (or physical icon) [10] that has a distinctive color that makes it easy to locate and track. The motion of the phicon is tracked using a color histogram tracker [7] in real time. Tracking is performed at roughly 30Hz. Since the tracking rate varies slightly, we resample the phicon locations at fixed time instants using linear interpolation. The horizontal and vertical velocity of the phicon is used for gesture recognition.

We define the following set of simple gestures which are useful for such a purpose (see Figure 3):

- **Start**: The start gesture tells the system to "pay attention" and start recognizing gestures. This gesture is simply a waving motion similar to what a person might do to get a human's attention.

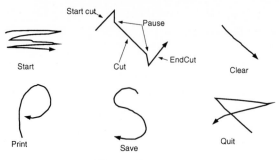

Fig. 3. Gestures.

- **Cut Region:** The cut gesture is used to indicate a region of the whiteboard to be scanned (possibly at higher resolution). This gesture consists of three primitive gestures with pauses in between of arbitrary duration. We refer to the complete cut gesture as a "parent" gesture that is made up of trajectory models.
  - **Cut-On**: The gesture begins with an upside-down "check mark." The end of this *cut-on* gesture marks the upper left corner of the scanning region.
  - **Cut**: The user then moves the phicon in a relatively straight line to the lower right corner of the region.
  - **Cut-Off**: To end the gesture and cut the image region the user makes a right-side-up "check mark".
- **Print**: To send a cut region to the printer, the user makes a gesture like the letter "P".
- **Save**: To save the region to a file, the user makes a gesture like the letter "S".
- **Clear**: A sharp diagonal motion "clears" the current stored whiteboard region. One can think of a cut region as being "stored" in the phicon. The gesture can be thought of as "throwing" the cut region away.
- **Quit**: The user makes a mark like an "X" when they wish to stop the gesture recognition function.
- **Stationary**: In addition to the gesture models we also represent when the phicon is stationary.

To construct models for the gestures, each gesture was performed approximately half a dozen times and the trajectories were saved. For a given gesture the training trajectories were manually aligned and the mean trajectories were computed. A standard deviation from the mean trajectory was also computed for each curve. The trajectory models for each gesture are shown in Figure 4. The initial alignment of the curves could be performed using DTW. In addition to computing just the mean curve, we could compute "EigenCurves" as in [22].

In our experiments we take $\mu_{max} = 9$ (there are nine primitive models), $\alpha_{max} = 1.3$, $\alpha_{min} = 0.7$ (we allow a 30% scaling), $\rho_{max} = 1.3$, $\rho_{min} = 0.7$ (a 30% temporal scaling). The standard deviations, σ_i, for the model trajectories were

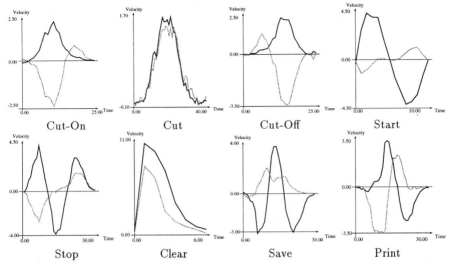

Fig. 4. Gesture Models. Temporal trajectories of horizontal (solid) and vertical (broken) velocity.

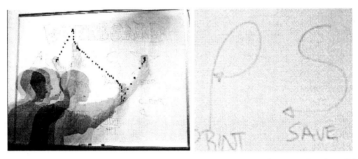

Fig. 5. Example of a "Cut" gesture. The user makes a gesture with the phicon. The image on the right is the region that is cut out of the larger image.

taken to be 1.0. Finally, the diffusion parameters were taken to be $\sigma_\rho = 0.01$ $\sigma_\phi = 0.05$ $\sigma_\alpha = 0.01$, and the temporal window was $w = 10$.

Figure 5 illustrates the performance of a "cut" gesture. We use a bright red block as our gesture phicon. The black dots in the figure represent tracked locations of the phicon. The image on the right is the region that is cut out by our algorithm.

Figure 6*a* shows the horizontal and vertical velocities of the phicon as a function of time. This is our input data to which we will incrementally match all our gesture models.

The estimated value of the horizontal and vertical velocity is taken to be

$$\mathbf{u}_t = \sum_{n=1}^{S} \pi_t^{(n)}(\alpha \mathbf{m}_\phi^{(\mu)})$$

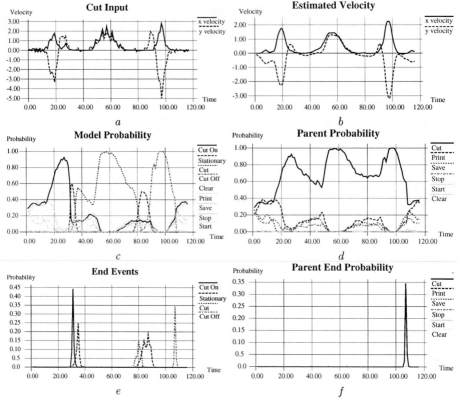

Fig. 6. "Cut" gesture. *(a)*, Input horizontal and vertical velocity; *(b)*, Estimated horizontal and vertical velocity; *(c)*, Probability of each model type; *(d)*, Probability of each parent gesture type; *(e)*, Probability that the current state is a model completion event; *(f)*, Probability that the current state is the completion of a parent.

where $\alpha\mathbf{m}_\phi^{(\mu)}$ is the estimated velocity for sample state $\mathbf{s}_t^{(n)}$. This represents the fit of the models to the data and is shown in Figure 6b.

Figure 6c shows the probability of each individual model as a function of time. Similarly Figure 6d shows the probability for the composite, parent, gestures. The probability of a particular model, μ, is taken to be the sum of the normalized probabilities $\pi_t^{(n)}$ for which $\mu \in \mathbf{s}_t^{(n)}$.

Figures 6e and f show the probability that the trajectory models or parent gestures have completed respectively. This probability is given by

$$p(\mu^*) = \sum_{n=1}^{S} \begin{cases} \pi_t^{(n)} & \text{if } \mu \in \mathbf{s}_t^{(n)} \text{ and } \phi + 1 > \phi_{\max} \\ 0 & \text{otherwise} \end{cases}$$

where a sample is considered completed if the estimated phase parameter, ϕ, is within one time instant of the maximum phase for that model/parent. The figures show clear spikes when the individual trajectory models ("Cut On", "Cut,"

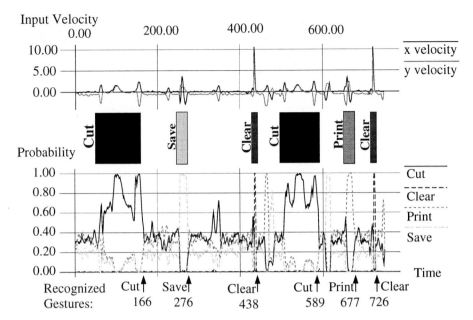

Fig. 7. Multiple-gesture experiment. *top:* Input horizontal and vertical velocity; *bottom:* Probability of each parent gesture type. The frame number at which the recognized gesture completes is given.

and "Cut Off") end. Similarly there is a spike when the parent cut gesture ends. If $p(\mu^*) > 0.1$ we consider μ to be recognized.

To actually cut the region (Figure 5) from the original image we must carry along with each state the time at which each trajectory model ended. This information is used at the end of the gesture to determine where the stationary mark points are located. The enclosed region of pixels is then extracted.

4.1 Multiple Gesture Experiment

We consider one more experiment that involves a series of gestures

Cut – Save – Clear – Cut – Print – Clear.

The input curves represent 850 samples of the horizontal an vertical velocities of the phicon (Figure 7 top). In this sequence, in addition to the actual gestures, the user moves the phicon between the gestures.

There are nine possible model types and six possible gestures. The input data at every frame is matched against these models and the data must be explained by some model. The normalized probabilities in Figure 7 (bottom) show that some of the non-gesture motions receive high normalized probabilities as we would expect. But using the probability for those gestures that actually are completed ($p(\mu^*) > 0.1$) we successfully recognize the completion of the gestures as shown along the bottom of Figure 7.

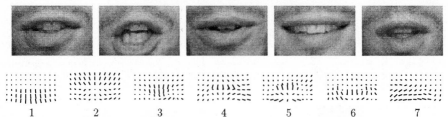

1 2 3 4 5 6 7

Fig. 8. Top: Example frames from the 600 image training set. Bottom: Basis flows for non-rigid mouth motion.

5 Facial Expressions

Parameterized models of optical flow provide a concise description of the image motion within a region in terms of a small number of parameters [2]. The evolution of these parameters over time can be used for motion-based recognition of facial expressions [3]. While here we consider optical flow, other authors have explored related approaches using deformable contours [1, 5, 12, 13, 15].

The horizontal and vertical image motion $\mathbf{u}(\mathbf{x}; \mathbf{a}) = (u(x, y), v(x, y))$ at a point $\mathbf{x} = (x, y)$ is represented as a linear combination of orthogonal basis flow fields, M_i

$$\mathbf{u}(\mathbf{x}; \mathbf{a}) = \sum_{i=1}^{k} a_i M_i(\mathbf{x}) \tag{3}$$

where $\mathbf{a} = (a_1, a_2, \ldots, a_k)^T$ are the coefficients of the model to be estimated.

Consider the example mouth images in Figure 8. To represent non-rigid motion of mouths we learn a parameterized model from example flow fields using principal component analysis (see [4]). Such a learned flow basis set is shown in Figure 8 for a training set that contained a variety of speech, a single smile, and four utterances of a test word. Since the image motion of the mouth is highly constrained, the optical flow structure can be modeled by a small number of principal component flow fields; in this case a seven parameter model is sufficient to account for 90% of the variance in the training data.

To recover the parameters we formulate an objective function to be minimized, namely

$$E(\mathbf{a}) = \sum_{\mathbf{x} \in R} \rho(I(\mathbf{x} + \mathbf{u}(\mathbf{x}; \mathbf{a}), t + 1) - I(\mathbf{x}, t), \ \sigma), \tag{4}$$

where ρ is a robust error function, R is a set of pixels in an image region, and $I(\mathbf{x}, t)$ is the image brightness at pixel $\mathbf{x}$ and time t. The motion coefficients are estimated between frames using a standard regression-based optical flow algorithm [4].

The learned model is used to estimate the motion in a 150-image test sequence in which the subject smiles and speaks a word that occured in the training set.

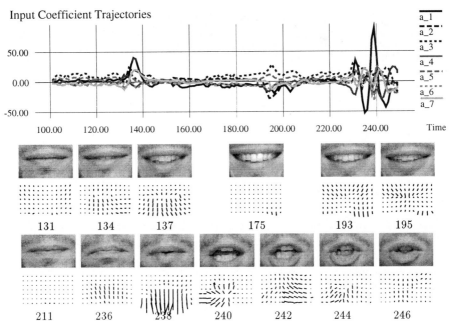

Fig. 9. Mouth motion experiment. Top: Recovered coefficients for the entire sequence. Below: Selected images and the corresponding estimated flow field are shown. Numbers under the images and flow fields correspond to frame numbers on the graphs.

A sample of the images from the sequence are shown in Fig. 9. Below each image is the estimated flow using the learned 7-parameter model.

The flow coefficients for the training sequence were computed and used to generate the trajectory models. The utterances of the test word were manually aligned and averaged to produce the trajectory models in Figure 10. Similarly, the single training smile was used to construct a compound model of a smile that is composed of primitive "onset," "apex," and "ending" models (cf. [3]). The apex is modeled as zero motion (all parameters zero) and may be of a prespecified or arbitrary duration. Given the small training set, we manually set σ to 20.0.

Figure 11 shows the results of the CTR algorithm applied to the test data. Figure 11 (top) shows the probability of each of the trajectory models (Constant (apex), Smile-Start (onset), Smile-Stop (ending), and Utterance) over the sequence. Figure 11 (middle) shows the probability of the composite parent models (Smile and Utterance). Finally Figure 11 (bottom) shows the estimated probability that each parent model has completed. The completion of the smile expression and the utterance are readily detected though the ending of the smile is located less precisely. As in the previous section a probability of greater than 0.1 is a reliable indicator of the end of an expression.

This simple, preliminary, experiment illustrates how the CTR algorithm can be used for on-line expression recognition with multi-variate optical flow data.

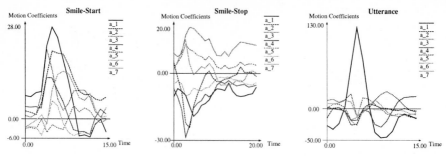

Fig. 10. Mouth expression models.

Our current research is exploring recognition with a richer set of facial expressions and speech acts. In particular, we are defining a vision-based user interface that uses mouth motions to control various computer screen functions.

6 Discussion and Conclusions

We have described an on-line, probabilistic, framework for matching temporal trajectories using the CONDENSATION algorithm. The framework extends previous work on CONDENSATION tracking to the problem of recognizing gestures based on stored temporal models. We have demonstrated how such a method can be used to recognize simple gestures and facial motions. In particular, we developed an augmented whiteboard application that allows users to interact with a whiteboard "scanner."

Note that in previous work [8,9], the CONDENSATION algorithm has been used to track objects with learned spatial and temporal dynamics. In this paper the tracking, or motion estimation, problem was solved separately and the CONDENSATION algorithm was used only to perform recognition given the temporal trajectories. In future research we will explore the integration of the motion estimation and recognition problems by using the probability distribution over states to help constrain the estimation problem. Note that for optical flow estimation this may prove more difficult than for the tracking applications in [9].

In the experiments presented here we took $S = 1000$ samples and the resulting experiments run significantly slower than real time. Blake and Isard have demonstrated real-time versions of a similar algorithm which suggests that our method might be suitable for real-time recognition (with appropriate optimizations). In particular, real-time performance is achieved when only 100 samples are used. The number of samples required for a particular problem is dependent on the number of models. We achieve real-time performance with the mouth example using only 100 samples with no reduction in accuracy. The gesture example, on the other hand, has a richer model-base and, hence, requires more samples.

In our current work, segmented and aligned training data was provided and transition probabilities between events in the parent models were set by hand.

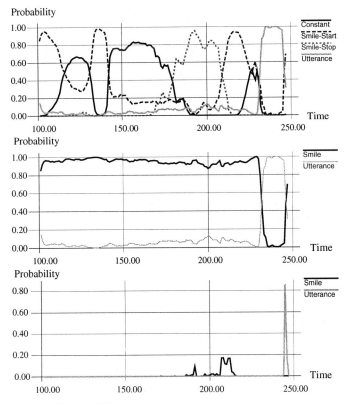

Fig. 11. Mouth expression recognition results.

While the method has very few parameters, it would be worth exploring how the techniques used for training HMM's might be used to generate the models automatically. Additionally, the size of the temporal window w might be learned from the training data.

In this paper we have explored the application of the CTR framework to the recognition of human motion (gestures and facial motions). The system could also be used to recognize other sorts of gestures as well as speech and on-line handwriting. In summary, random sampling techniques provide an interesting new framework for the automatic analysis of human motion.

Acknowledgements. We thank Francois Bérard for providing the real-time phicon tracking and Gudrun Socher for discussions about whiteboards and gesture interfaces.

References

1. A. Baumberg and D. Hogg. Learning flexible models from image sequences. *ECCV-94*, pp. 299–308, Stockholm, 1994.

2. M. J. Black and P. Anandan. The robust estimation of multiple motions: Parametric and piecewise-smooth flow fields. *CVIU*, 63(1):75–104, Jan. 1996.

3. M. J. Black and Y. Yacoob. Recognizing facial expressions in image sequences using local parameterized models of image motion. *IJCV*, 25(1):23–48, 1997.

4. M. J. Black, Y. Yacoob, A. D. Jepson, and D. J. Fleet. Learning parameterized models of image motion. *CVPR-97*, pp. 561–567, Puerto Rico, June 1997.

5. A. Blake, M. Isard, and D. Reynard. Learning to track the visual motions of contours. *Artificial Intelligence*, 78:101–134, 1995.

6. C. Bregler. Learning and recognizing human dynamics in video sequences. *CVPR-97*, pp. 568–574, Puerto Rico, June 1997.

7. J. L. Crowley and F. Berard, Multi-Modal Tracking of Faces for Video Communications, CVPR'97, pp. 640–645, Puerto Rico, June 1997.

8. M. Isard and A. Blake. Contour tracking by sotchastic propagation of conditional density. *ECCV-96*, pp. 343–356, Cambridge, UK, 1996.

9. M. Isard and A. Blake. A mixed-state Condensation tracker with automatic model-switching. *ICCV'98*, pp. 107–112, Mumbai, India, Jan. 1998.

10. H. Ishii and B. Ullmer. Tangible bits: Towards seamless interfaces between people, bits and atoms. *Proc. of CHI'97*, 1997.

11. K. Kanazawa, D. Koller, and S. Russell. Stochastic simulation algorithms for dynamic probabilistic networks. *Proc. of the Eleventh Conf. on Uncertainty in AI*, Montreal, 1995.

12. R. Kaucic, B. Dalton, and A. Blake. Real-time lip tracking for audio-visual speech recognition applications. *ECCV-96*, pp. 376–387, Cambridge, UK, 1996.

13. A. Lanitis, C. J. Taylor, T. F. Cootes, and T. Ahmed. Automatic interpretation of human faces and hand gestures using flexible models. *Int. Conf. on Automatic Face and Gesture Recognition*, pp. 98–103, Zurich, 1995.

14. L. R. Rabiner. A tutorial on Hidden Markov Models and selected applications in speech recognition. *Readings in Speech Recognition*, 1989.

15. D. Reynard, A. Wildenberg, A. Blake, and J. Marchant. Learning dynamics of complex motion from image sequences. *ECCV-96*, pp. 357–368, Cambridge, UK, 1996.

16. D. Sankoff and Eds. J. B. Kruskal. *Time warps, string edits, and macromolecules: The theory and practice of sequence compression.* Addison-Wesley Pub., Reading, Mass., 1983.

17. Q. Stafford-Fraser. Brightboard: A video-augmented environment. *Proc. of CHI'96*, 1996.

18. T. Starner and A. Pentland. Visual recognition of American Sign Language using Hidden Markov Models. *Int. Conf. on Automatic Face and Gesture Recognition*, pp. 189–194, Zurich, 1995.

19. R. Szeliski. Image mosaicing for tele-reality applications. *Second IEEE Workshop on Applications of Computer Vision*, pp. 44–53, Sarasota, Florida, 1994.

20. A. D. Wilson, A. F. Bobick, and J. Cassell. Temporal classification of natural gesture and application to video coding. *CVPR-97*, pp. 948–954, Puerto Rico, June 1997.

21. A. D. Wilson and A. F. Bobick. Recognition and interpretation of parametric gesture. *ICCV-98*, pp. 329–336, Mumbai, India, Jan. 1998.

22. Y. Yacoob and M. J. Black. Parameterized modeling and recognition of activities. *ICCV'98*, pp. 120–127, Mumbai, India, Jan. 1998.

23. Y. Yacoob and L. Davis. Parameterized modeling and recognition of activities. *ICCV'98*, pp. 446–453, Mumbai, India, Jan. 1998.

Author Index

Springer
and the
environment

At Springer we firmly believe that an international science publisher has a special obligation to the environment, and our corporate policies consistently reflect this conviction.
We also expect our business partners – paper mills, printers, packaging manufacturers, etc. – to commit themselves to using materials and production processes that do not harm the environment. The paper in this book is made from low- or no-chlorine pulp and is acid free, in conformance with international standards for paper permanency.

Springer

Lecture Notes in Computer Science

For information about Vols. 1–1340

please contact your bookseller or Springer-Verlag

Vol. 1377: H.-J. Schek, F. Saltor, I. Ramos, G. Alonso (Eds.), Advances in Database Technology – EDBT'98. Proceedings, 1998. XII, 515 pages. 1998.

Vol. 1378: M. Nivat (Ed.), Foundations of Software Science and Computation Structures. Proceedings, 1998. X, 289 pages. 1998.

Vol. 1379: T. Nipkow (Ed.), Rewriting Techniques and Applications. Proceedings, 1998. X, 343 pages. 1998.

Vol. 1380: C.L. Lucchesi, A.V. Moura (Eds.), LATIN'98: Theoretical Informatics. Proceedings, 1998. XI, 391 pages. 1998.

Vol. 1381: C. Hankin (Ed.), Programming Languages and Systems. Proceedings, 1998. X, 283 pages. 1998.

Vol. 1382: E. Astesiano (Ed.), Fundamental Approaches to Software Engineering. Proceedings, 1998. XII, 331 pages. 1998.

Vol. 1383: K. Koskimies (Ed.), Compiler Construction. Proceedings, 1998. X, 309 pages. 1998.

Vol. 1384: B. Steffen (Ed.), Tools and Algorithms for the Construction and Analysis of Systems. Proceedings, 1998. XIII, 457 pages. 1998.

Vol. 1385: T. Margaria, B. Steffen, R. Rückert, J. Posegga (Eds.), Services and Visualization. Proceedings, 1997/1998. XII, 323 pages. 1998.

Vol. 1386: T.A. Henzinger, S. Sastry (Eds.), Hybrid Systems: Computation and Control. Proceedings, 1998. VIII, 417 pages. 1998.

Vol. 1387: C. Lee Giles, M. Gori (Eds.), Adaptive Processing of Sequences and Data Structures. Proceedings, 1997. XII, 434 pages. 1998. (Subseries LNAI).

Vol. 1388: J. Rolim (Ed.), Parallel and Distributed Processing. Proceedings, 1998. XVII, 1168 pages. 1998.

Vol. 1389: K. Tombre, A.K. Chhabra (Eds.), Graphics Recognition. Proceedings, 1997. XII, 421 pages. 1998.

Vol. 1390: C. Scheideler, Universal Routing Strategies for Interconnection Networks. XVII, 234 pages. 1998.

Vol. 1391: W. Banzhaf, R. Poli, M. Schoenauer, T.C. Fogarty (Eds.), Genetic Programming. Proceedings, 1998. X, 232 pages. 1998.

Vol. 1392: A. Barth, M. Breu, A. Endres, A. de Kemp (Eds.), Digital Libraries in Computer Science: The MeDoc Approach. VIII, 239 pages. 1998.

Vol. 1393: D. Bert (Ed.), B'98: Recent Advances in the Development and Use of the B Method. Proceedings, 1998. VIII, 313 pages. 1998.

Vol. 1394: X. Wu. R. Kotagiri, K.B. Korb (Eds.), Research and Development in Knowledge Discovery and Data Mining. Proceedings, 1998. XVI, 424 pages. 1998. (Subseries LNAI).

Vol. 1395: H. Kitano (Ed.), RoboCup-97: Robot Soccer World Cup I. XIV, 520 pages. 1998. (Subseries LNAI).

Vol. 1396: E. Okamoto, G. Davida, M. Mambo (Eds.), Information Security. Proceedings, 1997. XII, 357 pages. 1998.

Vol. 1397: H. de Swart (Ed.), Automated Reasoning with Analytic Tableaux and Related Methods. Proceedings, 1998. X, 325 pages. 1998. (Subseries LNAI).

Vol. 1398: C. Nédellec, C. Rouveirol (Eds.), Machine Learning: ECML-98. Proceedings, 1998. XII, 420 pages. 1998. (Subseries LNAI).

Vol. 1399: O. Etzion, S. Jajodia, S. Sripada (Eds.), Temporal Databases: Research and Practice. X, 429 pages. 1998.

Vol. 1400: M. Lenz, B. Bartsch-Spörl, H.-D. Burkhard, S. Wess (Eds.), Case-Based Reasoning Technology. XVIII, 405 pages. 1998. (Subseries LNAI).

Vol. 1401: P. Sloot, M. Bubak, B. Hertzberger (Eds.), High-Performance Computing and Networking. Proceedings, 1998. XX, 1309 pages. 1998.

Vol. 1402: W. Lamersdorf, M. Merz (Eds.), Trends in Distributed Systems for Electronic Commerce. Proceedings, 1998. XII, 255 pages. 1998.

Vol. 1403: K. Nyberg (Ed.), Advances in Cryptology – EUROCRYPT '98. Proceedings, 1998. X, 607 pages. 1998.

Vol. 1404: C. Freksa, C. Habel. K.F. Wender (Eds.), Spatial Cognition. VIII, 491 pages. 1998. (Subseries LNAI).

Vol. 1406: H. Burkhardt, B. Neumann (Eds.), Computer Vision – ECCV'98. Vol. I. Proceedings, 1998. XVI, 927 pages. 1998.

Vol. 1407: H. Burkhardt, B. Neumann (Eds.), Computer Vision – ECCV'98. Vol. II. Proceedings, 1998. XVI, 881 pages. 1998.

Vol. 1409: T. Schaub, The Automation of Reasoning with Incomplete Information. XI, 159 pages. 1998. (Subseries LNAI).

Vol. 1411: L. Asplund (Ed.), Reliable Software Technologies – Ada-Europe. Proceedings, 1998. XI, 297 pages. 1998.

Vol. 1413: B. Pernici, C. Thanos (Eds.), Advanced Information Systems Engineering. Proceedings, 1998. X, 423 pages. 1998.

Vol. 1414: M. Nielsen, W. Thomas (Eds.), Computer Science Logic. Selected Papers, 1997. VIII, 511 pages. 1998.

Vol. 1415: J. Mira, A.P. del Pobil, M.Ali (Eds.), Methodology and Tools in Knowledge-Based Systems. Vol. I. Proceedings, 1998. XXIV, 887 pages. 1998. (Subseries LNAI).

Vol. 1416: A.P. del Pobil, J. Mira, M.Ali (Eds.), Tasks and Methods in Applied Artificial Intelligence. Vol.II. Proceedings, 1998. XXIII, 943 pages. 1998. (Subseries LNAI).

Vol. 1417: S. Yalamanchili, J. Duato (Eds.), Parallel Computer Routing and Communication. Proceedings, 1997. XII, 309 pages. 1998.

Vol. 1418: R. Mercer, E. Neufeld (Eds.), Advances in Artificial Intelligence. Proceedings, 1998. XII, 467 pages. 1998. (Subseries LNAI).

Vol. 1422: J. Jeuring (Ed.), Mathematics of Program Construction. Proceedings, 1998. X, 383 pages. 1998.

Vol. 1425: D. Hutchison, R. Schäfer (Eds.), Multimedia Applications, Services and Techniques – ECMAST'98. Proceedings, 1998. XVI, 531 pages. 1998.

Vol. 1427: A.J. Hu, M.Y. Vardi (Eds.), Computer Aided Verification. Proceedings, 1998. IX, 552 pages. 1998.

Vol. 1430: S. Trigila, A. Mullery, M. Campolargo, H. Vanderstraeten, M. Mampaey (Eds.), Intelligence in Services and Networks: Technology for Ubiquitous Telecom Services. Proceedings, 1998. XII, 550 pages. 1998.